The Coptic Encyclopedia

Editors and Consultants

The Coptic Encyclopedia

Aziz S. Atiya

EDITOR IN CHIEF

Volume 8

Macmillan Publishing Company
NEW YORK
Collier Macmillan Canada
TORONTO
Maxwell Macmillan International
NEW YORK · OXFORD · SINGAPORE · SYDNEY

Macmillan Publishing Company
866 Third Avenue, New York, NY 10022

Collier Macmillan Canada, Inc.
1200 Eglinton Avenue East, Suite 200, Don Mills, Ontario M3C 3N1

Library of Congress Catalog Card No.: 90-23448

Printed in the United States of America

printing number
1 2 3 4 5 6 7 8 9 10

Library of Congress Cataloging-in-Publication Data

The Coptic encyclopedia / Aziz S. Atiya, editor-in-chief.
p. cm.
Includes bibliographical references and index.
ISBN 0-02-897025-X (set)
1. Coptic Church—Dictionaries. 2. Copts—Dictionaries.
I. Atiya, Aziz S., 1898–
BX130.5.C66 1991 90-23448
281′.7′03—dc20 CIP

The preparation of this volume was made possible in part by a grant from the National Endowment for the Humanities, an independent federal agency.

Photographs on pages 567, 736, 754, 755, 790, 791, 876–878, 1284, 1311, and 2168 are reproduced courtesy of the Metropolitan Museum of Art. Photography by the Egyptian Expedition.

Contents of Volume 8

Errata	vi
Maps	1
Appendix: Linguistics	13
Index	229

Errata

Volume 1, page XXXIV:
In the List of Articles, Mounir Megally should be listed as the author of "Numerical System, Coptic."

Volume 1, page LIII:
In the List of Contributors, the following articles should be listed under the name of Mounir Megally: "Accounts and Accounting, History of Coptic"; "Bashmuric Revolts"; "Numerical System, Coptic"; "Toponymy, Coptic"; "Waq'at al-Kanā'is"; "Waq'at al-Naṣārā."

Volume 2, page 409:
The signature appearing with the article "Bookbinding" is incorrect. The author of the article is Jane Greenfield.

Volume 6, page 1822:
The signature appearing with the article "Numerical System, Coptic" is incorrect. The author of the article is Mounir Megally.

Further Acknowledgments

The editors wish to thank Nabil Selim Atalla, who graciously offered his services in taking photographs of objects in the Coptic Museum, Cairo. Thanks also to Charles Smith, Sirarpi Feredjian-Aivazian, Philip Friedman, Elly Dickason, Sylvia Kanwischer Miller, Jonathan Wiener, and others at Macmillan for their efforts on behalf of this encyclopedia.

Maps

1. Egypt: General Map
2. Egypt: Provinces
3. Alexandria in Late Antiquity
4. Monasteries in and around Cairo
5. Monasteries of the Delta
6. Monasteries of the Fayyūm
7. Monasteries of the Lower Ṣa'īd
8. Monasteries of the Middle Ṣa'īd
9. Monasteries of the Upper Ṣa'īd
10. Nubia
11. Oases
12. Pentapolis

Our thanks to Pierre Laferrière of the Institut français d'archéologie orientale, Cairo, and to Mark Hafey of Salt Lake City, for their work on the maps that follow.

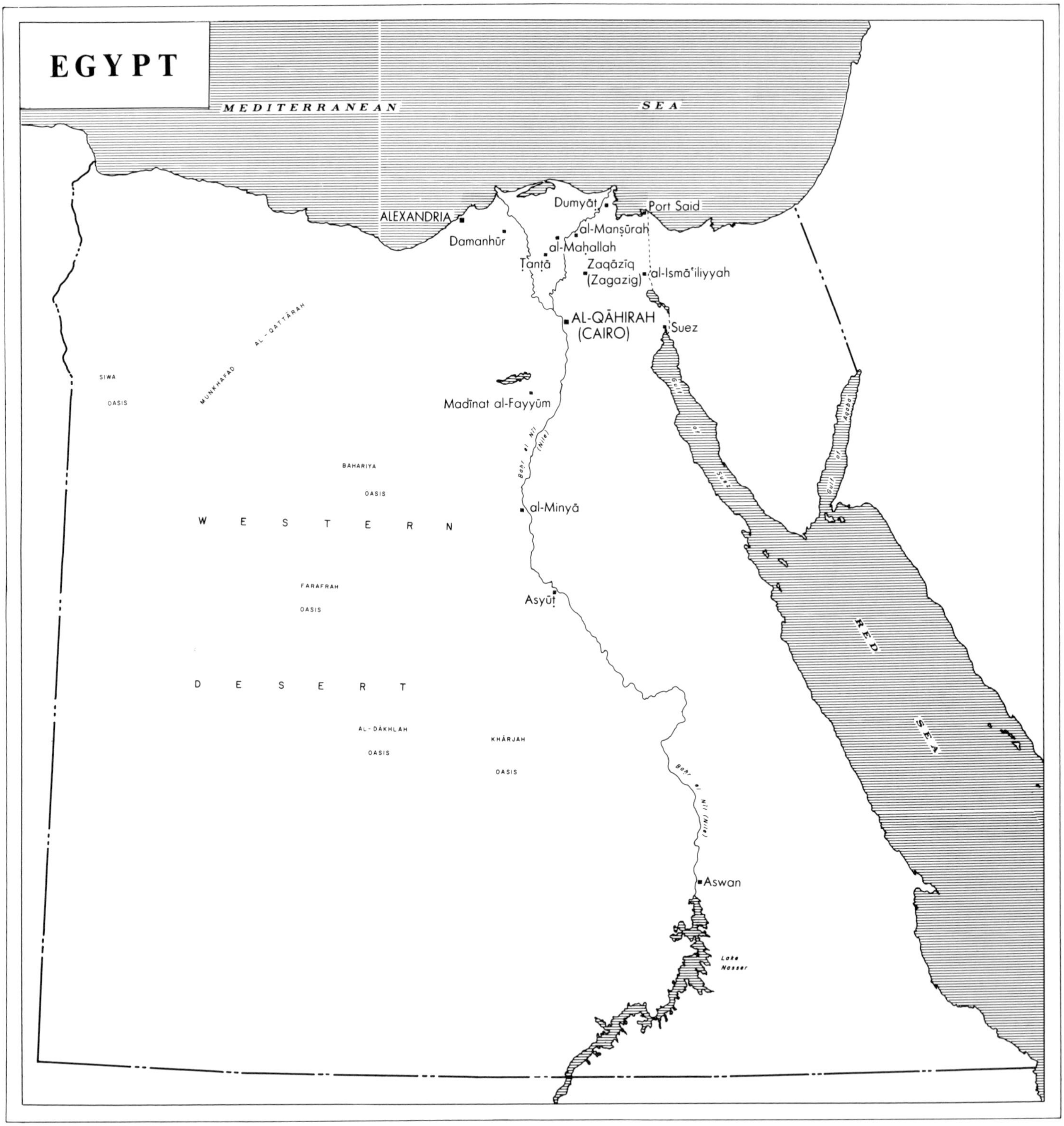

1. Egypt: General Map.

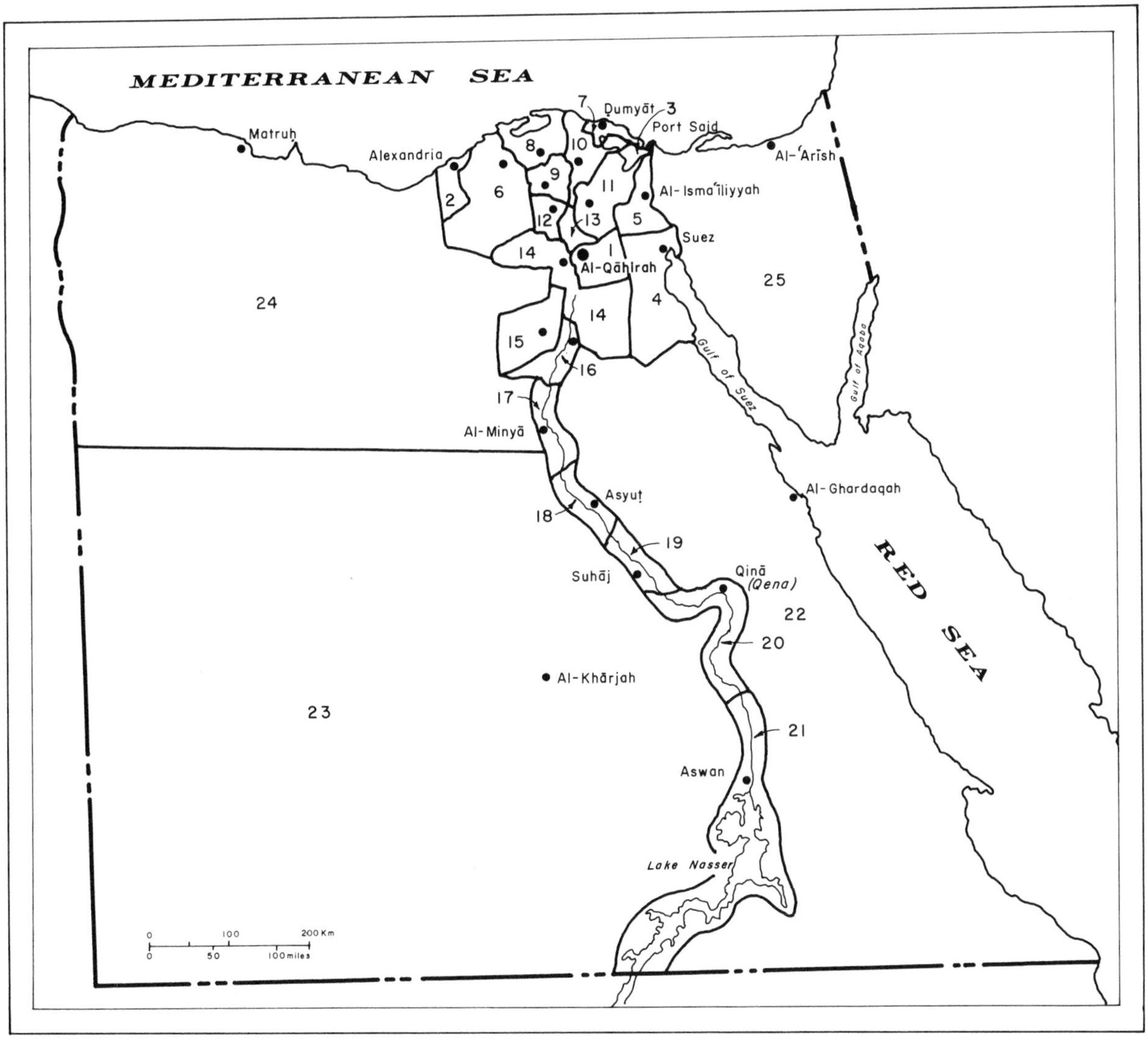

2. Egypt: Provinces.

City provinces: (1) Cairo (al-Qāhirah). (2) Alexandria (al-Iskandariyyah). (3) Port Said. (4) Suez (al-Suways).

Lower Egypt: (5) al-Ismā'iliyyah; capital, same. (6) Beheirah; capital, Damanhūr. (7) Damietta (Dumyāṭ); capital, same. (8) Kafr al-Shaykh; capital, same. (9) al-Gharbiyyah; capital, Ṭanṭā. (10) al-Daqahliyyah; capital, Mansura (al-Manṣūrah). (11) al-Sharqiyyah, capital, Zagazig (Zaqāzīq). (12) al-Minūfiyyah; capital, Shibīn al-Kom. (13) al-Qalyūbiyyah; capital, Banhā.

Upper Egypt: (14) Giza (al-Jizah); capital, same. (15) al-Fayyūm; capital, same. (16) Banī Suef (Banī Suwayf); capital, same. (17) al-Minyā; capital, same. (18) Asyūṭ; capital, same. (19) Suhāj; capital, same. (20) Qena (Qinā); capital, same. (21) Aswan; capital, same.

Frontier provinces: (22) Red Sea (al-Baḥr al-Aḥmar); capital, al-Ghardaqāh. (23) New Valley (al-Wādī al-Jadīd); capital, al-Khārjah. (24) Marsā Matrūḥ; capital, Matrūḥ. (25) Sinai; capital, al-'Arīsh.

The provincial boundaries shown reflect the divisions made by Muḥammad 'Alī in 1833, with additional provinces created after the Nasser revolution in 1953. The provinces are now formally known as governorates. (See also EGYPT, ADMINISTRATIVE ORGANIZATION OF.)

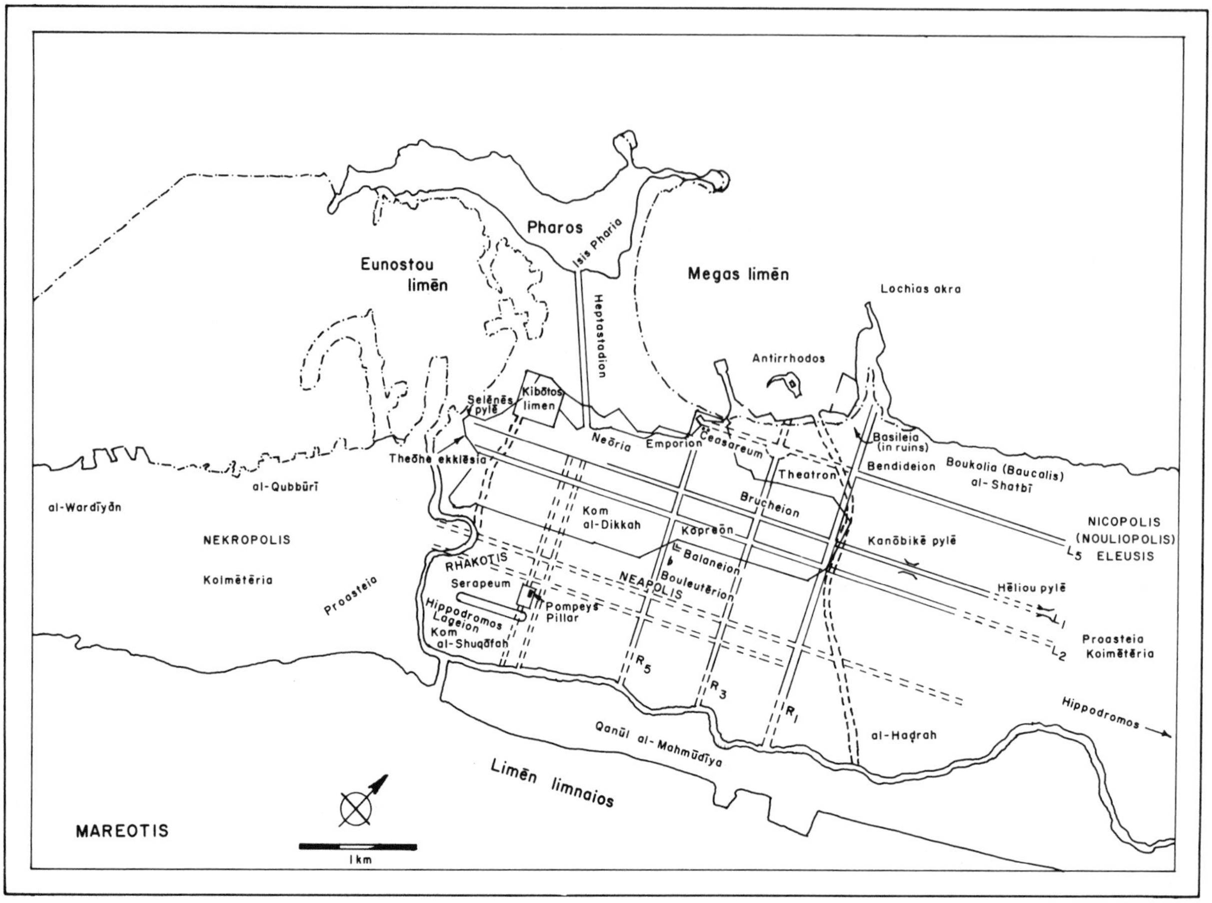

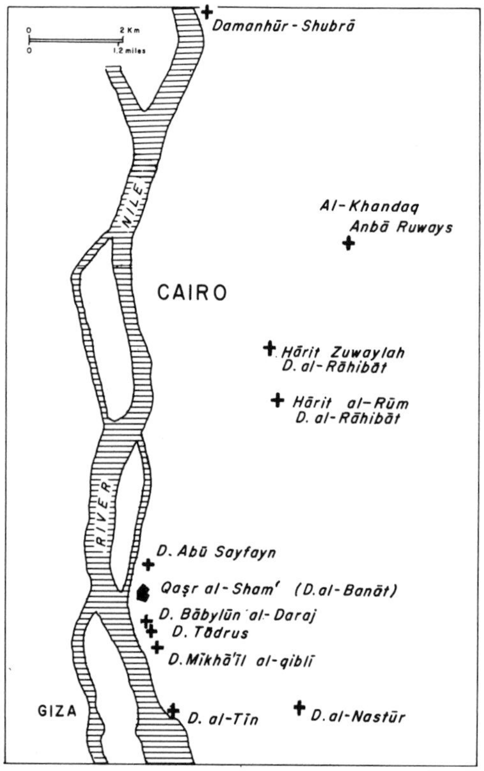

Above:

3. Alexandria in Late Antiquity. (See article, pp. 95–103.)

Left:

4. Monasteries in and around Cairo. (See article, pp. 1646–47.)

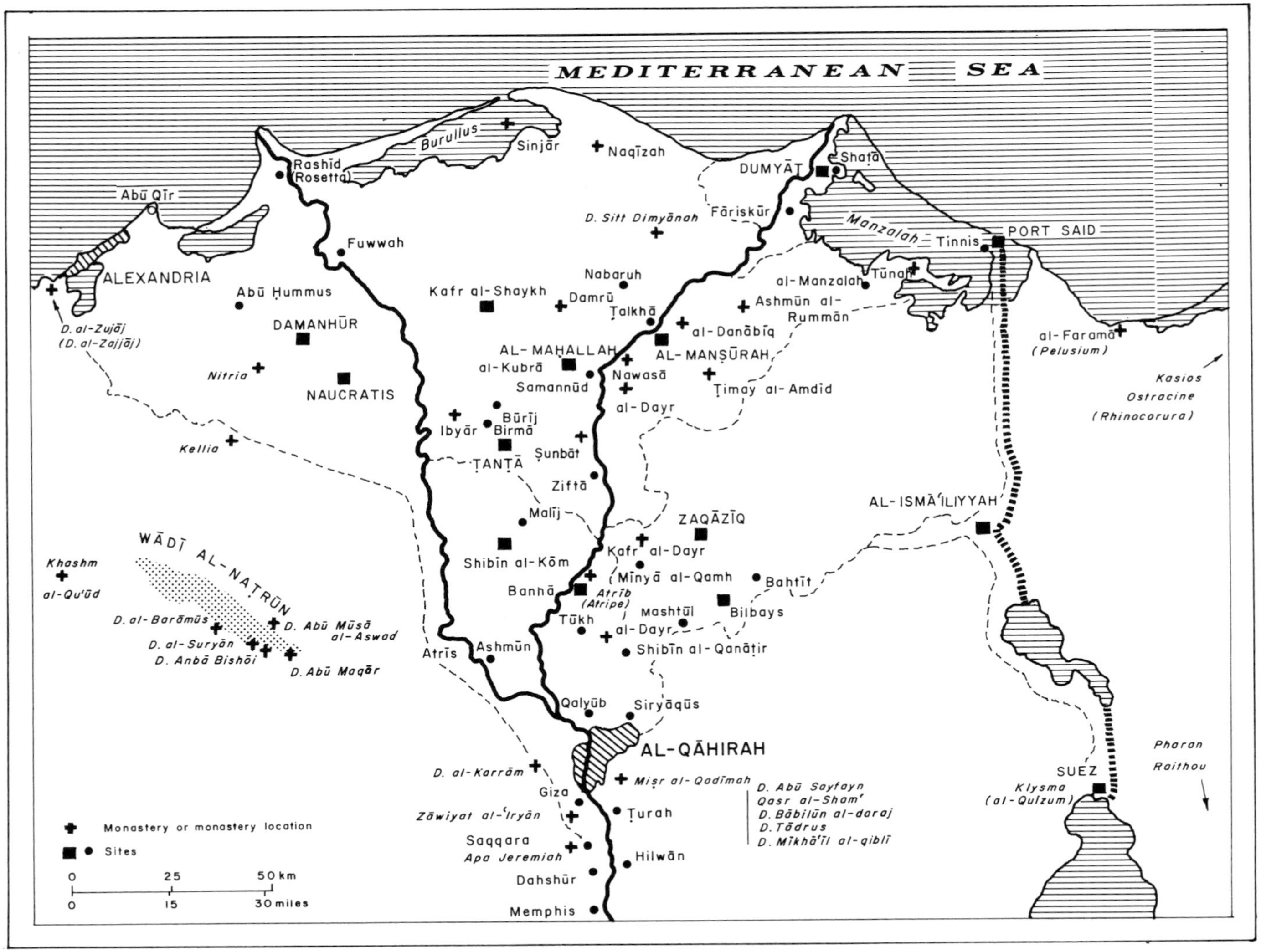

5. Monasteries of the Delta. Of the many monasteries in the Delta, some have vanished; some can still be identified by ruins, such as the innumerable sites excavated in the Kellia by the French and Swiss expeditions; and some have survived the Islamization of Egypt and the urbanization of the area. (See DAYR ANBĀ MAQĀR; DAYR AL-BARAMŪS; DAYR AL-SURYĀN; KELLIA; and articles on the Beheirah, Daqahliyyah, Gharbiyyah, Minūfiyyah, Qalyūbiyyah, and Sharqiyyah provinces under MONASTERIES.)

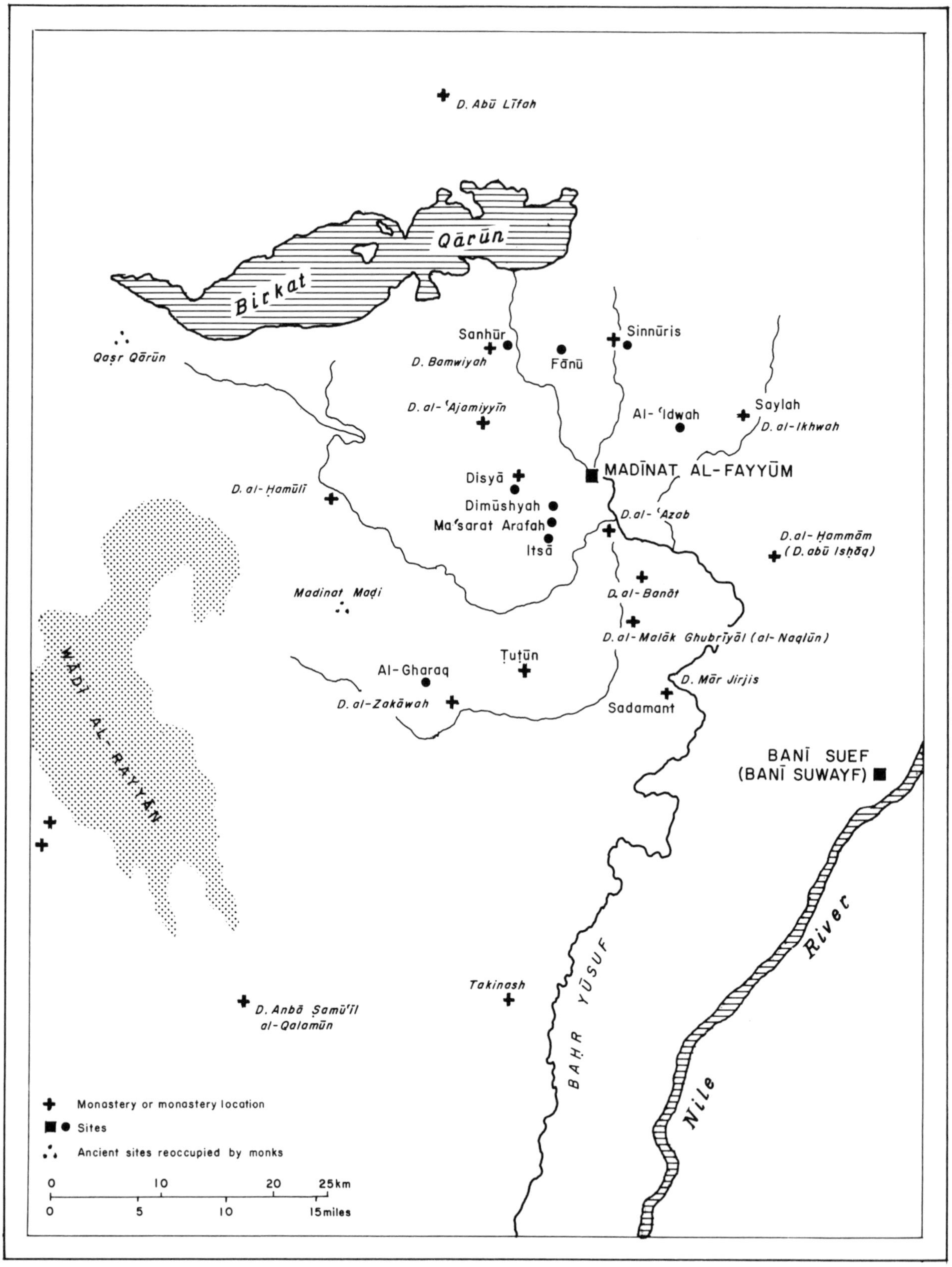

6. Monasteries of the Fayyūm. (See article, pp. 1650–51.)

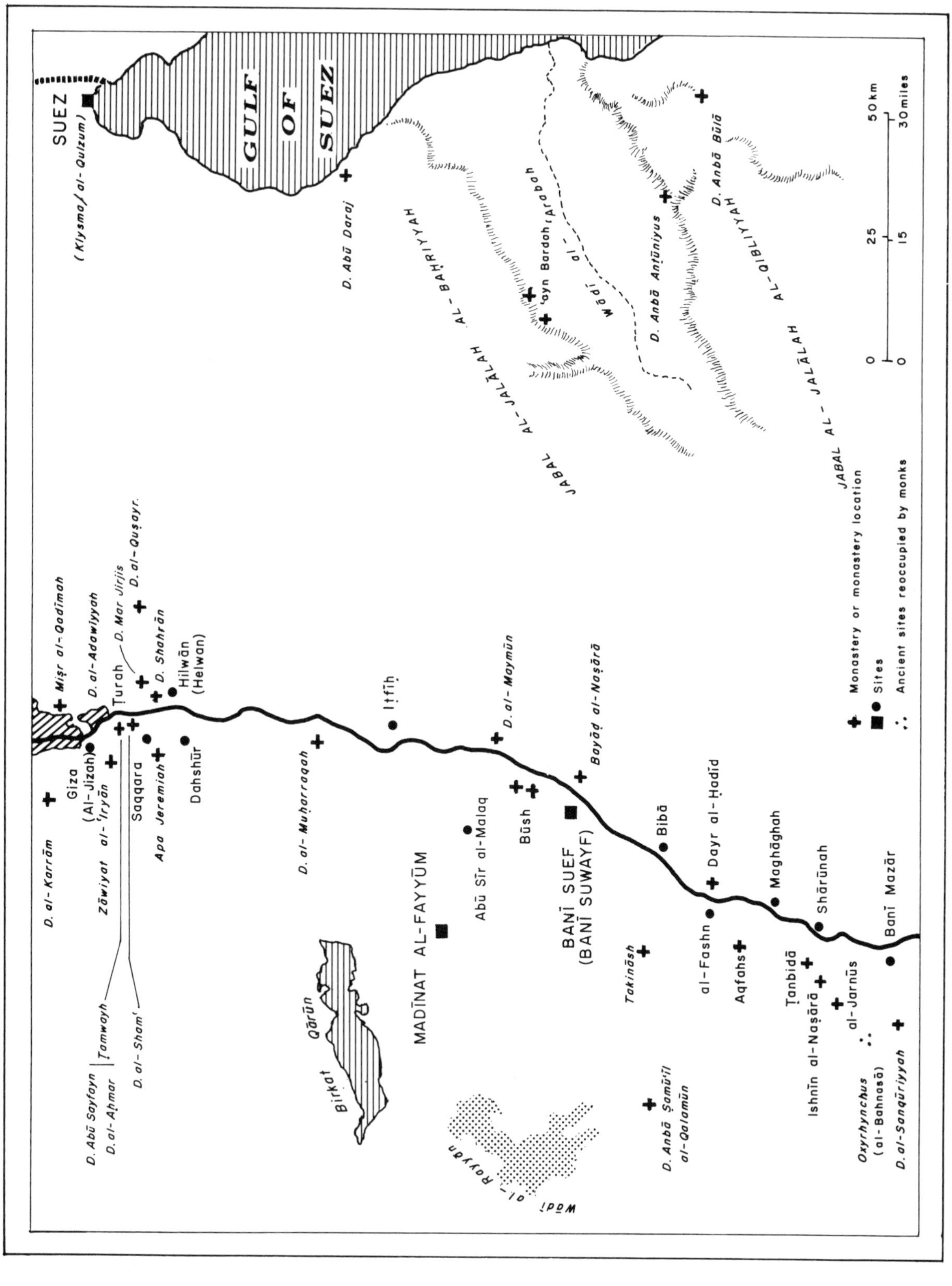

7. Monasteries of the Lower Ṣaʿīd. (See article, pp. 1652–53.)

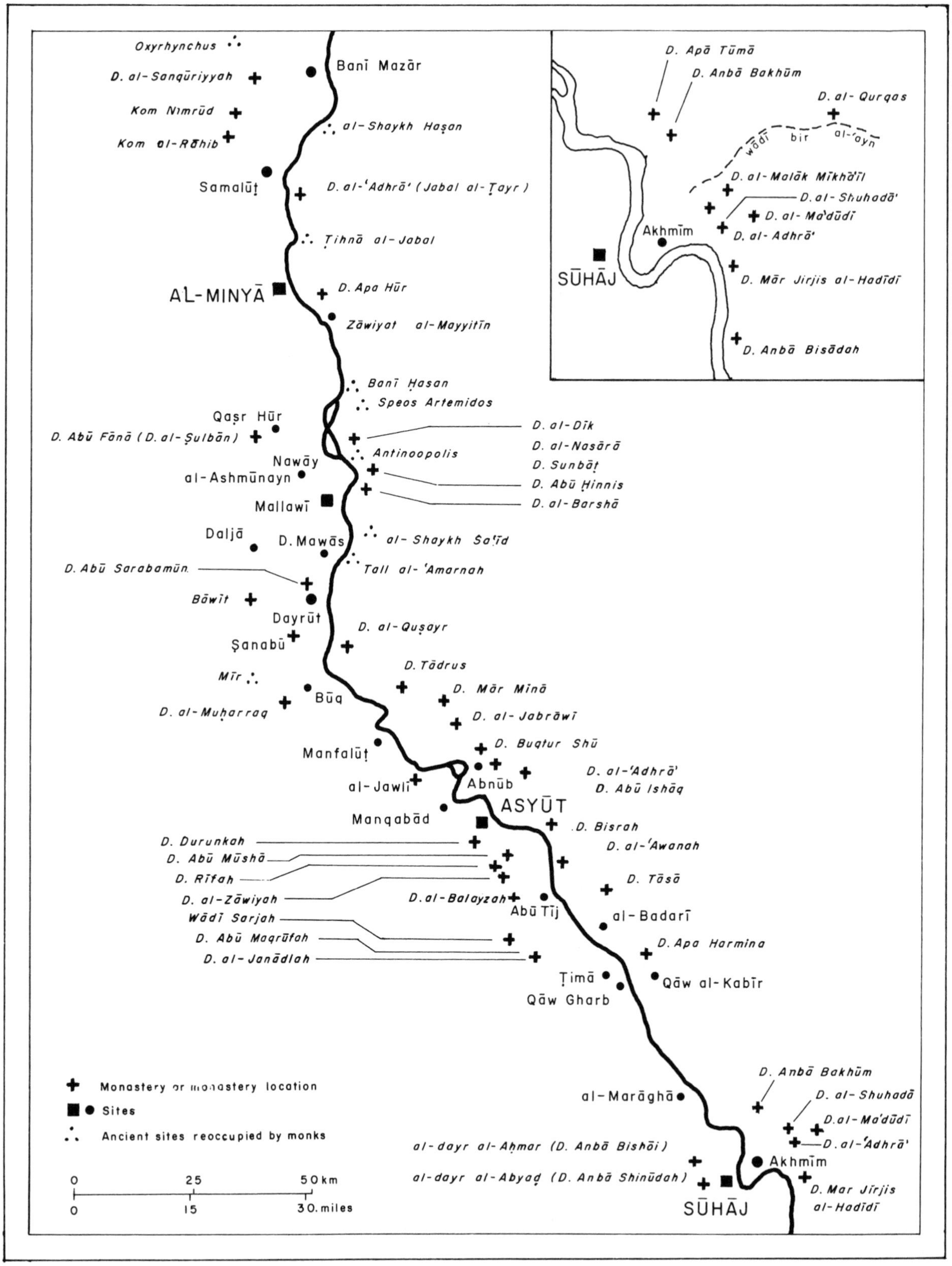

8. Monasteries of the Middle Ṣaʿīd. (See article, pp. 1654–55.)

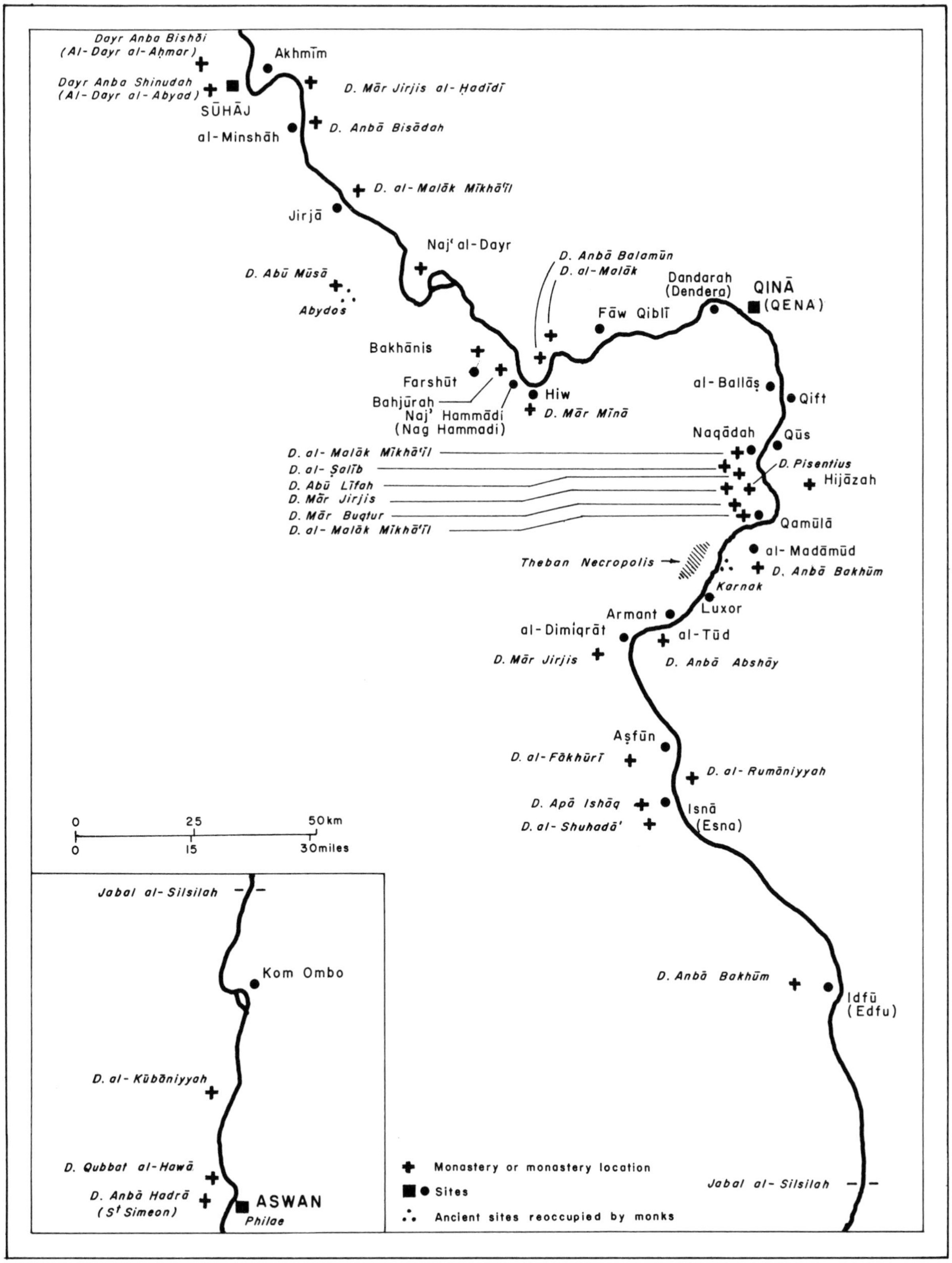

9. Monasteries of the Upper Ṣa'īd. (See article, pp. 1656–58.)

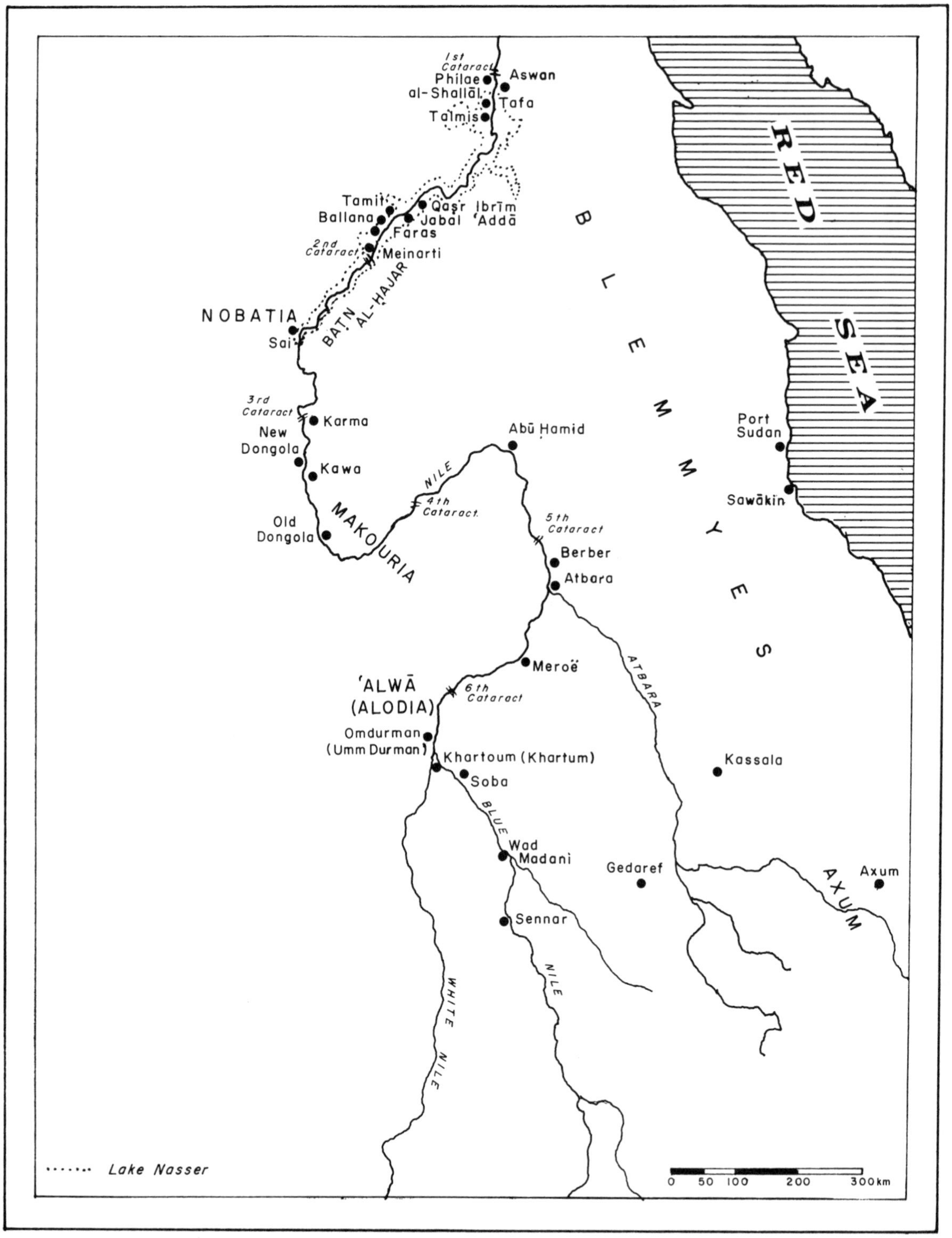

10. Nubia. The Nubians, speakers of the Nubian family of languages, in modern times have lived principally in the Nile Valley from Aswan, Egypt, to Debba (south of Old Dongola), Sudan. Much of this area was flooded by the building of the Aswan dams (1963–1969). In the Middle Ages the territory of the Nubians extended from Aswan to the confluence of the Blue and White Niles and comprised the kingdoms of NOBATIA, MAKOURIA, and 'ALWĀ. The Blemmye or BEJA TRIBES have occupied the Red Sea hills since pharaonic times. Area shown includes parts of modern-day Egypt, Sudan, and Ethiopia. (See NUBIA and related articles, pp. 1800–1820.)

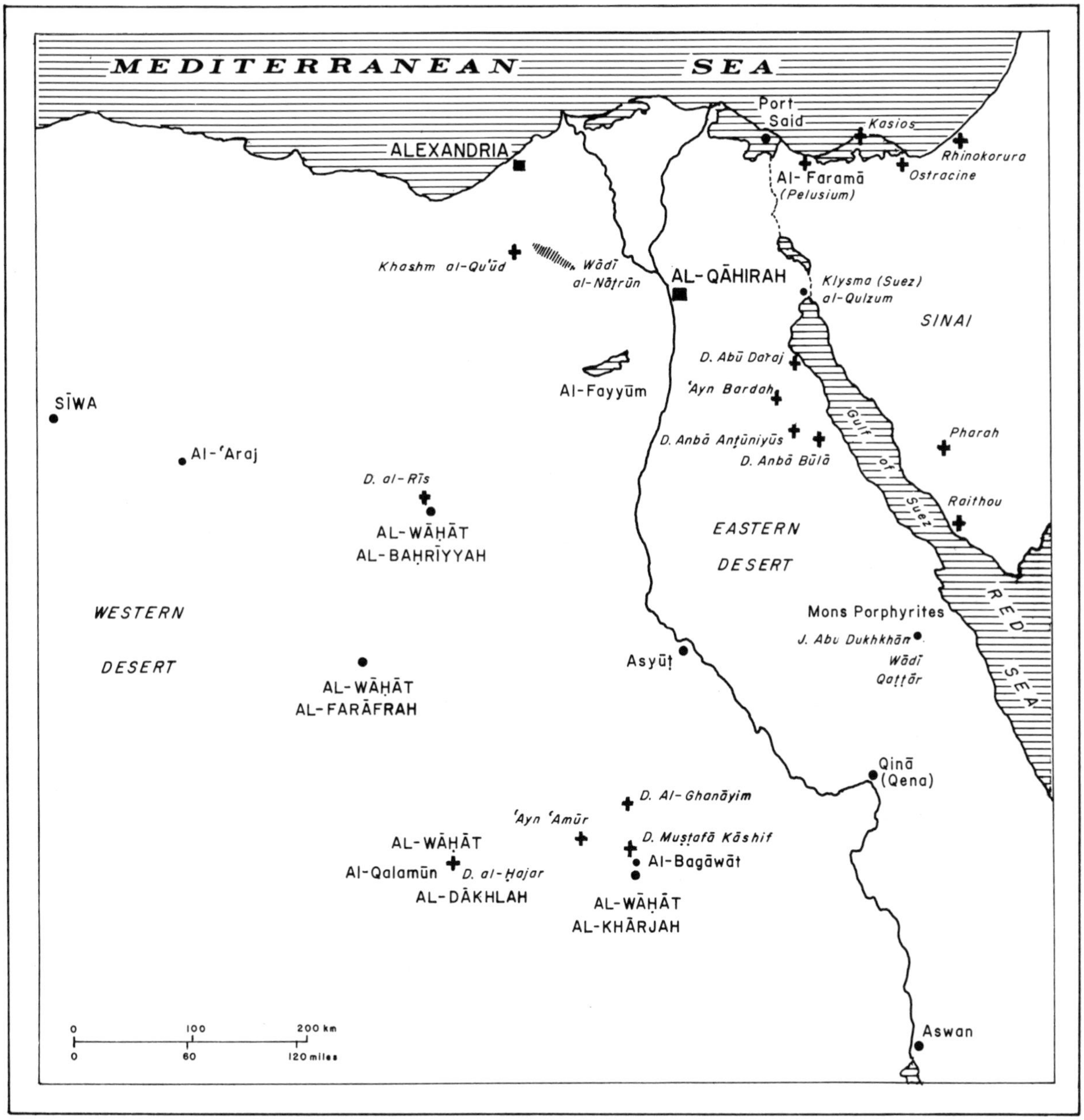

11. Oases. Christian ruins are still to be found in the oases located in the Western Desert. (See 'ARAJ, AL-; 'AYN AMŪR; BAGAWĀT, AL-; DAYR AL-GHANĀYIM; DAYR AL-ḤĀJAR; DAYR MUṢṬAFĀ KĀSHIF.)

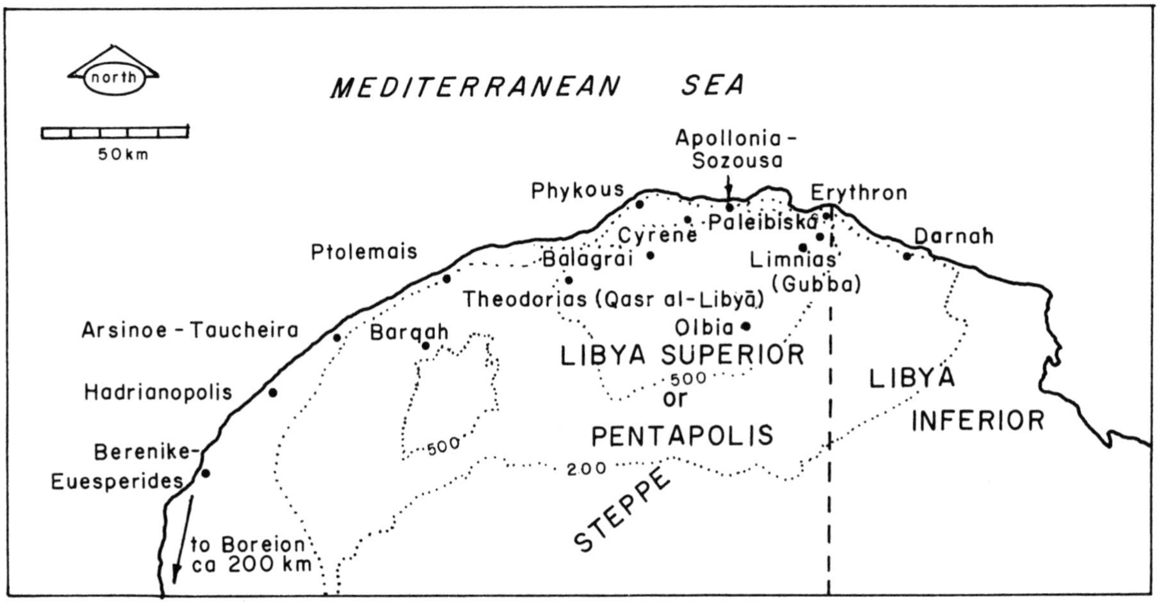

12. Pentapolis. (See article, pp. 1933–35.)

Appendix: Linguistics

List of Articles in the Appendix

Akhmimic
Aleph
Alphabet in Coptic, Greek
Alphabets, Coptic
Alphabets, Old Coptic
'Ayin
Bashmuric
Bodmer Papyri
Bohairic
Bohairic, Pronunciation of Late
Cryptography
Cryptophoneme
Dialect, Immigrant
Dialect, Sporadic
Dialect G (or Bashmuric or Mansuric)
Dialect H (or Hermopolitan or Ashmuninic)
Dialect İ (or Proto-Lycopolitan)
Dialect P (or Proto-Sahidic)
Dialects
Dialects, Grouping and Major Groups of
Dialects, Morphology of Coptic
Dictionaries
Djinkim
Egyptian Arabic Vocabulary, Coptic Influence on
Etymology
Fayyumic
Gemination
Geography, Dialectal
Greek Transcriptions
Idiolect
Language(s), Coptic
Lyco-Diospolitan
Lycopolitan (or Lyco-Diospolitan or Subakhmimic)
Memphitic
Mesodialect
Mesokemic
Metadialect
Muqaddimah
Old Coptic
Paleography
Phonology
Phonology of the Greek of Egypt, Influence of Coptic on the
Pre-Coptic
Pre-Old Coptic
Protodialect
Sahidic
Shenutean Idiom
Sullam
Syllabication
Vocabulary, African Contacts with Autochthonous Coptic
Vocabulary, Copto-Arabic
Vocabulary, Copto-Greek
Vocabulary, Cuneiform Transcriptions of Prototypes of Autochthonous Coptic
Vocabulary of Egyptian Origin, Autochthonous Coptic
Vocabulary of Semitic Origin, Autochthonous Coptic

Foreword

The greatest, but also the most fragile and delicate treasure of any highly developed civilization is its thought.

This is also true of the Egyptian pharaonic civilization, the most ancient among all exceptionally cultured civilizations.

The majority of today's tourists admire the Egyptian monuments covered with figures artistically drawn, carved, or painted, without really understanding them. Yet it is through these figures that the eternal soul of the Egyptians is expressed. These figures are a writing, or the essential illustrations to texts—texts written in the genuine Egyptian language, which hands down to us through the ages the mystery and profound essence of Egyptian thinking —through which humanity in its evolution completed a decisive stage in its history.

In the same way we can speak of the Egyptian Coptic civilization, direct descendant of the Egyptian pharaonic civilization. Its thinking, especially religious and Christian, but also Gnostic, Hermetic, and Manichaean, has come down to us through a rich literature. That literature is expressed in the different variations of the Coptic language, a language that is also a direct descendant of the Egyptian pharaonic language even if it is written in an alphabetical form (a writing for the most part renovated and simplified).

That is why the presentation of the Coptic language—with all its regional variations, orthographical, phonological, morphological, syntactic—is essential in an encyclopedia entirely devoted to all aspects of the splendid Coptic civilization, a living civilization that still remains flourishing today in Egypt.

Naturally in presenting the Coptic language—in its multiplicity—one cannot avoid some technical terminology without which it would have been difficult to treat correctly the subject in question. It is hoped that those readers who need such linguistic knowledge will make the effort necessary to understand this terminology. Other readers will consider the linguistics as useful tools ready to be used, perhaps rarely, but to hand whenever necessary.

Moreover, how could the Coptic language be omitted from the first Coptic encyclopedia when this language—more than 1500 years old, musically among the most beautiful, and rich in amazing subtleties (like those of the Egyptian Pharaonic language)—still resounds in the Coptic churches of today each time the holy liturgy is sung or recited there? This language goes on living through the adoration that human beings address to their eternal God, unique and permanent in its many forms and under its many names, multiple and various as it was revealed to humanity.

RODOLPHE KASSER

AKHMIMIC. The Akhmimic dialect (siglum *A*), along with the Sahidic (*S*) and the various vernaculars of the Lycopolitan dialect group (*L*), is one of the Upper Egyptian DIALECTS of Coptic. Its range of distribution extends from Aswan to Akhmīm (Coptic, ϣⲙⲓⲛ or ⲭⲙⲓⲛ; Arabic, *'Aḫmîm;* Greek, Panos or Panopolis). Thebes is considered the point of origin as well as the center of the Akhmimic-speaking region (Kahle, 1954, pp. 197–203; Vergote, 1973, Vol. la, p. 4). However, according to the former view of Kasser (1982a), the proto-Sahidic dialect (a reconstructed entity, symbol **pS*, very like DIALECT P) also began to develop in Thebes after having infiltrated from the north as early as the second half of the third century A.D. As a result, in the fourth century *A* and *S* were in concurrent use in the Upper Thebaid. While Akhmimic had not been uniformly standardized, it became a medium of writing as early as the fourth century and reached its zenith in the fourth and fifth centuries. Beginning in the fifth century, it was gradually displaced by the Upper Egyptian koine (*S*), although for its part *A* (besides *L?*) both influenced *S*—as seen in the Nag Hammadi texts and Shenute—in the fourth and fifth centuries and left traces in nonliterary texts from Thebes dating from the seventh and eighth centuries. These observations imply that even after being displaced by *S*, *A* was still in use as a spoken language.

1. General Characteristics

The dialectical features typical of *A* may be summarized in contradistinction to *S* (if necessary also to *P;* cf. Kasser, 1960) and to the group of dialects included under *L* (i.e., *L4* = Manichaean texts; *L5* = London Gospel of John, ed. Thompson, 1924, as well as the Dublin fragment of the Gospel of John and the Geneva fragment of the Acta Pauli, the latter two being unpublished; *L6* = Nag Hammadi texts of codices I, X, and XI, as well as the Heidelberg Acta Pauli, ed. Carl Schmidt, 1904 and 1909).

The textual citations below refer to editions and studies of the documents noted in the bibliography as follows: ApocSoph. = Steindorff, 1899; I Clem. = Schmidt, 1908; I Clem.(R) = Rösch, 1910 (pp. 1–87); Elias = Steindorff, 1899; EpAp. = Schmidt, 1919; Ex. = Lacau, 1911 (pp. 45–64); Herm. = Lefort, 1952 (pp. 1–18); Jn. = Rösch, 1910 (pp. 119–60); MinProph. (Minor Prophets) = Till, 1927b (for Obadiah 1–13; Amos 1:1–2:11; 6:3–10; 7:10–16; Habakkuk 1:7–2:2, 2:11–3:19; Haggai; Hosea; Joel 1:1–14, 2:19–3:21; Jonah 4:2–11; Malachi 1:1–7; 2:9–3:24; Micah 2:11–5:8; 6:1–7:20; Nahum 1:1–3:8, 3:14–19; Zephaniah; Zechariah 1:6–4:5, 7:14–14:21); MinProph. (Minor Prophets) = Malinine, 1950 (for Obadiah 13–21; Amos 8:11–9:15; Habakkuk 1:1–7, 2:2–17 (sic); Joel 1:14–2:19; Jonah 1:1–42; Micah 1:1–2:11, 5:8–6:1; Nahum 3:8–14; Zechariah 1:1–6, 4:6–7:14); Luke = Lefort, 1953; Ost. = Till, 1931 (text A); Prv. = Böhlig, 1958; Sir. = Lacau, 1911 (pp. 64–67); *P* (Papyrus Bodmer VI) = Kasser, 1960.

1.1 Grapheme Inventory. Beyond *S* and *L*, *A* adds the alphabetic symbol ⳉ, the postpalatal spirant /x/ (or h̠, [x_2] from the Egyptian *ḫ* or *h̠*); in *P*, the symbol for this is ϧ.

1.2 Phonetic Characteristics.

1.2.1. A, L /a/, *S* /o/ in a closed stressed syllable before a nonlaryngeal sound, e.g., *A, L* ⲥⲁⲛ, *S* ⲥⲟⲛ, brother.

1.2.2. A, L /e/, *S* /a/ in a closed stressed syllable, e.g., *A, L* ⲣⲉⲛ; *S* ⲣⲁⲛ, name.

1.2.3. A /i:/; *S* /ē/ before a laryngeal in the medial and final position, e.g., *A* ⲙⲉⲓϣⲉ, ⲙⲓϣⲉ, *S* ⲙⲏⲏϣⲉ, *L* ⲙⲏϣⲉ, crowd; *A* ⲟⲩⲓⲉⲓⲃⲉ, *S, L* ⲟⲩⲏⲏⲃ, priest; *A* ⲣⲓ, *S, L* ⲣⲏ, sun; *A* ⲟⲩⳉⲓ, *S, L* ⲟⲩϣⲏ, night.

1.2.4. A, (L5) /u:/, *S, L* /o:/ in a long final position or before a laryngeal, e.g., *A, (L5)* ⲕⲟⲩ, *S, L4, (L5)* ⲕⲱ, *L6* ⲕⲱⲉ, to place (< Egyptian *ḫ3ʿ*); *A, (L5)* ϭⲟⲩ, *S, L4 (L5)* ϭⲱ, to remain (< demotic *g3, gʿ* < *gr*); *A* ⲡⲣⲟⲩ, *S, L4, L5* ⲡⲣⲱ, winter; *A, (L5), L6* ϫⲟⲩ: *S, L4, L5* ϫⲱ, to say.

1.2.5. */ew/ in stressed final syllables: *A* /o/, *L* /eu̯/, *S* /au̯/, e.g., *A, L4* (ManiH=Manichaean Homilies) ⲛⲟ, *L* ⲛⲉⲩ, *S* ⲛⲁⲩ, to see; *A, L4* (ManiH) ⲉⲧⲙ̄ⲙⲟ, *L* ⲉⲧⲙ̄ⲙⲉⲩ, *S* ⲉⲧⲙ̄ⲙⲁⲩ, that (*literally*, which is there).

1.2.6.1. Typical of certain *A* texts (but not orthographically standardized throughout in *A*), insertion of a nasal before /t/ following /u:/ in open stressed syllables: *A* in I Clem., Herm., Prov. (minority), Jn. (minority) ⲙⲟⲩⲛⲧⲉ, *S, L,* etc., and elsewhere in *A* ⲙⲟⲩⲧⲉ, to call; *A* in I Clem., Herm., Prov. (majority) ⲛⲟⲩⲛⲧⲉ, *S, L,* etc., and elsewhere in *A* ⲛⲟⲩⲧⲉ, God.

1.2.6.2. In contrast, the inserted nasal (sonant) is missing in *A, L4, L5* (*L6* oscillating) in the posttonic syllable: /mt/, *A* ⳉⲁⲙⲧ, *L4, L5* ϣⲁⲙⲧ, *L6* ϣⲁⲙⲛ̄ⲧ, *S* ϣⲟⲙⲛ̄ⲧ, three; *A, L4, L5* ϩⲁⲙⲧ, *L6* ϩⲁⲙⲛ̄ⲧ, *S* ϩⲟⲙⲛ̄ⲧ, copper; *A, L4, L6* ⲥⲁⲙⲧ†, *S* ⲥⲟⲙⲛ̄ⲧ†, to be stretched.

1.2.7. Anaptyctic vowel [ə] as well as /e/ is written as ⲉ at the end of a word following a closed syllable of the pattern */voiceless consonant + voiced consonant or son(or)ant/*, by which *A* and *L4* form a group distinct from *L5, L6,* e.g., *A, L4* ⲥⲱⲧⲙⲉ, *S, (L4), L5, L6* ⲥⲱⲧⲙ̄, to hear; *A, L4* ⲧⲁϩⲙⲉ†, *S* ⲧⲁϩⲙ†, to be invited (versus *S, A, L* ⲧⲁϩⲙⲉ, to invite you [f.]), *A* ⳉⲧⲁⲣⲧⲣⲉ, *L* ϣⲧⲁⲣⲧⲣ̄, *S* ϣⲧⲟⲣⲧⲣ̄, to be amazed. Naturally, the consonant can also be /ʾ/, e.g., *A* ⲟⲩⲁⲁⲃⲉ†, *L4* ⲟⲩⲁⲃⲉ†, *S, L5, L6* ⲟⲩⲁⲁⲃ†, to be holy (< *wʿb*). Note that while the representation in spelling of the anaptyctic vowel ⲉ in the configuration */consonant + son(or)ant/*—not */laryngeal + son(or)ant/*—is not standardized in *L4,* the spelling with ⲉ predominates by far. Consistent spelling occurs only in ⲥⲁⲩⲛⲉ, to know (also *P* ⲥⲟⲟⲩⲛⲉ). The anaptyctic vowel noted here by /ə/ is phonemically relevant according to Hintze (1980).

1.3 Morphological Features.

1.3.1. Second present tense in *A, B*(!) ⲁϥ-, *S, L* ⲉϥ- (in affirmative sentences, it is homophonic with the circumstantial verbal prefix).

1.3.2. Imperfect: *A, B*(!) ⲛⲁϥ- (ⲡⲉ), *S, L* ⲛⲉϥ- (ⲡⲉ).

1.3.3. Second perfect: *A* ⲛⲁϥ-, *S, L* ⲛ̄ⲧⲁϥ-.

1.3.4. In the "ⲉⲧⲁϩ group" (see 3.2.1.1), the relative morpheme of the perfect remains invariably ⲉⲧⲁϩ- if the subject of the relative clause is identical to the antecedent in the main clause.

1.3.5. Homophony exists between the subject pronoun of the conjunctive tense and that of the first present, except the form of the first-person singular: first present *S, A, L* ϯ-; conjunctive *A* ⲧⲁ-, *S, L* (ⲛ̄)ⲧⲁ-.

1.3.6. Causative prefix *A* ⲧⲉ-, *S, L5, L6* ⲧⲣⲉ- (in *L4* the prefix is not standardized, ⲧⲉ- occurring alongside ⲧⲣⲉ-).

1.3.7. The qualitative form of ⲧ- causative verbs in *A* almost entirely ends in -ⲁⲉⲓⲧ.

1.3.8. The negation of the nominal sentence and the bipartite conjugation pattern in *A* is realized without ⲛ, i.e., only with ⲉⲛ (*S* ⲛ . . . ⲁⲛ): *A (L)* ⲉϥⲥⲱⲧⲙⲉ ⲉⲛ, *S* ⲉⲛϥ̄ⲥⲱⲧⲙ̄ ⲁⲛ, while he does not hear; *A* ⲉⲧⲥⲱⲧⲙⲉ ⲉⲛ, *S* ⲉⲧⲉ ⲛ̄ϥⲥⲱⲧⲙ̄ ⲁⲛ, who does not hear.

1.3.9. Definite articles in *A,* including those preceding double consonants and expressions of time, are ⲡ-, ⲧ-, and ⲛ- (without ⲉ).

1.3.10. The second-person feminine singular possessive articles in *A, B* are ⲡⲉ-, ⲧⲉ-, ⲛⲉ-, *S* ⲡⲟⲩ-, ⲧⲟⲩ-, ⲛⲟⲩ-.

1.3.11. The third-person plural possessive articles in *A, B* are ⲡⲟⲩ-, ⲧⲟⲩ-, ⲛⲟⲩ-, *S* ⲡⲉⲩ-, ⲧⲉⲩ-, ⲛⲉⲩ-.

1.4 Lexical Features (Akhmimic Isoglosses).

1.4.1. Significant function words:

1.4.1.1. A ⲗⲟⲩ, *S, L* ⲁⲩⲱ, and.

1.4.1.2. Directional preposition to or toward (< Egyptian *r*) *A, L* ⲁ-, *S* ⲉ-, including the adverbs containing the formative ⲁ/ⲉ, *A, L* ⲁⲃⲁⲗ, *P* ⲁⲃⲟⲗ, *S* ⲉⲃⲟⲗ, out of; *A* ⲁⳉⲟⲩⲛ, *L* ⲁϩⲟⲩⲛ, *P* ⲁϧⲟⲩⲛ, *S* ⲉϩⲟⲩⲛ, *B* ⲉϧⲟⲩⲛ, into.

1.4.1.3. Negative imperative *A* ⲙⲛ̄-, *S (L)* ⲙ̄ⲡⲣ̄-.

1.4.1.4. Lexical and functional distinction between conditional particles formed from -ⲡⲉ and -ϫⲉ: *A* ⲉⲓⳉⲡⲉ, ⳉⲡⲉ, if (in the sense "supposing it is true that") is to be differentiated from ⲉⲓⳉϫⲉ, ⳉϫⲉ, if (in the sense "as if it were"), the equivalent of ⲉϣϫⲉ in *S.* This distinction is found only in *L6* of those texts belonging to the *L* group: ⲉⲓϣⲡⲉ as opposed to ⲉⲓϣϫⲉ (Funk, 1985).

1.4.2. A number of nominal and verbal lexemes specific for *A* (cf. Till, 1928, pp. 276–78; Kasser, 1979a). While the vocabulary of Akhmimic has been treated throughout in Crum (1939), Kasser (1964), and Westendorf (1977), a fully documented lexicon of Akhmimic has not yet been compiled.

1.5 Syntactic Features.

1.5.1. Connecting objects.

1.5.1.1. Nonreduction of the stressed vowel of the infinitive occurs also when the object is attached directly to it. In such cases, the infinitive retains the form of the *status absolutus.* In the bipartite conjugation pattern this construction is possible only with objects not modified by a determinative (Shisha-Halevy, 1976).

1.5.1.2. There is a tendency toward placing a pronominal indirect object (dative) before the direct object (accusative) without an accusative particle, in the case of ϯ, to give; ⲕⲧⲟ, to bring back; and ϫⲡⲟ, to bring forth, which then take the respective forms ⲧⲉ ⲛⲉ⸗ accusative, ⲕⲧⲉ ⲛⲉ⸗ accusative, and ϫⲡⲉ ⲛⲉ⸗ accusative.

1.5.2. As in *L,* the affirmative final clause following ϫⲉ is almost always the second future (*S* third future, or *futurum energicum*).

As is apparent in sections 1–5 above, not all of the described features are exclusively characteristic of *A*. Further, it is the totality of all features (or, if not all features appear in a given text, the combination of sufficient individual features within a text) that assigns a document to the Akhmimic dialect.

The following sections will include a discussion of the phonemic inventory (2) and the conjugation system (3) of *A*, out of which the criteria for group classification (4) of Akhmimic texts will be derived. At the end (5), problems associated with a number of texts traditionally assigned to *A* will be treated.

2. The Phonemic Inventory of Akhmimic

As is traditional, consonants and vowels will be treated separately in this inventory.

2.1 Consonants.

2.1.1. Consonantal phonemes and graphemes are as shown in Table 1. The eighteen consonantal phonemes of *A* correspond to seventeen graphemes. The laryngeal stop /'/ does not have its own sign but is expressed, or may be recognized, by the following:

- graphic vowel doubling (or "breaking" of vowels) (e.g., ⲕⲁⲁ⸗ϥ, to place him)
- syllabic structure /*voiceless consonant* + *voiced consonant* + ə/ (cf. 1.2.7: ⲟⲩⲁⲁⲃⲉ†, ⲟⲩⲁⲃⲉ†, i.e., /wa'b(ə)/)
- vowel narrowing /ē/ > /i:/ (ⲣⲏ, ⲣⲓ; cf. 1.2.3), /ō/ > /u:/ (ⲕⲱ, ⲕⲟⲩ; cf. 1.2.4)
- the postconsonantal first-person singular suffix pronoun (ⲕⲁⲁ⸗ⲧ, to place me, i.e., /ka't/)

The phonetic articulation of /ƀ/ ⲃ is disputed; Vergote assigns it to the bilabial category, but see his *Grammaire copte* (1973, Vol. 1a, sec. 28).

ⲅ and ⲇ appear only in Greek loanwords. The replacement of ⲕ by ⲅ in the unstressed syllable ⲛⲅ (e.g., *S* ⲙⲟⲩⲛ̄ⲕ, ⲙⲟⲩⲛ̄ⲅ, to form) is foreign to *A*. Except in Greek loanwords, ⲍ is not represented in *A*, since ⲁⲛⲍⲏⲃⲉ (or variously ⲁⲛⲥⲏⲃⲉ), school, is not attested in Akhmimic.

ⲫ, ⲑ, and ⲭ are, as in *S* and *L*, monographic characters of the phoneme combinations /p + h/, /t + h/, and /k + h/. Only in Bohairic do aspirants corresponding to /p/, /t/, /k/ occur. The symbols ⲯ and ⲝ represent the phonemic combinations /p + s/ and /k + s/, e.g., ⲯⲓⲥ, nine, and ⲧⲉⲝⲉ (*S* ⲧⲁϭⲥⲉ, ⲧⲁⲕⲥⲉ), footprint. The graphemes (ⲟ)ⲩ and (ⲉ)ⲓ also serve to indicate those vowels, [u:] and [i:], which are homorganic with the voiced spirants.

Note that in causative verbs such as ϫⲡⲓⲟ, to cause to be ashamed (< *dj-špj*), ϫ may be interpreted in *A* as biphonemic /t + š/; compare *S*, *L* ϫⲡⲟ, *A* ⲧⳉⲡⲟ, *P* ⲧϧⲡⲟ, to bring forth (< *dj-ḫpr*).

2.1.2. Phonetic alterations of consonants.

2.1.2.1. Assimilation: *n* before *p* > *mp* is not standardized, e.g., *n-p* appears side by side with *m-p* (ϩⲛ̄ ⲡⲏⲉⲓ as well as ϩⲙ̄ ⲡⲏⲉⲓ [not in EpAp.], ⲉⲛ ⲡⲉ side by side with ⲉⲙ ⲡⲉ [rare, I Clem.]); *n* before *m* > *mm* (rare), ⲧⲙ̄ⲙⲟⲩϩ, and we fill (Prov. 13:1); *s* before *š* > *šš*, ⲥϣⲉ appears side by side with ϣϣⲉ, it is fitting.

2.1.2.2. Dissimilation: *mm* > *nm*, ⲙ̄ⲙⲁ⸗ (*status pronominalis* of ⲛ̄-) *A* (standard) versus ⲛ̄ⲙⲁ⸗ (EpAp.); *mp* > *np:* ⲙ̄ⲡⲉ- (negative first perfect) *A* (standard) versus ⲛ̄ⲡⲉ- (EpAp.).

2.1.2.3. Partial depalatalization: *k'* /c/ before *s* > *ks*, *S*, *L* ⲛⲟⲩϭⲥ, *A* ⲛⲟⲩⲕⲥ, to be wroth; *S* ϥⲟϭⲥ̄, *A* ϥⲁⲕⲥ̄, leap; *S* ⲧⲟϭⲥ̄, *A* ⲧⲁⲕⲥ̄, seat.

2.1.2.4. Metathesis: ⲡⲱϩⲥ̄ side by side with ⲡⲱⲥϩ̄, to bite; ⲱⳉⲥ̄ side by side with ⲱⲥⳉ̄, to reap.

2.2 Vowels.

2.2.1 The vocalic phoneme inventory. A new and comprehensive system of Coptic vowel phonemes, especially modified for the separate dialects, has been proposed by Vergote (1973, Vol. 1a, sec. 60–65, *A* sec. 62). According to the phonemic system developed by Satzinger (1979), vocalic phonemes appear always as carriers of the stressed syllable. "All vocalic articulation outside of the stressed syllable may be explained as consonantal phonemes or as anaptyctic vowels which emerge according to specific rules" (ibid. p. 344). While Satzinger's system has

TABLE 1. *Consonants of Akhmimic*

	BILABIAL	LABIO-DENTAL	DENTAL	PRE-PALATAL	POST-PALATAL	LARYNGEAL
Voiceless stops	/p/ ⲡ		/t/ⲧ	/č/,/c/ ϫ, ϭ	/k/ ⲕ	/'/ e.g., ⲁⲁ
Voiceless spirants		/f/ ϥ	/s/ⲥ	/š/ ϣ	/x/ ⳉ	/h/ ϩ
Voiced spirants	/w/ (ⲟ)ⲩ	/ƀ/ ⲃ		/j/ (ⲉ)ⲓ		
Nasals	/m/ ⲙ		/n/ ⲛ			
Laterals/vibrants			/l/ ⲗ,/r/ⲣ			

BASED ON: Vergote, 1973, Vol. 1a, pp. 13, 15.

the advantage of greater clarity, it ignores morphophonological connections. The result is that all morphemes that in the co-text do not function as the main stressed syllables remain unconsidered. The following summary relies on Vergote's analysis but does not treat all possible phonetic articulations. [ə] as an anaptyctic vowel in closed syllables, with or without a sonorant, is not considered a phoneme (otherwise Hintze, 1980; cf. 1.2.7).

2.2.1.1. Short vowels:

/a/ ⲁ: ⲃⲁⲧⲉ, abomination; ⲥⲁⲛ, brother. Articulated before laryngeals and in stressed final position as [ˈo] (ⲟ), as in ϩⲟ, thousand; ⲧⲉⲕⲟ, to destroy; ϩⲟⲟⲡ†, to be; ⲟⲟϩ, moon; but ⲟⲩⲁⲁⲃⲉ†, to be holy.

/e/ ⲉ: ⲡⲉϣⲉ, half; ⲣⲉⲛ, name. Articulated as [ə] before a sonorant concluding a syllable or before continuants, as in ⲃⲗ̄ϫⲉ, shard, pottery; ⲥⲃ̄ⲃⲉ, to circumcise; ⲧⲥ̄ⲧⲟ, to bring back.

/ə/ ⲉ: in unstressed initial, medial, and final sounds, but not as an anaptyctic vowel: ⲉⲁ́ⲩ, glory; ϭⲉⲥⲏ́ϭ, hunter; ⲣⲱ́ⲙⲉ, man, as opposed to ϩⲱⲧⲃⲉ /xōtb̩(ə)/, to kill; ⲧⲁϩⲙⲉ /tahmə/, to call you (fem. sing.), as opposed to ⲧⲁϩⲙⲉ† /tahm̩(ə)/ to be invited.

2.2.1.2. Long vowels:

/ī/ ⲓ, ⲉⲓ: ⲉⲓⲛⲉ, to bring; ⲙⲓⲥⲉ, to bear; ϫⲓ, to receive.

/ē/ ⲏ: ⲕⲏⲙⲉ, Egypt; ⲃⲏⲕ†, going; ⲛⲏⲧⲛⲉ, to you (pl.); ⲏⲣⲡ̄, wine. Articulated before laryngeals and at the ends of words as [i:]: ⲙⲓⲉ, truth; ⲟⲩϩⲓ, night; /hēp/ ϩⲏⲡ†, to be hidden, as opposed to /kē'/ ⲕⲉⲓ†, to be laid.

Note that according to Vergote, ⲏ [ˈe:] is an allophone of [i:] before and after sonorants (ϭⲉⲣⲏϭ, ⲛⲏⲧⲛⲉ).

/ō/ ⲱ: ⲕⲱⲧ, to build; ⲡⲱⲧ, to run; ⲣⲱⲕϩ̄, to burn; thereto the allophone [u:] (ⲟⲩ) after /m/ and /n/ before laryngeals and when final, as in ⲙⲟⲩ(ⲛ)ⲧⲉ, to call; ⲛⲟⲩ(ⲛ)ⲧⲉ, God; ⲕⲟⲩ, to place; ⲡⲣⲟⲩ, winter; but ⲙ̄ⲙⲱⲧⲛⲉ.

/ū/ ⲟⲩ: ϩⲟⲩⲛ, interior; ⲥⲟⲩⲣⲉ, thorn; ⲧⲟⲩⲛⲟⲩⲉⲓⲉⲧ⸗ (ⲁⲃⲁⲗ), to reveal (this last is different in Vergote, 1973, Vol. 1a, sec. 56).

2.2.1.3. Contraction vowel:

/ew/ ⲟ, ⲱ only in final sounds after /m/ and /n/: ⲙⲟ, ⲙⲱ mother; ⲛⲟ, to see; ⲙ̄ⲙⲟ, there. The written variations ⲙⲟ, ⲙⲱ do not indicate the neutralization of a supposed opposition *o versus ō, since in the *A* vocalic system [o] does not appear as a phoneme, but exists only as an allophone of /a/.

Note that ⲱ for ⲟ occurs occasionally as the final sound /-a'/ of the causative verb ⲧⲁϣⲱ, to increase (I Clem. 59:3, p. 77,9; Elias 33:9).

2.2.2. Vocalic opposition dependent upon syllabic structure (long-short opposition).

/ō/, /a/: /kōt/ ⲕⲱⲧ, to build, /katf/ ⲕⲁⲧϥ̄, to build it (masc.). /pōrx/ ⲡⲱⲣϩ̄, to spread out, /parxf/ ⲡⲁⲣϩⲉϥ, to spread it (masc.) out. /mōnk/ ⲙⲟⲩⲛⲕ̄, to form, /mankf/ ⲙⲁⲛⲕⲉϥ, to form it (masc.). /mōr/ ⲙⲟⲩⲣ, to bind, /marf/ ⲙⲁⲣϥ̄, to bind it (masc.). Before laryngeals: /xōpə/ ϩⲱⲡⲉ, to become, /xo'p/ ϩⲟⲟⲡ†, to be.

Note that in the *status nominalis*, /a/ before a sonorant is reduced to [ə]: ⲙⲣ̄, to bind someone/something; ⲡⲣ̄ϩ-, to spread out someone/something.

/ū/, /a/: /nhūt=/ ⲛ̄ϩⲟⲩⲧ⸗, to trust, /nhat/ ⲛ̄ϩⲁⲧ†, trusting (there are no further examples).

/ē/, /e/: /nētn̩(ə)/ ⲛⲏⲧⲛⲉ, to you (pl.), /nek/ ⲛⲉⲕ, to you (sing. masc.). /cərēc/ ϭⲉⲣⲏϭ, hunter, /cərecə/ ϭⲉⲣⲉϭⲉ, hunters.

/ī/, /e/: /mərit/ ⲙⲉⲣⲓⲧ, beloved (one), /məretə/ ⲙⲉⲣⲉⲧⲉ, beloved (ones). /mīsə/ ⲙⲓⲥⲉ, to bear, /mestf/ ⲙⲉⲥⲧϥ̄, to bear him. Before a sonorant, /ī/ disappears and the sonorant becomes sonant and syllabic: /cīnə/ ϭⲓⲛⲉ, to find, /cn̩təf/ ϭⲛ̄ⲧⲉϥ, to find him.

Vocalic opposition is summarized in Table 2.

3. The Conjugation System

The summary of the system is based on Polotsky (1960) and Funk (1981). Except in special instances (e.g., conjunctive), the form cited here is only the third-person masculine singular and the corresponding prenominal form (nom. = before nominal subject). The entire paradigm is not attested in all conjugations.

Unless specifically mentioned, the form is affirmative (neg. = negative). Every basic tense (abbreviated hereafter to "basic") is followed (if attested) by its satellites, after "And": circ. = circumstantial, rel. = relative, pret. = preterite, II = second tense. Forms

TABLE 2. *Summary of Vocalic Opposition*

LONG	SHORT	LONG
CLOSED/DARK	OPEN/CLEAR	OPEN/CLEAR
/ō/ⲱ	/a/ⲁ /e/ⲉ	/ī/ⲉⲓ, ⲓ
/ū/ⲟⲩ		/ē/ⲏ

between brackets [. . .] are reconstituted from very similar forms (zero = no verbal prefix, no particle, etc.).

3.1 Bipartite Pattern.

3.1.1. *Present* (basic) ϥ-, nom. zero. And circ. ⲉϥ-, nom. ⲉ- or ⲉⲣⲉ- (cf. Polotsky, 1960, sec. 55); rel. ⲉⲧ- or ⲉⲧϥ- resp., nom. ⲉⲧⲉ- or ⲉⲧⲉⲣⲉ-; pret. ⲛⲁϥ- . . . (ⲡⲉ; also ⲛⲉϥ-, Ex. 1:5, by influence of *S* ?), nom. ⲛⲁ- (Jn. 12,2; ⲛⲁ- see also second perfect) or ⲛⲁⲣⲉ- . . . (ⲡⲉ); II ⲁϥ- (with ϫⲉ, ϫⲁïⲛⲏⲩ, I Clem. 48:2), nom. ⲁ- or ⲁⲣ- or ⲁⲣⲉ- (cf. Polotsky, 1960, sec. 55).

3.1.2. Future (basic) ϥⲛⲁ-, nom. zero . . . ⲛⲁ-. And circ. ⲉϥⲛⲁ-, nom. ⲉ- . . . ⲛⲁ-; rel. ⲉⲧⲛⲁ- or ⲉⲧϥⲛⲁ-, nom. ⲉⲧⲉ- . . . ⲛⲁ-; pret. ⲛⲁϥⲛⲁ- . . . ⲡⲉ (in the apodosis of the hypothetical form = *Irrealis*); II ⲁϥⲛⲁ-, nom. ⲁ- . . . ⲛⲁ- or ⲁⲣⲉ- . . . ⲛⲁ- (second feminine singular ⲁⲣⲁ-, I Clem. 20:7, cf. Polotsky, 1960, sec. 59; second masculine singular also ⲉⲕⲛⲁ-, EpAp. 23,4; with ϫⲉ, ϫⲁϥⲛⲁ-, first plural ϫⲁⲛⲛⲁ-, I Clem. 58:1; second masculine singular also ϫⲉⲕⲛⲁ-, Prv. 5:2; nom. ϫⲁ- . . . ⲛⲁ-, Prv. 3:22, but ϫⲉ ⲁ- . . . ⲛⲁ-, Prv. 3:10; nom. ⲁ(ⲣⲉ)- . . . ⲛⲁ-; cf. Polotsky, 1960, sec. 55).

3.2 Tripartite Pattern.

3.2.1 Tenses with special negations (if not II). Independent (sentence) conjugations.

3.2.1.1. *Perfect* (basic) ⲁϥ- (second feminine singular ⲁⲣ-), nom. ⲁ-; neg. ⲙ̄ⲡϥ̄-, nom. ⲙ̄ⲡⲉ- (in EpAp. a dissimilative ⲛ̄ⲡϥ̄-, nom. ⲛ̄ⲡⲉ-). And circ. ⲉⲁϥ-, nom. ⲉⲁ-; neg. ⲉⲙⲡϥ̄-; rel. ⲉⲧⲁϥ- or ⲉⲧⲁϩ-, nom. ⲉⲧⲁ- (to the ⲉⲧⲁϩ-group belong EpAp.; Elias; Ex. 2:14, 4:11; I Clem.; Jn.; and Ost.; nevertheless, the inflected form ⲉⲧⲁ⸗ also appears in these texts under identical syntactic conditions; ⲡⲉⲛⲧⲁϥ-, Prv. 18:22, and ⲛ̄ⲧⲁϥ-, Elias 22:11, are to be considered as influenced by *S*); II ⲛⲁϥ-, nom. ⲛⲁ- (Polotsky [1937 and 1944] is to be credited with the discovery of the Akhmimic second perfect; it is found with a derivative of the second degree only in the protasis of the hypothetical form = *Irrealis,* ⲉⲛⲁⲩⲙⲁϩⲉ, if they had gone, Prv. 2:20), also ⲉⲁϥ- (I Clem. 31:3), [ⲉⲧⲁϥ-] (I Clem. 32:3, ⲛⲉï ϭⲉ ⲧⲏⲣⲟⲩ ⲉⲧⲁⲩϫⲓ ⲉⲁⲩ ⲁⲟⲩ ⲁⲩϫⲓⲥⲉ ⲁⲃⲁⲗ ϩⲓⲧⲟⲟⲧⲟⲩ ⲉⲛ ⲏ ϩⲓⲧⲛ̄ ⲛⲟⲩϩⲃⲏⲟⲩⲉ ⲛ̄ⲇⲓⲕⲁⲓⲟⲥⲩⲛⲏ ⲉⲧⲁⲩⲉⲩⲉ ⲁⲗⲗⲁ ϩⲓⲧⲙ̄ ⲡⲉϥⲟⲩⲱϩⲉ, "Now all of these are glorified and elevated, not through themselves nor through their works of righteousness which they did, but through his will"; cf. second perfect of *B*).

3.2.1.2. *Completive* (basic) (it is unknown whether the expected affirmative substitute *ⲁϥⲟⲩⲟⲩ ⲉϥ- is simply not attested or actually does not exist in *A;* the passage cited in Crum, 1937, 373b, Hos. 13:2, is not pertinent: ⲁⲩ⟨ⲟⲩ⟩ⲟⲩ, they perished, is a finite verb form in the first perfect; on the completive as a formal category, affirmative substitute *S* ⲁϥⲟⲩⲱ ⲉϥ-, has already . . . , neg. ⲙ̄ⲡⲁⲧϥ̄-, has not yet . . . , see Funk, 1981, pp. 191–94); neg. ⲙ̄ⲡⲁⲧϥ̄- (in EpAp. a dissimilative [ⲛ̄ⲡⲁⲧϥ̄-], third plural ⲛ̄ⲡⲁⲧⲟⲩ-), nom. ⲙ̄ⲡⲁⲧⲉ- (EpAp. [ⲛ̄ⲡⲁⲧⲉ-] not attested). And circ. neg. ⲉⲙⲡⲁⲧϥ̄-, nom. ⲉⲙⲡⲁⲧⲉ-.

3.2.1.3. *Aorist* (basic) ϩⲁⲣⲉϥ- (second plural ϩⲁⲣⲉⲧⲉⲧⲛ̄-, Hg. 2:16), nom. ϩⲁⲣⲉ-; neg. ⲙⲁϥ-, nom. ⲙⲁⲣⲉ- or ⲙⲁ- (cf. Polotsky, 1960, sec. 55). And circ. ⲉϩⲁⲣⲉϥ-, nom. ⲉϩⲁⲣⲉ-; neg. ⲉⲙⲁϥ-; rel. ⲉⲧϩⲁⲣⲉϥ-, nom. ⲉⲧϩⲁⲣⲉ-; neg. ⲉⲧⲉⲙⲁϥ- (Prv. 14:23); pret. [ⲛⲉϩⲁⲣⲉϥ-] third plural ⲛⲉϩⲁⲣⲟⲩ-; II ⲁϩⲁⲣⲉϥ- (Elias 38:13), nom. ⲁϩⲁⲣⲉ- (Prv. 11:10, 19:14, also ⲉϩⲁⲣⲉ-, Prv. 19:15 by influence of *S*?).

3.2.1.4. *Futurum energicum* (or third future) (basic) ⲁϥⲁ-, nom. ⲁ-; neg. ⲛⲉϥ- (also ⲉⲛⲉϥ-, Sir. 22,19), nom. ⲛⲉ-; with ϫⲉ, ϫⲁϥⲁ-, nom. ϫⲁ-; neg. [ϫⲛ̄ⲛⲉϥ-] (e.g., third feminine singular ϫⲛ̄ⲛⲉⲥ-, Lk. 18:5), nom. ϫⲛ̄ⲛⲉ- (Elias, I Clem.).

3.2.1.5. *Imperative,* e.g., ⲉⲛⲟ, see! (Ex. 4:13; for imperative with preformatives, see Till, 1928, sec. 147d); or infinitive; or ⲙⲁ + ⲧ-causative (no attestation among ⲧ-causative verbs of an imperative constructed simply from an infinitive); neg. ⲙⲛ̄- + infinitive; also ⲙ̄ⲡⲱⲣ ⲁ-, ApocSoph. 10,6. (this form is also common in *L4* and *L6* [Nag Hammadi]; ⲙ̄ⲡⲱⲣ ϩⲓⲛⲏⲃ, do not sleep (pl.), *A* Ost. A 10, is highly questionable, probably an erroneous writing of ⲙ̄ⲡⲱⲣ ⲁ-).

3.2.1.6. *Causative imperative* ⲙⲁⲣⲉϥ-, nom. ⲙⲁⲣⲉ-, absolute ⲙⲁⲣⲁⲛ (Mi. 4:2); neg. ⲙⲛ̄ⲧϥ̄-, nom. ⲙⲛ̄ⲧⲉ-.

3.2.2 Tenses with neg. ⲧⲙ̄(ⲛ̄)-. Subordinate (clause) conjugations.

3.2.2.1. *Conjunctive* (singular first, second masc./fem., third masc./fem., plural first, second, third) ⲧⲁ-, ⲕ-, ⲧⲉ-, ϥ- (also ⲛ̄ⲧϥ̄-, EpAp. 2,14), ⲥ-, ⲧⲛ̄-, ⲧⲉⲧⲛ̄-, ⲥⲉ- (or ⲥⲟⲩ-, EpAp. 6,7), nom. ⲧⲉ-.

3.2.2.2. *Future conjunctive* ⲧⲁⲣⲉϥ- (second plural ⲧⲁⲣⲉⲧⲉⲧⲛ̄-), nom. ⲧⲁⲣⲉ-.

3.2.2.3. *Temporal:* Group I ⲛ̄ⲧⲁⲣⲉϥ-, nom. ⲛ̄ⲧⲁⲣⲉ- (Jn.; Herm.; Prv.; ApocSoph. 11,2; Elias; EpAp. 3,14, 19,10); Group II ⲧⲁⲣⲉϥ-, nom. ⲧⲁⲣⲉ- (I Clem., Ex., EpAp., MinProph.).

3.2.2.4. *Limitative* ("until . . .") ϣⲁⲧϥ̄- (first singular ϣⲁϯ-), nom. ϣⲁⲧⲉ- (also ϣⲁⲛⲧⲉ-, ApocSoph. 18,5).

3.2.2.5. *First conditional* ⲁϥϣⲁ- (also ⲉϥϣⲁ-, I Clem.; second plural ⲁϣⲁⲧⲉⲧⲛ̄-, also I Clem., but once ⲉϣⲁⲧⲉⲧⲛ̄-, I Clem. 63:2), nom. ⲁϣⲁ- (also ⲉϣⲁ-, I Clem.).

3.2.2.6. *Second conditional* [ⲁϥ-] (only second plural ⲁⲧⲉⲧⲛ̄-, Zec. 6:15. The conjugation here referred to as second conditional is that termed "simple" conditional by Funk [1981, p. 197], in contrast to his "expanded" conditional constructed with ϣⲁ (*S* ϣⲁⲛ). That the "protatic" ⲉϥⲥⲱⲧⲙ̄ belongs to the tripartite conjugation was discovered by Shisha-Halevy, 1974. Affirmative forms are notoriously rare in literary texts. The protatic ⲁϥⲥⲱⲧⲙⲉ does not occur in clauses beginning with ⲉⲓϩⲡⲉ and is only to be distinguished from the second present when it may be defined by its syntactic behavior as a (tripartite) subordinate conjugation. Neg. first singular ⲁⲓⲧⲙ̄-, Mi. 3:8; second masculine singular ⲁⲕⲧⲙ̄ⲛ-, EpAp. 40,12,14; third plural ⲁⲩⲧⲙ̄-, Ex. 4:8).

3.2.2.7. *Causative infinitive* -ⲧⳉ-, nom. -ⲧⲉ- (second plural -ⲧⲉⲧⲉⲧⲛ̄-, Mal. 1,7, or -ⲧⲉⲧⲛ̄-, Mal. 2:17; ⲁⲡⲧⲉⲧⲛ̄-, Prv. 24:23; also -ⲧⲣⲉⲧⲉⲧⲛ̄-; concerning the second plural, see Polotsky, 1960, sec. 56; unique in *A* third masculine singular ⲁⲧⲣⲉ[ϥ-], Lk. 12:49, influenced by *L*).

4. Categorization Within Standard Akhmimic

The Akhmimic literary texts exhibit a high degree of standardization. Disregarding sporadic deviations which may occur within the same texts, four criteria may be taken for an attempt at classification:

1. dissimilation *m/m* and *m/p* → *n/m* and *n/p:* (1.1.1) ⲙ̄ⲙⲟ, there → ⲛ̄ⲙⲟ, EpAp. 12:13, 28:14, 29:7; (1.1.2) ⲙ̄ⲙⲁ⸗ → ⲛ̄ⲙⲁ⸗, EpAp. 1:5, 13; 19:1, 12; 17:7; 29:12; (1.2.1) ⲙ̄ⲡⲉ-, neg. perf. → ⲛ̄ⲡⲉ-, EpAp. (ⲙ̄ⲡⲟⲩ-, 25:3); (1.2.2) ⲙ̄ⲡⲁⲧⲉ-, neg. completive → *ⲛ̄ⲡⲁⲧⲉ-, EpAp. (ⲛ̄ⲡⲁⲧⲟⲩ-, 36:4)
2. the uninflected relative form of the perfect ⲉⲧⲁϩ- (as opposed to ⲉⲧⲁ⸗)
3. the temporal conjugation ⲧⲁⲣⲉ- (as opposed to ⲛ̄ⲧⲁⲣⲉ-)
4. the variant lexical appearance of the conditional particle "if (it happens that . . .)" ϩⲡⲉ, ⲉⲓϩⲡⲉ

The criterion noted first pertains only to EpAp. This phonetic feature is supplemented by the fact that the assimilation *n/p→m/p* very rarely occurs at morpheme junctures in this text, the standard for a morpheme juncture in EpAp. being the unassimilated form (ϩⲛ̄ ⲡⲏⲉⲓ, etc.).

The distribution of the remaining distinctive forms may be represented in Table 3. Where ⲉⲧⲁϩ- and ⲉⲧⲁ⸗, ⲧⲁⲣⲉ- and ⲛ̄ⲧⲁⲣⲉ-, occur simultaneously, the second form is to be considered as unmarked.

A special group is constituted by I Clem., Ex., EpAp., and Elias, which possess three common features. EpAp., moreover, is distinguished by dissimilation in its labial features. In I Clem., a distinction is still to be made between the conditional particle in Old Testament quotations and its form outside of such quotations (see footnote to Table 3). At the opposite end of the spectrum is Proverbs, which is the one Akhmimic text characterized only by the conditional particle ϩⲡⲉ while lacking ⲉⲧⲁϩ-, ⲧⲁⲣⲉ-, and ⲉⲓϩⲡⲉ. John and the Minor Prophets assume a middle position: ⲉⲓϩⲡⲉ occurs in both, but John also

TABLE 3.

	ⲉⲧⲁϩ-	ⲧⲁⲣⲉ-	ⲉⲓϩⲡⲉ	ϩⲡⲉ
I Clem.(R)	–	–	+	–
I Clem.	+	+	+[a]	+[a]
Ex.	+	+	+	–
EpAp.	+	+	+	–
Elias	+	+	+	–
Jn.	+	–	+	–
Prv.	–	–	–	+
MinProph.	–	+	+	–
Ost.	+	Temporal not attested	+	–

[a]The attestations of ⲉⲓϩⲡⲉ and ϩⲡⲉ are distributed in the *Berliner Handschrift* for I Clem. as follows:
ⲉⲓϩⲡⲉ: p. 36, 18 (I Clem. 27:7); p. 69, 8 (I Clem. 54:2).
ϩⲡⲉ: p. 11, 18 (I Clem. 8:4 = Is. 1:18); 13, 29 (I Clem. 10:5 = Gn. 13:16); p. 14, 5 (I Clem. 10:6 = Gn. 15:5); p. 23, 12 (I Clem. 16:16 = Ps. 21:9 LXX); p. 23, 14 (I Clem. 16:17).
The form ϩⲡⲉ is used in four out of five passages that cite the Old Testament, whereas ⲉⲓϩⲡⲉ occurs only outside of such quotations. The remaining form ϩⲡⲉ on p. 23,14 may have been attracted to the identical form on p. 23,12. In I Clem., therefore, two levels of language can be recognized in the case of the conditional particle.

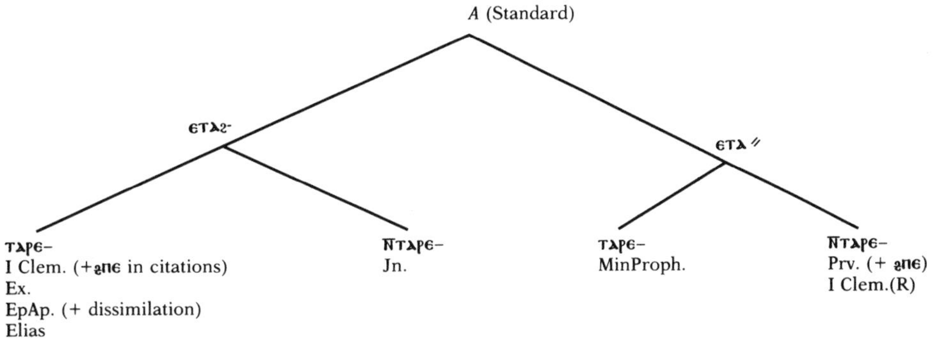

FIGURE 1. ⲉⲧⲁϩ, ⲉⲧⲁ⸗.

employs ⲉⲧⲁϩ- and ⲛ̄ⲧⲁⲣⲉ-, while the text of the Minor Prophets uses ⲉⲧⲁ⸗ and ⲧⲁⲣⲉ-. The position of Ost., which employs ⲉⲧⲁϩ- and ⲉⲓϩⲡⲉ, remains uncertain because of the lack of a form of the temporal. The most strongly neutralized document is I Clem. (R) in which no distinctive form (ⲉⲧⲁϩ-, ⲧⲁⲣⲉ-, or ϩⲡⲉ) appears.

A summary by morphological characteristics appears in Figures 1 and 2. Both types of morphological classification lead to the same "extreme" groups: I Clem., EpAp., Ex., and Elias, on the one hand, and I Clem.(R) and Prv., on the other. Jn. and MinProph. have no distinguishing features in common with the other main groups, but form a class of their own.

5. Akhmimoid Texts

5.1. A number of literary and nonliterary texts (e.g., letters, magical texts) have traditionally been designated Akhmimic:

5.1.1 Literary texts. The Ascension of Isaiah (AscIs.) = Lacau, 1946. The Berlin Genesis fragment, P. 8773 (Gn. 1:18–2:5, fragmentary) = Leipoldt, 1904. Gal. 5:11–6:1 = Browne, 1979 (pp. 19–21). The Hymn [of Hierakas] = Lefort, 1939. Ps. 46:3–10 LXX, a pupil's exercise on a wood tablet = Crum, 1934.

5.1.2 Letters. Listed by Simon, 1940, p. 201, with footnotes 30–31.

5.1.3 Magical texts. Same as above, with footnote 32; Ernštedt, 1959, no. 70.

5.2. The literary texts AscIs., Berlin Genesis, and the Hymn were previously described by Kahle (1954, pp. 203–205) as "Akhmimic with Subakhmimic [that is, *L*] influence," with AscIs. and Genesis forming a group of their own. The latter texts were shown by Kasser to be early forms of the dialect *L* (see especially Kasser, 1979b and 1982b, in which AscIs. and Genesis are referred to as *İ* and *İ7*, respectively; see also Funk, 1987). AscIs. and the Berlin Genesis have definitely to be eliminated from the body of Akhmimic texts, as does the Hymn of Hierakas, which corresponds more closely to *İ7* (and *L*) than to *A* ($\underline{h}$ > /š/ ϣⲱⲡⲉ : *h* > /x/ ϩⲛ̄-, without an anaptyctic vowel in the syllable /CR/ [= *voiceless consonant + voiced consonant or son(or)ant*], second perfect ⲛⲁⲩ-; vocalization of the stressed syllable as in *L*) or to Galatians (see Kasser and Satzinger, 1982).

5.3. Akhmimic Psalm 46, which is characterized by irregular orthography, is to be considered an early form of *L* rather than *A*, since none of the dialectical features of Akhmimic are distinctly marked: e.g., ⲁⲩⲱ, and not ⲁⲟⲩ (see 1.4.1.1); ⲃⲁⲁⲃ†, to be holy

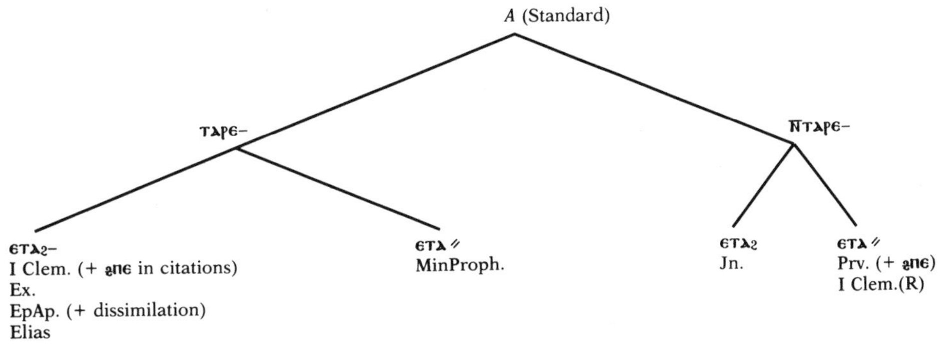

FIGURE 2. ⲧⲁⲣⲉ, ⲛ̄ⲧⲁⲣⲉ.

(for *ⲟⲩⲗⲁⲃ†) and not ⲃⲗⲁⲃⲉ† (see 1.2.7); ⲟⲩⲟⲧⲉ (for *ⲟⲩϩⲟⲧⲉ) and not ⲟⲩ(ϩ)ⲁⲧⲉ, (he is) fearful. In this connection, it is noteworthy that instead of the Akhmimic ϩⲛⲱ(ⲱ)ϩⲉ, fear, the *S (L)* lexeme ϩⲟⲧⲉ (ϩⲁⲧⲉ) is employed.

5.4. The nonliterary texts were delineated earlier by Simon (1940) as Akhmimic with Sahidic influence, or *As* (for the letters) and *"As vulgaire,"* or vulgar Akhmimic with Sahidic influence (for the magical texts). While detailed evidence cannot be offered here, it should be pointed out that the Meletian letter Pap. 1921 (between 330 and 340 A.D.; ed. Crum, in Bell, 1924) clearly belongs to *L*, as does the letter from the John Rylands Library, no. 396, which was claimed by Crum (1909, p. viii) as an example of "a practically pure Akhmimic" text.

5.5. It may be concluded that the more or less Akhmimoid texts should no longer be counted with the corpus of texts written in the Akhmimic dialect, not even with the mitigating addition of a small *s*, which is to indicate Sahidic influence. This means, furthermore, that the *A* dialect is only represented by literary texts (i.e., biblical, apocryphal, and patristic) and that, finally, "Akhmimic" is identical to "standard Akhmimic." The Akhmimic texts are exclusively documents translated from Greek or Sahidic. Just for the most comprehensive texts (MinProph., Prv.) it has been shown that they represent interlinear versions of Sahidic (Till, 1927b, p. xxx; Böhlig, 1936, p. 35).

BIBLIOGRAPHY

Bell, H. I. *Jews and Christians in Egypt.* London, 1924.

Böhlig, A. *Untersuchungen über die koptischen Proverbientexte.* Stuttgart, 1936.

______. *Der achmimische Proverbientext nach Ms. Berol. orient. oct. 987.* Munich, 1958.

Browne, G. M. *Michigan Coptic Texts.* Barcelona, 1979.

Crum, W. E. *Catalogue of the Coptic Manuscripts in the Collection of the John Rylands Library, Manchester.* Manchester, 1909.

______. "Un Psaume en dialecte d'Akhmîm." *Mémoires de l'Institut français d'archéologie orientale* 67 (1934):73–86.

______. *A Coptic Dictionary.* Oxford, 1939.

Ernštedt, P. V. *Koptskie teksty Gos. Ėrmitaža.* Moscow and Leningrad, 1959.

Funk, W. P. "Beiträge des mittelägyptischen Dialekts zum koptischen Konjugationssystem." In *Studies Presented to Hans Jakob Polotsky,* ed. D. W. Young, pp. 177–210. Beacon Hill, Mass., 1981.

______. "Koptische Isoglossen im oberägyptischen Raum 1, ⲉϣϫⲉ 'wenn', etc." *Zeitschrift für ägyptische Sprache und Altertumskunde* 112 (1985):19–24.

______. "Die Zeugen des koptischen Literaturdialekts İ7." *Zeitschrift für ägyptische Sprache und Altertumskunde* 114 (1987):117–33.

Hintze, F. "Zur koptischen Phonologie." *Enchoria* 10 (1980):23–91.

Kahle, P. E. *Bala'izah: Coptic Texts from Deir el-Bala'izah in Upper Egypt.* Oxford and London, 1954.

Kasser, R. *Papyrus Bodmer VI: Livre des Proverbes.* CSCO 194–195. Louvain, 1960.

______. *Compléments au dictionnaire copte de Crum.* Bibliothèque d'études coptes 7. Cairo, 1964.

______. "Un Lexème copte oublié, ⲧⲕⲏⲛ akhmîmique (Nahum 3,19)." *Bulletin de la Société d'égyptologie, Genève* 1 (1979a):23–25.

______. "Relations de généalogie dialectale dans le domaine lycopolitain." *Bulletin de la Société d'égyptologie, Genève* 2 (1979b):31–36.

______. "Le Dialecte protosaïdique de Thèbes." *Archiv für Papyrusforschung* 28 (1982a):67–81.

______. "Un Nouveau Document protolycopolitain." *Orientalia* 51 (1982b):30–38.

______. "Le Grand-Groupe dialectal copte de Haute-Egypte." *Bulletin de la Société d'égyptologie, Genève* 7 (1982c):47–72.

Kasser, R., and H. Satzinger. "L'Idiome du P. Mich. 5421 (trouvé à Karanis, nord-est du Fayoum)." *Wiener Zeitschrift für die Kunde des Morgenlandes* 74 (1982):15–32.

Lacau, P. "Textes coptes en dialectes akhmîmique et sahidique." *Bulletin de l'Institut français d'archéologie orientale* 8 (1911):43–81.

______. "Fragments de l'Ascension d'Isaïe en copte." *Muséon* 59 (1946):453–57.

Lefort, L. T. "Fragments d'apocryphes en copte-akhmîmique." *Muséon* 52 (1939):1–10.

______. *Les Pères apostoliques en copte.* CSCO 135–136. Louvain, 1952.

______. "Fragments bibliques en dialecte akhmîmique." *Muséon* 66 (1953):1–30.

[Leipoldt, J.]. *Aegyptische Urkunden aus den koeniglichen Museen zu Berlin, herausgegeben von der Generalverwaltung, koptische und arabische Urkunden.* Berlin, 1904.

Malinine, M. "Fragments d'une version achmimique des Petits Prophètes." *Bulletin of the Byzantine Institute* 2 (1950):365–415.

Polotsky, H. J. "Deux auxiliaires méconnus en copte." *Comptes rendus du Groupe linguistique d'études chamito-sémitiques* 3 (1937):1–3.

______. *Etudes de syntaxe copte.* Cairo, 1944.

______. "The Coptic Conjugation System." *Orientalia* 29 (1960):392–422.

Rösch, F. *Bruchstücke des ersten Clemensbriefes nach dem achmimischen Papyrus der Strassburger Universitäts- und Landesbibliothek, mit biblischen Texten derselben Handschrift.* Strasbourg, 1910.

Satzinger, H. "Phonologie des koptischen Verbs (sa'idischer Dialekt)." *Festschrift Elmar Edel,* ed. A. Wuckelt and K.-J. Seyfried, pp. 343–68. Bamberg, 1979.

Schmidt, C. *Acta Pauli aus der Heidelberger koptischen Papyrushandschrift Nr. 1.* Leipzig, 1904.

______. *Der erste Clemensbrief in altkoptischer Übersetzung.* Texte und Untersuchungen 32. Leipzig, 1908.

______. "Ein neues Fragment der Heidelberger Acta Pauli." In *Sitzungsberichte der Berliner Akademie der Wissenschaften, Philosophisch-Historische Klasse,* pp. 216–220. Berlin, 1909.

______. *Gespräche Jesu mit seinen Jüngern nach der Auferstehung.* Texte und Untersuchungen 43. Leipzig, 1919.

Shisha-Halevy, A. "Protatic ⲉϥⲥⲱⲧⲙ̄, a Hitherto Unnoticed Coptic Tripartite Conjugation-Form and Its Diachronic Connections." *Orientalia* 43 (1974): 369–81.

______. "Akhmimoid Features in Shenoute's Idiolect." *Muséon* 89 (1976):157–80.

Simon, J. "Note sur le dossier des textes akhmîmiques." *Cinquantenaire de l'Ecole biblique et archéologique de Jérusalem, Mémorial [Marie Joseph] Lagrange,* pp. 197–201. Paris, 1940.

Steindorff, G. *Die Apokalypse des Elias, eine unbekannte Apokalypse und Bruchstücke der Sophonias-Apokalypse.* Texte und Untersuchungen 17. Leipzig, 1899.

Thompson, H. *The Gospel of St. John According to the Earliest Coptic Manuscript.* London, 1924.

Till, W. C. "Die Stellung des Achmîmischen." *Aegyptus* 8 (1927a):249–57.

______. *Die achmimische Version der zwölf kleinen Propheten (Codex Rainerianus, Wien).* Coptica 4. Copenhagen, 1927b.

______. *Achmimisch-koptische Grammatik.* Leipzig, 1928.

______. *Osterbrief und Predigt im achmimischen Dialekt.* Leipzig, 1931.

______. "Coptic Biblical Texts Published After Vaschalde's List." *Bulletin of the John Rylands Library* 42 (1959–1960):220–40.

Vaschalde, A. A. "Ce qui a été publié des versions coptes de la Bible, quatrième groupe, textes akhmîmiques." *Muséon* 46 (1933):306–313.

Vergote, J. *Grammaire copte,* Vol. 1a, *Introduction, phonétique et phonologie, morphologie synthématique (structure des sémantèmes), partie synchronique.* Louvain, 1973. Vol. 1b, *Introduction, phonétique et phonologie, morphologie synthématique (structure des sémantèmes), partie diachronique.* Louvain, 1973. Vol. 2a, *Morphologie syntagmatique, syntaxe, partie synchronique.* Louvain, 1983. Vol. 2b, *Morphologie syntagmatique, partie diachronique.* Louvain, 1983.

Westendorf, W. *Koptisches Handwörterbuch, bearbeitet auf Grund des Koptischen Handwörterbuchs von Wilhelm Spiegelberg.* Heidelberg, 1977.

Worrell, W. H. *Coptic Sounds.* Ann Arbor, Mich., 1934.

PETER NAGEL

ALEPH. Not only in Coptic but in other languages also, aleph (= /'/) is a consonant of a very special kind: it is certainly a laryngeal occlusive, but is it really unvoiced? For some, it clearly is (e.g., Vergote, 1973, Vol. 1a, pp. 12–13), while others hesitate to place it either among the unvoiced or among the voiced sounds, or resign themselves to putting it somewhere between the two (e.g., Dieth, 1950, p. 98; Dubois et al., 1973, p. 25; Kasser, 1981a). It is best thought of as a stop followed by an abrupt emission of sound, especially a stop separating two adjacent vowels, for instance at the beginning of a syllable after a hiatus (e.g., in "reenter" or in French "la haine" [la 'ɛn]), or as a "glottal stop" replacing a consonant hurried over in pronunciation (e.g., "wa'er" for "water"; cf. the Arabic hamza).

In Coptic, so far as it is really preserved, it is in every case a CRYPTOPHONEME (that is, a phoneme not rendered by any written letter of its own), and it is no doubt for this reason that its existence in this language has long been ignored or disputed; even today it is not universally accepted. For this reason, it occupies a very special place in the Coptic phonological inventory.

It is true that pharaonic Egyptian, down to its last full manifestation prior to Coptic (i.e. demotic), possessed both the phoneme aleph = *3* and the corresponding grapheme (the "Egyptian vulture" of Gardiner, 1957, p. 27, a hieroglyph that, among other things, became in demotic; cf. du Bourguet, 1976, pp. 3, 75). Now this *3* was, on the one hand, almost everywhere muted and disappeared (cf. Vergote, 1945, pp. 80–98, and 1973, Vol. 1b, pp. 28–33; and 'AYIN); but, on the other hand, the aleph does indeed seem to have reappeared in Coptic as a phoneme /'/ and as a product of the transformation of various other consonants. It is appropriate in this connection to examine above all what can be observed in P. Bodmer VI, the sole witness to DIALECT P (which in its orthography and phonology often looks like what can be known about a primitive proto-

Sahidic, *ppS*, that became a more evolved proto-Sahidic, *pS*, a reconstructed proto-Sahidic, however, not situated in its region of origin but probably immigrant into the Theban region, where it was superimposed on *A* and probably also on some variety of *L;* cf. Vergote, 1973b, and Kasser, 1982). One can there see the scribe rendering what seems indeed to be /ʾ/ by a quite particular grapheme ⊥, but only sporadically, for in the same or similar cases he also, through confusion, uses – (normally equivalent to /n̩/); or again, as in *S* properly so called, he practices graphic vocalic gemination; or finally he omits any graphic proceeding that might render /ʾ/ and presents an orthography without vocalic gemination, in the manner of *M*, for example (where it is admitted that the phonological system has lost its primitive /ʾ/). Here are these unique vestiges of ⊥ (Kasser, 1981c, p. 35): ⲍⲁ⊥⫽ (to put) one case, but ⲍⲁ⫽ one case; ϣⲁ⊥ⲧ† (deficient) one case, but ϣⲁⲁⲧ† two cases, ϣⲁⲧ† one case; ϩⲟ⊥ⲛ† (being) two cases, but ϩⲟⲛ† one case; ϫⲟ⊥⫽ (to say) three cases, but ϫⲟⲟ⫽ one case, ϫⲟ⫽ one case; also ⲍⲉⲉ⊥ⲥ (sic) (bone) one case, but ⲍⲉⲉⲥ four cases. However, apart from these relatively weak and evanescent remains of an ancient usage (and those still more rare, vaguely similar, but, despite that, very uncertain, which one may eventually think to discover in rare Old Coptic texts; Kasser, 1980, pp. 258–59), one no longer finds any specific grapheme for /ʾ/ in the other Coptic DIALECTS and PROTODIALECTS at present known.

One notices, however, in some of them—especially in *A*, *pL* (= *İ*), *L4*, *L5*, *L6*, *V5*, *F5*, *S*, but not in *M*, *W*, *V4*, *F4*, *F7*, *B* and its subdialects, *G*—a graphic vocalic gemination (succession of two identical vowel graphemes; cf. GEMINATION, VOCALIC), of which the first element is, in phonology, an authentic tonic vowel, but the second seems manifestly to render a consonantal phoneme, to define, and itself replace, a vanished consonant such as *i͗*, *ʿ*, *r*, or *t*.

This substitute phoneme is consonantal for two reasons difficult to contest. First, in *A*, every final sonant placed after a consonant becomes a rising voiced consonantal phoneme: thus *S* ⲟⲩⲁⲁⲃ† (holy) = *A* ⲟⲩⲁⲁⲃⲉ†, just as *S* ⲥⲱⲧⲙ̄ (to hear) = *A* ⲥⲱⲧⲙⲉ, which proves that in ⲟⲩⲁⲁⲃ† or ⲟⲩⲁⲁⲃⲉ† the second vowel grapheme ⲁ phonologically renders a consonant, not a vowel. On the other hand, it is known that if the pronominal suffix of the first-person singular is always ⫽ⲓ after a single vowel, it is always ⫽ⲧ after a consonant and, likewise, after a succession of two identical vowel graphemes, of which the first and tonic element is, in phonology, manifestly a vowel, but the second element, although a vowel grapheme, is nevertheless phonologically clearly a consonant; thus, for example, *S* ⲕⲁⲁ⫽ⲧ, to leave me, like ϣⲟⲡ⫽ⲧ, to receive me, and not like ⲧⲁϩⲟ⫽ⲓ, to reach me. It is true that one finds likewise ⫽ⲧ and not ⫽ⲓ in similar cases in the dialects that do not have graphic vocalic gemination and for that reason are considered as having lost even this substitute /ʾ/ (e.g., *B* ϫⲁ⫽ⲧ, to leave me, I Tm. 1:12; *M* ⲕⲉ⫽ⲧ, Mt. 27:46); but this shows only that these dialects also possessed this substitute consonant in an earlier stage of the language and that they subsequently lost it, this phenomenon having come about before the time at which their orthographic system was fixed.

In a general way, it is admitted (Vergote, 1945, p. 71, etc.) that this substitute phoneme is /ʾ/ clearly and in all cases, and not now /ʾ/, now /ʿ/, as Till (1955, p. 46) expresses it, not without reservations and ambiguity: "ʾAleph and ʿAyin are still present in Coptic, although no separate letters exist for them. Both may have been pronounced alike (probably ʾ), even though ʿ in some circumstances exercises a different effect on the neighbouring vowel than *3*." Certainly, /ʿ/ is a voiced fricative, as are the glides /j/ and /w/, and like them, in Till's hypothesis, this fricative, although a consonant in phonology, would have been rendered by a vowel grapheme, while /ʾ/, on the contrary, is an occlusive considered as unvoiced (according to Vergote, 1973, Vol. 1a, pp. 12–13) and even as belonging to the category of the most unvoiced phonemes; from this point of view /ʿ/ rather than /ʾ/ would appear to be the more capable of playing the role of substitute consonant. (Stern also may have thought this; see Stern, 1880, pp. 29–30, 54–55.)

In spite of that, it is for various reasons proper to set aside this solution. First, ʿayin seems to have disappeared from Late Egyptian before the formation of literary Coptic and even PRE-COPTIC (Vergote, 1945, pp. 122–23, and 1973, Vol. 1b, pp. 31–32: after the sixth century A.D.). Second, as a consonant replacing *i*, *ʿ*, *r*, or *t* (or even *j* or *w;* see below), it is manifestly /ʾ/ rather than /ʿ/ that is the better suited to assume this manifold function: for example, *bi͗n* becomes in Coptic /bṓʾn/ ⲃⲱⲱⲛ, bad; *ḥfʿ* becomes (with metathesis) /kṓʾfə/ ⲕⲱⲱϥⲉ (or ⲕⲱⲱⲃⲉ), to constrain; *dr.t.f.* becomes /tṓʾtf/ ⲧⲟⲟⲧ⫽ϥ, his hand (cf. ibid., p. 35: "The tendency which contributed, in numerous words, to change proto-Semitic *r* and *l* into Egyptian *3* . . . continued to exercise a certain influence during the historical period"); *mútrat* becomes *múʾra*, then /mḗʾrə/ ⲙⲉⲉⲣⲉ, midday; *sꜣf*, to soil, qualitative *sáyfu* becomes *sáʾfu* and then /sṓʾf/

ⲥⲟⲟϥ†, soiled; and *wāgiwat* becomes *wágwat,* then *wáwga,* then *wa'ga,* and finally /wȯ'cə/ ⲟⲩⲟⲟϭⲉ, jaw, cheek (Vergote, 1973, Vol. 1b, pp. 36–37). In Dieth (1950, pp. 99–100) some similar modern examples will be found in which ['] replaces even occlusives other than /t/. The final and probably decisive argument is that the grapheme ⊥ in *P*, which seems to render /'/, resembles the demotic [demotic sign] = *3* in a rather striking manner (with eventual influence from [demotic sign] = *ỉ*), much more in any case than it does the [demotic sign] (or [demotic sign], [demotic sign], [demotic sign], [demotic sign], [demotic sign]) = demotic ʿ.

The graphic vocalic gemination attesting /'/ in Coptic occurs only within a word—that is, either within a final syllable where this /'/ is followed by another consonant (cf. ⲃⲱⲱⲛ above) or at the end of a penultimate syllable where this /'/ is followed by another consonant beginning the final syllable (cf. ⲕⲱⲱϥⲉ above). It is true that some ancient *S* manuscripts present spellings such as ⲛⲁⲁ /nȧ'/ (and not ⲛⲁ /nȧ[']/, pity) or ⲙⲉⲉ /mė'/ (and not ⲙⲉ /mė[']/, truth) and so on (cf. Polotsky, 1957a, p. 231, and 1957b, pp. 348–49); but this is always before the copula ⲡⲉ (masc.), ⲧⲉ (fem.), or ⲛⲉ (pl.) in such a way that one may suppose that the (atonic) copula was felt as forming part of the "word" that it immediately follows and that bears the tonic accent on the vowel of its last syllable, a vowel that is normally and graphically the last letter of the "word"; it is thus entirely legitimate to put, for example, ⲟⲩⲙⲉⲉ ⲧⲉ /umė'tə/, that is true, in parallel with ⲟⲩⲱⲱⲧⲉ /wȯ'tə/, to separate. Vergote (1973, Vol. 1a, p. 12) further considers that *A* and *L* "present an /'/ at the end of certain monosyllabic words, where it is marked by the hiatus *a–e:* ⲃⲁⲉ palm-tree; ⲛⲁⲉ to have pity; *A* ϩⲁⲉ to appear (of stars). In *B* [and] *F* it is transformed into /j/: *B* ⲃⲁⲓ, ⲛⲁⲓ, ϣⲁⲓ or *F* ⲃⲉⲓ, ϫⲉⲓ, ϣⲉⲓ" (cf. ibid. Vol. 1b, p. 31). However, even if it may find support in etymology, this phonological interpretation of the final letter of the *A* and *L* lexemes mentioned above seems likely to raise numerous questions; orthography, it must be remembered, expresses above all not the profound or semi-profound phonological structure of the word, but its most superficial structure (cf. Hintze, 1980, p. 49). Thus, one might ask how there can be hiatus if these lexemes are monosyllabic. Would they be monosyllabic in Pre-Coptic and polysyllabic, through their hiatus, in Coptic? Another question is, why must one in this case envisage the presence of a hiatus if the final ⲉ = /'/ and not /e/ or /ə/? Are there reasons based on etymology, and must these reasons be considered compelling? Finally, with regard to the *B* and *F* parallel forms, apparently also monosyllabic (by analogy with other Coptic finals of identical spelling, and whatever the conditions linked with etymology), would they not make the hiatus equally unlikely in *A* and *L*, even if the final there is /e/ or /ə/ and not /'/? The solution of this delicate problem will without doubt still require some supplementary investigations (cf. in particular Kasser, 1981b, p. 37).

[*See also:* Syllabication.]

BIBLIOGRAPHY

Dieth, E. *Vademekum der Phonetik.* Bern, 1950.

Dubois, J.; M. Giacomo; L. Guespin; C. Marcellesi; J.-B. Marcellesi; and J.-P. Mével. *Dictionnaire de linguistique.* Paris, 1973.

Bourguet, P. du. *Grammaire fonctionnelle et progressive de l'égyptien démotique.* Louvain, 1976.

Edgerton, W. Review of W. C. Till, *Koptische Grammatik (saïdischer Dialekt), . . . Journal of Near Eastern Studies* 16 (1957):136–37.

Gardiner, A. *Egyptian Grammar, Being an Introduction to the Study of Hieroglyphs.* 3d ed. Oxford, 1957.

Hintze, F. "Zur koptischen Phonologie." *Enchoria* 10 (1980):23–91.

Kasser, R. "Prolégomènes à un essai de classification systématique des dialectes et subdialectes coptes selon les critères de la phonétique, II, Alphabets et systèmes phonétiques." *Muséon* 93 (1980):237–97.

______. "Usages de la surligne dans le P. Bodmer VI, notes additionnelles." *Bulletin de la Société d'égyptologie, Genève* 5 (1981a):23–32.

______. "Voyelles en fonction consonantique, consonnes en fonction vocalique, et classes de phonèmes en copte." *Bulletin de la Société d'égyptologie, Genève* 5 (1981b):33–50.

______. "Syllabation rapide ou lente en copte, II, Aleph et 'voyelle d'aleph.'" *Enchoria* 11 (1981c): 39–58.

______. "Le Dialecte protosaïdique de Thèbes." *Archiv für Papyrusforschung* 28 (1982):67–81.

Nagel, P. "Der frühkoptische Dialekt von Theben." In *Koptologische Studien in der DDR*, pp. 30–49. Wissenschaftliche Zeitschrift der Martin-Luther-Universität Halle-Wittenberg, Sonderheft. Halle-Wittenberg, 1965.

Polotsky, H. J. Review of W. C. Till, *Koptische Grammatik (saïdischer Dialekt), . . . Orientalistische Literaturzeitung* 52 (1957a):219–34.

______. "Zu den koptischen literarischen Texten aus Balaizah." *Orientalia* 26 (1957b):347–49.

Stern, L. *Koptische Grammatik.* Leipzig, 1880.

Till, W. C. "Altes 'Aleph und ʿAjin im Koptischen." *Wiener Zeitschrift für die Kunde des Morgenlandes* 36 (1929):186–96.

———. *Koptische Grammatik (Saïdischer Dialekt), mit Bibliographie, Lesestücken und Wörterverzeichnissen.* Leipzig, 1955.

———. *Koptische Dialektgrammatik, mit Lesestücken und Wörterbuch.* 2d ed. Munich, 1961.

Vergote, J. *Phonétique historique de l'égyptien, les consonnes.* Louvain, 1945.

———. *Grammaire copte,* Vol. 1a, *Introduction, phonétique et phonologie, morphologie synthématique (structure des sémantèmes), partie synchronique,* and Vol. 1b, *Introduction, phonétique et phonologie, morphologie synthématique (structure des sémantèmes), partie diachronique.* Louvain, 1973a.

———. "Le Dialecte copte P (P. Bodmer VI: Proverbes), essai d'identification." *Revue d'égyptologie* 25 (1973b):50–57.

RODOLPHE KASSER

ALPHABET IN COPTIC, GREEK. The Greek alphabet is much in evidence in Coptic; in fact, among the various Coptic alphabets (cf. ALPHABETS, COPTIC), all have a considerable majority of Greek graphemes, or letters (cf. ALPHABETS, COPTIC, especially the synoptic table; Kasser, 1980b, pt. II, pp. 280–81). This majority varies from one dialectal alphabet to another. In the following calculation of the percentages, ϣ and ϣ̇, and ϩ and ϩ̇, have been considered, respectively, as one and the same grapheme, whether or not provided with a diacritical sign: *G* and *F9*, 100 percent; *J*, 92 percent; *F7, F8*, and *H*, 83 percent; *S* etc. (i.e., *S, K, K7, F4, F5, V4, V5, W, M, L4, L5*, and *L6*, together with their subdialects if there are any), with *B7, A, İ* (= *pL*), and *İ7* (= *p'L*), 80 percent; *B* etc. (i.e., *B4* and *B5*), 77 percent; *P*, 71 percent.

To this strong presence of the Greek alphabet, one may add that Coptic graphemes of demotic origin are assimilated to those of Greek origin, such as ϣ formed like ω with a tail, ϥ like ρ reversed and open at the top, and ϫ like ⲗ with two horns or ⲭ resting on a long horizontal bar underneath. This assimilation and this predominance are indeed such that a superficial observer might very well take an ancient Coptic manuscript for a contemporary Greek one, especially if it was a copy without any superlinear strokes (which may occur even in the dialects in which the use of such strokes is habitual).

Even if one recalls that Coptic is the final stage of the Egyptian language, which does not belong to the same family as Greek, this indisputable supremacy of the Greek alphabet in the Coptic ought not to occasion any undue surprise. When the first varieties of the Coptic alphabet were created in the course of the third (?) century A.D., Egypt had been wholly within the Hellenic sphere of influence for more than half a millennium, since the conquest of the country by Alexander the Great in 332 B.C. (Müller, 1969). This fact explains not only the presence of so many Greek graphemes (most frequently the entire Greek alphabet) in the Coptic alphabets but also the abundance of various Greek lexemes (words) used in Coptic. Some lexemes were used exceptionally or rarely in the texts that have survived, because they constituted a vocabulary of specialists and were scarcely employed outside their specialty; others were used more or less currently (even very currently) almost everywhere in Coptic literature, because they constituted a vocabulary so completely assimilated (mentally) by the mass of the autochthonous Copts that they considered it wholly Coptic as well as wholly Greek (cf. VOCABULARY, COPTO-GREEK).

Moreover, as can be seen from the texts, the Greek graphemes of the Coptic alphabet were in principle sufficient for transcribing into Coptic those lexemes which came from the Hellenic world. It is only rarely that one sometimes finds in addition, at the beginning of a word or replacing one of the two elements of a double ρ, a ϩ of demotic origin which seems to render normally the Greek rough breathing; it is also found occasionally in place of the smooth breathing of standard Greek orthography, which has been variously interpreted as a neutralizing of the contrast in pronunciation between the rough and smooth breathings in the Greek of contemporary Egypt (Böhlig, 1958, p. 111), a "hyperurbanism" (Vergote, 1973, p. 15), and a "secondary" or "vulgar" aspiration (Weiss, 1966, p. 204). Moreover, in the *L6* documents (and a group of *S* documents probably deriving from a region of Upper Egypt where *L6* was the autochthonous dialect; cf. Kasser, 1980a) there is ϣ, also of demotic origin, where one would expect to find an initial ϩ, in Copto-Greek words corresponding to Greek words beginning with ι or ει. It is not without interest to note further that several Greek graphemes of the Coptic alphabets are used exclusively, or nearly so, for the transcription of Copto-Greek words (e.g., ⲅ, ⲇ, ⲍ; cf. Vergote, 1973, p. 10). All these factors combined produce the result that in an average Coptic page about nine graphemes out of ten are of Greek origin (against one from demotic)—hence the "Greek" appearance, broadly speaking, of these Coptic copies.

The creators of these varieties of Coptic alphabets were by no means strictly "phonologists" in the modern sense of the term. Of course, like their modern counterparts, they seem to have striven to apply as strictly as possible the fundamental and general law according to which every phoneme should be rendered exclusively by a single grapheme, and this, just as exclusively, should render this one phoneme and no other. But, on the other hand, the means they employed and the criteria they applied evidently remained empirical. Above all, they were not always in a position to decide with complete freedom whether this sound or that deserved to be treated graphically as a distinct phoneme, in precise contrast to some other established phoneme; they could not in fact fail to take account of the work of their predecessors. No Coptic alphabet emerged completely new and original from an earlier vacuum.

The very fact that the greater part of the Coptic graphemes are Greek graphemes shows very well where lay the principal model that had to be taken into account, whence sprang the first source whose influence would make itself felt, more or less strongly, in the work of the inventors of Coptic alphabets —all the more because they, though coming from a native Egyptian milieu and carrying on their activity there, were always close to the Hellenic milieu of Egypt and found themselves forced, in reading or in writing, to practice frequently the Greek graphicophonemic system. It is worthy of note that the PRE-OLD COPTIC alphabet is the Greek alphabet, no more and no less, which was already used according to certain closely related rules for the transcription into Greek of the proper names of autochthonous Egyptians (cf. GREEK TRANSCRIPTIONS).

The OLD COPTIC alphabets, though still based on the Greek alphabet for the most part, admit a strong minority of graphemes of demotic origin. The Coptic alphabets eliminate several of these, above all for motives of simplification, and by that very fact the Greek alphabetic majority in them is reinforced. Hence, one may see that if the Coptic alphabets were created according to the principle of the fundamental law stated above, the strict application of this principle was limited in various ways, first by the empiricism of the methods employed by the creators, and later and above all by the Hellenic phonological heritage for which these alphabets were the vehicle and which they transmitted from one to the other.

In this process there intervened also a law of "economy," of which it will be necessary to speak again later. In a general way, one may say that the evolution and succession of these alphabets constitute a process of simplification: the number of the graphemes (and of the phonemes) diminishes rather than increases. It is true that this assertion appears at first to be in flat contradiction with the fact that the most ancient of these alphabets, the Pre-Old Coptic, is more simple than its immediate successors, the Old Coptic and Coptic alphabets. But the Pre-Old Coptic alphabet is only very imperfectly adapted to the transcription of Egyptian; certainly it could satisfy the Hellenic milieus of Egypt, not only in the Ptolemaic era but even down to the Byzantine epoch, because throughout this period it was an alphabet of this nature that sufficed for the transcription, in Greek documents, of autochthonous proper names. Going occasionally beyond its original frame, this type of alphabetic usage could even be applied (before the present era) to the transcription of some isolated Egyptian words (cf. Bilabel, 1938), and attempts were made (also before the present era), with some difficulty, to use it for a very brief and rudimentary text (cf. Lacau, 1934). It emerged anew in the Byzantine epoch in the nonliterary texts (above all private letters), which constitute the dossier for DIALECT G; but that alphabet, too exclusively Hellenic, always remained marginal so far as Coptic and its autochthonous antecedents are concerned.

To the mind of non-Greek Egyptians and possibly of some Greeks in Egypt who were "cross-bred" and strongly assimilated, a merely Greek alphabet would not suffice for the transcription of the language of the country, with its fundamental phonemic originalities; one could not make extensive and systematic use of it, first of all in Old Coptic texts (almost all of them magical texts, in which the correct pronunciation of the formulas played an essential role) and later in Coptic texts (where a vast and varied literary production makes its appearance). When they sought to effect a real transition to the literary stage for their language, the autochthonous men of letters engaged in this task of necessity had recourse to an autochthonous form of writing, that of demotic, and the Old Coptic alphabets that they created ought properly be considered not as successors to the Pre-Old Coptic alphabet (i.e., Greek) but as the results of a radical reform of the demotic "alphabet," with a massive infusion of Greek graphemes (Pre-Old Coptic), results that were eminently "economical," since demotic had many more graphemes than Old Coptic. It is thus, to say the least, a case of a "compromise" between the Greek system in Egypt and the autochthonous system, but one that, being alone fitted like the latter for rendering the idiom of the country, did so at much less cost (in terms of graphemes and soon of phonemes). The economizing process was continued in the proto-Coptic (cf.

PROTODIALECT) and then in the Coptic alphabets, in which (save for the exception in DIALECT H; cf. below) the total of graphemes of Greek origin remained stable, but the number of graphemes of autochthonous origin was gradually reduced: *S*, the most neutral Coptic idiom, has only six (ϣ, ϥ, ϩ, ϫ, ϭ, ϯ), and *H*, the most economical METADIALECT of all (probably twenty-three graphemes altogether; cf. *S*, with thirty, and *P*, with as many as thirty-five), has no more than four signs derived from demotic, ϣ, ϩ, ϫ, and ϭ, dispensing with the two autochthonous graphemes ϥ (> ⲃ) and ϯ (> ⲧⲓ), as it also does in principle with no fewer than three Greek graphemes, ⲅ (> ⲕ), ⲝ (> ⲕⲥ), and ⲯ (> ⲡⲥ), not to speak of two others whose use is considerably restricted, ⲟ (> ⲱ) and ⲩ (> ⲏ), both excluded except in the combination (ⲟ)ⲩ for /u/ and /w/.

BIBLIOGRAPHY

Barns, J. W. B. "Egyptians and Greeks." *Papyrologica Bruxellensia* 14 (1978):1–23.

Bataille, A. *Les Memnonia: Recherches de papyrologie et d'épigraphie grecques sur la nécropole de la Thèbes d'Egypte aux époques hellénistiques et romaines.* Cairo, 1952.

Bell, H. I. *Jews and Christians in Egypt.* London, 1924.

Bilabel, F. "Neue literarische Funde in der Heidelberger Papyrussammlung." In *Actes du Ve Congrès international de papyrologie,* pp. 72–84. Brussels, 1938.

Böhlig, A. *Die griechischen Lehnwörter im sahidischen und bohairischen Neuen Testament.* Munich, 1958.

Brunsch, W. "Untersuchungen zu den griechischen Wiedergaben ägyptischer Personennamen." *Enchoria* 8 (1978):1–142.

Chaîne, M. *Éléments de grammaire dialectale copte.* Paris, 1933.

Fraser, P. M. *Ptolemaic Alexandria.* Oxford, 1972.

Gignac, F. T. *A Grammar of the Greek Papyri of the Roman and Byzantine Periods,* Vol. 1, *Phonology.* Milan, 1976.

Kasser, R. "L'idiome de Bachmour." *Bulletin de l'Institut français d'archéologie orientale* 75 (1975):401–427.

______. "Expression de l'aspiration ou de la non-aspiration à l'initiale des mots copto-grecs correspondant à des mots grecs commençant par (E)I-." *Bulletin de la Société d'égyptologie, Genève* 3 (1980a):15–21.

______. "Prolégomènes à un essai de classification systématique des dialectes et subdialectes coptes selon les critères de la phonétique, I, Principes et terminologie." *Muséon* 93 (1980b):53–512. ". . . , II, Alphabets et systèmes phonétiques." *Muséon* 93 (1980b):237–97.

______. "Orthographe (sub)dialectale du vocabulaire copto-grec avant le VIIIe siècle de notre ère." *Museum Helveticum* 40 (1983):207–215.

Lacau, P. "Un Graffito égyptien d'Abydos écrit en lettres grecques." *Etudes de papyrologie* 2 (1934):229–46.

Mallon, A. *Grammaire copte, bibliographie, chrestomathie et vocabulaire,* 4th ed., rev. M. Malinine. Beirut, 1956.

Montevecchi, Orsolina. *La papirologia.* Turin, 1973.

Müller, C. D. G. *Grundzüge des christlich-islamischen Ägypten von der Ptolemäerzeit bis zur Gegenwart.* Darmstadt, 1969.

Peremans, W. "Über die Zweisprachigkeit im ptolemäischen Ägypten." In *Studien zur Papyrologie und antiken Wirtschaftsgeschichte, Friedrich Oertel zum achtzigsten Geburtstag gewidmet,* pp. 49–60. Bonn, 1964.

Plumley, J. M. *An Introductory Coptic Grammar (Sahidic Dialect).* London, 1948.

Préaux, C. *Le Monde hellénistique, la Grèce et l'Orient (323–146 av. J.-C.).* Paris, 1978.

Quaegebeur, J. "The Study of Egyptian Proper Names in Greek Transcription, Problems and Perspectives." *Onoma* 18 (1974):403–420.

Rémondon, R. "Problèmes du bilinguisme dans l'Égypte lagide." *Chronique d'Égypte* 39 (1964):126–46.

Steindorff, G. *Lehrbuch der koptischen Grammatik.* Chicago, 1951.

Stern, L. *Koptische Grammatik.* Leipzig, 1880.

Till, W. C. *Koptische Grammatik (saïdischer Dialekt), mit Bibliographie, Lesestücken und Wörterverzeichnissen.* Leipzig, 1955.

______. *Koptische Dialektgrammatik, mit Lesestücken und Wörterbuch.* 2d ed. Munich, 1961.

Vergote, J. *Grammaire copte,* Vol. 1a, *Introduction, phonétique et phonologie, morphologie synthématique (structure des sémantèmes), partie synchronique.* Louvain, 1973.

Weiss, H.-F. "Zum Problem der griechischen Fremd- und Lehnwörter in den Sprachen des christlichen Orients." *Helikon* 6 (1966):183–209.

RODOLPHE KASSER

ALPHABETS, COPTIC. Attentive study of the alphabet used in each of the various Coptic DIALECTS and subdialects obliges one to recognize that there was not a single Coptic alphabet, as is often believed, but several Coptic alphabets (or, to put it in a slightly different way, several varieties of the Coptic alphabet). Certainly, if one examines the Coptic texts themselves in their manifold variety, one finds that one of these alphabets, that of *S* etc., is employed almost everywhere (it is that of almost 92 percent of the total); it is therefore comprehensible enough that the alphabet of *S* should practically always be called "the Coptic alphabet," without further explanation, while the alphabetic variety of *B* etc. (almost 7 percent) is only very seldom mentioned, the existence of the twelve other varieties (about 1 percent only) being entirely neglected. However, all these fourteen alphabets, major and minor, will be accorded the place to which they have a right herein.

It will be convenient to recall in the first place that each type of Coptic dialect—whether a dialect in the narrow sense of the term or a PROTODIALECT, a MESODIALECT, a METADIALECT, or even a subdialect—is defined first and foremost as a phonological system, while morpho(phono)logy and morphosyntax intervene only secondarily in its definition (for want of evidence sufficiently frequently attested).

Coptic has been a dead language for several centuries, and its demise preceded the beginnings of Coptology as a modern discipline. Hence, Coptic PHONOLOGY can only be known today through the orthography of the Coptic texts that have survived, a very small number in comparison with the immense quantity of those that perished in the tempestuous and painful course of Coptic history; through their regular and systematic orthography only (that which we find in the texts of "good" quality), and not through the irregular and disordered graphical manifestations that may be observed in all sorts of careless and orthographically undisciplined copies.

Prudence certainly obliges one to remember that the analysis of a Coptic orthographic system is not automatically the analysis of a Coptic phonological system. One must always reckon with the possibility, however weak it may be, that the difference between the various Coptic alphabets may be not only a difference of quantity (phonemes and graphemes in more or less large numbers) but also, on some particular point, a difference of quality (a given grapheme rendering a given phoneme in one idiom, and the same grapheme rendering another phoneme in another idiom; or a given phoneme being rendered by a given grapheme in one idiom and by another grapheme in another idiom). However that may be, if one may sometimes doubt that such an original alphabetic system really attests a particular Coptic dialect, it nonetheless remains that each particular Coptic alphabetic system is a piece of evidence; and this reality, although superficial in relation to phonology, deserves to be recognized as such on its own (the alphabetic) level; this recognition, in fact, is not bound to the phonological interpretation, sometimes uncertain, of the graphemes that compose the alphabets.

The uncertainty of this interpretation at any given point often derives from a question of principle and from a methodological alternative of which one must be very conscious. In fact, the investigator who strives to rediscover and analyze the phonological systems of the Coptic dialects and subdialects through their orthographical systems is soon constrained to choose between two preliminary working hypotheses: each of these presents substantial advantages, but even in the better hypothesis, they remain limited and weakened by important disadvantages.

The first hypothesis consists in postulating a priori a phonological unity of the Coptic language, a unity practically absolute. In pushing this hypothesis to its extreme consequences, one would have to admit that despite the orthographical appearances, this language is by no means divided into a plurality of dialects. The differences that orthography seems to manifest would be only superficial, or to put it simply, the various schools of scribes would make use, in certain cases, of different graphemes to express the same phonemes. One should then observe in Coptic not various dialects but various "orthographic codes" applying to a language that is "one" and not divided on the phonological level.

This hypothesis is very seductive because, over against the various earlier stages of the Egyptian language (apparently homogeneous because dialectal multiplicity does not appear in it, or practically not), it sets not a group of Coptic phonological systems but a single Coptic phonological system (or, at the very most, a group of systems that differ among themselves only very rarely and on details that are truly exceptional). It seems to be confirmed by the fact that, if one compares with one another the different orthographical forms of the same autochthonous Coptic words, it appears evident that the ⲕ of the majority of dialects and the ⳅ of *P* render /k/; the ϣ of the majority and the cz of *G* render /š/; the ϥ of the majority and the ⲫ of *G* likewise render /f/; the ϧ of *P* and *B*, the ⳉ of *A* and *İ*, and finally even the ⲭ of *B7* and *G* (see below) render /x/; the ϭ of the majority and the ⲕ of *P* render /c/; and so on.

However, the limits of the efficacy of this explanation are reached when one is faced with problems such as these: when ⲗ in *F* corresponds to ⲣ in *S*, the phoneme cannot be either /l/ or /r/ uniformly for ⲗ and ⲣ at the same time; and likewise, when ⳉ in *A* corresponds to ϣ in *S* etc., the phoneme cannot be either /x/ or /š/ uniformly for ⳉ and ϣ at the same time. By themselves alone, these exceptions prove that there is in Coptic a dialectal plurality.

The second hypothesis consists in postulating that in Coptic, according to the unanimous intention of the creators of its alphabet, there is for each phoneme (or each combination of phonemes, should occasion arise; cf. /th/ etc. below) a single corresponding grapheme that can never serve to express another phoneme. This "law of exclusiveness" thus does not allow of any plurality of Coptic alphabets based on a difference of phonological "quality"; this plurality can only exist as a consequence of the "quantity" of the indissoluble phoneme-grapheme unities: certain Coptic idioms would make use of the Coptic series to the full (or nearly so), while other idioms would content themselves with a very diminished series (loss of /x/ or even /š/, /h/, or /c/, for example).

However, if this hypothesis gives very satisfactory results in regard to *F* ⲗ versus *S* etc. ⲣ or *A* ⳉ versus *S* etc. ϣ, for example, it seems to fail in other cases already mentioned above: in comparing the different orthographical forms of the same Coptic word, it is difficult to see what phoneme *P* ⳣ could render if not /k/ (/q/ seems excluded for solid reasons; cf. Kasser, 1980b, pp. 244–48); in the same way, it seems unlikely that, corresponding regularly to ϣ /š/ in *B* etc., the combination of graphemes ⲥⲍ in *G* should render /sz/ rather than /š/; and when the ⲫ of *G* corresponds to ϥ /f/ in *B* etc., would it be equivalent to /ph/ rather than to /f/? The rigid application of the law of exclusiveness would entail other phonological solutions that would be bizarre and difficult to accept. One must then resign oneself to some compromise between these two extreme hypotheses, a compromise to be negotiated and determined from case to case.

One particularly troublesome alphabetic fact (above all, in consequence of the second hypothesis and its law of "exclusiveness") is the use of (apparently) the same grapheme to express two different phonemes. When this phenomenon coincides with the opposition of two Coptic idioms, as with *S* ϭ /c/ versus *B* ϭ /čh/, one may attempt to explain it by referring to the divergent principles applied by two schools of scribes belonging to two different cultural ambiences. But what is one to say of this ambiguity when it appears within one and the same Coptic orthographical system (and probably idiom)?

Thus, in *P* (compared to *S* etc. in the orthography of their common vocabulary) ⲕ is assuredly /k/ in the Copto-Greek words, but it is /c/ in the autochthonous Coptic words. (It is difficult to imagine that *P*, by some palatalization, or "damping," applied to the Greek words, should have systematically replaced by /c/ all the /k/ in its Copto-Greek vocabulary.) One sees the same ambiguity in *G*, where one finds ⲫ both in the Copto-Greek words (for /ph/) and in the autochthonous Coptic words (for /f/, which could, however, at least locally, have become the articulation of ⲫ even in Copto-Greek). The same confusion is manifest in the Dublin *L5* (cf. below), *J* (sporadically), and *F9*, where ⲭ appears both in the Copto-Greek words (for /kh/) and in the autochthonous Coptic vocabulary (for /č/); there is furthermore the problem of the use of ⲭ even for /x/ or that of the inverse use of ϫ for ⲭ /kh/ in some Copto-Greek words in *L5*. (The relation of ϫ /č/ and ⲭ /kh/ or /x/ is probably of another order, or at least too subtle and complex to be summarily expounded here.) Finally, a similar ambiguity appears in *F7* and in some *L6* texts (cf. Kasser, 1984–1985), where the grapheme ϯ is both the "normal" Coptic ⲯ /ps/ and the "normal" Coptic ϯ /ti/. These are texts attested by manuscripts nearly all particularly ancient: *F7* is the language of the bilingual Papyrus No. 1 of Hamburg (Coptic and Greek, end of third century). *F9* is the language of Coptic glosses in a manuscript in the Chester Beatty collection (third century; cf. Kasser, 1981a, pp. 101–102). *J* is the language of a Coptic schoolboy's tablet (end [?] of third century; cf. ibid., pp. 113–15). An unpublished papyrus in Dublin (cf. Kasser, 1984, p. 274) seems to be contemporary with the preceding two or scarcely much later; it contains John 10:18–11:43 and 12:14–39 in a variety of *L5* with very particular orthographicophonological characteristics (Kasser 1981b, pp. 27–29).

The following hypothetical explanation could, however, to some extent resolve these diverse enigmas, except for the ambiguity of ⲫ in *G*. One should have in each instance, for two phonemes undoubtedly different, not a single grapheme considered (except for ϯ) as of Greek origin but two graphemes to be distinguished from one another, the one of Greek origin, the other of demotic—two graphemes distinct in their origin but in which the autochthonous Egyptian sign has gradually been so strongly influenced in its form by the Greek grapheme that it has become practically identical to the latter (whence the confusions that ensue). In what follows, except for special mention, references are made to du Bourguet (1976, p. 75), where the demotic signs are presented in their "usual" form on the left and then in certain of their "variants" on the right.

In *P*, the autochthonous ⲕ /c/ could be derived from a sign for *g*, the first of the variants, resembling a very "flattened" ⲕ; this ambiguous usage, alongside ⲕ /k/ in the Copto-Greek words, will have led to the usage in *S* of ⲕ (no longer ⳣ) for /k/ throughout, and ϭ (no longer ⲕ) for /c/.

In the Dublin *L5*, with *J* and *F9*, the autochthonous ⲭ /č/ could be descended from a sign for *d̲*, the first of the variants (it has the look of a slightly upturned ϫ, of which the first stroke, which in Greek goes from top left to bottom right, is near the vertical and the second stroke is consequently near the horizontal); confusions between the ϫ /kh/ and this ϫ /č/ will have led to the grapheme ϫ being soon preferred to it; this is also descended from a sign for $\underline{d}$, either the first usual sign (vaguely resembling an α the loop of which has been completely flattened) or the last of the variants (resembling a bulging α with the rounded part at the bottom and the two horns at the top).

In *F7* and some *L6* texts, the ϯ /ps/ is exactly identical with this grapheme as one sees it in the contemporary Greek manuscripts, which also makes it unfortunately almost identical with the autochthonous ϯ /ti/, habitually considered as derived from a demotic sign (cf., e.g., Steindorff, 1951, p. 12; but see also Kasser, 1984–1985); this ambiguity will have incited the Coptic scribes to modify into ⲯ the grapheme for /ps/ borrowed from the Greek alphabet.

With regard to the two ϭ (the *S* one for /c/ and the *B* etc. one for /čh/), one remains within the autochthonous Egyptian zone, without interference from the Greek alphabet. It is admitted that the ϭ /c/ derives from a demotic sign for *k*, the first usual one (which has the appearance of a ϭ the circle of which is very small, the stroke that escapes from it leaving at the summit and stretching horizontally at length to the right). The ϭ /čh/ could be descended from the demotic sign for $\underline{d}$, the last of the variants (the one that resembles a bulging α of which the rounded part would be at the bottom and the two horns at the top; cf. above with regard to ϫ and ϫ for /č/; the suppression of the left horn could well yield a kind of ϭ).

As can be seen, this compromise obliges one to renounce the thesis of the "absolute phonological unity" of the Coptic language; there are then several Coptic dialects, a fact that is incontestable. But this compromise probably also obliges one to consent to some detractions from the law of exclusiveness, which flows from the second hypothesis: if (admitting the duality of ⲕ, ϫ, ϯ, and ϭ, above) one is to see each grapheme always rendering the same phoneme, it may come about that a phoneme is rendered, according to the idiom, by two or even three different graphemes, as with ⳉ and ⲕ 2° for /k/; – and ⲛ for /n̩/˙; ϥ and ⲫ for /f/; ϫ and ϫ 1° for /č/; ⲕ 1° and ϭ 1° for /c/; ϧ and ϣ for /ç/; ϧ, ϩ, and ϫ 2° for /x/. In this last case, one might think of the influence of a local Greek articulation ϫ /x/ rather than ϫ /kh/ and extending to the pronunciation of the Copto-Greek words in *B7* and *F9* (cf. also the eventuality of ⲫ /f/ in *G* above). There are then in Coptic not only several Coptic dialects but also several Coptic alphabets employed to render these various dialects, the limits of the field of application of these alphabets not always coinciding with the phonological interdialectal limits.

From this perspective, a search through the most diverse Coptic texts finally ends in the identification of at least fourteen different Coptic alphabets. As was underlined at the beginning of this article, they vary considerably in their relative importance if one takes account of the number and the extent of the texts that employ each of them. One of these alphabets is supported by *S*, the vehicular language of the whole of the valley of the Egyptian Nile (the Delta excepted); it was also utilized by a large number of dialects and subdialects in the valley and even in the Fayyūm. Another alphabet is supported by *B*, the vehicular language of the Egyptian Delta. These are, one might say, the "classic alphabets" of the Coptic language. The other alphabets are supported only by a small number (on occasion even by a trifling number) of texts slight in extent and variety or even by a single small text, the sole representative of an idiom whose original character, on the level of the dialect and not simply on that of the IDIOLECT, remains open to discussion: hence, one may call them, respectively, "marginal" and "very marginal" alphabets.

An alphabet could be marginal for various reasons. It could be situated in the "preliminary historical margin" of Coptic literary life; this would be one of the various alphabets created by way of essays at the time when the pioneers of literary Coptic were attempting, as individuals or in small isolated groups, to forge the instruments indispensable for the realization of their enterprise; some of these alphabets would not have obtained the adhesion of a social or cultural group, so that they would very quickly have been abandoned, even by their few partisans. Or again, an alphabet could be marginal because it was descended from the inventive spirit of an individual or a small group living somewhat on the margin of the society that was contemporary with them, and this at least on the cultural or eventually the religious level; this alphabet would have known only an extremely restricted diffusion and an existence probably all too short. But whether "classic" or more or less "marginal," all the Coptic alphabets thus attested by the texts of this language will be of interest for the researcher.

A synoptic view of the fourteen Coptic alphabets mentioned above will be found in Table 1. Each of the alphabets is indicated either by the unique dialect or subdialect that attests it or by the principal idiom (language or dialect) that attests it. These are as follows:

(I) *P* (= a PROTODIALECT remarkably similar to **pS*, the latter being the tentatively reconstructed proto-Sahidic idiom; cf. DIALECT P), 0.1 percent of the whole Coptic textual surface.

(II) *İ* (= *pL*, proto-Lycopolitan dialect; cf. PROTODIALECT and DIALECT İ), 0.01 percent.

(III) *A* etc. (= *A*, Akhmimic dialect, with *İ7* = *p'L*, an evolved proto-Lycopolitan dialect; cf. AKHMIMIC and PROTODIALECT with DIALECT İ), 0.6 percent.

(IV) *B* etc. (= *B5*, the "classic" and relatively late BOHAIRIC language, commonly designated by *B*, with *B4*, the Bohairic dialect of "ancient" attestation, cf. Kasser, 1981a, pp. 92–93; *B4* texts published in Husselman, 1947; Quecke, 1974; Kasser, 1958, only p. 53 of Papyrus Bodmer III), in all, more than 6.5 percent (cf. LANGUAGE(S), COPTIC).

(V) *S* etc. (= *S* properly so called, the SAHIDIC language, with [a] the variety of the Fayyumic dialect showing lambdacism most recently attested, *F5* [cf. FAYYUMIC]; [b] *V5*, the least widely attested of the two mesodialectal varieties of the Fayyumic dialect without lambdacism (cf. FAYYUMIC); and [c] the three subdialectal varieties [or even dialects entirely apart, according to Funk, 1985] of *L*, the LYCOPOLITAN or LYCO-DIOSPOLITAN dialect), as a whole nearly 92 percent.

(VI) *M* etc. (= *M* properly so called, the MESOKEMIC dialect, with [a] the crypto-Mesokemic mesodialect called dialect *W* [published in Husselman, 1962]; [b] *V4*, the most widely attested of the two mesodialectal varieties of the Fayyumic dialect without lambdacism; [c] *F4*, one of the two varieties of the Fayyumic dialect with lambdacism and of ancient attestation [*F4* and *F7*]; and [d] the two very small mesodialects *K* and *K7(1)* [cf. Kasser and Satzinger, 1982]), in all 0.7 percent.

(VII) *B7* (cf. Kasser, 1981a, p. 93; subdialect), a little less than 0.001 percent.

(VIII) *L5* (Dub.) (= the particular subdialect of the Johannine fragment *L5* in Dublin), 0.015 percent (cf. LYCOPOLITAN or LYCO-DIOSPOLITAN).

(IX) *F7*(the FAYYUMIC subdialect *F7*, of ancient attestation; cf. Kasser, 1981a, pp. 97–100), 0.05 percent.

(X) *F8* (a very small subdialect; cf. Kasser, 1981a, p. 101), a little less than 0.001 percent.

(XI) *J* (very small subdialect; cf. Kasser, 1981a, pp. 113–15), 0.001 percent.

(XII) *G* (= DIALECT G or mesodialect [?]; cf. Crum, 1939; Kasser, 1975, and 1981a, pp. 102–103), 0.005 percent.

(XIII) *F9* (very small subdialect; cf. Kasser, 1981a, pp. 101–102), a little more than 0.0005 percent.

(XIV) *H* (= DIALECT H or metadialect; cf. Kasser, 1966; 1975–1976; and 1981a, pp. 104–112), 0.03 percent.

In the synoptic table (Table 1), everything has been grouped around *S* etc., the attestation of which, in relation to the other Coptic idioms, is very amply preponderant (92 percent). This is why (always with the exception of *P* ⲝ /k/ and – /n̩/˙; see below) the order of the phonemes (or combinations of phonemes, should occasion arise), along with the alphabetic order corresponding to them, is first of all the one habitually found in the Coptic grammars and lexicons (or dictionary elements) limited to Sahidic, *S:* (1) First come letters of Greek origin. (2) Next come letters of demotic origin (to the extent that they are in use in *S;* with regard to the debated origin of ϯ, see below; for details on the origin of these non-Greek graphemes, see ALPHABETS, OLD COPTIC). As regards the alphabetical order of the Coptic letters of demotic origin, it should be mentioned here that in some ancient documents showing that part of the Coptic alphabet, ϭ is placed before ϫ (e.g., Hall, 1905, pp. 35–36; Krall, 1888, pp. 129–30; question raised in di Bitonto Kasser, 1988). (3) Last come various "supplementary" phonemes (or combinations of phonemes), almost all descended from demotic (on their precise origins, see ALPHABETS, OLD COPTIC): deriving from pre-Coptic Egyptian, ALEPH = /ʾ/ is a CRYPTOPHONEME in *S*, as elsewhere in Coptic (except in *P*), and is therefore not rendered by any grapheme exclusively its own; also of autochthonous origin and pre-Coptic, /ç/, /x/, and eventually also /cə/ were abandoned in *S* etc., but have been preserved in other dialects or protodialects; /čh/ is specific to the Bohairic domain (*B* etc. and probably also *B7*); /v/ is the characteristic of a tendency that results in various manifestations of Coptic metadialects. In regard to the particularly varied graphemes that correspond to these supplementary phonemes, several will be noted in *P* that can be described as Old Coptic (so ⊥ /ʾ/, ९ /ç/, in addition to the ⲝ /k/ and – /n̩/˙, already mentioned above, which respectively in *P* alone replace the ⲕ and ⲛ of Greek origin); others (ϧ and ϭ, or ϣ̄ and ϩ with their diacritical signs, which, respectively, mark them off from, and oppose them to, ϣ and ϩ, which themselves belong in group 2) are simply of demotic origin; others finally (ⲃ and ϫ) are, or seem to be, Greek graphemes, but here play an unaccustomed role.

As regards the correspondence between the phonemes and the graphemes of the various Coptic alphabets, it will be noted that in this area the situation in Coptic is very similar to that in Greek. Thus, broadly speaking, for each Coptic alphabet there is a corresponding phonemic series made up of either (most frequently) isolated phonemes (e.g., /a/, /ƀ/, /g/, etc., the affricate /č/ = [tš] also being considered as a "single" phoneme) or of combinations of phonemes (/th/, /ks/, /ph/, /kh/, /ps/, /ti/).

Taking into account the total phonemic series resulting from the addition of all the particular phonemic series, each of which corresponds to one of the fourteen individual Coptic alphabets, one may establish, from case to case, the existence of one or another of the five following possibilities:

(1) In a given Coptic alphabet, a given phoneme (or combination of phonemes) is rendered by a grapheme that, according to a system of correspondence usual to this alphabet as well as to (almost) the whole of the Coptic dialects and subdialects, is peculiar to it and serves for its exclusive use: thus, for example, in *S* etc., ⲁ for /a/, ⲃ for /b/ etc., ⲑ for /th/ etc., ⲕ for /k/ etc. (It will be noted in this regard that, according to rules which cannot be set out here [cf. Kasser, 1983], /i/ may be rendered either by the grapheme ⲓ or by the combination ⲉⲓ, although the same ⲓ or ⲉⲓ may equally render /j/; and if /u/ is almost always rendered by the combination ⲟⲩ, nevertheless /w/, normally rendered by the same combination, often sees its initial ⲟ disappear in orthography after ⲁ, ⲉ, or ⲏ, which conveys the illusion of a correspondence ⲩ = /w/). This type of peculiar and exclusive phoneme-grapheme relationship is in the Coptic alphabets the most normal and widely favored possibility; every grapheme that attaches to it—and likewise the eventual combinations (ⲉ)ⲓ or (ⲟ)ⲩ—is then noted, just as it is in the synoptic table herein.

(2) In a given Coptic alphabet, a given phoneme is rendered by a given grapheme that, according to a system of correspondence usual to this alphabet, although not to the other Coptic dialects and subdialects, is peculiar to it and serves for its exclusive use: thus, for example, ⲕ for /c/ in *P*, although everywhere else ⲕ = /k/; ϭ for /čh/ in *B*, although everywhere else ϭ = /c/ (but see earlier discussion of law of exclusiveness). This possibility is not the most normal, but it remains very widely favored; this grapheme is then also noted, just as it is in the synoptic table.

(3) In a given alphabet, a given combination of phonemes, instead of being rendered by the grapheme usually peculiar to it, is rendered by each of the graphemes that habitually render each of the components of this combination: thus ⲧⲓ, and not ϯ, for /ti/ (one could likewise imagine ⲧϩ, and not ⲑ, for /th/, etc.). This possibility, scarcely less widely favored than the preceding ones, is marked by the symbol = in the synoptic table, the complementary explanations being found in the commentary following the table.

(4) In a given alphabet, a frankly more problematic case, the proper and exclusive grapheme for a given phoneme is missing; the phoneme, however, is reputed to be present despite this and is then said to be a CRYPTOPHONEME. This is, by definition, rendered by a grapheme or combination of graphemes each of which is normally appropriated to the proper and exclusive use of another phoneme: for example, in *S* ⲟ = /o/ in normal usage, and yet one may note the second element of ⲟⲟ (not ⲟ⊥) = /o'/ in graphic vocalic gemination (cf. ALEPH); or again in *G*, ⲥ = /s/ and ⲍ = /z/ in normal usage, and yet ⲥⲍ (not ϣ) = /š/. This possibility is indicated by the symbol =/= in the corresponding box in the synoptic table, the complementary explanations being found in the commentary following the table.

(5) Finally, in a given alphabet the absence of the usual grapheme (cf. point 1) signifies the absence of the phoneme concerned; this possibility, the only one that is really and fully negative, is marked by an empty shaded cell in the synoptic table.

In this table, any grapheme between parentheses is of considerably reduced usage (because it corresponds to a phoneme that is itself also of greatly reduced usage) in all of the dialect, subdialect, or group of idioms concerned (thus, e.g., the sonants /l̩/, /m̩/, /n̩/, /r̩/ in *B* etc.). This obviously does not apply to (ⲉ) in (ⲉ)ⲓ or to (ⲟ) in (ⲟ)ⲩ, which signify, respectively, the simultaneous existence of spellings in ⲉⲓ and in ⲓ, in ⲟⲩ and in ⲩ. Any grapheme between square brackets has had to be restored, taking account of the probabilities (the textual base being too narrow, there has been no occasion for this grapheme to appear). In line 31, "gem." signifies graphic vocalic gemination (see GEMINATION, VOCALIC), a way of rendering /'/ in writing as a cryptophoneme and not a phoneme in the ordinary sense.

For convenience, *S* has been assigned the function of a norm or standard; in relation to it the following phonemic and alphabetic differences will be noted (transformations and simplifications):

Lines 2a and 32: *J, G, F9, H* ⲃ /ƀ/ > /v/ (cf. l. 26): *B7* also has ⲃ /v/, but could well have preserved ⲃ /ƀ/ simultaneously.

Line 3: *H* ⲅ /g/ > ⲕ /k/.

Line 4: *H* ⲇ /d/ > ⲧ /t/.

Line 5a: *H* ⲉ /e/ > ⲏ /ē/.

Line 6: *H* ⲍ /z/ > ⲥ /s/.

Line 10: *P* ⲹ /k/ > *S* etc. (and all the other Coptic dialects etc.) ⲕ /k/ (cf. l. 29).

Line 15: *H* ⲟ /o/ > ⲱ /ō/.

Line 20a: *H* ⲩ /y/ > ⲏ /ē/.

Line 21: See line 26.

Line 22: See lines 28 and 35.

Line 25: *F9* ϣ /š/ > ⲥ /s/.

Line 26: *J, F9, H* ϥ /f/ > ⲃ /v/ (cf. l. 2a); *G* ⲫ probably /f/ rather than /ph/ (cf. l. 21).

Line 28: With regard to ϫ (*L5* Dub. and *J, F9*) for ϫ, see discussion above.

Line 29: *P* ⲕ /c/ > *S* etc. (and all the other dialects, etc., which have this phoneme) ϭ /c/ (cf. l. 10); note, however, that in *J* and *F9* ϭ /c/ > ⲕ /k/; *F7* ϭ /c/ > ϫ /č/.

Line 32: See line 2a.

Line 34: *P* ⳋ /ç/ and also *İ* ϣ /ç/ > *S* etc. (and *L* and all the other Coptic dialects, etc.) ϣ /š/.

Line 35: *P* (cf. *B*) ϧ /x/ and also *İ* (cf. *A*) with *J* ⳉ /x/ > *S* etc. (and *L* and all the other Coptic dialects, etc., except *A* etc. and *B* etc. with *B7* and *G*) ϩ /h/; note *B7, G* ⲭ probably /x/ rather than /kh/.

It is difficult to know with any precision the names of the letters of the various Coptic alphabets. Those proposed by modern or semimodern grammarians all rest upon relatively late traditions and represent not the primitive forms but forms already somewhat modified (Stern, 1880, p. 7; Mallon, 1907, p. 7; Steindorff, 1930, pp. 6–7, and 1951, p. 11; Plumley, 1948, p. 1; Worrell, 1942, pp. 314–27, taken up in Till, 1955, p. 40). To provide a useful,

TABLE 1. *Synoptic Table of Coptic Alphabets, with Commentary*

		P	*İ*	*A* etc.	*B* etc.	*S* etc.	*M* etc.	*B7*	*L5* (Dub.)	*F7*	*F8*	*J*	*G*	*F9*	*H*
1	/a/	ⲁ	ⲁ	ⲁ	ⲁ	ⲁ	ⲁ	ⲁ	ⲁ	ⲁ	ⲁ	ⲁ	ⲁ	ⲁ	ⲁ
2a	/ƀ	ⲃ	ⲃ	ⲃ	ⲃ	ⲃ	ⲃ	?	ⲃ	ⲃ	ⲃ				
2b	/ƀ̩/	ⲃ	ⲃ	ⲃ		ⲃ	ⲃ	[?]	ⲃ		[?]				
3	/g/	ⲅ	ⲅ	ⲅ	ⲅ	ⲅ	ⲅ	[ⲅ]	ⲅ	ⲅ	ⲅ	ⲅ	ⲅ	[ⲅ]	
4	/d/	ⲇ	ⲇ	ⲇ	ⲇ	ⲇ	ⲇ	[ⲇ]	ⲇ	ⲇ	[ⲇ]	[ⲇ]	ⲇ	[ⲇ]	
5a	/e/	ⲉ	ⲉ	ⲉ	ⲉ	ⲉ	ⲉ	[ⲉ]	ⲉ	ⲉ	ⲉ	ⲉ	ⲉ	ⲉ	
5b	/ə/	ⲉ	ⲉ	ⲉ	ⲉ	ⲉ	ⲉ	ⲉ	ⲉ	ⲉ	ⲉ	[ⲉ]	ⲉ	ⲉ	(ⲉ)
6	/z/	ⲍ	ⲍ	ⲍ	ⲍ	ⲍ	ⲍ	[ⲍ]	ⲍ	ⲍ	[ⲍ]	[ⲍ]	ⲍ	[ⲍ]	
7	/ē/	ⲏ	ⲏ	ⲏ	ⲏ	ⲏ	ⲏ	ⲏ	ⲏ	ⲏ	ⲏ	ⲏ	ⲏ	ⲏ	ⲏ
8	/th/	ⲑ	ⲑ	ⲑ	ⲑ	ⲑ	ⲑ	ⲑ	ⲑ	ⲑ	ⲑ	ⲑ	ⲑ	[ⲑ]	ⲑ
9a	/i/	(ⲉ)ⲓ	(ⲉ)ⲓ	(ⲉ)ⲓ	ⲓ	(ⲉ)ⲓ	(ⲉ)ⲓ	ⲓ	(ⲉ)ⲓ	ⲓ	ⲓ	(ⲉ)ⲓ	ⲓ	ⲓ	(ⲉ)ⲓ
9b	/j/	(ⲉ)ⲓ	ⲉⲓ	(ⲉ)ⲓ	ⲓ	(ⲉ)ⲓ	(ⲉ)ⲓ	ⲓ	(ⲉ)ⲓ	ⲓ	ⲓ	(ⲉ)ⲓ	ⲓ	ⲉⲓ	(ⲉ)ⲓ
10	/k/	ⲹ	ⲕ	ⲕ	ⲕ	ⲕ	ⲕ	ⲕ	ⲕ	ⲕ	ⲕ	ⲕ	ⲕ	ⲕ	ⲕ
11a	/l/	ⲗ	ⲗ	ⲗ	ⲗ	ⲗ	ⲗ	ⲗ	ⲗ	ⲗ	ⲗ	ⲗ	ⲗ	ⲗ	ⲗ
11b	/l̩/	ⲗ	ⲗ	ⲗ	(ⲗ)	ⲗ	ⲗ	[(ⲗ)]	ⲗ		?	?	?	ⲗ	
12a	/m/	ⲙ	ⲙ	ⲙ	ⲙ	ⲙ	ⲙ	ⲙ	ⲙ	ⲙ	ⲙ	ⲙ	ⲙ	ⲙ	ⲙ
12b	/m̩/	ⲙ	ⲙ	ⲙ	(ⲙ)	ⲙ	ⲙ	(ⲙ)	ⲙ	(ⲙ)	?	?	?	[ⲙ?]	
13a	/n/	ⲛ	ⲛ	ⲛ	ⲛ	ⲛ	ⲛ	ⲛ	ⲛ	ⲛ	ⲛ	ⲛ	ⲛ	ⲛ	ⲛ
13b	/n̩/	ⲛ	ⲛ	ⲛ	(ⲛ)	ⲛ	ⲛ	(ⲛ)	ⲛ	(ⲛ)	?	?	?	[ⲛ?]	
13c	/n̩/	–	ⲛ	ⲛ	(ⲛ)	ⲛ	ⲛ	(ⲛ)	ⲛ	(ⲛ)	?	?	?	[ⲛ?]	
14	/ks/	ⲝ	ⲝ	ⲝ	ⲝ	ⲝ	ⲝ	[ⲝ]	ⲝ	[ⲝ]	[ⲝ]	[ⲝ]	[ⲝ]	[ⲝ]	(ⲝ)
15	/o/	ⲟ	ⲟ	ⲟ	ⲟ	ⲟ	ⲟ	ⲟ	ⲟ	ⲟ	ⲟ	ⲟ	ⲟ	ⲟ	
16	/p/	ⲡ	ⲡ	ⲡ	ⲡ	ⲡ	ⲡ	ⲡ	ⲡ	ⲡ	ⲡ	ⲡ	ⲡ	ⲡ	ⲡ
17a	/r/	ⲣ	ⲣ	ⲣ	ⲣ	ⲣ	ⲣ	ⲣ	ⲣ	ⲣ	ⲣ	ⲣ	ⲣ	ⲣ	ⲣ
17b	/r̩/	ⲣ	ⲣ	ⲣ	(ⲣ)	ⲣ	ⲣ	(ⲣ)	ⲣ	?	?	?	?	[ⲣ?]	
18	/s/	ⲥ	ⲥ	ⲥ	ⲥ	ⲥ	ⲥ	ⲥ	ⲥ	ⲥ	ⲥ	ⲥ	ⲥ	ⲥ	ⲥ
19	/t/	ⲧ	ⲧ	ⲧ	ⲧ	ⲧ	ⲧ	ⲧ	ⲧ	ⲧ	ⲧ	ⲧ	ⲧ	ⲧ	ⲧ
20a?	/y/	ⲩ	ⲩ	ⲩ	ⲩ	ⲩ	ⲩ	[ⲩ]	ⲩ	ⲩ	[ⲩ]	ⲩ	ⲩ	[ⲩ]	
20b	/u/	ⲟⲩ	ⲟⲩ	ⲟⲩ	ⲟⲩ	ⲟⲩ	ⲟⲩ	ⲟⲩ	ⲟⲩ	ⲟⲩ	ⲟⲩ	ⲟⲩ	ⲟⲩ	ⲟⲩ	ⲟⲩ

TABLE 1. *Synoptic Table of Coptic Alphabets, with Commentary (continued)*

		P	*İ*	*A* etc.	*B* etc.	*S* etc.	*M* etc.	*B7*	*L5* (Dub.)	*F7*	*F8*	*J*	*G*	*F9*	*H*
20c	/w/	(ⲟ)ⲩ	(ⲟ)ⲩ	(ⲟ)ⲩ	(ⲟ)ⲩ	(ⲟ)ⲩ	(ⲟ)ⲩ	[(ⲟ)ⲩ]	(ⲟ)ⲩ	(ⲟ)ⲩ	(ⲟ)ⲩ	(ⲟ)ⲩ	ⲟⲩ	(ⲟ)ⲩ	(ⲟ)ⲩ
21	/ph/	ⲫ	ⲫ	ⲫ	ⲫ	ⲫ	ⲫ	ⲫ	ⲫ	ⲫ	ⲫ	[ⲫ]	?	[ⲫ]	ⲫ
22	/kh/	ⲭ	ⲭ	ⲭ	ⲭ	ⲭ	ⲭ	[ⲭ?]	ⲭ?	ⲭ	ⲭ	ⲭ?	?	ⲭ?	ⲭ
23	/ps/	ⲯ	[ⲯ]	ⲯ	ⲯ	ϯ/ⲯ	ⲯ	[ⲯ]	ⲯ	ϯ/ⲯ	[ⲯ]	ⲯ	[ⲯ]	ⲯ	(ⲯ)
24	/ō/	ⲱ	ⲱ	ⲱ	ⲱ	ⲱ	ⲱ	ⲱ	ⲱ	ⲱ	ⲱ	ⲱ	ⲱ	ⲱ	ⲱ
25	/š/	ϣ	ϣ	ϣ	ϣ	ϣ	ϣ	ϣ	ϣ	ϣ	ϣ	[ϣ?]	=/=		ϣ
26	/f/	ϥ	ϥ	ϥ	ϥ	ϥ	ϥ	ϥ	ϥ	ϥ	.ϥ		ⲫ⃞		
27	/h/	ϩ	ϩ	ϩ	ϩ	ϩ	ϩ	ϩ	ϩ	ϩ	ϩ				ϩ
28	/č/	ϫ	ϫ	ϫ	ϫ	ϫ	ϫ	ϫ	ⲭ⃞	ϫ	ϫ	ⲭ⃞	=/=	ⲭ⃞	ϫ
29	/c/	ⲕ⃞	ϭ	ϭ		ϭ	ϭ		ϭ		ϭ				ϭ
30	/ti/	ϯ	ϯ	ϯ	ϯ	ϯ	ϯ	ϯ	ϯ	ϯ	=	[=?]	=	=	=
31	/ʾ/	⊥⃞	gem.	gem.		gem.			gem.			gem.		gem.	
32	/v/							ⲃ				ⲃ	ⲃ	ⲃ	ⲃ
33	/ce/	ϗ⃞	[=]	=		=	=					[=?]		=	=
34	/ç/	ⳋ⃞	ϣ̇⃞												
35	/x/	ϧ	ⳉ⃞	ⳉ⃞	ϧ			ⲭ				ⳉ⃞	ⲭ		
36	/čh/				ϭ			[ϭ]					?		
Total		35	32	31	31	30	30	30	29	29	29	26	24	24	25

Lines 2a–2b: In phonology, /ƀ/ has the value of a consonant (voiced), and /ƀ̩/ of a vowel (sonant) (cf. Kasser, 1981c). In *B* etc. (and also in *F5, F4,* here included in *S* etc. and *M* etc., respectively) /ƀ̩/ > /əƀ/ (*F5, F4* also /yƀ/ in specific cases); in *F7* /ƀ̩/ > /əƀ/, /iƀ/, /oƀ/ or /yƀ/, each in specific cases.

Lines 5a–5b: /e/ tonic, /ə/ atonic.

Lines 9a–9b: In phonology, /i/ has the value of a vowel and /j/ of a consonant (glide). With regard to the rules of dialectal or subdialectal orthography that cause the writing of ⲉⲓ or ⲓ for /i/ or /j/, cf. Kasser (1983) and, more detailed and less systematic, Quecke (1984).

Lines 11a–11b: In phonology, /l/ has the value of a consonant (voiced), /l̩/ of a vowel (sonant), (cf. Kasser, 1981c). *H* /l̩/ > /ēl/. Almost always in *B* etc. (and also everywhere in *F5* and *F4*, here included in *S* etc. and *M* etc., respectively), /l̩/ > /əl/. In *F7* /l̩/ > /əl/ or /il/, each in specific cases (there is no possibility of /ol/); but in *F9* /l̩/ in ⲥⲧⲁⲧⲟⲗ† (= [ϣⲧⲉⲗⲧⲱⲗ†]), troubled.

Lines 12a–12b: In phonology, /m/ has the value of a consonant (voiced), and /m̩/ of a vowel (sonant) (cf. Kasser, 1981c). *H* /m̩/ > /ēm/. In *B* etc. (and also *F5* and *F4*, here included in *S* etc. and *M* etc., respectively), /m̩/ most often > /əm/; in *F7* /m̩/ most frequently > /əm/, /im/, or /om/, each in specific cases.

Lines 13a–13c: In phonology, /n/ has the value of a consonant (voiced), and /n̩/ and /n̩/* of a vowel (sonant, /n̩/* being at the beginning of a syllable and forming a syllable with the consonant that follows it; cf. Kasser, 1981c). *H* /n̩/ > /ēn/. In *B* etc. (and in *F5* and *F4*, here included in *S* etc. and *M* etc., respectively), /n̩/ most often > /ən/; in *F7* /n̩/ most frequently > /ən/ or /in/, each in specific cases (not /on/ apparently; cf. l. 31).

Line 14: *H* very often ⲝ /ks/ > ⲕⲥ /ks/.

Lines 17a–17b: In phonology, /r/ has the value of a consonant (voiced), and /r̩/ of a vowel (sonant). *H* /r̩/ > /ēr/. In *B* etc. (and in *F5* and *F4*, here included in *S* etc. and *M* etc., respectively), /r̩/ most often > /ər/; in *F7* /r̩/ most frequently > /ər/ or /ir/, each in specific cases (there is no possibility of /or/). Would *F9* have had ⲣ /r̩/ there as it has ⲗ /l̩/?

Lines 20b–20c: In phonology, /u/ has the value of a vowel, and /w/ of a consonant (glide): ⲟⲩ or ⲩ for /w/.

Line 22 (cf. l. 28): *L5* (Johannine fragments in Dublin), *J*, and *F9* regularly replace ϫ by a ⲭ that is very probably equivalent to /č/ and not /kh/; however, there is in various Copto-Greek words a ⲭ that is probably equivalent to /kh/. These two types of ⲭ may not be in origin the same grapheme (demotic ⲭ ≠ Greek *χ*).

Line 23: *F7* (not *B74*) and also some *L6* texts (under *S* etc.) write ϯ for ⲯ; *H* very often ⲯ /ps/ > ⲡⲥ /ps/.

Line 25: *G* ⲥⲍ very probably equivalent to /š/.

Line 28: *G* ⲧⲍ very probably equivalent to /č/.

Line 30: *F8*, [*J*?], *G*, *F9*, *H* ⲧⲓ /ti/; ϯ is generally considered a grapheme of demotic origin (cf., e.g., Mallon, 1907; Steindorff, p. 12); but other interpretations remain possible (cf. Kasser, 1984–1985).

Line 31: Gem. signifies that /ʾ/ is rendered not by a grapheme of its own but by the second element of a graphic vocalic gemination (see ALEPH); in fact, in Papyrus Bodmer VI, the sole witness of *P*, ⊥ /ʾ/ aleph tends to be replaced by gem. (although at the same time – /n̩/* tends to be replaced by ⊥!).

Line 33: The compendium P ϗ /cə/ (? Coptic autochthonous words *P* ϗ = *S* ϭⲉ, then; *P* ⲛ̄ϗ = *S* ⲛ̄ϭⲓ, the proleptic particle) also appears in some Copto-Greek words, in which it is almost always equivalent to ⲕⲁⲓ as in the Greek manuscripts (thus *P* ⲇⲓϗⲟⲥ *δίκαιος*, just, 85 percent of the cases; ⲇⲓϗⲟⲥⲩⲛⲏ *δικαιοσύνη*, justice, 86 percent of the cases; ⲛ̄ϗⲡⲉⲣ *καίπερ*, although, one case; ϗⲣⲉⲗ *κειρία*, bandage, one case).

rather standardized example, even if its value may be open to debate, here are presented first the names of the Coptic letters as in Plumley (1948), with some adaptation: while Plumley writes the names in Coptic letters, they are here transliterated, generally in accordance with Plumley's system of phonetic equivalents (e = short e; ē = long e; o = short o; ō = long o; ch = guttural ch as in German *Wehrmacht,* army; g' = hard g): ⲁ = alpha, ⲃ = bēta, ⲅ = gamma, ⲇ = dalda, ⲉ = ey (or ei), ⲍ = zēta, ⲏ = hēta, ⲑ = thēta, ⲓ = yōta, ⲕ = kappa, ⲗ = lauda (or lawda), ⲙ = mē, ⲛ = ne, ⲝ = ksi, ⲟ = ow, ⲡ = pi, ⲣ = rō, ⲥ = sēmma, ⲧ = tau (or taw), ⲩ = he, ⲫ = phi, ⲭ = khi, ⲯ = psi, ⲱ = ō, ϣ = shai, ϥ = fai, ⳉ = chai, ϩ = hori, ϫ = janjia (or janjya), ϭ = g(y)ima, ϯ = ti.

Coming closer to the testimony of the texts in their (quite confusing) manifold witness, see also, from various periods and in Coptic, the names of graphemes noted by Crum (1939), a list completed here by that of the names of autochthonous Coptic letters that appears at the end of the (unpublished) Bodmer papyrus of the Acta Pauli (fourth–fifth centuries, *L5,* siglum hereafter Bod.): ⲁ = ⲁⲗⲫⲁ, ⲃ = ⲃⲏⲧⲁ (or ⲃⲓⲇⲁ), ⲅ = ⲅⲁⲙⲙⲁ, ⲇ = ⲇⲁⲗⲇⲁ (or ⲇⲗ̄ⲇⲁ), ⲉ = ⲉⲓ (or ⲉⲓⲉ), ⲍ = ⲍⲏⲧⲁ (or ⲍⲓⲧⲁ, ⲍⲁⲧⲁ), ⲏ = (ϩ)ⲏⲧⲁ (or ⲏⲓⲧⲁ, ϩⲁⲧⲉ), ⲑ = ⲑⲏⲧⲁ (or ⲑⲓⲧⲁ, ⲑⲉⲧⲉ), ⲓ = ⲓⲱⲧⲁ (or ⲓⲟⲧⲁ, ⲓⲁⲩⲇⲁ), ⲕ = ⲕⲁⲡⲡⲁ (or ⲕⲁⲡⲁ), ⲗ = ⲗⲁⲩⲇⲁ (probably for ⲗⲁⲃⲇⲁ, or ⲗⲁⲩⲗⲁ, ⲗⲟⲗⲉ), ⲙ = ⲙⲏ (or ⲙⲉ, ⲙⲓ), ⲛ = ⲛⲉ (or ⲛⲓ), ⲝ = ⲝⲓ, ⲟ = ⲟⲩ (or ⲟ), ⲡ = ⲡⲓ, ⲣ = ⲣⲱ (or ϩⲣⲟ), ⲥ = ⲥⲏⲙⲙⲁ (or ⲥⲩⲙⲙⲁ, ⲥⲓⲙⲁ, ⲥⲙ̄ⲙⲁ), ⲧ = ⲧⲁⲩ, ⲩ = ϩⲉ (or ⲩⲉ, ⲩⲁ), ⲫ = ⲫⲓ, ⲭ = ⲭⲓ, ⲯ = ⲯⲓ, ⲱ = ⲱ (or ⲁⲩ, ⲱⲟⲩ); then ϣ = ϣⲁⲓ (or ϣⲉⲓ; Bod. ϣⲏⲉ̣[ⲓ]); ϥ = ϥⲁⲓ (or ϥⲉⲓ; Bod. ϥⲏⲉⲓ); ⳉ = ⳉⲁⲓ (or ⳉⲉⲓ); ϩ = ϩⲟⲣⲓ (Bod. ϩⲱⲣⲉⲓ); ϫ = ϫⲁⲛϫⲓⲁ (or ϫⲉⲛϫⲉ; Bod. probably ϫⲁⲛϫⲛ̣, but ϫⲁⲛϫⲓ̣ⲁ̣ not excluded); ϭ = ϭⲓⲙⲁ (Bod. ϭⲉ̣ⲓ̣ⲙ̣ⲉ̣ very uncertain); ϯ = Bod. ϯⲉⲓ.

(1) So far as the Coptic graphemes of Greek origin are concerned, one will probably be closer to their primitive names if one names them in the Greek fashion: ⲁ = alpha, ⲃ = beta, ⲅ = gamma, ⲇ = delta, ⲉ = epsilon, ⲍ = zeta, ⲏ = eta, ⲑ = theta, ⲓ = iota, ⲕ = kappa, ⲗ = lambda, ⲙ = mu, ⲛ = nu, ⲝ = xi, ⲟ = omicron, ⲡ = pi, ⲣ = rho, ⲥ = sigma, ⲧ = tau, ⲩ = upsilon, ⲫ = phi, ⲭ = chi, ⲯ = psi, ⲱ = omega.

(2) For the Coptic graphemes of demotic origin in *S,* the preference here is for the following forms (in the *S* vocalism): ϣ = shai, ϥ = fai, ϩ = hori, ϫ = janja, ϭ = gima (easier to pronounce than the more exact k(y)ima), ϯ = ti.

(3) For the supplementary graphemes, apart from ⳉ, their names are unknown, so that it was necessary to create them (if possible in relation with their written form, which is certain because it can be observed, rather than with their phonological value, which is sometimes less certain): ⲍ /k/ = zetoid kappa; - /ṇ/ = hyphen-shaped nu; ⲭ /č/ (for ϫ) = chioid janja; ⊥ /'/ = reversed-tau-shaped aleph; ϗ = kai compendium; 9 = 9-spiraled grapheme; ϣ = crossed shai; ⳉ = khai or ḥai; ϩ = barred hori; ϭ /čh/ in *B* etc. = aspirated janja.

BIBLIOGRAPHY

Bitonto Kasser, A. di. "Ostraca scolastici copti a Deir el Gizāz." *Aegyptus* 68 (1988):167–75.

Bourguet, P. du. *Grammaire fonctionnelle et progressive de l'égyptien démotique.* Louvain, 1976.

Crum, W. E. *A Coptic Dictionary.* Oxford, 1939.

Funk, W.-P. "How Closely Related Are the Subakhmimic Dialects." *Zeitschrift für ägyptische Sprache und Altertumskunde* 112 (1985):124–39.

Hall, H. R. *Coptic and Greek Texts of the Christian Period from Ostraka, Stelae etc. in the British Museum.* London, 1905.

Husselman, E. M. "A Bohairic School Text on Papyrus." *Journal of Near Eastern Studies* 6 (1947):129–51.

______. *The Gospel of John in Fayumic Coptic (P. Mich. Inv. 3521).* Ann Arbor, Mich., 1962.

Kasser, R. *Papyrus Bodmer III, évangile de Jean et Genèse I–IV,2 en bohaïrique.* CSCO 177–178. Louvain, 1958.

______. "Dialectes, sous-dialectes et 'dialecticules' dans l'Egypte copte." *Zeitschrift für ägyptische Sprache und Altertumskunde* 92 (1966):106–15.

______. "L'Idiome de Bachmour." *Bulletin de l'Institut français d'archéologie orientale* 75 (1975):401–27.

______. "A propos de quelques caractéristiques orthographiques du vocabulaire grec utilisé dans les dialectes H et N." *Orientalia Lovaniensia Periodica* (Miscellanea in honorem Josephi Vergote) 6–7 (1975–1976):285–94.

______. "Prolégomènes à un essai de classification systématique des dialectes et subdialectes coptes selon les critères de la phonétique, I, Principes et terminologie." *Muséon* 93 (1980a):53–112. ". . . , II, Alphabets et systèmes phonétiques." *Muséon* 93 (1980b):237–97. ". . . , III, Systèmes orthographiques et catégories dialectales." *Muséon* 94 (1981a):91–152.

______. "Usages de la surligne dans le P. Bodmer VI, notes additionnelles." *Bulletin de la Société d'égyptologie, Genève* 5 (1981b):23–32.

______. "Voyelles en fonction consonantique, consonnes en fonction vocalique, et classes de phonèmes en copte." *Bulletin de la Société d'égyptologie, Genève* 5 (1981c):33–50.

______. "EI ou I pour /i/ ou /j/ dans les dialectes coptes." *Bulletin of the American Society of Papyrologists* 20 (1983):123–26.

______. "Orthographe et phonologie de la variété

subdialectale lycopolitaine des textes gnostiques coptes de Nag Hammadi." *Muséon* 97 (1984):261–312.
______. "Psi en ti et ti pointé dans le P. Biling. 1 de Hambourg." *Bulletin de la Société d'égyptologie, Genève* 9–10 (1984–1985):135–40.
Kasser, R., and H. Satzinger. "L'Idiome du P. Mich. 5421 (trouvé à Karanis, nord-est du Fayoum)." *Wiener Zeitschrift für die Kunde des Morgenlandes* 74 (1982):15–32.
Krall, J. "Reste koptischer Schulbücherliteratur." *Mittheilungen aus der Sammlung der Papyrus Erzherzog Rainer* 4 (1888):126–35.
Mallon, A. *Grammaire copte, avec bibliographie, chrestomathie et vocabulaire.* 2nd ed. Beirut, 1907.
Plumley, J. M. *An Introductory Coptic Grammar (Sahidic Dialect).* London, 1948.
Quecke, H. "Ein altes bohairisches Fragment des Jakobusbriefes (P. Heid. Kopt. 452)." *Orientalia* 43 (1974):382–93.
______. "Zur Schreibung von i/j in der koptischen Buchschrift." In *Studien zu Sprache und Religion Ägyptens,* Vol. 1, *Sprache, zu Ehren von Wolfhart Westendorf überreicht von seinen Freunden und Schülern,* pp. 289–326. Göttingen, 1984.
Steindorff, G. *Koptische Grammatik, mit Chrestomathie, Wörterverzeichnis und Literatur.* Berlin, 1930.
______. *Lehrbuch der koptischen Grammatik.* Chicago, 1951.
Stern, L. *Koptische Grammatik.* Leipzig, 1880.
Till, W. C. *Koptische Grammatik (saïdischer Dialekt), mit Bibliographie, Lesestücken und Wörterverzeichnissen.* Leipzig, 1955.
Worrell, W. H. *Coptic Texts in the University of Michigan Collection.* Ann Arbor, Mich., 1942.

RODOLPHE KASSER

ALPHABETS, OLD COPTIC. The group of texts designated OLD COPTIC does not represent a linguistic unity, but on the contrary a motley collection of essays spaced out between the first and fourth centuries A.D. Chronologically they most frequently predate literary Coptic, but sometimes, though rarely, are contemporary with its beginnings. However that may be, through their character as isolated essays tentatively made, not very systematic or even practically unsystematic, and through their language, in which one observes a significant proportion of pre-Coptic features, they all logically represent a stage prior to that of literary Coptic, including proto-Coptic. The latter is already systematic and makes its appearance in the form of PROTODIALECTS, many of which have disappeared without leaving any traces, but two of which are nevertheless attested by Coptic documents that have survived the vicissitudes of the tormented history of the Copts: DIALECT İ (proto-Lycopolitan) and DIALECT P (an alphabetically and phonologically archaic idiom that often looks like what can be known about a proto-Sahidic, tentatively reconstructed and considered immigrant into the Theban region).

In these circumstances, it is scarcely surprising that each of the Old Coptic texts attests a particular Coptic alphabet (or if one prefers, a particular variety of Coptic alphabet). It is reasonable to suppose that all these alphabets included all the Coptic letters of Greek origin—a supposition and not a certainty, because these very ancient texts are generally too short for each to attest all these Greek graphemes. But there is no reason to suspect that one or more of these Greek letters was systematically eliminated in one or another of these alphabets, as is the case in the Coptic alphabet of a late text like that which attests DIALECT H (cf. ALPHABETS, COPTIC, synoptic table), which lacks the ⲅ, ⲇ, and ⲍ of Greek origin. All these Old Coptic alphabets included letters of demotic origin, generally in larger numbers than the Coptic alphabet properly so called, especially since the varieties of Old Coptic have at the same time a number of phonemes more significant than that of the Coptic idioms (the evolution proceeding logically toward phonological and graphical simplification and hence toward a reduction in the number of phonemes and graphemes). The synoptic table of Old Coptic alphabets (Table 1), which includes all the Old Coptic texts that are available and makes use of letters of demotic origin, will make this evident.

The sigla for the texts used in this table are as follows: Schm. = the Schmidt Papyrus (first–second century); Hor. = the London Horoscope Papyrus (first–second century); Mich. = the Michigan Horoscope Papyrus (second century); Mun. = the Munich Papyrus ([schoolbook?] second century); Ox. = the Egyptian Oxyrhynchus Papyrus (second century); Mum. = the two mummy labels in Berlin (second century); Mim. = the Mimaut Papyrus (third century); DMP = the Demotic Magical Papyrus of London and Leiden (third–fourth century); Par. 1 = first non-Greek section of the Paris Magical Papyrus (fourth century); Par. 2 = second non-Greek section (but not the third and last) of the Paris Magical Papyrus (fourth century).

To the alphabets of these ten texts properly designated Old Coptic are added here, by way of comparison, those of the only two protodialects surviving in Coptic, *P* and *İ*, because both have preserved certain phonemes of Old Coptic that later disappeared in

TABLE 1. *Synoptic Table of Old Coptic Alphabets, with Commentary*

		Schm.	Hor.	Mich.	Mun.	Ox.	Mum.	Mim.	DMP.	Par.1	Par.2	*P*	*İ*
1	/k/	ⲕ	ⲍ	ⲕ?	?	ⲕ	?	ⲕ	ⲍ	ⲕ	ⲕ	ⲍ	ⲕ
2	/ṇ/	ⲛ	–	ⲛ	?	ⲛ	ⲛ	ⲛ	ⲛ	ⲛ	ⲛ	–	ⲛ
3	/š/	/	3	ϣ	?	ϣ	3	ϭ	3	ϣ?	ϭ	ϣ	ϣ
4	/f/	ϥ	ϥ	ϥ	?	ϥ	?	ϥ	ϥ	ϥ	ϥ	ϥ	ϥ
5	/h/	ⲣ	9	ϩ	?	ⲣ	?	3	?	3	L	ϩ	ϩ
6	/č/	ɗ	ɗ	ɗ	?	ɗ	?	ш	ɗ	ɗ?	?	ϫ	ϫ
7	/c/	△	ⲕ	?	?	ϭ	?	?	ⲕ	?	?	ⲕ	ϭ
8	/ti/	=	=	=	?	=	?	=	=	=	=	ϯ	ϯ
9	/ʾ/		(⊥)?			?	?	?	?		gem.	⊥	gem.
10	/ç/		ϭ	(ȝ)?	ϭ	ϭ	?		ϭ	ϭ		9	ϣ̇
11	/x/	?	ϧ	ϧ	?	ϧ	?		?? ? ϧ/9/ϫ		(ϫ)	ϧ	ⳉ
12	/čh/									(ɗ)			
13	/ḥ/	3			ɩ	ɩϩ	?		ⲣⲩ?				
Total		31?	35	31	32?	33?	?	28?	34?	30?	27?	35	32

(In the following, "A.C. table" refers to the synoptic table in ALPHABETS, COPTIC.)

Line 1 (A.C. table, l. 10): Hor. generally has ⲍ /k/ and ⲕ /c/, but this text tends to confuse these two phonemes, since one also finds several ⲕ for /k/ and (more rarely) ⲍ for /c/. Mich. is so fragmentary that one cannot be sure here of its witness. Did Mim. also use, alongside ⲕ, a kind of ⲍ for /k/ (cf. Kasser, 1980, p. 265)? DMP generally has ⲍ /k/ and ⲕ /c/, but one also finds some ⲕ /k/ (confusion of the two phonemes).

Line 2 (A.C. table, ll. 13b–13c): Hor. has – for /ṇ/, while *P* has it rather for /ṇ/'.

Line 3 (A.C. table, l. 25): In Schm. the choice of / for /s/ is strange (in demotic / renders /r/ and also /f/; du Bourguet, 1976, p. 82). One of the texts of Mum. is written from right to left, with all but three of its letters equally turned from right to left, but 3 remains without inversion; the second text is written from left to right, with its 3 just as it is. In Mim., in one case, the editor of the text indicates the presence of an 9 (as in *P*) in place of ϭ, but it is preferable to take no account of this reading (at this point the text is almost entirely erased, and the photo shows no trace to allow us to confirm this assumption, however weakly). Par. 1, a single example, has perhaps the clumsy draft of a ϣ (rather than a 3, or still less a ϭ, Kasser, 1980, p. 267).

Line 4 (A.C. table, l. 26): Nothing.

Line 5 (A.C. table, l. 27): In Schm. generally, the ancient *h* is rendered by a ⲣ (of a very particular form; Kasser, 1980, p. 257), and the ancient *ḥ* by 3. In Ox., the ancient *h* is generally ⲣ, and the ancient *ḥ* is ɩ or ϩ. In DMP, for want of certain examples deriving from an ancient *h*, it is difficult to say whether there the ancient *ḥ* and *h* have reconciled their opposition to converge in a uniform /h/, rendered now by ⲣ, now by ⲩ, or whether eventually only the ancient *ḥ* is rendered by ⲣ or ⲩ, the ancient *h* having completely disappeared; this strange ⲩ of DMP is only there at the beginning of a word (but some other beginnings of words, more rare, also have ⲣ) and for preference before a vowel (supplementary details in Kasser, 1980, p. 268). In Par. 2, L is placed only rarely "before" the vowel that phonologically follows it; most often it is placed above it (like the Greek epigraphic rough breathing, which it much resembles and of which it might eventually be a variant); it also happens that the scribe replaces this L above the line by a simple "acute accent" or again that he forgets it altogether.

Line 6 (A.C. table, l. 28): In Schm. ɗ has the form of a large Greek *α*. In Mim. the regular form is decidedly ш (the two ϫ read by the editor of the text are extremely doubtful). In Par. 1, /č/ is normally rendered by ɗ (two cases), but also (through phonological confusion of /č/ and /ç/) by ϭ (two cases) or even by ϫ (one case, through the influence of the contemporary Coptic alphabet).

Line 7 (A.C. table, l. 29): Mich. very uncertain.

Line 8 (A.C. table, l. 30): Nothing.

Line 9 (A.C. table, l. 31): In Hor. three cases only, all rather doubtful (phoneme that could be /ʾ/, grapheme more or less resembling a ⊥ or a ɗ (Kasser, 1980, p. 264); in Ox. the possibility of a ⊥ remains too hazardous (ibid., p. 264).

Line 10 (A.C. table, l. 34): Hor. presents three cases where ϧ is written in place of ϭ and perhaps a further case where ϭ is written in place of ϧ (confusion between the phonemes /x/ and /ç/). The only ȝ of Mich. is in a context extremely (perhaps excessively) obscure. It is not very likely that ϭ of Ox. ever renders /x/ (Kasser, 1980, p. 267). In DMP there is eventually (?) a case where /ç/ is rendered by ȝ.

Line 11 (A.C. table, l. 35): In DMP there is an uncertain ϧ (two cases), a certain 9 (one case), and a probable ϫ (one case). In Par. 2, if L regularly renders /h/, it also renders /x/ two out of three times, ϫ rendering it (more correctly) one out of three times (tendency toward the neutralization of the opposition of the phonemes /h/ and /x/, in favor of the sole survival of a uniform /h/?).

Line 12 (A.C. table, l. 36): Mim. probably does not have this /čh/ (cf. Kasser, 1980, p. 269). With regard to the problem of the eventual existence of the phoneme /čh/ rather than /č/ in Par. 1, cf. Kasser (1980, p. 269).

Line 13 (no corresponding line in AC table): With regard to DMP, see above, line 5.

Coptic; *P* even has in its alphabet such a large number of letters typical of Old Coptic that it reaches a total alphabet of at least thirty-five graphemes. This is thus an alphabet as rich as the richest of the Old Coptic alphabets (excluding exceptional graphemes; see below), that of Hor., with its thirty-five letters; one might even say that *P* has thirty-six graphemes if one admits that the ⲕ /k/ of its Copto-Greek vocabulary is to be distinguished from the ⲕ /c/ of its autochthonous vocabulary, the first developing from the Greek *κ*, and the second from a demotic grapheme (see du Bourguet, 1976, p. 75, sign for *g*, first variant).

To facilitate comparison, the order of the phonemes is that of the final sections in the synoptic table of Coptic alphabets (only nos. 25–36 are concerned), except for /k/ and /ṇ/, placed right at the beginning, and /ḥ/, placed at the very end. In the table hereafter, the sign = indicates that instead of rendering /ti/ by a single grapheme, ϯ, the text in question renders it by two letters, ⲧⲓ; "gem." signifies that /'/ is rendered not by a grapheme of its own (like ⊥ in Hor. [?] and *P*) but by the second element of a graphic vocalic gemination (see ALEPH).

In this presentation of the graphemes typical of Old Coptic, each is given in a standardized form and no account is taken of its numerous particular graphic variants (sometimes very perceptibly remote from one another); so far as ϥ is concerned, it has been fixed in the form that it habitually has in Coptic, although in Old Coptic this form is generally much closer to that (the most usual) of the demotic grapheme for /f/ (du Bourguet, 1976, p. 3), especially with its stem strongly inclined toward the right. Furthermore, the signs are limited to those that appear regularly in these texts (or nearly so); it has not been judged indispensable to include also certain rare forms of Old Coptic graphemes whose use is occasional (or even, in most cases, exceptional) and does not seem to have any particular phonological significance (these unusual forms appear above all in Schm., Hor., Ox., DMP, and Par. 1; further details will be found in Kasser, 1980, pp. 256–57).

Right at the end, in the count of the total number of the graphemes of each Old Coptic alphabet (and of the two proto-Coptic alphabets *P* and *İ*), account is taken only of the graphemes of demotic origin that appear fairly regularly in these texts (as just explained), and it is assumed with regard to each text that the alphabet it uses had the full complement of the twenty-four letters of Greek origin, according to the assumption made above.

The majority of the graphemes of Old Coptic alphabets presented here are considered, as has been said, as being certainly of demotic origin; for others (especially ⲕ /c/, ⲩ /ḥ/, ⲭ /x/ and, above all, sometimes even /č/ in Coptic, if not in Old Coptic), even if their appearance is wholly that of graphemes of Greek origin, one may strongly suspect that it is a case of signs of demotic origin having been entirely assimilated graphically to Greek letters that resemble them and have influenced their graphic form.

This series of letters will now be reviewed in the following order: first the graphemes of Greek appearance; then the letters of demotic origin utilized in Coptic; and, finally, the graphemes of demotic origin (whether certain or possible), utilized only in Old Coptic, not in Coptic (the Coptic protodialect *P*, however, here rejoining the Old Coptic group).

In the enumeration of each of these signs below, there is first indicated, so far as possible, the precise demotic sign from which it derives or may be presumed to have derived; for these references to the demotic graphemes, the work cited will in each case be implicitly du Bourguet (1976, p. 75), where the "usual" graphic forms are presented on the left and their "variants" on the right. Thereafter, the name of the (Old) Coptic grapheme will be given: the name traditionally known in the case of the letters ϣ, ϥ, ϧ, ϩ, ϫ, ϭ, ϯ used in Coptic and a name unknown and to be created in the case of the other letters. The latter has been done, where possible, in relation to the graphic form (which is certain because it can be observed) rather than to the phonological value (sometimes very uncertain and above all very variable from one Old Coptic text to another).

1. ⲕ /c/ could strictly speaking be the same grapheme as ⲕ /k/ (of Greek origin), /k/ and /c/ being phonologically close to one another and hence liable to be confused; but if that was not the case, the demotic original of ⲕ /c/ (not /k/) could be the first variant of the sign for *g*. Name assigned: *kappaoid gima* (easier to pronounce than the more exact "kappaoid k(y)ima").

2. ⲩ /ḥ/ (or /h/?), always at the beginning of a word, is not very likely to be the same grapheme as ⲩ /y/ (of Greek origin), and this even if one must record that (with very rare exceptions in *F* and *M*) in Coptic ⲩ alone (hence not preceded by ⲁ, ⲉ, or ⲏ and not in any case ⲟⲩ) can only be found in a Copto-Greek word and that at the beginning of a word the Greek *υ* always has the rough breathing, equivalent (the most normal spelling in Sahidic, etc.) to ϩⲩ- in Coptic. This ⲩ could thus be a distortion of the Greek epigraphic rough breathing ⊢, placed above the ϒ and finally confused with it; but this ϒ /ḥ/ could better still have a demotic origin: see the third of the variants of the sign for *ḥ*. Name assigned: *Y-shaped grapheme.*

3. ϫ /x/ could strictly be the same grapheme as ϫ /kh/, corresponding to some local Greek pronunciation; if not, there is some chance that it issued from the fourth variant of the demotic sign for *ẖ*. Name assigned: *chioid ḥai* or *chioid khai.*

4. ϫ /č/ is phonologically so remote from ϫ /kh/ (of Greek origin) that their confusion appears very unlikely (even if one ventures to suppose a local Greek pronunciation in which [k] > [t] and [h] > [š], hence [kh] > [tš] > [č]); it is more reasonable to make this ϫ /č/ derive from the demotic sign for *ḏ*, first variant (slightly inclined to the left). Name assigned: *chioid janja.*

5. ʟ /h/ will evidently be interpreted first of all as a variant (in truth not rare) of the Greek epigraphic rough breathing (the more so since in Old Coptic one finds ʟ not only as a letter placed between the other graphemes of its line but also as an "accent" placed above graphemes in its line, as the rough breathing would be placed). One cannot, however, exclude a demotic origin for this sign also: see the grapheme for *h*, fifth or seventh variant (with the final "hook" cut off). Name assigned: *L-shaped grapheme.*

6. ϣ /š/ derives from the demotic sign for *š*, third usual form (see also the fifth and eighth variants). Traditional name: *shai.*

7. ϣ̄ /ç/ evidently derives from the same sign as ϣ, but completed by a diacritical element. Name assigned: *crossed shai.*

8. ϥ (Coptic graphic form) /f/ derives from the demotic sign for *f*, first variant (which is however clearly inclined toward the right, as is ϥ in its graphic form in Old Coptic; see above). Traditional name: *fai;* in Old Coptic it could also, if preferred, be called *inclined fai.*

9. ϧ /x/ derives from the demotic sign for *ẖ*, first usual form. Traditional name: *ḫai* or *khai.*

10. ϩ /h/ derives from the demotic sign for *h*, usual form (but not without some graphic evolution). Traditional name: *hori.*

11. ϩ̄ /x/ clearly derives from the same sign as ϩ but is completed by a diacritical element. Name assigned: *barred hori.*

12. ϫ /c/ derives from the demotic sign for *ḏ*, the first of the usual forms or the last of the variants (but in both with some graphic evolution). Traditional name: *janja.*

13. ϭ (Coptic graphic form) /c/ derives from the demotic sign for *k*, the first of the usual forms (which has, however, a very small loop and stretches its upper antenna at length to the right, as is the case also with ϭ in Old Coptic; see above). It is probable that this form of the Old Coptic ϭ should not lead one to confuse it with the graphically very similar one that Par. 1 eventually uses for /čh/ rather than for /c/ (see no. 30). Traditional name: *gima;* in Old Coptic one may also call it, if preferred, *stretched gima.*

14. ϭ /čh/ (only in *B*, etc.) could be derived not from the demotic sign for *k* (see above with reference to ϭ /c/), but from the demotic sign for *ḏ*, the last of the variants, which resembles a bulging *α* with the rounded part below and the two "horns" above (suppression of the left horn would in fact produce a kind of ϭ). Name assigned: *aspirated janja.*

15. ϯ /ti/ is generally considered as derived from the demotic sign for *t*, the second or eighth of the variants (with considerable graphic evolution). It will, however, be remarked that this Coptic letter has exactly the form of the ϯ in Latin epigraphy, a compendium for /ti/, more rarely for /it/ (cf. Kasser, 1984–1985); a strong graphic influence from the Latin compendium on the demotic sign, strangely absent from Old Coptic but adopted in Coptic, seems to be the least one can admit. Traditional name: *ti.*

16. ϯ /ps/ is the customary form of the grapheme psi in the Greek manuscripts contemporary with the oldest Coptic manuscripts; all the same, after the adoption of ϯ /ti/ (a non-Greek grapheme) in Coptic, it was necessary to modify the form of the psi, ϯ > ψ, to avoid confusion with ϯ /ti/. (The Coptic texts that still write ϯ /ps/, all very ancient, are rare.) Name assigned: *tioid psi.*

17. ⊥ /'/ derives from the demotic sign for *ỉ*, the third of the usual forms, perhaps also influenced by the demotic sign for *3*, the first of the usual forms or the first of the variants. Name assigned: *reversed tau-shaped aleph.*

18. ⳤ /k/ derives from the demotic sign for *ḳ*, the second of the usual forms. Name assigned: *zetoid kappa.*

19. - /n̩/ derives from the demotic sign for *n*, the first of the usual forms. Name assigned: *hyphen-shaped nu.*

20. 3, the equivalent in Old Coptic most often for /š/, but also sometimes for /h/ or /ḥ/, has particularly variable graphic forms (see above) and derives from the demotic sign for *š*, the second usual form (see also the thirteenth and the twenty-sixth variants for *ḥ*). Name assigned: *3-shaped grapheme.*

21. ϭ, the equivalent in Old Coptic most often for /ç/, but also sometimes for /š/, derives from the demotic sign for ẖ, the first usual form. Name assigned: *6-spiraled grapheme.*

22. ୨, the equivalent in Old Coptic (Hor.) of /h/ or (DMP and less clearly) /x/, but systematically equivalent to /ç/ in proto-Coptic *P* (an inversion of the ϭ presented just above?), derives from the demotic sign for *h*, the usual form (?) or first, third, or sixth variant (strongly developed on the graphic level), or eventually also from the demotic sign for *h*, tenth variant (?). Name assigned: *9-spiraled grapheme.*

23. ⁄ /s/ probably also derives from some variant of a demotic sign, but which? For phonological reasons, one cannot compare it with the sign for *r*, second usual form, or the sign for *f*, third variant, or the sign for *l*, second usual form, or even the sign for *ḥ*, fourth variant. Name assigned: *fraction-stroke-shaped grapheme.*

24. ϩ /ç/ (? in Mich.) does indeed seem to derive from the demotic sign for *ḥ*, second usual form. Name assigned: *stretched-capital-sigma-shaped grapheme.*

25. ρ, the equivalent in Old Coptic of /h/ (Schm. and Ox.), or again perhaps /ḥ/ (DMP), has particularly variable graphic forms: it may be almost vertical (Ox.) or more or less sloping (Schm.); its loop may be closed (Ox.) or less angular and largely open, in the manner of a demotic *h* (Schm., see further on). ρ derives from the demotic sign for *h*, the usual form or the first of the variants (with, probably, a fairly clear influence from the sign for *ḥ*, the second usual form; see also the fifth, sixth, and seventh variants, and again, phonologically incompatible, the sixth of the variants of the demotic sign for *w*). Name assigned: *P-shaped grapheme*, though one might specify in Ox. *three-corner P-shaped grapheme*, in Schm. *inclined-open-P-shaped grapheme*, or in a different way *demotic-h-shaped grapheme.*

26. ʕ /ḥ/ derives from the demotic sign for *ḥ*, the third of the usual forms (and fifth and sixth variants). Name assigned: *hook-shaped grapheme.*

27. ɑ /c/ derives from the demotic sign for *ḏ*, a compromise (clearly evolved) between the first usual form and the last variant. Name assigned: *minuscule-alpha-shaped grapheme.*

28. ꓕꓕ /c/ derives from the demotic sign for *ḏ*, second usual form (graphically evolved). Name assigned: *reversed-pi-shaped grapheme.*

29. ◭ /c/ perhaps derives from the demotic sign for *k*, the first or second variant (graphically evolved); it is difficult to see its origin in one or other of the variants of the sign for *g*. Name assigned: *divided-triangle-shaped grapheme.*

30. The grapheme of Mich. for /c/ (?) and that of Par. 1 for /čh/ (?) (see no. 13 and Kasser, 1980, p. 269) are decidedly too doubtful to merit being studied here and named, given present knowledge.

BIBLIOGRAPHY

Bourguet, P. du. *Grammaire fonctionnelle et progressive de l'égyptien démotique.* Louvain, 1976.

Kasser, R. "Prolégomènes à un essai de classification systématique des dialectes et subdialectes coptes selon les principes de la phonétique, II, Alphabets et systèmes phonétiques." *Muséon* 93 (1980):237–97.

______. "Psi en ti et ti pointé dans le P. Biling. 1 de Hambourg." *Bulletin de la Société d'égyptologie, Genève* 9–10 (1984–1985):135–40.

RODOLPHE KASSER

ʿAYIN. ʿAyin (= ʿ) is the voiced laryngeal fricative (Vergote, 1945, pp. 10, 72–76, 79–80), the Arabic ع . It belongs to the phonological inventory of ancient and also later Egyptian, perhaps even as far as the beginnings of demotic (cf. Vergote, 1945, pp. 122–23, and 1973, pp. 31–32; du Bourguet, 1976, pp. 3–4, 75). However, it probably does not belong any longer to the phonological inventory of Coptic or even Pre-Coptic, not even as a CRYPTOPHONEME, in contrast to ALEPH. (Hence, this discussion will set aside the hypothesis of those who have been tempted to see, or have actually thought to see, a phonemic survival of ʿ in the second element of the graphic vocalic gemination [see GEMINATION, VOCALIC] typical of certain lexemes belonging to *S* etc.)

Like the lost *3* or the revived /ʾ/ (cf. ALEPH), ʿayin nonetheless plays an important role in Coptic phonology; its presence, although anterior to Coptic, has not only influenced the vocalization of contemporary Egyptian but has also often left its mark in the vocalization of certain Coptic dialects and subdialects. On the other hand, it will be noted that in numerous cases ʿ itself has not entirely disappeared but has survived in some way, being transformed into /ʾ/, this phonological aleph (in tachysyllabication) normally appearing in orthography (as a phenomenon of bradysyllabication) through the graphic doubling of the phonologic tonic vowel preceding this /ʾ/ ("echo effect"), except in the final position (see below and SYLLABICATION).

Thus, according to Vergote (1973, pp. 30–33):

(1) At the beginning of the tonic syllable, both at the beginning and within the word, ʿ has disappeared in Coptic without leaving traces (e.g., *ʿānaḫ* /ṓnh/ ⲱⲛ̄ϩ, life; *waʿáb* > /wṓp/ ⲟⲩⲟⲡ, be pure) or, just as in the other positions (see below), the ʿ (after the general disappearance of *3)* has taken the value of the laryngeal occlusive /ʾ/, which is rendered by the first element (unstressed but the most-voiced) of a hiatus in the archaizing form of writing *rmt ʿ3* > languages or DIALECTS etc. *S* etc. /rm̥maṓ/ ⲣⲙ̄ⲙⲁⲟ, *B* /ramaṓ/ ⲣⲁⲙⲁⲟ, *M* /rm̥məá/ ⲣⲙⲙⲉⲁ, *F5* /ləmə̍a/ ⲗⲉⲙⲉⲁ, rich.

(2) At the beginning and end of the unstressed pretonic syllable and in the stressed final syllable, ʿ has generally disappeared, though leaving traces in the vocalization ("anteriorization" of the stressed vowel, or articulation of vowels more and more forward, /o/ > /a/ and /a/ > /e/, /o/ being less forward than /a/, and /a/ even less than /e/); thus atonic ⲁ; *S*, *B* tonic ⲁ instead of ⲟ; *F* tonic ⲉ instead of ⲁ, as in *ʿanáḫ(ḫa)* > /anáš/ ⲁⲛⲁϣ, etc., oath; *yaʿ-dá3t⸗* > /ja-tṓʾt⸗/ ⲉⲓⲁ ⲧⲟⲟⲧ⸗, etc., wash the hands. At the end of monosyllabic words the ʿ > /ʾ/ is sometimes preserved in some way (tachysyllabically) in *A* and *F* and there rendered (orthographically) by the second element (unstressed and the less-voiced) of a hiatus (where it plays the role of a "similiglide"; cf. Kasser, 1981b, p. 35), while in *B* this essentially vocalic linkage has become a veritable diphthong (its second element being the glide /j/), as in *baʿ* > baʾ > *S* /bá/ ⲃⲁ, *A*, *L* /báə/ ⲃⲁⲉ, *B* /báj/ ⲃⲁⲓ, *F* /béj/ ⲃⲉ(ⲉ)ⲓ, palm (cf. ALEPH, end of article); but note, on the other hand, *d̲abáʿ* > *S*, *A*, *L* /tbá/ ⲧⲃⲁ, *B* /thbá/ ⲑⲃⲁ, *F* /tbé/ ⲧⲃⲉ, ten thousand.

(3) At the beginning of the unstressed syllable before a consonant and in the unstressed final syllable of a word, ʿ has been preserved (in some way) in Coptic in the form of /ʾ/, except in *M*, *W*, *V4*, *F4*, *B* (and its subdialects), and *G*, as in *šaʿad* > /šṓʾt/ *S* ϣⲱⲱⲧ, *B* ϣⲱⲧ, to cut. When ʿ was the third radical, there was inversion (except in some particularly archaic idioms; see below), but the ʿ > /ʾ/ did not modify the "timbre" of the vowel, as in *múšʿu* > *S* /mḗʾšə/ ⲙⲏⲏϣⲉ, *B* /mḗš/ ⲙⲏϣ, crowd. Here, however, the archaic orthography will be noted (unstressed finals in -ⲁ instead of the usual -ⲉ or -ⲓ, with at the same time generally no graphic vocalic gemination), which attracts attention in some idioms: the PROTO-DIALECT *P* (in its most ancient form, phonologically very often similar to a reconstructed **ppS*, cf. DIALECT P) and the peripheral and often archaic subdialect *F7;* they are survivals from a stage in which the metathesis had not yet taken place and ʿ has retained its value, preserving the /a/ that derives from old *a* and *u* (which shows the late date of the change in question). *F5* and *V5* for their part present at once the gemination caused by ʿ > /ʾ/ and the peculiar atonic final vocalization (-ⲉ instead of the usual -ⲓ) resulting from the still active influence of ʿ. Finally, *F4*, *V4*, and *W* appear in a manner analogous to *P* and *F7*, with, however, in this case, as in *V5* and *F5*, an atonic final vowel in -ⲉ instead of the usual -ⲓ, as in *múšʿu* > *P* (and *F7*) /meḗša/ ⲙⲏϣⲁ, *W*, *F4* /mḗšə/ ⲙⲏϣⲉ, *F5* /mḗʾšə/ ⲙⲏⲏϣⲉ (*S*, *B* see above), crowd; *d̲úbʿu* > *P* /tḗba/ ⲧⲏⲃⲁ, *F5* /tḗʾbə/ ⲧⲏⲏⲃⲉ, cf. *S* /tḗʾbə/ ⲧⲏⲏⲃⲉ, *B* /tḗb/ ⲧⲏⲃ, finger (cf. Kasser, 1981a, 94–95). In the cases of /ʾ/ < ʿ at the end of a tonic syllable before a consonant, *S* presents an ⲁ instead of ⲟ; on the other hand, it has a tonic ⲟ before the /ʾ/ derived from other consonants, as in *d̲r.t.f.* > /tṓʾtf/ ⲧⲟⲟⲧ⸗ϥ, his hand. This proves that at the time of the general change at first in *B*, later in *S*, from /a/ to /o/ between the seventh and the sixth centuries A.D., ʿ had preserved its value as a voiced laryngeal fricative and had not yet become the unvoiced laryngeal occlusive /ʾ/ called ALEPH (Vergote, 1973, pp. 31–32). On the other hand, the presence of the tonic ⲁ in *B*, despite the disappearance of /ʾ/ < ʿ, shows that the latter phoneme is still later (e.g., *wáʿbu S* /wáʾb/ ⲟⲩⲁⲁⲃ†, *B* /wáb/ ⲟⲩⲁⲃ†, holy). When the ʿ precedes *ḥ*, *S* and *B* and even *A* and *L* present an ⲟ; it must be concluded that by differentiation ("dissimilation") between the two laryngeal frications, the voiced and the unvoiced, ʿ had already become /ʾ/ before the general change of /a/ to /o/ had come about (e.g., *yáʿḥu* > *S*, *A* /óʾh/ ⲟⲟϩ, *B* /jóh/ ⲓⲟϩ, moon). The ʿ that ends the atonic final syllable of a word has undergone a metathesis, without, however, modifying the quantity of the tonic syllable, which thereby became closed; when the second radical was *ḥ*, either ʿ disappeared or (after metathesis) it was entirely assimilated to this consonant; sometimes ʿ was changed into *ḥ* > ϩ; e.g. *pānaʿ* > *S* /pṓʾnə/ ⲡⲱⲱⲛⲉ, *B* /phṓnh/ ⲫⲱⲛϩ (cf. *F5* /pṓʾnə/ [ⲡⲱⲱ]ⲛⲉ), to change; *ʿāḥaʿ* > *S* /óhə/ ⲱϩⲉ, *B* etc. /óhi/ ⲟϩⲓ, etc., stand, stay; *d̲āmaʿ* > *S* /čṓʾmə/ ϫⲱⲱⲙⲉ (*F5* = *S*), *B* /čṓm/ ϫⲱⲙ, book (Vergote, 1973, pp. 30–33).

BIBLIOGRAPHY

Bourguet, P. du. *Grammaire fonctionnelle et progressive de l'égyptien démotique*. Louvain, 1976.

Kasser, R. "Prolégomènes à un essai de classification des dialectes et subdialectes coptes selon les critères de la phonétique, III, Systèmes orthographiques et catégories dialectales." *Muséon* 94 (1981a):87–148.

———. "Voyelles en fonction consonantique, consonnes en fonction vocalique, et classes de phonèmes en copte." *Bulletin de la Société d'égyptologie, Genève* 5 (1981b):33–50.
———. "Marius Chaîne et la thèse d'une relation phonologique privilégiée entre les langues coptes saïdique et bohaïrique." *Journal of Coptic Studies* 1 (1990):73–77.
Satzinger, H. "On the Origin of the Sahidic Dialect." In *Acts of the Second International congress of Coptic Studies, Roma 22–26 September 1980*, ed. T. Orlandi and F. Wisse, pp. 307–12. Rome, 1985.
———. "On the Prehistory of the Coptic Dialects." In *Coptic Studies, Acts of the Third International Congress of Coptic Studies, Warsaw, 20–25 August, 1984*, ed. W. Godlewski, pp. 413–16. Warsaw, 1990.
Stern, L. *Koptische Grammatik.* Leipzig, 1880.
Till, W. C. "Altes 'Aleph und 'Ajin im Koptischen." *Wiener Zeitschrift für die Kunde des Morgenlandes* 36 (1929):186–96.
———. *Koptische Grammatik (saïdischer Dialekt), mit Bibliographie, Lesestücken und Wörterverzeichnissen.* Leipzig, 1955.
Vergote, J. *Phonétique historique de l'égyptien, les consonnes.* Louvain, 1945.
———. *Grammaire copte,* Vol. 1b, *Introduction, phonétique et phonologie, morphologie synthématique (structure des sémantèmes), partie diachronique.* Louvain, 1973.

RODOLPHE KASSER

BASHMURIC. The history of the Bashmuric dialect is in large measure that of a "phantom dialect." Coptic Egypt had many more dialects than modern science has been able to identify from the texts discovered; but some of these never reached the literary stage. Others did (perhaps poorly enough), but none of their witnesses has been found as yet. Hence, they are as good as completely lost. Such might have been the fate of Bashmuric if it had not been saved from oblivion by a Coptic grammarian of the fourteenth century (Garitte, 1972), Athanasius of Qūṣ, who wrote in Arabic as follows (cf. Scala copte 44 in the National Library, Paris, p. 154, left column, ll. 14–22, trans. W. Vycichl; cf. Kasser, 1975, p. 403):

> . . . and you know that the Coptic language is distributed over three regions, among them the Coptic of *Miṣr* which is the Sahidic, the Bohairic Coptic known by the *Boḥaira,* and the Bashmuric Coptic used in the country of *Bashmur,* as you know; now the Bohairic Coptic and the Sahidic Coptic are (alone still) used, and they are in origin a single language.

The first scholars who in the seventeenth century set themselves to the serious study of Coptic had at their disposal only an extremely limited documentation—above all, Bohairic texts, some Sahidic, and Fayyumic texts in even smaller number. Hence, they had before their eyes three Coptic idioms or "dialects," and they knew the text of Athanasius of Qūṣ, who also spoke of three Coptic "dialects" and indicated their names and their location. These Coptologists thus sought to give to the "dialects" they knew the names mentioned by the bishop of Qūṣ.

For Sahidic and Bohairic, the identification was made without difficulty. The Sahidic and the Bohairic of Athanasius having been identified, there remained, on the one hand, the Fayyumic documents and, on the other, the mention of the "Bashmuric" dialect. How could they not yield to the temptation to confuse them—the more so since one then recovered the tripartite scheme dear to the Egyptologists, with the three chief regions marked by Egyptian history, Upper, Middle, and Lower Egypt?

In Tattam's grammar (1830) one sees that the texts of the third dialect, which could not be assimilated to those of the first (Bohairic "Coptic") or the second ("Sahidic"), are perforce those of "Bashmuric." Georgi (1789) affirmed that the region of Bashmur, of which the learned fourteenth-century grammarian spoke, is not the one in the eastern Delta but another Bashmur, deriving from the Coptic ⲡⲥⲁⲙⲏⲣ, territory "beyond the river," or the Egyptian oases of the Western Desert, including the Fayyūm (cf. Quatremère, 1808, pp. 147–228, for whom Fayyumic could not be the famous "Bashmuric" of the bishop of Qūṣ; hence, Quatremère gave to Fayyumic the name Oasitic). Champollion (1811, 1817) took up this terminology without contesting it; likewise Peyron (1835, 1841), Schwartze (1850), and others. Later still, at the time when the first Akhmimic texts appeared, Bouriant (1884–1889), by a very curious reasoning, identified them with Fayyumic and hence with Bashmuric, although recognizing very well the dialectal differences that rendered them fundamentally dissimilar (Kasser, 1975, p. 405).

Maspero (1899) was, it seems, the last author who called one *F* text Bashmuric, without explaining why he maintained such an opinion, although it had long been contested and become outmoded. In fact, some twenty years earlier, Stern (1880, p. 12, n. 1), following Quatremère (1808), had already categorically rejected this terminology: "It was not out of desire for novelty that I abandoned the usual designation for the dialects, once Bashmuric was no longer tenable." Shortly after, all Coptologists followed him, and since there was in fact no truly Bashmuric document, people ceased to speak of this dialect, to which only the mention made of it by Athanasius of Qūṣ could have drawn the attention of scholars; they became almost completely uninterested in it, if they did not reach the point of denying its existence as an authentic Coptic dialect. Thus, Steindorff (1951, p. 5) wrote: "According to Eutychius . . . the Bushmuric-speaking population was in origin Greek, not Egyptian; perhaps Bushmuric was a Greco-Egyptian gibberish and not a Coptic dialect at all." W. Crum, however, wondered if the medieval grammarian's famous "Bashmuric" was not the language (written, in principle, by means of an exclusively Greek alphabet, without graphemes of demotic origin) of which he published the principal texts in 1939. That is no doubt a hypothesis in whose favor several weighty and important arguments speak (cf. DIALECT G; Kasser, 1975).

BIBLIOGRAPHY

Bouriant, U. "Les Papyrus d'Akhmîm (fragments de manuscrits en dialectes bachmourique et thébain)." *Mémoires de la Mission archéologique française au Caire* 1 (1884–1889):243–304.

Champollion, J. F. "Observations sur le catalogue des manuscrits coptes du Musée Borgia à Velletri, ouvrage posthume de G. Zoega." *Magasin encyclopédique* 5 (1811):284–317.

———. "Observations sur les fragments coptes (en dialecte bachmourique) de l'Ancien et du Nouveau Testament à Copenhague." *Annales encyclopédiques* (1817):284–317.

Crum, W. E. "Coptic Documents in Greek Script." *Proceedings of the British Academy* 25 (1939):249–271.

Garitte, G. Review of G. Bauer, *Athanasius von Qūṣ Qilādat at-taḥrīr fi'ilm at-tafsīr, eine koptische Grammatik in arabischer Sprache aus dem 13./14. Jahrhundert. Muséon* 85 (1972):561–63.

Giorgi, A. A. *Fragmentum Evangelii S. Johannis Graeco-Copto-Thebaïcum.* Rome, 1789.

Kasser, R. "Dialectes, sous-dialectes et 'dialecticules' dans l'Égypte copte." *Zeitschrift für ägyptische Sprache und Altertumskunde* 92 (1966):106–115.

———. "L'Idiome de Bachmour." *Bulletin de l'Institut français d'archéologie orientale* 75 (1975):401–427.

Maspero, G. "Fragment de l'évangile selon S. Matthieu en dialecte bachmourique." *Recueil de travaux relatifs à la philologie et à l'archéologie égyptiennes* 11 (1899):116.

Peyron, V. A. *Lexicon Linguae Copticae.* Turin, 1835.

———. *Grammatica Linguae Copticae, Accedunt Additamenta ad Lexicon Copticum.* Turin, 1841.

Quatremère, E. M. *Recherches critiques sur la langue et la littérature de l'Egypte.* Paris, 1808.

Schwartze, M. G. *Koptische Grammatik . . . , herausgegeben nach des Verfassers Tode von Dr. H. Steinthal.* Berlin, 1850.

Steindorff, G. *Lehrbuch der koptischen Grammatik.* Chicago, 1951.

Stern, L. *Koptische Grammatik.* Leipzig, 1880.

Tattam, H. *A Compendious Grammar of the Egyptian Language as Contained in the Coptic and Sahidic Dialects, with Observations on the Bashmuric Together with Alphabets and Numerals in the Hieroglyphic and Enchorial Characters, with an Appendix Consisting of the Rudiments of a Dictionary of the Ancient Egyptian Language in the Enchorial Characters by Thomas Young.* London, 1830.

RODOLPHE KASSER

BODMER PAPYRI. The term "Bodmer papyri" is the conventional designation of an important group of manuscripts (75 percent on papyrus and 25 percent on parchment, at least 950 folios) held by the Martin Bodmer Foundation, at Cologny, near Geneva. There are good reasons for thinking that these manuscripts were found together as a complete collection (perhaps a private library) in Upper Egypt; the great majority of them (81 percent) was acquired by the learned Swiss collector Martin Bodmer, for his library. The percentages mentioned, like those below, are calculated, except in special instances, on the basis of folios the existence and location of which are known today. (Other folios may very likely have perished during the centuries or when their discovery took place.) The Bodmer collection, originally known as the Bibliotheca Bodmeriana, became, as of 1971, the Fondation Martin Bodmer. It is by no means limited to papyrology, and even in that field it has several manuscripts (on papyrus, such as P. Bodmer I, XVII, XXVIII, XLIII, and XLVII, or on parchment, such as P. Bodmer XXXIX, XLII, and XLIV) clearly distinct in origin from the Bodmer papyri proper. Information on this subject was collected from reliable informers at precisely the same time as these documents came to the Bodmer Foundation, that is, probably shortly after their discovery in the Egyptian sands.

All the Bodmer papyri are more or less complete codices (nineteen in all, according to an estimate confined only to reliable information), and these are works of very varied sizes and contents. They include, in Greek (39 percent), some pagan literary texts, some books of the Bible, some Apocrypha, and other documents from Christian literature (hagiography, liturgy, religious poems, etc.); in Coptic (58 percent), primarily biblical texts, an apocryphon, and two fragments of Christian literature; and, in Latin (3 percent), two pagan literary texts and a fragment of Christian literature. Here, of course, account is taken only of published texts and of some unpublished ones regarding which at least a minimum of indispensable information is available (such is not the case for the unpublished remainder Barc-LG = the Latin-Greek codex of Barcelona; cf. below).

There are some reasons for thinking that the Bodmer papyri were discovered some years after the end of World War II, in Upper Egypt, either near Asyūṭ or, more probably, in Debba, a few miles to the northeast of Nag Hammadi (cf. Kasser, 1988), thus in the same general region as the well-known Coptic NAG HAMMADI LIBRARY of Gnostic manuscripts, the remains of a library of thirteen papyrus codices of the fourth and fifth centuries, containing fifty-two distinct texts and amounting approximately to six hundred written folios fairly clearly identified as such. Although the place and time of these finds were more or less the same, it is impossible to group them together as one and the same discovery; while these two groups of manuscripts, which are very sizable, embrace, apart from a lot of more or less mutilated folios, a large number of tiny fragments, not a single shred belonging to the Gnostic library has been found among the Bodmer papyri and vice versa.

Thus, there are nineteen codices if one considers only the reliable information gathered by the Bodmer Foundation at the time the Bodmer papyri came to be included in the library. There are some scholars who, on the basis of much later research (some thirty years after the presumed date of the discovery of the Bodmer papyri), think that they can also include in the Bodmer papyri various other famous manuscripts such as the P. Palau-Ribes from Barcelona (the Gospels of Mark, Luke, and John in Sahidic Coptic, edited by H. Quecke), and, above all, various letters of PACHOMIUS, one of which is preserved in the Bodmer Foundation but with nothing to indicate that it might be part of the Bodmer papyri. Their suggestion is that the actual library of the famous Monastery of Saint Pachomius at Faw al-Qiblī has been rediscovered. This hypothesis is certainly very tempting, but the reliable information referred to above tends to weaken rather than strengthen it.

These nineteen codices are listed in Table 1. They contain in all fifty-four distinct texts and amount to 951 (?) preserved folios of which something short of 100 are seriously mutilated, incomplete, and fragmentary (this apart from a minimum of 213 folios lost, if one can trust the clues—and they are not absolutely precise—that the texts and their pagination provide). Of these nineteen codices, fourteen are still wholly in the Bodmer Foundation; a fifteenth (Divv-G) did until recently belong to the Bodmeriana in its entirety, but it was dismembered when Martin Bodmer made a gift of one of his texts (P. Bodmer VIII, 18 folios) to the Vatican Library; two (Jer-C and Jos-C) are partly in the Bodmer Foundation and partly in another library; and two (Barc-LG and Crosby-C) are entirely outside the Bodmer Foundation; eleven of these codices are Coptic, seven are Greek, and only one is Latin and Greek.

Following are the signs and abbreviations used in the chart of codices and list of papyri contents:

A = oldest witness; (A) oldest witness in that language; (A′) oldest witness in that Coptic idiom; A. oldest witness for almost the entire text; (A.) oldest witness in that language for almost the entire text; etc.; A: oldest witness for a large part of the text; etc.

a = one of the oldest witnesses; etc., as for A, mutatis mutandis

AP-C = P. Bodmer XLI (unpublished) (text no. 38)

B = Bohairic Coptic language

B74 and *B4* = Bohairic (sub)dialects (the latter attested only by Jo-C [imperfectly] and [better] by the Pap. Vat. Copto 9, manuscript of the Minor Prophets in the Vatican Library)

Barc-LG = Latin-Greek codex of Barcelona (partial publication: texts nos. 5, 6, 53; number of unpublished texts [= 22(?) folios] still unknown)

BF = Martin Bodmer Foundation

-C (at the end of the siglum) = in Coptic

cl. = classical version (in this or that Coptic language or dialect)

comp. = composition

corrupt = corrupt textual form

Crosby-C = Crosby Codex (unpublished) (texts nos. 12, 17, 32, 40, 42)

Ct-C = P. Bodmer XL (unpublished) (text no. 16)

Div-G = P. Bodmer XXVII, XLV, and XLVI (texts nos. 4, 23, 24)

TABLE 1. *The Nineteen Codices of the Bodmer Papyri*

Siglum here	Mat.	Format	Comp.	Age (century)	B.F.	Elsewhere	[Lost]	Sig.t.c.
AP-C	P	2/3	w	4th	mi (7)		[MA?]	
Barc-LG	P	1/1	V	4th		MA(54 ?)	[mi 2?]	
Crosby-C	P	1/1	w	4th		MA (59 ?)	[mi ?]	
Ct-C	m	1/1-	w	5th	mi (8)		[MA 71]	
Div-G	P	1/1-	w	3–4th	mi (12)		[MA]	
Divv-G	P	1/1	w	3–4th	MA (93)	mi (fr.)	[mi 2?]	(Rahlfs 2113)
					(-18)	(Mi +18)		(P 72)
Dt-C	P	1/1	w	4th	MA (48)			
Es-C	P	2/3	w	4th	MA (80)			
Ex-C	m	1/1	w	5(–6)th	MA (42)			
Jér-C	m	1/1	w	4th	MA (39)	Mi (34)	[mi 2]	
Jo-C	P	2/3	w	4th	MA (77)		[mi 5]	
Jo-G	P	1/1	w	2–3rd	MA (100)	mi (fr.)		P 66
Jos-C	P	2/3	w	5th	MA (21)	Mi (18)	[Mi?24??]	
LuJo-G	P	1/2	V	3rd	MA (48)		[Mi 17]	P 75
Men-G	P	1/2	V	3rd	MA (26)	mi (fr.)	[mi 6]	
Mt-C	m	1/1	w	4–5th	Mi? (48)		[MA? 70?]	
Ps-G	P	1/2	V	3–4th	MA (49)		[Mi 35]	Rahlfs 2110
Pv-C	m	1/1	w	3(–4)th	MA (66)		[mi 3]	
Vis-G	P	2/3	V	4–5th	MA (22)			

Divv-G = P. Bodmer V (text no. 35), X (no. 36), XI (no. 37), VII (no. 34), XIII (no. 39), XII (no. 41), XX (no. 43), IX (no. 14), VIII (nos. 31, 33)
Dt-C = P. Bodmer XVIII (text no. 9)
elsewhere = exists in some library or collection other than the Bodmer Foundation
Es-C = P. Bodmer XXIII (text no. 18)
Ex-C = P. Bodmer XVI (text no. 8)
fr. = fragment
-G (at the end of the siglum) = in Greek
Jer-C = P. Bodmer XXII (= Mississippi Coptic Codex II) (texts nos. 19, 20, 21, 22)
Jo-C = P. Bodmer III (texts nos. 7, 29)
Jo-G = P. Bodmer II (text no. 27)
Jos-C = P. Bodmer XXI (= Chester Beatty Library, Accession no. 1389) (texts nos. 10, 11)
L = Lyco-Diospolitan Coptic dialect (or cluster of dialects) (here of type *L5*)
-L (at end of siglum) = in Latin
[lost] = may exist in some unknown place, or no longer exists (having been destroyed)
LuJo-G = P. Bodmer XIV, XV (texts nos. 26, 28)
m = parchment (membrana)
MA = major part of codex (followed by the number of the folios, if known)
Men-G = P. Bodmer XXV, IV, XXVI (texts nos. 1, 2, 3)
mat. = material
mi = very small part of the codex (followed by the number of folios, if known)
Mi = relatively small but important part of the codex (followed by the number of folios, if known)
Mt-C = P. Bodmer XIX (texts nos. 25, 30)
N = completely new text; (N) completely new text in that language; (N′) completely new text in that Coptic idiom; N. new for almost the whole text; (N.) new in that language for almost the whole text; etc.; N: new for a large part of the text; etc.; N:. new for part of the text; etc.
or. = the original language of the text (the Greek of the Septuagint, though translated from Hebrew, is considered exceptionally here as the "original language" because very probably all the Coptic Old Testament versions were translated from one or other LXX text)
P = papyrus
P = DIALECT P (phonologically quite near to what can be known about **pS*, a tentatively reconstructed proto-Sahidic; remarkably archaic even in its alphabet, where ϭ is missing (replaced by ⲕ) and one finds the following demotic or Old Coptic letters: ⊥ /ʾ/, ⳝ /k/, – /n̩/, ၁ /ç/
precl. = preclassical version (in one Coptic dialect or another; what has remained of it is extremely rare, hence its exceptional interest)

Ps-G = P. Bodmer XXIV (text no. 13)
Pv-C = P. Bodmer VI (text no. 15)
S = Sahidic Coptic language
sig.t.c. = official siglum in Greek biblical textual criticism (of the Old Testament: Rahlfs . . . ; of the New Testament: P . . . ; this is placed in parentheses when only one part of the codex is biblical)
V = codex consisting of a single quire
Vis-G = Greek codex called (in the Bodmer Foundation) Codex Visionum (partial publication: P. Bodmer XXIX, text no. 44; unpublished are P. Bodmer XXX to XXXVIII, texts nos. 45–54)
w = codex made up of several quires
1/1 = folio almost square in shape (generally, however, a little taller than its width)
1/1- = roughly 1/1, although in a form tending toward 2/3
1/2 = folio of which the width is almost half the height
2/3 = folio of which the width is almost two-thirds of the height
[. .] = with various gaps

An outline of the fifty-four known texts of the Bodmer papyri follows:

I. Pagan Texts

1. Menander, *The Samian* (nearly three quarters), in Greek: P. Bodmer XXV in Men-G, third century [or. N:]
2. Menander, *The Dyskolos* (= *Knemon the Misanthrope*), in Greek: P. Bodmer IV in Men-G, third century [or. N.]
3. Menander, *The Shield* (=*Aspis*) (roughly half), in Greek: P. Bodmer XXVI, in Men-G, third century [or. N.]
4. Thucydides, *History* . . . 6.1.1–2.6, in Greek: P. Bodmer XXVII in Div-G, third–fourth centuries [or. A]
5. Cicero, *In Catilinam* 1.6–9, 13–33, 2.1–29, in Latin: in Barc-LG, fourth century [or. A]
6. Poem on the subject of the sacrifice of *Alcestis* in Latin: in Barc-LG, fourth century [or. N]

II. Christian Texts

A. Bible

7. Genesis 1:1–4:2 in *B74* (mixed with *B4*): in P. Bodmer III = Jo-C, fourth century [(A′) precl.]
8. Exodus 1:1–15:21 in *S*: P. Bodmer XVI = Ex-C, fifth(–sixth) century [(A:) cl.]
9. Deuteronomy 1:1–10:7 [. .] in *S*: P. Bodmer XVIII = Dt-C, fourth century, [(A:) cl.]
10. Joshua 1:1–11:23, followed immediately by 22:1-24:3, in *S*: in P. Bodmer XXI = Chester Beatty . . . 1389, in Jos-C, fifth century [(A) corrupt]
11. Tobit 14:13–15 (end) in *S*: in P. Bodmer XXI = Chester Beatty . . . 1389, in Jos-C, fifth century [(A) corrupt]
12. 2 Maccabees 5:27–7:41 in *S*: in Crosby-C, fourth century [(N:) cl.]; unpublished
13. Psalms 17:45–51:9[. .], 55:8–105:32 [. .], 106:28–118:44 [. .] in Greek: P. Bodmer XXIV = Ps-G, third–fourth centuries (= Rahlfs 2110) [a] (two-thirds of this text attest for the first time the type of Greek text from which the Sahidic version of the Book of Psalms is derived)
14. Psalms 33:2–34:16 in Greek: P. Bodmer IX in Divv-G, third–fourth centuries (= Rahlfs 2113) [a] (same type of text as no. 13 above)
15. Proverbs 1:1–2:9, 2:20–18:1, 18:9–20:9, 20:25–21:4, in *P*: P. Bodmer VI = Pv-C, third(–fourth) century [(N′) cl. *S*]
16. Song of Solomon 1:4–3.1, 4:2–8:12, in *S*: P. Bodmer XL = Ct-C, fifth century [(a) (N:.) cl.]; unpublished
17. Jonah, in *S*: in Crosby-C, fourth century [(a) precl.]; unpublished
18. Isaiah 47:1–66:24 (end), in *S*: P. Bodmer XXIII = Es-C, fourth century [(A′.) cl.]
19. Jeremiah 40:3–52:34 (end), in *S*: in P. Bodmer XXII = Mississippi Coptic Codex II = Jer-C, fourth century [(A) (N′.) cl.]
20. Baruch 1:1–5:5 in *S*: in P. Bodmer XXII = Mississippi Coptic Codex II = Jer-C, fourth century [(A)(N′.) cl.]
21. Lamentations, in *S*: in P. Bodmer XXII = Mississippi Coptic Codex II = Jer-C, fourth century [(A′)(N′:) cl.]
22. Epistle of Jeremiah in *S*: in P. Bodmer XXII = Mississippi Coptic Codes II = Jer-C, fourth century [(A)(N′.) cl.]
23. Susannah, in Greek (Theodotion): P. Bodmer XLV in Div-G, third–fourth centuries [or. A (or or. a)]
24. Daniel 1:1–20, in Greek (Theodotion): P. Bodmer XLVI in Div-G, third–fourth centuries [or. A (or or. a)]
25. Matthew 14:28–28:20 (end), in *S*: in P. Bodmer XIX = Mt-C, fourth–fifth centuries [(A′:.)(a′:.) cl.]
26. Luke 3:18–22, 3:33–4:2, 4:34–5:10, 5:37–18:18 [. .], 22:4–24:53 (end), in Greek: P. Bodmer XIV in LuJo-G, third century (= P 75) [or. A:, or. a]
27. John 1:1–6: 11 [. .], 6:35–7:52, immediately followed by 8:12–21:9 [. .], in Greek: P. Bodmer II = Jo-G, second–third centuries (= P 65) [or. A.]

28. John 1:1–7:52, immediately followed by 8:12–13:9 [. .], 14:8–15:8 [. .], in Greek: P. Bodmer XV in LuJo-G, third century (= P 75) [or. A:., or. a.]
29. John 1:1–25 [. .], 1:40–45 [. .], 2:9–16 [. .], 3:33, 4:5–7:52 [. .], immediately followed by 8:12–21:25 (end), in *B74* mixed with *B4*: in P. Bodmer III = Jo-C, fourth century [(A:.) (N′) precl.]
30. Romans 1:1–2:3 [. .], in *S:* in P. Bodmer XIX = Mt-C, fourth–fifth centuries [(A) cl.]
31. 1 Peter, in Greek: in P. Bodmer VIII in Divv-G, third–fourth centuries (=P 72) [or. A]
32. 1 Peter, in *S*: in Crosby-C, fourth century [(A)]; unpublished
33. 2 Peter, in Greek: in P. Bodmer VIII in Divv-G, third–fourth centuries (=P 72) [or. A]
34. Jude, in Greek: P. Bodmer VII in Divv-G, third–fourth centuries (=P 72) [or. A]

B. Apocrypha

35. Nativity of Mary (or Protevangelium of James), in Greek: P. Bodmer V in Divv-G, third–fourth centuries [or. A]
36. Apocryphal correspondence of the Corinthians and the Apostle Paul, in Greek: P. Bodmer X in Divv-G, third–fourth centuries [(or. N) or. A]
37. Eleventh Ode of Solomon, in Greek: P. Bodmer XI in Divv-G, third–fourth centuries [(or. N) or. A]
38. Acts of Paul, Ephesus episode [. .] [. .], in *L5*: P. Bodmer XLI = AP-C, fourth century [N: (A:)]; unpublished

C. Other Christian Literature

39. Melito of Sardis, Homily on Easter, in Greek: P. Bodmer XIII in Divv-G, third–fourth centuries [or. A, or or. a]
40. Melito of Sardis, Homily on Easter, in *S*: in Crosby-C, fourth century [(N)]; unpublished
41. Liturgical hymn, in Greek: P. Bodmer XII in Divv-G, third–fourth centuries [or. N]
42. Liturgical hymn, in *S*: in Crosby-C, fourth century [N]; unpublished
43. Apology of Phileas, bishop of Tmuis, in Greek: P. Bodmer XX in Divv-G, third–fourth centuries [or. (N)A]
44. Vision of Dorotheos, in Greek: P. Bodmer XXIX in Vis-G, fifth century [or. N]
45–52. Eight religious poems, in Greek, otherwise unknown, with the following titles: (45) Abraam (P. Bodmer XXX), (46) The Righteous (P. Bodmer XXXI), (47) [. . .] of the Lord Jesus (P. Bodmer XXXII), (48) The Murder of Abel by Cain (1°) (P. Bodmer XXXIII), (49) The Lord to the [. . .] (P. Bodmer XXXIV), (50) The Murder of Abel by Cain (2°) (P. Bodmer XXXV), (51) Poem with damaged title (P. Bodmer XXXVI), (52) Hymn (P. Bodmer XXXVII); all in Vis-G, fifth century, [or. N], unpublished
53. Psalmus Responsorius, in Latin: in Barc-LG, fourth century [or. N]
54. Hermas the Shepherd, the first three visions, in Greek: P. Bodmer XXXVIII, in Vis-G, fifth century [or. a]; unpublished

BIBLIOGRAPHY

P. Bodmer II

Martin, V. *Papyrus Bodmer II: Evangile de Jean chap. 1–14.* Cologny/Geneva, 1956.

______. *Papyrus Bodmer II, supplément: Evangile de Jean chap. 14–21.* Cologny/Geneva, 1958.

Martin, V., and J. W. B. Barns. *Papyrus Bodmer II, supplément: Évangile de Jean chap. 14–21, nouvelle édition augmentée et corrigée avec reproduction photographique complète du manuscrit (chap. 1–21).* Cologny/Geneva, 1962.

P. Bodmer III

Kasser, R. *Papyrus Bodmer III: Evangile de Jean et Genèse I–IV,2, en bohaïrique.* CSCO 177–178. Louvain, 1958.

P. Bodmer IV

Martin, V. *Papyrus Bodmer IV: Ménandre, Le Dyscolos.* Cologny/Geneva, 1958.

P. Bodmer V

Testuz, M. *Papyrus Bodmer V: Nativité de Marie.* Cologny/Geneva, 1958.

P. Bodmer VI

Kasser, R. *Papyrus Bodmer VI: Livre des Proverbes.* CSCO 194–195. Louvain, 1960.

P. Bodmer VII–IX

Testuz, M. *Papyrus Bodmer VII–IX: VII, L'Épître de Jude; VIII, Les Deux Épîtres de Pierre; IX, Les Psaumes 33 et 34.* Cologny/Geneva, 1959.

P. Bodmer X–XII

Testuz, M. *Papyrus Bodmer X–XII: X, Correspondance apocryphe des Corinthiens et de l'apôtre Paul; XI, Onzième Ode de Salomon; XII, Fragment d'un hymne liturgique, manuscrit du IIIe siècle*. Cologny/Geneva, 1960.

P. Bodmer XIII

Testuz, M. *Papyrus Bodmer XIII: Méliton de Sardes, Homélie sur la Pâque, manuscrit du IIIe siècle*. Cologny/Geneva, 1960.

P. Bodmer XIV–XV

Martin, V., and R. Kasser. *Papyrus Bodmer XIV: Évangile de Luc chap. 3–24, Papyrus Bodmer XV: Évangile de Jean chap. 1–15*. Cologny/Geneva, 1961.

P. Bodmer XVI

Kasser, R. *Papyrus Bodmer XVI: Exode I–XV,21 en sahidique*. Cologny/Geneva, 1961.

P. Bodmer XVIII

Kasser, R. *Papyrus Bodmer XVIII: Deutéronome I–X,7 en sahidique*. Cologny/Geneva, 1962.

P. Bodmer XIX

Kasser, R. *Papyrus Bodmer XIX: Évangile de Matthieu XIV,28–XXVIII,20; Épître aux Romains I,1–II,3, en sahidique*. Cologny/Geneva, 1962.

P. Bodmer XX

Martin, V. *Papyrus Bodmer XX: Apologie de Philéas, évêque de Thmouis*. Cologny/Geneva, 1964.

P. Bodmer XXI

Kasser, R. *Papyrus Bodmer XXI: Josué VI,16–25, VII,6–XI,23, XXII,1–2, 19–XXIII,7, 15–XXIV,23, en sahidique*. Cologny/Geneva, 1964.

P. Bodmer XXII

Kasser, R. *Papyrus Bodmer XXII et Mississippi Coptic Codex II: Jérémie XL,3–LII,34: Lamentations, Épitre de Jérémie, Baruch I,1–V,5 en sahidique*. Cologny/Geneva, 1964.

P. Bodmer XXIII

Kasser, R. *Papyrus Bodmer XXIII: Esaïe XLVII,1–LXVI,24 en sahidique*. Cologny/Geneva, 1965.

P. Bodmer XXIV

Kasser, R. and M. Testuz. *Papyrus Bodmer XXIV: Psaumes XVII–CXVIII*. Cologny/Geneva, 1967.

P. Bodmer XXV

Kasser, R. and C. Austin. *Papyrus Bodmer XXV: Ménandre, La Samienne*. Cologny/Geneva, 1969.

P. Bodmer XXVI

Kasser, R. and C. Austin. *Papyrus Bodmer XXVI: Ménandre, Le Bouclier; en appendice, compléments au Papyrus Bodmer IV*. Cologny/Geneva, 1969.

P. Bodmer XXVII

Carlini, A. "Il papiro di Tucidide della Bibliotheca Bodmeriana (P. Bodmer XXVII)." *Museum Helveticum* 32 (1975):33–40 and pl. 1–3.

P. Bodmer XXIX

Hurst, A.; O. Reverdin; and J. Rudhardt. *Papyrus Bodmer XXIX: Vision de Dorothéos, édité avec une introduction, une traduction et des notes*. With appendix by R. Kasser and G. Cavallo, "Description et datation du Codex des Visions." Cologny/Geneva, 1984.

P. Bodmer XLV–XLVI

Carlini, A. and A. Citi. "Susanna e la prima visione di Daniele in due papiri inediti della Bibliotheca Bodmeriana, P. Bodm. XLV e P. Bodm. XLVI." *Museum Helveticum* 38 (1981):81–120 and pl. 1–14.

Other Publications

Merkelbach, R. "Wartetext 2, P. Colon. Inv. 904. Komödienfragment." *Zeitschrift für Papyrologie und Epigraphik* 1 (1967):103–104.

Roca-Puig, R. *Himne a la Verge Maria, "Psalmus Responsorius," papir llatí del segle IV*. Barcelona, 1965.

______. "Fragment de 'La Sàmia' de Menandre, papir de Barcelona, inventari no. 45." *Boletin de la Real Academia de buenas letras de Barcelona* 32 (1967–1968):5–13.

______. *Ciceró, Catilinàries (I et II in Cat.), Papyri Barcinonenses*. Barcelona, 1977.

______. *Alcestis, Hexàmetres Llatins, Papyri Barcinonenses, Inv. no. 158–161*. Barcelona, 1982.

Shore, A. F. *Joshua I–VI and Other Passages in Coptic, Edited from a Fourth-Century Codex in the Chester Beatty Library, Dublin*. Dublin, 1963.

Willis, W. H. "A Papyrus Fragment of Cicero." *Transactions and Proceedings of the American Philological Association* 94 (1963):321–27.

RODOLPHE KASSER

BOHAIRIC, a major dialect of Coptic, called "MEMPHITIC," "the northern dialect," or "dialect of Lower Egypt" in earlier terminology, and simply "Coptic" in eighteenth- and nineteenth-century treatises, Bohairic being the first Coptic dialect with which Western scholarship became acquainted. "Bohairic" (*B*) was first used by Stern (1880, p. xii).

Originally the northern local dialect of the western Delta (Buhaira) and Wādī al-Naṭrūn, Bohairic spread dramatically (beginning after, and as an indirect result of, the ARAB CONQUEST OF EGYPT) eastward and southward. In the eighth and ninth centuries it broke the monopoly of Sahidic as a Pan-Coptic idiom and by the eleventh century had largely completed the process of becoming virtually the sole dialect of Coptic. Bohairic became the official ecclesiastical language, and the classical Bohairic version of the Scriptures, the official text. Bohairic, which survives only as a liturgical language, was the dialect that saw Coptic out as the living idiom of Egypt. The old controversial question of its prehistory—whether it was never a literary language before the Arab conquest (Stern, 1880, p. 1; Lefort, 1931) or was, on the contrary, an old literary dialect (Worrell's opinion) has not yet been settled. What survives in the way of Bohairic documentation consists, on the one hand, of manuscripts later than the ninth century with scriptural, homiletic, hermeneutic, hagiographical, and liturgical texts and, on the other, a much smaller collection of fourth- and fifth-century fragments, all biblical (see sec. 5 on the varieties of Bohairic).

Bohairic shares isoglosses with most other dialects of Coptic, mainly with Fayyumic, Middle Egyptian (MESOKEMIC), Sahidic, and, more subtly, certain Nag Hammadi varieties of Sahidic (especially some tractates in Codex VII), DIALECT G and DIALECT P. The persistent, somewhat biased impression of Bohairic as an innovating dialect is refuted by careful internal and contrastive examination, which shows it to be rather of a conservative nature (cf. Shisha-Halevy, 1981). Not only its grammatical minutiae but even some major issues are still obscure and in need of rigorous and methodologically careful investigation. Far from being "sufficiently well known" (Kahle, 1954, p. 232), it has, following Steindorff's *Grammatik* of 1894, been superseded by Sahidic as far as research and tuition are concerned. (For Stern, 1880, it was still the primary illustration dialect.) Since the 1890s "Coptic" par excellence has been Sahidic, and Bohairic has been suffering grave scholarly neglect (cf. Erman, 1915, p. 161). This article will attempt to provide a brief typological profile of Bohairic grammar. While details of phonology and nonsystemic morphology are relatively well known, its *système de valeur* and syntax still hold quite a few mysteries for the linguist. The account given here is predominantly synchronic and noncontrastive.

1. Phonology, Morphophonology, and Graphemics

1.1. Probably the most striking feature of Bohairic is the nonpertinent, allophonic status of consonant aspiration in words of native Egyptian stock. The aspirated allophone (ⲑ, ⲫ, ⲭ) occurs "combinatorily" before, and in contact with, a sonorant (any of /b/, /l/, /m/, /n/, /r/, /w/, and /j/) in initial clusters and elsewhere (ⲭⲗⲟⲙ, crown; ⲁⲑⲙⲟⲩ, immortal; ⲫⲙⲉⲛⲣⲓⲧ, the beloved) or "spontaneously" as the onset of a stressed syllable (indeed, "stress" is a feature equivalent to "sonority," and thus the "spontaneousness" is relative and only a manner of speaking). ϭ, the allophone of ϫ before sonorants (ϭⲗⲟϭ, bed), nonetheless constitutes a phoneme (ϭⲏ, quince, versus ϫⲏ, dish).

1.2. The *B* phonemic inventory features the opposition /x/ : /h/, graphemically ϧ : ϩ (ϧⲣⲏⲓ̈, lower part:ϩⲣⲏⲓ̈, upper part).

1.3. The open final unstressed (posttonic) vowel in *B* is /i/ (ⲣⲱⲙⲓ, man; ⲙⲉⲩⲓ, think, thought). Table 1 displays the facts in the case of closed unstressed syllables (cf. Polotsky, 1933).

1.4. Nonfinal historical laryngeals (primary and

TABLE 1. *Closed Unstressed Syllables in Bohairic*

	POSTTONIC			
	STRESS SYLLABLE CLOSED		STRESS SYLLABLE OPEN	
PRETONIC	SONORANT ONSET	NO SONORANT	SONORANT CODA	SONORANT ONSET/ NO SONORANT
e	*e*	*ø*	*e*	*ø*
ⲥⲉⲡⲥⲱⲡϥ ϣⲉⲣϣⲱⲣϥ	ⲥⲟⲑⲙⲉϥ	ⲥⲟⲧⲡϥ	ⲥⲱⲧⲉⲙ	ⲥⲱⲗⲡ ⲥⲱⲧⲡ
entreat/ destroy him	hear him	choose him	hear	break choose

secondary, evolved from *r* or *t*) are not realized in Bohairic: ϣⲟⲡϯ, in existence; ⲧⲏⲃ, finger; ⲥⲉⲡⲓ, remain over; ⲡⲉ-, thy- (second fem. sing.) Finally, one finds *i:* second fem. sing. ϩⲱⲓ, thou too; ⲧⲱⲟⲩⲛⲓ, stand thee up; masc. ⲟⲩⲁⲓ, one.

1.5. Palatal sibilant assimilation is the rule: ϣⲁⲛϣ, make live, nourish; ϣⲱϣ, despise.

1.6. Long diphthongs lengthened from short vowels occur with *w* and *j:* ⲱⲓⲕ, bread; ⲱ̀ⲟⲩ, honor.

1.7. The syllabicity of vowels and nasal sonorants is indicated by means of a superposed point (ϫⲓⲛⲕⲓⲙ; see DJINKIM). In classical usage (manuscripts prior to the fourteenth century), this applies to any vowel constituting by itself a syllable (ⲁϥⲓ ⲉ̀ⲃⲟⲗ, he went out; ⲁ̀ⲛⲓⲟⲩ̀ⲓ, bring [imp.]) and to ⲙ and ⲛ constituting a radical or a grammatical element and preceding another (ⲙ̀ⲧⲟⲛ, rest; ⲛ̀ⲑⲟϥ, he; ⲙ̀ⲫϯ, for God). This syllabicity is canceled in certain combinatory circumstances (cf. Polotsky, 1949). In later Bohairic, one finds the djinkim on other consonants (ⲥ̀ⲑⲟⲓ smell; ⲕ̀ⲛⲏⲟⲩ, you are coming).

1.8. Numbers are usually symbolized by letters and not written out (Dt. 34:8, ⲙ̀ⲗ̅ ⲛ̀ⲉ̀ϩⲟⲟⲩ, for thirty days; Mk. 6:40, ⲕⲁⲧⲁ ⲣ̅ ⲣ̅ ⲛⲉⲙ ⲕⲁⲧⲁ ⲛ̅ ⲛ̅, by hundreds and by fifties).

1.9. The phoneme /i/ is usually expressed by an iota, even when initial (ⲓ, come, go; ⲓⲃⲓ, thirst).

1.10. Proclitically weak elements are not always marked as such (Erman, 1915): ⲁ̀ⲛⲟⲕ-, ⲟⲩⲟⲛ-, ⲙ̀ⲙⲟⲛ-.

2. Morphology and Word Formation

2.1. There is superficial (structurally resolvable) coincidence of the perfect base with the second present/future converter, both ⲁ (opposed to the circumstantial ⲉ). *a*-vocalism characterizes the preterite converter ⲛⲁϥ- and the negative aorist ⲙ̀ⲡⲁϥ-.

2.2. The relative converter ⲉ̀ⲧⲉ is common to the bipartite and all tripartite conjugation forms (ⲉ̀ⲧⲁϥ-, relative perfect).

2.3. The relative and second perfect converters coincide, as ⲉⲧ-, with systemic consequences.

2.4. The relative converter ⲉⲧⲉ has no prenominal allomorph, thus differing from the other three converters before the bipartite pattern. ⲉⲣⲉ- is an alternant (variant?) of the circumstantial before the existential ⲟⲩⲟⲛ. The converters and some bases have a -ⲣⲉ- allomorph before the short second plural suffix: ⲁ̀ⲣⲉⲧⲉⲛ-, ⲛⲁⲣⲉⲧⲉⲛ-, ϣⲁⲣⲉⲧⲉⲛ-, (ⲉ̀ⲧ)ⲁⲣⲉⲧⲉⲛ-, etc.

2.5. The base of the conjuctive is ⲛ̀ⲧⲉ-, prenominally as well as presuffixally. In the first singular the base-plus-actor is ⲛ̀ⲧⲁ-; in the third plural it is ⲛ̀ⲧⲟⲩ-, which is opposed to ⲛ̀ⲥⲉ-, the sole representative in Bohairic of a syntagm (the Sahidic conjunctive) in which ⲛ̀- marks as modifier a nexus of "actor plus verb."

2.6. The so-called third future is largely convertible in Bohairic (Stern, 1880, sec. 418–19; Andersson, 1904, pp. 62ff.).

2.7. In one variety of Bohairic (see 5.3) there occurs a special negative-conditional base, ⲁⲛⲛⲉ- (discussed by Černý, 1963, and Kasser, 1963). -ϣⲁⲛ occurs only in the affirmative form of the conditional clause-tripartite conjugation form. The negatived base coincides with the second present (ⲁϥϣⲧⲉⲙ-), a coincidence that is diachronically significant but synchronically probably superficial.

2.8. The negative jussive (causative imperative) base is in Bohairic ⲙ̀ⲡⲉⲛⲑⲣⲉ-; its connection with the negative imperative characteristic ⲙ̀ⲡⲉⲣ- is thus severed.

2.9. The negative aorist base is ⲙ̀ⲡⲁ(-), showing diachronic affinities with the second tense.

2.10. ⲧⲉⲣⲁ- is the second singular feminine form of the future.

2.11. The first singular and third plural actor suffix pronouns are syllabic with the causative infinitive (ⲑⲣⲓ-, ⲑⲣⲟⲩ-) and negative third future (ⲛ̀ⲛⲓ-, ⲛ̀ⲛⲟⲩ-; cf. Polotsky, 1960, sec. 49).

2.12. Verb Lexeme/Stative Peculiarities. Historical *3ae infirmae -i* infinitives (Stern's class III) usually have no *-t=* in the pronominal state (ⲉⲛ⸗, bring; ⲙⲉⲥ⸗, give birth to; ϫⲉⲙ⸗, find; ϭⲁⲥ⸗, exalt). On the other hand, the imperative form marked by ⲁ often has *-t* = (ⲁ̀ⲣⲓⲧ⸗, do; ⲁ̀ⲛⲓⲧ⸗, bring). Verbs of Greek origin have in Bohairic the Greek infinitive form (-ⲓⲛ, -ⲉⲥⲑⲉ) and are integrated in the Coptic conjugation by means of the auxiliary ⲉⲣ- (ⲉⲣ ⲫⲟⲣⲓⲛ, bear; ⲉⲣ ⲁⲥⲡⲁⲍⲉⲥⲑⲉ, embrace, greet). The stative of the causative lexeme class ends in *-t* (-ⲏⲟⲩⲧ†, ⲑⲁⲙⲓⲏⲟⲩⲧ†, being created).

2.13. The imperative of "give" has three allomorphs: ⲙⲟⲓ, ⲙⲁ-, ⲙⲏⲓ⸗ (Polotsky, 1950, pp. 78ff.; 1971, 213ff.).

2.14. A verb-nominalization form in ϫⲓⲛ- is grammaticalized as ⲡϫⲓⲛⲧⲉ-/ⲑⲣⲉ- (Stern, 1880, sec. 470–72; Mk. 14:55, ⲉ̀ⲡϫⲓⲛϧⲟⲑⲃⲉϥ, to kill him).

2.15. The definite determinator pronoun {ⲡ} has only one form (with no special precluster allomorph).

2.16. Bohairic has a plural infix *-u-* (ⲁ̀ⲛⲁⲩϣ, oaths; ⲥⲛⲁⲩϩ, fetters).

2.17. The first plural object suffix is usually (postconsonantally) -ⲧⲉⲛ (rarely -ⲉⲛ).

2.18. Postadjunctive Greek-origin adverbial modifiers may be marked by ⲛ̀ (ⲛ̀ⲕⲁⲗⲱⲥ).

3. Syntagmatics, Paradigmatics (Role Relationship), and Prosody

3.1. Focalization Patterns. The second tense focalizes adverbs only, not actor or object (pro)nouns (except for ⲁⲣⲉⲧⲉⲛⲉⲣ ⲟⲩ, How are you?, cf. Polotsky, 1960, p. 409). Interrogative pronouns may be construed with an unmarked (basic tense) topic, especially the first perfect (Gn. 27:33, ⲛⲓⲙ ⲟⲩⲛ ⲁϥϫⲉⲣϫ ⲟⲩϫⲟⲣⲥ ⲛⲏⲓ, Who then hunted game for me?), but enter more usually the nominal cleft-sentence pattern. In the latter case, the topic constituent is either the invariable ⲡⲉⲧ- (Polotsky, 1962, pp. 419f. [=*CP* 424]), which differs from the "substantivized" relative ⲫⲏ ⲉⲧ- (the relative expanding a demonstrative and indefinite pronouns as well as proper names; cf. Polotsky, 1962, sec. 9; Shisha-Halevy, 1981, pp. 321f.): Mt. 3:14, ⲁ̀ⲛⲟⲕ ⲉⲧⲉⲣ ⲭⲣⲓⲁ̀ ⲉ̀ϭⲓ ⲱⲙⲥ, It is I who need to be baptized; Mt. 9:5, ⲟⲩ ⲅⲁⲣ ⲉⲑⲙⲟⲧⲛ ⲉ̀ϫⲟⲥ, What is it that is easy to say? Mt. 2:22 ⲁⲣⲭⲉⲗⲁⲟⲥ ⲉⲧⲟⲓ ⲛ̀ⲟⲩⲣⲟ, It is Archelaos that is king; Mk. 8:37, ⲫⲏ ⲅⲁⲣ ⲉ̀ⲧⲉ ⲡⲓⲣⲱⲙⲓ ⲛⲁⲧⲏⲓϥ ⲛ̀ⲧϣⲉⲃⲓⲱ̀ ⲛ̀ⲧⲉϥⲯⲩⲭⲏ, This is what a man will give in exchange for his soul.

3.2 Extraposition. Bohairic is strikingly topic-marking, favoring a front (topicalizing) extraposition as topic of a nominal sentence (Gn. 24:65, ⲡⲁⲓⲣⲱⲙⲓ ⲛⲓⲙ ⲡⲉ ⲉⲧⲧⲏ, Who is this man yonder?) and in other constructions (Shisha-Halevy, 1981, p. 321). The rear extraposition of a noun lexeme to an "interlocutive" (first-second person) pronoun is marked in Bohairic by ϧⲁ- (e.g., Acts 10:41, Jas. 4:12).

3.3 Nominal Syntagmatics. The Bohairic system of determinator nuclear pronouns ("articles") is quaternary: definite-deictic ({ⲡⲓ-}), definite nondeictic ({ⲡ-}), indefinite ({ⲟⲩ-}), generic, nonindividualizing (Ø-). Of these, the first two are interrelated in a complicated, still partly obscure set of factors, some external (cotextual), others internal (i.e., selection of {ⲡ-} by a special lexeme paradigm in a construction {ⲡ-} ⲛ̀- expressing inalienable possession, opposed to {ⲡⲓ-} ⲛ̀ⲧⲉ, which expresses noninherent "appurtenance"). Elucidating this issue is probably the most urgent single task to be undertaken by students of this dialect. ⲛ̀- is also used to add further lexemes to the determinator-plus-lexeme basic unit: ⲡⲓ= ⲟⲩⲟϩ ⲛ̀-, as in Mt. 23:17, 19, ⲛⲓⲥⲟϫ ⲟⲩⲟϩ ⲙ̀ⲃⲉⲗⲗⲉ, the stupid and blind; *Acta Martyrum* 1.21.2f., ⲟⲩⲣⲉϥϣⲉⲛϩⲏⲧ ⲟⲩⲟϩ ⲛ̀ⲛⲁⲏⲧ (nom. predicate) "pitiful and merciful."

3.4. The predication of possession is effected in Bohairic by a paradigm of adverbial-predicate patterns predicating ⲛ̀ⲧⲁ⸗ (Lk. 3:11), and not only by a verboid (ⲟⲩⲟⲛⲧⲁ⸗/ ⲙ̀ⲙⲟⲛⲧⲁ⸗, as in Gn. 16:1; cf. Shisha-Halevy, 1981, pp. 317f.). The pronominal *possessum* never occurs as object of the verboid, but as the subject of the adverbial predication (Dt. 4:38).

3.5. The pronominal subject of affirmative bimembral nominal sentences is sometimes zeroed when it is anaphoric to a determinator or an extraposed topic (Shisha-Halevy, 1981, pp. 328f.; I Cor. 5:18, ⲉ̀ϣⲱⲡ ⲉ̀ⲟⲩⲟⲛ ⲟⲩⲁⲓ ⲉⲩϯ ⲣⲁⲛ ⲉ̀ⲣⲟϥ ϫⲉ ⲥⲟⲛ ⲉ̀ⲟⲩⲡⲟⲣⲛⲟⲥ). The most common instance of this is the distinctively Bohairic possessive ⲡⲉⲧⲉⲫⲱ⸗ (ⲛ̀-) (Lk. 6:30, 16:12).

3.6. ⲑⲣⲟ, the grammatically operative causative infinitive of ⲓ̀ⲣⲓ, is in Bohairic subject to the Stern-Jernstedt Rule and thus incompatible with the mediate (ⲛ̀-/ⲙ̀ⲙⲟ⸗) direct-object construction in the bipartite pattern (Stern, 1880, p. 292; e.g., Mt. 5:32; De Vis, 1922–1929, 1.14.6).

3.7. The bipartite pattern predicating an adverb favors the intermediation of a copular stative (Gn. 26:24, ϯⲭⲏ ⲛⲉⲙⲁⲕ, I am with you).

3.8. Gender. The cataphoric gender in "impersonal" predications is as a rule the feminine. On the other hand, the pronominal subject of the predicate ("to the debit/obligation of . . .") is (at least as a variant) the masculine: Gal. 5:3, ϥⲉⲣⲟϥ ⲉ̀ⲉⲣ ⲫⲛⲟⲙⲟⲥ ⲧⲏⲣϥ, he is obliged to observe the whole Law.

3.9. Tempuslehre Idiosyncrasies. The so-called third future is in Bohairic a true tense, not a mode, in paradigm with the present-based imminent future marked by -ⲛⲁ-. The conjunctive has often a subjunctival or "that"-form value (Stern, 1880, sec. 442), such as expanding the cataphoric feminine in "impersonal" predications (Mt. 5:29, ⲥⲉⲣ ⲛⲟϥⲣⲓ ⲅⲁⲣ ⲛⲁⲕ ⲛ̀ⲧⲉ ⲟⲩⲁⲓ ⲛ̀ⲛⲉⲕⲙⲉⲗⲟⲥ ⲧⲁⲕⲟ, It is good for you that one of your members perish . . .). The second relative perfect form serves not only its topicalizing adnominal function but also as a temporal-protatic "temporalis" topic before a main clause (constituting a "topic-comment" nexus on a macrosyntactic level of analysis; Jn. 11:28, ⲫⲁⲓ ⲉ̀ⲧⲁⲥϫⲟϥ ⲁⲥϣⲉ ⲛⲁⲥ, Having said this, she went away). The temporal clause is thus not expressed by a specific clause-tripartite conjugation base. (Incidentally, the second perfect in Bohairic cannot be further converted by the circumstantial converter.) The final and conditional clause paradigms include in Bohairic the conjunctive (after Greek final conjunctions of ⲉ̀ϣⲱⲡ, respectively, I Cor. 12:25, Mt. 6:14ff.). The postimperative paradigm lacks in Bohairic a specific marked apodotic form (ⲧⲁⲣⲉϥ- in other dialects, especially Sahidic) and features, typically, imperative and jussive forms (Mt. 9:6; Lk. 7:7) beside the nonspecific conjunctive (Acts 6:3) and ⲟⲩⲟϩ plus future tense (Mt. 7:7; Prv. 4:6). The "ethical dative" is regular after ϣⲉ in the nondurative conjugation (ϣⲉ ⲛⲁ⸗).

3.10. Prosody and Juncture. Elements of relatively weak stress in the utterance (native Egyptian enclitic particles, augentia, ⲁⲛ, the "backgrounding" ⲡⲉ) tend to a sentence-posterior, "trailing" position (Shisha-Halevy, 1981, pp. 319f.; e.g., Mt. 23:4, 26:44; Jn. 5:30, Lk. 16:2).

The relative converter ⲉ̀ⲧⲉ, when expanding the formal demonstrative antecedent ⲫⲏ or ⲫⲣⲏϯ, may be separated from the converted conjugation-form by at least two adjacent paradigms ("slots"), the first (pro)nominal and the second adverbial (Shisha-Halevy, 1981, p. 318; e.g. Dt. 2:25, ⲛⲏ ⲉ̀ⲧⲉ ⲁⲩϣⲁⲛⲥⲱⲧⲉⲙ ⲉ̀ⲡⲉⲕⲣⲁⲛ ⲉⲩⲉ̀ϣⲑⲟⲣⲧⲉⲣ, they who shall tremble if they hear your name; Col. 3:7, ⲛⲁⲓ ⲉ̀ⲧⲉ ⲛ̀ⲑⲱⲧⲉⲛ ϩⲱⲧⲉⲛ ⲛⲁⲣⲉⲧⲉⲛⲙⲟϣⲓ ⲛ̀ϧⲣⲏⲓ ⲛ̀ϧⲏⲧⲟⲩ, those in which you too used to walk); this indicates that the converter/conjugation-form seam is juncturally open to a degree.

3.11. The functional range of the coordinating ⲛⲉⲙ- is considerably extended in Bohairic, entailing reduced functions for ⲟⲩⲟϩ. (ⲛⲉⲙ- is preferred as a coordinator of noun syntagms.)

4. Lexicon: Idiomatics

4.1. The Bohairic lexeme inventory, idiosyncratic to a considerable extent, has never been properly researched in respect of either its internal or its contrastive structure. In the unstructured lexicon peculiar to Bohairic, occasionally in common with Fayyumic (e.g., ⲙ̀ⲃⲟⲛ, be wroth; ⲟⲩⲱⲣⲡ, send; ⲕⲏⲛ, cease; ϭⲁⲗⲟϫ, foot; ⲥⲕⲉⲛ, side; ϫⲱϣ, pour; ⲉ̀ⲡϣⲱⲓ, up), one notes cases of 1:1 correspondence with Sahidic (ⲉⲙⲛⲟϯ : ⲉⲕⲓⲃⲉ, breast; ϫⲁϭⲏ : ϩⲃⲟⲩⲣ, left side; ⲑⲱⲟⲩϯ : ⲥⲱⲟⲩϩ, gather), 2:1 (ϣⲏⲣⲓ + ϧⲣⲟϯ : ϣⲏⲣⲉ, children; ϣⲁ- + ϩⲁ- : ϣⲁ-, unto), 1:2 (ⲕⲏⲛ : ⲟⲩⲱ + ϩⲱ, cease, have done), and so on.

4.2. Although no overall statistics are available on the Greek-origin component of the Bohairic lexicon (cf. Kasser, 1966, and Bauer, 1975), one impressionistically notes the higher frequency in Bohairic of the use of Greek loanwords as well as their broader semantic spectrum and their number in absolute terms, which is larger in comparison with Sahidic usage. Some loans (e.g., ⲉⲥⲧⲱ ⲇⲉ, ⲉⲛ ⲟⲓⲥ, ⲙⲉⲛ ⲟⲩⲛ ϭⲉ, ⲧⲟ ⲗⲟⲓⲡⲟⲛ, ⲟⲩ ⲡⲁⲣⲁ ⲧⲟⲩⲧⲟ, ⲟⲩ ⲅⲁⲣ) are exclusive to Bohairic and show to what extent it imported ready-made Greek phrases; others (e.g., ⲡⲱⲥ, ⲟⲩⲛ, ϩⲁⲣⲁ, ϩⲓⲛⲁ) do occur elsewhere, but are much more common in Bohairic.

4.3. Phraseology and idiomatics are again virgin fields of study. Peculiarly *B* are, for instance, ⲉⲣ ⲟⲩ (ⲛⲁ⸗), what for, to what purpose?; ⲛⲉⲙ-, ⲛⲉⲙⲁ⸗, together with; and ⲛ̀ⲟⲩⲕⲟⲩϫⲓ ⲁⲛ, not small, for *S* ⲛⲟϭ, ϩⲁϩ ⲛ̄-, ⲉⲙⲁⲧⲉ (Acts 12:18, 15:2, etc.).

5. Varieties of Bohairic

5.1. Without taking a stand on their relative status and relative chronology, one can point out the following main subdivisions, or *Gattungen*, that *B* texts fall into, from the grammatical point of view. Given the current state of knowledge, one can do no more; as more evidence comes in (e.g., following the publication and evaluation of the "Old Bohairic" Twelve Prophets, unbiased consideration of Nitrian sources) and as the general dialectological picture becomes clearer (as it surely will, following the publication and study of "Middle Egyptian" evidence), one may be able to integrate these types of Bohairic in a coherent system.

5.2. "Classical" scriptural Bohairic conventionally serves as a *point de repère* for judging other types and is usually used for "Bohairic proper." Although it is by no means homogenous (being often variously blended with Nitrian; see 5.4), it nevertheless represents an optimal *testo di lingua*, especially in "good" consistent manuscripts (such as Vat. copto 1 and Bibl. Nat. copte 1).

5.3. A group (again, not monolithic) of fourth- and fifth-century biblical texts—extremely early documentation in comparison with the bulk of Bohairic scriptural sources—differs sharply from the classical idiom in linguistic usage. The largest single document of this kind published to date is Papyrus Bodmer III, containing the Gospel of John (Kasser, 1958, and 1966, pp. 66ff; cf. DIALECTS); another extensive manuscript containing the Twelve Prophets in the Vaticana was studied by H. Quecke. In Bodmer III one finds, among others, the following idiosyncrasies: ⲙⲙⲁ, there; ⲥⲛⲁ, two (for the classical ⲙ̀ⲙⲁⲩ, ⲥⲛⲁⲩ); ⲟⲩⲟϩⲉ, and; the negative conditional ⲁⲛⲛⲉϥ-; the preterite relative converter ⲉⲣ- (known also in Gnostic Sahidic, Subakhmimic, and Middle Egyptian); absence of the djinkim; *flottement* of ϧ~ϩ, ϭ~ϫ, ⲫ~ⲡ. Under the same heading, one may also include some shorter biblical texts of approximately the same early dating, including passages from James (with the djinkim; Quecke, 1974) and a biblical anthology (Husselman, 1947). On some "Bohairic" elements in Old Coptic, see Kahle (1954, pp. 243f.).

5.4. Nitrian Bohairic is attested mainly in hagiographical, homiletic, and hermeneutical texts from the Nitrian Monastery of Macarius, where they are generally supposed to have been transposed from a Sahidic *Vorlage* in the ninth century, but is also found "seeping through" into classical sources. This idiom has not yet been redeemed from neglect due to the bias of "secondhandedness" and "tainting," and Nitrian grammar has not had the attention it deserves. Phonologically, one observes here ϧ fluctuating with ϩ (e.g., in ⲉ̀ϧⲣⲏⲓ, down) and ϭ with ϫ (in ⲥⲟϫ, fool; ϫⲁⲙⲟⲩⲗ, camel). Typically there are ϣϣⲏⲛ, tree; ⲥⲙⲟⲛⲧ, form; ⲧⲱⲟⲩⲛⲟⲩ, stand up; and ⲕⲟⲩⲓ, small. Sporadically, combinatory aspiration is absent. As regards morphology, one finds ⲁ~ⲉ for the second present converter; ⲉ̀ⲧⲉⲣⲉ- is found as a variant of prenominal ⲉ̀ⲧⲉ-; in certain classes the presuffixal allomorph of the verb lexeme is extended to the prenominal state, leveling simplification into two—absolute and preobject—allomorphs (see Polotsky, 1930, p. 875 [=*CP* 344]): ⲥⲟⲩⲱⲛ-, ⲧⲟⲩⲛⲟⲥ-, ϣⲟⲡ-, ⲧⲟⲙ-, ⲟϣ-, ϣⲟⲩⲟ̀-; typical are the conjugation bases ϣⲁⲛⲧⲉ- and ⲙ̀ⲡⲁⲛⲧⲉ- (first sing. ⲙ̀ⲡⲁⲛⲧⲁ-, ϣⲁⲛⲧⲁ-); ⲑⲏⲛⲟⲩ occurs for the second plural after ⲛ̀ⲧⲟⲧ-. One encounters the "freezing" of the possessive suffix in ⲡⲉϥⲣⲱϥ, ⲡⲓⲣⲱϥ (Polotsky, 1934, p. 61 [=*CP* 366)]; Greek loan verbs occur also without ⲉⲣ-. Syntactically, one finds the relative to be compatible with indefinite determination (ⲟⲩⲁⲓ ⲉ̀ⲧⲁϥ-, Balestri and Hyvernat, 1907–1950, 2.206.23; ⲣⲱⲙⲓ ⲉⲑⲛⲁⲛⲉϥ, *Homélies* 1.101.4) and the circumstantial expanding definite nouns (ⲡⲓⲙⲁ ⲉ̀ⲣⲉ ⲡ̅ⲭ̅ⲥ̅ ⲙ̀ⲙⲟϥ, Balestri and Hyvernat, 1907–1950, 2.184.22f.). As in Sahidic, the second tense may have a nonadverbial focus (Polotsky, 1944, pp. 22, n. 1, and 31; 1971, pp. 126, 135). The negator ⲁⲛ is compatible with independently negative elements: ⲙ̀ⲙⲟⲛ- ⲁⲛ (Balestri and Hyvernat, 1907–1950, 1.9.8), ⲙ̀ⲡⲉⲣ- ⲁⲛ (*ibid.* 216.3). The regulation of ⲡⲓ- ⲛ̀ⲧⲉ- versus ⲡ- ⲛ̀- adnominal expansion appears to be disrupted or changed. ⲡⲉ occurs (as a backgrounding of macrosyntactic subject) after verb forms other than the imperfect (Hyvernat, 1886–1887, 135.13f., ⲁϥ-; 146.6f., ⲉⲩ-, circumstantial; 150.13, ⲟⲩⲟⲛ). Although many of these traits are attributable to the influence of Sahidic, this is by no means true of all.

5.5. Liturgical Bohairic has never been especially considered from the grammatical point of view. The djinkim occurs over most consonants, including surds; phonetic spellings are very common. ⲛ̀- is often zeroed. Some of the syntactic characteristics of Nitrian Bohairic are in evidence; the word order is occasionally remarkable; "agrammatical" constructions (such as ϫⲉ + fut. I in a final clause, ϣⲉ ⲛⲁ⸗ in the durative conjugation) occur. Nominal sentences with zeroed ⲡⲉ are common; the conjunctive occurs in initial position.

5.6. Nonliterary Bohairic is still a complete mystery. The sixth–eighth-century inscriptions of Kellia in Wādī al-Naṭrūn belong here only in a sense (they include tombstone and other personal religious texts); they are interesting (and as yet unresearched) from the linguistic point of view. One finds here sporadic variation of ⲃ ~ ⲩ, ⲟ ~ ⲱ, ⲉⲙ ~ ⲙ; the conjunctive ⲧⲉ-; the spelling ⲉⲗⲁϧⲓⲥⲧⲟⲥ; sporadic absence of nasal-labial assimilation (ⲛ̀ⲡⲓⲁⲙⲏⲛ) and of combinatory aspiration (ⲡⲙⲉⲩⲓ). Proper names are expanded by ⲛ̀ⲧⲉ (ⲓⲱⲥⲏⲫ ⲛ̀ⲧⲉ ⲡⲧⲉⲗⲙⲉ). On the whole, the language conforms with the classical rather than the Nitrian standard of Bohairic.

5.7. Kahle's "semi-Bohairic" Bala'izah no. 19, a fourth-century papyrus text with passages from Philippians, shows some Fayyumic and Sahidic affinities.

6. Selected Bibliographical Information

6.1 Major or Comprehensive Text Editions. Biblical, hermeneutic: Tattam (1836, 1852 [Prophets]), de Lagarde (1867, 1886 [Pentateuch, New Testament Catena]), Burmester and Devaud (1925, 1930 [Psalms, Proverbs]), Porcher (1924 [Job]), Horner (1898–1905 [New Testament]). Patristic, hagiographical, homiletic: Hyvernat (1886–1887), Balestri and Hyvernat (1907–1950), de Vis (1922–1929).

6.2 Grammatical Discussion. Andersson (1904) contains, beside blatant errors, a few notable observations. Mallon (1956) is the only modern special grammar (cf. Polotsky, 1959, his major treatise concerning Bohairic, as well as 1930, 1934, 1944, 1950) with extensive bibliography, chrestomathy, and glossary; it leaves much to be desired. While Peyron's venerable grammar (1841) is still of value, Stern (1880) is still by far the best treatment of Bohairic (as of Sahidic) grammar; the Schwarze (1850) grammar is skeletal, but contains numerous important grammatical observations. Note also Schwarze's unwieldy work of 1843, and the early grammars by Tuki and by Scholtz and Woide (both 1778). Chaîne (1933), a detailed and extensive contrastive-dialectological grammar, has many merits and makes quite a few pioneering statements. Till (1931) is superficial and almost useless (cf. Polotsky, 1934). Finally, Erman's famous, yet unfollowed, contrastive study of juncture (1915) aims at reviving interest in Bohairic, and Shisha-Halevy (1981) dwells on some conservative characteristics of this dialect.

6.3 General Dialectological Discussion. Kahle (1954) is still the prime source of information (esp. pp. 231ff., 248ff.). Worrell (1934, esp. chaps. 1-2) treats Bohairic phonology and the general status of the dialect. Vergote (1973, Vol. 1b) discusses *B* phonology as a component in a panoramic presentation. Bohairic features in all of Kasser's important dialectological studies (see esp. 1981, pp. 92ff.).

6.4 Lexicology. Only Peyron and Tattam (both 1835) cater specially to *B*. The priceless information in Crum's *Dictionary* (1939) must yet be resolved for the individual dialects. G. Bauer's concordance (1975) of the invariable Greek elements in the Bohairic New Testament is a welcome tool of research, which, one hopes, is to be extended to the rest of the Greek, as well as the indigenous, lexicon.

BIBLIOGRAPHY

Andersson, E. *Ausgewählte Bemerkungen über den bohairischen Dialekt im Pentateuch koptisch.* Uppsala, 1904.

Balestri, G., and H. Hyvernat. *Acta Martyrum,* I. CSCO 43, 44. Paris, 1907, 1908. *Acta Martyrum,* II [Text]. CSCO 86. Paris, 1924. See also Hyvernat, 1950.

Bauer, G. *Konkordanz der nichtflektierten griechischen Wörter im bohairischen Neuen Testament.* Wiesbaden, 1975.

Burmester, O. H. E. and E. Dévaud. *Psalterii Versio Memphitica e Recognitione Pauli de Lagarde.* Louvain, 1925.

______. *Les Proverbes de Salomon (Ch. 1, v. 1-14, v. 26*, Ch. 24, v. 24—v. 29 et v. 50*—v. 77 et Ch. 29, v. 28—v. 38), texte bohaïrique du Cod. 8 de la Rylands Library, Manchester, du Cod. 53 et 98 de la Bibliothèque Vaticane et du Cod. 1051 du Musée Copte au Caire, avec les variantes de 24 autres manuscrits et index des mots coptes et des mots grecs.* Vienne, 1930.

Černý, J. "The Bohairic Verbal Prefix ⲁⲛⲛⲉϥ-." *Zeitschrift für ägyptische Sprache und Altertumskunde* 90 (1963):13-16.

Chaîne, M. *Eléments de grammaire dialectale copte.* Paris, 1933.

Crum, W. E. *A Coptic Dictionary.* Oxford, 1939.

Erman, A. "Unterschiede zwischen den koptischen Dialekten bei der Wortverbindung." *Sitzungsberichte der Preussischen Akademie der Wissenschaften, Berlin* 1 (1915):161-72.

Horner, G. W. *The Coptic Version of the New Testament in the Northern Dialect, Otherwise Called Memphitic and Bohairic.* London, 1898-1905.

Husselman, E. M. "A Bohairic School Text on Papyrus." *Journal of Near Eastern Studies* 6 (1947):129-51.

Hyvernat, H. *Les Actes des martyrs de l'Egypte.* Paris, 1886-1887.

______. *Acta Martyrum,* II [Translation], *Additis Indicibus Totius Operis.* CSCO 125. Louvain, 1950.

Kahle, P. E. *Bala'izah: Coptic Texts from Deir el-Bala'izah in Upper Egypt.* London, 1954.

Kasser, R. *Papyrus Bodmer III: Evangile de Jean et Genèse I-IV,2 en bohaïrique.* CSCO 177-178. Louvain, 1958.

______. "A propos des différentes formes du conditionnel copte." *Muséon* 76 (1963):267-70.

______. *L'Evangile selon Saint Jean et les versions coptes de la Bible.* Neuchâtel, 1966.

______. "Prolégomènes à un essai de classification systématique des dialectes et subdialectes coptes selon les critères de la phonétique, I, Principes et terminologie." *Muséon* 93 (1980a):53-112. ". . . , II, Alphabets et systèmes phonétiques." *Muséon* 93 (1980b):237-97. ". . . , III, Systèmes orthographiques et catégories dialectales." *Muséon* 94 (1981):91-152.

Lagarde, P. A. de. *Der Pentateuch koptisch.* Leipzig, 1867.

______. *Catenae in Evangelia Aegyptiacae Quae Supersunt.* Göttingen, 1886.

Lefort, L. T. "Littérature bohaïrique." *Muséon* 44 (1931):115-35.

Mallon, A. *Grammaire copte, bibliographie, chrestomathie et vocabulaire,* 4th ed. rev. M. Malinine. Beirut, 1956.

Peyron, V. A. *Lexicon Linguae Copticae.* Turin, 1835; repr., 1896.

______. *Grammatica Linguae Copticae.* Turin, 1841.

______. *Lexicon Copticum.* Berlin, 1896.

Polotsky, H. J. Review of H. de Vis, *Homélies coptes de la Vaticane. Orientalistische Literaturzeitung* 33 (1930):871-81.

______. "Zur koptischen Lautlehre II." *Zeitschrift für ägyptische Sprache und Altertumskunde* 69 (1933): 125-29.

______. Review of W. C. Till, *Koptische Dialektgrammatik, mit Lesestücken und Wörterbuch. Göttingische Gelehrte Anzeiger* 196 (1934):58-67.

______. *Etudes de syntaxe copte.* Cairo, 1944.

______. "Une question d'orthographe bohaïrique." *Bulletin de la Société d'archéologie copte* 12 (1949):25-35.

______. "Modes grecs en copte?" In *Coptic Studies in Honor of Walter Ewing Crum,* pp. 73-90. Boston, 1950.

______. "Zur Neugestaltung der koptischen Grammatik." *Orientalistische Literaturzeitung* 45 (1959): 453-60.

______. "The Coptic Conjugation System." *Orientalia* 29 (1960):392-422.

———. "Nominalsatz und Cleft Sentence im Koptischen." *Orientalia* 31 (1962):413–30.
———. *Collected Papers.* Jerusalem, 1971.
Porcher, E. "Le Livre de Job, version copte publiée et traduite." *Patrologia Orientalis* 18 (1924):209–239.
Quecke, H. "Ein altes bohairisches Fragment des Jakobusbriefes (P. Heid. kopt. 452)." *Orientalia* 43 (1974):382–92.
Scholtz, C. and Charles Godfrey Woide. *Grammatica Aegyptiaca Utriusque Dialecti.* Oxford, 1778.
Schwartze, M. G. *Das alte Ägypten, oder Sprache, Geschichte, Religion und Verfassung des alten Ägypten nach den altägyptischen Originalschriften und den Mittheilungen der nicht-ägyptischen alten Schriftsteller.* Leipzig, 1843.
Schwartze, M. G. *Koptische Grammatik . . . , herausgegeben nach des Verfassers Tode von Dr. H. Steinthal.* Berlin, 1850.
Shisha-Halevy, A. "Bohairic-Late-Egyptian Diaglosses." In *Studies Presented to Hans Jakob Polotsky,* ed. D. W. Young, pp. 314–38. East Gloucester, Mass., 1981.
Stern, L. *Koptische Grammatik.* Leipzig, 1880.
Tattam, H. *Lexicon Aegyptiaco-Latinum, ex Veteribus Linguae Aegyptiacae Monumentis, et ex Operibus La Crozii, Woidii, et Aliorum, Summo Studio Congestum, cum Indice Vocum Latinarum.* Oxford, 1835.
———. *Duodecim Prophetarum Minorum Libros in Lingua Aegyptiaca Vulgo Coptica seu Memphitica ex Manuscripto Parisiensi Descriptos et cum Manuscripto Johannis Lee . . . Collatos Latine Edidit.* Oxford, 1836.
———. *Prophetae Majores, in Dialecto Linguae Aegyptiacae Memphitica seu Coptica, Edidit cum Versione Latina.* Oxford, 1852.
Till, W. C. *Koptische Dialektgrammatik, mit Lesestücken und Wörterbuch.* Munich, 1931; 2nd ed., 1961.
Tuki, R. *Rudimenta Linguae Coptae sive Aegyptiacae.* Rome, 1778.
Vergote, J. *Grammaire copte,* Vol. 1a, *Introduction, phonétique et phonologie, morphologie synthématique (structure des sémantèmes), partie synchronique,* and Vol. 1b, *Introduction, phonétique et phonologie, morphologie synthématique (structure des sémantèmes), partie diachronique.* Louvain, 1973.
Vis, H. de. *Homélies coptes de la Vaticane.* Copenhagen, 1922–1929.
Worrell, W. H. *Coptic Sounds.* Ann Arbor, Mich., 1934.

ARIEL SHISHA-HALEVY

BOHAIRIC, PRONUNCIATION OF LATE.

The phonetics of a dead language can be determined in an indirect way only—namely, by a scrutinizing analysis of spelling irregularities that are based on phonetic phenomena and of transcriptions in the writing system and orthography of another language the phonetics of which are better known. Absolute proof of the issue can never be gained. But results obtained from different sources and by different methods are to be regarded as probable if they are consistent.

But is Coptic a dead language in respect to phonetics? Has not the Coptic liturgy been recited in a traditional way down to this day? Although some authors have claimed near-perfect authenticity for one or another modern tradition, it seems highly improbable that the mother tongue of the Copts has left no mark on the spelling of the liturgical language. It is, therefore, advisable to take a critical stand—that is, to reconstruct the pronunciation of ancient living Coptic from contemporary sources and to confront the issue of such an endeavor with modern evidence only as a last resort.

For the literary Coptic of the thirteenth century (which is, of course, the BOHAIRIC dialect), much elucidation can be gained from a codex of an Arabic version of the Apophthegmata Patrum that is entirely written in the Coptic alphabet (Casanova, 1901; Sobhy, 1926; Burmester, 1965–1966). Some remarks on the character of the Arabic idiom of the text are necessary. It has been plausibly classified by Blau (1979) as "Middle Arabic Substandard." He wrote, "Its author(s) intended to write Classical Arabic, but whether as a result of his (their) ignorance or negligence, elements of Neo-Arabic penetrated into it. Like Middle Arabic texts in general, our text is characterized by freely alternating features of Classical Arabic, Neo-Arabic and pseudo-corrections" (ibid., p. 215, sec. 2). The main features of its phonetics have been elaborated with a substantial degree of certainty. *q* was probably pronounced in the classical way (voiceless uvular plosive), although a pronunciation as [g] or [g] cannot be ruled out (ibid., p. 221, sec. 8; Satzinger, 1971, p. 61). *ǧ* was of palatalized articulation ([ǧ] or [ġ]). *ḍ* and *ẓ* had coalesced in an emphatic spirant, most probably *ḏ̣*. This pronunciation may also suggest that *ḏ* and *ṯ* had preserved their spirant articulation, although there is no direct evidence to exclude a plosive articulation *d* and *t*, respectively (Blau, 1979, p. 221, sec. 9; Satzinger, 1971, p. 52). The author generally preserves *aw* and *ay* in diphthong transcription, but in some cases slips to his Neo-Arabic vernacular monophthong articulation (ibid., p. 47). In forms of the verb *ǧā'a*, to come, he presents purely Neo-Arabic features, clearly eliding the glottal stop or *hamz* (*ğeyt*, I came, *ğeyyeh*, fem. sing. active participle; ibid., p. 52).

The main regular correspondences between the Arabic phonemes of the text and the Bohairic signs of the transcription are given in the following tables (ibid., pp. 49–50, but with observations of Blau, 1979, pp. 218–22, sec. 6–10):

1. The Consonants

ʾ	zero
b	ⲡ
t	ⲑ; in final position also ⲧ (see remarks)
ṯ	ⲑ
ğ	ϫ
ḥ	ϩ
ḫ	ϧ
d	ⲇ
ḏ	ⲇ
r	ⲣ
z	ⲍ
s	ⲥ
š	ϣ
ṣ	ⲥ
ḍ	ⲍ
ṭ	ⲧ; in nonfinal position also ⲑ (see remarks)
ẓ	ⲍ
ʿ	ϩ
ġ	ⲅ
f	ϥ
q	ⲕ
k	ϫ, more rarely ⲕ; in final position, exclusively ⲕ (see remarks)
l	ⲗ
m	ⲙ
n	ⲛ
h	ϩ
w	ⲃ
y	ⲓ

No use is made of the following Coptic letters for transcribing Arabic consonants: ⲝ, ⲫ, ⲯ, ϭ, consonantal ⲟⲩ.

Remarks. Arabic *t* is generally rendered by the aspirate, ⲑ. If in the final position, *t* may also be rendered by ⲧ.

Arabic *ṭ* is generally rendered by ⲧ; in nonfinal positions it may also be rendered by ⲑ.

Arabic *k* is rendered generally by ϫ or, more rarely, by ⲕ. In the final position, however, *k* is exclusively rendered by ⲕ. This letter is also used to render Arabic *q* (see Table 1).

It is remarkable that ⲧ is not used to render Arabic *t* (except in some cases where the latter is in the final position). This can be best explained by assuming a "soft" articulation [d̥] for ⲧ. Furthermore, three tendencies can be observed: (1) the use of aspirate signs for nonemphatic stops and of nonaspirate signs for emphatic stops, the reason for this being, in all probability, the notably nonaspirated character of the Arabic emphatics; cf. Kästner, 1981, p. 43); (2) the use of nonaspirate signs instead of aspirate signs for stops in the final position, such as ⲧ occasionally for ⲑ, and ⲕ regularly for ϫ, proving that Coptic nonaspirate stops were of soft articulation in nonfinal positions only; (3) the use of ⲕ rather than ϫ (Blau, 1979, pp. 218–20, sec. 6) (one may conclude from this that the articulation of ⲕ was less soft than that of ⲧ and ⲡ).

In the Arabic transcriptions of Coptic liturgical texts (of later date; cf. Worrell, 1934, pp. 5–6), nonfinal ⲧ is regularly rendered by Arabic *d* or *ḍ* (or *ẓ*, which had coalesced with *ḍ* in Arabic), though not in Greek words (صوتير, ⲥⲱⲧⲏⲣ; خرسطوس , ⲭ̄ⲥ̄; etc.). In what is probably the oldest transcription text preserved, an undated codex published in excerpts by Galtier (1905), final ⲧ is regularly rendered by Arabic *t*. The transcription that Sobhy (1940) published in excerpts—which is dated, according to him, A.M. 1438 (but this cannot be confirmed from the printed rendering; at any rate read "9" [= *ṭā*ʾ] instead of "8" [which would be *ḥā*ʾ])—is less consistent in this, as are the records by Petraeus (1659; cf. Galtier, 1905, pp. 109–110), de Rochemonteix (1892; taken down 1876–1877), and Sobhy (1915 and 1918; taken down early in this century). Modern reformed

TABLE 1.

ARABIC	COPTIC TRANSCRIPTIONS	
	NONFINAL POSITION	FINAL POSITION
t	ⲑ	ⲑ (ⲧ)
ṭ	ⲧ (ⲑ)	ⲧ
k	ϫ (ⲕ)	ⲕ
q	ⲕ	ⲕ

pronunciation does not articulate ⲧ "softly" at all; it is, rather, t or ṭ in all positions, in accordance with the Greek pronunciation.

2. The Vowels

a, ā if there is a *ḥarf mufaḫḫam* in the same syllable; otherwise, ⲉ (see Blau, 1979, p. 222, sec. 11, and remarks)
i ⲉ, occasionally ⲓ
ī ⲓ
u ⲟ, occasionally ⲟⲩ
ū ⲟⲩ, but also ⲟ if in the vicinity of a *ḥarf mufaḫḫam* (see remarks)
ay ⲁⲓ if preceded by a *ḥarf mufaḫḫam;* otherwise, ⲉⲓ or ⲏⲓ indiscriminately
aw ⲁⲩ

Remarks. *Tafḫīm*, or the glottalizing effect, is a characteristic of the emphatics *ṣ, ḍ, ṭ, ẓ*, uvular *q*, and, to a lesser extent, the postdorsal uvular consonants *ḫ* and *ġ*, the pharyngeal sounds of ʿ and *ḥ*, and in many instances *r*. Although, for example, both Arabic *s* and *ṣ* are rendered by Coptic ⲥ, the transcription differentiates in rendering *sa* by ⲥⲉ and *ṣa* by ⲥⲁ. This proves beyond doubt that ⲁ and ⲉ were pronounced differently in the Bohairic idiom, which underlies the Coptic transcription.

Similarly, the later Arabic transcriptions make use of the Arabic emphatics to distinguish Coptic vowels for which there are no distinct Arabic graphemes. In the text published by Galtier (1905), the reader can be sure that an Arabic *ṣā* renders ⲥⲁ, whereas the Arabic *sā* renders ⲥⲉ (or ⲥⲏ) rather than ⲥⲁ, more often than not. Similarly, both ⲥⲟ and ⲥⲱ are almost always rendered by *ṣū*, whereas *sū* is the regular equivalent of ⲥⲟⲩ. The writer of the text published by Sobhy (1918) does not proceed consistently, but a tendency toward distinguishing ⲁ and ⲉ is still clearly discernible. In the Coptic idioms underlying these transcriptions (though not necessarily the copies preserved, one of them perhaps from the early eighteenth century), the vowels ⲁ and ⲉ were obviously pronounced in a different way. But coalescence of these vowels is attested as early as the mid seventeenth century. In the record done by Petraeus (1659) both letters are regularly rendered by *a*. The same is found in de Rochemonteix's (1892) and Sobhy's (1915 and 1918) records of traditional pronunciation. It is only in the modern reformed pronunciation that ⲁ and ⲉ are again distinguished as *a* and *e* [ɛ], rendered by alif and yā', respectively, in the popular *khulagis* which have an Arabic transcription. Here, emphatics are only used to distinguish ⲧⲟ and ⲧⲱ (transcribed by *ṭū*) from ⲧⲟⲩ (transcribed by *tū*).

Conclusion

The evidence gained from the Bohairic transcription, the Arabic transcriptions of liturgical Bohairic, and transcriptions of this into the Latin alphabet from the mid seventeenth century onward corroborates many of the results that have been gained from other evidence (see BOHAIRIC).

The Bohairic consonants are voiceless, except ⲙ, ⲛ, ⲗ, ⲣ, and, if in a nonfinal position, ⲃ (see below).

A "soft" articulation of the nonaspirate plosives is assumed for all Coptic dialects. This has been corroborated by the evidence of the Arabic transcriptions: the usual equivalent of ⲧ is Arabic *d* or *ḍ*. It may, however, be assumed that ⲕ was not of the same "softness" as ⲡ, ⲧ, and ϫ; it is rather often used to render Arabic *k* instead of ϫ. Worrell (1934) thought it possible that Bohairic ⲡ, ⲧ, ϫ, and ⲕ were voiced whenever going back to Egyptian *b, d, d̲* (= ğ), and *g*, respectively. In the Coptic alphabet of the Arabic Apophthegmata, however, these signs represent voiceless stops: it is not ⲧ that is used for Arabic *d* but rather ⲇ (a letter of the alphabet of Coptic Greek). If ⲡ is used for Arabic *b* and ϫ for Arabic *ğ*, this may have been done by default, there being no voiced alternative available, in contrast to the case of ⲧ.

The problem of ϫ is rather one of Arabic dialectology, as this letter has by and large been identified with ğīm, a phoneme whose articulation varies greatly in the Arabic idioms of Egypt (see Woidich, 1980, pp. 207–208). De Rochemonteix's (1892) Upper Egyptian informants pronounced ϫ as ɟ (ġ), though one informant offered a free(?) variant *ž*. Sobhy (1918, p. 54), on the other hand, claimed that in Upper Egypt, ϫ is ɟ where it corresponds to Sahidic ϫ but *g* where it corresponds to Sahidic ϭ (but note that ϫⲉ in the text he reproduces is ϫⲉ, not ϭⲉ, in Sahidic). In Lower Egypt, ϫ preceding vowel *i* was pronounced as ǧ, but otherwise it was *g*, according to Sobhy (1915, p. 18). A very similar rule applies in modern reformed pronunciation, which has *ğ* before *i* and *e*. This is remarkable indeed. As it cannot be explained by Arabic influence, it is obviously a testimony to internal Coptic development.

In the final position, ⲡ, ⲧ, ϫ, and ⲕ seem to have coalesced with the aspirates, ⲫ, ⲑ, ϭ, and ⲭ, respectively. This, again, is corroborated by the evidence of the Arabic transcriptions.

As to aspirate stops, in the Arabic transcriptions, a (possibly late) tendency to pronounce ⲫ as a fricative, even in genuine Coptic words, is attested; it is sometimes rendered by Arabic *f* (corresponding evidence can be found with de Rochemonteix, 1892). ϭ is not used for transcribing Arabic. It is rendered by *š* in Arabic, although the assumed pronunciation is $\check{c}^h$. This can be explained by the fact that Arabic (both classical and Egyptian) has no *č* phoneme, and the device of rendering the Bohairic phoneme by two Arabic phonemes (and, by consequence, two graphemes), namely *t* plus *š*, met with reluctance. Compare this to the use in modern Egypt of *š* to render Turkish *č* (which is *ç* in the Turkish Latin alphabet; see Prokosch, 1983, p. 11). But somewhere the *č* articulation may have survived. Although both Petraeus (1659) and de Rochemonteix (1892) render ϭ by *š* exclusively, Sobhy (1915, p. 18, and 1918, p. 52) heard [č] (though obviously not in ⲟ̅ⲥ̅, which is *šois*). This could, however, be interpreted as a trait of the reformed pronunciation, which has the *č* sound (rendered *t̠* plus *s̠* in Arabic script), again with the exception of ⲟ̅ⲥ̅.

It is assumed that ⲃ was pronounced as a voiced bilabial fricative, *β* (= *b̠*). This articulation was still noticed by de Rochemonteix in 1876–1877; Sobhy (1915 and 1918) noted that nonfinal ⲃ is pronounced as vocalic *u*, and never like the rounded *w* of Arabic. The evidence of the Arabic transcriptions is in agreement with this: initial ⲃ is rendered, not by wāw but rather by alif plus wāw, and once in the syllable-initial position hamza with kasra plus wāw (امبرءوارءوورت , ⲙ̀ⲡⲉⲣⲃⲉⲣⲃⲱⲣⲧ): by indicating a short front vowel, the writer obviously hinted at a nonrounded articulation of the labial.

In the final position, however, ⲃ was not pronounced as a fricative (cf. Tuki, 1778, p. 3). This cannot be verified in the Apophthegmata transcription, as Arabic final *w* is realized as vocalic *u* in the pausal forms. But both in the transcriptions and in the records of traditional pronunciation, final ⲃ is rendered by the corresponding plosive (Arabic *b*). It is not possible to say whether final ⲃ fully coalesced with final ⲫ or the former remained softer and/or unaspirated.

It is a very remarkable fact that at the time the Arabic transcription of the Galtier (1905) text was produced, Copto-Greek words were mostly pronounced according to rules similar to those of late koine and modern Greek.

In many words, ⲧ is rendered by the Arabic voiceless stops *t* or *ṭ*. This indicates that it was not of soft articulation, as it was in autochthonous Coptic words.

The voiced stops of Greek had developed into the corresponding fricatives in late antiquity: *b* > *β* (*b̠*) > *v*; *d* > *δ* (*d̠*); and *g* before front vowels > ɟ (*ǵ*) > *y*, but otherwise > *γ* (*ḡ*).

The relevant correspondences with Arabic signs can be explained by assuming a similar pronunciation of the Copto-Greek words (see especially for ⲅ).

The aspirates of Greek had developed into the corresponding fricatives in late antiquity: p^h > *ϕ* (*p̄*) > *f*; t^h > *ϑ* (*t̠*); and k^h before front vowels > *ç* (*ś*), but otherwise > *χ* (*ḫ*).

For the Copto-Greek words in Bohairic, note especially that ⲫ was not rendered by Arabic *b*; ⲑ was apt to render Arabic *t̠*; and ⲭ was rendered by Arabic *š* (the sound value coming closest to *ç* in Arabic) if preceding a front vowel, but otherwise by *ḫ*.

One will be inclined to attribute the introduction of such "learned" usage to a rather late period of Coptic literacy—for example, a period of high philological interest, such as the thirteenth and fourteenth centuries. Note, however, that some of the misspellings in earlier Coptic (cf. Crum, 1939, pp. 48–49, 516, 540–41, 745) can hardly be explained otherwise than by assuming a tradition of "Neo-Greek" pronunciation. The question is, though, whether this pronunciation was applied to the Copto-Greek words in earlier times in the same matter-of-course way as in the Galtier (1905) text, for example.

Note that the informants of de Rochemonteix (1892) were not very consistent in the use of ⲅ, ⲇ, and ⲭ in Copto-Greek words, sometimes pronouncing them in the "Coptic" way, namely *ǵ* (< *g*?), even when preceding back vowels; *d* instead of *d̠*; *k* instead of *ḫ* or *ç*.

Present-day liturgical recitation follows the rules of a reformed pronunciation. It is mirrored in the Arabic transcriptions that have replaced the Coptic characters in the popular *khulagis*. The values attributed to the Coptic signs appear systematic and uniform, making transcription almost a transliteration. Consonants are more or less rendered according to the Neo-Greek values. ϫ is *ǧ* (spelled چ) before front vowels *i* and *e*, but otherwise *g* (spelled ج). Other values have been mentioned above. A conspicuous feature is the mechanical rendering of the *djinkim* by hamza: ⲉ̀ϩⲣⲏⲓ, *'e'ehrī*; ϣⲉⲡ̀ϩⲙⲟⲧ, *šep'ehmōt*, and so on.

These modern innovations represent the greatest break in the history of Coptic pronunciation. But

TABLE 2.

	ⲁⲣⲓⲧⲉⲛ	ⲛ̀ⲉⲙⲡϣⲁ	ⲛ̀ϫⲟⲥ	ϧⲉⲛ ⲟⲩϣⲉⲡ ϩ̀ⲙⲟⲧ
1.	*arī́den	ənəmbšá	əndšós	ḫen ušebəhmót
2.	aridān	enembša	eng̍os	ḫan ušabehmot
3.	aritēn	'en'empšā	'engōs	ḫen 'ušep'ehmōt

	ϫⲉ ⲡⲉⲛⲓⲱⲧ	ⲉⲧϧⲉⲛ ⲛⲓⲫⲏⲟⲩⲓ̀	ⲙⲁⲣⲉϥⲧⲟⲩⲃⲟ
1.	dšebeniṓt	etḫen nip^{h}éui	marefdubó
2.	g̍a baniōt	adḫan nifāui	marafdūo
3.	ǧe penyōt	'etḫen nifī'ui	mareftuvō

	ⲛ̀ϫⲉ ⲡⲉⲕⲣⲁⲛ	ⲙⲁⲣⲉⲥⲓ̀	ⲛ̀ϫⲉ ⲧⲉⲕⲙⲉⲧⲟⲩⲣⲟ
1.	əndše bek^{h}rán	maresī́	əndše dek^{h}meduró
2.	eng̍a bakrān	marasī	eng̍a dakmadūro
3.	'enǧe pekrān	mares'ī	'enǧe tekmet'urō

	ⲡⲉⲧⲉϩⲛⲁⲕ	ⲙⲁⲣⲉϥϣⲱⲡⲓ	ⲙ̀ⲫⲣⲏϯ
1.	bedehnák^{h}	marefšṓbi	əmp^{h}réi
2.	bedehnak	marafšōbi	emebrādi
3.	petehnāk	marefšōpi	'emefrīti

	ϧⲉⲛ ⲧⲫⲉ	ⲛⲉⲙ ϩⲓϫⲉⲛ	ⲡⲓⲕⲁϩⲓ
1.	ḫen tp^{h}é	nem hidšen	bikáhi etc.
2.	ḫan etba	nem hig̍an	ebkahi etc.
3.	ḫen 'etfī	nem hiǧēn	pi kāhi etc.

whereas present-day liturgical recitation would perhaps not be comprehensible to the ears of a medieval Copt, this would certainly not be true of traditional recitation even as it was heard in this century. Although it cannot be denied that changes had occurred—because of the influence of Arabic and internal development—the ancient tradition had been preserved in an astonishing measure. An example (Table 2) will serve best to clarify this.

The first line of the example is a reconstruction of what the beginning of the Lord's Prayer may have sounded like in classical times. But note that the phonetic rendering is quite imprecise. Voiceless stops [b̥, d̥] are meant by *b* and *d;* what is written *f* is thought to be a bilabial fricative [Φ]; short *e* and *o* are open vowels [ɛ, ɔ]; *ē* was rather an *ae* sound (or perhaps even *œ;* cf. Vycichl, 1936).

The second line renders Sobhy's (1915, p. 19) record in the conventions used here (*š* for *sh*, etc.). An Upper Egyptian pronunciation *g̍* has been assumed for ϫ.

The third line is a rendering of modern church recitation as it is transcribed in Arabic script in the popular *khulagis.*

BIBLIOGRAPHY

Blau, J. "Some Observations on a Middle Arabic Egyptian Text in Coptic Characters." *Jerusalem Studies in Arabic and Islam* 1 (1979):215–62.

Burmester, O. H. E. "Further Leaves from the Arabic MS. in Coptic Script of the Apophthegmata Patrum." *Bulletin de la Société d'archéologie copte* 18 (1965–1966):51–64, pl. I–V.

Casanova, P. "Un Texte arabe transcrit en caractères coptes." *Bulletin de l'Institut français d'archéologie orientale* 1 (1901):1–20, pl. I–II.

Crum, W. E. *A Coptic Dictionary.* Oxford, 1939.

Galtier, E. "Un Manuscrit copte en caractères arabes." *Bulletin de l'Institut français d'archéologie orientale* 5 (1905):91–111.

Kästner, H. *Phonetik und Phonologie des modernen Hocharabisch.* Leipzig, 1981.

Petraeus, T. *Psalmus Primus Davidis, Coptice, Arabice et Latine.* London, 1659.

Prokosch, E. *Osmanisches Wortgut im Ägyptisch-Arabischen.* Islamkundliche Untersuchungen 78. Berlin, 1983.

Rochemonteix, M. de. "La Prononciation moderne du copte dans la Haute Egypte." *Mémoires de la Société linguistique* 7 (1892):245–76. Repr. in de

Rochemonteix. *Oeuvres diverses,* pp. 95–129. Bibliothèque égyptologique 3. Paris, 1894.

Satzinger, H. "Zur Phonetik des Bohairischen und des Ägyptisch-Arabischen im Mittelalter." *Wiener Zeitschrift für die Kunde des Morgenlandes* 63–64 (1971):40–65.

Sobhy, G. P. G. "The Pronunciation of Coptic in the Church of Egypt." *Journal of Egyptian Archaeology* 2 (1915):15–20.

______. "La Prononciation moderne du copte dans l'Eglise." *Bulletin de l'Institut français d'archéologie orientale* 14 (1918):51–56.

______. "Fragments of an Arabic MS. in Coptic Script." In Hugh G. Evelyn-White. *The Monasteries of the Wadi 'n Natrūn,* Vol. 1, pp. 231–69. New York, 1926.

______. "The Traditional Pronunciation of Coptic in the Church of Egypt." *Bulletin de la Société d'archéologie copte* 6 (1940):109–117, pl. I–II.

Tuki, R. *Rudimenta Linguae Coptae seu Aegyptiacae.* Rome, 1778.

Vycichl, W. "Pi-Solsel, ein Dorf mit koptischer Überlieferung." *Mitteilungen des deutschen Instituts für ägyptische Altertumskunde in Kairo* 6 (1936):169–75.

Woidich, M. "Das Ägyptisch-Arabische." In *Handbuch der arabischen Dialekte,* ed. W. Fischer and O. Jastrow, pp. 207–248. Porta Linguarum Orientalium n.s. 16. Wiesbaden, 1980.

Worrell, W. H. *Coptic Sounds.* Ann Arbor, Mich., 1934.

HELMUT SATZINGER

CRYPTOGRAPHY. At times the Copts have felt the need to use cryptography in order to hide the contents of certain annotations, formulas, inscriptions, and messages. About thirty examples of this have been recorded. It would, however, be excessive to speak here of a "Coptic cryptography," for, as shall be seen, even in a Coptic context, the scribe used cryptographic systems borrowed from Greek and even preferred Greek over Coptic in formulas thus disguised. The cryptographic systems employed can be summarized within three types.

First Type

The two principal forms fully merit description as "encoding," for the Greeks took them not from the classical alphabet but from an archaic repertoire used in writing numbers: the first nine characters of the archaic Greek alphabet were used to express the units one through nine. The next set of nine were employed to express the tens: ten, twenty, thirty, and

TABLE 1.

1	α	10	ι	100	ρ
2	β	20	κ	200	σ
3	γ	30	λ	300	τ
4	δ	40	μ	400	υ
5	ϵ	50	ν	500	φ
6	ϛ	60	ξ	600	χ
7	ζ	70	ο	700	ψ
8	η	80	π	800	ω
9	ϑ	90	ϙ	900	ϡ or ⳁ

so on. The next set of nine letters were used to express the hundreds, as Table 1 illustrates. Here one can see three archaic letters that had fallen out of use: ϛ (stigma) for 6, ϙ (qoppa) for 90, and ϡ or ⳁ (sampi) for 900.

During the Hellenistic period, imitating a Jewish cryptographic process (called *atbash*), some Greek created a similar encoding based on that division of the former alphabet into three portions (or rows). This system consisted of inverting the letters of each row and replacing the normal row by the inverted row—for example, α β γ δ ϵ ϛ ζ η ϑ becoming ϑ η ζ ϛ ϵ δ γ β α, and normal α being replaced by ϑ, β by η, δ by ζ, and so on (see Gardthausen, 1913, p. 301; Wisse, 1979, pp. 119–20). As this system of inversion had the weakness of not being able to modify ⲉ (ϵ), ⲛ (ν), and ⲫ (φ), located at the center of each row, special cryptic symbols were fabricated for them. For instance, ⲉ was translated by ≡ and ⲛ by |||. When the Copts borrowed this system, the archaic letter ⳁ, which had the value of 900 and in such texts was written with the letter ρ, had fallen into disuse; it was thus rendered with some lack of precision, as if it were the well-known letters ⲩⲣ bound together. Such was the basis of the cryptography that the Copts mostly used (Table 2). It is noteworthy to remark that in Coptic the Greek ϙ is currently confused with ϥ, by which it is replaced.

TABLE 2.

ⲁ = ⲑ	ⲓ = ϙ	ⲣ = ⳁ
ⲃ = ⲏ	ⲕ = ⲡ	ⲥ = ⲱ
ⲅ = ⲍ	ⲗ = ⲟ	ⲧ = ⲯ
ⲇ = ϛ	ⲙ = ⲝ	ⲩ = ⲭ
ⲉ = ⲉ	ⲛ = ⲛ	ⲫ = ⲫ
ϛ = ⲇ	ⲝ = ⲙ	ⲭ = ⲩ
ⲍ = ⲅ	ⲟ = ⲗ	ⲯ = ⲧ
ⲏ = ⲃ	ⲡ = ⲕ	ⲱ = ⲥ
ⲑ = ⲁ	ϙ = ⲓ	ⳁ = ⲣ

This system was suitable for encoding a text written in Greek, and in fact, in encoding formulas, the Copts mostly used Greek formulas, even in the body of documents otherwise written completely in Coptic. However, when they wanted to hide a truly Coptic formula, they either did not modify the autochthonous graphemes (especially ϣ, ϥ, ϩ, ϫ, and ϭ), or they encoded them by means of conventional signs. Here are some examples of this system and some known variations of it:

1. From the Coptic treatise entitled "Zostrianos" (Nag Hammadi Library, Codex VIII [or IV, according to Doresse's numbering], p. 132) comes in Greek the following "colophon" at the tractate's end (first half of fourth century):

ⲟ̅ⲗ̅ⲍ̅ ⲗ̅ϥ̅ ⲑ̅ⲟ̅ⲃ̅ ⲁ̅ⲉ̅ϥ̅ [ⲑ̅] ϣ̣̅ⲅ̅ ⲥ̅ⲱ̅ϯ̅
ⲩ̅ⲣ̅ϥ̅ⲑ̅ ⲛ̅ⲗ̅ⲭ̅ ⲁ̅ⲉ̅ⲗ̅ϣ̣̅ ⲑ̅ⲟ̅ⲃ̅ⲁ̅ⲉ̣̅ϥ̅
ⲑ̅ⲱ̅ ⲟ̅ⲗ̅ⲍ̅ⲗ̅ϥ̅ ⲅⲥⲩⲣⲗ ⲑ̅ⲱ̅ψ̅ ⲩ̅ⲣ̅[ⲗ̅ⲭ̅]

λόγοι ἀληθεί[α]ς Ζωστ
ριανοῦ θεὸς ἀληθεί
ας λόγοι Ζωροάστρ̣[ου]

"Words of truth of Zostrianos, the God of truth, words of Zoroaster" (cf. Doresse, 1950; Wisse, 1979, no. 1; with some emendations).

2. A Greek graffito from the sixth century or later found in the Theban mountains (Crum and Evelyn-White, 1926, no. 701) reads thus:

ϯⲡ̅ⲉ̅ⲕⲑϥ{ⲭ}ⲋⲭⲛⲑⳅ̣ϥϣ̣
ϯⲥ̅ⲛ̅ⲑⲍϥⲗⲛⲉⲭⲩⲗⲛ
ϯⲥⲓⳅⲉⲍⲑⲗ̣ⲗ̣ⲛⲉⲭⲙⲑⲱ
ⲁⲑϥⲕⲉϡϥϯⲑⲱⲑ̣ⳅⲑϡϯ̣ϥⲑ
ⳅⲗⲭ̣ⲉⲅⲥⳅ[ⲃ]ⲛⲑⲱ{ⲥ}ⲗⳅⲑϡ
ϯⲗⲟⲱ ϯ ϥⲑ ϥ̅ⲑ̅ ϥⲑ ⲕ̅ⲉ̅ ϯ ⲓ̈ⲛⲇ ⲍ

κ̅ε̅ καὶ δύναμις
τῶν ἁγίον εὐχὸν
τῶν μεγάλ̣ο̣ν εὔξασ
θαι περὶ τὰς ἁμαρτία⟨ς⟩
μου ἐγὼ Μ[η]νὰς ὁ ⟨ἁ⟩μαρ
τωλ⟨ό⟩ς ϙθ ϙθ ϙθ κ̅ε̅ ινδ ζ

In lines 1 and 5, the marks in braces {. . .} are superfluous. In line 1, the first ϯ, and in line 6, the second and third ϯ are ordinary crosses. "Lord and power of the holy prayers of the great [monks], pray for my sins! I am Menas the sinner. Amen, Amen, Amen, Lord! Ind[iction] 7" (cf. Wisse, 1979, no. 2, which strongly improved the reading of this text, in an approximate Greek; formerly published in Crum and Evelyn-White, 1926, pp. 147, 330, 386). The sampi, a rarely used symbol, is sketched in some variable fashions. The siglum ϥ̅ⲑ̅ for "Amen" is the current Byzantine abbreviation based on the numerical value of the letters of this word:

ⲁ + ⲙ + ⲏ + ⲛ = 1 + 40 + 8 + 50 = 99.

3. Coptic formulas to protect oneself from dogs were not so much for the simple passerby as for lovers or thieves who would fear the dogs' barking and biting at night; the text shown below was edited by Erman (1895) from a fragment conserved in the British Museum (Or. 1013-A). The reading of the cryptographic formula was specified by Wisse (1979, no. 11). The revelation of this formula is attributed to Isis, an attribution that places it among the most archaic of Coptic formulas. Here are the most essential lines only:

[≡ϥ]ⳅⲗⲭⲣⳅⲕⲗⲭⲑⲣ||||||ϥⳅⲕϣⲃⲣ≡|||ψ≡ⲱϩϥⳅ≡
≡ψ≡ψ≡ϥ̣ⳅⲑ[ⲑⲭψ≡]

[ⲉⲓ]ⲙⲟⲩⲣ ⲙⲡⲟⲩⲁⲣ ⲛⲛⲓⲙ ⲡϣⲏⲣⲉ ⲛⲧⲉⲥϩⲓⲙⲉ
ⲉⲧⲉ ⲧⲉϥ̣ⲙⲁ[ⲁⲩ ⲧⲉ]

I bind the dog of [. . .], the son of the woman [. . .], who is his mother!

In this text, the three Coptic letters originated from demotic, ϣ, ϥ, and ϩ, are conserved just as they are, without encoding (cf. Erman, 1895; Kropp, 1930–1931, Vol. 2, no. 5, pp. 14–16, and Vol. 3, no. 249; see Wisse, 1979, no. 11, for review and comment).

4. In the Coptic medical papyrus published by Chassinat (1921), the names of a certain number of drugs are encoded in the same way. The manuscript can be dated from the ninth or the tenth century. Samples: ⳅⲇⲥϡ for ⲙϫⲱⲣ (or ⲙϫⲱⲗ), onion; ⲩⲑⲟⲡⲗⲱ for ⲭⲁⲣⲕⲟⲥ (or ⲭⲁⲗⲕⲟⲥ), bronze; ⳅⲑⲑⲱ≡ for ⲙⲁⲁⲥⲉ, calf.

5. During the Persian invasion at the beginning of the seventh century, the monks of the monasteries in the Theban mountains (in Dandarah as well as in Dayr al-Bahri) had to withdraw to the surrounding desert. Probably this temporary exile would account for the Coptic graffiti found in a hermitage in the region of Armant in 1947 by Bachatly (cf. Abd al-Masih et al., 1965). This graffito was written by a monk who came from the great Monastery of Phoebammon; only the first half is given here:

ⲑ|||ⲗⲡⲫⲉⲓⲟⲗⲁ≡ⲗⲱⲡϣⲃϡ≡|||ⲡⲗⲍ≡ⲱⲕ
ϯ≡ϥ≡ⲗⲁⲩ{ⲓ}ϥⲱϯⲗⲱ|||ⲧⲋⲁ
ⲡ̣ⲗ|||ⲗⲱ|||ψ≡ϡⲡⲥψⲕⲁⲭⲗ̣≡ϥⲱ̅
ϥ̅ⲱ̅ⲕ≡ⲩ̅ⲱ̅ⲑϡϥⲗ|||ⲑ̅|||ⳅ̅ⳅⲑϥ

ⲁⲛⲟⲕ ⲫⲉⲓⲗⲟⲑⲉⲟⲥ ⲡϣⲏⲣⲉ ⲛⲕⲟⲙⲉⲥ ⲡ
ⲉⲓⲉⲗⲁⲭⲓⲥⲧⲟⲥ ⲛⲇⲓⲁ
ⲕⲟⲛⲟⲥ ⲛⲧⲉⲣⲕⲱⲧ ⲡⲁϫⲟⲉⲓⲥ
ⲓ̅ⲥ̅ ⲡⲉⲭ̅ⲥ̅ ⲁⲣⲓ ⲟ⟨ⲩ⟩ⲛⲁ ⲛⲙⲙⲁⲓ

In line 2, the first ϯ is an ordinary cross. The sign in braces {. . .} is superfluous. In line 3, the scribe wrote the first ⲯ with the shape of an ankh. "I am Philotheos, the son of Komes, the insignificant deacon of Terkōt. My Lord Jesus Christ, have mercy on me . . ." The autochthonous coptic letters ϣ and ϫ remain without encoding (cf. ibid., p. 30; reviewed by Wisse, 1979, no. 12).

6. To disguise the autochthonous Coptic letters, the Copts tried employing conventional signs such as ∞̲ for ϣ and ⋈ for ϫ. The following example is a personal invocation inserted by a monk before the title of an epistle on virginity attributed to Saint Athanasius (Bibl. Nat. copte 131, fol. 2r, perhaps ninth or tenth century; cf. van Lantschoot, 1929, Vol. 1, App. 1; reviewed by Wisse, 1979, no. 14):

ⲫⲫϥⲕⲑⲝ≡ⲭ̣≡≡|||ⲑⲡ̣ⲑ̣[ⲕⲃ]
ⲗⲭⲥ||||||ϥⲝ≡ⲯ|||ⲑⲥ∞̲[ϩⲝ]
ⲕϥ̣⋈ⲥⲥⲝ≡|||ⲯ≡ⲯ|||∞̲[ⲟⲃⲟ]
≡⋈ⲥϥ

ⲁⲣⲓ ⲡⲁⲙⲉⲩⲉ ⲉⲛ ⲁⲕ̣ⲁ̣[ⲡⲏ]
ⲟⲩⲱⲛ ⲛⲓⲙ ⲉⲧⲛⲁⲱϣ [ϩⲙ]
ⲡⲓ̣ϫⲱⲱⲙⲉ ⲛⲧⲉⲧⲛϣ[ⲗⲏⲗ]
ⲉϫⲱⲓ

Remember me in love, everyone that will read in this book, and pray for me.

7. In a brief message of greeting written on a parchment scrap (B.M. Or. 4720[96]), the Coptic letters of demotic origin were encoded by Greek letters used as symbols for thousands: ⲁ̦ for 1,000; ⲃ̦ for 2,000; ⲅ̦ for 3,000; ⲇ̦ for 4,000; and ⲉ̦ for 5,000—this, respectively, for the letters ϣ, ϥ, ϩ, ϫ, and ϭ. These graphemes were conserved in their regular order.

	ⲑ	
Recto:	ⲥⲩ|||ⲯϥⲁ̦ϥ|||ϥ	ⲥⲩⲛ ⲑ⟨ⲉⲱ⟩ ⲧⲓϣⲓⲛⲓ
	ⲑⲭⲥⲯϥⲑⲧⲕⲑ	ⲁⲩⲱ ⲧⲓⲁⲥⲡⲁ
	ⲅ≡ⲝⲕⲗⲭⲁ̦ⲑϥ	ⲍⲉ ⲙⲡⲟⲩϫⲁⲓ
	ⲝⲕⲁⲝⲁϥ|||ⲗⲭⲧⲓ	ⲙⲡⲁⲙⲁⲓⲛⲟⲩⲧⲓ
Verso:	ⲁⲃⲃⲁ ⲡⲁⲡⲛⲟⲩϯ	ⲁⲃⲃⲁ ⲡⲁⲡⲛⲟⲩϯ

With God! I greet and salute the health of my pious Abba Paphnouti.

One can see that the name of the addressee, Abba Paphnouti, is written without code on the parchment's verso (cf. Crum, 1905, no. 669; reviewed by Wisse, 1979, no. 16).

Second Type

A second cryptographic system borrowed from Greek also uses the primitive alphabet divided into three rows of characters representing units of tens and hundreds. The units are represented by the letters ⲁ through ⲑ, the tens by the same ⲁ̇ through ⲑ̇ topped by a single dot, the hundreds by ⲁ̈ through ⲑ̈ topped by two dots. This system was perhaps borrowed from Arabic (Wisse, 1979, no. 18). Each set of the alphabet is encoded by the signs 1 to 9, 10 to 90, and 100 to 900, respectively, superimposed one on the other without resorting to an inversion, as was the case in the system described above, with the result that the letters ⲁ to ⲑ of the genuine text are not modified by this code at all (Table 3).

8. In a Bohairic Gospel book dated from 1327, an invocation is transcribed as follows:

ⲏ̇ⲁ̇ⲉ̣ⲃⲁ̇ⲏⲉ̇ ⲑⲏ̈ⲇ̇ⲁⲃ̈ ⲉ̈ϯ ⲉ̇ⲁⲁ̇ ⲉ̇ⲁⲑ̇
ⲁ̣ⲇ̇ⲏⲉ̇ ϥ̅ⲑ̅ ⲁ̇ⲝⲃ|||

ⲡⲓⲉⲃⲓⲏⲛ ⲑⲱⲙⲁⲥ ⲫϯ ⲛⲁⲓ ⲛⲁϥ
ⲁⲙⲏⲛ ϥ̅ⲑ̅ ⲁⲙⲏⲛ

The wretched Thomas, God be merciful to him! Amen, Amen, Amen.

An original peculiarity: each "Amen" is encoded in a different way. The first is represented by ⲁ̣ⲇ̇ⲏⲉ̇, corresponding to the later method illustrated by this invocation. The second is ϥ̅ⲑ̅ according to the isopsephic system already noted above in example 2. The third appears as ⲁ̇ⲝⲃ|||, according to the cryptographic process described at the beginning of this article (cf. Horner, 1898–1905, p. lxxi; Wisse, 1979, no. 18).

Third Type

A third system substituted for each letter of the normal alphabet the corresponding letter from another normal alphabet written beside it but shifted down by one or more letters, a process called in antiquity "Julius Caesar's method." If one shifts the second alphabet by one letter, starting with β replacing α, one has the following:

TABLE 3.

ⲁ = ⲁ	ⲓ = ⲁ̇	ⲣ = ⲁ̈
ⲃ = ⲃ	ⲕ = ⲃ̇	ⲥ = ⲃ̈
ⲅ = ⲅ	ⲗ = ⲅ̇	ⲧ = ⲅ̈
ⲇ = ⲇ	ⲙ = ⲇ̇	ⲩ = ⲇ̈
ⲉ = ⲉ	ⲛ = ⲉ̇	ⲫ = ⲉ̈
ⲋ = ⲋ	ⲝ = ⲋ̇	ⲭ = ⲋ̈
ⲍ = ⲍ	ⲟ = ⲍ̇	ⲯ = ⲍ̈
ⲏ = ⲏ	ⲡ = ⲏ̇	ⲱ = ⲏ̈
ⲑ = ⲑ	ϥ = ⲑ̇	ϡ = ⲑ̈

α β γ δ ϵ ζ η ϑ ι κ λ μ ν ξ ο π ρ σ τ υ φ χ ψ ω
β γ δ ϵ ζ η ϑ ι κ λ μ ν ξ ο π ρ σ τ υ ϕ χ ψ ω α

9. Here is an example attested in a Gospel text from the White Monastery dated 1112 A.D. The same process was only applied to the five Coptic letters ϣ through ϫ encoded by their own sequence being shifted by one letter:

ϣ ϥ ϩ ϭ ϫ
ϥ ϩ ϭ ϫ ϣ

The text reads:

ⲂⲜⲠⲖⲢⲔϬⲐⲖⲌⲄⲔⲖⲨⲀ̣[Ⲥ]
ⲪⲦⲜ̣ϤⲔⲜ̣ⲠⲪ[ⲨⲌ]Ⲗ̣ⲀⲜ̣ⲂⲔⲌ̣Ⲅ̣ⲠⲘ̣

ⲀⲚⲞⲔ ⲠⲒϨⲎⲔⲈ ⲂⲒⲔⲦⲰ̣[Ⲣ]
ⲨⲤ Ⲛ̣ϢⲒⲚ̣ⲞⲨ[ⲦⲈ] Ⲕ̣Ⲱ Ⲛ̣ⲀⲒ Ⲉ̣Ⲃ̣ⲞⲖ̣

I am the poor Victor, son of Shenoute. Forgive me!

(Cf. Crum, 1905, no. 489; van Lantschoot 1929, no. lxxx–h; Wisse, 1979, no. 19, settled the issue of its interpretation.)

These systems are the most current. The first, transmitted by the Coptic scribes to their Ethiopian colleagues, was even adapted to the Ge'ez language and used under the designation of the "learned language" or *naggara liqâwent* (Conti-Rossini, 1927, pp. 524–28; unfortunately notes written very hastily and imprecise).

Other Types

Were there other Coptic processes of encoding? One can suppose this, since several formulas still resist efforts to decode them, unless they are cryptogram imitations devoid of meaning. It must be pointed out that artificial alphabets existed and were used to hide astrological, alchemic, and magical formulas. Indeed, Hellenistic and Byzantine occultism produced many picturesque versions (Doresse, 1950–1951, pp. 221–26). Furthermore, the Arabs, not merely satisfied to revive such formulas, added a great number of fancies that spread throughout the Mediterranean world (among others, cf. Ibn Wahshīya, "Les Alphabets occultes dévoilés," in Hammer, 1806).

It is certain that through the Byzantines, the Copts learned the cryptographic method of transliterating the normal alphabet by a "long key"—that is, by a conventionalized phrase embodying all the letters of the alphabet out of alphabetical order, as suggested by repetitions in the artificial sentence

ⲀⲂⲢⲞⲬⲈⲒⲆⲰⲚ ⲦⲞ ⲪⲨⲖⲀⲜ ⲐⲎⲢⲀⲌⲨⲄⲰⲔⲀⲘⲮⲒⲘⲈⲦⲞⲠⲞⲤ,

to be compared with the alphabetic order transcribed as follows:

ⲐⲎⲌⲋⲈⲄⲂⲀϤⲠⲞⲜⲒ Ⲛ Ⲙ Ⲓ ⲖⲔ ⳨ Ⲱ Ⲯ Ⲭ Ⲫ Ⲩ Ⲧ Ⲥ Ⲣ

These two lines were found scribbled on a piece of wood recovered in the ruins of the Theban Monastery of Apa Epiphanius (Crum and Evelyn-White, 1926, no. 616). The grotesque formula

ἀβροχίτων δ'ὁ φύλαξ ϑηροζυγοκαμψιμέτωπος

was so well known that the Palatine Anthology (9.538) had included it. However, there survive no examples of either Coptic or Greek encoded texts employing it as a key. And yet, the cryptographic purpose of this mnemonic device seems to be indisputable, the normal alphabet being connected with it in the form of three inverted rows (from ⲑ to ⲁ, from ϥ to ⲓ, and from ⳨ to ⲣ), as in the first of the systems discussed above.

Purpose

One should ask what purpose these cryptograms served, for it is clear that such systems began virtually at the birth of the Coptic language (examples 1 and 3) and lasted at least until the fourteenth century (example 8). In answer, the limited number of examples so far identified, plus the fact that several cases remain unidentified and that it is impossible in other instances to decide whether the text is written in Greek or Coptic (e.g., the calamus box from Antinoë [ANTINOOPOLIS] in the ancient collection of the Guimet Museum kept today at the Louvre; cf. Doresse, 1951, pl. 1) allow just a few observations rather than true conclusions.

It seems that initially such systems served to hide the entire title of an apocryphal work, to disguise a magic formula or make it more mysterious, or to veil the exact identity of medical drugs from the knowledge of common people (examples 1, 3, and 4). For the rest, it became above all a guileful expedient of some literates to communicate among themselves only: an invocation inserted by a scribe at the end of a manuscript he has copied (examples 6, 8, and 9); a prayer of a monk scribbled on a wall (examples 2 and 5); a brief message, essentially a prayer, to another monk (example 7). All of this was at once naive in its process and impoverished in its content. Apparently, the worthiest things hidden in these cryptograms have been totally lost, except vague memories: "The Thebans tell of an angel giving the science of the mystic language to Pachomius, Cornelius and Syrus in such a way that they expressed themselves by means of a special alphabet which concealed the meaning in hidden signs and symbols" (*Praefatio ad regulas S. Pachomii*, in Migne, PL 23, p. 68). This would confirm a letter from Pachomius to Syrus (ibid., p. 100): "Animadverti enim terminos esse epistolae vestrae Heta et Theta," where *terminos* could specify a key to decode the order of those things of which one can only catch a glimpse.

BIBLIOGRAPHY

Abd al-Masih, Y.; W. C. Till; and O. H. E. Burmester. "Coptic Graffiti and Inscriptions from the Monastery of Phoebammon." In C. Bachatly, *Le Monastère de Phoebammon dans la Thébaïde*, Vol. 2, pp. 24–157. Cairo, 1965.

Chassinat, E. *Un Papyrus médical copte*. Cairo, 1921.

Conti-Rossini, C. "Di alcuni scritti etiopici inediti, 4, Il 'Nagara liqâwent,' scrittura convenzionale." *Rendiconti dell'Accademia nazionale dei Lincei, Classe di scienze morali, storiche e filologiche*, ser. 6, (1927):524–28.

Crum, W. E. *Catalogue of the Coptic Manuscripts in the British Museum*. London, 1905.

Crum, W. E., and H. G. Evelyn-White, eds. *The Monastery of Epiphanius at Thebes*, Pt. 2. New York, 1926.

Doresse, J. "'Les Apocalypses de Zoroastre, de Zostrien, de Nicothée, . . .' (Porphyre, Vie de Plotin, §16." In *Coptic Studies in Honor of Walter Ewing Crum*, pp. 255–63. Boston, 1950.

______. "Cryptographie copte et cryptographie grecque." *Bulletin de l'Institut d'Egypte* 33 (1950–1951):215–28 and pl. 1.

Erman, A. "Zauberspruch für einen Hund." *Zeitschrift für ägyptische Sprache und Altertumskunde* 33 (1895):132–35.

Gardthausen, V. *Griechische Paläographie*, Vol. 2, *Die Schrift, Unterschriften und Chronologie im Altertum und im byzantinischem Mittelalter*. Leipzig, 1913.

Hammer, J. *Ancient Alphabets and Hieroglyphic Characters*. London, 1806.

[Horner, G. W.] *The Coptic Version of the New Testament in the Northern Dialect, Otherwise Called Memphitic and Bohairic*. London, 1898–1905.

Kropp, A. M. *Ausgewählte koptische Zaubertexte*. Brussels, 1930–1931.

Lantschoot, A. van. *Recueil des colophons des manuscrits chrétiens d'Egypte*. Louvain, 1929.

Migne, J. -P., ed. *Patrologia Latina* 23. Paris, 1865.

Winkler, H. A. *Siegel und Charaktere in der muhammedanischen Zauberei*. Berlin and Leipzig, 1930.

Wisse, F. "Language Mysticism in the Nag Hammadi Texts and in Early Coptic Monasticism, I, Cryptography." *Enchoria* 9 (1979):101–120.

JEAN DORESSE

CRYPTOPHONEME. The term "cryptophoneme" designates any phoneme that appears not directly, through a grapheme (letter) exclusively its own in the superficial form of the language (its orthography), but indirectly, through some grapheme not its own and normally assigned to another phoneme. The existence of the cryptophoneme, superficially concealed, can be recognized at a deeper level (on the question of levels, see Hintze, 1980, pp. 111, 122), where it shows itself in indirect fashion by its influence on neighboring superficial phonological structures, in various lexemes, and the like.

If the grapheme that renders the cryptophoneme is normally allotted to another phoneme, it is nonetheless most often chosen because of the similarity of pronunciation between phoneme and cryptophoneme. Kasser (1982) thinks he can detect in Coptic the existence of at least three cryptophonemes in tachysyllabication (i.e., quick SYLLABICATION): the glide /j/ of tachysyllabication, rendered orthographically by (ⲉ)ⲓ (normally /i/ in tachysyllabication and always /i/ in bradysyllabication, slow syllabication); the glide /w/ in tachysyllabication, rendered orthographically by (ⲟ)ⲩ (normally /u/ in tachysyllabication and always /u/ in bradysyllabication); the enigmatic occlusive /'/ (cf. Dieth, 1950, p. 101; Kasser, 1981a, pp. 26–32; and ALEPH), which of necessity follows a tonic vowel, a chiefly vocalic link rendered graphically by vocalic gemination (see GEMINATION, VOCALIC), probably always equivalent to tonic vowel plus atonic vowel in bradysyllabication (cf. the problem of "glides" and "glidants" in phonology, Kasser, 1981b, pp. 37–38; and that of aleph, rather than 'AYIN, in relation to vocalic gemination).

In the Coptic idioms, dialects, and subdialects without graphical vocalic gemination, such as *B* and its subdialects, and *G*, *F4*, *V4*, *W*, and *M*, there are only the cryptophonemes /j/ and /w/, but not /'/, since even the borrowed grapheme that renders it in other dialects has disappeared, although in *B* etc., *G*, *F4*, *V4*, *W*, and *M* traces have survived of the influence formerly exercised by this cryptophoneme upon the neighboring superficial phonological structures (e.g., *S* ⲕⲁⲁ⸗ⲧ /ka't/, to leave me, *B* ⲭⲁ⸗ⲧ and not *ⲭⲁï).

Confronted by something that he has reason to think conceals a cryptophoneme, the phoneticist and philologist may seek to "decode" it, and thus demonstrate its existence, not by simple examination of graphemes with exclusive allocation but by a complex examination of graphemes with allocations that comparative and analogical analysis will show to be diverse. The possibility will always remain of contesting the existence of this or that cryptophoneme (cf. Edgerton, 1957, in regard to aleph and ʿayin, the survival of which [ʿayin only] in Coptic the author also contests).

Because of various factors that often make it very difficult, or even impossible, to achieve perfect correspondence between the phonological system of a language and its alphabetic and orthographical systems, practically every language has its cryptophonemes (cf. Dieth, 1950, pp. 36–43). It is therefore not surprising to find them also in Coptic.

BIBLIOGRAPHY

Dieth, E. *Vademekum der Phonetik. Phonetische Grundlagen für das wissenschaftliche und praktische Studium der Sprachen.* Bern and Munich, 1950.

Edgerton, W. F. Review of W. C. Till, *Koptische Grammatik (saïdischer Dialekt), mit Bibliographie, Lesestücken und Wörterverzeichnissen. Journal of Near Eastern Studies* 16 (1957):136–37.

Hintze, F. "Zur koptischen Phonologie." *Enchoria* 10 (1980):23–91.

Kasser, R. "Usages de la surligne dans le P. Bodmer VI, notes additionnelles." *Bulletin de la Société d'égyptologie, Genève* 5 (1981a):23–32.

______. "Voyelles en fonction consonantique, consonnes en fonction vocalique, et classes de phonèmes en copte." *Bulletin de la Société d'égyptologie, Genève* 5 (1981b):33–50.

______. "Syllabation rapide ou lente en copte, I, Les Glides /j/ et /w/ avec leurs correspondants vocaliques '/i/' et '/u/' (et phonèmes appariés analogues)" and "II, Aleph et 'voyelle d'aleph.'" *Enchoria* 11 (1982):23–27, 39–58.

Quecke, H. Review of J. Vergote, *Grammaire copte. Muséon* 91 (1978):476–80.

Stern, L. *Koptische Grammatik.* Leipzig, 1880.

Till, W. C. "Altes 'Aleph und ʿAjin im Koptischen." *Wiener Zeitschrift für die Kunde des Morgenlandes* 36 (1929):186–96.

______. *Koptische Grammatik (saïdischer Dialekt), mit Bibliographie, Lesestücken und Wörterverzeichnissen.* Leipzig, 1955.

______. *Koptische Dialektgrammatik, mit Lesestücken und Wörterbuch.* Munich, 1961.

Vergote, J. *Grammaire copte,* Vol. 1a, *Introduction, phonétique et phonologie, morphologie synthématique (structure des sémantèmes), partie synchronique,* Vol. 1b, *Introduction, phonétique et phonologie, morphologie synthématique (structure des sémantèmes), partie diachronique,* Vol. 2a, *Morphologie sytagmatique, syntaxe, partie synchronique,* Vol. 2b, *Morphologie syntagmatique, partie diachronique.* Louvain, 1973–1983.

RODOLPHE KASSER

DIALECT, IMMIGRANT. In Coptology, the term "immigrant dialect" means any idiom spoken outside its region of origin. The classic example is, of course, Sahidic, which in its farthest origin probably derives in some way from a regional dialect; afterward it spread upstream and downstream, and became gradually a supraregional language, the vehicular, or common, speech of the Nile Valley from Cairo to Aswan. It is reasonable to suggest that each Coptic idiom has, in principle, a territory of which it is, or originally was, the natural language (cf. GEOGRAPHY, DIALECTAL). The validity of this general statement is not affected by the fact that a dialect etc. known to scholars only in a more or less advanced stage of neutralization is evidence of a situation of compromise, which, in terms of logical and chronological evolution, is only secondary, not primary, a situation in which the more advanced the neutralization is, the more difficult it becomes to determine the geographical origin of its components.

The origin of *A, F, B,* and possibly *M* can be seen with some precision. That of *L*—or more precisely, that of each component of *L* (i.e., *L4, L5,* and *L6*) as a dialectal cluster, possibly evolved, collectively, if not degenerate, remains of the previous common speech of at least a large part of Upper Egypt—does not emerge so clearly (to the north and perhaps also to the south of *A*; cf. LYCO-DIOSPOLITAN). The origin of *S* is even more obscure, even if some arguments from its phonology (so far as it can be known from its orthography, which the majority of Coptologists think is possible) and especially from its morphosyntax suggest placing its origin in upper Middle Egypt, somewhere between the region of *M* and the area of which *L* was the current language. The reason is that the secondary components of *L* and their origin are still not known. This means that there is even greater ignorance of the precise character of its chief component, but there are good grounds for calling it, too, *L,* or pre-*L,* since it was from this above all that *L* emerged. The lack of knowledge of pre-*L* prevents location of its origin with any precision.

Even less is known about the secondary components of *S,* and hence about the precise character of its chief component, pre-*S,* so much so that some doubt whether it even existed and consider the search for it superfluous and illusory. From this point of view, *S* would not have any precise local origin; it would be a completely neutral and hybrid product, the result of a large number of compromises among the various Coptic dialects the whole length of the Nile, gathering up the results of earlier regional compromises. In this view, then, one would have to see in *S* ultimately some kind of a vast compromise embracing the whole "dialectal" panorama of the country, and hence a "language" in the broadest sense, not, strictly speaking, a "dialect" (cf. Kasser, 1980, pp. 103–104, n. 17).

When a local or regional dialect or idiom is spoken in the territory of its origin, it is the "autochthonous dialect" of that area. One may also use this term, by extension, for a somewhat neutralized dialect that has become regional (i.e., a large regional idiom originating in a compromise between the minor autochthonous dialect of one place and minor neighboring autochthonous dialects), so long as its use remains confined to the region in which it has established itself through these compromises.

Some Coptic idioms, each supported by an original milieu (geographical and, above all, social) more dynamic than that of its neighbors, progressively invaded neighboring territory, extending their own geographical area. This is true for *S* and, to a lesser but still considerable degree, possibly also for *L*, and was perhaps a tendency in *V* (rather than *M*). One calls these "immigrant dialects" when they are encountered outside the areas in which they are the autochthonous idioms.

The dialectal invasion, the most important cause of the formation of an IDIOLECT, can be seen most conveniently in what appears to have been the progress of *S*. It very soon, and probably a long time before the strictly Coptic epoch, became the common language of the whole Egyptian Nile Valley above the Delta. Beside it, of course, in all the important economic and political centers there was the Greek of Egypt, but this was a foreign language reserved for the Greek minority and a small elite of bilingual Egyptians. The consequences of this invasion of Sahidic, in the more or less long term, were disastrous for the other idioms, especially the autochthonous dialects of the areas involved; at least on the literary level, *S* progressively supplanted them and choked them off.

The Sahidic invasion could take effect in two main ways: (a) by a slow continuous progression, through direct contact along the roads by land, which produced a fairly homogeneous conquest and left behind various "pockets of resistance" in corners in the country, sometimes concentrated around small towns or (later) monasteries that were particularly conservative; or (b) by a more rapid discontinuous progression, along the line of the river from large port to large port, which led in the first place to the establishment of islands of the new idiom in certain social milieus of the most important towns, while the country areas and small towns (or small ports) in between remained practically unaffected in the short and middle term, and continued for a long time faithful to their autochthonous local dialect.

According to the social class or the level of culture of those who wished to speak it (the "social" aspect of the Coptic dialects; cf. GEOGRAPHY, DIALECTAL) and according to the time elapsed since its immigration, the immigrant dialect was itself inevitably, and in varying degrees, subject to the influence of the autochthonous dialect (cf. Vergote, 1973a, 2–3, 5). This hybridization may have been practically nonexistent in those milieus which had themselves immigrated from the region where *S* originated or among recent immigrants for whom *S* was their mother tongue. But from the second or third generation onward, even in cultivated circles, and with all the more reason in milieus of a low cultural level, it would be encouraged by continual contacts between autochthonous speakers and immigrants, or descendants of immigrants, and would sometimes have reached the level of orthography (especially in vowels), where it produced perceptible modifications.

In milieus of a low cultural level, this contamination was shown by the production, in quite anarchic fashion, of very diverse idiolectal forms. In cultivated milieus in which the immigrant dialect was spoken, resistance to contamination from the autochthonous dialect may have been effective for a short time after the immigration. Succeeding generations would eventually undergo contamination to some extent, despite their will to adhere to their own autochthonous dialectal system. They would gradually come to terms not with the idiolectal anarchy of the milieus of low culture but with a kind of systematic compromise that would emerge as, in some respects, a new dialectal system slightly different from the original system that had penetrated earlier into this area of immigration. This would be a system of hybrid origin, in which the immigrant phonemic component to a large extent predominates, but the autochthonous component, though very much in the minority, also has its part.

Such may have been the case with DIALECT P, in which some have seen a variety of proto-Sahidic (reconstructed, **pS*) immigrating into the Thebaid even before the Coptic period. Here, alongside a kind of **pS* vocabulary that would be the major element, there would be found also, among remains of some lost local dialect, several **pS* lexemes (i.e., proto-Sahidic with some phonemic characteristics that are Lycopolitan or, in a large number of cases, Akhmimic), but not $*pS^l$ (i.e., proto-Sahidic with Lycopolitan or other characteristics that are idiolectal or nonsystematic and thoroughly irregular; cf. Kasser, 1982).

Analysis of the numerous Sahidic texts found in Upper Egypt would probably allow one to discover, alongside those which are purely idiolectal and present S^l or S^a forms, others that systematically show their adoption of some Lycopolitan or Akhmimic phonemic characteristic, and hence present *Sl* or *Sa* forms.

Equally the product of cultivated Sahidic milieus in a region of which *L* is the autochthonous regional (or even local) dialect are some texts in immigrant *S* whose phonological system is entirely *S* (so far as one can judge from the orthography) but whose syntax and lexical stock are *L* rather than *S*. Mutatis mutandis, it could be *A* rather than *S*, if one is interested in the phenomena produced by immigration of *S* into an area of which the autochthonous dialect was akin to *A* (and no doubt very similar) and in which *L*, as an immigrant dialect, may have been the common speech even before the Sahidic invasion (as in the region of Nag Hammadi) and before the region was completely swamped by the immigration of *S*. Should one class these texts as evidence of *A* or, on occasion, of *L*, rather than of *S*? That would not be very reasonable, for if in theory syntactic and lexical criteria are at least as important as (or even more important than) phonological criteria in the analysis of a text, the fact remains that the last are the only ones which can in practice be applied in almost all circumstances, even if one is dealing with a trifling scrap of text in which the syntactic structures are not readily apparent and one can identify only a few isolated and not very specific words, and hence cannot find that rare word, or observe the characteristic syntactic construction, that belongs to *A* or *L* and not to *S*. It is, thus, to the phonological criteria that priority would ultimately be given, not in terms of any theoretical superiority but simply as a matter of convention, because these criteria are the most practical and, so to speak, universally applicable.

Therefore, these cases require the use of a siglum more complex than the earlier ones, to indicate a veneer of *S* phonology on either a lexical or a syntactical system that is non-*S*. This kind of siglum will designate either the non-*S* lexemes adopted into immigrant *S* (with a phonological orthography perfectly consistent with *S*) or Sahidic texts originating in another dialect, subsequently adopted into immigrant *S*, and clothed in an orthography perfectly consistent with *S*, but as a veneer on a non-*S* syntax. Cases of the latter sort may occur either because of mental habits due to the non-Sahidic mother tongue of the redactor (or the translator of the first Coptic version of a Greek original) or because these writings were first composed in another dialect and then translated into Sahidic. These complex sigla will be S^s/l, S^s/a, S^s/m, S^s/f, and so on, for Sahidic, showing its condition as an immigrant dialect in regions where *L*, *A*, *M*, *F*, or another dialect is the autochthonous dialect: they could also be L^l/a and so on if it was a case of Lycopolitan or Lyco-Diospolitan immigrating into the territory of autochthonous *A*, and so on.

Sahidic is the most neutral of the Coptic idioms and became the common speech of the entire Egyptian Nile Valley above the Delta. As noted above in the description of the origins of the phenomena indicated by the sigla *Sl* or S^s/l, there are all kinds of *S*, of which only one is an autochthonous *S* while the others are immigrant. Of the productions in immigrant *S*, some are as completely *S* as the autochthonous; these will be described as "atypical" immigrant *S*. Others will clearly betray their status as immigrant *S*; they will be called "typical" immigrant *S*. In a lexicon, the siglum *S* should be assigned only to lexemes attested by autochthonous *S* (and the witnesses of atypical immigrant *S*); the others (witnesses of typical immigrant *S*) should be given sigla such as *Sl* or S^s/l (cf. Kasser, 1980, pp. 108–109).

BIBLIOGRAPHY

Kahle, P. E. *Bala'izah: Coptic Texts from Deir el-Bala'izah in Upper Egypt.* Oxford and London, 1954.

Kasser, R. "Dialectes, sous-dialectes et 'dialecticules' dans l'Egypte copte." *Zeitschrift für ägyptische Sprache und Altertumskunde* 92 (1966):106–15.

______. "Prolégomènes à un essai de classification systématique des dialectes et subdialectes coptes selon les critères de la phonétique, I, Principes et terminologie." *Muséon* 93 (1980):53–112.

______. "Le Dialecte protosaïdique de Thèbes." *Archiv für Papyrusforschung* 28 (1982):67–81.

Nagel, P. "Der frühkoptische Dialekt von Theben." In *Koptologische Studien in der DDR*, pp. 30–49. *Wissenschaftliche Zeitschrift der Martin-Luther-Universität Halle-Wittenberg*, Sonderheft. Halle-Wittenberg, 1965.

Polotsky, H. J. "Coptic." In *Current Trends in Linguistics*, ed. T. Sebeok, Vol. 6, *Linguistics in South West Asia and North Africa*, pp. 558–70. The Hague and Paris, 1970.

Vergote, J. *Grammaire copte*, Vol. 1a, *Introduction, phonétique et phonologie, morphologie synthéma-*

tique (structure des sémantèmes), partie synchronique. Louvain, 1973a.

______. "Le Dialecte copte P (P. Bodmer VI: Proverbes), essai d'identification." *Revue d'égyptologie* 25 (1973b):50–57.

Worrell, W. H. *Coptic Sounds.* Ann Arbor, Mich., 1934.

RODOLPHE KASSER

DIALECT, SPORADIC. A "sporadic dialect" is any dialect attested by one or more texts that, while certainly idiolectal, are of a "transparent" IDIOLECT, allowing one to see clearly the greater part of the essential dialectal characteristics of the idiom; however, throughout the document(s), these characteristics are rivaled by those of another dialect that is continually more strongly attested. A sporadic dialect may be known only from almost pure witnesses that are not idiolectal, but are (like Husselman, 1947, and Quecke, 1974, for *B4*, a subdialect of *B*; cf. DIALECTS) probably (and unfortunately) too brief to provide a truly exhaustive description of most of its principal phonological and other characteristics.

Such was the case with *M* when Kahle (1954, pp. 220–27) described it before the discovery of the four great manuscripts known today: the Psalms (in rather good condition, but unpublished), the Gospel of Matthew (in perfect condition and carefully edited by Schenke, 1981), the first half of Acts (in perfect condition, but unpublished), and the Pauline epistles (with many lacunae, and rapidly published by Orlandi, 1974).

Such was also the case with *B74* (a southern [?] and slightly archaic [?] subdialect of *B*; cf. DIALECTS), which forms one of the components of the idiolect of P. Bodmer III (first hand), before the discovery of Pap. Vat. Copto 9, a papyrus codex of the Minor Prophets now in the Vatican Library but still unpublished (cf. Kasser 1958, and 1966, p. 66–76).

So it is, and even more evidently, with DIALECT i, a PROTODIALECT of *L*, for in *i*, where ϣ̈ may appear for /ç/ (60 percent of the cases), it is strongly rivaled by ϣ (40 percent; cf. Kasser, 1979; 1980b, pp. 83–84; 1981, pp. 112–13).

A partially sporadic dialect (or PROTODIALECT, METADIALECT, or subdialect) will, like *P*, for example, have some of its essential phonemic characteristics fully attested by orthography (thus ϧ = /ç/, ϧ = /x/), while others will be attested only in sporadic fashion (thus ⊥ = /ʾ/ in a primitive state of evolution only [graphic vocalic duplication in a secondary state, as in *S*, but also frequently omitted], and so on; cf. Kasser, 1980a).

BIBLIOGRAPHY

Browne, G. M. *Michigan Coptic Texts.* Barcelona, 1979.

Husselman, E. M. "A Bohairic School Text on Papyrus." *Journal of Near Eastern Studies* 6 (1947):129–51.

Kahle, P. E. *Bala'izah: Coptic Texts from Deir el-Bala'izah in Upper Egypt.* Oxford and London, 1954.

Kasser, R. *Papyrus Bodmer III: Evangile de Jean et Genèse I–IV,2, en bohaïrique.* CSCO 177–178. Louvain, 1958.

______. "A propos des différentes formes du conditionnel copte." *Muséon* 76 (1963):267–70.

______. *L'Évangile selon saint Jean et les versions coptes de la Bible.* Neuchâtel, 1966.

______. "Relations de généalogie dialectale dans le domaine lycopolitain." *Bulletin de la Société d'égyptologie, Genève* 2 (1979):31–36.

______. "Usages de la surligne dans le Papyrus Bodmer VI." *Bulletin de la Société d'égyptologie, Genève* 4 (1980a):53–59.

______. "Prolégomènes à un essai de classification systématique des dialectes et subdialectes coptes selon les critères de la phonétique, I, Principes et terminologie." *Muséon* 93 (1980b):53–112. ". . . , III, Systèmes orthographiques et catégories dialectales." *Muséon* 94 (1981):91–151.

______. "Un Nouveau Document protolycopolitain." *Orientalia* 51 (1982):30–38.

Lacau, P. "Fragments de l'Ascension d'Isaïe en copte." *Muséon* 59 (1946):453–57.

[Leipoldt, J.] *Aegyptische Urkunden aus den königlichen Museen zu Berlin, herausgegeben von der Generalverwaltung, koptische Urkunden.* Berlin, 1904.

Orlandi, T. *Papiri della Università degli Studi di Milano (P. Mil. Copti),* Vol. 5, *Lettere di San Paolo in copto ossirinchita, edizione, commento e indici di T. Orlandi, contributo linguistico di H. Quecke.* Milan, 1974.

Quecke, H. "Ein altes bohairisches Fragment des Jakobusbriefes (P. Heid. Kopt. 452)." *Orientalia* 43 (1974):382–93.

Schenke, H.-M. *Das Matthäus-Evangelium im mittelägyptischen Dialekt des Koptischen (Codex Scheide).* Texte und Untersuchungen zur Geschichte der altchristlichen Literatur 127. Berlin, 1981.

Worrell, W. H. *Coptic Texts in the University of Michigan Collection.* Ann Arbor, Mich., 1942.

RODOLPHE KASSER

DIALECT G (OR BASHMURIC OR MANSURIC). To judge by a rather curious orthographical-phonological system more or less adequately attested by a group of small, late nonliterary Coptic texts of the eighth century, of which the principal ones have been published by Krall (1887 [extracts]; 1892) and, most completely, by Crum (1939), there must have existed, probably in Lower Egypt, an idiom of Coptic conventionally called dialect *G*, occasionally called Bashmuric (Kasser, 1975, esp. pp. 406–407) or even Mansuric (Schüssler, 1969, p. 154). According to orthographical criteria, *G* should be included in the BOHAIRIC dialectal group (Kasser, 1981, pp. 102–103, 121–122), itself a subdivision of the northern (dialects and vehicular language)–southern (vehicular language) Coptic dialect major group (see DIALECTS, GROUPING AND MAJOR GROUPS OF; and Kasser, 1982, p. 51). Although it is difficult to locate this dialect geographically with any precision, several features would support assignment of it to the eastern Delta.

The most striking characteristic of the *G* texts is of an alphabetic nature (see ALPHABETS, COPTIC): the letters used in them are all of Greek origin. Thus, the alphabet of *G* does not include ϣ, ϥ, ϧ, ϩ, ϫ, ϭ, and ϯ (which does not mean the absence in *G* of all the phonemes normally used in other dialects by these graphemes of demotic origin, as will be seen). This alphabetic idiosyncrasy is glaringly evident, to the point of overshadowing other, nonalphabetic characteristics and with the consequence that the current view of the language of these texts is that it is, for all practical purposes, more or less pure Bohairic, even if a Bohairic disguised by a graphemic system different from that of Bohairic proper. This view has delayed the definition of *G*, although its main texts had been edited for over a century.

To compile the phonological inventory of *G*, it would be simplest to compare it with that of Bohairic, *B*, the idiom to which it is closest. If one studies mainly the manuscript K 1785 of the Austrian National Library in Vienna, one may have the impression that *G* lacks several phonemes occurring in the *B* system.

First, consider the phoneme series expressed in Coptic by letters of Greek origin, which may therefore be taken to match phonemes existing in Greek itself. After an unstressed vowel and before a stressed one, *G* replaces Bohairic ⲃ by ⲡ: thus, ⲉⲡⲟⲗ, out(ward), but ⲛⲓⲃⲉⲛ, every. Unfortunately, no lexeme beginning with ⲃ in *B* is attested in the *G* documents; elsewhere, however, *G* has ⲃ, which seems to have a /v/ rather than a /ƀ/ value (see below). Before the stress-carrying vowel and in word-initial position, *G* appears to replace Bohairic ⲇ /d/ by ⲧ /t/ fairly regularly (e.g., ⲧⲓⲁⲛⲟⲙⲏ, διανομή, sharing). *B* aspirates ⲕ /k/, ⲡ /p/, and ⲧ /t/ into ⲭ /kh/, ⲫ /ph/, and ⲑ /th/, respectively, in certain well-defined conditions (Stern, 1880, pp. 16–26; Mallon, 1907, pp. 17–18; Worrell, 1934, pp. 18–23; Till, 1961, p. 7), but *G* does not (see below, on the phonemes /f/, /x/, /č/, and also /čh/ of *B*). This can be stated in spite of the occurrence in *G* of ⲭⲱ etc., not ⲕⲱ etc., for "put", since this exceptional instance of what might, at first sight, be taken for the aspiration /kh/ of /k/ remains entirely isolated in *G;* and this ⲭ of *G* can be explained differently, on diachronic grounds: one may assume that the value of this ⲭ is not /kh/ as in *B* but /x/ as invariably elsewhere in *G*, for *S* etc. ⲕⲱ and *B* ⲭⲱ stem from Egyptian *ḫ3*ʿ, although for this lexeme alone, old *ḫ* has exceptionally evolved into /k/ or /kh/, whereas normally *ḫ* became /x/ > Coptic /h/, ẖ in a few cases similarly /x/, in most part /ç/ > /š/. On the other hand, Bohairic ⲧ /t/ corresponds to ⲇ /d/ in *G* when preceded by a stress-carrying vowel and followed by an unstressed one (e.g., ⲛⲟⲩⲇⲓ, God; ⲥⲟⲇⲉⲙ, hear; ⲧⲉⲕⲛⲓⲇⲉⲥ, τεχνίτης, artisan). Since ⲫ in *G* not only renders the Greek φ in Greco-Coptic words but also corresponds to Bohairic ϥ /f/ in the autochthonous Coptic vocabulary (e.g., ⲉⲧⲍⲟⲫ, [up]on him), one may assume that ⲫ in *G* was /f/ throughout and did not maintain the /ph/ value in the Greco-Coptic vocabulary. Similarly, since ⲭ in *G* not only renders Greek χ in Greco-Coptic but corresponds also to Bohairic ϧ /x/ in the autochthonous vocabulary (e.g., ⲭⲉⲛ-, in), it is a safe assumption that ⲭ in *G* had the value /x/ throughout and did not maintain the value /kh/ in Greco-Coptic—and that even in the apparently exceptional case of *G* ⲭⲱ, put (see above).

Turning now to the series of Coptic phonemes rendered by graphemes of demotic origin, one observes the following: Bohairic ϣ /š/ corresponds to ⲥⲍ /š/ in *G* (e.g., ⲥⲍⲁ-, until), Bohairic ϥ /f/ to ⲫ /f/ in *G* (see above), and Bohairic ϧ /x/ to ⲭ /x/ in *G* (see above); ϩ /h/ in *B* does not correspond to any *G* graphemes, which may give reason to assume that this phoneme has completely disappeared (leaving, however, some traces in neighboring vocalism; see below). Bohairic ϫ /č/ corresponds to ⲧⲍ in *G* (e.g., ⲧⲍⲟⲙ, power); Bohairic ϫ /čh/ also corresponds to ⲧⲍ in *G* (e.g., ⲧⲍⲓ-, take), from which one could conclude that *G* (probably) does not have the aspiration so typical of Bohairic (see above). Finally, *G* does not use the grapheme ϯ /ti/, expressing this combination of phonemes simply by ⲧⲓ (as is the case in all OLD COPTIC alphabets and in the Coptic DIALECT H as well as in the Fayyumic subdialects *F8* and *F9*). The foregoing gives some basic ideas of *G* consonantism; one should add that *G* replaces word-initial Bohairic ⲟⲩ /w/ by ⲃ /v/ (e.g., ⲃⲟⲩⲧⲍ, wish).

As for the vocalism (to give here but the most essential), *G* seems to treat what is in *B* rendered by ⲟ /o/ and ⲱ /ō/ as a single phoneme, expressed by ⲟ /o/ (e.g., ⲥⲟⲗⲉⲙ, hear) except in the following special cases: In closed syllable, after disappeared ϩ /h/, this vowel is ⲱ /ō/ in *G* (e.g., ⲱⲃ, thing); after ⲃ /v/ (replacing ⲟⲩ /w/ in *B*), this vowel is ⲟⲩ /u/ (see ⲃⲟⲩⲥⲍ, wish, above); and before ⲟⲩ /w/, this vowel is ⲱ /ō/ (e.g., ⲧⲱⲟⲩⲉⲓ, tomorrow). In open syllable, after disappeared ϩ /h/, this vowel is ⲱ /ō/ (e.g., ⲱ, face, person); and after ⲥⲍ /š/, this vowel is ⲟⲩ /u/ (e.g., ⲥⲍⲟⲩⲡⲓ, become, but ⲥⲍⲟⲣⲡ, first).

The *G* texts are too short and too unhomogenous to make possible a detailed and exhaustive observation on the morphosyntactic level. However, one may observe a negative imperative (or vetative) ⲙⲉⲛ-, most often followed by the negator particle ⲁⲛ, in a combination that is quite unusual elsewhere in Coptic (combining with the vetative ⲙⲛ̄-, normal in *A* and *P*, this negator particle that is not compatible with it, with some exceptions, very rare in *S*, less rare but not frequent in *B*, some indicated in Crum, 1939a, p. 10b, under ⲁⲛ, sec. d; others, particularly for *B*, indicated in Shisha-Halevy, 1981, pp. 324, 333 n. 51). Thus ⲙⲉⲛⲭⲁⲫ ⲉⲡⲟⲗ ⲁⲛ, Release him not; ⲙⲉⲛⲥⲍⲧⲟⲣⲓ ⲉⲧⲍⲟⲉⲓ ⲛⲉⲛ (?) ⲑⲉⲛⲛⲏⲥⲟⲩ, Take not surety of me for (?) Tinnis; ⲙⲉⲛⲥⲟⲗⲉⲙ ⲉⲛⲥⲟⲫ ⲁⲛ, Hearken not unto him; ⲙⲉⲛⲭⲁⲛⲧⲉⲫⲥⲁⲙⲕ ⲁⲛ ⲛⲁⲧⲥⲍⲧⲟⲣⲓ ⲉⲡⲉⲫⲱ, Suffer not that he quit (?) thee without undertaking for himself; ⲙⲉⲛⲡⲁⲉⲓⲥⲛⲁⲟⲩ ⲧⲉⲕⲛⲓⲁⲉⲥ ⲧⲁⲉⲓⲃⲟⲣⲡⲟⲩ ⲛⲁⲕ ⲙⲉⲛⲭⲁ ⲡⲉⲑⲱⲟⲩ ⲧⲉⲫⲧⲁⲱⲟⲩ ⲁⲛ, No, these two craftsmen that I have sent thee, suffer not evil to befall them.

Little is known of the *G* verbal prefixes, an ignorance due to the scarcity of texts in this dialect, all nonliterary, as well as too rare and too short. Given below will be the third-person singular masculine form and then the corresponding prenominal form (nom. = before nominal subject), if attested, the former in brackets, reconstructed where possible according to an associated form:

Bipartite pattern. Present I [ⲫ-], nom. zero (neg. [ⲫ-] . . . ⲁⲛ, nom. zero . . . ⲁⲛ); circumstantial of present I [ⲉⲫ-]; present II [ⲉⲫ-].

Tripartite pattern. Perfect I ⲁⲫ-, neg. [ⲙⲉⲫ-?]; relative perfect I ⲉⲧⲁⲫ-; perfect II [ⲧⲁⲫ-?]. Futurum energicum (or third future) ⲉⲫⲉ-. Imperative ⲁ- (in ⲁⲛⲁⲟⲩ, see), neg. (vetative) ⲙⲉⲛ- . . . (ⲁⲛ), see above. Causative imperative, nom. ⲙⲁⲣⲉ- (?). Conjunctive, 1st singular ⲧⲁ-, 2nd masc. ⲛⲕ- (or ⲧⲉⲕ-), 3rd masc. [ⲛⲫ-] (or ⲧⲉⲫ-), and so on (a morphological duality not unknown in *B*; see Shisha-Halevy, 1981, p. 324), nom. ⲧⲉ- (?) (or ⲉⲛⲧⲉ-); combined with ⲥⲍⲁ-, until (limitative) ⲥⲍⲁⲛⲧⲉⲫ-, nom. ⲥⲍⲁ⟨ⲛ⟩ⲧⲉ-; combined with ⲭⲁ-, let, allow, suffer, ⲭⲁⲛⲧⲉⲫ- (see above); combined with ⲉⲥⲍⲟⲩ-, if, a kind of conditional, ⲉⲥⲍⲟⲩⲧⲉⲫ-. Conditional [ⲁⲫⲥⲍⲁⲛ-].

It is hoped that one day the caprice of discovery may yield a literary *G* text, one more extensive than the small documents on which observations of the orthographical-phonological account of this dialect have perforce been based. Finally, as an illustration, the initial greeting in the text of Vienna K 1785 is presented here: ⲭⲉⲛ ⲡⲣⲁⲛ ⲉⲛⲡⲛⲟⲩⲁⲓ ⲉⲛⲥⲍⲟⲣⲡ ⲛⲱⲃ ⲛⲓⲃⲉⲛ ⲧⲓⲥⲭⲁⲉⲓ ⲧⲓⲉⲣ ⲁⲥⲡⲁⲍⲉⲥⲑⲉ ⲉⲛⲡⲁⲙⲁⲉⲓⲛⲟⲩⲁⲓ ⲉⲛⲥⲟ[ⲛ] ⲉⲧⲧⲁⲓⲏⲟⲩⲧ ⲕⲁⲧⲁ ⲥⲙⲟⲛⲧ ⲛⲓⲃⲉⲛ ⲛⲉⲙ ⲡⲉⲕⲏⲉⲓ ⲧⲏⲣⲫ ⲉⲓⲥⲍⲧⲍⲉⲛ ⲕⲟⲩⲧⲍⲓ ⲥⲍⲁ ⲛⲓⲥⲍⲧ(ⲓ) (In God's name. Before all things I write and I greet my God-loving brother, in all ways honored, and all thy house, from small to great).

BIBLIOGRAPHY

Crum, W. E. *A Coptic Dictionary.* Oxford, 1939a.

______. "Coptic Documents in Greek Script." *Proceedings of the British Academy* 25 (1939b):249–71.

Kasser, R. "L'Idiome de Bachmour." *Bulletin de l'Institut français d'archéologie orientale* 75 (1975):401–427.

______. "Prolégomènes à un essai de classification systématique des dialectes et subdialectes coptes selon les critères de la phonétique, III, Systèmes orthographiques et catégories dialectales." *Muséon* 94 (1981):91–152.

______. "Le Grand-Groupe dialectal copte de Haute-Egypte." *Bulletin de la Société d'égyptologie, Genève* 7 (1982):47–72.

Krall, J. "Aus einer koptischen Klosterbibliothek." *Mittheilungen aus der Sammlung der Papyrus Erzherzog Rainer* 1 (1887):62–72, and 2–3 (1887):43–73.

______. "Koptische Briefe." *Mittheilungen aus der Sammlung der Papyrus Erzherzog Rainer* 5 (1892):21–58.

Mallon, A. *Grammaire copte, avec bibliographie, chrestomathie et vocabulaire,* 2nd ed. Beirut, 1907.

Schüssler, K. *Epistularum Catholicarum Versio Sahidica.* Münster, 1969.

Shisha-Halevy, A. "Bohairic–Late-Egyptian Diaglosses." *Studies Presented to Hans Jakob Polotsky,* ed. D. W. Young, pp. 314–38. East Gloucester, Mass., 1981.

Stern, L. *Koptische Grammatik.* Leipzig, 1880.

Till, W. C. *Koptische Dialektgrammatik, mit Lesestücken und Wörterbuch.* 2nd ed. Munich, 1961.

Worrell, W. H. *Coptic Sounds.* Ann Arbor, Mich., 1934.

RODOLPHE KASSER
ARIEL SHISHA-HALEVY

DIALECT H (OR HERMOPOLITAN OR ASHMUNINIC). Among the manuscripts of the famous Pierpont Morgan collection in New York is a papyrus, M 636, of the ninth (or eighth–ninth) century, which contains mainly what are called *hermeneiai* (Quecke, 1970, pp. 97–100). A *hermeneia* is a liturgical text consisting of a mosaic of biblical quotations, chiefly from the Psalms, selected in relation to one word thought to be central and of prime importance, and so grouped. Drescher (1958–1960, p. 63) wrote:

> The Encyclopaedias in their articles 'Concordance' all have it that the first Biblical Concordance was made in the 13th century. . . . [F]or the Psalms the Copt had rudimentary Concordances before this. Coptic liturgical manuscripts from Upper Egypt show that the principle of verbal concordance was much followed in the liturgical use of the Psalms. The Pierpont Morgan manuscript M. 574 (895 A.D.) is entitled 'The Book of the Holy Hermeniae.' These Hermeniae are for the most part mere collections of versicles from the Psalms. Each Hermenia is based on a key-word—'king,' 'rise,' 'light,' 'house,' 'eye,' 'just,' etc.—and all the versicles in the Hermenia must contain this key-word. Common words have two or three Hermeniae. The word ⲥⲙⲟⲩ (bless, praise) has three, the first with 22 versicles, as well as Incipit and Explicit, the second with 46, the third with 13—in all, some 86 versicles, each containing the word ⲥⲙⲟⲩ. After the Hermeniae of this kind there follow in the manuscript what are called, 'The Little Hermeniae of the Church' but these seem rather to be for the most part short, continuous passages from the Psalms and they need not detain us.

Quecke (1978, p. 215) said:

> Although unfortunately we know very little about the Coptic "Hermeneiae," this designation still seems to be best suited as a brief and relatively clear indication of the kind of texts in question . . . The Copts collected quotations from the Psalter for particular purposes in the liturgy, with the same key-word occurring in each instance. And in any event there are instances where the description "Hermeneia" is connected with these quotations from the Psalter. So far we hardly have any reliable knowledge about the occasions when these Psalm quotations were used in the liturgy and about how they were used.

Papyrus M 636 is written in three different hands, one of which, hand α, is distributed in several sections and uses (regularly or almost so) a completely original spelling system. If it is accepted that this orthographical system is an adequate witness to the existence of a corresponding phonological system, one is led to think of the language of these sections of M 636 as a special Coptic dialect or subdialect, probably a METADIALECT, since it clearly gives the impression of being a much-evolved and, indeed, bastard and degenerate form of the Coptic language. These symptoms of degeneration, combined with a certain negligence in the use of the orthographic system, have encouraged Coptic experts previously concerned with this text to regard its language as a FAYYUMIC of a very special and highly peripheral type, or again, as an odd mixture, intermediate between *F* and *S:* thus, in Crum (1939), of the thirty-four words of M 636, hand α, that are quoted, twenty-three are classified under *F*, six under *S*^{f}, and five under *S*. The language to which M 636, hand α, testifies is today conveniently called dialect *H;* it is also termed Hermopolitan or Ashmuninic, since the ancient Hermopolis is the al-Ashmūnayn of modern Egypt, and according to Kahle (1954), in idiolectal *S* documents, most of the orthographic characteristics similar to those in *H* are mainly found in the region of Hermopolis. Apart from the Morgan manuscript, some other texts (quite as late) show a language close to that of *H*, although never as coherently and as regularly. Thus, phonological and other descriptions of *H* will be based, above all, on an examination of the orthography of M 636, hand α (cf. Kasser, 1966; 1975–1976; 1981, pp. 104–112).

In listing the phonology of *H*, it will be appropriate to compare it as far as possible with that of dialect *V* (or South Fayyumic), a type of Fayyumic without lambdacism (particularly as its *V5* variety has, like *H* generally, the graphic vowel gemination that testifies to the presence of /ʾ/ ALEPH as a CRYPTOPHONEME). Recourse will be had to *F*, *S*, or, where necessary, other Coptic idioms when such a word is not attested in *V* or when this additional reference seems to be of some use.

The order followed will be that of the series of phonemes of the alphabet most generally used in Coptic, that of *S* etc., which is also that of *F5*, *V5*, and almost all *L*, and which (except for aleph, which is graphically rendered by vowel gemination) is identical to the alphabet of *M* etc., which is also that of *W*, *V4*, and *F4* (cf. ALPHABETS, COPTIC). Any Coptic alphabet, as is well known, conventionally begins with those phonemes that are rendered by Coptic letters of Greek origin; it continues with phonemes rendered by Coptic graphemes of demotic origin. Aleph or the cryptophoneme /ʾ/, which was rendered by graphic vowel gemination, will be tackled at the very end.

ⲁ /a/: *H* greatly favors this phoneme (where it has the maximum presence among the Coptic dialects and subdialects, 35 percent; Kasser, 1966, p. 115); see below regarding tonic ⲉ /e/ and atonic ⲉ /ə/ in *V* etc.

ⲃ /ƀ/: *H* does not seem to have this phoneme (which is usual in *V* and in the great majority of the Coptic dialects and subdialects); the ⲃ of *H* is equivalent to /v/ rather than /ƀ/, since it also systematically replaces ϥ /f/ of *V* etc.; see below regarding ϥ /f/.

ⲅ /g/ (appears only in the Copto-Greek vocabulary): *H* does not have this ⲅ /g/ of *V* etc., and it replaces it by ⲕ /k/, for instance, *H* ⲕⲁⲣ, *V* ⲅⲁⲣ, for.

ⲇ /d/ (appears only in the Copto-Greek vocabulary): *H* does not have this ⲇ /d/ of *V* etc., and it replaces it by ⲧ /t/, for example, *H* ⲧⲓⲕⲏⲱⲥ *V* ⲇⲓⲕⲉⲟⲥ, righteous; *H* ⲧⲓⲕⲏⲱⲥⲏⲛⲓ (in one instance only), *V* ⲇⲓⲕⲉⲟⲥⲩⲛⲏ, justice.

Tonic ⲉ /e/ (except the ⲉ of the combination of graphemes ⲉⲓ for /i/ or /j/; see below under ⲓ): *H* always has ⲏ /ē/ where, according to the rules of *V* adapted to the system of *H*, one ought to find tonic ⲉ /e/ (in fact, only in the Copto-Greek vocabulary; see Till, 1948–1949, pp. 18–20), for example, ⲕⲏⲛⲱⲥ, *F* ⲅⲉⲛⲟⲥ, relationship, race, kind. As regards (tonic) vowel ⲉ /e/ in *V* etc., it will be seen again that on this point *H* does not have exactly the same vocalization as *V*, *F* etc.; in *H*, there is ⲁ /a/ also when it is so in *V* etc. while ⲟ /o/ in *S* (for example, *H*, *V*, *F* ⲥⲁⲡ, *S* etc. ⲥⲟⲡ, occasion; *H*, *V*, *F* ⲧⲁⲕⲁ, *S* ⲧⲁⲕⲟ, to destroy), when it is ⲁ /a/ in *S* etc. in opposition to ⲉ /e/ (or ⲏ /e/ before ⲓ /j/) in *V* etc. (especially for various reasons in relation to its position; Vergote, 1973–1983, Vol. 1a, pp. 24–25; Kasser, 1982, pp. 61–62), for example, *H* ⲁⲛ, *V* ⲉⲛ, the negative parti cle; *H* ⲙⲁ, *V* ⲙⲉ, place; *H* ⲉⲙⲕⲁϩ, *V* ⲙⲕⲉϩ, suffering; *H* ⲙⲁⲉⲓⲛ, *W* ⲙⲏⲓⲛ, sign; *H* ⲙⲁⲟⲩ, *V* ⲙⲉⲩ, (place) there; *H* ⲛⲁ, *F5* ⲛⲉⲉⲓ, pity; *H* -ⲛⲁ-, *V* -ⲛⲉ-, the future auxiliary; *H* ⲛⲏⲙⲁ⸗, *V* ⲛⲉⲙⲉ⸗, with; *H* ⲟⲩⲁⲃ†, *V* ⲟⲩⲉⲃ†, holy; *H* ϣⲁⲟⲩ, *V* ϣⲉⲩ, use; *H* ϣⲁϫⲓ, *W*, *V* ⲥⲉϫⲓ, *F (V)* ϣⲉϫⲓ, to talk; *H* ϩⲁⲓⲃⲏⲥ, *F* ϩⲏⲓⲃⲉⲥ, shade; *H* ϩⲏⲙϩⲁⲗ, *F* ϩ(ⲉ)ⲙϩⲉⲗ, slave; *H* ϩⲣⲁⲓ, *V* ϩⲣⲏⲓ, upper part or lower part.

Atonic ⲉ /ə/: When *V* etc. has atonic /ə/, *H* also has ⲏ /ē/ as a general rule but continues to retain ⲉ /ə/ in the following restricted area: in the initial syllable consisting of /ə/ followed by a consonant or consisting of /w/ followed by /ə/, followed by a consonant. In the first of these instances, if the "close liaison" phenomenon is produced (Polotsky, 1949, pp. 29–30), particularly by the attachment of the definite article (not of the possessive article!) before the word, what would otherwise be initial ⲉ is so no longer and returns to the ordinary category, being vocalized ⲏ as elsewhere; thus ⲉⲙⲧⲁ in ⲡⲏⲕⲉⲙⲧⲁ ⲃⲁⲗ, in thy presence, but ⲏⲙⲧⲁ in ⲡⲏⲙⲧⲁ ⲃⲁⲗ ⲡϫⲁⲉⲓⲥ, in presence of the Lord. It will also be noticed that *H*, even more than *F5*, finds it difficult to sustain the weight of two consecutive consonants within the one syllable and so separates them by inserting between them an atonic ⲏ (sometimes corresponding to atonic ⲉ in *F5*, not in *V*), except before ϩ, where in *H* the inserted vowel is then ⲁ; it thus divides the "heavy" syllable into two "lighter" syllables. Examples, which are particularly numerous, include *H* ⲁⲛⲕⲏⲗⲱⲥ, *V* ⲁⲅⲅⲉⲗⲟⲥ, angel; *H* ⲏⲃⲓⲏⲛ, *F* ⲉⲃⲓⲏⲛ, poor; *H* ⲏⲣⲏⲧ, *V* ⲉⲣⲏⲧ, promise; *H* ⲏⲥⲏⲧ, *V* ⲉⲥⲏⲧ, earth; *H* ⲏⲥⲁⲟⲩ, *W* ⲉⲥⲁⲩ, sheep; *H* ⲕⲏ-, *V* ⲕⲉ-, other, also; *H* ⲕⲏⲛⲧⲏ, *F* ⲕⲉⲛⲧⲏ, fig; *H* ⲙⲏⲛ-, *V* ⲙⲛ-, *F* ⲙⲙⲛ-, ⲙ(ⲉ)ⲛ, there is no; *H* ⲙⲏⲛ-, *V*, *F* ⲙⲛ-, more seldom *F* ⲙⲉⲛ-, with; *H* ⲙⲏⲧⲣⲏ, *V* ⲙⲉⲧⲣⲏ, witness; *H* ⲛⲟⲩϩⲏⲙ, *V* ⲛⲟⲩϩⲙ, *F5* ⲛⲟⲩϩⲉⲙ, to save; *H* poss. articles (masc. sing. etc.) sing. 2.m. ⲡⲏⲕ-, 3.m. ⲡⲏϥ-, 3.f. ⲡⲏⲥ-, plur. 1. ⲡⲏⲛ-, 3. ⲡⲏⲩ-, etc., and *V* etc., respectively, ⲡⲉⲕ-, ⲡⲉϥ-, ⲡⲉⲥ-, ⲡⲉⲛ-, ⲡⲉⲩ-, etc.; *H* ⲡⲏϫⲏ-, *V* ⲡⲉϫⲉ-, to say; *H* ⲣⲏⲕⲣⲓⲕⲓ, *F* ⲣⲉⲕⲣⲓⲕⲓ, sleep; *H* ⲣⲏⲙ-, *V* ⲣⲙ-, *F* ⲗⲉⲙ-, man of; *H* ⲣⲏϥ-, *V* ⲣⲉϥ-, maker of; *H* ⲥⲁⲣⲏⲝ, *V* ⲥⲁⲣⲝ, flesh; *H* ⲥⲱⲧⲏⲙ, *F* ⲥⲱⲧⲉⲙ, hear; *H* ⲧⲓⲕⲏⲱⲥ, *V* ⲇⲓⲕⲉⲟⲥ, righteous; *H* ⲧⲏⲗⲏⲗ, *F* ⲧⲉⲗⲏⲗ, joy; *H* ⲧⲏⲛⲧⲱⲛ†, *F* ⲧⲉⲛⲧⲱⲛ†, similar; *H* (except in the third personal pronoun) ⲧⲏⲣⲏ⸗, *V* ⲧⲏⲣ⸗, all; *H* ⲧⲁϣⲏ ⲁⲉⲓϣ, *F* ⲧⲁϣⲉ ⲁⲉⲓϣ, to preach; *H* ⲑⲏⲃⲃⲓⲁ, *V* ⲑⲉⲃⲓⲁ, to humiliate; *H* ⲟⲩⲱⲛⲁϩ, *V* ⲟⲩⲱⲛϩ, revelation; *H* ⲟⲩⲏⲣⲏⲧⲓ, *F* ⲟⲩⲉⲣⲏϯ, foot; *H* ⲱⲃⲏϣ, *V* ⲱⲃϣ, *F5* ⲱⲃⲉϣ, forgetting; *H* ⲱⲛⲁϩ, *V* ⲱⲛϩ, life; *H* ϣⲏⲗⲏⲧ, *F5* ϣⲉⲗⲏⲏⲧ, betrothed; *H* ϣⲁⲙⲏⲧ, *F* ϣⲁⲙⲧ, three; *H* ϣⲁⲣⲏⲡ, *V* ϣⲁⲣⲡ, *F5* ϣⲁⲣ(ⲉ)ⲡ, first; *H* ϩⲏⲃⲏⲥ, *F* ϩⲏⲃⲥ, lamp; *H* ϩⲏⲛ-, *V* ϩⲛ-, *F* ϩ(ⲉ)ⲛ-, in; *H* ϩⲁⲣⲏϩ, *V* ⲁⲣⲉϩ, *S* ϩⲁⲣⲉϩ, to guard; *H* ϩⲓϫⲏⲛ-, *V* ϩⲓϫⲛ-, *F* ϩⲓϫⲉⲛ-, on; *H* ϫⲏ, *V* ϫⲉ, that; *H* ϫⲏⲕⲁⲁⲥ, *V4* ϫⲉⲕⲉⲥ, *F5* ϫⲉⲕⲉⲉⲥ, in order that; *H* ϭⲏⲃⲁⲓ̈, *F* ϭⲃⲁⲓ̈, arm; *H* ϭⲱⲣⲏϭ, *F* ϭⲱⲣϭ, to hunt. On the other hand, ⲉ is in the relative particle (not preceded by the article as an antecedent) *H* ⲉⲧ- (but ⲡⲏⲧ-), *V* ⲉⲧ- (ⲡⲉⲧ-); *H* ⲉⲧⲃⲏ-, *V* ⲉⲧⲃⲉ-, because of; *H* ⲉϣϫⲏ, *V* ⲉϣϫⲉ, if; *H* ⲉⲙⲧⲁ (but ⲡⲏⲙⲧⲁ), *V* ⲙⲧⲁ, *F* (ⲉ)ⲙⲧⲁ face, presence; *H* ⲉⲛⲕⲁⲧⲕ, *V* ⲛⲕⲁⲧ, to sleep; *H* ⲟⲩⲉⲛ-, *V* ⲟⲩⲛ-, *F* ⲟⲩⲁⲛ, there is. On the almost total disappearance in *H* of the preposition "toward, for" etc., which is ⲉ- in *V* (pronominal forms *H* sing. 1. ⲣⲁϊ̈, 2.m. ⲣⲁⲕ, 3.m. ⲣⲁⲃ, etc.; cf. *V* etc. ⲉⲣⲁϊ̈, ⲉⲣⲁⲕ, ⲉⲣⲁϥ, etc., and *F* ⲉⲗⲁϊ̈, ⲉⲗⲁⲕ, ⲉⲗⲁϥ, etc.), see below.

ⲍ /z/ (appears only in the Copto-Greek vocabulary): *H* does not have this ⲍ /z/ of *V* etc. and replaces it by ⲥ /s/, for example, *H* ϫⲓⲑⲁⲣⲓⲥⲏ (one instance only), *S* ⲕⲓⲑⲁⲣⲓⲍⲉ, to make music (with the kithara, etc.).

ⲏ /ē/: As has been seen above regarding tonic ⲉ /e/ or atonic ⲉ /ə/, *H* greatly favors ⲏ /ē/ (tonic or atonic). Here it has the maximum presence among the Coptic dialects and subdialects, 34 percent (Kasser, 1966, p. 115). *H* even tends to substitute ⲏ for ⲓ as a final atonic vowel; see below regarding ⲓ (or ⲉⲓ) for /i/ vowel or /j/ consonant.

ⲓ (or ⲉⲓ) for /i/ vowel or /j/ consonant (except as regards the alternative ⲓ or ⲉⲓ, a problem too complex to go into here): *H* behaves very like *V* etc.; in particular, it has ⲓ /i/ as a final atonic vowel. In *H*, however, there exists a strong tendency toward the formation of a metadialect, which shows itself in the frequent replacement of final atonic ⲓ by a final atonic ⲏ. These ⲏ amount to 33 percent of all the atonic final letters, and among them may be noted a whole series of words with, in *H*, the final letter either always in -ⲏ or in -ⲏ more frequently than in -ⲓ (these last cases are shown below in parentheses): ⲕⲓⲃⲏ, pap; ⲉⲓⲙⲏ, to know; ⲉⲓⲛⲏ, to carry; (ⲉⲓⲣⲏ, to do); ⲉⲓϣⲏ, to hang, suspend; ⲕⲏⲙⲏ, Egypt; ⲙⲓⲥⲏ, to give birth; ⲧⲏ-, genitive preposition; ⲡⲱⲛⲏ, to move; ⲣⲓⲕⲏ, to bend; (ⲣⲱⲙⲏ, man); ⲣⲁϣⲏ, joy; ⲣⲱϣⲏ, sufficiency; ⲥⲱϣⲏ, field; ⲥϩⲓⲙⲏ, woman; ϣⲓⲛⲏ, to look for; ϣⲁϫⲏ, word; ϩⲏⲕⲏ, poor; ϩⲏⲛⲏ, incense, perfume; ϩⲓⲥⲏ, trouble; ϫⲱⲙⲏ, book; (ϫⲁϫⲏ, enemy;) ϭⲓⲛⲏ, to find (twenty-three words, against thirty-nine words where the atonic ending is either always -ⲓ or -ⲓ more frequently than -ⲏ, these latter cases being six in number). Finally, the final atonic vowel disappears completely after /w/; see below under ⲟⲩ /w/.

ⲝ /ks/ (occurs only in the Copto-Greek vocabulary): *H* sometimes keeps this letter, which, however, it tends to replace by ⲕⲝ, ⲕⲝⲥ, or ⲕⲥ /ks/, as in *H* ⲧⲱⲕⲥⲁ, *B* ⲇⲟⲝⲁ, glory; *H* ⲉⲕⲝⲟⲩⲥⲓⲁ, *V* ⲉⲝⲟⲩⲥⲓⲁ, authority; *H* ⲥⲁⲣⲏⲝ, *V* ⲥⲁⲣⲝ, flesh.

ⲟ /o/ (except for the ⲟ in the combination of graphemes ⲟⲩ for /u/ or /w/; see below under ⲩ): *H* has ⲱ /ō/ everywhere when, according to the rules of *V* adapted to the *H* system, one should find ⲟ /o/ (therefore, in fact, always in the Copto-Greek vocabulary): for example, *H* ⲁⲛⲕⲏⲗⲱⲥ, *V* ⲁⲅⲅⲉⲗⲟⲥ, angel; ⲧⲓⲕⲏⲱⲥ, *V* ⲇⲓⲕⲉⲟⲥ, just.

ⲩ /y/ (occurs only in the Copto-Greek vocabulary; ⲩ after ⲁ-, ⲉ-, or ⲏ- is a special case of ⲟⲩ /u/ or /w/, with loss of ⲟ, on which see below): *H* regularly replaces this ⲩ /y/ by ⲏ /e/: for example, *H* ⲧⲏⲛⲁⲙⲓⲥ, *F* ⲇⲩⲛⲁⲙⲓⲥ, power; *H* ⲝⲏⲗⲱⲛ, *S* ⲝⲩⲗⲟⲛ, wood.

ⲟⲩ (or ⲩ after ⲁ-, ⲉ-, or ⲏ-; see above) for /u/ vowel or /w/ consonant: *H* uses it without any special peculiarity, apart from the frequent disappearance of the final atonic vowel after ⲟⲩ /w/: for example, *H* ⲕⲁⲟⲩ, *V* ⲕⲁⲩⲓ, *F5* ⲕⲁⲟⲩⲓ, others; *H* ⲙⲏⲟⲩ, *V*, *F* ⲙⲏⲟⲩⲓ, thought; *H* ⲡⲏⲟⲩ, *V*, *F* ⲡⲏⲟⲩⲓ, heavens; *H* ϩⲓⲁⲟⲩ, *V*, *F* ϩⲓⲁⲩⲓ, roads; *H* ϩⲃⲏⲟⲩ, *V*, *F* ϩⲃⲏⲟⲩⲓ, works.

ⲯ /ps/ (occurs only in the Copto-Greek vocabulary): *H* sometimes keeps this letter, which, however, it tends to replace by ⲡⲯ /p(p)s/ (which could have ended up as ⲡⲯⲥ > ⲡⲥ): for example, *H* ⲡⲯⲏⲭⲏ (ⲯⲏⲭⲏ is clearly rarer), *V* ⲯⲩⲭⲏ, soul.

ϥ /f/: *H* always replaces ϥ /f/ by ⲃ /v/.

ϫ /č/: See ϭ /c/(?).

ϭ /c/(?): While generally *H* has ϫ and ϭ where *V* also has them, there are certain cases that may give the impression that while in *H* ϫ is the equivalent of /č/, ϭ has the value of some allophone of /č/ (difficult to define) rather than /c/. One may here compare in *H* ϫⲱⲣⲏⲡ, to stumble, with ϭⲣⲁⲡ, obstacle, and ϫⲱⲱⲣⲓ, strong, with ⲧⲁϭⲣⲁ, to make strong. See also the surprising *H* ϭⲡⲁ, give birth, and ϭⲡⲓⲁ, to insult, not to speak of ϭⲓϭ, hand, where this time there can be no question of the assimilation of the final consonant to the initial consonant (cf. *H* ϫⲁϫ, sparrow).

ϯ /ti/: *H* everywhere writes ⲧⲓ /ti/ where *V* has ϯ /ti/.

/ʾ/ or aleph: It will be noted that *H* generally has graphic vowel gemination testifying to the presence of aleph /ʾ/ as a cryptophoneme (even if this /ʾ/ tends to disappear there as it also does in other Coptic idioms).

Several observations could still be made regarding the morphosyntactic and other idiosyncrasies of *H*, as can be noted in manuscript M 636, hand *α*. These idiosyncrasies have at yet been little studied to date. It must be mentioned above all that *H* systematically omits both the preposition ⲉ-, toward, in relation to, or for, and the numerous prepositions or particles ⲛ-, all of them as initial ⲉ- (and ⲙ-) and ⲛ-. In relation to classical Coptic, the sentence in *H* from then on appears to be completely disarticulate and dismembered; for example, the infinitive absolute of a verb can no longer be distinguished from its prenominal infinitive. Other conditions might emerge through the falling away of the initial consonant of the "accusative" preposition in its pronominal form, which henceforth appears to be felt more or less as a secondary pronominal suffix, as in ⲡⲁⲣⲏⲃⲛⲟⲩϩⲏⲙⲁϊ̈, my Savior, and ϣⲁⲕⲛⲟⲩϩⲏⲙⲁϊ, Thou wilt save me, alongside ⲁⲕⲛⲁϩⲙⲏⲧ, Thou hast saved me.

In conclusion, there will be presented here the verbal prefixes attested to date in *H.* Except for special cases (conjunctive), the form cited here is only the third-person masculine singular, and its corresponding prenominal form (nom. = before nominal subject). The entire paradigm is not attested in all conjugations.

Unless specifically mentioned, the form is affirmative; neg. = negative. Every basic tense (abbreviated hereafter to "basic") is followed (if attested) by its satellites, after "And": circ. = circumstantial, rel. = relative, II = second tense; ant. = with pronominal antecedent. Forms between brackets [. . .] are reconstituted from very similar forms; zero = no verbal prefix.

Bipartite Pattern

Neg. zero particle . . . ⲁⲛ.

Present (basic) ⲃ-, nom. zero. And circ. ⲉⲃ-, nom. ⲉⲣⲏ-; rel. [(ⲛ)ⲧⲏⲃ-?].

Future (basic) ⲃⲛⲁ-, nom. zero . . . ⲛⲁ-. And II [ⲉⲃⲛⲁ-], nom. ⲉⲣⲏ- . . . ⲛⲁ-.

Tripartite Pattern

Tenses with special negation (if not II).

Perfect (basic) ⲁⲃ-, nom. ⲁ-; neg. [ⲡⲏⲃ-], nom. ⲡⲏ-. And circ. (ⲉ)ⲁⲃ- (?), nom. [(ⲉ)ⲁ-(?)]; rel. ⲧⲁⲃ-, nom. [ⲧⲁ-]; neg. with zero . . . ⲁⲛ.

Expectative (or completive) (basic = neg.) ⲡⲁⲧⲏⲃ-, nom. ⲡⲁⲧⲏ-.

Consuetudinal (or aorist) (basic) ϣⲁⲃ-, nom. ϣⲁⲣⲏ-; neg. ⲙⲏⲃ-, nom. [ⲙⲏⲣⲏ-]; rel. neg. [ⲉⲧⲏⲙⲏⲃ-], [ant. ⲡⲏⲧⲏⲙⲏⲃ-], nom. [ⲉⲧⲏⲙⲏⲣⲏ-], [ant. ⲡⲏⲧⲏⲙⲏⲣⲏ-].

Futurum energicum (or third future) (basic) [ⲉⲃⲏ-], (ϫⲏⲃⲃⲏ- with ϫⲏ, in order that, antecedent), nom. [ⲉⲣⲏ-]; neg. ⲛⲏⲃ-, nom. [ⲛⲏⲣⲏ-].

Causative imperative (basic) ⲙⲁⲣⲏⲃ-, nom. ⲙⲁⲣⲏ-; neg. [ⲛⲏⲕⲧⲣⲏⲃ-], nom. [ⲛⲏⲕⲧⲣⲏ-].

Tenses with neg. [ⲧⲏⲙ-].

Conjunctive (basic) (sing. 1.; 2.m./f.; 3.m.; plur. 2./3.) ⲧⲁ-, ⲕ-, ⲧⲏ-, ⲃ-, ⲧⲏⲧⲏⲛ, ⲥⲏ-, nom. ⲧⲏ-. And with ϣⲁ-, toward (= limitative), ϣⲁⲛⲧⲏⲃ-, nom. ϣⲁⲛⲧⲏ-.

Temporal (basic) ⲧⲏⲣⲏⲃ-, nom. ⲧⲏⲣⲏ-.

Conditional (basic) ⲉⲃϣⲁⲛ-, nom. ⲉⲣϣⲁⲛ-.

BIBLIOGRAPHY

Crum, W. E. *A Coptic Dictionary.* Oxford, 1939.

Drescher, J. "The Earliest Biblical Concordances." *Bulletin de la Société d'archéologie copte* 15 (1958–1960):63–67.

Kahle, P. E. *Bala'izah: Coptic Texts from Deir el-Bala'izah in Upper Egypt.* Oxford and London, 1954.

Kasser, R. "Dialectes, sous-dialectes et 'dialecticules' dans l'Egypte copte." *Zeitschrift für ägyptische Sprache und Altertumskunde* 92 (1966):106–115.

______. "A propos de quelques caractéristiques orthographiques du vocabulaire grec utilisé dans les dialectes H et N." *Orientalia Lovaniensia Periodica* 6–7 (1975–1976):285–94.

______. "Prolégomènes à un essai de classification systématique des dialectes et subdialectes coptes selon les critères de la phonétique, III, Systèmes orthographiques et catégories dialectales." *Muséon* 94 (1981):91–152.

Polotsky, H. J. "Une Question d'orthographe bohaïrique." *Bulletin de la Société d'archéologie copte* 12 (1949):25–35.

Quecke, H. *Untersuchungen zum koptischen Stundengebet.* Louvain, 1970.

______. "Koptische 'Hermeneiai': Fragmente in Florenz." *Orientalia* 47 (1978):215–19.

______. "Zwei Blätter aus koptischen Hermeneia-Typika in der Papyrussammlung der Österreichischen Nationalbibliothek (P. Vindob. K 9725 und 9734)." In *Festschrift zum 100-Jährigen Bestehen der Papyrussammlung der Österreichischen Nationalbibliothek, Papyrus Erzherzog Rainer (P. Rainer Cent.),* pp. 194–206. Vienna, 1983.

Till, W. C. "Betrachtungen zum Wortakzent im Koptischen." *Bulletin de la Société d'archéologie copte* 13 (1948–1949):13–32.

Vergote, J. *Grammaire copte,* Vol. 1a, *Introduction, phonétique et phonologie, morphologie synthématique (structure des sémantèmes), partie synchronique,* Vol. 1b, *Introduction, phonétique et phonologie, morphologie synthématique (structure des sémantèmes), partie diachronique,* Vol. 2a, *Morphologie syntagmatique, syntaxe, partie synchronique,* Vol. 2b, *Morphologie syntagmatique, partie diachronique.* Louvain, 1973–1983.

RODOLPHE KASSER

DIALECT İ (OR PROTO-LYCOPOLITAN OR PROTO-LYCO-DIOSPOLITAN). The siglum of dialect *İ* comes from the title of the text contained in the unique document attesting to its presence (Lacau, 1946), "The Ascension of Isaiah." This dialect (and partially its subdialects *İ7* and *İ74*) shows in its orthography phonological qualities that allow one to consider it a PROTODIALECT—more precisely, the protodialect corresponding to the former phonological level of some lost variety of the important dialect *L,* a collective entity whose chief manifestations are the subdialects *L4, L5,* and *L6* (cf.

LYCOPOLITAN and LYCO-DIOSPOLITAN). (Besides what makes *İ* etc. a protodialect, most of the phonological characteristics of this dialect and its subdialects are those of one or another of the branches of *L*, or at least resemble them more closely than those of all the other Coptic idioms.) These qualities cause each witness of *İ* in particular, but also of *İ7* and *İ74*, to be of greatest interest for Coptology. One must all the more regret that up to now the texts attested by these manuscripts have been extremely brief and full of gaps (the total amount of text expressing *İ*, *İ7*, and *İ74* is scarcely 0.01 percent of all the Coptic texts known nowadays and 0.6 percent of those of the *L* dialect). This excessive briefness prevents any observation in many important sectors of *İ*. Any possible observations elsewhere being too isolated, this textual poverty causes useful generalizations to be quite problematic, rendering difficult a comparative orthographic system of rules necessary to compare *İ* with *L4*, *L5*, *L6*, *A*, and so on.

It is fitting here to specify that despite the fundamental systematic elements that can be observed in the texts, particularly with regard to the protodialectal quality and the major characteristics of the dialectal group *L*, each of the small texts expressing *İ* etc. remains a separate and special case under other aspects (as are moreover, in a lesser but not negligible measure, each of the texts expressing *L4*, *L5*, and *L6;* cf. LYCOPOLITAN and LYCO-DIOSPOLITAN). Here are these protodialectal texts, each with its (sub)dialectal attribution.

İ (= *pL*): All of Lacau (1946; a manuscript from the fourth century at the latest), with the exception of several words that, through oversight or ignorance, the scribe wrote with ϣ instead of proto-Lyco-Diospolitan normal ϣ̈. (These words are considered to belong, then, to *İ7;* cf. infra.)

İ7 (=*p'L*): The few words of Lacau (1946) mentioned above, not really typical of *İ*; furthermore, the texts of Leipoldt (1904; fourth century), and Goehring (1984; fourth century) if ⲟⲩⲣⲉϯ (cf. *L6*, *L5* ⲟⲩⲣⲓⲧⲉ; *L4*, *A* ⲟⲩⲣⲏⲧⲉ) can (or could) be a case connected with the rule of Edel (1961). Possibly Browne (1979, no. 6; fourth or fifth century), though unfortunately no lexeme covered by the rule of Edel (1961) is present. If these two last texts are not *İ7*, they are *İ74* (cf. below). One can be tempted to relate to *İ7* in a way the text of Crum (1934; from the second half of the third century, bought in Luxor), which indeed presents, by at least one of the typical central characteristics of *İ7*, a vulgar orthography that appears rather strange (indicated by the siglum *J* in Kasser, pp. 113–15). Consonants: The initial consonant ⲟⲩ /w/ is replaced by ⲃ /v/, and likewise all ϥ /f/. Unfortunately this text has no example of ϣ, thus lacking proof that Crum's text belongs to *İ* etc. (Perhaps it is only a particularly aberrant form of *A*, although *A* does not have the -ⲓ of Edel, 1961, with certain exceptions [Lacau, 1911], ⲉⲓⲁϯ, ancestors, 2 Mc. 6:1, 6.) The consonant ϩ is always omitted. ⳉ is maintained in a series of cases where *İ* and *A* have ⳉ. ϫ is retained nine times and replaced three times by ⲭ (= /č/ rather than /x/; cf. ALPHABETS, COPTIC). ϭ is replaced by ⲕ. Stressed vowels: They frequently conform with those of *A* and *L* (56 percent), less often with those of *S* (44 percent). Unstressed vowels: Those of *L6* are preferred, since the -ⲓ of Edel (1961), missing in *L5* and *L4*, is regularly found in *İ* etc. and *L6*.

İ74 (= *p''L*): Possibly Goehring (1984) and Browne (1979, no. 6; cf. above); certainly Lefort (1939; from the fourth century at the latest). The text of Crum (1922; fourth or fifth century, origin unknown) could reasonably (in a sense) belong to *İ74* also because of certain chief characteristics, such as use of /x/ and /š/, as in *İ7* and *İ74* (cf. below). Yet one sees in it various spellings (sometimes systematic or nearly) that are very strange and far from *L* etc.; in Crum (1922) the normal ⲥ is replaced by ϣ (!) in six out of eight cases, such as ϩⲁϣⲉ†, painful. It also has a strong tendancy to replace the sonant (nasal) with /ē/ followed by the sonorant, having thus ⲏⲛⲧ⸗, to carry; ⳉⲏⲛ-, in; and the negation -ⲧⲏⲙ-.

One will additionally note that *İ* (with *İ7* and *İ74*) is a protodialect with an impoverished alphabet. Indeed, each supplementary phoneme characterizing *İ* as a protodialect, *pL*, with regard to *L*, is not written with a special grapheme but with a grapheme common to *L*, supplied, however, with a diacritical sign in *pL*. Thus, /x/ is ⳉ in *pL* (as it is in *A*), which is ϩ (the ordinary grapheme for /h/) supplied with a diacritical sign (and in fact, in the phonological evolution, *pL* > *L*, *pL* ⳉ > *L* ϩ), whereas in **pS* (reconstructed on the analogy of DIALECT P, an alphabetically rich protodialect), /x/ is ϧ, used for nothing else. (One will here notice that in *A* ⳉ /x/ and in *B* ϧ /x/ have no protodialectal function, since they belong to the alphabet and to the phonological stock of the dialect *A* and the language *B* themselves, according to their usual and traditional definition in Coptology.) Likewise, /ç/ is ϣ̈ in *pL*, which is ϣ (an ordinary grapheme for /š/) supplied with a diacritical sign (and in fact, in the phonological evolution *pL* > *L*, *pL* ϣ̈ > *L* ϣ), whereas in *P* (generally analogous to **pS*), /ç/ is ⳋ, used for nothing else.

The essential characteristics of *İ*, qualifying it as a protodialect, are (1) the survival of /ç/ (arising from majority x_3; cf. PROTODIALECT), written ϣ̈; (2) the survival of /x/ (arising from x_2, united with minority x_3; cf. PROTODIALECT), written ⳉ; (3) the survival of the final unstressed vowel -ⲓ in the cases described by Edel (1961; formerly *jw*), a survival also found in the *L6* branch of *L*.

One or more of these characteristics have disappeared in *İ7* or *İ74* (following an evolution that can summarily be represented as *İ* > *İ7* > *İ74* > *L*). *İ7* has the second and third characteristics only, while *İ74* has just the second.

The other phonological characteristics of *İ*, *İ7*, and *İ74* are not characteristics of protodialects but, rather, show their relation to (sub)dialects within the range of *L*'s subdialects (*L4, L5, L6;* cf. Kasser, 1984, p. 307). At this point, it will be interesting to add *A*, the Coptic language form whose vowels are the closest to *L*'s and *İ*'s vowels. *İ*, [*İ7*], *İ74*, *L6*, and *A* assimilate /s/ in /š/ before /č/: ϣⲉϫⲉ, *L4, L5* ⲥⲉϫⲉ, word. *İ*, [*İ7*, *İ74*], *L4*, and *A* have the potential final aleph: ⲟⲩⲉ, *L5* ⲟⲩⲉⲉ, *L6* ⲟⲩⲉⲉⲓ, one (masc.). Before the stressed vowel, *İ*, [*İ7*, *İ74*], *L5*, *L6*, and *A* have /f/: ϥ(ⲉ)ⲓ, *L4* ⲃⲓ, remove. *İ74*, *L5*, and *L6* have the final sonant, which on the contrary is the sonorant followed by /ə/ in *İ*, *L4*, and *A* [*İ7* lacks this form]: *İ*, *L4*, *A* ⲥⲱⲧⲙⲉ, *İ74*, *L5*, *L6* ⲥⲱⲧⲙ̄, to hear. *İ*, *İ7*, [*İ74*], *L44*, and *A* lose /w/ with metaphony in the end stressed syllable that in *L4* (except *L44*), *L5*, and *L6* is /-ew/: *İ*, *İ7*, [*İ74*], *L44*, *A* ⲛⲟ, *L4*, *L5*, *L6* ⲛⲉⲩ, to see. Where *İ* and *L4* have the stressed final vowel in /-ō/, *İ74*, *L6*, and *A* have /u/ (a situation quite unclear in *L5; İ7* lacks this form): *İ*, *L4* ϫⲱ, *L6*, *A* ϫⲟⲩ, to say, but *İ74* ϩϥⲟⲩⲟⲩ, *A* ϩⲃⲟⲩ, *L4* ϩⲃⲱ, serpent (fem.). The end syllable's vocalization of the prenominal form of causative verbs with *t*-initial, /-ə/ [*İ*], *İ7*, [*İ74*], (*L4*), *L6*, and /-a/ *L5: İ7* (?) ⲧ[ⲁ]ⲛⲉ-, to create; cf. *A* ⲧⲁⲛⲟ- or ⲧⲉⲛⲉ-, *L5* ⲧⲉⲛⲁ-. Peculiar lexemes: *İ74* ⲙⲉϩϫⲉ, *L44* (and *L4*, which is rare) ⲙⲉϫⲉ, *L6* ⲙⲉϣϫⲉ, *L5*, *L4* ⲙⲉϣⲧⲉ (cf. *P* ⲙⲁϣⲧⲁ), *A* ⲙⲉⲉϫⲉ, ear. The particle of the prolepsis *İ*, *İ7*, *İ74*, *L6*, (*L5*), *A* ⲛ̄ϭⲓ, (*L5*) ϫⲓ, *L4* ⲛ̄ϫⲓ, but (ⲛ̄)ϭⲉ or ϫⲉ (*A*) sometimes also. *İ*, [*İ7*, *İ74*], *L4*, *L5*, *A* ⲧⲟ, *L6* ⲧⲟⲛ, where (interrog.); *İ* (?), *İ7*, *L5*, *L6*, (*A*) ⲁⲣⲏϩ, *A* ⲉⲣⲏϩ (or ⲉⲣⲏϩⲧⲉ), but *L4* ϩⲉⲁⲏϭ (cf. *P* ϩⲉⲁⲁⲕ), to keep. Verbal prefixes: first future third sing. masc. etc. *İ*, *İ7*, [*İ74*], *L5*, *L6*, *A* ϥⲛⲁ-, *L4*, (*A*) ϥⲁ-. First perfect first sing. etc. *İ7*, *İ74*, *L4*, *L5*, *A* ⲁï-, *İ* ⲁ(ⲉ)ⲓ- or ϩⲁ(ⲉ)ⲓ- (cf. *V* hybrid also, *M* exclusively ϩⲁï-, etc.), *L6* ⲁⲉⲓ- or ⲁϩⲓ-. Relative perfect third sing. masc. etc. *İ*, *İ7*, [*İ74*], *L4*, *A* ⲉⲧⲁϥ-, *L5*, *L6* (ⲉ)ⲛⲧⲁϥ-.

The texts attesting *İ* etc. are unfortunately too brief to allow systematic observations in morphosyntactic and lexicologic fields. However, one should note forms such as *İ* ⲡⲁⲉⲓϭⲉ, mouth, which has no known Coptic equivalent except *A* ⲡⲁïϭⲉ; further, *İ* and *A* have ϭⲃⲓⲣ, left (hand) (cf. *P* ⲕⲃⲓⲣ), while *L4* and *L5* have ϭⲃⲟⲩⲣ, and *S*, *M*, and *F* have ϩⲃⲟⲩⲣ.

Finally, here are some typical examples of proto-Lycopolitan (*pL* or *İ* etc.): *İ7*, *L6* ⲕⲉⲕⲉⲓ, *L4*, *L5*, *A* ⲕⲉⲕⲉ obscurity; *İ*, *L44*, *A* ⲉⲧⲙ̄ⲙⲟ, *L4* (except *L44*), *L5*, *L6* ⲉⲧⲙ̄ⲙⲉⲩ, that (one) *İ7*, *L4*, *L6*, *S* ⲥⲁϣϥ seven (masc.) (*L5* etc. fem. ⲥⲁϣϥⲉ, *H* ⲥⲁϣⲃⲓ), *B* ϣⲁϣϥ, *M* ⲥⲉϣϥ (and ϣⲉϣⲃ special dialectal [?] variant of B.M.Or. 5300(27), between *M* and *H* rather than *F*), *A* ⲥⲁϩϥ, *P* ⲥⲁϩϥ; *İ7*, *A* ⲁⲛϩ†, *L4*, *L5*, *L6* ⲁⲛϩ̄† (and *L5* ⲁⲁⲛϩ̄†, John [Lond.], ⲁⲁϩ†, John [Dub.]), *B* ⲟⲛϧ† (cf. *P* ⲱⲓϧ), *S* ⲟⲛϩ̄†, *M*, *W*, *V*, (*F*) ⲁⲛϩ†, (*F*) *H* ⲁⲛⲁϩ†, living; *İ7*, *L4*, *L5*, *L6*, *S* etc. ϣⲏⲙ, *A* ⳉⲏⲙ, *P* ϣⲏⲙ, little, *İ* ϣⲱⲡⲉ, *P* ϣⲱⲡⲉ, *A* ⳉⲱⲡⲉ, *L4*, *L5*, *L6*, *S* etc. ϣⲱⲡⲉ, become; *İ7* ϩⲁⲗⲉϯ, *İ74*, *L4*, *A* ϩⲁⲗⲉⲧⲉ, *P* ϩⲁⲗⲁⲧⲉ, *S* etc. ϩⲁⲗⲁ(ⲁ)ⲧⲉ, birds; *İ*, *İ7*, *İ74*, *A* ⳉⲛ̄-, *P* ϧⲛ̄-, *B* ϧⲉⲛ-, *L4*, *L5*, *L6*, *S* etc. ϩⲛ̄-, in; *İ*, *L6* ϫⲁⲥⲓ†, *L4*, *L5*, *A*, *M* ϫⲁⲥⲉ†, *P*, *S* ϫⲟⲥⲉ†, *B* ϭⲟⲥⲓ†, *F*, *H* ϫⲁⲥⲓ† (from [*İ* etc.], *L4*, *L5*, *L6*, *A*, *S*, *M* ϫⲓⲥⲉ, metadialectal *H* ϫⲓⲥⲏ, *V*, *F* ϫⲓⲥⲓ, *B* ϭⲓⲥⲓ), exalted.

BIBLIOGRAPHY

Browne, G. M. *Michigan Coptic Texts.* Barcelona, 1979.

Crum, W. E. "La Magie copte: Nouveaux textes." *Bibliothèque de l'Ecole pratique des hautes études* 234 (1922):537–44.

______. "Un Psaume en dialecte d'Akhmîm." *Mémoires de l'Institut français d'archéologie orientale* 67 (1934):73–86.

Edel, E. "Neues Material zur Herkunft der auslautenden Vokale -E und -I im Koptischen." *Zeitschrift für ägyptische Sprache und Altertumskunde* 86 (1961):103–106.

Funk, W.-P. "Die Zeugen des koptischen Literaturdialekts İ7." *Zeitschrift für ägyptische Sprache und Altertumskunde* 114 (1987):117–33.

Goehring, J. E. "A New Coptic Fragment of Melito's Homily on the Passion." *Muséon* 97 (1984):255–60.

Kasser, R. "Relations de généalogie dialectale dans le domaine lycopolitain." *Bulletin de la Société d'égyptologie, Genève* 2 (1979):31–36.

______. "Prolégomènes à un essai de classification systématique des dialectes et subdialectes coptes selon les critères de la phonétique, I, Principes et terminologie." *Muséon* 93 (1980a):53–112. ". . . , II, Alphabets et systèmes phonétiques." *Muséon* 93 (1980b):237–97. ". . . , III, Systèmes orthographiques et catégories dialectales." *Muséon* 94 (1981):91–152.

______. "Un Nouveau Document protolycopolitain." *Orientalia* 51 (1982):30–38.

______. "Le Grand-Groupe dialectal copte de Haute-Egypte." *Bulletin de la Société d'égyptologie, Genève* 7 (1982):47–72.

———. "Orthographe et phonologie de la variété subdialectale lycopolitaine des textes gnostiques coptes de Nag Hammadi." *Muséon* 97 (1984):261–312.

———. "Encore un document protolycopolitain." *Muséon* 98 (1985):79–82.

Lacau, P. "Textes coptes en dialectes akhmîmique et sahidique." *Bulletin de l'Institut français d'archéologie orientale* 8 (1911):43–81.

———. "Fragments de l'Ascension d'Isaïe en copte." *Le Muséon* 59 (1946): 453–457.

Lefort, L. T. "Fragments d'apocryphes en copte-akhmîmique." *Muséon* 52 (1939):1–10.

[Leipoldt, J.]. *Aegyptische Urkunden aus den königlichen Museen zu Berlin, herausgegeben von der Generalverwaltung, koptische Urkunden.* Berlin, 1904.

Vergote, J. "Le Dialecte copte P (P. Bodmer VI: Proverbes), essai d'identification." *Revue d'égyptologie* 25 (1973):50–57.

———. *Grammaire copte,* Vol. 1a, *Introduction, phonétique et phonologie, morphologie synthématique (structure des sémantèmes), partie synchronique,* Vol. 1b, *Introduction, phonétique et phonologie, morphologie synthématique (structure des sémantèmes), partie diachronique,* Vol. 2a, *Morphologie syntagmatique, syntaxe, partie synchronique,* Vol. 2b, *Morphologie syntagmatique, partie diachronique.* Louvain, 1973–1983.

Worrell, W. H. *Coptic Sounds.* Ann Arbor, Mich., 1934.

RODOLPHE KASSER

DIALECT P (OR PROTO-THEBAN). The siglum for this dialect, *P,* comes from a Coptic biblical book of Proverbs in the form of a late-third-century parchment codex, P. Bodmer VI, the only existing document written in the dialect (Kasser, 1960). Its orthography exhibits phonological characteristics that allow one to consider it a PROTODIALECT. In brief though more precise terms, one could think of it as a proto-Theban that often resembles what can be known about a hypothetical proto-Sahidic, tentatively reconstructed (possibly a proto-Sahidic immigrant in the Theban region; cf. DIALECT, IMMIGRANT).

Alphabet of P

Even if it is of secondary importance to the study of dialects, it is worthwhile to examine the rather original alphabet used in *P,* which looks like the Old Coptic alphabets (see ALPHABETS, OLD COPTIC) and is incontestably the richest among the various Coptic alphabetic systems (many of the Coptic dialects and subdialects having their own varieties of the Coptic alphabet; see ALPHABETS, COPTIC and Kasser, 1980, pp. 280–81). Its thirty-five graphemes include three kinds of signs: (1) all twenty-four letters of the Greek alphabet, as in all Coptic dialects except *H;* (2) a ligature of Greek origin, ϗ /cə/, in autochthonous Coptic words such as *P* ⲛ̄ϗ = *S* ⲛ̄ϭⲓ, the proleptic particle, and *P* ϗ = *S* ϭⲉ, therefore; this interesting grapheme perhaps possesses the same phonological value in the Copto-Greek vocabulary, where it however may be also /kai/, /kaj/, or possibly even /ke/ or /kə/ (apparently the case also in various Greek and Coptic documentary texts where it occasionally appears, always optionally); and (3) no less than ten graphemes that originated in demotic. (In contrast, Bohairic has but seven demotic characters and Sahidic only six.)

The simplest way to describe the alphabet of *P* is to compare it with the alphabet of Sahidic (*S*). Many graphemes of demotic origin that belong properly to *P* obviously represent phonemes that *S* also possesses but expresses by other combined or single characters. For instance, /k/ in *S* is ⲕ, whereas for *P* it is ⲹ, a grapheme observed in two Old Coptic texts (Kasser, 1980, p. 259). However, /c/ in *S* is ϭ, while in *P* /c/ is ⲕ, for, as with virtually all Old Coptic texts, *P* refrains from using ϭ (Kasser, 1980, p. 258). Further, the two following signs of *P* no longer appear in P. Bodmer VI, except vestigially, being progressively forced out of usage by newer graphemic usages, in particular those of *S.* First, in a primitive state of evolution, *P* writes the sonant /n̩/ as –, like some Old Coptic texts (Kasser, 1963). Then it starts to write it as ⲛ̄, as in classical *S* later on. Also, in its primitive mode *P* appears to render graphically the tonic vowel as geminate (Kasser, 1985) and writes the voiceless laryngeal occlusive, aleph /ʾ/, as ⊥. It probably derives from a combination of both similar demotic signs for *3* and *ỉ* (du Bourguet, 1976, p. 3). Next, adopting the newer graphemic usages that will be those of *S* etc., *P* no longer geminates stressed vowels as such, but rather the tonic vowel is geminated when followed by aleph. For instance, for /taprȯ/, meaning "mouth," the primitive *P* has ⲧⲁⲡⲣⲟ̄ⲟ̄, while the logically secondary *P* and *S* have ⲧⲁⲡⲣⲟ; for /čȯʾf/, meaning "to say it," the primitive *P* has ϫⲟ⊥ϥ, whereas the secondary *P* and *S* have ϫⲟⲟϥ.

Other graphemes peculiar to *P,* however, constitute the written form of phonemes no longer in more evolved Coptic (*S* and most Coptic dialects). Therefore, in its usage of ϧ /x/, *P* comes into line with *B* etc., so *P* and *B* are graphemically opposed to *A* and *İ* where /x/ is ⳉ, but *P, B, A,* and *İ* (and the small subdialects *J* with ϩ, and *B7* and *G* with ⲭ) are phonologically opposed to all the rest of the Coptic languages, dialects, and subdialects, where /x/ disappeared previously and no longer exists at all. But above all, in still using ⳉ /ç/ (a sign found inverted in many Old Coptic texts; Kasser, 1980, pp. 258–60), *P* is phonologically opposed to all Coptic dialects and subdialects (except *İ* = *pL*, also a protodialect, where however /ç/ is ϣ̈). As for ⳉ, the graphemic combination ϫⳉ is still seen in the final position after the tonic vowel: ⲙⲟⲩϫⳉ, mix; ⲛⲟⲩϫⳉ, sprinkle; ⲡⲱϫⳉ, beat flat. This combination ϫⳉ could render a palatalized affricate /č2/ or /ç̌/ corresponding to /tç/ as /š/ corresponds to /tš/, rather than /čç/. In those three lexemes, the other Coptic dialects have, as the case arises (see below), -ϫϭ in *S* and sometimes *A;* -ϫⲕ in *S;* -ϫⲧ in *S, L,* and sometimes *A* and *B;* -ϫϩ in *A;* -ϫϧ in *B;* or simply -ϫ in *S*. This forms a range of possible phonemic combinations so open and diverse that the interpretation of *P* -ϫⳉ is scarcely made any easier.

Phonological and Morphological Peculiarities

As far as dialectology is concerned, the alphabet is a decisive indicator only insofar as its graphemes are able to reveal the nature of its phonemes. Thus, it is the phonology of *P* that enables one to see it as a type of protodialect often identical with a reconstructed proto-Sahidic. On this subject, it should be noted that nothing in the consonant system of *P* is incompatible with that of *S* (which is common, moreover, to many Coptic dialects, namely, those most neutralized in this respect, basically *L, M, W,* and *V*). A comparison of the consonant system of *P* with that of *S* is given below.

As regards vocalization, it is undoubtedly advisable to assign a preeminent importance to stressed vowels, which manifest most of the characteristics that allow one to distinguish between Coptic dialects or subdialects. One discovers that the vocabulary of *P* agrees thus in 97 percent of the cases with that of *S*. Nearly half of the remaining cases (*P* ⲛⲁⲕ, large; ⲣⲓⲛ, name; ⲟⲩϊ, one (masc.); ⲟⲩⲁϊ, rush; ⲁⳉⲙ⸗, quench; ϧⲣⲁⲩ, voice; and ⲉⲃⲁⲛ, wrath; cf. *B* ⲙ̇ⲃⲟⲛ, in Vycichl, 1983, p. 108b) can eventually be explained by etymology and the archaic state of the language rather than by the influence of other Coptic dialects, particularly from the south, such as *L* or *A*. (It will also be noted that the stressed-vowel agreement of *P* with *A* and *L*, when they are completely in accord, or with any special variety of *L* is only between 59 percent and 63 percent.)

In the remaining 1.5 percent of cases, the orthography of *P*, while distant from that of *S*, coincides with some other Coptic dialect (from Lower or Middle Egypt as well as Upper Egypt and thus having no particularly marked affinity with *L* or *A*). In class *i*, *P* always writes the stressed /ē/ before final /j/ (first-person singular pronoun suffix or any other element). Thus, *P* ⲛⲙ̄ⲙⲏϊ, with me, corresponds to ⲛⲙ̄ⲙⲏⲉⲓ in *L5* and *L6;* ⲛⲉⲙⲏϊ in *L4, F5, F56,* and *B;* ⲛⲉⲙⲉⲉⲓ in *A;* ⲛⲉⲙⲉϊ in *M* and *F4;* and ⲛⲙ̄ⲙⲁϊ in *S*. ⲛⲏϊ, to me, in *P, L4, W, V, F5, F56, F4,* (*F7*), and *B* corresponds to ⲛⲏⲉⲓ in *L5, L6,* and *F7;* ⲛⲉϊ in *M, F4,* and *F46;* ⲛⲉⲉⲓ in *A;* and ⲛⲁϊ in *S*. Also /j/ (not always final): for example, ⲁϊⲏ(ⲏ)ϊⲧⲉ in *P;* ⲁϊⲉϊ and ⲁ(ⲉ)ⲓⲉⲩ(ⲧⲉ), etc., in *A;* ⲁϊⲉⲩⲧⲉ in *A* and *L4;* ⲁⲉⲓⲉⲩ in *L6;* ⲁϊⲉⲉⲓ in *M;* ⲁϊⲉϊ in *F*, ⲁϊⲁϊ in *S* and *B* all mean "to grow." ⲁϣⲏ(ⲉ)ⲓⲧⲉ in *P;* ⲁϣⲉⲉⲓⲧⲉ in *A;* ⲁϣⲉϊ(ⲧⲉ) in *A* and *L4;* ⲁϣⲉⲉⲓ(ⲧⲉ) in *L6;* ⲁϣⲉⲉⲓ in *L5;* ⲁϣⲉϊ in *M, V,* and *F;* and ⲁϣⲁϊ in *S* and *B* all mean "to multiply." ⲙⲏⲉⲓⲛ in *P;* ⲙⲏϊⲛ in *W* and *F;* ⲙⲏϊⲛⲓ in *B;* ⲙⲉ(ⲉ)ⲓⲛⲉ in *A;* ⲙⲉϊⲛⲉ in *L4;* ⲙⲉⲉⲓⲛ in *M;* and ⲙⲁⲉⲓⲛ in *L5, L6,* and *S* all mean "sign." ⲥⲏⲉⲓⲛ in *P;* ⲥⲏϊⲛ in *F;* ⲥⲏϊⲛⲓ in *B;* ⲥⲉ(ⲉ)ⲓⲛⲉ in *A;* ⲥⲉϊⲛⲉ in *L4;* and ⲥⲉⲉⲓⲛ in *M* and ⲥⲁⲉⲓⲛ in *L6* and *S* all mean "doctor, physician." ⲟⲩϫⲏ(ⲉ)ⲓⲧⲉ in *P;* ⲟⲩϫⲉⲉⲓ in *A, L6,* and *L5;* ⲟⲩϫⲉϊ(ⲧⲉ) in *A* and *L4;* ⲟⲩϫⲉⲉⲓ(ⲧⲉ) in *L6;* ⲟⲩϫⲉϊ in *M* and *F;* ⲟⲩϫⲁϊ in *S* and *B* all mean "to be healed, saved." ϩⲣⲏϊ in *P, A, L, M, W, V,* and *B;* ϩⲗⲏϊ in *F;* and ϩⲣⲁϊ in *S* all mean "upper part." ϧⲣⲏϊ in *P* and *B;* ϩⲣⲏϊ in *A;* ϩⲣⲏϊ in *L, M, W,* and *V;* ϩⲗⲏϊ in *F;* and ϩⲣⲁϊ in *S* all mean "lower part." In this category alone, one finds that *P* reaffirms its originality. If one summarizes its points of contact with other Coptic dialects in the previous narrow category, one finds that its most pronounced affinities are with *B*, then with *F*, then with *L*, then with *A* and *M*, with *S* definitely coming last.

Some interesting observations can be made with unstressed vowels. -ⲉ is generally the unstressed vowel in *P*, as it is in *S*, but sometimes it is -ⲁ where the corresponding Egyptian word has a final ʿayin: for example, *P* ⲙⲏϣⲁ, *S* ⲙⲏⲏϣⲉ, crowd; *P* ⲙⲁϣⲧⲁ, *S* ⲙⲁⲁϫⲉ, ear; *P* ⲧⲏⲃⲁ, *S* ⲧⲏⲏⲃⲉ, finger; and *P* ⲕⲟⲟⲙⲁ†, *S* ϭⲟⲟⲙⲉ†, twisted, crooked, perverse, vicious. On the one hand, it would be permissible to consider this differentiated vocalization as an archaism typical of *P* when compared to the more neutralized *S*. On the other hand, one finds that the dialectal regions of Egypt where this phenomenon is manifest are precisely Lower Middle Egypt and Lower Egypt. In fact, *F* (except for *F7*) and *V, W* having -ⲓ as the normal unstressed final vowel, have -ⲉ (*F7* even has -ⲁ, like *P*) in the ʿayin position mentioned earlier, and *B* loses every final vowel in place of its normal -ⲓ (thus, *F7* ⲙⲏϣⲁ, *F5* ⲙⲏⲏϣⲉ, *W* ⲙⲏϣⲉ, *B* ⲙⲏϣ, crowd; *F7* ⲙⲉϫⲁ, *F5* ⲙⲉⲉϫⲉ, *V* ⲙⲉϫⲉ, *B* ⲙⲁϣϫ, ear; *F5* ⲧⲏⲏⲃⲉ, *B* ⲧⲏⲃ, finger; but, e.g., *F7*, *F* ⲗⲱⲙⲓ, *W*, *V*, *B* ⲣⲱⲙⲓ, man; cf. Polotsky, 1931; Vergote, 1945, p. 88).

But one must not forget that the categories where *P* moves farthest away from *S* to approach *B* and especially *F* (or perhaps other dialects) remain quite restricted (tonic vowels above, 1.5 percent of the *P* vocabulary; atonic above, 1 percent), so that the result could hardly call in question the striking affinity that *P* and *S* have almost everywhere else (97 percent) as well as certain disagreements between the two in unstressed pretonic vowels (thus, *P*, *L*, *A* ⲉⲙⲛ̄ⲧⲉ, *S* ⲁⲙⲛ̄ⲧⲉ, hell; *P*, *L*, *A* ⲉⲙⲁϩⲧⲉ, *S* ⲁⲙⲁϩⲧⲉ, seize; plur. *P* ⲉϩⲱ(ⲱ)ⲣ, *L*, *A* ⲉϩⲱⲣ, *S* ⲁϩⲱⲱⲣ, treasures; *P* ⲉϩⲟⲙ, *L*, *A* ⲉϩⲁⲙ, *S* ⲁϩⲟⲙ, sigh; *P*, *L*, *A* ⲁ-, *S* ⲉ-, toward; *P*, *L*, *A* ⲁⲛⲏϩⲉ, *S* ⲉⲛⲉϩ, eternity) or the fact that *P*, like *L5* and *L6*, writes /nə/ rather than final /n̩/ after /w/, but in this position only, while *A* and *L4* do not recognize this limitation (cf. *P* ⲥⲟⲟⲩⲛⲉ, *L*, *A* ⲥⲁⲩⲛⲉ, *S* ⲥⲟⲟⲩⲛ̄, to know). Nor, finally, does the situation change much from the fact that *P*, as opposed to *S* (and therefore coming close to *A*, *L*, and other dialects), readily replaces a potential aleph after the final stressed vowel with /j/ or /ə/ (similiglide, Kasser, 1981b, p. 35), while the *S* orthography will refrain from indicating it. For example, ⲙⲉⲉⲓ of *P;* ⲙⲉ(ⲉ)ⲓⲉ of *A;* ⲙⲉⲓ̈ⲉ of *L4;* ⲙⲁⲉⲓⲉ of *L5* and *L6;* ⲙⲏⲓ̈ⲉ of *M;* ⲙⲏⲓ̈ of *W*, *V*, *F*, and *B;* ⲙⲉⲓ̈ of *B;* and ⲙⲉ of *S* all mean "to love." ⲙⲏⲓ̈ of *P* and *B;* ⲙⲓⲉ of *A;* ⲙⲏⲉ of *L;* ⲙⲉⲉ̇ of *M;* ⲙⲉⲓ̈ of *W*, *V*, *B*, *F4*, and *F7;* ⲙⲉⲉⲓ of *F5* and *F56;* and ⲙⲉ of *S* all mean truth, justice. ⲛⲁⲉ of *P*, *A*, and *L;* ⲛⲉⲉ̇ of *M;* ⲛⲉⲓ̈ of *W;* ⲛⲉⲉⲓ of *F5* and *F56;* ⲛⲁⲓ̈ of *B;* and ⲛⲁ of *S* all mean "pity." ⲥⲁⲉ of *P;* ⲥⲁ(ⲉ)ⲓⲉ of *A* and *L;* ⲥⲉⲓ̈ of *F;* ⲥⲁⲓ̈(ⲉ) of *B;* and ⲥⲁ of *S* all mean "beauty." ⲟⲩⲉⲉ(ⲓ) of *P;* ⲟⲩⲉⲓ̈ⲉ of *A* and *L4;* ⲟⲩⲁⲉⲓⲉ of *L6;* ⲟⲩⲏⲓ̈ⲉ of *M;* ⲟⲩⲏⲏⲓ̈ of *F5;* ⲟⲩⲏⲓ̈ of *F7;* ⲟⲩⲉⲓ̈ of *B;* and ⲟⲩⲉ of *S* all mean "to be distant, far-reaching." ϩⲉⲉ(ⲓ) of *P;* ϩⲉ(ⲉ)ⲓⲉ of *A;* ϩⲉⲓ̈ⲉ of *L4;* ϩⲁⲉⲓⲉ of *L5* and *L6;* ϩⲏⲓ̈ⲉ of *M;* ϩⲏⲓ̈ of *V*, *F4*, and (*B*); ϩⲏⲏⲓ̈ of *F5*; ϩⲉⲓ̈ of *B*; and ϩⲉ of *S* all mean "to fall."

P's stressed vowels demonstrate, if not a complete identity with *S*, then at least a relationship close enough to consider it a regional dialectal variety very like a kind of "proto-Sahidic" (a reconstructed **pS*, cf. below). More precisely, it would be a **pS* that could have become a typical, local or regional variety of *S*, distinguished from classic *S* by only a few differences, but belonging, without doubt, to the Sahidic dialectal group (*P* is nearly as close to *S* as *L4* is to *L5* and *L6*, or *F4* to *F5*, *F7*, *F8*, and *F9* and conversely). Perhaps *P* was an immigrant variety of **pS*, some sort of **pS* from Thebes (cf. in some way the former hypothesis that *P* would be a Theban protodialect, Nagel, 1965; Kasser, 1982; on this, cf. especially *P* ϩⲉ-, on; ⲉⲥⲧⲉ, behold, here is; ⲣⲓⲛ, name; ⲁⲃⲟⲗ, outside; ⲃⲱϫ, to throw). More precisely, it would not be an indication that *S* was principally of Theban origin, but native to a place further north (between *L* and *M*). *S*, as a common language spreading (many centuries before Coptic times) southward (also northward) and through the whole valley of the Egyptian Nile above the Delta, would be implanted first of all, very early on, in some great urban centers, following the course of that river (Kasser, 1982). *P* (as a variety of **pS*) could only be "Theban" by means of immigration (cf. DIALECT, IMMIGRANT).

The close relationship of *P* and *S* is confirmed in the consonants, where the evidence of the protodialectal character is clear (cf. PROTODIALECT). In fact, the phonemes still present in *P* and absent in *S* follow exactly the well-known line of phonological evolution from pharaonic Egyptian to Coptic (Vergote, 1945, pp. 122ff.). Thus, *P* still has /ç/ (from predominant x_3) written ⳅ, and /x/ (from x_2, related to a minority x_3) written ⳋ. These two phonemes are also present in dialect *İ*, the only other Coptic protodialect known at present; this has an impoverished alphabet (/ç/ ⳃ; /x/ ⳉ, as in *A*). The development of *P* as a protodialect near to a kind of **pS* becoming *S* is as follows: ⳅ /ç/ > ϣ /š/, and ⳋ /x/ > ϩ /h/. For example, *P* ⳅⲟⲣⲡ, first, in *S* is ϣⲟⲣⲡ (*A* ⳉⲁⲣⲡ, *L* ϣⲁⲣⲡ, etc.); and *P* ⳋⲙ̄ⳋⲁⲗ, servant, is *S* ϩⲙ̄ϩⲁⲗ (*A* ⳉⲙ̄ⳉⲉⲗ, *L* ϩⲙ̄ϩⲉⲗ).

As far as the vowels are concerned, the verbal prefixes of *P* also have points in common with those of *S*, but even more with *L* (especially *L4*). This should not be too much of a surprise, since they are all directly or indirectly pretonic unstressed vowels, and it is specifically in the pretonic unstressed vowels that *P* is often closer to *L*, and sometimes *A*, than it is to *S* (perhaps an early characteristic neutralized later in *S* or the influence of native Thebes dialect on immigrant **pS*, in accordance with the hypothesis offered above). With the consonants, however, *P* sometimes exhibits original solutions approximating also to *A* or *L* (as the case arises) when disagreeing with *S*. (As regards the morphological peculiarities of *P*, see especially the conjugation system below.)

Conjugation System

Except in special instances (conjunctive, etc.), the form cited here is only the third-person masculine singular and the corresponding prenominal form ("nom." = before nominal subject). The entire paradigm is not attested in all conjugations.

Unless specifically mentioned, the form is affirmative; "neg." = negative. Every basic tense (abbreviated hereafter to "basic") is followed (if attested) by its satellites, after "And": "circ." = circumstantial, "pret." = preterite, "rel." = relative, "II" = second tense. Forms between brackets [. . .] are reconstituted from very similar forms; "zero" = no verbal prefix or no particle.

1. Bipartite Pattern.

Neg. zero . . . ⲁ or ⲁ̄ (sic) (ⲛ̅- . . . ⲁⲛ *S*, (ⲛ̅-) . . . ⲉⲛ *L*, zero . . . ⲉⲛ *A*).

1.1. *Present* (basic) ϥ- (= *S*, *L*, *A*), nom. zero (= *S*, *L*, *A*). And circ. ⲉϥ- (= *S*, *L*, *A*), nom. ⲉⲣⲉ- (= *S*, *L*, (*A*), ⲉ- *A*); rel. ⲉⲧ- (= *S*, *L*, *A*) or [ⲉⲧⲉϥ-] (= (*L5*), ⲉⲧϥ̅- *S*, *L*, *A*, nom. [ⲉⲧⲉⲣⲉ-] (= *S*, *L4*, (*L5*), *L6*, (*A*), ⲉⲧⲉ- *L5*, (*L6*), *A*); pret. ⲛⲉϥ- (= *S*, *L*, ⲛⲁϥ- (*L6*), *A*), nom. [ⲛⲉⲣⲉ-] (= *S*, *L*, ⲛⲁ(ⲣⲉ)- *A*); pret. rel. ⲉⲧⲉⲛⲉϥ- (= *S*, *L*, ⲉⲛⲉϥ- *S*, *L*, ⲉⲛⲁϥ- *A*), nom. [ⲉⲧⲉⲛⲉⲣⲉ-] (= *S*, *L*, ⲉⲛⲉⲣⲉ- *S*, *L*); II ⲉϥ- (= *S*, *L*, ⲁϥ- *A*), nom. ⲉ(ⲣⲉ)- (ⲉⲣⲉ- *S*, *L*, ⲁ(ⲣⲉ)- *A*).

1.2. *Future* (basic) with -ⲛⲁ-: ϥⲛⲁ- (= *S*, (*L4*), *L5*, *L6*, *A*), nom. zero . . . ⲛⲁ- (= *S*, *L*, *A*). And circ. ⲉϥⲛⲁ- (= *S*, (*L4*), *L5*, *L6*, *A*), nom. [ⲉⲣⲉ- . . . ⲛⲁ-] (= *S*, *L6*, ⲉ- . . . ⲛⲁ- *L5*, *A*); rel. ⲉⲧⲛⲁ- (= *S*, *L*, *A*) or ⲉⲧⲉϥⲛⲁ- (= (*L5*), (*L6*), ⲉⲧϥ̅ⲛⲁ- *S*, (*L4*), *L5*, *L6*, *A*), nom. ⲉⲧⲉⲣⲉ- . . . ⲛⲁ- (= *S*, *L4*, *L6*, (*A*), ⲉⲧⲉ- . . . ⲛⲁ- *L5*, *A*); II ⲉϥⲛⲁ- (= *S*, *L*, ⲁϥⲛⲁ- *A*), nom. ⲉⲣⲉ- . . . ⲛⲁ- (= *S*, *L*, ⲁ(ⲣⲉ)- . . . ⲛⲁ- *A*).

1.3. *Future* (basic) with -ⲁ-: ϥⲁ- (only Prv. 19:25) (= *L4*). And rel. (?) ⲉⲧⲉϥⲁ- (only Prv. 6:29) (ⲉⲧϥⲁ- *L4*).

2. Tripartite Pattern.

2.1 Tenses with special negations (if not II). Independent (sentence) conjugations.

2.1.1. *Perfect* (basic) ⲁϥ- (= *S*, *L*, *A*, but twice sing. 1. ϩⲓ- *P* = Prv. 7:15–16 [see Kasser, 1984], cf. ⲁϩⲓ- etc. *L6* sometimes), nom. ⲁ- (= *S*, *L*, *A*, except *L6* Acta Pauli from Heidelberg, ϩⲁ- [but ⲁϥ-, like *P*, *S*, *L4*, *L5*, *A*], (ⲁϩⲁ- rarely *L6*); neg. ⲙ̅ⲡϥ̅- (= *S*, *L*, *A*, ⲙ̅ⲡⲉϥ- (*L4*), (*L5*), (*L6*), nom. [ⲙ̅ⲡⲉ-] (= *S*, *L*, *A*, ⲛ̅ⲡⲉ- (*A*)). And circ. [ⲉⲁϥ-] (*S*, *L*, *A*), nom. [ⲉⲁ-] (= *S*, *L*, *A*, except *L6* Acta Pauli from Heidelberg, ⲉϩⲁ-); neg. [ⲉⲙⲡϥ̅-] (= *S*, *L*, ⲉⲙⲡⲉϥ- (*L4*), (*L6*)), nom. [ⲉⲙⲡⲉ-] (= *S*, *L*). Rel. ⲉⲧⲁϩ- (= *A*, (ⲉ)ⲛⲧⲁϩ- *L;* cf. Funk, 1984) or [ⲉⲧⲁϥ-] (= *L4*, *A*, ⲉⲛⲧⲁϥ- *S*, (*L6*), ⲛ̅ⲧⲁϥ- (*S*), *L5*, *L6*, (ⲉⲧⲉ(ϩ)ⲁϥ- *L6*)), nom. ⲉⲧⲁ- (= *L4*, (*L6*), *A*, ⲉⲛⲧⲁ- *S*, (*L6*), ⲛ̅ⲧⲁ- (*S*), *L5*, (*L6*), (ⲛ̅ⲧⲁϩⲁ-, ⲉⲧⲁ(ϩ)ⲁ-, ⲉⲛⲧⲁⲁ- *L6*)), neg. [ⲉⲧⲉⲙⲡϥ̅-] (= *S*, *L*, [*A*], ⲉⲧⲉⲙⲡⲉϥ- (*L6*)), nom. [ⲉⲧⲉⲙⲡⲉ-] (= *S*, *L*, *A*). II [ⲉⲧⲁϥ-] (= (*A*), ⲛ̅ⲧⲁϥ- *S*, *L*, ⲛⲁϥ- *A*, (ⲉⲁϥ- *L6*), also ⲉⲣⲉ(ⲛⲧ)ⲁϥ- with a causal sense *L6* Tractatus Tripartitus; cf. *P* ⲉⲣⲁⲍ- Prv. 6:3), nom. [ⲉⲧⲁ-] (ⲛ̅ⲧⲁ- *S*, *L*, ⲛⲁ- *A*); neg. zero . . . ⲁ (etc.).

2.1.2. *Completive* (basic) (affirmative substitute [ⲁϥⲟⲩⲱ ⲉϥ-] (= *S*, *L*, *A*); neg. (= *expectative*) ⲙ̅ⲡⲁⲧϥ̅- (= *S*, *L*, [*A*]), ⲙ̅ⲡⲁⲧⲉϥ- (*S*), (*L4*)), nom. [ⲙ̅ⲡⲁⲧⲉ-] (= *S*, *L*, *A*). And circ. ⲉⲙⲡⲁⲧϥ̅- (= *S*, *L*, *A*, ⲉⲙⲡⲁⲧⲉϥ- (*S*), (*L*)), nom. ⲉⲙⲡⲁⲧⲉ- (= *S*, *L*, *A*).

2.1.3. *Consuetudinal* (or *aorist*) ⳉⲁⲣϥ- (ϣⲁϥ- *S*, *L*, ϣⲁⲣⲉϥ- (*L5*), (*L6*), ϩⲁⲣⲉϥ- *A*), nom. ⳉⲁⲣⲉ- (ϣⲁⲣⲉ- *S*, *L*, ϩⲁⲣⲉ- *A*); neg. ⲙⲁϥ- (= *L*, *A*, ⲙⲉϥ- *S*), nom. ⲙⲁⲣⲉ- (= *L*, *A*, ⲙⲁⲣⲉ- *S*, ⲙⲁ- *A*). And circ. ⲉⳉⲁⲣϥ- (ⲉϣⲁϥ- *S*, *L*, [ⲉϣⲁⲣⲉϥ-] (*L5*), (*L6*), ⲉϩⲁⲣⲉϥ- *A*), nom. [ⲉⳉⲁⲣⲉ-] (ⲉϣⲁⲣⲉ- *S*, *L*, ⲉϩⲁⲣⲉ- *A*); neg. [ⲉⲙⲁϥ-] (= *L*, *A*, ⲉⲙⲉϥ- *S*), nom. [ⲉⲙⲁⲣⲉ-] (= *L*, [*A*], ⲉⲙⲉⲣⲉ-*S*). Rel. ⲉⲧⳉⲁⲣ- (without parallels elsewhere in Coptic) or ⲉⲧⲉⳉⲁⲣϥ- (ⲉ(ⲧⲉ)ϣⲁϥ- *S*, *L*, (ⲉⲧϣⲁϥ- *L6* once), ⲉⲧϩⲁⲣⲉϥ- *A*), nom. [ⲉⲧⲉⳉⲁⲣⲉ-] (ⲉ(ⲧⲉ)ϣⲁⲣⲉ- *S*, *L*, ⲉⲧϩⲁⲣⲉ- *A*); neg. ⲉⲧⲉⲙⲁϥ- (= *L*, *A*, ⲉⲧⲉⲙⲉϥ- *S*), nom. [ⲉⲧⲉⲙⲁⲣⲉ-] (= *L*, [*A*], ⲉⲧⲉⲙⲉⲣⲉ- *S*). Pret. [ⲛⲉⳉⲁⲣϥ-] (ⲛⲉϣⲁϥ- *S*, *L4*, (*L6*), ⲛⲉϣⲁⲣⲉϥ- (*L6*), [ⲛⲉϩⲁⲣⲉϥ-] *A*), nom. ⲛⲉⳉⲁⲣⲉ- (ⲛⲉϣⲁⲣⲉ- *S*, [*L*], [ⲛⲉϩⲁⲣⲉ-] *A*). II [ⲉⳉⲁⲣϥ-] (ⲉϣⲁϥ- *S*, *L*, [ⲉϩⲁⲣⲉϥ-] or ⲁϩⲁⲣⲉϥ- *A*), nom. ⲉⳉⲁⲣⲉ- (ⲉϣⲁⲣⲉ- *S*, *L*, ⲉϩⲁⲣⲉ- or ⲁϩⲁⲣⲉ- *A*).

2.1.4. *Futurum energicum* (or third future) ⲉϥⲁ- (probably so, not second future) (= *L*, ⲉϥⲉ- *S*, ⲁϥⲁ- *A*), nom. ⲉⲣⲁ- . . . ⲁ- (ⲉⲣⲉ- . . . zero *S*, *L*, ⲁ- . . . (ⲁ-) *A*); neg. ⲛϥ̅- (= (*L6*), ⲛⲉϥ- *L*, *A*, ⲛ̅ⲛⲉϥ- *S*), nom. ⲛⲉ- (= *L*, *A*, ⲛ̅ⲛⲉ- *S*). ⲉⲧⲉϥⲁ-: see 1.3.

2.1.5. *Imperative:* infinitive unaccompanied (= *S*, *L*, *A*) or else preceded by ⲙⲁ- (= *S*, *L*, *A*, always causative verbs) or by ⲉ- (= *L6*, *A*, ⲁ- *S*, *L4*, *L5*); neg. ⲙ̅ⲛ- (= *A*, *L4*, (*L6*), ⲙ̅ⲡⲣ̅- *S*, (*L4*), *L5*, *L6*, (*A*), ⲙ̅ⲡⲱⲣ- (*L4*), (*A?*), ⲙ̅ⲡⲱⲣ ⲁ- (*L6*), (*A*)).

2.1.6. *Causative Imperative* ⲙⲁⲣϥ- (ⲙⲁⲣⲉϥ- *S*, *L*, *A*), nom. ⲙⲁⲧⲉ- (ⲙⲁⲣⲉ- *S*, *L*, *A*); neg. [ⲙ̅ⲛ̅ⲧϥ-] (= *A*, ⲙ̅ⲛ̅ⲧⲣⲉϥ- *L6*, ⲙ̅ⲡⲣ̅ⲧⲣⲉϥ- *S*, *L5*, ⲙ̅ⲡⲱⲣ ⲁⲧⲣⲉϥ- *L6*, ⲙ̅ⲡⲣ̅[ⲧϥ]- *A*), nom. ⲙ̅ⲛ̅ⲧⲉ- (= *A*, ⲙ̅ⲛ̅ⲧⲣⲉ- *L6*, ⲙ̅ⲡⲣ̅ⲧⲣⲉ- *S*, *L5*, *L6*, ⲙ̅ⲡⲱⲣⲧⲉ- *L4*, *L6*, ⲙ̅ⲡⲣ̅ⲧⲉ- *A*).

2.2 Tenses with neg. -ⲧⲙ̅-. Subordinate (clause) conjugations.

2.2.1. *Conjunctive* (sing. 1., 2. masc., [fem.], 3. masc., fem.; plur. 1., 2., 3., nom.) ⲛ̅ⲧⲁ- (= *S*, *L*, ⲧⲁ- *S*, *L*, *A*), –ⲍ- or ⊥ⲍ- (ⲛ̅ⲅ- *S*, (*L4*), (*L6*), ⲛ̅ⲕ- *L*, ⲕ- (*L4*), (*L5*), *A*), -ϥ- or ⊥ϥ- (ⲛ̅ϥ- *S*, *L*, ϥ- (*L4*), (*L5*), *A*, (ⲛ̅ⲧϥ̅- *A* once)), ⊥ⲥ- (twice) (ⲛ̅ⲥ- *S*, *L*, ⲥ- *A*), ⲛ̅ⲧⲛ̅- (= *S*, *L*, ⲧⲛ̅- (*L4*), *A*), ⲛ̅ⲧⲉⲧⲛ̅- (= *S*, *L*, ⲧⲉⲧⲛ̅- (*L4*), (*L5*), *A*), ⲛ̅ⲥⲉ- (= *S*, *L*, ⲥⲉ- *A*, (ⲥⲟⲩ- *A* once)), nom. ⲛ̅ⲧⲉ- (= *S*, *L*, ⲧⲉ- *A*).

2.2.2. *Future Conjunctive* ⲛ̅ⲧⲁⲣϥ- (ⲧⲁⲣⲉϥ- *S*, *L*, *A*), nom. [ⲛ̅ⲧⲁⲣⲉ-] (ⲧⲁⲣⲉ- *S*, *L*, *A*).

2.2.3. *Temporal* ⲛ̅ⲧⲁⲣϥ- (ⲛ̅ⲧⲉⲣⲉϥ- *S*, ⲛ̅ⲧⲁⲣⲉϥ- *L*, (*A*), ⲧⲁⲣⲉϥ- *A*), nom. [ⲛ̅ⲧⲁⲣⲉ-] (= *L*, *A*, ⲛ̅ⲧⲉⲣⲉ- *S*, ⲧⲁⲣⲉ- *A*).

2.2.4. *Limitative* (or conjunctive with ϣⲁ-, until) ϣⲁⲛⲧϥ- (= *S*, (*L4*), (*L6*), ϣⲁⲛⲧⲉϥ- *L4*, (*L6*), ϣⲁⲧϥ- *A*), nom. ϣⲁⲛⲧⲉ- (= *S*, *L*, (*A* once), ϣⲁⲧⲉ- *A*).

2.2.5. *Conditional* ⲉϥϣⲁ- (= (*L4*), *L5*, (*L6*), (*A* once), ⲉϥϣⲁⲛ- *S*, *L4*, *L6*, ⲁϥϣⲁ- *A*), nom. ⲉϣⲁ- (=

(*L4*), (*A*), ⲉⲣϣⲁ- (*L4*), (*L5*), ⲉⲣϣⲁⲛ- *S*, ⲉⲣⲉϣⲁ- *L5*, (*L6*), ⲉⲣⲉϣⲁⲛ- *L6*, ⲁϣⲁ- *A*, ⲉϣⲁⲛⲧⲉ- *L4*).

Characteristic Lexemes

Lexicographically, *P*, on the one hand, displays various notable isolated orthographical peculiarities (apart from those that occur more systematically and have been already shown above) and, on the other, has some rare or otherwise unknown lexemes:

ⲁ or ⲁ̄ negative particle, cf. ⲁⲛ *S*, *B*, ⲉⲛ *A*, *L*, *M*, *W*, *V*, *F*.

ⲃⲉⲗⲗ (masc.) eyes, a plural not attested elsewhere in Coptic and corresponding to the singular ⲃⲁⲗ *P*, *S*, *B*, ⲃⲉⲗ *A*, *L*, *M*, *W*, *V*, *F;* ⲃⲁϩⲟⲩⲉ (masc.) eyelids, a plural not attested elsewhere in Coptic, corresponding to the singular ⲃⲟⲩϩⲉ *S*, ⲃⲱϩⲉ (*S*), *A*, ⲃⲟⲩϩⲓ *B*.

ⲉⲧⲃⲉ-: See ⲛ̄ⲧⲃⲉ-.

ⲑⲟⲩⲣⲉ-, more than, with no parallels elsewhere in Coptic (Prv. 9:3, κρείσσων . . . ἤ, ⲛⲁⲛⲉ- . . . ⲑⲟⲩⲣⲉ- *P*, ⲛⲁⲛⲉ- . . . ⲛ̄ϩⲟⲩⲟ ⲁ- *A*, ⲛⲁⲛⲟⲩ . . . ⲉϩⲟⲩⲉ- *S*, ϥⲥⲟⲧⲡ . . . ⲉϩⲟⲧⲉ- *B*).

ⲕⲃⲓⲣ, left; cf. ϭⲃⲓⲣ *A*, ϭⲃⲟⲩⲣ *L*, ϩⲃⲟⲩⲣ *S*, *M*, *F*.

ⲙⲁϣⲧⲁ, ear; cf. ⲙⲉϣⲧⲉ *L5*, *L4* (except the Manichaean Homilies, and more rarely, the Manichaean Psalms and Kephalaia, ⲙⲉϫⲉ), ⲙⲉϣϫⲉ *L6*, ⲙⲁϣϫ *B*, ⲙⲁⲁϫⲉ *S*, ⲙⲉϫⲉ *M*, *V*, ⲙⲉ(ⲉ)ϫⲉ *F;* ⲙⲉⳉⲏⲗ, to cure, without parallels elsewhere in Coptic (Prv. 12:18, ἰᾶσθαι, ⲧⲗ̄ϭⲟ *A*, ⲧⲁⲗϭⲟ *S*, *B;* cf. Bedja *mehēl*, to treat medically, Vycichl, 1983, p. 132a); ⲙⲟϩⲉ, to walk, go, cf. ⲙⲁ(ⲁ)ϩⲉ *A*, *L*, ⲙⲟⲟϣⲉ *S*, ⲙⲟϣⲓ *B*, ⲙⲁϣⲉ *M*, *W* (sic), ⲙⲁϣⲓ *V*, ⲙⲁⲁϣⲓ *F;* ⲙⲟⲩϫⳉ, to mix, cf. ⲙⲟⲩϫϭ *A*, *S*, *L6*, also ⲙⲟⲩϫⲧ *S*, *A*, (*L6*), *L4*, *B*, ⲙⲟϫⲕ *S* (cf. Hebrew *māzag* and the demotic *mdg*, container, wine-bowl, κρατήρ (?), Vycichl, 1983, p. 133b).

ⲛⲓⲃ, all; cf. ⲛⲓⲃⲓ *W*, *V*, *F*, ⲛⲓⲃⲉⲛ *B*, ⲛⲓⲙⲓ *F7*, ⲛⲓⲙ *A*, *S*, *L*, *M* (demotic *nb*, Vycichl, 1983, p. 142b); ⲛ̄ⲕ proleptic particle, cf. ⲛ̄ϭⲓ *S*, *A*, *L6*, (*M*) etc., ⲛ̀ϭⲏ *M*, ((ⲛ̄)ϭⲉ *A*), ⲛ̄ϫⲓ *L4*, (*L6*), *W*, ϫⲓ *L5* (Thompson, 1924), ⲛ̀ϫⲉ (*L6*), (*M*), *V*, *F*, *B;* ⲛ̄ⲕⲧⲟⲟⲕ or ⊥ⲕⲧⲟⲕ, premature(ly), with no parallels elsewhere in Coptic (Prv. 10:6, ἄωρος, ⲛ̄ϣⲁⲣⲁϩⲉ *A*, *S*, ⲙ̀ⲡⲁⲧⲉ ⲧϩⲟϯ ϣⲱⲡⲓ *B;* Prv. 11:30, ἄωρος, ϩⲛ̄ ⲟⲩⲙⲛ̄ⲧϣⲁⲣ ⲁϩⲉ *S*, ϩⲛ̄ etc. . . . *A*, ⲙ̀ⲡⲁⲧⲉ ⲧϩⲟϯ ϣⲱⲡⲓ *B*, cf. demotic *gtg*, sudden(ly); Vycichl, 1983, p. 168a); ⲛⲁⲣⲟ, to see, very probably a back formation from ⲛⲁⲣⲟ⸗, which is a contraction for ⲛⲁ(ⲩ ⲁ)ⲣⲟ⸗ (cf. Černý, 1971); ⲛ̄ⲧⲃⲉ- in ⲛ̄ⲧⲃⲉ ⲡⲁï ⲕ, so that is why, but elsewhere ⲉⲧⲃⲉ- (even ⲉⲧⲃⲉ ⲡⲁï, Prv. 7:15), cf. ⲉⲧⲃⲉ- *S*, *A*, *L*, *M*, *W*, *V*, *F*, ⲉⲑⲃⲉ- *B* (demotic *r db3* etc., Vycichl, 1983, p. 47b); ⲛⲟⲩϫⳉ, to sprinkle, cf. ⲛⲟⲩϫϩ *A*, ⲛⲟⲩϫⲕ̄, ⲛⲟⲩϫϭ̄, ⲛⲟⲩϫ *S*, ⲛⲟⲩϫϧ *B* (cf. demotic *ndh* etc., Vycichl, 1983, p. 152b).

ⲡⲱϫⳉ, to smother; cf. ⲡⲱϫϩ̄ *A*, ⲡⲱϫϭ̄, ⲡⲱϫⲕ̄, ⲡⲱϫⲧ̄ *S*, ⲡⲱϫ *S* (or S^f) (cf. demotic *pdh*, Vycichl, 1983, p. 168a).

The archaic ⲣⲙ̄ⲉϥ- (masc.), ⲣⲙ̄ⲉⲥ- (fem.), ⲣⲙ̄ⲉⲩ- (pl.), ⲣⲙ̄ⲉⲧ- (indefinite), and not (never) ⲣⲉϥ-, the agent prefix common to all the Coptic dialects (ⲗⲉϥ- *F*); such archaic forms only appear occasionally elsewhere or at least are always in a minority: ⲣⲙ̄(ⲙ)ⲉϥ- *A*, ⲣⲱⲙ(ⲉ)ⲉϥ-, ⲣⲙ̄ⲙⲉϥ-, ⲣⲱⲙⲉⲧ- *L6* (Tractatus Tripartitus).

ⲧⳉⲡⲟ etc., to beget, bring forth, acquire; cf. ⲧϩⲡⲟ *A*, ϫⲡⲟ *L*, *S*, ϫⲡⲁ *M*, (*W*), (*V*), *F*, ϫⲫⲟ *B*.

ⲱ⊥ϧ (rarely ⲱⲱ⊥ϧ or ⲱ(ⲱ–ϧ), life; cf. ⲱⲛϩ *A*, ⲱⲛϩ̄ *S*, *L4*, *W*, *V*, *F*, ⲱ(ⲱ)ⲛϩ̄ *L6*, *L5* (except ⲱⲱϩ in the unpublished Gospel of John manuscript from Dublin; cf. Kasser, 1981a), ⲟⲛϩ *M*, ⲱⲛϧ *B*.

ϧⲓⲏ etc., road; cf. ϩⲓⲏ *S*, *L*, *M*, *V*, *F*.

ϩⲓⲁ, something; cf. ϩⲗⲓ *B*, ϩⲗⲉⲓ *A*, *L6* (very rarely), ϩⲓ *M*, *W* (always "someone"); *P* uses also ⲗⲁⲁⲩ(ⲉ); ϩⲉⲗⲁⲕ, keep, the sole parallel for which in Coptic is ϩⲉⲗⲏϭ *L4* (neither *P* nor *L4* uses the lexeme ϩⲁⲣⲉϩ *S*, *M*, ⲉⲣⲏϩ *A*, ⲁⲣⲏϩ *L5*, *L6*, ⲁⲣⲉϩ *W*, *V*, *B*, ⲁⲗⲉϩ *F*); ϩⲓⲛⲏⲙ, sleep, cf. ϩⲓⲛⲏⲃ *S*, *A*, *L*, *M*, *V*, *F*, ϩⲓⲛⲓⲙ *B;* ϩⲏⲣ† in the expression ⲉϥϩⲏⲣ ⲁⲣⲟϥ ⲁ, unawares (Prv. 6:15 ἐξαπίνης, ϩⲛ ⲟⲩⲥϩ̄ⲛⲉ *A*, ϩⲛ̄ ⲟⲩϣⲥ̄ⲛⲉ *S*, ϧⲉⲛ ⲟⲩⲉ̀ⲝⲁⲡⲓⲛⲁ *B;* Prv. 13:23 reads rather ⲥⲉϩⲏⲧ[ϥ]; cf. Kasser, 1973–1975, Vol. 2, p. 324b), should be connected with *S* ϩⲱⲣ to guard against, take heed (Crum, 1939, p. 697b); ϩⲥⲓⲙⲉ, woman, cf. (ⲥ)ϩⲓⲙⲉ *S*, *A*, *L*, *M*, ⲥϩⲓⲙⲓ *V*, *F*, *B;* ϩⲱ(ⲱ)ⲧⲙ, wither, fade, expire, be quenched, extinguished (should be connected with ϩⲱϭⲃ̄, ϩⲉϭⲙ̄-, etc. *S* (ibid., p. 744b); Prv. 10:7 and 13:9 σβεννύναι, ⲃⲱⲕ *A*, ϫⲉⲛⲁ *S*, ϭⲉⲛⲟ *B;* this ϩⲱϭⲃ̄, *ϩⲱϭⲙ̄ could at a stretch have been confused with ϩⲱⲧⲡ̄ (ibid., p. 724b), in the sense of "be extinguished" like a star setting; *P* uses ϩⲱⲧⲡ only in the sense of "to be reconciled," Prv. 6:35 and 15:28a); connected with ϩⲟⲩⲟ is the expression corresponding to ⲛ̄ϩ(ⲟⲩ)ⲟⲉⲓⲧ ⲁ- or ⊥ϩ(ⲟⲩ)ⲟⲉⲓⲧ ⲁ-, more than, which corresponds to ⲛ̄ϩⲟⲩⲟ ⲁ- *A*, ⲉϩⲟⲩⲉ- *S*, ⲉ̀ϩⲟⲧⲉ- *B;* the *P* form seems close to ⲛ̀ϩⲟⲩⲁ̀ⲉⲓⲥⲧⲉ ⲉ-, ⲉ̀ϩⲟⲩⲁ̀ⲉⲓⲥⲧⲉ- *M*, ⲉϩⲟⲩⲁï̀ⲥⲧ(ⲉ)- *V*, *F*, ⲉϩⲟⲩⲁï̀ⲥⲧⲉ ⲉ- *F56*, ⲉϩⲟⲩⲁⲥⲧⲉ- *F7* (cf. exceptional ⲉϩⲟⲩⲟⲉⲓⲥⲧⲉ *S*, Crum, 1939, p. 736a).

BIBLIOGRAPHY

Allberry, C. R. C. *A Manichaean Psalmbook.* Stuttgart, 1938.

Attridge, H. W., ed. *Nag Hammadi Codex I (The Jung Codex), Introduction, Texts, Translations, Indices.* Nag Hammadi Studies 22. Leiden, 1985.

Böhlig, A. *Kephalaia: Zweite Hälfte* (Lieferung 11–12). Stuttgart, 1966.

[Böhlig, A., and H. J. Polotsky]. *Kephalaia: Erste Hälfte* (Lieferung 1–10). Stuttgart, 1940.

Bourguet, P. du. *Grammaire fonctionnelle et progressive de l'égyptien démotique*. Louvain, 1976.

Černý, J.; P. E. Kahle; and R. Parker. "The Old Coptic Horoscope." *Journal of Egyptian Archaeology* 43 (1957):86–100.

______. "Coalescence of Verbs with Prepositions in Coptic." *Zeitschrift für ägyptische Sprache und Altertumskunde* 97 (1971):44–46.

Crum, W. E. *A Coptic Dictionary*. Oxford, 1939.

Funk, W.-P. "Die Morphologie der Perfektkonjugation im NH-subachmimischen Dialekt." *Zeitschrift für ägyptische Sprache und Altertumskunde* 111 (1984):110–30.

Kasser, R. *Papyrus Bodmer VI: Livre des Proverbes*. CSCO 194–195. Louvain, 1960.

______. "Papyrus Londiniensis 98 (The Old Coptic Horoscope) and Papyrus Bodmer VI." *Journal of Egyptian Archaeology* 49 (1963):157–60.

______. "Prolégomènes à un essai de classification systématique des dialectes et subdialectes coptes selon les critères de la phonétique, II, Alphabets et systèmes phonétiques." *Muséon* 93 (1980):237–97.

______. "Usages de la surligne dans le P. Bodmer VI, notes additionnelles." *Bulletin de la Société d'égyptologie, Genève* 5 (1981a):23–32.

______. "Voyelles en fonction consonantique, consonnes en fonction vocalique, et classes de phonèmes en copte." *Bulletin de la Société d'égyptologie, Genève* 5 (1981b):33–50.

______. "Le Dialecte protosaïdique de Thèbes." *Archiv für Papyrusforschung* 28 (1982):67–81.

______. "Le parfait I copte ⲁ- et ⲁϩⲁ- et le langage de l'étrangère (Prov. 6,24–26 et 7,15–16)." *Aegyptus* 64 (1984):229–36.

______. "Gémination de voyelles dans le P. Bodmer VI." In *Acts of the Second International Congress of Coptic Studies, Rome 22–26 September 1980*, ed. T. Orlandi and F. Wisse, pp. 89–120. Rome, 1985.

Kasser, R.; M. Malinine; H.-C. Puech; G. Quispel; J. Zandee; W. Vycichl; and R. McL. Wilson. *Tractatus Tripartitus*, Vol. 1, *Pars I, De Supernis, Codex Jung f. XXVI^{r}–f. LII^{v} (p. 51–104)*, Vol. 2, *Pars II, De Creatione Hominis, Pars III, De Generibus Tribus, Codex Jung f. LII^{v}–LXX^{v}* (p. 104–140). Bern, 1973–1975.

Malinine, M.; H.-C. Puech; and G. Quispel. *Evangelium Veritatis, Codex Jung f. VIII^{v}–XVI^{v} (p. 16–32), f. XIX^{r}–XXII^{r} (p. 37–43)*. Zurich, 1956.

Malinine, M.; H.-C. Puech; G. Quispel; W. C. Till; R. McL. Wilson. *Evangelium Veritatis (Supplementum), Codex Jung f. XVII^{r}–XVIII^{v} (p. 33–36)*. Zurich, 1961.

Malinine, M.; H.-C. Puech; G. Quispel; W. C. Till; R. McL. Wilson; and J. Zandee. *De Resurrectione (Epistula ad Rheginum), Codex Jung f. XXII^{r}–f. XXV^{v} (p. 43–50)*. Zurich, 1963.

Nagel, P. "Der frühkoptische Dialekt von Theben." In *Koptologische Studien in der DDR*, pp. 30–49. *Wissenschaftliche Zeitschrift der Martin-Luther-Universität Halle-Wittenberg,* Sonderheft. Halle-Wittenberg, 1965.

Osing, J. *Der spätägyptische Papyrus B.M. 10808*. Wiesbaden, 1976.

Pearson, B. A., and S. Giversen. *Nag Hammadi Codices IX and X*. Nag Hammadi Studies 15. Leiden, 1981.

Polotsky, H. J. "Zur koptischen Lautlehre I." *Zeitschrift für ägyptische Sprache und Altertumskunde* 67 (1931):74–77.

______. *Manichäische Homilien*. Stuttgart, 1934.

Schmidt, C. *Acta Pauli aus der Heidelberger koptischen Handschrift Nr 1*. Leipzig, 1905.

______. "Ein neues Fragment der Heidelberger Acta Pauli." In *Sitzungsberichte der Berliner Akademie der Wissenschaften, Philosophisch-Historische Klasse*, pp. 216–20. Berlin, 1909.

Thomassen, E., and L. Painchaud. *Le Traité triparti (NH 1.5), texte établi, introduit et commenté par E. Thomassen; traduit par L. Painchaud et E. Thomassen*. Bibliothèque copte de Nag Hammadi, section "textes," 19. Québec, 1989.

Thompson, H. *The Gospel of St. John According to the Earliest Coptic Manuscript*. London, 1924.

Vergote, J. *Phonétique historique de l'égyptien, les consonnes*. Louvain, 1945.

Vycichl, W. *Dictionnaire étymologique de la langue copte*. Louvain, 1983.

RODOLPHE KASSER

DIALECTS. The geographical characteristics of the habitable area of Egypt favored the subdivision of its language. One may note first of all two linguistic entities, "languages" rather than "dialects," of very wide scope and more than local—indeed, more than regional—character. The first of these corresponds to the Nile Delta and the second to the Nile Valley above the Delta. These are in turn (probably in the Delta, certainly in the valley) subdivided into smaller linguistic units (see especially, although with partially divergent opinions, Kahle, 1954, pp. 193–278; Kasser, 1982; Krause, 1979; Layton, 1976; Vergote, 1973, pp. 53–59; Worrell, 1934, pp. 63–82; and DIALECTS, GROUPING AND MAJOR GROUPS OF and GEOGRAPHY, DIALECTAL).

It appears very likely that BOHAIRIC (*B*) was the indigenous language common to the whole of the Nile Delta. It is called a "vehicular," or supralocal, language because it permitted the inhabitants of the different regions of this Delta (where each spoke his local dialect) to understand one another. (These lo-

TABLE 1. *Characteristic Lexemes in the Principal Coptic Dialects and Subdialects*

	"LANGUAGE"	"WITHOUT"	"AND"
A	éspe	at-	aóu
pL	[éspe]	at-	aóu
L	éspe	at-	auṓ
M	éspe	a(ei)t-	auṓ
V	[éspi]	at-	auṓ
F	[éspi]	at-	auṓ
			(áha)
F56	[éspi]	at-	auṓ
F7	[éspi]	a(ie)t-	áha
			(auṓ)
H	[áspi]	at-	auṓ
P	[áspe]	at-	auṓ
S	áspe	at-	auṓ
B74!	[áspi]	at-	ouóhe
B	áspi	at-	ouóh
		ath-	

The following may be observed with regard to *L: auṓ L4, L5, L6,* but also (especially) *áhan* or *áhn L4, ouáha* or *ouáhn,* etc. *L6; petaf- L4* is *pentaf- L5, L6; kṓ L4, L5* is *kṓe L6; méie L4* is *máeie L5, L6; méeine L4* is *máein L5, L6,* with *S; nábe L4, L5* is *nábi L6,* with *[pL]; nji L4* is *ji L5, nci L6; péi L4* is *péei L5, L6; pei- L4* is *peei- L5, L6; ref- L4, L5, L6,* but also *rōmef- L6, rmmef- L6, rmef- L4* (rare) with *A* (rare) etc., and everywhere *rmef-*, etc. *P; sṓtme L4* is *sṓtm L5, L6; ouṓshe L4, L6* is *ouṓsh L5; ṓnh L4* is *ṓō(n)h L5, ṓ(ō)nh L6; séje L4, L5* is *shéje L6; shéi L4* is *shéei L5, L6; jṓme L4* is *jṓōme* [*L5*], *L6; jáse L4, L5* is *jási L6,* with *pL.*

With regard to *M: at-* before certain words (e.g., *shéu*), and a little more frequently still *aeit-* before other words (the case of *atnée* or *aeitnée* is not yet attested); *pethaf-* or sometimes *petehaf-; ncē,* but also (fairly rare) *nje,* etc.

With regard to *V: petaf-*, also *pentaf-*, more rarely [*petehaf-*] *V,* but also *petehaf-* (rarely *pethaf-*) *W;* sometimes *náj* also *V4* (idiolectal?); *nje* (rarely *nji*) *V* is *nji* W; *sháp V4, W, sháap V5;* fairly often *shéji* also in *V4* (idiolectal?); *jṓōme,* alone attested, but poorly, should be *jṓme V4, W, jṓōme V5.*

With regard to *F: auṓ F4, F5,* but also sometimes *áha F5; pentaf- F5, petaf- F4, (F5); méei F5* is *méi F4; nḗf F5* is *néf F4; péei F5* is *péi F4; tṓh F5, tóh F4; sháap F5* is *sháp F4; jṓōme F5* would be [*jṓme*] *F4.*

With regard to *F7: áha,* but also sometimes *auṓ.*

With regard to *H:* [*kḗmi*] *H* is *kḗmē H!; rṓmi H* is *rṓmē H!; shṓpi H* is *shṓpē H!; sháji H* is *shájē H!* ([*jṓmi*] or [*jṓōmi*]) *H* is *jṓmē H!; jási H* would be [*jásē*] *H!.*

With regard to *P: ō'ḥ* (ⲱ-ϧ) three cases, *ōō'ḥ* three cases, *ōōnḥ* (ⲱⲱ-ϧ) one case.

With regard to *B: ath- B* before the (autochthonous) voiced consonants (b, l, m, n, r) and before the glides (i and (o)u with the phonological value of a consonant, for example, at the beginning of the word *iṓt,* father, and ouṓsh, wish); but even in these cases *G* always has *at-; eból B* is *epól G; etemmáu B5* is *etemmá B4, B74; phái B* is *pái G; phḗ B* is *pḗ G; sṓtem B* is *sódem G; thṓh* or *thóh B* (two different etymologies; cf. Vycichl, 1983, p. 226); *ounóf B* is perhaps *ounṓph G* (idiolectal[?]; probably to be pronounced *ounṓf*); *ouṓsh B* is *bóusz G* (probably to be pronounced *vóush*); *ouóh B5* is *ouóhe B4, B74* (and also *G* apparently); *hṓb B* is *ṓb G; jhí B4, B5* is *jí B74.* The majority of the other specific forms of *G* (probably without phonological consequences) will be found in DIALECT G.

cal idioms very probably existed there, as elsewhere, even if the paucity of discoveries of texts in the soil of the Delta, which is too damp, prevents detection of these dialects; one among them could be the mysterious DIALECT G.) On the other hand, it is certain that the vehicular language of the whole valley of the Egyptian Nile above the Delta was SAHIDIC (*S,* accompanied for some time in the Theban region by DIALECT P, a PROTODIALECT that often looks like what can be known about the logical predecessor of *S,* a tentatively reconstructed **pS,* proto-Sahidic), an autochthonous language dominating (then tending gradually to stifle) the multiple local and regional dialects of this habitable zone, relatively narrow but

TABLE 1. *(continued)*

	"WHAT?"	FIRST PERFECT, SING.3.MASC.	"TO, FOR"	"OUT(WARD)" ETC.	RELATIVE PERFECT, SING.3.MASC.
A	éḥ	af-	a-	abál	etaf- petaf-
pL	[éç]	af-	a-	abál	[etaf-] [petaf-]
L	ésh	af-	a-	abál	e(n)taf- pe(n)taf-
M	ésh	haf-	e-	ebál	ethaf- pethaf-
V	ésh	(h)af-	e-	ebál	et(eh)af- etc. pet(eh)af- etc.
F	ésh	af-	e-	ebál	entaf- pentaf-
F56	ésh	af-	e-	ebál	entaf- pentaf-
F7	ésh	af-	e-	ebál	entaf- pentaf-
H	[ásh]	ab-	[zero]	bál	tab- pēntab-
P	áç	af-	a-	aból	etaf- petaf-
S	ásh	af-	e-	eból	(e)ntaf- pentaf-
B74!	ásh	af-	e-	eból	etaf- [pḗ] etaf-
B	ásh	af-	e-	eból	etaf- phḗ etaf-

extending for nearly five hundred miles.

Moving upstream from immediately above the Delta (the land of the Bohairic dialectal group), among the various local dialects of the valley that have left sufficient traces in extant texts, this article will follow the chain that runs from classical *B* (to the north) to *A* (the so-called AKHMIMIC dialect, which is frequently considered the ancient local dialect of Thebes and thus the most southerly of the known Coptic dialects). The first to call for mention will be the various subdialects of FAYYUMIC. Chief among those with lambdacism are *F7*, a kind of "north Fayyumic" presenting interesting consonantal similarities with the Bohairic subdialect *B74*, a kind of "south Bohairic," a transition between the dialects of lower Middle Egypt and *B4* (cf. Kasser, 1981, p. 92), and *B5*, called "classical Bohairic," still further to the north; *F5*, Fayyumic of classical type, abundantly attested but relatively late; and *F4*, of more ancient attestation, with some similarities with *V*. Chief among the forms without lambdacism are *V*, also called "south Fayyumic"; and, at the extreme southern limit of the "Fayyumic" group and almost in the MESOKEMIC dialectal group, the idiom *W* (or "Crypto-Mesokemic with South Fayyumic phonology"). With Mesokemic, or Middle Egyptian (*M*), located immediately to the south of *W*, one is no longer in the Fayyumic dialectal group, Mesokemic being an independent group.

Should one then locate on the south of *M* (between *M* and *L*) the strange DIALECT H (also known as Hermopolitan or Ashmuninic)? In truth, it is rath-

TABLE 1. *Characteristic Lexemes in the Principal Coptic Dialects and Subdialects (continued)*

	CIRCUM-STANTIAL PRESENT, SING.3.MASC.	"MAKE, DO"	"PLACE, LEAVE" ETC.	"EGYPT" AND "EGYPTIAN"	"GUILE"	"LOVE"
A	ef-	éire	kóu	kḗme rmnkḗme	kráf	mé(e)ie
pL	ef-	[éire]	[kṓ]	[kḗme] [rmnkḗme]	kráf	[m]éie
L	ef-	éire	kṓ(e)	kḗme rmnkḗme	kráf	méie máeie
M	ef-	éire	kṓ	kḗme rmnkḗme	kráf	mḗie
V	ef-	íri	kṓ	[kḗmi] rmn[kḗmi]	[kráf]	mḗi
F	ef-	íli	kṓ	kḗmi lemnkḗmi	kláf	mḗi
F56	ef-	íli	kṓ	kḗmi lemnkḗmi	[kláb]	[mḗi]
F7	ef-	(é)ili	kṓ	kḗmi [lemn]kḗmi	[kláf]	mḗi
H	eb-	íri	kṓ	[kḗmi] rēm[kḗmi]	kráb	[mḗi (?)]
P	ef-	(é)ire	k̈ṓ	k̈ḗme rmnkḗme	k̈róf	méei
S	ef-	éire	kṓ	kḗme rmnkḗme	króf	mé
B74!	ef-	íri	kṓ	kḗmi remnkḗmi	króf	méi
B	ef-	íri	khṓ	khḗmi remnkhḗmi	khróf	méi

er difficult to locate exactly, despite the hypothetical name assigned to it; one must recall that some of its characteristics caused it to be considered formerly as a kind of Fayyumic, certainly very barbaric and, in any case, without lambdacism; however, many of its features also bring it close to *S*, in addition to its very evolved if not decadent structures (see METADIALECT). It is also very likely that the regional dialect that became the classical *S*, the vehicular language of the whole valley of the Egyptian Nile above the Delta, originated between *M* and *L*.

However that may be, according to the most common opinion of Coptologists, one then finds, further to the north of *M*, in the region of Asyūṭ and upstream, the different varieties of LYCOPOLITAN, or Subakhmimic. "Subakhmimic" is a rather deceptive name and has been almost completely abandoned: it stemmed from the belief, held for some time at the beginning of the twentieth century and soon revealed to be untenable, that *L* was a kind of subdialect of Akhmimic, *A*, which it certainly is not, in any of its varieties. The varieties of *L* are *L4*, attested by the Manichaean texts; *L5*, found above all in an important Johannine manuscript, published by Thompson (1924); and *L6*, known from the published non-Sahidic Gnostic texts and from the Heidelberg manuscript of the Acta Pauli, published by Schmidt (1904, 1909). (With regard to these Lycopolitan or, better, LYCO-DIOSPOLITAN varieties, including DIALECT i, or proto-Lyco-(Dios)politan, *pL*, see

TABLE 1. *(continued)*

	"TRUTH" ETC. AND "THE TRUTH"	"THERE" AND "THAT"	"SIGN"	"PITY" AND "PITILESS"	"SIN"
A	míe	mmó	mé(e)ine	náe	nábe
	tmíe	etmmó		atnáe	
pL	míe	mmó	[méei]ne	[náe]	[nábi]
	tmíe	etmmó		at[náe]	
L	mḗe	mméu	méeine	náe	nábi
	tmée	etmméu	máein	atnáe	nábe
M	mée	mmé	méein	née	nábe
	tmée	etmmé		a(ei)tnée	
V	méi	mméu	mḗin	néi	nábi
	tméi	etmméu		atnéi	
	timéi				
F	mé(e)i	mméu	mḗin	néei	nábi
	tmé(e)i	etmméu		atnéei	
	timé(e)i				
F56	méei	mméu	[mḗin]	néei	nábi
	tméei	etmméu		atnéei	
	timéei				
F7	méi	mméu	[mḗin]	néi	nábi
	tméi	etmméu		a(ie)tnéi	
	timéi				
H	mḗei	máou	máein	ná	nábi
	tmḗei	etēmáou		atná	
	tēmḗei				
P	mḗi	mmáu	mḗein	náe	nóbe
	tmḗi	etmmáu		atnáe	
S	mé	mmáu	máein	ná	nóbe
	tmé	etmmáu		atná	
B74!	mḗi	mmá	mḗini	nái	nóbi
	tmḗi	etemmá		atnái	
	timḗi				
B	mḗi	mmáu	mḗini	nái	nóbi
	thmḗi	etemmáu		athnái	
	timḗi				

Kasser, 1984; Funk, 1985; and PROTODIALECT.)

Still further to the south, probably around Akhmīm and perhaps even as far as Thebes (if not Aswan), seems to be the domain of Akhmimic, which was perhaps outflanked on the south (at Thebes and with *P*?) by some variety of *L*, which tended to function as a semivehicular, or supralocal, language (see DIALECT, IMMIGRANT); of this function *L* was to be dispossessed by the most vigorous and active vehicular language of the whole Egyptian Nile Valley to the south of the Delta—*S*.

It would be tedious to describe afresh here all these dialects and subdialects, each of which is treated, separately or in groups, in one or other of the special linguistic articles of this encyclopedia. Here, however, is a list of the sigla of these idioms, in alphabetical order and with mention of the article in which it is presented.

TABLE 1. *Characteristic Lexemes in the Principal Coptic Dialects and Subdialects (continued)*

	"EVERY"	"OF" (GENITIVE PREP.)	"TO HIM" (DATIVE PREP., SING.3.MASC.)	"GREAT," LARGE"	"THAT IS" (PROLEPTIC PARTICLE)	"THIS"	"THIS . . ."
A	ním	nte-	néf	nác	nci	péi	pei-
pL	[ním]	nte-	néf	nác	nci	péi	pei-
L	ním	nte-	néf	nác	nji	pé(e)i	pe(e)i-
M	ním	nte-	néf	nác	ncē	péi	pei-
V	níbi	nte-	néf	náj̈	nje	péi	pei-
F	níbi	nte-	nḗf	náj̈	nje	péi	pei-
F56	níbi	nte-	nḗb	náj̈	nje	péi	pei-
F7	ními	nte-	néf	náj	nji	péi	pei-
H	ním	tē-	náb	náj̈	j̈i	pái	pēi-
P	níb	nte-	náf	nák	nk(e)	pái	pi-
S	ním	nte-	náf	nóc	nci	pái	pei-
B74!	níben	nte-	náf	níshti	nje	pái	pai-
B	níben	nte-	náf	níshti	nje	phái	pai-

A See AKHMIMIC.

B Equals *B5* in agreement with *B4;* see BOHAIRIC.

B4 Bohairic subdialect; see examples below and Kasser, 1981, p. 92.

B5 Classical Bohairic, in contrast to *B4* in the rare cases of disagreement between *B4* and *B5;* see BOHAIRIC.

B74 A kind of south Bohairic; see examples below and Kasser, 1981, pp. 93–94.

B74! See below.

F Equals *F5* in agreement with *F4;* see FAYYUMIC.

F4 Fayyumic subdialect, presented with *F.*

F5 Classical Fayyumic, in contrast to *F4* in cases of disagreement between *F4* and *F5;* see FAYYUMIC.

F56 A variety of *F5* very often replacing ϥ by ⲃ; presented with *F.*

F7 A kind of somewhat archaic "north Fayyumic"; presented with *F.*

G See DIALECT G.

H See DIALECT H.

H! See below.

i̇ See *pL.*

L Equals *L4* in agreement with *L5* and *L6;* see LYCOPOLITAN and LYCO-DIOSPOLITAN.

L4 Variety of *L* in the Manichaean texts; presented with *L.*

L5 Variety of *L* in the London papyrus of John, etc.; presented with *L.*

L6 Variety of *L* in the non-Sahidic Gnostic texts and the Heidelberg Acta Pauli; presented with *L.*

M See MESOKEMIC.

P See DIALECT P.

pL See DIALECT İ.

S See SAHIDIC.

V A kind of "south Fayyumic"; presented with *F.*

W A kind of "crypto-Mesokemic with South Fayyumic phonology"; presented with *F.*

To allow readers who are not Coptologists to sample in some way the "music," the sounds, of the Coptic language (truly an authentic form of the autochthonous Egyptian language) in its different dialectal varieties, it has seemed useful to present in Table 1 a list of some phonologically rather characteristic lexemes. These specimens illustrate the most striking characteristics of the dialects and subdialects. To make them more readily accessible, the Coptic is transliterated here, following the system chosen for the encyclopedia as a whole, but with the following remarks and adaptations.

The tonic accent of each word that has one is

TABLE 1. *Characteristic Lexemes in the Principal Coptic Dialects and Subdialects (continued)*

	COPULA SING. MASC.	POSSESSIVE ARTICLE: "HIS" (SING.MASC./SING. 3.MASC.), "THEIR" (SING.MASC./PL.3.)	"HE SAYS"	"MAN" "THE MAN" "THE MAN OF" "MAKER OF"	"NAME"	"VOICE"	"BROTHER"
A	pe	pf- pou-	pajéf	rṓme prṓme rm- ref-	rén	smí	sán
pL	pe	pf- pou-	pajéf	rṓme prṓme [rm-] ref-	[rén]	[smḗ]	[sán]
L	pe	pef- pou-	pajéf	rṓme prṓme rm- ref-	rén	smḗ	sán
M	pe	pef- peu-	pejéf	róme próme rm- ref-	rén	smḗ	sán
V	pe	pef- peu-	pejéf	rṓmi p(i)rṓmi rm- ref-	rén	smḗ	sán
F	pe	pef- peu-	pejéf	lṓmi p(i)lṓmi lem- lef-	lén	smḗ	sán
F56	pe	peb- peu-	pejéb	lṓmi p(i)lṓmi lem- lef-	lén	smḗ	sán
F7	pe	pef- peu-	[pejéf]	lṓmi p(i)lṓmi [lem-] lef-	lén	smḗ	sán
H	pē	pēb- pēu-	pējáb	rṓmi p(ē)rṓmi rēm- rēb-	rán	smḗ	[sán]
P	pe	pf- pou-	pajáf	rṓme prṓme rm- rmef-	rín	smē(́)	són
S	pe	pef- peu-	pejáf	rṓme prṓme rm- ref-	rán	smḗ	són
B74!	pe	pef- pou-	pejáf	rṓmi p(i)rṓmi rem- ref-	rán	smḗ	són
B	pe	pef- pou-	pejáf	rṓmi phrṓmi pirṓmi rem- ref-	rán	smḗ	són

TABLE 1. *Characteristic Lexemes in the Principal Coptic Dialects and Subdialects (continued)*

	"HEAR, LISTEN"	"WRITE"	"PURIFY"	"DISTURB, STIR"	"JOY"	"WILL" "THE WILL"
A	sṓtme	sẖéi	tbbouó	tṓḥ	ounáf	ouṓḥe pouṓḥe
pL	sṓtme	[sẖéi]	tb[bouó]	[tṓḥ]	[ounáf]	[ouṓçe] [pouṓçe]
L	sṓtm(e)	shéi	toubó	tṓh	ounáf	ouṓsh(e) pouṓsh(e)
M	sótm	shéi	toubá	tóh	ounáf	ouésh (pouésh (?))
V	sṓtm	shéi	tybbá	[tóh]	ounáf	ouṓsh p(i)ouṓsh
F	sṓtem	shéi	tybbá	tṓh	ounáf	ouṓsh p(i)ouṓsh
F56	sṓtm	shéi	tybbá	[tṓh]	ounáb	ouṓsh p(i)ouṓsh
F7	sṓtom	[shéi]	tybbá	tṓh	ounáf	ouṓsh p(i)ouṓsh
H	sṓtēm	[shái]	[tēbbá(?)]	[tṓh]	ounáb	ouṓsh p(ē)ouṓsh
P	sṓtm	sẖái	tbbó	tṓḥ	ounóf	ouṓç pouṓç
S	sṓtm	shái	tbbó	tṓh	ounóf	ouṓsh pouṓsh
B74!	sṓtem	shái	toubó	tṓh	ounóf	ouṓsh p(i)ouṓsh
B	sṓtem	sẖái	toubó	thṓḥ	ounóf	ouṓsh phouṓsh piouṓsh

noted by an acute accent placed above the vowel concerned. ⲃ b in *F56* and especially *H* is probably to be pronounced rather [v] (it is probably the same in *G*). ⲎⲎ and ⲞⲞ in *P* (when this vowel duplication indicates simply "one" vowel, but accentuated [see Kasser, 1985], and not the tonic vowel followed by /ʾ/ [see ALEPH]) are rendered respectively by ē(´) and o(´) and not by ḗē or ṓō as everywhere else. In the autochthonous Coptic vocabulary of *P*, ⲕ is rendered by k and ⲗ by k̈ (the first possibly to be pronounced a little more to the back of the throat, somewhat like q *qoph*, the second rather to the front of the throat; but it remains most probable that the k in the autochthonous vocabulary *P* has the value of c in the other dialects, and the k̈ of the autochthonous *P* (like the k of Copto-Greek *p*) that of k elsewhere. ꝁ in *P* is rendered by k(e). ϣ̈ in *pL* and ⳉ in *P* are rendered by ç (pronounced like the ch in German *ich*, or nearly like the initial h in English *human*, and thus to be distinguished from ϣ sh, German sch). ⊥ in *P* is rendered by ʾ (which one must beware of confusing with the apostrophe ʼ which serves to distinguish s'h ⲥϩ from sh ϣ). Finally, one cannot render the polyvalent ϭ of the various Coptic idioms uniformly by c, for though c fits for *A*, *L*, *M*, and *S*, ϭ in *W*, *V*, *F4*, *F5*, and *H* has probably the value of j̈ (to be distinguished in pronunciation, without one's knowing exactly how, from j ϫ), and ϭ in *B5* and *B4* has the value of jh. (*P*, *F7*, and *B74* do not have any ϭ.)

Only the thirteen principal Coptic idioms and (sub)dialects are presented in the table, some sup-

TABLE 1. *(continued)*

	"LIVE"	"BECOME" AND "BE"	"USE, VALUE"	"SAYING," WORD"	"SELF"	"WORK, THING"	"IN"
A	ṓnḥ	ḥṓpe ḥóop	shéu	shéje	hóuou ⸗	hṓb	ḥn-
pL	ṓnḥ	çṓpe çó⟨o⟩p	[shéu]	shéje	[hṓō ⸗]	[hṓb]	ḥn-
L	ṓ(ō)nh (ṓōh)	shṓpe shóop	shéu	séje shéje	hṓō ⸗	hṓb	hn-
M	ónh	shópe sháp	shéu	séje	hṓ ⸗	hób	hn-
V	ṓnh	shṓpi shá(a)p	shéu	séji (shéji(?))	hṓ[ō] ⸗	hṓb	hn-
F	ṓnh	shṓpi shá(a)p	shéu	shéji	hṓō ⸗	hṓb	hn-
F56	ṓnah	shṓpi sháap	shéu	shéji	hṓō ⸗	hṓb	hn-
F7	ṓnh	shṓpi sháp	[shéu]	shéji	hṓ ⸗	hṓb	hin-
H	ṓnah	shṓpi sháap	sháou	sháji	[hṓō ⸗]	hṓb	hēn-
P	ṓ'ḥ	çṓpe çó'p	sháu	sháje	(hṓ ⸗)	hṓb	ḥn-
S	ṓnh	shṓpe shóop	sháu	sháje	hṓō ⸗	hṓb	hn-
B74!	ṓnh	shṓpi shóp	sháu	sáji	hṓ ⸗	hṓb	hen-
B	ṓnḥ	shṓpi shóp	s̀háu	sáji	hṓ ⸗	hṓb	ḥen-

plementary linguistic forms appearing in addition in the footnotes to the table. Thus, *L4*, *L5*, and *L6* are noted in relation to one another (*L4* + *L5* + *L6* = *L*); *W* is noted in relation to *V* (= *V4* + *V5*); *F4* and *F5* are noted in relation to each other; *H!* is noted in relation to *H; B4* and *B74* (and even *G* when its forms are attested, in a few cases only) are noted in relation to one another and to *B*, which is almost always identical with *B5* (*B4* + *B5* = *B*). An exclamation mark indicates "metorthography"; thus, *H!* and *B74!* are, respectively, *H* and *B74* in metorthography. Metorthography is the new orthographic and phonological system toward which numerous copyists writing a dialect or subdialect are strongly tending; thus, in *H!* the final atonic vowel is ē rather than i; in *B74!* ḥ will be replaced by h and the aspiration typical of Bohairic, still vigorous in *B74* as in *B4* and *B5* (kh for k, ph for p, th for t, in certain well-defined conditions), will disappear (jh for j in *B4* and *B5* is already abandoned in *B74*).

BIBLIOGRAPHY

Funk, W.-P. "How Closely Related Are the Subakhmimic Dialects." *Zeitschrift für ägyptische Sprache und Altertumskunde* III (1984):110–30.

Kahle, P. E. *Bala'izah: Coptic Texts from Deir el-Bala'izah in Upper Egypt.* Oxford and London, 1954.

Kasser, R. "Prolégomènes à un essai de classification systématique des dialectes et subdialectes coptes selon les critères de la phonétique, III,

TABLE 1. *Characteristic Lexemes in the Principal Coptic Dialects and Subdialects (continued)*

	"THAT, BECAUSE"	"TAKE, RECEIVE"	"SAY"	"WRITTEN DOCUMENT, BOOK"	"BEGET, ACQUIRE"	"EXALT" AND "EXALTED, HIGH"
A	je	jí	jóu	jóu(ou)me	tḥpó	jíse jáse
pL	je	jí	jṓ	jṓme	[tçpó]	jíse jási
L	je	jí	jṓ	jṓme	jpó	jíse jási jáse
M	je	jí	jṓ	jóme	jpá	jíse jáse
V	je	jí	jṓ	jṓ(ō)me	jpá	jísi jási
F	je	jí	jṓ	jṓōme	jpá	jísi jási
F56	je	jí	jṓ	[jṓōme]	jpá	jísi [jási]
F7	je	jhí	jṓ	[jṓma]	jpá	jísi jási
H	jē	jí	jṓ	([jṓmi])	j̈pá	[jísi] jási
P	je	jí	jṓ	[jṓōma]	tçpó	jíse jóse
S	je	jí	jṓ	jṓōme	jpó	jíse jóse
B74!	je	jí	jṓ	jṓm	jpó	jísi jósi
B	je	jhí	jṓ	jṓm	jphó	jhísi jhósi

	"POWER, STRENGTH"	"VIOLENCE, INIQUITY"	"HAND"
A	cám	cáns	cíj
pL	[cám]	[cáns]	cíj
L	cám	cáns	cíj
M	cám	cáns	cíj
V	j̈ám	[j̈á]ns	j̈íj
F	j̈ám	j̈áns	j̈íj
F56	j̈ám	j̈áns	j̈íj
F7	jám	jás	jíjh
H	j̈ám	j̈ánēs	j̈íj̈
P	kóm	gko(-́)ns	kíj
S	cóm	cóns	cíj
B74!	jóm	jóns	jíj
B	jóm	jóns	jíj

Systèmes orthographiques et catégories dialectales." *Muséon* 94 (1981):91–152.

______. "Le Grand-Groupe dialectal copte de Haute-Egypte." *Bulletin de la Société d'égyptologie, Genève* 7 (1982):47–72.

______. "Orthographe et phonologie de la variété subdialectale lycopolitaine des textes gnostiques coptes de Nag Hammadi." *Muséon* 97 (1984):261–312.

______. "Gémination de voyelles dans le P. Bodmer VI." In *Acts of the Second International Congress of Coptic Studies, Rome, 22–26 September 1980,* ed. T. Orlandi and F. Wisse, pp. 89–120. Rome, 1985.

Krause, M. "Koptische Sprache." *Lexikon der Ägyptologie* 3 (1979):731–37.

Layton, B. "Coptic Language." In *Interpreter's Dictionary of the Bible,* Suppl. vol. pp. 174–79. Nashville, Tenn., 1976.

Schmidt, C. *Acta Pauli aus der Heidelberger koptischen Papyrushandschrift Nr. 1.* Leipzig, 1904.

______. "Ein neues Fragment der Heidelberger Acta Pauli." In *Sitzungsberichte der Berliner Akademie der Wissenschaften, Philosophisch-Historische Klasse,* pp. 216–20. Berlin, 1909.

Thompson, H. *The Gospel of St. John According to the Earliest Coptic Manuscript.* London, 1924.

Vergote, J. *Grammaire copte,* Ia, *Introduction, phonétique et phonologie, morphologie synthématique (structure des sémantèmes), partie synchronique.* Louvain, 1973.

Vycichl, W. *Dictionnaire étymologique de la langue copte.* Louvain, 1983.

Worrell, W. H. *Coptic Sounds.* Ann Arbor, Mich., 1934.

RODOLPHE KASSER

DIALECTS, GROUPING AND MAJOR GROUPS OF. The discovery of many Coptic manuscripts in the latter half of the twentieth century has led to a multiplication in the identification (sometimes disputed) of Coptic idioms, dialects, and subdialects, an identification based mainly on phonology, the most convenient and generally used criterion (see DIALECT, IMMIGRANT). The most likely working hypothesis that has been agreed upon is that the phonology of these idioms can be determined by analysis of their different orthographic systems; in practice, this is the only viable approach, since Coptic is a dead language. The increase in the number of known idioms is quite obvious: Stern (1880) has only three "dialects," *S, B,* and *F;* Crum (1939) has five, *S, B, F, A2 (= L),* and *A;* Kahle (1954) has six, *S, B, F, M, A2 (= L),* and *A;* Kasser (1964) has seven or eight, *S, (G?), B, F, M, A2 (= L), A,* and *P;* Kasser (1966), has nine, *S, G, B, F, M, A2 (= L), A,* and *P;* and Kasser (1973) reaches fifteen, of which, however, five are practically abandoned in Kasser (1981): *S, G, (D), B, (K), F, H, (N), M, L, İ, A, P, (C), (E).*

This multiplicity has led to revision of the very concept of "dialect" and "subdialect" (which should be rigorously distinguished from an IDIOLECT) so as to eliminate certain idioms that are possible but too poorly or too doubtfully attested and (despite Chaîne, 1934, pp. 2–3, and Kasser, 1974) to clarify dialectic filiations (Vergote, 1973b; Kasser, 1979; this concept should not be understood in too literal a way). Above all, the multiplicity has led to a classification of the different idioms into families or groups of dialects (Kasser, 1981, pp. 112–18) and then into major groups, to avoid complicating in the extreme the view of the phonetic and phonological facts of Coptic Egypt and to allow its more convenient integration into an analysis (synchronic and diachronic) of the Egyptian language as a whole. (On the terminology here employed, see IDIOLECT, PROTODIALECT, METADIALECT, and MESODIALECT.)

Although presented through the medium of another terminology, such groups of dialects were distinguished by Stern (1880) when he contemplated the existence of two clearly distinct dialects, the Lower Egyptian and the Upper Egyptian, which elsewhere he preferred to call Bohairic and Sahidic, respectively, and when he defined *F* as "the third dialect, only a variant of Sahidic" and "of less importance." In the same way, Steindorff (1951) presented two groups of dialects: Upper Egyptian *(S, A, L, F)* and Lower Egyptian (*B,* and Bashmuric, a dialect practically unknown).

The grouping of "dialects" set out below is quite similar to that of Kasser (1981) but with some significant differences, the most important of which is the new valuation of *S* and *B:* they are no longer considered as "dialects" (as are, e.g., *A, L,* and *M*) but as "Coptic languages," that is, "vehicular," or supralocal, even supraregional common languages, which permitted the inhabitants of numerous Egyptian regions, where each spoke his own local dialect, to communicate easily and to understand one another. So *S* is recognized as the common speech of the whole valley of the Egyptian Nile above the Delta, and *B* (more hypothetically but nevertheless rather likely) is considered the language of the whole Nile Delta. Coptic (supralocal etc.) languages (in touch with many local and regional dialects, which influence and neutralize them appreciably) cannot be compared without great caution with individual (local or regional) dialects.

According to this system, each group of dialects has a "chief," a dialect that is well represented in texts and is the one with the largest number of phonological (and, as far as possible, morphosyntactical) elements characteristic of its group. In principle, those idioms which have in common a large number of consonantal and vocalic isophones belong to the same dialectal group. Indeed, consonantal isophones are normally the same within a dialectal group, but they may sometimes differ, so long as the differences are tolerable and not decisive. Consonantal differences are tolerable if they fit into the pattern of the normal evolution of a dialect (progressive neutralization), as in ḫ > /ç/ > /š/ (the protodialect with /ç/ will belong to the same group as the dialect that has /š/ < /ç/ if their vocalic isophones are in large part the same; cf. Kasser, 1981, p. 114). On the other hand, a consonantal difference is not tolerable if it cannot be registered in a pattern of normal dialectal evolution. Thus, although the vocalic isophones of *A* and of some members of *L* are largely the same, the decisive difference between *A* and *L* consists in the striking fact that in *A* alone of all the Coptic dialects ḫ > /x/ everywhere and ẖ also > /x/ steadily, and thus ḫ and ẖ merge into ⳉ = /x/ constantly and everywhere, whereas in all the other dialects almost all the ḫ > /ç/ > /š/ (merging with the other /š/ < š) and all the ẖ (with a few ḫ) > /x/ > /h/ (merging with the other /h/ < h). This excludes any integration of *A* into the same schema as, for example, *P* and *S* (e.g., **A* > **P* > **S*). It is inconceivable that if in *A* ḫ and ẖ have merged into /x/, this distinction should reappear at a later stage, some of these /x/ > /ç/ > /š/ because they derive from ḫ and other /x/ > /h/ because they derive from ẖ.

The six groups of dialects are listed below in an order assumed to correspond to their geographical order, from south to north. As a whole, this schema corresponds to a conception of dialectal geography (see GEOGRAPHY, DIALECTAL) wherein the situation of the chief of each group, thanks to comparison of the isophones (Vergote, 1973, Vol. 1a, pp. 55–56), may be determined in relation to at least two of the other chiefs (those closest to it), all these chiefs being practically placed on an equal footing vis-à-vis the criterion of localization constituted by their isophones. Since the approximate geographical situation of at least three of these chiefs seems relatively well known (from south to north, *A*, *F*, and *B*, leaving out a fourth, *M*, which poses a more delicate problem), it appears possible to determine that of the remaining two, *L* and *S*, with a high degree of probability: *L* stands between *A* and *S*, and hence to the north of *A*; *S* is a vehicular language (the southern koine of Egypt) in contact (near Memphis) with the second Egyptian vehicular language, *B* (the northern koine), and hence a strong vocalic similarity between *S* and *B* (probably due to the influence of some pre-*B* on some pre-*S* in pre-Coptic time; see Chaîne, 1934, pp. 13–18, and Satzinger, 1985). Nevertheless, most of the typical phonological and morphosyntactical features of *S* suggest that the particular pre-Coptic idiom that became *S* as a widespread common language (see DIALECT, IMMIGRANT) was located not directly near the Delta and *B*, but rather more to the south, between *L* and *M*.

In the following list of six groups, **//S** means "everywhere in contact with *S* as a supralocal vehicular language"; and **//B** means "for the subdialects *B4*, *B7*, *B74*, and probably *G*, if not for *K* and *K7*, everywhere in contact with *B* as a supralocal vehicular language." The presence of a question mark (?) indicates strong doubt as to the dialectal identity (i.e., the possibility that one is dealing with a "dialectoid").

Akhmimic Group (//S)

A: Dialect; chief of the group; further research will possibly permit the definition of some subdialects of *A* (one might in particular consider that 2 Mc. 5:27–6:21 in Lacau, 1911, somewhat archaic in a few of its peculiarities, attests very sporadically a kind of proto-AKHMIMIC [*pA*], a practically missing protodialect). See AKHMIMIC.

Lycopolitan Group (//S)

İ (or *pL*): Partly sporadic protodialect of *L* (LYCOPOLITAN or LYCO-DIOSPOLITAN; cf. DIALECT İ).
- *İ7*: Subdialect of *İ*, through partial neutralization and evolution toward *L*.

L: Dialect; chief of group.
- *L4*: Subdialect of *L*.
- *L5*: Subdialect of *L*.
- *L6*: Subdialect of *L*.

Sahidic Group (//S)

P: Partially sporadic protodialect; it can be considered a regional dialectal variety very like a kind of (reconstructed) proto-Sahidic, probably immigrant into the region of Thebes (southern region of *A* also, probably, and perhaps of some variety of *L*). See DIALECT P.

S: Language; chief of group. Further research will perhaps permit the definition of some (sub)dialects of *S*. See SAHIDIC.

Mesokemic Group (//S)

M: Dialect; chief of group. Further research will perhaps permit the definition of some subdialects of *M*. One might in particular consider that P. Mil. Copti 1 and the codex of the Psalms attest a variety of *M* that could be denominated *M4* and that the subdialect of Codex Scheide and Codex Glazier is *M5*. See MESOKEMIC.

W: See Fayyumic group.

Fayyumic Group (//S)

F: Dialect; chief of group.

F4: Subdialect of *F*.

F5: Subdialect of *F*; classical FAYYUMIC.

F7: Eccentric and somewhat archaic subdialect of *F*; possibly a marginal northern protodialect of a variety of *F* ill known and not attested later.

F8: Eccentric subdialect of *F*.

F9: Eccentric subdialect of *F*.

F4, *F5*, *F7*, *F8*, and *F9* all have the typical Fayyumic lambdacism.

V: Without lambdacism; mesodialect (between a dominant *F* and *W*, and further *M*) and in some ways a subdialect of *F4* etc. by neutralization.

W: Without lambdacism; mesodialect (between *V* and *M*). Has a typical FAYYUMIC orthography, on the one hand, but a typical Mesokemic morphosyntax, on the other hand; hence its name "crypto-Mesokemic." One might also associate it with the Mesokemic group.

Bohairic Group (//B)

B: Language; chief of group.

B4: (Sub)dialect of *B*, possibly rather marginal and to the south.

B5: (Sub)dialect of *B*; classical Bohairic.

B7: Eccentric and partially sporadic subdialect of *B*.

B74: Eccentric (sub)dialect of *B*; in some way subdialect of *B4*, and perhaps more to the south.

K: Mesodialect (between a very dominant *B* and *V* [or *S*]).

K7: Eccentric subdialect of *K* (still further removed from *V* than *K* is).

G: Partially sporadic mesodialect (between a very dominant *B* and *S* [?], with probably also a third component, perhaps partly Hellenic and difficult to determine).

Difficult to classify in any group remains *H*: mesodialect, on the one hand (between *S* and *M*, or rather *S* and *V*, itself a mesodialect associated with the Fayyumic group); on the other hand, a typical metadialect, but too poorly represented to allow one to define it at an earlier (classical) period. See DIALECT H.

As seen above, the distribution of the Coptic idioms into six dialectal groups and their geographical localization in relation to one another are essentially based on the comparison of the isophones of these idioms, consonantal, on the one hand, and vocalic, on the other. If, however, one observes that there are very few consonantal differences between the varieties of Coptic, that several of these differences can be put down to various degrees of progression of the late Egyptian consonantal evolution (Vergote, 1945, pp. 122–23) in the various Coptic idioms, and that the most neutralized idioms (*V*, still more *L*, and above all *S*) are the most difficult to situate in Coptic dialectal geography, then another method can be envisaged, producing different results and manifesting a different system of dialect grouping.

Based again (for want of anything better) on phonology as it is revealed by the various orthographic systems employed, this method would rely particularly on vocalic phonology, and especially the phonology of the tonic vowels. It thereby relegates to the level of secondary importance certain spectacular phenomena, such as the sonant atonal finals (phonologically vowels) in *S*, *M*, *L*, *B*, and *F* or the voiced consonants followed by /ə/ in *A* and in the *L4* Manichaean witnesses (Kasser, 1982c, p. 49, n. 5), and above all the ordinary atonal final vowels /ə/ *S*, *M*, *L*, *A* versus /i/ *B*, *F*, phenomena upon which one might have been tempted in the first place to base the most general divisions of Egypt into large supradialectal geographical zones. The result is that, setting aside certain phenomena of extension generally more limited (ibid., p. 50, n. 7) than the phenomena given the primary diacritical function, the observation of the vocalic constants noted in the systematic cases considered to have priority leads to a grouping of the six "classical" entities (two "languages," *S* and *B*, and four "dialects," *A*, *L*, *M*, and

F) two by two, and thus to a subdivision of the linguistic totality of Coptic Egypt not into six "dialectal groups" but into three "major dialectal regions":

I. The southern (dialects) major region (Upper Egypt), including *A* and *L* (and their subdialects, etc.).
II. The middle (dialects) major region (middle and lower Middle Egypt and the Fayyūm), including *M* and *F* (and their subdialects, etc., among them *V* and *W*).
III. The northern (dialects and vehicular language)–southern (vehicular language) major region (Lower Egypt [or the Delta], Middle Egypt, and Upper Egypt), including *B* and *S* (and their subdialects etc.). See Kasser, 1989.

By this process, one could work out a Coptic dialectal geography at one and the same time perhaps less precise and more nuanced than that tied to the conception of the six dialectal groups above. Even if one admits that the most neutralized idioms (*V*, still more *L*, and above all *S*) of the Egyptian Nile Valley above the Delta each had as principal antecedent some idiom that was in origin a local dialect, this tripartite system would envisage each of them in the Nile Valley as the vehicular language (potentially or effectively) of a given major region, without further specifying their origin (in contrast to *A*, *M*, and *F*). Thus, major region I would have as its only local dialect known at the present time *A* (Akhmīm and environs, perhaps fairly far to the south) but would have *L* as the semineutralized vehicular dialect of this whole region (viz., the zone of *A* and other zones to the south and north of it). Major region II would have as a local dialect *M* (environs of Oxyrhynchus?) and *F* (with various subdialects, the Fayyūm) but would have *V* as a slightly neutralized dialect tending to become vehicular for the region (viz., the zone of *M* and *F*, and some zone between *M* and *F*, and to the east of *F*). Major region III, superposing itself partially on major regions I and II, would have all the local dialects of these regions and both their supralocal dialects (potentially or effectively, *V* and *L*) and, above all, both the major Coptic vehicular languages, *S* and *B* (further in the Delta, of course, the local dialects or subdialects of Lower Egypt, and *K* and *K7* of lower Middle Egypt; see above, Bohairic group). One must remember here that *S*, being dominant throughout the Egyptian Nile Valley above the Delta, progressively stifled there *A*, *L*, *M*, *W*, *V*, and finally *F*.

Both systems (six groups of dialects or three major regions of dialects) are to be considered in the present state of knowledge in this field.

BIBLIOGRAPHY

Chaîne, M. *Eléments de grammaire dialectale copte.* Paris, 1933.

______. *Les Dialectes coptes assioutiques A2.* Paris, 1934.

Crum, W. E. *A Coptic Dictionary.* Oxford, 1939.

Kahle, P. E. *Bala'izah: Coptic Texts from Deir el-Bala'izah in Upper Egypt.* Oxford and London, 1954.

Kasser, R. *Compléments au dictionnaire copte de Crum.* Bibliothèque d'études coptes 7. Cairo, 1964.

______. "Compléments morphologiques au dictionnaire de Crum, le vocabulaire caractéristique des quatre nouveaux dialectes coptes: P, M, H et G." *Bulletin de l'Institut français d'archéologie orientale* 64 (1966):19–66.

______. "Les Dialectes coptes." *Bulletin de l'Institut français d'archéologie orientale* 73 (1973):71–101.

______. "Y a-t-il une généalogie des dialectes coptes?" In *Mélanges d'histoire des religions offerts à Henri-Charles Puech,* pp. 431–36. Paris, 1974.

______. "Relations de généalogie dialectale dans le domaine lycopolitain." *Bulletin de la Société d'égyptologie, Genève* 2 (1979):31–36.

______. "Prolégomènes à un essai de classification systématique des dialectes et subdialectes coptes selon les critères de la phonétique, III, Systèmes orthographiques et catégories dialectales." *Muséon* 94 (1981):87–148.

______. "Le Grand-Groupe dialectal copte de Haute-Egypte." *Bulletin de la Société d'égyptologie, Genève* 7 (1982):47–72.

______. "Le Grand-Groupe dialectal copte de Basse-Egypte et son extension véhiculaire panégyptienne." *Bulletin de la Société d' égyptologie, Genève* 13 (1989):73–82.

Krause, M. "Koptische Sprache." *Lexikon der Ägyptologie* 3 (1979):731–37.

Lacau, P. "Textes coptes en dialectes akhmîmique et sahidique." *Bulletin de l'Institut français d'archéologie orientale* 8 (1911):43–81.

Layton, B. "Coptic Language." In *Interpreter's Dictionary of the Bible,* Suppl. vol., pp. 174–79. Nashville, Tenn. 1976.

Satzinger, H. "On the Origin of the Sahidic Dialect." In *Acts of the Second International Congress of Coptic Studies, Rome, 22–26 September 1980,* ed. T. Orlandi and F. Wisse, pp. 307–312. Rome, 1985.

Schüssler, K. *Epistularum Catholicarum Versio Sahidica.* Münster, 1969.

Steindorff, G. *Lehrbuch der koptischen Grammatik.* Chicago, 1951.

Stern, L. *Koptische Grammatik.* Leipzig, 1880.

Vergote, J. *Phonétique historique de l'égyptien, les consonnes.* Louvain, 1945.

______. *Grammaire copte,* Vol. 1a, *Introduction, phonétique et phonologie, morphologie synthématique (structure des sémantèmes), partie synchronique,* Vol. 1b, *Introduction, phonétique et phonologie, morphologie synthématique (structure des sémantèmes), partie diachronique.* Louvain, 1973a.

______. "Le Dialecte copte P (P. Bodmer VI: Proverbes), essai d'identification." *Revue d'égyptologie* 25 (1973b):50–57.

Westendorf, W. *Koptisches Handwörterbuch, bearbeitet auf Grund des Koptischen Handwörterbuchs von Wilhelm Spiegelberg.* Heidelberg, 1977.

Worrell, W. H. *Coptic Sounds.* Ann Arbor, Mich., 1934.

RODOLPHE KASSER

DIALECTS, MORPHOLOGY OF COPTIC.

The existence of quite a number of differential traits in the fields of morphology and morphosyntax may serve to show that the Coptic literary "dialects" comprise not just different pronunciations and spellings, supported by slightly differing vocabularies, of the same linguistic system but, in fact, different normative systems of written communication reflecting more or less directly some of the locally, regionally, or even sometimes nationally balanced spoken idioms. To be sure, these literary dialects cannot be conceived of as mere transcriptional records of the spoken dialects behind them. One may safely assume that each of them had undergone various stages of balance and adjustment—be it through its "natural" usage as a regional or supraregional vernacular or through the exertion of some standardizing force in scribal centers—before it was found worthy of being employed as the literary standard whose specimens have survived. Yet these dialectal varieties still reveal so many diverging traits—phonological, grammatical, and lexical—that only if considered in their sustained proximity to each other can they be identified as varieties of one language. If only the records of, say, Bohairic and Akhmimic had survived as the two extremes of this continuum, one would hardly be able to treat them as "dialects" but would rather classify them as distinct, though closely related, languages.

If, as is usually done, the term "dialect" is taken to cover several more or less closely related varieties of Coptic (i.e. the varieties of Bohairic, Fayyumic, etc.), it seems that on the morphological and morphosyntactic levels, in general, there is greater similarity between dialects, but a lower degree of consistency (i.e., less standardization) within each dialect than there is on the phonological level. Quite a number of morphemic elements that would be typical of dialect D_1 may be used more or less regularly in a single text of dialect D_2: they are easily understood in this context not so much because they are supposed to be "known" from D_1 but because they may represent basic options of the Coptic language as a "diasystem." The higher a given phenomenon ranks in the system of Coptic grammar (or the closer it is to the fundamentals of Coptic syntax), the more does it seem to be capable of neutralization in terms of dialectal distinction, its remaining variability being influenced by communicative perspective, text type, and individual style.

As for the linguistic value of a given text or variety, what counts is not primarily its degree of accordance with any standards known from other sources (often termed "standardization") but its degree of *internal* standardization, which might be more adequately termed "normalization." If one takes a closer look at the actual dialectal varieties (i.e., grammatically homogenous corpora) of Coptic, it is remarkable to see that even in minor or marginal dialects, the degree of normalization in the morphological field is enormous. Both in terms of morphemic (syntactic) usage and the phonological representation of grammatical morphemes, the greater number of literary manuscripts and groups of manuscripts reveal a degree of normalization that is in no way inferior to their observation of general (morpheme-independent) phonological and orthographic norms. This normalized usage (or *état de langue*), notwithstanding all the inconsistencies so often deplored by scholars, should be one of the primary subjects of study with both major and minor varieties. *External* standardization, on the other hand, may be measured in terms of both the amount of manuscripts available for one variety and the amount of neighboring varieties shading into another central "dialect." Investigations of the latter sort (for a beginning, see Kasser, 1980–1981), which seem to be most promising in particular within the multiple-centered Akhmimic/Subakhmimic southern area and the more clearly triangular Bohairic/Fayyumic/Middle Egyptian northern area, will eventually contribute a great deal to the historical understanding of the•dialect situation and development in Coptic Egypt and provide a safer ground for pertinent hypotheses (which they are so much in need of).

Taking into account the large number of "supplementing" dialectal varieties of Coptic that have become known through publications during the last few decades or still await publication, and considering the deficient supply of information about the actual morpheme-stock in many of the crucial text editions, a review of the morphological relationship of Coptic dialects at the present time cannot exhaust the whole scale of known varieties. As a matter of fact, comprehensive comparative analysis will have to start by grouping and classifying the smallest discernible units of texts that follow a distinct linguistic norm and joining them gradually together into natural groups (major dialects), with the crucial isoglosses and differential traits being broadly discussed and accurately accounted for. This is one of the tasks of future research. What can be done in an article of the present format, however, is to provide a selection of standard varieties that are more or less typical of the six major literary dialects accepted so far by a greater number of Coptic scholars, *A, B, F, L, M,* and *S*, and a list of traits exemplifying their isoglosses, in an attempt to point out the complexity of the task before scholars.

The varieties referred to are, for *A*, the AKHMIMIC "medial" group of Exodus (Lacau, 1911), Epistula Apostolorum (Schmidt, 1919), and the Strasbourg Codex (Rösch, 1910); for *B*, biblical BOHAIRIC (in order to facilitate roughly "synchronic" comparability, only such traits as are in concord with the usage of the "old-Bohairic" manuscripts will be accepted here); for *F*, some representatives of classical FAYYUMIC proper (*F5*, second group in Asmus, 1904) such as St. John ap. Zoega, St. Mark (Elanskaya, 1969), Agathonicus (Erichsen, 1932), insofar as they are not discordant with earlier Fayyumic proper (*F4*, see, e.g., Kahle, 1954, pp. 286–90); for *L*, the Nag Hammadi type *(L6)* of Subakhmimic (i.e., LYCOPOLITAN or LYCO-DIOSPOLITAN), exposing its most valuable representative in Codex I, 2, The Apocryphon of James (Malinine et al., 1968; Kirchner, 1977); for *M*, St. Matthew (Schenke, 1981; see MESOKEMIC); and for *S*, biblical (in particular, New Testament) SAHIDIC. In order to round off the picture and facilitate taxonomical operations, two other important varieties shall be added: DIALECT P, the idiom of P. Bodmer VI (Kasser, 1960) for its outstanding characteristics, and the Manichaean type of Subakhmimic (or Lyco-Diospolitan), hereafter referred to as *L4*, that is to say, one variety of the group symbolized formerly as *L4* in Kasser (1980a, pp. 68–69, to the exclusion, notably, of Thompson's Gospel of John, *L5*), for its abundant corpus, with its most normalized representative being the Homilies (Polotsky, 1934). Of all the minor varieties whose representatives have been published so far, the latter two are without any doubt the most interesting. (Perhaps somewhat "less interesting" for the network of isoglosses are varieties such as that represented by St. John, ed. Husselman, 1962 [the most important member of Kasser's former *V*, now *W*], which does not reveal any single trait that is not shared by either *F* or *M*.)

"Morphological" traits, in the sense in which the term will be applied here, fall into three groups: (i) variables in terms of different phonological representations of the same Pan-Coptic, transdialectal morpheme, or "diamorpheme," which may be called "diamorphemic variables"; (ii) variables in terms of a different handling of allomorphic rules, or "allomorphic variables"; (iii) morphosyntactic variables, including some idiosyncratic grammatical morphs. While the latter two items seem to be fairly conclusive, some words of explanation may be needed with regard to (i).

To begin with, it must be noted that the majority of formal grammatical devices used in given paradigms and/or for given purposes are either phonemically and graphemically invariable for all Coptic dialects (in clear contrast to the majority of lexical morphemes) or their varying phonemic/graphemic representations are conditioned by general phonological rules. Such items cannot be the subject of a special morphological comparison. For instance, the vocalization of the stressed "stem" vowel in some prepositions *(status pronominales)* and the stressed personal pronouns strictly follows the general rules governing the vocalization of short stressed syllables, dependent on the type of the following consonant. Thus, for example, one finds for ⲟ:ⲁ:

A, L6, L4, M, F	*S, B*	
ⲁ/ⲉⲣⲁϥ	ⲉⲣⲟϥ	cf. ⲥⲁⲛ:ⲥⲟⲛ
ⲙⲙⲁϥ	ⲙⲙⲟϥ	ϩⲁϥ : ϩⲟϥ
(ⲛⲧⲁϥ)	(ⲛⲧⲟϥ)	

But with the suffix of 2nd fem. sing. /ʾ/, one finds:

A, L6, L4, P/S, B	*F, M*	
ⲁ/ⲉⲣⲟ	ⲉⲣⲁ	cf. ϩⲟ : ϩⲁ
ⲙⲙⲟ	ⲙⲙⲁ	ⲧⲁⲕⲟ/ⲧⲉⲕⲟ : ⲧⲉⲕⲁ
(ⲛⲧⲟ)	(ⲛⲧⲁ)	ⲟ(ⲟ)ϩ : ⲁ(ⲁ)ϩ

Generally, with regard to suffixal pronouns, there is very little dialectal variation except for certain contexts (see the variables quoted below as nos. 6–10). Also, for instance, the different dialectal representations of such forms as ⲟⲩⲁ, one; ⲡⲁï, this one; ⲉϣⲱⲡⲉ, if; and other full-stress pronouns and particles can be easily reduced to general phonological rules.

The situation is thoroughly different with those morphemes that regularly occur in pretonic syllables, such as those establishing the basic syntactic relations in verbal sentences or connected in some way with the conjugation system. If used in pretonic positions, morphemes occupy slots that, with regard to vowel quality, are very little, if at all, determined by transparent (dialect-)phonological principles. It is rather the morpholexical identity of the form, usually balanced by a pan-Coptic norm, that determines the quality of these syllables. Compare for pretonic ⲉ in all dialects, the circumstantial converter; ⲉϣⲱⲡⲉ, if; ⲉⲧⲃⲉ-, because of; ⲉⲥⲏⲧ, ground; ⲉⲥⲟⲟⲩ, sheep; ϫⲉⲣⲟ, kindle; etc.; and for pretonic ⲁ in all dialects, the perfect and aorist conjugation bases; ⲁⲛⲟⲕ/ⲁⲛⲟⲛ; ⲧⲁïⲟ, honor; ⲁⲧ-, -less; ϣⲁ-, toward; -ϣⲁ(ⲛ)- condit. infix; etc.; but on the other hand, ⲉ *A*, *L6*, *L4*, *P* versus ⲁ *B*, *F*, *M*, *S* in certain *t*-causatives like ⲧⲁⲕⲟ, ⲧⲁⲗⲟ, ⲧⲁⲣⲕⲟ, ⲧⲥⲁⲃⲟ, ⲧⲁⲩⲟ, ⲧⲁϩⲟ, etc.; or ⲉ *A*, *L4*, *P* versus ⲁ *B*, *F*, *L6*, *M*, *S* in words like ⲁⲙⲁϩⲧⲉ, prevail, and ⲁϩⲟ, treasure. If the distribution, in terms of dialects, of ⲉ versus ⲁ in a particular grammatical morpheme, say, a conjugation or converter base, is found to follow one of these latter groupings, it may well be classified as determined by some phonological (though less transparent) ratio. But if it shows a grouping of its own, different from any other phonological trait (as is the case with almost all grammatical morphemes unless they are invariable), it may *cum grano salis* be counted as a "morphological" trait, although it still features not the morphological "system" but its phonological representation (or the *plan de l'expression*).

This comparison cannot be based on the phonemic system relations within each dialect (especially for the vowel system) or the phonological rules applying for the transition from one dialect to another, since this would not provide a common basis for the comparison. Thus, its validity largely rests on the overall assumption that the phonetic (!) values of the vowel graphemes are approximately the same in all dialectal writing systems, or at least that a Sahidic ⲁ, for example, is remarkably more similar in quality to an Akhmimic or Fayyumic ⲁ than it is to Akhmimic or Fayyumic ⲉ or Akhmimic ⲟ. This cannot be proved, even after a careful phonemic analysis of the respective graphemic systems; it simply has to be assumed.

i. Diamorphemic Variables

Diamorphemic variables are not classified in respect of the reasons for their variation, e.g., the issue of historical sameness or heterogeneity, unless this reason is synchronically to be seen as a difference in structural principles.

Basic Elements in Connection with the Conjugation.

(1) Operator of negative aorist, ⲙⲡⲁ⫽ *B;* ⲙⲁ⫽ *A*, *L6*, *L4*, *P*; ⲙⲉ⫽ *F*, *M*, *S*.

(2) Operator of affirmative perfect, ⲁ⫽ *A*, *B*, *F*, *L4*, *P*, *S*; ϩⲁ⫽ *M*; ⲁϩ(ⲁ)⫽, ⲁ⫽ *L6* (depending on the suffix chosen; but not fully normalized).

(3) Operator (initial vowel) of energetic future, ⲁ⫽ *A*; ⲉ⫽ *B*, *F*, *L6*, *L4*, *M*, *P*, *S*.

(4) Operator of conditional, homonymous with second present and coinciding with vocalization of "imperfect," ⲁ⫽ *A*, *B*, *F*, *M*; ⲉ⫽ *L6*, *L4*, *P*, *S*.

(5) "Causative infinitive," presence versus absence of -ⲣ- (-ⲁ-), presence *B*, *F*, *L6*, *S*; absence *A*; nonnormalized *L4*, *M*, *P*.

Vocalization of Pronominal Suffixes.

(6) First singular with negative energetic future, (ⲛ)ⲛⲁ- *A*, *B*, *M*, *S*; (ⲛ)ⲛⲓ- *L6*, *L4*; nonnormalized *F* (?) (unknown for *P*).

(7) First singular with "causative infinitive," ⲑ/ⲧⲣⲓ- *B*, *F*, *L6*; ⲧ(ⲣ)ⲁ- *A*, *L4*, *M*, *S* (unknown for *P*).

(8) Second feminine singular with possessive article, ⲡⲟⲩ- *M*, *S*; ⲡⲉ- *A*, *B*, *F*, *L6*, *L4* (unknown for *P*).

(9) Third plural with possessive article, ⲡⲉⲩ- *F*, *M*, *S*; ⲡⲟⲩ- *A*, *B*, *L4*, *P*; nonnormalized *L6*.

(10) Third plural with causative infinitive (similarly with the negative energetic future), ⲧ(ⲣ)ⲉⲩ- *M*, *S*; ⲑ/ⲧ(ⲣ)ⲟⲩ- *A*, *B*, *F*, *L6*, *L4*, *P*.

Formation of Qualitative (Stative) Verb Forms. What should not be neglected in this connection is the basic morphemic change concerning the verbal lexeme, that is, that between infinitive and qualitative (or more particularly, the formation of the qualitative form: "long" or "short" form; presence or absence of final /-t/, etc.). However, there appears to be but little normalization in this field for quite a number of varieties, so that it seems impossible to give distinct specimens of variables at the present state of research. A special case is the qualitative form of ⲉⲓⲣⲉ:

(11) Vowel quality /a/ ~ /o/ versus /e/, *B*, *F*, *L6*, *M*, *P*, *S* versus *A*; nonnormalized *L4*.

(12) Presence versus absence of /-i(e)/, presence *B*, *F*, *L6*; absence *M*, *P*, *S*; nonnormalized *A*, *L4*.

Miscellaneous Grammatical Forms of Transdialectal Identity.

(13) Postdeterminer "each," ⲛⲓⲙ *A, L6, L4, M, S*; ⲛⲓⲃⲉⲛ *B*; ⲛⲓⲃⲓ *F*; ⲛⲓⲃ *P*.

(14) Full-stress pronominal object of second plural, -ⲑ/ⲧⲏⲛⲟⲩ *B, F, M*; -ⲧⲏⲛⲉ *A, L6, L4, P*; -ⲧⲏⲩⲧⲛ *S*.

(15) Possessive pronoun, plural base, ⲛⲱ⸗ *A, F, L4*; ⲛⲟⲩ⸗ *B, L6, P, S*.

(16) Prefix negating infinitive, ⲧⲙ- (ⲧⲙⲛ-) *A, L6, L4, M, P, S*; ϣⲧⲉⲙ- *B, F*.

(17) Infinitive connector; interfix of affirmative energetic future; preposition (ⲉ-/ⲉⲣⲟ⸗ etc.), ⲉ- *B, F, M, S*; ⲁ- *A, L6, L4, P*.

(18) Marker (initial vowel) of "special" imperatives such as ⲁⲛⲓ-/ⲁⲛⲓ⸗, ⲁⲛⲁⲩ, ⲁⲣⲓ-/ⲁⲣⲓ⸗, ⲁϫⲓ⸗, etc., ⲉ(ⲣⲓ)- *L6, P*; ⲁ(ⲣⲓ)- *A, B, F, L4, M, S*.

(19) Proclitic particle of epistemic condition (ⲓⲥϫⲉ *B*, ⲉϣϫⲉ *S*, . . . (ⲉⲓ)ϩⲡⲉ *A*), second element, -ⲡⲉ *A, L6, P*; -ϫⲉ *B, F, L4, M, S*.

(20) Interrogative adverb of place, presence versus absence of -ⲛ, ⲑ/ⲧⲱⲛ/ⲧⲟⲛ *B, F, L6, M, S*; ⲧⲟ/ⲧⲟⲩ *A, L4, P*.

Miscellaneous "Nonidentical" Forms Filling the Same (or Partially Same) Paradigms, i.e., Lexicogrammatical Traits.

(21) Indefinite pronoun (NP equivalent in nonaffirmative contexts), ⲗⲁⲁⲩ(ⲉ)/ⲗⲁ(ⲟ)ⲩⲉ *A, L6, L4, P, S*; ϩⲗⲓ *B*; ⲗⲁⲡⲥ/ⲗⲁⲡϯ *F*; ϩⲓ (personal), ⲛⲓⲛⲉї (nonpersonal) *M*.

(22) Prefix forming negative imperative, ⲙⲛ- *A, P*; ⲙⲡ(ⲉ)ⲣ- etc. *B, F, L6, L4, M, S*.

(23) Proclitic relative converter preceding perfect conjugation operator, ⲉⲧ- *A, B, F, L4, M, P*; ⲛⲧ- *L6, S*.

(24) Presence versus absence of a special augens form ⲙⲁⲩⲁⲁ(ⲧ)⸗/ⲙ̇ⲙⲁⲩⲁⲧ⸗ beside the usual ⲟⲩⲁⲁ(ⲧ)⸗/ⲟⲩⲁⲉⲧ⸗, etc., presence *B, S*; absence *A, F, L6, L4, M, P*.

ii. Allomorphic Variables

Allomorphic Expansion of Conjugation Bases. Allomorphic expansion by -ⲣⲉ- in prenominal conjugation forms is handled very much alike in all dialects, allowing for frequent variation in nonnormalized manuscripts, and with striking deviations occurring only in Akhmimic (see Polotsky, 1960, sec. 52–56). Dialect-specific expansion of presuffixal bases may pertain either to the whole paradigm (e.g., the Akhmimic affirmative aorist, see ibid.) or to particular combinations, such as (a) all third-person forms (fluctuations in the affirmative aorist paradigm in *L6* and *M*), (b) the second-person feminine singular, and (c) the second-person plural. The rationale to be recognized behind the outstanding Akhmimic usage seems to be a different "signaling" function of -ⲣⲉ-. While in all other dialects it serves to expand a (greater) number of base morphemes so as to make them more "conspicuous" with regard to certain kinds of subject expressions that follow it (in particular, nominal and second feminine singular), in Akhmimic it tends to give up its expanding function and become an invariable part of the base morpheme for a (smaller) number of bases, the rest (in particular, present converted bases) being left without any expansion at all. The result is stronger morphemic uniformity and less submorphemic alternation. The following instances in terms of isoglosses may be typical of the situation:

(25) Circumstantial present, prenominal form, ⲉⲣⲉ- (ⲉⲗⲉ-) *B, F, L4, M, S*; ⲉ- *A*; nonnormalized ⲉ-, ⲉⲣⲉ- *L6, P*.

(26) Second present, prenominal form, ⲉⲣⲉ-/ⲁⲣⲉ- (ⲁⲗⲉ-) *B, F, L6, L4, M, P, S*; nonnormalized ⲁ-, ⲁⲣⲉ- *A*.

(27) Affirmative aorist, all third-person forms, ϩⲁⲣ(ⲉ)ϥ-, etc. *A*, ⳉⲁⲣϥ- *P*; ϣⲁϥ-, etc. *B, F, L4, S*; nonnormalized *L6, M* (both seem to prefer ϣⲁϥ- to ϣⲁⲣⲉϥ-).

(28) Circumstantial present, second present, imperfect, and conditional, before suffix of second plural (which then appears in different allomorphs accordingly), (ⲛ)ⲁⲣⲉ⸗/(ⲛ)ⲉⲣⲉ⸗ *B, L6*; (ⲛ)ⲁ⸗/(ⲛ)ⲉ⸗ *A, F, L4, M, P, S*.

Intradialectal Interference of Submorphemic Alternation. The generalization of an allomorph beyond the contextual scope it is otherwise strictly bound to is a phenomenon very close to grammatical error. In Coptic, as well as in other languages, it is rarely found to be characteristic of a literary standard variety of the language, within the same historical period. A case in point is the combination of the second-person plural pronominal (subject) suffix—that is, its two basic allomorphs -ⲧ(ⲉ)ⲛ and -ⲧⲉⲧ(ⲉ)ⲛ—with the various conjugation bases, which may be divided into "short" and "long" ones (depending on whether they contain -ⲣⲉ- or not). The general morphological rule of Coptic that says the short suffix only combines with the long bases and the long suffix only combines with the short bases is invalidated in dialects *A* and *M* in opposite directions (cf. Polotsky, 1960, sec. 56; Funk, 1981, sec. 1.4.1). This may be presented in terms of isoglosses as follows:

(29) Second plural suffix, short form: only with long bases *A, B, F, L6, L4, P, S*; also with short bases *M*.

(30) Second plural suffix, long form: only with short bases *B, F, L6, L4, M, P, S*; also with long bases *A*.

iii. Morphosyntactic Variables

Special "Portmanteau" Morphs.

(31) Special element /er-/ incorporating {rel} + {perf} + {third-person subj. pron.}, presence *M*; absence *A, B, F, L6, L4, P, S.*

(32) Special element /-ah-/ (preceded by relative converter ⲉⲧ-/ⲛⲧ-) incorporating {perf} + {third-person subj. pron.}, presence *A, L6, P*; absence *B, F, L4, M, S.*

(33) Special element -ϧⲁⲣ- /-çar-/ (phonologically corresponding in *P* to Sahidic -ϣⲁⲣ- /-šar-/ (preceded by relative converter ⲉⲧ-) incorporating {aorist} + {third-person subj. pron.}, presence *P*; absence *A, B, F, L6, L4, M, S.*

Special Conjugation Base.

(34) Presence versus absence of a special "temporalis" clause conjugation ⲛⲧⲉⲣⲉϥ-/ⲛⲧⲁⲣⲉϥ- ("absence" implies the use of rel. perf. in the same paradigm), presence *A, L6, L4, P, S*; absence *B, F, M* (Fayyumic proper is split here; this notation accounts for the usage of biblical manuscripts).

Use of Different (Coexistent) Forms in the Same Paradigm.

(35) Prefix deriving Greek-loaned verb stems, (ⲉ)ⲣ-/ⲉⲗ- *A, B, F*; zero *S, M*; nonnormalized *L6, L4, P.*

(36) Nuclear element of NP-equivalent relative clauses (not fully normalized), ⲡⲏ, etc. *B*; ⲡ-, etc. *A, F, L6, L4, M, P, S.*

(37) Element forming "instans" verb form (to be used in bipartite conjugation to express "future"), stative verb ⲛⲁ versus infinitive connector ⲉ-/ⲁ-, in particular after subject pronouns like ⲕ, ϥ, ⲥ, -ⲛⲁ-/-ⲛⲉ- *A, B, F, L6, M, P, S*; -ⲁ- *L4.*

(38) Prenominal form of the "causative imperative" operator: {ⲙⲁ-} + {causative infinitive} versus prenominal analogue to ⲙⲁⲣⲉϥⲥⲱⲧⲙ causative imperative, ⲙⲁ- ⲧⲉ- *P*; ⲙⲁⲣⲉ- *A, B, F, L6, L4, M, S.*

These dialectal isoglosses selected for a broad variety of morphological items may be used as a data basis to determine the degrees (and hierarchical order) of relationship between the eight dialectal varieties considered, by means of various "clustering" techniques supplied by modern numerical taxonomy. With a number of such methods having been applied successfully and yielding very similar results, a classification based on morphological traits might be suggested as shown in Figure 1 (neglecting, for the present purpose, the precise hierarchical level for the location of division nodes on the tree).

The primary division in the set of individual dialects turns out to be that between *A, L6, L4, P* and *B, F, M, S*, corresponding to only one trait (which then is the most typical differential trait), namely, the vocalic representation of the Egyptian preposition *r-* (as Coptic ⲁ- versus ⲉ-) in its various grammatical paradigms (cf. item 14 above). Although nonmor-

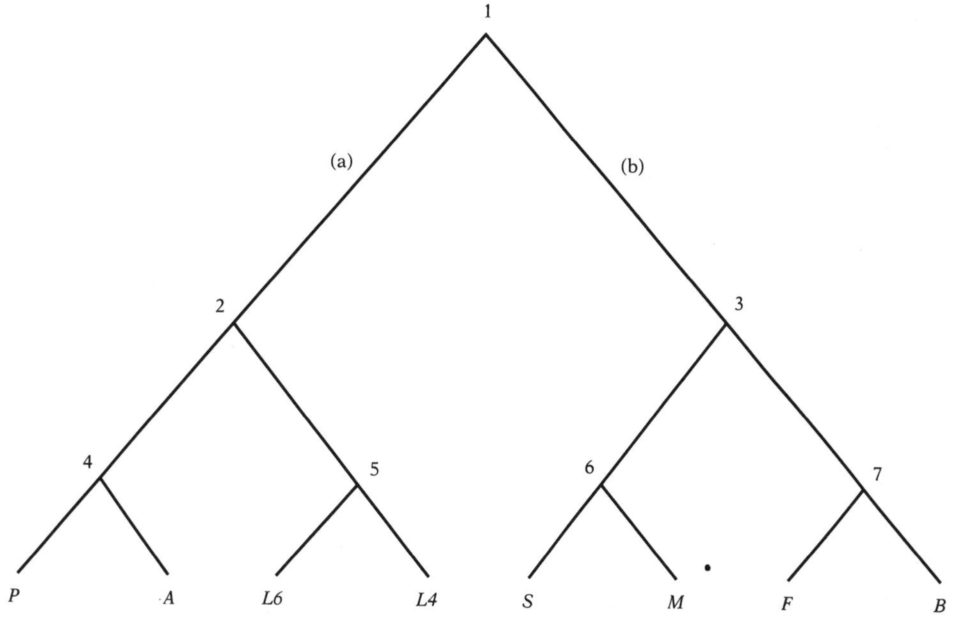

FIGURE 1. GROUPING OF EIGHT COPTIC LITERARY DIALECTS BASED ON MORPHOLOGICAL DATA.

phemic (and quasi-phonological) in nature, this trait seems to symbolize the most profitable division of the whole cluster of dialects into two subsets in terms of morphological isoglosses.

Some further traits of similarity along branch 1a are (14) -ⲧⲏⲛⲉ, (21) ⲗⲁⲁⲩ(ⲉ)/ⲗⲁ(ⲟ)ⲩⲉ (shared with *S*), (34) "temporalis" (shared with *S*), (16) ⲧⲙ- (shared with *M* and *S*), and (13) monosyllabic form of ⲛⲓⲙ/ⲛⲓⲃ (shared with *M* and *S*). Along branch 1b are (22) ⲙⲡ(ⲉ)ⲣ-, (27) aorist without -ⲣⲉ- extension (both shared with *L6* and *L4*), (20) ⲧⲱⲛ, etc. (shared with *L6*), (19) ⲉϣϫⲉ, etc. (shared with *L4*), and (18) ⲁⲣⲓ-, etc. (shared with *A* and *L4*).

The differential traits at node 2 are (22) ⲙⲛ- *A*, *P* versus ⲙⲡⲣ- *L6*, *L4*, plus, perhaps, the presence or absence of -ⲣⲉ- extension with the aorist base, (27) ϩⲁⲣ(ⲉ)⸗ *A*, ⳉⲁⲣ⸗ *P* versus ϣⲁ⸗ *L4*, *(L6)*. Some further traits of similarity within branch 2a are either shared with *L4*, as in (20) ⲧⲟ/ⲧⲟⲩ, (28) nonextended base (plus *F*, *M*, *S*), (2) perfect ⲁ⸗ (plus *B*, *F*, *S*), and (23) rel. ⲉⲧ- with perfect (plus *B*, *F*, *M*), or shared with *L6*, as in (19) ⲉⲓϩⲡⲉ, etc., and (32) -ⲁϩ-. Within branch 2b, some further concurring items are (6) (ⲛ)ⲛⲓ-, (41) nonnormalized use of ⲣ- (shared with *P*), (4) ⲉ-vocalization (shared with *P*, plus *S*), and some other traits shared with either *P* or *A* plus *B*, *F*, *M*, *S*, as in (3), (30), and (38).

The differential traits at node 3 are (35) zero *M*, *S* versus ⲉⲣ-/ⲉⲗ- *B*, *F*, (16) ⲧⲙ- versus ϣⲧⲉⲙ-, (7) ⲧⲣⲁ- versus ⲑ/ⲧⲣⲓ-, (8) ⲡⲟⲩ- versus ⲡⲉ-, (10) -ⲉⲩ versus -ⲟⲩ. Some further traits of similarity along branch 3a are (13) ⲛⲓⲙ (plus *A*, *L6*, *L4*), (1) ⲛⲉ⸗ (shared with *F*), (15) ⲛⲟⲩ⸗ (shared with *B*, plus *L6*, *P*), (6) (ⲛ)ⲛⲁ- (shared with *B*, plus *A*). Along branch 3b, most of the further concurring items are shared with *M*: (14) ⲑ/ⲧⲏⲛⲟⲩ, (34) rel. perf. for "temporalis," (23) rel. ⲉⲧ- with perf. (plus *A*, *L4*, *P*), (4) ⲁ-vocalization (plus *A*). Shared with none is (13) disyllabicity in ⲛⲓⲃⲉⲛ/ⲛⲓⲃⲓ; some traits are shared with *S* plus *A*, *(L6)*, *L4*, *P*, as in (2) and (29), or *S* plus *L6*, as in (5).

This classification based on morphological traits, perhaps in a more fully elaborated form, may be used to supplement and reinterpret the results of a classification based on purely phonological data (the more so, if any such classifications should be used as a guide to the geographical allocation of dialect centers). It is interesting to note that in terms of both serial and hierarchical order, the two sets of criteria lead to considerably different results. This is easily seen by comparing Figure 1 with what may be the result of a phonological classification. Depending on how much additional emphasis is put on the "natural" vocalization of stressed syllables (as compared with that of unstressed syllables and with consonant traits), either of the classifications shown in Figures 2 and 3 may be preferred. Since it has not yet been determined whether a binary division of the whole set of individuals is really appropriate here, even a third alternative might be worth considering, namely, that shown in Figure 4 (cf. also Hintze, 1984).

Irrespective of the actual hierarchy preferred, the difference between these classifications and the one based on morphological data is quite obvious. The most striking (though least surprising) detail is the differing allocation of *P*, not only changing its "nearest neighbor" affiliation but rather shuttling between poles (cf. earlier statements to similar effects in Polotsky, 1970, p. 561, n. 11; Kasser, 1960, pp. xxviii ff.). A satisfactory explanation of this phenomenon is not known to have been proposed so far. Of much greater bearing, however, taking into account the historical role of the various dialects and dialectal varieties, is the differing degree of relationship between Sahidic and Bohairic, on one hand (being remarkably stronger in the phonological than in the morphological field), and between either of these and Fayyumic or Mesokemic, on the other. Also, in terms of serial order, it is obvious that Sahidic is much closer to the southern dialects *(A, L6, L4)* in the morphological field than in the phonological, while the situation of *F* and *M* is the reverse. As far as Sahidic is concerned, it may well be the social nature and prehistory of this dialect as a supraregional vernacular rather than its geographical homeland that provides the clue to a greater part of its characteristics and its overall neutralizing behavior.

BIBLIOGRAPHY

The bibliography below has been compiled to satisfy two entirely different needs and thus comprises

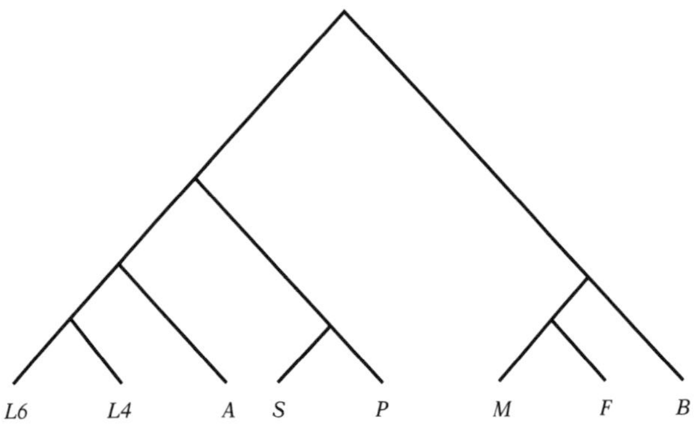

FIGURE 2. GROUPING BASED ON PHONOLOGICAL DATA, WITH EQUAL WEIGHTING FOR ALL VARIABLES.

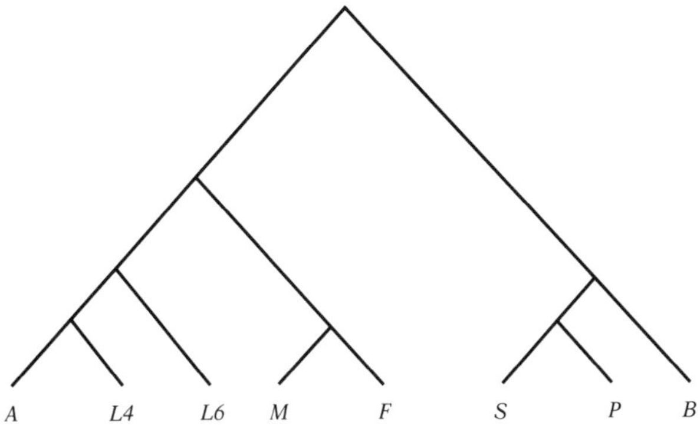

FIGURE 3. GROUPING BASED ON PHONOLOGICAL DATA, WITH HIGHER WEIGHTING FOR STRESSED VOWELS (BINARY SOLUTION).

references of two kinds: (a) a number of textbooks, research papers, and monographs providing basic information about the morphology of one or several Coptic dialects, and (b) editions of Coptic texts that have been used as main representative specimens of the dialectal varieties covered by this article, apart from "biblical" *B* and *S*. The latter group of items includes Elanskaya, Erichsen, Kahle (pp. 286–90), Kasser (1960), Kirchner, Lacau, Malinine et al., Polotsky (1934), Rösch, Schenke (1981), and Schmidt.

As to the particular dialects (especially the so-called minor dialects) covered by the present article, some basic information in the morphological field can be obtained from Till (1928) for *A;* from Asmus, and Till (1930), for *F;* from Chaîne (1934), Nagel, and Funk (1984) for *L4* and *L6;* from Quecke, Schenke (1978), and Funk (1981) for *M;* and from Kahle, Polotsky (1960), Kasser (1966), and Vergote for several of those dialects.

Apart from these works some of the older textbooks of Coptic grammar, dealing with several dialects, may still be used with profit to gain information about dialectal morphology. Among them are L. Stern, *Koptische Grammatik* (Leipzig, 1880, repr. Osnabrück, 1971), and G. Steindorff, *Lehrbuch der koptischen Grammatik* (Chicago, 1951). Still of basic relevance and indispensable for dialectological work in the field of morphology are W. E. Crum's *Coptic Dictionary* (Oxford, 1939) and R. Kasser's *Compléments au dictionnaire de Crum* (Cairo, 1964), as well as Kahle (1954). Westendorff's *Koptisches Handwörterbuch,* although offering an enormous amount of information based on more-recently published sources, does not in general guide the user back to the sources (as Crum does) and thus is informative on dialectal usage only for those who are content with the classification of dialects used therein. (Much the same applies to Till, 1961.) It should be noted that some of the text editions cited have introductory chapters providing useful information on the respective dialects.

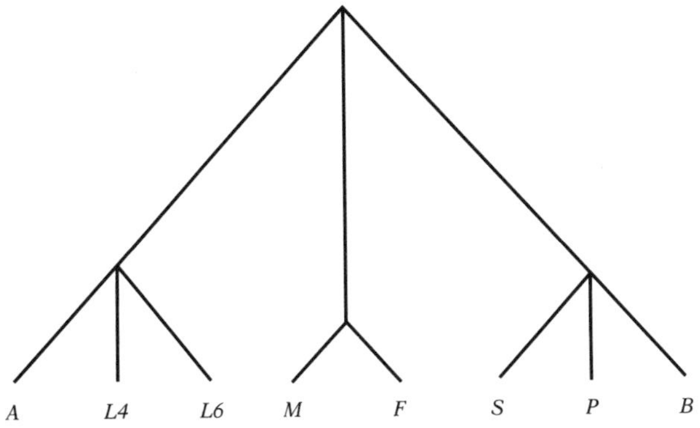

FIGURE 4. GROUPING BASED ON PHONOLOGICAL DATA, WITH HIGHER WEIGHTING FOR STRESSED VOWELS (NONBINARY SOLUTION).

BIBLIOGRAPHY

Asmus, H. *Über Fragmente im mittelägyptischen Dialekte.* Göttingen, 1904.

Chaîne, M. *Eléments de grammaire dialectale copte.* Paris, 1933.

______. *Les Dialectes coptes assioutiques A2.* Paris, 1934.

Elanskaya, A. I. "Rukopis' no. 53 koptskoĭ novoĭ serii (zaklyuchitel'nye glavy Evangeliya ot Marka na faĭyumskom dialekte)." In *Koptskie rukopisi Gosudarstvennoĭ Publičnoĭ Biblioteki imeni M. E. Saltykova-Ščedrina, Palestinskiĭ sbornik* 20, no. 83 (1969):96–120.

Erichsen, W. *Faijumische Fragmente der Reden des Agathonicus Bischofs von Tarsus.* Copenhagen, 1932.

Funk, W.-P. "Beiträge des mittelägyptischen Dialekts zum koptischen Konjugationssystem." In *Studies Presented to H. J. Polotsky,* ed. D. W. Young, pp. 177–210. East Gloucester, Mass., 1981.

______. "Die Morphologie der Perfektkonjugation im NH-subachmimischen Dialekt." *Zeitschrift für ägyptische Sprache und Altertumskunde* 111 (1984):110–30.

Hintze, F. "Eine Klassifizierung der koptischen Dialekte." In *Studien zu Sprache und Religion Ägyptens,* Vol. 1, *Sprache,* pp. 411–432. Göttingen, 1984.

Husselman, E.-M. *The Gospel of John in Fayumic Coptic (P. Mich. Inv. 3521).* Ann Arbor, Mich., 1962.

Kahle, P. E. *Bala'izah: Coptic Texts from Deir el-Bala'izah in Upper Egypt.* Oxford and London, 1954.

Kasser, R. *Papyrus Bodmer VI: Livre des Proverbes.* CSCO 194–195. Louvain, 1960.

———. "Compléments morphologiques au dictionnaire de Crum, le vocabulaire caractéristique des quatre nouveaux dialectes coptes: P, M, H et G." *Bulletin de l'Institut français d'archéologie orientale* 64 (1966):19–66.

———. "Prolégomènes à un essai de classification systématique des dialectes et subdialectes coptes selon les critères de la phonétique, I, Principes et terminologie." *Muséon* 93 (1980a):53–112. ". . . , II, Alphabets et systèmes phonétiques." *Muséon* 93 (1980b):237–97. ". . . , III, Systèmes orthographiques et catégories dialectales." *Muséon* 94 (1981):91–152.

Kirchner, D. *Epistula Jacobi apocrypha, neu herausgegeben, übersetzt und kommentiert.* Texte und Untersuchungen zur Geschichte der altchristlichen Literatur 136. Berlin, 1989.

Lacau, P. "Textes coptes en dialectes akhmîmique et sahidique." *Bulletin de l'Institut français d'archéologie orientale* 8 (1911):43–81.

Malinine, M., H.-C. Puech; G. Quispel; W. C. Till; R. Kasser; R. McL. Wilson; and J. Zandee. *Epistula Iacobi Apocrypha, Codex Jung f. Ir.—f. VIIIv. (p. 1–16).* Zurich and Stuttgart, 1968.

Nagel, P. "Untersuchungen zur Grammatik des subachmimischen Dialekts" (Ph.D. diss., Karl Marx University, 1964).

Polotsky, H. J. *Manichäische Homilien.* Stuttgart, 1934.

———. "The Coptic Conjugation System." *Orientalia* 29 (1960):392–422.

———. "Coptic." In *Current Trends in Linguistics,* Vol. 6, *Linguistics in Southwest Asia and North Africa,* ed. A. T. Sebeok, pp. 558–70. The Hague and Paris, 1970.

Quecke, H. "Il dialetto." In T. Orlandi, *Papiri della Università degli studi di Milano (P. Mil. Copti),* Vol. 5, *Lettere di San Paolo in copto ossirinchita, edizione, commento e indici di T. Orlandi, contributo linguistico di H. Quecke.* Milan, 1974.

Rösch, F. *Bruchstücke des ersten Clemensbriefes.* Strasbourg, 1910.

Schenke, H.-M. "On the Middle Egyptian Dialect of the Coptic Language." *Enchoria* 8 (Sonderband) (1978):43*(89)–(104)58*.

———. *Das Matthäus-Evangelium im mittelägyptischen Dialekt des Koptischen (Codex Scheide).* Texte und Untersuchungen zur Geschichte der altchristlichen Literatur 127. Berlin, 1981.

Schmidt, C. *Gespräche Jesu mit seinen Jüngern nach der Auferstehung.* Leipzig, 1919.

Till, W. C. *Achmîmisch-koptische Grammatik.* Leipzig, 1928.

———. *Koptische Chrestomathie für den fayumischen Dialekt, mit grammatischer Skizze und Anmerkungen.* Vienna, 1930.

———. *Koptische Dialektgrammatik, mit Lesestücken und Wörterbuch.* 2nd ed. Munich, 1961.

Vergote, J. *Grammaire copte,* Vol. 1a, *Introduction, phonétique et phonologie, morphologie synthématique (structure des sémantèmes), partie synchronique.* Louvain, 1973.

WOLF-PETER FUNK

DICTIONARIES. From the time when the Copts, like other nations or linguistic entities, felt the need to have at their disposal in writing the equivalents, exact or approximate, of the words of their language, attempts were made to compose modest lists of bilingual vocabulary; these may justly be considered the ancestors of modern Coptic dictionaries. In general, these lists follow either the order of the words as they are found in the particular text that had to be translated, or a more or less "logical" order, with lexemes classed by subject or themes. Thus, although the Coptic language was only at the beginning of its literary existence, when Christianity began to spread into the segment of the population that was almost exclusively Coptic and unfamiliar with Greek, there was need for Greco-Coptic glossaries. (At first Christianity was diffused through works in Greek, and chiefly in Greek-speaking milieus.)

The oldest extant Coptic glossary is in a manuscript in the MESOKEMIC dialect that seems to be from the second half of the third century (Bell and Thompson, 1925). Later, if use certainly continued to be made of such glossaries (Bell and Crum, 1925, manuscript of the sixth century, idiolectal $S = S^a$ or S^f), there may have been need also of Latin-Coptic or Latin-Greek-Coptic glossaries; one of them has been preserved by a manuscript of the first half of the sixth century (apparently Coptic language *S*; cf. Schubart, 1913).

In the middle of the seventh century, Egypt was invaded and occupied, once and for all, by the Arabs. This event was decisive for the future of the Coptic language. During the Byzantine period, in conjunction with the development of the Coptic church, this idiom consolidated its position on the literary level. A large number of literary texts were translated into one or another of the various dialects of Roman Egypt. Here and there bilingual Greco-Coptic manuscripts were also copied (Treu, 1965), but in comparison with the uniquely Coptic manuscripts, they are exceptions. Thus, on the arrival of the Arabs, Coptic was full of vigor. At first, the Arabs further enhanced its importance by proscribing the use of Greek in the Egyptian administration; and while from the seventh to the middle of the eighth century Greek progressively disappeared from Egyptian documents, Coptic took its place, and so it was down to the beginning of the ninth century. Then, in its turn, Arabic, already officially commissioned to replace Coptic in the administration for a hundred years and having for that reason continued to advance to the detriment of Coptic, soon supplanted it almost everywhere in administrative texts.

With this new orientation of Arab policy in Egypt, the ninth century thus saw the appearance of the first measures that threatened the very existence of the Coptic language. The latter at first resisted with some success, but under constant pressure its resistance gradually crumbled and came to nothing. In the tenth century Arabic was taught to the Coptic clergy (Casanova, 1901). From the eleventh century on, in some regions of Egypt, Coptic was understood only imperfectly, and from the eleventh century to the fourteenth, Coptic men of letters sought to make good this neglect by compiling grammars and, above all, Copto-Arabic vocabularies (more rarely Greco-Copto-Arabic, older Greco-Coptic ones adapted to Arabic). Such a vocabulary was called a SULLAM (plural, *salālim*) or scala, and without a *sullam* these grammars could only be used with difficulty by those to whom they were to teach the Coptic language. Most of them give only BOHAIRIC, notably the celebrated *Scala magna* of Abū al-Barakat (fourteenth century; cf. Mallon, 1906–1907; Munier, 1930; van Lantschoot, 1948). Others, however, set SAHIDIC beside Bohairic, above all the lexicons placed after the famous grammar of Athanasius of Qūṣ (fourteenth century) and that of Anbā Yūḥannā of Samannūd (thirteenth century) in the Coptic codex 44 in the National Library, Paris. These vocabularies, like the earlier glossaries, make no distinction between Coptic words of Egyptian origin and those of non-Egyptian origin (for the most part Greek). In so doing, they are in perfect harmony with the spirit of the Coptic language in which, except for certain very specialized lexemes of extremely rare usage, most of the words of Greek origin were felt to be not foreign words but genuinely Coptic, for the same reason as words of pharaonic origin (see VOCABULARY, COPTO-GREEK).

However, European scholars, who from the fifteenth century, and still more from the dawn of the seventeenth, took an interest in this language, looked at it from a very different point of view. It was not so much Coptic in itself, a language practically dead, that attracted their attention but rather Coptic as the only accessible form, however evolved (degenerate and impoverished), of the ancient Egyptian language. It was through Coptic that they hoped one day to reach an understanding of the hieroglyphs, and indeed it was this road that finally led to the success of Champollion in 1822.

After the *Lingua Aegyptiaca Restituta* of A. Kircher (1643) and the manuscript dictionary of Fell at the end of the seventeenth century (the first in which the words were arranged alphabetically; cf. Quatremère, 1808), several important lexicons and dictionaries saw the light in Europe in the eighteenth and nineteenth centuries (above all, Lacroze and Scholtz, 1775, *S* and *B*; Tattam, 1853, *S*, *B*, and a little *F*). A work of clearly superior quality to what had appeared before was by Peyron (1835, *S*, *B*, and a little *F*); this book represents a remarkable advance in Coptic lexicography. For the first time, the autochthonous Coptic words were classified like those in the majority of Semitic languages, taking account of the consonants in the first place and of the vowels only in secondary fashion. This system allows the placing together, quite naturally, of the various dialectal forms of a single Coptic word, since they most often differ in their vowels, not in their consonants. For another thing, it makes consultation of Coptic dictionaries easier for their principal users, Egyptologists familiar with the pharaonic language, in which in general only the consonants are expressed in writing.

However, parallel with the development of Coptic studies in Europe, and no doubt also encouraged by the contacts established in Egypt between the Egyptologists and the Copts, several Coptic personalities attempted to revive this ancient language in the form of its Bohairic variety. Their work essentially stands in the tradition of the autochthonous grammarians of the thirteenth and fourteenth centuries, but it could also render service to European Coptologists. The chief lexicons published within the frame of this genuinely Coptic activity appeared at the end of the nineteenth century and the beginning of the twentieth (Barsum, 1882; Labib, 1915).

The twentieth century in Europe saw the appearance of the first Coptic etymological dictionary, which firmly established the link between the Coptic lexicons and their counterparts for pharaonic Egyptian (Spiegelberg, 1921; *S*, *A*, *L* [called A^2], *F*, and *B*); but this dictionary, concentrating on etymology, gives only very summarily the various written forms and meaning of the words. One may assume that, knowing the preparations Crum was making for the publication of his great dictionary, Spiegelberg renounced in advance any thought of a work as rich as that of his rival.

Crum published his work in fascicles and completed it on the eve of World War II (1939; *S, A, L* [called A^2], *F,* and *B*). Although a little outmoded here and there (new and important manuscripts have been discovered since 1939), Crum's monumental work has scarcely aged, and one may affirm that it is even today by far the best Coptic dictionary (the richest and the most precise) at the disposal of Coptologists and Egyptologists. Thus, fifty years after its completion it has not yet been displaced. However, Coptic lexicographers have not remained inactive; they have sought in various ways to order the new material placed at their disposal since 1939 (through the Bodmer Papyri, the Nag Hammadi texts, and other Coptic witnesses of even greater interest, though less well known). This material reveals the existence of many dialects and subdialects hitherto quite unknown or known only in so deficient a way, so imprecise a form, that they could not be properly defined and systematically used before (Kasser, 1964, 1966). Spiegelberg's old *Handwörterbuch* has even been republished, though after a revision so thorough as to make of it practically a new work (Westendorf, 1977); this book, gathering up very completely, although sometimes without enough critical concern, the material available to its author, is of great service for rapid consultation. The fact remains that for those whose researches require consultation in somewhat greater depth, only Crum (1939) is really satisfactory. Coptology therefore has an urgent need for a new Coptic dictionary, complete and detailed, including autochthonous Coptic lexemes, Copto-Greek, and Copto-Arabic. Such a work is at present in preparation in Switzerland (Kasser, 1972). A new *Dictionnaire étymologique de la langue copte* (Vycichl, 1983) has also been prepared in Geneva and published in Louvain.

BIBLIOGRAPHY

Bachatly, C. *Le Monastère de Phoebammon dans la Thébaïde,* Vol. 2, pp. 33–34, 40–42. Cairo, 1965.

Barsum, I. *Al-Kharīdat al-Bahīyah fī Uṣul al-Lughat al-Kibtīyah.* Cairo, 1882.

Bell, H. I., and W. E. Crum. "A Greek-Coptic Glossary." *Aegyptus* 6 (1925):177–226.

Bell, H. I., and H. Thompson. "A Greek-Coptic Glossary to Hosea and Amos." *Journal of Egyptian Archaeology* 11 (1925):241–46.

Casanova, P. "Un Texte arabe transcrit en lettres coptes." *Bulletin de l'Institut français d'archéologie orientale* 1 (1901):1–20.

Černý, J. *Coptic Etymological Dictionary.* Cambridge, 1976.

Crum, W. E. *A Coptic Dictionary.* Oxford, 1939.

Kasser, R. *Compléments au dictionnaire copte de Crum.* Bibliothèque d'études coptes 7. Cairo, 1964.

______. "Compléments morphologiques au dictionnaire de Crum, le vocabulaire caractéristique des quatre nouveaux dialectes coptes: P, M, H et G." *Bulletin de l'Institut français d'archéologie orientale* 64 (1966):19–66.

______. "Les Dictionnaires coptes." In *Textes et langages de l'Egypte pharaonique: Hommage à Jean-François Champollion à l'occasion du cent-cinquantième anniversaire du déchiffrement des hiéroglyphes (1822–1972),* Vol. 1, pp. 209–216. Cairo, [1972].

Kircher, A. *Lingua Aegyptiaca Restituta, Opus Tripartitum. Quo Linguae Coptae sive Idiomatis Illius Primaeui Aegyptiorum Pharaonici, Vetustate Temporum Paene Collapsi, ex Abstrusis Arabum Monumentis, Plena Instauratio Continetur. Cui Adnectitur Supplementum Earum Rerum, quae in Prodromo Copto, et Opere Hoc Tripartito, vel Omissa, vel Obscurius Tradita Sunt.* Rome, 1643.

Krall, J. "Reste koptischer Schulbücherliteratur." *Mittheilungen aus der Sammlung der Papyrus Erzherzog Rainer* 4 (1888):126–35.

Labib, C. J. **ⲡⲓⲗⲉⲝⲓⲕⲟⲛ ⲛ̀ϯⲁⲥⲡⲓ ⲛ̀ⲧⲉ ⲛⲓⲣⲉⲙⲛ̀ⲭⲏⲙⲓ.** Cairo, 1895–1915.

Lacroze, M. V. de. *Lexicon Aegyptiaco-Latinum ex Veteribus Illius Linguae Monumentis Summo Studio Collectum et Elaboratum. Quod in Compendium Redegit Ita ut Nullae Voces Aegyptiacae, Nullaeque Earum Significationes Omitterentur Christ. Scholtz. Notulas Quasdam, et Indices Adjecit Carolus Godofredus Woide.* Oxford, 1775.

Lantschoot, A. van. *Un Précurseur d'Athanase Kircher, Thomas Obicini et la Scala Vat. copte 71.* Louvain, 1948.

Mallon, A. "Une École de savants égyptiens au moyen âge." *Mélanges de l'Université Saint-Joseph de Beyrouth* 1 (1906):109–131; 2 (1907):213–64.

Munier, H. *La scala copte 44 de la Bibliothèque Nationale de Paris,* Vol. 1, *Transcription.* Bibliothèque d'études coptes 2. Cairo, 1930.

Osing, J. Review of J. Černý, *Coptic Etymological Dictionary. Journal of Egyptian Archaeology* 64 (1978):186–89.

Parthey, G. F. C. *Vocabularium Coptico-Latinum et Latino-Copticum e Peyroni et Tattami Lexicis Concinavit G. Parthey. Accedunt Elenchus Episcopatuum Aegypti, Index Aegypti Geographicus Coptico-Latinus, Index Aegypti Geographicus Latino-Copticus, Vocabula Aegyptia a Scriptoribus Graecis Explicata, Vocabula Aegyptia a Scriptoribus Latinis Explicata.* Berlin, 1844.

Peyron, V. A. *Lexicon Linguae Copticae*. Turin, 1835.

Polotsky, H. J. Review of W. E. Crum, *A Coptic Dictionary*. *Journal of Egyptian Archaeology* 25 (1939):109–113.

Quatremère, E. M. *Recherches critiques et historiques sur la langue et la littérature de l'Egypte*. Paris, 1808.

Schubart, W. "Ein lateinisch-griechisch-koptisches Gesprächbuch." *Klio* 13 (1913):27–38.

Spiegelberg, W. *Koptisches Handwörterbuch*. Heidelberg, 1921.

Tattam, H. *Lexicon Aegyptiaco-Latinum, ex Veteribus Linguae Aegyptiacae Monumentis, et ex Operibus La Crozii, Woidii, et Aliorum, Summo Studio Congestum, cum Indice Vocum Latinarum*. Oxford, 1835.

Till, W. C. "Achmîmische Berichtigungen und Ergänzungen zu Spiegelbergs Koptisches Handwörterbuch." *Zeitschrift für ägyptische Sprache und Altertumskunde* 62 (1927):115–30.

Treu, K. "Griechisch-koptische Bilinguen des Neuen Testaments." In *Koptologische Studien in der DDR*, pp. 95–100. *Wissenschaftliche Zeitschrift der Martin-Luther-Universität Halle-Wittenberg*, Sonderheft. Halle, 1965.

Vycichl, W. *Dictionnaire étymologique de la langue copte*. Louvain, 1983.

Westendorf, W. *Koptisches Handwörterbuch, bearbeitet auf Grund des Koptischen Handwörterbuchs von Wilhelm Spiegelberg*. Heidelberg, 1977.

RODOLPHE KASSER

DJINKIM. The *djinkim* (حركة) is a Coptic reader's sign in the form of a point (derived from a much reduced supralinear stroke?) or, in BOHAIRIC (*B*) only, a grave accent, placed above a grapheme—a sign that is commonly found in *B* (cf. Polotsky, 1949) or in *M*, or Mesokemic (cf. Kasser, 1981; Schenke, 1981, pp. 26–30) and of which only a few traces have been discovered in *V*. (None are known in *F* or in any other of the Coptic dialects.) Polotsky (1949, p. 25, n. 1) wrote, "The name is inspired by the position of the point above some letters, superficially similar to that of the *ḥarakāt* in relation to the *ḥurūf* in Arabic writing. One cannot draw any conclusion from this regarding the significance of the point." In these various idioms the *djinkim* was used from the beginnings of their literary existence, but is employed in a way that differs from one dialect to another or even within the same dialect. Thus, one may distinguish at least four systems of its use, those of classical *B*, late *B*, pre-classical *M*, and classical *M*.

In classical *B* the only letters marked with a *djinkim* are (1) any vowel forming a syllable by itself, such as ⲁϥⲓ ⲉ̀ⲃⲟⲗ, he went out, and ⲁ̀ⲛⲟⲙⲓⲁ̀, sin; (2) the letters ⲙ and ⲛ when they are grammatical elements (prepositions, marks of the genitive, negation) or the first radical before another graphic consonant, as in ⲣⲉⲙⲛ̀ⲭⲏⲙⲓ, Egyptian; ⲙⲁⲛ̀ⲥⲱⲛϩ, prison; ⲙ̀ⲧⲟⲛ, repose; and ⲛ̀ⲑⲟⲕ, thee (Polotsky, 1949, pp. 25–29). These are then, in each case, either a graphic vowel = a vowel in phonology also, or a (nasal) graphic consonant = a vowel too in phonology, more precisely a nasal sonant. Hence, each letter marked with a *djinkim* in classical *B* is a phoneme with a vocalic function and forming a syllable by itself.

In late *B*, in addition to the syllabic vowels and sonant nasals of classical *B* (cases 1 and 2 above), the following four categories are also marked with the *djinkim*: (3) the first of two consecutive consonants at the beginning of a word or within the word when it is a case of Greek compounds, as in ⲥ̇ϩⲓⲙⲓ, woman; ⲭ̇ⲗⲟⲙ, crown; ϫ̇ⲫⲟ, engender; ⲉⲕ̇ⲕⲗⲏⲥⲓⲁ̀, church; ⲡⲁⲣⲁⲡ̇ⲧⲱⲙⲁ, offense; and ⲁ̀ⲡⲟⲅ̇ⲣⲁⲫⲏ, census; (4) the prefixes of the present I when they consist of a single consonant (2. masc. ⲕ̇-(ⲭ̇-), 3. masc. ϥ̇-, 3. fem. ⲥ̇-) both before a consonant and before a vowel, as in ⲕ̇ⲥⲱⲧⲉⲙ, you hear; ⲭ̇ⲛⲁⲩ, you see; ϥ̇ⲭⲏ, he is placed; ⲕ̇ⲉ̇ⲙⲓ, you know; and ⲥ̇ⲟ̇ⲛⲓ, she resembles; (5) the weak definite article masc. sing. ⲡ̇- (ⲫ̇-), fem. ϯ̇-(ⲑ̇-), both before a consonant and before a vowel, as in ⲡ̇ϣⲏⲣⲓ, the son; ⲫ̇ⲣⲱⲙⲓ, the man; ⲡ̇ⲱ̇ⲟⲩ, the glory; ϯ̇ⲫⲉ, heaven; ⲑ̇ⲙⲁⲩ, the mother; and ϯ̇ⲁ̀ⲫⲉ, the head; (6) the auxiliary ϣ̇, be able: ⲟⲩⲁⲧϣ̇ϯϣⲓ ⲉ̇ⲣⲟⲥ, which cannot be measured (Polotsky, 1949, pp. 25–26). In all these cases, which are late and probably influenced by Arabic, the consonant marked by the *djinkim* never forms a syllable by itself. One may thus with reason consider them suspect from the point of view of Coptic phonology and exclude them from a comparative analysis limited to the investigation of the general value and varieties of usage of the genuinely Coptic *djinkim*.

In preclassical *M* (fourth century; Orlandi, 1974) the letters marked with the *djinkim* (which might well have the same material aspect as the *djinkim* of classical *M*; see below) are as follows: (1) of vowels, only ⲉ when it forms a syllable by itself (equally within the word?) in bradysyllabication, as in ⲉ̇ⲧⲃⲉ, because of, 1 Thes. 3:1 (but ⲁⲛⲁⲕ, I, not ⲁ̇ⲛⲁⲕ, 1 Thes. 3:5); ⲡⲓⲥⲧⲉⲩⲉ̇, to believe, 1 Thes. 2:13 (but ⲡⲁⲣⲟⲩⲥⲓⲁ, advent, not ⲡⲁⲣⲟⲩⲥⲓⲁ̇, 1 Thes. 3:13); (2) (exactly as in point 2 of classical *B*) sonant ⲙ or ⲛ forming a syllable by itself (also within a compound word or at the end of a word?), as in ⲙ̇ⲙⲟⲧⲉⲛ, you, 1 Thes. 3:3; ⲛ̇ⲧⲉⲛ-, near to, 1 Thes. 2:13; ⲛ̇ⲛ̇ⲧⲟⲧⲉⲛ ⲉⲛ, not you, 1 Thes. 2:19 (Kasser, 1981).

In classical *M* (fifth-century, rather than sixth-century[?]) manuscripts, of which only one has been published so far (Schenke, 1981), the letters that use the *djinkim* (which has sometimes the appearance of a very short stroke, sometimes that of an actual point; Kasser, 1981, pp. 121–22) are as follows: (1) of vowels, only ⲁ and ⲉ when each forms a syllable by itself, in bradysyllabication, as in ⲁ̀ϩⲁ, treasure; ⲉⲓⲁ̀ⲡⲉ, trade, craft; ⲥⲟⲩⲁ̀, wheat; ⲉ̀ⲣⲁ, king; ⲓ̈ⲉ̀ⲣⲁ, river; and ϫⲓⲟⲩⲉ̀, steal; (2) (exactly as in point 2 in classical *B* and preclassical *M*) sonant ⲙ or ⲛ forming a syllable by itself, as in ⲙ̇ⲕⲉϩ, be sad; ⲛⲉⲙ̇ⲡϥ-, the verbal prefix of the preterite of the negative perfect (no cases attested for final ⲙ̇); ⲛ̇ⲕⲁⲧ, to sleep; ⲙⲛⲛ̇ⲥⲁ, after; ⲟⲩⲛ̇, there is (Kasser, 1981).

The only traces of the *djinkim* that have been found in *V* are at the beginning (Eccl. 1–4) of P. Mich. 3520 (unpublished) and appear, it seems, only over syllabic ⲙ or ⲛ (hence exactly and exclusively as in point 2 of classical *B* and preclassical and classical *M*). This would be a vestige of a usage that is elsewhere generalized but whose influence did not succeed in imposing itself in this dialect.

All that precedes gives support to Polotsky (1949, p. 27, speaking especially of the *djinkim* in classical *B*): this sign "relates to some phonetic character common to the vowels and to the nasals: one will think directly of sonority." Each of the graphemes that carry the *djinkim,* in *B* as in *M* (or *V*), forms a syllable by itself, often in tachysyllabication and always in bradysyllabication; they are sometimes graphic and concurrently phonologic vowels, sometimes sonant nasals (consonantal graphemes with vocalic function). And when, as in *M,* it is not just any vowel, it is certainly ⲁ and ⲉ, the most open (or voiced) and one of the most open (or voiced) among the vowels, but above all those most used in Coptic, whether each forms a syllable by itself or with another phoneme. Similarly, it is the sonant nasals, the most used among the sonants in Coptic, that carry the *djinkim* (in Coptic the voiced nasals are very frequent too). One may probably see in this the necessity for the use of the *djinkim,* particularly on ⲁ and ⲉ among the vowels and on ⲙ and ⲛ among the sonants.

BIBLIOGRAPHY

Kasser, R. "La Surligne a-t-elle précédé le 'djinkim' dans les textes bohaïriques anciens?" *Revue d'égyptologie* 24 (1972):91–95.

______. "'Djinkim' ou 'surligne' dans les textes en dialecte copte moyen-égyptien." *Bulletin de la Société d'archéologie copte* 23 (1981):115–57.

Mallon, A. *Grammaire copte, bibliographie, chrestomathie et vocabulaire,* 4th ed., rev. M. Malinine. Beirut, 1956.

Orlandi, T. *Papiri della Università degli Studi di Milano (P. Mil. copti),* Vol. 5, *Lettere di San Paolo in copto-ossirinchita, edizione, commento e indici di T. Orlandi, contributo linguistico di H. Quecke.* Milan, 1974.

Polotsky, H. J. "Une Question d'orthographe bohaïrique." *Bulletin de la Société d'archéologie copte* 12 (1949):25–35.

Schenke, H.-M. *Das Matthäus-Evangelium im mittelägyptischen Dialekt des Koptischen (Codex Scheide).* Texte und Untersuchungen der altchristlichen Literatur 127. Berlin, 1981.

Stern, L. *Koptische Grammatik.* Leipzig, 1880.

RODOLPHE KASSER

EGYPTIAN ARABIC VOCABULARY, COPTIC INFLUENCE ON. Coptic loanwords in Egyptian Arabic have been investigated to some extent by several writers, among them G. Sobhy, W. Vycichl, W. H. Worrell, W. B. Bishai, and E. Maher Ishaq.

Worrell included material collected by W. Vycichl and G. Sobhy. In his work, he lists 110 words, of which 83 are Coptic. Bishai collected 205 lexical items, all of which had been suggested by various scholars as Coptic loanwords in Egyptian Arabic. Of these only the 109 items treated in his article were considered by him as valid loanwords. At the end of his article he says, "Turkish, which was never a vernacular of Egypt, left more lexical items in Egyptian Arabic than Coptic did. This is indicated by a partial survey of Turkish loanwords in Egyptian Arabic by E. Littmann (1954, pp. 107–127; cf. Prokosch, 1983), which includes two hundred and sixty-four words." Bishai reached the conclusion that "the limited influence of Coptic on Arabic can only be explained as lack of widespread bilingualism in Egypt during the transition from Coptic to Arabic. . . . Again it may be said that Egyptian Muslims today are right in claiming a predominant Arab ancestory" (Bishai, 1964, p. 47).

E. Maher Ishaq has shown that, contrary to the opinion expressed by Bishai, a very great number of Coptic words have, in fact, survived in the modern colloquial Arabic of Egypt. Some of these items are listed below. Only the most conspicuous etymologies have been chosen (see Ishaq, 1975, for others).

It is to be assumed beyond reasonable doubt that there are many other Coptic words still surviving in remote villages that have not yet been surveyed. On the other hand, there are hundreds of colloquial words apparently of Coptic origin that cannot be identified at present because they have undergone significant change, such as by metathesis, by sound changes of a nonpredictable nature, or because their Coptic etymon has not yet been identified in any of the published documents.

Most of the Coptic words quoted are also attested in hieroglyphic (and/or demotic). For these etymologies see J. Černý (1976), W. Westendorf (1977), and W. Vycichl (1983).

In the following, Egyptian Arabic is rendered in a notation system that is phonological rather than phonetic. Thus, vowel length is often indicated where it is not realized, as in unstressed or in nonfinal closed stressed syllables. Note also that *q* is realized as [g] in Upper Egypt and as ['] in Cairo and large parts of Lower Egypt, and that *j* is realized as [g] in the latter areas.

The vocabulary items are discussed under the following headings:

I. Agricultural items: A. inundation, dams, and canals; B. lands, granaries, and stables; C. preparing the land; D. cultivating and reaping; E. interjections and work songs; F. tools; G. the plough; H. irrigating machines
II. Birds
III. Other animals
IV. Body: A. parts of the body; B. excretions of the body; C. diseases and swellings
V. Buildings and related terms
VI. Children: A. children's play; B. other words related to children
VII. Clothes
VIII. Ecclesiastic terms
IX. Fire, lamps, ovens, and related terms
X. Fish
XI. Food and drink
XII. Insects
XIII. Interjections and cries
XIV. Dry measures
XV. Nautical terms
XVI. Groups and sorts of people
XVII. Plants
XVIII. Sacks and baskets
XIX. Speech, bluffing, silence, and noise
XX. Sticks and tools
XXI. Vessels and utensils
XXII. Other items.

Uppercase letters indicate the various basic Coptic dialects, as follows:

S = Sahidic
B = Bohairic
A = Akhmimic
F = Fayyumic
L = Lycopolitan (or Lyco-Diospolitan)

I. Agricultural Items

A. Inundation, dams, and canals: (1) *damīra,* inundation, from *S* ⲉⲙⲏⲣⲉ, preceded by feminine article; (2) *ṭamy,* silt, deposit of the Nile, from *S* ⲟⲙⲉ, *B* ⲟⲙⲓ, mud, clay, preceded by feminine article; (3) *ishṭūm,* dam, from *S* ϣⲧⲟⲙ, *B* ϣⲑⲟⲙ, closure; (4) *libsh,* brushwood bundle, reed, etc. (with derivates *libsha,* sheaf, *labbish,* to stack with reeds), from *S* ⲗⲉⲃϣ, *B* ⲗⲉⲡϣ, fuel, brushwood; (5) *fayy,* canal, from *B* ϥⲟⲓ, *SB* ϥⲱⲓ (the regular *S* form is ϥⲟ).

B. Lands, granaries, and stables: (1) *barūbiyya,* plural *barāyib,* land used for grain, stubble, from *S* (ⲁ)ⲣⲟⲟⲩⲉ, *B* (ⲁ̀)ⲣⲱⲟⲩⲓ, stubble, preceded by masculine article; (2) *sharāqi,* fallow, *sharaq,* drought, *sharriq* or *sharraq,* to be dry (land), from *S, B* ϣⲁⲣⲕⲉ, lack of water, drought; (3) *shūna,* granary, from *B* ϣⲉⲩⲛⲓ, barn.

C. Preparing the land: (1) *bitn,* ridge (between furrows), from *S* ⲓⲧⲛ, ground, preceded by masculine article; (2) *sikāya,* ploughing, from *S* ⲥⲕⲁⲓ̈, to plough; (3) *ṭāsh,* border, boundary (with derivate *ṭawwish,* to make a boundary), from *S* ⲧⲟϣ, *B* ⲑⲟϣ, border, etc.; cf. *S* ⲧⲱϣ, *B* ⲑⲱϣ, to be boundary.

D. Cultivating and reaping: (1) *taqqā,* to sow (corn-seed), from *S* ⲧⲱ(ⲱ)ϭⲉ, to fix, to plant, or from *S, A, F* ⲧⲱⲕ, to throw; (2) *nabārī,* winter crop of maize (or other grains), from *S* ⲛⲁⲡⲣⲉ, grain, seed; (3) *waḥsa,* beams laid together, etc., from *A, L* ⲟⲩⲁϩⲥⲁ, *S* ⲟⲩⲉϩⲥⲟⲓ̈, *B* ⲟⲩⲁϩⲥⲟⲓ, roof; literally, addition of beams.

E. Interjections and work songs: (1) *ōni,* in the song *ōni ōni ya ṭaḥūn ir-riḥāya* (o mill of the hand mill), from *B* ⲉⲩⲛⲓ, nether millstone; (2) *ēla hōb, hēla hōb,* used when lifting heavy articles: second element from ϩⲱⲃ, thing, work, etc.; various explanations possible; (3) *shōb,* hot wind, also in the verse *hōb hōb qatalnī sh-shōb* (the heat has killed me), from *S* ϣⲱⲃϩ̄, ϣⲱϩⲃ̄, *B* ϣⲱϩⲡ, to be withered, hieroglyphic and demotic *šhb,* hot wind; (4) *hōb,* in the verse quoted above, item 3, and in *hōb ya hōb ya zarʿ in-nōb* (o sowing—seeds which bring forth—gold), from *S, B* ϩⲱⲃ, work, matter; the verse is said during the work of irrigating the field with the shadoof and is answered by the translation, *ya ḥāli ya ḥāli ya zarʿ id-dahab,* (o my business, o my business, o sowing gold); also cf. *hōb hōb ya shughl in-nōb* (o work of gold), sung while threshing wheat (Sobhy, 1950); (5) *nōb*, gold (see above, item 4), from ⲛⲟⲩⲃ.

F. Tools: (1) *bihnāw*, flowering branch of palm, used for sweeping the floor, from *B* ϩⲛⲁⲩ, preceded by masculine article; (2) *ṭūrya* and variants, pick, hoe, etc., from *S*, *A* ⲧⲱⲣⲉ, *B*, *F* ⲧⲱⲣⲓ, spade, pick; also borrowed by Old Nubian and Sīwa Berber; (3) *hawjal*, *hōjal*, *hōjan*, wooden or iron rake, etc., from *S* ϩⲁⲩϭⲁⲗ, *B* ⲁⲩϫⲁⲗ, anchor, hook.

G. The plough: (1) *bajrūm*, *bijrūm*, name of a pole, part of the plough, from *S*, *A*, *L*, *F* ϭⲉⲣⲱⲃ, *S*, *F* ϭⲁⲣⲱⲙ, staff; called *balanja* (cf. Latin *planca*, plank, pale) in the Delta; (2) *baskha*, *biskha*, part of the plough, share-beam, from *S* ⲥϩⲟ, *B* ⲥϧⲟ, plough-share, preceded by masculine article.

H. Irrigating machines: (1) *jabād*, part of the shadoof, consisting of stick or palm-leaf stalk fixed by palm-fibers, from *L* ϭⲁⲡⲉⲧ, *B* ϫⲁⲫⲁⲧ, fiber of palm tree; (2) *shalāw*, part of the shadoof, formed by a system of two ropes to which the buckets are fixed, from *S* ϣⲁⲗⲟⲟⲩ, ϣⲁⲗⲁⲩ, implement or mechanism which turns, water-wheel; (3) *harmīs*, central post of the water-wheel, is found in a Coptic text as *S* ϩⲉⲗⲙⲓⲥ (Crum, 1939, 671a, 780a).

II. Birds

(1) *basharōsh*, flamingo, probably from the Egyptian root *dšr*, red, flamingo, though not directly from *B* ⲉⲑⲏϣⲓ, flamingo; (2) *balshūm*, *balshūn*, *balashūn*, heron, from *S* ⲉⲗϭⲱⲃ, preceded by masculine article; (3) *hība*, *hēba*, ibis, from *S*, *F* ϩⲓⲃⲱⲓ̈, *S* ϩⲉⲃⲱⲓ̈.

III. Other Animals

(1) *baqrūr*, frog, from *S* ⲕⲣⲟⲩⲣ, *B* ⲭⲣⲟⲩⲣ, preceded by masculine article; (2) *timsāḥ*, 'crocodile,' from *S*, *B* ⲙ̄ⲥⲁϩ, preceded by feminine article (as in proper names Θεμσαις, Θομσαεις, Τομσαεις); (3) *ḥandūs*, lizard, gecko, used as nickname for children and as personal name, from *B* ⲁⲛⲑⲟⲩⲥ, lizard, also as personal name ϩⲁⲛⲧⲟⲩⲥ; (4) *shalla*, scorpion, from *B* ϭⲗⲏ.

IV. Body

A. Parts of the body: (1) *bahmōt*, middle finger, current among old people in Karnak (Worrell, 1942, p. 335), from ϩⲟⲙ̄ⲧ, a variant form, typical of nonliterary texts from Thebes, of *S* ϣⲟⲙⲛ̄ⲧ, three, preceded by masculine article; (2) *ṭōra*, variant *dōra* (Upper Egypt), tetrad, group of four; handful, etc., from *S*, *A*, *L* ⲧⲱⲣⲉ, hand; (3) *falt*, thighs, hips, anus, from *S* ⲃⲓⲗⲧⲓ; (4) *kās*, in swearing by the beloved dead, as in *wi-kās abūk*, by the . . . of your father, from *S*, *B* ⲕⲁⲥ, bone, or from *S* ⲕⲱⲱⲥ, corpse.

B. Excretions of the body: (1) *barbar*, to have a running nose, also *barbūr*, soft mucus of the nose, from *S* (ϩ)ⲃⲟⲣⲃⲣ̄, to be loosed, to fall to pieces, etc.; (2) *taff*, to spit, from *S* ⲧⲁϥ, *B* ⲑⲁϥ; (3) *taftaf*, *taftif*, to spit repeatedly, similarly *ṭafṭaf* (parallel to *rayyim*, to foam), from *B* ⲑⲟϥⲧⲉϥ, to let fall drop by drop; (4) *jukṣ*, crepitus ventris, from *B* ϫⲟⲕⲥⲓ; (5) *jīṣ*, (rectal) wind, and *jayyaṣ*, to break wind, probably from *B* ϭⲱⲥ, flatus ventris; (6) *zaraṭ*, to break wind, *zarraṭ*, to break wind repeatedly, *zurāt*, wind, from *S* ⲥⲣ̄-ⲣⲁⲧ, spread feet, so *ventrem purgare;* (7) *farr*, *farfar*, to cast off urine, from *B* ϥⲟⲣϥⲉⲣ, to cast off, to fall; (8) *naff*, to blow the nose, from *B* ⲛⲓϥⲓ, to blow, to breathe, to blow the nose.

C. Diseases and swellings: (1) *tāku*, as in *walad 'anduh tāku* (a boy who has . . .), used for acute cases of pneumonia among children (peasants in Minya), from *S*, *B* ⲧⲁⲕⲟ perdition; (2) *jiffa*, chill, from *S*, *B* ϫⲁϥ, *A*, *L* ϫⲉϥ, frost; (3) *kalaj*, to limp, from *S*, *B* ⲕⲱⲗϫ̄, to be bent, etc.; cf. proper name ⲕⲗ(ⲗ)ⲟⲩϫ, demotic *Ḳlwd*, whence Κολλουϑης; (4) *kalkū'a*, lump, bubo, tumor, also *kalkala*, callus, blister, from *S* ⲕⲗⲕⲗ, *B* ⲕⲉⲗⲕⲗ, *S* ⲕⲉⲗⲕⲟⲩⲗⲉ, lump, pustule; (5) *mitaltil*, dripping in coryza, from *S* ⲧⲗ̄ⲧⲗ̄, *B* ⲧⲉⲗⲧⲉⲗ, to drip, to let drop; (6) *mikhamkhim*, used of a feverish person, from *S* ϩⲙⲟⲙ, *B* ϧⲙⲟⲙ, to be hot; (7) *nōsha*, (typhoid) fever, cf. *S* ⲛⲟ(ⲟ)ϣⲉ, qualitative, said of diseases and wounds, and hieroglyphic *nwḫ*, to heat, to be scorched.

V. Buildings and Related Terms

(1) *birba*, ancient temple, from *S* ⲣⲡⲉ, temple, preceded by masculine article; (2) *janāfōr*, roof, from *S* ϫⲉⲛⲉⲡⲱⲣ, *B* ϫⲉⲛⲉⲫⲱⲣ; (3) *shūsha*, small window, from *S*, *B* ϣⲟⲩϣⲧ̄, window, niche; the final ⲧ was probably considered equivalent to the construct feminine ending in Arabic; (4) *ḍabba*, wooden lock, from *S* ⲉⲡⲟ, bolt, preceded by feminine article; (5) *ṭūba*, brick, Common Arabic, from Egyptian, cf. hieroglyphic *ḏbt* > *dbt*, demotic *tb*, Coptic *S* ⲧⲱⲱⲃⲉ, *S*, *A* ⲧⲱⲃⲉ; Arabic *al-ṭūba* passed into Spanish, etc., as *adobe*.

VI. Children

A. Children's play: (1) *all*, in *li'bit il-all*, a game with pebbles, from *S*, *A*, *B* ⲁⲗ, pebble, etc.; (2) *jull*, small ball, plural *jilūla*, probably from *B* ϭⲗⲟⲓ, ball, cf. *S* ϭⲱⲗ, to roll; (3) *sinnu*, the second round of the Egyptian peasant's ball game, from *S*, *B* ⲥⲛⲁⲩ, two; (4) *sīr*, a line drawn on the ground on which the children stand while playing with small balls, from *S* ⲥⲓⲣ, line, stripe, hair; (5) *minnāw,* (from) there, from *B* ⲙⲛⲏ, there, thither; the diphthong *āw* appears possibly under influence of *S, B* ⲙ̄ⲙⲁⲩ there; (6) *minnāy,* (from) here, from *B* ⲙⲛⲁⲓ, here, hence, hither.

B. Other words related to children: (1) *ala(h),* child, boy, e.g. *khud yala(h),* come on, o boy, from *A, B* ⲁⲗⲁⲩ, *S, B, F* ⲁⲗⲟⲩ, child; (2) *nannūs,* delicate, nice, mignonne, from *S* ⲛⲁⲛⲟⲩⲥ, it is nice (ⲛⲁⲛⲟⲩ⸗, plus suffix pronoun).

VII. Clothes

(1) *turāj,* piece of canvas used to cover the backs of asses (Dishna, Upper Egypt), from *B* ⲑⲟⲩⲣⲁϫⲓ, part of monastic costume, from Greek *ϑωράκιον*, literally, breastplate; (2) *jallābiyya* (Egypt and Syria), a kind of upper garment, gown, flowing outer garment, from *S* ϭⲟⲗⲃⲉ, *B* ϭⲟⲗⲃⲓ, garment of wool, or both from *κολόβιον*? (Černý, 1976); (3) *shintiyān,* plural *shanātīn,* woman's ample trousers (now out of fashion), probably from *S* ϣⲛ̄ⲧⲱ, sheet, robe of linen, cf. *σινδών*; (4) *farajiyya* (Post-Classical Arabic), loose robe, outer mantle of clerics and monks, probably from *B* ⲫⲱⲣⲕ, outer mantle of clerics, monks; (5) *fūṭah,* towel, napkin, apron, kerchief, *fūṭa* (Classical Arabic), waist-wrapper, cf. *S* ϥⲱⲧⲉ, to wipe, and also *S* ⲃⲁⲑⲱ, a garment or napkin, probably for *S, B* ϥⲁⲧ-ϩⲟ (from *S* ϥⲱⲧⲉ and *S, B* ϩⲟ, face), face-towel.

VIII. Ecclesiastic Terms

(1) *ajbiyya,* book of canonic hours, horologium, derived from *S, B* ⲁϫⲡ, hour; (2) *amnūt,* sexton (Worrell, 1942, p. 331), from *S, L, B, F* ⲙⲛⲟⲩⲧ, porter, doorkeeper; (3) *anbā,* pronounced *amba,* a title for Coptic clergy, from *B* ⲁⲃⲃⲁ; (4) *jābānyōt,* Our Father, is *B* ϫⲉ ⲡⲉⲛⲓⲱⲧ; (5) *daqq,* to bake, baking of the holy bread, from *S, F* ⲧⲱⲕ, ⲧⲱϭ, *B* ⲑⲱⲕ, kindle; bake; (6) *shūra, shūrya,* censer, from *S, B, F* ϣⲟⲩⲣⲏ, censer, brazier, altar; (7) *ṭubḥāt,* prayers, plural of *ṭubḥ, ṭubḥa* from *S, B* ⲧⲱⲃϩ̄, pray, prayer; (8) *hōs,* hymn, ode, from ϩⲱⲥ song, hymn, ode; (9) *arībāmāwi,* remember me (in your prayer)!, is *B* ⲁⲣⲓ ⲡⲁⲙⲉⲩⲓ, remember me!; (10) *ayārnūw(w)i,* ecclesiastic term as a confession, is *B* ⲁⲓⲉⲣⲛⲟⲃⲓ, I committed sin; (11) *kō nāy awōl,* forgive me!, is *B* ⲭⲱ ⲛⲏⲓ ⲉ̀ⲃⲟⲗ, forgive me!; (12) *shānrōmbi,* long live, is *B* ϣⲉ ⲛ̀ⲣⲟⲙⲡⲓ, hundred years.

IX. Fire, Lamps, Ovens, and Related Terms

(1) *takk,* to kindle, in *takk il-kibrīta,* he kindled the match, from *S, F* ⲧⲱⲕ, ⲧⲱϭ, *B* ⲑⲱⲕ, kindle; bake; (2) *rāyka,* burning coal, from *S* ⲣⲁⲕϩⲉ, *B* ⲣⲁⲕϩⲓ, fuel; cf. ⲣⲱⲕϩ, burning, fervor; fuel, firewood; (3) *fawwad,* to wipe, to clean the oven by rubbing (with a wet *fōda,* oven mop, or *fawwāda* [Upper Egypt]); also *fawwaṭ,* to wipe, clean or dry by rubbing, and *fawwāṭa,* oven mop, from ϥⲱⲧⲉ, to wipe.

X. Fish

(1) *būrī,* mullet, whiting, from *S* ⲃⲱⲣⲉ, *B* ⲫⲟⲣⲓ, a fish, *mugil cephalus, būrī;* (2) *rāy,* a kind of fish, *alestes dentex,* from *S, B* ⲣⲏⲓ, a fish, *alestes dentex*; (3) *shāl,* plural *shīlān,* a Nile fish, from *S* ϫⲏⲗ, a fish, *shīlān;* (4) *shabār,* a fish, *tilapia nilotica,* from *S* ϣⲁϥⲟⲩⲣ, *tilapia nilotica;* (5) *shilba,* a kind of Nile fish, bream, schilbe, *silurus mystus,* from *S* ϭⲗ̄ⲃⲟⲟⲩ, ϭⲉⲗⲃⲁⲩ, *B* ϫⲉⲗϥⲁⲩ, a fish, *silurus mystus;* (6) *ṣīr,* small fish, sardine, name of a fish species (Luxor), usually salted, from *S, B* ϫⲓⲣ, brine, small salted fish; (7) *qashu,* a fish (cf. Worrell, 1942, p. 338), from *S* ⲕⲁϣⲱ, *B* ⲕⲁϣⲟⲩ, among fish, *qashuwāt, qashwa* (Crum, 1939, 130b); possibly through iteration *qashqūsh,* a fish, sand smelt, silverside; (8) *qīl,* a kind of small fish, of species *shāl,* from *B* ⲕⲉⲗ, ⲕⲏⲗ, a fish (of species *shāl*); (9) *kalūj,* a kind of fish (cf. Worrell, 1942, p. 339), cf. *B* ⲕⲟⲩⲗⲁϫⲓ, a fish, *ἁβραμίς*; (10) *mishṭ,* plural *amshāṭ, tilapia nilotica, bulṭī* fish, from *S* ⲉⲙⲉϣϭⲉ, a Nile fish, *tilapia (chromis) nilotica.*

XI. Food and Drink

(1) *biṣāra, baṣāra,* puree of beans, from *S* ⲟⲩⲣⲱ, ⲁⲣⲱ, beans, preceded by *S* ⲡⲓⲥ(ⲉ), thing cooked, or *S* ⲡⲁⲥⲉ, cooked food, in construct state (?); (2) *bōsh, būsh,* porridge, gruel, from *S* ⲟⲟⲩϣ, *B* ⲱⲟⲩϣ, gruel of bread or lentils, etc., preceded by masculine article; (3) *dibdāb, dabdūb, dibdib,* a kind of unleavened bread, cf. *S* ⲧⲱⲡⲉ, to taste; *S* ⲧⲃ̄ⲧⲃ̄, mixed (?) food; (4) *samīṭ,* white baked stuff, often strewn with sesame seed, from *S, B, F* ⲥⲁⲙⲓⲧ, fine flour, *σεμίδαλις*, the finest wheaten flour; from the latter, probably also Classical and Egyptian Arabic *samīd,* white or whitened flour, fine bread; (5) *kunāfa,* (pastry made of sweet) vermicelli (Post-Classical Arabic), cf. hieroglyph *ḳfn* to bake, kind of bread, demotic *ḳfn, ḳnf,* kind of bread, *B* ⲕⲉⲛⲉⲫⲓⲧⲉⲛ, (from *ⲕⲉⲛⲉϥⲓ plus Greek ending *-τιον*?), kind of loaf or cake; ⲕⲉⲛⲉⲫⲓⲧⲏⲥ, baker; (6) *marīsa,* date-wine, barley-wine, zythum; in Nubian and Sudanese Arabic a kind of beer, from *S* ⲙ̄ⲣⲓⲥ, new wine, must; (7) *manjūj,* baked, roasted food, from *S* ⲙⲁ ⲛϭⲟϭ, baked, roasted food; (8) *takhkh,* be drunken, in locution *shirib lamma takhkh,* he drank till he became drunken, from *S* ϯϩⲉ, *B* ⲑⲓϩⲓ, to become, be drunken; (9)

shawwaḥ, to grill, broil, as in *shawwaḥ il-laḥma ʿala n-nār* (broiled the meat over fire), from *S* ϣⲱⲃϩ̄, ϣⲱⲟⲩϩ, to be withered, scorched, to scorch, wither.

XII. Insects

(1) *bība,* a biting insect, flea, from *B* ⲑⲏⲓ, flea, preceded by masculine article ⲡⲓ-; (2) *hallūs,* spider's web, from *S, L* ϩⲗⲗⲟⲩⲥ, *S, B* ϩⲗⲗⲟⲩⲥ, spider's web.

XIII. Interjections and Cries

(1) *is,* behold, lo!, from *S, A, L* ⲉⲓⲥ, *B* ⲓⲥ; (2) *ō, ōh,* oh, interjection of pain or disgust, from ⲱ, an exclamation expressing surprise, joy, pain; (3) *ō,* o!, mostly together with the vocative particle *ya,* as, e.g., *ō ya-brāhīm,* o Abraham!, from *S, B* ⲱ, a particle used with the vocative for address; (4) *ujāy* and *jāy,* a cry for help, from *S, B* ⲟⲩϫⲁï, to be whole, safe; (5) *shē,* shā, by, particle of swearing in vows, as in *shē-lla ya sitti ya ʿadra,* by God, o my Lady the Virgin, from *S, B, F* ϣⲉ, *S, B* ϣⲁ, by, in swearing; (6) *shī,* gee!, gee-up!, from ϣⲉ, to go.

XIV. Dry Measures

(1) *ardabb,* measure of grain, from *S* ⲣ̄ⲧⲟⲃ, cf. demotic *rtb,* ἀρτάβη, all from Aramaic *ardab,* this perhaps from Persian; (2) *rafṭāw, rifṭāw, rufṭāw,* a measure of grain, a quarter of a *wēba* = a half of a *kēla* = 1/24 of an *ardabb,* from *S* ⲣⲉ-ϥⲧⲟⲟⲩ, a fourth, one quarter; (3) *wēba,* Post-Classical Arabic *waybah,* a measure of grain, from *S* ⲟⲉⲓⲡⲉ, ephah.

XV. Nautical Terms

(1) *ramrūm,* raft, bark, from *S, B* ⲙ̀ⲣⲱⲙ, raft; also cf. *maramma,* raft (Colin, 1920, p. 77); (2) *ṭiyāb, ṭayāb,* east wind, north wind, from ⲧⲏⲩ (*S, A, F* ⲧⲟⲩ-, *B* ⲑⲟⲩ-) wind, and *S* ⲉⲓⲉⲃⲧ̄, east; (3) *marīsī,* southern, south wind, derived from *S, B* ⲙⲁⲣⲏⲥ, Southern country, Upper Egypt. See also Section I, items (D-3), (E-2), (E-3), and (F-3).

XVI. Groups and Sorts of People

(1) *shilla, shulla,* group, coterie, clique, plural *shilal, shulal,* probably from *B* ϣⲗⲟⲗ, plural ϣⲗⲱⲗ, folk, people; (2) *baẓramīt,* fool, silly, probably from *S* ⲥⲁⲣⲙ̄-ϩⲏⲧ, literally, he whose mind goes astray, preceded by masculine article; (3) *bōn,* bad, wicked, as in *da rājil bōn,* he is a bad man, from *S* ⲃⲱⲱⲛ, bad; (4) *tilim,* impudent, as in *mara matlūma,* woman of ill fame; *talāma,* forwardness, from *S, L* ⲧⲱⲗⲙ̄, *B* ⲑⲟⲗⲙ〃, to be defiled, to defile, and (noun) stain, pollution; (5) *kharyaṭ,* to be disordered in mind, from *S, B* ϣⲱⲣⲧ̄, to be demented, and *B* ϧⲟⲣⲧ, madman; (6) *nōsh,* enormous, something very big, as in *qadd in-nōsh* (as big or large as), *zayy in-nōsh* (like, as, such as), from *S* ⲛⲟϭ, great, large.

XVII. Plants

(1) *arw,* cypress, from *B* ⲁ̀ⲣⲟ, cypress; (2) *barsīm,* clover, from *S* ⲃⲉⲣⲥⲓⲙ, clover? (found once, in manuscript of ca. 730); (3) *barnūf, conyza odorata,* from *S* ⲡⲉⲣⲛⲟⲩϥⲉ, a plant?; cf. demotic *pr-nfr,* a plant; (4) *rīta,* a plant, *sapindus,* used for cleaning stained clothes, from *B* ⲣⲓⲧⲁ, a plant; (5) *sanṭa, acacia nilotica,* cf. hieroglyphic *šndt,* thorn tree, demotic *sntt, S* ϣⲟⲛⲧⲉ, thorn tree (*acacia nilotica*); passed as loanword into Akkadian, Hebrew, and Arabic (Černý, 1976); (6) *sawsan,* lily, iris, cf. hieroglyphic and demotic *sšn, B* ϣⲱϣⲉⲛ, lotus flower; also borrowed by Hebrew, Aramaic, Syriac, Greek (σοῦσον); (7) *shirsh,* spray, especially the green sprays of carrots, from *S, F* ϣⲣⲁϣ, bundle, cf. hieroglyphic and demotic *ḫrš* (Černý).

XVIII. Sacks and Baskets

(1) *buqūṭī,* a small basket made of palm leaves, straw basket, also *baqūṭī, baqūṭah,* from *S, B* ⲕⲟⲧ, basket, preceded by masculine article; (2) *janba,* basket for dates, from *S* ϫ(ⲉ)ⲛⲟϥ, ϫⲉⲛⲟⲃ, *B* ϭⲛⲟϥ, ϣⲛⲟ(ⲩ)ϥ, basket, crate; see also *shinf* (item 5 following); (3) *shalīta,* a large sack, probably through metathesis from *S* ϣⲁⲧⲓⲗⲁ, bag, etc.; (4) *shinda,* a grass mat or cloth in which curdled milk is kept to drain its whey and become cheese, from *S* ϣⲟⲛⲧⲉ, ϣⲛ̄ⲧⲉ, plaited work; (5) *shinf,* net sacks, singular *shinfa,* plural *shinaf; shanīf,* net sack for straw, from *B* ϭⲛⲟϥ, ϣⲛⲟϥ, *S* ϫ(ⲉ)ⲛⲟϥ, basket, crate.

XIX. Speech, Bluffing, Silence, and Noise

(1) *balham,* to bluff, to lie, to speak jargon, to speak fast, from the name of the Blemmye people, known for their bluffing, *S* ⲃⲗ̄ϩⲙⲟⲩ (cf. Vycichl, 1983, 28); (2) *matmata,* speech, prattle, argument; *matmat,* to argue, cf. *S, A, L* ⲙⲟⲩⲧⲉ, speak, call, or rather hieroglyphic *mtmt,* to discuss, discussion; (3) *hawwash, hawwish,* to bluff (mostly by talking roughly), to bully, from *S* ϩⲟⲟⲩϣ, *B* ϩⲱⲟⲩϣ, to abuse, to curse; (4) *wazz,* tinnitus; *washsh,* from *S* ⲟⲉⲓϣ, ⲟⲉⲓⲥ, cry.

XX. Sticks and Tools

(1) *shōda,* stick (al-Matīʿah), from *S, B, F* ϣⲃⲱⲧ, rod, staff; (2) *darafs,* awl, spike, from *B* ⲑⲣⲁⲡⲥ, ⲧⲣⲁⲡⲥ; (3) *shqāl,* bell (province of Suhāj); *shqilqīl,*

from *S* ϣⲕ(ⲉ)ⲗⲕⲓⲗ, ϣϭⲓⲗϭⲓⲗ, and cf. *S* ϣⲕⲏⲗ, anklet; (4) *shalīsh,* (iron) hook, from *S, A* ϣⲗⲓϭ, sharpened thing, spike; (5) *faṭs, fuṭs,* an iron wedge used by the carpenter in sawing, from *S* ⲡⲁⲧⲥⲉ, *B* ⲫⲁⲧⲥⲓ, piece, plank; (6) *qīl,* bell (Suhāj), cf. the reduplicated *B* ⲕⲁⲕⲓⲗ; (7) *washūr, warshūr,* saw, from *S, A, B* ⲃⲁϣⲟⲩⲣ.

XXI. Vessels and Utensils

(1) *baqlūla,* pot, from *S* ⲕⲉⲗⲱⲗ, *B* ϫⲗⲟⲗ, pitcher, jar, preceded by masculine article; (2) *bukla,* an earthenware vessel with two handles used for water, from *S* ⲕⲗⲏ, *B* ϫⲗⲏ, vessel for liquid, preceded by masculine article; (3) *makro,* mortar (Bagūr), from *B* ⲙⲁⲕⲣⲟ, trough, mortar.

XXII. Other Items

(1) *ishbār,* wonder, in *ishbār ʿalayya,* alas for me, from *S, A* ϣⲡⲏⲣⲉ, wonder, amazement; (2) *amandi,* in the imprecation *dāhya twaddīk l-amandi,* may a tragedy take you to hell, from *S, A* ⲁⲙⲛ̄ⲧⲉ, *B, F* ⲁⲙⲉⲛϯ, hades; (3) *ihniyy,* anything, from *S* ϩⲛⲁ(ⲁ)ⲩ, *A* ϩⲛⲉ, vessel, thing; (4) *bāb,* grave, as in the name of the Valley of the Kings, *bāb il-mulūk,* etc., from *S, A, B, F* ⲃⲏⲃ, cave; (5) *baḥat,* to dig (also in Sudan), and *faḥat,* from *S* ⲡⲱⲧϩ̄ (cf. qual. ⲡⲟϩⲧ̄), to carve; (6) *barash,* to squat, to lie down, from *S, A, F* ⲡⲱⲣϣ̄, to spread, to be spread; (7) *bursh,* mat, from *S* ⲡⲱⲣϣ̄; (8) *bary,* new, as in *warrāna bary wary,* literally, he showed us something always new, from *S, A, L* ⲃⲣ̄ⲣⲉ, *B, F* ⲃⲉⲣⲓ; (9) *bushla, bashla,* bundle, as e. g. *bashlit fijl,* a bundle of radishes, from *S* ⲡⲟϭⲗⲉ, *L* ⲡⲁϭⲗⲉ, art or quantity of vegetables, cluster of vegetables or fruit (Černý, 1976); (10) *bilbila,* pill, small ball, probably from *S, L* ⲃⲗ̄ⲃⲓⲗⲉ, a single grain of mustard, etc.; (11) *talla,* to lift, to carry, from *S, A, B* ⲧⲁⲗⲟ lift, etc.; (12) *tūt,* as in the expression *tūt ḥāwi,* gather, come together for the magician, from *S* ⲧⲟⲟⲩⲧⲉ, *B* ⲑⲱⲟⲩϯ, to gather, to be gathered; (13) *jarjar,* to frolic, from *S* ϫⲉⲣϫⲣ̄, *B* ϫⲉⲣϫⲉⲣ, to live luxuriously, to frolic; (14) *ḥadā,* before, in the presence of, as e.g. *ḥadāk,* before thee, in thy presence, from *S, A* ϩⲏⲧ〃, as ϩⲏⲧⲕ, before thee; (15) *dāḥa,* to beseech, from *B, S* ϯ ϩⲟ; (16) *daḥḥ,* to apply one's self to, from the preceding, meaning turn face, look; (17) *daghan,* to thrust, from *S* ⲧⲱϭⲛ, to push; (18) *daqq,* to hammer, to insist, etc., from *S, A, L, F* ⲧⲱⲕ to strengthen, to confirm, to drive, hammer; (19) *dihna, dihni,* forehead, in *dihn(a) il-jabal,* the front of the mountain, from *S, A* ⲧⲉϩⲛⲉ, *B, F* ⲧⲉϩⲛⲓ, forehead (the hieroglyphic prototype, *dhnt,* meaning also mountain ledge); (20) *rawash,* to hurry, to worry; *rawsha,* concern, worry, from *S* ⲣⲟⲟⲩϣ, *A* ⲣⲁⲩϣ, to have care for, concern, worry; (21) *sās,* oakum, tow, from *S* ⲥⲁ(ⲁ)ⲥⲉ, *B* ⲥⲁϩⲥ, tow; (22) *stīm,* stibium, antimon, kohl, from *S, B* ⲥⲧⲏⲙ, *B* ⲥⲑⲏⲙ; (23) *sakk,* to draw, to protract the fast (as, e.g., *ṣōm Niwa yākhdu sakk wara baʿd,* he passes [the three days of] the fast of Nineveh in a continuous fasting), from *S, L, B, F* ⲥⲱⲕ, to draw, to protract the fast; (24) *shakshik,* to prick repeatedly, from *S* ϫⲟⲕϫⲕ̄, *B* ϫⲟⲕϫⲉⲕ, to prick, brand; (25) *shaknan,* to be enthusiastic or zealous, to act with a forced hardness; *shaknana,* energy, zeal, from *B* ϣϭⲛⲏⲛ, to strive, contend; (26) *shalla,* skein, hank, probably from *S, B* ϣⲟⲗ *S, L, F* ϣⲁⲗ, bundle; (27) *shallūj* (South of Qena), *shallūd* (North of Qena, Farshūṭ), *shallūt* (Banī-Suef, Cairo), *sallūj* (Luxor through Aswan), kick; *shallat, shalli,* to kick, from *B* ϭⲁⲗⲟϫ, *F* ϭⲁⲗⲁϫ, foot, knee; (28) *shanaṭ,* to tie, knot (*shanaṭ dirāʿu f-mandīl,* he hung his arm in a sling), verbal noun *shanṭ; shinēṭa,* running-knot, slip-knot, from *S, B, F* ϣⲱⲛⲧ, to plait; *S* ϣⲟⲛⲧⲉ, ϣⲛ̄ⲧⲉ, plaited work; (29) *ṣarīf,* rope of twine, of *ḥalfa* or vine twigs, from *S* ⲥⲁⲣϥⲉ, ⲥⲁⲣϭϥ, vine twig; (30) *ṣafṭiyya,* ready, prepared, in *ṣafṭiyya n-nahār-da,* (our meal is already) preparing today, a polite way of refusing an invitation to lunch (Aswan), from *S* ⲥⲟϥⲧⲉ, to be ready; (31) *ṣann, sann,* to wait, as in *ṣinn ʿalēh ḥabba,* give him a little time, possibly from *S, A* ⲥⲓⲛⲉ, to pass by; (32) *ṭarash,* to throw one on his face; to oppress, as, e.g., *id-dinya ṭārshāni,* life is oppressing me, from *S* ⲑⲣ̄ϣⲟ, to make heavy, to terrify; (33) *ṭannish,* to remain silent; to feign not to hear; to give a deaf ear to, from *B* ⲑⲟⲛϣ (Crum, 1939, s.v. ⲑⲱⲃϣ), to be astonished, to stare with astonishment; (34) *ṭahma,* invitation, from *S* ⲧⲱϩⲙ̄, *B* ⲑⲱϩⲉⲙ, to invite; (35) *fāt, fawwat,* to putrefy (food), to taint, from *S* ⲃⲱⲧⲉ, ϥⲱⲧⲉ, to pollute, to befoul; (36) *kās,* pain, in *ya kāsi minnak,* o my pain from you; *kāyis,* run down, seedy, from *S, B* (ⲧ)ⲕⲁⲥ pain; (37) *karash,* to hurry; to flatter, to urge importunately (*id-dinya kārshāni,* life is hurrying me; *il-wiliyya di kārshāh . . . wākla dmāghu,* this woman is influencing him . . . she is eating his mind), from *S, A, B, F* ⲕⲱⲣϣ̄, to request, persuade, cajole; (38) *laqash,* to sneer, to ridicule, from *S* (ⲉ)ⲗⲕ-ϣⲁ, to turn up nose, to sneer; (39) *(i)mjakhkhim,* putrid, defiled, from *S, L* ϫⲱϩⲙ̄, *B* ϭⲱϧⲉⲙ, to be defiled; (40) *makmak,* to hesitate, be reluctant, and verbal noun *makmaka* (*balāsh makmaka, ma-tibqāsh bi-mīt niyya w-fikr,* don't hesitate, don't let yourself have a hundred aims and ideas), from *S, B* ⲙⲟⲕⲙⲉⲕ, to think, ponder; (41) *nabbit,* to sew fine stitches, from *B* ⲛⲟⲩⲃⲧ, to weave; (42) *hammas, hammis,* to sit, from *S* ϩⲙⲟⲟⲥ, *A, L* ϩⲙⲉⲥ, *B* ϩⲉⲙⲥⲓ, to sit, remain, dwell; (43) *hamsi,* sit down! (region of Balyana), from *B* ϩⲉⲙⲥⲓ, sit down!; (44) *wajba,* time, hour, period (*da qaʿad ʿindina wajba,* he

remained with us for a while), from *B* ⲁ̀ⲭⲛⲓ, ⲁ̀ⲭⲛ⸗, hour, preceded by indefinite article; (45) *waḥas,* to embarrass, *waḥsa,* confusion, from *S* ⲟⲩⲉϩ-ϩⲓⲥⲉ, to give trouble; (46) *wary,* new, as in *da-hu wary ʿalēna,* this is something new for us, and *wirwir,* plural *warāwir,* young, fresh (especially chicks, radishes), from *S, A, L* ⲃⲣⲣⲉ, *B, F* ⲃⲉⲣⲓ, new, young; see also *bary* (item 8, this section); (47) *waḍḍab,* to arrange, to put in order, to prepare, probably from *S* ⲟⲩⲱⲧⲃ, to change, remove, transfer; (48) *ya,* either, or (*ya dī ya dā,* either this or that, *ya tuqʿud ya timshi,* you must either sit down or go away), from *S* ⲉⲓⲉ *S, L, B, F,* ⲓⲉ, or, whether . . . or.

BIBLIOGRAPHY

Bishai, W. B. "Coptic Influences on Egyptian Arabic." *Journal of Near Eastern Studies* 23 (1964):39–47.

Černý, J. *Coptic Etymological Dictionary.* Cambridge, 1976.

Colin, G. S. "Notes de dialectologie arabe." *Bulletin de l'Institut francais d'archéologie orientale* 20 (1922):45–87.

Crum, W. E. *A Coptic Dictionary.* Oxford, 1939.

Ishaq, E. M. *The Phonetics and Phonology of the Bohairic Dialect of Coptic, and the Survival of Coptic Words in the Colloquial and Classical Arabic of Egypt, and of Coptic Grammatical Constructions in Colloquial Egyptian Arabic,* 2 vols. Doctoral dissertation, Oxford, 1975.

Littmann, E. "Türkisches Sprachgut im Ägyptisch-Arabischen." *Westöstliche Abhandlungen* (1954): 107–27.

Prokosch, E. *Osmanisches Wortgut im Ägyptisch-Arabischen.* Islamkundliche Untersuchungen 78. Berlin, 1983.

Sobhy, G. P. *Common Words in the Spoken Arabic of Egypt of Greek or Coptic Origin.* Cairo, 1950.

Vycichl, W. *Dictionnaire étymologique de la langue copte.* Louvain, 1983.

Westendorf, W. *Koptisches Handwörterbuch, bearbeitet auf Grund des Koptischen Handwörterbuchs von Wilhelm Spiegelberg.* Heidelberg, 1977.

Worrell, W. H. *Coptic Texts in the University of Michigan Collection, with a Study in the Popular Traditions of Coptic.* Ann Arbor, Mich., 1942.

EMILE MAHER ISHAQ

ETYMOLOGY. The Coptic language comprises an autochthonous vocabulary (see VOCABULARY OF EGYPTIAN ORIGIN and VOCABULARY OF SEMITIC ORIGIN) with an overlay of several heterogeneous strata (see VOCABULARY, COPTO-GREEK and VOCABULARY, COPTO-ARABIC). As a rule, etymologic research in Coptology is limited to the autochthonous vocabulary. Etymology (from Greek *etymos,* true, and *logos,* word) is the account of the origin, the meaning, and the phonetics of a word over the course of time and the comparison of it with cognate or similar terms.

In Coptic the basic vocabulary, as well as the morphology of the language, is of Egyptian origin. Egyptian shares many words and all its morphology (grammatical forms) with the Semitic languages.

Egyptian is transcribed with an alphabet of twenty-four letters in the following order: *3, ỉ, ʿ, w, b, p, f, m, n, r, h, ḥ, ḫ, ẖ, z, s, š, ḳ* (sometimes transcribed *q*), *k, g, t, ṯ, d, ḏ.* All these letters represent consonants. The sign *3* is the glottal stop heard at the commencement of German words beginning with a vowel (*die Oper*) or Hebrew aleph; *ỉ* is *y* in "yes," but sometimes pronounced like aleph; *ʿ* is called ʿayin, as in Hebrew, the emphatic correspondent to aleph (cf. Arabic *ʿAbdallāh*); *h* is the English *h*; *ḥ* is an emphatic *h*, as in Arabic *Muḥammad*; *ḫ* is the Scotch *ch* in *loch; ẖ* is like German *ch* in *ich* (between *ḫ* and *š*), and nearly like English *h* in human; *š* is English *sh* in "ship"; *ṯ* is *ch* in English "child"; and *ḏ* is English *j* in "joke."

The group *ỉỉ* is pronounced *y*. There is no particular sign for *l*; this sound is transcribed *3, r, n,* or *nr.* Late Egyptian uses the sign of a lion (*rw*) for *l.* There are no vowels written in Egyptian, but the original pronounciation may be reconstructed to some extent by the insertion of the Coptic vowels and by comparative studies. Thus, Egyptian *rmṯ,* man, which is *B* ⲣⲱⲙⲓ and *S* ⲣⲱⲙⲉ, is reconstructed **rōmeṯ* and was probably pronounced **rāmiṯ,* which is the form of a participle, as Egyptian Arabic **rāgil* (classical Arabic *rağul*).

Egyptian shares many words with the Semitic languages, including Akkadian (Assyrian in northern Mesopotamia, Babylonian in southern Mesopotamia), Hebrew (language of the Bible), Aramaic (language of Jesus Christ), Arabic (language of the Qur'ān), and Ethiopian (language of Menelik, the legendary son of Solomon and the Queen of Sheba, founder of the Ethiopian dynasty), among others.

Egyptologists pronounce Egyptian words by inserting *e* between the consonants: *sḏm,* to hear, is *sejem; ptr,* to look, is *peter.* The letters *3* and *ʿ* are pronounced *a*; *ỉ* is *i*; and *w* may be pronounced as *u.* Thus, *ḥ3p,* to hide, becomes *hap*; *ʿnḫ,* to live, is *ankh*; *ỉny,* to bring, is *ini*; and *mw,* water, is *mu. Ḫwfw,* the name of the builder of the Great Pyramid, becomes *Khufu* or, more often, *Cheops,* as the Greeks rendered it. This system provides an artificial pronunciation as a practical means to read an Egyptian text, but not the true phonetic value of the words.

The meaning of Egyptian words shows that the primitive vocabulary of the language was to a large extent identical with that of Semitic tongues: for example, *ỉb* (Arabic *lubb*), heart; *sp.t* (Arabic *šif-a.t*), lip; *ỉdn* (Arabic *3uḏn*), ear; *ls*, written *ns*, but *B*, *S las* (Arabic *lisān*), tongue; *d*, hand, as value of the hand hieroglyph (Arabic *yad*); *šdy*, to suckle (Arabic *ṯady*, woman's breast); *ḏbʿ* (Arabic *'iṣbāʿ*), finger; *gḥs*, gazelle (Arabic *ǧaḥš*, ass, gazelle); *ḳnd* (Arabic *ḳird*), ape; *z3b* (Arabic *ḏi3b*), *jackal*; *sfḫ* (Arabic *sabʿ-a*), seven; *wsḫ* (Arabic *wasiʿ*) to be wide; *ỉwn* (Arabic *lawn*), color; *ḥsb* (Arabic *ḥasab*), to calculate; *mwt* (Arabic *māt*, *yamūt* : *mawt*), to die; *ẖmm* (Arabic *ḥamm*, *yaḥumm* : *ḥamm*), to be hot.

There are also many words in Egyptian that are not found in any Semitic language. One might suppose that they belong to the African substratum of the language. Examples of such words are *ỉnʿ*, chin; *fnḏ*, nose; *ẖ.t*, belly; *ỉnm*, skin, hide; *3bw*, elephant; *mmy*, giraffe; *mzḥ*, crocodile; *št3*, turtle; *mnw*, dove; *bny*, date (fruit); *ḫt*, wood; *mḥʿ*, flax; *mdw*, to speak; *wnm*, to eat; *zwr*, to drink; *ḥmsy*, to sit; *wʿb*, to be pure; *ỉb3*, to dance; *wḥm*, to repeat; and *ẖdb*, to kill.

The grammatical elements of Egyptian correspond to those of the Semitic languages. The original form of some of them has been reconstructed, such as *-a.t*, ending of feminine nouns; *-ū* (not written in ancient texts, later indicated by *-w*), ending of the masculine plural; *-ay* (written *-y*), ending of the dual; *-īy* (written *-y*) adjective ending (cf. Arabic *-īy* as in *ʿarab-īy*, Arabic; *hind-īy*, Indian; *turk-īy*, Turkish). The endings of the personal pronouns resemble those of Semitic (particularly of Akkadian), with the sole exception of *-f* (probably *-fi*) for the pronoun of the third-person masculine singular "his." The verbal prefix *s-* (pronounced *sa-*) forms causative verbs, such as *wʿb*, to be pure, *s-wʿb* (**sawʿab*), to purify, also written *s-ʿb* (**sōʿab*); compare this with the causative prefix *ša-* in Babylonian, *sa-* (Assyrian). The prefix *m-* (with different vowels) forms names of place (*nomina loci*), names of instruments (*nomina instrumenti*), and passive participles, as in *m-ẖr*, low-lying land, from *ẖr*, under; *m-ḫ3.t*, balance, from *ḫ3y*, to weigh; *m-ḫtm.t*, closed receptacle, from *ḫtm*, to close, to seal; *m-ḥrỉ*, dung (cf. *S* ϩⲟⲉⲓⲣⲉ; **ḥair-a.t*, ancient **ḥarỉ-a.t*).

The position of Egyptian thus resembles that of Mbugu, a language spoken in Tanzania combining Bantu grammar with a largely non-Bantu vocabulary. In Mbugu "finger" is *ki-tshaa* (plural, *vi-tshaa*); in Bantu it is *ki-dole* (plural, *vi-dole*). The grammatical prefixes *ki-* (singular) and *vi-* (plural) are alike, but the words for "finger," *-tshaa* in Mbugu and *-dole* in Bantu (Swahili), are different. The specific Mbugu words derive from Somali, Iraqw, or other, still unknown languages (Tucker and Bryan, 1974).

Terminology

Coptic dialects are cited according to the system devised by Kasser (1980a–b, 1981): *A* is Akhmimic; *B* is Bohairic; *F* is Fayyumic; *L* is Lycopolitan or Lyco-Diospolitan; *M* is Mesokemic; *S* is Sahidic; and (not a dialect) O is Old Coptic.

"Radicals" are, as in the Semitic languages, the stem consonants of a word. Egyptian *wn*, to open, is a biradical verb, and *sḏm*, to hear, a triradical one. The radicals of a word are called a "skeleton": the skeleton of *B*, *S* ⲥⲱⲧⲡ, to choose, is *stp*. "Emphatic" as a phonetic term means articulated with an action of the tongue toward the soft palate combined with a contraction of the vocal cords. As a grammatical term, "emphatic" means a durative or repeated action, an action carried out by several subjects or on several objects. *B* ⲣⲁ, to do continually, is the emphatic form of *B* ⲓⲣⲓ, to do.

Egyptian reconstructed forms are preceded by an asterisk: **nátīr*, god; **naṯār-a.t*, goddess; **sāḏim*, to hear; **naḫát*, to be strong. Still older forms take a small circle: *°saḏm*, to hear; *°naḫāt*, to be strong. Archaic forms are preceded by quotation marks: *"saḏm-u*, to hear; *"naḫāt-u*, to be strong.

Periods of the Egyptian Language

The development of the Egyptian language comprises four main periods:

Proto-Egyptian (4000–3000 B.C.). Prehistoric civilizations of Amra (Negada I), Gerza (Negada II), Merimda, etc. Formation of the Egyptian language. No written documents.

Ancient Egyptian. Language of the Old Kingdom (approximately 3000–2100 B.C.). Short inscriptions, religious and biographic texts. The Pyramids, the most famous of which are those of Khufu (Cheops), Khafre (Chephren), and Menkure (Mykerinos), at Giza (2545–2457). Pyramid texts, beginning with Unas (Onnos) (2310–2290).

Middle Egyptian. Classical period of the Egyptian language, mainly during the Twelfth Dynasty (seven kings, called Amenemhet or Sesostris) (1991–1785 B.C.). After this dynasty, decline, invasion of the Hyksos (1650–1553 B.C.). The classical language remains in use for religious texts until the Roman period.

Late Egyptian, also called New Egyptian. Mainly the language of the Eighteenth Dynasty (kings named Thutmose and Amenophis, and queen named Hatshepsut or Ha-shpeswe) and the Nineteenth Dynasty. Late Egyptian shows more affinity with Coptic than the preceding periods of the language: definite and indefinite article, beginning of the analytic verbal forms. The Twenty-second Dynasty is Libyan (kings named Osorkon, Shoshenk, Takelot; 946–720); the Twenty-fifth Dynasty is from Kush, capital at Napata in Nubia, with small pointed pyramids (Shabako, Sebichos, Taharka; 713–655). Invasion of the Assyrians, then Persian domination (Cambyses, Darius I, Xerxes I, Darius II; 525–404) and, after a short period of independence, a second Persian domination (Artaxerxes III, Darius III; 342–332).

History of Coptic Etymology

The first attempts to establish the relations between Coptic and other languages were made by Ignazio Rossi (1808) before the decipherment of the hieroglyphs by Jean-François Champollion in 1823. Rossi, who was an excellent Semitist, compared Coptic words with related expressions in Semitic (Hebrew, Aramaic, Arabic), Latin, and Greek. The correspondence of *S, B las,* tongue, to Hebrew *lāšōn* and Arabic *lisān* was first noted by him.

The fundamental work was done by Champollion, whose *Grammaire égyptienne* (1836–1841) contains hundreds of etymologies. He even transcribed Egyptian words not with the Latin but with the Coptic alphabet. As the Egyptians wrote no vowels, the Egyptian form is often shorter than the Coptic one: Egyptian *rn,* but Coptic *ran,* name.

Champollion's successors transcribed Egyptian words with Latin letters, a system that was several times modified. The system presently used is the transcription system of the *Berlin Wörterbuch* (Erman and Grapow, 1926–1931), with the sole exception of the sibilants (*s* voiced = *z*, *ś* voiceless = *s*). Spiegelberg's *Koptisches Handwörterbuch* (1921) groups together all the then available etymologies. It is arranged in three columns. The first column contains the Coptic words and forms according to the different dialects (Old Coptic and four dialects: *A, B, F, S*); the second, the meaning, as well as the constructions and compositions; and the third, the hieroglyphic or demotic prototypes. So *B* ⲁⲫⲱⲫ (masc.), giant (plural, ⲁⲫⲟⲫⲓ) is derived from Egyptian *ʿ3pp,* Apophis dragon, in hieroglyphic script with the specific determinative (dragon with many twistings, each twisting cut by a knife).

Though Westendorf's *Koptisches Handwörterbuch* (1977) is just called a dictionary, it contains all the etymologies known at that time. It is far richer and more exact than Spiegelberg's work and distinguishes Old Coptic and five Coptic dialects (*A, B, F, A2, S*). Etymologies are given in Egyptian, demotic, Semitic languages (Akkadian, Hebrew, Aramaic, Arabic, etc.), and African languages (Nubian, Berber, Beḍauye, etc.) as well as in European languages.

Jaroslav Černý's *Coptic Etymological Dictionary* (1976) contains many new etymologies. The author was a well-known specialist in Late Egyptian and demotic. Exploring the countless works of early Egyptologists in order to find out who had first succeeded in identifying the ancient Egyptian or demotic ancestor of a Coptic word, Černý added Dévaud's notes to his own material. His guiding principle was to adopt only etymologies that he considered certain, probable, or at least possible.

Vycichl's *Dictionnaire étymologique de la langue copte* (1983) is mainly concerned with the phonetic and semantic changes that Coptic words have undergone during their history. Thus, *B* ⲙⲱⲟⲩ, and *S* ⲙⲟⲟⲩ, water, comes from Egyptian *mw,* which derives from the skeleton *m-w-y,* also found in all Semitic languages. *S, B* ⲥⲟⲛ, brother, is not considered a biradical noun (**san*), but a triradical one (**sany-aw*). So is *S* ϩⲟⲟⲩ, day, deriving from **harw-aw,* later **ha3w-aw* (cf. plural *A* ϩⲣⲉⲩ from **haríw-w-ū*). Reconstruction of the Egyptian prototypes of Coptic words: *S* ⲛⲟⲩⲧⲉ, god: **nátīr*, *S* ⲛ̄ⲧⲱⲣⲉ (fem.), goddess: **natā̱r-a.t,* a so-called "internal" feminine (vowel change *ī:ā* as in Ethiopian *ṭ'abīb,* wise, *ṭ'abbāb* [fem.]). Etymologies include Egyptian, Semitic, African, and some Greek and Latin.

Egyptian and Coptic Forms

Autochthonous Coptic words derive from Egyptian prototypes written in hieroglyphic script, as a rule without vowels. Coptic vowels help to reconstruct the ancient forms. Thus, *B, S* ⲣⲁⲛ, name, corresponds to Egyptian *rn* (written without vowel). But the primitive form was, it is now known, not **ran* but **rin,* as ancient *i* developed in closed syllables into *a* (cf. VOCABULARY OF SEMITIC ORIGIN). A comparison of some Egyptian and Coptic forms follows:

ỉr.t, eye	*L* ⲓⲉⲓⲣⲉ
ḏr.t, hand	*B* ⲧⲱⲣⲓ
Km.t, Egypt	*B* ⲭⲏⲙⲓ
ms(y).t, to give birth	*B* ⲙⲓⲥⲓ
zy.t-ḥym.t, woman	*B* ⲥ-ϩⲓⲙⲓ

nḫt, to be strong	*B* ⲛ̄ϣⲟⲧ
rmṯ, man	*B* ⲣⲱⲙⲓ
sn, brother	*B* ⲥⲟⲛ
sn.t, sister	*B* ⲥⲱⲛⲓ
znf, blood	*B* ⲥⲛⲟϥ

Sethe (1899, pp. 16–18) combined in his "Verbum" the Egyptian consonants and the Coptic vowels. This procedure allowed a better understanding of the primitive word forms. It must, however, be borne in mind that there may be a gap of more than three thousand years between the consonants and the vowels. The structure of the above words can be represented as follows: *ỉīre.t*, eye; *ḏōre.t*, hand; *Kēme.t*, Egypt; *mīse.t*, to give birth; *ḥ(y)īme.t*, woman; *ĕnḫót*, to be strong; *rōmeṯ*, man; *son*, brother; *sōne.t*, sister; *ĕznóf*, blood.

Long and Short Vowels: a and ā

Sethe discovered that there was a relation between vowel quantity and syllable structure—stressed vowels were long in open syllables and short in closed ones, thus:

OPEN	CLOSED
ḏō-re.t, hand	*ĕn-ḫót*, to be strong
rōmeṯ, man	*són*, brother
sō-ne.t, sister	*ĕz-nóf*, blood

B ϧⲱⲧⲉⲃ is "to kill" and *B* ⲁϥ-ϧⲟⲑⲃⲉϥ is "he killed him." *B* ϧⲱⲧⲉⲃ has a long *o* in an open syllable, and *B* ϧⲟⲑⲃⲉϥ a short one in a closed one. The vowels ⲟ and ⲱ derive from ancient *a*-sounds, as can be seen from cuneiform transcriptions of the Middle Babylonian period (before 1000 B.C.).

As a matter of fact, most of the examples quoted are more complicated to explain than they seem at first glance. Here one must just mention that the radicals of *ỉr.t*, *Km.t*, and *sn* were not simply *ỉr*, *km*, and *sn* but *ỉry*, *kmm*, and *sny*. ⲥⲟⲛ does not derive from **son*, ancient **san*, but from **sanyaw*, and so on.

The i-Vowels

Another correspondence of short and long vowels is found in the following cases:

(a) short *a*: long *ē*:

ḥr-k, thy face: *S* ϩ̄ⲣⲁⲕ	*ḥr-ṯn*, your face: *S* ϩⲣⲏⲧⲛ̄
n-k, to thee: *S* ⲛⲁⲕ	*n-ṯn*, to you: *S* ⲛⲏⲧⲛ̄
ỉrm-k, with thee: *S* ⲛⲙ̄ⲙⲁⲕ	*ỉrm-ṯn*, with you: *S* ⲛⲙ̄ⲙⲏⲧⲛ̄

(b) short *a*: long *ī*:

ms.t-f, to give him birth: *S* ⲙⲁⲥⲧϥ̄	*ms.t*, to give birth: *S* ⲙⲓⲥⲉ
rn, name: *S* ⲣⲁⲛ	*rn-f*, his name: *S* ⲣⲓⲛϥ̄
ṯz.t-f, to lift him: *S* ϫⲁⲥⲧϥ̄	*ṯz.t*, to lift: *S* ϫⲓⲥⲉ

Tentative reconstructions: **eḥ-rak*, thy face, and **eḥ-rē-ṯen*, your face; **nak*, to thee, and **nē-ṯen*, to you; **nem-mák*, with thee, and **nem-mē-ṯen*, with you; **más-tef*, to give him birth, and **mī-set*, to give birth; **rán*, name, and **rī-nef*, his name; **ṯáz-tef*, to lift him, and **ṯī-zet*, to lift.

The difference between ⲏ = *ē* and ⲓ = *ī* has to be explained, as both vowels stand in open syllables. ⲏ = *ē* derives from ancient *ī*, as in the ending of the nisba-adjectives, while ⲓ = *ī*, equally long, was primarily a short vowel and but secondarily lengthened in open syllables.

There is no doubt that the vowel was primarily not *a*, as ancient *a* is represented by *o* in closed syllables and by *ō* in open ones. It is now known that the primitive vowel was (1) long *i*, (2) short *i*. It was a long *i* as in the ending of the nisba-adjectives: *ḥ3.t-y*, heart: *S* ϩⲏⲧ; *ḥ3.t-y-f*, his heart: *S* ϩⲧⲏϥ (cf. Arabic ending *-īy*). On the other hand, *S* ⲥⲓϥⲉ, pitch, derives from **zīfet*, ancient form *zift* (cf. Arabic *zift*). The Egyptian word *zft* is not attested, but is found in Berber languages, for example, Kabyle *ṯi-zefṯ*, pitch (Algeria), from ancient **ṯa-zift* (*ta-* former definite article, with metaphony *ti-*).

The u-Vowels

The vowels corresponding to ancient *u* were more difficult to detect, but it is certain that *S*, *B* ⲙⲏⲧ, ten, corresponds to cuneiform *mu-ṭu*. The real pronunciation of the *u* in this word must have been *ö* as in German *höflich*, *eu* as in French *feu*, or *ir* as in British *bird*. Another case of an ancient *u* is found in the word for "woman," **ḥ(y)ū-me.t* (plural, **ḥyúm-we.t*), cf. *S* ⲥ-ϩⲓⲙⲉ (plural, ϩⲓⲟⲙⲉ). The *ū* in the singular was pronounced like *ü* in German *für* and *u* in French *pur*. Another good example is *S* ⲧⲣⲓⲣ, oven (cf. Akkadian *tinūr-u*, from **tirūr-u* or sim.). *Rmy-y.t*, tear, is *S* ⲣⲙ̄ⲉⲓⲏ, the plural of which is ⲣⲙ̄ⲉⲓⲟⲟⲩⲉ with ⲟ and, in *A*, ⲣⲙ̄ⲉⲓⲉⲩⲉ with ⲉ, probably an old *ö* (short). These examples show that *u*-vowels can be represented in Coptic by ⲉ, ⲟ, ⲏ, and ⲓ.

Semantic Changes

In many cases, the meaning of a word changes in the course of time; thus, *B* ⲁ̀ⲙⲉⲛϯ and *S* ⲁⲙⲛ̄ⲧⲉ, which always appear without an article as a proper noun to mean "hell," derive from Egyptian *ỉmn.t-y.t* (probably **yamín.t-ī.t*), west, where the sun sets, site of the underworld, the empire of the deceased, the realm of Osiris, judge of souls. In Coptic the word is employed in the Christian sense of "hell." In Egyptian *ỉmn* signifies "right, dexter" and "western," while *ỉ3b.t-y* is "left, sinister" and "eastern": the Egyptians looked southward to take their bearings.

Old Coptic ⲃⲁⲓ, soul, and *S, B* ⲃⲁⲓ̈, night raven (*nycticorax*) or screech owl, derive from Egyptian *b3* (probably **bi3*, then **bē*), soul, represented by the hieroglyph of the *jabiru* (*Mycteria ephippiorhynchus senegalensis*), a big storklike bird now found in the Sudan and recognizable by his wattles. This notion of "soul" was so closely connected with Egyptian paganism that the word was replaced in Christian times by *S, B* ⲯⲩⲭⲏ (as in Greek), traditionally pronounced *ebsīka*.

B ⲭⲏⲙⲉ, *S* ⲕⲏⲙⲉ (fem.), Egypt, always without a definite article, is related to *B* ⲭⲙⲟⲙ, *S* ⲕⲙⲟⲙ, become black. Thus, Egypt is the "black one," that is, the "black land," so called after the black Nile mud of the inundation, as opposed to *dšr.t*, the "red one" or "the red land," meaning the desert. The radicals of the verb were *k-m-m*, and *B Khēmi* or *S Kēme* derives from the adjective **kumm-a.t* or **kömm-a.t*, then **Kōm-a.t* (fem.), black. The name of the desert was probably **dašr-a.t* (fem.), red.

B ⲙⲁϣϫ, *S* ⲙⲁⲁϫⲉ (masc.), ear, derives from Egyptian *m-sḏr*, ear, from the verb *sḏr*, to sleep, because it is on the ear that one sleeps. *M-sḏr* employs the prefix *m*, which is used to signify place (*nomina loci*), as in Semitic languages (Arabic *maktab*, office, from *katab*, he wrote). The primitive word for "ear" still occurs in the Coffin Texts as *ỉdn* (cf. Arabic *'uḏn*, Hebrew *'ózen*, Aramaic *'eḏn-ā*).

B, S ⲙⲉϣⲁⲕ, perhaps, comes from Egyptian *bw rḫ-k*, thou dost not know, later pronounced *m(w) 3ḫ-k*.

B ⲛⲟⲩϥⲓ, *S* ⲛⲟⲩϥⲉ, good (adj.), derives from Egyptian *nfr*, beautiful, good. The word is written with the hieroglyph for "the *heart* and the *windpipe*" (Gardiner, 1927, p. 465, Sign list F 36). Horapollon, a Greek author who wrote a book on hieroglyphs, explains the sign as *kardía* and *pharynx* (*Hieroglyphica* 2.4). The author is not sure that Gardiner's translation is correct. In Greek, *kardía* signifies the "heart" or "the upper opening of the stomach," and *pharynx*, "esophagus" or "windpipe." Gardiner's translation is improbable, as there is in fact no connection between the heart and the windpipe, while "esophagus" and "(upper opening of) stomach" makes good sense. In spite of this, it is possible that *nfr* may have meant "windpipe" too because a similar word is found in Arabic, *nafīr* meaning "trumpet," this latter term being related to Akkadian *nipru*, which means "offshoot, sprout" or "descendant, son." *Nfr* primarily meant "young"; note *nfr-w* adolescents, and *nfr.t*, maiden; in Berber (Shilḥa, southwestern Morocco) *šbāb*, beautiful, come from Arabic *šabāb*, youth.

B nūfi and *S nūfe* derive from **nāfir*, **nāfiì* (verbal adjective = present participle). One might expect *B *nōfi*, and *S *nōfe*, but the vowel (*ū* instead of *ō*) is due to postnasalization. The feminine form is *B nofri* or *S nofre*, advantage, from *°nāfir-a.t*, then **nafr-a.t* (neutral meaning of the feminine form).

B ⲉⲣⲫⲉⲓ, *S* ⲣ̄ⲡⲉ (masc.), temple, today *birbā* in Egyptian Arabic (plural, *barābī*), derives from *r3-pr* or, more exactly, from **r3pr(y.t)*, door of coming out (i. e. the "false door" of Egyptian mastabas representing the deceased coming out of his tomb to receive the offerings brought by his relatives). The verbal noun *B -pei*, *S -pe* is the regular form of **piry-a.t*, coming out, later pronounced **pi3y-a.t*. Coptic has two forms: (1) *B* ⲫⲓⲣⲓ, *S* ⲡⲉⲓⲣⲉ from **pīri.t*, (2) *S* ⲡ̄ⲣⲣⲉ from **piry-a.t* where the *r* has been reconstituted by analogy. The original meaning of the word is "funerary temple" with a "false door," and not the *ḥw.t nṯr*, god's house.

S, B ⲥⲉ, yes, derives from Egyptian *s.t*, it (neuter pronoun), probably derived from *sy* (**siya*), she. One may compare Provençal *oc*, yes, in southern France from Latin *hoc*, that one. Also French *oui*, yes, derives from *hoc illud* or a similar form (Dauzat, 1938, p. 520).

B ⲟⲩⲏⲃ, *S* ⲟⲩⲏⲏⲃ (masc.), priest, comes from Egyptian *w'b*, priest, from *w'b*, to be pure, which equals *S, B* ⲟⲩⲟⲡ from *°wa'āb*, **wa'áb*. The *w'b* priests were the lower priests and the *ḥm nṯr*, god's servant, was a "prophet." *B* ⲟⲩⲏⲃ and *S* ⲟⲩⲏⲏⲃ are Christian priests, while *B, S* ϩⲟⲛⲧ̄ is but a pagan priest.

B ⲟⲩⲓⲛⲁⲙ *S* ⲟⲩⲛⲁⲙ (fem.), right hand (noun), right, dexter (adj.), is from the old verb *wnm*, to eat, which is in Coptic *B, S* ⲟⲩⲱⲙ. The primitive meaning of the word was the "eating hand" as opposed to the left hand, which was used for unclean purposes. There are two different nominal forms in Coptic: *B* ⲟⲩⲓⲛⲁⲙ derives from an emphatic participle *°wanīm*, then **wanním*, while *S* ⲟⲩⲛⲁⲙ derives from a simple participle *°wanīm*, then **waním*, eating (hand). There are many African languages that call the right hand the "eating hand," such as Logone *zëmi*, right, from *zëm*, to eat, Fulani *dyuṅgo nyamo*, eating hand (i.e., the right hand), Ewhe *ṅu-ḍu-si*, right hand (literally, the hand [*si*] that eats [*ḍu*] something [*ṅu*]), Swahili *mkono wa kulia*, right hand (literally, hand of eating).

B ϩⲏⲕⲓ, *S* ϩⲏⲕⲉ, poor (adj), derives from Egyptian *ḥkr*, to be hungry, which is *B*, *S* ϩⲕⲟ. A "hungry man" is a "poor man." In Egyptian Arabic one finds the same idea: *nās ǧaʿānīn*, hungry people, are the "poor" and *nās šabʿānīn*, satiated people, are the "rich." The form *ǧaʿānīn* stands for **ǧōʿānīn* (*ǧawʿānīn*).

B ϩⲑⲟ, *S* ϩⲧⲟ (masc.), horse, comes from Egyptian *ḥtr*, which primarily means a "yoke of oxen," from *ḥtr*, to fix, to attach; compare Arabic *ḥatar*, to tighten (a knot, etc.). After the Hyksos period, *ḥtr* signifies also a pair of horses and even a horse. The radicals of the word were *ḥtr*, then *ḥtỉ*, hence *B* ϩⲑⲟ. An older form, **ḥty*, has been kept in Beja, a Hamitic language spoken between the Nile Valley and the Red Sea, as *hatāy*.

Some Examples of Phonetic Changes

Influence of ỉ, ʿ, ḥ, ḫ, ẖ. The preceding short vowel is always *a*, as in *S* ⲥⲁⲁⲛϣ̄, to bring up, nourish, Egyptian **saʿnaḫ*, to make live (*s-ʿnḫ*); compare *S* ⲥⲟⲟⲩⲧⲛ̄, to erect, Egyptian **sadwan*, to make stretch (*s-dwn*, then *s-wdn*, with metathesis).

Nasalization. In most cases the groups ⲙⲱ and ⲛⲱ are replaced in Coptic by ⲙⲟⲩ and ⲛⲟⲩ. This is due to the nasalizing influence of *m* and *n* in an earlier period of the language, as in Vai, a language now spoken in Liberia. In many languages, nasalized *ã* becomes *o*, as in Provençal *femo*, wife, and *vaco*, cow, from Latin *feminam* (acc.) and *vaccam* (acc.). The intermediary forms were **femã*, **vacã*, or sim. In Coptic, exceptions are rare, among them *S* ⲣⲁⲙⲱⲛⲉ, door post, from Egyptian **rammān-a.t* (fem.), carrier; and the *S* ending -ⲱⲧⲛ̄, you, as in ⲛ̄ⲙⲱⲧⲛ̄, you (acc.).

Influence of Final -r. In most cases late Egyptian *-ār* corresponds in Coptic, not, as one might expect, to -ⲱⲣ, but to -ⲟⲩⲣ, as in *S* ϩⲣⲟⲩⲣ, to be quiet, from **harāraw;* compare *B* ϩⲉⲣⲓ, to be quiet, qual. *B* ϩⲟⲩⲣⲱⲟⲩ, from **harw-āw-ey*, then **hawr-āw-ey*. Exceptions due to dialectic influences include *S* ϩⲱⲣ, Horus; *S* *ⲡⲱⲣ, house, in *S* ϫⲉⲛⲉⲡⲱⲣ, roof (literally, head of house); and verbal nouns such as *S* ⲥⲱⲣ, to display, spread out.

Influence of Final ḥ. In Bohairic, sometimes also in other dialects, final -ⲏϩ and -ⲱϩ are replaced by -ⲉϩ and -ⲟϩ with long and open vowels, here transcribed ɛ̄ and ɔ̄, as in *S* ⲡⲱϩ, *B* ⲫⲟϩ, to reach, arrive, qual. *S* ⲡⲏϩ, *B* ⲫⲉϩ.

Influence of w and y in Diphthongs.

S ⲛⲁϊ, to me = *nay: B* ⲛⲏⲓ = *ney* (with short *e*)
S ⲙⲁⲉⲓⲛ, sign = *mayn: B* ⲙⲏⲓⲛⲓ = *meyni* (with short *e*)
S ⲙⲟⲉⲓⲧ, way = *mɔyt: B* ⲙⲱⲓⲧ = *moyt* (with short *o*)
S ⲙⲟⲟⲩ, water = *mɔw: B* ⲙⲱⲟⲩ = *mow* (with short *o*)

Note that final *-ɔy* remains unchanged: *S* ⲉⲣⲟϊ, to me = *erɔy* = *B* ⲉⲣⲟⲓ = *erɔy* (with ɔ = short open o). The case of *S* ϩⲟⲟⲩ, day, is different. This word derives from Egyptian **harwaw* (written *hrw*), then *ha3waw*. In this case, *a* and *w* were not in *direct contact* and therefore *B* ⲉϩⲟⲟⲩ, (probably ⲉ-, to + *B* ϩⲟⲟⲩ) = phon. *ho3w*.

Change from n to y. The group *ns* or *nš* may be replaced by *ys* or *yš*, as in *S* ⲡⲣⲁⲛϣ̄ = *S* ⲡⲣⲁⲉⲓϣ, from Egyptian *pr ʿnḫ*, usually translated "house of life" but probably "house of documents." Also, *S* ϩⲛⲏⲥ, Ahnās (*nomina loci*); compare modern *Ahnāsīya al-Madīna*, the ancient *Ḥw.t nn Ny-sw.t*, House of the Prince, Assyrian cuneiform (*ālu*) *Ḫī-ni-in-ši* = phon. **Ḫininsi*, then **Ḫiniysi* = *Ḫinīsi* = *S* ϩⲛⲏⲥ.

Metathesis (Change of Position: AB:BA). Examples are Egyptian **sadwan*, to make stretch, then **sawdan* = *S* ⲥⲟⲟⲩⲧⲛ̄, to erect, *"ridy-u-fi*, his foot, then *°rid(y)-u-f* = *S* ⲣⲁⲧϥ̄, his foot. But *A* ⲣⲏⲧϥ̄, his foot, derives from *°riyd-u-f* = *°rīd-u-f* and the variant *A* ⲣⲉⲉⲧϥ̄, from *°ridy-u-f*, *°ridd-u-f*, then **ri3d-u-f*.

Diphthong development in Coptic feminine and plural forms. *B* ϫⲁⲙⲟⲩⲗ (masc.), camel, *B* ϫⲁⲙⲁⲩⲗⲓ (fem.), she-camel, *B* ⲥⲛⲁϩ, bond, fetter, plural, ⲥⲛⲁⲩϩ. *B* ⲃⲏϫ, (masc.), falcon, had a feminine form **bayki;* compare the feminine proper noun *Thbaikhis* (Θβαΐχις) in Greek. The plural of *S* ⲛⲟⲩⲧⲉ, god, Egyptian *nāṯir*, is *S* ⲉⲛⲧⲏⲣ and ⲉⲛⲧⲁⲓⲣ, from **naṯir-ū*.

The Group tr After Stressed Vowels. Examples of the development of Egyptian *tr*, *rr*, *3r* follow:

ỉtrw, canal: *B* ⲉⲓⲟⲣ, *S* ⲉⲓⲟⲟⲣ
mtr.t, noon: *B* ⲙⲉⲣⲓ, *S* ⲙⲉⲉⲣⲉ
ptr-f, to see him: *B* ⲫⲟⲣϥ, *S* *ⲡⲟⲟⲣϥ

Reconstruction: **yatraw*, then **yarraw* (written *yrw* in the Eighteenth Dynasty), then **ya3raw* or sim., **mitr-a.t*, then **mirr-a.t*, then **mi3r-a.t*, **patr-u-f*, then **parr=u-f*, **pa3r=u-f*, or sim. *B* ⲫⲱⲣ, *S* ⲡⲱⲱⲣⲉ, to dream, is a reconstitution after **patr-*, the *status pronominalis*.

[*See also:* VOCABULARY, AFRICAN CONTACTS WITH AUTOCHTHONOUS COPTIC; VOCABULARY, COPTO-ARABIC; VO-

CABULARY, COPTO-GREEK; VOCABULARY, CUNEIFORM TRANSCRIPTIONS OF PROTOTYPES OF AUTOCHTHONOUS COPTIC; VOCABULARY OF EGYPTIAN ORIGIN, AUTOCHTHONOUS COPTIC; VOCABULARY OF SEMITIC ORIGIN, AUTOCHTHONOUS COPTIC.]

BIBLIOGRAPHY

Brugsch, H. K. *Grammaire démotique.* Paris, 1855.

Černý, J. *Coptic Etymological Dictionary.* Cambridge, 1976.

Champollion, J. F. (the Younger). *Grammaire égyptienne.* 2 vols. Paris, 1836–1841.

Dauzat, A. *Dictionnaire étymologique.* Paris, 1938.

Dévaud, E. *Etudes d'étymologie copte.* Fribourg, 1922.

Edel, E. *Altägyptische Grammatik.* Rome, 1955–1964.

Erman, A. and H. Grapow. *Wörterbuch der ägyptischen Sprache.* 5 vol. Leipzig, 1926–1931.

Erman, A. *Ägyptische Grammatik,* 4th ed. Berlin, 1928.

______. *Neuägyptische Grammatik,* 2nd ed. Leipzig, 1933.

Gardiner, A. *Egyptian Grammar, Being an Introduction to the Study of Hieroglyphics.* 3rd ed. London, 1927.

Horapollon. *Hieroglyphica,* ed. F. Sbordane. Naples, 1940.

Junker, H. *Grammatik der Denderatexte.* Leipzig, 1906.

Kasser, R. "Prolégomènes à un essai de classification systématique des dialectes et subdialectes coptes selon les critères de la phonétique, I, Principes et terminologie." *Muséon* 93 (1980a):53–112. ". . . , II, Alphabets et systèmes phonétiques." *Muséon* 93 (1980b):237–97). ". . . , III, Systèmes orthographiques et catégories dialectales." *Muséon* 94 (1981):91–152.

Korostovtsev, M. A. *Egipetskij jazyk.* Moscow, 1961.

Lefebvre, G. *Grammaire de l'égyptien classique,* 2nd ed. Cairo, 1955.

Rossi, I. *Etymologiae Aegyptiacae.* Turin, 1808.

Sethe, Kurt. *Das Aegyptische Verbum im Altaegyptischen, Neuaegyptischen und Koptischen,* Vol. 1. Leipzig, 1899.

Spiegelberg, W. *Koptisches Handwörterbuch.* Heidelberg, 1921.

______. *Demotische Grammatik.* Heidelberg, 1925.

Tucker, A. N. and M. A. Bryan. "The Mbugu Anomaly." *Bulletin of the School of Oriental and African Studies* 37, no. 1 (1974):188–207.

Vergote, J. *Grammaire copte,* Vol. 1a, *Introduction, phonétique et phonologie, morphologie synthématique (structure des sémantèmes), partie synchronique.* Louvain, 1973. Vol. 1b, *Morphologie synthématique (structure des sémantèmes), partie diachronique.* Louvain, 1973. Vol. 2a, *Morphologie syntagmatique, syntaxe, partie synchronique.* Louvain, 1983. Vol. 2b, *Morphologie syntagmatique, partie diachronique,* Louvain, 1983.

Vycichl, W. *Dictionnaire étymologique de la langue copte.* Louvain, 1983.

Westendorf, W. *Koptisches Handwörterbuch, bearbeitet auf Grund des Koptischen Handwörterbuchs von Wilhelm Spiegelberg.* Heidelberg, 1977.

WERNER VYCICHL

FAYYUMIC. The name "Fayyumic dialect" (*F*) is usually given to a typical variety of the Coptic language belonging with *M, W,* and *V* to the middle Coptic major group (see DIALECTS, GROUPING AND MAJOR GROUPS OF and MESOKEMIC). Contrary to many others, this dialectal variety appears to be located geographically with some certainty, in the region of the ancient oasis of the Fayyūm (hence its name; cf. GEOGRAPHY, DIALECTAL). This terminology was inaugurated by Stern (1880), but only became established in the course of the first decades of the twentieth century. Before Stern, this idiom was readily described as BASHMURIC when it appeared in a "pure" state, while the preference was to designate it "Middle Egyptian" when its forms were less typical and could be considered the hybrid result of contamination by some neighboring dialect, above all SAHIDIC (*S*) (this is particularly frequent within *F5,* the chief subdialect of *F,* four-fifths of the whole). It was then supposed that Bashmuric was more especially the language of the central and western part of the Fayyūm, while to Middle Egyptian was attributed perhaps the eastern fringe of the Fayyūm and still more probably the portion of the Nile Valley to the east of the Fayyūm (also to the northeast and southeast). After Stern, the term "Bashmuric" rapidly fell into disuse, but "Middle Egyptian" (designating from that time the whole of *F*) maintained itself for some time longer, until the beginning of the twentieth century; then it gave way to the present terminology.

The study of Fayyumic is unfortunately seriously complicated by the fact that its texts are published in the most widely dispersed places. In addition, as will be seen later and as was already remarked at the dawn of this century (Asmus, 1904), central *F* itself is manifold and multiform, just as much as the editions mentioned above, at least if one takes into account some of its secondary characteristics, so that modern research distinguishes in it several subdialects (which, if need be, may be subdivided in turn). There can be no question of entering into all these details here, and this article will confine itself to presenting the chief varieties of *F:* these are *F4* (of limited attestation and the oldest, fourth–sixth [seventh?] century; principal texts published in Crum and Kenyon, 1900; Gaselee, 1909; some *F46* fragments, among others, in Stern, 1885, pp. 30, 34, 35, 39, and *F8*, p. 42); and *F5*, habitually considered by the grammarians as Fayyumic par excellence (e.g., Till, 1930), a variety very widely attested (four-fifths of all *F* = *F4* + *F5*) but the documents of which are relatively late (sixth–eighth [ninth?] century; editions are very scattered and numerous; only some appear in the bibliography below; for *F56*, see Müller, 1962). Anyone who wishes information on the subdivisions of *F4* and *F5* (*F46;* and *F55, F56, F58*, respectively) or on the minuscule and very marginal *F8* and *F9*, which will be mentioned only exceptionally below, will find some rudiments on the subject in Kasser (1981, pp. 101–102) and, above all, in Diebner and Kasser (1989).

It is appropriate to distinguish from "central" *F* (= *F4* + *F5*) the following entities (which some persist in indiscriminately calling "Fayyumic"): the subdialect *F7* (sometimes called "ancient Fayyumic," as in Crum, 1939, p. vi, n. 3), which is clearly peripheral in relation to central *F* (edition of its sole witness, Diebner and Kasser, 1989) and, if not specifically protodialectal as a whole, at least somewhat archaic in a few of its peculiarities. Dialect *V*, or Fayyumic without lambdacism (sometimes also called "South Fayyumic"), is still more remote from *F* because it does not show lambdacism, the chief characteristic of *F* (important text published in Lefort, 1952, pp. 32–34; the longest witness of *V*, P. Mich. Inv. 3520, is still unpublished). Dialect *W* (or "crypto-Mesokemic with South Fayyumic phonology") is without lambdacism, like *V*, and presents close morphosyntactic affinities with *M* (edition of its only text, Husselman, 1962). Finally, DIALECT H (or Hermopolitan or Ashmuninic; its sole witness, P. Morgan M 636, is unpublished) is an entity more outside than inside the Fayyumic dialectal group, being at once a MESODIALECT (between *V* and *S*?) and a METADIALECT (a manifestation of the Coptic language typically evolved to the extreme). This advice will not appear useless to one who notes that several authors, still following Crum (1939), continue to describe indiscriminately as "Fayyumic" a vocabulary that it would be preferable to classify under the rubrics *F7, V, W* and *H*.

As for *M* (MESOKEMIC, or Middle Egyptian), the vocabulary of which was also formerly confused with that of *F* etc., but which saw its dialectal originality and identity recognized by Kahle (1954, pp. 220–27), no one today thinks any longer of making it Fayyumic (after the lexicographical publications of Kasser, 1964 and 1966, and, above all, the meticulous dialectal studies of Quecke in Orlandi, 1974, pp. 87–108, and Schenke, 1978 and 1981).

1. Phonology

In Fayyumic, as in other dialects of the Coptic language (a dead language and hence known today only from the texts), the majority of the characteristics perceptible appear at the level of phonology, which is expressed through orthography.

1.1 Consonants (Not Including Glides). The stock of the consonants in Fayyumic is that of the majority of the Coptic idioms (*S* with *L* and *M;* see ALPHABETS, COPTIC, Synoptic Table). In its autochthonous vocabulary, *F* thus does not have the /ç/ of *P* and *İ*; the /x/ of *P, İ, A*, and *B;* or the aspirated occlusives /kh/, /ph/, and /th/, and the aspirated affricate /čh/, all typical of *B*. It will be noted that some subdivisions of *F* (*F56* in a majority of cases, *F46* everywhere, as in *H*) replace ϥ /f/ by a ⲃ, which probably has the value of /v/ rather than /ƀ/ (see several examples further on). Furthermore, *F* (with *V* but not *M;* no example in *W*) assimilates /s/ to /š/ before /š/, as in *F, V* ϣⲱϣⲓ, field, but *M* ⲥⲟⲱⲉ (and *S* etc. ⲥⲱϣⲉ); *F, V* ϣⲉϣⲓ†, bitter (cf. *B* ϣⲁϣⲓ†), but *M* (and *S* etc.) ⲥⲓϣⲉ bitterness. *F* (contrary to *V, W, M*, with *L4, L5, B*) assimilates /s/ to /š/ before /č/, as in *F* ϣⲉϫⲓ, to speak (cf. *S* ϣⲁϫⲉ, *A, L6,* ϣⲉϫⲉ), but *V, W* ⲥⲉϫⲓ, *M* (and *L4 L5*) ⲥⲉϫⲉ (*B* ⲥⲁϫⲓ).

F as well as *V, W, M*, and *H* (and almost all the other Coptic idioms; see ALPHABETS, COPTIC) have in their alphabet at once ϫ /č/ and ϭ /c/ (*B, B7* ϭ /čh/); however, *F7* has only ϫ everywhere, even sometimes writing ϫϩ where the rest of Fayyumic etc. writes ϫ (for example, *F, V, W, M, H* ⲛⲁϭ, large, but *F7* ⲛⲁϫ; *F, V, M* ϭⲓϫ, hand, but *F7* ϫⲓϫ(ϩ) [and sometimes also ϫⲓϫ in *V*, it is true; then one will note the surprising ϭⲓϭ of *H*]; see Diebner and Kasser, 1989). However, the truly typical characteristic of *F* is its lambdacism: while in the autochthonous vocabulary of all the other Coptic idioms (including *V, W*, and *H*) the proportion of use of ⲗ /l/ and ⲣ /r/ is /l/ 30 percent and /r/ 70 percent, in *F* (with *F7*) it is /l/ 80 percent and /r/ 20 percent. This means that many words written with ⲣ in *S, M, W, V* etc. are written with ⲗ in *F4, F5, F7*, (and *F8, F9*) alone, as in *S* ⲣⲱⲙⲉ, *M* ⲣⲟⲙⲉ, *W, V* ⲣⲱⲙⲓ, man, but *F4, F5, F7,* ⲗⲱⲙⲓ and *F8* ⲗⲟⲙⲓ; (cf. *F9* ⲥⲧⲗⲧⲟⲗ†, troubled, from *F5* ϣⲧⲁⲗⲧⲉⲗ, *M* ϣⲧⲁⲣⲧⲣ, *S* etc. ϣⲧⲟⲣⲧⲣ̅, to trouble).

As regards the presence or absence of ALEPH (presence marked by vocalic gemination in the orthography; see GEMINATION, VOCALIC), *F* and the subdialects of its group are profoundly divided: *F5, F56, F58, F46*, with *V5, H* (and *İ, L* etc., *A, P, S*) have aleph; *F4, F55, F7*, with *V4, W*(?) (and *M, B* etc., *G*) do not have it (see various examples further on).

1.2 Glides. The glides are the least consonantal of the consonants. Fayyumic has /j/ and /w/, as do all the Coptic dialects. In any position /j/ is written ⲓ in *F* (cf. Kasser, 1983a), as in ⲓ̈ⲱⲧ, father; ϩⲓⲏ, way, road; ⲗⲓ̈ⲕ, bread; ϩⲗⲓ̈ⲛⲓ, some; ⲧⲗⲓ̈ⲗ, to honor; ⲗⲓ†, being. However, /w/ is always written ⲟⲩ at the beginning, as in ⲟⲩⲱⲙ, to eat; but elsewhere orthographic procedures diverge, and now ⲟⲩ will be written, now ⲩ (see Diebner and Kasser, 1989): *F* ⲉⲗⲩ, glory; *F* ⲧⲗⲟⲩⲗ (more often than ⲧⲗⲩⲗ), to produce; *F* ⲥⲗⲟⲩⲛ, to know; *F4, F5, F56* (more rarely *F46, F5* ⲙⲙⲉⲟⲩ) ⲙⲙⲉⲩ, there; *F* ⲙⲉⲟⲩ, mother; *F4* ϭⲉⲩϫ, hands; *F* ⲗⲗⲏⲟⲩ, each other; *F* ⲙⲏⲟⲩⲓ̈, to think; *F* ⲥⲛⲏⲟⲩ, brothers; *F* ⲉⲣ(ⲣ)ⲱⲟⲩ, kings.

1.3. Tonic Vowels (Not Including Sonants). As a general rule, when the tonic vowels are long, the orthography of *F* is no different from that of the other Coptic dialects (e.g., ⲗⲱⲙⲓ, man; ⲙⲟⲩⲛ, to rest; ⲕⲓⲙ, to move; ⲕⲏ†, being; an exception is *F, F7, V, M* ⲣⲉ, sun, but *S, L, B* ⲣⲏ and *A* ⲣⲓ). On the contrary, *F* is more clearly distinct in the orthography of the short tonic vowels, as outlined below.

Class o. Short normal when not final, e.g., ⲥⲗⲛ, brother *F*, with *F7, V, W, M* (and *L, A*, but ⲥⲟⲛ *S, B*); before /ʾ/ not final (in the dialect or subdialect that preserves it), e.g., ϣⲗⲗⲡ†, being *F5, F56, F46*, with *V5* and *H* (without /ʾ/ ϣⲗⲡ† *F4*, with *F7, V4, W*, and *M;* but ϣⲟⲟⲡ† *L, S*, ϩⲟⲟⲡ† *A*, and without /ʾ/ ϣⲟⲡ† *B*); ⲟⲩⲉⲉⲃ†, holy *F5, F56* (without /ʾ/ ⲟⲩⲉⲃ† *F4*, with *F7* and *V, M;* but ⲟⲩⲗⲗⲃ†, *H* and *L5, L6, S*, ⲟⲩⲗ(ⲗ)ⲃⲉ† *L4, A* and without /ʾ/ ⲟⲩⲗⲃ† *B*); before final /h/, e.g., (ⲉ)ⲙⲕⲉϩ, pain *F* with *F7, V*, and *M* (but ⲉⲙⲕⲗϩ *H* and ⲙ̄ⲕⲗϩ *L, A, S, B*); before (potential) final /ʾ/, e.g., ⲙⲉ, place *F*, with *F7, V, W*, and *M* (but ⲙⲗ ⲛ-, place of *F, F7*, [*V*], *W, M;* ⲙⲗ *H* and *L, A, S, B*) before /(ʾ)/ or /ʾ/ or /ʾj/ ϣⲉⲉⲓ, to rise (of a star), festival *F5* (ϣⲉⲉ̇, *M*, without /ʾ/ but with /j/ ϣⲉⲓ *F7, V, W*; but ϣⲗ(ⲉ)ⲓⲉ *L*, ϩⲗⲉ *A*, ϣⲗⲓ *B*, ϣⲗ *S*). As a final (esp. causative verbs), e.g., ⲧⲗⲕⲗ, destroy *F* with *F7, V, W*, and *M, H* (but ⲧⲉⲕⲟ *L, A*, ⲧⲗⲕⲟ *S, B*).

Class i. Short normal, e.g., ϩⲉⲧ, silver *F* with *F7, V*, and *M* (and *L, A*, but ϩⲗⲧ *S, B*); before pronominal suffix /j/ (first-person sing.), e.g., ⲛⲏⲓ̈, to me *F4*(?), *F5, F56, V, W*(?) (with *P, B*, and ⲛⲏ(ⲉ)ⲓ *L*), but ⲛⲉⲓ̈ *F46* with *M* (and *A*, and ⲛⲗⲓ̈ *H* and *S*); all the other persons of this preposition with its suffixes, except the second- and third-person plural, being vocalized, however, in /ē/ *F5*, /e/ *F4, V, W, M, L, A*, /a/ *H, S, B*: thus *F5* (and *F56*) ⲛⲏⲓ̈, ⲛⲏⲕ, ⲛⲏ, ⲛⲏϥ (ⲛⲏⲃ *F56*), ⲛⲏⲥ, ⲛⲏⲛ, ⲛⲏⲧⲉⲛ, ⲛⲏⲟⲩ, *F4* ⲛⲏⲓ̈, ⲛⲉⲕ, ⲛⲉ, ⲛⲉϥ, ⲛⲉⲥ, ⲛⲉⲛ, ⲛⲉⲧⲉⲛ, ⲛⲉⲩ, *F46* similarly (but very incomplete) ⲛⲉⲓ̈, ⲛⲉⲕ, [. . .], ⲛⲉⲃ, ⲛⲉⲥ, [. . .], *V, W*(?) ⲛⲏⲓ̈ (*M* ⲛⲉⲓ̈), *V, W, M* ⲛⲉⲕ, ⲛⲏ (*M* alone), ⲛⲉϥ, ⲛⲉⲥ, ⲛⲉⲛ, ⲛⲏⲧⲉⲛ, *V, M* ⲛⲉⲩ (*W* ⲛⲗⲩ), *H* ⲛⲗⲓ̈, ⲛⲗⲕ, [. . .], ⲛⲗⲃ, ⲛⲗⲥ, ⲛⲗⲛ, [. . .], ⲛⲗⲟⲩ; likewise, *F5* ⲛⲉⲙⲏ⸗, with, *F4* ⲛⲉⲙⲉ⸗, etc.; before /j/ followed by another consonant, most often /n/, e.g., ⲙⲏⲓ̈ⲛ, sign *F, W*, cf. ⲙⲏⲉⲓⲛ *P*, ⲙⲏⲓ̈ⲛⲓ *B* (but ⲙⲉⲉⲓⲛ *M*, ⲙⲉⲓ̈ⲛⲉ *L4*, ⲙⲉ(ⲉ)ⲓⲛⲉ *A*, and ⲙⲗⲉⲓⲛ *H, L5, L6, S*; a case apart is ϩⲗⲏⲓ̈, upper part (or also "lower" except in *A, P, B*) *F, F7*, ϩⲣⲏⲓ̈ *V, W, M, L, A, P, B*, ϩⲣⲗⲓ̈ *H* and *S;* before /h/, e.g., ⲛⲉϩⲥⲓ *F* (with *B*, and ⲛⲉϩⲥⲉ *L, A, S;* cf. ⲛⲏϩⲥⲥ[ⲓ] and [ⲛⲏ]ϩⲥⲥⲓ *F7*).

Class e. Short normal (including final), e.g., ϣⲏⲗⲓ, daughter *F5*, ϣⲏⲗⲓ (or ϣⲏⲗⲉ?) *F7*, cf. ϣⲏⲣⲉ *M* (but ϣⲉⲉⲣⲉ *L5, L6, A, S*, ϣⲉⲣⲉ *L4*, ϣⲉⲣⲓ *B*); ⲙⲉⲧⲣⲏ, witness *F, V, W, M* (and ⲙⲏⲧⲣⲏ *H*, but ⲙⲛ̄ⲧⲣⲉ *L, A, S*, ⲙⲉⲑⲣⲉ *B*); before /h/, e.g., ⲙⲉϩ†, full *F5, F4, F46, F7, V4* (with *B*, and sometimes *S*), but ⲙⲏϩ† *F56* (with *H* and *M, L, A, S*); ⲉⲛⲉϩ, eternity *F, F7, V, W* (with *M, S, B*, but ⲉⲓⲛⲏϩ *H* and ⲗⲛⲏϩⲉ *L, A, P*).

1.4 Tonic Sonants. The sonants (/ḇ̩/, /l̩/, /m̩/, /n̩/, /r̩/) are the least vocalic of the vowels. At the beginning, *F* has no tonic sonant, and it is replaced by its phonematic substitute, the corresponding sonorant (/ḇ/, /l/, /m/, /n/, /r/), preceded by ⲉ; it is the same in *V*, partly also in *F7;* the case is not attested in *W;* this sonant is, however, characteristic of *M* (thus, *F, V* ⲉⲛⲧϥ, to carry it; *F7* ⲛ̇ⲧϥ or ⲉⲛⲧϥ, *H* ⲏⲛϥ, *M* ⲛ̇ⲧϥ). Elsewhere it will be found that *F5* (like *F7* and *H, B* but differing from *V, W, M* and of course from *L, A, S*) has no tonic sonant. *F4* shows a single case of ϣⲙϣⲓ, to serve (without inverse cases clearly belonging to *F4*), which leads one to think that on this point *F4* occupies a position intermediate between *F5* (without this sonant) and *V, W* (which have now the sonant, and now its substitute; thus, *V* ⲗⲙⲛϯ, hell; *W* ϣⲙ̄ϣⲓ or ϣⲉⲙϣⲓ, serve; *W* ⲃⲣ̄ⲣⲓ, new; *V* ϭⲛ̄ⲧ⸗, to find; *V* ⲕⲉⲙⲧⲥ or ⲕⲙⲧⲥ obscurity; *W* ⲕⲣⲉⲙⲣⲉⲙ, grumble, murmur).

1.5 Atonic Vowels (Not Including Sonants). These vowels are evidently always short. In several categories of the atonic vowels, significant differences appear between *F* and *F7* and between *F* and *V, W*, without mentioning *H* and *M* and the other Coptic idioms.

The case of the initial atonic vowel does not call for any particular commentary: e.g., *F, F7, V;* ⲗⲗⲟⲩ, child; *F5* ⲗⲙⲏⲛϯ, hell, *F7* ⲗⲙⲓⲛϯ (ⲓ by assimilation?), *V* ⲗⲙⲛϯ, *H* ⲗⲙⲏⲛⲧⲓ, *M* ⲗ̇ⲙⲛⲧⲉ; *F, F7, V, W, M* ⲉⲥⲏⲧ lower part, ground, *H* ⲏⲥⲏⲧ (always in close liaison ⲡⲏⲥⲏⲧ).

More instructive and interesting are certain cases of the vocalization of the atonic syllable when its vowel is neither initial nor final (this vocalization may occur by means of a sonant in place of a corresponding voiced sonorant preceded by a vowel, graphically most often ⲉ; see below); it may be remarked here that several of the atonic "syllables" in question are in fact "subsyllables" (i.e., syllables only in bradysyllabication; see SYLLABICATION).

One will notice below only the cases that manifest differences between *F*, *F7*, *V*, *W*, and *M* (manuscripts of the Gospel of Matthew and of Acts, here always making use of the sonant; *M* of the Pauline letters has for its part some ⲉ followed by the sonorant; see Kasser, 1987; with regard to the characteristics of *H*, see DIALECT H).

After an open tonic syllable, in a closed atonic syllable with a sonorant as the final, *F* vocalizes with ⲉ, *F7* probably also (except for some cases where it uses ⲓ), except when this syllable follows tonic ⲱ and ends in ⲃ or ⲙ (*F7* then vocalizes in ⲟ, e.g., ⲥⲱⲧⲟⲙ, to hear, and ϩⲱⲧⲟⲃ, to kill). *V*, *W*, *M* make use of the sonant (e.g., *V*, *W* ⲥⲱⲧⲙ̄, *M* ⲥⲟⲧⲙ, *M* ϩⲟⲧⲃ; likewise, *V* ⲥⲱⲣⲙ, to go astray; it will be noted that *F56* also sometimes uses Ø, e.g., ⲥⲱⲧⲙ and, likewise, ⲧⲱϩⲙ, to summon).

After a closed tonic syllable, in a closed atonic syllable with a sonorant as the initial only, *F*, *F7*, *V*, and *W* vocalize in ⲉ, while *M* has the sonant (thus, e.g., *F*, *V*, *W* ϩⲁⲧⲃⲉϥ, to kill him, and likewise, *F7* ⲛⲉϩⲃⲉϥ, yoke).

After a closed tonic syllable, in a closed atonic syllable with a sonorant as the final, *F* and *F7* vocalize in ⲉ, while *M*, *W*(?), and *V* have the sonant (thus, e.g., *F5* ⲕⲗⲉⲙⲗⲉⲙ, to grumble, murmur, *W* ⲕⲣⲉⲙⲣⲉⲙ or [ⲕⲣⲉ]ⲙⲣ̄ⲙ̄, *M* ⲕⲣⲙⲣⲙ; *F5* ϣⲧⲗⲁⲧⲉⲗ, to trouble, *H* ϣⲧⲁⲣⲧⲏⲣ, *V*, *M* passim ϣⲧⲁⲣⲧⲣ, except for a *M* ϣⲧⲁⲣⲧⲉⲣ in Acts 9:22).

Before a tonic syllable, in a closed syllable with a sonorant as the final, *F* vocalizes in ⲉ, except between ⲧ and ⲃ, where *F5* vocalizes in ⲩ (*F4* is lacking); *F7* vocalizes rather in ⲓ (it also has several ⲉ), except before ⲃ (but not specially after ⲧ), where it generally writes ⲩ; *W* and *M* (most often), and probably also *V*, have the sonant (thus, e.g., *F5* ⲃⲉⲗⲗⲏ, blind, *W*, *M* ⲃⲗⲗⲏ; *F* ⲗⲉⲙϩⲏ, free, *M* ⲣⲉⲙϩⲏ (sic); *F5* ⲗⲉⲙ(ⲙ)ⲉⲗ, rich, *F7* ⲗⲓⲙⲙⲗ or ⲗⲉⲙ(ⲙ)ⲗⲗ, *V* ⲣⲙ(ⲙ)ⲗⲗ; *F5* ⲧⲩⲃⲛⲏ, cattle, *F7* ⲧⲉⲃⲛⲏ (sic), *M* plural ⲧⲃⲛⲗⲟⲩⲉ̀; *F5* ϩⲉⲃⲥⲱ, clothing, *F7* ϩⲩⲃⲥⲱ, *M* ϩⲃⲥⲱ).

Generally speaking, the final atonic vowel is ⲓ in *F* as it is in *F7*, *V*, *W*, and *H* (and finally in *B*), while it is ⲉ in *M* (as in *L*, *A*, *S*). This rule however knows a significant systematic exception in Fayyumic, with or without lambdacism. When this final corresponds to an ancient Egyptian ʿ (ʿAYIN), we find final ⲉ in *F*, *V*, *W* (and semievolved and logically secondary *F7*), final ⲗ in *F7* (primitive), as in DIALECT P; *B* then omits any vowel. It may, however, happen that we find, above all in *F5* (where this is among others the chief characteristic of the subdialect *F58*), more rarely in more evolved *F7* and evolved *F4*, *V*, forms of this category which have levelled their atonic final in ⲓ (thus e.g. from *mšʿ* *F5* ⲙⲏⲏϣⲉ, crowd, *F4*, *F7*, (semievolved) *W* ⲙⲏϣⲉ, *F7* [ⲙⲏ]ϣⲗ (like *P* ⲙⲏϣⲗ), and finally *B* ⲙⲏϣ; from *mšdʿ* *F5* ⲙⲉⲉϫⲉ, ear, *F4*, *V* ⲙⲉϫⲉ, *F7* (primitive) ⲙⲉϫⲗ (compare *P* ⲙⲗϣⲧⲗ), finally *B* ⲙⲁϣϫ).

1.6 Atonic Sonants. In an initial position, if they are systematically absent from *F5*, the atonic sonants appear in *F4* as in *F7*, and in *V*, *W* as in *M* (and in *S*, *L*, *A*, even *B*). But if, in the area of Middle Egypt, they appear immutable in *V*, *W*, they may still be replaced by their substitute, the corresponding sonorant preceded by a vowel (ⲉ everywhere except in *F7*, which prefers here ⲓ), when the phenomenon of "close liaison" (Polotsky, 1949, pp. 29–30) is produced. This takes place in *F4* (as in *F7*, *M*, also in a certain fashion in *H*) only when the word, beginning with the sonant is preceded by the definite article (ⲡ- etc.), which is so closely linked with what follows that the sonant is no longer considered as an initial, and the corresponding sonorant preceded by ⲉ (etc.) is substituted for it (in *B* the possibilities for "close liaison" are much more numerous). One will then have *F4*, *F7*, *M* ⲙⲡⲉϥⲉⲙⲧⲗ ⲉⲃⲗⲗ, in his presence (and immutable, *F5* ⲙⲡⲉϥⲉⲙⲧⲗ ⲉⲃⲗⲗ, on the one hand, *V* [*W* probably the same] ⲙⲡⲉϥⲙⲧⲗ ⲉⲃⲗⲗ, on the other); in close liaison one finds, in contrast, *F4*, *F5*, *M* ⲙⲡⲉⲙⲧⲗ ⲉⲃⲗⲗ ⲛ-, in presence of, *F7* ⲙ̀ⲡⲓⲙⲧⲗ ⲛ̀- . . . (ⲉⲃⲗⲗ) (and immutable, *F5* ⲙⲡⲉⲙⲧⲗ ⲉⲃⲗⲗ ⲛ-, on one hand, *V* ⲙⲡⲙⲧⲗ ⲛ [- . . . ⲉⲃⲗⲗ], on the other; and similarly *W* ⲡⲙϩⲉⲩ, the tomb, John 11:38, according to what the manuscript itself shows).

As regards the atonic sonants within a word or as finals, see what was said above with reference to the atonic vowels in these positions: such sonants are systematically lacking in *F4*, as in *F5* and *F7* (and also in *H* and *B*), but they appear regularly in *M*, very often in *W* also, and in *V* finally more frequently than their substitute (ⲉ followed by the corresponding sonorant).

2. The Conjugation System

Except in special cases (conjunctive, etc.), the form cited here is the third-person singular masculine only, as well as its corresponding prenominal form (nom. = before nominal subject). The complete paradigm is not attested in all conjugations. Only the most specific form(s) for each dialect (*F, V, W, H*) or subdialect (*F4, F46, F5, F56, F7*) are given here.

Except where specially mentioned, the form is affirmative (neg. = negative). Every basic tense (hereafter abbreviated "basic") is followed (if attested) by its satellites, after "And": circ. = circumstantial, rel. = relative, pret. = preterite, II = second tense; ant. = with pronominal antecedent. Forms between brackets [. . .] are reconstructed from very near forms; zero = no verbal prefix. Except where specially mentioned, *F56* (not *F46*) is included in *F5; F4* and *F5* together are *F*.

2.1 Bipartite Pattern. Neg. ⲛ- . . . ⲉⲛ *F, F46, F7, V, W*, zero particle . . . ⲁⲛ *H*.

2.1.1. Present (basic) ϥ- *F, F7, V, W*, ⲃ- [*F46*] *H*, nom. zero. And circ. ⲉϥ- (neg. ⲉⲛϥ- . . . ⲉⲛ etc.) *F, F7, V, W*, ⲉⲃ- *F46, H*, nom. ⲉⲗⲉ- *F, F46, F7*, ⲉⲣⲉ- [V], W, ⲉⲣⲏ- H; rel. ⲉⲧⲉϥ- *F5*, [*F56*], *F7*, ⲉⲧϥ- *F4*, (*F7*), [*V*], *W*, nom. ⲉⲧⲉ(ⲗⲉ)- *F*, ⲉⲧⲉ- *F7, V*, ⲉⲧⲉⲣⲉ- *W;* pret. (= imperfect) ⲛⲁϥ- *F, F7*, [*V*], *W*, [ⲛⲁⲃ- *F46*], nom. ⲛⲁⲗⲉ- *F*, ⲛⲁⲣⲉ- *V, W;* II ⲁϥ- *F, F7, V, W*, [ⲉⲃ- *H*], nom. ⲁⲗⲉ- *F, F7;* ⲁⲣⲉ- [*V*], *W*.

2.1.2. Future (basic) ϥⲛⲉ- *F, F7, V, W* [ⲃⲛⲉ- *F46*], ⲃⲛⲁ- *H*, nom. zero . . . ⲛⲉ- *F, F46, F7, V, W*, zero . . . ⲛⲁ- *H*. And circ. ⲉϥⲛⲉ- (neg. ⲉⲛϥⲛⲉ . . . ⲉⲛ etc.) *F*, [*F7, V*], *W*, nom. ⲉⲗⲉ- . . . ⲛⲉ- *F;* rel. ⲉⲧⲉϥⲛⲉ (neg. ⲉⲧⲉⲛϥⲛⲉ . . . ⲉⲛ etc.) *F*, ⲉⲧϥⲛⲉ- [*F4*], *F7*, [*V, W*], nom. ⲉⲧⲉⲗⲉ- . . . ⲛⲉ- *F*, ⲉⲧⲉ- . . . ⲛⲉ- *F7*, [*V*], (*W*), [ⲉ]ⲧⲉⲣⲉ- . . . [ⲛⲉ-] (*W*); pret. ⲛⲁϥⲛⲉ- *F4*, nom. ⲛⲁⲣⲉ- . . . ⲛⲉ- *W;* II ⲁϥⲛⲉ- *F*, [*F7*], *V*, (*W*), nom. [ⲁⲗⲉ- . . . ⲛⲉ- *F, F7*], ⲁⲣⲉ- . . . ⲛⲉ- *V*, [*W*], ⲉⲣⲏ- . . . ⲛⲁ- *H*.

2.2 Tripartite Pattern.

2.2.1. Tenses with special negations (if not II):

2.2.1.1. *Perfect* (basic) ⲁϥ- *F, F7, V*, ⲁⲃ- *F46, H*, ϩⲁϥ- (*V*), *W*, nom. ⲁ- *F, F46, F7, V*, ϩⲁ- (*V*), [*W*]; neg. ⲙⲡⲉϥ- *F, F7, V*, ⲙⲡⲉⲃ- *F46*, [ⲡⲏⲃ- *H*], nom. ⲙⲡⲉ- *F*, [*F46*], *F7*, [*V*], *W* [ⲡⲏ- *H*]. And circ. ⲉⲁϥ- *F, F7*, [(*V*)], ⲉⲁⲃ- [*F46*] *H*, ⲉϩⲁϥ- [(*V*)], *W*, nom. ⲉⲁ- *F*, [*F46, F7*, (*V*)], [ⲉϩⲁ- (*V*), *W*]; neg. ⲉⲙⲡⲉϥ- *F*, [*F7, V, W*], nom. [ⲉⲙⲡⲉ- *F, F7, V, W*]; rel. ⲛⲧⲁϥ- (ant. ⲡⲉⲛⲧⲁϥ-) *F5, F7*, (*V*), ⲛⲧⲁⲃ- *F46*, ⲧⲁⲃ- (ant. ⲡⲏⲛⲧⲁⲃ-) *H*, ⲉⲧⲁϥ- *F4*, (*F7*), (*V*), ⲉⲧ(ⲉ)ϩⲁϥ- *W;* nom. ⲛⲧⲁ- (ant. ⲡⲉⲛⲧⲁ-) *F5*, ⲛ̈ⲧⲁ- *F7*, [*V*], ⲧⲁ- (ant. ⲡⲏⲛⲧⲁ-) *H*, ⲉⲧⲁ- *F4*, [(*V*)], ⲉⲧ(ⲉ)ϩⲁ- *W;* neg. ⲉⲧⲉⲙⲡⲉϥ- *F5, F7*, nom. [ⲉⲧⲉⲙⲡⲉ- *F5, F7*]; II ⲁⲁϥ- *F5*, [ⲛⲧⲁⲁϥ- *F4*? ⲛⲁϥ- *F4*?], ⲛⲧⲁϥ- *F5*, [*V*?], ⲧⲁⲃ- *H* (ⲁϥ- *F7*?), ⲁϩⲁϥ- *W;* nom. ⲁⲁ- *F5*, (ⲛⲧⲁⲁ- *F4*?), ⲛⲁ- *F4*, (*V*?), [ⲧⲁ- *H*], (ⲁ- *F7*?), [ⲁϩⲁ- *W*]; neg. with ⲛ- . . . ⲉⲛ *F, F46, F7, V, W*, zero . . . ⲁⲛ *H*.

2.2.1.2. *Expectative* (or completive) (basic = neg.) ⲙⲡⲁⲧ(ⲉ)ϥ- *F5, V*, [*W*], ⲡⲁⲧⲏⲃ- *H*, [ⲙⲡⲁϥ- *F7*], nom. ⲙⲡⲁⲧⲉ- *F5*, [*V, W*]. ⲡⲁⲧⲏ- *H*, ⲙ̈ⲡⲁ- *F7*.

2.2.1.3. *Consuetudinal* or *aorist* (basic) ϣⲁϥ- *F, F7, V*, [*W*], ϣⲁⲃ- *F46, H*, nom. ϣⲁⲗⲉ- *F*, [*F46*], *F7*, ϣⲁⲣⲉ- *V, W*, ϣⲁⲣⲏ- *H;* neg. ⲙⲉϥ- (*F4*), [*F5*], *F7, V, W*, ⲙⲙⲉϥ- (*F4*), (*F7*?), [ⲙⲉⲃ- *F46*], ⲙⲏⲃ- *H*, nom. ⲙⲉⲗⲉ- (*F4*), *F5*, [*F46, F7*], ⲙⲉⲣⲉ- [*V*], *W*, [ⲙⲏⲣⲏ- *H*]. And circ. ⲉϣⲁϥ- [*F*], *F7*, [*V, W*], [nom. ⲉϣⲁⲗⲉ- etc.]; rel. ⲛϣⲁϥ- *F*, (ⲉϣⲁϥ- *F5*? *V*?), ⲉⲧⲉϣⲁϥ- (*F5*), *F7*, [ⲉϣⲁⲃ-] (ant. ⲡⲏϣⲁⲃ-) *H*, nom. [ⲛϣⲁⲗⲉ- *F*], [(ⲉϣⲁⲗⲉ- *F5*? *V*?)], ⲉⲧⲉϣⲁⲗⲉ- (*F5*), *F7*, [ⲉϣⲁⲣⲉ- *V*?, ⲉϣⲁⲣⲏ- *H*]; neg. ⲉⲧⲉⲙⲉϥ- *F5, F7*, ([ant. ⲡⲏⲧⲏⲙⲏⲃ- *H*]), [nom. ⲉⲧⲉⲙⲉⲗⲉ-, etc.]; pret. [ⲛⲛⲉϣⲁϥ- *F5*], nom. ⲛⲛⲉϣⲁⲗⲉ- *F5;* II [ⲛϣⲁϥ- *F5*, nom. ⲛϣⲁⲗⲉ- *F5*].

2.2.1.4. *Futurum energicum* or *third future* (basic) ⲉϥⲉ- *F, F7*, [*V*], *W*, ⲉⲃⲉ- *F46*, [ⲉⲃⲏ-] (ϫⲏⲏⲃⲏ- with ϫⲏ, in order that, ant.) *H*, nom. ⲉⲗⲉ- *F*, [*F46*], *F7*, [ⲉⲣⲉ- *V, W*, ⲉⲣⲏ- *H*]; neg. ⲛⲛⲉϥ- *F*, (*F7*), *V*, [*W*], ⲛⲉϥ- *F7*, ⲛⲏⲃ- *H*, nom. ⲛⲛⲉ- *F*, (*F7*), [*V*], (*W*?).

2.2.1.5. *Causative imperative* (basic) ⲙⲁⲗⲉϥ- *F, F7*, [ⲙⲁⲗⲉⲃ- *F46*], ⲙⲁⲣⲉϥ- *V, W*, ⲙⲁⲣⲏⲃ- *H*, nom. ⲙⲁⲗⲉ- *F*, [*F46, F7*], ⲙⲁⲣⲉ- *V, W*, ⲙⲁⲣⲏ- *H;* neg. ⲙⲡⲉⲗⲧⲣⲉϥ- *F5*, [ⲙ̈ⲡⲓⲗⲧⲗⲉϥ- or ⲙ̈ⲡⲉⲗⲧⲗⲉϥ *F7*], [ⲙⲡⲉⲗⲧⲉϥ- *F46*], ⲙⲡⲉⲣⲧⲉϥ- *V*, [*W*?], [(ⲙⲉⲛⲧ(ⲉ)ϥ- *F7*)], [ⲛⲏⲕⲧⲣⲏϥ- *H*], nom. ⲙⲡⲉⲗⲧⲣⲉ- *F5*, [ⲙⲡⲉⲗⲧⲉ- *F4*], ⲙ̈ⲡⲓⲗⲧⲗⲉ or ⲙ̈ⲡⲉⲗⲧⲉ- *F7*, ⲙⲡⲉⲣⲧⲉ- *V*, [*W*?], [ⲛⲏⲕⲧⲣⲏ- *H*].

2.2.2. Tenses with neg. ϣⲧⲉⲙ- *F* or ⲧⲙ- *V*, W, ⲧⲓⲙ- or ⲧⲉⲙ- *F7*:

2.2.2.1. *Future conjunctive* (basic) [ⲧⲁⲗⲉϥ-] or ⲛⲧⲁⲗⲉϥ- *F5*, [ⲧⲁⲗⲉϥ- F4], nom. ⲧⲁⲗⲉ- [or ⲛⲧⲁⲗⲉ-] *F5*, [ⲧⲁⲗⲉ- *F4*].

2.2.2.2. *Conjunctive* (basic) (sing. 1., 2. masc., 3. masc., fem., pl. 1., 2., 3.) (ⲛ)ⲧⲁ-, ⲛⲕ-, ⲛⲧⲉ-, ⲛϥ-, ⲛⲥ-, ⲛⲧⲉⲛ-, ⲛⲧⲉⲧⲉⲛ-, ⲛⲥⲉ- *F, F7, V, W*, ⲧⲁ-, ⲧⲉⲕ-, [ⲧⲉ-], ⲛⲃ-, [ⲛⲥ-], ⲧⲉⲛ-, [ⲧⲉⲧⲉⲛ-], ⲧⲟⲩ- *F46*, [ⲧⲁ-], ⲕ-, ⲧⲏ-, ⲃ-, [ⲥ-], [ⲧⲏⲛ-], (ⲧⲏⲧⲛ-?), ⲥⲏ- *H*, nom. ⲛⲧⲉ- *F, F7, V, W*, ⲧⲉ- *F46*, [ⲧⲏ- *H*]. And with ϣⲁ-, toward (= limitative) ϣⲁⲛⲧⲉϥ- *F*, [*F7*], *V*, [W], ϣⲁⲛⲧⲏⲃ- *H*, nom. ϣⲁⲛⲧⲉ- *F*, *F7*, [V, W], ϣⲁⲛⲧⲏ- *H*.

2.2.2.3. *Temporal* (basic) ⲛⲧⲉⲗⲉϥ- *F5*, [*F7*?], ⲛⲧⲉⲣⲉϥ- [*V*?] *W*, ⲧⲏⲣⲏⲃ- *H*, ⲉⲧⲁϥ- *F4*, ⲉⲧⲉⲁϥ- (*F5*?), [ⲉⲧϩⲁϥ- (*W*)], nom. ⲛⲧⲉⲗⲉ- *F5*, [*F7*?], ⲛⲧⲉⲣⲉ- [*V*?], *W*, ⲧⲏⲣⲏ- *H*, ⲉⲧⲁ- *F4*, [ⲉⲧⲉⲁ- *F5*?], ⲉⲧϩⲁ- *W*.

2.2.2.4. *Conditional* (basic) ⲁϥ- [*F4*, (*F5*) with neg.], *F7*, [*V, W*] with neg.], ⲁϥϣⲁⲛ- *F4*, [(*F56*)], (*F7*), (*V*), [*W*], ⲁϥϣⲁ- (*F7*), (*V*), ⲉϥϣⲁⲛ- *F5*, ⲉⲃϣⲁⲛ- *H*, nom. ⲁⲗⲉ- [*F4*, (*F5*) with neg.], *F7*, [(*V*) with neg.], *W* with neg., ⲁⲗⲉϣⲁⲛ- [*F4*], (*F56*), ⲁⲣⲉϣⲁ- *V*, ⲁⲣϣ[ⲁ]ⲛ- *W*, ⲁϣⲁ- (*F7*), ⲉⲗ(ⲉ)ϣⲁⲛ- *F5*, ⲉⲣϣⲁⲛ- *H*.

3. Vocabulary

The lexical stock of *F4, F5, F7, V*, and *W* (not to speak of *H*) presents a certain number of units not found elsewhere in Coptic (or only in a single idiom, or only in two, etc.). They cannot all be presented here (cf. Crum, 1939, and Westendorf, 1977), and only some examples will be listed.

F5, F46, F7 ⲁϩⲁ, and, to be compared with *B4, B74, G* ⲟⲩⲟϩⲉ (and *B* ⲟⲩⲟϩ), etc., *L6* ⲟⲩⲁϩⲁ, *L4* ⲁϩⲛ̄, ⲁϩⲁⲛ (Kasser 1983b). *F7* ⲁϫⲱ (pl. ⲁϫϩⲁⲩⲓ̈) viper, serpent, cf. ⲁ̀ϫⲱ *B* (the other Coptic dialects prefer ϩⲟϥ, a word that *F7* also knows).

ⲃⲱⲕ, servant, once in *F5*, a word current in *B* (which does not have ϩⲙϩⲁⲗ, a word current, with ϩⲉⲗ, in *F5*); ⲃⲱⲕ is absent from the other Coptic dialects. *F7* ⲃⲱⲣⲉ, ⲃⲁⲣⲉ, repulse, cf. *S* ⲃⲱⲱⲣⲉ, ⲃⲟⲟⲣ⸗, etc.

F ⲉⲙⲉϣⲏⲓ̈ ⲉ-, except, is lacking elsewhere in Coptic. Note *F5, S* ⲉⲣⲡⲱ, branch (?), Isaiah 34:4.

F5 ⲕⲁⲥ, roaring, clamor, is lacking elsewhere in Coptic (Epistle of Jeremiah 31).

F ⲗⲁⲡⲥ, something, is lacking elsewhere in Coptic, but may be compared with *B* ⲗⲁⲡⲥⲓ, to bite, a mouthful; on the other hand, one can only make the same comparison for *F, F7, V* ⲗⲁⲡϯ, something (cf. ⲗⲁⲡⲧ once or twice in *F7*) if one supposes a ⲗⲁⲡϯ derived graphically from ⲗⲁⲡⲯ, an explanation that remains doubtful (ϯ /ti/ confused with the ancient ϯ = ⲯ /ps/; see ALPHABETS, COPTIC).

F5 ⲙⲟⲩⲟⲩⲓ̈, *F4, V* ⲙⲟⲩⲓ̈, new, has its only correspondent in ⲙⲟⲩⲓ̈, which appears once only in *S* (Kahle, 1954, p. 701, 11), if the etymology sometimes suggested (e.g., Černý, 1976, p. 79) from *S, B* ⲙⲟⲩⲓ̈, island is set aside (Vycichl, 1983, pp. 108–109). The parallel with *M* ⲙⲁⲓ̈ (Husselman, 1965, p. 85) remains very doubtful. *F5* ⲙⲁⲧⲉⲙ, winnowing fan, is lacking elsewhere in Coptic (Is. 30:24). *F* ⲙϣⲓϣ, vengeance, appears also in *B*, but not elsewhere.

F7 ⲛⲏⲛⲓ, honeycomb, cf. *B* ⲛⲏⲛⲓ (a rare word). *W* ⲛⲓⲛⲉⲓ̈, nothing, cf. *M* ⲛⲓⲛⲉⲓ̈. ⲛⲟⲩⲉ-, see ⲟⲩⲉ-, against, below. *F7* ⲛⲟⲩϣⲥ, strike with amazement, cf. *S* ⲛⲟⲩϣⲥ etc.

F7 ⲡⲓⲁ⸗, awaken, unknown elsewhere in Coptic (Sg. 2:7 and 8:5). *F7* ⲡⲁⲣⲕ†, chiseled, cf. *B* ⲫⲱⲛⲕ with the same significance (in truth, rather remote from those of *S* etc. ⲡⲱⲛⲕ̄ etc., draw, heap up, etc.). *F7* ⲡⲁⲛⲁⲗⲉⲥϥⲓ, dream(er) (Eccl. 5:2), is probably to be resolved into ⲗⲉⲥϥⲓ, cf. *F5* ⲗⲉⲥⲃⲓ, *S* ⲣⲁⲥⲟⲩ, dream, and ⲡⲁⲛⲁ- cf. *S* etc. ⲡⲱⲛ etc. *B* ⲫⲉⲛ ⲣⲁⲥⲟⲩⲓ, Crum, 1939, p. 263b,3; 268a,15). Vulgar *F5* ⲡⲉⲧⲃⲓ, avenger, *F46* ⲡⲉⲧⲃⲏ, cf. *S* ⲡⲉⲧⲃⲉ.

F5 ⲥⲁⲕⲃⲓ, sprinkle (?), unknown elsewhere in Coptic. *F5* ⲥⲛⲁⲧ, to fear, cf. *S* ⲥⲛⲁⲧ. *F7* ⲥⲓⲧⲃⲉⲓϩ, tool, utensil, weapon, etc., Eccl. 9:18, cf. *S* ⲥⲧⲉⲃⲁⲉⲓϩ, *B* ⲥⲉⲃⲁⲓϩ etc., is a rare word.

F5 ⲧⲕⲁⲛ, impulse, force (?), cf. *M* ⲧⲕⲁⲛ, *A* ⲧⲕⲏⲛ (Kasser, 1979). *F7* ⲧⲁⲓ̈ⲙ to aid, *V* ⲧⲁⲉⲓⲙ, cf. *M* ⲧⲁⲉⲓⲙ. *W* ⲧⲣⲟⲩⲣ, haste, cf. *M* ⲧⲣⲟⲩⲣ.

F5 ⲟⲩⲉ- in (ⲛ)ⲛⲟⲩⲉ- etc., against, cf. *M* and *S* ⲛ̄ⲟⲩⲉ- etc., alongside ⲟⲩⲃⲉ- etc. in *S* and other Coptic idioms (including *F7*).

ϣⲕⲓⲗ, curl (of hair), cf. *S* ϣⲕⲓⲗ. *V5* ϣⲉⲉⲣ, price, cf. *S* ϣⲁⲁⲣ. *F5, F7* ϣⲧⲁ, thicket, copse, cf. eventually *S* also? (Crum, 1939, 595a). *F7* ϣⲱϫⲓ, whisper, whistle (?), Eccl. 2:15–16, is probably found nowhere else in Coptic and could be onomatopoeia.

F5 ϩⲉⲓ, here, behold, cf. *M* ϩⲓ and perhaps also *F* ϩⲉⲓⲧⲉ, *F5* etc. ϩⲉⲓⲧⲉⲥ. ϩⲗⲁⲗ, darkness, cf. *B* ϩⲗⲟⲗ etc. *F4, F7* ϩⲗⲁϯ, descendants, children, Lam. 4:10, *V* ϩⲣⲁϯ, 1 Jn. 3:7, 18, cf. *B* ϧⲣⲟϯ. *F5* ϩⲧⲉⲓ in ϩⲓ ϩⲧⲉⲓ, deceive, cf. *S* ϩⲓ ϩⲧⲁⲓ̈.

F7 ϫⲓⲗⲗⲉⲓ, shield, buckler, cf. *S* ϭϫ̄. *F5* ϫⲁⲟⲩⲧ†, base, without value, cf. *S* ϫⲟⲟⲩⲧ†, e.g., 2 Cor. 13:5–6.

F5 ϭⲉⲗⲃⲉⲥⲓ, purple, *F7* ϫⲉⲗⲃⲉⲥⲓ, appears nowhere else in Coptic. *F5* ϭⲉⲗⲙⲁⲉⲓⲛ, pitcher, *H* ϭⲏⲗⲙⲁⲓ, cf. *S* ϭ(ⲉ)ⲗⲙⲁ(ⲉ)ⲓ(ⲛ) etc. *F5, V4* ϭⲁⲗⲁϫ, foot, *F* pl. ϭⲁⲗⲁⲩϫ, *F7* ϫⲁⲗⲁⲩϫ(ϩ), cf. *B* ϭⲁⲗⲟϫ, pl. ϭⲁⲗⲁⲩϫ.

One may finally recall here various lexical or morphological peculiarities that make *W* (as distinct from *V*) very close to *M*: the first perfect prefix (nom., etc.) *W, M* ϩⲁ- (rare in *V*) in opposition to *V, F* ⲁ-, etc.; *W, M* ⲛⲓⲛⲉⲓ, nothing; only *M* ⲉⲓⲣⲉ ⲙ̀ⲙⲁ⸗, to do that, or *W* ⲓⲣⲓ ⲙ̄ⲙⲁ⸗ in opposition to *V, F*, where there is a choice between ⲓⲣⲓ ⲙⲙⲁ⸗ and ⲣⲁ ⲙⲁ⸗; ϣⲉ ⲛⲉ⸗, to go, so almost always in *W, M*, while *V*, like *F*, writes simply ϣⲏ (without the "dative" preposition); in *W* and *M* the Copto-Greek verbs are not preceded by the auxiliary (ⲉ)ⲣ, etc., and do not have the Greek final -ⲛ, which sets them against those of *V* or above all *F*, where one may observe rather the contrary.

4. Grammar

The Fayyumic subdialects are either too poorly attested or attested in too irregular a fashion (this is especially the case with *F5*) for one to be able to establish with any ease or precision the syntax characteristic of each of them or even what might be more modestly and vaguely considered the "Fayyumic syntax" in general. At least, investigations in this area have not as yet been sufficiently advanced for a *status quaestionis* to be given here (what can be found in Till, 1930 and 1961, remains very elementary and not distinctive).

BIBLIOGRAPHY

Asmus, H. *Über Fragmente im Mittelägyptischen Dialekte*. Göttingen, 1904.

Bouriant, U. "Fragments bachmouriques." *Mémoires de l'Institut d'Egypte* 2 (1889):567–604.

Černý, J. *Coptic Etymological Dictionary*. Cambridge, 1976.

Chassinat, E. "Fragments de manuscrits coptes en dialecte fayoumique." *Bulletin de l'Institut français d'archéologie orientale* 2 (1902):171–206.

Crum, W. E. *A Coptic Dictionary*. Oxford, 1939.

Crum, W. E., and F. G. Kenyon. "Two Chapters of Saint John in Greek and Middle Egyptian." *Journal of Theological Studies* 1 (1900):415–33.

Diebner, B. J.; R. Kasser; A. M. Kropp; C. Voigt; and E. Lucchesi. *Hamburger Papyrus Bil. 1. Die alttestamentlichen Texte des Papyrus bilinguis 1 der Staats- und Universitätsbibliothek Hamburg. Canticum Canticorum (coptice), Lamentationes Ieremiae (coptice), Ecclesiastes (graece et coptice)*. Cahiers d'orientalisme 18. Geneva, 1989.

Elanskaya, A. I. "Rukopis' no. 53 koptskoĭ novoĭ serii (zaklyuchitel'nye glavy Evangeliya ot Marka na faĭyumskom dialekte)." In *Koptskie rukopisi Gosudarstvennoĭ Publičnoĭ Biblioteki imeni M. E. Saltykova-Ščedrina, Palestinskiĭ sbornik* 20, no. 83 (1969):96–120.

Engelbreth, W. F. *Fragmenta Basmurico-Coptica Veteris et Novi Testamenti qui in Museo Borgiano Velitris Asservantur, cum Reliquis Versionibus Aegyptiis Contulit, Latine Vertit nec non Criticis et Philologicis Adnotationibus Illustravit*. Copenhagen, 1811.

Erichsen, W. *Faijumische Fragmente der Reden des Agathonicus Bischofs von Tarsus*. Copenhagen, 1932.

Gaselee, S. "Two Fayoumic Fragments of the Acts." *Journal of Theological Studies* 11 (1909):514–17.

Husselman, E. M. *The Gospel of John in Fayumic Coptic (P. Mich. Inv. 3521)*. Ann Arbor, Mich., 1962.

———. "The Martyrdoms of Cyriacus and Julitta in Coptic." *Journal of the American Research Center in Egypt* 4 (1965):79–86.

Kahle, P. E. *Bala'izah: Coptic Texts from Deir el-Bala'izah in Upper Egypt*. Oxford and London, 1954.

Kasser, R. *Compléments au dictionnaire copte de Crum*. Cairo, 1964.

———. "Compléments morphologiques au dictionnaire de Crum, le vocabulaire caractéristique des quatre nouveaux dialectes coptes: P, M, H et G." *Bulletin de l'Institut français d'archéologie orientale* 64 (1966):19–66.

———. "Un lexème copte oublié, ⲧⲕⲏⲛ akhmimique (Nahum 3, 19)." *Bulletin de la Société d'égyptologie, Genève* 1 (1979):23–25.

———. "Prolégomènes à un essai de classification systématique des dialectes et subdialectes coptes selon les critères de la phonétique, III, Systèmes orthographiques et catégories dialectales." *Muséon* 94 (1981):91–152.

———. "ⲉⲓ ou ⲓ pour /i/ ou /j/ dans les dialectes coptes." *Bulletin of the American Society of Papyrologists* 20 (1983a):123–26.

———. "Les Conjonctions coptes dérivées de la racine de ⲟⲩⲱϩ 'mettre,' 'ajouter.'" *Göttinger Miszellen* 69 (1983b):43–44.

———. "Subdialectes en mésokémique?" *Miscel'lània Papirologica Ramon Roca-Puig en el seu vuitantè aniversari*, ed. S. Janeras, pp. 159–70. Barcelona, 1987.

Lefort, L. T. *Les Pères apostoliques en copte*. CSCO 135–136. Louvain, 1952.

Müller, C. D. G. *Die Bücher der Einsetzung der Erzengel Michael und Gabriel*. CSCO 225–226. Louvain, 1962.

Orlandi, T. *Papiri della Università degli Studi di Milano (P. Mil. Copti)*, Vol. 5, *Lettere di San Paolo in Copto ossirinchita, edizione, commento e indici di T. Orlandi, contributo linguistico di H. Quecke*. Milan, 1974.

Polotsky, H. J. "Une Question d'orthographe bohaïrique." *Bulletin de la Société d'archéologie copte* 12 (1949):25–35.

Quatremère, E. *Recherches critiques et historiques sur la langue et la littérature de l'Egypte*. Paris, 1808.

Schenke, H.-M. "On the Middle Egyptian Dialect of the Coptic Language." *Enchoria* 8 (Sonderband) (1978):43*(89)–(104)58*.

———. *Das Matthäus-Evangelium im mittelägyptischen Dialect des Koptischen (Codex Scheide)*. Texte und Untersuchungen zur Geschichte der altchristlichen Literatur 127. Berlin, 1981.

Simon, J. "Note sur le dossier des textes fayoumiques." *Zeitschrift für die Neutestamentliche Wissenschaft* 37 (1939):205–211.

Stern, L. *Koptische Grammatik*. Leipzig, 1880.

———. "Faijumische Papyri im Ägyptischen Museum zu Berlin." *Zeitschrift für ägyptische Sprache und Altertumskunde* 23 (1885):23–44.

Till, W. C. *Koptische Chrestomathie für den fayumischen Dialekt, mit grammatischer Skizze und Anmerkungen*. Vienna, 1930.

———. *Koptische Dialektgrammatik, mit Lesestücken und Wörterbuch*. 2nd ed. Munich, 1961.

Vycichl, W. *Dictionnaire étymologique de la langue copte*. Louvain, 1983.

Wessely, K. "Ein Sprachdenkmal des mittelägyptischen (baschmurischen) Dialekts." *Sitzungsberichte der königlichen Akademie der Wissenschaften in Wien, Philosophisch-historische Klasse* 158 (1908):1–46.

Westendorf, W. *Koptisches Handwörterbuch, bearbeitet auf Grund des Koptischen Handwörterbuchs von Wilhelm Spiegelberg*. Heidelberg, 1977.

Worrell, W. H. *Coptic Sounds*. Ann Arbor, Mich., 1934.

———. "Fayumic Fragments of the Epistles." *Bulle-*

tin de la Société d'archéologie copte 6 (1940):127–39.

RODOLPHE KASSER

GEMINATION, VOCALIC. Fairly frequently, Coptic manuscripts present examples of graphic vocalic gemination (duplication of various graphV= graphemes called "vowels": ⲁ, ⲉ, ⲏ, ⲓ, ⲟ, (ⲟ)ⲩ, and ⲱ; to be distinguished from V = vocalic phonemes, which, in addition to /a/, /e/, /ə/, /ē/, /i/, /u/, and /ō/, include the sonants /b̩/, /l̩/, /m̩/, /n̩/, and /r̩/). This article will ignore the nonsystematic cases, arising from causes that produced the IDIOLECT of some scribe insufficiently trained and incapable of adhering unreservedly to *one* well-defined orthographic system, to *one* dialect (cf. Worrell, 1934, pp. 110–11; Kasser, 1980, pp. 78–82). The discussion here is restricted to the series of cases that have a systematic cause.

Two types of graphic vocalic gemination are found (graphV + same graphV), each belonging to certain particular dialect(s) or subdialect(s), of which it is one of the fundamental characteristics.

The first of these types of gemination is exceptional. It may be observed in the examples of the most archaic orthography of the text of P. Bodmer VI, the only existing witness of DIALECT P, which is either possibly a kind of proto-Sahidic according to Vergote (1973b), or (looking indeed often very like a kind of reconstructed proto-Sahidic) is rather another variety of Coptic PROTODIALECT, perhaps some sort of proto-Theban (Nagel, 1965; Kasser, 1982a), if not a kind of proto-Sahidic immigrant in the Theban region and strongly influenced by the local (nonliterary) Theban idiom (see Kasser, 1985, and DIALECT, IMMIGRANT). Whatever it may be, that type of gemination only appears sporadically in these examples, being always under strong competition from examples of a more evolved orthography (see below).

There, the tonic vowel of the lexeme is systematically duplicated. (These forms remain very much in the minority, about 2 percent of the whole, to which may be added 3 percent of forms in which an unusual gemination of the consonant immediately preceding or following the tonic vowel or the first consonant of the syllable containing the tonic vowel seems to have been produced through negligence instead of the vocalic gemination mentioned above.) Contrary to what happens in regard to the second type of vocalic gemination (see below), the first is not motivated by any etymological factor; the formula for this first type is thus graphV + same graphV = tonic V. Here are some characteristic examples: *P* ⲁⲁϩⲉ, existence; ⲟ̅ⲟ̅ⲥⲉ (sic), loss; plur. ⲏ̅ⲏ̅ⲩ̅ (sic), houses; plur. ⲓ̈ⲟ̅ⲟ̅ⲧⲉ (sic), fathers, parents; ⲓ̈ⲱⲱⲧⲉ, dew; ⲗⲟⲟⲉⲓⲅⲕⲉ, pretext; ⲡⲱⲱϫϩ, to smooth; ⲁⲡⲉ̅ⲉ̅ (sic) or ⲁⲡⲉⲉ, head; ⲃⲉⲕⲉⲉ, wages; ⲥⲙⲏ̅ⲏ̅ (sic), voice; ϧⲓⲏ̅ⲏ̅ (sic), road, way; ⲧⲉⲩⲟ̅ⲟ̅ (sic), to produce; ϣⲟⲩⲱ̅ⲱ̅ (sic), to empty; and even the Copto-Greek ⲡⲛⲟⲏⲏ (= *πνοή*), breath.

Readers will have noted the supralinear stroke that quite often joins the top of these graphV; appearing perhaps at a late stage to distinguish (in *P*) these geminations from those of the second type (see below), which are phonologically very different, this stroke could well have here, as it usually does elsewhere in Coptic, a syllabic significance, indicating that this gemination of graphV does not express a "broken vowel," a "hiatus," or any analogous phenomenon, and this no more in bradysyllabication (corresponding to slow speech) than in tachysyllabication (corresponding to natural, rapid speech; see SYLLABICATION); it expresses a single V (= vocalic phoneme) simply tonic (= stressed).

The second, much more common type of vocalic gemination appears systematically (or nearly so) in the least archaic forms of the dialect *P*, as well as the dialect *İ* (= *pL*, protodialect of *L*), and especially the idioms *A*, *L4*, *L5*, *L6*, *V5*, *F5*, and *S* (but not in *M*, *W*, *V4*, *F4*, *B* and its subdialects, and *G*). The purely vocalic aspect of this gemination is deceptive, since its formula is graphV + same graphV = tonic vowel + consonant (the demonstration will be found under ALEPH). Those who have sought to analyze this gemination phonologically have in fact very soon realized that its appearance in Coptic most often coincides with the disappearance of an older Egyptian radical consonant. (Some lexemes not affected by this disappearance later took on the vocalic gemination by simple analogy with lexemes that were superficially similar.) However, the conclusions of these investigators have not, from the outset, been unanimous (Kasser, 1982c).

Stern (1880, p. 54): "We understand it [the duplication] as a breaking of the vowel, and compare the stem affected with the Semitic roots expanded by א י ו (mediae quiescentis)." But if one notes that for this author the Coptic "breaking of the vowel" seems indeed to be a kind of diphthongizing; that for him (pp. 34–35) the diphthong is the (syllabic) combination of a vowel with (after it) a semivowel (= glide); that he states (pp. 29–30) that ancient Egyptian had three semivowels (*j* = Coptic /j/ = (ⲉ)ⲓ, *w* = Coptic /w/ = (ⲟ)ⲩ, and finally ʿ), which often became the second element of a vocalic gemination in written Coptic; and that, broadly speaking, one may thus say that all these semivowels appear as graphV in Coptic, then one may suppose that Stern tended, if not always, at least frequently, to identify the second element of the vocalic gemination in Coptic phonologically as an /ʿ/. Lacau (1910, pp. 77–78), while analyzing the phenomenon with much finesse and perspicacity, nevertheless seems to have admitted tacitly that the duplication of the vowel caused by the dropping of the consonant *i*, ʿ, *r*, or *t* is equally a vocalic duplication on the level of superficial phonology, the second V of this gemination replacing those consonants which have effectively disappeared and for which nothing has been substituted, not even some /ʾ/ derived from them (which seems acceptable in bradysyllabication, but debatable in tachysyllabication).

Steindorff (1930, pp. 34–35) presented a distinctly different position: "In Sahidic, in those syllables which have been opened through the suppression of a following consonant . . . , the short medial vowel is frequently doubled: . . . *šeere* "daughter" for **šer-ἰᵉt*, **šer-ʾᵉt*, **še-rᵉ(t)* . . . This process is called a compensating duplication; it is a substitute for the lengthening of a short vowel which appears in an open syllable." Later Steindorff (1951, pp. 34–35) adopted a less clear position, apparently seeking to harmonize his earlier explanation, in modified form, with other explanations that come into play; thus, he subsequently distinguished the cases of compensating duplication from those of "vowel assimilation," on the one hand, and those of "breaking the vowel," on the other (see above).

Kuentz (1934) examined these various possibilities and finally proposed the idea of a compensating (vocalic) lengthening (*Ersatzdehnung*, not *Ersatzverdoppelung*); in reply to the objection that in Coptic ⲱ and ⲏ are the long forms of ⲟ and ⲉ, and hence that instead of, for example, ⲙⲟⲟⲛⲉ, pasture, feed, one ought to find *ⲙⲱⲛⲉ, Kuentz supposed that "at some undetermined period the old opposition of quality became an opposition of timbre; no doubt ⲱ and ⲏ, representing old long vowels, became closed vowels, while ⲟ and ⲉ were open vowels. Thenceforth the graphic duplication of the various vowels examined is naturally interpreted as a notation for long vowels, whether open or closed, at the period when this system of writing was put into use."

Till (1929) was the first to express clearly the idea that the second element (graphV) of the graphic vocalic gemination examined here must represent a consonantal phoneme, without, however, venturing to say which. Later Till (1955, p. 46) became more precise (though still ambiguous): "'Aleph and ʿAjin are still present in Coptic, although no special letters for them exist. Both may have been expressed alike (probably ʾ), although ʿ in some circumstances has a different effect on neighbouring vowels from *3*." And Till (1961, p. 10) wrote that "the vowel written double is to be understood as a simple vowel + Aleph or Ajin." This author (perhaps under the influence of Vergote, 1945, pp. 89–91) thus very clearly comes close to the solution most generally admitted today, according to which it is always ALEPH that the second element in the vocalic gemination renders (Till seems to have seen there sometimes /ʾ/, sometimes /ʿ/, but then it is a /ʿ/ practically pronounced /ʾ/); however, the ambiguity of his position suddenly appears again in a different fashion in his suggestion (Till, 1955, p. 46) that this /ʾ/ "was evidently no longer felt to be a consonant" and in his transcription of ⲃⲱⲱⲛ by *bōʾn* (p. 46) but of ϩⲓⲧⲟⲟⲧϥ by *hitoᵒtĭf* (p. 259).

Edgerton (1957, pp. 136–37) adopted a position resolutely opposed to that of Till, refusing to admit the phonological survival of /ʾ/ or /ʿ/ in Coptic, from the time when they were not represented by any grapheme of their own (the problem of the CRYPTOPHONEME): "It seems simplest to explain the nonexistence of signs for 'aleph and ʿajin in Coptic writing by assuming the non-existence of these phonemes in Coptic speech."

Finally, Vergote (1945, pp. 87–96; 1973, Vol. 1a, pp. 12–15, and Vol. 1b, pp. 31–37) clearly demonstrated that aleph is the consonantal phoneme best suited for replacing ancient ἰ, ʿ, *r*, and *t* (and even *j* or *w*), which have disappeared. His opinion was entirely shared by Kasser (1982c), who, however, thought that the graphic aspect (graphV + same graphV) of this gemination (the orthography corresponding largely to br/syl. = bradysyllabication, an artificially slow articulation, in which this gemination is effectively vocalic even in phonation [V tonic + same V atonic]) is to be distinguished radically from its phonetic and phonological expression in normal articulation (in t/syl. = tachysyllabication, where this gemination renders a tonic vowel followed by /ʾ/): thus, ⲕⲁⲁϥ, to put it, t/syl. ʻ/kȧʾf/ʼ (monosyllabic, cf. Vergote, 1973, Vol. 1a, p. 45), but br/syl. /kȧaf/ (disyllabic); or ⲙⲁⲁϫⲉ, ear, /mȧʾče/ (disyllabic) but ʻ/mȧače/ʼ (trisyllabic). The transition from t/syl. to br./syl. would entail a kind of "echo effect" resulting in this vocalic gemination which appears in Coptic orthography: thus, for example, /mȧʾče/ > */mȧʾače/ > ʻ/mȧ a če/ʼ (an idea the first expression of which could already be found in

Vergote, 1945, p. 91, and which, taken up a little differently, is developed in Kasser, 1981, pp. 7–9; 1982b, p. 29, n. 23; 1982c, pp. 33–34).

BIBLIOGRAPHY

Edgerton, W. F. Review of W. C. Till, *Koptische Grammatik (saïdischer Dialekt). Journal of Near Eastern Studies* 16 (1957):136–37.

Hintze, F. "Noch einmal zur 'Ersatzdehnung' und Metathese im Ägyptischen." *Zeitschrift für Phonetik und allgemeine Sprachwissenschaft* 2 (1948):199–213.

Kasser, R. "Prolégomènes à un essai de classification systématique des dialectes et subdialectes coptes selon les critères de la phonétique, I, Principes et terminologie." *Muséon* 93 (1980):53–112.

______. "Usages de la surligne dans le P. Bodmer VI, notes additionnelles." *Bulletin de la Société d'égyptologie, Genève* 5 (1981):23–32.

______. "Le Dialecte protosaïdique de Thèbes." *Archiv für Papyrusforschung* 28 (1982a):67–81.

______. "Syllabation rapide ou lente en copte, I, Les Glides /j/ et /w/ avec leurs correspondants vocaliques '/i/' et '/u/' (et phonèmes appariés analogues)." *Enchoria* 11 (1982b):23–37. ". . . , II, Aleph et 'voyelle d'aleph.'" *Enchoria* 11 (1982c): 39–58.

______. "Gémination de voyelles dans le P. Bodmer VI." In *Acts of the Second International Congress of Coptic Studies, Rome, 22–26 September 1980,* ed. T. Orlandi and F. Wisse, pp. 89–120. Rome, 1985.

Kuentz, C. "Quantité ou timbre? A propos des pseudo-redoublements de voyelles en copte." *Groupe linguistique d'études chamito-sémitiques* 2 (1934–1937):5–7.

Lacau, P. "A propos des voyelles redoublées en copte." *Zeitschrift für ägyptische Sprache und Altertumskunde* 48 (1910):77–81.

Nagel, P. "Der frühkoptische Dialekt von Theben." In *Koptologische Studien in der DDR*, pp. 30–49. *Wissenschaftliche Zeitschrift der Martin-Luther-Universität Halle-Wittenberg,* Sonderheft. Halle-Wittenberg, 1965.

Steindorff, G. *Koptische Grammatik, mit Chrestomathie, Wörterverzeichnis und Literatur.* Berlin, 1930.

______. *Lehrbuch der koptischen Grammatik.* Chicago, 1951.

Stern, L. *Koptische Grammatik.* Leipzig, 1880.

Till, W. C. "Altes 'Aleph und 'Ajin im Koptischen." *Wiener Zeitschrift für die Kunde des Morgenlandes* 36 (1929):186–96.

______. *Koptische Grammatik (saïdischer Dialekt), mit Bibliographie, Lesestücken und Wörterverzeichnissen.* Leipzig, 1955.

______. *Koptische Dialektgrammatik, mit Lesestücken und Wörterbuch.* 2nd ed. Munich, 1961.

Vergote, J. *Phonétique historique de l'égyptien, les consonnes.* Louvain, 1945.

______. *Grammaire copte,* Vol. 1a, *Introduction, phonétique et phonologie, morphologie synthématique (structure des sémantèmes), partie synchronique,* Vol. 1b, *Introduction, phonétique et phonologie, morphologie synthématique (structure des sémantèmes), partie diachronique.* Louvain, 1973a.

______. "Le Dialecte copte P (P. Bodmer VI: Proverbes), essai d'identification." *Revue d'égyptologie* 25 (1973b):50–57.

Worrell, W. H. *Coptic Sounds.* Ann Arbor, Mich., 1934.

RODOLPHE KASSER

GEOGRAPHY, DIALECTAL. A description of Egypt in terms of dialectal geography must take as its basis its physical and especially hydrogeographical characteristics. Egypt is most commonly divided geographically into two elements comparable in area, number of inhabitants, and economic and political importance, but starkly contrasted on the political and linguistic levels. On the one hand, there is the Nile Delta, the vast triangle, practically flat and often marshy, about 125 miles (200 km) on each side and bordered by the sea along its whole northern flank; its geographically open configuration favored a rather undivided (or at least not much divided) linguistic shape. On the other hand, there is the long, threadlike valley of the Nile upstream from the Delta as far as the First Cataract, a little to the south of Aswan, extending nearly 560 miles (900 km), a strip of fertile ground about 8–12 miles (12–20 km) wide in the north, but only 0.6–3 miles (1–5 km) wide in the south; it is locked between two desert plateaus of rock and sand that differ in height. The ancient oasis of the Fayyūm may be considered an appendage of the valley, since an irrigation canal from the Nile could have been dug as early as the pharaonic period. Such a geographical configuration could not but favor the development of divergent dialects within the Egyptian language, whether ancient (pharaonic) or more recent (Coptic).

In traditional terminology, the Delta is generally called "Lower Egypt," and the valley upstream from the Delta either is called as a whole "Upper Egypt" or is subdivided into "Middle Egypt" (roughly from Cairo [Heliopolis-Memphis] to al-Ashmūnayn [Hermopolis] or somewhat further south) and "Upper Egypt" (comprising everything south of Middle

Egypt from Dayrūṭ or possibly Asyūṭ [Lycopolis], or even Ṭimā and Qaw, south of Asyūṭ, as far as Aswan). Clearly this terminology is not without ambiguity.

It has also been suggested (Kasser, 1980a, pp. 74–76) that Egypt be divided, moving downstream, into five regions: (1) the Upper Valley, or the upper and middle parts of Upper Egypt in the strictest sense of the term (that is, from about Aswan and Philae to Ṭahṭā, north of Akhmīm [Panopolis]); (2) the Middle Valley, or the lower part of Upper Egypt, in the strictest sense, and the upper part of Middle Egypt (from about al-Badārī [Qaw] to north of al-Bahnasā [Oxyrhynchus]); (3) the Center (so called because its situation makes it a crossroads between the Middle Valley, the Fayyūm, and the Delta), or the middle and lower parts of Middle Egypt (from south of Banī Suef, to the west of which is Heracleopolis, to north of Cairo [Heliopolis], i.e., all the territory of the Nile Valley to the east and a little to the northeast and the southeast of the Fayyūm); (4) the Fayyūm; and (5) the Delta.

Since Coptic, like pharaonic Egyptian, is a dead language, it is not possible to know its dialects by direct observation of the language as it is spoken, as would be done for a living language. Only texts allow one to attain ultimately a knowledge of the dialects of a dead language. One may observe, whenever occasion affords, systematic morphosyntactical and lexical differences linked to this or that region; as regards Coptic, these differences certainly seem to exist, but for the most part they remain very modest, to the point that they do not of themselves convey the impression of true dialectal differences. But it is known that the most striking divergences between the dialects are generally of a phonological kind. To observe them in a dead language, one must admit (as the majority of linguists do) that the orthography of the language has a phonological value sufficiently precise to allow one to discover, from the various systematic graphic variants, various dialectal phonological systems. Certainly pharaonic Egyptian, in its various written forms, allows one to know the consonantal structure of the ancient Egyptian lexemes but scarcely or not at all their vocalic structure. The latter appears very clearly in Coptic, in which all the graphemes called vowels, or graphV (ⲁ, ⲉ, ⲏ, ⲓ, ⲟ, (ⲟ)ⲩ, and ⲱ), are of Greek origin. This allows one to observe in the Coptic texts divergent orthographic systems, which have always been considered by Coptologists (with some modern exceptions) as having put into writing their phonological systems in a manner still perceptible. Without this working hypothesis, by far the most probable, it seems impossible to work out any dialectal geography of Coptic Egypt whatsoever. On this basis, various systems of dialectal geography have been elaborated; mention will be made here only of those that have been set out in extenso and chiefly the most recent among them (cf. Vergote, 1973, Vol. 1a, pp. 53–59, and the maps herein).

Worrell (1934) divided Egypt into six dialectal regions: (1) the Delta (at least the western Delta), the land of BOHAIRIC, or *B*; (2) the valley from Cairo as far as the Fayyūm (to north of Heracleopolis), SAHIDIC, or *S*; (3) the Fayyūm, FAYYUMIC, or *F*; (4) the valley from the Fayyūm as far as Qaw and Ichqau (south of Ṭimā, to the south of Asyūṭ), also *S* (Worrell did not yet know the existence of MESOKEMIC, or *M*, called by some "Oxyrhynchite"); (5) the valley from Qaw to Thebes, AKHMIMIC, or *A*; and (6) the valley south of Thebes, *A* again. As for LYCOPOLITAN, or *L*, Worrell placed it, rather vaguely, north of *A* and south of *S* (region of Asyūṭ and Ṭimā?).

The distribution proposed by Kahle (1954) is often different: (1) the Delta, land of *B* (properly speaking), except for Alexandria, which could possibly have been the homeland of *S*; (2) Worrell's region 2 (to Heracleopolis), a variety of *B* particularly close to *S* ("semi-Bohairic"; cf. ibid., pp. 377–80; Kasser and Satzinger, 1982); (3) the Fayyūm, *F*; (4) the valley, from Heracleopolis to the north of al-Ashmūnayn, *M*; (5) the valley from Ashmūnayn to the north of Nag Hammadi, *L*; and (6) the valley from Nag Hammadi as far as the region to the south of Thebes, *A* (which very soon advanced toward the north, establishing itself in particular at Akhmīm).

Vergote (1973, Vol. 1a) proposed a solution that on certain points may be considered a compromise between the two preceding: (1) the Delta, *B*; (2) the valley from Cairo to Heracleopolis, *S*; (3) the Fayyūm, *F*; (4) the valley from Heracleopolis to the north of al-Ashmūnayn (a little farther to the north than for Kahle), *M* (called *O*, or Oxyrhynchite, by this author); (5) the valley from al-Ashmūnayn to a zone between Qaw and Akhmīm, *L* (called *A2*, or Subakhmimic, by this author); and (6) the valley from Akhmīm as far as the regions to the south of Thebes, *A*.

It can be seen that Coptology is still far from having reached any certainty concerning all points of its dialectal geography. It is therefore not unreasonable to take up again briefly the various problems of this domain. One may recall first of all (an obvious fact, the full implications of which are not, however, always drawn) that Coptic is now a dead language, so that the investigator must adapt himself to the inconvenience linked to this fact. Moreover, it has been a dead language for a very long time, unfortunately from a period largely prior to the first attempts at observation and scientific study of its philology (seventeenth century). Under these conditions, it is very often extremely difficult to localize its dialects, known almost solely from the evidence of literary manuscripts. These are liable to travel far, and since the majority have survived as the result of clandestine excavation one cannot even know exactly where they were found. (The place where they were sold is often very distant from that of their discovery, precisely to discourage investigation, whether by the police or by scholars: the "laws" of this illegal traffic require that the sources be shrouded in the most absolute secrecy, so that the stories of discovery which some inquirer thinks he has been fortunate enough to gather may well be no more than fables intended to lull his indiscreet curiosity; and if by chance one actually comes to know the place of discovery, it may well not be the place where the manuscript was copied and such an idiom was in use.)

Further, traditional data are too often vague and uncertain. Thus, the fourteenth-century grammarian Athanasius of Qūṣ wrote of knowing the existence of three Coptic idioms: (1) "the Coptic of Miṣr, which is Sahidic" (Miṣr is Cairo, and for Arabic-speaking Egyptians the *sa'id* is all Upper Egypt, in the widest sense of the term, and hence the whole Nile Valley south of the Delta as far as Aswan; the Sahidic country is thus by no means restricted to southern Upper Egypt, the region of Thebes, as numerous Coptologists have believed); (2) "the Bohairic Coptic known by the Boḥaira" (this is the province occupying the greater part of the north-central western Delta); and (3) "the Bashmuric Coptic used in the country of Bashmur" (north-central eastern Delta).

Athanasius located *B* with relative precision. (Bohairic is a well-known idiom, whose localization is now confirmed by hundreds of parietal inscriptions found in the monastic site of Kellia, some of which are also in Greek; no one attests *S* or any dialect of the Nile Valley above the Delta.) He also located, to a certain degree, BASHMURIC (of which unfortunately practically nothing remains: two perhaps doubtful words in all). As for *S*, he said only that its territory is somewhere to the south of the Delta.

One must therefore have recourse to other means of locating the majority of the Coptic dialects, but unfortunately such indicators are often lacking. Certainly, the large quantity of nonliterary *F* texts found in this region allow one to believe that the cradle of this dialect is the Fayyūm. Various phonemic and graphic resemblances between an Old Coptic manuscript (Osing, 1976) and the *M* texts have led some to locate the land of *M* in the region of Oxyrhynchus and thus call this dialect "Oxyrhynchite," but this too-precise localization has been contested with serious arguments (Osing, 1978), which leads one to think that *M* should perhaps be located not exactly at Oxyrhynchus but a little farther north (or south?). Finally, it does indeed seem from graffiti found in situ that *A* was spoken very early, and probably from the beginning, at Akhmīm (whose name in its present Arabic form with /x/ after the initial /a/ seems to reflect an ancient dialectal orthography *ϩⲙⲓⲙ, differing from *S* ϣⲙⲓⲙ, but also written ⲭⲙⲓⲛ or ⲭⲙⲓⲙ, cf. Westendorf, 1977, p. 481; *B* ϣⲙⲓⲛ is certainly a simple orthographical revival of *S* ϣⲙⲓⲛ). But the arguments (e.g., Kahle, 1954, pp. 198–99) according to which *A* was at first the idiom of Thebes, before being driven out, especially by *S*, are not entirely convincing. (Crum and Kahle knew neither DIALECT i as a dialect, proto-Lycopolitan, nor DIALECT P, also a typical PROTODIALECT, which often looks like what can be known about the logical predecessor of *S*, a tentatively reconstructed proto-Sahidic; a protodialect that, Nagel, 1965, has shown, had some affinities with the language of Thebes and which could, as much as *A* or *L*, or at least along with them, have influenced the orthography of the local nonliterary texts.)

There remain *L* and especially *S*, the most neutral classical Coptic idioms, the localization of each being particularly difficult to determine. The area within which *L* manuscripts have been found extends apparently from the Fayyūm to the region near Thebes (perhaps even farther south, as far as Aswan; Worrell, 1934, p. 74). The area of the attested existence of *S* is even larger, since it is certain that it covers all the Egyptian Nile Valley above the Delta. One must therefore have recourse to other methods, especially the comparative analysis of isophones (phonemic isoglosses), in the attempt to locate *L* and *S* in relation to the dialects already more or less exactly localized: *B* in the Delta (probably at first the western Delta); *F* in the Fayyūm (and *V*, or "Fayyumic without lambdacism," a semineutralized variety of *F* or a MESODIALECT between dominant *F*, and *W* and *M*, probably in the east or southeast [?] of the Fayyūm and somewhere in the Nile Valley immediately to the east or southeast [?] of the Fayyūm); *M* in the neighborhood of Oxyrhynchus in Middle Egypt; *A* in the center (and south) of Upper Egypt.

To turn to the phonemic isoglosses (or isophones) is to admit as a general principle (Vergote, 1973, Vol. 1a, p. 56) that "the numbers of isophones are

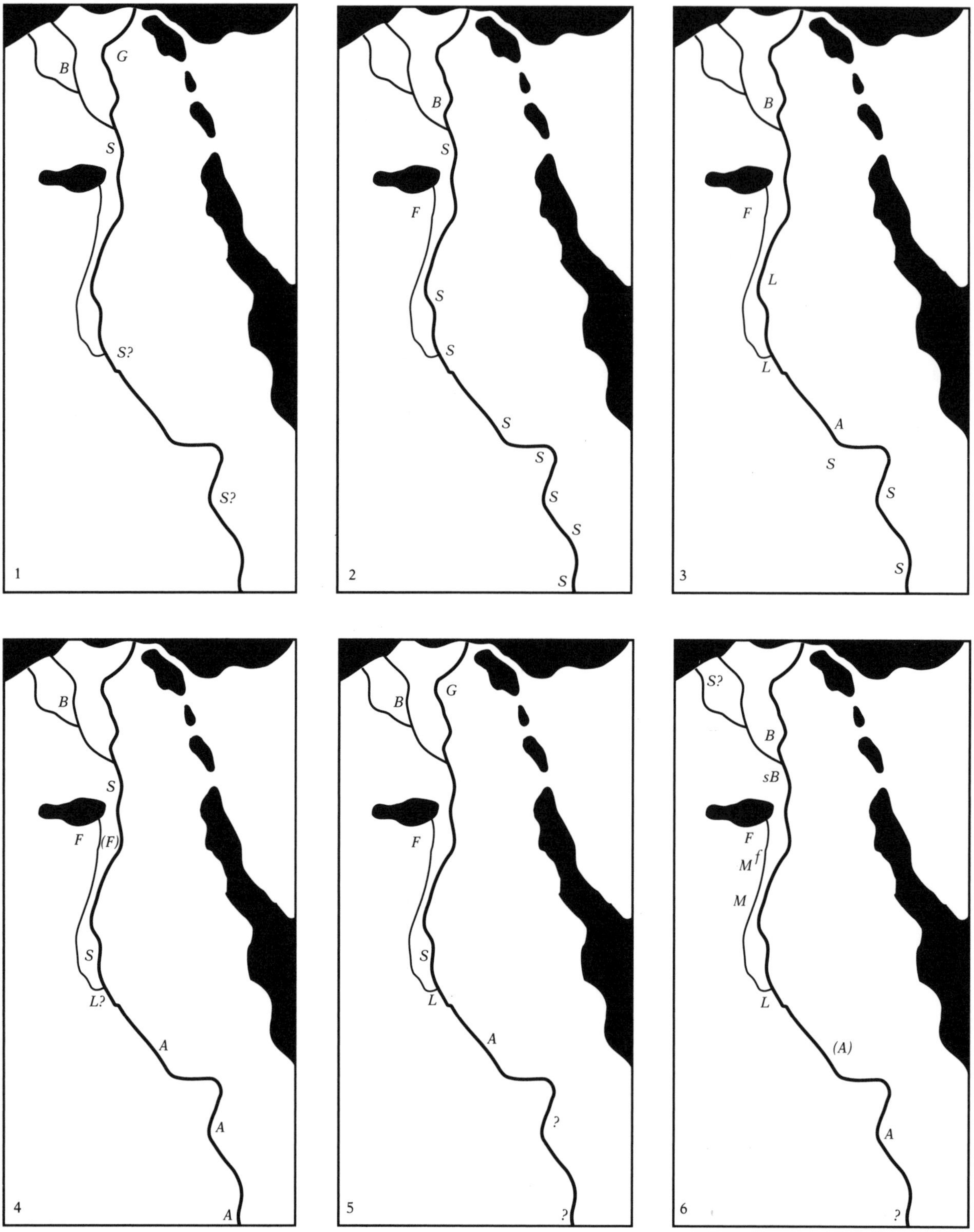

PROPOSED DIALECTAL GEOGRAPHIES OF COPTIC EGYPT: **1.** Athanasius of Qūṣ, fourteenth century. **2.** Stern, 1880. **3.** Chaine, 1934. **4.** Worrell, 1934. **5.** Steindorff, 1951. **6.** Kahle, 1954. **7.** Nagel, 1965 and 1972. **8.** Vergote, 1973a. **9.** Layton, 1976. **10.** Krause, 1979. **11.** Kasser, 1982. **12.** Funk, 1988, and Kasser, 1989. (In parentheses: sigla for rather problematically located dialects etc.) [In brackets: supplementary sigla for dialects etc. accepted by Kasser, 1989,

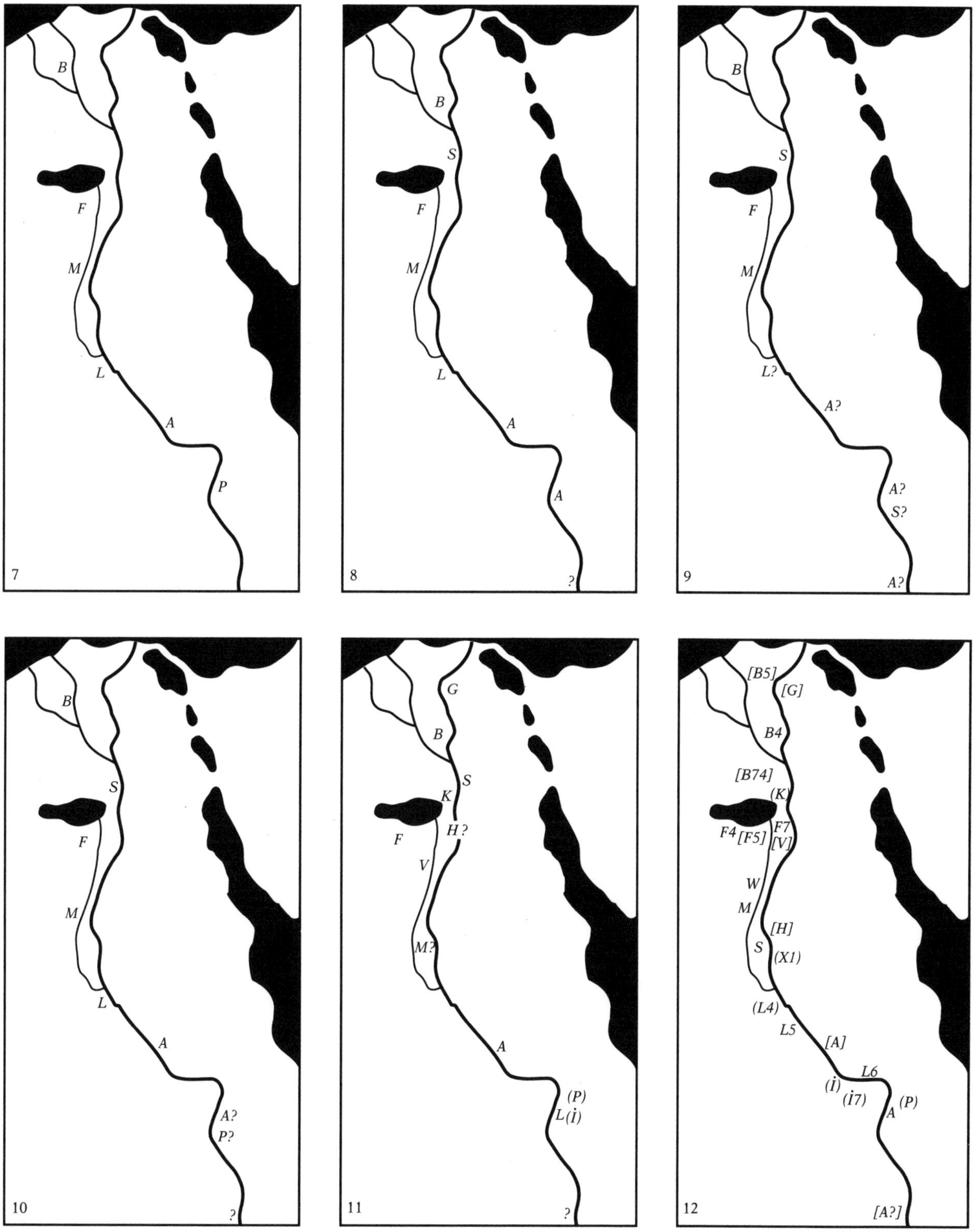

not by Funk, 1988.] Funk, not Kasser, takes account of the "early varieties of Coptic" only (dialects, etc., attested by manuscripts no later than the sixth century), putting provisionally aside the "later" but sometimes very abundantly attested varieties of Coptic (*B5* or "classical" Bohairic, *F5* or "classical" Fayyumic, etc.).

proportional to the distances between the dialectal areas" (the greater the distances between two dialects, the smaller the number of isophones shared by them). One must note the use of the same principles and similar methods in Hintze (1984) and Kasser (1981, pp. 124–31), and a more developed process (with a copious set of phonemic isoglosses completed with various morphophonological and morphosyntactic isoglosses) in Funk (1988).

However, one must also "take account of the relative importance of the phenomena" (Vergote, 1973, Vol. 1a, p. 56), particularly the isophone (which is the most convenient and generally used criterion; see DIALECT, IMMIGRANT); there (Kasser, 1987) some priority might be reasonably granted to the consonantal (and among the consonantal to the general) variables, excluding the cases in which the oppositions are not synchronic but diachronic (e.g., ⳓ /ç/ *P* versus ϣ /š/ *S, L, M* etc., according to the consonantal late Egyptian evolution *ḫ* > /ç/ > š/; ⳉ /x/ *P* versus ϩ /h/ *S, L, M* etc., according to *ẖ* > or = /x/ > /h/; see Vergote, 1945, pp. 122–23).

An additional restriction may be added here: the preceding rules only have their full value if one compares idioms that are really all of the same nature—that is, local dialects (and not, like *S* and *B*, "vehicular," supraregional common languages; see DIALECTS, GROUPING AND MAJOR GROUPS OF), these local dialects being generally not neutralized (or only slightly neutralized)—for it is evident that an idiom whose expansion always remained strictly limited to its local area will normally have undergone only the influence of similar and neighboring local dialects, those who speak it belonging chiefly to a social level where professional occupation (agriculture, minor trades, etc.) and often modest way of life do little to encourage travel. This is a social aspect of the Coptic languages and dialects, which no doubt existed, frequently and secondarily, alongside their geographical aspect. An idiom of strong expansion, a vehicular language, will be much more neutralized by its repeated contacts, accompanied by reciprocal influences, not only with neighboring local dialects but also with more distant regional dialects and probably with one or another common language from even farther afield (cf. Chaîne, 1934, pp. 17–18), because those who speak a vehicular language, normally rather neutralized in its zone of expansion (hence outside its region of origin), belong chiefly to a social level where professional occupation (major trades, industry, commerce, higher administration, etc.) and a relatively comfortable way of life encouraged travel.

Consider now a semitheoretical example. Suppose the geographical chain of idioms 1, 2, 3, 4, 5, and 6, moving from south to north in this order the length of the Nile Valley. Of these, 2 and especially 1, 4, and 5 are typically regional dialects, not neutralized (or only slightly neutralized); and 3 and 6 are clearly supraregional idioms and are neutral (or at least more neutralized than the local dialects with which they are in touch, as immigrant dialects or vehicular languages). Of course, 3 will have isophones, among other things, in common not only with its neighbors 2 and 4, but also with the farther idiom 6, because, in spite of the remoteness of their geographical origin, both "common languages" are in touch on a higher (supralocal, social, etc.) level. Thus, it would be incautious to draw geographical conclusions too mechanically, by only counting the various isophones, many of which seem to locate 3 near 6. Both vehicular languages, as a result of their wide expansion, have been brought into contact, and this contact has made them influence one another, even if they may have been in their origin very far apart; in fact, their isophones (at least) bring them notably closer. One might easily take for geographical proximity what is probably no more than a sign of their similar nature as common languages and as neutral (or semineutral) idioms.

Consequently, it will be prudent to submit to critical reexamination the conclusion (Worrell, 1934; Kahle, 1954; Vergote, 1973, Vol. 1a, p. 59) that sought to locate the dialects of the Nile Valley and the Delta by their isophones in the following order, moving downstream and leaving *F* aside in its corner (and remembering that Worrell did not know *M*): *A, L, (M), S, B*. This order has today become almost conventional, but one may prefer an order more in conformity with the theoretical schema set out above, placing *A* in 1, *L* in 2, but *S* (not *M*) in 3, *M* (not *V*) in 4, *V* (not *S*) in 5, and finally (as in every scheme of dialectal geography) *B* in 6.

But perhaps such a division of Coptic Egypt is still too detailed and too precise according to the present state of knowledge? One way of doing justice to the reservations that this skepticism implies would be, for example, to classify the dialects not in groups (six in number) but in "major groups" (the number limited to three; see DIALECTS, GROUPING AND MAJOR GROUPS OF) and, in dialectal geography, to divide Egypt into three main regions only (cf. Kasser, 1982); this would be a way of returning, by and large, to the tripartite division most commonly accepted as regards Egypt in general.

According to this schema, major region I would be the land of the "major (dialectal) group I" and would correspond to Upper Egypt (including Asyūṭ and maybe upper Middle Egypt). It would probably take in several local dialects, little neutralized, of which only *A* is known today, used in any case in the region of Akhmīm and probably in other areas further south (e.g., the region of Thebes). In addition, major region I would include *L* (= *L4* + *L5* + *L6*) as a fairly neutralized cluster of (sub-)dialects, used regionally at least in the area of Asyūṭ (= Lycopolis) and widespread as a second vehicular language by the side of *S*, over the same area, of course, and further south over the various areas of *A*, and possibly, though more discreetly and weakly, even further north (in parts of upper and a part of middle Middle Egypt?), temporarily and everywhere in rivalry with *S*. Gradually confronted by its most serious rival, *S*, invading from the north (and possibly also from Thebes, where *S* could have infiltrated very early, by way of the river), *L* finally perished, a little before *A*, both being stifled by *S*.

Major region II would be the land of the "major (dialectal) group II" and would correspond, if not to upper Middle Egypt, at least to middle and lower Middle Egypt and the Fayyūm. This region would include several local dialects, little neutralized, of which the only ones known are *F* (located in the Fayyūm and relatively little neutralized) and *M* (to be placed in the neighborhood of Oxyrhynchus or perhaps a little further north), in some respects a little better neutralized than *F*. Hemmed in between major regions I and III, and perhaps culturally less active, major region II would find itself invaded very early and traversed throughout, above all from the south, by the vehicular language *S* (and perhaps partially by *L*, the most neutralized dialect of the neighboring major region), which would leave but little chance of development for its own most, if little, neutralized Fayyumic subdialect *V*, which would possibly have tried to gain acceptance as the vehicular language over the greater part of this territory. Finally, *V* would have perished, with *W* and *M* and probably before *F* (which was better fitted to resist in its remote corner of the Fayyūm), all stifled by *S*.

Major region III would correspond to the Delta (or Lower Egypt). This region would probably include several local dialects, neutralized to different degrees, in which *B* (as a supralocal and supraregional vehicular language rather than a regional dialect; see LANGUAGE(S), COPTIC) is sufficiently known (from the first, well established in the western Delta, and then gradually penetrating throughout the Delta). Major region III would be essentially that of "major group III," connecting dialects (those of the Delta) and, above all, two large vehicular languages, of which one (*B*) is that of the Delta also, and the other one (*S*) is used only outside of Lower Egypt, being superposed on all the regional dialects and local subdialects of the Egyptian Nile Valley above the Delta (i.e., chiefly *A, L, M, W, V*) in the whole of major regions I and II.

As is shown by the majority of the typical (nonvocalic!) *S* phonological features and by the most numerous morphosyntactical variables (see Funk, 1988), it is at least most likely that *S* derives from some local dialect of upper Middle Egypt (between a kind of pre-*L* and a kind of pre-*M*) in pre-Coptic times. This pre-*S*, whose tonic vowels were generally like those of pre-*L* and pre-*M*, became, probably very early on, the southern koine of Egypt, that of the whole Egyptian Nile Valley between the Delta and Aswan. As a vehicular language, it came in contact (near Memphis) with the second vehicular language, *B*, the northern koine—hence, a strong vocalic

	[SOUTH]		UPPER EGYPT				/			MIDDLE EGYPT				/ LOWER EGYPT			[NORTH]
								Schema I (fourth century)									
Lang.	*S*	*S*	*S*	*S*	*S*	*S*	/	*S*	*S*	*S*	*S*	*S*	*S*	*S/B5*	*B5*	*B5*	*B5*
s-Lang.	*L?*	*L*	*L*	*L*	*L*	*L*		*S*	*L?*	*L?*	*L?/V*	*V*	*V?/?*			*B5*	
dial.	?	*A*	*A*	*L6*	*L5*	*L4*		*S*	?	*M*	*W*	*V*	*K*	*B74*	*B4*	*B5*	?
								Schema II (eighth century)									
Lang.	*S*	*S*	*S*	*S*	*S*	*S*	/	*S*	*S*	*S*	*S*	*S*	*S*	*S/B5*	*B5*	*B5*	*B5*
dial.	—	?	—	—	—	—		*S*	*H*	—	—	?	—	—	?	*B5*	*G*

Lang., common language; s-Lang., semicommon language; dial., local dialect or subdialect.

(stressed vowels) similarity between *S* and *B* (probably the influence of some pre-*B* on some pre-*S* about five centuries B.C.; cf. Chaîne, 1934, pp. 13–18, and, more clearly, Satzinger, 1985). One might also suppose that *S* penetrated very soon, by way of the river traffic, to Thebes, where it would have established a center of expansion more and more active into the very heart of major region I (developing at the same time a variety of proto-*S* moving into the Theban region and bearing the phonological marks of this implantation, according to a former hypothesis; cf. Nagel, 1965, and Kasser, 1982).

The sequel seems better known and may be deduced from what is recorded of *S* in the classical Coptic period: pre-*S*, if not *S* itself, would have ended by occuping the whole Nile Valley (but not the Delta) to the detriment of its local dialects, invading in particular major region I from the north (and possibly from Thebes; cf. above), eliminating *L* and then *A*, and finally reducing the last pockets of resistance in major region II by the elimination of *V*, *W*, and *M*.

BIBLIOGRAPHY

Chaîne, M. *Eléments de grammaire dialectale copte.* Paris, 1933.

______. *Les Dialectes coptes assioutiques A2.* Paris, 1934.

Funk, W.-P. "Dialects Wanting Homes: A Numerical Approach to the Early Varieties of Coptic." In *Historical Dialectology, Regional and Social,* ed. J. Fisiak, pp. 149–92. Berlin, New York, and Amsterdam, 1988.

Hintze, F. "Eine Klassifizierung der koptischen Dialekte." In *Studien zu Sprache und Religion Ägyptens, zu Ehren von Wolfhart Westendorf überreicht von seinen Freunden und Schülern,* Vol. 1, pp. 411–32. Göttingen, 1984.

Kahle, P. E. *Bala'izah: Coptic Texts from Deir el-Bala'izah in Upper Egypt.* Oxford and London, 1954.

Kasser, R. "Dialectes, sous-dialectes et 'dialecticules' dans l'Égypte copte." *Zeitschrift für ägyptische Sprache und Altertumskunde* 92 (1966):106–115.

______. "Dialectologie." In *Textes et languages de l'Egypte pharaonique, hommage à Jean-François Champollion à l'occasion du cent-cinquantième anniversaire du déchiffrement des hiéroglyphes (1822–1972),* Vol. 1, pp. 107–115. Cairo, [1972].

______. "Les Dialectes coptes." *Bulletin de l'Institut français d'archéologie orientale* 73 (1973):71–101.

______. "L'Idiome de Bachmour." *Bulletin de l'Institut français d'archéologie orientale* 75 (1975):401–427.

______. "Prolégomènes à un essai de classification systématique des dialectes et subdialectes coptes selon les critères de la phonétique, I, Principes et terminologie." *Muséon* 93 (1980a):53–112. ". . . , II, Alphabets et systèmes phonétiques." *Muséon* 93 (1980b):237–97. ". . . , III, Systèmes orthographiques et catégories dialectales." *Muséon* 94 (1981):91–152.

______. "Le Grand-Groupe dialectal copte de Haute-Egypte." *Bulletin de la Société d'égyptologie, Genève* 7 (1982):47–72.

______. "OTUs et OTUs, taxonomie, discernement et distinction des catégories en dialectologie et géographie dialectale coptes." *Bulletin de l'Institut français d'archéologie orientale* 87 (1987):225–53.

______. "Le Grand-Groupe dialectal copte de Basse-Egypte et son extension véhiculaire panégyptienne." *Bulletin de la Société d'égyptologie, Genève,* 13 (1989):73–82.

Kasser, R., and H. Satzinger. "L'Idiome du P. Mich. 5421 (trouvé à Karanis, nord-est du Fayoum)." *Wiener Zeitschrift für die Kunde des Morgenlandes* 74 (1982):15–32.

Krause, M. "Koptische Sprache." *Lexikon der Ägyptologie* 3 (1979):731–37.

Layton, B. "Coptic Language." In *Interpreter's Dictionary of the Bible,* Suppl. Vol., pp. 174–79. Nashville, Tenn., 1976.

Lefort, L. T. "Littérature bohaïrique." *Muséon* 44 (1931):115–33.

Mallon, A. *Grammaire copte, avec bibliographie, chrestomathie et vocabulaire.* 2nd ed. Beirut, 1907.

______. *Grammaire copte, bibliographie, chrestomathie et vocabulaire,* 4th ed., rev. M. Malinine. Beirut, 1956.

Nagel, P. "Der frühkoptische Dialekt von Theben." In *Koptologische Studien in der DDR,* pp. 30–49. *Wissenschaftliche Zeitschrift der Martin-Luther-Universität Halle-Wittenberg,* Sonderheft. Halle-Wittenberg, 1965.

______. "Die Bedeutung der Nag Hammadi-Texte für die koptische Dialektgeschichte." In *Von Nag Hammadi bis Zypern,* pp. 16–27. Berliner Byzantinische Arbeiten 43. Berlin, 1972.

Osing, J. *Der spätägyptische Papyrus B. M. 10808.* Wiesbaden, 1976.

______. "The Dialect of Oxyrhynchus." *Enchoria* 8 (1978):29*(75)–36*(82).

Satzinger, H. "On the Origin of the Sahidic Dialect." In *Acts of the Second International Congress of Coptic Studies, Rome, 22–26 September 1980,* ed. T. Orlandi and F. Wisse, pp. 307–312. Rome, 1985.

Simon, J. "L'Aire et la durée des dialectes coptes." In *Acts of the Fourth International Congress of Linguists,* pp. 182–86. Copenhagen, 1936.

Steindorff, G. *Koptische Grammatik, mit Chresto-*

mathie, Wörterverzeichnis und Literatur. Berlin, 1930.
______. *Lehrbuch der koptischen Grammatik.* Chicago, 1951.
Stern, L. *Koptische Grammatik.* Leipzig, 1880.
Till, W. C. *Koptische Grammatik (saïdischer Dialekt), mit Bibliographie, Lesestücken und Wörterverzeichnissen.* Leipzig, 1955.
______. *Koptische Dialektgrammatik, mit Lesestücken und Wörterbuch.* 2nd ed. Munich, 1961.
Vergote, J. *Phonétique historique de l'égyptien, les consonnes.* Louvain, 1945.
______. *Grammaire copte,* Vol. 1a, *Introduction, phonétique et phonologie, morphologie synthématique (structure des sémantèmes), partie synchronique,* Vol. 1b, . . . , *partie diachronique.* Louvain, 1973a.
______. "Le Dialecte copte P (P. Bodmer VI: Proverbes), essai d'identification." *Revue d'égyptologie* 25 (1973b):50–57.
Westendorf, W. *Koptisches Handwörterbuch, bearbeitet auf Grund des Koptischen Handwörterbuchs von Wilhelm Spiegelberg.* Heidelberg, 1977.
Worrell, W. H. *Coptic Sounds.* Ann Arbor, Mich., 1934.

RODOLPHE KASSER

GREEK TRANSCRIPTIONS. The rendering of Egyptian proper names into Greek characters was a first step toward the writing of Egyptian in an alphabetical script, that is, toward the creation of the Coptic script (see PRE-COPTIC). These proper names are mainly thousands of Egyptian anthroponyms, toponyms, and temple names, as well as names of gods, divine epithets, and sacerdotal titles, written in the Greek alphabet in order to adapt them to, and insert them into, a Greek context.

Apart from Homer (ninth century B.C.), where one finds, for instance, the first mention of the term Αἴγυπτος, the oldest real examples are from the Saite period (Twenty-sixth Dynasty), when Greek mercenaries and merchants were present in Egypt. To this early period belongs the famous Greek graffito of Abu Simbel (on Egypt's southern border), which dates back to 589 B.C. and which contains, among other things, the name of a well-known Egyptian general, rendered as Ποτασιμτο (see Dittenberger, 1915, no. 1). As early as Herodotus, who must have visited Egypt around 430, the language problem the Greeks had to cope with in Egypt appears clearly in the evidence. Writing for Greeks, Herodotus gave several Egyptian gods the names of Greek counterparts (e.g., "Hephaestos" for "Ptah," and "Aphrodite" for "Hathor"), but he had to transcribe the "barbarian" personal names into Greek characters. Apart from a number of words adopted in the Greek vocabulary (e.g., ἶβις, ἔβενος, ὄασις; see Pierce, 1971), there are only a few, quite exceptional cases of indigenous generic names that are transliterated into Greek, such as πιρωμις (Herodotus 2.143), corresponding to the Bohairic **ⲡⲓⲣⲱⲙⲓ**, the man, the human being.

Following the conquest of Egypt by Alexander the Great (332 B.C.), a large number of Greeks settled in the Nile Valley, and with the establishment of Ptolemaic rule, Greek became, along with Egyptian, a commonly spoken tongue. The increasing contact between natives and Greek-speaking people in everyday life and on a more intellectual level led to rather widespread bilingualism on the upper levels of native Egyptian society (see, e.g., Peremans, 1982). A number of Greek words were even adopted by demotic (see Clarysse, 1984); they can be considered distant forerunners of the Copto-Greek vocabulary (see VOCABULARY, COPTO-GREEK). Throughout the Roman occupation (from 30 B.C. onward) and until the ARAB CONQUEST OF EGYPT (640 A.D.), Greek remained the language of the administration.

The innumerable Greek documentary texts from the end of the fourth century B.C. and later (contracts, letters, tax lists, inventories, etc., written mostly on papyrus, ostraca, or wooden tags) contain numerous Egyptian proper names written in Greek letters, usually provided with a Greek ending to integrate them better into the Greek context. It is clear that the Greek phonological system was quite different from the Egyptian and that the Greek alphabet was not an ideal means to render Egyptian. Thus, the schwa had to be rendered by ϵ or ο (see Lacau, 1970, pp. 131–36) and consonants such as $\underline{d}$ or $\underline{t}$, unknown in Greek, were written in various ways (see Quaegebeur, 1973, p. 99). Although the graphic transposition can vary widely, detailed study clearly reveals some systemization in the transliterations. Many of the scribes of Greek documents were Egyptians, so one need not be surprised that attempts were made to write sequences of words, short sentences, or formulas in the Greek alphabet. Since the intention here is less restricted than, and different from, the purpose of the Greek transcriptions of Egyptian proper names, and since it concerns here only a temporary stage in an evolution, these cases merit separate treatment (see PRE-OLD COPTIC).

From the first century A.D. onward, there appeared Egyptian texts, most of a magical or related nature, in which the Greek alphabet was enlarged with a varying number of supplementary signs derived from demotic (see OLD COPTIC). One can also notice in Greek transcriptions of Egyptian proper names, especially from the later Roman period, that occasionally supplementary signs were used to render phonemes that do not occur in Greek, such as *š* and *ḥ*. Since they were incorporated in Greek texts (often without Grecization), these cases are also regarded as Greek transcriptions. Greek texts containing transcriptions of Egyptian proper names continued to appear along with Coptic until about the eighth century (i.e., even after the Arab conquest).

A special case is the collection of texts published by Crum (1939b). These documents of the eighth century or later in the Coptic language are written in a cursive hand making exclusive use of the Greek alphabet. They are much too late to be considered Pre-Old Coptic and seem to represent a particular idiom related to BOHAIRIC (see DIALECT G).

The importance of the Greek transcriptions for the study of Coptic is apparent from, among others, Crum (1939a), Černý (1976), and Vycichl (1983). The toponyms in Greek transcription mentioned by Crum have also been registered in a separate index (see Roquet, 1973), but for the numerous anthroponyms incorporated in his dictionary, there is no index. In this field, indeed, much work remains to be done (see, e.g., Quaegebeur, 1981). A comparison of Coptic with the data of the Greek transcriptions can be important for various research aspects. Thus, for instance, Coptic orthography sometimes reveals the influence of Greek transcriptions, such as ⲯ for *pš* (ⲡϣ). As for the study of phonetics, the occasional rendering of *f* by (*o*)*υ* can be mentioned: for example, -*ευτημις* alongside -*νεφθιμις*, and ϩⲓⲡⲡⲉϥ for *ἱππεύς* (see Quaegebeur, 1974, p. 417, and 1978, p. 255). With Coptic and, for much earlier periods, cuneiform transcriptions, Greco-Egyptian onomastics also supply interesting information on the vocalization of Egyptian, which in its own written form noted only the consonants; mention can be made of research on word accent and word formation (see Fecht, 1960; Vergote, 1973; Osing, 1976). Finally, the study of spoken dialects and their dispersion must be undertaken for the Pre-Coptic period in the light of present knowledge of Coptic dialects. A methodical investigation in this field (of which the first results, Quaegebeur, 1975, were challenged by Brunsch, 1978, on—in the view of this author—inadequate and insufficient grounds) is being continued.

BIBLIOGRAPHY

Brunsch, W. "Untersuchungen zu den griechischen Wiedergaben ägyptischer Personennamen." *Enchoria* 8 (1978):1–142.

Černý, J. *Coptic Etymological Dictionary*. Cambridge, 1976.

Clarysse, W. "Greek Loan-Words in Demotic." In S. P. Vleeming, ed., *Aspects of Demotic Lexicography. Acts of the Second International Conference for Demotic Studies, Leiden, 19–21 September 1984*. Studia Demotica 1, pp. 9–33. Louvain, 1987.

Crum, W. E. *A Coptic Dictionary*. Oxford, 1939a.

______. "Coptic Documents in Greek Script." *Proceedings of the British Academy* 25 (1939b):249–71.

Dittenberger, G. *Sylloge Inscriptionum Graecarum*, Vol. 1. Leipzig, 1915.

Fecht, G. *Wortakzent und Silbenstruktur*. Ägyptologische Forschungen 21. Glückstadt, Hamburg, and New York, 1960.

Lacau, P. *Etudes d'égyptologie*, Vol. 1, *Phonétique égyptienne ancienne*. Bibliothèque d'étude 41. Cairo, 1970.

Osing, J. *Die Nominalbildung des Ägyptischen*. Mainz, 1976.

Peremans, W. "Sur le bilinguisme dans l'Egypte des Lagides." In *Studia P. Naster Oblata*, Vol. 2, *Orientalia Antiqua*, ed. J. Quaegebeur, pp. 143–54. Louvain, 1982.

Pierce, R. H. "Egyptian Loan-Words in Ancient Greek." *Symbolae Osloenses* 46 (1971):96–107.

Quaegebeur, J. "Considérations sur le nom propre égyptien Teëphthaphônukhos." *Orientalia Lovaniensia Periodica* 4 (1973):85–100.

______. "The Study of Egyptian Proper Names in Greek Transcription: Problems and Perspectives." *Onoma* 18 (1974):403–420.

______. *Le Dieu égyptien Shaï dans la religion et l'onomastique*. Orientalia Lovaniensia Analecta 2. Louvain, 1975.

______. "Sénénouphis, nom de femme et nom d'homme." *Chronique d'Egypte* 56 (1981):350–59.

______. "De la préhistoire de l'écriture copte." *Orientalia Lovaniensia Periodica* 13 (1982):125–36.

Roquet, G. *Toponymes et lieux-dits égyptiens enregistrés dans le Dictionnaire copte de W. E. Crum*. Bibliothèque d'études coptes 10. Cairo, 1973.

Vergote, J. *Grammaire copte*, Vol. 1a, *Introduction, phonétique et phonologie, morphologie synthématique (structure des sémantèmes), partie synchronique*, Vol. 1b, . . . , *partie diachronique*. Louvain, 1973.

Vycichl, W. *Dictionnaire étymologique de la langue copte*. Louvain, 1983.

JAN QUAEGEBEUR

IDIOLECT. An "idiolect" is, by definition, a linguistic entity that may be contrasted with the "dialect." Dubois et al. (1973, p. 144) wrote, "The 'dialect' is a form of a language which has its own lexical, syntactic and phonetic system, and which is used in a more restricted environment than the language itself." Thus, every dialect appears in the form of a "system." On the other hand, they added (p. 249, slightly modified on the suggestion of Vergote; cf. Kasser, 1980, p. 78), "By 'idiolect' we denote the totality of the data produced by a single person, established by reference to linguistic constants which subtend them, and which are envisaged as specific idioms or systems; the idiolect is then the totality of the uses of a language peculiar to a given individual at a fixed time." Thus, despite the preferential uses that can be observed in it, always fluctuating and essentially transitory, the idiolect does not present itself to the observer in the form of a stable system; it is, rather, the accidental and nonsystematic combination, by a single individual at a fixed time, of elements deriving from authentic systems (dialects). One may then say that these systems "subtend" the idiolect, but they never succeed in really regularizing its expression to the point of making a system of it.

To grasp firmly the phenomena "idiolect" and "dialect" in their apparent complexity, one must endeavor to perceive the chief psychological motivations of their users. It is known that a language is essentially an instrument of social relations, a means of communication between people; that is why the users of a language try in principle to speak or write an idiom comprehensible to their interlocutors, as far as possible the same idiom, the very language of the group to which the latter belong, and this all the more when the interlocutor in view is not simply the intended recipient of a letter (i.e., an individual whose idiolect is possibly to some extent known) but is, on the contrary, indeterminate or collective, as is the totality of the readers of a book, for which its author wishes a very wide diffusion. Of course, each individual, tempted to obey the "principle of least effort," will have a natural tendency to express himself in an idiolectal manner, but he will combat that tendency as soon as he wishes to facilitate the effective diffusion of his thought, conscious of the fact that in intellectual communication between people the dialect is a road where the idiolect is an obstacle. One could not then imagine that a reasonable author would voluntarily choose to express himself in an idiolect, which is peculiar to himself alone, rather than in the dialect of his interlocutors (a dialect that may on occasion be the idiom of a quite small group, like the semisecret language that allows the members of a minority to communicate among themselves, sheltered from the indiscretions and the threats of the surrounding world, but nonetheless a dialect because it is the language of a group in the course of a period of its history and not simply the idiolect of a strictly unique individual at a strictly unique moment of his life).

Thus, even if each or nearly every person at certain moments of his daily life, following unconsciously his natural tendency, in speaking or even in writing, departs more or less seriously from the dialect to fall into the idiolect, this deviation is rarely conscious and in all cases always involuntary.

Several causes may provoke the formation of idiolects (Chaîne, 1933, p. xxiii; Till, 1955, pp. 36–37; Kasser, 1964, pp. xi–xiv). Probably among those most current in Coptic Egypt (and even in the modern world) was the literary productions of a man of letters speaking from birth a certain dialect and then carrying on his activity in a region where another dialect was the natural speech. In a more general way, one may recall the phenomena of linguistic hybridization that irresistibly develop in any territory that has its own autochthonous dialect, on which is superimposed (in certain social classes, generally influential) an immigrant dialect (see DIALECT, IMMIGRANT), dominating its area, and becoming in a way there and in the adjacent regions their vehicular language.

If, then, the dialect is a linguistic phenomenon whose immediate origin is collective and relatively simple—a convention that is fixed by a group and to which the individual adheres insofar as he is capable of overcoming his individual tendencies by means of sufficient intelligence and an effort of his will—the idiolect is, in contrast, a phenomenon whose immediate origin is strictly individual and clearly complex; that is, it arises from the relative and involuntary incapacity of an individual to overcome his individual tendencies in order to adhere to a given dialectal convention, whether from serious intellectual inadequacy, which prevents him from mastering even his mother dialect, at least in its conventional written expression and apart from any influence of other dialects, or from a moderate inadequacy, in the context of an insufficient knowledge of various dialects (his mother dialect, that of his place of work, that of the text to be copied, etc.), which prevents him mastering them so that he does not confuse them in oral or written expression.

In either case, what subtends the idiolect is the elements that are opposed one to another, whose presence creates a state of tension in the text (whether oral or in writing). In fact, if it has been thought possible to differentiate two "dialects" from one another in Coptic, a dead language, it is because in them can be distinguished two (orthographic, morphosyntactic) systems, which because of their reciprocal oppositions cannot as a whole be reduced one to another, and the copyist who is subjected (unconsciously) to the contradictory influence of these two dialects finds himself in a state of tension, of linguistic instability (and so also if he attempts to conform to a single standardized dialect, but does not know very well the standardized orthography of this dialect). One might then say that "the idiolect is the result of a tension provisionally resolved." It is a point of balance achieved today (different from the balance achieved yesterday or the one that will be achieved tomorrow) between (1) what the individual has of necessity had to learn, or may have learned, of the dialect of the society in which he lives (a dialect related to his mother dialect and in which he intends and thinks to express himself) and (2) what he has for the moment ceased to learn, because his vernacular form of expression (his mother dialect) is sufficient for him to make himself understood by the society, to some extent alien, in which he lives.

Most frequently, this state of tension remains unknown to the conscious subject, so that it should rarely be understood as a state of crisis, painful and dramatic. Indeed, with a Shenute, a very strong personality, one may imagine a calm assurance and a kind of pride in speaking and writing Sahidic with some touches of Akhmimic, which make this language, already vigorous on his lips, even more lively. Each case of an idiolect is the result of a personal situation, and there are as many such situations as there are individuals. If, then, the language of Shenute is an idiolect (weakly idiolectal), so is that (often very idiolectal) of many nonliterary documents of the Theban region and of the copies of literary works that have survived; for example, the majority of the Bodmer papyri are not very idiolectal, but the Nag Hammadi manuscripts and other literary copies from the fourth and fifth centuries are generally much more so. At any rate, the orthographic anomalies in these copies (in relation to one or another of the dialects that have been, or are on the way to being, standardized) are never truly systematic, so that it would be a mistake to classify the linguistic expression of these texts among the "dialects" or subdialects, all of which require the presence of a minimum of systematization.

Thus, an idiolect by its nature has several components, of which one is the mother dialect of the individual. Another may be either his profound ignorance of any particular dialectal orthographic convention (including that of his mother dialect) or his knowledge of other dialects combined with his inability to master this knowledge to the point of sufficiently distinguishing them in their conventional written expression.

Theoretically, the oral and written expression of an individual can only be idiolectal, in varying degree. But in texts written by individuals with adequate intellectual capacity and strength of will, the idiolectal proportion (in relation to the dialect chosen as the means of expression) is so weak that it may be neglected; there the idiolect in no way obscures the dialect, which can be sufficiently known through these texts (if they are long enough and varied enough). Here one may speak of a "transparent" idiolect.

In other texts, the idiolectal expression is more "opaque." It then demands from the investigator an effort of analysis to decode what is hidden by the phenomena of hypocorrection and hypercorrection, in particular, and to succeed in identifying the components of the idiolect, among which he will be specially interested in the dialects that subtend the idiolect.

It will be convenient to designate idiolectal lexemes by indicating, first, their principal component with an italic capital and then their secondary component(s) with an italic lower-case superscript; for example, S^a signifies Sahidic influenced phonetically (and to some extent, but irregularly, phonologically) by Akhmimic.

BIBLIOGRAPHY

Chaîne, M. *Eléments de grammaire dialectale copte.* Paris, 1933.

Dubois, J.; M. Giacomo; L. Guespin; C. Marcellesi; J.-B. Marcellesi; and J.-P. Mével. *Dictionnaire de linguistique.* Paris, 1973.

Kasser, R. *Compléments au dictionnaire copte de Crum.* Cairo, 1964.

______. "Prolégomènes à un essai de classification systématique des dialectes et subdialectes coptes selon les critères de la phonétique, I, Principes et terminologie." *Muséon* 93 (1980):53–112.

Till, W. C. *Koptische Grammatik (saïdischer Dialekt), mit Bibliographie, Lesestücken und Wörterverzeichnissen.* Leipzig, 1955.

RODOLPHE KASSER

LANGUAGE(S), COPTIC. Coptic is the last stage of the Egyptian language in the course of its very long existence and slow evolution (we can observe it over a period of more than four thousand years, a quite exceptional phenomenon in linguistics). Since Coptic is today a dead language, and has been for several centuries, the death of Coptic has therefore meant the death of ancient Egyptian. Will the Copts of today have enough faith, devotion, perseverance, and perspicacity to succeed in reviving the glorious language of their ancestors, one of the most beautiful, most cleverly structured, and most musical in the world? Those inspired by the love of Egypt can only hope so.

Although people habitually speak of "the" Coptic language, it must be stated that in reality there are two Coptic languages (cf. Kasser, 1984a, pp. 261–62; Vycichl, 1987, pp. 67–68), each of which is accompanied by various regional dialects, themselves the successors in some fashion of the dialects of PRE-COPTIC.

The first is Sahidic (*S*), which is the common speech, or "vehicular language," supralocal and supraregional, of the valley of the Egyptian Nile above the Delta, after having probably (but in what distant past?) itself been a local dialect that may have issued from some region of upper Middle Egypt without direct contact with the second language, Bohairic (*B*), as a local dialect, but probably in touch with Bohairic in the region of Memphis as a common language reaching the boundary of the neighboring common language (see DIALECTS, GROUPING AND MAJOR GROUPS OF). The most ancient *S* manuscript is of the end of the third century A.D.; the latest are of the fourteenth century, a period at which Sahidic (as indeed already from the eleventh century) was no longer anything more than a language virtually dead, surviving only artificially in the ecclesiastical milieus of some communities in Upper Egypt which had not yet been won to the exclusive use of Bohairic.

The Bohairic language is the supraregional vehicular language of the Nile Delta, having been, it seems, the principal regional dialect of the western Delta. Like Sahidic, Bohairic ceased to be a truly living language from the eleventh century. Its survival in the course of the following centuries remains a phenomenon in large part artificial, a means of communication particularly esteemed among clerks of the church (a very closed institution, turned in upon itself and much preoccupied, and indeed with good reason, with its survival in the midst of a hostile environment), a language above all religious. In this regard the testimony of the writer al-Maqrīzī (fifteenth century) is not very significant: he affirmed that in his time the Christians of Upper Egypt still spoke Coptic (and even Greek!) among themselves; one may receive with the same circumspection what is reported by the Jesuit Vansleb (seventeenth century), who said he met in Egypt an old man who still knew how to express himself in Coptic. For a long time, in fact, and throughout the country, Arabic had become the only living language and the sole means of communication among all its inhabitants, Christian as well as Muslim.

It is stated that the oldest *B* manuscripts are of the fourth century A.D.; the latest are of the nineteenth (!) century, and one might even say of the twentieth if one admitted to this category the copies of old Coptic manuscripts made by Copts to study them or to aid them in one way or another to save their ancestral language from oblivion. Bohairic was the living language of the Delta exclusively before the eleventh century, a period after which Coptic as a whole became a dead language among the Egyptian people, even Christians, and survived only in purely ecclesiastical milieus and usages. Bohairic then spread rapidly throughout the valley, as far as the southern extremities of Upper Egypt, but as a liturgical language, artificially practiced by the clergy alone (and the officiants who accompanied them). Even so, Bohairic's very restricted role does allow the ear to hear the sounds of the Coptic language, expressed by Coptic mouths and throats, beneath the ceilings and the domes of the Coptic churches. Bohairic is a survival, then, of ancient Egyptian in a very particular form, regrettably restricted and deprived of its original life and creative capacity, but despite everything a survival. However, even this feeble remnant of the ancient treasures of Coptic intellectual life is threatened in modern Egypt. In fact, from one side certainly and for more than a century, certain Copts inspired by their faith have been working with an admirable perseverance and devotion to revive *B*, teaching it to the Coptic people (Vycichl, 1936; Vergote, 1973, Vol. 1a, pp. 1–2; Barsum, 1882; Labib, 1915; cf. the work of the modern teachers, among whom the admirable popular savant Emile Maher stands out). But, from another side, some partisans of a religious renewal in the ancient Coptic church are pressing the church to Arabize its whole liturgy, in which, alongside brief Greek passages, some fairly long sections in Bohairic have survived: the essential thing is, they say, that the people of the church, who know only Arabic, should understand "everything" that is said and chanted in the liturgy. One may understand and approve this reasoning on the religious level, but unfortunately its consequences deal a mortal blow to what, after ten centuries of exhaustion, had in some fashion survived of the public use of the Coptic language. Egyptologists and Coptologists cannot but deplore this complete effacement (projected or realized) of liturgical Coptic.

The word "Coptic" thus describes, especially today, the totality of Sahidic and Bohairic, as well as the local dialects that they cover (Kahle, 1954; Kasser, 1980–1981). There is no need to repeat here all that has been written elsewhere in this regard; see in general DIALECT, IMMIGRANT; DIALECTS; DIALECTS, MORPHOLOGY OF COPTIC; GEOGRAPHY, DIALECTAL; META-DIALECT; OLD COPTIC; PRE-COPTIC; PRE-OLD COPTIC; PROTODIALECT; and in particular AKHMIMIC; BOHAIRIC; DIALECT G (OR BASHMURIC OR MANSURIC); DIALECT H (OR HERMOPOLITAN OR ASHMUNINIC); DIALECT İ (OR PROTO-LYCOPOLITAN); DIALECT P (OR PROTO-THEBAN); FAYYUMIC; LYCOPOLITAN (OR SUBAKHMIMIC); MESOKEMIC (OR MIDDLE EGYPTIAN); and SAHIDIC.

The word "Copt" itself derives from the same word as "Egypt" and "Egyptian," a term the origin of which appears to be authentically Egyptian: *Ḥt k3 Ptḥ* (Vycichl, 1983, p. 5) or *Ḥwt k3 Ptḥ* (Krause, 1979, p. 731), "the house of the spirit of [the god] Ptah" (that is, Memphis, several kilometers south of modern Cairo). This *Ḥt k3 Ptḥ* became in Greek Αἴγυπτος, Egypt, whence Αἰγύπτιος, Egyptian. Ptah was the god of the town of Memphis, and the local theology considered him the creator of the world. Distorting to some extent Αἰγύπτιος (the name of the ancient inhabitants of the country, then of those among them who remained Christians), the Arabs (conquerors of Egypt from 642) made of it *(Ai)gypti(os)*; then *gypti* became *qubṭi* (Vergote, 1973, Vol. 1a, pp. 1–6; Stern, 1880, pp. 1–6, who cites the Coptic forms of this name **ΓΥΠΤΙΟΣ**, **ΚΥΠΤΑΙΟΣ**; cf. also Gardiner, 1957, pp. 5–6; Layton, 1976; Mallon, 1907, pp. 1–7; Steindorff, 1930, pp. 1–5, and 1951, pp. 1–6; Till, 1955, pp. 29–39). Krause (1979, p. 731) notes that the form *gibtith* is already found in various passages of the Talmud in the second century A.D.

The Copts of the classical period (before the Arab invasion) called themselves by another name in Sahidic: **ⲣⲙ̄ ⲛ̄ⲕⲏⲙⲉ** (transcribed in Greek ἐρμοχύμιος), which means "the inhabitants [or "men," **ⲣⲙ̄-**] of the Black Land [**ⲕⲏⲙⲉ**]," an allusion to the dark color of the sediment which forms the cultivable and habitable land along the Nile and in its Delta, in opposition to the yellowish or reddish colors of the deserts, sterile and uninhabitable areas where the Egyptian did not feel in any way at home.

How can one affirm that Coptic is authentically Egyptian, when it has so much a Greek air at first sight? In fact, anyone not forewarned who approaches a Coptic text for the first time notices at once that its alphabet is four-fifths Greek in *S*, indeed a little less (68 percent) in dialect *P* or proto-Theban but actually much more in other idioms (up to 100 percent in dialect *G*, or Bashmuric or Mansuric, and up to 83 percent in dialect *H*, or Hermopolitan or Ashmuninic; cf. ALPHABET IN COPTIC, GREEK and ALPHABETS, COPTIC). Furthermore, one encounters many Copto-Greek words in the Coptic texts (cf. VOCABULARY, COPTO-GREEK). Nevertheless, these appearances ought not to deceive: Coptic in all its essential structures (Polotsky, 1950) and at a profound level (syntax, etc.) is an authentic form of the Egyptian language.

Building above all on Gardiner (1957, p. 5), one may distinguish five successive stages in the long evolution of this language over several thousand years: (1) Ancient Egyptian (from the First to the Eighth Dynasty, about 3180–2240 B.C., or 940 years); (2) Middle Egyptian (from the Ninth to the Eleventh Dynasty fully, to the Eighteenth Dynasty less clearly, about 2240–1570 B.C., or 670 years); (3) Neo-Egyptian (from the Eighteenth to the Twenty-fourth Dynasty, about 1570–715 B.C., or 855 years); (4) demotic (from the Twenty-fifth Dynasty to the third century A.D., Egypt being from this time Roman after having been Greek, and even as far as the reign of the Byzantine emperor Leo I if one takes account of certain sporadic extensions of the use of demotic during the first Coptic centuries, hence from about 715 B.C. to 470 A.D., or 1185 years, or only 965 years if we stop at the beginning of the Coptic period); (5) Coptic (not counting Old Coptic, which preceded it and was not yet properly Coptic), a stage that one might arbitrarily and approximately reckon to begin in the middle of the third century A.D. and the end of which is difficult to fix with any precision (there are no nonliterary Coptic documents from the eleventh century on, and it is artificially that this language still survived for some time, say to the thirteenth century if one may fix a limit there, again arbitrarily, for convenience in chronological evaluation, and even though the slow agony of Coptic during the Middle Ages is difficult to discern with precision); one may thus admit that the Coptic stage could have lasted approximately a thousand years (cf. Kasser, 1989).

However that may be, Coptic (in its two principal forms, *S* and *B*) is indeed the last state of the Egyptian language. It might have been the last but one, as some investigators would have it, if the Coptic language had not failed, for want of vigor, in the last of the metamorphoses it was undergoing locally and endeavoring to undertake from the eighth century on.

On the basis of Gardiner's scheme, one may try to imagine more concretely the succession of these stages of the Egyptian language. It is known that every language constantly evolves, and it is very probable that Egyptian is no exception to this rule. But if the spoken language is in perpetual evolution, the written language, on the contrary, strives to remain stable—or rather, the intellectual class, that of the scribes, which could not carry out its work in conditions of unduly accentuated orthographic (chiefly), lexical, and morphosyntactic instability, strives for a clear definition and fixing of orthography and related matters, for a strict control of all impulses toward evolution, to immobilize them as far as possible. The result is that although the orthography corresponds fairly well to the pronunciation of the spoken language at the time the rules of orthography become fixed, it is no longer the same after a number of centuries; then the distance between the written and the spoken languages becomes ever greater, and the orthography becomes more and more arbitrary in relation to what is spoken; it thus becomes more and more difficult to learn, to the point where the difficulty becomes intolerable and the tension leads to rupture. People then proceed to a reform of the orthography, adapting it to the contemporary spoken language.

When the language studied is a language entirely dead, as is Egyptian, a language known only from texts that no modern scientific observer has ever heard pronounced by a man who spoke it as his proper living language, then the scheme sketched above remains a hypothesis, however probable it may be. The investigator, instead of being able to grasp the spoken language in its constant evolution, lays hold only of the texts, showing that the first stage of the Egyptian language (Ancient Egyptian) is quite suddenly succeeded by the second (Middle Egyptian), then the third (Neo-Egyptian, rather different from Middle Egyptian), then the fourth (demotic, rather different from Neo-Egyptian), and finally the fifth (Coptic, rather different from demotic). But by comparison with what he can observe in other languages, today still living, he knows that the evolution of the spoken language (which is the "true" language) ought not to be confused with the irregular progress shown by the written language, with its abrupt mutations.

The result of these considerations may be a slightly more nuanced vision of this evolution. The one that Vergote (1973, Vol. 1b, pp. 3–4) presents is very illuminating. First of all, he admits (with B. H. Stricker [1945]) that Middle Egyptian is further removed from Neo-Egyptian that it is from Ancient Egyptian, so that one may bring together Ancient Egyptian and Middle Egyptian in a "line I"; similarly, Neo-Egyptian is further removed from Middle Egyptian than it is from demotic, so that one may bring Neo-Egyptian and demotic together in a "line II"; Coptic, by itself, forms "line III." (Vergote adds a line IV, of which no account will be taken here: it is the Greek of Egypt, contemporary with the autochthonous stages of the Egyptian language from about the sixth and seventh centuries B.C.).

On the other hand, Vergote considers that at the time when the orthography and related matters become remote from the spoken language to such a point that the rupture takes place, entailing a reform of the orthography, this reform is never accepted at a stroke by the whole intellectual class, in all its milieus and in all the literary genres. There are then always some more conservative circles which, at least for some very particular usages to which an archaizing style is especially appropriate, tend to make the ancient state of the language endure, and for as long as possible and as intact as possible in the midst of an environment henceforth greatly changed. Thus, an ancient stage of a language may survive for several centuries, or even millennia, alongside stages that logically have succeeded it (somewhat as, in Coptic, a protodialect may have survived for some time alongside the dialect that, in the logic of dialectal evolution, has succeeded it).

The scheme that results from these considerations (Vergote, 1973, Vol. 1b, p. 3) thus shows a line I ("written classical Egyptian" is equated with Ancient Egyptian followed by Middle Egyptian) which starts from the beginnings of the third millennium B.C. (or even a little earlier), deviates perceptibly from the line of the spoken language toward [-2400], and nevertheless extends down to the middle of the third century A.D. (+250). Next is a line II ("written vulgar Egyptian" being Neo-Egyptian followed by demotic) starting from the middle of the second millennium B.C. (or even a little earlier, toward [-1800]), which deviates perceptibly from the line of the spoken language toward [-1200], and nevertheless extends beyond the middle of the fifth century A.D. (+470). Finally, there is a line III (Coptic), a simple prolongation of the line of the earlier spoken language (after its separation from line II), starting from the middle of the third century A.D. (+250), which no doubt also deviated to some extent from the line of the spoken language at a certain point (but this does not appear in Vergote's scheme) and which extends approximately down to the end of the first millennium. In this scheme, then, in the third century A.D. the three stages of Egyptian happen to exist simultaneously: line I (very close to extinction), line II (on the way to decline, but still capable of enduring for another two centuries), and line III (still very close to its birth).

This very nuanced conception of the evolution of the Egyptian language, from Ancient Egyptian down to Coptic (the Coptic languages *S* and *B*, with the various regional dialects that accompany them) appears the most probable in the present state of knowledge in this field. It may be represented as in Figure 1.

The "Coptic" of this scheme is in fact the totality of the two "Coptic languages" (*S* and *B*) with the various regional dialects which accompany them (*A*, *L*, *M*, *W*, *V*, *F*, *H*, *G*, not to speak of the protodialects *P* and *İ*). Does this signify that each of these idioms is the direct prolongation of a like earlier dialectal form which existed in Egypt already in Neo-Egyptian and in demotic (not to speak of Ancient and Middle Egyptian)? A "prolongation" probably yes, but perhaps not quite "direct," in the sense that one might be tempted to give it in a rather simplistic fashion (cf. Chaîne, 1933, p. xviii, and 1934, pp. 2–3, which must, however, be adapted to the present knowledge of matters of Coptic dialectology). The Coptic dialects (and languages) are idioms of late Egyptian that appeared in the middle of the Greco-Roman period and are particularly perceptible thanks to the Coptic documents, which in contrast to the older Egyptian documents provide information not only about the consonants but also about the vowels. It is thus extremely difficult to compare these idioms with this or that orthographic or semisystematic variant encountered in the Pre-Coptic Egyptian texts, in the hope of thus effecting a comparison between the Coptic and the Pre-Coptic Egyptian dialects.

Certainly the latter must have existed; that is highly probable. But how is one to know them? Prudence in any case advises one to keep some distance from the optimistic hypothesis that would consider each Coptic dialect as the direct descendant of a pharaonic Egyptian dialect corresponding to it. Certainly each historical period in Egypt must have seen the manifestation of numerous local idioms existing side by side (a circumstance evidently favored by the geographical conditions of the country), but one cannot simply affirm that each of them was content to perpetuate itself, if it could, in a linear fashion, reappearing from one period to another in rejuvenated form. Considering the relative orthographic uniformity of the successive pharaonic Egyptian languages, in all probability Egypt also knew periods in which there was something like a linguistic leveling; as a result of reciprocal interferences that had accrued or under the constraining action of a "dia-

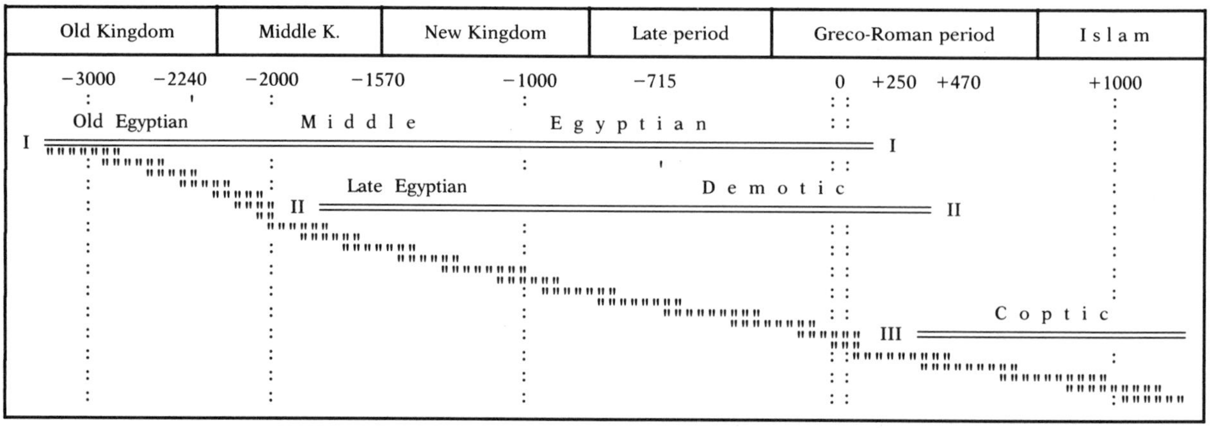

FIGURE 1. EVOLUTION OF THE EGYPTIAN LANGUAGE. Adapted and simplified from Vergote, 1973, Vol. 1b, p. 3, and Lüddeckens, 1980, p. 251.

lect" that had acquired some supremacy in its field of influence (geographic or social)—for example, becoming a supraregional vehicular language—there must have been formed several times over in the course of Egyptian history a kind of koine whose influence extended itself over the greater part or even the whole of one or the other of the halves of Egypt (the Nile Delta, on the one hand, and the valley of the Egyptian Nile above the Delta, on the other). This koine may have been able to eliminate certain local idioms, profoundly inhibiting and radically modifying the others in such a way as to efface the greater part of the differences that constituted their originality. Thus, each local dialect when it reappears after such a leveling is the synthesis of two different currents. Like a son in whom one finds certain features of his father associated with others coming from his mother, the reemergent dialect has quite certainly something of the dialect formerly used in the same region but also bears very strongly the mark of the koine that, at least on the literary level, has supplanted the earlier dialect. The relation between the Coptic idiom and its putative ancestor cannot then be other than ambiguous.

Anyone who examines the scheme above will note that the passage from language I (Ancient Egyptian and Middle Egyptian) to language II (Neo-Egyptian and demotic) represents a "leap" much less great than that from language II to language III (Coptic). Despite their by no means negligible differences, II is easily compatible with I, and there is no doubt the reason for their long coexistence (over about two millennia). III, on the contrary, is much less easily compatible with II (and with I), and that no doubt is the cause of the rapid and, so to speak, catastrophic disappearance of II as soon as III has reached its zenith (reducing their coexistence to some two centuries only; the coexistence of III with I was chronologically zero, or nearly so).

The writing expressing I and II is purely Egyptian and, on the level of phonology, shows only the consonants. The writing of III, on the contrary, is about four-fifths Greek and, in comparison with I and II, presents the immense advantage of showing not only the consonants but also the vowels. The slight inconvenience linked to this advantage is that henceforward the same orthography can no longer, as formerly, be common to all the dialects, thus veiling their existence on the level of writing.

It is thought that the idea of writing Egyptian by means of graphemes fixing not only the consonants but also the vowels could have been born in the bosom of certain bilingual social groups in Egypt who desired to practice magic with greater security. The majority of the texts called Old Coptic are in fact magical texts, disparate essays from the first to the fifth centuries A.D. that logically, if not always chronologically, preceded the first truly Coptic texts.

Certainly the idea of using, even for Egyptian, an alphabet showing the vowels also had already been in the air for several centuries. More than once, and above all from the second century A.D., some man of letters had tried to apply it for his personal use, and this evidently with recourse to Greek, a script with which every Egyptian was confronted every day (and whose convenience he well knew), since it was that of the Greek language, the administrative language of the country over a very long time and thus omnipresent in the innumerable documents that one of necessity had to have written or be able to read to get out of difficulty in the face of the authorities in everyday life.

Such initiatives were taken in the Greco-Egyptian milieus in Egypt above all when it was a case of writing in a manner comprehensible for a Greek some magic formula that brought healing or life to oneself or a friend or suffering and death to a hated enemy. A Greek in Egypt endeavoring to read aloud a text in Ancient Egyptian would perhaps have pronounced his consonants correctly, but he would probably have been mistaken several times in articulating his vowels, since they do not appear in the hieroglyphs or in demotic. Now the demons whom the magician invokes to employ positively in his service or to unleash against an enemy are like fierce dogs accustomed to obeying precise orders. If the formula is ill pronounced, however slightly, their reflexes make them act in a manner impossible to foresee. If they are content to remain asleep and inactive, that is still a lesser evil; but the far worse risk is that they may awake, excited and bewildered by the incomprehensible order, the magic phrase ill pronounced: in fury, they will turn against their bungling master and tear him to pieces. Egyptian written in Greek letters (consonants and vowels, with some additional letters for special sounds) permitted a much more sure pronunciation and thus seemed to protect the Greco-Egyptian magician against regrettable "technical accidents."

Taking up and systematizing better the idea of these isolated predecessors (each of whom had invented his own recipe without knowing too much of those of others), the Copts then decided to adopt the popular Egyptian of their time, and since their language had some phonemes that did not exist in Greek, they completed their alphabet by adding some supplementary graphemes (between six and ten, depending on the Coptic dialects; cf. ALPHABETS, COPTIC).

An admirable reform of the orthography, one will say, but why did no one think of it sooner? Yes indeed, but a reform as dangerous as it was admirable. In fact, in any language, the more fundamental a reform of the orthography is, the more it produces revolutionary and destructive effects, including above all a radical incision in the very heart of the national culture. The "old" literature, that from before the reform, becomes immediately incomprehensible, hence more than difficult, impossible of access, for all those who have been intellectually molded according to the "new" principles (to the exclusion of the old principles, quickly fallen into desuetude and forgotten). We know how many projects for reform of the orthography of numerous modern languages have failed in the face of this formidable obstacle.

The obstacle can only be surmounted if the partisans of fundamental reform are animated by a revolutionary spirit, little disposed to be hampered by scruples about a despised and hated past. If the champions of the new system are ready without regret to see the ancient literature of their people sink into oblivion and disappear, its centuries-old or millennial traditions (at that period evidently above all religious traditions), they will not hesitate to sacrifice to the "progress" that they proclaim a whole cultural heritage; not only have they no esteem whatever for its value, but they probably even judge it inauspicious, dangerous, deserving of being destroyed.

So aggressive and destructive an attitude is evidently very remote from the more respectful state of mind that animated the promoters of the cultural reform which permitted the Egypt of the second millennium B.C. to create its language II and to use it in parallel with its language I (in no way threatened with disappearance on the occasion of the birth of this rival); it was no doubt found convenient and appropriate to be able to employ II alongside I for certain preferential usages, but nobody desired the death of I on the occasion of this innovation.

This revolutionary and iconoclastic attitude appears, on the contrary, to have been that of the promoters of the cultural reform which in the third century A.D. provoked the birth and the prompt flowering of III, on the one hand, and the rapid decadence and soon the extinction of I and II, on the other. The partisans of the old system of Egyptian writing, the "conservatives," were the pagans of Egypt, particularly attached to their thousand-year-old traditions of a dazzling richness. But over against them were arrayed, in ever-increasing numbers, the creators and partisans of the new system of Egyptian writing, the Coptic alphabet; for these Christians of Egypt, revolutionaries so convinced that they scarcely troubled themselves with nuances, the whole pagan past of their country was not only without value, but also inauspicious, diabolical, to be extirpated from their civilization for reasons of mental hygiene. The Copts then did not shed a single tear, rather the contrary, over the death of the hieroglyphic Egyptian preserved in the written cultural language I or over the definitive disappearance of Neo-Egyptian, above all in its demotic form as it then still appeared in the written cultural language II. For them, these means of expression were indissolubly linked to the manifold and at all points monstrous phenomenon of a diabolical and detested paganism, which struck fear into the simple soul and provoked the horror of the Christian. Far from regretting the treasures of their own civilization sinking henceforth into general incomprehension and oblivion, the Copts on the contrary applauded what they considered a salutary intellectual cleansing: the triumph of the Truth.

One must keep equally present in memory this dramatic aspect of a choice now seventeen centuries old, brutal as every revolutionary choice is; a cruel choice, but nonetheless one of genius, since it was only through Coptic that Egyptology was able in 1822, thanks to the perspicacity of Champollion, to attain to a real knowledge of the ancient Egyptian (pharaonic) language, and it is through Coptic that even now Egyptology can "hear" in a manner certainly approximate but nevertheless concrete and, beyond hypothesis and the dry conventional notation, nevertheless gripping, the true "sounds" of a mysterious language, the voice of antique Egypt.

BIBLIOGRAPHY

Barsum, I. *Al-Kharīdat al-Bahīyah fi Uṣul al-Lughat al-Ḳibṭīyah.* Cairo, 1882.

Chaîne, M. *Éléments de grammaire dialectale copte.* Paris, 1933.

———. *Les Dialectes coptes assioutiques A2, les caractéristiques de leur phonétique, de leur syntaxe.* Paris, 1934.

Gardiner, A. *Egyptian Grammar, Being an Introduction to the Study of Hieroglyphs,* 3rd ed. Oxford, 1957.

Kahle, P. E. *Bala'izah: Coptic Texts from Deir el-Bala'izah in Upper Egypt.* Oxford and London, 1954.

Kasser, R. "Prolégomènes à un essai de classification systématique des dialectes et subdialectes coptes selon les critères de la phonétique, I, Principes et terminologie." *Le Muséon* 93 (1980):53–112. ". . . , II, Alphabets et systèmes phonétiques." *Muséon* 93 (1980):237–97. ". . . , III, systèmes orthographiques et catégories dialectales." *Muséon* 94 (1981):91–152.

______. "Orthographe et phonologie de la variété subdialectale lycopolitaine des textes gnostiques coptes de Nag Hammadi." *Muséon* 97 (1984):261–312.

______. "Le copte vraiment vivant, ses idiomes écrits (langues, dialectes, subdialectes) au cours de leur millénaire (IIIe–XIIe siècles environ)." *Bulletin de la Société d'archéologie copte* 28 (1989):11–50.

Krause, M. "Koptische Sprache." *Lexikon der Ägyptologie* 3 (1979):731–37.

Labib, C. J. ⲡⲓⲗⲉⲝⲓⲕⲟⲛ ⲛ̀ϯⲁⲥⲡⲓ ⲛ̀ⲧⲉ ⲛⲓⲣⲉⲙⲛ̀ⲭⲏⲙⲓ. Cairo, 1895–1915.

Layton, B. "Coptic Language." In *Interpreter's Dictionary of the Bible,* Supp. vol., pp. 174–79. Nashville, Tenn., 1976.

Lüddeckens, E. "Ägypten." In *Die Sprachen im römischen Reich der Kaiserzeit,* pp. 241–65. Beihefte der Bonner Jahrbücher 40. Cologne, 1980.

Mallon, A. *Grammaire copte, avec bibliographie, chrestomathie et vocabulaire,* 2nd ed. Beirut, 1907.

______. *Grammaire copte, bibliographie, chrestomathie et vocabulaire,* 4th ed., rev. M. Malinine. Beirut, 1956.

Nagel, P. "Der Ursprung des Koptischen." *Das Altertum* 13 (1967):78–84.

Polotsky, H. J. "Modes grecs en copte?" In *Coptic Studies in Honor of W. E. Crum,* pp. 73–90. Boston, 1950.

Steindorff, G. *Koptische Grammatik, mit Chrestomathie, Wörterverzeichnis und Literatur.* Berlin, 1930.

______. *Lehrbuch der koptischen Grammatik.* Chicago, 1951.

Stern, L. *Koptische Grammatik.* Leipzig, 1880.

Stricker, B. H. *De indeeling der Egyptische taalgeschiedenis.* Leiden, 1945.

Till, W. C. *Koptische Grammatik (saïdischer Dialekt), mit Bibliographie, Lesestücken und Wörterverzeichnissen.* Leipzig, 1955.

Vergote, J. *Grammaire copte,* Vol. 1a, *Introduction, phonétique et phonologie, morphologie synthématique (structure des sémantèmes), partie synchronique,* Vol. 1b, *Introduction, phonétique et phonologie, morphologie synthématique (structure des sémantèmes), partie diachronique.* Louvain, 1973.

Vycichl, W. "Pi-Solsel, ein Dorf mit koptischer Überlieferung." *Mitteilungen des deutschen Instituts für ägyptische Altertumskunde in Kairo* 6 (1936):169–75.

______. *Dictionnaire étymologique de la langue copte.* Louvain, 1983.

______. "Étude sur la phonétique de la langue bohaïrique." *Discussions in Egyptology* 8 (1987):67–76.

RODOLPHE KASSER

LYCO-DIOSPOLITAN. A new dialectological designation connected to the siglum *L* (see LYCOPOLITAN [OR LYCO-DIOSPOLITAN OR SUBAKHMIMIC]), now considered as appropriate and accepted by several Coptologists. Indeed, not only Lycopolis (Asyūṭ) and its area but virtually every place between this area in the north and the area of Diospolis Magna (Thebes, Luxor) in the south must be taken into consideration as a possible home of the *L* dialects (*L4*, the Mani dialect; *L5*, the John dialect; *L6*, the Nag Hammadi non-Sahidic dialect).

RODOLPHE KASSER
WOLF-PETER FUNK

LYCOPOLITAN (OR LYCO-DIOSPOLITAN OR SUBAKHMIMIC). The traditional view of the "Lycopolitan dialect" (also called "Subakhmimic") has become increasingly disputed in recent years, and the question arose if Lycopolitan in fact existed as a distinct dialect.

1. Research History and Problems

1.1 Attempted Definition. A group of Coptic subdialects (or, better, dialects) is usually classed together as Lycopolitan or Lyco-Diospolitan (siglum *L* or, in earlier years and even sometimes today, *A2*) or Subakhmimic (more rarely and in former times Asyutic). Each Coptic (sub)dialect is composed of a number of individual texts (see IDIOLECT) and groups of texts whose uniform designation (linguistically and in terms of dialectal geography; see GEOGRAPHY, DIALECTAL) seems somewhat difficult. The entire group of *L* (sub)dialects and connected idiolects can justifiably be given a collective description only in terms of the linguistic center stretching from Qaw to Asyūṭ (Lycopolis), with various possible extensions to the south and north, and in terms of the linguistic traits that place *L* among the dialects of Upper Egypt but that both as a whole and in relation to their distribution cannot be assigned either to Akhmimic (*A*) or to Sahidic (*S*). Furthermore, because of diversification and subdivision within *L*, it cannot be described as a "neutral" dialect.

1.2 Unity or Diversity of L. The original assumption of relative uniformity of *L* (or *A2*) has been called into question by the increasing number of texts, some of which await publication. The first textual witness to become known was the Acta Pauli (AP. Heid.), which Carl Schmidt published from the Heidelberg Papyrus Collection (1904 and a further folio in 1909). In 1924 Sir Herbert Thompson published extensive fragments of St. John's Gospel in a dialect very close to the AP. Heid. but showing some characteristic peculiarities. In the same year, a letter of the Meletian archives (Crum, in Bell, 1924, no. 1921), the sole nonliterary text thus far known in *L*, was edited and was considered by the editors as belonging to "the later type of Achmimic [Acta Pauli]." Since 1933 the comprehensive corpus of Coptic-Manichaean texts from Madīnat Māḍī has become known and has been published to a great extent. This was followed in 1945 by the discovery of the Nag Hammadi library, of which the codices I, X, and XI once again reveal a new variety of Subakhmimic. Publication began in 1956 with the Gospel of Truth (Evangelium Veritatis) from Codex I. While publication of the Nag Hammadi finds has almost been completed, a wide range of Coptic Manichaean texts is still unpublished. Fragments outside the Nag Hammadi library, but belonging to it in content, were published in 1975; the Sahidic parallel version to these is in Nag Hammadi Codex II, 5. In 1978 fragments of the Letter to Philemon and of Hebrews from the Sir Herbert Thompson Collection (now in Cambridge University library) were published (but these are peculiar in their dialect and seem to be wrongly described as Subakhmimic). One text from the Sir Chester Beatty Collection in Dublin (parts of the Gospel of John) and one from the Bibliotheca Bodmeriana in Geneva (parts of the Acta Pauli, or AP. Bod.) are still unpublished. These two texts are not identical either codicologically or linguistically with the texts published by Sir Herbert Thompson and Carl Schmidt.

1.3 Texts and Editions. The *L* texts now known are almost without exception literary and belong to various categories.

1.3.1. Biblical texts:

JoL = Gospel of John, London manuscript (Thompson, 1924). Provenance: Qaw, fourth century.

JoD = fragments from the Gospel of John (10:18–11:43), Dublin manuscript (unpublished). Transcript: R. Kasser. End of the third century.

Yet a little different from every (sub)dialect of *L* (i.e. *L4*, *L5*, or *L6*, see below) and not too far from *M* and *V* is the dialect of the following fragments of the Pauline Epistles (ed. Bellet, 1978, pp. 45–47; perhaps provenance Suhāj [Dayr al-Abiad], end of fifth century; see Funk, 1986, and Kasser, 1986):

Hbr = fragment of Hebrews (Heb. 5:5–9, 11–14).

Phm = fragment of Philemon (Phlm. 6:15–16).

The language of Hbr and Phm is not taken into account here.

1.3.2. Apocrypha:

AP. Heid. Acta Pauli manuscript in Heidelberg (Schmidt, 1904, 1909). Source: Akhmīm antique dealer; perhaps from Edfu, fifth century.

AP. Bod. = Acta Pauli manuscript fragments in Bibliotheca Bodmeriana, Geneva (unpublished). Incomplete transcript: R. Kasser. Provenance: east of Nag Hammadi (but not with Nag Hammadi library or near Dishnā), fourth century.

1.3.3. Coptic Manichaean texts:

ManiH = Manichaean Homilies (Polotsky, 1934). Provenance: Madīnat Māḍī, in the Fayyūm (but perhaps from Lycopolis[?]; see 1.4), fifth century.

ManiK = Manichaean Kephalaïa (Polotsky and Böhlig, 1940; Böhlig, 1966). Provenance: same as for ManiH, fourth–fifth century.

ManiP = Manichaean Psalter (Allberry, 1938). Provenance: same as for ManiH, fourth–fifth century.

1.3.4. Coptic Gnostic texts:

With one exception (OW; see below) all these texts are Nag Hammadi texts (NagH), so called because they were discovered east of Nag Hammadi but not in the same place as AP. Bod: Their numeration follows that of the Nag Hammadi codices and the sequence of the individual tractates in each codex:

I,1 = Prayer of the Apostle Paul (Kasser et al., 1975b; Attridge, 1985). Fourth century.

I,2 or EpJac = Apocryphal Letter of James (Malinine et al., 1968; Kirchner, 1977; Attridge, 1985). Fourth century.

I,3 or EV = Gospel of Truth (Malinine et al., 1956 and 1961; Till, 1959; Attridge, 1985). Fourth century.

I,4 or Rheg = Tractate on the Resurrection or Letter of Rheginos (Malinine et al., 1963; Layton, 1979; Attridge, 1985). Fourth century.

I,5 or Trip. = Tripartite Tractate (Kasser et al., 1973a, 1975a, and 1975b; Attridge, 1985). Fourth century. The folio with the Prayer of the Apostle Paul later turned out to be a flyleaf of Codex I and is now reckoned as NagH I,1. The language of Trip. is taken into account here only with regard to morphology, not orthography and phonemics, as it is clearly a unique phenomenon (wild orthography, oscillation between *S* and *L*, a series of syntactical errors that are not only irregularities or exceptions) and is perhaps not the work of someone whose mother tongue was Coptic.

X,1 or Mar = Marsanes (Pearson, 1981). Fourth century.

XI, 1 or Inter = Interpretation of Gnosis, pp. 1–32. Copied by W.-P. Funk. Fourth century.

XI, 2 or Exp = Valentinian Exposition, pp. 33–39. Copied by W.-P. Funk. Fourth century.

Appendix = five Valentinian prayers, pp. 40–44.

RhInEx = collective designation for Rheg, Inter, and Exp (NagH I, 4—XI,1.2.).

OW = On the Origin of the World (Oeyen, 1975). Provenance: unknown. According to Oeyen (p. 134) the London fragment shows an older stage in the development of the text than the Sahidic version of NagH II,5, but this does not allow one to draw any direct conclusions as to the age of the manuscript, which Kenyon (in Crum, 1905, no. 522) puts in the fourth century.

1.3.5. Nonliterary texts:

Mel = Letter of the Meletian Archive, no. 1921 (Crum, in Bell, 1924, pp. 94–97). Provenance: antique trade; approx. 330–340 A.D.

Note that there is still a number of texts that are closely related linguistically to the *L* texts but use the grapheme ϩ for /x/; for this reason, they were previously—and wrongly—described as "Akhmimic" or "Akhmimic with Sahidic influences" because they use this ϩ only in part, as *A* does. These preliminary stages (to some extent) in the development of *L* (Kasser, 1979 and 1982a) are dealt with under DIALECT i (with its subdialects, especially *İ7;* see also Funk, 1987).

1.4 Date, Place of Discovery, and Place of Origin. The *L* texts for the most part date from the fourth and fifth centuries (Nag Hammadi and JoL, fourth century; ManiK and ManiP, fourth–fifth centuries; ManiH and AP. Heid., fifth century). On the other hand, the unpublished Gospel of John in Dublin (JoD) seems to be much earlier, even from the end of the third century. It is interesting to see that the witnesses of *L* are written on papyrus, whereas the fragments with the Pauline Epistles (Hbr and Phm), which are to be excluded from *L* for linguistic reasons, are written on parchment.

In some cases (Nag Hammadi and Mani texts, and JoL), the place of discovery is certain, but Crum's dictum is to be kept in mind: "Place of finding is not necessarily place of origin." The Mani texts were discovered in Madīnat Māḍī, a place where the *L*-dialect never had been spoken. Rather, the place of origin of the Coptic Manichaean texts seems to have been Lycopolis (Asyūṭ). For a long time it was regarded as a hiding place for the Manichaean "heresy" (Schmidt and Polotsky, 1933, pp. 12–14). In the case of JoL, there is no compelling reason why the place of discovery should not be considered the same as the place of origin (Qaw/Antaiopolis). As the Nag Hammadi Library resulted from the purposeful collection of various texts, the place of origin of the *L* texts of Nag Hammadi is not guaranteed. As they, however, represent a different type of *L* from Mani and JoL, they should be placed further south.

After the fifth century no textual witness of *L* is attested, and one may conclude that by that time *L* had gone out of use as a literary language.

1.5. Descriptions of Dialect and Geographical Location. The alternating descriptions of "dialect" *L* throw light on the history of the problem of *L* and on Coptic dialectology as a whole. Carl Schmidt, the editor of AP. Heid., characterized the dialect of this manuscript as "a dialect related to the Akhmimic texts." Its consonants are consistently identical with those of the Sahidic, while the vowels show the peculiarities of Akhmimic (Schmidt, 1904, p. 14). Rösch (1909) interpreted this observation to the effect that the AP. Heid. represented the transitional stage from the (older) Akhmimic to the (later) Sahidic ("late" or "new" Akhmimic; similarly, Crum, in Bell, 1924, p. 94, wrote of "the younger type of Achmimic" with regard to the Meletian letter no. 1921). H. Thompson grouped the dialects of AP. Heid. and JoL under the designation "sub-achmimic," which established itself subsequently (JoL, p. xx). He subscribed to Schmidt's view that Subakhmimic stood between Akhmimic and Sahidic, but he raised the fundamental question whether that intermediate position should be interpreted in terms of chronology or dialectal geography. Chaîne (1934) preferred the geographical view, describing the dialect as "Assiutic" (Asyutic, siglum *A2*). The view that Akhmimic was replaced by Sahidic by way of Subakhmimic had already been dismissed by Till (1928, p. 3), who said that *A*, *A2*, and *S* had "basically come into being independently of each other . . . and [had been] spoken at an earlier period simultaneously, and alongside each other, in various districts of Upper Egypt." Nevertheless, the term "Subakhmimic" was retained (Till, *passim;* Schmidt and Polotsky, 1933; Worrell, 1934; Kahle, 1954; and even Vergote, 1973–1983, Vol. 1a).

Worrell (1934, pp. 63–74, map p. 65, region V), assumed that the region of Pbow in the south as far as the al-Ashmūnayn–Antinoë line in the north was the area in which *A* and *A2* spread, but rejected the idea of a more circumscribed localization. Kahle (1954, pp. 206ff.) placed *A2* between Akhmimic and MESOKEMIC, or Middle Egyptian, and considered the region from Abydos to al-Ashmūnayn to be the original area in which *A2* spread (basically in agreement with Worrell). He envisaged for the first time a grouping within *A2* on a broader textual basis, leading to three main groups: (1) JoL, AP. Heid, Mel, OW (Kahle partly other sigla: OW = BM522; Mel = J. & C. 1921); (2) the Mani texts; and (3) the Nag Hammadi texts (still unpublished at the time and not taken further into account by Kahle). *A2*-Mani was, according to him, characterized by Akhmimic influences, while *A2*-AP. Heid. and *A2*-JoL represented "much more truly the ancient Subachmimic" (p. 219). Polotsky (in Schmidt and Polotsky, 1933, p. 11) had already noted that the Manichaean *A2* was closest to the Akhmimic and also drew attention to agreements of Mani-JoL against AP. Heid. These observations were not taken into account by Kahle. Although Kahle's first main group cannot stand up to scrutiny, one is nevertheless indebted to him for many fine individual observations on *A2*.

According to Vergote, 1973–1983, Vol. 1a, p. 4, sec. 5), *A2* was spoken in a region stretching from Akhmīm-Eshqāw in the south to al-Ashmūnayn–Antinoë in the north with Asyūṭ (Lycopolis) as center. As against Kahle, it may be regarded as a backward step that *A2* is treated by Vergote as a dialectal unity. From Worrell to Vergote, there is agreement that the al-Ashmūnayn–Antinoë line is the northern frontier while the frontier for expansion southward remains open, so to speak.

Recognition that *A2* is an independent "dialect" in relation to *A* and *S* is contradictory to the still rather widely current description of the dialect as "Subakhmimic," which, like the siglum *A2*, tends to lead one to assume a subdialect or collateral dialect of Akhmimic, or *A*, even if the terminology is only used conventionally. Hence, in a series of publications since 1972, Kasser has proposed instead of "Subakhmimic" the dialectal designation "Lycopolitan" (*L*), to correspond to the linguistic center of this dialect, or, more exactly, of an important branch of this dialect (see especially Kasser, 1982b and 1984). This description adapts a variant of Chaîne's "Assiutic" and has the advantage that the siglum consists of just one sign, corresponding to the signs of the other main dialects of Coptic. For a rather long time, various indices were used to designate the individual branches or types of *L*. Since 1986, however, a general agreement has been reached among Coptologists. Now numerical indices are preferred: thus, *L4* rather than *L*-Mani, *L5* rather than *L*-JoL, *L6* rather than *L*-NagH (see also LYCO-DIOSPOLITAN).

Far more important is the question of the particular type of *L* to which the textual witnesses can be allotted, the more so since practically every manuscript exhibits peculiarities and even inconsistencies, as *L* in fact is not a thoroughly standardized dialect in any of its branches. The individual groups will be denoted below in accordance with their main characteristics.

1.6 Means of Dialectal Subdivision. Like the Coptic dialects in general, the individual representatives and branches of *L* (as an *L* group) are also mainly distinguished from each other phonetically (insofar as this can be recognized from the orthography) and in specific areas of morphology. Except for Funk (1985), where some primary elements of the kind are already shown, there have been until now no available investigations for differences in the lexical and syntactical field (see, however, DIALECTS, MORPHOLOGY OF COPTIC and AKHMIMIC). These *L* branches are designated as follows:

L4 (or *L*-Mani) (all Mani texts)
L5 (or *L*-JoL) (JoL, JoD and AP. Bod.)
L6 (or *L*-NagH) (all Nag Hammadi *L* texts, and also AP. Heid)

2. The Phonemic Inventory of Lycopolitan

As usual, consonants and vowels will be treated separately.

2.1 Consonants. The *L* consonantal phonemes and graphemes (according to Vergote, 1973–1983, Vol. 1a, p. 13) are those of most Coptic dialects and therefore also of *S*, *M*, *W*, *V*, and *F* (apart from *F7*) (see Table 1). There are sixteen graphemes matching the seventeen consonantal phonemes of Lycopolitan. The laryngeal stop phoneme /'/ has no sign of its own but is expressed, or is recognizable, by the break in the vowels (e.g., **ⲕⲁⲁ**⸗**ϥ**, to place him *or* it), as in *S* (with *pS*) and also *A*, as in most of the *F* branches.

The use of some of these consonants, especially **ⲃ**/**ϥ** and **ⲥ**/**ϣ**, is indicative of a difference within the *L* dialect (see 2.3.1.3 and 2.3.2.1).

2.2 Vowels. A comprehensive description of the vowel phonemes of Lycopolitan can be found in Vergote, 1973–1983 (Vol. 1a, p. 41). The vowel indicators of Lycopolitan are important because they

TABLE 1. *Consonantal Phonemes and Graphemes*

	BILABIALS	LABIODENTALS	DENTALS	PREPALATALS	POSTPALATALS	LARYNGEALS
Voiceless stops	/p/ ⲡ		/t/ ⲧ	/č/:/c/ ϫ:ϭ	/k/ ⲕ	/ʾ/ e.g., ⲁⲁ
Voiceless spirants		/f/ ϥ	/s/ ⲥ	/š/ ϣ		/h/ ϩ
Voiced spirants	/w/ (ⲟ)ⲩ	/ƀ/ ⲃ		/j/ (ⲉ)ⲓ		
Nasals	/m/ ⲙ		/n/ ⲛ			
Laterals/vibrants			/l/ ⲗ, /r/ ⲣ			

often show and clarify relationships with *A* and deviations from, on the one hand, *M*, *F*, etc. and, on the other, *S*, *B*, etc. (see Till, 1961, pp. 8–11; Kasser 1982b, p. 58) and because they emphasize differences within *L* and so are indispensable in defining *L4*, *L5*, and *L6*, as the case may be.

2.3 Indicators of Differences Within Dialect L. These differential markers between *L4*, *L5*, and *L6* are mostly vocalic but sometimes can be consonantal.

2.3.1. L4 versus L5 and L6:

2.3.1.1. The characteristic that most clearly distinguishes *L4* from the other *L* branches is the treatment of the syllable /CR/ (= voiceless consonant + voiced consonant or son[or]ant) and /i̯/ + voiced consonant, or /ʾR/ (= /ʾ/ + voiced consonant or son[or]ant), in the final position after an open tonic syllable. In these cases, as in Akhmimic, an anaptyctic vowel -ⲉ /(ə)/ follows the voiced consonant at the end of the syllable:

MANI =*L4*	*L5, L6*	
ⲥⲱⲧⲙⲉ	ⲥⲱⲧⲙ̄	to hear
ⲙⲉⲓ̈ⲛⲉ	ⲙⲁⲉⲓⲛ	sign
ⲟⲩⲁⲓ̈ⲛⲉ	ⲟⲩⲁⲉⲓⲛ	light
ⲟⲩⲁⲃⲉ†/waʾb(ə)/ (rarely ⲟⲩⲁⲁⲃⲉ†)	ⲟⲩⲁⲁⲃ	to be holy

Only when /wn/ closes a syllable is the anaptyctic vowel found in all the *L* texts: ⲥⲁ(ⲟ)ⲩⲛⲉ (cf. ⲥⲟⲟⲩⲛⲉ), recognize. Note also that in the spelling of the Mani texts, the anaptyctic vowel after /CR/ is not completely standardized. Listing the lexeme "to hear" in ManiK I, the results are ⲥⲱⲧⲙⲉ (seventy-four) and ⲥⲱⲧⲙ̄ (twenty-four). In all comparable instances, the orthography with the anaptyctic vowel predominates.

After a closed tonic syllable /CR/ does not produce any anaptyctic vowel: *L* ⲧⲁⲛⲧⲛ as opposed to *A* ⲧⲁⲛⲧⲛⲉ, to be equal to. The orthography ϣⲧⲁⲣⲧⲣⲉ in ManiK 4,3 is unique (ϣⲧⲁⲣⲧⲣ̄ twenty-five times in ManiK I).

2.3.1.2. The short tonic vowel before the /i̯/ opening a syllable appears in *L4* as ⲉ and in the other *L* branches as ⲁ:

MANI = *L4*	*L5* AND *L6*	
ⲙⲉⲓ̈ⲉ	ⲙⲁⲉⲓⲉ	to love
ϩⲉⲓ̈ⲉ	ϩⲁⲉⲓⲉ	to fall

When /i̯/ closes the syllable, then ⲉ appears uniformly: ⲥϩⲉ(ⲉ)ⲓ, to write; ϩⲉ(ⲉ)ⲓ, husband.

2.3.1.3. The labial spirant at the beginning of words before the tonic vowel becomes in *L4* voiced ⲃ /ƀ/ and in the other *L* branches voiceless ϥ /f/:

MANI = *L4*	*L5* AND *L6*	
ⲃⲓ	ϥⲓ	to carry
ⲃⲱⲉ	ϥⲱⲉ	hair
ⲃⲱⲧⲉ	ϥⲱⲧⲉ	to annihilate
ⲃⲱϭⲉ	ϥⲱϭⲉ	to jump

2.3.1.4. With the verb ⲛⲁ, ⲛⲏⲩ†, to come, the non-Manichean texts (*L5*, *L6*) show nasal gemination: ⲛ̄ⲛⲁ, ⲛ̄ⲛⲏⲩ.

2.3.2 L4 and L5 Versus L6. In a number of phonological phenomena *L4* and *L5* stand together as against *L6*.

2.3.2.1. The alveolar spirant is shown as ⲥ /s/ or ϣ /š/ when ϫ /č/ is involved:

L4 AND *L5*	*L6*	
ⲥⲉϫⲉ	ϣⲉϫⲉ	to speak
ⲥⲁϫⲛⲉ	ϣⲁϫⲛⲉ	counsel
ⲥⲱϫⲡ̄	ϣⲱϫⲡ̄ (b)	to be left over
ⲥⲁⲓ̈ϫ (a)	ϣⲁⲉⲓϫ (b)	warrior

(a) no evidence for JoL; (b) no evidence for AP. Heid.

2.3.2.2. In the unstressed syllabic finale a significant difference occurs between the two groups. Wherever the old initial *j* has become syllabic (vocalic) *-i* through the dropping of the ending *-w*, -ı is retained at the end of the word in *L6* (*t̠ˊsjw* > ϫⲁⲥⲓ[†]); if, on the other hand, another weak consonant has fallen out, then -ⲉ appears in this position. This Edel's law of finales (Edel, 1961) takes effect only in *L6;* in *L5* and *L4* one also finds -ⲉ in the conditions formulated by Edel (see Table 2).

2.3.2.3. In the case of ⲕⲱ, to set, to place < *h̯3ʿ*, the original laryngeal finale in *L6* (NagH, AP. Heid.) is retained as the anaptyctic vowel -ⲉ: ⲕⲱⲉ (likewise OW 3,3). In *L4* and *L5* (Mani JoL) the anaptyctic vowel (or laryngeal) does not emerge, and the long back vowel is shown differently: ManiHK ⲕⲱ, ManiP ⲕⲟⲩ (1), JoL ⲕⲱ (5), ⲕⲟⲩ (9).

The stable opposition is the presence of the anaptyctic vowel (AP. Heid. and NagH = *L6*) as against its absence (Mani = *L4*, JoL = *L5*). There is no other example of that kind available in Coptic lexicography.

From the above, one should distinguish the syllabic finale /sibilant or labial consonant + long back vowel/, where an original nonlaryngeal consonant has fallen out. The vowel in finale is shown consistently as -ⲟⲩ only in *L6* (NagH), whereas otherwise no uniform group formation is recognizable (for texts other than NagH, cf. Kahle, 1954, p. 209):

ⲥⲱ < *swr*, to drink:
ⲥⲱ JoL(9), ManiP (7), ManiHK;
ⲥⲟⲩ JoL(1), ManiP (4), AP. Heid. NagH
ⲥⲃⲱ < *sb3w.t*, teaching:
ⲥⲃⲱ JoL (4), Mani, AP. Heid. (!);
ⲥⲃⲟⲩ JoL (4), NagH
ϫⲱ < *d̠d*, say:
ϫⲱ JoL (plur.), ManiP (plur.), ManiHK;
ϫⲟⲩ JoL (2), ManiP (1), AP. Heid., NagH
ϩⲃ̄ⲥⲱ < *ḥbsw.t*, garment:
ϩⲃ̄ⲥⲱ Mani;
ϩⲃ̄ⲥⲟⲩ JoL, NagH < ϩϥ̄ⲥⲟⲩ Inter 11,38.

2.3.3 L6 Versus L4 and L5. The feature of *L6* that most strikingly distinguishes it from the other branches of *L* is on the morphematic level, especially in the perfect conjugation (both affirmative and relative), where the *L6* texts (including Trip.) exhibit ϩ before prenominal ⲁ- and the pronominal actor expressions (see 3.2.1.1 and Funk, 1984).

3. The Conjugation System

The summary of the system is based on Polotsky (1960) and Funk (1981). Except in special instances (such as the conjunctive), the form cited here is only the third-person masculine singular and the corresponding prenominal form (nom. = before nominal subject). The entire paradigm is not attested in all conjugations.

TABLE 2.

L4 (MANI)	L5 (JOL)	L6 (AP. HEID.)	NAGH	
ⲁⲥⲉ	—	ⲁⲥⲓ	ⲁⲥⲓ	damage
ⲉⲃⲉⲧⲉ	—	—	ⲉ[ⲃ]ⲁϯ	months (OW 3, 6)
—	—	—	ⲉⲕⲉⲓⲁϯ	drachmae (EpJac 8, 9)
ⲕⲉⲕⲉ	ⲕⲉⲕⲉ	ⲕⲉⲕⲉⲓ	ⲕⲉⲕ(ⲉ)ⲓ	darkness
ⲗⲁⲃⲉ[†]	—	—	ⲗⲁⲃⲓ[†]	to be mad (Inter 20, 39)
ⲛⲁⲃⲉ	ⲛⲁⲃⲉ	ⲛⲁⲃⲓ	ⲛⲁⲃ(ⲉ)ⲓ	sin
ⲥⲁⲛⲉ	ⲥⲁⲛⲉ	ⲥⲁⲛⲓ	ⲥⲁⲛⲓ	robber
ⲥⲁϣⲉ[†]	—	ⲥⲁϣⲓ[†]	ⲥⲁϣⲓ[†]	to be bitter
ϫⲁⲥⲉ[†]	—	ϫⲁⲥⲓ[†]	ϫⲁⲥⲓ[†]	to be high, sublime
ϩⲁⲥⲉ[†]	—	ϩⲁⲥⲓ[†]	ϩⲁⲥⲓ[†]	to be suffering
ϩⲁⲗⲉⲧⲉ	—	—	ϩⲁⲗⲉϯ	birds
but:				
ⲟⲩⲉ	ⲟⲩⲉⲉ (passim)	ⲟⲩⲉⲉⲓ	ⲟⲩⲉⲉⲓ	one (numeral)
	ⲟⲩⲉ (2)			
	ⲟⲩⲉⲉⲓ (2)			

Unless specifically mentioned, the form is affirmative; neg. = negative. Every basic tense (abbreviated hereafter to "basic") is followed (if attested) by its satellites, after "And": circ. = circumstantial, rel. = relative, pret. = preterite, II = second tense. Forms between brackets [. . .] are reconstituted from very similar forms; zero = no verbal prefix; 1.sg. = first-person singular, 2.m.sg. = second masculine singular, 3.f.sg. = third feminine singular, 1.pl. = first plural, 2.pl. = second plural, 3.pl. = third plural; *L* = *L4* with *L5* and *L6*. AP. Heid. = Schmidt (1904 and 1909); Trip. = Kasser et al. (1973 and 1975a); *L6*(. . .) = *L6* without AP. Heid. and Trip.

3.1 Bipartite Pattern: Neg. ⲛ̄- . . . ⲉⲛ.

3.1.1. *Present* (basic) *L* ϥ-, nom. *L* zero. And circ. *L* ⲉϥ- (twice *L6* Trip. ⲁϥ-, and 1.sg. *L4* ⲉⲓ̈-, *L5, L6* ⲉⲉⲓ-, 2.pl. *L4, L5* ⲉⲧⲉⲧⲛ̄-, (*L5*), *L6* ⲉⲣⲉⲧⲛ̄), nom. *L* ⲉⲣⲉ- (also sometimes *L5, L6* ⲉ-, once *L6* Trip. ⲁⲣⲉ-); rel. *L* ⲉⲧϥ̄- (also sometimes *L* ⲉⲧⲉϥ-, once *L6* Trip. ⲉⲧⲁϥ-, and 2.pl. *L* ⲉⲧⲉⲧⲛ̄-), nom. *L4*, (*L5*), *L6* ⲉⲧⲉⲣⲉ- (twice *L6* Trip. ⲉⲧⲁⲣⲉ-), (*L4*), *L5*, (*L6*) ⲉⲧⲉ-; pret. ⲛⲉϥ- ((*L6*) Trip. ⲛⲁϥ-, and 1.sg. *L4* ⲛⲉⲓ̈-, *L5, L6* ⲛⲉⲉⲓ-, 2.pl. *L5* ⲛⲉⲧⲉⲧⲛ̄-, *L6* ⲛⲉⲣⲉⲧⲛ̄-, no attestation of 2.pl. in *L4*), nom. ⲛⲉⲣⲉ-; pret. circ. *L* ⲉⲛⲉϥ- (1.sg. *L6* ⲉⲛⲉⲉⲓ-, 2.pl. *L5* ⲉⲛⲉⲣⲉⲧⲛ̄-); pret. rel. *L* ⲉⲧⲉⲛⲉϥ- ((*L6*) Trip. ⲉⲧⲉⲛⲁϥ-, and 1.sg. *L4* ⲉⲧⲉⲛⲉⲓ̈-); II *L* ⲉϥ- (1.sg. *L4* (*L6* Trip. once) ⲉⲓ̈-, *L5, L6* (without Trip.) ⲉⲉⲓ-, 2.pl. *L4* (*L5*) (*L6*) ⲉⲧⲉⲧⲛ̄, (*L5*), (*L6*) ⲉⲣⲉⲧⲛ̄-), nom. *L* ⲉⲣⲉ-.

3.1.2. *Future* (basic) (*L4*), *L5, L6* ϥⲛⲁ-, *L4* ϥⲁ- (2.pl. *L4, L5*, (*L6*) ⲧⲉⲧⲛⲁ-, (*L6*) ⲧⲉⲧⲛ̄ⲛⲁ-), nom. *L* zero . . . ⲛⲁ-. And circ. (*L4*), *L5, L6* ⲉϥⲛⲁ-, *L4* ⲉϥⲁ- (1.sg. *L5* ⲉⲉⲓⲛⲁ-, 2.pl. *L4* ⲉⲧⲉⲧⲛⲁ-), nom. *L6* ⲉⲣⲉ- . . . ⲛⲁ-, *L5* ⲉ- . . . ⲛⲁ-; rel. (*L4*), *L5, L6* ⲉⲧϥ̄ⲛⲁ-, (*L5*), (*L6*) ⲉⲧⲉϥⲛⲁ-, *L4* (*L6* once) ⲉⲧϥⲁ- ((*L6*) Trip. ⲉⲧⲁϥⲛⲁ-, and 2.pl. *L4, L5* ⲉⲧⲉⲧⲛⲁ-), nom. *L4, L6* ⲉⲧⲉⲣⲉ- . . . ⲛⲁ- ((*L6*) Trip. ⲉⲧⲁⲣⲉ- . . . ⲛⲁ-), *L5* ⲉⲧⲉ- . . . ⲛⲁ-; pret. (*L4*), *L5, L6* ⲛⲉϥⲛⲁ-, (*L4*) [ⲛⲉϥⲁ-] (1.sg. *L5, L6* ⲛⲉⲉⲓⲛⲁ-, 2.m.sg. *L4* ⲛⲉⲕⲁ-, 2.pl. *L5* ⲛⲉⲧⲉⲧⲛⲁ- or ⲛⲉⲣⲉⲧⲛⲁ-), nom. *L4, L5* ⲛⲉⲣⲉ- . . . ⲛⲁ-; pret. circ. *L6* Trip. once ⲉⲛⲉϥⲛⲁ-, but once also 3.f.sg. ⲉⲛⲁⲥⲛⲁ- . . . ⲡⲉ; II *L* ⲉϥⲛⲁ-, (*L4*), (*L5*) ⲉϥⲁ- (1.sg. *L4*, (*L5*) ⲉⲓ̈ⲛⲁ-, *L5, L6* ⲉⲉⲓⲛⲁ-, (*L4*) ⲉⲓ̈ⲁ-, 3.m.sg. *L6* with Trip. ⲉϥⲛⲁ-, *L6* Trip. once ⲁϥⲛⲁ-, 1.pl. *L* ⲉⲛⲁ-, 2.pl. *L4, L5* ⲉⲧⲉⲧⲛⲁ-, *L5, L6* ⲉⲣⲉⲧⲛⲁ-), nom. *L* ⲉⲣⲉ- . . . ⲛⲁ-.

3.2 Tripartite Pattern.

3.2.1 *Tenses with special negations (if not II).* Independent (sentence) conjugations.

3.2.1.1. *Perfect* (basic) *L* ⲁϥ- (1.sg. *L4* ⲁⲓ̈-, *L5, L6* ⲁⲉⲓ-, also *L6*(. . .) ⲁϩⲓ-, 1.pl. *L* ⲁⲛ-, also *L6*(. . .) ⲁϩⲛ̄-, 2.pl. *L* ⲁⲧⲉⲧⲛ̄-, 3.pl. *L* ⲁⲩ-, also *L6*(. . .) ⲁϩⲟⲩ-; cf. Shisha-Halevy, 1977, p. 113), nom. *L* ⲁ- (but *L6* AP. Heid. prefers ϩⲁ-, once also in Trip., also rarely *L6*(. . .) ⲁϩⲁ-); neg. *L* ⲙ̄ⲡϥ̄- or ⲙ̄ⲡⲉϥ- (2.pl. *L* ⲙ̄ⲡⲉⲧⲛ̄-), nom. ⲙ̄ⲡⲉ-. And circ. *L* ⲉⲁϥ- (1.sg. *L4* ⲉⲁⲓ̈-, *L5* ⲉⲁⲉⲓ-, *L6*(. . .) once ⲉⲁϩⲓ-, 1.pl. *L* [ⲉⲁⲛ-] no attestation, *L6*(. . .) once ⲉⲁϩⲛ̄-, 2.pl. *L4* ⲉⲁⲧⲉⲧⲛ̄-, 3.pl. *L* ⲉⲁⲩ-, *L6*(. . .) once ⲉⲁϩⲟⲩ-), nom. *L* ⲉⲁ- (but *L6* APh. ⲉϩⲁ-, perhaps once also in Trip., *L6*(. . .) once ⲉⲁϩⲁ-); neg. *L4, L6* ⲉⲙⲡϥ̄- or ⲉⲙⲡⲉϥ- (2.pl. *L6* once ⲉⲙ[ⲡ]ⲉⲧⲛ̄-), nom. *L* ⲉⲙⲡⲉ-; rel. *L4* (and (*L6*) Trip.) ⲉⲧⲁϥ-, *L5, L6* ⲛ̄ⲧⲁϥ-, *L6* Trip. (and (*L6*) elsewhere) ⲉⲛⲧⲁϥ-, (also (*L6*) Trip. ⲉⲧⲉⲁϥ-, once ⲉⲧⲉϩⲁϥ-) (1.sg. *L4* ⲉⲧⲁⲓ̈-, *L6* Trip. ⲛ̄ⲧⲁⲓ̈- or ⲉⲛⲧⲁⲓ̈-, (*L6*) ⲉⲛⲧⲁⲓ̈-, *L5, L6* ⲛ̄ⲧⲁⲉⲓ-, also *L6*(. . .) ⲛ̄ⲧⲁϩⲓ-, 2.f.sg. *L4* ⲉⲧⲁⲣⲉ-, *L5* ⲛ̄ⲧⲁ-, *L6*(. . .) ⲛ̄ⲧⲁϩⲁ-, 1.pl. *L4* (and (*L5*), *L6* Trip.) ⲉⲧⲁⲛ-, *L5, L6* ⲛ̄ⲧⲁⲛ-, (*L4*), (*L6*) ⲉⲛⲧⲁⲛ-, (also (*L6*) Trip. ⲉⲧⲉⲁⲛ-), also *L6*(. . .) ⲛ̄ⲧⲁϩⲛ̄-, 2.pl. *L4* ⲉⲧⲁⲧⲉⲧⲛ̄-, *L5, L6* ⲛ̄ⲧⲁⲧⲉⲧⲛ̄-, also *L6*(. . .) once ⲛ̄ⲧⲁϩⲁⲧⲉⲧⲛ̄-, 3.pl. *L4* (and (*L6*) Trip.) ⲉⲧⲁⲩ-, *L5, L6* ⲛ̄ⲧⲁⲩ-, (*L4*), (*L6*) ⲉⲛⲧⲁⲩ- (also (*L6*) Trip. ⲉⲧⲉⲁⲩ-), also *L6*(. . .) ⲛ̄ⲧⲁϩⲟⲩ- (or ⲉⲛⲧⲁϩⲟⲩ-)), nom. *L4* (and (*L6*) Trip.) ⲉⲧⲁ-, *L5*, (*L6*) ⲛ̄ⲧⲁ-, *L6* Trip. (and (*L6*) elsewhere) ⲉⲛⲧⲁ-, *L6* AP. Heid. sometimes ⲛ̄ⲧⲁϩⲁ- but prefers ⲛ̄ⲧⲁ- (also (*L6*) Trip. ⲉⲧⲉⲁ-, once each one ⲉⲧⲁϩⲁ-, ⲉⲧⲁⲁ-, ⲉⲛⲧⲁⲁ-), also *L6*(. . .) ⲛ̄ⲧⲁϩⲁ- (or ⲉⲛⲧⲁϩⲁ-); neg. *L4, L6* ⲉⲧⲉⲙⲡϥ̄- or ⲉⲧⲉⲙⲡⲉϥ- (2.pl. *L6* ⲉⲧⲉⲙⲡⲉⲧⲛ̄-), nom. *L6* ⲉⲧⲉⲙⲡⲉ-; pret. *L5, L6* ⲛⲉⲁϥ-, nom. *L5* ⲙⲉⲁ-, *L6* AP. Heid. ⲛⲉϩⲁ-; neg. (3.pl. *L6* ⲛⲉⲙⲡⲟⲩ-), nom. *L6* ⲛⲉⲙⲡⲉ-; pret. circ. = Irrealis *L4, L6* ⲉⲛⲉⲛⲧⲁϥ- (2.pl. *L5* ⲉⲛⲉⲛⲧⲁⲧⲉⲧⲛ̄-); neg. = Irrealis (1.sg. *L5* ⲉⲛⲉⲙⲡⲓ-, 3.pl. *L4* ⲉⲛⲉⲙⲡⲟⲩ-), nom. *L5* ⲉⲛⲉⲙⲡⲉ-; II *L* ⲛ̄ⲧⲁϥ- (also (*L6*) Trip. once ⲉⲛⲧⲁϥ-, twice ⲉⲁϥ-, and 1.sg. *L4* ⲛ̄ⲧⲁⲓ̈-, *L5* ⲛ̄ⲧⲁⲉⲓ-, *L6*(. . .) perhaps once ⲛ̣̄[ⲧ]ⲁϩⲓ̈-, 2.pl. *L5* ⲛ̄ⲧⲁⲧⲉⲧⲛ̄- (or ⲉⲛⲧⲁⲧⲉⲧⲛ̄-)), nom. *L* ⲛ̄ⲧⲁ-.

3.2.1.2. *Completive* (basic) (affirmative substitute *L* ⲁϥⲟⲩⲱ ⲉϥ-, nom. ⲁ- . . . ⲟⲩⲱ ⲉϥ-); neg. *L* ⲙ̄ⲡⲁⲧϥ̄- (also *L4* ⲙ̄ⲡⲁⲧⲉϥ-, and 2.pl. *L5* ⲙ̄ⲡⲁⲧⲉⲧⲛ̄-), nom. *L5, L6* ⲙ̄ⲡⲁⲧⲉ-. And circ. neg. *L4, L6* ⲉⲙⲡⲁⲧⲉϥ-, *L5, L6* ⲉⲙⲡⲁⲧϥ̄-, nom. *L* ⲉⲙⲡⲁⲧⲉ-; rel. neg. *L6* ⲉⲧⲉⲙⲡⲁⲧϥ̄ nom. *L6* ⲉⲧⲉⲙⲡⲁⲧⲉ-; pret. neg. *L5, L6* ⲛⲉⲙⲡⲁⲧϥ̄-, nom. *L6* ⲛⲉⲙⲡⲁⲧⲉ-.

3.2.1.3. *Aorist* (basic) *L4*, (*L5*), *L6* ϣⲁϥ-, *L5*, (*L6*) ϣⲁⲣⲉϥ- (1.sg. *L4* ϣⲁⲓ̈-, 2.pl. *L6* ϣⲁⲣⲉⲧⲛ̄-), nom. *L* ϣⲁⲣⲉ-; neg. *L* ⲙⲁϥ- (1.sg. *L4* ⲙⲁⲓ̈-), nom. *L* ⲙⲁⲣⲉ-. And circ. *L4*, (*L6*) ⲉϣⲁϥ-, *L5*, (*L6*) [ⲉϣⲁⲣⲉϥ-] (1.sg. *L4* ⲉϣⲁⲓ̈-, 3.f.sg. *L6* ⲉϣⲁⲥ-, 3.pl. *L5*, (*L6*) ⲉϣⲁⲣⲟⲩ-), nom. *L4* ⲉϣⲁⲣⲉ-; neg. *L4*, [*L5, L6*] ⲉⲙⲁϥ- (3.f.sg. *L5, L6* ⲉⲙⲁⲥ-), nom. *L4* ⲉⲙⲁⲣⲉ-; rel. (*L4*), [*L5*], *L6* ⲉϣⲁϥ- (*L6* once ⲉⲧϣⲁϥ-), *L4*, ([*L5*]), [*L6*] ⲉⲧⲉϣⲁϥ- (1.sg. *L4* ⲉⲧⲉϣⲁⲓ̈-, 3.f.sg. *L6* once ⲉⲧⲉϣⲁⲥ-, 3.pl. (*L4* once), (*L6* once) ⲉϣⲁⲩ-, *L4*, (*L5* once?) *L6* ⲉⲧⲉϣⲁⲩ-, *L5* (*L6*) ⲉϣⲁⲣⲟⲩ-, (*L6* Trip. ⲉⲧϣⲁⲣⲟⲩ- once, ⲉⲧⲉϣⲁⲣⲟⲩ- once), nom. (*L4* once?) *L5* ⲉϣⲁⲣⲉ-, *L4, L6* ⲉⲧⲉϣⲁⲣⲉ-; neg.

(*L6*) [ⲉⲙⲁϥ-], *L4, L6* ⲉⲧⲉⲙⲁϥ- (3.pl. *L6* once ⲉⲙⲁⲩ-, *L4, L6* ⲉⲧⲉⲙⲁⲩ-, (*L6* once) ⲉⲧⲉⲙⲁⲣⲟⲩ-), nom. *L4, L6* ⲉⲧⲉⲙⲁⲣⲉ-; pret. (3.pl. *L4, L6* [no attestation Trip.] ⲛⲉϣⲁⲩ-, *L6* Trip. ⲛⲉϣⲁⲣⲟⲩ- once); II *L4, L6* ⲉϣⲁϥ- (3.pl. *L4* ⲉϣⲁⲩ-, *L6* Trip. ⲉϣⲁⲣⲟⲩ- once), nom. *L4* ⲉϣⲁⲣⲉ-.

3.2.1.4. *Futurum energicum* (or third future) (basic) *L* ⲉϥⲁ- (1.sg. *L4, L5* ⲉï̈ⲁ-, (*L5*), *L6* ⲉⲉⲓⲁ-, 2.pl. *L6* once ⲉⲣⲉⲧⲛⲁ-, once ⲉⲣⲉⲧⲛ̄-, 3.pl. *L* (without Trip.) ⲉⲩⲁ-, *L6* Trip. once ⲁⲩ(ⲁ)-), nom. *L4, L5* ⲉⲣⲉ-; neg. *L4, L5,* (*L6*) ⲛⲉϥ-, (*L6*) ⲛϥ̄-, (*L6* AP. Heid.) ⲉⲛⲉⲣ- (1.sg. *L5* ⲛⲁ-, *L6* AP. Heid. ⲉⲛⲉⲉⲓ- or ⲛ̄ⲛⲓ-, *L6* also ⲛⲓ-, 2.pl. *L5* ⲛⲉⲧⲛ̄-, 3.pl. *L* ⲛⲟⲩ- but *L4* also ⲛ̄ⲛⲟⲩ-, ⲛⲉⲩ-, ⲛ̄ⲛⲉⲩ-, *L6* AP. Heid. ⲉⲛⲟⲩ-), nom. *L4, L5* ⲛⲉ-; rel. (3.pl. *L6* Trip. once ⲉⲧⲁⲩⲁ-).

3.2.1.5. *Imperative,* e.g., *L4, L5* ⲁⲛⲉⲩ (*L4* no attestation from Polotsky, 1934), *L6* once ⲉⲛⲉⲩ, see; or *L* infinitive; or *L* ⲙⲁ + ⲧ-causative; neg. (*L4?*), (*L6* once) ⲙⲛ̄-, *L* ⲙ̄ⲡⲣ̄- (*L4* once, Polotsky, 1934, p. 5, 20) ⲙ̄ⲡⲱⲣ-, *L6*(. . .) ⲙ̄ⲡⲱⲣ ⲁ-.

3.2.1.6. *Causative imperative L4, L5,* (*L6?*) ⲙⲁⲣⲉϥ-, nom. *L* ⲙⲁⲣⲉ-; neg. *L5* ⲙ̄ⲡⲣ̄ⲧⲣⲉϥ-, *L6* once ⲙ̄ⲡⲱⲣⲁⲧⲣⲉϥ-, once ⲙⲛ̄ⲧⲣⲉϥ-, (*L4* 1.sg. ⲙ̄ⲡⲣ̄ⲧⲁ-, 1.pl. ⲙ̄ⲡⲱⲣⲧⲛ̄-), nom. *L4* ⲙ̄ⲡⲱⲣⲧⲉ-, *L5, L6* (AP. Heid.) ⲙ̄ⲡⲣ̄ⲧⲣⲉ-, *L6* (not AP. Heid.) once ⲙⲛ̄ⲧⲣⲉ-.

3.2.2 Tenses with neg. ⲧⲙ̄-. Subordinate (clause) conjugations.

3.2.2.1. *Conjunctive* (singular 1., 2. m., f., 3. m., f., plural 1., 2., 3.) *L4, L5* ⲛ̄ⲧⲁ- or ⲧⲁ-, *L* ⲛ̄ⲕ- (or (*L4*), *L6* ⲛ̄ⲅ-, (*L4*), (*L5*) ⲕ-), *L* ⲛ̄ⲧⲉ- (or *L4* ⲧⲉ-), *L* ⲛ̄ϥ- (or (*L4*), (*L5*) ϥ-, (*L4* once), (*L6* once) ⲛ̄ⲧϥ̄-), *L* ⲛ̄ⲥ-, *L* ⲛ̄ⲧⲛ̄- (or (*L4*) ⲧⲛ̄-), *L* ⲛ̄ⲧⲉⲧⲛ̄- (or (*L4* once), (*L5* once) ⲧⲉⲧⲛ̄-, *L* ⲛ̄ⲥⲉ-, nom. *L* ⲛ̄ⲧⲉ-.

3.2.2.2. *Future conjunctive L4* ⲧⲁⲣⲉϥ- (1.pl. *L4* ⲧⲁⲣⲛ̄-), nom. *L4* ⲧⲁⲣⲉ-.

3.2.2.3. *Temporal L* ⲛ̄ⲧⲁⲣⲉϥ- (1.pl. *L4, L6* ⲛ̄ⲧⲁⲣⲛ̄-, (*L6* once) ⲛ̄ⲧⲁⲣⲉⲛ-), nom. ⲛ̄ⲧⲁⲣⲉ-.

3.2.2.4. *Limitative* ("until . . . ") *L4,* (*L6* Trip. once) ϣⲁⲛⲧⲉϥ-, (*L4*), (*L6* AP. Heid.) ϣⲁⲛⲧϥ̄-, (*L6* Trip. ϣⲁⲧⲉϥ- twice?), (1.pl. *L4* once ϣⲁⲧⲛ̄-, 2.pl. *L4* once ϣⲁⲧⲉⲧⲛ̄-, 3.pl. *L* ϣⲁⲛⲧⲟⲩ- (*L4* once) ϣⲁⲧⲟⲩ-), nom. *L* (with Trip.) ϣⲁⲛⲧⲉ- (*L6* Trip. once ϣⲁⲧⲉ-).

3.2.2.5. *First conditional L4, L6* ⲉϥϣⲁⲛ-, (*L4*), *L5,* (*L6*) ⲉϥϣⲁ- (1.sg. *L4* ⲉï̈ϣⲁⲛ-, *L5* ⲉⲉⲓϣⲁ-, *L6* ⲉⲉⲓϣⲁ(ⲛ)-, 2.pl. *L4* ⲉϣⲁⲛⲧⲉⲧⲛ̄-, *L5* ⲉⲧⲉⲧⲛ̄ϣⲁ-, (*L5*) ⲉⲣⲉⲧⲛ̄ϣⲁ-, *L6* ⲉⲣⲉⲧⲛ̄ϣⲁⲛ-), nom. *L4* ⲉϣⲁⲛⲧⲉ-, (*L4*), (*L5*) ⲉⲣϣⲁ-, (*L4* Psalms of Thomas) ⲉϣⲁ-, *L5,* (*L6*) ⲉⲣⲉϣⲁ-, *L6* ⲉⲣⲉϣⲁⲛ-.

3.2.2.6. *Second conditional L6* [ⲉϥ-], neg. *L4* ⲉϥⲧⲙ̄- (1.sg. neg. *L5* ⲉⲉⲓⲧⲙ̄-, 3.pl. *L6* ⲉⲩ-, neg. *L5, L6* ⲉⲩⲧⲙ̄-), nom. *L6* ⲉⲣⲉ-, neg. *L5* ⲉⲣⲉⲧⲙ̄-.

3.2.2.7. *Causative infinitive L* -ⲧⲣⲉϥ-, *L4,* [(*L6*)] -ⲧϥ̄-, (1.sg. [*L4*], *L5,* (*L6* AP. Heid. once?) -ⲧⲣⲁ-, *L4* -ⲧⲁ-, *L6* APh. -ⲧⲣⲓ-, 1.pl. *L* -ⲧⲣⲛ̄-, 2.pl. *L6* -ⲧⲣⲉⲧⲛ̄-, 3.pl. *L* -ⲧⲣⲟⲩ-, *L4,* (*L6*) -ⲧⲟⲩ-), nom. *L* -ⲧⲣⲉ-, *L4* -ⲧⲉ-.

BIBLIOGRAPHY

Allberry, C. R. C. *A Manichaean Psalmbook.* Stuttgart, 1938.

Attridge, H. W., ed. *Nag Hammadi Codex I (The Jung Codex): Introduction, Texts, Translations, Indices.* Nag Hammadi Studies 22. Leiden, 1985.

Bell, H. I. *Jews and Christians in Egypt.* London, 1924.

Bellet, P. "Analecta Coptica." *Catholic Biblical Quarterly* 40 (1978):37–52.

Böhlig, A. *Kephalaia: Zweite Hälfte.* Stuttgart, 1966.

Chaîne, M. *Les Dialectes Coptes Assioutiques A2, les caractéristiques de leur phonétique, de leur syntaxe.* Paris, 1934.

Crum, W. E. *Catalogue of the Coptic Manuscripts in the British Museum.* London, 1905.

Edel, E. "Neues Material zur Herkunft der auslautenden Vokale -E und -I im Koptischen." *Zeitschrift für ägyptische Sprache und Altertumskunde* 86 (1961):103–106.

Funk, W. P. "Beiträge des mittelägyptischen Dialekts zum koptischen Konjugationssystem." In *Studies Presented to Hans Jakob Polotsky,* ed. D. W. Young, pp. 177–210. East Gloucester, Mass., 1981.

______. "Die Morphologie der Perfektkonjugation im NH-subachmimischen Dialekt." *Zeitschrift für ägyptische Sprache und Altertumskunde* 111 (1984): 110–30.

______. "How Closely Related Are the Subakhmimic Dialects?" *Zeitschrift für ägyptische Sprache und Altertumskunde* 112 (1985):124–39.

______. "Zur Frage des Dialekts der koptischen Paulus-Fragmente der Thompson-Sammlung in der Universitätsbibliothek Cambridge." *Hallesche Beiträge zur Orientwissenschaft* 8 (1986):45–61.

______. "Die Zeugen des koptischen Literaturdialekts İ7." *Zeitschrift für ägyptische Sprache und Altertumskunde* 114 (1987):117–33.

Hedrick, C. W., ed. *Nag Hammadi Codices XI, XII, XIII.* Nag Hammadi Studies 28. Leiden, 1990.

Kahle, P. E. *Bala'izah: Coptic Texts from Deir el-Bala'izah in Upper Egypt.* Oxford and London, 1954.

Kasser, R. "Relations de généalogie dialectale dans le domaine lycopolitain." *Bulletin de la Société d'égyptologie, Genève* 2 (1979):31–36.

______. "Un Nouveau Document protolycopolitain." *Orientalia* 51 (1982a):30–38.

______. "Le Grand-Groupe dialectal copte de Haute-Egypte." *Bulletin de la Société d'égyptologie, Genève* 7 (1982b):47–72.

______. "Orthographe et phonologie de la variété subdialectale lycopolitaine des textes gnostiques coptes de Nag Hammadi." *Muséon* 97 (1984):261–312.

______. "L'Identité linguistique du Ms. Cambridge Univ. Lib. Or. 1700.1 à la périphérie de l'aire lycopolitaine." *Muséon* 99 (1986):221–27.

Kasser, R.; M. Malinine; H.-C. Puech; G. Quispel; J. Zandee; W. Vycichl; and R. McL. Wilson. *Tractatus Tripartitus, Pars I, De Supernis, Codex Jung f. XXVI r.-f. LII v. (p. 51–104).* Bern, 1973. . . ., *Pars II, De Creatione Hominis, Pars III, De Generibus Tribus, Codex Jung f. LII v.-LXX v. (p. 104–140).* Bern, 1975a.

______. *Oratio Pauli Apostoli, Codex Jung, f. LXII? (p. 143?–144?),* Bern, 1975b.

Kirchner, D. *Epistula Jacobi Apocrypha, neu herausgegeben und kommentiert.* Texte und Untersuchungen zur Geschichte der altchristlichen Literatur 136. Berlin, 1989.

Layton, B. *The Gnostic Treatise on Resurrection from Nag Hammadi.* Harvard, 1979.

Malinine, M.; H.-C. Puech; and G. Quispel. *Evangelium Veritatis, Codex Jung f. VIII v.-XVI v. (p. 16–32), f. XIX r.-XXII r. (p. 37–43).* Zurich, 1956.

Malinine, M.; H.-C. Puech; G. Quispel; W. C. Till; and R. McL. Wilson. *Evangelium Veritatis (Supplementum), Codex Jung f. XVII r.-f. XVIII v. (p. 33–36).* Zurich, 1961.

Malinine, M.; H.-C. Puech; G. Quispel; W. C. Till; R. McL. Wilson; and J. Zandee. *De Resurrectione (Epistula ad Rheginum), Codex Jung f. XXII r.-f. XXV v. (p. 43–50).* Zurich, 1963.

Malinine, M.; H.-C. Puech; G. Quispel; W. C. Till; R. Kasser; R. McL. Wilson; and J. Zandee. *Epistula Iacobi Apocrypha, Codex Jung f. I r.-f. VIII v. (p. 1–16).* Zurich, 1968.

Oeyen, C. "Fragmente einer subachmimischen Version der gnostischen 'Schrift ohne Titel.'" In *Essays on the Nag Hammadi Texts, in Honour of Pahor Labib,* ed. M. Krause, pp. 125–44. Leiden, 1975.

Pearson, B. A., ed. *Nag Hammadi Codices IX and X.* Nag Hammadi Studies 15. Leiden, 1981.

Polotsky, H. J. *Manichäische Homilien.* Stuttgart, 1934.

Polotsky, H. J., and A. Böhlig. *Kephalaia: 1. Hälfte (Lieferung 1–10).* Stuttgart, 1940.

______. "The Coptic Conjugation System." *Orientalia* 29 (1960):392–422.

Rösch, F. *Vorbemerkungen zu einer Grammatik der achmimischen Mundart.* Strasbourg, 1909.

Schmidt, C. *Acta Pauli aus der Heidelberger koptischen Papyrushandschrift Nr. 1.* Leipzig, 1904.

______. "Ein neues Fragment der Heidelberger Acta Pauli." *Sitzungsberichte der Berliner Akademie der Wissenschaften, Philosophisch-historische Klasse* (1909):216–20.

Schmidt, C., and H. J. Polotsky. "Ein Mani-Fund in Ägypten: Originalschriften des Mani und seiner Schüler." In *Sitzungsberichte der Berliner Akademie der Wissenschaften, Philosophisch-historische Klasse,* pp. 4–90. Berlin, 1933.

Shisha-Halevy, A. "Bohairic ⲧⲱⲟⲩⲛ (ⲧⲱⲛ⸗): A Case of Lexemic Grammaticalisation." *Enchoria* 7 (1977):109–113.

Thompson, H. *The Gospel of St. John According to the Earliest Coptic Manuscript.* London, 1924.

Till, W. C. *Achmimisch-koptische Grammatik.* Leipzig, 1928.

______. "Die kairener Seiten des 'Evangeliums der Wahrheit.'" *Orientalia* 28 (1959):167–85.

______. *Koptische Dialektgrammatik, mit Lesestücken und Wörterbuch.* 2nd ed. Munich, 1961.

Vergote, J. *Grammaire copte,* Vol. 1a, *Introduction, phonétique et phonologie, morphologie synthématique (structure des sémantèmes), partie synchronique,* Vol. 1b, *Introduction, phonétique et phonologie, morphologie synthématique (structure des sémantèmes), partie diachronique,* Vol. 2a, . . . , *morphologie syntagmatique, syntaxe, partie synchronique,* Vol. 2b, . . . , *morphologie syntagmatique, partie diachronique.* Louvain, 1973–1983.

Worrell, W. H. *Coptic Sounds.* Ann Arbor, Mich., 1934.

PETER NAGEL

MEMPHITIC. What was formerly called the Memphitic dialect (an appellation now abandoned) was one that Egyptologists and Coptologists long sought to identify and get to know, thinking that it must have been one of the principal dialects of Coptic Egypt. It was in fact known that Memphis had been one of the two very great metropolises of pharaonic Egypt; it was therefore natural that, soon after the beginnings of the science which was to become Coptology and which was at first considered essentially an auxiliary of Egyptology, attempts were made to discover the idiom of ancient Memphis and that scholars endeavored to identify this dialect with one of the dialects found in those texts believed to have been found at Memphis, or at least in a region not too distant from it.

ATHANASIUS OF QŪṢ, a grammarian of the fourteenth century, in listing the Coptic dialects known in his time, spoke of "Sahidic," "Bohairic," and "Bashmuric" (Kasser, 1973, pp. 76–77). Since the first Coptologists were above all Egyptologists, they naturally sought to find in the Coptic idioms attested by the documents at their disposal a reflection of Egyptian "dialects," which corresponded to the two (or three) centers of the political and cultural life of pharaonic Egypt: Upper Egypt (Thebes) and Lower Egypt (Memphis), with sometimes the intermediate region of Middle Egypt. In trying to superimpose these two triads, scholars had no difficulty in understanding the "Coptic of Miṣr" or "Sahidic" as *S*, and they soon located it in the upper third of Upper Egypt (the upper Nile Valley; cf. GEOGRAPHY, DIALECTAL), in the region of Thebes. Likewise, "Bohairic" was evidently *B*, and if the center of this dialect was the western Delta, it was conjectured that its region could be practically identified with the whole of the Delta; to meet the needs of the case, Lower Egypt could even annex to itself lower Middle Egypt (the region of Memphis). Along the same lines, "Bashmuric" was identified with *F*. The first of these identifications still has its defenders today, for it is certain that *S* was spoken at Thebes, if not probably at the origins of this dialect, at least in the period of its greatest extension (classical Coptic; see DIALECT, IMMIGRANT). The third identification quickly encountered great difficulty and was already rejected by Quatremère (1808, pp. 147–228).

Since the second identification (of *B* as "Memphitic") is more probable, although also erroneous, it endured for a little more than a century (1777–1908). It was proposed for the first time by Woide in 1777 (according to Stern, 1880, p. 12, n. 1) and Tuki in 1778, after whom we may mention Mingarelli (1785), Quatremère (1808), Zoega (1810), Engelbreth (1811), Peyron (1835 and 1841), Schwartze (1850), Tattam (1852), Uhlemann (1853), Abel (1876), Rossi (1878), and finally Stern. (Stern, however, expressly rejected it (1880, p. 12): "Earlier scholars called Lower Egyptian 'Coptic' *κατ' ἐξοχήν* and when Upper Egyptian gained in significance for scholarship Woide 1777 proposed for it the name Memphitic. This name is not appropriate, because the language of Memphis, which is preserved, e.g., in the papyri from the monastery of Abba Jeremias and the Bible translation of which Tuki still knew and cited as *Memphiticus alter*, is rather 'Middle Egyptian.' I would have no objection to the description of the Lower Egyptian dialect as Bohairic, since it bears this name in Arabic, while the Coptic texts themselves call it ϯⲁⲥⲡⲓ ⲛⲣⲉⲙⲡⲉⲙϩⲓⲧ 'the northern language.'" Moreover, he required the siglum *M* for "Middle Egyptian," which is Fayyumic in the widest sense of the term; Fayyumic in the strict sense (with regular lambdacism, etc.) was for him "*F* (fayyûmisch)." But it took a dozen years before other Coptologists (Krall, 1892) followed Stern's example, so that one finds Maspero (1886) and Ciasca (1889), among others, still calling *B* "Memphitic."

It was apparently Steindorff (1894) who succeeded in persuading the majority of Coptologists to give up calling Bohairic pure and simple "Memphitic," no doubt by presenting to them a siglum *M* corresponding to a "Memphitic" that was certainly the language of Memphis but quite different from *B*, and in fact an idiom that corresponds rather well with Stern's "Middle Egyptian" *M*, either F^s in modern terminology or F^b (?) or even S^f. After him, the use of the term "Memphitic" in Wessely (1908, p. 185) appears as no more than an isolated survival. The siglum *M* is used today for the MESOKEMIC dialect, at least by those who have not been put off by the recollection of the diverse significance formerly given to this siglum in Coptic dialectology and who distrust the identification, still disputed, of Mesokemic and the autochthonous speech of Oxyrhynchus.

BIBLIOGRAPHY

Abel, K. *Koptische Untersuchungen.* Berlin, 1876.

Ciasca, A. *Sacrorum Bibliorum Fragmenta Copto-sahidica Musei Borgiani Iussu et Sumptibus S. Congregationis de Propaganda Fide Studio . . . Edita.* Vols. 1 and 2. Rome, 1885 and 1889. And [without author or ed.]: *SS. Bibliorum Fragmenta Copto-Sahidica Musei Borgiani, Vol. 1–2. Tabulae.* Rome, [1904].

Engelbreth, W. F. *Fragmenta Basmurico-coptica Veteris et Novi Testamenti quae in Museo Borgiano Velitris Asservantur, cum Reliquis Versionibus Aegyptiis Contulit, Latine Vertit nec non Criticis et Philologicis Adnotationibus Illustravit.* Copenhagen, 1811.

Kasser, R. "Les Dialectes coptes." *Bulletin de l'Institut français d'archéologie orientale* 73 (1973):71–101.

Krall, J. "Koptische Briefe." *Mittheilungen aus der Sammlung der Papyrus Erzherzog Rainer* 5 (1892):21–58.

Maspero, G. "Notes sur différents points de grammaire et d'histoire." *Recueil de travaux relatifs à la philologie et à l'archéologie égyptiennes* 8 (1886):179–92.

Peyron, V. A. *Lexicon Linguae Copticae.* Turin, 1835.

______. *Grammatica Linguae Copticae.* Turin, 1841.

Quatremère, E. M. *Recherches critiques et historiques sur la langue et la littérature de l'Egypte.* Paris, 1808.

Rossi, F. *Grammatica copto-gieroglifica con un'appendice dei principali segni sillabici e del loro significato.* Rome, 1877.

Schwartze, M. G. *Koptische Grammatik . . . herausgegeben nach des Verfassers Tode von Dr. H. Steinthal.* Berlin, 1850.

Steindorff, G. *Koptische Grammatik mit Chrestomathie, Wörterverzeichnis und Literatur.* Berlin, 1894.

Stern, L. *Koptische Grammatik.* Leipzig, 1880.

Tattam, H. *Prophetae Majores, in Dialecto Linguae Aegyptiacae Memphitica seu Coptica, Edidit cum Versione Latina.* Oxford, 1852.

Uhlemann, M. A. *Linguae Copticae Grammatica in Usum Scholarum Academicarum Scripta, cum Chrestomathia et Glossario: Insertae Sunt Observationes Quaedam de Veterum Aegyptiorum Grammatica.* Leipzig, 1853.

Wessely, K. "Les Plus Anciens Monuments du christianisme écrits sur papyrus." *Patrologia Orientalis* 4 (1908):95–210; 18 (1924):341–511.

Zoega, G. *Catalogus Codicum Copticorum Manuscriptorum qui in Museo Borgiano Velitris Adservantur.* Rome, 1810.

RODOLPHE KASSER

MESODIALECT. If the term "dialect" is confined to idioms whose originality, when compared to others, is strongly characterized (by a large number of phonological and morphosyntactical oppositions of a cogent quality) and if the term "subdialect" is confined to idioms whose originality in relation to others is but weakly characterized (by a small number of oppositions of uncompelling or inconclusive quality) (cf. DIALECTS, GROUPING AND MAJOR GROUPS OF), there would still remain a residue of idioms that one would hesitate to class either with the independent dialects proper (because their originality seems too weak) or with the subdialects (because their originality seems too strongly pronounced). One could thus (Kasser, 1980, p. 103) call this last group mesodialects—that is, quasi-dialects, situated almost midway, phonologically and perhaps also geographically, between other dialects—and assign them, following due consideration, to the dialect group to which they nevertheless stand closest.

In view of the unidimensional dialectal configuration of the Nile Valley, in which the local dialects are strung out like pearls on a necklace, a mesodialect will be encountered most often between two dialects; however, there are certain regions (such as the Nile Valley near the Fayyūm or in the Delta) where dialectal geography admits of a second dimension, and there a mesodialect may consequently lie enclosed between three (or, theoretically, even more than three) dialects, linguistically and geographically speaking. Should one assign to a given dialect a particular territory in Egypt, one would apparently be attributing the same territory to the whole dialectal group of which the said dialect is part, so that this territory could be subdivided and parceled among the various member dialects or subdialects of the group; in such a case, the district of the mesodialect would logically lie near the dialectal frontier, adjoining the territory or territories of the neighboring dialect(s), with which it would share affinities (characteristics that are, however, less important than those it shares with the core dialect of its group).

A typical example of a mesodialectal text is the papyrus Mich. 3521. Kahle (1954, pp. 224–25) considered it "Middle Egyptian with Fayyumic influence" and therefore to be attached to the *M* dialectal group rather than to the *F* group, but Husselman published it as belonging to the "Fayumic dialect of Coptic" (1962, pp. vii, 11–18). This judgment was confirmed on the whole by Polotsky (1964, p. 251): "Although the dialect of the MS does not share in the shibboleth of Fayyumic, viz. its lambdacism, anyone previous to Kahle would have unhesitatingly characterized it as 'not quite pure' Fayyumic. Kahle calls it 'Middle Egyptian with Fayyumic influence.' The editor, however, maintains (11) that the basis of the dialect appears to be typical Fayyumic nonetheless, in which I must agree with her. On the other hand, Kahle is certainly right in that the non-Fayyumic infusion is 'Middle Egyptian.' . . . One could perhaps compromise on 'Fayyumic with Middle Egyptian influence.'" P. Mich. 3521, one sees, illustrates well the properties necessary for defining a mesodialect.

It has been suggested that the same term be applied to DIALECT G (or Basmuric, or Mansuric, partly sporadic, belonging to the dialectal group *B*, situated between *S* and a highly dominant *B*, with a probable third component that is perhaps partly Hellenic but difficult to determine; see DIALECT, SPORADIC) and to *K* (situated between *V* or *S* and a highly dominant *B*).

When a mesodialect does not contribute any important original element, one not found in its classic neighbor dialects, it may conveniently be neglected in a systematic and general study of Coptic dialects.

BIBLIOGRAPHY

Browne, G. M. *Michigan Coptic Texts.* Barcelona, 1979.

Chaîne, M. *Eléments de grammaire dialectale copte.* Paris, 1933.

Crum, W. E. "Coptic Documents in Greek Script." *Proceedings of the Britich Academy* 25 (1939):249–71.

Funk, W.-P. "Eine frühkoptische Ausgleichsorthographie für Unter- und Mittelägypten? *Bulletin de la Société d'égyptologie, Genève* 4 (1980):33–38.

Husselman, E. M. *The Gospel of John in Fayumic*

Coptic (P. Mich. Inv. 3521). Ann Arbor, Mich., 1962.
Kasser, R. "Les Dialectes coptes." *Bulletin de l'Institut français d'archéologie orientale* 73 (1973):71–101.
Kahle, P. E. *Bala'izah: Coptic Texts from Deir el-Bala'izah in Upper Egypt.* Oxford and London, 1954.
______. "L'Idiome de Bachmour." *Bulletin de l'Institut français d'archéologie orientale* 75 (1975):401–427.
______. "Prolégomènes à un essai de classification systématique des dialectes et subdialectes coptes selon les critères de la phonétique, I, Principes et terminologie." *Muséon* 93 (1980):53–112.
Polotsky, H. J. Review of E. M. Husselman, *The Gospel of John in Fayumic Coptic (P. Mich. Inv. 3521). Orientalistische Literaturzeitung* 59 (1964):250–53.
Worrell, W. H. *Coptic Sounds.* Ann Arbor, Mich., 1934.

RODOLPHE KASSER

MESOKEMIC (OR MIDDLE EGYPTIAN).

The Mesokemic or Middle Egyptian dialect, siglum *M* (also called Oxyrhynchite), belongs to the Coptic dialects of Middle Egypt. It is one of the relatively minor Coptic idioms and probably flourished only briefly in the early period of the Coptic language (fourth and fifth centuries), but nevertheless developed in this period into a highly standardized written dialect.

Both according to its theoretical system and according to the probable geography of the Coptic dialects (see GEOGRAPHY, DIALECTAL), *M* lies between FAYYUMIC (siglum *F*) and LYCOPOLITAN (siglum *L*). Its homeland may have been the region of Oxyrhynchus.

It is to the abiding credit of P. E. Kahle that on the basis of a very few small fragments he was the first to postulate *M* as an independent dialect (1954). Since then, three larger manuscripts written in this dialect have come to light. These three primary witnesses for this dialect are P. Mil. Copti 1, a fragmentary papyrus codex containing the whole Corpus Paulinum (Pauline Epistles), and Codex Scheide and Codex Glazier, two small parchment codices preserved complete, the first containing the Gospel of Matthew with the so-called Great Doxology, the second containing the first half of Acts (1:1–15:3). Another parchment codex containing the Psalms has since been excavated in Egypt.

1. Characteristics

In comparison with other dialects, *M* in its general outward form comes closest to Fayyumic, not to Fayyumic's central variety, *F* (characterized by its lambdacism), but to varieties like *V* (defined as Fayyumic without lambdacism) or even better *W* (said to be a kind of crypto-Mesokemic with a rather Fayyumic phonology, although without lambdacism; see below).

Indeed, the phonology of *M* shows its most important affinities with that of *W* and *V*. Its consonants are those of every Coptic dialect, except *P*, *İ*, *A*, and *B*. (Like *F*, *V*, *W*, *L*, *S* etc., dialect *M* does not have the /x/ of *P*, *İ*, *A*, and *B*, or the /ç/ of *P* and *İ*.) And like *F4*, *V4*, *W*, *B* etc., *M* does not show the graphic vocalic gemination meaning phonologically /'/ (see ALEPH and GEMINATION, VOCALIC).

The stressed vowels of *M* are most frequently those of Fayyumic, as in **ⲥⲁⲛ**, brother *M*, *W*, *V*, *F* etc. with *A*, *L* (not **ⲥⲟⲛ** *S*, *B*); **ⲙ̇ⲕⲉϩ**, pain *M*, [*W*], *V*, *F* etc. (not **ⲙ̄ⲕⲁϩ** *S*, *A*, *L*, *B*); **ⲧⲁⲕⲁ**, destroy *M*, *W*, *V*, *F* etc. (not **ⲧⲁⲕⲟ** *S*, *B*, **ⲧⲉⲕⲟ** *A*, *L*); **ⲣⲉⲛ**, name *M*, *W*, *V* with *A*, *L*, **ⲗⲉⲛ** *F* etc. (not **ⲣⲁⲛ** *S*, *B*). The unstressed final vowel is **ⲉ** (as in *S*, *A*, *L*), not **ⲓ** (as in *W*, *V*, *F* etc., *B*), as in **ⲉⲓⲣⲉ**, to do *M*, *L*, *A*, *S* (compare with **ⲓⲣⲓ** *W*, *V*, *B*, **ⲓⲗⲓ** *F* etc.). Also characteristic of *M* are some endings with (graphic) vocalic gemination of **ⲉ** (difficult to interpret phonemically, e.g., **ⲙⲉⲉ̇**, truth *M;* compare this with **ⲙⲉⲓ̈** *W*, *V*, *F4*, (*B*), **ⲙⲉⲉⲓ** *F5*, **ⲙⲏⲓ̈** *B*, **ⲙⲏⲉ** *L*, **ⲙⲓⲉ** *A*, **ⲙⲉ** *S*) or endings in **-ⲏⲓ̈ⲉ** (e.g., **ⲉⲣⲡⲏⲓ̈ⲉ**, temple *M;* compare this with [**ⲣ**]**ⲡⲏⲓ̈** *W*, **ⲉⲗⲡⲏⲏⲓ̈** *F5*, **ⲉⲣⲫⲉⲓ** *B*, **ⲣ̄ⲡⲉⲉⲓ** *L6*, **ⲣ̄ⲡⲉ(ⲉ)ⲓ̈ⲉ** *A*, **ⲣ̄ⲡⲉⲉ** *L5*, **ⲣ̄ⲡⲉ** *L4*, *S*).

Mesokemic agrees with SAHIDIC in its full integration of the Greek verb and with BOHAIRIC in that the *M* system of the supralinear point is very closely connected with the older Bohairic system concerning the placing of the DJINKIM. There are two main characteristics peculiar to *M.* First, the letter omicron is used in the stressed syllable, where all other Coptic dialects have omega, as in the infinitive **ⲥⲟⲧⲡ**, to choose. This omicron does not, however, represent a short *o* sound, as was at first uncritically assumed, but, as H. Quecke was the first to recognize, a (long and) open *o* sound. The second characteristic is the perfect in **ϩⲁ-**, together with all the satellites (perfect I **ϩⲁϥ-**; circumstantial **ⲉ̇ϩⲁϥ-**; relative **ⲉ̇ⲑⲁϥ-**; perfect II **ⲉ̇ϩⲁϥ-**; preterite **ⲛⲉϩⲁϥ-**). This form produces the most important morphological peculiarity of the *M* conjugation system, the complete differentiation between circumstantial first present (**ⲉϥ-**), present II (**ⲁϥ-**), and perfect I (**ϩⲁϥ-**).

Another point to be emphasized in regard to the conjugation system is that the peculiar morphology carries with it the existence of a circumstantial of present and future II, but not of perfect II. Of the individual tenses, the affirmative simple conditional is the most striking. It has the same form as the present II, but its syntax shows that it belongs to the verbal sentence (tripartite pattern). The "energetic" future (ⲉ̀ϥⲉ-, negative ⲛ̀ⲛⲉϥ-) can also be used in either form with a relative converter (ⲉ̀ⲧⲉϥⲉ-, negative ⲉ̀ⲧⲉ ⲛ̀ⲛⲉϥ-), while combination with the circumstantial converter is documented only for the negative form. *M* has only four subordinate clause conjugations; the fifth, the temporal, is missing. Instead, the dialect makes use of the subordinate temporal function of the relative converter, which the latter may have in past tenses. Among individual forms in the paradigms, the form of the third-person plural in present and future relative clauses (ⲉ̀ⲧⲥⲉ- or ⲉ̀ⲧⲥⲉⲛⲉ-) is especially typical for *M*.

2. The Conjugation System

Except in special instances (e.g., conjunctive), the form cited here is only the third-person masculine singular and the corresponding prenominal form (nom. = before nominal subject). The entire paradigm is not attested in all conjugations.

Unless specifically mentioned, the form is affirmative; neg. = negative. Every basic tense (abbreviated hereafter to "basic") is followed (if attested) by its satellites, after "And": circ. = circumstantial, pret. = preterite, rel. = relative, II = second tense. Forms between brackets [. . .] are reconstituted from very similar forms; zero = no verbal prefix.

2.1 Bipartite Pattern. Neg. ⲛ̀- . . . ⲉⲛ.

2.1.1. *Present* (basic) ϥ-, nom. zero. And circ. ⲉϥ-, nom. ⲉ̀ⲣⲉ-; rel. ⲉⲧ- or ⲉ̀ⲧϥ-, nom. ⲉ̀ⲧⲉ- (for the third-person plural the standard form here is ⲉ̀ⲧⲥⲉ-, although ⲉ̀ⲧⲟⲩ- may also be found; nom. only once appears ⲉ̀ⲧⲉⲣⲉ-, Acts 7:48); pret. ⲛⲁϥ- . . . (ⲡⲉ), nom. ⲛⲁⲣⲉ- . . . (ⲡⲉ); pret. circ. ⲉⲛⲛⲁϥ-, nom. ⲉⲛⲛⲁⲣⲉ- (introduces the protasis of an irreal clause); pret. rel. ⲉ̀ⲧⲛⲁϥ-, nom. ⲉ̀ⲧⲛⲁⲣⲉ- (there also appears once a form with the ⲉ̀ⲧⲉ- converter: third-person plural ⲉ̀ⲧⲉ ⲛⲁⲩ-, Mt. 26:35); II ⲁϥ-, nom. ⲁ̀ⲣⲉ-; II circ. [ⲉ̀ⲁϥ-], nom. ⲉ̀ⲁ̀ⲣⲉ-.

2.1.2. *Future* (basic) ϥⲛⲉ-, nom. zero . . . ⲛⲉ-. And circ. ⲉϥⲛⲉ-, nom. ⲉ̀ⲣⲉ- . . . ⲛⲉ-; rel. ⲉ̀ⲧⲛⲉ- or ⲉ̀ⲧϥⲛⲉ-, nom. ⲉ̀ⲧⲉ- . . . ⲛⲉ (for the third-person plural the standard form here is ⲉ̀ⲧⲥⲉⲛⲉ-, although ⲉ̀ⲧⲟⲩⲛⲉ- may also be found occasionally); pret. ⲛⲁϥⲛⲉ- . . . (ⲡⲉ), nom. ⲛⲁⲣⲉ- . . . ⲛⲉ- . . . (ⲡⲉ); pret. rel. ⲉ̀ⲧⲛⲁϥⲛⲉ- (Acts 12:6), nom. [ⲉ̀ⲧⲛⲁⲣⲉ- . . . ⲛⲉ-] (in Acts 12:6 that relative has also a temporal [accessory] function); II ⲁϥⲛⲉ-, nom. ⲁ̀ⲣⲉ- . . . ⲛⲉ-; II circ. [ⲉ̀ⲁϥⲛⲉ-], nom. [ⲉ̀ⲁ̀ⲣⲉ- . . . ⲛⲉ-] (for [. . .] first-person plural ⲉ̀ⲁⲛⲛⲉ-, Acts 4:12).

2.2 Tripartite Pattern.

2.2.1 Tenses with special negations (if not II). Independent (sentence) conjugations.

2.2.1.1. *Perfect* (basic) ϩⲁϥ-, nom. ϩⲁ- (occasionally, especially in the Glazier codex, also written without ϩ); neg. ⲙ̀ⲡϥ-, nom. ⲙ̀ⲡⲉ-. And circ. ⲉ̀ϩⲁϥ-, nom. ⲉ̀ϩⲁ- (once appears also the third-person plural form ⲉ̀ⲁⲩ-, Acts 2:22); neg. ⲉⲙⲡϥ-, nom. ⲉⲙⲡⲉ-; rel. ⲉ̀ⲑⲁϥ- or ⲉ̀ⲧⲉ ϩⲁϥ-, nom. ⲉ̀ⲑⲁ- or ⲉ̀ⲧⲉ ϩⲁ- (but ⲉⲣ-, participial prefix, may be used in the cases where the pronominal suffix of the third person, singular or plural, is identical with the antecedent; once appears, moreover, the relative perfect also in the *S* form [third-person plural] ⲉⲛⲧⲁⲩ-, Acts 5:9); neg. ⲉ̀ⲧⲉ ⲙ̀ⲡϥ-, nom. ⲉ̀ⲧⲉ ⲙ̀ⲡⲉ-; pret. ⲛⲉϩⲁϥ- . . . (ⲡⲉ), nom. ⲛⲉϩⲁ- . . . (ⲡⲉ); neg. ⲛⲉ ⲙ̀ⲡϥ-, nom. ⲛⲉ ⲙ̀ⲡⲉ-; II ⲉ̀ϩⲁϥ-, nom. ⲉ̀ϩⲁ- (but in the P. Mil. Copti 1 ⲁϩⲁϥ-, nom. ⲁϩⲁ-, Col. 1:16, 1. Thes. 2:3, cf. Heb. 7:14); neg. ⲛ̀ⲉ̀ϩⲁϥ- . . . ⲉⲛ, nom. ⲛ̀ⲉ̀ϩⲁ- . . . ⲉⲛ.

2.2.1.2. *Completive* (basic) (affirmative substitute ϩⲁϥⲟⲩⲱ ⲉϥ-, nom. ϩⲁ- . . . ⲟⲩⲱ ⲉϥ-); neg. ⲙ̀ⲡⲁⲧϥ-, nom. ⲙ̀ⲡⲁⲧⲉ-. And circ. ⲉⲙⲡⲁⲧϥ-, nom. ⲉⲙⲡⲁⲧⲉ-; pret. ⲛⲉ ⲙ̀ⲡⲁⲧϥ- (Acts 8:16), nom. ⲛⲉ ⲙ̀ⲡⲁⲧⲉ-.

2.2.1.3. *Aorist* (basic) ϣⲁϥ-, nom. ϣⲁⲣⲉ- (the enlarged form [converted or not] ϣⲁⲣⲉϥ- may also be found); neg. ⲙⲉϥ-, nom. ⲙⲉⲣⲉ-. And circ. ⲉ̀ϣⲁϥ-, nom. ⲉ̀ϣⲁⲣⲉ-; neg. ⲉ̀ⲙⲉϥ-, nom. ⲉ̀ⲙⲉⲣⲉ-; rel. ⲉ̀ⲧϣⲁϥ-, nom. ⲉ̀ⲧϣⲁⲣⲉ-; neg. ⲉ̀ⲧⲉ ⲙⲉϥ-, nom. ⲉ̀ⲧⲉ ⲙⲉⲣⲉ-; pret. ⲛⲉϣⲁϥ- . . . (ⲡⲉ), nom. ⲛⲉϣⲁⲣⲉ . . . (ⲡⲉ); II ⲉ̀ϣⲁϥ-, nom. ⲉ̀ϣⲁⲣⲉ- (twice however appears also a form with ⲛ̀-converter, third-person plural ⲛ̀ϣⲁⲩ-, Heb. 6:16, and nom. ⲛ̀ϣⲁⲣⲉ-, Mt. 6:32); neg. ⲛ̀ⲉ̀ϣⲁϥ- . . . ⲉⲛ, nom. ⲛ̀ⲉ̀ϣⲁⲣⲉ- . . . ⲉⲛ.

2.2.1.4. *Futurum energicum (or third future)* (basic) ⲉ̀ϥⲉ-, nom. ⲉ̀ⲣⲉ- . . . (ⲉ̀-) (in the present state of knowledge of *M* texts, the coalescence of the *futurum energicum* with ϫⲉ- to ϫⲉϥⲉ-, nom. ϫⲉⲣⲉ- . . . (ⲉ̀-) is typical for a variety of *M* represented, for example, by the P. Mil. Copti 1; further ⲉϥ- in Matthew 3:12, instead of normal ⲉ̀ϥⲉ-, is possibly not a spelling mistake, but may be the short form of the *futurum energicum* [apodotic *efsōtm*]; the standard spelling of the Scheide codex is ⲉ̀ⲟⲩⲉ̀- for the third-person plural, in spite of 5 ⲉⲩⲉ̀-, and the same spelling appears in the P. Mil. Copti 1; in the Glazier codex one finds only ⲉⲩⲉ̀-; in the case of a nominal subject, the form with the element ⲉ̀- between the nominal subject and the infinitive appears only in the Scheide codex and as a less-used form (three times with ⲉ̀-, seven times without ⲉ̀-); neg. ⲛ̀ⲛⲉϥ-, nom. ⲛ̀ⲛⲉ-. And circ. neg. ⲉⲛⲛⲉϥ-, nom. ⲉⲛⲛⲉ-; rel. ⲉ̀ⲧⲉϥⲉ-, nom. ⲉ̀ⲧⲉⲣⲉ- . . . (ⲉ̀-); neg. ⲉ̀ⲧⲉ ⲛ̀ⲛⲉϥ-, nom. ⲉ̀ⲧⲉ ⲛ̀ⲛⲉ-.

2.2.1.5. *Imperative,* e.g., ⲁ̀ⲛⲉ(ⲩ), see; or infinitive; neg. ⲙ̀ⲡ(ⲉ)ⲣ- + infinitive; ⲙⲁ + ⲧ-causative; ⲙⲉ + ϣⲉ ⲛⲉ⫽, go.

2.2.1.6. *Causative imperative* ⲙⲁⲣⲉϥ-, nom. ⲙⲁⲣⲉ-, absolute ⲙⲁⲣⲁⲛ; neg. ⲙ̀ⲡ(ⲉ)ⲣⲧⲉϥ-, nom. ⲙ̀ⲡ(ⲉ)ⲣⲧⲉ-.

2.2.2 Tenses with neg. ⲧⲙ-. Subordinate (clause) conjugations.

2.2.2.1. *Conjunctive* (singular 1., 2. m., [f.], 3. m., f., plural 1., 2., 3.) ⲛ̀ⲧⲁ-, ⲛⲕ-, [ⲛ̀ⲧⲉ-], ⲛϥ-, ⲛⲥ-, ⲛ̀ⲧⲛ-, ⲛ̀ⲧⲉⲧⲛ- (P. Mil. Copti 1 chiefly ⲛ̀ⲧⲉⲧⲉⲛ-), ⲛ̀ⲥⲉ-, nom. ⲛ̀ⲧⲉ-.

2.2.2.2. *Future conjunctive* ⲛ̀ⲧⲁⲣⲉϥ-, nom. ⲛ̀ⲧⲁⲣⲉ-.

2.2.2.3. *Temporal,* elsewhere normal, appears only sporadically and seems to be a foreign body in *M*: ⲛ̀ⲧⲉⲣⲉϥ-, Acts 10:10; ⲛ̀ⲧⲉⲣⲟⲩ-, Matthew 11:7. Its function is covered by the relative form(s) of the first perfect ⲉ̀ⲑⲁϥ- or ⲉ̀ⲧⲉ ϩⲁϥ-, nom. ⲉ̀ⲑⲁ- or ⲉ̀ⲧⲉ ϩⲁ-; the form with the converter ⲉ̀ⲧⲉ appears only as a secondary form (in that function) and only in the Glazier codex.

2.2.2.4. *Limitative* ϣⲁⲛⲧϥ-, nom. ϣⲁⲛⲧⲉ-.

2.2.2.5. *First conditional* ⲁϥϣⲁⲛ-, nom. ⲁ̀ⲣⲉϣⲁⲛ- (neg. always second conditional).

2.2.2.6. *Second conditional* ⲁϥ-, nom. ⲁ̀ⲣⲉ-.

2.2.2.7. *Causative infinitive* -ⲧ(ⲣ)ⲉϥ-, nom. -ⲧ(ⲣ)ⲉ- (neg. -ⲧⲙⲧⲣⲉϥ-, etc., only once appears a form without ⲣ, -ⲧⲙⲧⲉⲩ-, Acts 4:18).

3. Vocabulary

Other characteristics of the dialect include the combination ⲛ̅ⲧ̅, that is, the use of the word ⲛⲟⲩϯ, God, from the neighboring (Fayyumic) dialect to reproduce the *M* word ⲛⲟⲩⲧⲉ by a contraction; the form ⲛ̀ⲉⲏ for the particle that introduces the subsequent noun identifying the pronominal subject of a conjugation; the indefinite pronouns ϩⲓ, anyone, and ⲛⲓⲛⲉï, anything; the perfect participial prefix ⲉⲣ-; the modal verb ⲛⲉϣ, to be able; the interjection ϩⲓ, ϩⲉ̈ⲓ̈ⲡⲉ, and (in combination) ϩⲉ̈ⲓ̈ⲡⲉ ϩⲓ, lo, see; the form of the compound preposition ⲛ̀ⲟⲩⲉ-, ⲛ̀ⲟⲩⲏ⫽ with its wide range of application; the rich use of the noun ⲁ̀ⲉⲧ in itself and for the formation of the preposition (ⲉ̀)ⲡⲁⲉⲧ ⲛ̀-, beyond, and of the adverb ⲉ̀ⲡⲁⲉⲧ, over; the substantival infinitive ⲙⲏⲧ ⲉ̀ⲃⲁⲗ as a constituent of the prepositional expression ⲙ̀ⲡⲙⲏⲧ ⲉ̀ⲃⲁⲗ ⲛ̀-, ⲙ̀ⲡⲉ⫽ ⲙⲏⲧ ⲉ̀ⲃⲁⲗ, before; the compound verbs ϫⲉⲟⲩⲱ, answer, ⲁϣ (-ϣ)ⲧⲁⲡ ⲉ̀ⲃⲁⲗ, cry out, and ϩⲛⲧⲟⲩⲟ⫽, recline (or sit) at table; the form and syntax of the verb form ϫⲉϩ, touch, which appears as an active infinitive (to which the object is linked by ⲉ̀-) and for which there is no evidence in the present (bipartite pattern); the qualitative forms ϣⲏⲡⲧ† and ϩⲏⲡⲧ† (from ϣⲟⲡ, receive, or ϩⲟⲡ, hide); the use of the noun ⲏⲣ, companion (the singular of the familiar plural ⲉⲣⲏⲩ), to express reciprocal relationships ("one another"); the omission of the final (ⲟ)ⲩ in the verb ⲛⲉ, see, and the adverb ⲙ̀ⲙⲉ, there.

4. Syntax

The syntax of *M* also has some special features. The most characteristic is a type of sentence in which the relative particle ⲉ̀ⲧⲉ appears to take the position of the copula in a nominal sentence, such as ⲛ̀ⲧⲁⲕ ⲉ̀ⲧⲉ ⲡⲉⲭ̅ⲣ̅ⲥ̅ ⲡϣⲏⲣⲉ ⲙ̀ⲡ̅ϯ̅ ⲉ̀ⲧⲁⲛϩ, "Thou art the Christ, the son of the living God," Matthew 16:16. In reality, however, this is the special form of an abbreviated cleft sentence.

BIBLIOGRAPHY

Barns, J. W. B., and R. Kasser. "Le Manuscrit moyen-égyptien B. M. Or. 9035." *Muséon* 84 (1971):395–401.

Funk, W. P. "Beiträge des mittelägyptischen Dialekts zum koptischen Konjugationssystem." In *Studies Presented to Hans Jakob Polotsky,* ed. D. W. Young, pp. 177–210. East Gloucester, Mass., 1981.

Husselman, E. M. "The Martyrdom of Cyriacus and Julitta in Coptic." *Journal of the American Research Center in Egypt* 4 (1965):79–86.

Kahle, P. E. *Bala'izah: Coptic Texts from Deir el-Bala'izah in Upper Egypt.* Oxford and London, 1954.

Orlandi, T. *Papiri della Università degli Studi di Milano (P. Mil. Copti),* Vol. 5, *Lettere di San Paolo in copto ossirinchita, edizione, commento e indici di T. Orlandi, contributo linguistico di H. Quecke.* Milan, 1974.

Osing, J. *Der spätägyptische Papyrus B.M. 10808.* Wiesbaden, 1976.

Schenke, H.-M. "On the Middle Egyptian Dialect of the Coptic Language." *Enchoria* 8 (1978):43*(89)–(104)58*.

______. *Das Matthäus-Evangelium im mittelägyptischen Dialekt des Koptischen (Codex Scheide).* Texte und Untersuchungen zur Geschichte der altchristlichen Literatur 127. Berlin, 1981.

HANS-MARTIN SCHENKE

METADIALECT. By common consent the term "dialect" is used by Coptologists for those idioms whose originality, in relation to one another, is very strongly marked. The basis for judgment is, of course, on the lexical and morphosyntactical levels, but also and above all, using the most convenient and practical criterion, on the phonological level, through the number of phonemic oppositions, their quality, and the clarity of their representation in their respective orthographic systems. This originality is, however, located at the very heart of the classical Coptic stage of evolution, and not at the immediately anterior stage (that of the PROTODIALECT) or at any stage immediately posterior. On this basis, if such a posterior stage of evolution should manifest itself clearly enough in one text or another (normally late), one might call the language of this text a "metadialect" (Kasser, 1980a, p. 112).

It is in fact known that after the beginnings of the history of literary Coptic and long before the extinction of the language and its reduction to the status of a fossil piously preserved as a purely liturgical language, all the Coptic idioms except for *B*, and perhaps to some extent *F*, were progressively stifled by the most tenacious among them, *S*, the "vehicular language" of the whole Nile Valley above the Delta.

One can detect more or less the point at which they were stifled on the literary level. But no doubt they survived for some time further on a strictly oral level, though undergoing very profoundly the contamination imposed upon them by the dominant language, *S*. This survival can be seen (through orthography and its deviations) from the phonological idiolectalism of many copies of *S* written in the region of the old lapsed dialect: in these IDIOLECTS undeniable influences from the defeated idiom continually appear, in varying degree, alongside typically Sahidic forms (Chaîne, 1933, pp. xv–xxiii, and 1934, pp. 1–9). Such are the peculiarities of numerous documents found in the Theban region, in which a subterranean *L* (or *A*) through under- or overcorrection succeeds in disturbing very effectively the vocalization of copies that are theoretically *S* (or eventually S^s/l, more often than S^s/a, from their lexemes) but in any case are generally characterized by the presence in greater or smaller number of lexemes strongly idiolectalized into S^l or S^a (on the phonological level).

It is not inconceivable that as a result of particularly favorable general circumstances (e.g., weakening of the dominant "language") or of the obstinacy of a scribe deeply attached to his local patois long after the apparently final extinction of a dialect on the literary level, this dialect, considered dead, should surface again in one isolated copy or another. It could then be a case not of the reappearance of the dialect in its ancient form but of an avatar of the dialect, a rather different and, in some ways, developed form of it, an original form that clearly shows the effects of the influence of *S* but one in which can be found, nonetheless, several of the characteristics of the old dialect, which had not quite died out. This late, postclassical form of a dialect, surviving in a developed condition (or degenerate, according to the criterion by which one judges it), could be described as a "metadialect."

It is also not inconceivable that in the Arab period, at the time of the decline of the dominant neutral Coptic idioms *S*, some minor dialect that was not quite stifled by *S* should have come to life for some time in a very poor and mediocre fashion on the literary level, profiting from the space it could briefly occupy in those times of cultural anarchy when *S* had lost its supremacy and Arabic had not yet conquered it absolutely (enough to make impossible the survival of any remnant of Coptic cultural life in the depths of some remote district). The cultural anarchy itself, and perhaps the influence of Arabic, which gave this linguistic renaissance an original character, may give the impression, on the one hand, of decadence in the language and, on the other, of the birth, still vague and confused, of a new form of the Egyptian language, in some ways "post-Coptic." Even if such a phenomenon did not have an opportunity to display itself in full bloom, even if it was reduced perforce to a timid and rather clumsy essay, it remains nonetheless very interesting for the linguist analyzing "le fait copte" diachronically and in its various dialects. Here one might by analogy call this new idiom, even poorly outlined, a "metadialect."

The only metadialectal Coptic idiom actually well enough known to allow one to study the phenomenon is DIALECT H (or Hermopolitan, or Ashmuninic). Since metadialectalism shows itself, above all, through phonological and morphosyntactical impoverishment, it is possible that it will scarcely afford any significant original elements on these levels. In such a case, it will be legitimate to concede that the incorporation of the metadialect into a general and systematic study of the Coptic dialects is not indispensable.

BIBLIOGRAPHY

Chaîne, M. *Eléments de grammaire dialectale copte.* Paris, 1933.

______. *Les Dialectes coptes assioutiques A2, les caractéristiques de leur phonétique, de leur syntaxe.* Paris, 1934.

Kasser, R. "Dialectes, sous-dialectes et 'dialecticules' dans l'Egypte copte." *Zeitschrift für ägyptische Sprache und Altertumskunde* 92 (1966):106–115.

______. "Prolégomènes à un essai de classification systématique des dialectes et subdialectes coptes selon les critères de la phonétique, I, Principes et terminologie." *Muséon* 93 (1980a):52–112. ". . . , II, Alphabets et systèmes phonétiques." *Muséon* 93 (1980b):237–97. ". . . , III, Systèmes orthographiques et catégories dialectales." *Muséon* 94 (1981):87–148.

RODOLPHE KASSER

MUQADDIMAH. *Muqaddimah* is the Arabic term for a grammar of the Coptic language in Arabic. When the Coptic language was facing extinction in the thirteenth century, Coptic scholars began to fix the rules of their own national and religious language in order to enable the reader to understand the Coptic of biblical and liturgical texts. These grammars, called *muqaddimah* (plural, *muqaddimāt*), meaning primarily "introduction" or "preface" but also "account" or "statement," were written in Arabic and used Arabic grammatical terminology. There is no reference to earlier Greek authorities, such as Aristarchos of Samothrace (217–145 B.C.), the creator of grammatical terminology, who lived in Alexandria, or to his pupil Dionysos Thrax, the author of the first Greek grammar, in only twenty-five paragraphs, a model for countless later treatises.

The creation of an appropriate grammatical terminology for Coptic was the work of several scholars using terms of the Arabic national grammar and adapting others to the spirit of the Coptic language. When comparing the different authors, one sees that there was a continuous progress in exactitude that reached its peak with the *Qilādah* of Athanasius of Qūṣ, the longest and most elaborate such treatise that survives. The term *muqaddimah* has been retained by Arabic and Western scholars for independent treatises, such as Ibn Khaldūn's historical work. There is, however, a different form, *muqaddamah,* meaning literally "what has been proposed", used in the sense of "preface [of a book]" (de Biberstein-Kazimirski, 1868, Vol. 2, p. 692) or "first chapter" (Al-Munjid, 1962, p. 613). In some dictionaries both forms (*muqaddimah, muqaddamah*) occur (Wehr, 1952, p. 669).

The first of these grammars is the *Muqaddimah* of Ambā Yuḥannā as-Samannūdī (laic name al-As'ad ibn ad-Duhayri) who was consecrated bishop of Samannūd (western Delta) in 1235 by Patriarch Cyrillus in Old Cairo (Graf, 1947, Vol. 2, pp. 371–75). There are two versions: the Bohairic one (Codex Vaticanus Copt. 71) was published and translated into Latin by Athanasius Kircher (1643, pp. 2–20). A translation into French was done by E. Dulaurier, professor of Malay and Javanese and author of different publications on the Coptic language (*Catalogue,* 1849, pp. 360–64, 718–39); this (partial) publication brillantly illustrates the work accomplished by the Coptic scholar.

In Ambā Yuḥannā as-Samannūdī's work one can observe the birth of new grammatical studies. Some definitions seem to be somewhat primitive, but they nevertheless led to development of a real grammatical terminology. Thus, it is true that "words beginning with ⲡⲓ" are masculine, those "beginning with ϯ" are feminine, and those "beginning with ⲛⲓ" are plurals. He observed that masculine words in Coptic may be feminine in Arabic and vice versa, as with the Coptic feminine ϯⲃⲁϣⲟⲣ, fox or vixen, and the Arabic masculine *ath-tha'lab,* fox; conversely, the masculine ⲡⲓⲕⲁϩⲓ, earth, is the feminine *al-arḍ* in Arabic. There is almost no theory concerning the prefix conjugation, but the examples quoted are nevertheless helpful: ⲙⲁⲣⲉⲛⲥⲁϫⲓ = *li-kay natakallama,* that we may speak; ⲁϥⲥⲁϫⲓ = *takallama,* he has spoken; ⲉϥⲉ̀ⲥⲁϫⲓ = *yatakallamu,* he will speak; etc. At the end of the *Muqaddimah* there is a list of similar words: the reader has to distinguish between ⲥⲟⲛ, brother; ⲥⲟⲛⲓ, robber; and ϯⲥⲱⲛⲓ, the sister.

The different chapters are reproduced and translated, sometimes accompanied with linguistic notes, so that the logical structure of the treatise becomes fully apparent. Dulaurier admired the logical composition of the Coptic possessive pronouns consisting of the definite article and the suffix pronouns: "C'est une idée très logique qui a conduit les Egyptiens à former leur pronoms possessifs de l'article déterminatif accru des marques des personnes" (e.g., ⲡⲉϥ-, his, = article ⲡ and suffix ⸗ⲉϥ).

When reading Ambā Yuḥannā's *Muqaddimah* one is well aware that his work was a *creatio ex nihilo,* as there was no tradition of linguistic studies. He had to use grammatical terms of the Arabic national grammar and, when necessary, adapt them to the need of Coptic. His language is medieval Egyptian

Arabic: *mudakkar,* masculine (= *mudakkar*), and *muwannat,* feminine (= *mu'annath*). Coptic words beginning with ⲟⲩ are "indeterminate singulars" (*mufrad bi-ghayr al-alif wa-l-lām,* literally "singular without the letters *al-,*" i.e., without the Arabic definite article).

The postscript reads as follows: "This is the end of the *Muqaddimah.* Whoever will remark a mistake may note and correct it and in return for this service he may receive the retribution and the recompense that he merits" (Dulaurier's text; omitted by Kircher, 1643). A Sahidic version of Ambā Yuḥannā's *Muqaddimah,* probably the work of another scholar whose mother language was Sahidic, has been published in Arabic and Coptic, but without translation, by Munier (1930, pp. 46–64).

Al-Wajīh Yuḥannā al-Qalyūbī (from Qalyūb, north of Cairo) wrote a Coptic grammar to fulfil a wish of his friend Abū Isḥāq ibn al-'Assāl. He was still living in 1271, for in that year he composed a funeral oration for Patriarch Gabriel. Instead of using the paradigmatic method of Ambā Yuḥannā as-Samannūdī's work, he began to establish rules for the morphology of Coptic. His introduction has been translated by Mallon (1906, pp. 126–29). Abū Isḥāq mentions him in his own grammar as "the estimable, learned, venerable Sheikh al-Wajīh Yuḥannā, son of the Priest Michael, son of the Priest Ṣadqah al-Qalyūbī" (Mallon, 1907, pp. 222–29).

Ath-Thiqah ibn ad-Duhayri was the author of a grammar in which he tried to improve on the works of Ambā Yuḥannā and al-Qalyūbī. When he saw Ibn Kātib Qayṣar's *Tabṣira,* he noticed how it depended on the *muqaddimāt* of as-Samannūdī and al-Qalyūbī. His *Muqaddimah* follows the Arabic categorization of words: *ism* (noun = substantive, adjective, numeral, pronoun), *fi'l* (verb), and *ḥarf* (particles, such as prepositions and conjunctions). Its appendix discusses some statements of Ibn Kātib Qayṣar's grammar. It is now known that Ibn Kātib Qayṣar wrote an explanation of the Revelation of John 20:4 in A.M. 983/A.D. 1266–1267, but after this passage the manuscript breaks off. It is thus certain that Ath-Thiqah's *Muqaddimah* was written after that year, probably the year in which Ibn Kātib Qayṣar died.

Al-As'ad Abū al-Faraj Hibat-Allāh ibn al-'Assāl was a member of a famous family of Coptic scholars, the 'Assālids (Mallon, 1906, pp. 109–131; 1907, pp. 213–64), being al-Ṣafī's brother and al-Mu'taman Abū Isḥāq's half brother; he lived in the first half of the thirteenth century. He, too, intended to improve as-Samannūdī's work. Bohairic and Sahidic are described in the same book.

An-Nushū' Abū Shākir ibn Buṭrus ar-Rāhib was the son of an archon and administrator of the Sarga Church in Cairo. The name an-Nushū' is in full Nushū' al-Khilāfah, which means "growth of the caliphate." His activity in A.D. 1249 and 1264–1282 is known (Graf, 1947, p. 428). He was deacon at the Church of al-Mu'allaqah in Cairo and wrote two voluminous theological treatises and a grammar. He endeavored to be more pedagogic than his predecessors, explaining the meaning of monoliteral prefixes (ⲁ, ⲉ, ⲓ, ⲙ, ⲛ, ⲡ, ϣ, ⲱ, ϫ, ϯ) and translating complex word forms and sentences collected from the works of "the bishop of Sakhā" and Ibn Raḥāl or Raḥḥāl, as well as from biblical and liturgical books, hagiographic texts, and St. Cyrillus' "Book of Treasures." The introduction to his *Muqaddimah* has been translated by Mallon (1907, pp. 230–58). The origin of his biblical quotations is always indicated by sigla.

A grammar called *At-Tabṣirah* (The Enlightment) is the work of Ibn Kātib Qayṣar, literally "son [in fact, grandson] of [the Emir] Qayṣar's secretary." His full name (with genealogy) is Abū Isḥāq 'Alam ar-Ri'āsah Ibrahīm ibn ash-Shaykh Abū Th-Thanā ibn ash-Shaykh Ṣāfī ad-Dawlah Abū l-Faḍā'il Kātib al-Amīr 'Alam ad-Dīn Qayṣar (i.e., his grandfather was secretary to Emir 'Alam ad-Dīn Qayṣar). His grammar, though appreciated by Abū Isḥāq ibn al-'Assāl, depends both on as-Samannūdī's *Muqaddimah* and on Arabic grammar. Thus, he distinguished three numbers of the noun (singular, dual, plural) as in Arabic, while there are only two numbers in Coptic (singular, plural). Nouns are either primitive (ⲡⲓⲕⲁϩⲓ, the earth) or composed (ϯⲙⲉⲑⲙⲏⲓ, the truth). If the pronouns are numbered 1–5 (singular) and 6–8 (plural), he gave the following order: 12674358. Also the relative pronouns are quoted as ⲑⲏ, ⲫⲏ, ⲛⲏ. His examples are not always correct: ϩⲁⲛⲭⲏⲙⲓ, Egyptians, = *Miṣrīyūn* (Kircher, 1643, p. 27). In spite of this, Ibn Kātib Qayṣar was an authority in the exegetic field (Commentary on the Apocalypse, the Corpus Paulinum, the Catholicon, etc.; cf. Graf, 1947, p. 379).

Athanasius, bishop of Qūṣ (Upper Egypt, north of Luxor), the author of the last and most complete Coptic grammar, was born near Qamūlah (north of Luxor, but on the western bank of the Nile). His father, called Ṣalīb, was a priest and Athanasius became a monk in the nearby Monastery of St. Victor. His grammar, which has been transmitted in two versions, Sahidic and Bohairic, bears a rhymed title: *Qilādat at-Taḥrīr fī 'Ilm at-Tafsīr* (Necklace of Redaction in the Science of Explanation), inspired by Arabic models. Nothing is known of his life, but there is a detailed study on his work by Gertrud Bauer

(1972), who was able to collect some data on the time in which he lived. He mentioned a vocabulary called *As-Sullam al-Kanā'isī,* by Yuḥannā as-Samannūdī, who died after 1257, so it is certain that he lived in the second half of the thirteenth century. It may even be that he lived into the fourteenth century, as there was then a bishop of Qūṣ called Athanasius who was the author of several writings, including "History of the Myron-Consecration Under the Patriarch Gabriel IV" (ibid., pp. 11–12). That these two authors were the same person is probable but not absolutely certain, for Athanasius is even today a common name among Copts.

The *Qilādah* uses, as do earlier *muqaddimāt,* Arabic grammatical terminology. In many cases, expressions occur with different meanings to meet the necessities of Coptic. In her study Bauer presented an exhaustive catalogue of Arabic grammatical terms used by Athanasius, in which she specified whether each was used in the sense of the Arabic authors or in a special sense for Coptic.

A *ḥarakah* (movement) is in Arabic a vowel sign placed over or under a consonant; in the superior position it signifies *a* or *u,* and in the inferior, *i.* A *muḥarrak* is a consonant bearing such a vowel sign and is pronounced with a following vowel (*a, i, u*): *ba, bi, bu.* In Coptic the *muḥarrak* means something different, the auxiliary vowel preceding a word, such as the name **ⲅⲣⲏⲅⲟⲣⲓⲟⲥ**, Gregorios (pronounced with a short central vowel, *Ĕghrēghōriyōs,* written اغريغوريوس), in order to facilitate the pronunciation of a consonant cluster at the beginning of the word (ibid., p. 40).

In Arabic *al-ḥurūf az-zawā'id* (additional letters) are the consonants ', *t, s, l, m, n, h, w,* and *y* used as prefixes, infixes, and suffixes. In Coptic the same expression means the additional letters at the end of the Greek alphabet, that is, the letters of demotic origin, such as ϣ (ibid., p. 123). *Murakkab* (composed) is a term created by Athanasius for the three letters ⲝ (*ks*), ⲯ (*ps*), and ϯ (*ti*) (ibid., p. 124). *Taksīr jam' al-asmā'* is not the phenomenon of broken plurals, as in Arabic (e.g., *bayt,* house, plural, *buyūt*), but the normal plural form of Coptic nouns (ibid., p. 125). The *jazm,* in Arabic the *modus apocopatus* (as in *lam yaktub,* he did not write, not *yaktubu,* he writes)—that is, the vowelless form (third-person singular *yaktub*)—is in Coptic the imperative or the prohibitive (ibid., p. 126). *Tashdīd* is in Arabic a gemination (double *ll* as in *Allāh,* God), but in Coptic (Sahidic only) it means ⲑ = ⲧϩ and ⲫ = ⲡϩ (ibid., p. 127).

Like other Coptic grammarians, Athanasius adopted the classification of words in three categories: *ism,* noun; *fi'l,* verb; and *ḥarf,* particle. It is astonishing that there is not the slightest trace of the famous grammatical school in Alexandria. There are only four expressions derived from Greek terms: *aḥruf ṣawtīyah,* vowels (*φωνήεντα*); *aḥruf nawāṭiq,* vowels (another translation of the preceding term); *al-aḥruf an-niṣf nawāṭiq,* semivowels (*ἡμίφωνα*), in Arabic a postclassical formation; and *aḥruf ṣawāmit,* voiceless consonants (*ἄφωνα,* scil. *στοιχεῖα*; ibid., pp. 147–48).

Almost all quotations in the *Qilādah* are of biblical or liturgical origin, including even the beginning of Genesis in Sahidic, otherwise not conserved: ϩⲛ̄ ⲧⲉϩⲟⲩⲉⲓⲧⲉ ⲁⲡⲛⲟⲩⲧⲉ ⲧⲁⲙⲓⲉ ⲧⲡⲉ ⲙⲛ̄ ⲡⲕⲁϩ, "In the beginning God made the heaven and the earth" (ibid., p. 197). In any case, Athanasius did not wish to teach his readers Coptic as a spoken language.

Quite new are the phonetic paragraphs at the end of the book, where one finds, for example, the pronunciation of ⲃ as *wīṭah* (*-w*), except at the end where it is *bīṭah,* as in ⲡⲓⲟⲩⲏⲃ, the priest (ibid., p. 230). Likewise, ϫ is pronounced *sh* in four (or five) words, such as ϫⲉⲣⲉ, a greeting (*χαῖρε*), which survives even today in *shāra,* but elsewhere it is *k,* as in ⲯⲩⲭⲏ, soul, and ⲉⲩⲭⲏ, prayer, today pronounced *ebsīka* and *awka* at Zainīyah Qiblī, a village north of Luxor, and in other places.

At the end of his *Qilādah,* Athanasius spoke of the Coptic dialects still spoken in his time. There were still two dialects alive: (1) Sahidic, spoken from Aswan to Munyat al-Qays (i.e., Munyat Banī Khaṣīb, today Minyah), and (2) Bohairic, spoken in the "Bohairah" (Buḥairah), probably the northwestern Delta, in Old and New Cairo. A third, Bashmūric, formerly spoken in "the region of Bashmūr" (probably the eastern Delta), was extinct.

Athanasius also spoke of Coptic words that sounded alike but were written differently (ibid., p. 306). He had decided to write a kind of poem called *muthallath* (threefold) to teach them to his readers. This verse form is Arabic and has been used in Coptic only once, in the so-called Triadon, the "swan-song of Coptic literature." It employs strophes of four lines; the first three rhyme with each other, but the last one rhymes with other last lines, producing the scheme aaab, cccb, dddb, and so on. There are some anonymous *muqaddimāt* (Graf, 1947, Vol. 2, p. 446) not yet edited. Two scholars known to have written grammars are "the bishop of Samannūd" and Ibn Raḥāl or Raḥḥāl, both mentioned by an-Nushū'.

Together with the Coptic scalas (see SULLAM), the *muqaddimāt* proved extremely important for the study of Coptic and Egyptian in Europe. Thanks to Athanasius Kircher's *Lingua Aegyptiaca Restituta* (1643), Jean François Champollion was able to recognize the partly phonetic character of the Egyptian hieroglyphs, mainly because of the monoliteral pronominal suffixes, and to achieve their decipherment in a relatively short time. On the other hand, a Coptic priest, RŪFĀ'ĪL AL-ṬŪKHĪ (1695–1787), used Yuhannā as-Samannūdī's *Muqaddimah* for his *Rudimenta Linguae Coptae sive Aegyptiacae ad Usum Collegii Urbani de Propaganda Fide* (Rome, 1778).

BIBLIOGRAPHY

'Abd al-Masīḥ, Y. "Al-Muqaddimāt wa-s-Salālim." In *Risālat [Jam'īyat] Mār Mīnā*, Vol. 2, pp. 59–68. Alexandria, 1947.

Al-Munjid fī-l-lugha al-'Arabīyah. Beirut, 1969.

Bauer, G. *Athanasius von Qūṣ, Qilādat at-Taḥrīr fī 'Ilm at-Tafsīr: Eine koptische Grammatik in arabischer Sprache aus dem 13./14. Jahrhundert.* Freiburg im Breisgau, 1972.

Biberstein-Kazimirski, A. de. *Dictionnaire arabe-français.* Paris, 1868.

Catalogue général des manuscrits des bibliothèques publiques des départements, Vol. 1, Paris, 1849.

Graf, G. "Die koptische Gelehrtenfamilie der Aulād al-'Assāl und ihr Schrifttum." *Orientalia* 1 (1932):34–56, 129–48, 193–204.

______. *Geschichte der christlichen arabischen Literatur,* Vol. 2. Vatican City, 1947.

Kircher, A. *Lingua Aegyptiaca Restituta, Opus Tripartitum.* Rome, 1643.

Lantschoot, A. van. *Un Précurseur d'Athanase Kircher, Thomas Obicini et la Scala Vat. copte 71.* Louvain, 1948.

Mallon, A. "Ibn al-'Assāl, les trois écrivains de ce nom." *Journal asiatique* 6 (1905):509–529.

______. "Une Ecole de savants égyptiens au moyen âge." *Mélanges de la Faculté orientale de l'Université Saint-Joseph de Beyrouth* 1 (1906):109–131; 2 (1907):213–64.

______. "Catalogue des scalas coptes de la Bibliothèque Nationale de Paris." *Mélanges de la Faculté orientale de l'Université Saint-Joseph de Beyrouth* 4 (1910):57–90.

Munier, H. *La Scala copte 44 de la Bibliothèque Nationale de Paris,* Vol. 1, *Transcription.* Bibliothèque d'études coptes 2. Cairo, 1930.

Sidarus, A. "La Philologie copte arabe au moyen âge." In *Actes du 8ᵉ Congrès de l'Union européenne des arabisants et islamisants,* pp. 267–81. Aix-en-Provence, 1978.

Wehr, H. *Arabisches Wörterbuch für die Schriftsprache der Gegenwart.* Wiesbaden, 1952.

WERNER VYCICHL

OLD COPTIC. Although Coptic dictionaries use the abbreviation *O* (or, in German, *Ak,* or *Altkoptisch*) in the same manner as the initials of the Coptic dialects (*A, L* [= *A2*], *S, M, F, B,* etc.), Old Coptic is not the name of a specific dialect. The term *OC* is used for the language and script of a number of pagan texts that are earlier than, or contemporary with, the oldest texts in Coptic proper—that is, the oldest Coptic texts of Christian or Gnostic (including Manichaean) contents (Haardt, 1949; Kahle, 1954; Vergote, 1973). Not unlike "demotic," *OC* may be primarily regarded as a term for the writing systems or ALPHABETS of the respective texts, rather than for their language. Secondarily, it may refer to the respective idioms. Thus, one may speak of a text written in OC script, but not in OC language (see below, 2.7).

The more important OC texts may be grouped, according to their character, into pagan magical texts and pagan astrological texts. In addition to texts entirely written in OC, some OC passages or shorter texts are embedded in Greek contexts. Furthermore, one has to take into account the OC glosses in several demotic magical papyri. There are a number of other attempts to write Egyptian (Late Egyptian or contemporary vernacular) in Greek letters, with or without addition of demotic signs. This material may be adduced for comparison, but it should not be labeled OC (cf. Quaegebeur, 1982). The texts that have hitherto been regarded as OC (cf. Kammerer, 1950; Steindorff, 1951; Mallon, 1956; Vergote, 1973; Osing, 1976, p. 128, n. 3; the glosses on Isaiah in Kammerer, 1950, no. 1756, are here excluded, since they are of Christian context and of pure Fayyumic phonology) may, in respect to their contents, be classified as follows:

1. Main Group: Old Coptic Texts

Prayer, or plea, to an Egyptian god (Osiris):

1.1. The OC Schmidt Papyrus (present location unknown); first to second century A.D. Perhaps from the Hermopolitan area (Satzinger, 1975).

Horoscopes:

1.2. The London Horoscope Papyrus (P. London 98); first or second century A.D. (Černý, 1957; cf.

Kammerer, 1950, nos. 1761, 1762, 1763, 1766; Kasser, 1963).

1.3. The Michigan Horoscope Papyrus (P. Michigan 6131); second century A.D. From excavations at Soknopaiou Nesos (Worrell, 1941).

Magical spells and prescriptions:

1.4. The OC passages of the Mimaut Papyrus (P. Louvre 2391); late third century A.D. (Preisendanz, 1973, pp. 30ff.; cf. Kammerer, 1950, no. 1776).

1.5. The OC passages of the Paris Magical Papyrus (P. Bibl. Nat. suppl. gr. 574); fourth century A.D. Acquired at Thebes (Preisendanz, 1973, pp. 66–77; cf. Kammerer, 1950, nos. 1732, 1758, 1759, 1760, 1762, 1763, 1767, 1772, 1776; Kahle, 1954, Vol. 1, pp. 242–45; Roeder, 1961, pp. 218–22).

1.6. The OC insertion in the Berlin Magical Papyrus (P. Berlin P 5025); fourth to fifth century A.D. Perhaps from Thebes. This very short text (fifteen words) contains no demotic signs. A sign for *f* is expected as a suffix pronoun attached to the last word, but it is omitted. Hence, the text may be considered an example of Greek TRANSCRIPTION rather than OC.

2. Comparative Material

Under this heading are grouped isolated words, such as glosses, and a text written in the OC script, but in an idiom that is considerably older than that of the other OC texts. For the rendering of Egyptian in Greek letters from an earlier period, see PRE-OLD COPTIC.

OC glosses on magical names and the like written in demotic or in cipher:

2.1 In a demotic magical papyrus of the British Museum (P. Brit. Mus. 10 588); third century A.D. (Bell et al., 1931). (*Note:* The glosses of 2.1, 2.3, and 2.4 are on magical names and the like only and do not contain any true Egyptian. They do not make use of any letters of demotic origin. It is only for their close relationship to the truly OC glosses of 2.2 that they are here taken into account.)

2.2. In the demotic Magical Papyrus, or "(Bilingual) Gnostic Papyrus," of London and Leiden (P. Brit. Mus. 10 070, formerly P. Anastasi 1072, and P. Leiden I. 383, formerly P. Anastasi 65); third century A.D. Acquired at Thebes (Griffith and Thompson, 1904–1909; cf. Kammerer, 1950, nos. 1763, 1769, 1779; Roeder, 1961, pp. 185–213).

2.3. In a demotic papyrus of Leiden (P. Leiden I.384); third century A.D. or slightly later; written by same scribe as 2.2 (Johnson, 1975).

2.4. In a demotic papyrus of the Louvre Museum (P. Louvre E 3229, formerly P. Anastasi 1061); third or fourth century A.D. (Johnson, 1977).

Glosses on a hieratic onomasticon, in both demotic and OC:

2.5. In a Copenhagen papyrus (P. Carlsberg 180; further fragments are preserved in Berlin and Florence); about 180 A.D. From Tebtunis (Osing, 1989).

Demotic name list with OC glosses:

2.6. A Munich papyrus (schoolbook?); second century A.D.

A magical text written in the OC script but in the late classical Egyptian language:

2.7. The Egyptian Oxyrhynchus Papyrus (P. Brit. Mus. 10808); second century A.D. From the Oxyrhynchus excavations (Crum, 1942; Osing, 1976).

Bilingual mummy labels (Greek and OC):

2.8. Two mummy labels in Berlin; second century A.D. From Akhmīm (Kammerer, 1950, nos. 1770, 1775).

The OC texts and the comparative material are presented in chronological order in Table 1.

It can be seen from the chronological arrangement that in spite of the scarcity of the material, and allowing for the random nature of the sample, there is a development in the use of the OC language and script. One of the oldest texts, the Schmidt Papyrus (1.1), is from the realm of Egyptian popular beliefs: just as early Egyptians who found themselves in desperate situations would have recourse to dead persons by writing "letters to the dead," they would later address their pleas to gods (especially, perhaps, those of the necropolis; see Satzinger, 1984). But whereas earlier pleas (Saite to Ptolemaic periods) were written in demotic, around 100 A.D. OC was chosen for a similar purpose.

Two more of the earliest OC texts (1.2–3) are horoscopes apparently connected with the activities of bilingual astrologers. Other texts of the second century (2.5, 2.6, 2.8) served practical purposes. None of the texts mentioned here is of magical character,

Table 1. Old Coptic Texts and Comparative Material

First to second century A.D.	1.1	prayer
	1.2	horoscope
Third century A.D.	1.3	horoscope
	2.6	glosses on demotic name list
	2.7	Egyptian magical text
	2.8	mummy labels
About 180 A.D.	2.5	glosses on hieratic onomasticon
Third century A.D.	1.4	magical text
	2.1	glosses on demotic magical text
Third or third to fourth century A.D.	2.2	glosses on demotic magical texts
	2.3	glosses on demotic magical texts
	2.4	glosses on demotic magical texts
Fourth century A.D.	1.5	magical text
Fourth to fifth century A.D.	1.6	magical text

but about the same time, OC was being applied to magical texts. The oldest of the texts preserved is written in the classical Egyptian language (strongly influenced by Late Egyptian) but in the OC script (2.7). From a later date there are demotic magical texts in which names and certain terms are glossed in OC script. Magical texts in the OC language seem to be the latest stage of this development. When they were produced, Coptic writing was already in full use in the Egyptian church as well as among copyists of Gnostic and Manichaean texts. It may be assumed that some inconsistencies in the latest OC texts are due not so much to a lack of practice in a pioneering stage as to a reluctance to use the conventions of the Christian scribes or even deliberate choice of forms that were thought to give to the texts an archaic appearance. Another significant feature of many OC texts is their connection with Greek texts or even with Greek language (Satzinger, 1984). Both horoscopes are written on scrolls that also contain Greek texts (cf. Kammerer, 1950, nos. 1766, 1778). The OC London horoscope is appended to a horoscope written in Greek; the verso of the papyrus bears the famous funeral oration of Hyperides. The OC magical texts are just parts of larger bodies, the greater part being written in Greek. Some peculiarities of writing and alphabet may point to writers of the Greek tradition as compilers of these Egyptian texts. The demotic magical texts with OC glosses seem to be, partly at least, translations from the Greek. Some Greek spells and several Greek words occur in these texts, written in Greek or OC and occasionally in the alphabetic demotic script. Phonological evidence has been adduced for assuming that the glosses were aimed not at a speaker of Coptic but rather at a Greek-speaker (Satzinger, 1984).

The Writing System of the OC Texts

OC texts are written with Greek characters supplemented by a number of signs of demotic origin that resemble rather closely their demotic prototypes. This is the most conspicuous feature of OC. The systems of the individual texts are inconsistent insofar as more than one sign may be used for the same phoneme. In some cases, historical phonology may account for this. By analogy to the demotic spelling, an attempt may have been made to distinguish sounds that had once been different but had coincided by the time the respective OC texts were written. Thus, in some texts (1.1, 2.2, 2.7) a distinction is made between [demotic sign] *h* and [demotic sign] *ḥ* (or variants), according to etymology, no less carefully than in contemporary (Roman period) demotic. The London horoscope (1.2) once (l. 142) uses a demotic *m*-sign in [demotic sign]**cωoγ** (i.e., **n̄cωoγ**, Egyptian *m s3.w*), where the element *n* goes back to Middle Egyptian *m*. In the same text, **z** is used for an *s*-sound that goes back to ancient — (Černý et al., 1957, p. 92, n. 149), which is, however, coincidence. The use of - (a demotic *n*-sign) for an initial *n* of syllabic quality, in the London Horoscope Papyrus (1.2), offers a clue to the origin of the supralinear stroke of Coptic proper (Crum, 1942, p. 22, n. 2; in other texts, i.e., 1.4 and 1.5, the stroke is still used in connection with **n** only). The Paris Magical Papyrus (1.5) makes use of the Greek spiritus asper for *h* (originating both from Egyptian *h* and *ḥ*). In some texts whole words are written with demotic ligatures or ideograms (1.2; 2.2; cf. 1.1).

The principal *OC* signs of demotic origin are presented in Figure 1.

The Question of Dialects

The OC magical texts were written down at a time when the standardization of the Coptic dialects had just started. Other OC texts were written considerably earlier. In general, the language of many Christian and Gnostic Coptic texts of the fourth century shows an admixture of elements of other dialects, but also mistakes (e.g., overcorrections) that arose from the fact that the writer used a dialect other than the one he was most familiar with.

Similar observations can be made in the OC texts. None of them is written in an idiom that does not show the influence of one or more of the other dialects. Furthermore, one text has obviously to be regarded as an attempt to display several different dialects at the same time (see below, on the second part of the OC texts in the Paris Magical Papyrus).

Generally speaking, it can be said that the OC prayer (Schmidt Papyrus, 1.1) and the OC magical texts (1.4–6) display a kind of Sahidic, whereas the glosses on the demotic magical papyri (2.1–4) can be identified as a kind of Akhmimic (Satzinger, 1984). Of the two horoscopes, the language of the Oxford example (1.3) is close to Akhmimic, whereas the Michigan papyrus (1.2) shows typical Fayyumic features.

Too little of such comparative material as the glosses on the demotic Munich papyrus (2.6) and the mummy labels (2.8) exists to allow for a more precise labeling than "Upper and/or Middle Egyptian." (To put it more exactly, they hardly digress from the characteristics of *A*, *L*, and *M*, but differ in various details from *S*, *F*, and *B*.) The language of the Egyptian Oxyrhynchus Papyrus (2.7) is not Coptic. An attempt has been made, however, to establish the position of the phonological system of this text among the Coptic dialects (Osing, 1978). The results (namely, an intermediary position between *M* and *L/A*?) would be invalidated if it turned out that the crucial features are due to a tradition of pronouncing classical texts in a more conservative way than contemporary vernacular speech. At any rate, the phonological system of this text differs considerably from *S* and *B*.

The Schmidt Papyrus (1.1), written in *S*, has, however, ⲛⲙ-, with (*S* ⲙ̄ⲛ̄-, *B* ⲛⲉⲙ-), and ⲙⲟⲛⲉ, nurse (*S*, ⲙⲟⲟⲛⲉ; *B*, ⲙⲟⲛⲓ), thus perhaps proving a certain affinity to *B*. On the syntactic level, note the use of the third future in a relative clause (as in *B*), where *S* would have the first future.

In the Akhmimic London Horoscope Papyrus (1.2), a few forms agree with *S* and *B*, contrary to the *A* characteristics that are found in the remaining material: ⲡⲟⲣϫ (qual.), to be separated; ϩⲁⲡ, law; ⲛⲁϥ, to him; ϭⲧⲁⲙ, closing; ⲛⲁⲟⲩ, to see; ⲥⲛⲁⲟⲩ, two.

Lack of vowel-doubling produces an agreement with *B* and *M* only in ⲃⲱⲛ, evil. The preformatives of the conjunctive display the full *B* forms, contrary to all the other dialects: –ⲧⲉ- (read ⲛ̄ⲧⲉ-) before noun, –ⲧϥ-, –ⲧⲥ-, –ⲧⲟⲩ-. But this may be due to an archaistic attitude. The syntax shares certain features with late demotic (conditional constructions).

In the few intelligible remains of the Michigan Horoscope Papyrus (1.3), the following forms diverge from *F*: ⲙⲁ, give (as *S*, *A*, *L*, *M*; cf. *B* ⲙⲟⲓ, ⲙⲁ-); ⲡⲁⲓ-, this (as in *B*). This may point toward an influence from *K/K71* (Kasser and Satzinger, 1982), intermediary idioms between *B* and *V* (Kasser, 1980, p. 69, under sy: *V*).

In a very corrupt passage of the Sahidic Mimaut Papyrus (1.4), a ⲣⲉⲛ, name, occurs (ll. 347 ff.), whereas in ll. 396ff., 418, and 633ff. definite non-*S* features are lacking.

The invocations of the Paris Magical Papyrus (1.5), recto and verso of fol. 2, are *S* except for ⲉⲃⲱⲧ, Abydos; ⲉⲙⲟⲩ, come (imperative), l. 76, but ⲁⲙⲟⲩ, l. 92; ⲉⲛⲓ-, bring (imperative), ll. 14 and 16, but ⲁⲛⲓ-, passim; ⲣⲉⲛ, name, ll. 21, 22, and 84; ⲙⲉ𝔷ⲭ (read ⲙⲉⲕϩ), neck, l. 76; ⲟï, to be (qual. of ⲉⲓⲣⲉ), l. 17; ⲁⲫⲱⲃ, about the matter, l. 25, may correspond either to *S* ⲉⲡϩⲱⲃ (*A* and *L*, ⲁ-) or to ϩⲁ ⲡϩⲱⲃ. All these non-*S* features could be expected in an *L*-like idiom.

L. 94 is the beginning of a mythological story of Isis. At this point, the character of the idiom changes. A distinction is made between *h* (ʽ, ˪, etc.) and *ḫ* (ⲭ), as in *B* (ϩ and ϧ, respectively) and *A* (ϩ and ⳉ, respectively); the text has, however, the *š*-sign where *A* would have ⳉ, contrary to the ϣ of the other dialects: ϭⲟïϭ, dust, ll. 95 and 97 (cf. *A*, ⳉⲁⲉⲓⳉ).

The aspirate consonants of *B* are alien to the phonological system of the papyrus. The glottal stop, lacking in *B* and *M*, is indicated by doubled vowels when following an O-sound (ϭⲟⲟⲙⲉ, slim, l. 111; ⲧⲟⲟⲧ⫽, hand, l. 120 bis), but never when following an A- or E-sound (ïⲁⲧ⫽, ïⲉⲧ⫽, eye, ll. 95 and 97; ⲙⲉⲣⲉ, noon, l. 94; ϭⲉⲣⲓ, daughter, passim; ⲙⲉⲩⲓ, to think, l. 152; ⲙⲉⲟⲩ, mother, l. 102). There is no

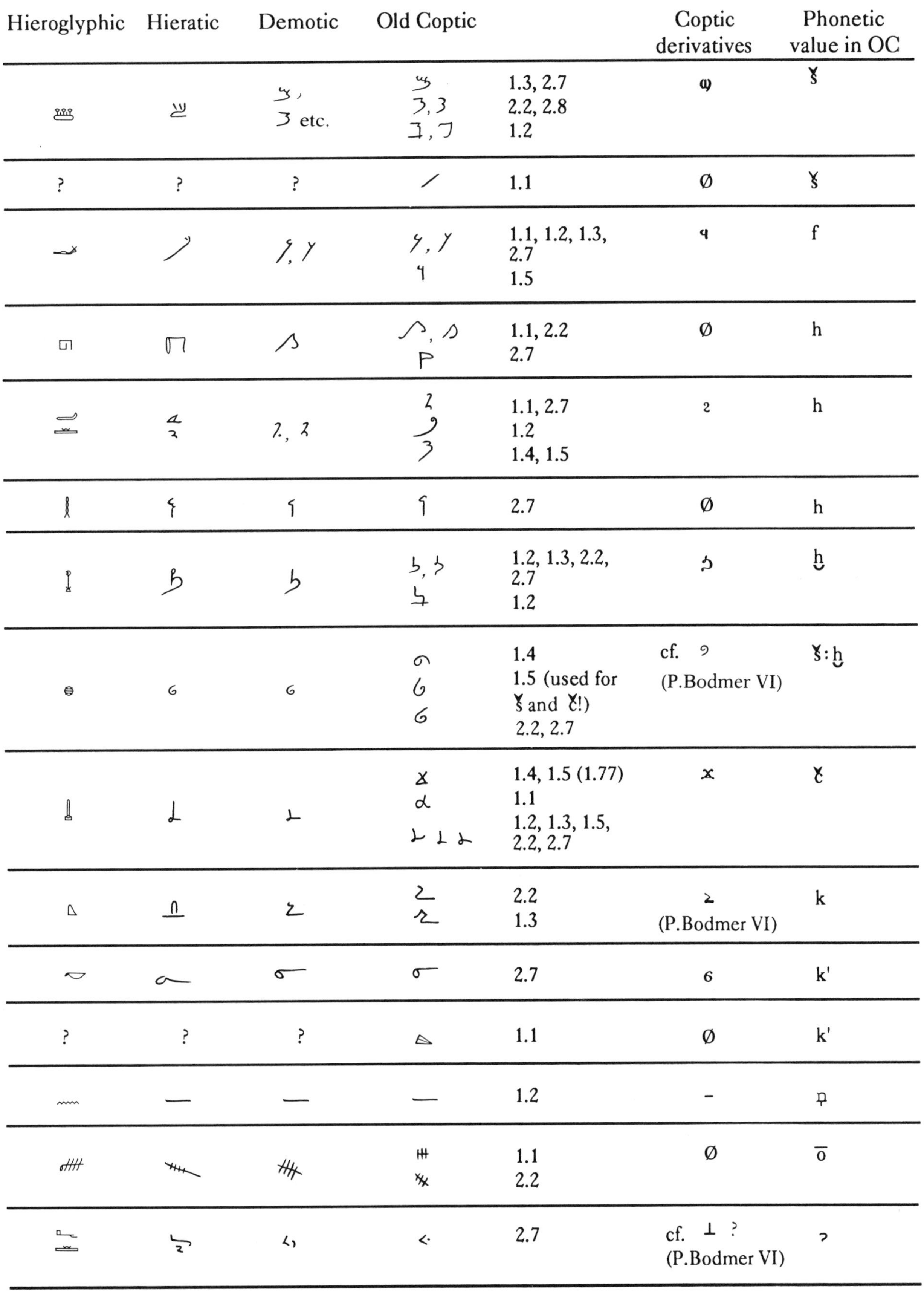
Hieroglyphic
Hieratic
Demotic
Old Coptic
Coptic derivatives
Phonetic value in OC
etc.
1.3, 2.7
2.2, 2.8
1.2
ϣ
?
?
?
1.1
Ø
1.1, 1.2, 1.3, 2.7
1.5
ϥ
f
1.1, 2.2
2.7
Ø
h
1.1, 2.7
1.2
1.4, 1.5
ϩ
h
2.7
Ø
h
1.2, 1.3, 2.2, 2.7
1.2
ϧ
1.4
1.5 (used for š and č!)
2.2, 2.7
cf.
(P.Bodmer VI)
1.4, 1.5 (1.77)
1.1
1.2, 1.3, 1.5, 2.2, 2.7
ϫ
č
2.2
1.3
(P.Bodmer VI)
k
2.7
ϭ
k'
?
?
?
1.1
Ø
k'
1.2
-
1.1
2.2
Ø
ō
2.7
cf.
(P.Bodmer VI)

FIGURE 1 PRINCIPAL OLD COPTIC SIGNS OF DEMOTIC ORIGIN. Numbers refer to the classification of texts given above.

trace of the *F* lambdacism. As regards vocalism, many words are provided with glosses, indicating variant dialect forms of words or parts of words. (The glosses are hardly corrections, as Erman [cf. Kammerer, 1950, no. 1759] calls them.) But neither the main text nor the glosses retain the same dialect. Even when a word is repeated, it may assume a different form—for example, ⲉⲭⲉⲛ ⲧⲓⲟⲧⲓ ⲧⲓⲁⲧⲉ, in the moment, the moment, ll. 121–22. In this way, three or four known dialects are indicated simultaneously (not to speak of forms that are alien to any known idiom): *B, S, L,* and perhaps *F.*

Examples of words of pure *B* phonology are (ⲁⲃ)ϭⲉⲛⲥ, (he) found her, l. 96; ⲧⲱⲟⲩⲛⲓ, rise, l. 106; ⲥⲁⲧⲓ, flame, ll. 114 and 115; ⲁïⲧⲟⲩ, to do them, ll. 116 and 117; ⲱⲟⲩ, glory, l. 127; cf. ⲑⲱⲩⲑ, Thoth, l. 139. Some words of pure *S* phonology are ⲧⲟⲟⲩ, mountain, l. 94; ϭⲟïϭ, dust, ll. 95 and 96; ⲑⲟⲟⲩⲧ, Thoth, ll. 96, 99, and 105; ⲉϭⲟⲩⲛ, in (adverb), l. 96; ⲁⲣⲟ⸗, what is the matter with, ll. 96 and 99; ⲟⲩⲟïⲛ, light, l. 142. Some words of pure *L* phonology are ïⲉⲧⲉ, your (fem.) eye, l. 98; ⲛ̄ⲙⲉⲟⲩ, there, l. 108 (ⲛ̄ presents both Coptic ⲙ̄ and ⲛ̄); ⲣⲉⲧ⸗, foot, l. 111; ⲥⲉⲧⲉ, flame, l. 114 (gloss); ⲥⲛⲉⲟⲩ, two, l. 140; ⲟⲩⲉ, one (masc.), l. 148. Some words indicate mixed features (*L* versus *S* and *B*): ⲉϭⲟⲙ, sigh, ll. 95, 97, and 115; ⲡⲉϭⲉⲥ, she said, l. 98. A few words appear in a form that is attested only in *F*: ⲛⲓⲃⲓ, every, ll. 115 and 116 (var. ⲛⲓⲃⲉ); ⲟⲩⲏï, to be remote (?), l. 151; ⲓⲙⲓ, to know, l. 151 (but ⲉⲙⲙⲓ, l. 130). But perhaps *F* (as well as *V* and *M*) has to be discarded, since none of its most characteristic features can be found (ⲗ for ⲣ; ⲏ for *B, S, L,* and *A* ⲉ; ⲏ for *B* ⲉ and for *S, L,* and *A* ∅). *ō* may appear as ⲟⲩ, but not only in the cases where *L* has ⲟⲩ: ïⲟⲩⲧ, father, ll. 95 (gloss), 99, 100, 104, and 105. It may appear as ⲟ, but not only in the cases where *M* has ⲟ: ⲥⲟ, to drink, l. 147. It may also appear as ⲟⲓ (no dieresis!): (ⲁⲃ)ⲟⲓ(ⲧ), Abydos, l. 107 (gloss); (ⲁⲭ)ⲟⲓ(ï), l. 114 (gloss); ⲉϭⲟⲓï, over me, l. 125; ⲃⲟⲓⲟⲓⲑ (gloss [ⲃ]ⲱⲱ[ⲑ]), l. 116; ⲕⲁⲧⲁⲕⲟⲓⲧⲓ (gloss [-ⲕ]ⲱⲧⲉ), l. 117; ⲉϭⲟⲓⲡⲉ, if, l. 147 *ter;* ⲟⲩⲟⲓⲙ, to eat, l. 147.

Summing up, it may be said that in ll. 97ff. an attempt was made to encompass several Coptic dialects simultaneously. It may be assumed that this was to serve a practical purpose. The individual reader should be placed in a position to be able to use the spells in his own vernacular idiom. It should be remembered that the text was most probably put down by a Greek compiler. If he found the source of the text written (or recited) in an Egyptian idiom other than the one(s) he was most familiar with, he may have changed it—partly in the main text and partly in the glosses, though retaining the original version. He may also have substituted vowel signs according to their sound values in contemporary Greek, if such differed from the Coptic graphic tradition (e.g., ⲟⲩ and ⲟⲓ, respectively, for Coptic ⲱ, thus indicating a pronunciation [o], not [ɔ], and [ø] (?), not [o], respectively).

Pre-Coptic Features

Because of their pagan background, OC texts employ many names, epithets, and terms that are not found in Coptic proper, such as ⲧⲃⲁⲓⲧⲱⲩ, who is on (his) mountain, an epithet of Anubis (Egyptian, *tpy-ḏw.f*); ⲥⲓ- or ⲥⲓ ⲛ-, son of (Egyptian, *z3, z3 n*); and ⲧⲏ, underworld (Egyptian, *d3t*). Apart from that, words are used that have become obsolete in standard Coptic, such as ⲁⲟⲉⲓⲙ, help 1.1, l.8 (Coptic ⲃⲟⲏⲑⲓⲁ); *ⲛⲓⲕⲉ (?), to copulate, 1.1, l.6 (Coptic, ⲣ̄-ⲛⲟⲉⲓⲕ); ⲙⲁⲟⲩⲥⲉ, liver (?), 1.5, l.117; ϭⲟï, rise (?, imperative), 1.5, ll.123, 138, etc.; ϭⲁϥ, strong, 1.5, l.15; ⲏⲟⲩ, limbs (?), 1.5, l.122; ⲡⲉⲉⲣ, enchant, 1.5, l.149–150); ⲕⲉⲡ-, fumigate, 1.4, l.665; ⲥⲟⲩⲛⲟⲩϥⲉ, good star (*sb3 nfr*), ⲥⲟⲩϧⲁⲛ (cf. demotic *ḫn*, prefer), agreeable (?) star, ⲥⲟⲩⲃⲱⲛ, evil star, ⲥⲟⲩϫⲁϫⲉ, hostile star, 1.2 passim; ⲁϩⲏϥ, ⲁϩⲉϥ (?), period of his life (?), 1.3 and 1.2, l.164). A conspicuous feature is the almost complete lack of Greek words. Exceptions are ⲁⲅⲅⲉⲗⲟⲥ, messenger, 1.5, l.16; and ⲁⲏⲣ, air, 1.5, l.23.

Other pre-Coptic features can be found in the morphology of the verb, such as residues of the demotic relative form (Haardt, 1963–1964; Satzinger, 1975, pp. 42f.) or the form –ⲡⲣⲧⲟⲩ-, before they, 1.3, l.153 (Coptic, ⲙ̄ⲡⲁⲧⲟⲩ-).

A rather strange feature is ⳁⲛⲟⲩ-, in (1.2, passim), since the *w* of Egyptian *m-ẖnw* had already been dropped in the second millennium B.C.; possibly the form is influenced by the *nw* sign of the traditional Egyptian spellings on a purely graphic level. Syntactic uses of a pre-Coptic nature in the London Horoscope Papyrus (1.2) include lack of an indefinite article (ⲁⲥ ⲓⲙⲉ ⲁϭⲱⲡⲉ ⲛⲁϥ, a woman shall be to him, third future, l.144); possessive use of suffix pronouns with a word like ϧⲣⲁ⸗, voice (l.141); and conditional construction ⲁϥϭⲱⲡⲉ ⲁ- (a construction found in Roman-period demotic). Nevertheless, the OC texts are definitely not transcriptions in OC script of demotic texts; their morphology and syntax are essentially Coptic.

BIBLIOGRAPHY

Bell, H. I.; A. D. Nock; and F. H. Thompson. "Magical Texts from a Bilingual Papyrus in the British

Museum, Edited with Translations, Commentary and Facsimile." *Proceedings of the British Academy* 17 (1931):235–86.

Černý, J.; P. E. Kahle; and R. Parker. "The Old Coptic Horoscope." *Journal of Egyptian Archaeology* 43 (1957):86–100.

Crum, W. E. "An Egyptian Text in Greek Characters." *Journal of Egyptian Archaeology* 28 (1942):20–31.

Griffith, F. L., and H. F. H. Thompson. *The Demotic Magical Papyrus of London and Leiden.* 3 vols. London, 1904–1909.

Haardt, R. "Versuch einer altkoptischen Grammatik" (Ph.D. diss., University of Vienna, 1949).

______. "Zum Gebrauch des präteritalen Relativums '-'r (ϵⲣ-) im Altkoptischen und Koptischen." *Wiener Zeitschrift für die Kunde des Morgenlandes* 57 (1961a):90–96.

______. "Das Tempus *w3ḥ=f sdm* im altkoptischen Text des Pariser Zauberpapyrus." *Wiener Zeitschrift für die Kunde des Morgenlandes* 57 (1961b):96–97.

______. "Residuale Relativformen im Altkoptischen." *Wiener Zeitschrift für die Kunde des Morgenlandes* 59/60 (1963–1964):95–98.

Johnson, J. H. "The Demotic Magical Spells of Leiden I 384." *Oudheidkundige Mededelingen uit het Rijksmuseum van Oudheden te Leiden* 56 (1975):29–64.

______. "Louvre E 3229: A Demotic Magical Text." *Enchoria* 7 (1977):55–102.

Kahle, P. E. *Bala'izah: Coptic Texts from Deir el-Bala'izah in Upper Egypt.* Oxford and London, 1954.

Kammerer, W. *A Coptic Bibliography,* esp. pp. 100–101. Ann Arbor, Mich., 1950.

Kasser, R. "Papyrus Londiniensis 98 (the Old Coptic Horoscope) and Papyrus Bodmer VI." *Journal of Egyptian Archaeology* 49 (1963):157–60.

______. "Prolégomènes à un essai de classification systématique des dialectes et subdialectes coptes selon les critères de la phonétique, I, Principes et terminologie." *Muséon* 93 (1980):53–112.

Kasser, R., and H. Satzinger. "L'idiome du p. Mich. 5421 (trouvé à Karanis, nord-est du Fayoum)." *Wiener Zeitschrift für die Kunde des Morgenlandes* 74 (1982):15–32.

Mallon, A. *Grammaire copte, bibliographie, chrestomathie et vocabulaire,* 4th ed., rev. M. Malinine, esp. pp. 288–89. Beirut, 1956.

Morenz, S. "Das Koptische." In *Ägyptische Sprache und Schrift.* Handbuch der Orientalistik I/I/1. Leiden and Cologne, 1959; 2nd ed., 1973, p. 92.

Osing, J. *Der spätägyptische Papyrus BM 10808.* Wiesbaden, 1976.

______. "The Dialect of Oxyrhynchus." *Enchoria* 8 (Sonderband) (1978):29*(75)–(82)36*.

______. "Ein spàthieratisches Ostrakon aus Tebtunis." *Studien zur altägyptischer Kultur,* Beihefte, 3 (1989):183–87.

Preisendanz, K. *Papyri graecae magicae, die griechischen Zauberpapyri,* Vol. 1. Leipzig, 1928; 2nd ed., rev. A. Henrichs, Coptic texts by G. Möller, Stuttgart, 1973.

Quaegebeur, J. "De la préhistoire de l'écriture copte." *Orientalia Lovaniensia Periodica* 13 (1982):125–36.

Roeder, G. *Der Ausklang der ägyptischen Religion mit Reformation, Zauberei und Jenseitsglaube,* Zurich, 1961.

Stazinger, H. "The Old Coptic Schmidt Papyrus." *Journal of the American Research Center in Egypt* 12 (1975):37–50.

______. "Die altkoptischen Texte als Zeugnisse der Beziehungen zwischen Ägyptern und Griechen." In *Graeco-Coptica,* ed. Peter Nagel, pp. 137–46. Wissenschaftliche Beiträge der Martin-Luther-Universität Halle-Wittenberg. Halle-Wittenberg, 1984.

Steindorff, G. *Lehrbuch der koptischen Grammatik,* esp. pp. 2–3. Chicago, 1951.

Vergote, J. *Grammaire copte,* Vol. 1b, *Introduction, phonétique et phonologie, morphologie synthématique (structure des sémantèmes), partie diachronique,* esp. pp. 12–13. Louvain, 1973.

Worrell, W. H. "Notice of a Second-Century Text in Coptic Letters." *American Journal of Semitic Languages and Literatures* 58 (1941):84–90.

For further references, see especially Kammerer, 1950.

HELMUT SATZINGER

PALEOGRAPHY. Paleography, the science of the critical analysis of ancient scripts, not only makes it possible to read, date, and fix the provenance of documents produced by scribes but also draws out other information of extreme value for the knowledge of the history of culture. In analyzing ancient scripts critically, one has to trace the history of graphic forms and to determine all the special features that characterize the individual scripts, thus making it possible to classify them by age, origin, and function.

Furthermore, this science also includes the study of the materials with which the scribes did their work (and how they used them), such as ink, calamus (reed pen), and the medium on which the text is written. This last would include (a) pliant material, like papyrus, parchment (seldom leather), and (later) paper; (b) rigid materials, such as wood (for mummy labels), potsherds of terra-cotta when suitable (ostraca), and flaked stone of appropriate quality or shape (ostraca); (c) stone or terra-cotta from which a stela or a dedicatory, commemorative, or funerary inscription could be made; (d) the rock wall of a tomb or the like with some inscription carved on it; and (e) an adequately smooth, brightly polished coating of mortar on a wall, representing a whitish surface on which some text or other has been traced on with a brush.

When the medium is a material sufficiently pliable and appropriate (papyrus, parchment, etc.) to take a literary text, either as a scroll, or *volumen* (but this is uncommon in Coptology), or as a book, or *codex* (almost always in fact), modern paleography cannot fail to base its findings on those of at least one accessory discipline. For example, codicology analyzes the various processes of codex manufacture, whether as a single quire or as several gathered quires, and studies the way in which the folios were sewn into quires and the quires were sewn together. Codicology also examines such features as the quality of the thread that was used to sew the quires, the presence or absence of tabs, and the binding.

It is easy to understand that the philological study of the Coptic language and its literature (not to mention everything relative to Coptic history) must be based on a chronology of the manuscripts and other written documents that is as precise as possible. However, despite these desiderata, despite the worthy efforts of isolated researchers who edited newly discovered texts and who drew mostly on Greek paleography to resolve the problems encountered case by case, and despite the more systematic efforts of the few Coptologists who have attempted to arrive at a unified view of Coptic writings as a foundation for paleography, at least in outline, this science is still far from reaching the maturity needed to satisfy the most demanding among specialized users. All Coptologists recognize this one fact: Coptic paleography is still a new field.

At the present time, Coptologists have at their disposal three monographs on Coptic paleography. Each one has been more or less useful. They will be reviewed hereafter in chronological order.

As clearly indicated by the title of his work, Hyvernat (1888) never made any attempt to cover the entire field of documents written in Coptic. Therefore, he should not be blamed for giving only one manuscript from the fourth or fifth century (which he placed, moreover, in the sixth) or for providing a very substantial number of specimens dating from the sixth century to the eighteenth century, which most often were produced in beautiful full-page plates. His plates show complete pages of the manuscripts (and thus naturally take up whole pages in his publication). Further, unlike more modern paleographers, Hyvernat never worked properly by analyzing the details of the various scripts; he merely presented and rapidly identified manuscripts he was interested in.

As the length of its title indicates, the work of Stegemann (1936) was a great deal more ambitious (even though in his foreword he gave a very modest estimate indeed of the value of his work). Stegemann tried to include the whole field of strictly Coptic writing in his analysis. He studied both literary scripts and documentary ones, from the earliest uncertain beginnings of Coptic (third century) through the start of its decline (eleventh century) to its death as a living language (fourteenth century). Taking into consideration both the available manuscripts and the state of Greek paleography when Stegemann wrote, one must recognize that this worthy paleographer mostly achieved his goals. Even though some of his conclusions, deductions, and classifications of writing styles might now be contested, no one can deny that he did sterling service for Coptology and that his work is still of substantial use. His *Koptische Paläographie* remains a necessary reference tool for researchers and will continue to be so as long as Coptology remains without a more effective, fully developed working tool, the product of a modern paleographer expert in Greek and Latin and familiar with discoveries made in these various fields since 1936.

On the one hand, Stegemann compared Coptic manuscripts from the third century to the eighth (which never expressly give their dates) with contemporary Greek manuscripts, thus producing a Coptic paleographic chronology much less rough-and-ready than Hyvernat's. On the other hand, specimens of Coptic dated (by colophons) are to be found from the ninth century onward, and this enables the paleographer to establish his chronology on a more dependable basis. Simultaneously he tried to analyze and to follow the successive Coptic writing styles in their development. Modern scholars may now censure his tendency to analyze isolated graphemes and to compare them with one another. When he gave more extensive samples, they were nothing more than small rectangles cut out from the middle of a manuscript page. The above-mentioned limitations were the results of inadequate resources for the production of his edition, rather than of his free choice of a particular working principle. That same kind of constraint is naturally experienced by any compiler of contributions to encyclopedias, which explains why this article is also illustrated by extracts from pages rather than whole pages, as is frequently the case in Hyvernat (1888) and Cramer (1964), despite the undoubted fact that a scribe's handwriting would be much better studied on a whole page. But one must admit that despite these limitations and constraints, Stegemann made the most of the material he sought to organize.

The same cannot be said about the monograph on Coptic paleography by Cramer (1964). Failing to assimilate the progress made in this field after 1936 and too often providing inadequately checked information, this work has not fulfilled Coptologists' needs; thus, it has been rather disappointing (cf. M. Krause, 1966, an extremely circumstantial report on this subject).

The present article makes no attempt to present a complete survey of the state of Coptic paleography. It is written merely for those of the educated public at large who want to know about the many facets of Coptic civilization in all its brilliance, pending the publication of more-specialized studies. Medieval or Byzantine Coptic writing, which is beautiful even simply as a majuscule script (capitals) and is sometimes, in later periods, illuminated, represents an important mark of civilization to which the reader's attention must without fail be drawn. Without this, one would have an incomplete, distorted view of this culture.

From the time when Coptic (as the latest form of the Egyptian language) adopted all the signs of the Greek alphabet, augmented by a few additional symbols borrowed from demotic script (cf. ALPHABET IN COPTIC, GREEK; ALPHABETS, COPTIC; LANGUAGE(S), COPTIC), this language expressed itself through the graphic styles specific to Greek writing during late antiquity. Two graphic styles in particular were employed for Coptic (at least for writing books and formal documents): biblical majuscule, or capital letters (see figures 1c, 2a, 2b, 3b, and 4b); and Alexandrian majuscule. Within those two styles of script, two kinds are distinguishable: first, script in letters of uniform character (see figures 2c, 3c, and 4a), and, second, script in letters of contrasted character, wherein broad and narrow graphemes are both found (see figures 5a, 5b, and 5c).

A phenomenon even more peculiar to Coptic graphic usages, although occasionally found in other texts (Greek or bilingual), is the existence of mixed types of script that are a kind of compromise between biblical majuscule and Alexandrian majuscule (see figures 3a and 4c). Other graphic styles borrowed from Greek script can be found (see figures 1a and 1b). Here, however, discussion can suitably be confined to standard categories and fundamental phenomena.

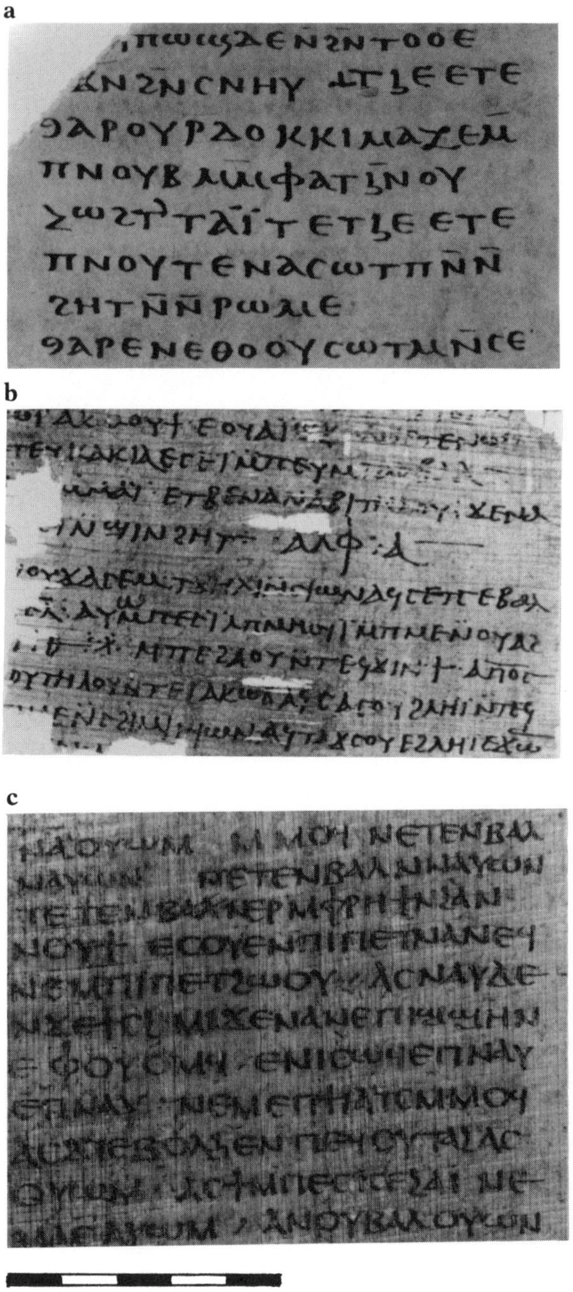

FIGURE 1. **(a)** THIRD–FOURTH CENTURY: P. BODMER VI (PARCHMENT). Published by Kasser (1960). Dialect: *P*. **(b)** THIRD–FOURTH CENTURY: P.BIL. 1 OF HAMBURG (PAPYRUS). Published by Diebner and Kasser (1989). Dialect: *F7*. **(c)** FOURTH CENTURY: P. BODMER III (PAPYRUS). Published by Kasser (1958). Dialect: *B4* with *B74* (idiolectal mixture; see DIALECT, SPORADIC and IDIOLECT). Scale bar = 5 cm. *Courtesy Rodolphe Kasser.*

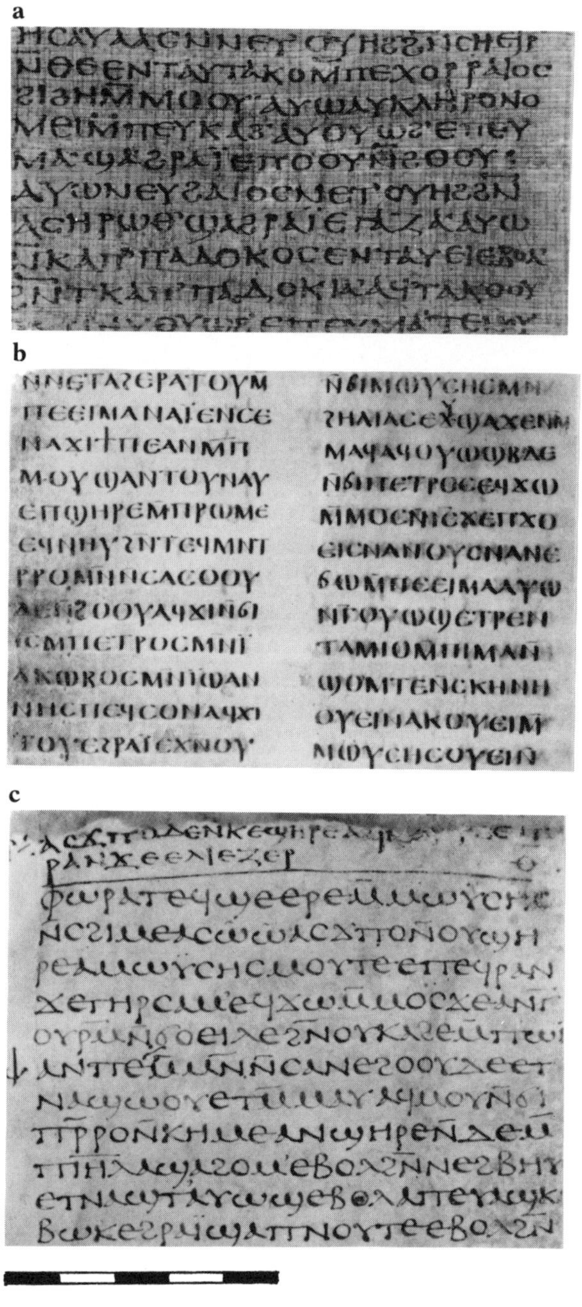

FIGURE 2. **(a)** FOURTH CENTURY: P. BODMER XVIII (PAPYRUS). Published by Kasser (1962a). Language: *S.* **(b)** FIFTH CENTURY: P. BODMER XIX (PARCHMENT). Published by Kasser (1962b). Language: *S.* **(c)** LATE FIFTH CENTURY: P. BODMER XVI (PARCHMENT). Published by Kasser (1961). Language: *S.* Scale bar = 5 cm. *Courtesy Rodolphe Kasser.*

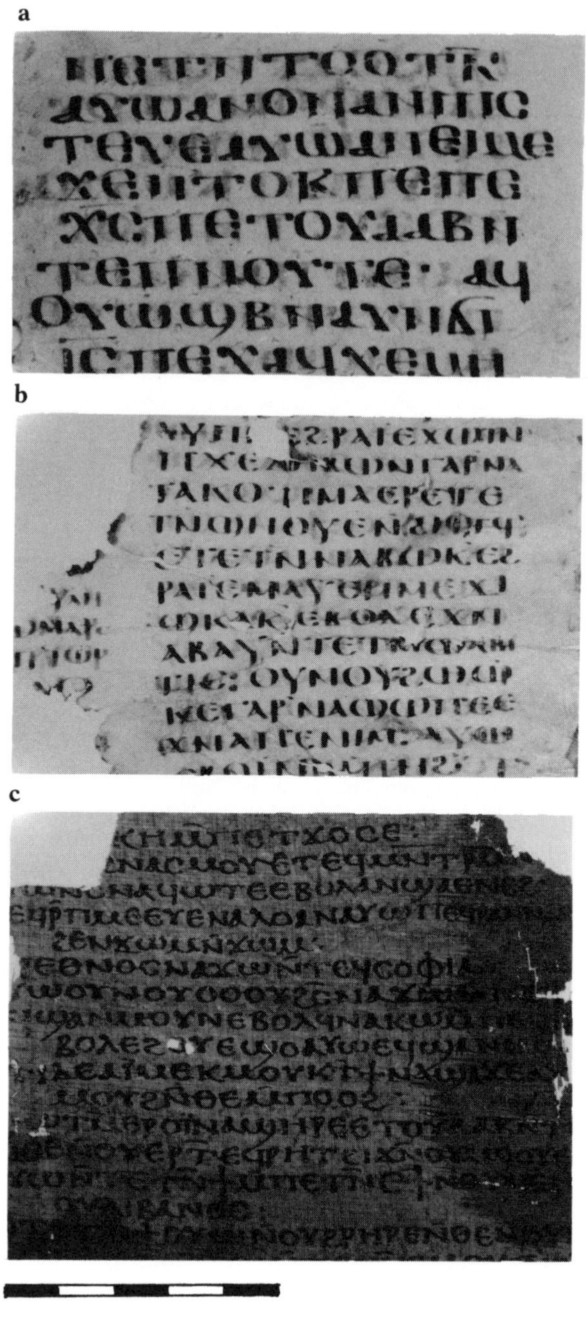

FIGURE 3. **(a)** SIXTH CENTURY: VIENNA K. 15 (PARCHMENT). Published by Wessely (1911), and photograph in Cavallo, 1967, pl. 104. Language: *S.* **(b)** SIXTH CENTURY: VIENNA K. 2713 (PARCHMENT). Published by Till (1937). Language: *S.* **(c)** SIXTH–SEVENTH CENTURY: B.M.OR. 5984 (PAPYRUS). Published by Thompson (1908). Language: *S.* Scale bar = 5 cm. *Courtesy Rodolphe Kasser.*

Any attempt to date Coptic scripts by comparing them to Greek scripts raises quite a critical problem. This approach, which may have seemed at first glance the obvious one and which Stegemann (1936) raised to the rank of methodological principle, can hold its own when applied to bilingual (Greek and Coptic) manuscripts. But with manuscripts written

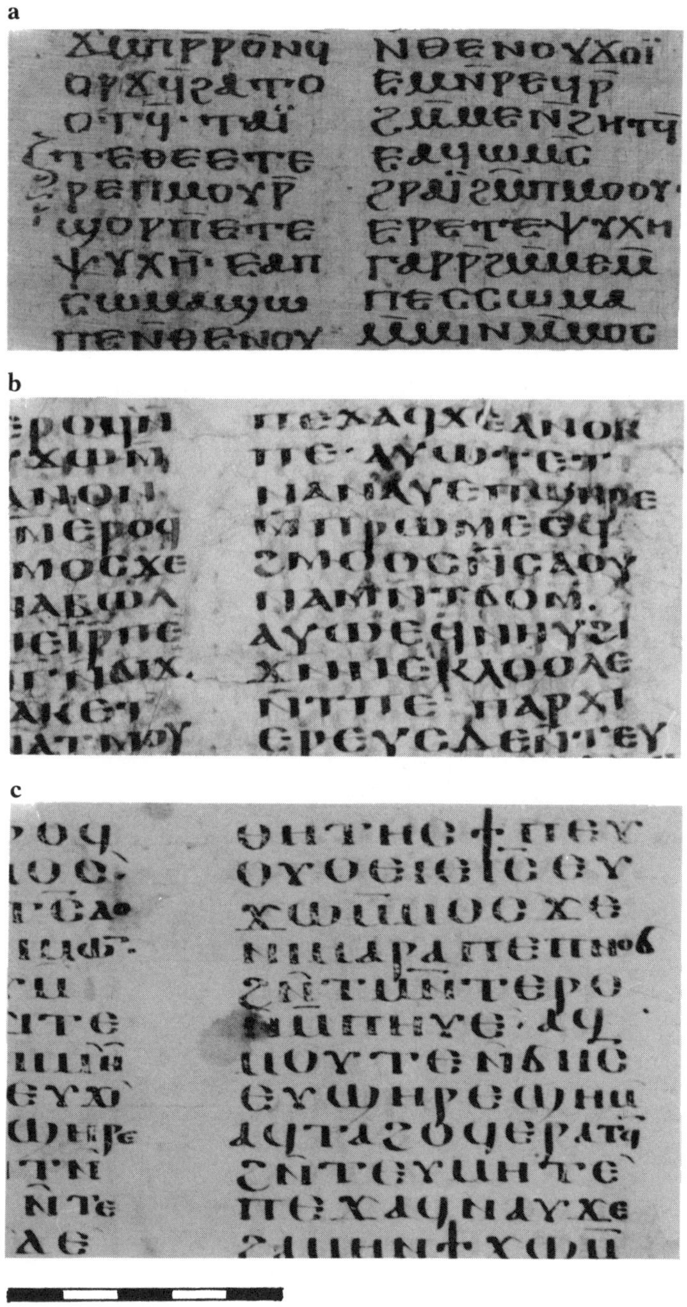

FIGURE 4. **(a)** SEVENTH CENTURY: B.M.OR. 5001 (PAPYRUS). Published by Budge (1910). Language: *S.* **(b)** SEVENTH CENTURY: VIENNA K. 9095 (PARCHMENT). Published by Wessely (1912). Language: *S.* **(c)** EIGHTH CENTURY: VIENNA K. 9062 (PARCHMENT). Published by Wessely (1911). Language: *S.* Scale bar = 5 cm. *Courtesy Rodolphe Kasser.*

only in Coptic, one should be very cautious when making such comparisons. Kahle (1954, Vol. 1, pp. 260–61) rightly noted that "texts which can be dated either on external evidence . . . or on the basis of Greek texts in the same manuscripts . . . reveal a rather different picture from that which we obtain from early Coptic manuscripts which have been dated purely on the basis of Coptic supported by Greek paleography."

Indeed, one finds that in Coptic practice Greek scripts appear as a borrowed element and are frequently related diachronically to the same scripts evolving in Greek usage, so a Coptic script that possesses the same graphic characteristics as a Greek

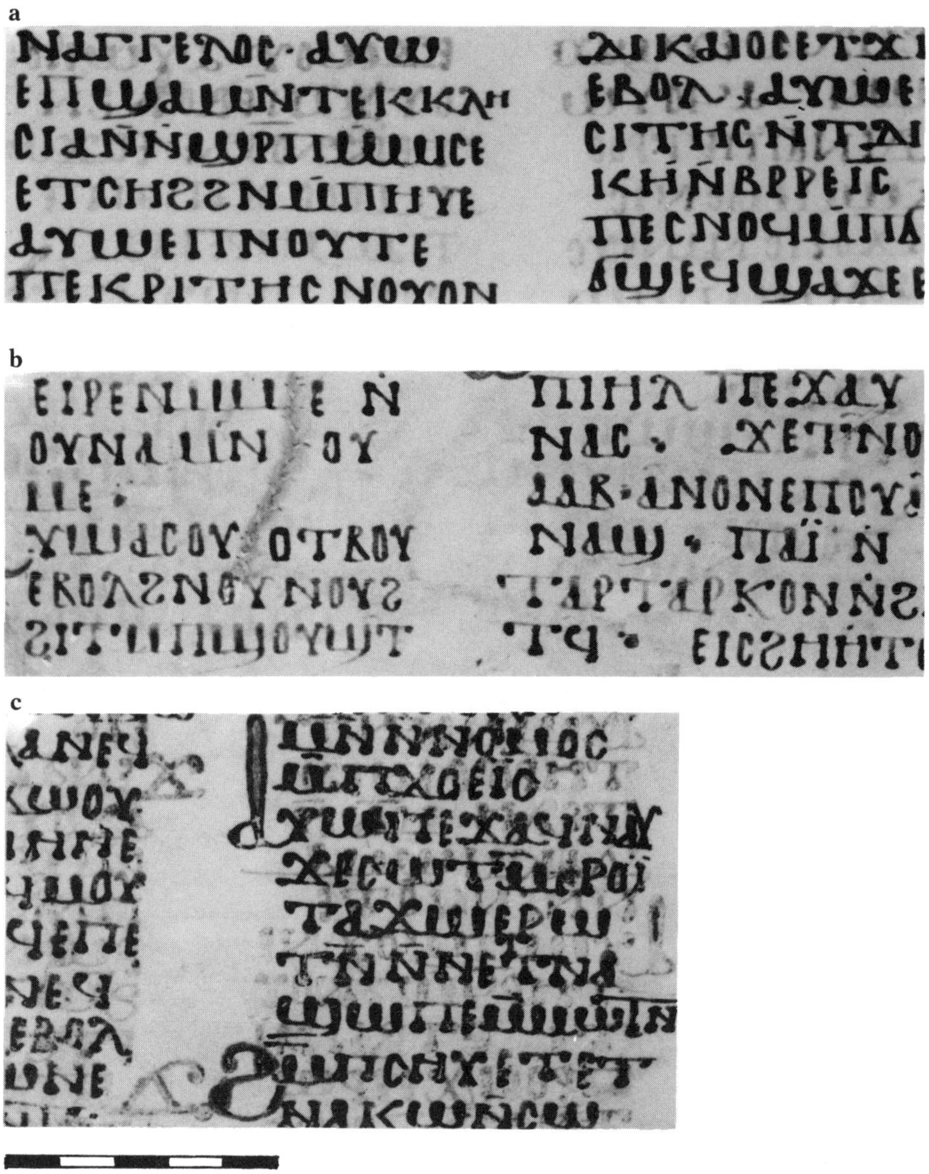

FIGURE 5. **(a)** NINTH CENTURY: VIENNA K. 9791 (FORMERLY K. 9712) (PARCHMENT). Published by Wessely (1912). Language: *S.* **(b)** TENTH CENTURY: VIENNA K. 9390 (PARCHMENT). Published by Wessely (1914). Language: *S.* **(c)** ELEVENTH CENTURY: VIENNA K. 9761 (PARCHMENT). Published by Campagnano (1985). Language: *S.* Scale bar = 5 cm. *Courtesy Rodolphe Kasser.*

one may nevertheless be of clearly later date. It is possible in this way to explain the contradictions noted by Kahle with their attendant substantial risk that some perspectives may not be correct. Moreover, various hybrids were created by the Copts as they developed many types of script, each of which united characteristics borrowed from several kinds of Greek scripts (especially by mixing biblical and Alexandrian majuscules). This makes a whole series of comparisons and additional contrasts necessary when discussing "mixed" materials of this kind, where the two types of script are present at the same time. As mentioned above, this is especially relevant to the script in books. But clearly, in working out a complete Coptic paleography, it will be essential to examine also the documentary (that is, in some sense informal) scripts—an undertaking beyond the scope of the present encyclopedia.

To enhance the understanding of the above observations, the author has thought it useful to include

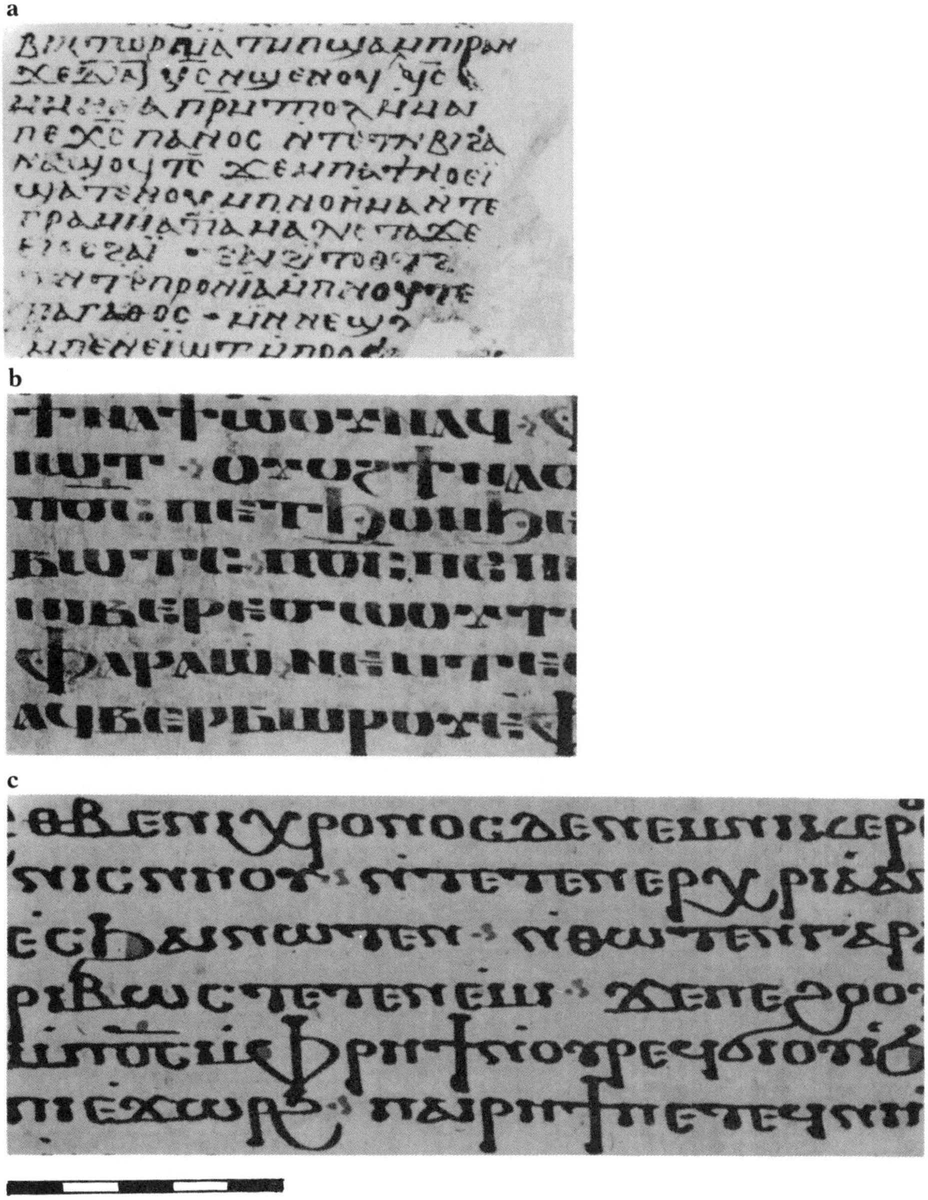

FIGURE 6. **(a)** TWELFTH CENTURY (A.D. 1112): B.M.OR. 3581B(69) (PARCHMENT). Published by Crum (1905). Language: *S*. **(b)** TWELFTH–THIRTEENTH CENTURY: VATICAN COPT. 5 (PARCHMENT). Unpublished. Language: *B5*. **(c)** FOURTEENTH CENTURY (A.D. 1339): PARIS COPT. 21 (PAPER). Unpublished. Language: *B*. Scale bar = 5 cm. *Courtesy Rodolphe Kasser.*

herein some specimens of Coptic majuscules, while making a very limited selection from what was available and abandoning any attempt to give the reader a complete range of paleography. These specimens, without paleographic comments, are in chronological order. Although restricted, this will constitute a useful visual basis for what could be a small album of Coptic paleography in outline.

Those who need to investigate the subject in a more thorough way should consult Stegemann (1936) and (mostly for medieval manuscripts) Hyvernat (1888), but in view of their relative age they should be handled with caution. Moreover, there is important systematic information in Till (1940) on the Coptic biblical parchments of the Austrian National Library in Vienna; and in Kahle (1954, pp. 269–78) can be found a list of all the Coptic manuscripts from the third–fifth centuries known at that date. However, it must be noted that Till's work is not illustrated, and Kahle's, poorly so.

Finally, it is important not to neglect Greek paleographies, among them the chief production of a scholar working particularly in Greek and Greco-Latin paleography and now entering the Coptic paleographic field, G. Cavallo (1967 and 1975).

A great deal of complementary information may be gleaned from numerous Coptic text editions illustrated by photographic plates or by other plates of the same quality, although the dating systems proposed by such different authors cannot be used without extreme caution. Even if one does not consider the real possibility of varying quality levels in the information provided, each author has his own personal tendencies concerning the importance given to the various criteria and his own paleographic sensitivity. Consequently, the accumulation of all these isolated dates is far from constituting a coherent whole and is useful only within the broad outline of a relative chronology.

In the following list, which is no more than a selection of what seems to be most significant, the editions giving the complete photographic reproduction of a manuscript are marked by an asterisk. Such editions are certainly the most useful in every way, paleographically and otherwise, for they not only preserve entirely such fragile witnesses from further destruction but also permit each researcher to check on the details in which he is most interested and which might have been left out of account by the author of the editio princeps.

In order not to encumber the bibliography below with too many items, all the titles that can be found in *A Coptic Bibliography* (Kammerer, 1950) are excluded and only the names of the authors in alphabetical order and the year of publication appear here, followed by the number in parentheses assigned by Kammerer, now standard: Allberry, 1938 (1665); [Böhlig and Polotsky], 1940 (1700); Böhlig, *[1963]; Budge, 1910 (1097) and 1912 (775); Ciasca and Balestri, 1885–1904 (779; has numerous plates of excellent quality that reproduce full pages of medieval manuscripts); Crum, 1893 (718), 1905 (147), 1909 (170), and 1926 (749); Daumas et al., 1969; Farid et al. *1972–1979; Hall, 1905 (1907); Husselman, 1962; Hyvernat, *1922 (726); Kasser, 1958, 1960, *1961, *1962a, *1962b, *1963, *1964, and *1965; Kasser et al., 1972, *1973, *1975; Leroy, 1974; Malinine et al., *1956, *1963, and *1968; Michałowski, 1965; Monneret de Villard, 1933 (1980); Orlandi, 1974a–b; Plumley, *1975; Polotsky, 1934 (1693); Quecke, 1972, 1977, and 1984; Satzinger, 1967–1968; Schenke, 1981; Schiller, 1973; Schmidt, *1904 (1033), 1908 (1140), and 1919 (1094); Thompson, 1908 (810) and *1924 (980); Wessely, 1915 (890); Worrell, 1923 (751) and 1931 (869); Zoega, 1810 (753).

A selection mainly from idioms other than classical Sahidic (*S*) and Bohairic (*B*) includes the following: *A*: Böhlig *[1963]; Schmidt, 1908 (1140) and 1919 (1994). *B* (prior to the eighth century): Daumas et al., 1969; Kasser et al., 1972. *B74*: Kasser, 1958; *F*: Hyvernat, *1922. *L4*: Allberry, 1938 (1665); [Böhlig and Polotsky], 1940 (1700); Polotsky, 1934 (1693). *L5*: Thompson, *1924 (980). *L6*: Kasser et al., *1973 and *1975; Malinine et al., *1956, *1963, and *1968. *M*: Orlandi, 1974; Schenke, 1981. *P*: Kasser, 1960. *W*: Husselman, 1962 (see DIALECTS; LANGUAGE(S), COPTIC).

A variety of illustrated complementary paleographic information can be found in various articles in journals giving space to Coptology (e.g., *Bulletin de l'Institut français d'archéologie orientale. Bulletin of the American Society of Papyrologists, Bulletin de la Société d'archéologie copte, Enchoria, Journal of Coptic Studies, Journal of Egyptian Archeology,* and *Le Muséon*).

The parts of manuscripts reproduced in the six figures here are published with the kind permission of their respective owners, to whom the author tenders warmest thanks: the Vatican Apostolic Library in Vatican City; the National Library in Paris, France; the Martin Bodmer Foundation in Cologny/Geneva, Switzerland; the British Library in London, England; the Austrian National Library in Vienna; and the State and University Library in Hamburg, West Germany.

BIBLIOGRAPHY

Böhlig, A. *Proverbien-Kodex.* Leipzig [1963].

Budge, E. A. T. W. *Coptic Homilies in the Dialect of Upper Egypt, Edited from the Papyrus Codex Oriental 5001 in the British Museum.* London, 1910.

Campagnano, A. *Preliminary Editions of Coptic Codices, MONB.GB, Life of Manasses, Encomium of Moses, Encomium of Abraham.* Unione Accademica Nazionale, Corpus dei manoscritti copti letterari, Centro Italiano Microfiches. Rome, 1985.

Cavallo, G. *Ricerche sulla maiuscola biblica.* Florence, 1967.

———. "Γράμματα ἀλεξανδρῖνα." *Jahrbuch der österreichischen Byzantinistik* 24 (1975):23–54.

Cramer, M. *Koptische Paläographie.* Wiesbaden, 1964.

Crum, W. E. *Catalogue of the Coptic Manuscripts in the British Museum.* London, 1905.

Daumas, F.; A. Guillaumont; J.-C. Garcin; J. Jarry; B. Boyaval; R. Kasser; J.-C. Goyon; J.-L. Despagne; B. Lentheric; and J. Schruoffeneger. *Kellia I, kôm*

219, fouilles effectuées en 1964 et 1965. Cairo, 1969.

Diebner, B. J.; R. Kasser; A. M. Kropp; C. Voigt; and E. Lucchesi. *Hamburger Papyrus Bil. l. Die alttestamentlichen Texte des Papyrus bilinguis l der Staats- und Universitätsbibliothek Hamburg. Canticum Canticorum (coptice), Lamentationes Ieremiae (coptice), Ecclesiastes (graece et coptice)*. Cahiers d'orientalisme 18. Geneva, 1989.

Farid, S.; G. Garitte; V. Girgis; S. Giversen; A. Guillaumont; R. Kasser; M. Krause; P. Labib; G. Mehrez; G. Moktar; H.-C. Puech; G. Quispel; J. M. Robinson; H.-M. Schenke; T. Säve-Söderbergh; and R. McL. Wilson. *The Facsimile Edition of the Nag Hammadi Codices*. Leiden, 1972–1979.

Husselman, E. M. *The Gospel of John in Fayumic Coptic (P. Mich. Inv. 3521)*. Ann Arbor, Mich., 1962.

Hyvernat, H. *Album de paléographie copte pour servir à l'introduction paléographique des Actes des martyrs de l'Egypte*. Paris and Rome, 1888.

Kahle, P. E. *Bala'izah: Coptic Texts from Deir el-Bala'izah in Upper Egypt*. Oxford and London, 1954.

Kammerer, W., *A Coptic Bibliography*. Ann Arbor, Mich., 1950.

Kasser, R. *Papyrus Bodmer III: Evangile de Jean et Genèse I–IV,2 en bohaïrique*. CSCO 177–178. Louvain, 1958.

______. *Papyrus Bodmer VI: livre des Proverbes*. CSCO 194–195. Louvain, 1960.

______. *Papyrus Bodmer XVI: Exode I–XV,21 en sahidique*. Geneva, 1961.

______. *Papyrus Bodmer XVIII: Deutéronome I–X,7 en sahidique*. Geneva, 1962a.

______. *Papyrus Bodmer XIX: Évangile de Matthieu, XIV,28–XXVIII,20, Épître aux Romains I,2–II,3, en sahidique*. Geneva, 1962b.

______. *Papyrus Bodmer XXI: Josué VI,16–25, VII,6–IX,23, XXII,1–2, 19–XXIII,7,15–XXIV,23, en sahidique*. Geneva, 1963.

______. *Papyrus Bodmer XXII et Mississippi Coptic Codex II: Jérémie XL,3–LII,34, Lamentations, Epître de Jérémie, Baruch I,1–V,5, en sahidique*. Geneva, 1964.

______. *Papyrus Bodmer XXIII: Esaïe XLVII–LXVI en sahidique*. Geneva, 1965.

Kasser, R., ed. *Kellia, topographie*. Recherches suisses d'archéologie copte 2. Geneva, 1972.

Kasser, R.; M. Malinine; H.-C. Puech; G. Quispel; J. Zandee; W. Vycichl; and R. McL. Wilson. *Tractatus Tripartitus, Pars I, De Supernis, Codex Jung f. XXVI r.–f. LII v. (p. 51–104)*. Bern, 1973.

______. *Tractatus Tripartitus, Pars II, De Creatione Hominis, Pars III, De Generibus Tribus, Codex Jung f. LII v.–LXX v. (p. 104–140)*. Bern, 1975.

Krause, M. Review of M. Cramer, *Koptische Paläographie*. *Bibliotheca Orientalis* 23 (1966):286–93.

Leroy, J. *Les Manuscrits coptes et coptes-arabes illustrés*. Paris, 1974.

Malinine, M.; H.-C. Puech; and G. Quispel. *Evangelium Veritatis, Codex Jung f. VIII v.–XVI v. (p. 16–32), f. XIX r.–XXII r. (p. 37–43)*. Zurich, 1956.

Malinine, M.; H.-C. Puech; G. Quispel; W. C. Till; R. McL. Wilson; and J. Zandee. *De Resurrectione (Epistula ad Rheginum), Codex Jung f. XXII r.–f. XXV v. (p. 43–50)*. Zurich, 1963.

Malinine, M.; H.-C. Puech; G. Quispel; W. C. Till; R. Kasser; R. McL. Wilson; and J. Zandee. *Epistula Iacobi Apocrypha, Codex Jung f. I r.–f. VIII v. (p. 1–16)*. Zurich, 1968.

Michałowski, K. *Faras, fouilles polonaises 1961–1962, avec des contributions de T. Dzierżykray-Rogalski, S. Jakobielski, H. Jędrzejewska, Wł. Kubiak, M. Marciniak*. Warsaw, 1965.

Orlandi, T. *Koptische Papyri theologischen Inhalts*. Vienna, 1974a.

______. *Papiri della Università degli Studi di Milano (P. Mil. Copti)*, Vol. 5, *Lettere di San Paolo in copto-ossirinchita, edizione, commento e indici di Tito Orlandi, contributo linguistico di H. Quecke*. Milan, 1974b.

Plumley, J. M. *The Scrolls of Bishop Timotheos: Two Documents from Medieval Nubia*. London, 1975.

Quecke, H. *Das Markusevangelium saidisch: Text der Handschrift PPalau Rib. Inv.-Nr. 182 mit den Varianten der Handschrift M 569*. Barcelona, 1972.

______. *Das Lukasevangelium saidisch: Text der Handschrift PPalau Rib. Inv.-Nr. 181 mit den Varianten der Handschrift M 569*. Barcelona, 1977.

______. *Das Johannesevangelium saidisch: Text der Handschrift PPalau Rib. Inv.-Nr. 183 mit den Varianten der Handschriften 813 und 814 der Chester Beatty Library und der Handschrift M 569*. Rome and Barcelona, 1984.

Satzinger, H. *Koptische Urkunden, III*. 2 vols. Berlin, 1967–1968.

Schenke, H.-M. *Das Matthäus-Evangelium im mittelägyptischen Dialekt des Koptischen (Codex Scheide)*. Texte und Untersuchungen zur Geschichte der altchristlichen Literatur 127. Berlin, 1981.

Schiller, A. A. *Ten Coptic Legal Texts*. New York, 1973.

Stegemann, V. *Koptische Paläographie: 25 Tafeln zur Veranschaulichung der Schreibstile koptischer Schriftdenkmäler auf Papyrus, Pergament und Papier für die Zeit des III.–XIV. Jahrhunderts, mit einem Versuch einer Stilgeschichte der koptischen Schrift*. Heidelberg, 1936.

Thompson, H. *The Coptic (Sahidic) Version of Certain Books of the Old Testament, from a Papyrus in the British Museum*. London, 1908.

Till, W. C. "Saidische Fragmente des Alten Testamentes". *Muséon* 50 (1937):175–237.

Wessely, K. *Griechische und koptische Texte theologischen Inhalts II, III, IV*. IX., XII., XV. Studien zur

Palaeographie und Papyruskunde. Leipzig, 1911, 1912, 1914.

RODOLPHE KASSER

PHONOLOGY. In Coptic, as in any other language, it is vital to distinguish carefully between phonology and phonetics. According to Dubois (1973, p. 373), "Phonetics studies the sounds of language in their concrete realization, independently of their linguistic function." Phonetics is thus a science concerned with a phenomenon purely material and physical, and therefore measurable by means of instruments of physics, sensitive and especially adapted for this delicate task. Consequently, phonetics does not treat the semantic use of these sounds or of their combinations; it is concerned neither with their signification nor with the message they take part in expressing.

On the other hand, "phonology is the science that studies the sounds of language from the point of view of their function in the system of linguistic communication. It studies the phonic elements that distinguish, within one and the same language, two messages of different meaning" (ibid., p. 375). Thus, in English, for instance, it is only the difference between the phonemes /d/ and /t/ that distinguishes the two words, entirely different in meaning, "doodle" (scrawl) and "tootle" (toot repeatedly). Of course, both of these words could be pronounced in a great many different ways and with nuances that may be studied, measured, or defined, according to the speaker's linguistic habits or to the conditions in which he pronounces them at any given time (local, dialectal, personal habits, or possibly the pronunciation arising from a physical malformation, an occasional cold, a broken tooth, a mouth full of food, a state of fatigue making for negligent elocution, and so on). Yet, on the phonological level, these nuances are in no way taken into account: each of these two words is subject to but a single interpretation, /'du:dl/ and /'tu:tl/, respectively. Practically speaking, whatever the speaker's accent (provincial, negligent, or obstructed, within certain limits), the listener will usually decode the message in the same way.

In ALPHABETS, COPTIC, the synoptic table gives (on the extreme left) the phonological value of the various Coptic graphemes, a value well known or at least sufficiently well known or probable. This value occasionally varies from one dialect or subdialect to another; one even observes certain idioms wanting one or several phonemes present in others. However, the present article will not treat these dialectal differences but present a complete inventory of Coptic phonemes (Table 1), "Coptic" considered comprehensively, as a total phenomenon comprising all particular idiomatic, dialectal, and subdialectal diasystems (cf. Stern, 1880, p. 7; Mallon, 1907, p. 7; Chaîne, 1933, pp. 2–3; Worrell, 1934, pp. 83–98; Vergote, 1945, p. 10; Steindorff, 1951, p. 11; Till, 1955, p. 40, and 1961, p. 3, and especially Vergote, 1973, pp. 7, 13, 18, and Kasser, 1981).

The synoptic table gives only the graphemes of four Coptic idioms—vehicular languages *S* and *B*, dialect *A*, and protodialect *P*—considered here as the most typical phonologically and alphabetically. (More details can be found in the synoptic table in ALPHABETS, COPTIC; gem. = graphic vocalic gemination; the phoneme /v/ is found only in the subdialects *B7*, *J*, *G*, *F9*, and *H* [grapheme ⲃ]; [wa] = phoneme wanting in this dialect).

From the following list of Coptic phonemes must be removed, of course, the phoneme combinations rendered in the script by a single grapheme—/ks/ (14), /ps/ (23), /ti/ (30), /cə/ (33), and, in all Coptic idioms except *B* and its subdialects, /th/ (8), /ph/ (21), and /kh/ (22). In *B* etc. they are, respectively, aspirated allophones of /t/ (19), /p/ (16), /k/ (k), as /čh/ is the aspirated allophone of /č/ (28) (see BOHAIRIC).

Coptic has eight (or perhaps nine) *vowels* proper, namely /a/ (1), /e/ (5a), /ə/ (5b), /ē/ (7), /i/ (9a), /o/ (15), /u/ (20b), /ō/ (24), and perhaps /y/ (20a). /ə/ is a medial vowel, /a/ is the most open (or most voiced) vowel, and /i/ and /u/ (and, as the case may be, /y/; see below), the most close (or least voiced): the gradation from most open to most close being /a/, /e/, /ē/, /i/ for the palatal and anterior series, and /a/, /o/, /ō/, /u/ for the velar or posterior one.

Coptic has five (perhaps even six) *sonants* (of truly vocalic value, although expressed in the script by an apparently consonantal grapheme), namely /ƀ̩/ (2b), /l̩/ (11b), /m̩/ (12b), /n̩/ (13b), /r̩/ (17b), and possibly /y̩/.

All the above Coptic phonemes are thus, on the phonological level, vowels. On the other hand, all other phonemes of Coptic presented below are, phonologically considered, consonants.

Coptic has probably only two *glides*, or semivowels (or voiced fricatives; see below), which are voiced consonants (their consonantal value is certain, although they are rendered by apparently vocalic graphemes): /j/ (9b) and /w/ (20c). It is possible to conceive that Coptic might have a third glide, /ɥ/, in some very rare Copto-Greek words, such as *S*, *B* ϩⲩⲁⲕⲓⲛⲑⲓⲛⲟⲛ (ὑακίνθινος), hyacinth-coloured, written

TABLE 1. *Synoptic Table of Coptic Phonemes*

		P	*S*	*B*	*A*
1	/a/	ⲁ	ⲁ	ⲁ	ⲁ
2a	/ƀ/	ⲃ	ⲃ	ⲃ	ⲃ
2b	/ƀ̩/	ⲃ	ⲃ	[wa]	ⲃ
3	/g/	ⲅ	ⲅ	ⲅ	ⲅ
4	/d/	ⲇ	ⲇ	ⲇ	ⲇ
5a	/e/	ⲉ	ⲉ	ⲉ	ⲉ
5b	/ə/	ⲉ	ⲉ	ⲉ	ⲉ
6	/z/	ⲍ	ⲍ	ⲍ	ⲍ
7	/ē/	ⲏ	ⲏ	ⲏ	ⲏ
8	/th/	ⲑ	ⲑ	ⲑ	ⲑ
9a	/i/	(ⲉ)ⲓ	(ⲉ)ⲓ	ⲓ	(ⲉ)ⲓ
9b	/j/	(ⲉ)ⲓ	(ⲉ)ⲓ	ⲓ	(ⲉ)ⲓ
10	/k/	ⲕ	ⲕ	ⲕ	ⲕ
11a	/l/	ⲗ	ⲗ	ⲗ	ⲗ
11b	/l̩/	ⲗ	ⲗ	(ⲗ)	ⲗ
12a	/m/	ⲙ	ⲙ	ⲙ	ⲙ
12b	/m̩/	ⲙ	ⲙ	(ⲙ)	ⲙ
13a	/n/	ⲛ	ⲛ	ⲛ	ⲛ
13b–c	/n̩/	– / ⲛ	ⲛ	(ⲛ)	ⲛ
14	/ks/	ⲝ	ⲝ	ⲝ	ⲝ
15	/o/	ⲟ	ⲟ	ⲟ	ⲟ
16	/p/	ⲡ	ⲡ	ⲡ	ⲡ
17a	/r/	ⲣ	ⲣ	ⲣ	ⲣ
17b	/r̩/	ⲣ	ⲣ	(ⲣ)	ⲣ
18	/s/	ⲥ	ⲥ	ⲥ	ⲥ
19	/t/	ⲧ	ⲧ	ⲧ	ⲧ
20a	/y/?	ⲩ	ⲩ	ⲩ	ⲩ
20b	/u/	ⲟⲩ	ⲟⲩ	ⲟⲩ	ⲟⲩ
20c	/w/	(ⲟ)ⲩ	(ⲟ)ⲩ	(ⲟ)ⲩ	(ⲟ)ⲩ
21	/ph/	ⲫ	ⲫ	ⲫ	ⲫ
22	/kh/	ⲭ	ⲭ	ⲭ	ⲭ
23	/ps/	ⲯ	ⲯ	ⲯ	ⲯ
24	/ō/	ⲱ	ⲱ	ⲱ	ⲱ
25	/š/	ϣ	ϣ	ϣ	ϣ
26	/f/	ϥ	ϥ	ϥ	ϥ
27	/h/	ϩ	ϩ	ϩ	ϩ
28	/č/	ϫ	ϫ	ϫ	ϫ
29	/c/	ⲕ	ϭ	[wa]	ϭ
30	/ti/	ϯ	ϯ	ϯ	ϯ
31	/'/	⊥	gem.	[wa]	gem.
32	/v/	[wa]	[wa]	[wa]	[wa]
33	/cə/	ⲕ̡	ϭⲉ etc.	[wa]	ϭⲉ etc.
34	/ç/	ɘ	[wa]	[wa]	[wa]
35	/x/	ϧ	[wa]	ϧ	ⳉ
36	/čh/	[wa]	[wa]	ϭ	[wa]

frequently ϩⲩⲁ̀ⲕⲓⲛⲑⲓⲛⲟⲛ or even *B* ϩⲓⲁ̀ⲕⲓⲛⲑⲓⲛⲟⲛ, probably pronounced /hy a kin thi non/ or even more likely /hi a kin thi non/; however, hɥa kin thi non/ seems not inconceivable.

Coptic has six *sonorants,* or voiced consonants: /ƀ/ (2a), /l/ (11a), /m/ (12a), /n/ (13a), /r/ (17a), and /v/ (32), of which /l/ is a lateral, /r/ is a vibrant trill, /m/ and /n/ are nasals, /ƀ/ and /v/ are, like the glides, voiced fricatives.

All the other consonants below are unvoiced. Note that the Greek voiced fricative /z/ (6) and the Greek voiced stops /g/ (3) and /d/ (4) occur practically only in Copto-Greek words (cf. VOCABULARY, COPTO-GREEK), in which, however, they have probably lost their original (Greek) voicing; thus, as elements of Coptic, /z/ = /s/ (18), /g/ = /k/ (10), and /d/ = /t/ (19).

Coptic has 6 *fricatives:* /s/ (18), /š/ (25), /f/ (26), /h/ (27), /ç/ (34), and /x/ (35).

According to the traditional Coptic grammar, Coptic has only a single *affricate,* /č/ (28). However, DIALECT H (and perhaps even *F* and the subdialects of the Fayyumic dialectal group, except *F7*) may also have /ç̌/ (/č/ being pronounced nearly like [tš], and /ç̌/ nearly like [tç]).

Coptic has five *stops:* /k/ (10) (and /c/ (29), which is a palatalized /k/ corresponding approximately to [kj]); /p/ (16); /t/ (19); and /'/ (31) (see ALEPH; CRYPTOPHONEME; and GEMINATION, VOCALIC). For the aspirated affricate and stops in *B* etc. (/čh/, /kh/, /ph/, /th/), see above.

BIBLIOGRAPHY

Chaîne, M. *Eléments de grammaire dialectale copte.* Paris, 1933.

Dubois, J.; M. Giacomo; L. Guespin; C. Marcellesi; J.-B. Marcellesi; and J.-P. Mével. *Dictionnaire de linguistique.* Paris, 1973.

Kasser, R. "Voyelles en fonction consonantique, consonnes en fonction vocalique, et classes de phonèmes en copte." *Bulletin de la Société d'égyptologie, Genève* 5 (1981):33–50.

Mallon, A. *Grammaire copte, avec bibliographie, chrestomathie et vocabulaire.* 2nd ed. Beirut, 1907.

Steindorff, G. *Lehrbuch der koptischen Grammatik.* Chicago, 1951.

Stern, L. *Koptische Grammatik.* Leipzig, 1880.

Till, W. C. *Koptische Grammatik (saïdischer Dialekt), mit Bibliographie, Lesestücken und Wörterverzeichnissen.* Leipzig, 1955.

______. *Koptische Dialektgrammatik, mit Lesestücken und Wörterbuch.* 2nd ed. Munich, 1961.

Vergote, J. *Phonétique historique de l'égyptien, les consonnes.* Louvain, 1945.

______. *Grammaire copte,* Vol. 1a, *Introduction, phonétique et phonologie, morphologie synthématique (structure des sémantèmes), partie synchronique.* Louvain, 1973.

Worrell, W. H. *Coptic Sounds.* Ann Arbor, Mich., 1934.

RODOLPHE KASSER

PHONOLOGY OF THE GREEK OF EGYPT, INFLUENCE OF COPTIC ON THE. The main source for the Greek language in Egypt is the mass of nonliterary papyri, ostraca, and inscriptions from the Ptolemaic, Roman, and Byzantine periods, a total of almost fifty thousand documents. An analysis of the orthographic variations in these documents indicates that the pronunciation of the Greek koine spoken and written within the confines of Greco-Roman Egypt reflects to a large extent a transitional stage between that of the classical Greek dialects and that of modern Greek. But there is also extensive evidence of bilingual interference in its phonology by Coptic.

As regards consonants, there is some evidence from as far back as the early Roman period for the shift of the classical voiced stops /b/, /g/, and /d/, represented by β, γ, and δ, to fricatives, as in modern Greek. But there is abundant evidence from documents of the same period and place that these sounds were still stops, for γ and δ interchange very frequently, and β occasionally, with the symbols for the corresponding voiceless stops κ, τ, and π, respectively. Similarly, χ, ϑ, and φ, the symbols for the aspirated stops /kh/, /th/, and /ph/, also interchange frequently in the same documents with κ, τ, and π. This confusion, found extensively only in Egypt and paralleled in the spelling of Greek loanwords in Coptic, has no satisfactory explanation in terms of Greek phonology, for although both the voiced and aspirated stops have shifted to fricatives in modern Greek, they have never merged with those of another order but have remained distinct to the present day.

In Coptic, however, there was no phonemic distinction between voiced and voiceless stops in any dialect. But the sound represented by ⲃ occurs as a distinct phoneme, pronounced during the Greco-Roman period as a voiced bilabial fricative [β]; hence, the symbols for the labial stops are not so frequently confused. Similarly, the unconditional interchange of aspirated and voiceless stops is caused by bilingual interference. In Coptic, aspirated stops were phonemic only in the BOHAIRIC dialect, where the opposition occurred only in accented syllables and the aspirates were lost in late Byzantine times.

In addition, the voiced bilabial fricative quality postulated for Greek β especially when it interchanges with ου /w/ or υ /y/ coincides with that of Coptic ⲃ, and the fricative quality of intervocalic Greek γ in connection with rounded back vowels may represent the labiovelar fricative quality of the Coptic ⲟⲩ /w/.

There is also widespread confusion of λ and ρ. Although in Greek the phonetic quality of these liquids varied considerably, nowhere outside Egypt was there an identification of the two sounds. In the FAYYUMIC dialect of Coptic, however, from which area most of the documents showing this interchange come, there may have been only one liquid phoneme /l/, for most words spelled with ⲣ in other dialects show ⲗ in Fayyumic, although ⲣ is retained in many words.

The final nasal is frequently dropped in pronunciation, a tendency that has continued in spoken Greek to the present day. In addition, medial nasals are frequently lost, especially after stops. This is also the result of bilingual interference, for in Coptic a voiceless stop had a voiced allophone following a nasal. This fact, combined with the underdifferentiation of voiced and voiceless stops, made *ντ*, *τ*, *δ*, and *νδ*, for example, simply orthographic variants of the same sound /t/.

Initial aspiration is frequently dropped. This represents a phonetic tendency within Greek itself, in which aspiration was generally lost during the period of the koine. Aspiration was also lost in some Coptic dialects in Byzantine times.

In vowels, the classical long diphthongs were reduced to simple vowels by the end of the first century B.C. The short diphthongs in -*ι* became identified with simple vowels, *ει* with *ι* in /i/ already in the third century B.C., *αι* with *ϵ* in /ϵ/ in the second century B.C., and *οι* (and *υι*) with *υ* in /y/ by the first century A.D.

The short diphthong *ου* had become a simple vowel /u/ before the beginning of the Ptolemaic period. In the Roman and Byzantine periods, it interchanged occasionally with *ω* and *ο*, both representing /o/. Since this interchange was rare elsewhere in Greek but was paralleled in Greek loanwords in Coptic, it may rest on bilingual interference. In Coptic, ⲟⲩ is a reflex of ⲱ and ⲙ and ⲛ, and it has been proposed that ⲱ after ⲟⲩ represented the same sound; but a phonemic opposition between /o/ and /u/ seems well established.

By the second century B.C. the short diphthongs *αυ* and *ϵυ* were showing evidence of the reduction of their second element to a consonantal sound [w], which closed to a bilabial fricative [β] in Byzantine times. This corresponds to the known historical development of these diphthongs from original /au eu/ to /av ϵv/ or /af ϵf/ in modern Greek. Parallel orthographic variations in Coptic suggest that Greek *αυ* and *ϵυ* may have been identified with Coptic ⲁⲩ and ⲉⲩ, both arising frequently from contraction from ⲁⲟⲩ and ⲉⲟⲩ, which also represented a vocalic plus a consonantal element.

The simple vowels for the most part preserved their classical Greek pronunciation, but itacism was more advanced because of the nature of the Coptic vowel system, in which there were only three front vowel phonemes corresponding to the four Greek front vowels. In addition, *η* seems to have been bivalent, since throughout the Roman and Byzantine periods it was confused sometimes with the /i/ sound represented primarily by *ι* and *ει*, and sometimes with the /ϵ/ sound represented by *ϵ* and *αι*, as well as frequently with *υ*. In Coptic, ⲏ occurred only in accented syllables and was bivalent. In all dialects it represented an allophone of /i/ before or after sonants. In Bohairic, it also represented an allophone of /ae/.

The simple vowel represented by *υ* was particularly unstable. In the koine where the diphthong *ου* came to represent /u/, *υ* apparently represented the Attic value /y/, until it finally merged with /i/ about the ninth century A.D. The interchange of the symbols for /y/ and /i/ possibly indicates the unrounding of the /y/ and its merger with /i/ in Egypt during Byzantine times. But the constant confusion of *υ* with other vowel symbols, especially *η*, suggests underdifferentiation of phonemes through bilingual interference, since Coptic had no /y/ sound. There are parallel interchanges of ⲩ with ⲓ and ⲏ in Greek loanwords in Coptic.

There is also a frequent interchange of *α* with *ϵ* and *ο*, mainly in unaccented syllables but occasionally in accented syllables as well. This is also the result of bilingual interference, for in no dialect of Coptic were there more than two phonemes corresponding to the three Greek phonemes represented by *α*, *ϵ*, and *ο*.

Finally, all quantitative distinction has been lost. This in turn reflects a change in the nature of the Greek accent from pitch to stress, which came about in Egypt, as generally throughout the koine, through the transfer by nonnative Greek-speakers of their own accentual patterns to their Greek.

The possibility of the influence of Coptic on the phonology of the Greek of Egypt has long been recognized but usually not invoked to explain more than isolated phenomena in documents clearly emanating from the Egyptian element of the population. But the evidence of bilingual interference in the nonliterary papyri, ostraca, and inscriptions, especially from the Roman and Byzantine periods, is so extensive that Coptic influence must have fairly permeated the Greek language in Egypt.

BIBLIOGRAPHY

Czermak, W. *Die Laute der ägyptischen Sprache: Eine phonetische Untersuchung*. Schriften der Arbeitsgemeinschaft der Ägyptologen und Afrikanisten in Wien 2, 3. Vienna, 1931–1934.

Gignac, F. T. "Bilingualism in Greco-Roman Egypt." In *Actes du Xe Congrès international des linguistes,* pp. 677–82. Bucharest, 1970a.

______. "The Language of the Non-Literary Greek Papyri." *American Studies in Papyrology* 7 (1970b):139–52.

______. *A Grammar of the Greek Papyri of the Roman and Byzantine Periods,* Vol. 1, *Phonology,* Vol. 2, *Morphology.* Testi e documenti per lo studio dell'antichità 55. Milan, 1976–1981.

Kahle, P. E. *Bala'izah: Coptic Texts from Deir el-Bala'izah in Upper Egypt,* Vol. 1. Oxford and London, 1954.

Kasser, R. "Prolégomènes à un essai de classification systématique des dialectes et subdialectes coptes selon les critères de la phonétique, I, Principes et terminologie." *Muséon* 93 (1980a):53–112. ". . . , II, Alphabets et systèmes phonétiques." *Muséon* 93 (1980b):237–97. ". . . , III, Systèmes orthographiques et catégories dialectales." *Muséon* 94 (1981a):91–152.

______. "Voyelles en fonction consonantique, consonnes en fonction vocalique, et classes de phonèmes en copte." *Bulletin de la Société d'égyptologie, Genève* 5 (1981b):33–50.

______. "Syllabation rapide ou lente en copte, I, les glides /j/ et /w/ avec leurs correspondants vocaliques '/i/' et '/u/' (et phonèmes appariés analogues)." *Enchoria* 11 (1982):23–37.

Knudsen, E. E. "Saidic Coptic Vowel Phonemes." *Acta Orientalia* 26 (1961):29–42.

Lambdin, T. O. "The Bivalence of Coptic Eta and Related Problems in the Vocalization of Egyptian." *Journal of Near Eastern Studies* 17 (1958):177–93.

Mayser, E. *Grammatik der griechischen Papyri aus der Ptolemäerzeit, mit Einschluss der gleichzeitigen Ostraka und der in Ägypten verfassten Inschriften,* Vol. 1, *Laut- und Wortlehre.* Leipzig, 1906. 2nd ed. of Pt. 1, *Einleitung und Lautlehre,* rev. Hans Schmoll. Berlin, 1970.

Šmieszek, A. *Some Hypotheses Concerning the Prehistory of the Coptic Vowels.* Mémoires de la Commission orientaliste de l'Académie polonaise des sciences. Kraków, 1936.

Vergote, J. "Het probleem van de Koine volgens de laatste historisch-philologische bevindingen." *Philologische Studiën* 4 (1932–1933):28–32; 5 (1933–1934):81–105; 6 (1934–1935):81–107.

______. *Phonétique historique de l'égyptien, les consonnes.* Louvain, 1945.

______. "Les Dialectes dans le domaine égyptien." *Chronique d'Egypte* 36 (1961):237–51.

______. *Grammaire copte,* Vol. 1a, *Introduction, phonétique et phonologie, morphologie synthématique (structure des sémantèmes), partie synchronique,* Vol. 1b, . . . , *partie diachronique,* Vol. 2a, . . . , *morphologie syntagmatique, syntaxe, partie synchronique,* Vol. 2b, . . . , *morphologie syntagmatique, partie diachronique,* Louvain, 1973–1983.

Worrell, W. H. *Coptic Sounds.* Ann Arbor, Mich., 1934.

FRANCIS THOMAS GIGNAC, S.J.

PRE-COPTIC. This general term indicates different stages of script or script forms that to a greater or lesser extent prepared or influenced the creation of the Coptic script. Since the use of the Greek alphabet is essential to the definition of Coptic, it is obvious that one must go back to the first more or less regular contacts between Greeks and Egyptians —such as the foundation of the Greek colony of Naucratis in the Twenty-Sixth Dynasty (seventh–sixth century B.C.)—to search for the very beginnings of Egyptian written with Greek letters. Indeed, the transliterations of Egyptian proper names in Greek texts (GREEK TRANSCRIPTIONS) are the first seeds of Pre-Coptic. But an occasional rendition of a Greek name in hieroglyphs can also be encountered, such as *3rksk3rs* for Alexicles (Quaegebeur, 1976, pp. 50–51; cf. de Meulenaere, 1966, pp. 42–43). In the same period (Twenty-sixth Dynasty, sixth and seventh centuries B.C.) demotic script came into general use in the administration. Demotic scribes regularly employed phonetic, instead of etymological, orthographies. This phenomenon and its effect on phonetic orthographies in hieroglyphic merit more detailed study (Quaegebeur, 1980, pp. 68–69). Some authors even think that phonetic and, in particular, alphabetic spellings in hieroglyphic texts from late pharaonic times onward are to be explained as tendencies toward simplification caused by the advantages recognized in the simple Greek script system (e.g., Brunner, 1965, p. 767). But we must not overlook that in this period Aramaic texts too are known in Egypt. An example is the notation of the word *ntr* (god) by means of the uniliteral signs *n* + *t* (compare ⲛⲟⲩⲧⲉ) on the Naucratis stela (1. 5; Nectanebo I; cf. Lichtheim 1980, p. 87, for bibliography).

From the late fourth and early third centuries B.C., when after the conquest of Alexander the Great many Greeks settled in Egypt, one finds an enormous number of Egyptian proper names integrated into Greek texts. On the other hand, many Greek anthroponyms, such as those of eponymous priests and priestesses, were rendered alphabetically in demotic documents (Clarysse et al., 1982). In both kinds of transliteration a measure of systematization occurs with local characteristics.

Apart from the custom of writing Egyptian proper names in Greek documents in the alphabet used, there survives evidence from Greco-Roman times of a few isolated attempts to transcribe Egyptian generic names or somewhat longer texts by making exclusive use of the Greek alphabet. In such cases, one speaks of PRE-OLD COPTIC.

The last stage of Pre-Coptic, then, is OLD COPTIC. From the first century A.D. onward, attempts to write Egyptian (Late Egyptian or contemporary vernacular) with Greek characters to which were added a varying number of supplementary signs derived from demotic became more numerous and more systematic. Moreover, it is interesting to see that in the same period demotic scribes were making ever greater use of alphabetic orthographies (Spiegelberg, 1901, pp. 18–19; Lüddeckens, 1980, p. 256). Unique of their kind are the demotic ostraca of Narmuthis (Madīnat Māḍī) from the second century A.D., school exercises of a sort (Bresciani et al., 1983), in which Greek is mixed with demotic; not only are Greek words in Greek script integrated into demotic texts, but also some attempts are made to write native words in an alphabetical way, combining Greek and demotic signs (Pernigotti, 1984).

The transition from the Egyptian scripts to Old Coptic was fostered by circumstances: first of all, mention should be made of the decline of the temple scriptoria, which put an end to the tradition of complex hieroglyphics and of the difficult demotic script, which was also used for religious, literary, and scientific works. (The last hieroglyphic inscription, found at Philae, dates from 393–394 A.D.; demotic survives in graffiti at Philae until the fifth century, the last dated example belonging to 452–453. This southern center of the Isis cult was only closed, by a decree of Justinian, in 550.) Further, it should be borne in mind that from Ptolemaic times onward the bearers of the pharaonic heritage often knew Greek or even had a Hellenistic education, as is apparent from Greek translations of demotic literature.

The abandonment of such a characteristic script system implies a fundamental change in cultural traditions. (That is why the *Lexikon der Ägyptologie* does not devote an article to the Coptic script.) The national language survives, but tainted by a large number of Greek words (see VOCABULARY, COPTO-GREEK). The transition from the demotic to the Coptic language is difficult to date precisely (Sethe, 1925; Vergote, 1973, Vol. 1b, pp. 1–4). Nor is the relation between the Coptic DIALECTS and any dialectal differentiation in the earlier, Pre-Coptic and in particular Pharaonic, language phases definitely clear (Osing, 1974).

BIBLIOGRAPHY

Bresciani, E.; S. Pernigotti; and M. C. Betrò. *Ostraka demotici da Narmuti,* Vol. 1. Quaderni di Medinet Madi 1. Pisa, 1983.

Brunner, H. "Die altägyptische Schrift." *Studium Generale* 18, no. 12 (1965):756–69.

Clarysse, W.; G. van der Veken; and S. P. Vleeming. *The Eponymous Priests of Ptolemaic Egypt.* Papyrologica Lugduno-Batava 24. Leiden, 1982.

De Meulenaere, H. "La mère d'Imouthès." *Chronique d'Egypte* 41 (1966):42–43.

Gessmann, A. M. "The Birthdate of Coptic Script." *University of South Florida Language Quarterly* 14, nos. 2–3 (1976):2–4.

Grapow, H. "Vom Hieroglyphisch-Demotischen zum Koptischen." *Sitzungsberichte der Preussischen Akademie der Wissenschaften, Philosophisch-historische Klasse,* 28 (1938):322–49.

Kasser, R. "Prolégomènes à un essai de classification systématique des dialectes et subdialectes coptes selon les critères de la phonétique, I, Principes et terminologie." *Muséon* 93 (1980):53–112. ". . . , II, Alphabets et systèmes phonétiques." *Muséon* 93 (1980):237–97. ". . . , III, Systèmes orthographiques et catégories dialectales." *Muséon* 94 (1981):91–152.

Lichtheim, M. *Ancient Egyptian Literature,* Vol. 3, *The Late Period.* Los Angeles and Berkeley, 1980.

Lüddeckens, E. "Ägypten." In *Die Sprachen im römischen Reich der Kaiserzeit,* pp. 241–65. Beihefte der Bonner Jahrbücher 40. Cologne, 1980.

Morenz, S. "Das Koptische." In *Ägyptische Sprache und Schrift: Handbuch der Orientalistik,* pp. 241–65. Leiden and Cologne, 1959.

Osing, J. "Dialekte." In *Lexikon der Ägyptologie,* Vol. I, Lief. 7, pp. 1074–75. 1974.

Pernigotti, S. "Il 'Copto' degli ostraka di Medinet Madi." In *Atti del XVII Congresso Internazionale di Papirologia,* pp. 787–91. Naples, 1984.

Quaegebeur, J. "De Griekse weergave van korte Egyptische dodenteksten." *Phoenix* 22 (1976):49–59.

______. "Une épithète méconnaissable de Ptah, Livre du Centenaire." *Mémoires de l'Institut français d'archéologie orientale* 104 (1980):61–71.

______. "De la préhistoire de l'écriture copte." *Orientalia Lovaniensia Periodica* 13 (1982):125–36.

Sethe, K. "Das Verhältnis zwischen Demotisch und Koptisch und seine Lehren für die Geschichte der ägyptischen Sprache." *Zeitschrift der deutschen morgenländischen Gesellschaft* 79 (1925):290–316.

Spiegelberg, W. *Aegyptische und griechische Eigen-*

namen aus Mumienetiketten der römischen Kaiserzeit. Demotische Studien 1. Leipzig, 1901.

Vergote, J. *Grammaire copte,* Vol. 1a, *Introduction, phonétique et phonologie, morphologie synthématique (structure des sémantèmes), partie synchronique,* Vol. 1b, . . ., *partie diachronique,* Louvain, 1973.

JAN QUAEGEBEUR

PRE-OLD COPTIC. Pre-Old Coptic is a component of PRE-COPTIC, more specifically the stage preceding OLD COPTIC. It differs from the latter preparatory stage mainly in that no supplementary signs borrowed from demotic were used to transliterate phonemes that did not exist in Greek. GREEK TRANSCRIPTIONS of proper names had demonstrated the possibility of writing Egyptian in an alphabetical script, even though a number of sounds could not be rendered adequately. In Greco-Roman times there are, in addition to the Greek transcriptions of proper names, a number of other attempts to render Egyptian by means of the Greek alphabet. The aim of these instances, which can be individually different, is most of the time not very clear. But the motive has to be different from that of the usual Greek transcriptions of proper names integrated in a Greek context.

Fairly well known are a Heidelberg papyrus and a graffito from Abydos, both of the earlier Ptolemaic period. A number of other cases can be added, but several remain uncertain because of difficulties in the interpretation. Here is a short survey:

(1) P. Heid. inv. no. 414 verso (mentioned as P. Heid. inv. 413 by Pack, 1965, no. 2157; the recto is a grammatical treatise), extracted from mummy cartonnage from el-Hiba (Teudjoi), is a list of Greek words with their Egyptian counterparts written in the Greek alphabet. Bilabel (1937, pp. 79–80), who described a few extracts of the text, dates it to the middle of the third century B.C. Because this text is not well known (not incorporated in Černý, 1976, or Westendorf, 1977), the available data are presented here: *λεκάνιον–κρωρι; ἀξίνη–κολεβειν; μάχαιρα–σηφι; μόσχος–αγ́ολ* (the accentlike mark above the *γ* apparently indicated that the consonant did not correspond exactly to the Greek gamma, which equals the Bohairic **ⲁϭⲟⲗ**). The text now appears to have been lost (Quaegebeur, 1982, p. 129, n. 18). In Bilabel's view, the lexicon itself reveals its purpose: "Der Text zeigt . . . dass auch in den Kreisen der herrschenden Griechenschicht das Interesse an der alteinheimischen Sprache aus dem praktischen Bedürfnis heraus bestand." On the other hand, it cannot be ruled out that it was a manual for Egyptians to learn Greek.

(2) Graffito from Abydos (Temple of Sethi I), edited by P. Perdrizet and G. Lefebvre (1919, no. 74), which is discussed by P. Lacau (1933–1934); new edition with commentary in P. W. Pestman et al. (1977, doc. no. 11). Of the seven lines of Greek letters, only four can be interpreted with sufficient certainty. The interrupted first line is repeated in full in line two. After the regnal year, given in the Greek manner (Ἔτους) *ϵ* (= 5), we read: Π*ορω* Υ*ρ-γοναφορ μηι* Ε*σι νομ* Ο*υσιρι μηι* Ε*μουνλασοντηρ πνοτω*, which is to be regarded as transcribed Egyptian: "Pharaoh Hyrgonaphor, beloved by Isis and Osiris, beloved by Amun, king of gods, the great god." Because this pharaoh is identified with the indigenous rebel king whose name should be read Ḥr-wn-nfr (Clarysse, 1978, pp. 243–53), the graffito can now be exactly dated to 202–201 B.C. (Vandorpe, 1986, pp. 299–300). Apart from the dating formula, the content of the text is not clear. Yet it remains an important historical and linguistic piece of evidence, which raises the question why a scribe would write such a long Egyptian text in Greek characters. Was he an Egyptian who could read and write Greek but had not mastered demotic script?

(3) Greek papyrus UPZ I no. 79 (Wilcken, 1927), dated to 159 B.C., known as the dream of Nektembes. In a dream the latter is told (lines 4–5): *φαφϵρϵ σι ϵυρϵηξ . . . χμϵννι . . . πϵλ λϵλ χασον χανι.* Though the attempts to understand the text by way of Egyptian were unsuccessful, the editor writes, "Diese barbarischen Lautgruppen . . . können nach Lage der Dinge nichts anderes sein als griechische Transkriptionen von ägyptischen Wörtern."

(4) Greek inscription from Hermopolis Magna (al-Ashmūnayn) preserved in Alexandria, Greco-Roman Museum no. 26.050. The document was published by V. Girgis (1965, p. 121) and again in P. W. Pestman et al. (1977, doc. no. 12). This dedication by priests of Thoth in honor of a *strategos* is to be dated at the end of the second or beginning of the first century B.C. After the name ΘΩΥΘ follows Ω Ω Ω NOBZMOYN. If taken as Egyptian, this means "Thoth, trismegas, lord of Ashmūnayn/Hermopolis." Since it is the name of a god followed by epithets, this example could be treated as a special case among the Greek transcriptions.

(5) For Roman times two particularly interesting mummy labels in the Louvre (inv. 532 and 550) are noteworthy; they contain the same demotic religious formula in Greek transcription: Α*νχη βιου ομμα* Ο*υσορχοντϵμοντ νοντω νοβηβωτ*, to be translated as "May his *ba* [soul] live before Osiris, foremost in the

West, great god, lord of Abydos" (Quaegebeur, 1978, pp. 254–55). Notwithstanding the synchronism (2nd or 3rd century A.D.) with Old Coptic, this text belongs rather to the stage of Pre-Old Coptic because of the exclusive use of the Greek alphabet. An interesting feature is that *νουτ(ω)* = *ntr* (*ˁ3*) seems to correspond to the Akhmimic form ⲛⲟⲩⲛⲧⲉ (= Sahidic ⲛⲟⲩⲧⲉ).

(6) Perhaps a Munich papyrus may also be mentioned here, regarded by the editor as a kind of schoolbook (Spiegelberg, 1928, pp. 44–49) with short demotic sentences, among which are personal names; for a few expressions, a Greek transcription appears between the lines. Because of the use of additional signs, making comparison possible with the Old Coptic glosses, this item should rather be treated as an example of Old Coptic.

(7) The demotic ostraca of Narmuthis (Madīnat Māḍī), which are essentially school exercises from the second century A.D., also deserve special mention. Besides using Greek names and words written in Greek, they contain some attempts to render Egyptian terms by means of Greek letters combined with demotic signs.

(8) An uncertain instance from the beginning of the Roman period is P. IFAO III 34, dating to 32 B.C. (Schwartz and Wagner, 1975), an extremely difficult text of which, apart from the name of a prefect and a few elements pointing to Greek, one cannot make sense. Presumably, the scribe was a native who did not know Greek very well at all, but the question was put whether Egyptian was not inserted, written in Greek characters.

(9) Finally, the two lines (9–10) of text in P. Hamb. II 187 (Morenz, 1959, p. 92, n. 1) from 246–245 B.C. have wrongly been considered as Egyptian transcribed in Greek characters, as was shown by E. van 't Dack (1964, pp. 62–63). The two Oxyrhynchus texts referred to in this edition (P. Hamb. II 167), P. Oxy. 90 (not 40!), ll. 6–7, and 287 (second hand), both from Roman times, were rightly not interpreted as grecized demotic by their editors.

BIBLIOGRAPHY

Bilabel, F. "Neue literarische Funde der Heidelberger Papyrussammlung." In *Actes du Ve Congrès international de papyrologie, Oxford 30 août–3 septembre 1937*, pp. 72–84, especially pp. 79–80. Brussels, 1938.

Černý, J. *Coptic Etymological Dictionary.* Cambridge, 1976.

Clarysse, W. "Hurgonaphor et Chaonnophris, les derniers pharaons indigènes." *Chronique d'Egypte* 53 (1978):243–53.

Girgis, V. "A New Strategos of the Hermopolite Nome." *Mitteilungen des deutschen archäologischen Instituts, Abteilung Kairo* 20 (1965):121 and pl. 39.

Kasser, R. "Prolégomènes à un essai de classification systématique des dialectes et subdialectes coptes selon les critères de la phonétique, I, Principes et terminologie." *Muséon* 93 (1980):53–112. ". . . , II, Alphabets et systèmes phonétiques." *Muséon* 93 (1980):237–97. ". . . , III, Systèmes orthographiques et catégories dialectales." *Muséon* 94 (1981):91–152.

Lacau, P. "Un graffito égyptien d'Abydos écrit en lettres grecques." *Etudes de papyrologie* 2 (1933–1934):229–46.

Morenz, S. "Das Koptische." In *Ägyptische Sprache und Schrift: Handbuch der Orientalistik,* pp. 241–65. Leiden and Cologne, 1959.

Pack, R. A. *The Greek and Latin Literary Texts from Greco-Roman Egypt,* especially p. 117. Ann Arbor, Mich., 1965.

Perdrizet, P., and G. Lefebvre. *Les Graffites grecs du Memnonion d'Abydos.* Paris, 1919. Repr. as *Inscriptiones Graecae Aegypti III, Inscriptiones "Memnonii" Besae Oraculi ad Abydum Thebaidis.* Chicago, 1978.

Pestman, P. W.; J. Quaegebeur; and R. L. Vos. *Recueil de textes démotiques et bilingues.* Leiden, 1977.

Quaegebeur, J. "Mummy Labels: An Orientation." In *Textes grecs, démotiques et bilingues,* pp. 232–59. Papyrologica Lugduno-Batava 19. Leiden, 1978.

______. "De la préhistoire de l'écriture copte." *Orientalia Lovaniensia Periodica* 13 (1982):125–36.

Schwartz, J., and G. Wagner. *Papyrus grecs de l'Institut français d'archéologie orientale,* Vol. 3. Bibliothèque d'étude 56. Cairo, 1975.

Spiegelberg, W. "Demotica II." In *Sitzungsberichte der Bayerischen Akademie der Wissenschaften,* Pt. 2, pp. 44–49. Munich, 1928.

Vandorpe, K. "The Chronology of the Reigns of Hurgonaphor and Chaonnophris." *Chronique d'Egypte* 61 (1986):294–302.

Van 't Dack, E. "Coniecturae Papyrologicae." In *Studien zur Papyrologie und Antiken Wirtschaftsgeschichte Fr. Oertel zum 80. Geburtstag gewidmet,* pp. 62–63. Bonn, 1964.

Westendorf, W. *Koptisches Handwörterbuch, bearbeitet auf Grund des koptischen Handwörterbuchs von Wilhelm Spiegelberg.* Heidelberg, 1977.

Wilcken, U. *Urkunden der Ptolemäerzeit,* Vol. 1. Berlin and Leipzig, 1927.

JAN QUAEGEBEUR

PROTODIALECT. From the earliest time that its existence is attested (before 3000 B.C.) until its most recent form, prior to its extinction as a living tongue, the Egyptian language has evolved somewhat in its phonology. To be sure, while this language was still alive, Coptology had not yet been born, so that no phonologist possessing modern scientific skills could, by hearing the language pronounced as it was spoken, note precisely its articulation. However, there exist thousands of Egyptian texts, both pharaonic and Coptic, that record the existence of diverse orthographies. If they are simultaneous, they are considered dialectal orthographies synchronically. If they are successive, they are considered to indicate various evolutionary stages of the language.

Even though orthography is merely a conventional system with an essentially practical usage and therefore a system with rather empirical foundations, and though it is very far from answering all theoretical questions asked by phonologists and from satisfying the concerns, curiosity, and needs of the researcher, one cannot deny that orthography has some capacity to inform one of the nature of a language's phonology. This is particularly true either when the vocabulary of this language has adopted lexemes of other languages whose phonology is better understood or when various lexemes of the language in question have been cited, if not adopted, in texts from a neighboring language with a better-known phonology. To a certain extent, such is the case with pharaonic Egyptian and, to an even greater degree, Coptic, because of the close coexistence of Coptic and Greek in Roman-Byzantine Egypt, in which the autochthonous majority who spoke Coptic were politically dominated by the Hellenized minority, even within the framework of the imperial Roman administration. Thus, one finds many Egyptian proper nouns transcribed into Greek, and vice versa, as well as numerous Greek words adopted into Coptic, a language whose alphabet is in fact mostly Greek (see VOCABULARY, COPTO-GREEK and ETYMOLOGY; also ALPHABET IN COPTIC, GREEK, and ALPHABETS, COPTIC).

The phonological evolution observable in Egyptian before the Coptic era is unfortunately limited to consonants since pharaonic writing exhibited no vowels. In Coptic, on the other hand, the vowels were written along with the consonants. Concerning Egyptian, one should not be surprised to observe some phonological evolution, since the language can be analyzed today on the basis of texts covering more than three thousand years. Coptic, however, existed for scarcely a millennium, and even less if one stops with the epoch in which it ceased to be both productive in the literary field and truly living as a spoken language among Egyptians, surviving with difficulty and increasing artificiality for several centuries only within the closed and conservative milieu of the Coptic clergy. Consequently, one might expect to observe no evolution within Coptic and to see here only one stage, the single and final stage in the evolution of the Egyptian language. At most, by comparing the idioms of Coptic with each other, one finds that some, particularly Akhmimic (*A*) and Bohairic (*B*), have a phonemic inventory slightly richer than certain others, such as Sahidic (*S*), Lyco-(Dios)politan (*L*), Mesokemic (*M*), crypto-Mesokemic (*W*), South Fayyumic (*V*), and Fayyumic (*F*). For example, *A* and *B* have retained phonemes such as /x/ from pharaonic Egyptian, which classical *S* and *L* have lost. This is, of course, an interesting phenomenon. But the phenomenon is even more remarkable when the presence and disappearance of such a phoneme can be noticed in the documents of a single dialect, as it evolves from a formative archaic stage, relatively rich in phonemes, to a more recent, neutralized and impoverished state.

Such observations can also be made here or there in the study of vowels (Kasser, 1984, pp. 246ff.), where the phenomenon remains strictly confined to Coptic because pharaonic Egyptian texts exhibit no written vowels. One must admit that, if one finds in the same position and quality (i.e., long stressed, short stressed, unstressed) a greater variety of vocalic usage, this is a sign of archaism. This vocalic archaism is frequently confirmed by consonantal archaic phonology (see below). Thus, for example, insofar as final unstressed vowels are concerned, *A*, *L4*, *L5*, *M*, and *S* have only one (-ⲉ), while *L6* still possesses two (-ⲉ and -ⲓ), as do *V* and *F* (-ⲓ and -ⲉ). *F7* also has two (-ⲓ and -ⲁ). One could also say that *B* retains two (-ⲓ and Ø, that is, zero vowel, no vowel at all). Further, one also sees two in proto-Lyco-(Dios)politan (*pL*, -ⲉ and -ⲓ) and in proto-Theban (*P*, -ⲉ and -ⲁ), dialects whose consonantic inventory is very archaic (see below).

It can thus be observed that almost all Coptic dialects have adopted only one or the other of the two vowels -ⲉ or -ⲓ in the unstressed final position, the second tightly closed and the first less closed or more or less medial. But the archaic *P* and *F7* show in that position a very open, unstressed final vowel, -ⲁ, an unusual and remarkable phenomenon in Coptic.

The study of Egyptian phonological evolution remains most fruitful when dealing with consonants, which have been transcribed over a period of approximately four thousand years, from the most ancient of pharaonic texts to the later Coptic documents. In fact, the result of such an analysis can be a synoptic table like that published by Vergote

(1945, pp. 122–23), which expanded Worrell's study (1934). As far as Coptic is concerned, however, this table shows only synchronic and interdialectal differences, except in the cases of silencing (disappearance of phonemes).

Nevertheless, some thirty years later, Vergote (1973–1983, Vol. 1a, p. 57) discovered some rare archaic documents in Coptic that attest and manifest the existence of a "proto-Subakhmimic" or rather (in present Coptological terminology) "proto-Lyco-(Dios)politan" (see DIALECT I and Kasser, 1990), and of a "proto-Sahidic" (according to Vergote's terminology, now rather to be considered a "proto-Theban" very similar to some reconstructed "proto-Sahidic"; see DIALECT P and Kasser, 1990), sigla respectively *pL* and *P*. These remarkable idioms had conserved up to the third–fourth centuries two phonemes that can reasonably be considered archaic in the Lyco-(Dios)politan cluster, and also in comparision with Sahidic. Still surviving in *pL* and *P*, they have disappeared from *L*, and also cannot be found in *S*. The first is /x/, which is derived from ẖ = /x_2/ (rarely from ḫ = /x_3/). The second is the phoneme /ç/, which is the principal intermediate form in the evolution that starts with ḫ = /x_3/ and finally ends at /š/ in all Coptic dialects, except for Akhmimic (*A*), which has /x/ in its place. This /x/ is apparently identical to the /x/ derived from /x_2/. Therefore, even within Coptic, in the consonants there is a small segment where a modest but significant phonological evolution in the Egyptian language can be observed.

Present terminology is that of Kasser (1980a, pp. 109–111), who called proto-Theban (considered more precisely a kind of proto-Sahidic) and proto-Lycopolitan "protodialects." When, through the very rare discovery of archaic texts, protodialects appear in Coptology, the protodialect exists as an entity logically anterior to the Coptic "dialects" that have been defined and named according to the habitual and traditional criteria. It is anterior not exactly in the same way that a father is anterior to his son, but as someone of the father's generation, perhaps the father's brother or cousin, is logically anterior to the father's son. Concerning the dialects, their character as "dialects" came to be recognized because their differentiating traces were observed throughout the known Coptic texts. Furthermore, these dialects represented, each in its own way, the state of the phonological evolution of the Egyptian language in the various regions of the country. This held true during the entire Coptic era, or at least for *A*, *L*, *M*, *W*, *V*, and possibly *F* until they were smothered by *S*. Therefore, in contrast to these various idioms in general, but more particularly in contrast to *L* and also *S*, respectively, proto-Lycopolitan (*pL*) and proto-Theban (*P*) are called "protodialects." A specific protodialect of *B*, *F*, *V*, *W*, *M*, or *A* may yet come to light, should new texts be discovered with such archaic phonological features.

Concerning *L* and also *S*, it is known that these idioms lost /ç/ and even /x/ at the termination of a well-known phonological evolution: the majority of x_3 > /ç/ > /š/, while x_2, linked to a minority of x_3, > /x/ > /h/. Consequently, it is the survival of /ç/ and /x/ in *pL* and *P* very similar to some reconstructed "proto-Sahidic") that makes the former a protodialect of *L* and the latter a protodialect that looks very like a tentatively reconstructed protodialect of *S*, *pL* in the rest of its phonological system being very Lycopolitan and *P* being more often than not identical with *S*. In *A* and *B*, on the other hand, one can see in the mass of their manuscripts from each period that /x/ was always present, so that this phoneme plays a role in the definition of *A* and *B* as dialects and has nothing of a protodialectal stage.

A protodialect, therefore, can exist only in relationship to a dialect to which it is extremely similar, if not identical, in most of its phonological traits. This dialect, however, shows a phonological evolution in some precise point—almost always in its consonants—away from its protodialect. This type of relationship of protodialect to dialect is also that which exists, in a reversed sense, between a dialect and a METADIALECT, with this latter showing a state of evolution posterior to that of the dialect to which it corresponds.

For reasons tied to the status of the present knowledge of Coptic, which is based on documentation known to the present day, the presence or absence of /ç/—or even /x/ in a dialect other than *A* or *B*—in the graphicophonological system of one of the varieties of the Coptic language forms the only certain criterion that will permit one to distinguish between a protodialect and a dialect.

As for the age of these protodialectal documents. one will note that they are among the most ancient Coptic manuscripts, an observation that seems logically normal. However, occasionally a certain "dialectal" document will slightly predate a particular "protodialectal" document (just as the father's son may be, in certain cases, a little older than his uncle or some relative from his father's generation), indicating that the protodialect survived in one region of Egypt longer than in another. And when it vanished, its disappearance would probably be progressive, with a certain period of contemporaneous usage of the protodialect by the conservatives and of the dialect by the innovators in the same area (see LANGUAGE(S), COPTIC).

It will be instructive here to borrow some component parts from the synoptic table of Vergote in a slightly modified order, adapting and illustrating each one with an example and choosing in particular those components that are useful in the definition of a protodialect.

The abbreviations and adaptations employed are as follows: for periods, MK = Middle Kingdom, NK = New Kingdom, pC = Saitic and Greco-Roman (or proto-Coptic) period, C = Coptic period; for dialects, *L* = *A2* of Vergote; *S* . . . = *S*, *F*, and its subdialects, as well as *M* and *V*, which were still unknown to Vergote in 1945; *L* . . . within the pC period = *pL* (and through *P* a reconstructed **pS*). Without postulating or defining any phonological difference between them, two varieties of /x_3/ will henceforth be distinguished here: the major form whose evolution was /ç/ > /š/ in *L* . . . is /x_{33}/; and the minor form that evolved into /h/ in *L* . . . is /x_{32}/.

(MK) *ḥ* > (NK) *ḥ* > (pC) /h/ > (C) /h/; for example, *ḥḳr* > ϩⲕⲟ *L*, *S* . . . , *B*, *A*, to be hungry.

(MK) *h* > (NK) *h* > (pC) /h/ > (C) /h/; for example, *hb* > ϩⲱⲃ *L*, *S* . . . , *B*, *A*, thing.

(MK) x_2 > (NK) x_2 > (pC) /x_2/ [*A*], /x/ *L* . . . , [*B*] > /x_2/ *A*, /x/ *B*, but /h/ *L*, *S* . . . ; for example, *ẖnw* ϧⲟⲩⲛ *B*, *P* (and a reconstructed **pS*), ⳉⲟⲩⲛ *A*, *pL*, but ϩⲟⲩⲛ *L*, *S* . . . , inside part.

x_3 = (MK) x_{32} > (NK) x_{32} > x_2 = (pC) /x_2/ [*A*], /x/ *L* . . . , [*B*] > /x_2/ *A*, /x/ *B* but /h/ *L* . . . ; for example, *ʿnḫ* ⲱⲛϧ *B*, ⲱ⊥ϧ *P* and a reconstructed **pS*, ⲱⲛⳉ̄ *A* (and *pL* through ⲁⲛⳉ̄† *pL*), but ⲱⲛ̄ϩ *L*, *S* . . . , to live.

x_3 = (MK) x_{33} > (NK) x_{33} > (pC) /ç/ *L* . . . , [*B*], but /x_{33}/ [*A*], then (pC) /ç/ *L* . . . , [*B*] > (C) /š/ *L*, *S* . . . , *B*, and (pC) /x_{33}/ [*A*] > /x/ *A*; for example, *ḫpr* > ϣⲱⲡⲉ *P* and a reconstructed **pS*), ϣ̈ⲱⲡⲉ *pL*, [etc., and /çōpi/ *pB*] > ϣⲱⲡⲉ *S*, *L*, ϣⲟⲡⲉ *M*, ϣⲱⲡⲓ *W*, *V*, *F*, *B*, but [/xōpə/ *pA*] > ⳉⲱⲡⲉ *A*, to become.

(MK) *š* > (NK) *š* > (pC) /š/ > (C) /š/; for example, *šp*, ϣⲱⲡ *L*, *S* . . . , *B*, *A*, to receive.

[*See also:* Dialect İ; Dialect P.]

BIBLIOGRAPHY

Černý, J. *Coptic Etymological Dictionary.* Cambridge, 1976.

Edel, E. "Neues Material zur Herkunft der auslautenden Vokale -ⲉ und -ⲓ im Koptischen." *Zeitschrift für ägyptische Sprache und Altertumskunde,* 86 (1961):103–106.

Kasser, R. *Papyrus Bodmer VI: livre des Proverbes.* CSCO 194–195. Louvain, 1960.

______. "Prolégomènes à un essai de classification systématique des dialectes et subdialectes coptes selon les critères de la phonétique, I, Principes et terminologie." *Muséon* 93 (1980a):53–112. ". . . , II, Alphabets et systèmes phonétiques." *Muséon* 93 (1980b):237–97. ". . . , III, Systèmes orthographiques et catégories dialectales." *Muséon* 94 (1981):91–152.

______. "Orthographe et phonologie de la variété subdialectale lycopolitaine des textes gnostiques coptes de Nag Hammadi." *Muséon* 97 (1984):261–312.

______. "A Standard System of Sigla for Referring to the Dialects of Coptic." *Journal of Coptic Studies* 1 (1990):141–151.

Lacau, P. "Fragments de l'Ascension d'Isaïe en copte." *Muséon* 59 (1946):453–57.

Polotsky, H. J. "Zur koptischen Lautlehre I." *Zeitschrift für ägyptische Sprache und Altertumskunde* 67 (1931):74–77.

Vergote, J. *Phonétique historique de l'égyptien, les consonnes.* Louvain, 1945.

______. "Le Dialecte copte P (P. Bodmer VI: Proverbes), essai d'identification." *Revue d'égyptologie* 25 (1973):50–57.

______. *Grammaire copte,* Vol. 1a, *Introduction, phonétique et phonologie, morphologie synthématique (structure des sémantèmes), partie synchronique,* Vol. 1b, *Introduction, phonétique et phonologie, morphologie synthématique (structure des sémantèmes), partie diachronique,* Vol. 2a, *Morphologie syntagmatique, syntaxe, partie synchronique,* Vol. 2b, *Morphologie syntagmatique, partie diachronique.* Louvain, 1973–1983.

Vycichl, W. *Dictionnaire étymologique de la langue copte.* Louvain, 1983.

Worrell, W. H. *Coptic Sounds.* Ann Arbor, Mich., 1934.

RODOLPHE KASSER

SAHIDIC. Sahidic (siglum *S*) is a major Coptic dialect, earlier known as Upper Egyptian, Theban, or the southern dialect; the term "Sahidic," used by Athanasius of Qūṣ, was adopted by Stern (1880). In twentieth-century Coptology, *S* has been the main dialect of study and research—indeed Coptic *par excellence,* today totally supplanting BOHAIRIC in this respect (compare, for instance, its precedence in Crum, 1939, to that of Bohairic in Stern, 1880). This process, virtually complete by 1915 (cf. Erman, 1915, pp. 180f.), may be said to have been initiated by Steindorff's grammar of 1894; yet note early statements favoring Sahidic as "older," "richer," and "purer" (Stern, 1880, p. 1; Sethe, in Kahle, 1954, p. 202), and "magis regularis atque ad analogiam exacta" (Peyron, 1841, p. xix), the earliest observation of its relatively innovating, leveling nature. Indeed, the reputation of *S* as "old," or at least "older" than Bohairic, is due rather to its early documentation and its chronological precedence over Bohairic, which replaced it as the Coptic koine, than to typological fact.

Still the prestige of Sahidic is certainly justified by its rich literature, both original and translated, scriptural and nonscriptural (homiletic, patristic, monastic, Gnostic, magical, poetic), religious and nonreligious (epistolary, documentary, legal, medical). Sahidic was probably the first Coptic dialect into which the Scriptures were translated, apparently in the third century; by the fourth, the translation was completed. Almost all original Coptic literature was written in Sahidic (see ANTONY OF EGYPT, SAINT; PACHOMIUS, SAINT; SHENUTE, SAINT). By the ninth century, *S* had become the official dialect of the Coptic church, but as early as the fourth century, perhaps even earlier, it was a common Pan-Egyptian written literary dialect, spread at least from Heliopolis to Aswan. In subsequent centuries, it completely replaced the minor dialects (*A, L, M*) as a colloquial idiom. By the time of the ARAB CONQUEST OF EGYPT, *S* was the sole literary dialect beside northern Bohairic. From the ninth century onward, *S* gradually receded before Bohairic, a process much accelerated from the eleventh century on.

Sahidic occupies "a position apart from all other dialects" (Polotsky, 1970, p. 560) in that, first, it is "neutral" (Worrell, 1934, p. 73; Kahle, 1954, p. 241) or, better, most leveled, dialectologically speaking; it is the dialect most difficult to characterize distinctively, a "mean" dialect, the one with the fewest exclusive traits and the most isoglosses shared with others. Second, it raises (1) the diachronic, nondescriptive question of its local origin and "proper domain" (the statement by Athanasius of Qūṣ that Sahidic is "the dialect of Miṣr" is not helpful here) and (2) the synchronic question of its integration in the overall dialectological scheme. Question 1 is controversial: Worrell (1934, pp. 68ff.) considered its initial range to have been Oxyrhynchus and the lower valley (his "region IV" or perhaps an area even more northerly); Vergote (1973b, Vol. 1a, pp. 2f.) and Kasser (1980a, pp. 103ff.) suggested it spread southward from around Saqqara-Memphis (perhaps Worrell's "region II"); Polotsky (1970, p. 561) considered Thebes as a possible point of origin. Rather extreme appear Kahle's thesis (1954, pp. 256ff.) tentatively identifying its point of origin in Alexandria, and Schenke's denying Sahidic any original local basis, considering it to be a koine type of idiom born out of contacts, interaction, and leveling of local dialects (1981, pp. 349ff.); Vergote's conception seems to be the most plausible.

In any case, the characterization, still encountered, of Sahidic as "artificial" to a degree is descriptively irrelevant. It is true that standard literary Sahidic is largely "a gift" of the translation of the Bible (and in this sense many literary languages are "artificial") and that Sahidic probably owes its drastic expansion to the progressive suppression of distinctive phenomena. What specific traits Sahidic has, it shares most usually with Akhmimic and Subakhmimic in contrast to Bohairic and Fayyumic. ("Middle Egyptian" really occupies a roughly middle position between the two dialect clusters.) This is, however, no more than an impression and may be proved erroneous by a precise investigation.

Although standard, or "pure," Sahidic is more of a construct, an idealized average, a research *point de repère* than linguistic reality, some varieties of the dialect approach it more closely than others (see below); Sahidic is a *Mischdialekt,* an aggregation of linguistic habits only imperfectly and variously standardized (cf. Mink, 1978, pp. 91ff.; his statement that "die Annahme von Dialekten ist . . . sprachwissenschaftlich ein Konstrukt" is especially cogent when applied to Sahidic). However, extreme cases of "tainting" (e.g., by Fayyumic, Bohairic, Subakhmimic) must be specially treated. The dialect *P*, documented in the Papyrus Bodmer VI text of Proverbs published by Kasser (1960), is held by Vergote (1973a, p. 57) and Kasser (1980a, pp. 62ff.) to be a "protodialect of Sahidic," with non-Sahidic (Theban or Subakhmimic) traits; according to Nagel (1965), it represents early Theban.

1. Standard Sahidic

1.1 Phonology, Morphophonology, and Orthography. As a rule, *S* agrees with Bohairic in points of vocalism, while sharing its consonantism with *A–L* —according to Kasser, in a way reflecting an evolutive scale (see Vergote, 1973b, sec. 60 p. 58, and Kasser, 1981, sec. 25, for lists of "isophones").

1.1.1. Sahidic has no aspirate phonemes: ⲑ, ⲫ, and ⲭ are (in native words) monogram graphemes representing a combination of two phonemes. (They may have a different standing in the system of Greek-origin phonology.)

1.1.2. Sahidic has only one unvoiced laryngeal spirant (ϩ /h/).

1.1.3. ϫ and ϭ represent distinct phonemes (velopalatal or palatalized stop and alveolar affricate, respectively, ϫⲉ and ϭⲉ, as in ϫⲱ, say, and ϭⲱ, remain).

1.1.4. Sahidic has at least one laryngeal stop phoneme (/X/ = Vergote's and Kasser's /'/), synchronically suprasegmental: "(proneness to) vocalic reduplication." Its distribution is complex (see Satzinger, 1979), with the allophones "zero" (e.g., nonsyllabic /X/ in the final position and pausal junctive: ⲙⲉ, truth) and ⲁ (syllabic, pretonic /X/: ⲧⲁⲙⲟ, inform). In *P*, the laryngeal stop has its own sporadic grapheme (⊥).

1.1.5. In Sahidic there is no progressive sibilant assimilation to /s/ (ⲥⲁⲁⲛϣ̄, make live, nourish), but progressive sibilant assimilation to /c/ does take place (ϣⲁϫⲉ, speak).

1.1.6. Sonorants (/b/, /l/, /m/, /n/, and /r/) closing the tone syllable are graphically "reduplicated," occurring in two neighboring syllables as syllabic and nonsyllabic (onset): ϩⲃ̄ⲃⲉ, plow; ϩⲗ̄ⲗⲟ, old; ⲥⲙ̄ⲙⲉ, report; ⲕⲛ̄ⲛⲉ, be fat; ⲃⲣ̄ⲣⲉ, new.

1.1.7. The Sahidic vowel in the unstressed syllable (after Polotsky, 1933) is outlined in Table 1.

1.1.8. Stressed ⲁ represents the allophone of /o/ before /h/ and /X/ (ⲙ̄ⲕⲁϩ, be pained; ⲧⲃⲁ, ten thousand). In similar prelaryngeal environments, ⲉ represents /a/ (ⲥⲉⲉⲡⲉ, be left over; ϩⲉ, way).

1.1.9. Orthography (see in exhaustive detail Kasser, 1980a). Diagrams: ⲉⲓ, ⲟⲩ. Monograms: ⲑ, ⲫ, ⲭ, ϯ, ⲯ. ⲡⲛⲟⲩⲧⲉ, God, is not included among the *nomina sacra* abbreviations. The superlinear stroke occurs above one or more nonvocalic elements, signaling their syllabic phonological status (not their phonetic value or manner of actualization; see Polotsky, 1957a, pp. 221ff., 1971, pp. 227ff.). Proclitic prosodic: relative weakness is fully reflected in the standard orthography; see 1.3.7.

1.2 Morphology (Systemic and Nonsystemic) and Word Formation.

1.2.1. A superficial vocalic *e*-merger of the four converters (ⲉ- circ., ⲉ- second present, ⲛⲉ- preterite, ⲉⲧ(ⲉ)- relative) is characteristic of Sahidic; of these, the first two are actually homonymous. The relative and second perfect forms are not homonymous in the best standard orthography (ⲉⲛⲧ-ⲁ- versus ⲛ̄ⲧ-ⲁ-, respectively); the second perfect may be further circumstantially converted (ⲉ-ⲛ̄ⲧ-ⲁ-; Polotsky, 1957a, pp. 232ff., 1971, p. 232, 1960, sec. 11 obs., e.g., Mt. 20:28 and Eccl. 19:15).

1.2.2. The Sahidic future tense is the extended bipartite ϯⲛⲁⲥⲱⲧⲙ̄; the so-called third future (ⲉϥⲉ-/ⲛ̄ⲛⲉϥ-) is a mode rather than a tense (cf. Polotsky, 1950, pp. 34ff., 1971, pp. 219ff.) and has very limited convertibility (only circ. of the negative base: Polotsky, 1957a, p. 233, 1971, p. 233, 1960, pp. 400, 401, 1971, pp. 246ff.). ⲧⲉⲣⲁ- is a special second-person singular feminine future form.

1.2.3. The *S* conjunctive presuffixal base consists of a nasal (ⲛ̄) and no dental, except for the first-person singular (ⲛ̄ⲧⲁ-, ⲛⲧⲁ-). The conjunctive is in *S* a conjugation form apart, standing midway between the tripartite and bipartite patterns, with ⲛ̄- (prenominally ⲛ̄ⲧⲉ-) marking the modifier status of a nexus of (pro)noun and infinitive; morphologically, this special status is manifested in the pronominal elements, which are (with a single exception in the

TABLE 1.

PRETONIC		POSTTONIC			
FINAL SONORANT	NO SONORANT, INITIAL SONORANT	AFTER CLOSED STRESS SYLLABLE		AFTER OPEN STRESS SYLLABLE	
		INITIAL SONORANT	NO SONORANT, FINAL SONORANT	INITIAL OR FINAL SONORANT	NO SONORANT
∅	ⲉ	ⲉ	∅	∅	∅
ϣⲣ̄ϣⲱⲣϥ	ⲥⲉⲡⲥⲱⲡϥ	ⲥⲟⲧⲙⲉϥ	ⲥⲟⲧⲡ̄ϥ	ⲥⲱⲗⲡ̄	ⲥⲱⲧⲡ̄
	ⲟⲩⲉϭⲟⲩⲱϭϥ	ⲙⲟⲕⲙⲉⲕ	ϣⲟⲣϣⲣ̄	ⲥⲱⲧⲙ̄	
		(var. ∅)			
		ϩⲟⲧⲃ̄ϥ		(var. ⲉ)	

first singular) identical with the bipartite actor pronouns (prefix pronouns).

1.2.4. ⲧⲁⲣⲉϥⲥⲱⲧⲙ̄, the causative or "future" conjunctive, a specific postimperative, postinterrogative form with a first singular causation or guarantee seme (Polotsky, 1944, pp. 1ff., 1971, pp. 106ff.), is a typically Sahidic form. The causative infinitive is used as a noncausative "that" form after several prepositions (but less usually after others).

1.2.5. Sahidic employs a specific "temporal" clause conjugation, tripartite pattern form (ⲛ̄ⲧⲉⲣⲉϥ(ⲧⲙ̄)ⲥⲱⲧⲙ̄) distinct from the second and relative perfect forms.

1.2.6. The negatived conditional conjugation form has in Sahidic two variants (alternants), namely ⲉϥϣⲁⲛⲧⲙ̄ⲥⲱⲧⲙ̄ and ⲉϥⲧⲙ̄ⲥⲱⲧⲙ̄.

1.2.7. A special prenominal allomorph of all converters and some tripartite conjugation bases is characterized by the ending -ⲣⲉ.

1.2.8. Verbs of Greek origin occur in Sahidic in a zero-stem form (usually identical with the Greek imperative) and are directly incorporated in the conjugation and generally grammatical forms without the intermediation of an auxiliary: ⲁϥⲡⲓⲥⲧⲉⲩⲉ, ⲡⲉⲧⲉⲛⲉⲣⲅⲉⲓ, ϩⲟⲙⲟⲗⲟⲅⲉⲓ (imperative/infinitive).

1.2.9. The verb ϯ, give, has in *S* two imperatives, ϯ and ⲙⲁ (Polotsky, 1950, pp. 76ff., 1971, pp. 211ff.).

1.2.10. Pronominals: Sahidic has a ternary determination category—definite, indefinite, and zero ({ⲡ}, {ⲟⲩ-}, Ø-) determinators, expanded by noun lexemes. The proclitic form of the demonstrative ⲡⲏ, namely ⲡⲓ-, has (wherever distinct from ⲡⲉⲓ-, the proclitic allomorph of ⲡⲁї) affective and specially designative value (Polotsky, 1957a, pp. 229ff., 1971, pp. 231ff.).

1.2.11. Numbers are expressed as a rule by number words, not letters (e.g., Acts 23:23).

1.2.12. The first-person singular suffix-pronoun -ⲓ- has the allomorphs -ⲁ- (ⲛ̄ⲛ-ⲁ-, ⲧⲣ-ⲁ-) and -ⲧ (as object of infinitives following a consonant or /X/ or prepositions in similar environments). The second-person singular feminine suffix-pronoun consists of the allomorphs -Ø-/-ⲣⲉ after conjugation bases -Ø-/-ⲉ-/-ⲧⲉ as object of infinitives. The second-person plural suffix-pronoun consists of the allomorphs -ⲧⲛ̄- and -ⲧⲉⲧⲛ̄-. The third-person plural suffix-pronoun is nonsyllabic after ⲛ̄ⲛⲉ-, ⲧⲣⲉ-, ⲡⲉ- (possessive article). A special objective pronoun-paradigm is characterized by the third-person plural term -ⲥⲉ/-ⲥⲟⲩ. (This paradigm occurs mostly after another pronoun, e.g., as pronominal object of the possession verboid ⲟⲩⲛ̄ⲧⲁϥ.)

1.2.13. ϭⲓⲛ- forms in Sahidic lexical (nongrammatical) action nouns.

1.3 Syntagmatics and Prosody.

1.3.1. Focalization patterns: The second tense focalizes in Sahidic not only adverbials but also actor and object (pro)nouns, and may even be autofocal, that is, with the verb lexeme or predicative adverb itself the information focus (see Polotsky, 1944, pp. 51ff., 1971, pp. 155ff., 1960 sec. 32 obs., 1971, pp. 408ff., as in Lk. 20:13, ⲉⲓⲛⲁⲣ ⲟⲩ, "What shall I do?"; Sir. 5:4, ⲛ̄ⲧⲁⲟⲩ ϣⲱⲡⲉ ⲛⲁї, "What has happened to me?"; Acts 12:15, ⲉⲣⲉⲗⲟⲃⲉ, "Thou art mad"; Ps. 67:28, ⲉϥⲙ̄ⲙⲁⲩ, "Ibi est"). The cleft sentence with (pro)nominal focus (*vedette*; Polotsky, 1962) has the form "(pro)noun-ⲡⲉⲧ- (etc.)," with the *glose* marker ⲡ- tending to be invariable, and omissible only after a personal-pronoun focus (Polotsky, 1962, p. 420, 1971, p. 421).

1.3.2. Nominal syntagmatics: The nominal expansion of a noun syntagm is effected by ⲛ̄-/ⲛ̄ⲧⲉ- regulated by the determination of the nuclear noun and/or other expansions thereof, apparently with no lexical considerations involved.

1.3.3. -ⲙⲛ̄- is limited to coordinating non-zero-determinated nouns; the range of ⲁⲩⲱ is accordingly extended. (Zero-determinated nouns are coordinated by means of -ϩⲓ-.)

1.3.4. After converters, an indefinite or zero-determinated actor noun does not necessarily condition a ⲟⲩⲛ̄-/ⲙⲛ̄- allotagm of the bipartite pattern (Polotsky, 1960, sec. 21 and 35).

1.3.5. Final clauses are expressed by the conjunctions ϫⲉ, ϫⲉⲕⲁ(ⲁ)ⲥ followed by future III or the second future (circ. negative future III following ϫⲉⲕⲁⲁⲥ; Polotsky, 1957a, p. 233, 1971, p. 233) and not by means of the conjunctive (which does, however, resume ϫⲉⲕⲁⲁⲥ after an interposition; Lefort, 1948). The *S* conjuctive occurs after a limited number of conjunctions (the consecutive ϩⲱⲥⲧⲉ and ⲙⲏⲡⲱⲥ [ⲙⲏⲡⲟⲧⲉ], both of Greek origin) and does not usually function as a "that" form or expand impersonal verb predications (Stern, 1880, p. 275, sec. 445).

1.3.6. The possession-predicating ⲟⲩⲛ̄ⲧⲁϥ and ⲙⲛ̄ⲧⲁϥ have in Sahidic verboid status—that is, partake of all syntactic properties of verbal predications (conjugation forms): the *possessum* may be expressed pronominally as an object adjacent of the pronominal possessor (Acts 3:6, ⲡⲉⲧⲉⲟⲩⲛ̄ⲧⲁⲓϥ, "that which I have"; see ibid., sec. 316).

1.3.7. Prosody: Prosodic proclitic weakness is consistently reflected in the standard *S* orthography (see Erman, 1915: ⲟⲩⲛ̄-/ⲙⲛ̄-; ⲁⲛⲅ̄-/ⲛ̄ⲧⲕ̄ . . . ; ⲡⲉї-; ⲟⲩⲛ̄ⲧϥ̄-; ⲥϯ-; etc.). The relative converter joins in Sahidic in close juncture with the converted conjugation form (e.g., Lk. 12:5). Vowel reduplication occurs sporadically in monosyllabic, final-laryngeal words before an enclitic (ⲟⲩⲙⲉⲉ ⲡⲉ; Polotsky, 1957a, p. 231, 1971, p. 232, 1957b, pp. 348ff., 1971, pp. 390ff.).

1.4 Lexicon. As a rule, Sahidic shares lexical isoglosses at least with Akhmimic and/or Lycopolitan (or Subakhmimic), such as ⲃⲱⲱⲣⲉ, push, protrude. (This, however, may be refuted by further, more sophisticated investigation.) Lexemes not occurring in Bohairic seem relatively more common than exclusive *S* + *B* ones (e.g., ϣⲱⲱϭⲉ, wound; ⲃⲱⲕ, go; ⲧⲱⲕ, throw; ϩⲱⲛ, approach; ⲡⲱⲱⲛⲉ, turn; ⲕⲱⲙϣ̄, sneer; ⲟⲩⲱϣⲃ̄, answer; ϩⲱⲱϥ (particle), on the other hand; ϫⲟⲟⲩ-ⲧⲛ̄ⲛⲟⲟⲩ, send). Relatively few conjunctions of Greek origin are found in Sahidic.

2. Varieties of Sahidic

2.1 Classical, or Scriptural, Sahidic. As a rule, classical Sahidic conforms to the standard described above. However, more-precise scanning is called for in this case, differentiating between the Old and New Testaments, between various parts thereof, and even between the various manuscripts. Sahidic boasts more early (fourth or fifth century) manuscript sources than any other dialect of Coptic, and in this corpus many idiosyncrasies are observable, which may be subsumed together under the heading of "early Sahidic." The grouping of manuscripts in this category is helpful: the British Library Deuteronomy-Jonah and Psalms (Budge, 1898, 1912); the Bodmer Papyri, complemented by Chester Beatty and University of Mississippi fragments (Kasser, 1961, 1962, 1964, 1965) with linguistic introductions (note the forms ⲛ̄ⲇⲉ, ⲛ̄ⲅⲁⲣ; ⲛⲙ̄-, with; the rarity of the preterite relative prefix ⲉⲣ-, Dt. 4:42; total assimilation of nasals to sonorants; omission of nasals, etc.); the Turin Wisdoms (de Lagarde, 1883); the Berlin Psalter (Rahlfs, 1901); and recently the Palau Ribes Gospels (Quecke 1972, 1977; note the idiosyncrasies pointed out in the editor's extraordinary introductions: ⲛⲙ̄-, ⲙⲁϥ- (negative aorist), ⲧⲏⲛⲟⲩ second-person plural object, variation of ⲉⲧⲉ- ~ ⲉⲧⲉⲣⲉ-, ⲧⲉϥ- ~ ⲧⲣⲉϥ, sporadic omission of adverbial ⲛ̄- (ⲧⲉⲩⲛⲟⲩ, ⲥⲁ, ⲟⲩⲱⲧ), even some special lexemes). See in general Kahle's (1954, p. 233) discussion of this kind of manuscript; "Old Coptic" similarly presents mainly Sahidic traits (ibid., pp. 242ff., 252ff.).

2.2 "Gnostic" Sahidic. One must distinguish here between the Gnostic texts with no special dialectological problem (the Pistis Sophia, the Bruce Codex, some of the Nag Hammadi tractates) and such Nag Hammadi tractates as exhibit non-Sahidic traits. The former group conforms by and large to the early-Sahidic type, with some idiosyncrasies (total nasal assimilation, ⲉⲣ- relative prefix, ⲛ̄ⲧⲁⲣⲉϥ- for the classic ⲧⲁⲣⲉϥ-, ⲁ-future ⲥⲟⲩⲱⲛ-, ϩⲉⲱⲥ ϣⲁ(ⲛⲧⲉ-) [PS 178f., 313]), perhaps a more pronounced tendency to resume a converter/conjugation base after a nominal extraposition (PS 31, 173, 275f., 320). A profile of the Nag Hammadi idiom(s) or idiolect(s) will eventually be achieved on the basis of a series of monographs (cf. Nagel, 1969; Layton, 1973, 1974). The Nag Hammadi grammatical systems, which vary from one text to another, often seem inconsistent even in one and the same text. One encounters tractates written by a "speaker of some form of dialect A^2" (Layton, 1974, p. 379, Codex II). Certain texts (notably in codices III, V, and especially VII, tractates 2, 3, and 5) reveal Bohairic or "Middle Egyptian" (morpho-)syntactic traits, e.g., open juncture of the relative converter (III, 42.5f.), interrogative pronouns before basic tenses (VII, 103.3f.), the conjunctive a "that" form (VII, 80.13, 99.29f.), the relative compatible with indefinite determinators (ϩⲉⲛ-ⲉⲑⲟⲟⲩ, VII, 85. 11f.), relative conversion of the future III (III, 114.2f.), and, most striking, a four-term determination category with consequences for the expansion of the noun syntagm (ⲡⲓ- ⲛ̄ⲧⲉ-). Codices II and V reflect early Sahidic with non-Sahidic traits, mostly Akhmimoid (*A*, *L*, and, in the case of Codex V, Middle Egyptian as well). Note the following ⲁ-coloring in varying ratios: *A* forms of lexemes and morphs (ϩⲙⲁⲥⲧ, ⲕⲱⲉ, ϫⲉⲕⲁⲥⲉ, ⲧⲱⲱⲛ, ϫⲟⲩ); lexical Akhmimicisms (e.g., ϩⲣ̄ⲧⲉ, fear; ⲗⲁϭⲉ, cease [also Pistis Sophia]; ⲧⲁⲛⲟ, make, create); ⲙⲛ̄- ~ ⲙ̄ⲡⲣ̄- (negative imper.); ⲣ̄ ~ Ø- with Greek loan-verbs; ⲡ- ~ ⲡⲉ- for the definite article before a consonant cluster; ⲡⲉ- (possessive article second singular feminine), ⲡⲟⲩ-, ⲧⲣⲟⲩ- (third plural); the perfects ⲁϩⲁ-, ⲁϩ⸗, ⲉⲧⲁϩ-, ϩⲁϥ-.

2.3 Nonliterary, Postclassical, and Late Sahidic. These terms, often confused (if only by implication), demand clear definition. On the one hand, there are late literary texts, especially hagiographical, martyrological, and liturgical, but also popular literature and poetry (Drescher, 1947; Till, 1935–1936; Erman, 1897; Junker, 1908; etc.), mostly posterior to the Arab conquest. This corpus has to be carefully distinguished from the extremely important one, of high standardization, of postclassical literary Sahidic of the fourth, fifth, and sixth centuries (note especially Pachomius' writings and, above everything, the linguistic usage in Shenute's works, considered by the present writer at least as significant for the description of Sahidic grammar as is the scriptural idiom).

On the other hand, there is the immense body of nonliterary sources of late documentation, largely overlapping the late-*S* corpus in its grammatical norm. This category includes letters (private, formal, official), documents (receipts, contracts and agreements, demands, testaments), magical and medical recipes and spells (see, e.g., Chassinat, 1921), and so on. This corpus has had very scant attention hitherto (see Crum, 1926, Vol. 1, chap. 10; Kahle, 1954, chap. 8), and grammatical investigation of this area is still a future goal—perhaps the greatest challenge before Coptic linguistics today.

The overpowering impression conveyed by these texts, apart from their sheer numbers (major collections have been found at Thebes, al-Ashmūnayn, Wādī Sarjah, Dayr al-Bala'izah, Armant, and Aphrodito), is their bewildering variety and degrees of deviation from the classical standard; but therein lies their value. The letters (eighth–eleventh centuries in all catalogic collections, e.g., the British Library and the John Rylands Library ones, by Crum; Berlin, by Satzinger; Vienna, by Krall and Till) and documentary legal texts (again, in most collections) are to a large extent characterized by formulas. The poetic (tenth–eleventh centuries), magical (seventh–tenth centuries; Kropp, 1930–1931; Stegemann, 1934), and liturgical (see Quecke, 1970, pp. 350–89, M 574, a ninth-century manuscript) all to a lesser or greater extent exhibit non-Sahidic characteristics (Akhmimoid, Fayyumic, Bohairic). Striking are the following traits:

Phonological (if not dialectal) *and orthographic:* Vocalic and (to a lesser extent) consonantal variation is common; note especially the vocalic (ⲉ-) treatment of syllabic nasals (ⲙⲉ-, with; ⲉⲧⲟϥ, he) and the fluctuations ⲉ ~ ⲁ, ⲉ ~ ⲏ ~ Ø, ⲟ ~ ⲱ, ϭ ~ ⲕ, ⲃ ~ ϥ, voiced ~ unvoiced, aspirated ~ unaspirated. Many magical texts show Fayyumicism (stressed ⲁ for ⲟ, ⲉ for ⲁ, ⲏ for ⲉ and even Ø, and ⲃ for ϥ), although some (e.g., Kropp's A and B) are pure standard Sahidic; so on the whole is the Bala'izah collection. Some texts (e.g., Till's Martyrdoms) show a mixture of the *S* superlineation and Bohairic DJINKIM. Observe that incomplete or hesitant standardization must on no account be taken for "misspelling" (cf. Kahle, 1954, p. 254, n. 5; Kahle's lists [chap. 8] constitute an unsurpassed, indeed unparalleled description of the phonologic-orthographic usage of the Theban nonliterary sources).

Morphological. First-person singular ϣⲁⲛⲧⲁ-; second plural ⲧⲉⲧⲛⲉ- (Theban); second singular feminine ⲉⲣ- (converter), ⲁⲣ- (perfect) (Polotsky, 1960, p. 422, obs. 1); ⲛ̄ϣⲁϥ-, relative aorist, ⲛⲉ- future (*F*); ⲧⲉϥ- conjunctive (especially Theban, but also elsewhere; also ⲛ̄ⲧⲉϥ-); ⲉϥⲁ- future, ⲟⲩⲁ- future base, ⲙⲛ̄(ⲧ)- conditional (all Theban); verb lexeme sporadically unreduced before the direct nominal object; verb-lexeme morphology—(Theban) ⲟⲩⲱϣⲉ, ⲙⲟⲩⲛⲉ, ⲧⲓ⸗.

Tempuslehre and syntax. A future-eventual use of ϣⲁϥ-; a final-"subjunctive" use of the conjunctive (e.g., Martyrdoms 1.8.1, Ryl. 290, 321, also Theb., Kahle, 1954, pp. 160ff.), also in a "that"-form role, as direct object (Martyrdoms 1.5.9), even with past tenses; future final-consecutive use of ⲧⲁⲣⲉϥⲥⲱⲧⲙ̄ (Ryl. 316, Martyrdoms 1.5.29, Epiph. 162.26); ϣⲁⲛⲧϥ̄- (also final) and ϫⲉⲕⲁⲁⲥ acquire the value of content-clauses (cf. ἵνα). The second tense is used as a "that" form outside the cleft sentence (BKU 335 ⲁ ⲡⲉⲛⲥⲟⲛ ⲧⲁⲙⲟï ⲛ̄ⲧⲁϭⲛ̄ⲧϥ, "Our brother has told me that you found him." The circumstantial occurs adnominally, attributive to a definite nucleus (Kropp D 20 ⲡⲛⲟϭ ⲛ̄ⲁⲉⲧⲟⲥ ⲉⲣⲉ ⲛⲉϥⲧⲛ̄ϩ ⲡⲟⲣϣ̄ ⲉⲃⲟⲗ, "The great eagle whose wings are spread"); the circumstantial as *glose* in a cleft sentence (Kropp D ⲧⲟⲕ ⲡⲉ ⲉⲕϯ ϩⲛ̄ ⲡⲗⲡⲟⲧ, "It is you who pour"); the possessive ⲉⲡⲱ⸗ ⲡⲉ (e.g., Ryl. 325, 341), also ⲡⲱ⸗ as an augens of the possessive article ⲡⲉϥ- (KRU 36 ⲧⲛ̄ⲁⲓⲧⲏⲥⲓⲥ ⲧⲱⲛ ⲙ̄ⲙⲓⲛ ⲙ̄ⲙⲟⲛ). Note such Bohairic-like features as ⲟⲩⲁ ⲛ̄ⲧⲁϥ- (Martyrdoms 1.58.1, a generic relative, an indefinite ⲡⲉⲛⲧⲁϥ-), ⲛ̄ⲧⲁϥⲥⲱⲧⲙ̄ (relative/second perfect) used as a temporal clause, ⲛⲓⲙ ⲁϥ- (Martyrdoms 1.3.7); also ⲛ̄ⲥⲁ- ⲛ̄ⲧⲟϥ (ibid. 1.34.3).

2.4 Sahidic Alloyed with Other Dialects (cf. Crum's S^a and S^f). This is, in view of the reservations and observations made above, to be understood as an ad hoc text-specific descriptive appellation (IDIOLECT) rather than a clear, definable dialectological phonomenon. The quality and degree of component admixture vary considerably from one case to another, and it is doubtful whether dialectologically meaningful classification and gradation are at all feasible. For instance, the Fayyumicisms peculiar to many *S* manuscripts in the Morgan collection are neither predictable nor uniformly distributed. In "Pseudo-Shenute," M 604 (Kuhn, 1960), the *F* element consists of sporadic grammatical characteristics -ϣⲧⲉⲙ-, negative conditional ⲁⲣⲉϣⲧⲉⲙ-, second singular feminine possessive article ⲡⲉⲣ-, and lexical-phonological

Fayyumicisms: ⲥⲱⲡⲧ, ⲟⲩⲛ, what (interrogative). In the unpublished parallel source, B. L. Or. 12689, the vocalism and generally the phonological shape of words is drastically affected.

3. Bibliographical Information

3.1 Major, Comprehensive, or Authoritative Bible Editions. Old Testament: de Lagarde, 1883 (Wisdom of Solomon, Ecclesiasticus); Ciasca, 1885–1904 (Old Testament fragments, a basic edition); Maspero, 1892–1897 (a complementary edition of Old Testament fragments); Budge, 1898 and 1912 (Psalms, Deuteronomy, Jonah); Rahlfs, 1901 (Psalms); Thompson, 1908 (Job, Proverbs, Ecclesiastes, Song of Solomon, Wisdom of Solomon, Ecclesiasticus) and 1911 (Joshua, Judges, Ruth, Judith, Esther); Worrell, 1931 (Proverbs); Shier, 1942 (Ruth, Ecclesiastes, Song of Solomon, fragments of Genesis, Jeremiah, Baruch); Kasser, 1961, 1962, 1964, and 1965 (the Bodmer manuscripts: Exodus, Deuteronomy, Isaiah, Jeremiah, Lamentations, Epistle of Jeremiah, Baruch). New Testament: Horner, 1911–1924 (authoritative critical edition of the New Testament); Balestri in Ciasca and Balestri, 1885–1904, Vol. 3 (Borgia New Testament fragments); Budge, 1912 (Acts, Revelation); Thompson, 1932 (Acts, Pauline Epistles); Kasser, 1962 (Matthew, Romans); Quecke, 1972, 1977, and 1984 (Mark, Luke, John).

3.2 Grammars and Grammatical Monographs. Stern, 1880 (best grammar yet); Steindorff, 1894, 1904 (reprint 1930), and 1921; Till, 1961 (still the most commonly used, for its convenience rather than for descriptive merit); Plumley, 1948, and Walters, 1972, are rather sketchy. Dialect comparative grammars: Stern 1880; Till, 1961; Chaîne, 1933 (very detailed); Steindorff, 1951; Vergote, 1973b, Vol. 1a. Special studies: Erman, 1897; Levy, 1909; Wilson, 1970; Kickasola, 1975.

3.3 Dictionaries. There is no special Sahidic lexicon, but the Sahidic component of Crum's *Dictionary* (also Spiegelberg and Westendorff's *Handwörterbuch*) is certainly adequate. Wilmet's invaluable *Concordance* (1957–1959) covers the Sahidic New Testament. Many text editions include special glossaries.

BIBLIOGRAPHY

Balestri, G. *Sacrorum Bibliorum Fragmenta Copto-Sahidica Musei Borgiani.* Vol. 3, *Novum Testamentum.* Rome, 1904. See also Ciasca, A.

Budge, E. A. W. *The Earliest Known Coptic Psalter.* London, 1898.

———. *Coptic Biblical Texts in the Dialect of Upper Egypt.* London, 1912.

Chaîne, M. *Eléments de grammaire dialectale copte.* Paris, 1933.

Chassinat, E. *Un Papyrus médical copte.* Cairo, 1921.

Ciasca, A. *Sacrorum Bibliorum Fragmenta Copto-sahidica Musei Borgiani Iussu et Sumptibus S. Congregationis de Propaganda Fide Studio . . . Edita.* Vols. 1 and 2. Rome, 1885 and 1889. And [without author or ed.]: *SS. Bibliorum Fragmenta Copto-Sahidica Musei Borgiani. Vol. 1–2. Tabulae.* Rome, [1904]. See also Balestri, G.

Crum, W. E. "The Language of the Texts." In *The Monastery of Epiphanius at Thebes,* Part 1, *The Archaeological Material by H. E. Winlock, The Literary Material by W. E. Crum,* pp. 232–56. New York, 1926.

———. *A Coptic Dictionary.* Oxford, 1939.

Drescher, J. *Three Coptic Legends.* Cairo, 1947.

Erman, A. *Bruchstücke koptischer Volksliteratur.* Berlin, 1897.

———. "Unterschiede zwischen den koptischen Dialekten bei der Wortverbindung." *Sitzungsberichte der Preussischen Akademie der Wissenschaften* 1 (1915):161–72.

[Horner, G. W.] *The Coptic Version of the New Testament in the Southern Dialect, Otherwise Called Sahidic and Thebaic.* Oxford, 1911–1924.

Junker, H. *Koptische Poesie des 10. Jahrhunderts.* Berlin, 1908.

Kahle, P. E. *Bala'izah: Coptic Texts from Deir el-Bala'izah in Upper Egypt.* Oxford and London, 1954.

Kasser, R. *Papyrus Bodmer VI: livre des Proverbes.* CSCO 194–195. Louvain, 1960.

———. *Papyrus Bodmer XVI: Exode I–XV,21 en sahidique.* Cologny/Geneva, 1961.

———. *Papyrus Bodmer XVIII, Deutéronome I–X,7 en sahidique.* Cologny/Geneva, 1962.

———. *Papyrus Bodmer XXII et Mississippi Coptic Codex II: Jérémie XL,3–LII,34, Lamentations, Epître de Jérémie, Baruch I,1–V,5, en sahidique.* Cologny/Geneva, 1964.

———. *Papyrus Bodmer XXIII: Esaïe XLVII–LXVI, en sahidique.* Cologny/Geneva, 1965.

———. "Prolégomènes à un essai de classification systématique des dialectes et subdialectes coptes selon les critères de la phonétique. I, Principes et terminologie." *Muséon* 93 (1980a):53–112. ". . . , II, Alphabets et systèmes phonétiques." *Muséon* 93 (1980b):237–97. ". . . , III, Systèmes orthographiques et catégories dialectales." *Muséon* 94 (1981):91–152.

Kickasola, J. N. *Sahidic Coptic (*ⲛ̄*) . . .* ⲁⲛ *Negation Patterns: A Morpho-syntactic Description of Sentences and Adjuncts.* Ann Arbor, Mich., 1975.

Kropp, A. M. *Ausgewählte koptische Zaubertexte.* Brussels, 1930–1931.
Kuhn, K. H. *Pseudo-Shenoute on Christian Behaviour.* CSCO 206–207. Louvain, 1960.
Lagarde, P. A. de. *Aegyptiaca.* Göttingen, 1883.
Layton, B. "The Text and Orthography of the Coptic Hypostasis of the Archons." *Zeitschrift für Papyrologie und Epigraphik* 11 (1973):173–200.
______. "The Hypostasis of the Archons or the Reality of the Rulers: A Gnostic Story of the Creation, Fall, and Ultimate Salvation of Man, and the Origin and Reality of His Enemies, Newly Edited from the Cairo Manuscript with a Preface, English Translation, Notes, and Indexes." *Harvard Theological Review* 67 (1974):352–425; 69 (1976):31–101. Particularly "Preface," 67 (1974):351–94.
Lefort, L. T. "ϫⲉⲕⲁⲥ dans le NT sahidique." *Muséon* 61 (1948):65–73.
Levy, A. *Die Syntax der koptischen Apophthegmata Patrum Aegyptiorum.* Berlin, 1909.
Maspero, G. *Fragments de la version thébaine de l'Ancien Testament.* Mémoires de l'Institut français d'Archéologie orientale 6. Cairo, 1892–1897.
Mink, G. "Allgemeine Sprachwissenschaft und Koptologie." In *The Future of Coptic Studies,* ed. R. McL. Wilson, pp. 71–103. Leiden, 1978.
Nagel, P. "Der frühkoptische Dialekt von Theben." in *Koptologische Studien in der DDR,* pp. 30–49. *Wissenschaftliche Zeitschrift der Martin-Luther-Universität Halle-Wittenberg,* Sonderheft. Halle-Wittenberg, 1965.
______. "Grammatische Untersuchungen zu Nag H. Codex II." In *Die Araber in der alten Welt,* ed. F. Altheim and R. Stiehl, Vol. 5, *Nachträge, Das christliche Aksūm.* Berlin, 1969.
Peyron, V. A. *Grammatica Linguae Coptae.* Turin, 1841.
Plumley, J. M. *An Introductory Coptic Grammar (Sahidic Dialect).* London, 1948.
Polotsky, H. J. "Zur koptischen Lautlehre II." *Zeitschrift für ägyptische Sprache und Altertumskunde* 69 (1933):125–29. Repr. in *Collected Papers,* pp. 358–62. Jerusalem, 1971.
______. *Etudes de syntaxe copte.* Cairo, 1934. Repr. in *Collected Papers,* pp. 102–207. Jerusalem, 1971.
______. "Modes grecs en copte?" In *Coptic Studies in Honor of W. E. Crum,* pp. 73–90. Boston, 1950. Repr. in *Collected Papers,* pp. 208–225. Jerusalem, 1971.
______. Review of W. C. Till, *Koptische Grammatik (saïdischer Dialekt). Orientalistische Literaturzeitung* 52 (1957a):219–34. Repr. in *Collected Papers,* pp. 226–33. Jerusalem, 1971.
______. "Zu den koptischen literarischen Texten aus Balaizah." *Orientalia* 26 (1957b):347–49. Repr. in *Collected Papers,* pp. 389–91. Jerusalem, 1971.
______. "The Coptic Conjugation System." *Orientalia* 29 (1960):392–422. Repr. in *Collected Papers,* pp. 238–68. Jerusalem, 1971.
______. "Nominalsatz und Cleft Sentence im Koptischen." *Orientalia* 31 (1962):413–30. Repr. in *Collected Papers,* pp. 418–35. Jerusalem, 1971.
______. "Coptic." In *Current Trends in Linguistics,* Vol. 6, *South West Asia and North Africa,* ed. T. A. Sebeok, pp. 558–70. The Hague, 1970.
Quecke, H. *Untersuchungen zum koptischen Stundengebet.* Louvain, 1970.
______. *Das Markusevangelium saidisch: Text der Handschrift PPalau Rib. Inv.-Nr. 182 mit den Varianten der Handschrift M 569.* Barcelona, 1972.
______. *Das Lukasevangelium saidisch: Text der Handschrift PPalau Rib. Inv.-Nr. 181 mit den Varianten der Handschrift M 569.* Barcelona, 1977.
______. *Das Johannesevangelium saidisch: Text der Handschrift PPalau Rib. Inv.-Nr. 183 mit den Varianten der Handschriften 813 und 814 der Chester Beatty Library und der Handschrift M 569.* Rome and Barcelona, 1984.
Rahlfs, A. *Die Berliner Handschrift des sahidischen Psalters.* Berlin, 1901.
Satzinger, H. "Phonologie des koptischen Verbs (sa'idischer Dialekt)." In *Festschrift E. Edel, 12 März 1979,* pp. 343–68. Bamberg, 1979.
Schenke, H.-M. Review of Joseph Vergote, *Grammaire copte. Orientalistische Literaturzeitung* 76 (1981):345–51.
Shier, L. A. "Old Testament Texts on Vellum." In William H. Worrell. *Coptic Texts in the University of Michigan Collection,* pp. 23–167. Ann Arbor, Mich., 1942.
Stegemann, V. *Die koptischen Zaubertexte der Sammlung Erzherzog Rainer in Wien.* Heidelberg, 1934.
Steindorff, G. *Koptische Grammatik.* Berlin, 1894.
______. *Koptische Grammatik.* Berlin, 1904. Repr. Berlin, 1930.
______. *Kurzer Abriss der koptischen Grammatik.* Berlin, 1921.
______. *Lehrbuch der koptischen Grammatik.* Chicago, 1951.
Stern, L. *Koptische Grammatik.* Leipzig, 1880.
Thompson, H. *The Coptic (Sahidic) Version of Certain Books of the Old Testament from a Papyrus in the British Museum.* London, 1908.
______. *A Coptic Palimpsest Containing Joshua, Judges, Ruth, Judith and Esther in the Sahidic Dialect.* Oxford, 1911.
______. *The Coptic Version of the Acts of the Apostles and the Pauline Epistles in the Sahidic Dialect.* Cambridge, 1932.
Till, W. C. *Koptische Heiligen- und Martyrerlegenden.* Rome, 1935–1936.
______. *Koptische Grammatik (saïdischer Dialekt), mit Bibliographie, Lesestücken und Wörterverzeichnissen.* Leipzig, 1955.

———. *Koptische Dialektgrammatik, mit Lesestücken und Wörterbuch.* 2nd ed. Munich, 1961.
Vergote, J. "Le dialecte copte P (P. Bodmer VI: Proverbes), essai d'identification." *Revue d'égyptologie* 25 (1973a):50–57.
———. *Grammaire copte,* Vol. 1a, *Introduction, phonétique et phonologie, morphologie synthématique (structure des sémantèmes), partie synchronique,* Vol. 1b, *Introduction, phonétique et phonologie, morphologie synthématique (structure des sémantèmes), partie diachronique.* Louvain, 1973b.
Walters, C. C. *An Elementary Coptic Grammar of the Sahidic Dialect.* Oxford, 1972.
Wilmet, M. *Concordance du Nouveau Testament sahidique,* II, *Les Mots autochthones.* CSCO 173, 183, 185. Louvain, 1957–1959.
Wilson, M. R. *Coptic Future Tenses: Syntactical Studies in Sahidic.* The Hague, 1970.
Worrell, W. H. *The Proverbs of Solomon in Sahidic Coptic According to the Chicago Manuscript.* Chicago, 1931.
———. *Coptic Sounds.* Ann Arbor, Mich., 1934.

ARIEL SHISHA-HALEVY

SHENUTEAN IDIOM. "Shenutean Coptic" is the term applied to the idiom, including the grammatical norm and stylistic-phraseological usage, observable in the corpus of writing by the archimandrite Apa Shenute (334–451), outstanding among Coptic literary sources in that it constitutes the single most extensive homogenous and authentic *testo di lingua* for Sahidic and Coptic in general. This corpus provides the linguist with a precious opportunity to achieve a consistent and complete description of a grammatical system. The other extensive corpus, that of the Scriptures, although somewhat earlier and so enjoying the prestige of a "classical" *état de langue,* has the disadvantage of being translated from the Greek; its native Coptic constituent element can be properly determined only after a complete structural description of the grammatical system of its *Vorlage,* precise knowledge of the quality and degree of its dependence upon this *Vorlage,* and diacritical-contrastive application of an independent, untranslated grammatical system such as that abstractable from Shenute's works. The desirability of such a grammar makes an early analysis of this corpus of paramount importance.

Compilation of the Corpus

Although only slightly more than half of all known or surmised Shenute sources have been edited to date (1982), there is no great difficulty about compiling most of the extant corpus: the task of isolating unattributed Shenute fragments from the host of homiletic and rhetoric-epistolary ones is largely technical. Linguistic (grammatical and stylistic-phraseological) data extractable from the unambiguously Shenutean sources in the three major editions (Amélineau, 1907–1914; Leipoldt and Crum, 1908–1913; Chassinat, 1911) and the many minor ones—mostly in catalogic collections (by Crum, Munier, Pleyte-Boeser, Rossi, Wessely, and Zoega) and occasionally in special publications (e.g., by Guérin, Lefort, Teza, Young, and the present writer), as well as unpublished sources—serve as probes for locating other sources. Identification on the basis of stylistic impression alone, although certainly unavoidable as a practical guide, is not always adequate, especially when the style is untypically pedestrian rather than in the usual powerful, involved vein. The main unedited collections of Sinuthiana are those in Paris and Vienna repositories and in British libraries (Oxford, Cambridge, and Manchester).

Linguistic Characterization

Shenute's dialect is what is conventionally conceived of as high-standard literary Sahidic, albeit with distinct Akhmimoid traces (Shisha-Halevy, 1976a), which are probably due to his native Akmimic background and consist mainly of (morpho)-phonologic, morphologic, idiomatic, and lexical features, with more elisive syntactic affinities. (Present-day knowledge of Akhmimic syntax is notoriously inadequate, because of insufficient evidence.) Some of the more striking phenomena in Shenute's grammatical usage are the idiosyncratic use of the conjunctive and of object constructions and the favoring of one of the "mediators" or lexeme premodifiers (ⲣ̄ ϩⲟⲩⲉ-, ⲣ̄ ⲡⲕⲉ-, ϣⲣ̄ⲡ (ⲛ̄)-). Note two (of several) distinctive nominal-sentence patterns, namely # Ø -ⲡⲉ # (e.g., Leipoldt, 1908–1913, IV, 23.22, ⲙ̄ⲕⲁϩ ⲛ̄ϩⲏⲧ ⲡⲉ ⲥⲱⲧⲙ̄ ⲉⲛⲉϊϣⲁϫⲉ; Amélineau 1907–1914, I, 228, ϣⲗⲟϥ ⲡⲉ ϫⲟⲟⲩ, ϣⲓⲡⲉ ⲡⲉ ⲥⲱⲧⲙ̄ ⲉⲣⲟⲟⲩ) and a hyperbatic construction with a demonstrative subject (Chassinat, 1911, 150.3ff., ⲛ̄ⲛⲟⲩϩ ⲛⲉ ⲛⲁϊ ⲛ̄ⲧⲁⲩⲥⲱⲗⲡ̄, "These are 'the cords which broke'"); ϫⲉ, used adnominally (ibid., 125.38ff., ⲙ̄ⲙⲛ̄ ϭⲉⲡⲓⲥⲧⲓⲥ, ⲙ̄ⲙⲛ̄ ϭⲉϩⲉⲗⲡⲓⲥ ⲛ̄ϩⲱⲃ ⲛ̄ⲁⲅⲁⲑⲟⲛ ϫⲉ ⲛϥϣⲟⲟⲡ ⲛⲁⲥ ⲁⲛ, "There is no faith, there is no hope of goodness that does not belong to it").

As regards the use of the second tenses, one finds numerous distinctive figures and constellations variously combining topicalizations and foci. Striking is the cleft sentence with the circumstantial topic (ⲉⲁϥ-, ⲉⲛϥ̅- . . . ⲁⲛ, ⲉ- + nominal sentence). Negative second-tense topics seem to be avoided. This list can be much extended with numerous other minutiae as well as central issues of grammar, which still await monographic study (for some discussions and exemplifications, see Jernstedt, 1949; Morenz, 1952; Rudnitzky, 1956–1957; Young, 1961, 1962, and 1969; and Shisha-Halevy, 1975 and 1976a–b). It must be stressed that idiosyncratic stylistic syntax (e.g., "rhetorical figures" [see below], typical word-order and context patterns) is at present indistinguishable from syntax *tout court*. Note also that although most of the above traits are met with elsewhere, their cumulative and pronounced reoccurrence and distribution in Shenute is syndromic, and therein lies their diagnostic value.

Shenute's "style" (between which and syntax there exists no clear-cut objective boundary) has been described, at its most characteristic, as fervent, passionately eloquent, full of pathos, and often argumentative, polemic, occasionally ironic. Still, placid and pedestrian passages are not uncommon (cf. Leipoldt, 1903, sec. 11, 13, and 15). The long, involved, occasionally convoluted sentence complexes, sometimes anacoluthic, are well known. Similarly distinctive are a number of exclusive or near-exclusive Shenutean idiomatic expressions, such as ⲧⲱ ⲉⲧⲱ, "how can one compare . . ."; ϣⲁⲛⲧⲉ ⲟⲩ ϣⲱⲡⲉ, "*Quousque tandem . . .*"; ⲉⲓ̈ϫⲱ ⲙⲡⲁⲓ̈ ϫⲉ, "by which I mean to say"; ϫⲉ ⲛ̅ⲛⲁϫⲟⲟⲥ, "*pour ne pas dire*"; and many others. Probably the best-known typically Shenutean turn of phrase, the quintessential "*figura Sinuthiana*" par excellence, is the apparently tautological, often disjunctive repetition of an idea with a slight variation in this form: ⲥⲉⲣⲏⲥ ⲁⲩⲱ ⲥⲉⲣⲟⲉⲓⲥ, ⲡⲁⲥⲟⲛ ⲏ ⲛⲁⲥⲛⲏⲩ, ϯⲕⲱⲗⲩⲉ ⲏ ϯⲛⲁⲕⲱⲗⲩⲉ, ⲁϥⲟⲩⲱⲛ ⲏ ⲁⲩⲟⲩⲱⲛ ⲙ̅ⲙⲟϥ, ⲁ ⲡⲁϩⲏⲧ ⲟⲩⲱϣⲥ̅ ⲏ ⲁϥⲟⲩⲱϣⲥ̅ ϩⲣⲁⲓ̈ ⲛ̅ϩⲏⲧ, ⲁⲩⲙⲟⲟⲩⲧϥ̅ ⲏ ⲁⲩⲧⲁⲁϥ ⲉⲧⲟⲟⲧϥ̅ ⲙ̅ⲡⲙⲟⲩ . . .

Vocabulary

The Shenutean lexicon—which constitutes a considerable part of the Sahidic evidence in Crum's *Coptic Dictionary* (1939) and is still in need of determination and structural-semantic resolution—is perhaps most idiosyncratic in the favoring of certain words, some of which have acquired a Shenutean flavor and association: ⲕⲣⲟϥ, guile; ⲗⲟⲓⲙⲟⲥ, pestilence; ⲕⲱⲙϣ̅, mock; ⲃⲟⲗⲃⲗ̅, burrow; ⲗⲱⲙⲥ̅, ⲗⲱⲱⲙⲉ, filth, be foul; ⲗⲓⲃⲉ, be mad; ⲙⲟⲩϩ, look; ⲗⲉⲯⲉ, fragment; ⲱⲣϫ̅, be firm, secure; ⲣⲱϣⲉ, have authority, be responsible. There are some exclusively Shenutean lexemes, a few with obscure meanings: ⲕⲱⲱⲗⲉ ⲉⲃⲟⲗ (Crum, 1939, p. 102b); ⲕⲟⲛ (part of vine? ibid. p. 111b); ⲗⲱⲡⲥ̅ (ibid., p. 144a); ⲕⲱⲣⲙ̅, smoke; ⲗⲁⲁⲗⲉ, teem; ⲛⲟⲩⲥ, term of abuse; also some common to Shenute (the sole representative for Sahidic) and Akhmimic or Subakhmimic (Shisha-Halevy, 1976a, pp. 364ff.). There are forms and functions attested only in Shenute: ⲃⲗ̅ⲗⲏ, blind (fem.); ⲛⲓϥⲉ, blow (trans.); ⲣⲟⲉⲓⲥ ⲟⲩⲃⲉ-, keep watch against; ⲣⲱϩⲧ̅ ⲉϩⲣⲁⲓ̈, be struck down. Some lexemes are typically Shenutean in collocation (ⲣⲟⲉⲓⲥ + ⲣⲏⲥ, ⲛⲁ + ⲛⲏⲩ) and some in their morphology (e.g., ⲕⲧⲟⲉⲓⲧ†, returned; ⲛⲟⲩϭⲧⲉ ~ ⲛⲟϭ, big; ⲉⲗⲙⲱ, sycamore fruit; ⲧⲛⲟⲙ, furrow).

BIBLIOGRAPHY

Amélineau, E. C. *Oeuvres de Schenoudi.* Paris, 1907–1914.

Chassinat, E. *Le Quatrième Livre des entretiens et épîtres de Shenouti.* Mémoires de l'Institut français d'archéologie orientale 23. Cairo, 1911.

Crum, W. E. *A Coptic Dictionary.* Oxford, 1939.

Frandsen, P. J., and E. Richter-Aeroe. "*Shenoute: A Bibliography.*" In *Studies Presented to Hans Jakob Polotsky,* ed. D. W. Young, pp. 147–76. East Gloucester, Mass., 1981.

Guérin, H. "Sermons inédits de Senouti." *Revue égyptologique* 10 (1902):148–64, and 11 (1905):15–34.

Jernstedt, P. V. "K determinacii v koptskom jazyke." *Sovetskoje Vostokovedenije* 6 (1949):52–62. Translated by Peter Nagel as "Zur Determination im Koptischen." *Wissenschaftliche Zeitschrift der Martin-Luther-Universität Halle-Wittenberg* 27 (1978): 95–106.

Leipoldt, J. *Schenoute von Atripe und die Entstehung des nationalägyptischen Christentums.* Leipzig, 1903.

Leipoldt, J., and W. E. Crum. *Sinuthii Archimandritae Vita et Opera Omnia.* CSCO 42 and 73. Paris, 1908–1913.

Morenz, S. "Die ⲛ̅ϭⲓ-Konstruktion als sprachliche und stilistische Erscheinung des Koptischen." *Annales du Service des antiquités de l'Egypte* 52 (1952):1–15.

Rudnitzky, G. "Zum Sprachgebrauch Schenutes." *Zeitschrift für ägyptische Sprache und Altertumskunde* 81 (1956):45–58, and 82 (1957):143–51.

Shisha-Halevy, A. "Two New Shenoute-Texts from the British Library, II (Commentary)." *Orientalia* 44 (1975):469–84.

______. "Akhmîmoid Features in Shenoute's Idiolect." *Muséon* 89 (1976a):157–80.

______. "Commentary on Unpublished Shenoutiana in the British Library." *Enchoria* 6 (1976b):29–61.

______. *Coptic Grammatical Categories, Structural Studies in the Syntax of Shenoutean Sahidic.* Analecta Orientalia 53. Rome, 1986.

Young, D. W. "On Shenoute's Use of Present I." *Journal of Near Eastern Studies* 20 (1961):115–19.
______. "Ešōpe and the Conditional Conjugation." *Journal of Near Eastern Studies* 21 (1962):175–85.
______. "Unfulfilled Conditions in Shenoute's Dialect." *Journal of the American Oriental Society* 89 (1969):399–407.

ARIEL SHISHA-HALEVY

SULLAM (or *scala*). The Arabic term for a Coptic-Arabic dictionary is *sullam* (ladder; plural *salālim*), because the words are arranged to the left (Coptic) and the right (Arabic) in a manner that gives the impression of a ladder (Latin *scala;* Coptic ⲙⲟⲩⲕⲓ *B*, ⲧⲱⲣⲧⲉⲣ or ϭⲗⲟⲟϭⲉ *S*).

Coptic lexicography started at the same time as Coptic grammar. Anbā Yūḥannā al-Samannūdī, the author of the first grammar, also wrote the first known Coptic dictionary. Anbā Yūḥannā, who was bishop of Samannūd (western Delta) in the middle of the thirteenth century, wrote *Al-Sullam al-Kanā'isī* (or *Scala Ecclesiastica*), of which two versions survive, Sahidic (Munier, 1930, pp. 1–43) and Bohairic, both found in many manuscripts (Graf, 1947, pp. 372–74). It is not a dictionary but a glossary of terms in biblical and liturgical books, mainly the New Testament, a portion of the Old Testament, and some liturgical texts. The words are given with their Arabic translation in the order in which they occur, except repetitions. The *sullam* begins with the Gospel of St. John because of its easy style. Anba Yūḥannā did not intend to write a dictionary in the modern sense of the term but a manual for his readers, to enable them to understand religious texts. The beginning of St. John's Gospel runs as follows: ϩⲛ̄ = *fi*, in; ⲧⲉ-ϩⲟⲩⲉⲓⲧⲉ = *al-bady,* the beginning; ⲛⲉϥϣⲟⲟⲡ = *kān, kāyin,* was; ⲡϣⲁϫⲉ = *al-kalimah,* the word (Munier, 1930, p. 1). In the preface of his *Bulghat al-Ṭālibīn* (freely translated as "What Seekers Find"; Bauer, 1972, pp. 303–306) he announced his intention to write a poem of the *muthallath* kind (strophes with three rhymes) on words pronounced in the same way but written differently, but this has not survived.

Abū Isḥāq ibn al-'Assāl (full name al-Mu'taman Abū Isḥāq Ibrāhīm ibn al-'Assāl), a member of the famous 'Assāl family (Mallon, 1906–1907), wrote a "rhymed" dictionary called *al-Sullam al-Muqaffā wa-l-Dhahab al-Muṣaffā* (The Rhymed Dictionary and the Purified Gold; Kircher, 1643, pp. 273–495, not quite complete). Words are classified by the last letter, as in Arabic dictionaries (e.g., the *Ṣiḥāḥ* of al-Jawharī; Sidarus, 1978, p. 129). The order is last letter, then first letter, and then second letter, as in ϫⲁⲥ, leave her; ϫⲗⲁⲙⲓⲥ, shirt (= ϫⲗⲁⲙⲩⲥ); ϫⲟⲣⲟⲥ, tambourine; ϫⲣⲟⲛⲟⲥ, time; (. . .) ϫⲱⲣⲓⲥ, except (Kircher, 1643, p. 443). Also words with affixes are listed; thus, ⲁⲓϫⲁⲕ, I have put thee, and ⲧⲏⲣⲉⲛ, all of us, are found under *-k* and *-n*. As a matter of fact, their are no "rhymes" in his dictionary, as only the last letter is taken into consideration. His vocabulary is limited to religious texts (Graf, 1947, pp. 407–411).

Abū Shākir ibn al-Rāhib (full name al-Nushū' Abū Shākir ibn Buṭrus al-Rāhib, author of a grammar (MUQADDIMAH), wrote another "rhymed" scala, which he finished in 1263–1264. He used a larger number of liturgical books and two ancient scalae, as is revealed in the preface of his book. His scala is lost. As a *sullam muqaffā,* or rhymed scala, it was arranged after the last letter of the words. It comprised two parts: simple word forms and words with prefixes and suffixes (Sidarus, 1978, p. 130).

An independent work is the anonymous Sahidic-Arabic *Daraj as-Sullam* (Book of Steps), called in Greek Βιβλίον τῶν βαθμῶν and in Sahidic ⲡⲧⲱⲣⲧⲣ̄ ⲛ̄ⲧⲉϭⲗⲟⲟϭⲉ (The Rung of the Ladder; Munier, 1930, pp. 67–249). Its contents are as follows: chapter 1, miscellanea, as particles, prepositions, nouns, and verbal forms; chapters 2–19, a classified part beginning with God, good qualities of men, the heavens, the earth, the sea and mountains, the whole universe; chapters 20–23, various subjects; chapters 24–26, words and sentences of the Old Testament (lacking in al-Samannūdī's scala); chapter 27, "difficult" words (ϩⲛ̄ⲗⲉⲝⲓⲥ ⲉⲩⲙⲟⲕϩ; ibid., pp. 135–36).

An anonymous Greek-Bohairic-Arabic vocabulary of the Vatican Library (Hebbelynck and van Lantschoot, 1937–1947, Vol. 2, 82–85) arranges the words by first letter, as the oldest Greek alphabetical dictionaries do: ⲁ, letter a; ⲁⲃⲗⲁⲃⲏ, ⲁⲃⲗⲏ (sic), unharmed; ⲁⲇⲓⲕⲓⲁ, injustice. There are two other copies in the National Library in Paris (Mallon, 1910, pp. 87–88), the first dated 1318 and the second from the fourteenth or fifteenth century.

Greek lexicography, like the Coptic, began with the explanation of difficult passages as they occurred in the text. Alphabetical arrangement was a relatively late development. The first alphabetical dictionary in the world was perhaps Glaukias' lexicon, dating from 180 B.C. In the beginning, the alphabetical order was not strictly observed, for only the first letter was taken into consideration, and later the second and even the third. The lexicon by Hesychius Alexandrinus (fifth or sixth century A.D.) was entirely alphabetical (Schwyzer, 1939, p. 29). So it seems that the alphabetical arrangement in Coptic lexicography was an independent attempt to arrange words in alphabetical order. Furthermore, the demotic "alphabetical" word list had nothing to do with Coptic classification, as there was no real alphabet with a fixed order of signs in demotic (Volten, 1952, pp. 496–508).

The scalae hitherto published are not free of mistakes—mistakes of the author, the copyist, the editor, and the printer. Here are but two examples: ϯⲧⲁⲣⲉϫ, lioness (*B*) = *al-labwa*, which elsewhere (*S*, *B*) is ⲁⲣϫ, bear (fem.), from Greek ἄρκος (masc./fem.) (Vycichl, 1983, p. 16), a confusion due to the fact that there were no bears in Egypt. In this case the definite article has been put in twice: ϯ-ⲧ-ⲁⲣⲉϫ, Bohairic ϯ and Sahidic ⲧ. *S* ⲯⲉⲣⲛⲓⲯ, basin for ablutions (?) = *al-kirnīb* (Munier, 1930, p. 174)—between *al-maṭhara*, vessel for ablutions, and *ṣaṭl* (= *saṭl*), bucket, pail—should be spelt ⲭⲉⲣⲛⲓⲯ = Greek χέρνιψ, water for ablution (χειρ, hand, before consonant χερ-, νιβ, to clean, from a pre-Greek root **nigw*-).

In other cases, such as Coptic manuscripts from the eighth century, the spelling of Copto-Greek (chiefly) words reflects phonetic changes of the spoken language. Three well-known cases need to be mentioned. ⲏ and ⲩ are interchangeable: *S* ϩⲩⲡⲁⲣ, liver = ϩⲏⲡⲁⲣ (ἧπαρ). Copto-Greek ⲁⲓ = ⲉ, and sometimes vice versa: ⲭⲉⲣⲉ, welcome (greeting) = χαῖρε, be happy, and *S* ⲯⲁⲓⲧⲁⲥⲉ, 96 (Crum, 1939, p. 273) = phonetically **pset-asé*. ⲅ and ⲇ often interchange with transcribed ⲕ and ⲧ: thus, ⲧⲉⲙⲟⲛ, demon, genius = δαίμων, and ⲕⲣⲁⲙⲃⲏ (Munier, 1930, p. 165) = *S* ⲅⲣⲁⲙⲃⲏ (ibid., p. 167) = κράμβη, cabbage. But there are other cases as well, such as insertions of an auxiliary vowel (written ⲉ) in a three-consonant cluster: thus, *S* ⲥⲉⲕⲣⲟⲫⲁ, sow (ibid., p. 113) = Latin *scrofa*, and *S* ⲥⲉⲫⲉⲣⲁ, vault of heaven = Greek σφαῖρα, ball, vault of heaven. Also στρουθος, sparrow, appears as *S* ⲥⲉⲧⲣⲟⲩⲑⲟⲥ, bird = عصفور (*'uṣfūr*) (ibid., p. 114).

The group *ks* (ϫ) was often pronounced *nks* in the final position and later, with an auxiliary vowel, *-niks*: μάστιξ, whip, appears as *S* ⲙⲁⲥⲧⲓⲅϫ (ibid., p. 171), still without auxiliary vowel, but μύρμηξ, ant, appears as *S* ⲙⲉⲣⲙⲉⲛⲓϫ (ibid., p. 116), and σφῆξ, wasp, is *S* ⲥⲫⲓⲛⲓϫ instead of *S* ⲥⲫⲏⲛϫ (ibid., p. 115).

A similar case is *S* ⲁⲡⲟⲕⲁⲗⲩⲙⲯⲓⲥ, apocalypse, from ἀποκάλυψις, today pronounced *abū ghalamsīs*. The group ⲗⲗ is often written ⲗⲗⲗ, probably influenced by ⲁⲗⲗⲁ (ἀλλά), but, a frequent conjunction. Thus, one finds *S*, *B* ⲡⲁⲗⲗⲁϯⲟⲛ, palace, from παλάτιον = Latin *palatium*. *S* ⲗⲗⲟⲩ, *B* ⲗⲗⲗⲟⲩ, pupil of the eye, is nothing else than *S*, *B* ⲗⲗⲟⲩ, child, in this case the "girl of the eye" as in Egyptian *ḥwn.t im.t ir.t*, the girl in the eye, or Greek κόρη, girl, pupil of eye (Vycichl, 1983, p. 7).

The Copto-Greek words of the scalae often represent Greek postclassical forms. *B* ⲟⲕⲧⲟⲙⲃⲣⲓⲟⲥ, October, is neither Latin, nor modern 'Οκτώβριος or a similar form, but a postclassical form. One can compare Armenian *Hoktember* and Russian *Oktyabr'* (**Oktembri*). There are four *S* words for "water": ⲩⲇⲱⲣ (ὕδωρ), ⲛⲉⲣⲱⲛ (νερόν), ⲛⲁⲙⲁ (νᾶμα), and ⲡⲙⲟⲟⲩ (Munier, 1930, p. 109). Ὕδωρ (*hydōr*) is the classical word; νερόν (*nerón*), literally "the new, fresh one," is the current expression in modern Greek; νᾶμα (*nâmā*) is "running water"; and ⲡ-ⲙⲟⲟⲩ is the autochthonous Coptic word for "water" (*S*). ⲯⲓⲥⲙⲟⲥ and ⲡⲕⲙⲧⲟ are translated الزّلزلة (*az-zalzalah*), the earthquake (ibid., p. 107). The etymologies are quite clear: ⲡ + σεισμός, earthquake, and the autochthonous Coptic form derives from *S* ⲕⲓⲙ, to move, and the old word *S* ⲧⲟ, earth. This *S* ⲕⲙⲧⲟ is another word than Old Coptic ⲕⲙⲧⲱ, creator of the earth (Vycichl, 1983, p. 82).

S ⲛ̄ⲗⲓⲙⲏⲛ, the pictures = Arabic الصّور (*aṣ-ṣuwar*) (Munier, 1930, p. 122) derives from Greek λαιμίον, little picture (Stephanus, 1831–1865, Vol. 4, p. 42: "imaguncula vel protome"). The Copto-Greek form is influenced by Greek λιμήν, harbor.

Another problem is ⲕⲁⲓⲧⲟⲩⲣⲓⲛ, he-ass = *al-ḥimār*, and ⲅⲉⲇⲁⲣⲓⲟⲛ, she-ass = *al-atānah* (Munier, 1930, p. 112). The normal spelling of these words would be *ⲅⲁⲓⲇⲟⲩⲣⲓⲛ (accusative) and *ⲅⲁⲓⲇⲁⲣⲓⲟⲛ (neuter nominative or accusative); compare modern Greek γάϊδαρος, ass, and γαϊδουράκι, little ass (Demetrakos, 1936, Vol. 3, p. 1535). The word occurs in Egyptian Greek as γαϊδάριον, donkey, in a text of the sixth or seventh century A.D. (Grenfell and Hunt, 1901, p. 153). Also γαϊδοῦρι occurs in modern Greek (ibid.).

Coptic vocabularies reveal that in some cases names of animals are derived from names of the corresponding Egyptian (theriomorphic) gods. A name of the crocodile was ⲉⲫⲱⲧ (Crum, 1939, p. 63) = *at-timsāḥ*, wrongly = *at-tirsah*, turtle (Kircher, 1643, p. 171), but the same word occurs as βαινεφωθ, soul of Ephōt, in a Greek-Coptic glossary = ⲙⲥⲁϩ (Bell and Crum, 1925, p. 197). According to Epiphanius, the Egyptians called crocodiles νεφῶθ from Egyptian *Nfr ḥtp*, epithet of several gods, not only Suchos (Vycichl, 1983, p. 49). The initial ⲛ was considered the plural article—thus, *B* ⲉⲫⲱⲧ, crocodile.

In the chapter on languages and peoples one reads *B* ⲁⲥⲥⲩⲣⲓⲟⲥ (*Assyrios*) = سرياني (*Suryānī*), Syrian, (Kircher, 1643, p. 80). This translation is due to an old confusion between Syria and Assyria (Cannuyer, 1985, p. 133) and not to a misunderstanding, for as with Armenian *Asorikh, Asorestan* is northern Syria, because of the "Assyrian Christians" in the region of Edessa (Froundjian, 1952, p. 58), so called after their coreligionists in Assyria, the northern part of Mesopotamia. Another strange term is ⲟⲩⲃⲉⲣⲟⲥ, Armenian (Kircher, 1643, p. 80). This is of course a mistake. The preceding word is كرجى = *Kurjī*, Georgian (compare Persian *Gurjī*). So *B* ⲟⲩⲃⲉⲣⲟⲥ stands for *ⲟⲩ-ⲓⲃⲉⲣⲟⲥ, an Iberian, because Ἴβερες, a people of the Caucasus, are considered the ancestors of the Georgians. They descend from *Ibēr*, and *Iberos* is attested as a personal name (Ἴβερος). One must read ⲟⲩ-ⲓⲃⲉⲣⲟⲥ, a Georgian.

Coptic glossaries were highly appreciated in the Middle Ages and even in modern times as they permitted their readers access to the sense of the Holy Scriptures in Coptic. The situation is however somewhat different for modern scholars. They prefer to collect words in religious sources from original texts and not from secondhand glossaries. But ordered lexicons containing words from daily life are constantly referred to, mainly for natural history, geography, and, of course, dictionaries (Crum, 1939; Vycichl, 1983). These lexicons were written at a time when Coptic, both Sahidic and Bohairic, had undergone major changes, phonetically and lexically. The spoken language was full of Arabic words, as one can see from a medical papyrus (Chassinat, 1921) or a treatise on alchemy (Stern, 1885). There seem to be only very few words of Arabic origin in the scalae; for example, *B* ⲡⲓⲁⲣⲣⲟⲥ, rice (Kircher, 1643, p. 194) = modern Arabic *ar-ruzz*, a medieval and modern form of *urz* (with many variants) from Greek ὄρυζα. Another word is *S* ϭⲉⲗⲗⲟⲟⲩⲍ, almond (Munier, 1930, p. 164), from Arabic *jillawz*, kind of hazel nut; compare Tunisian *zellūz*, almond, from *jillawz*. *S* ⲃⲩⲣⲓⲕⲟⲕⲗ, apricot (ibid., p. 164), derives from Latin *praecox*, accusative *praecoce(m)*, precocious; hence Greek πραικόκια and Arabic *barqūq*, apricot (Near East), plum (North Africa) with a change *p:b*.

In this context one must mention Kircher's *Lingua Aegyptiaca Restituta* (1643). Although it certainly does not meet modern standards, it was for its time excellent and marks the very beginning of Coptic studies in Europe. Champollion used it 180 years later for deciphering the hieroglyphs.

BIBLIOGRAPHY

ʿAbd al-Masīḥ, Y. "Al-Muqaddimāt wa-s-Salālim." In *Risālat [Jamʿīyat] Mār Mīnā*, Vol. 2, pp. 59–68. Alexandria, 1947.

Bauer, G. *Athanasius von Qūṣ, Qilādat at-Taḥrīr fī ʿIlm at-Tafsīr: Eine koptische Grammatik in arabischer Sprache aus dem 13./14. Jahrhundert.* Freiburg im Breisgau, 1972.

Bell, H. I. and W. E. Crum. "A Greek-Coptic Glossary." *Aegyptus* 5 (1925):176–226.

Cannuyer, C. "À propos du nom de la Syrie." *Journal of Near Eastern Studies* 44 (1985):133–137.

Catalogue général des manuscrits des bibliothèques publiques des départements, Vol. 1. Paris, 1849.

Chabot, J.-B. "Inventaire sommaire des manuscrits coptes de la Bibliothèque nationale." *Revue des bibliothèques* 6 (1906):351–67.

Chassinat, E. *Un Papyrus médical copte.* Cairo, 1921.

Crum, W. E. *Catalogue of the Coptic Manuscripts in the British Museum*, especially nos. 920–931. London, 1905.

———. *A Coptic Dictionary.* Oxford, 1939.

Demetrakos, D. *Mega Lexikon tēs Hellenikēs Glōssēs*, Vol. 2. Athens, 1936.

Froundjian, D. *Armenisch-deutsches Wörterbuch.* Munich, 1952.

Graf, G. *Geschichte der christlichen-arabischen Literatur*, Vol. 2. Vatican City, 1947.

Grenfell, B. P., and A. S. Hunt. *The Amherst Papyri*, Vol. 2. London, 1901.

Hebbelynck, A., and A. van Lantschoot. *Codices Coptici Vaticani, Barberiniani, Borgiani, Rossiani*, Vol. 1, *Codices Coptici Vaticani.* Rome, 1937. See also van Lantschoot.

Kircher, A. *Lingua Aegyptiaca Restituta, Opus Tripartitum.* Rome, 1643.

Lantschoot, A. van. *Codices Coptici Vaticani, Barberiniani, Borgiani, Rossiani*, Vol. 2, *Pars Prior, Codices Barberiniani Orientales 2 et 17, Borgiani 1–108.* Rome, 1947. See also Hebbelynck.

———. *Un Précurseur d'Athanase Kircher, Thomas Obicini et la "Scala" Vat. Copte 71.* Louvain, 1948.

Mallon, A. "Une Ecole de savants égyptiens au moyen âge." *Mélanges de la Faculté orientale de l'Université Saint-Joseph de Beyrouth* 1 (1906):109–131; 2 (1907):213–64.

———. "Catalogue des scalae coptes de la Bibliothèque nationale de Paris." *Mélanges de la Faculté orientale de l'Université Saint-Joseph de Beyrouth* 4 (1910):57–90.

Munier, H. *La Scala copte 44 de la Bibliothèque nationale de Paris*, Vol. 1, *Transcription.* Bibliothèque d'études coptes 2. Cairo, 1930.

Schwyzer, E. *Griechische Grammatik*, Vol. 1. Munich, 1939.

Schubart, W. "Ein lateinisch-griechisch-koptisches Gesprächbuch." *Klio* 13 (1913):27–38.

Sidarus, A. Y. "Coptic Lexicography in the Middle Ages." In *The Future of Coptic Studies*, ed. R. McL. Wilson, pp. 125–42. Leiden, 1978.

Stephanus, H. *Thesaurus Linguae Graecae.* Paris, 1831–1865.

Stern, L. "Fragment eines koptischen Traktates über

Alchimie." *Zeitschrift für ägyptische Sprache und Altertumskunde* 23 (1885):102–119.

Volten, A. "An 'Alphabetical' Dictionary and Grammar in Demotic." *Archív orientální* 20 (1952):496–508.

Vycichl, W. *Dictionnaire étymologique de la langue copte*. Louvain, 1983.

WERNER VYCICHL

SYLLABICATION. It is common knowledge that the syllabication of a language is always closely related to its phonology. This appears at once in the definition of "syllable" given by the phonologist Grammont (1939, pp. 99–103): "A syllable . . . is a sequence of increasing apertures followed by a sequence of decreasing apertures." This occurs without the degree of aperture necessarily increasing to the point where the decrease begins or diminishing from this point to the end of the syllable; in both increase and decrease two phonemes of the same aperture may follow one another (cf. below). Grammont then added: "Moreover, a phoneme of given aperture may be followed by a phoneme of smaller aperture in the increasing part, and by one of greater aperture in the decreasing part. . . . There is no syllable without a vocalic point, and in phonology there is no syllable without a vowel. . . . This vowel always appears at the vocalic point, and . . . when it is the only one, it is always the phoneme of maximum aperture in the syllable and the first the tension of which is decreasing. But it is not uncommon to find in phonetics, that is, in languages, syllables which have no vowel [such as] the French interjection *pst*!" Here *s* is increasing since some pronounce this word [*psit*] while the pronunciation [*pist*] never appears in French; the vocalic point of this word therefore lies between *s* and *t*, for "the vocalic point always appears at the transition from the last increasing phoneme to the first decreasing phoneme. . . . Every time the phoneme which has the largest aperture in the syllable is not a vowel, it does not become a vowel through its position, but it has the vocalic point beside it, and is itself now increasing, now decreasing."

Grammont extended this principle even to the sonorants (= consonant[s] on the level of phonological function) /ƀ/, /l/, /m/, /n/, and /r/, to which he refused to attribute any capacity for becoming vowels on the level of phonological function, and hence sonant (/ƀ̩/, /h̩/, /m̩/, /n̩/, and /r̩/), according to the terminology of Kasser, following Dieth (1950, pp. 379–80). It will be noted that even in these definitions appear the data essential for solving the problems of Coptic syllabication.

In any discussion of a dead language like Coptic, which can only be known from written texts, to say that its syllabication is always closely related to its phonology is to make a gratuitous statement that leads to nothing if it is not admitted that the phonology can be determined with considerable clarity through the various orthographic systems (generally considered dialectal) of the texts in the dead language. This is admittedly a working hypothesis, but is still very widely accepted because it is much more probable and fruitful than the contrary hypothesis (Loprieno, 1982). It is therefore permissible to lay down here the principle that the syllabication of Coptic (or, rather, that of its various "dialects," in the traditional sense of the term) is to be found in a rather close relationship with its orthography (or the various dialectal orthographic systems).

Before going further in the examination of Coptic syllabication, it is appropriate to recall that the normal phonology of a language is evidently that which governs the language in its most natural spoken utterance, hence in rapid speech. There are in any language two kinds of utterance (cf. Kasser, 1982a–b). Rapid speech is characterized by, among other things, the use of the glides (/j/ and /w/ in Coptic) and ALEPH (except in the idioms *M, W, V, F4*, and *B*, which have completely abandoned it). The syllabication that rapid speech entails is "tachsyllabication" (producing tachysyllables, siglum t/syl.). Slow speech is characterized by, among other things, the abolition of the glides and aleph, the first being replaced respectively by /i/ and /u/, the second by an atonic vowel identical with the tonic vowel that precedes it; this speech is clearly artificial, but if it is not that of normal phonology, it has nevertheless contributed powerfully to the shaping of the orthography, the only surviving witness (unfortunately indirect) for tachysyllabic phonology. The syllabication that slow speech entails is "bradysyllabication" (producing bradysyllables, siglum br/syl.).

Certainly the tachysyllables (the only ones truly interesting for phonology) ought to be the syllables of Coptic as a living language, in its most common use in ordinary "prose." Since Coptology came into existence as a science, it has never been possible to make them the object of direct investigation, because Coptic has been too long since a dead language. Thus, the grammarians (e.g., Stern, 1880, p. 39; Till, 1955, pp. 49–50; Vergote, 1973–1983, Vol. 1a, p. 44) have reconstructed it, for want of anything better, on the basis of theoretical and analogical reasoning (in some cases comparative), by taking into consideration the vocalic and consonantal phonemes (including eventual CRYPTOPHONEMES), taking account of the graphemes not merely according to their graphic kind ("vowel" or "consonant" graphemes) but according to their phonological function (vocalic or consonantal) (Marouzeau, 1951, p. 209; Kasser, 1981c), and by observing their syllabic combinations in various living languages or in dead ones phonologically better known than Coptic.

The bradysyllables, as the result of artificial and abnormally slow enunciation, could be, among other things, the syllables of recited Coptic "poetry," but like the t/syl. they equally evade direct observation. But, above all, it seems probable that the br/syl. were those of the syllabication practiced by the scribes in their work, since bradysyllabication (alongside other factors) to a large extent conditions the orthography; in fact, the creation and fixation of an orthography is of necessity accompanied by an intense effort of reflection and phonemic analysis, which goes hand in hand with an artificially slow articulation.

The majority of t/syl. phonemes could have remained identical br/syl. phonemes, but a minority of them was modified for this purpose. In fact, it seems (in Coptic and in various other languages, at least modern ones) that a glide can exist only in t/syl., and if it is necessary to pass to br/syl., one passes immediately and of necessity from the glide to the corresponding glidant (Kasser, 1981c, pp. 37–38): for example, ⲉⲓⲱⲧ, father, t/syl. /jṓt/ (monosyllabic), but br/syl. '/(ə)i ṓt/' (disyllabic); ⲟⲩⲱⲙ, to eat, t/syl. /wṓm/ (monosyllabic), but br/syl. '/u ṓm/' (disyllabic); and aleph, which survives only in t/syl. and becomes an "aleph vowel" in br/syl., as in ϣⲟⲟⲡϯ, being, t/syl. /šóʼp/ (monosyllabic), but br/syl. '/šó op/' (disyllabic). At the same time, since orthography and the signs it uses are strongly influenced by br/syl., one should not be astonished if the different varieties of the Coptic alphabet are found to correspond in principle only to the phonemes found in br/syl. and these alphabets (except for ⊥ = /ʼ/ in *P*) are found to lack the graphemes that might render the cryptophonemes, or phonemes that have disappeared in the transition t/syl.>br/syl.

One must now return to tachysyllabication, which alone is really important in phonology. In regard to the latter, it may be said that the way in which various Coptologists have considered it is, in general, somewhat variable, the various theses being supported by divergent arguments, none of which can be lightly set aside.

Some phonologists, perhaps moved more than others by a concern to facilitate comparison of Coptic (the latest form of Egyptian) with pharaonic Egyptian, accord to Coptic orthography only a rather approximate indicative value. This relative imprecision affords them the appreciable advantage of, to some extent, "unifying" the Coptic language (as opposed to ancient Egyptian as it is known through its writings, a language also considered "one" and not divided dialectally in its literary form); they consider as phonologically insignificant certain graphic differences that belong to the domain of the various "dialects," in the traditional sense of the term (cf. Loprieno, 1982, p. 79: "The methodology applied can for example show that the phonological structure /sōtəm/ is common Coptic, and that differences like *S* ⲥⲱⲧⲙ̄, *B* ⲥⲱⲧⲉⲙ, and *A* ⲥⲱⲧⲙⲉ are purely graphic variants"). Another by no means negligible advantage is that it brings Coptic phonology (thus neatly "unified") closer to pharaonic Egyptian (which is unified to the extent that hieroglyphs and the like allow one to know it).

Other phonologists tend to consider Coptic orthography as a much more precise criterion of phonological knowledge, which has, as a result, somewhat increased the distance established between Coptic phonology (thus conceived) and the phonology of pharaonic Egypt.

Hintze (1980, p. 58) had the great merit of attempting what may appear as a way of reconciling these divergent positions, by presenting his conception of a Coptic phonology *on several levels,* a phonology in some sense "stratified" (cf. Kasser, 1984b), the term "Coptic" being understood in a very wide sense, including also proto-Coptic and pre-Coptic. In this passage Hintze distinguished with great perspicacity the successive layers of Coptic phonology as they can be reconstructed on the basis of the traces they have left in the surface layer (the most recent layer, attested in the strict sense by the various Coptic "dialectal" orthographic systems) and on the basis of what is known of pharaonic Egyptian phonology; among those layers that may be called "underlying," it is evident that the highest (the most recent) will be the most similar to the surface layer, with its diversity of dialectal phonology, while at the deeper levels the dialectal phonological differences do not yet appear.

Relying on this attractive conception of a Coptic phonology on several levels, one may, among other things, present side by side (without the opposition synonymous with exclusion) a "superficial syllabication" (siglum syl/sup.), corresponding to the superficial phonology, and an "underlying syllabication" (siglum syl/und.), corresponding to the underlying phonology. On numerous points these two types of syllabication are in complete accord. Elsewhere, however, they diverge. On the one hand, in syl/sup., autosyllabic ⲃ, ⲗ, ⲙ, ⲛ, and ⲣ (generally marked with a stroke—or in the case of ⲙ and ⲛ, with a DJINKIM or some other sign—as ⲃ̄, or ⲛ̄ etc., or ⲛ̇ etc.) or ⲃ, ⲗ, ⲙ, ⲛ, and ⲣ capable of forming the apex of a syllable (by themselves as sonants, according to Polotsky, 1933, p. 126 [probably]; Dieth, 1950, pp. 379–80; and Kasser, 1981c; or through their vocalic point, according to Grammont, 1939, pp. 99–103) have the phonological value v (vowel). But the phonemes rendered by these graphemes are assimilated to voiced c (consonants) preceded by /ə/, and hence have the value vc (vowel plus consonant, respectively /əb/, /əl/, /əm/, /ən/, /ər/) in syl/und. (Vergote, 1973–1983, Vol. 1a, pp. 45–46). Vergote gave to this vocalic point, in the absence of a vowel grapheme, the same phonological value as atonic ⲉ = /ə/): for example, ⲣ̄ (in ⲣ̄(ⲧⲟⲃ), artabe) syl/sup. v /r/, syl/und. vc /ər/; ⲡϥⲛ̄ⲧ, the worm, syl/sup. ccvc /pfn̩t/, syl/und. ccvcc /pfənt/.

On the other hand, in syl/sup., it is permissible to think that certain groups of consonants cannot, in the absence of v, properly speaking form a syllable together (at least in tachysyllabication, although they have probably acquired this capacity in bradysyllabication); according as these c are together increasing or decreasing, they will be attached to the following or preceding v to form a syllable. (It is here understood that a c certainly increasing followed by one certainly decreasing could form a syllable with a vocalic point not marked by a vowel grapheme, cf. Grammont, 1939, p. 102, and below; this case is practically always improbable in syl/sup.—bradysyllabication excluded—comparison of the different "dialectal" orthographies being of no use in this matter, since, with equal lexemes, the same phoneme may well be increasing in one idiom but decreasing in another—this inversion of aperture being precisely one of the criteria for possible distinction between the dialects, such as /m/ decreasing in *S* ⲥⲱⲧⲙ̄, to hear, increasing in *A* ⲥⲱⲧⲙⲉ.) But these groups of c most often form a syllable (syl/und.) in underlying syllabication (as also in bradysyllabication; cf. above), because etymology or interdialectal comparison (some other idiom having a vowel grapheme there) invites one to consider the first of these c as increasing and the following as decreasing, so that there is a vocalic point there that in syl/und. will be marked by /ə/ even in the absence of any vowel grapheme (cf. above with reference to Vergote, 1973–1983, Vol. 1a, pp. 30–32) in the orthography: for example, ⲥⲱⲧⲡ̄, to choose, monosyllabic syl/sup. cvcc /sṓtp/, disyllabic syl/und. cv cvc /sṓ tĕp/.

All that precedes is based on the principle according to which a syllable cannot exist without an apex around which the elements of the syllable gather. On the one hand, this apex may be its phoneme of strongest sonority; on the other, the syllable (then called a "syllable of junction"; Kasser, 1982a, n. 7 and 26) may regroup, disregarding the limits of the lexemes, various graphemes and phonemes that belong to several different "words" (semantemes and morphemes), such as ⲟⲩⲁϣ ⲁϩⲟⲙ, a sigh, semantically ⲟⲩ ⲁϣ ⲁϩⲟⲙ, but syllabically rather t/syl. ⲟⲩⲁ ϣⲁ ϩⲟⲙ /wa ša hóm/.

None will dispute that the apex of the syllable may be a v = vowel grapheme (which is by far the most common case in Coptic, as in most other languages). In Coptic again it will be noted that this role of v may be played fairly often by a sonant (= v, according to Polotsky, 1933, p. 126, Dieth, 1950, pp. 379–80, Kasser, 1981c; = decreasing [voiced] c, having then beside it or in front of it the vocalic point that serves as v, according to Grammont, 1939, pp. 99–103, Vergote, 1973–1983, Vol. 1a, pp. 31–32, 45–46). Opinions are most at variance when the presumed apex of the syllable, assumed to be formed solely of consonantal graphemes, is not a voiced c but a fricative or, worse still, an occlusive. Polotsky (1933, p. 128) seemed to admit the possibility that these voiceless c (sometimes even voiceless stops) may play the role of sonants: "In and for itself it is a peculiarity of Coptic that in atonic and especially posttonic syllables it admits simply any consonant as the apex of the syllable." (Dieth, 1950, pp. 379–80, did not exclude this in theory, although he limited to the extreme the realization of such an eventuality: "Practically excluded are the poorest in sound"—i.e., the stops.) Vergote (1973–1983, Vol. 1a), following Grammont (1939), arrived at almost the same conclusion, although he placed the apex of the syllable not on the fricative or stop but on the vocalic point, which phonologically (though not graphically) exists alongside them. However that may be, the admission of this possibility ought not to be widely opened except in syl/und. and should not be a motive for unduly limiting, or even eliminating, the possibility of having two successive c at the beginning and/or end of a syllable in syl/sup. (Steindorff, 1951, p. 36, excluded it, however, at the end of a syllable).

Those who consider Coptic orthography as a relatively and sufficiently precise criterion for phonological knowledge will naturally tend to admit in syl/sup. the minimum of possible cases of syllables called "surdisonant" (cf. Kasser, 1981c, p. 43) or even practically to exclude them. In this respect, they will be able to draw support, in all cases partially, from Stern (1880, p. 39), whose statement, however, seems ambiguous: "The syllable [in Coptic] is either open, ending in a vowel or dipthong, or closed by one or more consonants. Where it ends in two or three consonants, pronunciation is sometimes facilitated by the insertion of an ⲉ without signification, a *sh*ᵉ*wa mobile,* although this is usually left unwritten, as in ⲥⲟⲧⲡϥ, presumably pronounced *sotpef.* A syllable may begin with one or more consonants; but later pronunciation usually prefixes an *e* to the opening double consonant, and this is sometimes also written, e.g. . . . ⲉϣⲧⲉⲕⲟ for ϣⲧⲉⲕⲟ. . . . Beginning with three consonants, as in ⲥϫⲣⲉϩⲧ : ⲥⲉⲣⲁϩⲧ (to rest) is an abnormality." From this passage it clearly emerges that for Stern there are syllables beginning or ending in cc or ccc, even if the latter are rare and indeed exceptional, and even if the difficulty of pronouncing them soon gave birth to a tendency to divide them into several syllables less awkward to pronounce by adding an ⲉ (or phonetically a kind of [ə], which did not appear in writing) as the apex of a supplementary syllable (a relief syllable, one might say); such a tendency is phonetic and not phonological in origin, and is realized phonologically only at a second, logical stage.

In what follows (in the main, after Vergote, 1973–1983, Vol. 1a, an excellent work of synthesis) the Coptic syllable will be presented as a late-Egyptian syllable, under its various forms. It will be seen that some types of Coptic syllables are identical in syl/sup. and in syl/und. The presentation of other types will have to mark clearly the distinction between what is syl/sup. and what (in strict conformity with the principles of Vergote, ibid., pp. 45–46) is syl/und. The list of types of syllables that is found in Vergote will even be extended to make room for some of the most complex syl/sup. (and nearly always not syl/und.) types (also admitted by Stern, 1880, p. 39; cf. above).

In comparing pharaonic Egyptian syllabication with that of its last avatar, Coptic, one may establish obvious constants, but one is nonetheless struck by significant differences, the result of the evolution and profound transformation of the language. It is admitted (Vergote, 1973–1983, Vol. 1a, p. 53) that only the following syllables existed in Egyptian prior to Coptic: 1a v̄̍, 1b v̆; 2a v̆̍c, 2b v̆c; 3a cv̄̍, 3b cv̆; 4a cv̆̍c, 4b cv̆c (c = consonantal phoneme, v = vowel phoneme; ¯ long, ˘ short, ˈ tonic accent). "According to the theories of Sethe, only types 3a, 4a, 4b, and perhaps 2b in its later conception exist in the most ancient form of Egyptian" (ibid., Vol. 1b, p. 53). In this pattern, as can be seen, only the tonic v in an open syllable are long; all the rest are short. On the other hand, it will be noted, there is no syllable beginning or ending in several consonants.

The rules for the formation of the syllable in Coptic are clearly rather different. The example ⲫⲙⲱⲓⲧ /phmō̍jt/, the way, clearly monosyllabic, ccv̄̍cc (in which Bohairic /ph/ is one phoneme, not two, i.e., aspirated /p/), already shows that the Coptic syllable may very well (and probably not only in *B* but also in the other idioms) have several consonants at the beginning and/or end.

Some authors (according to Vergote, ibid., Vol. 1b) seem to have admitted that a Coptic syllable, like a pharaonic syllable, ought always to begin with a consonant (Steindorff, 1951, p. 36, and Till, 1955, p. 46, however, expressed themselves on this subject in nuanced fashion). The result would be that despite appearances (i.e., orthography) lexemes such as ⲱⲡ, to count, and ⲉⲧⲡⲱ, burden, would in reality begin phonologically with /ʼ/, hence with a c (unvoiced laryngeal stop): thus */ʼō̍p/ and */ʼətpō̍/, respectively. Vergote contested this interpretation, because of "the way in which, for example, the article is joined to the substantive in . . . ⲡⲏï, the house." He added, "The presence of the decreasing laryngeal occlusive is always marked by the doubled vowel, and one does not see why it could not be noted in an increasing position." Certainly there is nothing to prevent one thinking that in principle it could be, but that people were not prompted to mark the presence of /ʼ/ in that position, where its presence did not produce the "echo effect" in bradysyllabication (cf. below). However that may be, it seems reasonable to admit with Vergote that in Coptic there are syllables beginning with a v (which apparently pharaonic Egyptian did not have).

Here, then, is the list of the types of Coptic syllables (cf. above). On the left are placed the tonic syllables, and on the right, the atonic. Each type is illustrated by a few examples; unless otherwise identified, they are chosen from *S*; the part of the "word" that is not involved in the example is placed between parentheses; ˘ or ¯ above vowels indicates respectively their brevity or length, and ˈ marks the tonic accent. It will be noted that long v can only be found in tonic syllables (open or closed), while short

1a. v́: ⲉⲓ /í/, to go; ⲟ† /ó/, being	1b. v: ⲁ(ⲙⲟⲩⲛ)/ă(mún)/, (god) Ammon; syl/sup. ⲙ̄(ⲧⲟⲛ)/m̥(tón), rest (but syl/und. vc /əm(tón)/)
2a. v́c: ⲱϣ /óš/, to cry; ⲁϣ /áš/, what (interrogative)	2b. vc: ⲉⲗ(ϭⲱⲃ)/əl(cób), heron; syl/und. /əm(tón)/; cf. 1b
3a. cv́: ⲥⲱ /só/, to drink; ⲡⲉ /pé/, heaven; syl/sup. ϣⲙ̄(ϣⲉ) /šḿ(šə)/, to serve, (but syl/und. cv́c /šə́m(šə)/)	3b. cv: ϭⲉ(ⲡⲏ) /cə(pé)/, haste; (ⲛⲟⲩ)ⲧⲉ /(nú)tə/, god; syl/sup. ⲡⲣ̄(ⲣⲟ) /pr̥(ró)/, the king (but syl/und. cvc /pər(ró)/); syl/sup. (ⲥⲱ)ⲧⲙ̄ /(só)tm̥/, to hear (but syl/und. cvc /(só)təm/)
4a. cv́c: ⲕⲱⲧ /kót/, to build; ⲥⲟⲡ /sóp/, time; syl/sup. ϥⲛ̄ⲧ /fń̥t/, worm (but syl/und. cv́cc /fə́nt/)	4b. cvc: ⲡⲉⲣ(ⲕⲓⲃⲉ) /pər(kíbə)/, breast; *H* (ⲱ)ⲛⲁϩ /(ó)năh/, life; syl/sup. ⲙⲛ̄ⲧ(ⲛⲟⲩⲧⲉ) /mn̥t(nútə)/, divinity (but syl/und. cvcc /mənt(nútə)/); syl/sup. (ϣⲟ)ⲙⲛ̄ⲧ /(šó)mn̥t/, three (but syl/und. cvcc /(šó)mənt/)
5a. ccv́: ⲥⲙⲟⲩ /smú/, to bless; ϩⲧⲟ /htó/, horse	5b. ccv: ⲡⲣⲉ(ⲙⲏⲧ) /prə(mét)/, the tithe; *A* (ϩⲱ)ⲧⲃⲉ /(xó)tbə/, to kill; syl/sup. ⲡⲣⲙ̄(ⲣⲁϣ) /prm̥(ráš)/, the mild man (but syl/und. ccvc /prəm(ráš)/); syl/sup. (ⲛⲁ)ϩⲙⲛ̄ /(ná)hmn̥/, to save us (but syl/und. ccvc /(ná)hmən/)
6a. ccv́c: ⲥϭⲏⲣ /scér/, to navigate; ϣⲧⲁⲙ /stám/, to close; syl/sup. ⲡϥⲛ̄ⲧ /pfń̥t/, the worm (but syl/und. ccv́cc /pfə́nt/)	6b. ccvc: ⲡⲣⲉϥ(ϫⲱ) /prəf(čó)/, the singer; (ϩⲟ)ⲧⲃⲉϥ /(hó)tbəf/, to kill him; syl/sup. ⲧⲙⲛ̄ⲧ(ⲛⲟⲩⲧⲉ) /tmn̥t(nútə)/, the divinity (but syl/und. ccvcc /tmənt(nútə)/); syl/und. /prəm(ráš)/; cf. 5b
7a. v́cc: *B* ⲱⲓⲕ /ójk/, bread; ⲉⲉⲧ† /é't/, pregnant (woman); syl/sup. ⲛ̄ⲧⲥ̄ /ń̥ts/ monosyllabic, to carry her (but syl/und. disyllabic /ə́n təs/)	7b. vcc: nothing in syl/und.; syl/sup. ⲉⲧⲡ̄- /ətp/ monosyllabic, to shut up (but syl/und. disyllabic /ə təp/); syl/sup. ⲛ̄ⲧϥ̄ /n̥tf/ monosyllabic, he (but syl/und. disyllabic /ən təf/)
8a. cv́cc: ⲃⲱⲱⲛ /bó'n/, bad; ⲙⲁⲉⲓⲛ /májn/, sign; syl/sup. ϭⲛ̄ⲧⲥ̄ /cń̥ts/ monosyllabic, to find her (but syl/und. disyllabic /cə́n təs/)	8b. cvcc: ⲡⲉⲥⲧ(ⲥⲟϭⲛ̄) /pəst(sócn̥)/, perfumer; (ⲥⲟ)ⲗⲉⲡϥ̄ /(só)ləpf/, to break it; syl/sup. ⲙⲛ̄ⲧϥ̄(ⲛⲟⲩⲥ) /mn̥tf(nús)/ a disyllabic expression, he has no intelligence (but syl/und. trisyllabic /mən təf (nús)/); syl/sup. (ⲥⲟ)ⲙⲛ̄ⲧϥ̄ /(só)mn̥tf/ disyllabic, to stretch him (but syl/und. trisyllabic /(só)mən təf/)
9a. ccv́cc: ⲡⲥⲱⲱϥ /psó'f/, the pollution; ⲥⲛⲁⲉⲓⲛ /snájn/, to loiter	9b. ccvcc: ⲡⲙⲁⲥⲧ(ⲣⲱⲙⲉ) /pmăst(rómə)/, the misanthrope

v, which may also be found in tonic syllables (open or closed), are the only ones that can appear in atonic syllables (open or closed).

Beyond point 9, for practical purposes, the only cases to be found (more and more rare because increasingly difficult to articulate) belong to syl/sup. (to the almost complete exclusion of syl/und.), and present conglomerations of four c or (at any rate in theory) even more, to the point at which one may ask if their difficult phonological structure was always truly realized in phonetics and if the speaker did not often readily have recourse to the "relief" /ə/, not written in orthography, of which Stern (1880, p. 39) spoke: for example, cccv́: syl/sup. ϣϫⲣⲟ /ščró/ monosyllabic, be able to be victorious (but syl/und. disyllabic /əš čró/); cccv: syl/sup. ϣϫⲣⲉ- /ščrə/ monosyllabic, be able to be victorious (but syl/und. disyllabic /əš črə/); cccv́c: syl/sup. ϣⲥⲧⲱⲧ/šstót/ monosyllabic, be able to tremble (but syl/und. disyllabic /əš stót/); cccv́cc: ⲥϭⲣⲁϩⲧ̄/scráht/, tranquillity; ccv̍ccc: syl/sup. ϣⲥⲟⲧⲡϥ /ššo̍tpf/ monosyllabic, be able to choose it (but syl/und. trisyllabic /ə̆š so̍t pə̆f/); cv̍ccc: syl/sup. ⲥⲟⲧⲡϥ, cf. above; v̍ccc: syl/sup. ⲟⲧⲡϥ/o̍tpf/ monosyllabic, to load it (but syl/und. disyllabic /o̍t pə̆f/); and even ccccv̍: syl/sup. ϥⲧⲥ̄ⲧⲟ /ftsto̍/ monosyllabic, he turns aside (but syl/und. at least disyllabic /ftə̆s to̍/). One can, however, find similar homosyllabic conglomerations of consonants in modern languages too (e.g., German *(du) hältst*, you hold, monosyllabic /h'ltst/, cvcccc; or French [from English] *script*, monosyllabic /skri̍pt/, cccvcc).

One may also, in a more general fashion, describe the Coptic syllable (in syl/sup. above all, but often also in syl/und.) by resorting to the idea of a phonemic link increasing or decreasing as a whole, and hence taking account not only of the aperture, increasing or decreasing, but also of the global increase in the degree of sonority of the phonemes up to the apex of the syllable and the general decrease in this degree from the apex to the end of the syllable, it being understood that it is a matter of tachysyllabication (cf. above) and that this increase or decrease, uninterrupted as a whole, may be irregular, since two phonemes of the same sonority or resonance may follow one another in the increase or decrease or a less-voiced or less-resonant phoneme may follow a more-voiced one in the increase and a more-voiced or more-resonant phoneme follow a less-resonant one in the decrease (in each case with appropriate aperture; cf. Grammont, 1939, pp. 100–101).

Phonemes may be classified, as is well known, in increasing order of sonority (cf. Dieth, 1950, p. 166; Nagel, 1965, p. 76; Kasser, 1981c, p. 3) from the unvoiced occlusives to the unvoiced fricatives, then the sonorants (otherwise called voiced consonants), the glides (or voiced fricatives, Vergote, 1973–1983, Vol. 1a, pp. 13, 18), the sonants, the glidants, and the nonglidant vowels, of which /a/ is finally the most strongly voiced phoneme (see PHONOLOGY). On the other hand, if no syllable can exist without a syllabic apex, which is its most strongly voiced phoneme (Dieth, 1950, pp. 377–79; the syllable may naturally have only one phoneme and hence comprise only its "apex" or "top" without "slopes" that lead the speaker to it in voiced increase or after which the speaker comes down again in voiced decrease), it is equally evident that no syllable can have more than one syllable apex. (Two successive v, nonglidant or sonant, cannot exist together in the same syllable, and, separated by a hiatus, they are automatically assigned to two different syllables, e.g., ⲡⲁⲁϩⲉ /pă a̍ hə̆/, my existence; here one must, of course, understand two authentic v, and not, for example, a tonic v followed by the second element of a vocalic gemination in writing, which is phonologically a c: /'/.)

One may therefore say, broadly speaking, that there are four categories of syllables in Coptic, plus five subcategories:

I. The single phoneme syllable, the single phoneme of which is at the same time its apex, such as ⲁ /a/ in ⲁ(ⲃⲱⲕ) /ă bo̍k/, crow.

IIa. The regularly increasing syllable, consisting only of an increasing phonemic link of which each phoneme is more strongly voiced than the previous one and hence a syllable in which the last and most strongly voiced phoneme is the apex, such as ⲡⲥⲟ /pso̍/ in ⲡⲥⲟ(ⲧⲉ) /pso̍(tə̆)/, the arrow. (The presence of another syllabic apex, for preference a vocal grapheme v, immediately before the increasing chain does not attract to itself the first c of the chain, since Coptic has no aversion to open syllables.)

IIb. The irregularly increasing syllable, consisting of a phonemic link that is increasing as a whole but of which each phoneme is not more strongly voiced than the preceding one (this irregularity does not however interrupt the total voiced increase or invert the aperture and split the syllable), such as ⲧⲡⲱ /tpo̍/ in (ⲉ)ⲧⲡⲱ/(ə̆)tpo̍/, burden; ⲥϣⲓ(ⲛⲉ) /ssi̍(nə)/, she seeks; or even ⲥⲕⲱ(ⲧⲉ)/sko̍(tə)/, she turns.

IIIa. The regularly decreasing syllable, consisting of a decreasing phonemic link of which each phoneme is less voiced than the previous one and hence a syllable in which the first phoneme, the most strongly voiced, is the apex, as in ⲱⲙⲥ/o̍ms/, immerse. (The presence of another syllabic apex, for preference a vowel grapheme v, immediately after what would seem at first to be a decreasing link, deprives it by syllabic annexation of its last c, since Coptic has a distinct aversion to syllables beginning with a v; hence ⲟⲙⲥⲟⲩ, to immerse them, /o̍m sū/ and not */o̍ms ū/.)

IIIb. The irregularly decreasing syllable, consisting of a phonemic link that is decreasing as a whole but in which each phoneme is not less strongly voiced than the previous one (this irregularity does not, however, interrupt the overall decrease or invert the aperture and split the syllable), as in ⲱⲧⲡ /o̍tp/, to load; ⲟϣⲥ̄ /o̍šs/, read it; or even ⲱⲧϩ̄ /o̍th/, to weave.

IVa. The regularly increasing and decreasing syllable, composed of a regularly increasing phonemic link (cf. IIa) articulated (by the apex phoneme) with a regularly decreasing link (cf. IIIa), such as ⲡⲥⲟⲣⲧ /pso̍rt/ monosyllabic, the wool (same final handicap as in IIIa).

IVb, IVc, and IVd. The irregularly increasing and decreasing syllable, composed respectively of an irregularly increasing link combined with a regularly decreasing one, a regularly increasing link combined with an irregularly decreasing one, and an irregularly increasing link combined with an irregularly decreasing one, such as ⲡⲧⲱⲃϩ̄ /pto̍bh/ the prayer; ⲥⲧⲱⲃϩ̄ /sto̍bh/, she prays; ⲡⲥⲱⲧⲡ̄ /pso̍tp/, the elect; ⲧⲥⲁⲣⲝ /tsa̍rks/, the flesh; ϣⲥⲱⲧⲡ̄ /šso̍tp/, to be able to choose; and ϥⲡⲱⲧⲥ̄ /fpo̍ts/, he splits.

As can be seen, the problems posed by Coptic syllabication are very complex, and those who have dealt with them are far from being at one. No doubt the last word has not yet been spoken on this matter.

BIBLIOGRAPHY

Allen, W. S. *Vox Graeca: A Guide to the Pronunciation of Classical Greek.* Cambridge, 1974.

Böhlig, A. *Die griechischen Lehnwörter imsahidischen und bohairischen Neuen Testament.* 2nd ed. Munich, 1958.

Černý, J. *Coptic Etymological Dictionary.* Cambridge, 1976.

Chaîne, M. *Eléments de grammaire dialectale copte, bohaïrique, sahidique, achmimique, fayoumique.* Paris, 1933.

Dieth, E. *Vademekum der Phonetik.* Bern, 1950.

Dubois, J.; M. Giacomo; L. Guespin; C. Marcellesi; J.-B. Marcellesi; and J.-P. Mével. *Dictionnaire de linguistique.* Paris, 1973.

Edgerton, W. F. Review of W. C. Till, *Koptische Grammatik (saïdischer Dialekt). Journal of Near Eastern Studies* 16 (1957):136–37.

Gardiner, A. *Egyptian Grammar, Being an Introduction to the Study of Hieroglyphs.* 3rd ed. Oxford, 1957.

Gignac, F. T. *A Grammar of the Greek Papyri of the Roman and Byzantine Period,* Vol. 1, *Phonology,* Vol. 2, *Morphology.* Testi e documenti per lo studio dell'antichità, 55. Milan, 1976 and 1981.

Grammont, M. *Traité de phonétique, avec 189 figures dans le texte.* 2nd ed. Paris, 1939.

Hintze, F. "Zur Struktur des Wortes im Ägyptischen ('Ersatzdehnung' und Metathese)." *Zeitschrift für Phonetik und allgemeine Sprachwissenschaft* 1 (1947):18–24.

______. "Noch einmal zur 'Ersatzdehnung' und Metathese im Ägyptischen." *Zeitschrift für Phonetik und allgemeine Sprachwissenschaft* 2 (1948):199–213.

______. "Zur koptischen Phonologie." *Enchoria* 10 (1980):23–91.

Kahle, P. E. *Bala'izah: Coptic Texts from Deir el-Bala'izah in Upper Egypt.* Oxford and London, 1954.

Kasser, R. "Usages de la surligne dans le Papyrus Bodmer VI." *Bulletin de la Société d'égyptologie, Genève* 4 (1980a):53–59.

______. "Prolégomènes à un essai de classification systématique des dialectes et subdialectes coptes selon les critères de la phonétique, I, Principes et terminologie." *Muséon* 93 (1980b):53–112. ". . . , II, Alphabets et systèmes phonétiques." *Muséon* 93 (1980c):237–97. ". . . , III, Systèmes orthographiques et catégories dialectales." *Muséon* 94 (1981a):91–152.

______. "'Djinkim' ou 'surligne' dans les textes en dialecte copte moyen-égyptien." *Bulletin de la Société d'archéologie copte* 23 (1981b):115–57.

______. "Voyelles en fonction consonantique, consonnes en fonction vocalique, et classes de phonèmes en copte." *Bulletin de la Société d'égyptologie, Genève* 5 (1981c):33–50.

______. "Syllabation rapide ou lente en copte, I, Les Glides /j/ et /w/ avec leurs correspondants vocaliques '/i/' et '/u/' (et phonèmes appariés analogues)." *Enchoria* 11 (1982a):23–37. ". . . , II, Aleph et 'voyelle d'aleph.'" *Enchoria* 11 (1982b):39–58. ". . . , III, Syllabes ou sous-syllabes non vocalisées en orthographe saïdique." *Enchoria* 12 (1984a):15–26.

______. "Phonologie superficielle et sous-jacente en copte." *Bulletin de la Société d'archéologie copte* 26 (1984b):43–49.

______. "Gémination de voyelles dans le P. Bodmer VI." In *Acts of the Second International Congress of Coptic Studies, Roma, 22–26 September 1980,* ed. T. Orlandi and F. Wisse, pp. 89–120. Rome, 1985.

Kuentz, C. "Quantité ou timbre? A propos des pseudo-redoublements de voyelles en copte." *Groupe linguistique d'études chamito-sémitiques* 2 (1934–1937):5–7.

Lacau, P. "A propos des voyelles redoublées en copte." *Zeitschrift für ägyptische Sprache und Altertumskunde* 48 (1910):77–81.

Loprieno, A. "Methodologische Anmerkungen zur Rolle der Dialekte in der ägyptischen Sprachentwicklung." *Göttinger Miszellen* 53 (1982):75–95.

Mallon, A. *Grammaire copte, avec bibliographie, chrestomathie et vocabulaire.* 2nd ed. Beirut, 1907.

Marouzeau, J. *Lexique de la terminologie linguistique, français-allemand-anglais-italien.* Paris, 1951.

Nagel, P. "Zum Problem der konsonantischen Silbenträger im Koptischen." *Zeitschrift für ägyptische Sprache und Altertumskunde* 92 (1965):76–78.

Polotsky, H. J. "Zur koptischen Lautlehre I." *Zeitschrift für ägyptische Sprache und Altertumskunde* 67 (1931):74–77.

———. "Zur koptischen Lautlehre II." *Zeitschrift für ägyptische Sprache und Altertumskunde* 69 (1933):125–39.

———. "Une Question d'orthographe bohaïrique." *Bulletin de la Société d'archéologie copte* 12 (1949):25–35.

Robert, P. *Dictionnaire alphabétique et analogique de la langue française.* Paris, 1970.

Steindorff, G. *Koptische Grammatik, mit Chrestomathie, Wörterverzeichnis und Literatur.* Berlin, 1930.

———. *Lehrbuch der koptischen Grammatik.* Chicago, 1951.

Stern, L. *Koptische Grammatik.* Leipzig, 1880.

Till, W. C. "Altes 'Aleph und 'Ajin im Koptischen." *Wiener Zeitschrift für die Kunde des Morgenlandes* 36 (1929):186–96.

———. *Koptische Grammatik (saïdischer Dialekt), mit Bibliographie, Lesestücke und Wörterverzeichnissen.* Leipzig, 1955.

———. *Koptische Dialektgrammatik, mit Lesestücken und Wörterbuch.* 2nd ed. Munich, 1961.

Vergote, J. *Phonétique historique de l'égyptien, les consonnes.* Louvain, 1945.

———. *Grammaire copte,* Vol. 1a, *Introduction, phonétique et phonologie, morphologie synthématique (structure des sémantèmes), partie synchronique,* Vol. 1b, *Introduction, phonétique et phonologie, morphologie synthématique (structure des sémantèmes), partie diachronique,* Vol. 2a, *Morphologie syntagmatique, syntaxe, partie synchronique,* Vol. 2b, *Morphologie syntagmatique, partie diachronique.* Louvain, 1973–1983.

RODOLPHE KASSER

VOCABULARY, AFRICAN CONTACTS WITH AUTOCHTHONOUS COPTIC.

There were doubtlessly close contacts between Egyptian or Coptic and the neighboring African languages. The latter have almost entirely disappeared in Egypt, and the three languages still spoken there are of relatively recent date: (1) Berber, the language subfamily of the Berbers of Siwa Oasis in the west, near the Libyan border, who settled there in the Middle Ages, though the people of the oasis itself were Berber-speaking from the oldest times; (2) Nubian, the tongue of the Nubians in the Nile Valley from Aswan southward, who penetrated there after the fall of the Meroitic empire, probably in the fourth century A.D.; and (3) Beḍawīye, the language of the Beja of the Eastern Desert, between the Nile Valley and the Red Sea, approximately south of the desert road from Qifṭ to Qoṣeir, who seem to be the oldest inhabitants of their territory, though they are mentioned farther south in an inscription of Ezana, king of Ethiopia (fourth century A.D.).

Berber

In all these cases, one must distinguish between Hamito-Semitic words and loanwords. Hamito-Semitic are the words for "tongue" (Arabic *lisān*, Egyptian *ls* = Bohairic (*B*) and Sahidic (*S*) ⲗⲁⲥ, Berber *i-les*, and Chadic *lisi* in Mubi) and "to die" (Arabic *māt*, *yamūt* : *mawt*, Egyptian *mwt* = *S* ⲙⲟⲩ : ⲙⲟⲟⲩⲧ†, Berber *emmet*, Chadic *mutu* in Hausa). Berber shares several words with Egyptian that are not Hamito-Semitic, such as *uššen*, jackal (Shilha in Morocco, Kabyle in Algeria): *wnš* = *B*, *S* ⲟⲩⲱⲛϣ; *ab̲ēna*, date (fruit) (Ghadames in Libya), Egyptian *bny* = *B* ⲃⲉⲛⲓ, *S* ⲃⲛ̄ⲛⲉ; also *S* ⲕⲟⲩⲕ, fruit of the dum palm (*Hyphaene thebaica*), corresponds to Tuareg *a-kūka*. A Berber loanword of the Libyan period (Twenty-second Dynasty) is *B*, *S* ⲙⲟⲣⲧ, beard, Berber *tamart* (Shilha of Morocco), with variants, in almost every dialect.

Beḍawīye

In Beḍawīye, the language of the Beja in the Eastern Desert, the horse is called *hatāy* (plural, *hatáy*). This word derives from Egyptian *ḥtr*, yoke of oxen, later pronounced *ḥtỉ* = *B* ϩⲑⲟ, *S* ϩⲧⲟ. Yet *hatāy* does not derive from *ḥtr* or *ḥtỉ* but from a third form, *ḥty* (probably pronounced **ḥatáy*), not found in Coptic dialects.

Beḍawīye *san*, brother, looks like *B*, *S* ⲥⲟⲛ. In spite of the similarity, the words are of different origin. This can be seen from the different derivations. Coptic has *B* ⲥⲱⲛⲓ, sister, and the plural *B* ⲥⲛⲏⲟⲩ, brothers, while the Cushitic languages have different forms: Beḍawīye *kwa*, sister, and in Dembea *zän*, in Khamir *zin*, in Bilin *dan*, brothers.

Mehēl, to treat medically, is probably of Coptic or Egyptian origin; compare *P* ⲙⲉϩⲏⲗ, to heal, apparently an emphatic verbal noun (**maḫḫīlaw* or similar).

Nubian

Nubian is not a Hamito-Semitic language. In the Middle Ages there were several Christian kingdoms in Nubia and the old-Nubian texts contain a certain number of Coptic and Greek loanwords, such as ⲁⲣⲫⲗ, temple: *B* ⲉⲣⲫⲉⲓ, *S* ⲣ̄ⲡⲉ; ⲟⲣⲡ, wine: *S*, *B* ⲏⲣⲡ̄, probably **ìōrep* or similar; and ⲥⲓⲗⲉⲗ, pray, with which compare *B*, *S* ϣⲗⲏⲗ, to pray, and Beḍawīye *silēl*, pray, prayer. In modern Nubian one finds *adīr*, winter = the month Hathor or, more exactly its

Greek form ⲁⲑⲩⲣ, pronounced *Atīr* (without *h*); and *bogon*, a month name (Arabic *Bašans*) from Greek ⲡⲁⲭⲱⲛ, pronounced *Pakōn* (without *h*).

Kam, camel, derives not directly from *B* ϫⲁⲙⲟⲩⲗ, *S* ϭⲁⲙⲟⲩⲗ, camel, but from an earlier form, **ḳamūli*. There were no camels in pharaonic Egypt unless in the last centuries B.C., but Cambyses' expedition to Siwa Oasis is unthinkable without camels; it took place shortly after 525 B.C. But the name of the animal, which is of Semitic origin (Akkadian *gammalu-m*, Hebrew *gāmal*, Aramaic *gaml-ā* but *gĕmal-* before a genitive, Arabic *gamal, ǧamal*), must have been known in Egypt a long time before, as the shift from *ā* to *ō* (*gamāl-i : gamōl-i*) took place before 1000 B.C. The Coptic forms derive from *ḳamūli*, *ū* being due to postnasalization, and the same form is the ancestor of various forms in Berber, such as Kabyle *a-lġʷem*, plural *i-leġʷman*, where *a-* and *i-* are the old singular and plural articles and *ġ* is Arabic ghayn, a fricative *g* as in the modern Greek *gála*, milk. The Berber form derives from **ḳalūmi* (metathesis for **ḳamūli*), and similar forms are found in numerous languages in the western Sudan, such as Hausa *ṛāk'umi*, camel, Kanuri *ka-ḷigimo* (prefix *ka-*), probably also Fulani *ṅ-geloba*, camel, and so on. In Nubian the word has lost its last part (*kam* instead of *kamūl*), but the plural is still *kaml-i* (plural ending *-i*).

BIBLIOGRAPHY

Vycichl, W. *Dictionnaire étymologique de la langue copte*. Louvain, 1983.

WERNER VYCICHL

VOCABULARY, COPTO-ARABIC.

No language is entirely homogeneous, and so it is with Coptic. There is a majority of autochthonous words deriving from pharaonic Egyptian, but after the conquest of Egypt by Alexander the Great (332 B.C.) many Greek words were adopted. And, later on, after the end of the Byzantine domination, Egypt, subdued by the Arabs (A.D. 641), began to undergo their influence, at first imperceptibly but later more obviously. Thus, Arabic loanwords were extremely rare in Coptic immediately after the ARAB CONQUEST OF EGYPT, comprising but a few personal names and some substantives. They became more numerous in the very last period of Coptic, as evidenced by Stern's text (1885) on alchemy and Chassinat's medical papyrus (1921), both probably translated from the Arabic. In the former, most nouns are preceded by *al-* or an assimilated form:

S ⲁⲗⲕⲁⲣⲟⲟⲣⲉ (fem.), bottle:Arabic *al-ḳarūra*.
S ⲁⲗⲕⲁⲧⲁϩ (masc.), beaker:Arabic *al-ḳadaḥ*.
S ⲁⲗⲃⲁϩⲙ (masc.), coal:Arabic *al-faḥm*.
S ⲁⲗⲭⲓⲡⲣⲓⲧ (masc.), sulphur:Arabic *al-kibrīt*.
S ⲁⲗⲭⲉⲛⲟⲩⲛ (masc.), oven:Arabic *al-kānūn*.
S ⲁⲗⲭⲁⲣⲣⲟⲟⲡⲉ (fem.), carob bean:Arabic *al-ḫarrūba*.
S ⲁⲥⲥⲉⲃⲏϩⲉ (fem.), sheet of metal:Arabic *aṣ-ṣafīḥa*.
S ⲁⲥⲥⲉⲣⲛⲏϩ (masc.), arsenic:Arabic *az-zirnīḫ*.
S ⲁⲥⲥⲓⲡⲁⲕ (masc.), mercury:Arabic *az-zaybaḳ*.

There are forms without article, such as *S* ⲧⲉⲣϩⲁⲙ (masc.), *dirham* (unit of weight); *S* ⲧⲁⲛⲁⲕ (masc.), *dānaḳ* (unit of weight); and *S* ⲁⲡⲓⲁⲧ, white, from Arabic *'abyaḍ*, white.

BIBLIOGRAPHY

Chassinat, E. *Un Papyrus médical copte*. Mémoires publiés par les membres de l'Institut français d'archéologie orientale du Caire 32. Cairo, 1921.

Stern, L. "Fragment eines koptischen Traktates über Alchimie." *Zeitschrift für ägyptische Sprache und Altertumskunde* 23 (1885):102–119.

WERNER VYCICHL

VOCABULARY, COPTO-GREEK.

The reader who has not been warned in advance, approaching a Coptic text, will probably be struck by its "Greek" appearance. But even if its superficial appearance is almost entirely Greek, the body thus clothed remains authentically Egyptian. Furthermore, the proportion of elements of Greek appearance to those of Egyptian aspect may vary from one Coptic text to another (because of the DIALECTS, the subjects treated, the stylistic and linguistic preferences of the authors, not to mention the level of their culture, etc.), as will be seen further on. The two following examples, in which will be found either Sahidic (*S*), Mesokemic (*M*), "classical" Fayyumic (*F5*), "classical" Bohairic (*B5*), on the one hand, or Akhmimic (*A*), on the other, will show this summarily and in a preliminary way.

First is the best known of the Gospel prayers (Mt. 6:9–13), attested as it happens in four different Coptic idioms (Exhibit 1). The proportions cited here are calculated chiefly on the basis of the Sahidic text. In *S* this passage requires 219 letters, of which 204 (95 percent) are Greek (see on this subject ALPHABET IN COPTIC, GREEK). If one counts the "words" (following the conventional procedures and omitting the articles and various prefixes, which are always of Egyptian origin), one finds here 41 words, of which

EXHIBIT 1.

	Our Father who art in heaven,	hallowed be thy name;
S	ⲡⲉⲛⲉⲓⲱⲧ ⲉⲧϩⲛ̄ ⲙ̄ⲡⲏⲩⲉ	ⲙⲁⲣⲉ ⲡⲉⲕⲣⲁⲛ ⲟⲩⲟⲡ
M	ⲡⲉⲛⲉⲓⲟⲧ ⲉⲧϩⲛ ⲙ̇ⲡⲏ	ⲡⲉⲕⲣⲉⲛ ⲙⲁⲣⲉϥⲧⲟⲩⲃⲁ
F5	ⲡⲉⲛⲓ̈ⲱⲧ ⲉⲧϩⲛⲛ ⲙⲡⲏⲟⲩⲓ̈	ⲡⲉⲕⲗⲉⲛ ⲙⲁⲗⲉϥⲧⲩⲃⲃⲁ
B5	ⲡⲉⲛⲓⲱⲧ ⲉⲧϧⲉⲛ ⲛⲓⲫⲏⲟⲩⲓ	ⲙⲁⲣⲉϥⲧⲟⲩⲃⲟ ⲛ̇ϫⲉ ⲡⲉⲕⲣⲁⲛ

	(10) thy kingdom come;	thy will be done
S	ⲧⲉⲕⲙⲛ̄ⲧⲣ̄ⲣⲟ ⲙⲁⲣⲉⲥⲉⲓ	ⲡⲉⲕⲟⲩⲱϣ ⲙⲁⲣⲉϥϣⲱⲡⲉ
M	ⲧⲉⲕⲙⲛⲧⲉⲣⲁ ⲙⲁⲣⲉⲥⲉⲓ	ⲡⲉⲧⲉϩⲛⲉⲕ ⲙⲁⲣⲉϥϣⲟⲡⲉ
F5	ⲧⲉⲕⲙⲉⲧⲉⲣⲣⲁ ⲙⲁⲗⲉⲥⲓ̈	ⲡⲉⲧⲉϩⲛⲏⲕ
B5	ⲙⲁⲣⲉⲥⲓ ⲛ̇ϫⲉ ⲧⲉⲕⲙⲉⲧⲟⲩⲣⲟ	ⲡⲉⲧⲉϩⲛⲁⲕ ⲙⲁⲣⲉϥϣⲱⲡⲓ

	on earth as it is in heaven;	(11) give us this day our daily bread;
S	ⲛ̄ⲑⲉ ⲉⲧϥ̄ϩⲛ̄ ⲧⲡⲉ ⲙⲁⲣⲉϥϣⲱⲡⲉ ⲟⲛ ϩⲓϫⲙ̄ ⲡⲕⲁϩ	ⲡⲉⲛⲟⲉⲓⲕ ⲉⲧⲛⲏⲩ ⲧⲁⲁϥ ⲛⲁⲛ ⲙ̄ⲡⲟⲟⲩ
M	ⲛ̇ⲑⲏ ⲉⲧϣⲁⲡ ϩⲛ ⲧⲡⲏ ⲙⲁⲣⲉⲥϣⲟⲡⲉ ϩⲓϫⲛ ⲡⲕⲉϩⲉ	ⲡⲉⲛⲁ̇ⲉⲓⲕ ⲛ̇ⲣⲉⲥⲧⲉ ⲙⲁⲉⲓϥ ⲛⲉⲛ ⲙ̇ⲡⲁⲟⲩ
F5	ϩⲛ ⲧⲡⲏ ⲙⲁⲗⲉϥϣⲱⲡⲓ ϩⲓϫⲉⲛ ⲡⲕⲉϩⲓ	ⲡⲉⲛⲁⲓ̈ⲕ ⲛⲗⲉⲥϯ ⲙⲁⲓ̈ϥ ⲛⲏⲛ ⲙⲡⲁⲟⲩ
B5	ⲙ̇ⲫⲣⲏϯ ϧⲉⲛ ⲧⲫⲉ ⲛⲉⲙ ϩⲓϫⲉⲛ ⲡⲓⲕⲁϩⲓ	ⲡⲉⲛⲱⲓⲕ ⲛ̇ⲧⲉ ⲣⲁⲥϯ ⲙⲏⲓϥ ⲛⲁⲛ ⲙ̇ⲫⲟⲟⲩ

		(12) and forgive us our trespasses	as we forgive those
S		ⲕⲱ ⲛⲁⲛ ⲉⲃⲟⲗ ⲛ̄ⲛⲉⲧⲉⲣⲟⲛ	ⲛ̄ⲑⲉ ϩⲱⲱⲛ ⲟⲛ ⲉⲧⲛ̄ⲕⲱ ⲉⲃⲟⲗ
M		ⲕⲱ ⲉ̇ⲃⲁⲗ ⲛ̇ⲛⲉⲧⲉⲣⲁⲛ	ⲛ̇ⲑⲏ ϩⲱⲛ ⲉⲧϣⲁⲛⲕⲱ ⲉ̇ⲃⲁⲗ
F5		ⲕⲱ ⲛⲛⲉⲧⲉⲗⲁⲛ ⲛⲏⲛ ⲉⲃⲁⲗ	ⲛⲧϩⲏ ⲛⲧⲁⲛⲕⲱ ⲉⲃⲁⲗ
B5	ⲟⲩⲟϩ	ⲭⲁ ⲛⲉⲧⲉ̇ⲣⲟⲛ ⲛⲁⲛ ⲉ̇ⲃⲟⲗ	ⲙ̇ⲫⲣⲏϯ ϩⲱⲛ ⲉ̇ⲧⲉⲛⲭⲱ ⲉ̇ⲃⲟⲗ

	who trespass against us;	(13) and lead us not into temptation [*πειρασμός*]	
S	ⲛ̄ⲛⲉⲧⲉ ⲟⲩⲛ̄ⲧⲁⲛ ⲉⲣⲟⲟⲩ		ⲛ̄ⲅⲧⲙ̄ϫⲓⲧⲛ̄ ⲉϩⲟⲩⲛ ⲉⲡⲉⲓⲣⲁⲥⲙⲟⲥ
M	ⲛ̇ⲛⲉⲧⲉ ⲟⲩⲛⲧⲉⲛ ⲉ̇ⲣⲁⲩ	ⲁⲩⲱ	ⲙ̇ⲡⲣ̇ⲛⲧⲛ ⲉ̇ϩⲟⲩⲛ ⲉⲡⲡⲓⲣⲁⲥⲙⲟⲥ
F5	ⲛⲛⲉⲧⲉ ⲟⲩⲁⲛⲧⲏⲛ ⲉⲗⲁⲩ	ⲁⲩⲱ	ⲙⲡⲉⲗⲉⲛⲧⲉⲛ ⲉϩⲟⲩⲛ ⲉⲡⲡⲓⲣⲁⲥⲙⲟⲥ
B5	ⲛ̇ⲛⲏ ⲉ̇ⲧⲉ ⲟⲩⲟⲛ ⲛ̇ⲧⲁⲛ ⲉ̇ⲣⲱⲟⲩ	ⲟⲩⲟϩ	ⲙ̇ⲡⲉⲣⲉⲛⲧⲉⲛ ⲉ̇ϧⲟⲩⲛ ⲉ̇ⲡⲓⲣⲁⲥⲙⲟⲥ

	but [*ἀλλά*] deliver us from evil [*πονηρός*].			
S	ⲁⲗⲗⲁ	ⲛ̄ⲅⲛⲁϩⲙⲉⲛ	ⲉⲃⲟⲗ ϩⲓⲧⲙ̄	ⲡⲡⲟⲛⲏⲣⲟⲥ.
M	ⲁⲗⲗⲁ	ⲛⲉϩⲙⲛ	ⲉ̇ⲃⲁⲗ ⲛ̇ⲧⲁⲧϥ	ⲙ̇ⲡⲡⲟⲛⲏⲣⲟⲥ.
F5	ⲁⲗⲗⲁ	ⲛⲉϩⲙⲉⲛ	ϩⲁⲃⲁⲗ	ⲙⲡⲡⲉⲧϩⲁⲩ.
B5	ⲁⲗⲗⲁ	ⲛⲁϩⲙⲉⲛ	ⲉ̇ⲃⲟⲗ ϩⲁ	ⲡⲓⲡⲉⲧϩⲱⲟⲩ.

only 3 (7 percent) are of Greek origin (in *M* likewise 3 words out of 40, in *F5* 2 out of 35 = 6 percent, in *B5* 2 out of 46 = 4 percent; if instead of considering Mt. 6:9–13 one considered only 6:9–12, one would find in all these idioms no word of Greek origin). This text, as can be seen, is particularly sober in its use of the Copto-Greek vocabulary.

The First Epistle of Clement 42.4 in *A* (Exhibit 2) is as far as can be from this sobriety. This passage uses 108 letters, of which 103 (95 percent) are Greek. If one counts the words, there are 17, of which 12 (71 percent) are of Greek origin.

These two examples are probably extreme cases, and the great mass of the Coptic texts lies somewhere between them, readily making use of this Hellenic material, without parsimony or anti-Greek purism but also without falling into "Hellenomania."

There can be no question here of examining in every detail the problem posed by the variable usage of the Copto-Greek words in the various Coptic texts (the most detailed study of the subject, although limited to the New Testament and to the "languages," rather than "dialects," *S* and *B*, is Böhlig, 1958; with regard to the Coptic dialects outside *S* and *B*, see Kasser, 1983). This discussion will therefore be confined to the most important facts.

Every language carries words borrowed from neighboring languages; in English, for example, there are many words deriving from French, in particular because the political history of England was often and over long periods closely interlocked with that of France. However, the proportion of the Greek words in Coptic (rarely of words that passed into Greek from Semitic languages or from Latin,

EXHIBIT 2.

They preached [κηρύσσειν] in every [κατά] city [πόλις] and in every [κατά] country [χώρα],

ⲁⲩⲣ̄ ⲕⲏⲣⲩⲥⲥⲉ ϭⲉ ⲕⲁⲧⲁ ⲡⲟⲗⲓⲥ ⲁⲟⲩ ⲕⲁⲧⲁ ⲭⲱⲣⲁ

they installed [καθιστάναι] [in office] their first-fruit [ἀπαρχή, i.e., those who were to be the first among them],

ⲁⲩⲣ̄ ⲕⲁⲧϩⲓⲥⲧⲁ ⲛ̄ⲛⲟⲩⲁⲡⲁⲣⲭⲏ

they proved [δοκιμάζειν] by the [Holy] Spirit [πνεῦμα] bishops [ἐπίσκοπος] and deacons [διάκονος]

ⲁⲩⲣ̄ ⲇⲟⲕⲓⲙⲁⲍⲉ ϩⲙ̄ ⲡⲡ̅ⲛ̅ⲁ̅ ⲛ̄ⲛ̄ⲉⲡⲓⲥⲕⲟⲡⲟⲥ ⲙⲛ̄ ϩⲉⲛⲇⲓⲁⲕⲟⲛⲟⲥ

capable [now and in the future] of having [and preserving] the faith [πιστεύειν].

ⲛⲉⲧⲛⲁϩ ⲣ̄ ⲡⲓⲥⲧⲉⲩⲉ.

Persian, or other tongues) is enormous—about 40 percent. This is, of course, counting each lexeme as a unit, for it happens that very often the Copto-Greek words are of rarer usage (because more specialized) in ordinary Coptic texts (not those devoted to law, theology, medicine, etc.), so that their presence there is more modest (about 20 percent on average).

This very evident and massive presence of the Greek element in the Coptic language (as an Egyptian language) has no doubt some relation to the fact that the majority of the Coptic texts preserved today were translated from the Greek. The translations were generally carried out in a rather free manner in *S*, rather literally in *B*, where the Greek term of the original was readily taken up into Copto-Greek, especially where the term was difficult to understand, whereas in *S*, the effort was made to interpret, by means of a more accessible vocabulary, at the cost of departing somewhat from the Greek.

However, that is not the chief cause of what appears as a kind of Hellenization of Egyptian. It results in fact, above all, from a process of linguistic interference, in which Greek naturally most often plays the role of the "donor" and Egyptian that of the "recipient" (Brunsch, 1978, pp. 60–61). This phenomenon is the inevitable result of the Hellenic grip on Egypt during the five centuries or so that preceded the formation of Coptic as a literary language (see ALPHABET IN COPTIC, GREEK). Since Greek had been so long in a dominant position in Egypt, a country of which it became the administrative language from the beginning of the Ptolemaic period and in which there was a strong Greek colony, there gradually came about, of necessity and also through mixed marriages (e.g., between Greek soldiers and Egyptian women), a bilingual milieu, which facilitated the smooth functioning of this heterogeneous social whole, and the diffusion of numerous words from the Greek koine of Egypt (with certain rudimentary concepts that accompanied them) into the widest circles of the native population, which in the beginning did not know Greek.

Furthermore, this diffusion could only have been accelerated and extended by the diffusion of new ideas brought by Greek texts (Judeo-Christianity, Gnosticism, Hermeticism, Manichaeism, etc.). These ideas first took root among the Greek minority in Egypt; later they contaminated the bilingual milieu and then the milieu in which only the native (Coptic) language was spoken. It may be remarked in this connection that, on the one hand, the Coptic words deriving from Greek are for the most part so well assimilated into the Coptic language that it is appropriate to call them "Copto-Greek" rather than "Greek" (they were probably no longer felt to be "Greek," and thus foreign, by the Copts who used them); but, on the other hand, these Copto-Greek lexemes only rarely play a truly indispensable role in Coptic, for in the majority of cases one could without serious inconvenience replace them with some almost synonymous autochthonous equivalent. (The old Egyptian language was supple enough and rich enough to be able to face up to these diverse new situations, to answer these "modern" needs and adapt itself, as it did several times in the course of a history of several thousand years.) The use of the Copto-Greek vocabulary thus remains very often optional, this aspect of "free choice" being further underlined, more than once, by the fact that the writer apparently delighted in placing side by side the Copto-Greek word and the native Coptic word (redundancy in some sort, as in ϩⲓⲛⲁ ϫⲉ, in order that; ⲟⲩⲭ ⲟⲧⲓ ϫⲉ, not because; ⲡⲁⲗⲓⲛ ⲟⲛ, again; ϫⲉ ⲅⲁⲣ, because; or in tautologies like ⲁⲅⲁⲑⲟⲥ ⲁⲩⲱ ⲉⲛⲁⲛⲟⲩϥ in the Pistis Sophia; cf. Schmidt and MacDermot, 1978, p. 550). But it is evident that other factors in practice limited this theoretical liberty. In fact, the use of the Copto-Greek vocabulary may be imposed by certain conventions, such as those of some specialized milieu or other. It may be linked also to the personal taste of some author or translator for a given terminology, some writers probably putting on a certain affectation of Hellenizing their discourse while others, for other ideological motives (purism, desire to safeguard an ethnic and religious particularism, etc.), reacted negatively in face of this inclination, which tended progressively to assimilate Egypt to the somewhat hybrid Hellenism of the other provinces of the Byzantine Orient.

In short, one may think that certain ecclesiastical milieus in the third and fourth centuries encouraged the Hellenization of the native Egyptian idioms: Greek was the language common to all parts of the church, it was the language of the theologians after having been that of the Septuagint version (Greek Old Testament) and of the entire New Testament, and so of the Gospel itself. Certainly, it was considered necessary to translate the Bible into Coptic, but this was above all to answer a transitory need, that of the Christianization of the rural masses of Egypt. Once this end had been attained, the partisans of Greek thought that the sooner the Coptic church became Hellenized, the better: by this means they would avoid a dangerous particularism, productive of schisms. And, in fact, it was well recognized that by the force of events the Greek vocabulary of the Copts was becoming richer from generation to generation; it would suffice to accelerate this movement further by multiplying the borrowings from the Hellenic patrimony. From this point of view, every Greek word used in Egypt already belonged by right to the Coptic language and could find its place one day or another in a Coptic sentence; every word in the koine was in some sort potentially a Coptic word. Thus, one may observe here or there the appearance of some Greek word, new in Coptic, used in a moment of audacity or with an urge to emphasis, according to the temperament or the whim of an author.

This movement of openness to Greek was opposed very early by a reaction of native particularism, growing ever stronger, which prevented many Greek words newly introduced into Coptic from becoming profoundly assimilated to it and so becoming part of common usage. Besides, in the third century A.D. the preponderance of Greek in the Roman empire, at least in the principal ports and in wide areas of its eastern part, and in Rome, had been breached, especially by Latin but also, more regionally, by other cultural particularisms. One might thus define Coptic, as it presents itself to the observer in all its diversity, as the fluctuating result of a very incomplete Hellenization of the popular Egyptian language. Certain Greek words were thoroughly assimilated to it, in all levels of the population; others were part of the current professional baggage of specialists (jurists, theologians, physicians, etc.) within their specialization, while remaining foreign to those who did not know sufficiently well the science expressed by this particular learned terminology; still others remained true foreign bodies in Coptic, being used only exceptionally, by an author who did not know how to translate them or took delight in the mystery of a term understood by him alone (or by a very few initiates). Therefore, one cannot describe all these Coptic words derived from Greek uniformly as "assimilated," "borrowed," or "foreign."

A very small part of the Copto-Greek vocabulary appears to have entered into the Egyptian language a very long time before the beginnings of literary Coptic, and probably even before the Ptolemaic period, at a time when Greek had not yet acquired the preponderant role that it later played there for close to a thousand years. One can recognize these words from their orthography, often somewhat distorted in Coptic in comparison with their Greek orthography. Thus, for example (Böhlig, 1958, pp. 6, 80), *ἄγκυρα*, anchor, *S* **ϩⲁⲩϭⲁⲗ**, *F5* **ϩⲁⲩϭⲏⲗ**, *B* **ⲁⲩⲭⲁⲗ**; *μηλωτή*, skin garment, *B* **ⲙⲉⲗⲱⲧⲏ** but again *S* **ⲙⲉⲗⲱⲧ**, *S* **ⲙⲁⲗⲗⲱⲧ**, and above all *S* **ⲃⲁⲗⲟⲧ**, *A*, *F5* **ⲃⲁⲗⲁⲧ**; *πέλεκυς*, ax, *S*, *B* **ⲕⲉⲗⲉⲃⲓⲛ**; *πίναξ*, plate, dish, *S*, *M* **ⲡⲓⲛⲁⲝ** but *F5* **ⲡⲓⲛⲉϭ**, *B* **ⲃⲓⲛⲁⲭ**; *σινδών*, linen cloth (or garment), *S*, *A*, *M* **ⲥⲓⲛⲇⲱⲛ** but also *S* **ϣⲛ̄ⲧⲱ**, *B* **ϣⲉⲛⲧⲱ**; *στατήρ*, stater (weight or coin), *S*, *L5* **ⲥⲁⲧⲉⲉⲣⲉ**, *L5* **ⲥⲧⲁⲧⲉⲉⲣⲉ**, *L4* **ⲥⲧⲁⲧⲉⲉⲣ**, *M* **ⲥⲧⲁⲧⲏⲣⲉ**, *F5* **ⲥⲁⲧⲏⲏⲗⲓ**, *B* **ⲥⲁⲑⲉⲣⲓ**.

However, the majority of the other words derived from Greek in the Ptolemaic period or even later ("derived from Greek" here may also signify "derived from other languages via Greek," as is the case, for example, with the Latin *census*, which became *κῆνσος*, taxation, *S* **ⲕⲏⲛⲥⲟⲥ**, *M* **ⲕⲏⲛⲥⲟⲛ**, or with *λίβανος*, incense, *S*, *A*, *L*, *M*, *F*, *B* **ⲗⲓⲃⲁⲛⲟⲥ**, *F7* **ⲗⲉⲃⲉⲛⲟⲩⲥ**, derived from the Semitic linguistic domain, and with *νάρδος*, nard, *S*, *A*, *W*, *F*, *F7*, *B* **ⲛⲁⲣⲇⲟⲥ**, derived from Persian, etc.; Böhlig, 1958, pp. 8–11). In all the Coptic dialects except *H* (which follows its own ways; see Kasser, 1975–1976, and DIALECT H, OR HERMOPOLITAN OR ASHMUNINIC), these words of Hellenic origin have preserved their original orthography, either exactly or nearly so (perhaps thanks to the bilingualism of the majority of the copyists, who knew well the form of the same terms in the Greek of Egypt). Of course, since Coptic syntax is entirely and radically Egyptian, the Copto-Greek substantives are freed from any Greek declension (they remain in principle invariably in the nominative singular), and the verbs are equally freed from any Greek conjugation (remaining, as a general rule, fixed in a form of the infinitive or, according to the dialects and with loss of the final -ν of the infinitive, in a form identical with that of the imperative), as will be seen further on.

Systematic consonantal modifications are rare and very limited. Considering only the principal characteristics, one may mention here above all -ⲕⲓ- becoming -ϭⲓ- (by palatalization) in *S, A, L,* and *M* (but not in the other Coptic idioms, which leads one to think that there ϭ had a phonological value other than /c/): for example, κακία, wickedness, *S, A, L* ⲕⲁⲕⲓⲁ but also *S, M* ⲕⲁϭⲓⲁ; κίνδυνος, danger, *S, A, L* ⲕⲓⲛⲇⲩⲛⲟⲥ or *S, A, L, M* ϭⲓⲛⲇⲩⲛⲟⲥ. It is probably a more complex phenomenon, in which, however, palatalization also plays a certain role, which produces in the case of χι the mutation of ⲭⲓ into ϫⲓ in *S, A, L,* and *M* (/khi/ > */kçi/ > */tçi/ > */tši/ > /či/ [?]; see further on with regard to ἱ- ϩⲓ- sometimes becoming ϣⲓ-); thus ἀρχιερεύς, high priest, *S, A, F, B* ⲁⲣⲭⲓⲉⲣⲉⲩⲥ, *L* ⲁⲣϫⲓⲉⲣⲉⲩⲥ; ἀρχιμάγειρος, chief cook, *S, B* ⲁⲣⲭⲓⲙⲁⲅⲓⲣⲟⲥ, *S* ⲁⲣϫⲓⲙⲁⲅⲉⲓⲣⲟⲥ; χιών, snow, *S, A, L, F, B* ⲭⲓⲱⲛ, *S, A, M* ϫⲓⲱⲛ; and so on.

It is legitimate to include in the consonantal domain the rough or smooth breathing at the beginning of Greek words starting with a vowel. Very often (and in *S* more often than in *B*) the rough breathing is rendered by ϩ and the smooth breathing by the absence of any special grapheme before the initial vowel. One dare not speak of a rule here, for there are too many exceptions, proving that at the dawn of literary Coptic the Greek of Egypt no longer made any difference in pronunciation between the rough and the smooth breathing (what continued in the texts and left its reflection in Coptic is only the more or less complete survival of a more or less intact Greek orthographical tradition; see Böhlig, 1958, p. 111, etc.): for example, ἄδικος, unjust, *S, A, L, F5, B* ⲁⲇⲓⲕⲟⲥ; ἅμα, simultaneously, *S, L* ϩⲁⲙⲁ, *B* ⲁⲙⲁ; ὅταν, when, *S, A, L, M, W, V, F5, B* ϩⲟⲧⲁⲛ; εἰκών, image, *S, A, L, M, F5, B* ϩⲓⲕⲱⲛ. It will be noted that in a narrow idiomatic (and archaic) Coptic sector (especially *L6* and *S* of the Coptic Gnostic texts from Nag Hammadi in Upper Egypt; Kasser, 1980), the initial Greek ἱ- has as its equivalent ϣⲓ rather than ϩⲓ (a phenomenon of palatalization, in which /ši/ would derive from an ancient */çi/ issuing from /hi/ [?]): for example, ἱκανός, sufficient, *S, A, L4, B* ϩⲓⲕⲁⲛⲟⲥ, *S, L6* ϣⲓⲕⲁⲛⲟⲥ. On the other hand, it may happen that the Greek -ῤῥ- is rendered by -ⲣϩ- rather than by -ⲣⲣ-, as in παρρησία, freedom of speech, *S, A, L, F5, B* ⲡⲁⲣⲣⲏⲥⲓⲁ, *S, A, L, M, W* ⲡⲁⲣϩⲏⲥⲓⲁ, *V* ⲡⲁⲣϩⲉⲥⲓⲁ (idiolectal).

In the area of the vowels, various idiolectal modifications appear (above all confusions between ⲏ, ⲓ, and ⲩ, sometimes also between ⲉ and ⲏ, ⲟ and ⲱ, etc.); they will not surprise anyone who deals with the texts of the koine (contemporary with the genesis of Coptic literature) in Egypt and has noted its graphic fluctuations, particularly in vowels (Böhlig, 1958, pp. 91–106; Gignac, 1976–1981; and PHONOLOGY OF THE GREEK OF EGYPT, INFLUENCE OF COPTIC ON THE); being too numerous and not systematic, they cannot be set out here. However, the substitution of ⲉ for Greek αι in *B, F, V,* and *W* is very general and regular; thus αἵρεσις, heresy, *S, L, M* ϩⲁⲓⲣⲉⲥⲓⲥ, *B* ϩⲉⲣⲉⲥⲓⲥ (also here and there in *S* and *L*); αἴσθησις, intuition, *S, A, L* ⲁⲓⲥⲑⲏⲥⲓⲥ, *F, B* ⲉⲥⲑⲏⲥⲓⲥ (also here and there in *S* and *L*); δίκαιος, just, *S, A, L, M* ⲇⲓⲕⲁⲓⲟⲥ, *V, F, B* ⲇⲓⲕⲉⲟⲥ (also here and there in *S* and *M*). *L4* often replaces a verbal final -ειν, normally -ⲉⲓ in *L*, by -ⲏ, as in ἐπιθυμεῖν, to desire, *S, A,* ⲉ̀ⲡⲓⲑⲩⲙⲉⲓ, *L6, M* ⲉⲡⲓⲑⲩⲙⲓ, *L4* ⲉⲡⲓⲑⲩⲙⲏ (with regard to *F5, B* ⲉ̀ⲡⲓⲑⲩⲙⲓⲛ, see further on).

In a general way, Coptic invariably uses the Greek substantives in the nominative singular, as with Matthew 24:7, ἔθνος (nominative singular), a people, *S* ⲟⲩϩⲉⲑⲛⲟⲥ; Matthew 6:32, τὰ ἔθνη (nominative plural), the Gentiles, *S* ⲛ̄ϩⲉⲑⲛⲟⲥ; Romans 11:13, ἐγὼ ἐθνῶν ἀπόστολος (genitive plural), I, the apostle of the Gentiles, *S* ⲁⲛⲅ̄ ⲡⲁⲡⲟⲥⲧⲟⲗⲟⲥ ⲛ̄ⲛ̄ϩⲉⲑⲛⲟⲥ. Other forms are quite exceptional, as in Luke 1:3, the vocative κράτιστε, *S, B* ⲕⲣⲁⲧⲓⲥⲧⲉ, or the nominative plural of σκεῦος, object, vase, plural σκεύη, regularly attested in *S, A,* and *L*, as in Romans 9:22, σκεύη ὀργῆς, vessels of wrath, *S* ϩⲉⲛⲥⲕⲉⲩⲏ ⲛ̄ⲟⲣⲅⲏ but *B* ϩⲁⲛⲥⲕⲉⲩⲟⲥ ⲛ̀ⲧⲉ ⲡϫⲱⲛⲧ. One may note finally that Coptic tends to impose its own native plural endings, in *S* -/ówə/ etc., on Copto-Greek words ending in tonic -ⲏ, as with ψυχή, soul, plural ψυχαί, Coptic plural *S* ⲯⲩⲭⲟⲟⲩⲉ, *P* ⲯⲩⲭⲏⲩ, *L6* (?) ⲯⲩⲭⲏⲟⲩ, *L4* ⲯⲩⲭⲁⲩⲉ, *M* ⲯⲩⲭⲁⲟⲩⲉ̀, *F56* ⲯⲩⲭⲁⲩⲓ, *B* ⲯⲩⲭⲱⲟⲩⲓ̀; compare *S* etc. ⲧⲃ̄ⲛⲏ, cattle, plural *S* ⲧⲃ̄ⲛⲟⲟⲩⲉ, *B* ⲧⲉⲃⲛⲱⲟⲩⲓ̀, *A* ⲧⲃ̄ⲛⲉⲩⲉ, *L4* ⲧⲃ̄ⲛⲁⲩⲉ, *M* ⲧⲃⲛⲁⲟⲩⲉ̀, *H* ⲧⲃⲛⲁⲟⲩ, *F5* ⲧⲩⲃⲛⲁⲩⲓ. Should one be surprised that Coptic did not likewise use its plurals *S* etc. -ⲟⲓ (plurals of words in final tonic *S* etc. -ⲟ) for Copto-Greek words ending in -ⲟⲥ, which would have corresponded to the Greek plural (nominative), such as νομός, plural νομοί? See for comparison, *S, L,* etc.

ϩⲗ̄ⲗⲟ, old man, *S* plural ϩⲗ̄ⲗⲟⲓ̈, and *B* ϧⲉⲗⲗⲟⲓ̈, *A* ϩⲗ̄ⲗⲁⲓ, *L* ϩⲗ̄ⲗⲁⲓ̈, *M* ϩⲁⲗⲗⲟⲩⲓ̈ (*F5*? ϩⲉⲗⲗⲟⲩⲓ̈). This is not the place for an answer to so delicate a question. One may note finally that, Coptic having only two genders (masculine and feminine, not neuter), a Copto-Greek word corresponding to a Greek neuter is masculine in Coptic, as in Romans 1:32, *τὸ δικαίωμα*, the act of judgment, the verdict, *S* ⲡⲇⲓⲕⲁⲓⲱⲙⲁ.

In regard to the Copto-Greek forms corresponding to the Greek adjective, it may be noted that the usages of Coptic are clearly different from those of Greek. The feminine form is rarely preserved: it is most often replaced by the masculine form. In any case, the allocation of these forms (always in the nominative singular) is as follows: the masculine (or on occasion the feminine, when it has survived in Coptic) for persons, the neuter in all other cases. Thus Matthew 12:35, *ὁ ἀγαθὸς ἄνθρωπος*, the good man, *S* ⲡⲣⲱⲙⲉ ⲛ̄ⲁⲅⲁⲑⲟⲥ; Titus 2:4–5, *νέας . . . εἶναι . . . οἰκουργοὺς ἀγαθάς*, the young women . . . (are to be) . . . domestic, kind, *S* ⲛ̄ϣⲉⲉⲣⲉ ϣⲏⲙ (ⲉⲣ̄ . . .) . . . ⲛ̄ⲣⲉϥⲧⲉϣ ⲙⲁ ⲛ̄ⲁⲅⲁⲑⲟⲥ, *B* ⲛⲓⲁⲗⲱⲟⲩⲓ̀ ⲛ̀ϩⲓⲟⲙⲓ (ⲉⲉⲣ . . .) . . . ⲛ(ⲓ)ⲣⲉϥⲥⲉϩⲛⲉ ⲡⲟⲩⲏⲓ ⲛ̀ⲁⲅⲁⲑⲏ; Philippians 4:8, *ὅσα δίκαια*, whatever is just, *S* ϩⲱⲃ ⲛⲓⲙ ⲛ̄ⲇⲓⲕⲁⲓⲟⲛ, *B* ⲛⲏ ⲉ̀ⲧⲉ ϩⲁⲛⲇⲓⲕⲉⲟⲛ ⲛⲉ; Romans 7:12 *ἡ ἐντολή . . . δικαία*, the commandment (is) just, *S* ⲧⲉⲛⲧⲟⲗⲏ . . . ⲟⲩⲇⲓⲕⲁⲓⲟⲛ ⲧⲉ. According to the adjectives and the use that may be made of them in the text, it may evidently happen that only their "masculine" or "neuter" form is attested; thus, for example, in the Coptic texts at present known, there is always *αἱρετικός*, heretic, *S* ϩⲁⲓⲣⲉⲧⲓⲕⲟⲥ, *B* (ϩ)ⲉⲣⲉⲧⲓⲕⲟⲥ (it is difficult to imagine a heretical "thing," although it could be a dogma, a book, etc.), and *τετράγωνος*, quadrangular, *S*, *B* ⲧⲉⲧⲣⲁⲅⲱⲛⲟⲛ (a quality that one can scarcely conceive as applied to a person).

In the area of the Copto-Greek verbs (considering only the most important facts) two different usages can be observed (varying with the idioms). First of all, they are only fully felt as verbs (and used as such on the same basis as the native Coptic verbs) in *S*, *M*, *W*, and *F56*, while in *A*, *L*, and *B*, like any substantive that one wishes to make into a "pseudo-verb," they are preceded by an auxiliary (the prenominal state of the verb *S* etc. ⲉⲓⲣⲉ), *A*, *L* ⲣ̄-, *B* ⲉⲣ-; in *V* and *F*, however, there is a variation: about 50 percent with ⲉⲗ- and 50 percent without in *F*, and a majority of cases with ⲉⲣ- and a minority without it in *V*; one may observe the same fluctuation in *P*.

On the other hand, if the form of the Copto-Greek verb is similar to that of the Greek infinitive in *B*, and often in *F* and *V*, it is without the final -ⲛ everywhere else in Coptic. So far as the vocalization of this final syllable *-́ειν* or *-εῖν* in Greek is concerned, it is invariably -ⲓⲛ in *B* (*F* etc.), while it is ⲉ for *-́ειν* and -(ⲉ)ⲓ for *-εῖν* elsewhere; for example, Copto-Greek pseudo-verbs in Galatians 4:19, *μορφοῦσθαι*, to be formed, *S* ϫⲓ ⲙⲟⲣⲫⲏ; Baruch 2:18, *λυπεῖσθαι*, be sorrowful, *S* ⲣ̄ ⲗⲩⲡⲏ; and then Copto-Greek verbs, such as *πιστεύειν*, believe, *S*, *M*, *W*, (*V*?), (*F*) ⲡⲓⲥⲧⲉⲩⲉ, *A*, *L* ⲣ̄ ⲡⲓⲥⲧⲉⲩⲉ, (*V*? ⲉⲣ ⲡⲓⲥⲧⲉⲩⲉ), (*F* ⲉⲗ ⲡⲓⲥⲧⲉⲩⲉ), *V*, *B* ⲉⲣ ⲡⲓⲥⲧⲉⲩⲓⲛ, *F* ⲉⲗ ⲡⲓⲥⲧⲉⲩⲓⲛ; *αἰτεῖν*, ask, *S* ⲁⲓⲧⲉⲓ, (*S*) *M* ⲁⲓⲧⲓ, *A*, *L* ⲣ̄ ⲁⲓⲧ(ⲉ)ⲓ, *B* ⲉⲣ ⲉⲧⲓⲛ, *F* ⲉⲗ ⲉⲧⲓⲛ. Other verbal terminations include *πλανᾶν*, go astray, *S*, *M*, *W*, *F5*, *F56* ⲡⲗⲁⲛⲁ, *A*, *L5*, *L6* ⲣ̄ ⲡⲗⲁⲛⲁ, *L4* ⲣ̄ ⲡⲗⲁⲛⲏ, *B4* ⲉⲣ ⲡⲗⲁⲛⲁⲛ; *μαστιγοῦν*, whip, scourge, *S* ⲙⲁⲥⲧⲓⲅⲟⲩ, *M* ⲙⲁⲥⲧⲓⲅⲅⲟⲩ or ⲙⲁⲥⲥⲓⲅⲅⲟⲩ, *A*, *L* ⲣ̄ ⲙⲁⲥⲧⲓⲅⲟⲩ, *B5* ⲉⲣ ⲙⲁⲥⲧⲓⲅⲅⲟⲓⲛ, *B4* ⲉⲣ ⲙⲁⲥⲧⲓⲅⲟⲓⲛ. One may note finally (Böhlig, 1958, pp. 136–37) that *B* especially has preserved several Greek deponents, such as *ἀσπάζεσθαι*, to salute, *S*, *M*, *V*, *F5*, *F56* ⲁⲥⲡⲁⲍⲉ, *A*, *L* ⲣ̄ ⲁⲥⲡⲁⲍⲉ, *B* ⲉⲣ ⲁⲥⲡⲁⲍⲉⲥⲑⲉ.

As a general rule, when Greek words were being carried over into Coptic and becoming Copto-Greek, relatively simple ones were given preference, substantives above all and then verbs (although still treated as substantives by about half of the Coptic idioms). Despite appearances, this does not prevent one from finding in Coptic some adjectives (e.g., *ἀγαθός*, good, ⲁⲅⲁⲑⲟⲥ), derivative substantives signifying some abstraction (e.g., *εὐσέβεια*, piety, ⲉⲩⲥⲉⲃⲉⲓⲁ, but also, and most often, ⲙⲛ̄ⲧⲉⲩⲥⲉⲃⲏⲥ from *εὐσεβής*, pious; see below), and even a small number of adverbs (e.g., *καλῶς*, well, ⲕⲁⲗⲱⲥ).

All the same, Coptic more frequently manufactures its Copto-Greek derivatives by adding some prefix or similar auxiliary element in front of the simple Copto-Greek term. Examples here are restricted to *S* alone (and above all from the New Testament; see Draguet, 1960).

A Copto-Greek pseudo-verb is created by addition of a verb such as ⲣ̄-, ϯ-, or ϫⲓ-, before a Copto-Greek substantive, its complement as a direct object; thus *λυπεῖσθαι*, to be sad, is rendered now by ⲗⲩⲡⲉⲓ, now by ⲣ̄ ⲗⲩⲡⲏ (see below, from *λύπη*, sorrow).

A Copto-Greek pseudo-adjective is created by the addition of the genitive preposition and the article before the Copto-Greek substantive; thus Romans 16:26, *διά . . . γραφῶν προφητικῶν*, through prophetic writings, ϩⲓⲧⲛ̄ ⲛⲉⲅⲣⲁⲫⲏ ⲙ̄ⲡⲣⲟⲫⲏⲧⲓⲕⲟⲛ, but 1 Peter 1:19, *ἔχομεν . . . τὸν προφητικὸν λόγον*, we have . . . the prophetic word, ⲟⲩⲛ̄ⲧⲁⲛ ⲙ̄ⲙⲁⲩ ⲙ̄ⲡϣⲁϫⲉ ⲙ̄ⲡⲉⲡⲣⲟⲫⲏⲧⲏⲥ (from *προφήτης*, prophet). This pseudo-adjective, when it includes a Greek negative prefix *ἀ(ν)*-, will again spring from a Copto-Greek substantive preceded by a Coptic negative prefix such as ⲁⲧ- or ⲁϫⲛ̄- or from a verb preceded by a negative verbal prefix: thus ἄκαρπος, without fruit, barren, ⲁⲧⲕⲁⲣⲡⲟⲥ or ⲁϫⲛ̄ ⲕⲁⲣⲡⲟⲥ (from καρπός, fruit). This pseudo-adjective is created also by the addition of a circumstantial prefix in front of a Copto-Greek verb; thus Philemon 6, ἐνεργής, efficacious, ⲉϥⲉⲛⲉⲣⲅⲉⲓ (from ἐνεργεῖν, to be efficacious).

A Copto-Greek pseudo-substantive signifying an abstraction, a trade, or the like is created from a Copto-Greek adjective or verb, in front of which are placed one or more prefixes. Thus, ἀπιστία, unbelief, may be rendered either by ⲁⲡⲓⲥⲧⲓⲁ or by ⲙⲛ̄ⲧⲁⲡⲓⲥⲧⲟⲥ (from ἄπιστος, unbelieving); κολλυβιστής, money-changer, is in *S* ⲣⲉϥϫⲓ ⲕⲟⲗⲩⲙⲃⲟⲛ or ⲉⲧϫⲓ ⲕⲟⲗⲩⲙⲃⲟⲛ (from κόλλυβος, small piece of money; *B* and *M* have adopted ⲕⲟⲗⲩⲃⲓⲥⲧⲏⲥ and ⲕⲟⲗⲗⲩⲃⲓⲥⲧⲏⲥ, respectively); εἰδωλολατρία, idolatry, never appears as a Copto-Greek word in Coptic and is replaced (e.g., 1 Cor. 10:14) by *S* ⲙⲛ̄ⲧⲣⲉϥϣⲙ̄ϣⲉ ⲉⲓⲇⲱⲗⲟⲛ, *B* ⲙⲉⲧϣⲁⲙϣⲉ ⲓⲇⲱⲗⲟⲛ (from εἴδωλον, idol).

A Copto-Greek pseudo-adverb is created most often by placing ϩⲛ̄ ⲟⲩ-, in a, by a, in front of a substantive; thus Luke 7:4, σπουδαίως, zealously, is ⲥⲡⲟⲩⲇⲉⲱⲥ in *B* but ϩⲛ̄ ⲟⲩⲥⲡⲟⲩⲇⲏ in *S* (literally "in a zeal," from σπουδή, zeal).

It is fitting to mention here in addition some Greek prepositions that became Copto-Greek. Most notable is κατά, according to (distributive), *S, A, L, H, M, W, V, F, B* ⲕⲁⲧⲁ, which even has a pronominal form in the native Coptic manner, *S, B* ⲕⲁⲧⲁⲣⲟ⸗, but ⲕⲁⲧⲁⲣⲁ⸗ in the other idioms except for *F* ⲕⲁⲧⲁⲗⲁ⸗ (in fact a combination of the Copto-Greek ⲕⲁⲧⲁ with the native preposition *S, B* ⲉ-, ⲉⲣⲟ⸗, *M, W, V* ⲉ-, ⲉⲣⲁ⸗, *F* ⲉ-, ⲉⲗⲁ⸗, *A, L* ⲁ-, ⲁⲣⲁ⸗), used in particular in expressions such as κατὰ γένος, (each) according to its species (e.g., Gen. 1:25), *S, pL, B, B74* ⲕⲁⲧⲁ ⲅⲉⲛⲟⲥ, or again κατὰ τὴν σάρκα, according to the flesh (e.g., Jn. 8:15) *S, L5, B, B74* ⲕⲁⲧⲁ ⲥⲁⲣⲝ. One also finds παρά, more than, beyond, against, *S, A, L, H, M, V, F, B* ⲡⲁⲣⲁ, then (in the native fashion) *S, B* ⲡⲁⲣⲁⲣⲟ⸗, *A, L* ⲡⲁⲣⲁⲣⲁ⸗; πρός, to, for, *S, A, L, M, F, B* ⲡⲣⲟⲥ, used most frequently in the expression *S* ⲡⲣⲟⲥ ⲟⲩⲟⲉⲓϣ, *L, M, F* ⲡⲣⲟⲥ ⲟⲩⲁ(ⲉ)ⲓϣ, *L, B* ⲡⲣⲟⲥ ⲟⲩⲥⲏⲟⲩ, for a moment (only), ephemeral; χωρίς, except, apart from, *S, L, V, F, B* ⲭⲱⲣⲓⲥ, then in *B* alone ⲭⲱⲣⲓⲥ⸗ (Prv. 7:1, πλήν . . . αὐτοῦ, except for him, *B* ⲭⲱⲣⲓⲥϥ but *P, S* ⲙ̄ⲃⲗ̄ⲗⲁϥ, *A* ⲙ̄ⲃⲗ̄ⲗⲉϥ); and so on.

Other grammatical elements passed into Copto-Greek only in stereotyped expressions such as ἀπὸ μέρους, partially, *S* ⲁⲡⲟ ⲙⲉⲣⲟⲩⲥ, *S, B* ⲁⲡⲟ ⲙⲉⲣⲟⲥ; διὰ τοῦτο, that is why, *S* (especially in Gnostic texts) ⲇⲓⲁ ⲧⲟⲩⲧⲟ (alternating with ⲉⲧⲃⲉ ⲡⲁï); καὶ γάρ, and besides, *S, A, L, M* ⲕⲁⲓ ⲅⲁⲣ, *V, F, B* ⲕⲉ ⲅⲁⲣ; καίπερ, although, *S, A, L* ⲕⲁⲓⲡⲉⲣ, *F, B* ⲕⲉⲡⲉⲣ; καίτοιγε, and yet, *S, L* ⲕⲁⲓⲧⲟⲓⲅⲉ, *V, F, B* ⲕⲉⲧⲟⲓⲅⲉ; μὴ γένοιτο, God forbid, *S, L* ⲙⲏ ⲅⲉⲛⲟⲓⲧⲟ, *S* (idiolectal) ⲙⲉ ⲅⲉⲛⲉⲧⲟ, *B* ⲙⲏ ⲅⲉⲛⲉⲧⲟ; οὐκ ἔξεστιν, it is not permitted, *L5* ⲟⲩⲕ ⲉⲝⲉⲥⲧⲓⲛ, *S, M, F* ⲟⲩⲕ ⲉⲝⲉⲥⲧⲓ, *F56* ⲟⲩⲕ ⲉⲝⲉⲥϯ; and so on.

One may also note here, above all in the legal documents (*S*, see Crum and Steindorff, 1912), some even longer Greek formulas, so long that one may perhaps hesitate to consider them as Copto-Greek and not quite simply Greek (islets of Hellenism preserved by the notaries, who considered them truly indispensable in a context that had become Coptic after the Arab invasion). Thus (ibid., text 48, l. 60) ἐν πάσῃ ἀκολουθίᾳ, with all due (legal) conformity, ⲉⲛ ⲡⲁⲥⲏ ⲁⲕⲟⲗⲟⲩⲑⲉⲓⲁ; (text 98, l. 36) ἐπὶ πάσῃ καλῇ προαιρέσει, with every good intention, ⲉⲡⲓ ⲡⲁⲥⲏ ⲕⲁⲗⲏ ⲡⲣⲟⲉⲓⲣⲏⲥⲉⲓ; (text 39, l. 52) κατὰ πᾶσαν νομὴν καὶ δεσποτείαν, with full right of free conduct and decision, ⲕⲁⲧⲁ ⲡⲁⲥⲁⲛ ⲛⲟⲙⲏⲛ ⲕⲁⲓ ⲇⲉⲥⲡⲟⲧⲉⲓⲁⲛ; (text 44, l. 96) πρὸς πᾶσαν τελείαν ἀπαλλαγήν, in every operation of definitive division, ⲡⲣⲟⲥ ⲡⲁⲥⲁⲛ ⲧⲉⲗⲉⲓⲁⲛ ⲁⲡⲁⲗⲗⲁⲅⲏⲛ.

In any case, certain words of late Bohairic (Stern, 1880, p. 78) are Greco-Coptic rather than Copto-Greek; the preponderant element is autochthonous, but they have been superficially Hellenized by the addition of a Greek ending: thus, for example, ⲕⲉⲛⲉⲫⲓⲧⲏⲥ, baker, from ⲕⲉⲛⲉⲫⲓⲧⲉⲛ, bread baked under the ashes (Vycichl, 1983, pp. 83–84).

There remains to be examined the semantic aspect of the use of Copto-Greek words in Coptic. Apart from various words in common use and of very general sense, there is the matter of the technical terminology of special fields (sometimes partly unknown to pre-Greek Egypt): religions and philosophies newly introduced into the country, political or military life, administration, weights and measures, law, medicine, pharmacology, magic, botany, zoology, mineralogy (including the famous precious stones), clothing, household or agricultural implements, sports, theater, and much else. Appreciation of what was required may thus vary from one idiom to another. Limiting oneself to the two main "languages" of Coptic Egypt, *S* and *B* (see DIALECTS), one may note, for example, that in the New Testament both *B* and *S* render σταυρός, cross, by ⲥⲧⲁⲩⲣⲟⲥ; but when it is a question of translating σταυροῦν, crucify, *S* has opted everywhere for ⲥⲧⲁⲩⲣⲟⲩ (save one case of ⲉⲓϣⲉ, hang, suspend), while *B* has thought it possible to use the native ⲱϣⲓ, suspend, without inconvenience throughout (but in other literary texts in *B* one may also find the Copto-Greek verb ⲉⲣ ⲥⲧⲁⲩⲣⲱⲛⲓⲛ).

In a general way, and as is usually the case with any vocabulary borrowed by one language from another, the Copto-Greek terms are used in a much more restricted sense than the Greek terms from which they derive. For example, if in Greek ἄγγελος designates all kinds of "messengers," including "angels," in Coptic ⲁⲅⲅⲉⲗⲟⲥ means only "angels," while the ordinary messenger is ϥⲁïϣⲓⲛⲉ in *S* and ⲣⲉⲙ ⲛ̀ϩⲱⲃ in *B*. If in Greek πρεσβύτερος designates any aged person, any "old man," in Coptic an ordinary old man is *S* etc. ϩⲗ̄ⲗⲟ, while only the "elder" (member of the ruling council of a religious community, etc.) is ⲡⲣⲉⲥⲃⲩⲧⲉⲣⲟⲥ. If in Greek εὐχαριστία is "gratitude" in a very general manner, in *S* (New Testament) ⲉⲩⲭⲁⲣⲓⲥⲧⲓⲁ seems to describe more particularly (Rev. 4:9, 7:12) a service of thanksgiving or "eucharist," while elsewhere (in a nonritual expression of thanksgiving, even if it is effusively addressed to God) *S* contents itself with ϣⲡ̄ ϩⲙⲟⲧ, render thanks, or ϩⲙⲟⲧ, grace (Acts 24:3; 1 Cor. 16:16; 2 Cor. 4:15, 9:11–12; Eph. 5:4; Phil. 4:6; Col. 2:7; 1 Thes. 3:9; 1 Tm. 2:1, 4:3). Many other cases of this kind could be mentioned.

BIBLIOGRAPHY

Böhlig, A. *Die griechischen Lehnwörter im sahidischen und bohairischen Neuen Testament.* 2nd ed. Munich, 1958.

Brunsch, W. "Untersuchungen zu den griechischen Wiedergaben ägyptischer Personennamen." *Enchoria* 8 (1978):1–142.

Crum, W. E., and G. Steindorff. *Koptische Rechtsurkunden des achten Jahrhunderts aus Djême (Theben).* Leipzig, 1912.

Draguet, R. *Index copte et grec-copte de la Concordance du Nouveau Testament sahidique (CSCO 124, 173, 183, 185).* CSCO 196. Louvain, 1960.

Ernstedt, P. V. "Graeco-Coptica." *Zeitschrift für ägyptische Sprache und Altertumskunde* 64 (1929): 122–35.

Gaselee, S. "Greek Words in Coptic." *Byzantinische Zeitschrift* 30 (1929–1930):224–28.

Gignac, F. T. *A Grammar of the Greek Papyri of the Roman and Byzantine Periods,* Vol. 1, *Phonology,* Vol. 2, *Morphology.* Testi e documenti per lo studio dell'antichità 55. Milan, 1976–1981.

Hopfner, T. *Über Form und Gebrauch der griechischen Lehnwörter in der koptisch-sa'idischen Apophthegmenversion.* Vienna, 1918.

Kasser, R. "La Pénétration des mots grecs dans la langue copte." *Wissenschaftliche Zeitschrift der Martin-Luther-Universität, Halle-Wittenberg* 15 (1966): 419–25.

______. "A propos de quelques caractéristiques orthographiques du vocabulaire grec utilisé dans les dialectes H et N." *Orientalia Lovaniensia Periodica* 6–7 (1975–1976):285–94.

______. "Expression de l'aspiration ou de la non-aspiration à l'initiale des mots copto-grecs correspondant à des mots grecs commençant par (E)I-." *Bulletin de la Société d'égyptologie, Genève* 4 (1980):53–59.

______. "Orthographe (sub)dialectale du vocabulaire copto-grec avant le VIIIe siècle de notre ère." *Museum Helveticum* 40 (1983):207–215.

Lefort, L. T. "Le Copte, source auxiliaire du grec." *Annuaire de l'Institut de philologie et d'histoire orientales de l'Université libre de Bruxelles* 2 (1934):569–78.

______. *Concordance du Nouveau Testament sahidique,* Vol. 1, *Les Mots d'origine grecque.* CSCO 124. Louvain, 1950a.

______. "Gréco-copte." In *Coptic Studies in Honor of Walter Ewing Crum,* pp. 65–71. Boston, 1950.

Nagel, P. "Die Einwirkung des Griechischen auf die Entstehung der koptischen Literatursprache." In *Christentum am Roten Meer,* ed. F. Altheim and R. Stiehl, Vol. 1., pp. 327–55. Berlin, 1971.

Rahlfs, A. "Griechische Wörter im Koptischen." In *Sitzungsberichte der Preussischen Akademie der Wissenschaften,* pp. 1036–1046. Berlin, 1912.

Schmidt, C., and V. MacDermot. *Pistis Sophia.* Leiden, 1978.

Stern, L. *Koptische Grammatik.* Leipzig, 1880.

Vycichl, W. *Dictionnaire étymologique de la langue copte.* Louvain, 1983.

Weiss, H.-F. "Zum Problem der griechischen Fremd- und Lehnwörter in den Sprachen des christlichen Orients." *Helikon* 6 (1966):183–209.

______. "Ein Lexikon der griechischen Wörter im Koptischen." *Zeitschrift für ägyptische Sprache und Altertumskunde* 96 (1969):79–80.

Wessely, K. *Die griechischen Lehnwörter der sahidischen und boheirischen Psalmenversion.* Denkschriften der kaiserlichen Akademie der Wissenschaften in Wien 34, no. 3. Vienna, 1910.

RODOLPHE KASSER

VOCABULARY, CUNEIFORM TRANSCRIPTIONS OF PROTOTYPES OF AUTOCHTHONOUS COPTIC. Fully vocalized prototypes of Coptic words are found in cuneiform transcriptions. Thus, it is known that the month name *B* ⲭⲟⲓⲁⲕ (*S* ⲕⲟⲓⲁϩⲕ and many variants) was pronounced in Late Egyptian **ku-iḫ-ku,* or something close to it. These transcriptions are often preceded by determinatives, such as (*ilu*), god; (*m*), male person; (*ālu*), town; and (*mātu*), country.

Three periods have to be distinguished (all dates according to Beckerath, 1971):

1. Middle-Babylonian transcriptions: the so-called Tell el-Amarna Letters, which comprise the correspondence of Amenophis II (1439–1413 B.C.) and Amenophis IV (Akhenaton) (1365–1349 B.C.) with their allies and vassals in Asia, tablets found in the foreign-office archives at Tell el-Amarna (central Egypt), and letters and documents of the Hittite royal archives of Boghazkeui (Asia Minor) of the time of Ramses II (1290–1224 B.C.).

2. Assyrian transcriptions: inscriptions, annals, and commercial documents from the time of Sargon II (722–705 B.C.), who conquered Palestine and received tribute from Bukurninip (Bocchoris in Greek), king of Egypt in 714 B.C.; of Assarhaddon (conquest of Memphis, 671 B.C.), and of Assurbanipal (conquest of the Delta, 667 B.C.).

3. New-Babylonian and Persian transcriptions: mainly commercial documents of the time of Cambyses (525–522 B.C.), Darius I (521–486 B.C.), Artaxerxes I (464–424 B.C.), and Artaxerxes II (404–359 B.C.).

Some examples are given below.

Middle-Babylonian Transcriptions

(*ilu*) *A-ma-a-na*, (*ilu*) *A-ma-na*: the god Amun, *B* ⲁⲙⲟⲩⲛ; (*m*) *A-ma-an-ḫa-at-pi*, n. pr. m. Amenophis, where the group *ḫa-at-pi* corresponds to the qualitative *B* ϩⲟⲧⲡϯ; (*alū*) *A-na:* n. loc. Heliopolis, Egyptian *'Iwnw*, Hebrew *'Ōn*: *B* ⲱⲛ; (*m*) *Ri-a-na-pa*: n. pr. m. Ranofer, literally "the good Sun" or similar, where according to Edel the name was pronounced *Rēʿ-nāfe* or similar, but in any case with *Rēʿ* and not with *Rīʿ*, sun = *S*, *B* ⲣⲏ; (*ilu*) *Ḫa-a-ra*: the god Horus, *S*, *B* ϩⲱⲣ.

Assyrian Transcriptions

(*m*) *U-na-mu-nu:* n. pr. m. Wen-Amun or similar, which contains the name of Amun, *B* ⲁⲙⲟⲩⲛ; (*m*) *Bu-kur-ni-ni-ip*: n. pr. m. Bocchoris, Egyptian *B3k n rn-f*, literally "servant of his name," where the Coptic form would be *B* *ⲃⲱⲕ ⲛ̀ⲣⲓⲛϥ (the transcription should read *(*m*) *Bu-ku-un-ri-ni-ip*); (*m*) *Ḫu-u-ru*: n. pr. m. Horus, *S*, *B* ϩⲱⲣ; (*ālu*) *Me-im-pe*: n. loc. Memphis, *B* ⲙⲉⲛϥⲓ.

New-Babylonian and Persian Period

(*m*) *A-mu-nu-ta-pu-na-aḫ-ti*: n. pr. m. *Amon tef-naḫte*, literally "Amon is his strength," with *Amunu* = **Amōn* or *Amūn*, *B* ⲁⲙⲟⲩⲛ; (*m*) *Na-'a-* (*ilu*) *E-si* n. pr. m. literally "Great is Isis," where the Coptic form would be *B* *ⲛⲁⲁ-ⲏⲥⲓ.

Commentary

Middle-Babylonian *ā* corresponds to later (i.e., Assyrian or Neo-Assyrian or Persian) *ū* (see Table 1). This comparison shows that long *ā* before 1000 B.C. is transcribed as long *ū* after 1000 B.C. This long *ū* must be read *ō*, as the Coptic has *ō* in two cases (*Ōn* and *Hōr*). After a nasal in *A-mu-nu* and in *nu-u-pi* (reconstructed), the Coptic has ⲟⲩ *ū*, which is due to postnasalization. As a matter of fact, it is not known if *A-mu-nu* and *nu-u-pi* were still pronounced **Amōn* and **nōfi* or already *Amūn* and *nūfi*.

BIBLIOGRAPHY

Beckerath, J. von. *Abriss der Geschichte des alten Ägypten.* Munich and Vienna, 1971.

Edel, E. "Neue keilschriftliche Umschreibungen ägyptischer Namen aus den Bogazköytexten." *Journal of Near Eastern Studies* 7 (1948):11–24.

______. *Die Ortsnamenlisten aus dem Totentempel Amenophis III.* Bonner biblische Beiträge 25. Bonn, 1966.

______. "Der Brief des ägyptischen Wesirs Pašijāra an den Hetiterkönig Ḫattusili und verwandte Keilschriftbriefe." *Nachrichten der Akademie der Wissenschaften in Göttingen, Philosophisch-historische Klasse* 1, no. 4 (1978):117–58.

______. "Neue Deutungen keilschriftlicher Umschreibungen ägyptischer Wörter und Personennamen." In *Sitzungsberichte der Österreichischen Akade-*

TABLE 1.

Middle-Babylonian	Assyrian or Neo-Assyrian and Persian	Coptic
A-ma-a-na (**Amān*)	*A-mu-nu* (*Amōn*)	*B* ⲁⲙⲟⲩⲛ
A-na (**Ān*)	*U-nu* (*Ōn*)	*B* ⲱⲛ
Ka-si (**Kās*)	*Ku-u-si* (*Kōš*)	—
Ḫa-a-ra (**Ḫār*)	*Ḫu-u-ru* (*Ḫōr*)	*S*, *B* ϩⲱⲣ
-na-pa (**-nāfe*)	**-nu-u-pi* (**nōfi*)	*B* ⲛⲟⲩϥⲓ

mie der Wissenschaften, Philosophisch-historische Klasse, Sitzungsberichte, p. 175. Vienna, 1980.

Lambdin, T. O. "Another Cuneiform Transcription of Egyptian msḥ 'crocodile.'" *Journal of Near Eastern Studies* 12 (1953a):284–85.

———. "Egyptian Words in Tell el Amarna Letter No. 14." *Orientalia* 22 (1953b):362–69.

Ranke, H. "Keilschriftliches Material zur ägyptischen Vokalisation." In *Anhang zu den Abhandlungen der Königlichen Preussischen Akademie der Wissenschaften, Philosophisch-historische Klasse,* Abhandlung 2. Berlin, 1910.

Smith, S., and C. J. Gadd. "A Cuneiform Vocabulary of Egyptian Words." *Journal of Egyptian Archaeology* 11 (1925):230–38.

Vittmann, G. "Zu einigen keilschriftlichen Umschreibungen ägyptischer Personennamen." *Göttinger Miszellen* 70 (1984):65–66.

WERNER VYCICHL

VOCABULARY OF EGYPTIAN ORIGIN, AUTOCHTHONOUS COPTIC. Coptic is the autochthonous language (or languages, *S* and *B*) spoken and written in Egypt from the third century A.D. down to the Middle Ages (eleventh century or a little later). Moreover, it is the latest and most developed form of the Egyptian language itself (known at first in the form called "pharaonic"; cf. LANGUAGE(S), COPTIC). In these circumstances, one is not in the least surprised to observe that the greater part of the Coptic vocabulary is of Egyptian origin (pharaonic more or less ancient, down to demotic), so that one might justly describe it as "autochthonous Coptic of Egyptian origin," and this even if one observes in the Coptic language the not insignificant presence—indeed rather conspicuous and impressive but nonetheless in a minority—of words of non-autochthonous origin (above all of Greek origin; cf. VOCABULARY, COPTO-GREEK).

This autochthonous preponderance in the Coptic vocabulary is illustrated below by two brief Sahidic texts, one written directly in Coptic by Shenute (Exhibit 1), the other probably translated from the Greek (Exhibit 2). Examining the total of the vocabulary of these two texts and taking no account either of the various articles, the prepositions, or the autochthonous adverbs, one counts, in terms of lexemes, fifty-eight units. Among them is one proper noun, ⲁⲅⲁⲑⲱⲛ, and then seven Copto-Greek words: ⲇⲉ, now, then, from *δέ*; ⲇⲓⲁⲕⲟⲛⲉⲓ, to serve, from *διακονεῖν*; ⲇⲣⲁⲕⲱⲛ, serpent, from *δράκων*; ⲉⲓⲧⲉ, whether, from *εἴτε*; ⲏ, or, from *ἤ*; ϩⲟⲗⲱⲥ, absolutely, altogether, from *ὅλως*; ⲥⲩⲛⲁⲅⲱⲅⲏ, community, from *συναγωγή*.

Among the fifty other lexemes, all to be considered as autochthonous in the broad sense of the

EXHIBIT 1.

Everything excellent, everything mediocre, whether of bread or any (other) nourishment,
ϩⲛⲁⲁⲩ ⲛⲓⲙ ⲉϥⲥⲟⲧⲡ̄ ϩⲛⲁⲁⲩ ⲛⲓⲙ ⲉϥϭⲟϫⲃ̄ ⲉⲓⲧⲉ ⲟⲉⲓⲕ ⲉⲓⲧⲉ ϩⲛⲁⲁⲩ ⲛ̄ⲟⲩⲱⲙ

whether any vegetable or salted things or cooked (foods) or cucumbers or any other thing of any kind,
ⲉⲓⲧⲉ ⲟⲩⲟⲟⲧⲉ ⲉⲓⲧⲉ ϩⲉⲛϩⲛⲁⲁⲩ ⲉⲩⲙⲟⲗϩ̄ ⲏ ⲉⲩⲡⲟⲥⲉ ⲏ ϩⲉⲛϯϭⲉ ⲏ ⲕⲉⲗⲁⲁⲩ ⲛ̄ϩⲛⲁⲁⲩ ϩⲟⲗⲱⲥ

(all) will be for us such as the Lord has prepared them or will prepare them (for us). Those who dwell
ⲉⲩⲛⲁϣⲱⲡⲉ ⲛⲁⲛ ⲛ̄ⲑⲉ ⲉⲛⲧⲁ ⲡϫⲟⲉⲓⲥ ⲥⲃ̄ⲧⲱⲧⲟⲩ ⲙ̄ⲙⲟⲥ ⲏ ⲉⲧⲉϥⲛⲁⲥⲃ̄ⲧⲱⲧⲟⲩ. ⲉⲣⲉ ⲛⲉⲧⲟⲩⲏϩ

in these (monastic) communities, at all times, will eat (all these foods, good or less good) with one another.
ϩⲛ̄ ⲛⲉⲓⲥⲩⲛⲁⲅⲱⲅⲏ ⲛ̄ⲟⲩⲟⲉⲓϣ ⲛⲓⲙ ⲛⲁⲟⲩⲟⲙⲟⲩ ⲙⲛ̄ ⲛⲉⲩⲉⲣⲏⲩ

And let there not be anyone or any people who eat the excellent things
ⲁⲩⲱ ⲛ̄ⲛⲉ ⲟⲩⲁ ⲏ ϩⲟⲉⲓⲛⲉ ⲟⲩⲉⲙ ⲛⲉⲧⲥⲟⲧⲡ̄

at all times, or the good things, while (on the contrary) another or some others eat the mediocre or
ⲛ̄ⲟⲩⲟⲉⲓϣ ⲛⲓⲙ ⲏ ⲛⲉⲧⲛⲁⲛⲟⲩⲟⲩ ⲛ̄ⲧⲉ ⲕⲉⲟⲩⲁ ⲏ ϩⲉⲛⲕⲟⲟⲩⲉ ⲟⲩⲉⲙ ⲛⲉⲧϭⲟϫⲃ̄

despised things. And the fault (in respect) of those who (always) eat the good things
ⲏ ⲛⲉⲧⲥⲟϣϥ̄. ⲁⲩⲱ ⲉⲣⲉ ⲡϣⲱⲱⲧ ⲛ̄ⲛⲉⲧⲛⲁⲟⲩⲱⲙ ⲛ̄ϩⲉⲛϩⲛⲁⲁⲩ ⲉⲛⲁⲛⲟⲩⲟⲩ

or the bad will fall upon those who serve (at table) or those who distribute the rations.
ⲏ ⲉⲩϩⲟⲟⲩ ⲛⲁⲉⲓ ⲉϩⲣⲁⲓ̈ ⲉϫⲛ̄ ⲛⲉⲧⲇⲓⲁⲕⲟⲛⲉⲓ ⲏ ⲛⲉⲧⲛⲁⲡⲱϣ ⲛ̄ϩⲉⲛⲧⲟ.

SOURCE: Leipoldt and Crum, 1913, pp. 87–88 (Coptic orthography corrected).

EXHIBIT 2.

It is related with regard to Apa Agathon that he (installed himself to) live in a cave, once, in the desert.
ⲁⲩϫⲟⲟⲥ ⲉⲧⲃⲉ ⲁⲡⲁ ⲁⲅⲁⲑⲱⲛ ϫⲉ ⲁϥⲟⲩⲱϩ ϩⲛ̄ ⲟⲩⲃⲏⲃ ⲛ̄ⲟⲩⲥⲟⲡ ϩⲙ̄ ⲡϫⲁⲓ̈ⲉ.

Now there was a great serpent in it. Then the serpent decided to go out (from the cave) to go off (and live
ⲉⲩⲛⲟϭ ⲇⲉ ⲛ̄ⲇⲣⲁⲕⲱⲛ ⲛ̄ϩⲏⲧϥ̄. ⲡϩⲟϥ ⲇⲉ ⲁϥⲧⲟϣϥ̄ ⲉⲙⲟⲟϣⲉ ⲉⲃⲟⲗ ⲉⲃⲱⲕ ⲛⲁϥ.

elsewhere). Apa Agathon said to it: "If you go out (to go and live elsewhere), I shall not stay in (the cave)."
ⲡⲉϫⲉ ⲁⲡⲁ ⲁⲅⲁⲑⲱⲛ ⲛⲁϥ ϫⲉ ⲉⲕϣⲁⲛⲙⲟⲟϣⲉ ⲉⲃⲟⲗ ⲛ̄ϯⲛⲁϭⲱ ⲁⲛ ⲛ̄ϩⲏⲧϥ̄.

Then the serpent remained (there), it did not go away. Now there was a sycamore in that (place of the) desert.
ⲡϩⲟϥ ⲇⲉ ⲁϥϭⲱ ⲙ̄ⲡⲉϥⲃⲱⲕ ⲉⲛⲉⲟⲩⲛ̄ ⲟⲩⲛⲟⲩϩⲉ ⲇⲉ ϩⲙ̄ ⲡϫⲁⲓ̈ⲉ ⲉⲧⲙ̄ⲙⲁⲩ

They went out (then) together but Apa Agathon made a mark (incised) in the sycamore, he (thus) divided it
ⲛⲉϣⲁⲩⲉⲓ ⲉⲃⲟⲗ ⲙⲛ̄ ⲛⲉⲩⲉⲣⲏⲩ. ⲁⲡⲁ ⲁⲅⲁⲑⲱⲛ ⲇⲉ ⲁϥϯ ⲛ̄ⲟⲩϣⲱⲗϩ ⲉⲧⲛⲟⲩϩⲉ ⲁϥⲡⲟϣⲥ̄

between himself (Agathon) and it (the serpent), that the serpent might eat on (one) side of the sycamore,
ⲉϫⲱϥ ⲛ̄ⲙ̄ⲙⲁϥ ϫⲉⲕⲁⲁⲥ ⲉⲣⲉ ⲡϩⲟϥ ⲛⲁⲟⲩⲱⲙ ⲛ̄ⲥⲁ ⲥⲡⲓⲣ ⲛ̄ⲧⲛⲟⲩϩⲉ

and the old (hermit) himself eat on another side (of the tree); (this) until they had finished
ⲛ̄ⲧⲉ ⲡϩⲗ̄ⲗⲟ ϩⲱⲱϥ ⲟⲩⲱⲙ ⲛ̄ⲥⲁ ⲡⲕⲉⲥⲡⲓⲣ ϣⲁⲛⲧⲟⲩⲟⲩⲱ

eating, and returned within their (shelters in the) caves, both of them.
ⲉⲩⲟⲩⲱⲙ ⲛ̄ⲥⲉⲃⲱⲕ ⲉϩⲟⲩⲛ ⲟⲛ ⲛ̄ⲛⲉⲩⲃⲏⲃ ⲙ̄ⲡⲉⲥⲛⲁⲩ.

SOURCE: Chaîne, 1960, p. 69 (Coptic orthography corrected).

term (according to Vycichl, 1983; Černý, 1976; Vergote, 1945 and 1973; and Westendorf, 1977), three appear to be of Semitic origin (cf. VOCABULARY OF SEMITIC ORIGIN, AUTOCHTHONOUS COPTIC): **ⲁⲡⲁ** /apa̍/, abbot (*B* **ⲁⲃⲃⲁ**), cf. Aramaic *3abbā* (in Greek ἄββας); **ⲙⲟⲩⲗ̄ϩ̄** /mu̍lh/, to salt, cf. Hebrew *mèlaḥ*, Arabic *milḥ*; **ϭⲱϫⲃ̄** /cō̍čḇ/, to diminish, cf. Hebrew *ḳāṣab*, Arabic *ḳaṣab*.

For all the rest (apart from three cases, indicated by a question mark, where the etymology is either unknown or appears too uncertain), an authentically Pharaonic etymology (more or less ancient, or demotic) is known: **ⲃⲏⲃ** /bē̍b/, cave, from *b3b3* etc.; **ⲃⲱⲕ** /bō̍k/ to go, from (?); **ⲉⲣⲏⲩ** /ərē̍w/, the companions, mutually, from *i͗r(y)*; **ⲉⲓ** /i̍/, to go, from *i͗*, etc.; **ⲕⲉ-** /kə/, another, from *ky*, etc.; **ⲗⲁⲁⲩ** /la̍'w/, something, from (?); **ⲙ̄ⲙⲁⲩ** /m̩ma̍w/, there, from *n-i͗m-w;* **ⲙⲟⲟϣⲉ** /mo̍'šə/, to walk, go, from *mšʿ*, etc.; **ⲛⲓⲙ** /ni̍m/, each, every, from *nb*; **ⲛⲁⲛⲟⲩ-** /nanu/, to be good, from **wnn ʿny*; **ⲛⲟⲩϩⲉ** /nu̍hə/, sycamore, from *nhy*; **ⲛⲟϭ** /no̍c/, large, from (?); **ⲟⲉⲓⲕ** /o̍jk/, bread, from *ʿḳ*, etc.; **ⲡⲓⲥⲉ** /pi̍sə/, cause to be cooked, bake, from *ps(y)*, etc.; **ⲡⲱϣ** /pō̍š/, to share, distribute, from *pš*; **ⲡⲉϫⲉ-** /pəčə/, to say, from *p3y ḏd*; **ⲥⲟⲃⲧⲉ** /so̍btə/, to prepare, from *spdd*, etc.; **ⲥⲛⲁⲩ** /sna̍w/, two, from *sn-wy*; **ⲥⲟⲡ** /so̍p/, time, from *sp*; **ⲥⲡⲓⲣ** /spi̍r/, side, rib, from *spr*; **ⲥⲱⲧⲡ̄** /sō̍tp/, to choose, from *stp*; **ⲥⲱϣϥ̄** /sō̍šf/, despise, judge vile, base, etc., from *sḫf*, etc.; **ϯ** /ti̍/, to give, make, etc., from *ti*, etc.; **ⲧⲟ** /to̍/, part, share, from *tny.t*, etc.; **ⲧⲱϣ** /tō̍š/, to delimit, decide, from *tš*, etc.; **ϯϭⲉ** /ti̍cə/, cucumber, from *tgy*, etc.; **ⲟⲩⲁ** /wa̍/, one, from *wʿ*; **ⲟⲩⲱ** /wō̍/, to cease, finish, from *w3ḥ*; **ⲟⲩⲱⲙ** /wō̍m/, to eat, from *wnm*; **ⲟⲩⲛ-** /wn/, there is, from *wn*, etc.; **ⲟⲩⲟⲟⲧⲉ** /wo̍'tə/, vegetable, from *w3ḏ.t*; **ⲟⲩⲟⲉⲓϣ** /wo̍jš/, time, from *wrš*; **ⲟⲩⲱϩ** /wō̍h/, to inhabit, from *w3ḥ*; **ϣⲱⲗ̄ϩ̄** /šō̍lh/, to impress a mark, etc., from *šlḥ*, etc.; **ϣⲱⲡⲉ** /šō̍pə/, to become, from *ḫpr*, etc.; **ϣⲱⲱⲧ** /šō̍'t/, to cut, curtail, diminish, from *šʿt*, etc.; **ϩⲉ** /he̍/, way, manner, from *ẖ*, etc.; **ϩⲱⲱ⸗** /hō̍'/, (one)self, from *ḥʿ*, etc.; **ϩⲗ̄ⲗⲟ** /hl̩̍lo/, old man, from *ẖlʿ3*; **ϩⲟⲉⲓⲛⲉ** /ẖo̍jnə/, some, from *hyn*; **ϩⲛⲁⲁⲩ** /hna̍'w/, thing, from *ḥnw*; **ϩⲟⲟⲩ** /ho̍'w/, to be bad, from *ḥw*, etc.; **ϩⲟϥ** /ho̍f/, serpent, from *ḥf*, etc.; **ϫⲱ** /čō̍/, to say, from **ḏid;* **ϫⲁⲓ̈ⲉ** /ča̍jə/, desert, from *ḏʿ*; **ϫⲟⲉⲓⲥ** /čo̍js/, lord, from *ṯzw*; **ϭⲱ** /cō̍/, to rest, remain, from *gr*.

What is presented above is only a modest couple of examples. The matter is examined more systematically in ETYMOLOGY.

BIBLIOGRAPHY

Černý, J. *Coptic Etymological Dictionary*. Cambridge, 1976.

Chaîne, M. *Le Manuscrit de la version copte en dialecte sahidique des Apophthegmata Patrum.* Bibliothèque d'études coptes 6. Cairo, 1960.

Leipoldt, J., and W. E. Crum. *Sinuthii Archimandritae Vita et Opera Omnia.* CSCO 42 and 73. Paris, 1908 and 1913.

Vergote, J. *Phonétique historique de l'égyptien, les consonnes.* Louvain, 1945.

———. *Grammaire copte,* Vol. 1b, *Introduction, phonétique et phonologie, morphologie synthématique (structure des sémantèmes), partie diachronique.* Louvain, 1973.

Vycichl, W. *Dictionnaire étymologique de la langue copte.* Louvain, 1983.

Westendorf, W. *Koptisches Handwörterbuch, bearbeitet auf Grund des Koptischen Handwörterbuchs von Wilhelm Spiegelberg.* Heidelberg, 1977.

RODOLPHE KASSER

VOCABULARY OF SEMITIC ORIGIN, AUTOCHTHONOUS COPTIC. Every country has relations with its neighbors (commercial relations, military relations, mainly when it is conquered, etc.), and in the course of time its language adopts foreign words. Egypt is no exception to this rule. At a relatively recent epoch of their history, the autochthonous Egyptians adopted a great number of Greek words (among them a certain number of Greco-Latin origin), and, later on, some Arabic words (see VOCABULARY, COPTO-GREEK and VOCABULARY, COPTO-ARABIC). But even the Egyptian vocabulary of the pharaonic period, which later became Coptic and is considered autochthonous with regard to these Greek and Arabic additions, is not entirely homogeneous, as attentive etymological studies reveal. Several components may be distinguished, such as an old Semitic layer that is far from being negligible (for a more recent Semitic component, see VOCABULARY, COPTO-ARABIC).

Semitic loanwords made their first appearance in Egyptian in texts of the Eighteenth and Nineteenth Dynasties (1554–1305 and 1305–1196 B.C.). Being foreign personal names and place-names, they are written in the so-called syllabic orthography.

Syllabic orthography was used in Egyptian mainly to distinguish foreign names and words from Egyptian ones. In many cases, an *3* is added to the consonants: *d̲3* may be read *d̲a, d̲i,* or *d̲u.* In other cases, *y* and *w* are added: *ny* is read *ni̲, dw* is read *du.* In particular cases, short words are used: *t3,* land, was pronounced *ta3* in the New Kingdom, and so the word is used for the syllable *ta. Sw,* he, and *sy,* she, were probably pronounced **suwa* and **siya* (as in Assyrian), and later, in the New Kingdom, *su* and *si.* Therefore, *sw* and *sy* were used for the syllable *su* and *si.* In two cases, syllabic orthography indicates consonants without vowels: the group *r3-y* was pronounced *-r* (at the end of a syllable); and *-n* (suffix of the first-person plural) represented final *-n.* The system has been explained by W. F. Albright (1934). Later it was strongly attacked by W. F. Edgerton (1940), but E. Edel (1949), who adopted an intermediary position, laid down the rules governing this system in different periods of the language. Syllabic orthography is more useful for reading ancient personal names and place-names than for Coptic etymology, as true Egyptian words are rarely written syllabically. Nevertheless, it is known that *B, S* ⲛⲓⲙ, who?, derives from **ni-m,* and not from **nū-m, nū-m,* thanks to syllabic writings, and that *S* ⲙ̄ϣⲓⲣ, Meshir, a month name, derives from **m-ḫi-r. Š-ba-d,* staff, is the prototype of *B, S* ϣⲃⲱⲧ, and **ba-n-r* = **ba-l* the prototype of *B, S* ⲃⲟⲗ outside, as in *B, S* ⲉⲃⲟⲗ, out (Arabic *barra*).

It is not always easy to assign a definite origin to the Semitic loanwords in Egyptian and particularly in Coptic: most of them may be compared with Hebrew, Aramaic, or Arabic forms, but some of them seem to derive from extinct languages and dialects:

ⲟⲉⲓⲗⲉ (*S* masc.), ram; compare Hebrew *'áyil;* probable origin pre-Hebrew **'ayl-a* (accusative)

ⲛⲟϣⲣ̄ (*S* masc.), vulture, hawk; compare Hebrew *nèšer,* hawk, eagle; Akkadian *našru,* eagle; Arabic *nasr,* vulture, eagle; probably from **našr-i* (genitive)

ϣⲁⲁⲣ (*S* masc.), price; compare Hebrew *šá'ar,* measure, price; probably from pre-Hebrew **ša'r-i* (genitive)

ϫⲁⲡⲧ (*S* in ⲗⲁⲙϫⲁⲡⲧ, also ⲗⲁⲙϫⲁⲧⲡ, masc.), pitch, a composed word: *lam* + ϫⲁⲡⲧ; compare Arabic *zift,* pitch; probably from **zift-i* (genitive); Hebrew has *zèfet,* pitch, from ancient **zaft-i* (genitive)

ⲥⲓⲣ (*S*), ⲥⲉⲉⲣⲉ (*A* masc.), leaven; compare Arabic *su3r,* rest, remainder; ⲥⲓⲣ from **sūr-i, *sūr-i* (genitive); ⲥⲉⲉⲣⲉ from **su3r-i, *sö3r-i* (genitive)

ϩⲙ̄ϫ (*S* masc.), vinegar; compare Hebrew *ḥómeṣ,* vinegar, from pre-Hebrew **ḥumṣ-i* (genitive)

ϫⲟⲉⲓⲧ (*S* masc. and fem.), olive, olive tree; compare Hebrew *záyit,* Arabic *zayt,* oil, probably from **zayt-i* (genitive)

ϭⲁⲗⲁϩⲧ (*S* fem.), ϭⲁⲗⲁϩⲧⲉ (*S* fem.), pot; compare Hebrew *kallaḥat,* cooking pot, cauldron; probably from **ḳallaḥt-i* (genitive)

ⲓⲟⲙ (*B* masc.), sea, wine-press, oil-press, plural ⲁⲙⲁⲓⲟⲩ; compare Hebrew *yām* (fem.), sea, basin (plural *yammīm*), and Arabic *yamm*, sea; probably from **yamm-i* (genitive); the plural ⲁⲙⲁⲓⲟⲩ derives from *yammi*, considered ancient adjective **yamm-īy: *ʾiammīy-ū*, then **ʾiammīw-ū* (regressive assimilation *-īy-ū:-īw-ū*) (This is the one case where it is certain that the Coptic form derives from an ancient [i.e., pre-Hebrew] genitive.)

ⲃⲁϣⲟⲩⲣ (*B, S* masc. and fem.), saw; comp. Hebrew *maśśōr*, Arabic *minšār*; apparently from pre-Hebrew **maśśār-i* (genitive)

ϫⲉⲫⲣⲟ (*B*), ϫⲉⲡⲣⲟ (*S* fem.), farm, small village; compare Aramaic *kafr-ā*, village; the ending *-ā* is the Aramaic definite article, still in use in biblical Aramaic; the Coptic form survives in the place-name *Shubra*, Arabic *Šubrā* (The correct form would be **Šibra*. The modern pronounciation *Šubrā* is vulgar; compare *Quft̩* n. loc., Koptos, for *Qift̩*; *Qubt̩-īy*, Copt, for *Qibt̩-īy*, from Greek *Aigypti-os*.)

ⲃⲁϣⲟⲩϣ (*B* masc.), rue (*Ruta graveolens sive montana*), demotic *bšwš*, Aramaic *baššāš-ā, baššūš-ā*

ⲙⲁⲧⲉϭⲧⲉ (*L* subst.), army; compare Akkadian *madakt-u* (fem.), camp (military); compare also demotic *mtgt*

BIBLIOGRAPHY

Albright, W. F. *The Vocalization of the Egyptian Syllabic Orthography*. American Oriental Series 5. New Haven, Conn., 1934.

Burchardt, M. *Die altkanaanäischen Fremdworte und Eigennamen im Ägyptischen*, Vols. 1–2. Leipzig, 1909–1910.

Edel, E. "Neues Material zur Beurteilung der syllabischen Orthographie des Ägyptischen." *Journal of Near Eastern Studies* 8 (1949):44–47.

______. *Die Ortsnamenlisten aus dem Totentempel Amenophis III*. Bonner biblische Beiträge 25. Bonn, 1966.

Edgerton, W. F. "Egyptian Phonetic Writing from Its Invention to the Close of the Nineteenth Dynasty." *Journal of the American Oriental Society* 60 (1940):473–506.

Müller, M. W. *Asien und Europa nach altägyptischen Denkmälern*. Leipzig, 1893.

______. "Spuren der babylonischen Weltschrift in Ägypten. *Mitteilungen der vorderasiatischen Gesellschaft* 17, no. 3 (1912):1–90.

Stricker, B. H. "Trois Études de phonétique et de morphologie coptes." *Acta Orientalia* 15 (1936–1937):1–20.

Ward, W. A. "Notes on Egyptian Group Writing." *Journal of Near Eastern Studies* 16 (1957):198–203.

WERNER VYCICHL

Index

*Page numbers in **boldface** indicate a major discussion. Page numbers in italics indicate illustrations.*

A

Aaron at Philae, Apa, 1955
Ababius, Saint, **1**, 2081
ʻAbādah ibn al-Ṣāmit, 1528
Abadion, Bishop of Antinoopolis, 1551
Abadir. *See* Ter and Erai, Saints
Abadyus. *See* Dios, Saint
Abāmūn of Tarnūṭ, Saint, **1**, 1551
Abāmūn of Ṭūkh, Saint, **1–2**, 1551
Abarkah. *See* Eucharistic wine
Abbā
  origin of term, 2–3
  see also Proestos; specific name inverted
Abbā Maqārah. *See* Macarius II
ʻAbbās Ḥilmī I, Khedive, 1467, 1636, 1692
ʻAbbās Ḥilmī II, Khedive, 1693, 1694, 1988
Abbasids
  compared with Umayyad administration, 2287
  and Islamization, 937
  Tulunid and Ikhshid rule, 2280–2281
Abbaton, **2**, 1368, 1619
Abbot, **2–3**
  hegumenos and, 1216
  provost and, 2024
  see also Abbā; specific names inverted
ʻAbdallāh, **3**
ʻAbdallāh Abū al-Suʻūd, 1993
ʻAbdallāh ibn Mūsā, **3–4**
ʻAbdallāh ibn al-Ṭayyib, 6, 1777
ʻAbdallāh Nirqī, **4**
  evidence of Nubian liturgy at, 1817
  example of Byzantine cross-in-square building at, 661
  Nubian church art at, 1811–1812
ʻAbd al-ʻAzīz, Sultan, 893
ʻAbd al-ʻAzīz ibn Marwān (Arab governor of Egypt), 85, 709, 1303
ʻAbd al-ʻAzīz ibn Saʻd al-Dīn, **5**
Abdelsayed, Father Gabriel, 1621
ʻAbd al-Malāk, Saint, 840
ʻAbd al-Malik ibn Marwān, Caliph, 239, 937
ʻAbd al-Malik ibn Mūsā ibn Nāṣir, Caliph, 1411
ʻAbd al-Masīḥ (manuscript), **5**
ʻAbd al-Masīḥ, Yassā, 1911
  doxologies studied by, 1728
ʻAbd al-Masīḥ ibn Isḥāq al-Kindī, **5**
ʻAbd al-Masīḥ al-Isrāʼīli al-Raqqī, **5–7**
ʻAbd al-Masīḥ, known as Ibn Nūḥ, **7**
ʻAbd al-Masīḥ Ṣalīb al-Masūʻdī, **7**, 14, 1461
  on Dayr al-Jarnūs, 813
  on Dayr al-Khādim and Dayr al-Sanqūriyyah, 814
  on Dayr Sitt Dimyānah, 870, 871
  and Iqlādiyūs Labīb, 1302
  and Isidhūrus, 1307
  on Jirjis al-Jawharī al-Khanānī, 1334
  on monastery of Pisentius, 757
ʻAbd al-Rāziq, ʻAlī, 1996
ʻAbd al-Sayyid, Mīkhāʼīl, 1465, 1994
ʻAbduh, Muḥammad, 1995
Abednego, 1092
Abfiyyah (martyr), 1552
Abgar, King of Edessa, **7–8**, 1506
Abīb. *See* Phib, Saint
Abīb (eleventh month of Coptic calendar), 439, 443
  in Copto-Arabic Synaxarion, 2187–2189
Abīb ibn Naṣr, **8**, 1775
Abilius, Saint and Patriarch, **8**, 2081
  dates of patriarchy, 1913
Abishkhīrun, Saint, 2036
Abiskharūn al-Qallīnī al-Muqtadir, 752
Abī Sulaymān Dāwūd ibn Abī al-Munā ibn Abī Fānah, 1691
Ablanathanalba (palindrome), 1500
Ablution, **8–9**
  basin and ewer for, 1469
Abnūb
  monasteries at, 703, 714, 881, 1655
  pilgrimages to, 1971
Abraam I, Saint and Bishop of Fayyūm, **10**, 845, 2081
  pilgrimages to tomb of, 784
Abracas, Saint, 2081
Abraham (Old Testament patriarch)
  Archangels' visits to, 1136, 1618
  and circumcision practice, 1106

Abraham (Old Testament patriarch) (*cont.*)
paintings of, 793–794, *793*, 1660
sacrifice of Isaac. *See* Biblical subjects in Coptic art
Testament of, 164, 165
Abraham, Saint and Patriarch, **10–11**, 14, 321, 1534, 1593, 1999, 2081
and chrism consecration, 521
and Church of al-Mu'allaqah (Old Cairo), 558
and condemnation of *cheirotonia*, 517
dates of patriarchy, 1916
and Ethiopian prelates, 1001–1002
and Fast of Jonah, 1094
patriarchal residence, 1912
Abraham I, Archbishop of Jerusalem, 1325
Abraham bar Kaili, Bishop, 1675
Abraham of Farshūṭ, **11–12**, 1518, 1656, 1679
Coptic accounts of, 1455
and monasteries at Farshūṭ, 1092–1093
and monastery of Apa Moses, 1680
and Pbow monastery, 1448, 2154
Abraham and George of Scetis, Saints, **12–13**, 69, 2081, 2368
Abraham of Hermonthis, Bishop, **13**, 779, 1639
archives of, 227
correspondence of, 400–401
on defrocking of priests, 891
on excommunication grounds, 1079–1080
and mummification, 1697
on ordination, 564, 1844
portrait of, 402
Abraham and Isaac, depicted in Coptic art, 382–383
Abrahamites, 1533, 1534
Abraham of Luxor, Apa, icon of, *1277*
Abraham of Minūf, Saint, **13–14**, 1633, 2081
Abraham Persa, **14**
Abraham of Phelbes. *See* John the Hegumenos
Abraham of Qifṭ, Bishop, 730
Abrahat. *See* Preht
Abrākiyūs. *See* Abracas, Saint
Abrāshit the magician (Coptic legend), 845
Abraxas, **14**, 1500, 2173
Abrīm al-Qibṭī, Anbā, **14**
Abrimus. *See* Primus
Absaliyyah. *See* Music, Coptic, corpus and present practice
Absalmudiyyah. *See* Music, Coptic, corpus and present practice
Abshay, Saint, 719
Absolution, **15–17**
penance and, 1932
of women in baptismal liturgy, 339
Abstinence, **17**, 2308
see also Fasting
Abū. *See* Apa; specific names inverted
Abū al-'Alā' Fahd ibn Ibrahim, **17–18**, 1098, 1202
Abū 'Awn, Caliph, 1411–1412
Abū Bakr al-Akhram, 1098
Abū al-Barakāt. *See* Ibn Kabar
Abū al-Barakāt ibn al-Mabatt, Shaykh, 1128
Abū al-Barakāt Yuḥannā ibn Abī Layth, 1097
Abū al-Faḍl ibn Abī Sulaymān, 1691, 1749
Abū al-Faḍl ibn Isḥāq ibn Abī Sahl ibn Abī Yūsr Yuḥannā ibn al-'Assāl. *See* Fakr al-Dawlah
Abū al-Faḍl 'Īsā ibn Nasṭūrus, **18–19**
Abū al-Fakhr ibn Azhar, 1535
Abū al-Fakhr al-Masīḥī, **19**
Refutation of the Jews, 1779
Abū al-Faraj 'Abdallāh ibn Ṭayyib, 1089
Abū al-Faraj Ya'qūb ibn Killis, 1097
Abū al-Ghālib, 18
Abū Ḥabīb Mīkhā'īl ibn Badīr al-Damanhūrī, 1573
Abū Ḥulayqah, **19**, 1691, 2055
Abū Isḥāq. *See* Mu'taman Abū Isḥāq Ibrāhīm ibn al-'Assāl
Abū Isḥāq (ascetic), 1924
Abū Isḥāq ibn Faḍlallāh, **19–20**, 2075
Abū Ja'far al-Manṣūr, Caliph, 1631, 1632
Abū Jirjah, **20**
Abū al-Khayr al-Rashīd ibn al-Tayyib, **20**
Abū al-Majd ibn Abī Ghālib ibn Sāwīrus, 1391
Abū al-Majd ibn Yu'annis, **21–23**
Abū al-Makārim, **23**, 346
and Abū Ṣāliḥ the Armenian, 33
on ancient Alexandrian churches, 92
and Copts in Jerusalem, 1324
on Dayr Abū Qarqūrah, 708–709
on Dayr Anbā Anṭūniyūs, 724
on Dayr Anbā Būlā, 741
on Dayr Asfal al-Arḍ, 783
on Dayr Ebifania, 800
on Dayr al-Maghṭis, 818
on Dayr Maṭrā, 837
on Ibyār, 833
on patriarchal election, 1911
works of, 33, 1462
Abū al-Manṣūr ibn Būlus, Shaykh, 848
Abū al-Manṣūr ibn Fatḥ al-Dimyāṭī, 2079
Abū Maqrūfah. *See* Macrobius, Saint
Abū Mīnā, **24–29**, 1541
altars, 106, 107
ampullae from, 534, 537, 541
and Bahīj, 330
baptistery of Martyr Church, 197, *198*
basilica, 263–264, 355
cathedral, 707
ceramics of. *See* Ceramics, Coptic
church finished by Timothy II Aelurus, 2266
church in Hiw, 1242–1243
church started by Theophilus, Patriarch, 2248
and Coptic sculpture in stone, 2112
excavations, 1394
Great Basilica, 107, *198*
lamps and ampullae collection (State Museum of Berlin), 2146
as laura of hermitages, 1224–1225
Martyr Church, 24–29, *25–28*, 38, 94, 197
and Menas the Miracle Maker, 1590
monastic murals at, 1874
paintings of, 727
parekklesia addition, 1903
pilgrimages to, 24, 1550, 1969

settlement, 24–25
Tomb of the Martyr, 24
transept compared with church at Hawwāriyyah, 1212
see also Dayr Abū Mīnā
Abū Mīnā, Saint. *See* Menas the Miracle Maker, Saint
Abū al-Misk Kāfūr, 1632
Abū al-Mufaḍḍal ibn Amīn al-Mulk, **29**
Abū al-Munā (16th-century parish priest), **29**
Abū al-Munā (17th-century deacon), **30**
Abū al-Munā ibn Nasīm al-Naqqāsh, **30**
Abū Mūsā. *See* Dayr Abū Mūsā; Moses of Abydos; Moses the Black
Abun, **30–31**
and anointing Ethiopian emperor, 141
and *eččagē*, 930
and Ethiopian prelates, 980, 999–1044, 1613
and Ethiopian Synaxarion, 2190–2191
Abūnā Mīnā al-Barāmūsī. *See* Cyril VI, Pope
Abūnā Murqus of Maṭāy. *See* Murqus of Maṭāy
Abū Naṣr ibn Hārūn ibn ʿAbd al-Masīḥ, **31**
Abūnā Taklā. *See* Taklā, Abūnā
Abū Nofer (Nūfar). *See* Onophrius, Saint
Abū al-Qāsim, Caliph, 1410
Abūqīr (Canopus), **31**
Franciscan church, 1123
Abū Rakwah, 1099
Abū Saʿīd ibn Abī Sulaymān, 1749
Abū Saʿīd ibn Qurqah, 1097–1098
Abū Saīd ibn Sayyid al-Dār ibn Abī al-Faḍl al-Masīḥī, **32**
Abū Saʿīd ibn al-Zayyāt, 1536
Abū Ṣāliḥ the Armenian, **33**, 37, 38, 1462
on Abāmūn, 2
on administrative organization of Egypt, 934–936
on ʿAlwā, 110
on Antinoopolis, 144–145
on al-Bashmūr, 349
on churches and monasteries of Victor Stratelates, Saint, 2307–2308
on Dayr Abū Mūsā, 707
on Dayr al-ʿAdawiyyah, 712
on Dayr al-ʿAdhrā (Samālūṭ), 715
on Dayr al-Aḥmar (Giza), 716–717
on Dayr Anbā Abshāy, 718–719
on Dayr Anbā Bākhūm, 729
on Dayr Anbā Bishoi, 738
on Dayr Anbā Hadrā, 745
on Dayr Anbā Sāwīrus, 761
on Dayr Anbā Shinūdah, 764
on Dayr al-ʿAsal, 782
on Dayr Bālūjah, 788
on Dayr al-Ḥammām, 806
on Dayr al-Ikhwah, 808
on Dayr al-ʿIẓām (Asyūṭ), 809
on Dayr al-Malāk Mīkhā'īl (Qamūlah), 827
on Dayr al-Maymūn, 838
on Dayr al-Muḥarraqah, 841
on Dayr al-Naqlūn, 845, 846
on Dayr al-Nastūr, 848, 862
on Dayr al-Shamʿ, 863
on Dayr al-Ṭīn, 881
on Fatimids and Copts, 1098
on Febronia, Saint, 1109–1110
on Giza monasteries, 1142
and al-Ḥamīdāt, 1205
and Ibn Salīm al-Aswānī, 1272
on Iṭfīḥ, 1313
on Memphis, 1587
on monasteries of Upper Ṣaʿīd, 1657–1658
on monastery of Saint Pisentius, 757, 819–820
on Nubian matrilineal succession, 1514
on Nubian monasteries, 1817
on places dedicated to Theodorus, Saint, 797
on Soba, 2141
on Tafa, 2198
on Talmīs, 2200
Abū Sayfayn. *See* Church of Abū Sayfayn; Dayr Abū Sayfayn; Mercurius of Caesarea
Abū Shaʿār, castrum of, 468, *468*
Abū Shākir ibn Abī Sulaymān, 1691
Abū Shākir ibn Buṭrus al-Rāgub, 548
Abū Shākir ibn al-Rāhib, **33–34**, 1095, 1463
Abūṣīr (modern village), **34**
Abūṣīr (Taposiris Magna), **34**, *35*, *36*, 925
castrum of, 465
Abūṣīr Banā, **36–37**, 2272
Abūṣīr al-Malaq, **37**, 2272
monasteries in, 695–696
Abū Tarbū. *See* Magic
Abū Tīj, **38**
Dayr Abū Maqrūfah and Dayr al-Janādlah at, 704
Dayr Anbā Abshāy at, 718–719
Dayr Tāsā at, 881
on martyrs of Isnā, 866
pilgrimages to, 1971
Abū al-Yumn ibn al-Bazzāz, 718
Abū al-Yumn ibn Quzmān ibn Mīnā, 11
Abū Zakariyyā, 1097
Abwāb, Al-, **38**
Abyār, **38**
Abydos, **38–42**, *39*, *40*
antipaganism in, 1870
buildings, 41–42
monasteries at, 40, 707, 729, 1656
oracle of Bes at, 1869
see also Moses of Abydos
Abyssinia, 1517, 1536
Acacian schism, **42–47**, 594, 1671–1672, 1673
Acephaloi and, 55
Henoticon and, 1218
impact on Alexandria, 102
Justin I and, 1383–1384
and Ulphilas, 2285
Acacius, Bishop of Caesarea, **48–49**, 1948
and Acacian schism, 42–47, 1671, 1673
and Eusebius of Caesarea, 1070–1071
and Henoticon, 1217–1218
as leader of Homoeans, 1252
on Mercurius of Caesarea, 1592, 1593
Accounts and accounting, history of Coptic, **49–54**
see also Numerical system, Coptic
Acephaloi, 44, **55**, 347, 689, 1218, 1337, 1533–1534
Achaemenid dynasty, 1174
Acheronian Sea, 1499
Achillas, Saint (monk), **56**, 2239
Achillas, Saint and Patriarch, **55–56**, 2081
and Arius, 81, 231
dates of patriarchy, 1914
death, 81
and Melitian schism, 1584

Achillas, Saint and Patriarch (*cont.*)
successor, 81
Achilles (mythological figure), 1768
Achilleus of Thebaid, 2245
Acrostics, 1986
Acta Alexandrinorum, **56**, 1889
Acta apocrypha. *See* Acts of the Apostles
Acta sanctorum, **56–57**, 405, 1445
Actius, 230
Act of Peter, **57**, 59
Acts, Michigan Papyrus of, **58**
Acts of the Alexandrian Martyrs. *See Acta Alexandrinorum*
Acts of Andrew, 59
Acts of the Apostles, **58–60**
on catechumenization, 473
on miraculous healings, 1433
on Stephen, Saint, 2153
Acts of John, 59
Acts of the Martyrs. *See Acta Alexandrinorum*
Acts of Paul, 59–60
Coptic translations, 1451
Acts of Peter, 57, 59, 63
Acts of Peter and the Twelve Apostles, 57, **61–63**
Acts of Thomas, 59, 1635
Act of Union, 609–610, 797–798, 810
Adam, 2, 1618, 1619
Apocalypse of, 156–157, 166
Gabriel, Archangel, and, 1136
in Manichaeism, 1520
see also Adam and Eve; Apocalypse of Adam
Adām (Coptic melody type), **63**, 901, 1425, 1479, 1722, 1724, 1726, 1727, 1728, 1986
Adam and Eve, 1542, 1544, 1868
depicted in Coptic art, *384*, 384
in *Hypostasis of the Archons*, 1261
Norea as daughter of, 2257
Origen on, 1849
Paradise abode, 1900–1901
Pelagianism on, 1929, 1930
Adamnan, Saint (Ireland), 418
Adam Qadmon, 1150
ʿAdawiyyah, Al-. *See* Dayr al-ʿAdawiyyah
Adayma. *See* Isnā
Addas, 1521
Ad filios Dei (Macarius the Egyptian), 1491
ʿAdhrā, al-, Church (Dayr al-Majmaʿ), 820, *821*, 821
ʿAdhrā, al-, Church (Scetis), 791–794, *792*
ʿĀḍid, al-, Caliph, 1097, 1099
ʿAdil Ayyūb ibn Abū Bakr, al-, Sultan, 783
Adjudication by bishops. *See Audientia episcopalis*
Admon (martyr), 1554
Adonis (pagan deity), cult of, 1866
Adoption, 1942
Adoptionists. *See* Dynamic Monarchians; Unction of Christ
Adoration of the Magi, 527
Adrībah (town), 762
Adrūsīs. *See* Atrasis (martyr)
Advent, **63**
Aeneas of Paris, 1115
Aengus, Saint (anchorite), 253
Aesculapius. *See* Dioscorus and Aesculapius (martyrs)
Aesi (martyr), 1551, 1553
Aetius of Antioch, 141, 230, 1442, 1522
Afāṣim, Saint (Ethiopia). *See* Afṣē
Afḍal ibn Shāhinshāh, al-, 1097, 1488
Affagart, Greffin, 1977
Afghānī, Jamāl al-Dīn, al-, 1994, 1995
Aflaḥ al-Zaytun. *See* Monasteries of the Fayyūm
Aflāqah, **64**
Afrājūn, Al- (Phragonis), **64**
Afrām ʿAdad ("The Monk of Baramūs"), 791
African Independent Churches, 1622
Afrūnyah. *See* Febronia
Afṣē, Ethiopian saint, 1046
Afterlife
Abbaton's role, 2, 1619
eschatology, 973–974
Gabriel's and Michael's role, 1136–1137
heaven concepts, 1214
hell concept, 974
Paradise, 1900–1901
Rapahel's role, 2053
see also Hades; Judgment, Last; Purgatory
Afthīmī al-Miṣrī, **64**
Against the Definition of the Council of Chalcedon (Timothy II Aelurus), 2266–2267
Against the Galileans (Julian), 177
Against the Manichaeans (Didymus), 900
Aga Khan, mausoleum of, 745
Agapetae (beloved), 114
Agapetus, Pope (Rome), 1674
Agathammon, Bishop of Chora, 686
Agathangelo of Vendôme, Father, 610
Agathodorus (martyr), 1554
Agathon, Saint (anchorite), **64–65**, 2081
Agathon of Alexandria, Patriarch, **65–66**, 1999
dates of patriarchy, 1915
feast day, 2081
and John III, 808, 1337
on the Kellia, 1397
and Mareotis, 1527
panegyrics by, 1456
on Psote/Diocletian relationship, 2032
and Saint Mark's Cathedral, 1532
Agathon and his brothers (saints and martyrs), **66–67**, 1551
Agathon of Ḥomṣ, Bishop, 29, **67–68**
Agathonicus of Tarsus, **69–70**, 1185, 1453
Agathon the Stylite, Saint, 3, 12, **68–69**, 749, 2081
Agāthūn ibn Faṣīḥ al-Tūrsīnī, **70**
Agency (legal term), 1430
Agharwah, **70**
Agnoetae, **70–71**
Agnus Dei, **71**
Agricultural calendar. *See* Calendar and agriculture; Calendar, seasons, and Coptic liturgy; Calendologia
Agriculture
annona, 135–136
calendar, 440–443
commodities as loans, 1429
Dayr Anbā Maqār, 756
Ibn Mammātī work on, 1461
Nile valley crops, 440–443
Umayyad land policies, 2287–2288
see also Kharāj (land tax)

Agrippida. *See* Diocletian, Emperor
Agrippinus, Patriarch, **72**
dates of patriarchy, 1914
Ahālī, Al- (publication), 1990
Ahāywah Sharq, Al-, Dayr Anbā Bisādah in, 732–733
'Ahd al-'Umar. See Covenant of 'Umar
Ahīb. *See* Phib, Saint
Ahl al-Dhimmah, **72–73**
and Covenant of 'Umar, 655–656
and Ḥisbah, 1236–1237
and Ibn Qayyim Islamic law encyclopedia, 1269–1270
and Islamization, 189, 655–656, 939
millet system, 1631
Ottoman persecution during John XIII patriarchy, 1346
taxation of. *See Jizyah; Kharāj*
Ahl al-Kitāb, 72
Aḥmad Fatḥī Zaghlūl, 1994
Aḥmad ibn al-Afḍal Shāhinshāh, Caliph, 1128
Aḥmad ibn al-Maridānī, 1412
Aḥmad ibn Ṭūlūn, 939
Aḥmad Luṭfī al-Sayyid, 1987, 1988
Ahnās, **73–76**
and Apion family, 155
Fayyūm Gospel fragment found in, 1100
sculptures at, 74–76, 2112, 2116
Ahrūn ibn A'yan al-Qass, **77**
Aion (pagan deity), 1866
Aisle, 194
Ajā, 1648
Ajbiyah. See Canonical Hours, Book of
Akhbār, Al- (publication), 1990
Akhbariyyah, Al-. *See* Karm al-Akhbariyyah
Akhbār Qibṭ Miṣr (Maqrīzī), 1525
Ākhir Sā'ah (publication), 1991
Akhmīm, **78–80**, 946, 1089
antipaganism in, 1870
churches, 78–80
Dayr Abū Ḥalbānah near, 700
Dayr al-'Adhrā at, 78, 79, 80, 713
Dayr Anbā Bākhūm at, 731
Dayr al-Malāk Mīkhā'īl at, 78, 823
Dayr al-Qurqāṣ at, 78, 852
Dayr al-Shuhadā' at, 865
gravestone prayer inscriptions, 1294
monasteries, 78–79, 1654, 1655, 1661; *see also* specific names
papyrus collections, 80, 1891
papyrus discoveries, 1898
remains and representations of Coptic clothing. *See* Costume, civil
stelae from, 2161, 2162
and Thomas, Saint, 2256
Akhmīm fragments, **80**
Akhmimic dialect
Coptic translations of Old Testament, 1837–1838
Hermas codex in, 1223
see also Appendix; New Testament, Coptic versions of the
Aksum. *See* Axum
'Alā' al-Dīn ibn 'Alī ibn al-Kūrānī (governor of Cairo), 882
Alam, Al- (title), 80
'Alam al-Dīn Shākir, 1616
'Alam Ṣalīb al-Ibnāsī, Al-, **80**
'Alam Shaltūt, 81, 1874
Albertus a Sarthiano, 1119
Alcuin, 1112
Alēf, Ethiopian Saint, 1046
Aleph. *See Appendix*
Aleppo, 1098
Alexander, Bishop of Cappadocia (martyr), 1551
Alexander, Bishop of Jerusalem (martyr), 889–890, 1551, 1881
Alexander I, Patriarch, **81–85**, 93, 101, 1089, 1584, 1617
and Arius, 81–84, 609, 1790, 2156, 231–232
and Athanasius I, 298
dates of patriarchy, 1914
and Eusebius of Caesarea, 1070–1071
and first usage of *Theotokos* term, 2255
literature and works of, 84–85
on Peter I, 1943–1944, 1945
and Sabellianism, 2072
Alexander II, Patriarch, 37, **85–87**, 1589
dates of patriarchy, 1915
at the Enaton, 957–958
and Ḥilwān, 1233
and Theodorus, Patriarch, 2237
Alexander the Egyptian (martyr), 1551
Alexander the Great, 1166, 1174–1175, 1179, 1758, 2063
Alexander Romance, 2059
tomb of, 2065
Alexander of Lycopolis, **87–88**, 1149, 1521
Alexander of Maro, 46, 1673
Alexander Romance, 2059
Alexander Severus, Emperor, 892
patriarch under, 1914
Alexandra, Saint, **88**, 1663, 2055, 2082
Alexandria, **95–102**
Antony of Egypt visits to, 150
as apostolic see, 180
apostolic succession, 181
Arab conquest of, 100, 655, 683
and Arius's teachings, 231–232
bishopric, 892, 911
castrum of, 465
ceramics of, 483
Christian catacombs and chapels, 1873
Christianity introduced into, 1866
Christian and medieval era, 88–92
churches consecrated by Christodoulus, Patriarch, 92, 544
churches in, 92–95, 101–102
church relations with Church of Rome, 608–611
church restoration in, 11; *see also subhead* historic churches
cult of Homeric gods in, 1865
Damian and, 688, 689
Dayr Maṭrā at, 837
Dayr Qibriyūs at, 850
Easter date-setting, 1904–1905, 1105
ecumenical disputes, 688, 1138; *see also* Chalcedon, Council of; Monophysitism
as Egyptian mint site, 574, 575, 944
and the Enaton, 954–955
end to institutionalized paganism in, 1870
Franciscan friary and churches, 1122, 1123
French governor, 1417

Alexandria (*cont.*)
glassmaking, 1142, 1143
gnosticism, 1148, 1149–1150
Great Persecution of Christians (303–312), 907–908
Greek founding and influence in, 1174–1175, 1179, 1180
Greek language use in, 1167
Islamic period. *See* Alexandria, Christian and medieval
Jewish ascetics, 1661
Jewish community, 91, 97, 1175, 1180, 1865–1866
Jewish rebellion, 97, 1947, 2016
in late antiquity, 95–102, *96*
library of, 100, 1447
Mark, Saint, journeys to, 1529–1530
Mark, Saint, martyrdom in, 1531
martyrs, 1, 890, 1554, 1558, 1559; *see also* specific names
martyrs' shrines, 1976
medicine in, 91, 2065
metropolitan see, 913–914, 915, 1612–1614
monasteries, 101, 707, 837, 850, 1467, 1645–1646
monastic murals at, 1874
monophysitism in, 913–915
paganism in, 946, 1870
Pantaenus' school in, 1881
patriarchal residences, 689, 1912–1913
as patriarchate of Coptic Catholic Church, 601
patriarchs in, 689
persecutions in, 907–909, 1868–1869, 1936, 1937; *see also subhead* martyrs
Persian capture of, 131–132, 1938–1939, 1940
Philo (Jewish philosopher), 1956–1957
pilgrims and travelers to, 1977, 2065
pope designation in, 1998–1999
power of see, 913–914, 915
prefect, 2023
revolt against Arab conquerors, 187–188
rival patriarchs, 1138
Roman emperors in, 2061–2063
Roman political impact, 1177, 1180
Roman travelers to, 2065
uprising against Peter II, 1947
Alexandria, Christian and medieval, **89–92**
Alexandria, historic churches in, **92–95**
Alexandria in late antiquity, **95–102**
Alexandrian Monastery of the Metanoia. *See* Metanoia, Monastery of the
Alexandrian theology, **103–104**
apologia, 176
and Arianism, 232
Communicatio idiomatum, 578–579
patristic writings, 1921
see also Catechetical School of Alexandria
Alexandria, treaty of (641), 682, 931
Alḥān (songs), 1744
ʿAlī, Sayyid, 1990
ʿAlī (Bey) al-Dimyāṭī, 1538
ʿAlī ibn Rabbān al-Ṭabarī, al-Ṣafī ibn al-ʿAssāl reply to, 2078
ʿAlī al-Ikhshīd, 1098
ʿAli Shaʿrāwī Pasha, 1987
ʿAlī Yūsuf, 1988
Allādyūs (martyr), 1551
Allah ist gross (Kaufmann), 1394
Allberry, Charles Robert Cecil Austin, **104**
Allegory, 62, 104
see also Symbols in Coptic art
Alleluia, **104**, 109, 1731
Allenby, Lord, 1992
Allogenes, **105**
and *Valentinian Exposition*, 2295
and *Zostrianus*, 2372
Almanacs, 440–443
Alodia. *See* Alwā
Alphabet, Coptic
and letters of Pachomius, 1863
see also Appendix
Alphabet, Greek, 1501, 1749–1750
acrostics, 1986
alpha and omega symbols, 2160–2163
and Coptic numerical system, 1820–1821
use in Coptic illuminated manuscripts, 1282–1283
see also Appendix; Greek language
Alpha and omega, 2160–2163
Altaner, B., 1921
Altar, **105–107**, 221
and antimension use, 144
ban on wooden, 580
basin and ewer, 1469
Christian, 106–107
in eastern end of churches, 1846
pagan, 105–106
wooden, 2328, *2328*
see also Communion table
Altar, consecration of, **108–109**
see also Church, consecration of
Altar-board, **109**; *see also* Antimension
Altar lights, **109–110**
see also Candles
Altar veil. *See* Eucharistic veils
ʿAlwā, 38, **110–111**, 1420
described by Ibn Ḥawqal, 1266
described by Ibn Salīm al-Aswānī, 1272
and Nubian evangelization, 1801–1802
and Nubian Islamization, 1803
as Nubian kingdom, 1797, 1800
and Nubian languages and literature, 1815–1816
Soba as capital city of, 110, 111, 2141–2142
Alypios of Alexandria, 1731
A.M. (*anno martyrum*), 434, 972
Ama. *See* Apa
Amadeus VIII of Savoy, 1572
Amasis (Egyptian leader), 1166
Amazons, as subjects in Coptic art, 1750–1752
Ambo, **111**
Ambrose, Saint and Bishop of Milan, 1378, 1921
on age for admission to convent, 1822
on discovery of the Holy Cross, 1243
and Lord's Prayer, 1481
on marriage, 1542
patristic writings, 1920
on remarriage of widows, 901
Theodorus of Mopsuestia and works attributed to, 2239
Ambrosian Library (Milan), 782
Ambrosius (companion of Hor), 1254
Ambrosius (patron of Origen), 1847
Ambulatory, 195, 222
Amélineau, Emile Clement, **112**
on Buṭrus al-Sidmantī, 431
on Hilaria, Saint, 1231

on Paul of Thebes, 1926
Shenute text-editing, 1452
and study of hagiographical cycles, 666
Amenemhet III, 1210, 1497
Amenhotep (pagan deity), 439
Amenophis III, 1484
Amīn, Qāsim, 1465, 1994
Amīn al-Dīn ʿAbd-Allāh ibn Tāj al-Riyāsah al Qibṭī, **112–113**
Amīr bi-Aḥkām Allāh, Al-, 843
Amīr al juyūsh (title of Badr al-Jamālī), 324
Amjad Abū al-Majd ibn al-ʿAssāl, Al-, 1748
Amma, origin of term, 2, 3
Ammianus Marcellinus, 99, 100
Ammon. *See* Letter of Ammon
Ammon, Saint. *See* Amun, Saint
Ammonas, Saint, **113**, 2082
and Antony, Saint, 150
Ammonia. *See* Paraetonium
Ammonius (monk of Canopus), on martyrs of Raithou, 2050
Ammonius, Bishop of Isnā, 1312
and founding of Dayr al-Shuhadā', 866, 869–870, 1551
Ammonius of Aswan, Saint, 2082
Ammonius of Kellia, 32, **113–114**, 1397, 1490, 2082
and desert fathers, 894
and Dioscorus, 686, 916
and Evagrius Ponticus, 1076
on keeps, 1395, 1396
and Kellia community, 1397
Ammonius Saccas, 470, 1981
Ammonius of Ṭūkh. *See* Abāmūn of Ṭūkh
Ammonius of Tūnah, **114**, 1543, 2082
Amoi (father of Abba Yuḥannis), 883
Amos, 22
Amphilochius of Iconium, **114–116**
Amphorae, 490
cosmetic box design, *2339*
found at Monastery of Mark the Evangelist (Qurnat Marʿī), 2046
stoppers for, 499, *499*
Amplissima, 1523
Ampulla, **116–118**, *116–118*, 534, 537, 541, 1603
ʿAmr ibn al-ʿĀṣ (Arab general), 100, 183–189, 749, 783
ʿAmriyyah (Maryūt), **118**, *118*
Amsah of Qifṭ (martyr), 1551
Amshīr (6th month of Coptic calendar), 439, 441–442, 2180–2181
Amulets, 14, 1499, 1504, 1506, 1508, *1508*, 1509, 1606
Nubian, 1814
Amun (martyr). *See* Krajon and Amun, Saints
Amun (pagan deity), 1392, 1484–1485
Amun, Saint, **119**
and cenobitic monasticism, 1138
feast day, 2082
as founder of Nitria, 1794
in Letters of Saint Antony, 150
and Pambo, Saint, 1877–1878
Amun, Saint (martyr). *See* Krajon and Amun, Saints
Anachoresis, **118–120**, 1320–1321, 1661, 1958
see also Anchorites; Reclusion
Anamnesis, **120–121**, 964, 1566
Ananius (martyr), 1552
Anaphora of Saint Basil, 71, **121–123**, 124
see also Canons of Saint Basil; Liturgy of Saint Basil
Anaphora of Saint Cyril, 71, **123–124**, 352, 988–990, 1066–1067, 1539
see also Liturgy of Saint Cyril
Anaphora of Saint Gregory, 71, **124–125**, 968, 1066, 1733
see also Liturgy of Saint Gregory
Anargyroi, 638–639
Anastasia, Saint (martyr), **125**, 692, 955, 1552, 1931, 2082
Anastasius, Abbot, **126**, 720, 721
Anastasius, Emperor, 1934, 1962
exile of, 773
Formula of Satisfaction, 44, 1672
and Monophysites, 44, 2124, 1671, 1672, 1673
patriarch under, 1915
Anastasius of Eucaita, **127**, 2237
Anastasius, Patriarch, 95, **125–126**
concordat between Copts and Syrians, 688
dates of patriarchy, 1915
Anathema, 82, 84, **127–128**, 589–590
Twelve Anathemas of Cyril, 1671
Anatolius (Dioscorus' deacon), 1441, 1442
Anatolius, Patriarch of Constantinople, 512–515
Anatolius, Saint, **128**, 892, 1552, 2237–2238
Anawati, G. C., 918
Anbā. *See* Apa; personal name inverted
Anbā Bimānun. *See* Epima, Saint
Anbā Bisādah. *See* Dayr Anbā Bisādah; Psote of Psoï, Saint
Anbā Bishoi. *See* Dayr Anbā Bishoi; Pshoi of Scetis
Anbā Būlā. *See* Paul of Thebes, Saint
Anbā Furayj. *See* Anbā Ruways
Anbā Maqārah. *See* Macarius I, Saint
Anbā Mīnā. *See* Menas the Miracle Maker, Saint; Sanctuary of Saint Menas
Anbā Ruways
monastery and Clerical College, 564
as patriarchal seat, 2000
Anbā Ruways, Saint, **128–129**, 2082
Anbā Yusāb. *See* Joseph the Bishop, Saint
Anchorites, **129–130**, 724–725, 737, 795, 800–801, 1491, 1661–1662
Agathon, Saint, 64–65
Claudius, Saint, 561
in Diolkos province, 908
folklore, 130
history, 129–130
Isaiah of Scetis, 1305–1306
Kom Namrūd settlement, 1418
Mary the Egyptian, 129, 130, 1560
Moses the Black, 1681
Onophrius, Saint, 1841–1842
Pambo, Saint, 1877–1878
Pamin, Saint, 1878
Paphnutius the Hermit, Saint, 1882–1883
Patape, 1907
Paul of Thebes, 129–130, 1925–1926
in Pharan oasis, 1953
Poemen, Saint, 1983–1984
at Raithou, 2049–2050
and sabbath observance, 1099

Anchorites (*cont.*)
Sisoēs, 2141
Theodorus of Pherme, 2239
Thomas, Saint, 2256–2257
Timotheus, Saint, 2262–2263
see also Anachoresis; Asceticism; Desert fathers; Hermits; Monasticism, Pachomian
Ancient Coptic Churches in Egypt (Butler), 2000
Andreas, Abbot. *See* Andrew, Abbot
Andrew (martyr). *See* Eunapius and Andrew (martyrs)
Andrew, Abbot of Dayr Anbā Antūniyūs, 722, 1119
Andrew, Abbot of Dayr al-Salīb, 703–704
Andrew, Saint, and Dayr al-Ṣalīb, 859
Andrew of Crete, Saint, **130–131**, 2082
Andronicus, Patriarch, **131–132**, 1940, 1978, 1999
and Benjamin I as successor, 375
dates of patriarchy, 1915
Angel, **132**
cherubim and seraphim, 518
depicted in Coptic art, 270
depicted with demons at Bāwīṭ, 370–371
depicted on wood panel, *2346*
role of guardian angel, 1186
subdivisions analogous to priesthood, 2015–2016
see also Archangel; Cherubim and seraphim; Demons; Guardian angel
Angel, Feast of, 1111
Angelic Worship, The, 1565–1566
Anglican church
on canon of Scripture, 2110
creeds, 179
Anglican church in Egypt, **133**
Anianus, Patriarch (the Cobbler), 94, **133–134**, 1530, 1612, 1911
dates of patriarchy, 1913
Animals
depicted in paintings at Bāwīṭ, 371–372
depicted on wood column, *2345*
Egyptian worship of, 1867, 2065
lamps in shapes of, 1598
Physiologos on, 1965, 1966
Ankh, **134–135**, 281
depicted in Coptic art, 270, *272*, 276
as Nubian Meroitic pottery decoration, 1806
see also Crux ansata; Symbols in Coptic art
Annales ecclesiastici, 1523
Annali dell'Islam (Caetani), 433
Anna (martyr), 1554
Anna (prophetess), 1107
Anno martyrum (A.M.), 434, 972
Annona (wheat crop), **135–136**, 2203
Annunciation
Hail Mary prayer, 1199
as subject in Coptic art, 282, 528–529, *2346*
Annunciation, Feast of the, 1102, 1103, 1111, 2256
Anointing, **137–140**
and confirmation, 138, 586
and consecration of buildings and objects, 139–140
and consecration of vessels and icons, 140
and Coptic doctrine of the Holy Spirit, 1250
of heretics, 138–139
and Holy Matrimony, 139
in Judaism, 137
of kings, 139
and unction of the sick, 139, 2291–2292
see also Chrism
Anointing of the Ethiopian emperor, **140–141**
Anomoeans, **141–142**
Ansate cross. *See* Ankh
Anselm of Canterbury, 1113
Anṣinā, **142–143**
see also Antinoopolis; Dayr al-Dīk; Dayr al-Naṣāra; Dayr Sūnbat; Shaykh Sa'īd
Anṭākiyah, 1098
Anthimus, Patriarch of Constantinople, 1674, 1679–1680, 2241
Anthony Fulayfil, 610
Anthropomorphism, **143**
Cassian on, 461
Cyril I warning against, 758
Gnostic rejection of, 1151
Theophilus, Patriarch, campaign against, 154, 1884, 2103, 2249–2250
Anthropos, 1148, 1150
see also Gnosticism
Antichrist, **143**
in *Concept of Our Great Power*, 583
Nero seen as, 1785
Antimension, **144**
see also Altar-board
Antinoë. *See* Antinoopolis
"Antinoë veil", 1482
Antinoopolis, **144–148**
Ammonius (martyr) buried at, 866
Anṣinā, 142–143
architecture, 146–147, *146*, *147*
Bishoi in, 734, 795
and castrum of Dayr al-Dīk, 465
ceramics of. *See* Ceramics, Coptic
Dayr Abū Ḥinnis linked with, 701
Dayr al-Dīk near, 798–799
Dayr al-Naṣārā, 847
Dayr Sunbāṭ near, 875–876
excavations, 416, 1481–1482, 2049
founding of, 1179, 1181, 2062, 2066
glass intarsia, 1145–1146, *1145*
Greek influences in, 1174, 1179, 1181
literary and archaeological sources, 144–145, *145*
martyrs at, 1–2, 696, 893, 1551, 1552, 1553, 1554, 1555, 1556, 1557
monasteries around, 1654; *see also* specific names
monastic murals at, 1874
Panine and Paneu legend, 1881
pen cases found at, 1933, 1961
remains and representations of Coptic clothing. *See* Costume, civil
rock churches, 716
ruins in southeast quarter of, 146–148, *147*
shrines, 1976
site of tribunal of Victor Stratelates, Saint, 2304
Ter and Erai, Saints, visit to, 2209
textile production, 257
textile production, Sassanid influences, 2097–2098
tomb mural paintings, 1873
tombstone inscriptions, 1293, 1294

woman's monastery at, 1663
Antinous (favorite of Hadrian), 142, 2062, 2066
see also Antinoopolis
Antioch
Anastasius and, 125
as apostolic see, 180
apostolic succession, 181
Arius and theology of, 231–232
Christology, 547, 578
Demetrius (fictional character), 893–894
Isidorus, Saint, martyrdom, 1307
Julian the Apostate efforts to restore paganism in, 1382
Lucian, 1484
Mark II relations with patriarchy, 1536
martyrs, 1555
Paul the Black as patriarch, 688, 689
Philotheus of, 1960–1961
Severus, 2123–2125
theological opposition to Apollinarianism, 174
Theophilus, Patriarch, as theological schism mediator, 2248–2249
Antioch, Council of (341)
on archbishops, 190
and Holy Communion, 579
Lucian and, 1484
on metropolitan, 1612
Antiochus, Bishop of Memphis, 1587
Antiphon, **148–149**, *1717*, 1732, 1733, 2024
Antiphonary. *See Difnār*
Antiquities Museum (Leiden). *See* National Antiquities Museum
Antoninus (martyr), 741, 1552, 1868
Antonius of Banah, 1089
Antonius Marcus, Bishop, 1622
Antonius Pius, Emperor
patriarch under, 1914
temples, 863
Anton and Paul, Saints, 1733
Antony of Egypt, Saint, 2, 31, 88, **149–151**, 114, 697, 1190, 1477, 1522
abstinence of, 17
and Ammonas, Saint, 113, 2082
Ammonius's vision of, 114
Amun, Saint, 119
and anachoresis, 119, 120, 1661–1662, 1663
and Anbā Būlā, 129
and Athanasius I, 300, 1921
and Besa, Abbot, 378–379
and Bessarion, Saint, 2082
biographies of, 116, 149, 1663; *see also Life of Saint Antony*
on canonical hours, 449
as "carrier of the Spirit," 1249
cave, 725
chapels of, 753, 754
compared with Irish monastic saints, 418
on costume of the religious, 652, 654
and Cronius of Nitria, Saint, 2083
in Dalās, 685
depicted in Coptic art, 270, 385–386
as desert father, 894
and Didymus the Blind, 900
disciples of, 1923
and Ethiopian monasticism, 990
as father of monasticism, 1668
and Fayyūm monasteries, 1100
Fayyūm visit by, 845
feast day, 2082
on Gabriel VII, Patriarch, 1133
and Hilarion, Saint, 1232
John of Shmūn on, 1369
and Kellia, 1397
letters in Coptic text, 1451
letters translated from Coptic into Arabic, 721
and Macarius the Egyptian, 1491
monasteries of, 719–729, 838, 839, 1658, 1664
and Old Testament, Coptic translations of, 1836
paintings of, 727, 754
and Pambo, Saint, 1878
panegyrics on, 1456
and Paul the Simple, Saint, 2086
and Paul of Thebes, Saint, 741, 1925–1926
and Pior, Saint, 2086
and Poemen, Saint, 1983
reclusion of, 2055
and Sarapion of Tmuis, Saint, 2096
veneration of, 728
and women's religious communities, 1822, 2325
writings, 150–151
writings and *Teachings of Silvanus*, 2207
see also Dayr Anbā Anṭūniyūs
Antony the Great. *See* Antony of Egypt, Saint
Anṭūn Abū Ṭaqiyyah, 1688
Anṭūniyūs Mulūkhiyyah, **151–152**
Anūb, Apa. *See* Dayr Apa Anūb
Anub, Saint, **152**, 705, 1552, 2090
Bāwīṭ founding, 843
martyrdom in Atrīb, 307
and Poemen, 1983, 1984
see also Nob
Apa, **152–153**
see also Abbā; specific names inverted
Apaiule and Tolemaeus, Saints (martyrs), **153**, 1552
see also Tolemaeus, Saint
Apa Jeremiah Monastery. *See* Dayr Apa Jeremiah (Saqqara)
Apa Kīr. *See* Cyrus (martyr)
Apater. *See* Ter and Erai, Saints
Apa Til. *See* Til
Aper, 904
Aphraam. *See* Abraam I, Saint and Bishop of Fayyūm
Aphrodite (pagan deity)
depiction in Coptic art, *266*, *1752*, 1752–1753, *1753*
see also Hathor
Aphrodite Anadyomene tapestry, *2225*
Aphrodito, **153–154**, 227, 1642, 1659, 2205
archive of Basilios, 226, 228, 229, 358–359
Aphroditopolis. *See* Iṭfīḥ
Aphthartodocetae. *See* Julian
Aphthonius, 1522
Aphu (monk and bishop), **154**
Apion, family of, **155–156**, 1871
Apocalypse of Adam, **156–157**
as Old Testament apocrypha, 166
Apocalypse of Bartholomew, 2
Apocalypse of Daniel, 165
Apocalypse of Elias, 165
Apocalypse of Elijah, 165
Apocalypse of Ezra, 165, 2053
Apocalypse of James, First, **157–158**, 160
Apocalypse of James, Second, **158–159**
Apocalypse of Moses, 165

Apocalypse of Paul, **159–160**, 1782
Apocalypse of Peter, **160–161**, 917
Apocalypsis Heliae, Coptic translations, 1451
Apocalyptic literature
of Abū Isḥāq ibn Faḍlallāh, 20
Antichrist and, 143
Concept of Our Great Power, 583
Melchizedek in, 1583–1584
Old Testament apocrypha, 164–166
predictions, 1867
Pseudo-Pisentius of Qifṭ, 2028
Apocryphal literature, **161–166**
Acts of the Apostles, 58–60
Akhmīm fragments, 80
as canon of Scripture, 2108
condemnation of, 162
Coptic translations of, 1454
Gospel of Thomas, 1162, 1163
Gospel of Truth, 1163–1164
in Ireland, 418
on Joseph the Carpenter, 1372–1373
on Michael, archangel, investiture in Heaven, 1618
National Library, Paris, manuscripts, 1777
Apocryphon of James, 569, **169–171**
Apocryphon of Jeremiah, **170–171**
Apocryphon of John, **171–172**
comparison with *Sophia of Jesus Christ*, 1068–1069
comparison with *Trimorphic Protennoia*, 2276
parallels with *Zostrianus*, 2372
Apoli, Saint (martyr), 1413, 1552
"Apollinarian Forgeries," 961
Apollinarianism, **173–174**, 1669, 1670, 1673
Cappadocian counter to, 114–115
Cyril I opposition to, 1262
and Ephesus, First Council of, 959–960
on nature of Christ, 547
Theodoret and, 2236
Theodorus of Mopsuestia opposition to, 2239
Timothy I opposition to, 2263
Apollinaria, Saint, 2082
Apollinaris, Bishop of Laodicea, 173–174, 1669, 1674
Apollinopolis Parva. *See* Qūṣ
Apollo (martyr), 1551, 1552
Apollo (priest), 927
Apollo of Bāwīṭ, Saint, 1448, 1976, 2082
and Ammonius, 114
and Bāwīṭ founding, 362–363, 843
Phib, Saint, associated with, 1953
see also Bāwīṭ; Phib, Saint
Apollo and Daphne, depicted in Coptic art, 1753–1754, *1754*, 1757
Apollonia, 1934
see also Sozousa
Apollonius of Nitria, Saint, 2082
Apollonius and Philemon, Saints, **174–175**, 231, 1552, 1733, 1880, 2082
Apollonopolis Magna. *See* Idfū
Apollonopolis Minor. *See* Qūṣ
Apollo the Shepherd, Saint, **175–176**
Apologetic literature. *See* Apologist
Apologia de incredulitate (Agathonicus of Tarsus), 69–70
Apologist, **176–177**, 1920–1921
ʿAbd al-Masīḥ ibn Isḥāq al-Kindī, 5
Abū al-Khayr al-Rashīd ibn al-Ṭayyib, 20–21
Agathonicus of Tarsus, 69–70
Butrus Sāwīrus al-Jamīl, 431
Eusebius of Caesarea, 1071
manuscripts in National Library, Paris, 1777, 1779, 1780, 1782
al-Ṣafī ibn al-ʿAssāl, 2076–2079
Theodoret, 2236
Yūḥannā al-Ḥādhiq al-Qibṭī, 2357
Apology for Origen (Pamphilus), 1879
Apology for Origen (Rufinus translation), 2068
Apomea, shrine to Michael, Archangel, 1616
Apophthegmata patrum, 56, **177–178**, 894, 1136, 1663
on Ammonas, Saint, 113
on Antony, Saint, 149, 1491
on Bessarion, Saint, 379
Coptic translations of, 1454
on al-Faramā, 1089
on Isaac, Saint, 1304
Isaiah of Scetis and, 1305–1306
on Isidorus of Scetis, Saint, 1310
John Colobos, Saint, and, 1359
on Kellia, 1397
on Macarius, 1490, 1491
on Maximus and Domitius in Scetis, 789, 790
on Pambo, Saint, 1878
on Paphnutius of Scetis, 1884
on Paul the Simple, 1923
on Poemen, Saint, 1983–1984
ranking of Arsenius of Scetis and Ṭurah, 240
on reclusion, 2055
on sayings attributed to Abbā Bane, 698
on Theodorus of Pherme, Saint, 2239
Theophilus, Patriarch, and, 2249
on Timotheus, Saint, 2262
word *apa* in, 152
Zacharias, Saint and, 2368
Apostates, Dionysius the Great and, 910, 912
Apostatized Coptic dignitaries. *See* Professional activities of Copts in medieval Egypt
Apostles
Acts of the Apostles, 58–60
Acts of Peter and the Twelve Apostles, 57, 61–63
on circumcision, 1106
and descent of the Holy Spirit, 1446
Didascalia on, 899–900
and evangelists, 529, 1078
fast of the, 1093
and first seven deacons, 885
and Holy Ghost, 1105–1106
and laying-on of hands, 1432, 1433
Mark I, Saint and Patriarch, 1528–1533
and priesthood, 2015
see also Canons, Apostolic; Christian subjects in Coptic art; specific names
Apostles' Creed, **178–179**, 2069
Apostles Peter and Paul, Feasts of the. *See* Festal days, monthly
Apostolic Canons. *See* Canons, Apostolic
Apostolic Church Order, 454–455, 898
Apostolic Constitutions, 178, **179–180**, 454–455, 898, 899, 1235

and bishops, 393–395
on celebration of feasts, 1101, 1102, 1432
on church architecture, 216
on confession and penitence, 584
on deaconesses, 888
doxology, 923
on fasting on Saturday, 2098
on fasting on Sunday, 2159
and intercession for the dormant, 889
on morning prayers, 1568
on Nativity date, 1102
and the Octateuch of Clement, 1824
on orientation toward the East during prayers, 1846
on prostration during prayer on Sunday, 2159
and use of oil prior to baptism, 340
Apostolic fathers, **180**, 1920
Apostolic See, **181**
see also Metropolitan Sees; Patriarch
Apostolic succession, **181**
Apostolic Tradition (Hippolytus), **182**, 454–455, 1235–1236
and *Canons of Hippolytus*, 485
on Holy Trinity, 178
on laying-on of hands, 1432
on offertory, 1824
Apparel. *See* Costume, civil; Costume, military; Costume of the religious; Liturgical vestments
Apparition of the Holy Light, 1248–1249
Apparition of the Virgin Mary, 2308–2309
Appenzell I, 1572
Apse, 195–196, 221
iconography, 555
Aptia (martyr), 1552
Aqbāṭ, al- (Lacbat), **182–183**
Aqfahṣ, **183**
Aqmar, al-, mosque of, 810, 814
ʿArab al-ʿAwāmir, 703
Arab conquest of Egypt, 20, **183–189**, 1667
Abraham, Patriarch, and, 10, 11
and Abūṣīr Banā, 37
administrative organization of Egypt under, 934–936
Agathon and, 65
Ahl al-Dhimmah and, 72–73
Alexander II patriarchy during, 85–87
Alexandria under, 88–92, 96, 100
attack on ʿAlwā, 110–111
Ayyubid dynasty, 314–315, 1534, 1535, 2037
and al-Banāwān, 334
Bashmuric revolts, 349–351
Benjamin I and, 375
Bilbeis and, 391
Burullus and, 427
and "Christian encounter," 2316–2317
and church architecture, 553
coinage, 575–576
and Coptic art and architecture, 131–132, 274–275
and Coptic literature, 1456, 1458, 1460–1467
and Coptic magic, 1504–1506
and Coptic martyrs, 1550–1551, 1557, 1558, 1559, 1589
and Coptic music, 1734–1736
and Coptic population decline, 1857
and Coptic public law, 1430
and Coptic textiles iconography, 2230
and Covenant of ʿUmar, 655–656
Cyrus al-Muqawqas role, 682–683
Dayr Anbā Maqār under, 749
Dayr Epiphanius under, 801
Enaton under, 957–958
Greek culture and, 1168, 1178
John of Nikiou chronicles of, 655, 977, 1366
Makourian annexation attempts, 1514
Mamluks and the Copts, 1517–1518
al-Maqrīzī history of, 1525
monasteries active during, 709
and monastic life in Scetis, 2104
and monastic population decline, 1663, 1857
pagarch system, 189. 1871–1872
patriarchs under, 1915–1918
and Paul of Aigina's medical texts, 1922
Pentapolis and, 1934, 1935
personal status law under, 1941
Peter V patriarchy under, 1948–1949
and pilgrimages, 1975
provincial absence of arabization, 2289
Qaṣr al-Sham and, 2038
Qūṣ and, 2043–2044
Roman decentralization facilitating, 2008
and Roman taxation measures, 2204
and secular confirmation of patriarchal election, 1911
and spread of circumcision among Ethiopians, 1001
Umayyad arabization, 2289
waqf system and land tenure, 2319
see also Islam; Literature, Copto-Arabic; Mamluks and the Copts; Ottomans, Copts under the; Persians in Egypt; Taxation; Umayyads, Copts under the
ʿArabī, Maḥmūd Ḥusnī, al-, 1996
Arabic Canons of Nicaea, 1789–1790
Arabic language
Abū Isḥāq ibn Faḍlallāh's writings in, 19
Barlām and Yuwāṣaf fables, 346
Canons, Apostolic, 452
canons, ecclesiastical, 454
catena, 475
Coptic dictionaries, 34, 1267, 1302, 1748
Coptic legal sources, 1438
Coptic literature, 1459, 1460–1467
Coptic magic, 1504
Coptic music and, 1727, 1731, 1734–1736
Coptic service translation, 1630
correspondence, 970–971
French-Arabic dictionary, 1284, 1285
homilies on Gabriel, archangel, 1136
homilies of Mark II, 1534
homilies of Proclus, 2019
Ibn Kabar theological encyclopedia, 1634–1635
inscriptions in, 1290
Life of Pachomius in, 1860, 1861
medical texts in, 1922
al-muʿaqqab term, 1687

Arabic language (*cont.*)
Nubians' use of, 1816
Old Testament version, 1827–1835
papyrus collections, 1890–1896
Psalis in, 1727
Pseudo-Cyril of Alexandria and, 2025
Qusṭanṭīn translation of *Typikon of Saint Sabas*, 2046–2047
al-Ṣafī ibn al-ʿAssāl works, 2075–2079
traditions on John Colobos, Saint, 1361
use in Egyptian government administration, 1168
words designating administration of Egypt, 935
see also Toponymy, Coptic
Arab League, 1694
ʿArab Mitīr (village), 703
Aragāwi, Ethiopan Saint, 1046
ʿAraj, Al- (oasis), **189–190**, 1659
Arbitration, Coptic, 1430, 1431
Arcadia. *See* Lower Ṣaʿīd
Arcadius, Emperor, 93, 789–790, 2033
and Dayr al-Quṣayr (Turah)
patriarch under, 1914
and Theophilus, Patriarch, church-building, 2248
Archaelaus (martyr), 1552
Archaeological and Anthropological Museum, France, 1187
Archaeological digs. *See* Excavations
Archaeologists
Clarke, Somers, 560
Hauser, Walter, 1210
Kaufmann, Carl Maria, 1394
Omar Toussoun, 1841
Sāmī Gabrā, 2090
Seyffarth, Gustavus, 2125
see also Society of Coptic Archaeology; specific subjects and sites
Archangel, **190**
Coptic art and portraiture, 270, 2004
icons of, 1278
priesthood structure analogy, 2015
see also Gabriel; Michael; Raphael; Suriel
Archbishop, **190–191**
in church hierarchy, 1229
Coptic in Jerusalem, 1325–1326
Archdeacon, **191**
in church hierarchy, 1229
ordination of, 887–888
Archebius, Saint, 2082
Archelaus of Neapolis, Bishop, **192**, 1136, 1575
Archellides, Saint, **192**, 2082
poetry on, 1985
Archimandrite, **192–194**
and *hegumenos* title, 1215
see also Proestos
Archippus (martyr), 1552
Architectural elements of churches, **194–225**
aisle, 194
ambulatory, 195, 222
apse, 195–196, 221
atrium, 195
baptistery, 197–200, *198*, *199*
cancelli, 200–201, 217
ceiling, 201–202
choir, 202
ciborium, 202
coffer, 203
colonnade, 204
column, 202–207, *205*, *206*, *207*
crypt, 208–209
diaconicon, 209
dome, 209–210
gallery, 210
Greco-Roman influence, 260
horseshoe arch, 211
iconostasis, 211–212
khūrus, 212–213, 218, 221, 223, 552, 553, 554, 555, 661
maqṣūrah, 213
naos, 213, 221, 222
narthex, 213–214, 222
nave, 215
niche, 215–216, *215*
pastophorium, 216
pillar, 217
porch, 217
presbytery, 217–218, 220
prothesis, 218
prothyron, 218
return aisle, 218
roof, 218
sacristy, 219
saddleback roof, 220
sanctuary, 220–221
synthronon, 221–222
tetraconch, 222
tribelon, 222
triconch, 222–223
triumphal arch, 223–224
vault, 224–225
see also Altar; Architecture; Basilica; Church architecture in Egypt; Church art; Nubian church architecture; Sculpture in stone; specific churches and monasteries (Dayr)
Architectural elements of monasteries. *See* Architecture; Refectory; specific Dayr headings
Architectural fragments, preservation of Coptic, 280
Architectural sculpture
at Ahnās, 74–76, 2112, 2116
at al-Ashmūnayn, 287–288
church at Dayr Anbā Bishoi (Suhāj), 739–740, 770
church at Dayr Anbā Shinūdah, 769–770
at Dayr Anbā Bishoi (Suhāj), 739–740, 770
at Dayr Apa Jeremiah (Saqqara), *776*, 776–777
made of wood, 2341–2347, *2342–2346*
ornamentation, 275
preservation, 280
in stone, 2112–2117
Architecture
Antinoopolis, 146–147, *146*, *147*
Arab conquest impact on, 275
al-Ashmūnayn, 285–287, *286*
al-Bagawāt, 326
Bāwīṭ, 364–366
Dayr Abū Fānah, 699–700, *699*
Dayr Abū Mattā, 706, *706*
Dayr al-ʿAdhrā, 713, *713*, 715, *715*
Dayr Anbā Bākhūm (al-Ṣawāmʿah Sharq), 730–731, *731*
Dayr Anbā Bisādah, 733
Dayr Anbā Bishoi (Scetis), 735–736, 2056
Dayr Anbā Hadrā, 745–746, *746*
Dayr Anbā Ṣamū'īl of Qalamūn, 760
Dayr Anbā Shinūdah, 766–769, *767*, *768*
Dayr al-ʿAzab, 784
Dayr al-Bakhīt, 786
Dayr al-Balaʿyzah, 787, *787*
Dayr al-Baramūs, 791–794, *792*, *793*, 2056
Dayr al-Barshah and Dayr al-Nakhlah, 795–796, *796*
Dayr al-Biṣrah, 797

Dayr al-Dīk, 799
Dayr al-Fakhūrī, 803–805, *803*, *804*
Dayr al-Ḥammām, 807, *807*
Dayr al-ʿIẓām (Asyūṭ), *809*, 809–810
Dayr al-Jabrāwī, 811–812, *811*, *812*
Dayr al-Janādlah, 705–706
Dayr al-Kubāniyyah, 815–816, *816*
Dayr al-Madīnah, 817–818
Dayr al-Majmaʿ, 820–821, *820*, *821*
Dayr al-Malāk Mīkhā'īl, 823, *823*
Dayr al-Malāk Mīkhā'īl (Qamūlah), 827, *828*
Dayr Mār Buqṭur (Qamūlah), 829–830, *830*
Dayr Mār Jirjis al-Jadīdī, 832–833, *832*
Dayr al-Maṭmar, 836–837
Dayr al-Maymūn, 839, *839*
Dayr al-Nāmūs, 844
Dayr al-Naqlūn, 845–846
Dayr al-Naṣārā, 847
Dayr Qaṣriyyah, 850
Dayr Qubbat al-Hawā, 851–852
Dayr al-Quṣayr (Ṭurah), 854–855, *855*
Dayr al-Rūmī, 857
Dayr al-Sabʿat Jibāl, 858
Dayr al-Ṣalīb, 860
Dayr al-Shuhadā' (Akhmīm), 865–866
Dayr al-Shuhadā' (Isnā), 869
Dayr Sitt Dimyānah, 872
Dayr al-Suryān, 879–880
earliest Coptic, 269
Ethiopian church, 998, 1425–1426
Ethiopian Orthodox Church, 998
Hathor temple (Dandarah), 690–691, *691*
Kellia site, 1401–1405
Kom Namrūd, 1418
Monastery of Mark the Evangelist (Qurnat Marʿī), 2042
Mount Sinai Monastery of Saint Catherine, 1682–1685
Nubian Christian, 1807–1810
octagon-domed church, 1823–1824
ornamentation, 275
Ramses Wissa Wassef, 2051
Roman, 907
see also Architectural sculpture; Art, historiography of Coptic; Art and architecture, Coptic; Basilica; Church architecture in Egypt; Sculpture in stone
Archives, **226–227**
of Basilios, 358–359
from Qaṣr Ibrīm, Nubia, 227
see also Libraries; Ostracon; Papyrus collections; Papyrus discoveries
Archives of Papas (pagarch), 226, **228–229**
Archon, 89, 94, **229**
in *Concept of Our Great Power*, 583
Hypostasis of the Archons, 1261
and John XI, Patriarch, 1344
and selection of patriarch, 1341, 1344, 1998, 1999
Argentina, Coptic collections, 1701
Ari, Saint (martyr), **229**, 1552
Ariadne, depicted in Coptic art, 1754, *1755*
Arianism, 115, **230**, 1385, 1669
Alexander I and, 82–84
in Alexandria, 97, 99
Anomoeans, 141–142
Antony of Egypt opposition to, 150
and *Apostolic Constitutions* authorship, 179
Athanasius I and, 298–302
Basil the Great opposition to, 351–352
Constantine, Bishop of Asyūṭ, and, 591–592
Constantine I and, 589–590
Constantinople, First Council of and, 593–595
and Cyril of Jerusalem, 681
Ethiopian opposition to, 995–997, 999–1000
Exoucontians and, 1081–1082
filioque and, 1112
Gregory of Nyssa opposition to, 1184
Hamai of Kahyor opposition to, 1204
homoiousion and, 1253
hymn collection, 1733
and hypostasis controversy, 1260
and Jacobite rebellion, 93–94
Jerome, Saint, opposition to, 1323
and Melitian schism, 591–592, 1584, 1878
and Nicaea, Council of, 1791–1792
in Pentapolis, 1934
and persecutions in Alexandria, 99
and Peter II, 1947
subordinationism and, 1484
Theodoret on, 2236
and Ulphilas' conversion of the Goths, 2285
see also Arius; Melitian schism; Semi-Arians
Arianus, Saint, **230–231**
and Ascla, Saint, 283
and Herpaese and Julianus, Saints, 1225
and Lacaron, Saint, 1424
and Lycopolis martyrdoms, 296
martyrdom of, 1552
and Nabraha, Saint, 1770
and Panine and Paneu legend, 1880, 1881
persecutions by, 296, 1551, 1552, 1553, 1554, 1555, 1557, 1559
and Psote of Scetis, 2031, 2032
and Ter and Erai, Saints, 2209
and Tolemaus, Saint, 2271
Aripsima (martyr), 1552
ʿArīsh, Al-, treaty of (1800), 1688
annulment, 1417
Aristages, Bishop, 1183
Aristarchus, 1618
Aristotelian category of relation, 1114–1115
Arius, 55, 81–85, 230, **231–232**
Alexander I and, 81–85
anathema declared against, 589–590
Eusebius of Caesarea and, 232, 1070–1071
hymns of, 1733
influence on Ethiopian theology, 984
on Logos, 1791
on Lucian of Antioch, 1484
on nature of Christ, 173, 232, 547
opposition to *homoousion* concept, 1253
Peter I and, 1944
seen as Antichrist, 143
and semi-Arians, 2119
and subordinationism, 2156–2157
see also Arianism

Arius of Shetnusi (martyr), 1552
Ark, as Eucharistic vessel, 1064
Arles, Council of (314), paschal controversy, 1906
Armada (martyr), 1553
Arman (martyr), 1554
Armant (Hermonthis), **233-234**, *233*
Abraham, Bishop of, 13
ceramics of. *See* Ceramics, Coptic
inscription list of bishops, 1291
John, Saint and Bishop of, 1353-1354
monasteries in region of, 839-840, 844, 847-848, 849, 863, 1656, 1657, 1658, 2069
papyrus collection, 1895
Pisentius of, 1978
stelae from, 2149, 2150, 2151, 2161-2162, 2168
tombstone material and shape, 1295
Armanus. *See* Armenius and his mother (martyrs)
Armanyus, Muʿallim, 1737
Armenian language
inscriptions in, 1290
manuscripts and documents, 235
Armenians and Copts, **234-235**, 764, 782
Gregory the Illuminator evangelization, 1183
monophysitism, 547-548
Armenius and his mother (martyrs), 1552, 1555
Army, Roman, **235-238**
ammona provisions for, 135-136
and taxation in Eqypt, 2203
and Theban Legion, 2231-2233
see also Castrum; Costume, military
Arnobius, on incense use, 1472
Arrowheads, 1605
Arsānī al-Miṣrī (Melchite monk), **239**
Arsenal of Tunis, **239**, 2286
Arsenius (martyr of Diocletian era), 1552
Arsenius and Eulogius (martyrs), 831, 1554
Arsenius of Scetis and Ṭurah, Saint, 32, 65, **240-241**, 789, 790, 1976
feast day, 2082
hymns attributed to, 1726
and John Colobos, Saint, 1360
at Monastery of Metanoia, 1608
on mummification, 1697
retirement and death near Dayr al-Quṣayr, 853-854
and Theodorus of Pherme, Saint, 2239
and Theophilus, Patriarch, 2249
Arsinoë. *See* Fayyūm, City of
Art, Byzantine influences on Coptic, **241-243**, 260, 2319
see also Islamic influences on Coptic art
Art, church. *See* Art and architecture; Church art; Monastery paintings; Painting, Coptic mural; Sculpture in stone; specific churches and monasteries
Art, Coptic. *See* Art headings; Icons; Illumination; Monastery paintings; Museums; Painting, Coptic mural; Portraiture; Sculpture in stone
Art, Coptic influence on European, **243-250**
Ascension and Triumph of Christ, 244-247, *245-247*
devil, 247-248, *249*
Michael, Saint, **250**
Virgo lactans, 243-244, *243*
see also Art, Coptic and Irish
Art, Coptic and Irish, **251-254**, 418-419
Art, Ethiopian. *See* Ethiopian art
Art, historiography of Coptic, **254-261**
Art, Irish. *See* Art, Coptic and Irish
Art, Nobatian kingdoms, 1675
Art, Sassanid influences on Coptic. *See* Sassanid influences on Coptic art
Art, Syrian influences on Coptic. *See* Syrian influences on Coptic art
Art and architecture, Coptic, 255, **261-278**, *262-278*
church art, 355-356
Coptic Museum (Old Cairo) collection, 607-*608*, *607*
historical origins, 261-262
hunting theme, 1258-1259
Islamic influences on, 1310-1312
Louvre (Paris) collection, 1483
at Mareotis, 1527-1528
monastery paintings, 1659-1660
problems of dating, 693-694
State Museum of Berlin collection, 2146-2147
warrior depiction, 2319-2320
see also Architectural elements of churches; Biblical subjects; Bone and ivory carving; Book decoration; Ceramics; Christian subjects; Church architecture in Egypt; Cross, Triumph of; Glass; Metalwork; Monastery paintings; Mythological subjects; Painting, Coptic mural; Portraiture; Sculpture in stone; Statuary; Stela; Symbols in Coptic art; Textiles; Woodwork
Artemius (martyr), 1120
Artemon, 1638
Artemus, 1869
Art History Museum, Vienna, 1891
Artifact dating, 693-694
Artisan-service occupations. *See* Copts in late medieval Egypt
Artophorion, as Eucharistic vessel, 1064-1065
Art preservation, **278-280**
Art survivals from ancient Egypt, **280-282**
Asʿad, Al-. *See* al-Maqrīzī
Asʿad Abū al-Faraj Hibat Allāh ibn al-ʿAssāl, Al-, **282-283**, 1462, 1748, 2075
see also Awlād al-ʿAssāl
Aṣbagh, Al- (governor of Egypt), 85
Asbah (martyr), 1552
Ascension, Feast of the, 1105, 1125, 1904
Ascension of Christ
iconography of, 244-247, *245-247*, 555, 556, 558
and orientation toward the East, 1846
Origen on, 1850
pilgrimages and, 1968
Triumph of Christ, 525-526
Ascension of Isaiah, 166
Ascension of Mary. *See* Assumption

Asceticism
  Abraam I, Saint, 10
  and abstinence, 17
  Achillas, Saint (monk), 56
  Ammonius of Kellia, 113
  Aphu, 154
  Arsenius of Scetis and Ṭurah, 240–242
  Basil the Great, 351
  celibacy, 1543
  and Coptic doctrine of the Holy Spirit, 1249
  Ebionites, 929
  Egyptian monasticism compared with Syrian, 1662
  and Egyptian monasticism origins, 1661
  Elias of Bishwāw, 952–953
  Encratites, 958–959
  Ethiopian monastic, 993–994
  Evagrius Ponticus on, 1076
  Gangra, Council of, on, 1138
  Hieracas of Leontopolis, 1229
  Isaiah of Scetis on, 1306
  Isidorus of Pelusium on, 1310
  James, Saint, 1320–1321
  John Calybites, 1357
  John Sabas, 1369
  Palamon, Saint, and, 1876
  Pambo, Saint, 1877–1878
  Paul of Tamma, Saint, 1924, 1925
  Pidjimi, Saint, 1966–1967
  pilgrimages linked with, 1968
  Poemen, 1984
  Pshoi of Scetis, 2029
  Pshoi of Ṭūd, 2030
  Sara, Saint, 2094
  seven ascetics of Tūnah, 2122
  see also Anachoresis; Anchorites; Manichaeism; Monasticism, Pachomian
Ascetic Sermon (Stephen the Theban), 2155
Ascla, Saint (martyr), **283**, 1552
Asclepiades, **283**
  as brother of Heraiscus, 1221–1222
  as father of Horapollon, 1255–1256
Asclepius 21–29, **284**
Asfal al-Arḍ. *See* Dayr Asfal al-Arḍ
Aṣfūn al-Maṭā'nah, 802
Ashmūn, **285**, 635
Ashmūnayn, Al- (Hermopolis Magna), 37, 114, **285–288**
  atrium of great church of, 196
  basilica, 264
  church architecture, 552–553
  and Coptic scupture in stone, 2117
  Dayr Abū Anūb at, 696
  Dayr Abū Fānah at, 698
  Dayr Apa Anūb at, 770
  as early bishopric, 1866
  and excavations of Sāmī Gabrā, 2090
  and flight into Egypt, 233, 841, 1976
  history and architecture, 285–287, *286*, *287*
  monasteries at, 1654; *see also* specific monasteries
  monastic murals at, 1874
  papyrus collections, 1891, 1893
  Sāwīrus ibn al-Muqaffa' and, 2100
  sculpture, 287–288
  shrines and pilgrimages to, 1976, 1977
  transept, 1212
Ashmūn Ṭanāh, **288**
Ashraf Khalīl, Al-, 1517
Askinah, **288**
Aspasmos. *See* Kiss of Peace
Asqalun (martyr), 1552
Asqīt. *See* Scetis
Asra. *See* Pihour, Pisouri, and Asra (martyrs)
Assemani, Joseph Aloysius, 289
Assemani, Joseph Simeonis, 289
  and 'Abd al-Masīḥ manuscript attributions, 6
  Chronicon Orientale translation by, 548
Assemani, Simon, 289
Assemani, Stephen Evodius, 289
Assemani family, **289**
Association of Schools of Upper Egypt, 1330
Assumption, **289–293**, 1096
  Arabic tradition, 293
  Coptic tradition, 290–292
Assumption, Feast of the, 2256
Assumption of the *Theotokos*, Fast of the, 1094
Astarte (pagan deity), 1150, 1866
Asṭāsī al-Rūmī (Eustathius the Greek), **293–294**, 1279
Asterisk, as Eucharistic vessel, 1065
Asterius
  and Lucian of Antioch, 1484
  Marcellus and, 1526
Astrolate (magician and martyr), 1552
Aswan, **294–296**, *294*, *295*
  gravestone prayer inscriptions, 1294
  inscriptions, 764
  monasteries near, 850, 870, 1657
  Philae and, 1855, 1954
  tombstone material, 1295
Aswan, Saint, 2083
Aswan Dam, 1484, 1955
Aswan ware. *See* Ceramics, Coptic, types
Asyūṭ (Lycopolis), 114, **296–297**, 1976, 2029
  and Banī Kalb, 335
  as birthplace of John of Lycopolis, Saint, 1363
  Dayr Abū Bifām at, 696, 697
  Dayr Abū Maqrūfah and Dayr al-Janādlah in, 704
  Dayr al-'Adhrā, 714
  Dayr al-'Awanah near, 784
  Dayr Anbā Sāwīrus, 760–761
  Dayr al-Biṣrah, 796–797
  Dayr Harmīnā, 808
  Dayr al-'Iẓām, 809–810
  Dayr al-Jabrāwī, 810–812
  Dayr al-Muṭṭin, 842–843
  Dayr al-Naṣārā, 848
  Dayr Rīfah, 855–856
  Dayr al-Shalīd near, 861
  Holy Family visit to, 927
  icons of Asṭāsī al-Rūmī at, 293–294
  as Manichaean center, 1521
  Melitian bishopric, 1585
  monasteries in region of, 1654–1655, 1658; *see also* specific monasteries
  soldier-martyrs at, 1964
  see also Coptic Congress of Asyūṭ
Asyūṭī, Naṣr Lūzah, al-, 1466, 1467
'Aṭallah, Philip, 1466
'Atallāh, Wahīb, 1911
Atargatis (pagan deity), 1866
Aṭfīḥ (bishopric), 849
Athanasia of Mīnūf, Saint, 31, 1554, 2082
Athanasian Creed, **297–298**, 1112
Athanāsī al-Misrī (monk), **297**
Athanasius I, Apostolic Saint and Patriarch, 82, 84, 99, **298–302**, 686, 926, 1456, 1478, 1559, 1610, 1666, 1669, 1863, 2032

Athanasius I, Apostolic Saint and Patriarch (*cont.*)
Abraham of Farshūṭ support of, 12
and Aetius, 141–142
and Alexander I, 84
on anathema, 127–128
and Ansinā (Antinoopolis), 142–143
anti-Manichaeism, 1522
and Antony of Egypt, 149–150
Apollinarianism refutation by, 173
on Apostolic Canons, 453
as archdeacon, 191
and Arianism, 232, 590, 609, 1792
and Arianist Exoucontians, 1081–1082
on baptism, 337
and Basil the Great, 351–352
and Besa, Abbot, 378–379
bilingualism in Greek and Coptic, 1178
and bishop's translation, 398
on canon of the Scripture, 2109
on celibacy, 476, 478
Christology. *See subhead* nature of Christ
on *communicatio idiomatum*, 578
on communion of the sick, 580
on congregational participation in responsory, 2058
consecration as bishop at age 23, 393–395
on consubstantiation, 597–598
Coptic hymn texts attributed to, 1726, 1733
Coptic text on life of, 1455
on costume of religious, 652
cycle of, 666–667
dates of patriarchy, 1914
and *Didascalia*, 900
and Didymus the Blind, 900
and doxology, 923
and Epistle to Marcellinus, 567
and Ethiopian Christian conversion, 312–313
and Ethiopian church ties, 980, 995–997, 999–1000
and Ethiopian monasticism, 990–991
on Eucharist, 597–598
and Eusebius of Caesarea, 1070–1071
exile, and aid from unnamed virgin, 2324
exile in Ethiopia, 984
feast day, 2082
and *filioque* justification, 1115
five exiles of, 299–301
on Gabriel, Archangel, 1136
and *Gloria in Excelsis*, 1147
on the Holy Spirit, 1249–1250
and *homoousion* concept, 1253–1254
and hypostatic union, 1262
on Incarnation, 1287, 1288–1290
on Iṭfīḥ bishopric, 1313
Jerusalem visit, 1324
and John the Baptist relics, 1355
Jovian, Emperor, support for, 1376–1377
and Julian the Apostate, 1381, 1382
and Kallinikos, Bishop, 1089
letters of, 2008
and *Life of Antony*, 116, 149, 150–151, 728, 1663
on Mareotis, 1527
on martyrology, 1549
and Melitian schism, 1584
on Michael, Archangel, 1619
on miracle of the cross, 660
on musical instruments' symbolism, 1738
on nature of Christ, 523, 1638, 1669
on New Testament, 2109–2110
on Nikiou bishops, 1793
and Origen, 471, 1855
and Pambo, Saint, 1878
patristic writings, 1920, 1921
Philostorgius on, 1959
poetry on, 1985, 1986
and power of Alexandrian See, 913, 914
on Psoï, 2030
and Sabellianism, 2072
and Sakhā, 2087
on Samannūd, 2090
and Sarapion of Tmuis, Saint, 2087, 2095–2096
successor, 1947
and Theodorus of Alexandria, Saint, 2055, 2238
and Theophilus, Patriarch, 2248
and Timothy I, 2263
and Western monasticism, 417
on wooden altar, 580
writings, 301–302, 1920, 1921
Athanasius II, Saint and Patriarch, **302**, 2082
and Acacian schism, 44
dates of patriarchy, 1915
Athanasius III, Saint and Patriarch, 33, **302–303**
burial site, 848
contemporaries, 686
dates of patriarchy, 1917
and Yūsāb, Bishop, 2359
Athanasius I (1725–1766), Archbishop of Jerusalem, 1325
Athanasius, Bishop of Jerusalem, and Coptic relations with Rome, 610
Athanasius of Anazarbus (Collucianist), 1484
Athanasius of Antioch (Jacobite patriarch), **304**
Athanasius of Clysma (martyr), **304–306**, 1140, 1552
Athanasius of Qūṣ, Bishop, **303–304**, 829, 1106, 1132, 2045
Athenaeus (2nd-century author), on Church of Saint Michael, 1617
Athenagoras, 1472, 1867
Atheniensis, 1445
Athom (martyr), 1558
Athribis. *See* Atrīb
Atiya, Aziz S., 1230
Atnātēwos, Ethiopian prelate, 1036–1037
Atonement, **306–307**, 1287
Atrasis (martyr), 1552
Atrīb, **307**
Greek inscriptions found at, 1292
toponymy, 2272
Atripe. *See* Suhāj
Atrīs, **307–308**
Atrium, 195, 1414
Atticus, Patriarch of Constantinople, 2033
Audians, 143
Audientia episcopalis, **308**
ancient correspondence on, 401
curtailments, 945
on penalization, 1931
see also Interdict
Augury. *See* Lecanoscopy
Augustine, Saint, 921, 1921
on archdeacon rank, 191
on baptism and immersion, 1286

on canon of Scripture, 2110
and conversion, 151
description of heaven, 1214
on Egyptian worship, 1867
on incense use, 1472
and Joseph the Carpenter, Saint, 1371
on Kiss of Peace, 1416
on Last Judgment, 1379
and Lord's Prayer, 1481
on marriage, 1543
on mummification, 1697
Neoplatonist influence on, 1982
patristic writings, 1920, 1921
and Pelagius, 1929, 1930
on Trinity, 1114–1115
Augustus. *See* Octavian Augustus
Aūr (Coptic legend), 845
Aurelianus, Emperor, 1556
patriarch under, 1914
Aurelius Achilleus, 906
Aurelius of Carthage, Bishop, 921
Aurelius Victor, 907
Australia
Coptic churches, 1622–1623
Coptic collections, 1701
Austria
Coptic churches, 1624
Coptic collections, 1702, 2049
papyrus collections, 1891
Authentikos Logos, **309**
and *Interpretation of Knowledge*, 1301
'Awaḍ, Aḥmad Ḥāfiẓ, 1990
'Awaḍ, Jirjis Philūthāwus, 1911
'Awaḍ, Louis, 1995
Awlād al-'Assāl, family of, **309–311**
and al-Ṣafī ibn al-'Assāl, 2075
works of, 1462–1463
see also Fakhr al-Dawlah Abū al-Mufaḍḍal ibn al-'Assāl
Awshīm. *See* Karanis
Awshiyah, **311**
Awshiyah, melodies of. *See* Music, Coptic
Awsīm, **311–312**
Axum (Aksum), **312–313**, 1802
Aybak, Sultan, 1517
'Ayin. *See Appendix*
'Ayn 'Amūr (ruins), **313**, 1658
'Ayn Bardah, 728
see also Monasteries of the Eastern Desert
'Ayn al-Ghazāl, 1517
'Ayn Murrah, **314**
inscription list of monks, 1291
'Ayn Nisīmah. *See* Qasr Nisīmah
Ayrout, Habib, Father, 1330
'Ayyād Bishāy, 1465
Ayyubid dynasty and the Copts, **314–315**, 1534, 1535, 2037
and Islamization, 940
Azarī, **315–316**, 1649, 1652
Azhar 'Abdallāh al-Shabrūhī, Al-, Shaykh, 1538
Azhar University, Al-, 1465
'Azīz, Al-, Caliph, 1097, 1098, 1461, 1524
'Azmī, Maḥmūd, 1995

B

Baalsemes (pagan deity), 1500–1501
Ba'arāt, 800
Bābah (second month of Coptic calendar), 438, 440, 2175–2176
Babīj, **317**
Babluhiyyah. *See* Tanis
Babnūda. *See* Paphnutius the Hermit, Saint
Babylas, Bishop of Antioch, 889, 1552
Babylon, 92, **317–323**
Arab seizure of, 100, 185–187, 655
castrum of, 465
metropolitan see of, 1613
Qaṣr al-Sham' fortress, 2038
on route of flight into Egypt, 1118
as shipbuilding center, 89
see also Church of al-Mu'allaqah; Miṣr
Bacchus (martyr), 1558
Bacchylides, 1889
Bachatly, Charles, **323**, 779
Bacheus, **324**
Badāri, Al-
monasteries at, 1655
pilgrimages to, 1971
Badasius (martyr), 1552
Badet, Louis, 1743
Badr al-Jamālī, **324–325**, 782, 1099, 1128, 1535, 1574
Bagawāt, Al-, **326–329**, *327*, *328*
inscriptions found at, 1290, 1291
necropolis at, 1873
Baghām ibn Baqūrah al-Ṣawwāf, **329–330**, 329–330
Baḥariyyah, al-, 1658
Bahīj, **330**
Bahjūrah, **330**
Bahnā (martyr), 1552
Bahnām and Sarah (martyrs), 1552
Bahnasā, Al-, **330**, 808
and Banī Suef, 335
and Butrus, Bishop, recasting of Holy Week Scripture readings, 1251
Coptic sculpture in stone at, 2112, 2116
remains and representations of Coptic clothing. *See* Costume, civil
Bahnasāwī, Al-. *See* Latson, Saint
Bahram I, 1519
Bahrām, Vizier, 702, 764, 782, 1128
Bahrein, Coptic churches in, 1621
Bahri Mamluks, 750
Bahr Yūsuf, Dayr Bālūjah and, 788
Baḥṭīṭ (village), 1655
Bā'issah. *See* Athanasia of Mīnūf, Saint
Bajūj (martyr), 1552
Bajūrī, Shaykh Ibrāhīm, al-, **330–331**, 1636
Bajush (martyr), 1552
Bakhānis-Tmoushons, **331**, 731–732, 1656
Bakharas. *See* Faras
Bakhumius of Beheira, Bishop, 1624
Bākhūm, Saint. *See* Pachomius, Saint
Bakr al-Shadhlī, Abū, 884
Bakwa. *See* Menarti
Balāgh, Al- (publication), 1990
Balānā (martyr), 1552
Balances. *See* Weights and balances
Baldachin, **332**
Baldwin (Bardawīl) (crusader), 1090, 1488
Balestri, Giuseppe, **332**
Ballana kingdom and culture, **332–333**
Nubian evangelization, 1802
and royal tombs of Nobatae kings, 1797
and Talmīs, 2200
Ballāṣ, Al-, **333**
Bālūjah. *See* Dayr Bālūjah

Balyanā, Al-, Dayr Anbā Bākhūm near, 729
Bamhā, 1653
Banā, **333–334**, 925
Banāwān, al-, **334**
Bane, Abbā, 698
Banī Ezra (synagogue), 320
Banī Ḥasan and Speos Artemidos, **334–335**
Banī Kalb, **335**
Banī Khaṣīb. *See* Minyā
Banī Murr, pilgrimages to, 1971
Banī Mūsā. *See* Dayr Abū Mūsā
Bāninā (martyr), 1552
Banī Riḍah, Dayr al-'Adhrā, 714
Banī Suef, **335**
  Dayr al-Sanqūriyyah, 861
  women's religious community, 2325
Banū al-Kanz, **335–336**, 344, 1955
  and Nubian Islamization, 1803
Banū al-Muṭī (Christian clan), 1959
Bapheús (Coptic textile term), 2221
Baptism, **336–338**, 1699
  and absolution of women, 339
  administration of, 336–338
  Apostles' Creed during, 178–179
  awshiyahi recited during, 311
  candle use during, 446
  circumcision relationship with, 1106
  and confirmation, 585–586
  deaconesses' assistance at, 888
  Dialogue of the Savior on, 898
  Didache on, 898
  Dionysius the Great on rebaptism of repentant apostates, 910
  and Epiphany, 1103
  and Eucharist, 1056
  features of, 336–338
  Hippolytus on, 182
  and immersion, 1285–1286
  importance in Coptic family life, 1087
  of infants, 338
  instruction for. *See* Catechumen
  Monophysites on, 1673
  and Nicene Creed, 1792–1793
  origin of, 336–338
  Paraphrase of Shem on, 1902
  and Paul's laying-on of hands, 1433
  Pelagianism on, 1930
  and pilgrimages, 1968
  poem in *Ordo* on, 1132
  rite of, 137–138
  ritual books for, 1729
  statements of faith, 178–179
  turning toward the East during, 1846
Baptismal font. *See* Baptistery
Baptism of Jesus
  depicted in Coptic art, 529–530, 537
  see also Epiphany
Baptistery, 197–200, *198*, *199*
Baptistery, consecration of, **342–343**
Baqīrah (deacon), 1573
Baqṭ Treaty, **343–344**, 547, 1099, 1514, 2037
  Ibn Salīm al-Aswānī and, 1271
  and Nubian independence, 921, 1800, 1802
Baramhāt (seventh month of Coptic calendar), 439, 442, 2181–2183
Baramūdah (eighth month of Coptic calendar), 439, 442, 2183–2184
Baramūn, al-, **344–345**, 1556
Baramūsī, Father Antonios, al-, 1622
Barārī, al-. *See* Pilgrimages
Barbara (martyr), 1552–1553
Barbarikários (Coptic weaving term), 2221
Barbīsh, **349**
Barbiyyah, 1649
Bardenhewer, Otto, **345**, 1921
Bardesanes (Syrian writer), 1635
Bar Hebraeus, **345–346**, 1923
Bari, Council of (1098), 1113
Barjanūs, Dayr Anbā Bākhūm, 729
Barjawān (tutor to al-Ḥākim), 18
Barkalas (martyr), 1553
Barlām and Yuwāṣaf, **346**
Barmius. *See* Primus
Barnabas (Judaic-Christian missionary in Alexandria), 1150
Barnabas, Saint, 1529, 2082
  and laying-on of hands, 1432
Barns, John Wintour Baldwin, **347**
Baronius, Cesare Cardinal, **347**
Barqah, 1934
Barqūq, Sultan, 1570
Barsanuphians, **347–348**, 1553–1534
  at Rashīd, 2054
  Simon I on, 2139
Barsanuphius, Saint, **348–349**, 1553
Barsbay, Caliph, 1130 1130
Barsuma. *See* Barsūm the Naked, Saint
Barsūm the Naked, Saint, **348–349**, 550, 1626, 2082
  at Dayr Shahrān, 862, 863
  hagiographical collection, 1780
  laura of, 718
  predictions about Benjamin II, 377
Bartalomēwos, Ethiopian prelate, 1012–1013, 1054
Bartholomew, Saint, 764, 1183
Baruch, in Apocryphon of Jeremiah, 170
Baruh Ahtah Adonai (Jewish benediction), 1731
Bashans (ninth month of Coptic calendar), 439, 442–443, 2184–2186
Bashmūr, al-, **349**
Bashmuric dialect. *See Appendix*
Bashmuric revolts, **349–351**, 1411
  affected by Islamization, 938
  and burning of Rashīd, 2054
Bashrudat, al-. *See* Bashmūr, al-
Bashrut. *See* Bashmūr, al-
Basidi (martyr), 1553
Basil (martyr), 1553
Basil II, Emperor, 1098
Basil of Ancyra, 1254
Basil (Basilios), Bishop (martyr), 1553
Basil of Caesarea. *See* Basil the Great
Basil the Great, Saint and Archbishop, 114, **351–352**, 1183, 1184, 1309
  anaphora, 71, 121–123, 124, 1066–1067
  anaphora used in Ethiopian liturgy, 988–990
  on angels, 132
  and the Anomoeans, 142
  on Athanasius I, 298
  and baptism, 337
  on canonical hours, 449
  on celibacy, 476
  condemnation of *cheirotonia*, 517

and Constantine of Asyūṭ, 592
cycle of, 667
on Eucharist, 1060
and Evagrius Ponticus, 1076–1077
and *filioque* justification, 1115
and Greek monasticism, 1663
on incense use, 1472
and Julian the Apostate, 1380
and liturgical music, 1733; *see also* Liturgy of Saint Basil
on matins, 1568
on Mercurius of Caesarea, 1592, 1593
on Michael, Archangel, 1619
on Monarchianism, 1638
on nature of Christ, 523
as older brother of Saint Gregory of Nyssa, 1184
on orientation toward the East during prayers, 1846
and Origen, 1854, 1855
patristic writings, 1920, 1921
on regulations for nuns, 1822
on Sabellianism, 2072
and use of compline, 582
and Western monasticism, 417
see also Anaphora of Saint Basil; Canons of Saint Basil

Basilica, 269, **353–355**
at al-Bagawāt, 326
function replaced by Bayt al-Nisā', 373
Greco-Roman influence on Coptic, 260, 264
at Hawwāriyyah, 1211–1212, *1211*
at Ḥilwān, *1233*
Nubian, 1807–1810, *1808*, *1809*

Basilidas (martyr), 14, 127, 892, 1553

Basilides, **356–357**, 1148, 1151, 1307, 1866
and Besamon, Saint, 379
as heretic, 1222
and Justus, Saint, 1386
and Ter and Erai, Saints, 2209
and Theodorus, Saint, 2238
and Victor Stratelates, Saint, 2303

Basilides, Bishop of the Pentapolis, 912, 1612

Basilides, family of (martyrs), 1553, 1554, 1556, 1559
see also Basilidas (martyr)

Basilides the General. *See* Basilidas (martyr)

Basilios, archive of, 226, 228, 229, **358–359**

Basilios I, Archbishop of Jerusalem, 872, 1325

Basilios II, Archbishop of Jerusalem, **358**, 873, 1246, 1325, 1614

Basilios III, Archbishop of Jerusalem, **358**, 1246, 1325

Basilios IV, Archbishop of Jerusalem, 873–874, 1245, 1326, 2049

Basilios the Great. *See* Basilios II, Archbishop of Jerusalem

Basiliscus, 1671

Basilius, Abuna (20th-century Ethiopia), 1613

Basilius, Bey, **359–360**, 1636

Basil of Nikiou, Bishop, 1794

Basil of Oxyrhynchus, **360**, 1778

Basin and ewer, 1469, 1601–1602

Basket, eucharistic bread, 1473

Basketmaking, 1640, 1662

Basset, René, **360**

Bassos, Bishop, 925

Basṭah, **360–361**

Batanūn, Al-, 361
pilgrimages to, 1971

Bath of the Infant Jesus, depicted in Coptic art, 530–531, *530*

Baths, 690

Baṭn al-Ḥajar, **361–362**
and Nubian archaeology, 1805
and Nubian islamization, 1804
Nubian monasteries in, 1817

Batos (melody type), 1986
see also Wāṭus

Batra (martyr), 1553, 1556

Baumeister, T., as Coptic hagiographer, 1192

Baumstark, Anton, on use of *Hōs*, 1726

Ba'ūnah (tenth month of Coptic calendar), 439, 443, 2186–2187

Bavarian State Library, Munich, 1893

Bāwīṭ, **362–372**, *365*, *366*
Abraham of Hermonthis portrait found at, 402
Apollo of, 1953
archive, 226–227
art at, 2004–2005
cells, 270
ceramics of. *See* Ceramics, Coptic
and Christian subjects in Coptic art, 533
church artwork, 406
and Coptic scupture in stone, 2117
Dayr Bālūjah and, 788, 1654
decoration of monastery cells at, 525, 555, *556*
examples of hunting theme in Coptic art at, 1258–1259
excavation at, 256, 694, 700, 1482, 1483
founders of, 362–363, 843
fresco depicting magical objects, 1509–1510
frescoes, Islamic-influenced, 1311
frescoes of the Virgin Enthroned at, 542, 543
fresco of Phoibammon at, 1965
iconographical paintings at, 245–247, *246*, *250*
inscriptions found at, 193, 1291, 1292
Islamic-influenced Coptic art, 1311, *1311*
Menas, Saint, at, 1588–1589
monastery mural painting at, 1874, 1875; *see also* frescoes subheads
paintings at, 272–273, 402, 1588–1589, 1660
remains and representations of Coptic clothing. *See* Costume, civil
representation of military costumes at, 650
sculpture in stone at, 2112, 2115
wood carvings at, 1753

Bayaḍ al-Naṣārā
monasteries at, 714, 1653
pilgrimages to, 1971

Bayahū, Al-, pilgrimages to, 1972

Baybars, Sultan, 1517–1518, 1588

Bayt al-'Ajīn, **372**

Bayt al-Nisā', **373**
in Babylonian church, 322
at Dayr Abū Ḥinnis, 373, 703

Beatty, Chester, 518–519, 1885, 1894
see also Chester Beatty Biblical Papyri; Chester Beatty Coptic Papyri; Chester Beatty Library

Beckwith, John, 257, 258

Bede (8th-century historian), 418–419

Bedouins
and fugitive Mamluks, 1538
sacking of Dayr Anbā Antūniyūs, 720, 722
sacking of Dayr Anbā Būlā, 742, 1134
sacking of Dayr Anbā Maqār, 750
sacking of Dayr Anbā Ṣamū'īl of Qalamūn, 758
sacking of Dayr Mar Maryam, 835
sacking of Scetis, 1534
sackings of monasteries, 1449; *see also* specific names
Beheirah Province
Damanhūr as capital, 686–687
monasteries in, 1646
Beinecke Library (Yale University)
and Nag Hammadi Codices, 1771
papyrus collection, 1895
Beirut, Lebanon, 1098
Beja tribes, **373**, 905
and Axum, 312
Ibn Ḥawqal on, 1266
Ibn Salīm al-Aswānī on, 1272
influence on Ballana kingdom and culture, 332
influence on Banū al-Kanz, 335
and Nabis, Bishop, 1769
and Nestorius, 1786
Qaṣr Ibrīm seizure by, 2037
Bejrash. *See* Faras
Bekkos, John, 1114, 1115, 1116
Belgium
Coptic collections, 1702
papyrus collections, 1891
Belial. *See* Antichrist; Satan
Belisarius (Byzantine general), 1385, 1675, 2019, 2020
Bell, Harold Idris, **374**
Bellerophon and the Chimera, depicted in Coptic art, 1754–1755
Bells, 1605, *1605*, 1738, 1739
Belts, 645
Beltz, W., 1893
Benam and Sarah (martyrs), 1553
Benedict, Saint (monk), 417
Benedict VIII, Pope (Rome), 1113
Bénédite, George, 1481
Benevolent societies, Coptic, **374–375**
Benevolent societies, Coptic, role in education, 933
Benjamin (monk of Nitria), 915
Benjamin I, Saint and Patriarch, 94, 102, **375–377**, 926, 1609, 1667, 1940, 1979
Agathon of Alexandria as successor to, 65
and Arab conquest of Egypt, 188, 682
and Arab rule, 656, 947
Cyrus al-Muqawqas persecution of, 682–683
dates of patriarchy, 1915
Dayr Maṭrā residence, 837
feast day, 2082
and forty-nine martyrs of Scetis, 1120
and John, Hegumenos of Scetis, 1362
and the Kellia, 1397
panegyrics by, 1456
refuge at Dayr Qibriyūs, 850
Saint Mark's Cathedral construction, 1531–1532
sanctuary at Dayr Anbā Maqār, *751*, 751, *752*
Benjamin II, Patriarch, **377–378**
burial at Dayr Shahrān, 378, 862
dates of patriarchy, 1917
and Ethiopian Sabbath controversy, 993, 1050–1051
and Ēwosṭātēwos, Ethiopian saint, 1050–1051
and reconstruction of Dayr Anbā Bishoi, 734
successor, 1948
visit to Dayr Yuḥannis Kama, 883
Benjamin and Eudoxia (martyrs), 1553
Berbers
capture of Christodoulus, 1573
in Pentapolis region, 1933, 1934
plunder of Damrū, 689
plunder of Dayr Anbā Maqār, 750, 753, 1652
plunder of Dayr Yuḥannis al-Qaṣīr, 884
plunder of Scetis monasteries, 1120
Berlin, Germany. *See* State Museum of Berlin
Bermudez, João, and first Portuguese mission to Ethiopia, 1017–1018
Bernard the Wise, 783, 1089, 1646
Bert, Alexis, 700
Bertrada, Queen, 2293, 2302
Beryllus, Bishop of Bostra, 1638
Bes (pagan deity), 1869, 1870
Besa, Abbot, **378–379**, 737, 1448
as desert father, 894
and Shenute, Saint, 762, 2131
and Zenobios, 2371
Besamon, Saint, **379**, 1553, 1880
Bess (pagan deity), 134
Bessarion, Saint, **379**, 1114, 2082
Bessus, Saint, 2082
Bethlehem. *See* Holy Land
Betrothal customs, **379–380**, 1481
see also Marriage
Beṭrus Aghā Armāniyūs, 1636
Bi-Amr-Illāh Abū 'Alī Manṣūr, 939
Bibāwī, Ibrahīm Ḥunayn, al-, 1465
Bible
Arabic, 80; *see also* Old Testament, Arabic versions of the
canon of the Scripture, 2108–2111
Coptic version. *See* Old Testament, Coptic translation of; New Testament, Coptic versions
Greek. *See* Bible manuscripts, Greek
Hesychian, 1226
Latin translation by Jerome, Saint, 1323
lectern, 1434–1435
lectionary, 1435–1437
Lucianic texts, 1484
manuscripts in National Library, Paris, 1776–1783
multilingual, 782
Polyglot and Arabic versions of Old Testament, 1827, 1829–1830, 1832, 1835
Polyglot of London, 80
see also New Testament; Old Testament
Bible manuscripts, Greek, **380–381**, 566–567
Acts, Michigan papyrus of, 58
see also Codex Alexandrinus; Codex Ephraemi Syri; Codex Sinaiticus; Codex Vaticanus
Bible text, Egyptian, **381–382**
Biblical subjects in Coptic art, **382–390**, *384*, *387*, *388*
and hunting theme, 1259
icons of, 1276–1279
Roman influence on, 270
types, 2283–2284
see also Art and architecture,

Coptic; Christian subjects in Coptic art; Illumination; Mythological subjects in Coptic art
Biblical subjects in Coptic poetry, 1985
Biblioteca Medicea Laurentiana, Florence, Italy, 1894
Bibliotheca Bodmeriana (Bodmer Library), Zurich, Switzerland, 404
Bidaba. *See* Patape, Bishop of Coptos (martyr)
Biet Giorgios (house of George) (Lālibalā church), 1425
Biet Maryam (house of Mary) (Lālibalā church), 1425
Bifām, Saint, 696, 697
Bijīj. *See* Jabal Khashm al-Qu'ud
Bikabes. *See* Pihebs (martyr)
Bikawarnidās (*Lōbsh*), 1479
Bi Khā Īsūs. *See* Dayr al-Maghṭis
Bīkhībis. *See* Pihebs (martyr)
Bilabel, Friedrich, **390–391**
Bilad, **391**
Bilbeis, **391**
  Dayr Mart Maryam, 835
  and flight into Egypt, 1118
Biljāy, **391**
Bilqās
  Dayr Sitt Dimyānah, 870
  monasteries near, 783, 818, 838
  pilgrimages to, 1968, 1969, 1970
Bima. *See* Epima, Saint
Bimīn, Saint. *See* Pamin, Saint
Bīmīn. *See* Poemen, Saint
Bināyin. *See* Tayaban (martyr)
Bīr al-ʿAẓāmah. *See* Dayr al-ʿIẓām (Monastery of the Bones)
Birmā, **392**
  churches dedicated to Saint George at, 1140
Birth of Christ. *See* Nativity
Birth rites and customs, **392–393**
Bisadah. *See* Psoï
Bisādah, Anbā, 1973
  see also Dayr Anbā Bisādah; Psote
Bīsah (martyr), 718, 719
Bishāy. *See* Bishoi (desert father)
Bishāy, Basṭā, 1465
Bishoi, Anbā. *See* Dayr Anbā Bishoi; Pshoi of Scetis
Bishoi, Anūb of Naesi (martyr), 1553
Bishoi, Saint. *See* Pshoi, Saint
Bishoi, Hor, and Diodora (martyrs), 1553
Bishop, **393–395**
  apostles and, 2015
  and apostolic succession, 181
  and Chalcedon, Council of, 914–915
  chorepiscopus, 520–521
  in church hierarchy, 1229
  consecration of liturgical vestments by, 1475–1476
  and defrocking of priests, 891
  Didascalia on, 899
  Dionysius the Great's epistles to, 911
  in ecclesiastical hierarchy, 2015
  election of, 1934
  Eucharist officiation, 1061
  excommunication powers of, 1079–1080
  Gabriel II antisimony policy, 1128
  interdicts by, 1299
  laying-on of hands by, 1432
  liturgical insignia, 1468–1469
  liturgical vestments, 1476–1478
  and Nicene Creed, 1792
  and ordination of deacons and priests, 885, 886–888, 1844–1845, 2013–2015
  penalization powers, 1931–1932
  rules on election as patriarch, 1911
  and selection of patriarch, 1998, 1999, 2000
  throne in sanctuary, 221–222
  see also Metropolitan; specific bishoprics and bishops
Bishop, consecration of, 394, **395–398**
  and Kiss of Peace, 1416–1417
  at Qaṣr Ibrīm, 2037
Bishop, translation of, **398–399**
Bishop of Alexandria. *See* Patriarch; Pope in the Coptic church
Bishopric. *See* Eparchy
Bishops
  Abraam I, 10
  Abraham of Hermonthis, 13
  Basil the Great, 351–352
  Buṭrus, 428
  Buṭrus ibn al-Khabbāz, 429
  Butrus Sāwīrus al-Jamīl, 431
  Constantine of Asyūṭ, 590–593
  Dioscorus, 915–916
  from al-Faramā, 1089–1090
  Flavian of Ephesus, 1117
  in Giza, 1142
  Hadrā of Aswan, Saint, 1190
  Ḥasaballāh, 1209–1210
  Hesychius, 1226
  Ibn al-Dahīrī, 1266
  Ignatius of Antioch, 1281–1282
  John of Antioch, 1354
  John of Mayuma, 1366
  John of Nikiou, 1366–1367
  John of Shmūn, 1369
  Judas Cyriacus, Saint, 1377–1378
  Julian, 1379
  Macrobius, Saint, 1494
  Marcellus, 1526
  Marquṣ, 1541–1542
  Melitius, 1585
  of Memphis, 1587
  Mena, 334
  Mīkhā'īl of Atrīb and Malīj, 1625–1627
  Mīkhā'īl of Damietta, 1625–1625
  Moses of Aw Sīm, 1678–1679
  of Nikiou, 1793–1794
  Paphnutius, 1882
  Patape, 1907–1908
  Paul of Bahnasā, 1922
  and Pentapolis, 1934
  Philip of Anatolia, 1956
  Pisentius of Armant (Hermonthis), 1978
  Pisentius of Qifṭ, 1978–1980
  Polycarp, 1997–1998
  Psote of Psoï, 2031–2032
  Synesius, 2192
  Theodosius of Jerusalem, 2242
  Theodotus of Ancyra, 2242–2243
  Theophilos I, 2247
  Timotheos I, 2262
  Yacobos II, 2349
  Yu'annis, 2355
  Yūḥannā, 2355–2356
  Yūsāb (13th-century), 2359
  Yūsāb (15th-century), 2359
  Yūsāb (18th-century), 2360
  Zacharias, Saint, 2368
  see also Ethiopian prelates; specific names
Bishops, biographies of, **399–400**
Bishops, correspondence of, **400–402**
Bishops, Nubian, 1813
Bishops, portraits of, **402–403**
Bistizzi, Vespasiano da, 1119

Bisūrah al-Ḥarīrī, **403**
Bisūs (monk), 1574
Bitimios, Abbot, 1967
Biuka (martyr), 1553
Biyūkhah. *See* Biuka (martyr)
Black Book (Makram), 1515–1516
Black Death, 708, 750, 877
  see also Plagues
Blake, William, 1149
Blemmye. *See* Beja tribes
Blessing, **403–404**
  see also Laying-on of hands
Blind singers. *See* Cantors
Blin, Jules, 1743
Blue turbans, 1535
Bochtor, Ellious. *See* Ilyās Buqṭur
Bodleian Library (Oxford University), 1894
Bodmer, Martin, **404–405**
Bodmer papyri, 1885, 1894, 1895, 1899
  and Coptological studies, 615
  of Egyptian Bible texts, 381–382
  of Greek Bible manuscripts, 380–381
  see also Appendix
Body and Blood of Christ. *See* Communion; Concomitance; Consubstantiation; Sacrament, reservation of the blessed
Boehme, Jacob, 1149, 1151
Boeser, Pieter Adriaan Art, **405**
Bogdanoff, Pierre de, 1666
Bohairic dialect, 605, 606, 613
  Alexander's encomium on Peter I, 1943–1944
  Canons, Apostolic, 451–452
  canons, ecclesiastical, 454
  and Coptological studies, 613
  Life of Pachomius in, 1860
  New Testament in, 1788, 2107
  in Old Testament, Coptic translations of, 1837–1838
  poetry and hymns, 1986
  Psalis in, 1727
  see also Appendix
Bollandists, 56–57, **405**, 1929
Bone and ivory carving, Coptic, 280, **405–407**, *406*, *407*
Bonhome, Alphonse, 1647
Bonifacius (legate), 914
Bonnets. *See* Headdress, Coptic women
Bookbinding, **407–409**, *407–409*, 573
Book of Canonical Hours. See Canonical hours, book of
Book of Canon Law (Ibn al-ʿAssāl), on use of candles in church, 445
Book on the Christian Religion, 1626
Book of Chronicles, 19, 1460, 1463
Book of the Consecration of the Sanctuary of Benjamin, on the Kellia, 1397
Book of the Councils (Severus of al-Ashmūnayn), 1779
Book of the Dead, 573
Book of Dialectic (ʿAbd al-Masīḥ al-Isrāʾīli al-Raqqī), 5, 6
Book of Epact, **409–411**
Book of the Exposition of the Union, 1626
Book of the Foundation (Mani), 1520–1521
Book of the Hidden Pearls
  on Dayr Abū Līfah, 704
  on Dayr al-Ballās, 788
  on Dayr al-Ḥammām, 806
  on Dayr Manṣūr (Dayr al-Malāk Mīkhāʾīl, Idfū), 825
  on Dayr al-Maymūn, 838
  on monasteries of the Fayyūm, 1651
  on monasteries of the Sharqiyyah Province, 1655, 1656
Book of the Hours. See Horologion
Book of the Investiture of Michael (John the Apostle), 1618, 1619
Bookkeeping. *See* Accounts and accounting, history of Coptic
Book of the Miracles of Mary, 818–819, 840
Book of the Rolls (Pseudo-Clement of Rome), 1782
Books. *See* Archives; Bookbinding; Illumination; Lectern; Lectionary; Libraries; Literature; Manuscripts; specific titles
Books of Chronicles, Arabic versions of, 1827–1829
Books of Enoch, 162–163
Books of Maccabees, 166
Book of Spiritual Medicine, 1089, 1626
Book of Thomas the Contender, **411–412**, 897
Book of the Tower (Mārī ibn Sulaymān), 1779
Boots. *See* Costume, civil
Boreaux, Charles, 924
Borgia, Stefano Cardinal, **412**, 1448, 1894
Borsai, Ilona, 1726, 1732, 1741, 1743
"Bosnians". *See* Qaṣr Ibrīm
Bostra affair (394), 2249
Bottles. *See* Glass, Coptic; Metalwork, Coptic
Bouclé technique of linen weaving, *2211*, *2217*
Boule, **413–414**
Bourguet, Pierre du, S. J., **414**
Bouriant, Urbain, **414–415**
Boutos. *See* Ibṭū
Boutros Ghālī, 375, **415–416**, 580, 1466
  assassination of, 416, 603
  and Cyril V, Patriarch, 677
  and Egyptian national unity, 950–951
  role in British occupation of Egypt, 420
  role in Muḥammad ʿAlī dynasty, 1693
  and Saʿd Mīkhāʾīl ʿAbdū, 2074
  and Saʿd Zaghlūl, 2074
Boxes
  bone and ivory carvings, 407
  wooden, 2328–2330, 2337–2338, *2338–2339*
Bracelets, 1606
Brakários (Coptic weaving term), 2221
Branding of Copts, 87
Braziers, 1601, *1601*
Bread, consecrated. *See* Fraction
Bread, Eucharistic. *See* Eucharistic bread
Bread and wine, donation of. *See* Offertory
Breccia, A. Evaristo, **416**, 1527
Brendan, Saint (Ireland), 418
Bricks, in Kellia construction, 1401, 1402
Bridal chamber, 898
Brienne, Jean de, 783
Brightman, Frank Edward, **416**
Britain. *See* British Isles, Coptic influences in the; British occupation of Egypt; Great Britain
British Isles, Coptic influences in the, **416–419**
  Irish harp, 1734, 1740

British Library, London, 780, 825, 876, 899, 1427
papyrus collections, 1893
British Museum, London, 780, 1136, 1410, 1508, 1592, 1708–1709
collection of Coptic manuscripts, 612
Coptic Street, 611–612
papyrus collections, 1893
British occupation of Egypt, **419–422**, 1466, 1627–1628, 1637, 1693–1694, 1748
Boutros Ghālī and, 415–416
Coptic press on, 2010–2011
and Dayr al-Sulṭān, 873–874
and Egyptian national identiy, 949, 950
political thought under, 1993, 1994–1995
Sa'd Zaghlūl and, 2074–2075
Salāmah Mūsā and, 2089
Wafd party independence movement, 1989–1990
and Wissa Wassef, 2323–2324
Bronze, 1596–1597, 1599
Brooklyn Museum, New York City, papyrus collection, 1895
Browne, G. M., 1894
Bruce, James, **422**
Brugsch, Heinrich Ferdinand Karl, **422**
Bryennios, Metropolitan, 898
"Bubal". *See* Paphnutius of Scetis, Saint
Buckets, 1601–1602
Bucolic iconography, 1766–1767
Buddhism, 1520, 1521
Budge, Ernest Alfred Thompson Wallis, **422–423**, 614, 1449
Buildings (Procopius), 2019, 2020
Bukharas. *See* Faras
Būkhīshā, heretical sect at, 94–95
Būlā, Anbā. *See* Dayr Anbā Būlā; Paul of Thebes, Saint
Bulāq Museum and Service des Antiquités, 693, 1561
Bulāq printing press, 1993
Bulbinus and Pupienus, Emperors, patriarch under, 1914
Būlus al-Būshī, 29, 32, **423–424**, 1613
Būlus Ghubriyāl al-Muḥarraqī. *See* Abraam I
Būlus al-Ḥabīs, Saint (Paul the Solitary), **424–425**
feast day, 1553, 2086
at Ḥilwān, 1233
as rescuer of *Dhimmis*, 424–425, 1517
Buqayrah al-Rashīdī the Deacon. *See History of the Patriarchs*
Buqṭur. *See* Dayr Buqṭur of Shū; Victor, Saint
Būrah, **425**
Bureaucratic offices in the Mamluk state. *See* Copts in late medieval Egypt
Burgundians, 1572
Burial rites and practices, **425–426**, 1901
and Egyptian tunic finds, 648
Gabriel II, Patriarch, policy, 1128
see also Funerary customs; Mourning in early Christian times; Mummification; Stela; Tombs
Buried Monastery. *See* Dayr al-Maṭmar
Būrīj, 1652
Burkitt, Francis Crawford, **426**
Burmester, Oswald Hugh Edward, **426**
Burning bush, site of the, 1681–1682, 1683, 1684
Burullus, Al-, **427**
Būsh, **427**
Būṣir Qūrīdus (Busiris). *See* Abūṣir al-Malaq
Busts. *See* Portraiture, Coptic
Butcher, Edith L., **428**
Butler, Alfred Joshua, **428**, 2000
Būtros, Nabīl Kamāl, 1743
Buṭrus I and II, Archbishops of Jerusalem, 1325
Buṭrus, Basīlī, 374–375, 1124
Buṭrus, Bishop of al-Bahnasā, 1251
Buṭrus, Bishop of Cairo, 1614
Buṭrus, Bishop of Miṣr (Melchite), **428**, 1613
Buṭrus ibn 'Abd al-Sayyid, **428–429**, 1614
Buṭrus ibn al-Khabbāz, Metropolitan of Ethiopia, **429**
Buṭrus ibn Ṣahyūn al-Ghannāmī, **430**
Buṭrus ibn Sālim al-Sunbaāṭī, **430–431**
Buṭrus al-Jawlī. *See* Peter VII
Buṭrus Sāwīrus al-Jamīl, **431**
Buṭrus al-Sidmantī, **431–432**, 831, 1974
Byzantine church architecture, cross-and-square building, 660–661
Byzantine Empire
and Alexandrine See, 913–914, 915
Coptic patriarchs contemporary with, 688–689
Dayr Abū Isḥāq's importance during, 703
and Egyptian government, 2063
and Egypt in late antiquity, 942–947
icon-painting stylistic rules, 1277
impact on Egypt and the Copts, 942–947
monenergism and, 1666–1667
and taxation in Egypt, 2204
see also Constantinople; Eastern Orthodox churches; Fatimids and Copts; Jerusalem
Byzantine influences on Coptic art. *See* Art, Byzantine influences on Coptic; Islamic influences on Coptic art
Byzantium. *See* Constantinople

C

Cabalistic amulets, 1508
Caecilian, Bishop, 920, 921
Caesarea
library, 1447
Mercurius, Saint, 1592–1594
see also Basil the Great; Eusebius of Caesarea
Caesarion. *See* Church of Saint Michael
Caetani, Leone, **433**
Cailliaud of Nantes, 927
Cairensis Gnosticus. *See* Nag Hammadi Library
Cairo
Babylon, 317
Coptic burning of (1320), 1518
Coptic churches' legal status in, 687
founding, 810
Franciscan churches, 1123
monasteries in and around, 1646–1647
patriarchal residence at, 1913
as patriarchal seat, 689, 1999–2000

Cairo (*cont.*)
pilgrims and travelers to, 1977
tombstone material, 1295
see also Babylon; Fusṭāṭ, al-
Cairo Museum. *See* Coptic Museum (Old Cairo)
Cairo University, 1141, 1423
Calamus. *See* Jabal Khashm al-Qu'ud; Kalamon
Calendar and agriculture, **440–443**
Calendar, Coptic, 19, 430, **433–436**, *435*
Advent, 63
Anno Martyrum, 1549
fast days, 1093–1096
lectionary and, 1435–1437
Paschal controversy, 1905–1906
and Shamm al-Nasīm feast day, 2126
see also Calendar, months of Coptic; Synaxarion, Copto-Arabic
Calendar, Gregorian, **436–437**
Calendar, Julian, **437**
Calendar, months of Coptic, **438–439**
Calendar, seasons, and Coptic liturgy, **443–444**
Calendologia, **444–445**
Caligula, Emperor (Gaius), 2062
Philo of Alexandria and, 1956
Calixtus, Bishop of Rome, 1638
Calligraphy, at Dayr al-Baramūs, 791
Callinicum, Conference of (568), 1676
Callinicus, Bishop of Syene (martyr), 1553
Calotychius, 2241
Cambridge University, 1138, 1893
Cambyses Romance, 2060
Camoul, Saint, **445**, 1553
Camp (castrum) of Hierakion. *See* Dayr al-Jabrāwī
Campaign to Save the Monuments of Nubia, 1090, 1091
Canada
Coptic churches in, 1621
Coptic collections, 1702–1703
papyrus collections, 1891
Cancelli, 200–201, 217
Candelabrum, 1469
see also Candles; Lighting equipment; Liturgical instruments; Metalwork, Coptic
Candlemas, 1106–1107
Candles, **445–446**
as altar lights, 109–110
during consecration of church, 548
Canons of Ammonius, 32
Canon, derivation of term, 2108–2109
Canonical Hours, Book of, **446–449**, 1724, 1733
Agathon the Stylite and, 69
compline, 582–583
and Coptic doctrine of the Holy Spirit, 1250
and Giyorgis, 1052
and Holy Week Scripture readings, 1251
hymns. *See* Music, Coptic, description
liturgy of matins, 1568–1569
Lord's Prayer, 1481
vespers, 2301
Canonical Letter (Peter I), 1944–1945, 1946
Canonization, **449**
Canon law, **449–451**
and Cyril III ibn Laqlaq, 310–311
Kitāb al-Burhān fī al-Qawānīn, 33, 1463
al-Ṣafī ibn al-'Assāl works on, 2076
Canons, Apostolic, 179–180, **451–453**
on confession and penitence, 585
on fasting on Saturday, 1248, 2098
on immersion, 1286
on incense use, 1472
see also Canons, ecclesiastical
Canons of Clement, **456**
copied by Ibrāhīm ibn Sulaymān al-Najjār al-Mīrī, 1273
Canon of the Scripture. *See* Scripture, canon of the
Canons, ecclesiastical, **453–455**
on clerical instruction, 564
on clerical ordination, 1844
Canons of Epiphanius, **456–457**
Canons of Eusebius, 32
Canons of Gregory of Nyssa, **457**
Canons of Hippolytus, **458**, 1235, 1455
Canons of Pseudo-Athanasius, **458–459**
Canons of Saint Basil, **459**
in condemnation of *cheirotonia*, 517
see also Anaphora of Saint Basil
Canons of Saint John Chrysostom, **459–460**
Canopus. *See* Abūqīr; Dayr Qibriyūs; Metanoia, Monastery of the
Canopy. *See* Baldachin
Cantate Domino, 1119
Canticles, 1729, 1733
Cantor, **460**, 1732, 1736–1738, 1742
antiphon, 148–149
Clerical College, 564
Mu'allim Mīkhā'īl Jirjis, 1629–1630
responsory, 2058
see also Chant
Cap, bishops', 1476
Cape, priests' and bishops', 1476
Capital
Coptic sculpture in stone, *2114*
Saqqara South, *776*, 777
see also Column; Corinthian capital
Cappadocian fathers, 44, 114–116, 351, 1183, 1184, 1310, 1921, 1982
Caracalla, Emperor
and massacre of Alexandria, 97, 1177
patriarch under, 1914
visit to Egypt, 2063, 2066
Caraccioli, Clement, **461**
Carausius, 904, 905
Carbon-14 dating method, 694
Carinus, 904
Carion of Scetis. *See* Zacharius of Scetis
Carolingians, patron saint of, 1572
Carolingian theologians, controversy over *filioque*, 1115
Carpentry, 2326–2327
Carpocrates, **460–461**, 1222, 2118
Carthage
Arsenal of Tunis, 239
rivalry with Numidia, 920, 921
sacrifice to Roman gods at, 890
Carthage, Council of (397), on regulations for nuns, 1822
Carus, Emperor, 904
patriarch under, 1914
Caskets, wooden, 2328–2330, *2329*

Cassian, Saint John, **461–463**, 2024, 2082
on anchorites in Diolkos, 908
on canonical hours, 449
Conferences and *Cenobitic Institutes*, 1663
and costume of the religious, 650
on devil as black, 248
in France, 1623
on genuflection, 1139
on Jabal Khashm al-Quʿūd, 1316
and John Colobos, Saint, 1359
on John of Lycopolis, Saint, 1364
on matins, 1568
on the monks of Scetis, 2103
and Paphnutius of Scetis, 1884
on respect for one's body, 958–959
on Sarapion, 2094, 2095
Castanets, 1604–1605, 1739–1740
wooden, 2333, *2334*
Castle of the two gates. *See* Qalʿat al-Bābayn
Castrum, **464–468**, *466*, *467*, *468*
at Abūṣīr (Taposiris Magna), 34
at Najʿ al-Ḥajar, 1774
see also Qaṣr headings
Castrum Memnonium, 1657
Catecheses (Cyril of Jerusalem), 667, 681
Catechesis (Pachomius), 1862–1863
Catechetical Lectures
on finding Holy Cross, 1243
on prayers for the dead, 889
Catechetical School of Alexandria, 55, 77, 100–101, 103, **469–472**, 474, 1533
and Athanasius I, 298
and Clement of Alexandria, 562–563
Clerical College in footsteps of, 563
Demetrius I and, 892, 893
Didymus the Blind and, 900
Dionysius of Alexandria and, 909
Eusebius of Caesarea and, 1070–1071
Heraclas, Saint, and, 909, 911, 1219
influence on Coptic education, 931–932
Jerome, Saint, and, 1323
library, 1447
Origen and, 176, 1847, 1852
Theonas, Patriarch, and, 2245, 2246
use of Egyptian Bible text, 381–382
Catechumen, 103, **473–474**, 1473
and Holy Communion, 578
liturgy of the, 1715
and Lord's Prayer, 1480–1481
Mass of the. *See* Mass of the Catechumens
oil of the, 522, 523
Catena, Arabic tradition of, **475**
Cathedral Church of Abū Sayfayn (Saint Mercurius), 1535
Cathedral Church of the Jacobites (Alexandria), 93–94
Cathedral of Faras, 1090, 1091–1092
Cathedral of Heliopolis, 2051
Cathedral of Nicomedia, 907
Cathedral of Qaṣr Ibrīm, 2037
Cathedral of Saint Mark (Alexandria), 1531–1532
papal investiture at, 1999
restoration of, 1303
Cathedral of Saint Mark (al-Azbakiyyah), 1538
Cathedral of Saint Mark (Cairo), 1434, 2091
consecration of patriarchs in, 1909, 1913
master chanter, 1629
Cathedral of Saint Mark (Venice), 1532
Cathedral of Zamalek, 2051
Catherine of Alexandria, Saint
cult of, 1976, 1977
martyrdom of, 2325
monastery of, 1681–1685, 2325
Catholic church, Coptic. *See* Coptic Catholic church
Catholicism. *See* Coptic Catholic church; Coptic relations with Rome; Eastern Orthodox churches; Franciscans in Egypt; Jesuits and the Coptic church; Oriental Orthodox churches; Roman Catholic church
Catholicos (title), **475**
Catholic University of America, Washington, D.C., 1951
Cauldrons, 1601, 1602
Caves
Abū Ḥinnis, 703
at Abydos, 39, 41–42
of Barsūm the Naked, 348
and cells, 477
Dayr Abū Līfah, 704
Dayr Anbā Anṭūniyūs, 725
Dayr Anbā Hadrā, 746
Dayr al-Dīk, 799
Dayr al-Janādlah, 705
Dayr Mār Mīnā (Jabal Abū Fūdah), 834
Dayr al-Naqlūn, 845, 846
Dayr al-Naṣārā, 847
and hermits' cells, 477
of Saint Paul of Thebes, 741
Wādī al-Nakhlah, 795
Caxo, Saint, 1151–1152
Ceiling, 201–202
Celadion, Saint and Patriarch, **475**, 2082
dates of patriarchy, 1914
Celestinus of Rome, Bishop, **475–476**
and Coptic tradition of Victor Stratelates, Saint, 2303
and Copto-Arabic tradition of Victor Stratelates, Saint, 2305–2306
Celestius (disciple of Pelagius), 1930
Celibacy, 84, 88, **476–477**, 1543
Encratites, 958
Hieracas of Leontopolis on, 1229
Cell, **477–478**, 1403
Celsus, **478–479**, 1868
refuted by Origen, 176–177, 1847, 1854
Cemeteries
ʿAbdallāh Nirqī, 4
Alexandria, 96–97
Anbā Ruways, 2000
Asyūt region, 1654
Coptic mummification, 1697
Damrū, 690
Dayr Abū Isḥāq, 703
Dayr Abū Qarqūrah, 709
Dayr Abū al-Sayfayn (Qūṣ), 711
Dayr al-Amīr Tadrūs, 717, 718
Dayr Anbā Abshāy (near al-Tūd), 719
Dayr Apa Phoibammon, 780
Dayr al-ʿAzab, 785
Dayr Epiphanius, 801
Dayr al-Ḥammām, 807
Dayr al-ʿIẓām, 809
Dayr al-Janādlah, 705
Dayr al-Khandaq, 814–815

Cemeteries (*cont.*)
Dayr al-Madīnah, 817
Dayr al-Malāk Mīkhā'īl (Jirjā), 825
Dayr al-Nasṭūr, 848
Dayr al-Quṣayr, 853
Dayr al-Shuhadā', 867
Dayr al-Zāwiyah, 884
Faras, 1091
funerary customs concerning, 1125
Kom al-Rāhib, 1418
Nubian, 1805
Qarārah grave sites, 2036
Quṣūr 'Īsā 1, 1405
see also Burial rites and practices; Stela; Tombs
Cenobites. *See* Monasticism, Pachomian; Pachomius of Tabennēsē, Saint
Cenobitic Institutes (John Cassian), 1663
Censer, 1469–1472, *1470*, *1471*
Centre national de la recherche scientifique, Paris, 924, 1419
Ceramics, Coptic, 267–268, **480–503**, *484*, *485*, *486*
as dating tool at Kellia site, 1400–1401, 1402, 1407
decorative techiques and motifs, 483–487, *483*, *484*, *485*, *486*
Faras, 1090, 1091
figurines, **500–503**, *501*, *502*, *503*
manufacturing techniques, **480–482**
from Monastery of Mark the Evangelist (Qurnat Mar'ī), 2042
preservation of terra-cotta, 278–279
statuary, 2147–2148
types of ceramic ware, **487–499**, *489*, *491*, *492*, *496*, *499*
see also Art, historiography of Coptic
Ceramics of the late Coptic period, **504–510**, *505-510*
Ceramics, Nubian, 1806–1807
Cerdon, Saint and Patriarch, **511**, 2082
dates of patriarchy, 1913
Ceremony of the Holy Light, 1248–1249
Cerinthus, **511**, 917, 1222, 1288
Černý, Jaroslav, **511**
Chaeremon, Bishop of Neilopolis/Dalāṣ, 685
Chaîne, Marius Jean Joseph, **511–512**
Chairemon of Alexandria, **512**
Chalcedon, Council of (451), 20, 37, 88, 102, 126, **512–515**, 914–915
and Abraham of Farshūṭ, 11–12
and Acacian schism, 42–47, 102
Acephaloi opposition to, 55
and Agathon of Alexandria, 65
aims, 1670
and Antioch, Council of, 190
and Armenian church, 234
Christological definition of, 523, 547, 578, 1638, 2255
on clerical ordination, 1844
on *communicatio idiomatum*, 578
and Constantinople, First Council of, 594
and Constantinople, Second Council of, 595–596
and Coptic art and architecture, 269–270
Coptic music post, 1734
Coptic music prior to, 1732–1734
and Coptic relations with Rome, 609, 661–662
and Cyrus al-Muqawqas, 682–683
Dayr Maṭrā monks' resistance to dogma of, 837
on deaconesses, 888
and divisions among monks of the Kellia, 1397
and ecclesiastical use of eparchy, 959
Enaton monks' opposition to dogma of, 956–957
and Ephesus councils, 960, 961, 962
and Eutyches, 1075
and Henoticon edict, 1217–1218, 2370
and homilies on Michael, Archangel, 1618–1619
and hypostatic union, 1262
and iconoclasm, 1276
impact on Coptic literature and thought, 1454–1455
impact on Copts, 66, 146, 661–662, 693, 943, 1211; *see also subhead* reactions to
Isidorus of Pelusium role, 1308
and John II, 1337
and John I, 1337
and John of Lycopolis, Saint, 1365
and Julian, Bishop, 1379
and Justin I, 1383
and Justinian, Emperor, 1385, 1386
and Leo I the Great, 1441–1442
and Macarius of Tkow, 1556
and Mark II, 1533, 1534
and Melchite-Coptic split, 1583
and Monastery of the Metanoia, 1609–1610
monenergism and, 1666–1667
and monenergist formula, 1666
and monophysitism, 1575–1576, 1669–1670; *see also* Monophysitism
on nature of Christ. *See subhead* Christological definition of
and Nicene Creed, 1793
and nine saints from Ethiopia, 1045–1047
on *oikonomos*, 1825
and the Oriental Orthodox churches, 1845–1846
and Pachomian-Shenutean traditions, 1453
and Peter III Mongus, 1947, 1948
and Philoxenus of Mabbug, 1962
and Pulcheria, Empress, 513–514, 1441, 1442, 1670, 2033
reactions to, 1670–1671, 1672
and saints recognized by Ethiopian church, 1044–1045
and Severus of Antioch, 2124
and Simon I, 2139
and Theodoret, 2236
and Theodosius of Jerusalem, 2242
and Theopistus of Alexandria, 2254
and *Theotokos*, 1218, 2255; *see also subhead* Christological definition of
and Timothy II Aelurus, 2264–2267
and Western alienation of Copts, 661–662
and Zeno, Emperor, 1217–1218, 2369–2370
see also Nestorians and Copts

Chalcedonians. *See* Chalcedon, Council of; specific issues
Chaldaean Oracles, **516**
Chalice, as Eucharistic vessel, 1065
Chalice veil. *See* Eucharistic veils
Chamoul. *See* Camoul, Saint
Champollion, Jean François, **516**, 614, 1424, 1440, 1445, 2073, 2125
Chanazhum (martyr), 1553
Chancel. *See* Cancelli
Chandeliers. *See* Lighting equipment; Metalwork
Chants, 63, 1721
  Adām, 63, 1722
  and Agnus Dei, 71
  antiphon, 148–149, *1717*, 1732
  Coptic poetry, 1985
  responsory, 2058
  wāṭus, 1722, 1724, 2320–2321
  see also Choral singing
Chapel 180 (al-Bagawāt), *327*
Chapel of Anbā Anṭūniyūs (Saint Antony), 753, 754
Chapel of the Archangel Michael, 753, 754, *755*
Chapel of the Exodus (al-Bagawāt), 1873
Chapel of the Forty-nine Martyrs (Dayr al-Suryān), 876, 880
Chapel of the Hermits, 753, 754
Chapel of Mār Jirjis, Dayr Anbā Bishoi, 736
Chapel of Peace (al-Bagawāt), 1873
Chapel of Saint Michael (Dayr Anbā Anṭūniyūs), 721
Chapel of the Virgin, Dayr Anbā Maqār, 754
Charisios, **516**
Charlemagne, 1110, 1112
Charles of Anjou, 1114
Chassinat, Emile Gaston, **516–517**, 1561–1562, 1579
  Daumas, François, association, 695
Cheirotonia, **517**
  Abraham, Patriarch, suppression of, 10
  and Būlus al-Būshī, 423
  and Cyril III, Patriarch, 677
  and Cyril II, Patriarch, 676
  and John VI, Patriarch, 1342
  Mark III, Patriarch, abolished by, 1536
  and Philotheus' patriarchy, 1959, 1960
  revival of, 1413
  and Shenute I, Patriarch, 2134
Chenoboskion, as burial site of Nag Hammadi codices, 1771
Chenoboskion Sheneset. *See* Pachomius of Tabennēsē, Saint
Cherubic Hymn, 518, 1565
Cherubim and seraphim, **518**, 1875, 2015
  oldest-known painting of, 751
Chester Beatty Biblical Papyri, 380–382, **518–519**, 1899–1900
Chester Beatty Coptic Papyri, **519**
Chester Beatty Library, Dublin, 1894
Chiftichi, Yuḥanna, **519–520**
  see also Yaʿqūb, General
Children
  Coptic family life, 1086–1088
  donation to monasteries, 918–919
  infant baptism, 338
  martyrs, 1553, 1556, 1557, 1960–1961
  sacrament administration to, 2072
  see also Education; Toys and games; Youth of Egypt; Youth movements
Chillebert de Lannon, 720
Chironomy system, 1730
Chitty, D. J., on Letter of Ammon, 1445
Choir, 202
  wood carvings on enclosures, *2342*
  see also Khūrus
Choirs. *See* Choral singing
Chora, Alexandrian exemptions, 1180
Choral singing
  antiphonal, 148–149, *1717*, 1732
  cantors, 1736–1738
  responses, 1719, *1720*, 1721
  unison, *1718–1719*, 1721
  vocalise, *1720*, 1721, 1732
Chordophones, 1738, 1740–1741
Chorepiscopus, **520–521**
  in ecclesiastical hierarchy, 2015
  Neocaesarea, Council of, on, 1785
Chosroes II Parvēz, 1243, 1676, 1938
Chotsko, 1519
Chrism, **521–522**, 1473, 1474
  and Benjamin II, Patriarch, 377
  at Church of Abū Sayfyn, 550
  Damanhūr bishops at preparation of, 686
  and Jesuits, 1330
  and John XVI, Patriarch, 1348
  use in confirmation, 586
  use in consecration of new church, 548–549
Chrism, consecration of the, **522–523**, 580
  Giza bishops at, 1141–1142
  Jirjis al-Jawhari translation, 1334
  manuscript copied by Ibrāhīm ibn Sulaymān al-Najjār al-Mīrī, 1273
Chrismatory, **523**, 1473
Christ, nature of, **523–525**
  ʿAbd al-Masīḥ al-Isrāʾīli al-Raqqī on, 6–7
  Abū Shākir ibn al-Rāhib on, 33
  Agnoetae on, 70–71
  in Alexandrian theology, 103–104
  and alpha and omega symbol, 2151
  Apollinarianism and, 173–174
  Arius on, 230, 232, 597
  Chalcedon, Council of, on, 512–515, 523, 547, 1638, 1670
  and church art, 555–556
  communicatio idiomatum, 578–579
  Coptic church–Roman Catholic church statement (1988), 1786
  Cyril I, Patriarch, on, 913–914, 1669
  Docetists on, 917
  ecthesis formula, 682, 931
  Ephesus councils on, 959–962
  Ethiopian controversy, 1033
  Eutyches on, 913–914, 1074–1075, 1669–1670, 2267
  gnosticism on, 1301, 2256
  Henoticon on, 1671
  Homoeans on, 1252–1253
  homoiousion and *homoousion* concepts, 1253–1254, 2096
  and hypostatic union, 1262
  and Incarnation, 1287–1290

illustration of "two-finger blessing" at, 404
liturgical instruments, 1473
patriarchal seat at, 1912, 1913
restoration of, 11
see also Architectural elements of churches; Christian subjects in Coptic art
Church of al-ʿAdhrāʾ, *736*, *878*, 879–880, *880*
see also Balyanā, al-; Dayr al-ʿAdhrāʾ; Jabal al-Tayr
Church of Anbā Bishoi. *See* Dayr al-Barshah and Dayr al-Nakhlah
Church of Anbā Ruways, 815
Gabriel VI buried in, 1133
Church of the Angelion (Alexandria), 93
Church of the Apparition of the Holy Virgin (Jerusalem), 1327
Church of Arcadius, 1870
Church architecture in Egypt, **552–555**
octagon-domed church, 1823–1824
see also Architecture; Art and architecture; Coptic; specific churches
Church architecture in Nubia. *See* Nubian Christian architecture
Church art, **555–556**
see also Art and architecture, Coptic; Cross, triumph of the; Christian subjects in Coptic art; Symbols in Coptic art
Church art, Nubian, 1811–1812
Church of the Ascension (Jerusalem), 1328–1329
Church of Cosmas and Damian (Alexandria), 93, 2017
Church of Creniua (Alexandrian Melchite church), 94
Church of Dandarah, 690, *691*
Church doors, wood, 2331–2333, *2332–2333*
Church of Emperor Arcadius (Alexandria), 93
Church of England. *See* Anglican Church in Egypt
Church of the Epiphany (Dayr Sitt Dimyānah), 872
Churches
at ʿAbdallāh Nirqī, 4
Abraham, Patriarch, restoration of, 11
Abū al-Makārim listing of, 92–94, 1462
at Abū Mīnā, 24–29
Akhmīm, 78–80
Alexandria, 101–102
Alexandria, historic, 92–95
altar, 105–110
altar form and location, 106–107
ambo, 111
Antinoopolis, 145
architectural elements, 194–225
Babylonia, 318–323, *319*
Bayt al-Nisāʾ (area reserved for women), 373
Chalcedonian. *See* Eastern Orthodox churches
in Daqādūs, 692
at Dayr Abū Fānah, 698, 699–700
at Dayr Abū Ḥinnis, 701, 702–703
at Dayr Abū Ishāq, 703
at Dayr Abū Mattā, 706
at Dayr Abū Mūshā, 708
at Dayr Abū Qarqūrah, 709
at Dayr Abū al-Sayfayn (Qūṣ), 711
at Dayr al-ʿAdawiyyah, 712, 713
at Dayr al-ʿAdhrāʾ, 713, 714, 715
at Dayr al-ʿAdhrāʾ (al-Ruzayqāt), 2069
at Dayr al-ʿAdhrāʾ (Samālūṭ), 716
at Dayr al-Aḥmar (Giza), 716–717
at Dayr al-Amīr Tadrūs, 717, 718
at Dayr Anbā Anṭūniyūs, 720–721, 724–727, *725*
at Dayr Anbā Bākhūm, 730–731, *731*
at Dayr Anbā Bisādah, 733
at Dayr Anbā Bishoi (Scetis), 735–736, *736*
at Dayr Anbā Bishoi (Sūhaj), 739–740
at Dayr Anbā Bulā, 741, 742–744
at Dayr Anbā Hadrā, 746, 747, 855
at Dayr Anbā Helias (Naqādah), 747
at Dayr Anbā Maqār, 749, 750–756
at Dayr Anbā Palaemon, 757
at Dayr Anbā Ṣamūʾīl of Qalamūn, 758, 759, 760
at Dayr Anbā Shinūdah (Suhāj), 761, 763, 768–770
at Dayr Apa Hor (Sawādah), 770–771
at Dayr Apa Isḥāq, 772
at Dayr Apa Jeremiah (Saqqara), 773, 774–776, *775*
at Dayr Apa Thomas, 781
at Dayr Asfal al-Arḍ, 783
at Dayr al-ʿAwanah (Asyūt), 784
at Dayr al-ʿAzab, 784, 785
at Dayr al-Balaʿyzah, 787
at Dayr al-Banāt, 788–789
at Dayr al-Baramūs, 791–794, *792*, *793*
at Dayr al-Barshah and Dayr al-Nakhlah, 795–796, *796*
at Dayr al-Biṣrah, 797
at Dayr Buqṭur of Shū, 797–798
at Dayr Durunkah, 799, 856
at Dayr al-Fakhūrī, 803–805, *804*
at Dayr al-Ḥammām, 806, 807
at Dayr Harmīnā, 808
at Dayr al-Ikhwah, 808
at Dayr al-ʿIẓām, 810
at Dayr al-Jabrāwī, 810, 811–812
at Dayr al-Janādlah, 704, 705–706
at Dayr al-Jarnūs, 813
at Dayr al-Khandaq, 815
at Dayr al-Kubāniyyah, 815–816, *816*
at Dayr al-Madīnah, 817, 818
at Dayr al-Majmaʿ, 820–821
at Dayr al-Malāk Mīkhāʾīl (Jirjā), 713, 823, 825–826
at Dayr al-Malāk Mīkhāʾīl (Naqādah), 827
at Dayr al-Malāk Mīkhāʾīl (Qamūlah), 828
at Dayr Mār Buqṭur (Qamūlah), 829–830
at Dayr Mār Jirjis (Sadamant-Fayyūm), 831
at Dayr Mār Jirjis al-Hadīdī, 713
at Dayr Mār Tumās, 835–836
at Dayr al-Maṭmar, 836–837
at Dayr al-Maymūn, 838, 839
at Dayr al-Muḥarraq, 1969
at Dayr al-Naqlūn, 845–846
at Dayr al-Naṣara, 848
at Dayr al-Qaṣriyyah, 849–850
at Dayr Qubbat al-Hawā, 851–852

Churches (*cont.*)
at Dayr al-Quṣayr (Ṭurah), 854–855
at Dayr Rīfah, 855–856
at Dayr al-Sanqūriyyah, 860
at Dayr al-Shahīd Tadrus al-Muḥārib, 862
at Dayr al-Sham', 863, *864*, 865
at Dayr al-Shuhadā' (Akhmīm), 865–866
at Dayr al-Shuhadā' (Isnā), 868–870
at Dayr Sitt Dimyānah, 713, *871*, 872
at Dayr al-Sulṭān, 872
at Dayr al-Suryān, 876, *878*, *880*
at Dayr Tāsā, 881
at Dayr al-Ṭīn, 881
at Dayr al-Zāwiyah, 884
dedicated to Victor Stratelates, Saint, 2307
in Dinūshar, 903
donations to, 1430
in Dumyāṭ, 926
in al-Faramā, 1089
in Faras, 1090, 1091
Franciscan in Egypt, 1123
Gabriel II prohibition against burial within, 1128
Gospel caskets in sanctuary, 1153
at Hawwārah, 1210–1211
at Hawwāriyyah, 1211–1212
historic Alexandrian, 92–95
in Holy Land, 1244–1247
icon placement in, 1276
icons, post-17th-century, 1270
inscriptions, 192–193
in Jerusalem, Coptic see of, 1326–1329
at Karm al-Akhbāriyyah, 1391–1392
at Karnak, 1393, *1394*, 1394
of Kellia, 1404–1405, 1406–1407
at Khirbat al-Filūsiyyah, 1414
at Kom Namrūd, 1418
at Lālibalā, 1425–1426
lecterns, 1434–1435
at Luxor temples, 1485
at Madamūd, 1494–1495
at Madīnat Hābū, 1497
at Madīnat Māḍī, 1498
at Makhūrah, 1512–1513
Mamluk destruction of, 1518
at Manqabād, 1523
Maqrīzī history on, 1525
at Mareotis, 1527
Mark's home as first, 1529
in Memphis, 1587
at Mīt Damsīs, 1970–1971
at Mount Sinai Monastery of Saint Catherine, 1682–1684, *1683*, 1902
murals in, 1874–1875
at Musṭurud, 1970
non-Chalcedonian. *See* Oriental Orthodox churches
Nubian architecture, 1807–1810, *1808*, *1809*, *1810*
Nubian art, 1091–1092
octagon-domed, 1823–1824
parekklesia (subsidiary), 1902
at Pbow, 1927–1929, *1928*
at Philae, 1956, *1955*
at Qal'at al-Bābayn, 2035
at Qaṣr Ibrīm, 2037
at Qaṣr Nisīmah, 2038
at Qaṣr al-Sham', 2038
at Qifṭ, 2039–2040
in Qūṣ, 2043, 2045
restorations under Mark III, 1535
rock, 716, 747, 770, 771, 798, 853, 1425–1426, *1426*, 1656
Saladin decree for painting black, 1535
Shams al-Dīn, 2127, *2127*
Shaykh 'abd al-Qurnah, 2128, *2129*
status during Muslim domination, 687, 693–694, 1098, 1535
at Ṭūd, 2279–2280, *2280*
at Umm al-Barakāt, *2290*, 2290
see also specific church and saint names
The Churches and Monasteries of Egypt and Some Neighbouring Countries Attributed to Abū Ṣāliḥ (Abū al-Makārim), 23, 33, 856, 1462
Church of the Forty-nine Martyrs (Ḥārit al-Rūm), 753, 2046
Church of the Four Beasts of the Revelation (Jerusalem), 1328
Church hierarchy. *See* Ecclesiastical hierarchy; Hierarchy, church
Church historians. *See* Historians; specific names
Church of the Holy Apostles Peter and Paul (Dayr Anbā Anṭūniyūs), 720, 722, 724
Church of the Holy Sepulcher (Jerusalem), 1097, 1098, 1099
destruction of, 1203
Church of the Holy Virgin (Dayr Anbā Anṭūniyūs), 721
Church of the Holy Virgin Mary (Dayr Anbā Būlā), 741
Church of the Island (Pharos), 93
Church of Jesus Christ of the Latter-day Saints, 2108
Church of John the Baptist (Alexandrian Melchite church), 94
Church of John the Baptist and the Prophet Elijah (Alexandria), 93
Church of Joseph (the Prophet) (Alexandria vicinity), 94
Church of al-Khandaq. *See* Dayr al-Khandaq
Church manual. *See Didache*
Church of Mār Jirjis (Saint George) (Old Cairo), 2038
Church of Mark the Evangelist (al-Qamḥah) (Alexandria), 94
Church of Mār Mīna (Babylon), 320, *321*
Church of Mār Sābā (Alexandria), 92
Church of the Martyr Abiskharūn, 752
Church of Mercurius. *See* Church of Abū Sayfayn
Church of Michael the Archangel, *see also* Church of Saint Michael
Church of Michael the Archangel (Alexandria), 92, 93
dedication of, 1617–1618
Church of Michael the Archangel (Durunkah), 927
Church of Michael the Archangel (Jerusalem), 1328
Church Missionary Society (CMS), 131
Church of al-Mu'allaqah (Alexandria), 93, 94
Church of al-Mu'allaqah (Old Cairo), **557–560**, *557*, *559*, 1207, 1208–1209, 1532, 1536, 2038
ambo in, 111
convent at, 2325
destruction of portions during patriarchy of John XI, 1345
Gabriel II anointed in, 1128

Gabriel V as *hegumenos of*, 1130
iconography of Ascension of Christ, 244, 558
lintel, 244–245, *245*
and Nasīm Abū Sa'd ibn 'Abd al-Sayyid, 1775
as patriarchal seat, 92, 558, 1912, 1999, 2159–2160
repairs and restoration, 11, 558
wood lintel, *2343*
Church of the Nativity (Bethlehem), 1244–1245
Church of Niederglatt (Saint Gall), 1110
Church of Saint John (Alexandria), 93, 94
Church of Saint John (Dayr al-Majma'), 820, *821*
Church of Saint John (Dayr al-Suryān), 879
Church of the Holy Virgin in Gethsemane. *See* Jerusalem, Coptic See of
Church of Our Lady (Dayr al-Muḥarraq), 1969
Church of Our Lady (Martmaryam) (Alexandria), 93
Church of Our Lady (Old Cairo). *See* Church of al-Mu'allaqah
Church of Our Lady (Shubra), 882
Church of Qasriyat al-Rihan. *See* Babylon
Church of the Qayṣāriyyah (Alexandrian Melchite church), 94
Church of Queen Helena (Jerusalem), 1327
Church of the Resurrection (Jerusalem), 446, 1326, 1328
Church of Rome. *See* Roman Catholic church
Church of Saint Ammonius and the Martyrs (Dayr al-Shuhadā'), 869
Church of Saint Andrew (Jericho), 1245
Church of Saint Antony (Dayr Anbā Anṭūniyūs), 720, 722, 724, 725
Church of Saint Antony (Dayr al-Mayūn), *839*, 839
Church of Saint Antony (Jaffa), 1246–1247
Church of Saint Antony (Jericho), 1246
Church of Saint Antony (Jerusalem), 1327
Church of Saint Colluthus (Antinoopolis), 1874
Church of Saint Gabriel (al-Naqlūn), 845
Church of Saint George (Alexandria), 92, 94
Church of Saint George (Jerusalem), 1327–1328
Church of Saint George (Old Cairo), 881, 1207, 1208–1209
Church of Saint George (Ṭurah), 1536
Church of Saint John the Baptist (Alexandria), 101, 1870
Church of Saint John the Baptist (River Jordan), 1246
Church of Saint John the Baptist (Scetis), 792
Church of Saint John the Evangelist (Alexandria), 92
Church of Saint John of Sanhūt (Damanhūr Shubra), 882
Church of Saint Joseph (Cairo), 1123
Church of Saint Macarius, 749, 750–751, 754
Church of Saint Mark (Dayr Anbā Anṭūniyūs), 720–721, 722
Church of Saint Mark (Dayr Asfal al-Arḍ), 783
Church of Saint Mary (Philae), 1954
Church of Saint Menas (Abū Mīnā) (Alexandria), 92, 94
Church of Saint Mercurius (Alexandria), 92
Church of Saint Mercurius (Dayr Anbā Būlā), 743
Church of Saint Mercurius (Dayr al-Maymūn), *839*, 839
Church of Saint Mercurius (Old Cairo). *See* Church of Abū Sayfayn; Dayr Abū Sayfayn
Church of Saint Michael (Babylon), 323
Church of Saint Michael (al-Bharī), 815
Church of Saint Michael (Dayr Anbā Bishoi), 736
Church of Saint Michael (Dayr Anbā Būlā), 741
Church of Saint Michael (Dayr al-Majma'), 820, 821
Church of Saint Michael (Dayr al-Naqlūn), 845
Church of Saint Michael (Kafr al-Dayr), 1656
Church of Saint Nicholas (Alexandria), 94
Church of Saint Palaemon. *See* Dayr Sitt Dimyānah
Church of Saint Paul of Thebes, 721, 741
Church of Saint Peter the Apostle (Alexandria), 94
Church of Saint Raphael at Tamīt, **2201**
Church of Saint Sanutius (Alexandria), 94
Church of Saint Sergius, 318, *319*, *320*
altar made of wood, *2328*
as patriarchal site, 1912
Church of Saints Felix and Regula (Zurich), 1110
Church of Saint Shenute, 768–769, 1875
Church of Saint Sinuthius, 321–322, *322*, 321–322, *322*
Church of Saint Sophia (Constantinople), 2143, 2144
Church of Saints Sergius and Bacchus (Church of the Nativity) (Cairo), 1875
Church of Saints Sergius and Wachas (Alexandria), 94
Church of Saint Stephen (Philae), 1870
Church of Saint Theodorus (Shubra), 882
Church of Saint Thomas, 835–836
Church of Santa Maria Novella (Florence), 1119
Church of the Saviour (Alexandria), 94
Church of the Sepulcher of the Holy Virgin (Jerusalem), 1328
Church of Sitt Barbārah (Old Cairo), 318–319, 2038
door, *2332*
screen, *2335*
Church of Sitt Dimyānah, 872
Church of Sitt Maryam, 319–320, 879, 880
Church of Thaddaeus (Alexandria), 93
Church of Thalwil (Zurich), 1110
Church of Theodosius (Alexandria), 94
Church of the Three Peasants (Dayr al-Shuhadā'), 870

Church of the Tomb of the Prophet Jeremiah (Alexandria vicinity), 94
Church of the Virgin (Babylon), 320, 323
Church of the Virgin in the Desert of Apa Shenute, 763
Church of the Virgin Mary (Alexandria), 93
Church of the Virgin Mary (Dahshūr), 685
Church of the Virgin Mary (Dayr al-ʿAdhrā'), 927
Church of the Virgin Mary (Dumyāṭ), 925
Church of the Virgin (Old Cairo), 1207, 1208–1209
Church of Wattwil (Saint Gall), 1110
Ciasca, Agostino, **560**
Ciborium, 202
Circumcellion movement, 920
Circumcision, 1581, 1699
Circumcision, Feast of, 1106
Cities
  Abūqīr, 31–32
  Abūṣīr (Taposiris Magna), 34
  Abyār, 38
  al-Afrājūn, 64
  Alexandria, 95–102
  Anṣīna, 142–143
  Armant, 233–234
  Ashmūn, 285
  al-Ashmūnayn, 285–288
  Atrīb, 307
  Babylon, 317
  al-Bahnasā, 330
  al-Balyanā, 333
  Banā, 333
  Banī Suef, 335
  al-Baramūn, 344–345
  Basṭah, 360–361
  al-Batanūn, 361
  Bilbeis, 391
  Dongola, 921–922
  Dumyāṭ, 925–926
  Durunkah, 926–927
  al-Faramā, 1089–1090
  Fayyūm, 1100
  Fuwwah, 1125–1126
  Giza, 1141–1142
  Greek in Egypt, 1179–1181
  Ḥārit al-Rūm section of Old Cairo, 1206–1207
  Ḥārit Zuwaylah section of Old Cairo, 1207–1209
  Hiw, 1242–1243
  Ibṭū, 1275
  Idfā, 1280
  Idkū, 1280–1281
  Isnā, 1312
  Iṭfīḥ, 1313
  Luxor, 1484
  al-Maḥallah al-Kubrā, 1510
  al-Manṣūrah, 1524
  Mareotis, 1526–1527
  Memphis, 1586–1587
  Minūf al-ʿUlyah, 1633
  Minyā, 1634
  Naqādah, 1774
  Naucratis, 1783–1784, 1783–1784
  Nikiou, 1793
  Pimandjoili, 1977
  Qallīn, 2036
  Qalyūb, 2036
  al-Qays, 2038
  Qifṭ, 2038–2040
  Qinā, 2040
  Rashīd, 2054
  Samannūd, 2090
  Soba, 2141–2142
  Tinnis, 2269
  Tmuis, 2270
  see also Toponymy, Coptic; Towns and settlements; specific cities
Civil law. *See* Law, Coptic
Clapper (castanet), 1739, 2333, *2334*
Claremont Institute for Antiquity and Christianity, 1899
Clarinet, 1740
Clarke, Somers, **560**
  on Dayr al-Majmaʿ, 820, 821
  on Dayr al-Malāk Mīkhā'īl (Idfū), 825
  on Dayr al-Malāk Mīkhā'īl (Jirjā), 825–826
  on Durunkah, 926
Classical subjects. *See* Mythological subjects in Coptic art; specific pagan deities
Claude of Antioch, Saint, 592, 701
Claudian (poet), 100
Claudius II, Emperor, 1377, 1378, 1530, 1914
Claudius Labīb. *See* Iqlādyūs Labīb
Claudius, Saint, **561**, 732
  paintings of, 727, 869
Claudius Ptolemy, 1731
Claudius Stratelates (martyr), 1456, 1553
Cleansing. *See* Ablution
Clédat, Jean, **561**, 1482
Clement, Canons of. *See* Canons of Clement
Clement I, Saint, **561–562**, 2083
  as apostolic father, 180
  patristic writings, 1920
  see also Octateuch of Clement
Clement VIII, Pope (Rome), signing of Act of Union, 716, 810
Clement of Alexandria, Saint, **562–563**, 1096
  and Alexandrian theology. *See subhead* Catechetical School
  on angels, 132
  apologia, 176
  and baptism, 337
  and Basilides, 356–357
  on Carpocratian sect, 460–461
  and Catechetical School, 100–101, 103–104, 470, 474, 892, 893, 931
  on celibacy, 476
  and Chairemon of Alexandria, 512
  on Clement I, Saint, 561
  and Coptic education, 932
  in defense of the faith, 176–177
  docetism and, 917
  on ecclesiastical hierarchy, 2016
  on Egyptian religion, 1867
  on encratites, 958
  and eschatology, 973
  on Eucharist, 597, 1065
  feast day, 2083
  and Gnostic-related concepts, 470, 1076, 1148, 1150, 1163
  on Gospel of Saint Mark, 1158, 1161
  and Heracleon, 1219
  on incense use, 1472
  in Jerusalem, 1324
  and liturgical music, 1732, 1733
  on marriage, 1542, 1543
  on mixing Eucharistic wine with water, 1065
  on Nativity date, 1102
  Pantaenus' influence on, 1881
  Philo and, 1957
  and Secret Gospel of Saint Mark, 2118–2119
  on symbolism of women's headdress, 641

and *Teachings of Silvanus*, 2207
and *Testimony of Truth*, 2210
and *Theotokos*, 2255
Clement of Rome. *See* Clement I, Saint
Cleopas, Saint, 2083
Cleopatra, Queen, 90, 1617
Cleopatra (town), 695–696
Clerestory. *See* Basilica
Clerical College (Cairo), **563–564**, 1302, 1397, 1737, 1962
and Anbā Ruways Monastery, 129
and Cyril V, 679
and Ḥabib Jirjis, 1189
and Higher Institute of Coptic Studies, 1230
and inception of Coptic youth movements, 2354
and Iqlādiyūs Labīb, 1302
reforms in, 1465
role in Coptic education, 931–933
and Samuel, Bishop, 2090–2091
and Sarjiyūs, Malatī, 2096
and Shenouda III, 567, 2130
and Tādrus Shinudah al-Manqabādī, 2197–2198
and Yacobos II, 2349
and Yassa ʿAbd al-Masīḥ, 2353
Clerical instruction, **564–565**, 1844
Clermont-Tonnerre, Amédée de, 1285
Cleveland Museum of Art, Ohio, 1764
Clodius Culcianus, Prefect, 1937, 1963–1964, 2009
Cloister. *See* Atrium
Clothing. *See* Costume, civil; Costume, military; Costume of the religious; Textiles, Coptic
Clysma, **565**
chapels marking Exodus, 1976
as John Colobos refuge, 701, 795
as shipbuilding center, 89
Coats. *See* Costume, civil
Codex, **565–566**, *566*, *567*
bookbinding, 407–409
see also Codicology; Manuscripts; Nag Hammadi Library
Codex Alexandrinus, **566–567**
Codex Askewianus, 1148
Codex Brucianus, 1148
Codex cover, *409*
Codex Ephraemi Syri, 566, **568**
Codex Jung, **568–569**
Codex Justinianus, **569–570**, 1889, 1385
Codex Sinaiticus, 566, 567, **570–571**, 1222, 1900
Codex Theodosianus, 1889
Codex Vaticanus, 566, 567, **572**
Codex VII. *See Second Treatise of the Great Seth*
Codicology, **572–573**
Coffer, 203
Coffins, wood, 2330–2331
Cohort. *See* Army, Roman
Coinage in Egypt, **573–576**
Byzantine, 53, 574
Coptic, 944
Dayr Abū Qarqūrah excavation, 709
Islamic period, 575–576
Roman Empire, 905, 907
Colcasia antiquorum (vegetable), 1103
Collège de France, 1440
Collucianists. *See* Lucian of Antioch
Colluthus, **577**
Colluthus, Saint, 771
martyrdom of, 701, 702, 1554
Colobos, John. *See* John Colobos, Saint
Cologne Mani Codex, 1899
Colonnade, 204
Colophon, **577**
Columbia University, New York City, 780, 1895
Column, 202–207, *205–207*, *2167*
woodwork, 2345
Combs
ivory artwork, 406–407, *406*
weaver's wooden, 2340–2341, *2341*
woodwork, 2327, 2336–2337, *2337*
Comintern, 1996
Commentaries of ʿAbdallāh ibn al-Ṭayyib, manuscripts in National Library, Paris, 1777
Commentaries on Corinthians (Origen), 1847
Commentaries on the Creed (medieval)
of Abū al-Majd, 22–23
of Ibn Kabar, 21
of Sāwīrus ibn al-Muqaffaʿ, 21
Commentaries on the Gospels, manuscripts in National Library, Paris, 1777, 1778
Commentaries on Job (Didymus), 900
Commentaries of Origen, 1847, 1852–1853
Commentary on the Apocalypse, 1268
Commentary on the Creed (Abū al-Majd), 21–23
Commentary on Ecclesiastes (Gregory of Nyssa), 1184–1185
A Commentary on Psalms XX–XLXI (Didymus), 900
Commentary on Saint John's Gospel (Origen), 1847
Commission for the Preservation of Arab Monuments, 1700
Commodus, Emperor, 892, 1914
Communicatio idiomatum, **578**, 1441, 2255
Communion, **578–579**, 1567–1568
ablution before and during, 8–9
and absolution, 17
and baptism, 339
baptism prerequisite, 1106
concomitance belief, 584
and confirmation, 586
consubstantiation doctrine, 597–598
excommunication from, 1079–1080
liturgical instruments, 1472–1473
in marriage ceremony, 1543
and pilgrimages, 1968
and reservation of the blessed sacrament, 2073
on Saturday, 2098–2099
see also Eucharist
Communion of the sick, **579–580**, 2073
see also Unction of the sick
Communion table, **580**
Communion vessels
chalice, 1065
Coptic glass, 1146
Community Council, Coptic, **580–581**
and Boutros Ghālī, 416
and Clerical College founding, 563
defense of, 1962, 1963
formation of, 1941–1942
and Ḥabīb Jirjis, 1189

Community Council, Coptic (*cont.*)
and Higher Institute of Coptic Studies founding, 1230
and John XIX, 1351
and Sa'd Mīkhā'īl 'Abdū, 2073–2074
and Sarjiyūs, Malatī, 2097
and Tādrus Shinudah al-Manqabādī, 2198
and *waqf*, 2319
and Ya'qūb Nakhlah Rufaylah, 2353
Compline, **582–583**, 900
Concept of Our Great Power, **583**
Conch shell, as Coptic art symbol, 2163–2164
Concomitance, **584**
Concordat of 616, 688
Conferences (John Cassian), 1663
Confession and penitence, **584–585**
absolution, 15–17
penance, 1932
Confessions (Augustine), 1929, 1982
Confessions of the Fathers (anthology), 21
Confirmation, **585–586**
anointing and, 138, 586
Confraternity, **586–587**
Congregatio de Propaganda Fide, 1122
Congress of Asyūṭ, Coptic. *See* Coptic Congress of Asyūṭ
Conon. *See* Qūnā (martyr)
Consecration, **588**
of altar, 108–109
of baptistery, 342–343
of bishop, 394, 395–398
of building and objects, 139–140
of church. *See* Church, consecration of
of liturgical instruments, 1469
of liturgical vestments, 1475–1476
of patriarch, 1909–1910, 1912
prayers for, 1566–1567
of vessels and icons, 140; *see also* Eucharistic vessels
Constans, Emperor, 150, 1678
Constantine I, Emperor, **588–590**, 920, 1618, 2063
and Alexandria, 101
antipaganism of, 1869
and Antony of Egypt, Saint, 150
and Athanasius exile, 299
and *audientia episcopalis*, 308
and canon law, 1941
and Church of the Nativity (Bethlehem), 1244–1245
conversion of, 1551
on Easter designation, 1104
and Eudoxia, 1067
and Eusebius, 1071
and Eusignius, Saint, 1072
and holy places rediscovered in Jerusalem, 1324
and *homoousion* controversy, 1253
and Nicaea, Council of, 81, 83, 232, 589–590, 1791, 1792
patriarch under, 1914
reforms in Egypt, 943, 944
and Theodotus of Ancyra, 2243
vision of the cross of Christ, 1072, 1243–1244, 1377
Constantine II, Emperor
and Melchite patriarchy, 93
patriarch under, 1914
Constantine V, Emperor, and iconoclasm, 1275, 1276
Constantine VI, Emperor, 1275
Constantine VII, Emperor, 1098
Constantine IX, Emperor, 1099
Constantine of Asyūṭ, Bishop, 84, 296, **590–592**
Basil of Oxyrhynchus writings and, 360
on Coptic hagiography, 1192–1193
panegyrics by, 1456
Constantine the Great. *See* Constantine I, Emperor
Constantinople
Acacian schism with Rome, 42–47
administrative organization of Egypt, 934
Alexandria and, 98–99
Antiochene problem, 688
Arab naval assault on (717–718), 85, 2286
Byzantine influences on Coptic art, 241–243
and Egyptian *annona*, 135
founding of, 590, 943
patriarchs, 2016–2017
see of, 913
Tall Brothers exile in, 916
Theotokos as protector of, 1276
Constantinople, First Council of (381), 230, **593–595**, 1671
on anointing of heretics, 138–139
on Apollinarianism, 174, 1669
and *Apostolic Constitutions*, 179
and Arian controversy, 230
bishop's consecration affirming, 394, 396
on confirmation, 586
and ecclesiastical use of eparchy, 959
and Gregory of Nyssa, 1184
Henoticon edict affirming, 1217
on the Holy Spirit, 1250
and *homoiousion* controversy, 1253
homoousion reinstatement, 1253
on nature of Christ, 525
and Nicene Creed, 1116, 1793
on Origen, 1850
on Sabellianism, 2072
and semi-Arians, 2118
and Timothy I, 2263
and Zeno, Emperor, 2370
Constantinople, Second Council of (553), **595–596**, 1676
and Didymus the Blind, 900
on Origen, 1851, 1855–1856
and Theodorus of Mopsuestia's writings, 2239
on three-immersion baptism, 1286
Constantinople, Third Council of (680–681), 1678, **596–597**
Constantius II, Emperor, 2, 101, 102, 150, 904, 1380, 1381, 1869, 1959
Constitutions of the Holy Apostles. *See Apostolic Constitutions*
Consubstantiation, 590, **597–598**
see also Homoiousion; *Homoousion*
Consultative Council, **598**
Contra Celsum (Origen), 176–177, 1847, 1854
Contra Julianum (Cyril of Alexandria), 177
Convents. *See* Women's religious communities
Conversion of dates, 435–436
Conversion to Christianity. *See* Baptism; Catechumen; Missionaries
Conversion to Islam. *See* Egypt, Islamization of
Cooking vessels. *See* Ceramics, Coptic

Copper coins, 575, 576
Copres, Saint (monk and martyr), **598**, 1554
Copt, definition of, **599–601**
Coptic archbishops in Jerusalem, 1325–1326
Coptic art. *See* Art headings; Art and architecture; Christian subjects in Coptic art; Church art; Monastery paintings; Mythological subjects in Coptic art; Painting, Coptic mural; Portraiture; Statuary; Sculpture in stone; Symbols in Coptic art
Coptic Catholic Church, **601–602**
  and Coptic relations with Rome, 611
  and Jesuits in Egypt, 1330
  and monophysitism, 547–548
  and Sicard, Claude, 2137
  in the Sudan, 2157–2158
  see also Coptic relations with Rome
Coptic Clerical College (Cairo). *See* Clerical College
Coptic collections. *See* Museums, Coptic collections in; Papyrus collections; specific museums
Coptic Community Council. *See* Community Council, Coptic
Coptic Congress of Asyūṭ (1911), **602–603**, 1465, 1466, 1627, 1693, 1911, 2011
  and Egyptian Conference of Heliopolis, 948
  and Egyptian national unity, 950–951
  and Wissa Wassef, 2323
Coptic correspondence, 970–971
Coptic Dictionary (Crum), 614, 661
Coptic Dictionary (Spiegelberg), 2145
Coptic Evangelical Church, **603–604**
  in the Sudan, 2158
Coptic Grammar (Steindorff), 2148
Coptic history. *See* Hagiography, Coptic; Historians; specific aspects
Coptic Horologion, 4
Coptic Hospital, 1693
Coptic language. *See* Language, Coptic; specific dialects and *Appendix*
Coptic language, spoken, **604–606**
Coptic Legion, 1206, 1512, 1524, 2089, 2137
  establishment of, 1417
  study sources, 2350
  see also Ya'qūb, General
Coptic Life of Maximus and Domitius. *See* Maximus and Domitius
Coptic literature. *See* Literature, Coptic
Coptic martyrs. *See* Martyrs
Coptic Museum (Old Cairo), 4, 8, 74–76, *208*, **607–608**, *607*, 710, 776, 777, 800, 824, 844, 1138, 1427, 1449, 1698, 1701, 2040
  Coptic metalwork examples, 1596, 1598, 1599–1601, *1599*, 1602
  and Coptological studies, 615–616
  founder of, 1700
  manuscript on life of Paul of Tamma at, 1925
  and Nag Hammadi codices, 1771–1773
  papyrus collection, 1892
  pen cases at, 1933
Coptic Nation Association (Jamā'at al-Ummah al-Qibṭiyyah), 1694
Coptic Orthodox Church, History of. *See History of the Patriarchs of Alexandria*
Coptic Orthodox Hermitage of Saint Mark (Toulon), 1623
Coptic Patriarchate (Cairo), 1892
Coptic Reform Society, **608–609**
Coptic relations with Rome, **609–611**
  see also Roman Catholic church; Trent, Council of
Coptic See of Jerusalem. *See* Jerusalem, Coptic See of
Coptic Street, London, **611–612**
Coptic studies. *See* Coptological studies; Coptology; Scholars
Coptic Testament of Isaac, 164, **612**
Coptic Trading Corporation, 2198
Copto-Armenian relations. *See* Armenians and the Copts
Copto-Ethiopian church negotiations. *See* Ethiopian Church Autocephaly
Coptologia (journal), **613**
Coptological studies, **612–616**
  Awlād al-'Assāl family and, 310–311
  Chaîne, Marius Jean Joseph, 511–512
  Chassinat, Emile Gaston, 516–517
  Ciasca, Agostino, 560
  Clédat, Jean, 561
  Cramer, Maria, 656–657
  Crum, Walter Ewing, 663
  Gaselee, Stephen, 1136
  Heuser, Gustav, 1227
  international congresses and associations, 1299–1301
  Jernstedt, Peter Viktorovich, 1323
  Jesuit contributions, 1330
  Junker, Hermann, 1383
  and Nag Hammadi Library, 1770–1773
  O'Leary, De Lacy Evans, 1840
  Omar Toussoun, 1315–1316
  Rösch, Friedrich, 2067
  Saint-Paul-Girard, Louis, 2081
  Schmidt, Carl, 2106–2107
  Scholtz, Christian, 2107
  Schwartze, Moritz Gotthilf, 2107
  Simon, Jean, 2140
  Stegemann, Viktor, 2148
  Steindorff, Georg, 2148
  Thompson, Henry Francis Herbert, 2257
  Till, Walter, 2261
  value of inscriptions, 1291
  Vansleb (Wansleben), Johann Michael, 2299
  Worrell, William Hoyt, 2348
  see also Archaeologists; Archives; Coptology; Excavations; Libraries; Manuscripts; Museums; Papyrus collections; Scholars; Society of Coptic Archaeology; specific countries, personal names, and subjects
Coptology, **616–618**
Coptos. *See* Qifṭ
Copts in late medieval Egypt, **618–634**
Copts and Moslems Under the British Control (Mikhail), 1627
Corbels, wood, 2344–2345, *2344*
Corinthian capital, 205–206, *205*, *206*, 739, 760
  at al-Ashmūnayn, *287*
  church at Dayr Anbā Bishoi (Sūhaj), 739

Corinthian capital (*cont.*)
church at Dayr Anbā Ṣamū'īl of Qalamūn, 760
church at Dayr al-Maymūn, 839
Cornelius, **635**, 1618
Cornelius the Centurion, Saint, 2083
Corpus, Apollo, and Peter, Saints, 2083
Corpus Hermeticum. *See* Hermes Trismegistus
Corpus Scriptorum Christianorum Orientalium edition. *See* Synaxarion, Copto-Arabic
Correspondence. *See* Epistolography
Cosmas I, Patriarch, 334, **636**, 1589, 2083
dates of patriarchy, 1915
Cosmas II, Patriarch, **636–637**, 902, 903, 2083
dates of patriarchy, 1916
Yuḥannā biography of, 2356
Cosmas III, Patriarch, **637–638**, 2083
dates of patriarchy, 1916
Cosmas and Damian, Saints (martyrs), **636–640**, 1554, 1576, 1973
churches dedicated to, 93, 126, 716–717, 2017
as doctors, 1213
Cosmas Indicopleustes, **640–641**, 1635
and Timothy III, 2268
Cosmos. *See* Quzmān of Ṭaḥā and his companions (martyrs)
Cosson, A. F. C., de, 1397, 1402
Costume, civil, **641–648**, *643*, *644*, *645*, *646*, *647*
belts and handbags, 645
dalmatic, 647–648
Dhimmis requirements, 72
distinguishing Copts, 1535
headdresses, 641–642
hides and skins, preservation of, 280
leather sandals and shoes, 1433
Nubian, 1820
scarves, 643–644
shawls, 642–643
socks, sandals, and shoes, 645–647
tunics, 644–645
undergarments, 645
see also Textiles, Coptic
Costume, military, **649–650**, *649*
Costume of the religious, **650–655**
anchorites, 130
bishop's consecration, 395–396
see also Liturgical vestments
Cotton, used in Coptic textiles, 2213
Councils, ecumenical. *See* name inverted, e.g., Chalcedon, Council of
Courts. *See* Law; Personal status courts
Covenant of 'Umar, **655–656**, 1570
and Cosmas I, 636
Ibn Qayyim al-Jawziyyah commentary on, 1269–1270
and Incident of the Churches, 2314
and John VIII patriarchy, 1343–1344
and John XI patriarchy, 1345
and Mamluks, 2318
renewal of, 1518
Cramer, Maria, **656–657**, 1727
Credit. *See* Law of obligation
Creed. *See* Apostle's Creed; Athanasian Creed; Constantinople, First Council of; Nicene Creed
Crete, 1098
Cromer, Lord (British High Commissioner), 1693
Cronius of Nitria, Saint, 149, 2083
see also Antony of Egypt, Saint
Cronus (pagan god), 1617
Crops. *See* Agriculture
Crosby Schøyen Codex, **656–658**
Cross
ankh shape, 134–135
on antimension, 144
apparitions of sign of the, 1243–1244
Constantine the Great vision, 1072, 1243–1244, 1377
Coptic, *406*, *407*
Coptic colored glass inlays, 1146
Coptic metalwork, *1595*, 1596, 1597, *1597*, 1606
Holy Cross Day, 1243–1244
illuminated manuscript depiction, 1284
intersected, 252
Lālibalā church in shape of, 1425
legends on discovery of, 1377–1378; *see also* Constantine, Emperor; Helena, Saint
liturgical insignia, 1468–1469
manual, liturgical use of, 1472
in mural paintings, 1875
pectoral. *See* Liturgical insignia
as primary motif in the Kellia, 1409
processional. *See* Liturgical insignia
Saladin's decrees against, 1535
sculpture in stone depictions, *2114*, *2116*
as symbol in Coptic art, 2164–2166
wall painting depictions, 779, 1660, 1875
woodworked, 2331, *2331*
Cross, sign of the, **658**
see also Holy Cross Day
Cross, Triumph of the, **658–659**, *659*
Cross, veneration of the, **660**
Cross of Christ. *See* Holy Cross Day
Cross-in-square, **660–661**
in Nubian Christian architecture, 661, 1810
see also Architectural elements of churches
Cross with tapers, 1469
Cross vault. *See* Vault
Crotalum, 1604–1605, 1740
Crowns. *See* Diadems; Miter
Crucifixion. *See* Cross; Good Friday; Holy Cross Day; Incarnation
Cruet, 1472–1473, 1598
Crum, Walter Ewing, 614, **663**, 780, 806, 1448, 1726, 1892, 1893, 1894, 1895
and Erman, Adolf, 973
and identity of Hor, 1254
and identity of John of Armant, 1354
on Latson, Apa, 1427
on Severian of Jabalah, 2123
and Shenute text-editing, 1452
Crusades, Copts and the, 314–315, **663–665**
alliances with Fatimids and Byzantines, 1099
in Apocryphal Apocalypse of Daniel, 165
and Athanasius III patriarchy, 303
and Ayyubid dynasty, 314–315
Coptic view of, 1488, 1615

and Dayr al-ʿAdhrā (Samālūṭ), 716
and Dayr Asfal al-Arḍ, 783
and Dayr al-Sultān, 872
defeat at al-Manṣūrah, 1524
and Dumyāṭ destruction, 925
and al-Faramā destruction, 1090
Muslim view of, 939
Peter I (Pierre) de Lusignan, 1537, 1569–1570
and pilgrimages to Christian Egypt, 1975
Crux ansata
in Triumph of the Cross tapestry, 659
see also Ankh
Crypt, 208–209
Saint Sergius, 318, *320*
Cryptograms, 1863
Cryptography. *See Appendix*
Cryptophoneme. *See Appendix*
Cultural Center of the Villa Hügel (Essen), 257
Cups, 1601–1602
Currency. *See* Coinage in Egypt
Curses, 1931–1932
Curzon, Robert, **665–666**, 879, 1448
Cuthbert, Saint (British Isles), 419
Cycle, **666–668**, 1457–1458
Anub, 152
Archelaus of Neapolis, 192
Bacheus, 324
Basilidas, 1553
Basil of Oxyrhynchus, 360
and Coptic hagiography, 1191–1193, 1196
Demetrius of Antioch, 893
Eustathius of Thrace, 1073
John Chrysostom, 1358
Theodosius of Jerusalem, 2242
see also Hagiography; Literature, Coptic; specific cycles
Cycle of Athanasius, 666–667
Cycle of Basil of Caesarea, 667
Cycle of Basilides. *See* Basilides; names of specific martyrs and saints
Cycle of Cyril of Jerusalem, 667
Cycle of Evodius of Rome, 667–668
Cycle of John Chrysostom and Demetrius, 667
Cycle of Julius of Aqfahṣ, and martyrdom of Saint Ari, 229
Cycle of Theodores, 668
Cycle of Theophilus, 667
Cycle of Victor, Claudius, and Cosmas and Damian, 668
Cymbals, 1604–1605, 1738, *1738*, 1739, 1740, 1968
Cyriacus and Julitta, Saints (martyrs), **671**, 1554
Cyprian of Carthage, 890
Cyprian the Magician, Saint, **668–669**, 1504, 1945, 1946
Cyprus, monasteries in, 1647–1648
Cyrenaica. *See* Pentapolis
Cyriacus, Bishop of al-Bahnasā, **669–670**, 813, 2305
Cyriacus, King of Nubia, 1411
Cyril I, Saint and Patriarch, 20, 44, 55, 71, 93, **671–675**, 926, 1674, 1676, 1921, 2083
anaphora, 71, 123–124, 352, 988–990, 1066–1067, 1539
on anathema, 127–128, 1217
anathemas accepted at Ephesus, Second Council of, 961–962
on Assumption, 292
and bishop's translation, 399
and Celestinus, 475
and Chalcedon, Council of, 512–515
Christology, 514–515, 523, 547, 596, 913, 914, 1669, 1672
on *communicatio idiomatum*, 578
contra Julianum, 177
and Coptic Catholic Church, 601–602
and Cycle of Athanasius, 666
Cyrillian mass, 1532
dates of patriarchy, 1915
in defense of the faith, 176–177
and Dioscorus I, 912–913
and Egyptian paganism, 1868
and Ephesus, First Council of, 762, 959–960
on the Eucharist, 597
and Eutyches, 1074–1075
and *filioque* justification, 1115
and Henoticon edict, 1217
Hesychius of Alexandria and letters of, 1227
homily on John Chrysostom and Theophilius, 1358
homily on Raphael, Archangel, 2053
homily on the Three Hebrews in the Furnace, 2258
and hypostatic union, 1262
on Incarnation, 1287
and John of Antioch, Bishop, 1354
and Leo I the Great, 1440, 1441
liturgical authorship, 1733
on marriage, 1542–1543
on musical instruments, 1738
on nature of Christ. *See subhead* Christology
and Nestorians, 609, 1785–1786
opposition to anthropomorphism, 758, 1652
on paschal controversy, 1906
patristic writings, 1921
and Pelagianism, 1930
and Pulcheria, 2033
and Shenute, Saint, 2131–2132
and Susinius, Saint, 2087
and Theodoret, 2236
and Theodotus of Ancyra, Bishop, 2242
and Theophilus, Patriarch, 2247, 2248
on *Theotokos*, 270, 542, 2255
on unction of the sick, 2292
Cyril II, Patriarch, **675–676**
and Alexandrian historic church restoration, 94
and Badr al-Jamālī, 325
biography, 1573, 1574
and canons of Coptic law, 450
and Church of al-Muʿallaqah (Old Cairo), 558
condemnation of *cheirotonia*, 517
consecration of Sāwiros as Ethiopian metropolitan, 1005
Dahlak refuge, 685
dates of patriarchy, 1917
feast day as saint, 2083
and Ghuzz plunder, 689
and James of Scetis, 1322
and liturgical language, 1734
Cyril III ibn Laqlaq, Patriarch, 38, **677**, 1009, 1207, 1209, 1613
and Basilios I as Jerusalem archbishop, 1325
and Būlus al-Būshī, 423
church law codification, 1942
and Coptic relations with Rome, 609
and Damanhūr bishops, 686
dates of patriarchy, 1917
and Dayr al-Nastūr, 848
death and burial at Dayr al-Shamʿ, 865
and Epiphany tanks, 968

Cyril III ibn Laqlaq, Patriarch (*cont.*)
  and Joseph, Bishop of Fuwwah, 1126
  and al-Ṣafī ibn al-ʿAssāl, 2075, 2078
Cyril IV, Patriarch, 358, **677–679**, 1613, 1614, 1693, 1993
  and cantorial training, 1736–1737
  and Coptic Clerical College founding, 1962
  dates of patriarchy, 1919
  and Dayr Anbā Anṭūniyūs, 723
  educational reforms, 932–933
  Ethiopian visit, 1035
  icon destruction by, 293, 1278
  and ʿIryān Jirjis Muftāḥ, 1302–1303
  patriarchal residence, 1206, 2000
  and printing of Bohairic-Coptic Bible, 564
  reforms of, 580–581, 932–933, 1465, 1466
  and Saʿd Mīkhāʾīl ʿAbdū, 2073
  and Tādrus al-Mashriqī as historian of, 2197
Cyril V, Patriarch, **679**, 1465, 1629, 1647
  and ʿAbd al-Masīḥ Ṣalīb al-Masūʿdī, 7
  and Abraam I, 10
  and apocryphal literature, 161
  and baptismal prayer wording, 343
  and Boutros Ghālī, 416
  and British occupation of Egypt, 420–422
  and cantorial training, 1737
  and Clerical College founding, 563
  condemnation of apocrypha, 161
  and Coptic community council, 580, 1693
  and Coptic Congress of Asyūṭ, 602–603
  and Coptic education, 932–933
  and Coptic Museum (Old Cairo), 607
  dates of patriarchy, 1919
  Dayr al-Amīr Tādrūs as retirement site, 718
  and Dayr Shahrān, 863
  and Ethiopian church autocephaly, 980
  and Ethiopian church controversies, 986–987
  and Ḥabib Jirjis, 1189
  and Haile Selassie I, 1198
  and inception of Coptic Youth movements, 2354
  and Iqlādiyūs Labīb scholarship, 1302
  and Isidhūrus, 1307
  and John XIX, 1351
  and Mātēwos, Ethiopian prelate, 1038
  as monk at Dayr al-Baramūs, 791
  and Pēṭros IV, Ethiopian prelate, 1038
  and Saʿd Mīkhāʾīl ʿAbdū, 2073–2074
  and Sarjiyūs, Malaṭī, 2096
  and Timotheos I, 2262
  and ʿUrābī's revolt, 1693
Cyril VI, Patriarch, **679–681**, *680*, 1621, 1942
  and Community Council, 582
  dates of patriarchy, 1919
  and Dayr Abū Mīnā, 706–707
  and Dayr al-Baramūs, 791
  and Dayr al-Sulṭān, 873, 874
  on divorce, 1943
  early monastic life, 1541
  and Ethiopian church autocephaly, 983
  and Makāri al-Suryānī, 2091
  and relics of Mark, Apostolic Saint, 1532
  and Sarjiyūs, Malaṭī, 2097
  successors, 1911
Cyril of Alexandria. *See* Cyril I, Saint and Patriarch
Cyril of Antioch, and hypostasis controversy, 1260
Cyril of Alexandria, Pseudo-. *See* Pseudo-Cyril of Alexandria
Cyril the Father of Reform. *See* Cyril IV, Patriarch
Cyril the Great. *See* Cyril I, Saint and Patriarch
Cyril of Jerusalem, Saint, **681–682**, 2083
  on ablution, 9
  on angels, 132
  anti-Manichaeism, 1522
  on Bacheus, 324
  and baptism, 337
  on candle use at Easter, 446
  on celibacy, 476
  cycle of, 667
  on Easter designation, 1104
  on Eucharist, 1056–1057, 1061
  on Gospel of Saint Mark, 1161
  on hand position for receiving Eucharist, 1065–1066
  on Holy Cross of Christ, 1243, 1244
  on *homoiousion*, 1253
  and Judas Cyriacus legend, 1378
  on Kiss of Peace, 1416
  on prayers for the dead, 889
  and rite of baptism, 138
  on second marriage, 901, 1545
Cyril Maqār. *See* Cyril I, Saint and Patriarch
Cyril of Scythopolis, 894, 1560
Cyril the Syrian, Bishop of Jerusalem, 1131
Cyrus, Anbā, marital chastity of, 1543
Cyrus (Apa Kīr) of Alexandria (martyr), 31, 1554
Cyrus (Apa Kīr) of Damanhūr (martyr), 688, 1554
Cyrus the Caucasian (Chalcedonian patriarch), 1609, 1666–1667, 1676, 2092
Cyrus al-Muqawqas, 90, 102, **682–683**, 1528, 1610
  and Arab conquest of Egypt, 184–188
  tomb in Alexandria, 94
Cyrus of Phasis, 2241
Czechoslovakia
  Coptic collections, 1703
  papyrus collections, 1891

D

Dabamun (martyr), 1554
Dābbah, Al-, Dayr al-Malāk, 822
Dabra Libanōs, eččagē title, 930
Dabra Metmāq. *See* Dayr al-Maghṭis
Dado, Saint, 1151–1152
Daff (musical instrument), 1738
Dafʿ al-Hamm (Elias of Nisibis), 1779
Dahlak, **685**
Dahshūr, **685**, 1653
Daidasa (martyr), 1554
Dākhlah Oasis, monasteries at, 706, 822, 1658
Dalās, **685**
Dalasina (martyr), 1553

Dalmatic, 647–648
Dālūshām (martyr), 730
Damallu, **686**
Damanhūr, **686–687**
  bishops of, 915–916
  martyrs, 1554
Damanhūrī, Shaykh Aḥmad, al-, **687**
Damanhūr Shubra, Dayr Yūḥannā at, 882
Damanhūr al-Waḥsh, **688**
Damascius, 1221, 1222
Damasus I, Pope (Rome), 1323, 1947
Damian, Saint (martyr). *See* Cosmas and Damian
Damian, Saint and Patriarch, **688–689**
  Anastasius as successor, 125
  Benjamin I and policies of, 376
  churches dedicated to, 716–717
  and Constantine of Asyūṭ, 592
  Coptic texts of, 1455
  dates of patriarchy, 1915
  and the Enaton, 956
  feast day, 2083
  Jacob Baradaeus on, 1319
  and John of Parallos, 1368
  and John of Shmūn, 1369
  Pisentius consecrated by, 1979
Damiana. *See* Dimyānah
Damnas (martyr), 1554
Damrū, **689–690**, 1652
  patriarchal seat at, 1912, 1959
  visited by Christodoulus, 545
Danābīq, al-. *See* Tambūq
Dancers
  Coptic art depictions, *537*, 1755–1757, *1756*
  Coptic embroidery, *2223*
  resist-dyed tapestry, *2228*
  tapestry with busts of, *277*, *2230*
  woven textile, *2226*
Dandarah, 553, **690–691**, *691*, 1657
  martyrs of, 1554
  monastic murals at, 1874
  pharaonic-style temples at, 1865
D'Andilly, Arnaud, 894
Dān'ēl, Ethiopian prelate, 1002
Danfiq (village), 1922
D'Anglure, Baron, 1977
Daniel (Old Testament), 22, 1618
  Apocryphal Apocalypse of, 165
  see also Daniel in the Lion's Den; Three Hebrews in the Furnace
Daniel, Hegumenos of Scetis, 125
Daniel in the Lion's Den
  depicted in Coptic art, 384–385
  Gabriel, Archangel, and, 1135, 1136, 1137
Daniel and Moses (hermits), **691–692**
Daniel of Scetis, Saint, **692**, 1648, 2083
  and legend of Mark the Simple, 1540–1541
Daniel the Stylite, 1671
Daphne, depicted in Coptic art, 1753–1754, *1754*, 1757–1758, *1758*
Daqādūs, **692**
  pilgrimages to, 1970, 1971
Daqahlah, **693**, 2270
Daqahliyyah Province, monasteries, 1648–1649
Daraj al-Haykal. *See* Architectural elements of churches
Darb al-Ḥīn, 687
Daressy, Georges Emile Jules, 693
Dār al-harb, 72
Dār al-Islām, 72–73
Darrāj, Aḥmad, on Egyptian persecutions of Christians and Jews, 1130
Darwāt Sarabām. *See* Dayr Abū Sarabām
Dasyah (martyr), 1554
Dating (Coptic monuments and artifacts), **693–694**
  Dayr Anbā Bākhūm (al-Ṣawām'ah Sharq), 731
  gravestones, 1293–1294
  Kellia excavations, 1400, 1401, 1407
  sculpture in stone, 2112–2113, 2117
  textiles, 255, 257
Daughters of Saint Mary (Banī Suef), 2325
Daumas, François, **694–695**, 1316
David (martyr), 1554
David at court of Saul, Coptic art depiction, 385
Dawlah, Al-. *See* Mu'taman Abū Isḥāq Ibrāhīm ibn al-'Assāl
Dāwūd, Ethiopian sovereign, 1570
Dawūd, Qusṭandī, 1466
Dāwūd-Shāh, Syrian patriarch, 878
Day of Atonement (Old Testament), 306, 1101
  see also Atonement
Day of Judgment. *See* Judgment, Last
Dayr, al-, **695**, 856, 1657, 1648, 1658
  see also Monasteries; specific monasteries
Dayr Abīrūn, **695–696**, 1650
Dayr Abū Anūb (Nūb), **696**
Dayr Abū Baghām. *See* Dayr Abū Bifām
Dayr Abū Banūkh. *See* Dayr Abū Līfah
Dayr Abū Bifām (Asyūṭ), **696**, 697, 1654
Dayr Abū Bifām (Samālūt), **696–697**
Dayr Abū Bifām (Timā), **697**
Dayr Abū Daraj, **697–698**, 728, 1649
Dayr Abū Fānah, **698–700**, *699*, 1654
  apse of, 196
Dayr Abū Ḥalbānah, **700**
  see also Dayr al-Sab'at Jibāl
Dayr Abū Ḥinnis (Mallawī), **701–703**, *701*, 794, 1654
  and Christian subjects in Coptic art, 533
  inscriptions found at, 1292
  John Colobos, Saint, and, 1360
  murals, 270, 1874
  representation of military costumes at, 650
  seal for stamping eucharistic bread, 1062
Dayr Abū Hurmus, 1652
Dayr Abū Isḥāq (Abnūb), **703**, 1655
Dayr Abū Isḥāq (Fayyūm). *See* Dayr al-Ḥammām
Dayr Abū Ja'rān, 1651
Dayr Abū Jirjā, 927, 1527–1528
Dayr Abū al-Līf, **703–704**, 1656
Dayr Abū Līfā, **704**, 1644, 1650
Dayr Abū Maqrūfah, **704–706**, 1654
Dayr Abū Mattā (Dākhlah Oasis), **706**
Dayr Abū Mīnā (Maryūt), **706–707**, 724, 1527
Dayr Abū Mūsā, 40, **707**, 1656, 1680
Dayr Abū Mūsā al-'Aswad, **708**
Dayr Abū Mūshā, **708**, 1654
Dayr Abū al-Ni'nā'. *See* Dayr Abū Ḥinnis

Dayr Abū Nūb (Dayr Apā Anūb), 770, 1654
Dayr Abū Qarqūrah, **708–709**
  and excavations by Zaki Yusef Saad, 2017
  and Simon I, 2139
Dayr Abū al-Ṣādir, 797
Dayr Abū Sarabām (Minyā), **709–710**, 718, 1654
Dayr Abū al-Sarī, 797
Dayr Abū Sayfayn (Akhmīm). *See* Akhmīm
Dayr Abū Sayfayn (Nag Hammadi). *See* Dayr Anbā Palaemon
Dayr Abū Sayfayn (Old Cairo), **710–711**, 1427, 1647, 1973
  Bayt al-Nisā' location, 373
  churches, 320
  as convent, 2325
  Epiphany tank use, 968
  murals, 1875
  pilgrimages to, 1972
  see also Church of Abū Sayfayn
Dayr Abū al-Sayfayn (Qūṣ), **711**, 1657
Dayr Abū al-Sayfayn (Tamwayh), **711–712**, 1652
Dayr Abū Shinūdah. *See* Dayr Anbā Shinūdah (Fayyūm)
Dayr Abū Ṣurrah (Asyūṭ region), 1655
Dayr al-Abyaḍ (Armant). *See* Dayr al-Maṭmar
Dayr al-Abyaḍ (Suhāj). *See* Dayr Anbā Shinūdah (Suhāj)
Dayr al-ʿAdawīyyah, **712–713**, 1535, 1653
Dayr al-ʿAdhrā' (Akhmīm), 78, 79, 80, 700, **713**, *713*, 823, 833, 836, 865, 927, 1654, 1655
Dayr al-ʿAdhrā' (Asyūṭ), **714**, 927, 1655
Dayr al-ʿAdhrā' (Fayyūm), **714**, 808, 1650
Dayr al-ʿAdhrā' (near Bayaḍ al-Naṣārā), **714**
Dayr al-ʿAdhrā' (near Jabal al-Tayr), **715**, *715*, 717
Dayr al-ʿAdhrā' (Qifṭ). *See* Monasteries of the Upper Ṣaʿīd
Dayr al-ʿAdhrā' (Samālūṭ), **715–716**
Dayr al-Aḥmar (Giza), **716–717**, 1652
Dayr al-Aḥmar (Suhāj). *See* Dayr Anbā Bishoi
Dayr al-ʿAjamiyyīn (Fayyūm), 1651
Dayr al-ʿĀmil, 1651
Dayr al-Amīr Tadrūs (Cairo). *See* Babylon
Dayr al-Amīr Tadrūs (Jabal Abū Fūdah), **717**
Dayr al-Amīr Tadrūs (Luxor), **717**, 1656
Dayr al-Amīr Tadrūs (Munā al-Amīr), **718**
Dayr Anbā Abshāy (Abū Tīj), **718–719**, 1654, 1978
Dayr Anbā Abshāy (near al-Ṭūd), **719**, 1657, 2030
Dayr Anbā al-Abyaḍ. *See* Dayr Anbā Shinūdah (Suhāj)
Dayr Anbā Anṭūniyūs, **719–728**, *724*, *725*, *726*, *727*, 841, 869, 871, 877–878, 1122, 1532, 1615, 1658, 1875
  and Athanasius III, 303
  Basilios II at, 358
  Basilios III at, 358
  Byzantine-influenced art at, 241, 242, 275
  as center of Eastern Desert monasteries, 1649
  chronology, 721–723
  Cyril IV and, 677, 1035
  and Dayr Anbā Bulā, 741
  and Dayr al-Mayūn, 838
  described by Vansleb (Wansleben), Johann Michael, 2299
  difnār found at, 1728
  and Ethiopian monks, 2191
  food supplied from Būsh, 427
  Gabriel VI, Patriarch, as monk in, 1133
  Gabriel VII, Patriarch, death at, 1134
  Gabriel VII, Patriarch, restoration of, 1133, 1134
  ḥiṣn at, 1237
  history, 720–721
  and homily on Saint Justus, 668
Dayr Anbā Anṭūniyuṣ, John XV at, 1347
Dayr Anbā Anṭūniyūs
  John XVI at, 1348
  John XVIII at, 1350
  layout of, 723–725
  Macarius III retreat to, 1489
  manuscript on life of Paul of Tamma at, 1925
  Mark VII as monk at, 1538
  Mārqos III, Ethiopian prelate, from, 1022
  Marqus al-Antūnī chapel at, 1699
  Mātēwos, Ethiopian prelate, from, 1039
  Matthew I as deacon at, 1569
  Menas, Saint, at, 1589
  Ottoman impact on, 1857
  painting of Abraham and Isaac at, 383
  papyri collection, 1892
  Peter VII at, 1950
  and Ṗēṭros I, Ethiopian prelate, 1001–1002
  pilgrims and travelers to, 1976–1977
  pillage of, 720, 722
  region of, 728
  role in Coptic education, 932
  scriptorium of, 2108
  and Theophilos I, 2247
  and Timotheos I, 2262
  and Yacobos II, 2349
  Yesḥaq I, Ethiopian prelate at, 1008
  and Yūsāb II, 2363
Dayr Anbā Anṭūniyūs (Qifṭ). *See* Monasteries of the Upper Sa'īd
Dayr Anbā Bākhūm, *see also* Dayr al-Malāk Mīkhā'īl (Idfū); Dayr al-Shuhadā'
Dayr Anbā Bākhūm (Abydos), 40, **729**, 1680
Dayr Anbā Bākhūm (Barjanūs), **729**
Dayr Anbā Bākhūm (Medamud; al-Madāmūd), **729–730, 1657**
Dayr Anbā Bākhūm (al-Sawāmʿah Sharq), 78, **730–731**, *731*
Dayr Anbā Bīḍābā, **731–732**, 1656
Dayr Anbā Bisādah, 78, 731, **732–733**, *733*, 883, 1657, 1973, 2030
  Idfā location, 1280
Dayr Anbā Bishoi (Barshah-Minyā). *See* Dayr al-Barshah
Dayr Anbā Bishoi (Scetis), **734–736**, *735*, *736*, *749*, 876, 879, 883, 884, 1623, 1972, 2029, 2103, 2104, 2105
  keep construction, 1395–1396
  pilgrimages to, 1970
  Pshoi of Scetis relics at, 2029

refectories, 735–736, 2056
restored by Benjamin II, 377
Dayr Anbā Bishoi (Suhāj), **736–740**, 1654, 1875, 2117
apse of, 196
architectural sculpture and paintings, 739–740, 764, 770
buildings, 740
history, 736–738
inscriptions found at, 1291
murals, 1875
Pococke visit, 1349
Dayr Anbā Būlā, **741–744**, *743*, *744*, 878, 1653, 1875, 1925
Būlus al-Būshī and, 423
as center of Eastern Desert monasteries, 1649
and Coptic art, 390, 541
food supplied from Būsh, 427
Gabriel VII, Patriarch, restoration of, 1133, 1134
historical landmarks, 741
inscriptions, 1292
and John XVII, 1348
and John XIX, 1351
Mark VII as monk at, 1537–1538
old church, 742–744
paintings at, 1659
papyri collection, 1892
Peter VI at, 1949
pilgrims and travelers to, 1976–1977
travelers' reports on, 722, 741, 742
Dayr Anbā Daryūs, **744**, 840, 848, 1658, 2358
Dayr Anbā Hadrā, **744–747**, *746*, 851, 855, 870, 919, 1190, 1295, 1657
ambulatory of, 195
art and murals, 541, 747, 1874
church architecture, 554
inscriptions found at, 1291, 1293, 1295
keep construction, 1396
octagon-domed church at, 1823
refectory, 2056
see also Hadrā of Aswan, Saint
Dayr Anbā Helias (Naqādah), **747**
Dayr Anbā Helias (Wādī al-Natrūn), **747–748**
Dayr Anbā Ḥiziqyāl (Armant), **748**
Dayr Anbā Maqār, 12, 20, 37, 307, **748–756**, *749*, *750–756*, 789, 790–791, 808, 824, 825, 835, 927, 1122, 1397, 1491, 1533, 1571, 1615, 1616, 1625, 1972
Abraham and George of Scetis at, 12–13
Agathon of Alexandria at, 66
Agathon the Stylite at, 69
art depicting Daniel at, 384–385
Benjamin I canon for, 376
and Catechetical School of Alexandria, 931–932
as center of Coptic ecclesiastical culture, 1459
and Christodoulus, 545
consecration of oil (*myron*) at, 770
and Cosmas I, 636
and Cosmas II, 636
and Cyril I, 671
and Cyril II, 675
and Demetrius II, 892
encomium on Gabriel, Archangel, in codex of, 1136
Ephraem Syrus, Saint at, 963
Gabriel I at, 1127
Gabriel II at, 1128
Garden of the Monks daily readings at, 178
Giyorgis I, Ethiopian prelate at, 1006
grave of Sāwiros, Ethiopian prelate, at, 1006
ḥiṣn at, 1237
History of Joseph the Carpenter manuscript at, 1373
illuminated manuscript, *1284*
Isaac, Patriarch, as monk at, 1303
Islamic-influenced Coptic art, 1311
Jacob, Saint at, 1318
James of Scetis at, 1321
and John I, 1337
and John III, the Merciful, 1337
and John IV, 1338
and John VI, 1342
and John of Parallos, 1367
and John of Scetis, 1362
keep construction, 1395–1396
Khā'īl I at, 1410
Khā'īl II burial site, 1412
library, 1449
Macarius I as monk at, 1487
Macarius II as monk at, 1487
manuscript on life of Paul of Tamma at, 1924, 1925
Mīnā I as monk at, 1631
Mīnā II as monk at, 1632
Onophrius, Saint, portrayed at, 1842
Ottoman impact on, 1857
papyri collection, 1892
as patriarchal residence, 1912
Peter V and, 1948, 1949
Philotheus as monk at, 1959
rebuilding of, 1535
relics of forty-nine martyrs of Scetis at, 1121
relics of Ishkirūn, Saint, at, 758
relics of John Colobos at, 1361
relics of Mark, Apostolic Saint at, 376, 1532
reliefs of, 275
revival of, 755–756
Shenute I at, 2133
synod at, 360–361
and *tafsīr*, 2198
and Testaments of the Patriarchs, 163–164
and woman monk Nabdūnah, 1769
and Yūḥannā, Bishop, 2355
Yūsāb I at, 2362
Zeno, Emperor, endowment of, 749, 1462
Dayr Anbā Matiyas. *See* Dayr al-Fakhūr
Dayr Anbā Orion, 12
Dayr Anbā Palaemon, **757**, 822, 1657
Dayr Anbā Pisentius, **757**, 819, 1656
Dayr Anbā Ruways. *See* Dayr al-Khandaq
Dayr Anbā Ṣamū'īl (Naqādah). *See* Dayr al-Sanad
Dayr Anbā Ṣamū'īl of Qalamūn, 130, **758–760**, 806, 845, 1615, 1650
Isaac of Qalamūn and, 1304
keep construction, 1396
relics from Birmā, 392
and Wādī al-Rayyān, 2311
Dayr Anbā Sāwīrus (Asyūṭ), **760–761**, 927, 1615, 1654
Dayr Anbā Shinūdah. *See* Dayr al-Ṣalīb
Dayr Anbā Shinūdah (Fayyūm), 1651
Dayr Anbā Shinūdah (Qūṣ), 1657, 1658
Dayr Anbā Shinūdah (Suhāj), 60, 69, 705, 708, 734, 736, 737, **761–770**, *767*, 804, 836, 884,

Dayr Anbā Shinūdah (Suhāj) (*cont.*)
1092, 1654, 1679, 1875, 1908, 1921, 1968, 1969
Agathonicus of Tarsus treatises at, 69–70
Alexander Romance fragment found at, 2059
apse of, 196
architecture, 617, 766–769, *767*, *768*
art, 617
assets, 1641, 1642
Besa, Abbot, 378–379
codex on Gabriel, Archangel, at, 1136
codex of Gregory of Nyssa at, 1184–1185
codex on Heraclides, Saint, at, 1220
codex of Theodosius of Jerusalem at, 2242
codices on John of Lycopolis at, 1365
codices on Raphael, Archangel, at, 2053
Coptic sculpture in stone, 2117
Coptic text of prayer from *Apostolic Tradition* (Hippolytus) at, 1235
Coptic texts at, 1452–1453, 1456; *see also* specific names
Coptic translations of Old Testament at, 1837–1838
cultic niches at, 553
deuterarios of, 895
and Hamai of Kahyor, Saint, 1204
history, 761–765
inscriptions at, 1291, 1292, 1448
khizānahs at, 1414
and legend of Eusignius, Saint, 1071–1072
and legend of Panine and Paneu, 1880
library, 1448, 1452
manuscript on Eustathius of Thrace at, 1073
manuscript of Evodius of Rome homily at, 1078–1079
manuscript fragments of John Chrysostom at, 1358
manuscript of *History of Joseph the Carpenter* at, 1373
manuscript on life of Paul of Tamma at, 1925
manuscript mention of Gregory of Nazianzus at, 1183–1184
manuscript on Philip of Anatolia at, 1956
and miracles of Mercurius of Caesarea, 1592
Pamin, Saint, honored at, 1878
Paphnutius celebrated at, 1882
papyrus collection, 1891, 1892, 1893, 1894, 1895
papyrus discoveries, 1900
Pococke visit to, 1349
Seth as archimandrite of, 2121
Shenute as archimandrite of, 2131–2133
Shenute iconography at, 538–539, *539*
Thomas, Saint, *typika* at, 2256
and Victor of Tabennēsē, Saint, 2308
visited and described by Vansleb (Wansleben), Johann Michael, 2299
Zenobios burial site at, 2371

Dayr Anbā Yuḥannis, Khā'īl II as monk at, 1412
Dayr Andarawus. *See* Dayr Abū al-Līf
Dayr Apa Agenios, 1657
Dayr Apa Anūb (al-Ashmūnayn). *See* Dayr Abū Nūb
Dayr Apa Anūb (Wādī al-Naṭrūn), **770**
Dayr Apa Apollo. *See* Bāwīṭ
Dayr Apa Hor (Sawādah), **770–771**, 1974
Dayr Apa Hor (Siryāqūs), **771–772**
Dayr Apa Isḥāq (Isnā), **772**, 1656
Dayr Apa Jeremiah (Damietta). *See* Monasteries of the Daqahliyyah Province
Dayr Apa Jeremiah (Jirjā), 1657
Dayr Apa Jeremiah (Saqqara), 34, *262*, 718, **772–779**, 918, 1587, 1642, 1649, 1653, 1888
archaeology, 773–776, 777, 778, 2040
archimandrite at, 193
architectural sculpture, 776–777, *776*, 1753; *see also subhead* sculpture in stone
art at, 389, 2004; *see also* related subheads
art depicting Abraham and Isaac, 383
and Byzantine influences on Coptic art, 241
and Christian subjects in Coptic art, 532–533
Coptic glass excavations, 1143, 1144, 1145, *1146*
deuterarios at, 895
founder of, 193, 532–533
frescoes of Virgin Enthroned at, 542, 543
fresco of Onophrius, Saint, at, 1842
hall from in Coptic Museum (Old Cairo), *608*
hegumenos title used at, 1216
and Hor, 1254
inscriptions found at, 1291, 1293
murals, 1875
musical instruments, 1739, 1740
paintings, 777–779, 1659, 1660
proestos at, 2021
sculpture in stone at, 2117
stelae from, 2149

Dayr Apa Macarius. *See* Monasteries of the Upper Ṣa'īd
Dayr Apa Nob. *See* Monasteries of the Upper Ṣa'īd
Dayr Apa Phoibammon, **779–781**, 786, 857, 918, 1093, 1656, 1657, 1874
Abraham of Hermonthis as abbot of, 13
ancient correspondence found at, 400–401
archives of, 226, 227
excavations directed by Bachatly, Charles, 323
library, 1448
papyri collection, 1891
Pisentius of Qifṭ as monk at, 1979

Dayr Apa Psote. *See* Monasteries of the Upper Ṣa'īd
Dayr Apa Sergius. *See* Monasteries of the Upper Ṣa'īd
Dayr Apa Thomas, **781**, 1655, 1654
Dayr al-'Arabah. *See* Dayr Anbā Anṭūniyūs
Dayr al-Arba'ī Shahīd (Dayr Theophilus), 1658
Dayr Arḍ al-Ḥājiz, 927
Dayr Arganūs. *See* Dayr al-Jarnūs (Maghāgha)
Dayr al-Arman, **782**
Armenian inscriptions, 1290

Dayr Arsāniyūs. *See* Dayr al-Quṣayr (Ṭurah)
Dayr al-ʿAsal (Minyat Banī Khaṣīb), **782**, 784, 1654
Dayr Asfal al-Arḍ, 95, **782–783**, 1646
Dayr al-ʿAskar, **783**, 818, 837, 871, 1649, 1652
Dayr ʿAtiyyah, 782, **784**, 1653, 1655
Dayr al-ʿAwanah (Asyūṭ), **784**, 1655, 1971
Dayr al-ʿAyn. *See* Dayr al-Malāk Mīkhā'īl (Qamūlah)
Dayrayn (village), 1652
Dayr al-ʿAysh. *See* Dayr al-Malāk Mīkhā'īl
Dayr al-ʿAzab (Fayyūm), **784–785**, 1650, 1651
  Abraam I, Saint, gravesite, 10
Dayr Azilun. *See* Monasteries of the Middle Ṣaʿīd
Dayr Babilūn al-Daraj, 1647
Dayr al-Badla. *See* Dayr al-Maymūn
Dayr al-Baghl. *See* Dayr al-Quṣayr (Tūrāh)
Dayr al-Baḥrī. *See* Dayr Apa Phoibammon
Dayr al-Bakarah. *See* Dayr al-ʿAdhrā' (Jabal al-Tayr); Dayr al-ʿAdhrā' (Samālūṭ); Dayr Mār Mīnā (Jabal Abū Fūdah)
Dayr al-Bakhīt (Luxor), 728, 779, **785–786**, 849, 1655, 1656
Dayr Bakhūm (Akhmīm), 1655
Dayr Bakhūm (Idfū). *See* Dayr al-Malāk Mīkhā'īl
Dayr al-Balaʿyzah, 50, **786–787**, 1073, 1389, 1539, 1654
  refectories of, 2056
Dayr al-Ballāṣ (Qifṭ), **787–788**, 1656
Dayr Bālūjah, **788**, 1654
Dayr Bamwiyyah, 1651
Dayr al-Banāt, **788–789**, *789*, 1647, 1651
  church of Mercurius of Caesarea, 1594
  as convent, 2325
Dayr Banūb. *See* Dayr Abū Nūb
Dayr al-Baramūs, 7, 10, 12, **789–794**, *790*, *791*, *792*, 1395–1396, 1576, 2103, 2105
  Abraam I at, 10
  architecture, 791–794, *792*, *793*, 2056
  Christodoulus at, 544
  and Cyril V, 677, 1693
  and Cyril VI, 678
  and Dayr Abū Mūsā al-ʿAswad, 708
  Isidhūrus at, 1307
  John XIV at, 1347
  John XVI at, 1347
  John XIX at, 1351
  Matthew III at, 1571
  Matthew IV at, 1571
  Moses the Black's relics at, 1681
  and reconstruction of Dayr Anbā Ṣamū'īl of Qalamūn, 759, 760
  Scetis location, 2102, 2105
  sculpture in stone at, 2113, 2116–2117
  Yoḥannes I, Ethiopian prelate, at, 1001
  Yūḥannā al-Maqsī at, 2358
  see also al-Baramūsī, Father Antonios
Dayr Barjanūs. *See* Dayr Anbā Bākhūm (Barjanūs-Minyā)
Dayr al-Barshah and Dayr al-Nakhlah, 771, **794–796**, 1255, 1654
Dayr Bawlos. *See* Monasteries of the Upper Ṣaʿīd
Dayr Bayt Isūs. *See* Dayr al-Jarnūs (Maghāgha)
Dayr bi'l-Habash, **796**
Dayr al-Biṣrah (Buṣrah) (Asyūṭ), **796–797**, 1655
Dayr Bisūs. *See* Dayr al-Jarnūs (Maghāgha)
Dayr Bū Baghām, 927
Dayr Bū Maghām. *See* Dayr Abū Bifām (Ṭimā)
Dayr Buqṭur of Shū, **797–798**, 811, 1655
Dayr Bū Sawīrus, 927
Dayr Buṭrus Wa Būlus. *See* Dayr al-Qaṣrīyyah
Dayr Colluthus. *See* Monasteries of the Upper Ṣaʿīd
Dayr Dhāt al-Ṣafā, 1651
Dayr al-Dīk, **798–799**, 847, 1654
  and Christian subjects in Coptic art, 533
  foundations of, 146
Dayr Dimūshiyyah, 1651
Dayr Disyā, 1651
Dayr Durunkah, **799**, 855, 856, 1654
  pilgrimages to, 1970
Dayr Ebifania, **800**
Dayr Epiphanius, **800–802**, 817, 857, 1078, 1656
  church at Shaykh ʿAbd al-Qurnah, 2128
  inscriptions found at, 1291
  mummification, 1697
  Pisentius archives at, 1456
  wall inscriptions, 689
  weaving, 1641
Dayr al-Fakhūrī, **802–805**, *803* *804*, 1653, 1656, 1875, 2056
Dayr al-Ganadlah, 1654
Dayr al-Ghanāyim, **805**, 1658
Dayr Ghubriyāl, **805**, 1658
Dayr al-Ḥabash, Peter V burial at, 1949
Dayr al-Ḥabīs (Monastery of the Hermits), 38
Dayr al-Ḥadīd, **805**, 1653
Dayr al-Ḥajar, **806**, 1658
Dayr al-Ḥamāmah. *See* Dayr Abū Sayfayn (Qūṣ)
Dayr Hamas. *See* Dayr al-ʿAwanah
Dayr al-Ḥamidāt, 1109
Dayr al-Hammām (Dayr Abū Isḥāq), 37, **806–807**, 1650
Dayr al-Hanādah. *See* Monasteries of the Middle Ṣaʿīd
Dayr al-Haraqal. *See* Dayr al-Quṣayr (Ṭurah)
Dayr Harmīnā (Asyūṭ), **808**, 1655
Dayr al-Hawā. *See* Dayr al-Naṣārā (Antinoopolis); Dayr Sunbāṭ
Dayr Helias. *See* Scetis
Dayr Ibsidiyyah. *See* Monasteries of the Middle Ṣaʿīd
Dayr al-Ikhwah, **808**, 1651
  Dayr al-ʿAdhrā' as duplicate of, 714
  John III at, 1337
Dayr Isidorus. *See* Dayr al-Madīnah
Dayr Isūs. *See* Dayr al-Jarnūs (Maghāgha)
Dayr al-ʿIẓām (Monastery of the Bones) (Asyūṭ), **809–810**, *809*, 842, 1654
Dayr Jabal al-Ṭayr. *See* Dayr al-ʿAdhrā' (Samālūṭ)
Dayr al-Jabrāwī (Asyūṭ), 114, **810–812**, *811*, *812*, 853, 1653
Dayr al-Janādlah. *See* Dayr Abū Maqrūfah
Dayr al-Jarādāwī, 788

Dayr al-Jarnūs (Maghāgha), **813**, 1972
Dayr al-Jawlī, **814**
Dayr al-Jazīrah (Monastery of the Island). *See* Dayr al-Rūmāniyyah
Dayr Jimyānah. *See* Dayr Sitt Dimyānah
Dayr al-Jizāz. *See* Dayr al-Sanad
Dayr al-Jū', **814**, 1654
Dayr al-Jūd. *See* Dayr al-Mayūn
Dayr al-Jummayzah. *See* Dayr Anbā Antūniyūs; Dayr al-Maymūn
Dayr al-Kahmas. *See* Dayr al-Ballās
Dayr Karfūnah, 927
Dayr al-Karrām. *See* Dayr Nahyā
Dayr Katreh. *See* Dayr al-Shalwīt
Dayr al-Khādim, 145, **814**, 860, 861
Dayr al-Khandaq, 23, **814–815**, 1517, 1647
  Anbā Ruways buried at, 129
  contemporary patriarchal residence at site of, 1913
  Gabriel VI buried at, 1133
  Matthew I tomb at, 1570
  relics of Mark, Apostolic Saint, at, 1532
Dayr al-Kharbah, 1655, 1656
Dayr Kharfūnah. *See* Dayr al-Muṭṭin
Dayr al-Khasab. *See* Dayr al-Naqlūn
Dayr al-Kubāniyyah, **815–816**, *816*, 851, 1657
  ambulatory of, 195
  and church architecture in Egypt, 554
  octagon-domed church at, 1823
Dayr al-Kulah. *See* Dayr Mār Buqṭur (Qamūlah)
Dayr Kyriakus. *See* Dayr Epiphanius
Dayr al-Madīnah, **816–818**, 857, 1620, 1656, 1874
  Černý, Jaroslav, and, 511
  and costume of the religious, 653
  excavated under du Bourguet, Pierre, 414
Dayr al-Ma'dūdī. *See* Dayr Abū Ḥalbānah
Dayr al-Madwid. *See* Dayr al-Sab'at Jibāl
Dayr Maghārat Shaqalqīl, 1974
Dayr al-Maghṭis, **818–819**, 870, 1649, 1652
  destroyed during patriarchate of John XI, 1345
  Zar'a Yā'qob's grief at destruction of, 1053
Dayr al-Majma', 757, **819–821**, 1656
Dayr al-Malāk, **822**, 1657
Dayr al-Malāk al-Baḥrī (Cairo). *See* Dayr al-Khandaq
Dayr al-Malāk (Dākhlah Oasis), **822**, *822*
Dayr al-Malāk Ghubriyāl. *See* Dayr al-Naqlūn
Dayr al-Malāk Mīkhā'īl (Akhmīm), 78, **823**, *823*, 1655, 1974
Dayr al-Malāk Mīkhā'īl (Fayyūm), 713, 815, 820, 821, **824**, 865
Dayr al-Malāk Mīkhā'īl (Fayyūm), papyrus collection, 1899
Dayr al-Malāk Mīkhā'īl (Idfū), **825**, 1656
Dayr al-Malāk Mīkhā'īl (Jirjā), **825–826**, 1657
Dayr al-Malāk Mīkhā'īl (Marāghah), **826**, 1654
Dayr al-Malāk Mīkhā'īl (Naj al-Dayr), **826–827**, *827*
Dayr al-Malāk Mīkhā'īl (Naqādah), **827**
Dayr al-Malāk Mīkhā'īl (Qamūlah), **827–828**, *828*, 1656, 1658
Dayr al-Malāk Mīkhā'īl (Qinā), 1656, 1657
Dayr al-Malāk Mīkhā'īl (Quṣ), 1656, 1657, 1658
Dayr al-Malāk Mīkhā'īl (al-Rayramūn), **828–829**, 1654
Dayr Manāwus. *See* Dayr al-Shuhadā' (Isnā)
Dayr Manṣūr. *See* Dayr al-Malāk Mīkhā'īl (Idfū)
Dayr Maqrūfiyus, 705
Dayr Mār Buqṭur (Jeme). *See* Monasteries of the Upper Ṣa'īd
Dayr Mār Buqṭur (Naqādah). *See* Dayr al-Malāk Mikhā'īl (Qamūlah)
Dayr Mār Buqṭur (Qamūlah), 554, **829–830**, *830*, 1656, 1657
Dayr Mār Buqṭur (Qūṣ). *See* Dayr Abū Sayfayn (Qūṣ)
Dayr Mār Ḥannā. *See* Dayr al-Ṭīn
Dayr Mār Jirjis (Dimiqrāṭ), **830–831**, 1650, 1656
  pilgrimages to, 1972
Dayr Mār Jirjis al-Ḥadīdī, 78, 713, **831–833**, 1657
Dayr Mār Jirjis (Naqādah). *See* Dayr al-Majma'
Dayr Mār Kyriakos, 1657
Dayr Mār Mīnā (Gharbiyyah), 707, **833**, 1652
Dayr Mār Mīnā (Hiw/Nag Hammadi), 717, **833–834**, 1656
Dayr Mār Mīnā (Ibyār), 1652
Dayr Mār Mīnā (Jabal Abū Fūdah), **834**
Dayr Mār Murqus al-Rasūlī. *See* Qurnat Mar'i
Dayr Marqūrah, 1654
Dayr Marqūryus. *See* Dayr Abū Sayfayn (Cairo); Dayr al-Malāk Mīkhā'īl (Idfū)
Dayr Mār Stefanos, 1657
Dayr Mart Maryam, **835**, 1655
Dayr Mār Tumās, 78, **835–836**, *835*
Dayr al-Maṭmar, **836–837**, *836*, 1656
Dayr Maṭrā, **837**
Dayr Mawās. *See* Monasteries of the Middle Ṣa'īd
Dayr al-Maymah (Gharbiyyah), 783, **837–838**, 871, 1652, 1649
Dayr al-Maymūn, **838–839**, *839*, 1653
  pilgrims and travelers to, 1977
  restoration of, 1134
Dayr al-Maẓall, 843
Dayr al-Mighṭās, 871
Dayr Mīkhā'īl al-Qiblī, 927, 1647
Dayr Minyat Ṭānah. *See* Dayr al-Maghṭis
Dayr al-Misaykrah, **839–840**, *840*
Dayr al-Muḥārib. *See* Dayr al-Amīr Tadrūs (Luxor)
Dayr al-Muḥarraq, 784, **840–841**, 1118, 1654, 1736
  Abraam I, Saint, vows at, 10
  Clerical College at, 564
  Ethiopian monks at, 765, 1039, 2191
  Gabriel IV as monk at, 1130
  Gabriel VII restoration of, 1134
  icons of Asṭāsī al-Rūmī at, 294
  Iqlādiyūs Labīb and, 1302
  Isidhūrus, Bishop, at, 1307
  John XII at, 1346
  John XIII at, 1346

keep construction, 1395
manuscript on Macrobius at, 705
and Mātēwos, Ethiopian prelate, at, 1039
Matthew I at, 1569
pilgrimages to, 1969
Dayr al-Muḥarraqah, **841–842**, 1653
Dayr Mūsā. *See* Dayr Sitt Dimyānah
Dayr Muṣṭafā Kāshif, **842**, 1658
Dayr al-Muṭṭin, **842–843**, 1654
Dayr Nahyā (Giza), **843**, 1652
Dayr al-Nakhlah. *See* Dayr al-Barshah and Dayr al-Nakhlah
Dayr al-Nāmūs (Armant), **844**, 1656
Dayr al-Naqlūn, 758, 788, **845–846**, 1650, 1651
pilgrimages to, 1972
Yūnā (Jonas) of Armant at, 2358
Dayr al-Naṣārā (Antinoopolis), **847**, 1654
confused with Dayr al-Dīk, 798
foundations of, 146
Dayr al-Naṣārā (Armant), **847–848**, 1656
confused with Dayr al-Misaykrah, 839–840
Dayr al-Naṣārā (Asyūṭ), **848**
Dayr al-Nasṭūr, 712, 796, **848**, 862, 1647
Theodosius II buried at, 2242
Dayr Nujtuhur. *See* Monasteries in the Province of Qalyubiyyah
Dayr al-Numurah. *See* Dayr Anbā Būlā
Dayr al-Nuzhah, 1647
Dayr Onophrios. *See* Monasteries of the Middle Ṣaʿīd
Dayr Pampane. *See* Monasteries of the Middle Ṣaʿīd
Dayr Papnute. *See* Monasteries of the Upper Ṣaʿīd
Dayr Patermuthius. *See* Monasteries of the Upper Ṣaʿīd
Dayr Pei-Isus. *See* Dayr al-Jarnūs (Maghāgha)
Dayr Philemon. *See* Monasteries of the Middle Ṣaʿīd
Dayr Philūthawus. *See* Dayr al-Nasṭūr
Dayr Pisentius (Luxor). *See* Monasteries of Upper Egypt
Dayr Pisentius (Naqādah). *See* Dayr al-Malāk Mīkhā'īl (Naqādah)
Dayr Posidonios, **849**, 1656
Dayr al-Qalamūn. *See* Dayr Anbā Ṣamū'īl of Qalamūn
Dayr Qamūlah al-Qiblī. *See* Dayr al-Malāk Mīkhā'īl (Qamūlah)
Dayr al-Qaṣanūn, 1653
Dayr al-Qaṣrīyyah, **849–850**, 1653
Dayr Qaṭṭān, 1658
Dayr Qibriyūs, **850**, 1646
Dayr al-Qiddīs Yuhannis. *See* Dayr al-Sāqiyah
Dayr Qubbat al-Hawā, **850–852**, *851*, *852*, 1657
octagon-domed church at, 1823
Dayr Qurnat Marʿī. *See* Qurnat Marʿī
Dayr al-Qurqāṣ, 78, **852**, 1655
Dayr al-Quṣayr, **853**, 1653, 1654
Murqus ibn Qanbar at, 1699
octagon-domed church at, 1823–1824
Dayr al-Quṣayr (Ṭurah), **853–855**, *855*, 1395, 2358
Dayr al-Rāhibāt, 1647
Dayr Rīfah, 1654
Dayr al-Rīs, 1658
Dayr al-Rūm, 1680
Dayr al-Rūmāniyyah, **856**, 1657
Dayr al-Rūmī, 729, **856–857**, 1656
Dayr al-Rusul. *See* Monasteries of the Middle Ṣaʿīd
Dayr al-Sabʿat Jibāl, 78, 700, 852, **857–858**, 1655
Dayr Ṣabrah. *See* Dayr al-Malāk Mīkhāʾīl
Dayr al-Ṣafṣāfah. *See* Dayr al-Sabʿat Jibāl
Dayr Ṣaft al-Khammār. *See* Dayr ʿAtiyyah
Dayr al-Ṣalīb, 703, 704, **858–860**, *859*, 1656
Dayr al-Sanad, **860**
Dayr Sannūris, 1651
Dayr al-Sanqūriyyah, **860–861**, 1653, 1974
Dayr al-Khādim link with, 814
Dayr al-Sāqiyah, **861**, 1656
Dayr Anbā Ḥiziqyāl link with, 748
Dayr Sawādah. *See* Dayr Apa Hor (Minyā)
Dayr Saylah. *See* Dayr al-ʿAdhrā' (Fayyūm); Dayr al-Ḥammām
Dayr al-Shahīd Philūthāwaus (Jirjā), **861–862**
Dayr al-Shahīd Tadrus al-Muḥārib, **862**, *862*
Dayr al-Shahīd Tadrus (Qamūlah). *See* Monasteries of the Upper Ṣaʿīd
Dayr al-Shahīd Tadrus (Qifṭ). *See* Monasteries of the Upper Ṣaʿīd
Dayr Shahrān, **862–863**, 1570, 1653
and Barsūm the Naked, Saint, 348–349
burial of Benjamin II at, 378
Mark IV as monk at, 1536
Peter V as abbot of, 1948
Dayr al-Shallā, 788, 1651
Dayr al-Shalwīt, **863**, *864*, 1656
hermitages found nearby, 1225
Dayr al-Shamʿ, **863**, **865**, 1652
Paphnutius the Hermit death and relics at, 712, 1883
Dayr al-Shaykhah. *See* Dayr al-Ḳubāniyyah
Dayr al-Shayyāṭīn (Monastery of the Demons), 863
Dayr Shubrā Kalsā, 1652
Dayr al-Shuhadā' (Akhmīm), 78, 713, 823, **865–866**, *866*, 1655
Dayr al-Shuhadā' (Isnā), 772, **866–870**, *867*, *870*, 1656, 1875
pilgrimages to, 1972
Dayr Simʿān, **870**
see also Dayr Anbā Hadra
Dayr Sitt Dimyānah, 40, 79–80, *79*, 707, 729, 818, 819, 838, **870–872**, *871*, 1649, 1652, 2325
Christian altars, 107
churches of, 713, 757
pilgrimages to, 1968, 1969
Dayr al-Sulṭān (Jerusalem), 358, **872–874**, 1327
and Ceremony of the Holy Light, 1248
and Haile Selassie I, 1198
and Mātēwos, Ethiopian prelate, 1039
represented at Florence, Council of, 1119
Dayr Sunbāṭ, **875–876**, 1654
Dayr al-Suryān, 23, 107, 791, **876–881**, 883, 884, 1532, 1646, 2105–2106
art at, 527, 1311, 2195

Dayr al-Suryān (*cont.*)
church altar, 107
church architecture, 554
Dayr Anbā Bishoi counterpart, 734
Gabriel VII as priest in, 1131
Isidhūrus as abbot at, 1307
Islamic-influenced Coptic art, 1311, *1311*
khizānah in church at, 1415
library, 1449
and Makāri al-Suryānī, 2091
pilgrimages to, 1972
and Shenouda III, 2130
and Simon I, 2138
Syriac inscriptions, 1290
Dayr Tādrus, 1647, 1654
Dayr Tāsā, **881**, 1351, 1655, 1971
Dayr al-Tayr. *See* Dayr al-'Adhrā' (Jabal al-Jayr)
Dayr Theophilus, 1658
Dayr al-Ṭīn, 796, **881–882**, 1647
Dayr al-Tinādah. *See* Dayr Abū Bifām (Asyūṭ)
Dayr Ton Ethiopon. *See* Dayr al-Muḥarraq
Dayr Ṭurah. *See* Dayr al-Quṣayr (Ṭurah)
Dayr al-Ṭurfah, **882**
Dayr Umm 'Ali. *See* Dayr al-Rūmāniyyah
Dayr al-Wusṭānī. *See* Dayr al-Shuhadā'
Dayr Yūḥannā (Damanhūr Shubra), **882**
Dayr Yuḥannis (al-Minshāh), **883**, 1657
Dayr Yuḥannis Kama, **883**, 1412
Dayr Yuḥannis al-Qasīr (Asyūṭ). *See* Dayr al-'Iẓam (Asyūṭ)
Dayr Yuḥannis al-Qaṣīr (Wādi al-Naṭrūn), **883–884**
Dayr al-Yunān. *See* Dayr al-Quṣayr (Ṭurah)
Dayr al-Zakāwah, 1651
Dayr al-Zāwiyah, **884**, 1654
Dayr al-Zaytūn (Sharūnah), 2128
Dayr al-Zujāj. *See* Enaton, the
Days, epagomenal (intercalary), 439
Days of the week
Saturday, 2098–2100
Sunday, 2159–2160
Days of the year, Abraxas, 14
Dayumīdis. *See* Diomede (martyr)
Dayūt, Dayr Abū Sarabām in, 709–710
Day of worship. *See* Sabbath
Deacon, **885–886**
apostles and, 2015
Didascalia on, 899
fan use by, 1473
and laying-on of hands, 1432
and liturgical music, 1719, 1721, 1729, 1737, 1738
and liturgical vestments, 1477, 1478
musical role, 1910
origination of rank, 885, 886–887
place in ecclesiastical hierarchy, 1229, 2016
ritual book for, 1729, 1737
see also Subdeacon
Deacon and archdeacon, ordination of, **886–888**
Deaconess, **888**
Didascalia on, 899
Dead, prayer for the, **889**
Dead Sea Scrolls of the Essenes, 1148
De anima et resurrectione (Gregory of Nyssa), 1184–1185, 1958
Death
funerary murals, 1873
gnosticism on, 1156
mourning customs, 1686
mummification, 1696–1697, 1865
mummy labels, 1698
netherworld, 1499
prayer for the dead, 889
tombstone inscriptions with lamentations, 1293–1294
see also Afterlife; Burial rites; Cemeteries; Funerary customs; Martyrs; Mummification; Stela; Tombs
Debt. *See* Law of obligations
Decius (martyr), 1554, 1559
Decius, Emperor, **889–891**
Encomium of Claudius on persecutions of, 1193
and martyrdom of Mercurius of Caesarea, 1592
patriarch under, 1914
persecutions under, 909, 911, 1868, 1936
successor, 2298
Decius, governor of Turicum (Zurich), 1082, 1110, 2057
and martyrdom of Exuperantius, Saint, 1082
Decoration, Coptic interlacing motif, 251–252
De deitate Filii et Spiritus Sancti (Gregory of Nyssa), 1184
Defense of Origen (Eusebius and Pamphilus), 471, 1071, 1879
Defensor ecclesiae, **891**
De fide (Agathonicus of Tarsus), 69, 70
Defrocking of priests, **891**, 1931
De haeresibus, 71
Deir Omali. *See* Dayr al-Rūmāniyyah
De Legatione ad Gaium (Philo of Alexandria), 1956
Delehaye, H., as Coptic hagiographer, 1191
Della Valle, Pietro. *See* Pietro delle Valle
Demel, H., 815
Demetrius I, Patriarch, **891–893**, 1471, 1866, 1999, 2083
and baptism of Dionysius the Great, 909
Book of Epact, 409–411
dates of patriarchy, 1914
on Easter date-setting, 1104
encomium in honor of, 1117
and Heraclas, Saint, 1219
marital chastity of, 1543
and nuns, 1822
and Origen, 470, 609, 1219, 1847, 1851, 1855
and orthodox Christianity in Egypt, 1222
and Pantaenus, 1881
recognition of Coptic fasts, 1094
Demetrius II, Patriarch, 713, **893**
Demetrius II, Patriarch
and Atnātēwos, Ethiopian prelate, 1037
and Cyril V, Patriarch, 677
dates of patriarchy, 1919
election of successor, 1911
and founding of Coptic school at Asyūṭ, 2197
and Sa'd Mīkhā'īl 'Abdū, 2073
Tādrus al-Mashriqī as historian of, 2197
Demetrius of Antioch, **894–895**, 1961
and *Cycle of John Chrysostom and Demetrius*, 667, 1358
and John Chrysostom, 1358
in Nubian liturgy, 1816
and Victor Stratelates, Saint, 2305, 2306–2307

Demon possession
  and healings in Coptic community, 1212–1214
  James, Saint, power to exorcise, 1320
  Paul the Simple's power over, 1923
Demons, depiction in Coptic art, 370–371, 385–386
Demosthenes, 1889
Demotic writing, 1169
De Nativitate (Demetrius of Antioch), 894
Dendera. *See* Dandarah
Den Heijer, J., 1573
Denis of Paris, Saint, 908
Denmark, Coptic collections, 1703
De placitis Manichaeorum (Alexander of Lycopolis), 87–88
Deposit. *See* Law, Coptic: Private Law
De principiis (Origen), 1847, 1852, 1853–1854, 1855
De processione Spiritus Sancti (Anselm of Canterbury), 1113
Derdekeas, 1901–1902
Dermataus of Pemje, Saint, 2083
Dermatāwūs. *See* Patermuthius, Saint
A Description of the East and Some Other Countries (Pococke), 1983
Description de l'Egypte (Villoteau), 1742, 1977
Desert. *See* Caves; Hermits; Kellia; Monasteries of the Eastern Desert; Monasteries of the Western Desert; Nitria; Oasis; Scetis
Desert fathers, **894**
  Ammonius of Kellia, 113–114, 894
  Apophthegmata patrum on, 177–178
  Armenian settlement, 234
  Arsenius of Scetis and Ṭurah, 240–241
  and British Isles Christian converts, 417–418
  Copres, Saint, on, 598
  exclusion of women, 1663
  John Colobos, Saint, 1359–1361
  Onophrius, Saint, 1841
  see also Asceticism; Anchoresis; Monasticism, Pachomian
De spiritu et littera (Saint Augustine), 1930
De trinitate (Augustine), 1114–1115
Deuterarios, **895**
Deuterocanonical books. *See* Apocryphal literature
Dévaud, Eugène Victor, **895**
Devil
  iconography of, 247–248, *249*
  renunciation in baptismal liturgy, 339–340
  see also Antichrist; Demon possession; Satan
"Devil traps", 1508
De viris illustribus (Saint Jerome), 1920, 1921
Dhimmis. *See Ahl al-Dhimmah*
Diaconia, 209, **895–896**, 1826
Diadems, marriage, 1544
Dialects. *See Appendix*
Dialogue of the Savior, **897–898**
Diapolis Magna. *See* Karnak; Luxor
Diatonic progression, 1721–1722, *1722*
Dictionaries
  Arabic-French, 1284–1285
  Armenian, 1424
  Coptic, 614, 661, 1424, 2107, 2145
  Copto-Arabic, 34, 1267, 1302, 1748
  Greek, 1227
  see also Appendix; Coptological studies; Grammars
Didache, 179, 180, **898–899**
  on absolution, 17
  on confession, 584
  hosanna in, 1258
  on immersion, 1285–1286
Didascalia, 898, **899–900**
  Arabic translation, 20
  as basis for the *Apostolic Constitutions*, 179
  and bishops, 394
  copied by Ibrāhīm ibn Sulaymān al-Najjār al-Mīrī, 1273
  on Eucharistic fast, 1063
  on Holy Communion on Saturday, 2098
  on the seven canonical hours, 446–448
  on use of candles in church, 445
Didaskaleion (Alexandria), 231
Didius Julianus, Emperor, patriarch under, 1914
"Didymian Comma" (musical tonal interval), 1731
Didymus the Blind, **900**, 1448, 1876, 1885
  anathematization, 1076–1077
  anti-Manichaeism, 1522
  Antony of Egypt and, 150
  and Catechetical School of Alexandria, 100–101, 470, 471, 564, 931
  Coptic liturgy authorship, 1733
  and *filioque* justification, 1115
  and identity of Heraclides in Passion, 1220–1221
  and Origen, 1855
  and papyrus discoveries, 854, 1899
  translated by Jerome, Saint, 1323
Didymus Institute for the Blind, 564, 1737, 2091
Didymus of Tarshjebi, Saint, 2083
Dier. *See* Dayr
Diethart, J. M., 2022
Difnār, 63, **900–901**, 1728, 1986
  and celebration of Suriel the Trumpeter, 2160
  and the Copto-Arabic Synaxarion, 2174
  on flight into Egypt, 1117–1118
  and *wāṭus*, 2320
Digamy, **901**, 1544–1545
Dikaion, **901–902**
Dikhaylah, al-. *See* Enaton, the
Dikirnis, 1649
Dimayrah, **902–903**
Dimiqrāṭ. *See* Dayr Mār Jirjis (Dimiqrāṭ)
Dimyānah, Saint, 819, 838, 871
  icon of, *1279*
  see also Dayr Sitt Dimyānah; Dimyānah and her forty virgins
Dimyānah and her forty virgins, **903**, 1087, 1554, 2324
Dīn, Fu'ād Sirāj, al-, 1991
Dinūshar, **903**
Diocletian, Emperor, 24, 55, 93, **904–908**, 1485
  and Alexandria, 96
  Anatolius under, 128
  and beginning of Byzantine era in Egypt, 942
  and dating of Coptic artifacts, 694

Diocletian, Emperor (*cont.*)
- and destruction of Qifṭ, 2038
- and George, Saint, 1139–1140
- and Great Persecution, 88, 379, 730, 845, 903, 919, 1424, 1489, 1548, 1549, 1552, 1553, 1554, 1555, 1556, 1557, 1558, 1559, 1865, 1869, 1936–1937, 1943, 1944, 1960–1961, 1963–1964, 1969, 1971, 1973, 2031
- impact on Greek language and culture in Egypt, 1167–1168, 1171, 1179, 1180
- Justus, Saint, on, 1386
- Manichaeism edict, 1521
- and martyrdom of Apaiule and Tolemaeus, Saints, 153
- and martyrdom of Ascla, Saint, 283
- and martyrdom of Epimachus of Pelusium, Saint, 965
- and martyrdom of Epima, Saint, 965
- and martyrdom of Hesychius, Saint, 1226
- and martyrdom of Nabraha, Saint, 1770
- and martyrdom of Olympius, Saint, 1840
- and martyrdom of Shenufe, Saint, 2130
- martyrdoms under, 1305, 1307; *see also subhead* Great Persecution; specific martyrs
- and martyrdom of Ter and Erai, Saints, 2209
- and martyrdom of Theban Legion, 2231
- and martyrdom of Til, 2261
- and martyrdom of Tolemaus, Saint, 2271
- and martyrdom of Victor of Solothurn and Geneva, Saint, 2302
- and martyrdom of Victor Stratelates, Saint, 2303
- and martyrs at al-Bahnasā, 330
- military reforms of, 236–237
- patriarch under, 1914
- persecutions chronicled by Eusebius of Caesarea, 1069–1070, 1071
- and Psote of Psoï, 2031–2032
- reforms of, 135, 236–237, 943, 2007–2008, 2009, 2022–2023
- Socrates as historian of, 2142
- and taxation reforms, 135
- and Theban Legion, 2231
- Theodotus of Ancyra on, 2243
- Theonas patriarchy and initial tolerance of Christianity by, 2245–2246
- visits to Egypt by, 2063, 2066

Diocletian Era, 434, 972

Diocletianopolis. *See* Qūṣ

Diodora (martyr), 1553

Diodore of Tarsus, 174, 1672, 2017

Diogenes, 1944, 1958

Diolkos, 461, **908**

Diomede (martyr), 1554

Dionysiaka (Nonnos of Panopolis), 1759, 1799, 1865

Dionysian Era of the Incarnation, in the Coptic calendar, 434

Dionysius (anchorite), 1650

Dionysius, Antiochene Patriarch of Syria, 1534

Dionysius, Bishop of Corinth (circa 170), 908

Dionysius the Areopagite, **908–909**

Dionysius Exiguus (Scythian monk), 1103, 1906
- Latin translation of Life of Pachomius by, 1861

Dionysius the Great, Patriarch, 81, **909–912**, 1638, 1934, 1936
- and burial, 425–426
- and Catechetical School of Alexandria, 472, 2245
- dates of patriarchy, 1914
- on Easter observance date, 81, 912, 1905
- epistles to Basilides, 1612
- and Heraclas, Saint, 1219
- and *homoousion* concept, 1253
- on Mareotis, 1526
- on martyrdoms, 1549
- and Origen, 1851
- and persecutions of Decius, Emperor, 890, 1936
- poetry on, 1985, 1986
- successor, 1574–1575

Dionysius the Pseudo-Areopagite, on censer use, 1472

Dionysus (pagan deity)
- depicted in tapestry, *2222, 2224*
- depiction in Coptic art, 73, 1758–1760, *1759, 1760*

Dioscorus I, Saint and Patriarch, 93, **912–915**, 1583, 2033
- and Chalcedon, Council of, 512–515, 1673, 1786, 1787, 2236
- Christology, 524–525, 1699
- Coptic texts on, 1455
- dates of patriarchy, 1915
- encomium on Macarius, 400, 1882
- and Leo I the Great, 1440, 1441, 1442
- on nature of Christ. *See subhead* Christology
- and Peter III Mongus, 1947
- sainthood and feast day, 2083
- supported by monks at the Enaton, 956
- support for Eutyches's anti-Nestorianism, 961–962, 1074–1075
- and Timothy II Aelurus, 2264

Dioscorus II, Patriarch, **915**
- and Acacian schism, 45–46
- dates of patriarchy, 1915

Dioscorus, Bishop of Damanhūr, 113, 686, **915–916**

Dioscorus and Aesculapius (martyrs), 1554

Dioscorus of Aphrodito, **916**, 1644, 1731
- archives of, 226
- as exponent of Greco-Coptic society, 946–947, 1168, 1178, 1181

Dios, Saint, **912**, 1120, 1554

Diptychs, 1567

Dirā' Abū al-Najā, plateau of, 786

Disciples. *See* Apostles; specific disciples

Discourse against Arius and Sabellius (Didymus), 900

Discourse on the Eighth and Ninth, **916–917**

Diseases. *See* Communion of the sick; Black Death; Healings in Coptic literature; Medicine; Plagues; Unction of the sick

Dishes. *See* Missoria; Tableware

Dispute with the Cilicians (Agathonicus of Tarsus), 69

Dispute with Justin the Samaritan about the Resurrection (Agathonicus of Tarsus), 69

"A Dissertation on the Falsifications by Heretics of the Works of Origen" (Rufinus), 2068

Dissolution of marriage. *See* Divorce; Marriage; Personal status law
Divine Liturgies of Coptic Orthodox Church, 120–121
Divine Logos. *See* Christ, nature of; Logos
Divinity of Christ. *See* Christ, nature of
Divjak, Johannes, and Pelagianism, 1930
Divorce, 1119, 1462
  civil regulations, 1088
  Coptic justifications for, 1542, 1543
  Coptic law on, 1088, 1428, 1942–1943
Diyāb, Tawfiq, 1990
Djeme
  papyrus collection, 780, 1895
  see also Madīnat Hābū; Memnonia
Djinkim. *See Appendix*
Docetism, **917**, 1583
  and Cerinthus, 511
  and Julian, Bishop, 1379
  on nature of Christ, 547
Doctors. *See* Medicine, Coptic
Doctrina apostolorum, 898
Dodekaschoenus Kingdom (Nubia)
  Greek language use, 1170, 1171
  see also Nubia
Dolls
  made of wood, *2340*
  for magical spells, 1509, *1510*
Dolphins, as symbols, 1598, 2166–2167, *2169*
Dome, 209–210
Dominican Institute of Oriental Studies, Cairo, 918
Dominicans in Egypt, **918**
Domitian, Emperor, 1375
Domitius, Saint. *See* Maximus and Domitius, Saints
Domitius Celsus, Emperor, 906
Domnus, Archbishop of Antioch, 1074, 1670
Donation of children, **918–919**
Donations, 1430
  see also Law, Coptic: Private law
Donatism, **919–921**, 1935
  Constantine I and, 589
Donatus, Bishop, 920–921
Dongola, **921–922**
  and Baqṭ Treaty, 343
  basilica, 1807, 1808–1809, *1808*
  as episcopal see of Nubia, 1813
  and Islamization of Nubia, 1803–1804
  as medieval city, 1514
  and Nubian archaeology, medieval, 1805
  Nubian Christian architecture in, 1807–1809
  visited by Ibn Salīm al-Aswānī, 1271
Doors, wooden, 2331–2333, *2332–2333*
Doresse, J., 726, 849, 1899
Dormition of the Virgin Mary, Feast of the. *See Theotokos*, Feast of the
Dorotheus (elder), and Gabriel, Archangel, 1127
Dorotheus (Theban ascetic), 1931
Dorotheus, Bishop of Isnā, 772, 866
Dorotheus, Bishop of Pelusium, 1089
Dorotheus, Bishop of Thessalonica, 45
Dorotheus and Theopista, and Michael, Archangel, 1618, 1619
Doss Khillah family, 1991
Dotawo, **922–923**
  and Islamization of Nubia, 1803
  and Jabal ʿAddā, 1315
  and Nobatia, 1797
  Nubian church organization at, 1813
  and Nubian languages and literature, 1816
  Qaṣr Ibrīm as center, 2037
Double-entry bookkeeping, 54
Doxology, **923–924**, 1727–1728
  Gloria in excelsis, 1147
  honoring Raphael, Archangel, 205
  and *sabʿah wa-arbaʿah*, 2071
  and *wāṭus*, 2321
Draguet, René, **924**
Drawloom, 2216
Dream of Nectanebo (first Greek prose fiction), 1169
Drescher, James Anthony Bede, **924**
Drioton, (Chanoine) Etienne Marie Felix, **924**
Drovetti, B., 1894
Drum, 1738
Dualism, 1519, 1521
Dubernat, Father, 1330
Duchesne, Louis, **925**
Duke Street (London). *See* Coptic Street
Duke University, 1895
Dukṣār. *See* Porch
Dulaurier, Jean Paul Louis François Edouard Leuge, **925**
Du Mans, Belon, 1977
Dumbarton Oaks Collection, Washington, D.C., 1596, 1598, 1600, 1714
Dumerah. *See* Dimayrah
Dumyāṭ, 89, **925–926**
  bishops of, 1541–1542
  Crusades and, 314–315
  Dayr Apa Jeremiah, 1649
  Franciscan friary, 1121, 1122, 1123
  French governor, 1417
  Metropolitan See of, 1613–1614
Dürer, Albrecht, 1532
Durr al-Thamīn, al-, 431, **926**
Durunkah, **926–927**
  Dayr Abū Bifām in, 697
  monasteries in region, 799, 856
Dūsh, **927–928**
Duwayr, al-, **928**
Dyeing, in manufacture of Coptic textiles, 2214–2215
Dynamic Monarchians, 1637–1638
Dyophysites, vs. Monophysites in Alexandria, 97, 99, 101

E

Eagle, as Coptic art symbol, 2167–2169, *2170*
Early History of the Christian Church (Duchesne), 925
Earrings, 1606, *1606*
Earthquakes, 1487–1488
East, orientation toward the, 1846
East Bank. *See* Monasteries of the Upper Ṣaʿīd
Easter, 1104–1105, 1904
  date-setting. *See Book of Epact*; Paschal controversy
  Didascalia on, 899
  Dionysius the Great on, 912
  Eusebius of Caesarea work on, 1071
  Good Friday and, 1152–1153
  Mark, Apostolic Saint, martyrdom on, 1531

Easter (*cont.*)
Melito of Sardis homily on, 1585–1586
Proclus homily on, 2017
and Shamm al-Nasīm feast day, 2126
use of candles for, 446
Eastern Desert
monasteries of the, 1649–1650
Rufinus history of hermits in, 2068
see also Scetis
Eastern Orthodox churches
and Acacian schism, 42–47
baptismal creeds, 178–179
canon of Scripture, 2108
Chalcedon, Council of, 1670, 1671, 1673, 1674
consubstantiation doctrine rejection, 597–598
fan use, 1474
Henoticon, 1671
Iconoclastic controversy, 1275–1276, 1277
Immaculate Conception doctrine repudiation, 1285
al-Istifhām Ba'd al-Istibhām, 1312–1313
and Leo I the Great, 1440–1442
Monophysite rift, 1669–1677
penance, conception of, 1932
see also Constantinople; Jerusalem; Oriental Orthodox churches
Eastern Roman Empire. *See* Constantinople; Roman Empire
Easter Sunday. *See* Easter; Paschal controversy
'Ebeid, Makram. *See* Makram 'Ebeid
Ebionites, **929–930**
on Incarnation, 1288
on the nature of Christ, 547
Eççagē, **930**
and abun, 30–31
and anointing the Ethiopian emperor, 141
and Ethiopian church autocephaly, 980
and power to ordain priests and deacons, 1021
role in Ethiopian Orthodox Church, 997
and Salāmā III, Ethiopian prelate, 1034
Ecclesiastes. *See* Old Testament, Coptic translations of the
Ecclesiastical canons. *See* Canons, ecclesiastical
Ecclesiastical hierarchy, 1229–1230, 2015–2016
Ecclesiastical history of Egypt
late antiquity, 944–945
see also Patriarchs; specific names and issues
Ecclesiastical History (Eusebius). *See Historia ecclesiastica*
Ecclesiastical History (Evagrius Scholasticus), on Nestorius, 1786–1787
Ecclesiastical History (Rufinus), 2068, 2069
Ecclesiastical punishment. *See* Excommunication; Penalization
Ecdicius Olympus (prefect), 2009
Echoi (*oktoechos*), 1735
Echos. *See* Music, Coptic: description; Music, Coptic: history
Economy
of Egypt in late antiquity, 945
of the Enaton, 956
monastic, 802, 1638–1645, 1662
Pachomian monastic, 1665
Qūṣ as prosperous center, 2043–2044
Ecthesis, 682, **931**, 1667, 168
Edessa, Persian school of, 1962
Edicts. *See* name inverted
Education, Coptic, **931–933**
Clerical College (Cairo), 563–564
and Coptic Community Council, 582
and Jesuits in Egypt, 1330
reforms, 676, 1465
schools, 1488–1489
under Ottoman rule, 1465
see also Catechetical School of Alexandria; Christian religious instruction in Egyptian public schools; Clerical College; Clerical instruction; Higher Institute of Coptic Studies
Education, Ethiopian, 997–998, 1591
Egerton Gospel, **933–934**
Egypt
administrative organization of, **934–936**
ancient funerary customs, 1125
Anglican Church in, 133
Coptic collections. *See* Coptic Museum (Cairo)
Coptic equal rights movement, 1465–1466
Coptic period, 600
Copts and independence of, 1466
Copts in late medieval, 618–634
Diocletian era, 905–908
economy and monasteries in, 1643–1645
eighteenth-century politics, 1274
family life, 1086–1088
Franciscans in, 1121–1123
French expedition, 1284, 1416–1417
glassmaking, 1142
gods and religion, 1150, 1154, 1292
government under Romans, 2007–2009, 2022–2023
Greek presence and language use in, 1165–1169, 1174–1178, 1179–1181
Holy Family in, 1117–1118
Islamization of, **936–941**
Kellia archaeological activity, 1406–1407
in late antiquity, 942–947
libraries, 1447–1449
links with Jerusalem, 1325
modern Coptic family life, 1088
modern era patriarchs, 1918–1919
modern political thought in, 1993, 2074–2075
monasticism's origins in, 1661–1664
mourning customs, 1686
Muḥammad 'Alī dynasty, 1691–1694
mummification, 1696–1697, 2001–2003
music, 1732, 1739–1741
Muslim–Christian relations, 1098–1099
mythological subjects in Coptic art, 1751–1768
nineteenth-century administration of, 1141
nineteenth-century politics, 1636–1637
paganism and Christianity in, 1865–1870

pagarch system, 1871–1872
papyrology, 1888–1889
papyrus collections, 1891–1892
persecution of Christians in, 1936–1937; *see also* Martyrs; Persecutions
Persians in, 1938–1940
personal status law in, 1941–1943
pilgrimages to, 1968–1976
pilgrims and travelers in, 1975–1977, 2064, 2066
political parties in, 1986–1996
provincial organization of, 943–944, 2007–2009, 2022–2023
Roman emperors in, 2061–2063
Roman policies in, 1167–1168
Roman taxation in, 2202–2206
Roman travelers in, 2064–2066
twentieth-century nationalism, 1515–1516
twentieth-century patriarchs, 1919
twentieth-century politics, 1627–1628, 1637, 1748
and veneration of Antony, Saint, 728
see also Arab conquest of Egypt; British occupation of Egypt; Flight into Egypt; Islam; Ptolemy dynasty; specific places and subjects
Egypt Exploration Fund, 780
Egypt Exploration Society, 1893
Egyptian accounting. *See* Accounts and accounting, history of Coptic
Egyptian Antiquities Organization, 768, 1299, 1300, 1418
Kellia excavations, 1406–1407
Egyptian Antiquities Service, 924, 1485
Egyptian Arabic vocabulary, Coptic influence. *See* *Appendix*
Egyptian Christians, as "Copts," 599–600
Egyptian Church Order, 454–455
Egyptian church order. *See* *Apostolic Tradition*
Egyptian Communist Party, 1996
Egyptian Conference of Heliopolis (1911), **948**, 1466, 1693–1694, 1988
and Egyptian national unity, 950–951
Egyptian Democratic Party (al-Ḥizb al-Dīmūqrātī al-Miṣrī), 1989
Egyptian Institute, 1396
Egyptian Museum, Berlin, 1596, 1597, 1598, 1600, 1892
Egyptian Museum, Cairo, 4, 1700, 1899
papyri collections, 1891–1892
Egyptian Museum, Turin, 1598, 1601, 1894
Egyptian Museum of the Vatican, 1559
Egyptian national identity, **948–949**
Egyptian national unity, **950–951**
Egyptian Newsletter, 1628
Egyptian Party, 1988–1989
Egypt in late antiquity, **942–947**
Egyptology
and Coptology, 616
see also Coptological studies; Excavations; Scholars
Eikoston, **951**
Eirene (martyr), 1552, 1554, 1559
Elephantine, **951–952**, *952*
and Aswan, 294
castrum of, 467
ceramics of. *See* Ceramics, Coptic
Elias (ascetic), 1663
Eliano, Giambattista, **952**, 1329–1330
Elias (biographer of John of Tella), 1674
Elias (martyr), 840, 1656
Elias, Apocalypse of, 165
Elias, Patriarch of Jerusalem, 44, 45, 1672, 1673
Elias of Bishwāw, Saint, **952–953**, 1371, 2083
Elias the Eunuch (martyr), 1554
Elias of Jeme, Saint, 2083
Elias of Nisibis, collected works of, 1779
Elias of Samhūd, Saint, **953**, 2083
Elias of Scetis, Saint, 747–748
Elijah, Apocalypse of, 165
Elim, twelve springs of, 2050
Elisha, Prophet, 1646
Elizabeth, Saint, 102
Elkasites, **953–954**, 1519
Elpidios of Tamiathis, Bishop, 925
Elpidius (martyr), 1554
Embroidery, *2214*, 2218
Emerson, Ralph Waldo, 1149
Empaiat. *See* Mareotis
Enanisho, 3
Enaton, the, 95, 101, 102, 129, **954–958**, *957*
Alexander II as monk at, 85
Basil of Oxyrhynchus on, 360
Christodoulus as monk of, 544
Damian at, 688, 689
foreign monks at, 956
hegumenos at, 1216
John II at, 1337
as laura of hermitages, 1224–1225
monasteries, 1931
name derivation, 951
organization of, 955–956
Persian destruction of, 131
Peter IV as monk at, 1948
pilgrims and travelers to, 1976
proestos at, 2021
religious history of, 956–957
Theophilus, Saint, as monk at, 2253
and Victor as abbot of, 2301
Encomia, role in Coptic hagiography, 1196–1197
Encomium on the Archangel Michael (Peter I), 1946
Encomium of Benjamin (Agathon of Alexandria), 2032
Encomium of Claudius (Constantine of Asyūṭ), 1192–1193
Encomium in Gabrielem Archangelum (Celestine I of Rome), 1136
Encomium in Philotheum, Miracula Philothei (Demetrius of Antioch), 893–894
Encomium of Theodorus Anatolius (Theodorus of Antioch), 2032
Encomium in Victorem (John Chrysostom), 893
Encomium of the Virgin Mary (Philip of Anatolia), 1956
Encratite, **958–959**
Encyclopedias
Coptic religious, 1267
Islamic law pertaining to *Dhimmis*, 1269–1270
theological, 1634–1635
England. *See* British headings; Great Britain
Ennodius, Bishop of Ticinum (Pavia), 45

Enoch
  aprocryphal literature of, 162–163
  and Gabriel, Archangel, 1133, 1135
  and Raphael, Archangel, 2053
Enoch, Saint. *See* Dayr Apa Jeremiah
Enthronement of Abbaton (homily), 2
Entombment. *See* Good Friday
Epacts. *See Book of Epact*
Eparchy, **959**, 2023
  Vansleb list of, 686
Ēpētēs (Coptic textile term), 2221
Ephesus, First Council of (431), 37, 48, 74, 127, 913, **959–960**, 1453, 2033
Ephesus, First Council of (431)
  affirmed by Henoticon edict, 1217
  on archdeacon rank, 191
  and Armenian synod profession of faith, 234
  and Celestinus deposition, 475
  on Christology, 547, 1699
  condemnation of Pelagianism, 1930
  and Cyril I, 673
  on divine maternity. *See subhead* on *Theotokos*
  Eutyches and, 1074–1075
  Ibṭū bishop at, 1275
  Isidorus of Pelusium role, 1308
  and John of Antioch, 1354
  on the nature of Christ. *See subheads* Christology; on *Theotokos*
  on Nestorius, 1786
  and Nicene Creed, 1116
  and Oriental Orthodox churches, 1846
  participants, 1089, 762
  Pseudo-Macarius and, 2027
  and Shenute, Saint, 2131–2132
  Tarnūṭ bishop at, 2202
  Theodoret and, 2236
  on *Theotokos*, 244, 270, 525, 528, 542, 547, 2255
  Tinnis bishops at, 2269
  and Victor of Tabennēsē, 2308
  and Zeno, Emperor, 2370
  see also Nestorians and Copts
Ephesus, Second Council of (449), 515, 913, 914, 915, **961–962**, 1075, 1947–1948, 2236
  and Chalcedon, Council of, 512–513
  and hypostatic union, 1262
Ephesus, Third Council of (476), **962**
Ephraem. *See* Mercurius and Ephraem
Ephraem the Syrian. *See* Abraham, Saint and Patriarch
Ephraem Syrus, Saint, **963**, 2083
  collected homilies of, 1778
  on Eastern orientation during prayers, 1846
  on incense use, 1472
  Theotokia texts ascribed to, 1726
Epiclesis, 120–121, 125, **964**, 1566
  and Coptic doctrine of the Holy Spirit, 1250
  during confirmation, 586
Epigraphy. *See* Inscriptions
Epigraphy of the Kellia. *See* Kellia
Epima, Apa, on glass communion vessels, 1146–1147
Epima, Saint, **965**, 1554
Epimachus and Gordian (martyrs), 1554
Epimachus of Pelusium, Saint, 835, 902, **965–966**, 1089, 1554
Epima of Pshante, Saint, 824
Epimarchus of Arwāṭ, Bishop of Pelusium, 835
Epiphania, Saint, 2083
Epiphanius (hermit), 800–801
Epiphanius (monk of Jerusalem), 749
Epiphanius, Canons of. *See* Canons of Epiphanius
Epiphanius of Salamis, Bishop of Cyprus, 1456, 1534, 1638
  feast day, 2083
  and Gospel of Philip, 1156
  and John Chrysostom, 2250–2251
  on marriage, 1543
  on Nativity date, 1103
  patristic writings, 1921
  see also Dayr Epiphanius
Epiphany, Feast of the, 1102, 1103
  and agricultural calendar, 441
Epiphany, liturgy of the, **967–968**
Epiphany tanks, **968**
Episcopacy. *See* Bishop
Episcopal churches. *See* Anglican Church in Egypt
Epistemun (Epistamon) (martyr), 1553, 1558
Epistle of Barnabas, 898
Epistle on the Eight Modes of Speech (al-Marṣafī), 1994
Epistles of Clement, 898
Epistles of Dionysius the Great, 911–912
Epistolography, **968–972**
  Arabic correspondence, 970–971
  of Athanasius I, 2008
  correspondences of bishops, 400–402
  of Ignatius of Antioch, 1281–1282
  of Isidorus of Pelusium, 1309–1310
  letters, of Ammonas, 113, 150
  letters of Antony of Egypt, 150
  letters of Dionysius, 911–912
  of Murqus al-Mashriqī al-Mallāwanī, 1700
  of Pachomius, Saint, 1863
  of Peter I, 1944, 1945, 1946
  of Pisentius, Saint and Bishop of Qifṭ, 1979–1980
  of Theodoret, 2236
  see also Epistles; Letters headings
Epistula Ammonis. *See* Letter of Ammon
Epistula apostolorum, Coptic translations, 1451
Epistula fundamenti (Mani), 1521
Epitome (Hippolytus), 1235–1236
Epitrachelion, 1476
Epiuse. *See* Epima, Saint
Equal rights movement, Coptic, 1465–1466
Era of Diocletian, in the Coptic calendar, 434, 972
Era of the Incarnation, in the Coptic calendar, 434
Erai. *See* Ter and Erai (martyrs)
Era of the Martyrs, **972**
  in the Coptic calendar, 434
  and Diocletian's ascension, 908
Eremika. *See* Pempton
Erescentius Alexander, 81
Erichsen, Wolja, **972–973**
Eric VII, King of Denmark, 1130
Eriokártēs (Coptic textile term), 2221
Erman, Adolf, **973**, 1165, 1965, 1966

and Boeser, Pieter Adriaan Art, 405
and Černý, Jaroslav, 511
and Crum, Walter Ewing, 661
and Sethe, Kurt Heinrich, 2121
Esaias. *See* Prayer of Esaias
Eschatology, **973–974**
Esdras, 22
see also Old Testament, Arabic versions of the
Esna. *See* Isnā
Esṭifānos, Ethiopian saint, 1053–1055
Esṭifānosites, 984–985
Etheria (Egeria)
on feast of the Ascension, 1105
on incense use, 1472
Ethiopia, *see also* Ethiopian headings
Ethiopia
anointment of emperor, 140–141
Axum as capital, 312–313
Christian conversion, 312–313
Franciscan prefecture in, 1122
Haile Selassie I, Emperor of, 1197–1199
and Mamluks and Copts, 1517
Menelik II, Emperor of, 1590–1591
Metropolitan See of, 1613, 1614
and Saladin, 1536
twentieth-century government, 1394
Ethiopia francescana (Somigli and Montano), 1122
Ethiopian art, Coptic influence on, **975**
Ethiopian Christian literature, **975–978**
on the Assumption, 290
and Salāmā II, Ethiopian prelate, 1011–1012
Synaxarion, 2190–2191
Ethiopian church autocephaly, 547–548, **980–984**, 1040–1044, 1909
catholicos title, 475
and Cyril II, Patriarch, 676
and Cyril VI, Patriarch, 678
eččage under, 930
Egyptian Coptic church relations, 1394
and Gabriel II, Patriarch, 1129
and Gabriel V, Patriarch, 1130–1131
and Haile Selassie I, 1198
selection of own patriarch, 1911
Ethiopian heresies and theological controversies, **984–987**
role of Bartalomēwos, Ethiopian prelate, 1012–1013
role of Zar'a Yā'qob, 1052–1053
Ethiopian liturgy, **987–990**, 997–998
Ethiopian monasticism, **990–994**
claims for Dayr al-Sulṭān, 872–874
Coptic church and Dayr al-Muḥarraq, 841
Isaac as *abūna*, 722
Lālibalā community, 1425–1426
monks in Egypt, 747–748, 765, 841
Rule of Pachomius use, 1862
Ethiopian Orthodox church, 30, **995–998**
canon of Scripture, 2108, 2109
and Haile Selassie I, 1198
"Ethiopian" pharaohs. *See* Kush, Empire of
Ethiopian prelates, **999–1044**, 1570
abūna title, 153
and Athanasius I, 300
Ethiopian saints, **1044–1055**
and Ashmūn church, 285
Ethiopian Synaxarion on, 2191
see also Ethiopian monasticism
Etymology. *See Appendix*
Eucharist, **1056–1061**, 1715
ablution in, 9
and absolution prayers, 16, 17
altar, 106
celebration at beginning of each month, 1112
Didache on, 898, 899
epiclesis limited to, 964
Gloria in excelsis and, 1147
Liturgy of Saint Mark, 1539
and Lord's Prayer, 1480–1481
Manichaean, 1520
Mass of the Catechumens, 1562–1565
Mass of the Faithful, 1565–1568
Maundy Thursday and, 1107
preparation in pastophorium, 216
reception in the apse, 200–201
rite of fraction in, 1121
Trisagion introduced into, 2017
use in antimension, 144
water into wine miracle and, 1107
see also Communion; Excommunication; Sacrament, reservation of the blessed
Eucharistic bread, **1062**, *1062*, 1472–1473
baked at Bayt al-'Ajīn, 372
leavened vs. unleavened, 1060–1061
seals for marking, *2336*
Eucharistic bread basket. *See* Liturgical instruments
Eucharistic bread trough. *See* Eucharistic bread
Eucharistic fast, **1063**
Eucharistic literature, 121–125
Eucharistic veils, **1063–1064**, 1252, 1472
Eucharistic vessels and instruments, **1064–1066**
cruet, 1472
deacon's role, 885
role of Eucharistic veils, 1063–1064
see also Antimension
Eucharistic wine, **1066**, 1472
Eucherius, Saint, 2231, 2303
Euchologion, **1066–1067**
see also Mark, Liturgy of Saint
Euchologion stand, **1067**
Euctemon, Bishop (Smyrna), 890
Eudamon (martyr), 233, 1554, 1558
Eudocia, 2033
Eudorus, 1149
Eudoxia. *See* Benjamin and Eudoxia (martyrs)
Eudoxia, Empress, **1067**, 1618
and the Assumption of Mary, 292
and council on Theophilus, Patriarch, 2250–2251
and John Chrysostom, 667, 1357, 2250, 2251
Eugenius. *See* Eusignius (martyr)
Eugenius IV, Pope, 1119
Eugenius, Agathodorus, and Elpidius (martyrs), 1554
Eugnostos the Blessed and The Sophia of Jesus Christ, 897, **1068–1069**, 1301
Euhemerism, 1867
Eulogius (Chalcedonian), 126
Eulogius (martyr), 831, 1554
Eulogy of Origen (Gregory Theodorus), 1848

Eumenius, Saint and Patriarch, **1069**, 1618, 2083
dates of patriarchy, 1914
Eunapius and Andrew (martyrs), 1555
Eunomius, 114, 115, 141, 142
Eunomius of Cyzicus, 230, 1959
Euphemia, Saint (martyr), 1073, 1111, 1555, 1617, 1618
Euphemia, Saint. *See* Epiphania, Saint
Euphrasia, Saint, 2083
Euphrosinus, 1881–1882
Euphrosyna, Saint, **1069**, 2083
Eupropious (martyr), 1554
Euripides, 1889
European art. *See* Art, Coptic influence on European
Eusebius (Tall Brother), 113
Eusebius, Bishop of Armenia, 1619
Eusebius, Saint (martyr), **1069–1070**, 892, 1555
Eusebius of Caesarea, 83, **1070–1071**, 1489
on Abgar legend, 8
on Abilius, Saint, 8
and Arianism, 230, 232, 1791
and Arius, 230, 231
and Basilides, 356–357
on candles, 446
on canonization, 449
canons of, 32
and Christianity in Anṣinā (Antinoopolis), 142
on Constantine the Great's vision of the Holy Cross, 1243–1244
and Constantine's edict, 944–945
on Decius, 889
on Easter designation, 1104
on epistles of Dionysius the Great, 911–912
and "godly monarch" concept, 1957
Historia ecclesiastica continued by Jerome, Saint, 1323
and Jerome, Saint, 1323
on Judas Cyriacus, 1377
on Mark, Saint, 1530
on martyrdoms, 1548–1549
on Melito of Sardis, 1585
on Nativity date, 1103
and Nicaea, Council of, 83
on Origen, 893, 1071, 1846, 1851, 1853
on Origen's *Hexapla and Tetrapla*, 1227
and Pamphilus, Saint, 1071, 1879
on Pantaenus' mission to India, 892
on patriarchal election, 1911
patristic writings, 1920, 1921
on persecution of Christians, 906–908
on Psalms, use of, 448
Rufinus' translations of, 2068
on subordinationism, 2157
see also Historia ecclesiastica
Eusebius of Dorylaeum, Bishop, 913, 914, 962, 1074
Eusebius Hieronymus. *See* Jerome, Saint
Eusebius of Nicomedia, Bishop
and Arianism, 84, 231, 298, 299, 1790
and Lucian of Antioch, 1484
Eusebius of Pelusium, Bishop, 1089
Eusegnius. *See* Eusignius
Eusignius, Saint (martyr), **1071–1072**, 1555
Eustathius, Bishop of Sebaste (Armenia), 1138
Eustathius the Greek. *See* Asṭāsi al-Rūmī
Eustathius and Theopista, Saints, **1072–1073**, 1555
Eustathius of Thrace, **1073**
Euthymius (Tall Brother), 113
Eutyches, 45, **1074–1075**, 1671, 1672, 1674, 2033
and Apollinarianism, 174
and Ephesus, Second Council of, 913, 914, 961–962, 1670
and Ethiopian theology, 984
on Incarnation, 1288
and Justinian's edict, 1674
and Leo I the Great, 1440–1441
on nature of Christ, 524–525, 1669–1670, 2267
and Nestorianism, 913, 1074–1075, 1440–1441, 1786
Eutychius. *See* Ibn al-Biṭrīq, Sa'īd
Evagrius (prefect under Theodosius), 2009
Evagrius Ponticus, 113, 120, **1076–1077**, 1453, 1490, 1976, 2020
and costume of the religious, 650
as desert father, 894
on the eight capital vices, 463
and Encratite view of body, 958–959
and Isaiah of Scetis, 1306
on Isidorus of Pelusium, 1308
and John Colobos, Saint, 1359
and Kellia and Nitria communities, 1397, 1796
and Macarius the Egyptian, 1491
manuscript in Paris, 1779
Palladius as disciple of, 1876, 1877
and Theophilus, Patriarch, 2249
and Timothy II Aelurus, Patriarch, 2264
Evagrius Scholasticus (536–600), on exile of Nestorius, 1786–1787
Evangeliary, **1077–1078**
Evangelical Church, Coptic. *See* Coptic Evangelical Church
Evangelical Theological Seminary, Cairo, 603
Evangelist, **1078**
animal symbols of, 244–247, *247*, 1812
see also Missionaries
Eve. *See* Adam and Eve
Evelyn-White, Hugh Gerard, **1078**, 1449
on Dayr Anbā Helias
on Dayr Apa Anūb, 770
on Dayr al-Arman, 782
on duplicate monasteries, 714
and identification of Kellia site, 1397
and identification of Nitria site, 1794–1795
and identity of Hor, 1254
on Jabal Khashm al-Qu'ud, 1316
on Pidjimi, Saint, 1966, 1967
Evening Offering of Incense, music with, 1719, 1721, 1725
Evetts, Basil Thomas Alfred, **1078**, 1462
Evil, Origen on, 1849
Evodius of Rome, **1078–1079**
cycle of, 667–668
Ewer. *See* Basin and ewer
Ēwosṭātēwos, Ethiopian saint, 1050–1051
Ēwosṭātēwosites, 985
Excavations
Abū Mīnā, 24–29, 1394
Abūṣīr al-Malaq, 37

Abūṣīr (Taposiris Magna), 34, *35, 36*
Abydos, 38–42
Ahnās, 73, 74–75
ʿAlam Shaltūt, 80
Alexandria, 96–97, 1180
'Amriyyah (Maryūt), 118, *118*
Antinoopolis, 145, 146–148, 1933, 1961, 2049
al-ʿAraj, 190
archives, 226–227
al-Ashmūnayn, 74, 2090
Bāwīṭ, 74, 256, 363–364
Clysma, 565
Coptic glass evidence, 1143, 1144
Coptic mummies, 1697
Coptic sculptures in stone, 2112–2113
dating of Coptic monuments, 693–694
Dayr Abū Ḥalbānah, 700
Dayr Abū Jirjā, 1527
Dayr Abū Līfah, 704
Dayr Abū Mattā, 706
Dayr Abū Qarqūrah, 708–709
Dayr Anbā Abshāy (near al-Tūd), 719
Dayr Anbā Shinūdah, 766, 768
Dayr Apa Jeremiah, 773–776, 777, 778, 1143, 2040
Dayr Apa Phoibammon, 13, 779, 780–781
Dayr al-Balaʿyzah, 786–787
Dayr al-Baramūs, 792
Dayr al-Barshah and Dayr al-Nakhlah, 795
Dayr al-Dīk, 798, 847
Dayr Epiphanius, 800–801
Dayr Harmīnā, 808
Dayr al-Janādlah, 705
Dayr al-Kubāniyyah, 815–816
Dayr al-Madīnah, 817
Dayr al-Malāk Mīkhāi'īl, 824
Dayr al-Malāk Mīkhā'īl (Jirjā), 825–826
Dayr al-Midīnah, 1620
Dayr Muṣṭafā Kāshif, 842
Dayr Nahyā, 843
Dayr al-Naqlūn, 846
Dayr al-Naṣārā (Antinoopolis), 847
Dayr al-Quṣayr, 853
Dayr al-Rūmāniyyah
Dayr al-Sāqiyah, 861
Dongola, 922
al-Duwayr, 928
the Enaton, 101
Faras, 1091–1092
Fayyūm Gospel fragment, 1100
French, 693, 694–695, 724, 924, 927
al-Fusṭāt, 188
Ḥājir Idfū, 1200
Hawwāriyyah, 1211–1212
inscriptions, value of, 1291
Jabal Khashm al-Quʿūd, 1315–1316
Karanis, 1390
Karm al-Akhbāriyyah, 1391–1392
Karnak, 1392–1393
Kellia, 1398–1407, 2103, 2104–2105
Khash al-Quʿūd, 1658
Khirbat al-Filūsiyyah, 1414
at Kom al-Dikka, 90, 97, 116–118, *116, 117, 118*
Kom Namrūd, 1418
Luxor temples, 1485
Madamūd, 1494–1495
Madīnat Ghurān, 1651
Madīnat Hābū, 1496–1497
Madīnat Māḍī, 1498
Memnonia, 1586
Menarti, 1588
monastery of Saint Menas, 707
mural painting examples, 1872–1873
Najʿ al-Ḥajar, 1773–1774
in Nubia, 1185, 1804–1806, 2071, 2142; *see also* Nubian archaeology, medieval; Nubian ceramics; Nubian Christian architecture; Nubian Christian survivals; Nubian church art; Nubian inscriptions, medieval; Nubian monasteries
as nucleus of Louvre Coptic section, 1481
at Oktokaidekaton monastery, 118
of Oxyrhynchus Papyri, 1857–1858
papyrology, 1888–1889
papyrus discoveries, 1898–1900
Pbow, 1927–1929
pottery kilns, 481–482
Qaṣr Ibrīm, 2037
Qurnat Marʿī, 2041, 2042
Sai Island, 2080–2081
Saqqara, 74
at Soba in ʿAlwa, 2141–2142
Tall Atrīb, 1620
Tall al-Faramā, 1090
Upper Egypt, 1668–1669
Wādī al-Rayyān, 2311
Wādī Sarjah, 2312
Wādī Shaykh ʿAlī, 2312–2313
see also Ceramics, Coptic; Ceramics of the late Coptic period; Costume, civil; Society of Coptic Archaeology
Excommunication, **1079–1080**, 1931
and anathema, 55
and *audientia episcopalis*, 308
and clerical instruction, 565
Exegesis on the Soul, 898, **1080–1081**
and *Authentikos logos*, 309
and Encratites, 958–959
and *Interpretation of Knowledge*, 1301
Exhibitions of Coptic art. *See* Museums
The Exhortation to Martyrdom (Origen), 1847
Exodus to Sinai, 1976
Exorcism
pilgrimages and, 1968, 1970, 1971, 1973, 1974
Pisentius, Saint and Bishop of Qifṭ, powers, 1979
Raphael, Archangel, role in, 2053
Exoucontians, **1081–1082**
Exultate Deo, 1119
Exuperantius, Saint, **1082**, 1555, 2057, 2232
Eye diseases, 1579, 1581
Ezekiel, Anbā, 748, 861, 1923–1924, 1925
Ezekiel of Armant, Saint, 2083
Ezekiel Tragicus, 1150
Ezr (catholicus of Armenian church), 1666
Ezra, Apocalypse of, 165

F

Fabian, Pope, 889
Fabian Society, 2088
Fabius, Bishop of Antioch, 909, 911, 912
Fabrics. *See* Textiles, Coptic
Facsimile Edition of the Nag Nammadi Codices (ARE-UNESCO), 1771–1773

Faḍl ibn Abī al-Faḍā'il, 1463
Fā'iz, al-, Caliph, 1099
Fakhr al-Dawlah Abū al-Mufaḍḍal ibn al-'Assāl, **1085**, 1748
False doctrine. *See* Heresy
Family law, Coptic, 1942
 see also Personal status law
Family life, Coptic, **1086–1088**
 see also Children; Marriage
Family Life Education Program (FLEP), 1088
Famines, 693, 708, 750, 877, 1633
Fan, 1473–1474
Fānah, Saint, 698
 see also Dayr Abū Fānah
Fānūs, Akhnūkh, 1988, 1989
Fānūs, Louis, 1627
Fārābī, Al-, 6
Faraj, Ibrāhīm, 1991
Faraj Aghā, 1636
Farajallāh al-Akhmīmī, **1089**, 1780
Faramā, al- (Pelusium), **1089–1090**, 1650
 on route of flight into Egypt, 1118
Fārān. *See* Pharan
Faras, 114, **1090–1091**, 1675
 and classic Christian Nubian pottery, 1806
 as episcopal see of Nubia, 1813
 evidence of Nubian liturgy at, 1816–1817
 fresco of Onophrius, Saint, at, 1842
 and Jabal 'Addā, 1315
 as Nobatian capital, 1797, 1798
 Nobatian royal headquarters at, 2037
 and Nubian archaeology, medieval, 1804
 and Nubian Christian architecture, 1807–1809
 and Nubian inscriptions, medieval, 1814–1815
 and Nubian studies, 615
 portraits of bishops, 402
Faras Cathedral, 1090, 1091–1092
Faras murals, **1091–1092**, *1092*, 1811–1812, 1819
 and the eparchs of Nobatia, 1798
Farīd, Muḥammad, 1994
Fāriskūr, 1649
Farouk I, King, 1694, 1990, 1992
Farshūṭ, 11, 12, 331, **1092–1093**, 1656
Fast of the Apostles, 1093
Fast of Heraclius, 1093–1094
Fasting, **1093–1096**, 1699
 abstinence differentiated from, 17
 communion and, 579
 Didache on, 898
 Didascalia on, 899
 Eucharist, 1063
 as funerary custom, 1125
 Good Friday, 1152
 and Holy Saturday, 1247–1248
 and Holy Week, 1251
 Lent, 1437
 liturgical ritual books for, 1729
 marriage ceremonies proscribed during periods of, 1545
 monthly festal days and, 1111
 and *Paramone*, 1901
 Saturday, 2098, 2099
 Sunday, 2159–2160
Fast of Jonah, 1094
Fast of the Nativity, 1095–1096
Fast of the Virgin Mary, 1096
Fatḥ, Maḥmūd Abū, al-, 1990
Father of the Monks. *See* Antony of Egypt, Saint
Father of Two Swords. *See* Mercurius of Caesarea
Fatimid dynasty, **1097–1099**, 1271, 1488, 1632–1633
 Abū al-Faḍl 'Īsā ibn Nasṭūrus financial role, 18
 coinage, 576
 Coptic church under, 1574
 Copto-Muslim art, 1311–1312
 al-Ḥākim prohibitions and persecutions, 1201–1203
 Islamization, 939, 940
 Qūṣ prosperity under, 2043
Fāw al-Qiblī (Fāw of the South). *See* Pbow
Fayyūm (region)
 Abraam I, Bishop of, 10
 Coptic glass excavations, 1143
 cult of Homeric gods, 1865
 funerary portraits, 2001
 Greek settlements in, 1175
 inscriptions found in, 1292
 monasteries of, 1650–1651; *see also* specific monasteries
 monastery libraries, 1449
 papyrus collections, 1389, 1891, 1895
 stelae from, 2162
 tombstone material and shapes in, 1295
Fayyūm, city of, **1100**
Fayyūm Gospel Fragment, **1100**
Fayyumic dialect
 New Testament in, 1788
 see also Appendix
Fayyumic Papyrus. *See* Hamburg Papyrus
Fayyūm paintings. *See* Portraits and funerary masks
Feast, **1101–1109**
 monthly festal days, 1111–1112
Feast of the Angel, festal day, 1111
Feast of Blowing of the Trumpets, 1101
Feast of the Martyrs, 1547–1548
Feast of Saints Peter and Paul, *awshiyahi* during, 311
Feasts of the Cross, 1469
Feast of Shamm al-Nasim, 2126
Feasts, Latin, in the Coptic Catholic Church, 601
Feasts, major, 1101, 1102–1106, 1904
 anaphora of Saint Gregory use, 124–125
 Assumption of the Virgin Mary, 290, 1096, 2256
 Epiphany liturgy, 967–968
 liturgical ritual books, 1715–1716, 1729
 pilgrimages linked with, 1968, 1970
Feasts, minor, 1101, 1106–1109
 liturgical ritual books for, 1729
Feasts, movable, in the Copto-Arabic Synaxarion, 2190
Feasts of the *Theotokos*, 2256
Feast of the Tabernacles, 1101
Feast of the Virgin, 1111
Feast of Weeks, 1101
Febronia, Saint (martyr), **1109–1110**, 1555
Federal Republic of Germany. *See* Germany
Feet, washing of, 8–9, 1107–1108, 1252, 1426–1427
 laqqān tank, 1426–1427
 Maundy Thursday, 311
Felix III, Pope (Rome), 43, 1218
Felix, Saint, 1082, **1110**, 1555, 2057, 2086, 2232, *2233*
Felix of Aptunga, 920
Festal days, monthly, **1111–1112**
Festival of Saint Michael, 1617, 1618
Festugière, A.-J., 1445

Feudal system, Coptic control of, 1535
Fibers used in Coptic textiles, 2211–2213
Figurines
metal, 1607
terra-cotta, 500–503, *501–503*
Fikrī, ʿAbdallāh, 1994
Filatis (martyr), 1555
Filioque, **1112–1116**, 1119
in Coptic Catholic church, 601
and Coptic doctrine of the Holy Spirit, 1250
history of controversy, 1112–1114
theological background and interpretation, 1114–1116
Filtā'ūs Malaṭī, 1688
Filya (martyr), 688
Fiqṭor, Ethiopian prelate, 1002–1003
The First Book of Jeu, 897
First Principles (Origen). *See De principiis*
Fīs, Saint, 716, **1116**, 2083
Fish, as symbol in Coptic art, 2170–2171, *2171*
Fīshah, **1117**
Flasks, 1602–1603
Flavian, Archbishop of Constantinople, 44, 893, 913, 1440, 1441, 1672, 1948
and Eutyches, 1074, 1670
and Evagrius Ponticus, 2249
and John Chrysostom, 893, 1357
and Theophilus, Patriarch, 2249
Flavian of Ephesus, Bishop, **1117**
Flavio, Biondo, 1119
Flavius Eutolmius Tatianus (prefect), 2009
Flavius Honorius, Emperor, 921
Flavius Philagrius (prefect), 2009
Flavius Strategius Apion, 155
Flight into Egypt, **1117–1118**
and Armant, 233
and al-Ashmūnayn, 233, 841
and Asyūṭ, 927
and Basṭah, 360–361
and Bilbeis, 391
and al-Burullus, 427
and al-Faramā, 1089
Feast of the, 1107
and Ḥārit Zuwaylah, 1207–1209
martyrdoms linked with, 1554
monastic sites associated with, 712, 716, 813, 818, 840, 841, 1653
and Nikiou, 1793
pilgrimage sites associated with, 1969, 1970, 1972, 1973, 1976, 1977
traditions about, 841–842
Flinders Petrie, W. M., 705, 1090
Florence, Copts at the Council of (1439–1443), 722, **1118–1119**
on canon of New Testament, 2110
filioque debate, 1114, 1115–1116
and relations with Rome, 609
and Zar'a Yāʿqob of Ethiopia, 1052–1053
Florentinus, 1445
Florentius (patrician), 1074
Florianus, Emperor, patriarch under, 1914
Florus (prefect), 2009
Flowers, woven textile, *2226*
Flute, 1740, *1740*
Flute of the Holy Spirit. *See* Jacob of Sarūj
Fogg Art Museum, Cambridge, Massachusetts, 1713
Fontaine, A. L., 1090
Food and diet
abstinence, 17
Dayr Anbā Bishoi refectory, 735–736
Dayr Epiphanius (Pachomian monks), 801–802
Epiphany feast, 1103
fasting prohibitions, 1093
funerary customs, 1125
Shamm al-Nasīm feast day, 2126
see also Famines; Refectory
Foot washing. *See* Ablution; Feet, washing of
Formosus of Porto, Bishop, 1113
Formula of Satisfaction (Anastasius), 44, 1672
Fortescue, Adrian, **1120**
Fortress of Babylon, 317–320, *318*
and Coptic Museum (Old Cairo), 607–608
Fortress of Candles. *See* Qaṣr al-Shamʿ
Fortresses
ḥiṣn, 1237
Jabal ʿAddā, 1315
Qalʿat al-Bābayn, 2035
Qaṣr Ibrīm, 2036–2037
Qaṣr Nisīmah, 2038
Qaṣr al-Shamʿ, 2038
Talmīs, 2200
Umm Dabadīb, 2291
see also Castrum
Fortress of Mount Sinai Monastery of Saint Catherine, 1684
Forty-nine martyrs of Scetis, 12, **1120–1121**
and Bilbeis, 391
buried at al-Batanūn, 361
chapel at Dayr al-Suryān, 876, 880
church of (Ḥārit al-Rūm), 753, 2046
and John of Scetis, 1362
Fouad, King, 1694, 1990, 1992
Foucart, G., 924
Four Living Creatures in Coptic Art. *See* Christ, Triumph of
Fourth Eclogue (Virgil), 1867
Fra Bartolomeo, 1532
Fraction, **1121**, 1567
and Epiphany, liturgy of the, 967–968
and Lord's Prayer, 1481
prayers, 17, 71
France
archaeological activity, 1398–1400, 1402
archaeological activity in the Kellia, 1398
Archaeological and Anthropological Museum, 1187
Coptic churches in, 1623
Coptic collections, 1701, 1705–1707; *see also* Louvre Museum
influence on Egyptian political parties, 1987–1988
Louvre Museum, 1481–1483
Mauritius, Saint, veneration, 1572
papyri collections, 1892
see also Coptological studies; French expedition in Egypt; Scholars
Franciscan Center for Christian Oriental Studies, founding of, 1123
Franciscan Mission of Upper Egypt, 1123
Franciscans in Egypt, **1121–1123**, 1699

Frankish kingdoms, 1112
Fraumünster, Zurich, 1082, 1110, 2057
Freer Collection, Washington, D.C., 843, 1136, 1895–1896
Free will, 1929
French expedition in Egypt, 1141, 1206, 1284, 1511–1512
  and administrative organization of Egypt, 935, 1516
  Coptic Legion, 1524; *see also* Coptic Legion
  Coptic officials, 1687–1688
  influence on Egyptian political thought, 1993
  Jirjis al-Jawharī and, 1332–1334
  Kléber, Jean Baptiste, participation, 1416
  Mark VIII patriarchy during, 1538–1539
  military leadership, 1417, 1591–1592
  and Muḥammad ʿAlī dynasty, 1691–1692
  Muḥammad al-Muhdī support, 1696
  scholarship and, 1526, 1977
  Shukrallāh Jirjis and, 2136
  Yaqūb, General, 2349–2352
French Institute of Oriental Archaeology, Cairo, 256
French language, Arabic-French dictionary, 1284, 1285
French Oriental Army, 1417
French School, Rome, 925
Frescobaldi, 1977
Frescoes. *See* Painting, Coptic mural
Friars Minor of the Observance, 610
Friday. *See* Wednesday and Friday fast days
Friedrich Schiller University, Jena, 1893
Friends of the Bible, **1124**
Friezes, 1873, 2341–2342, *2342*
Frumentius. *See* Salāmā I
Fugas, Bishop of Bontos (martyr), 1555
Fulvius Asticus, 906
Funeral masks, 2001
Funerary customs, **1124–1125**
  mourning, 1686
  murals and portraiture, 1873, 2001–2003
  objects, 263
  rites, 425–426, 1128, 1901
  stela, 2149–2152
  see also Burial rites; Mourning in early Christian times; Mummification
Furayj Ruways, hagiographical collection of, 1780
Fusṭāṭ, Al- (Old Cairo)
  and Arab conquest of Egypt, 188
  Coptic churches' legal status in, 687
  Dayr Abū Sayfayn, 710–711
  Dayr bi'l-Habash, 796
  foundation of, 188
  Ḥārit al-Rūm section, 1206–1207
  Ḥārit Zuwaylah section, 1207–1209
  and Islamization, 937
  as site of Egyptian mint, 575–576
  transfer of Egyptian capital to, 88–89, 91, 96
Fusṭāṭ Expedition of the American Research Center in Egypt. *See* Ceramics of the late Coptic period
Futūḥ Miṣr (ʿAbd al-Hakam), on the Arab conquest of Egypt, 183–189
Fuwwah, **1125–1126**

G

Gabra Manfas Qeddus, Ethiopian saint, 1055
Gabra Masqal, Ethiopian saint, 1047–1048
Gabr'ēl, Ethiopian prelate, 1014–1015, 1054
Gabriel (monk-priest of Dayr al-ʿAdhrā', Samālūṭ), 716
Gabriel (qummus of Dayr al-Muḥarraq), 840
Gabriel, Archangel, 190, **1135–1137**
  and the Annunciation, 528–529, 1102, 1199, 2256
  and the Assumption of Mary, 292, 293, 2256
  churches dedicated to, 845, 860, 1137
  festival of, 845–846
  and Herpaese and Julianus, Saints, 1226
  monasteries dedicated to, 814, 845, 1654
  paintings of, 868, 869
  and *Theotokos*, feasts of the, 2256
Gabriel, Bishop of Atfīh (Aphroditopolis), 726
Gabriel I, Archbishop of Jerusalem, 1325
Gabriel I, Saint and Patriarch, **1127**, 2083
  dates of patriarchy, 1916
  as monk of Dayr Anbā Antūniyūs, 722
Gabriel II ibn Turayk, Patriarch, 881, **1127–1128**, 1613, 2083
  and Apostolic Canons, 453
  and canons of Coptic law, 450
  on *Canons of Epiphanius*, 457
  and *Canons of Hippolytus*, 458
  compilation of *difnār* by, 1728
  condemnation of *cheirotonia*, 517
  dates of patriarchy, 1917
  on Dayr Anbā Būlā, 741
  and Dayr al-Shamʿ, 863
  and Ethiopian church autocephaly, 980
  and Holy Week scripture readings, 1251
  imprisonment, 1129
  and Mikā'ēl I, Ethiopian prelate, 1006
  successor, 1615
Gabriel III, Patriarch
  dates of patriarchy, 1917
  and Ḥasaballah, 1209
  as monk at Dayr Anbā Anṭūniyūs, 722
Gabriel IV, Patriarch, **1129–1130**
  dates of patriarchy, 1918
  successor, 1569
  and Timotheus, 1845
Gabriel V, Patriarch, 392, **1130–1132**
  dates of patriarchy, 1918
  as monk at Dayr Anbā Ṣamū'īl of Qalamūn, 759
Gabriel VI, Patriarch, **1133**
  dates of patriarchy, 1918
  successor, 1616
  writings copied by Jirjis Makramallāh al-Bahnasāwī, 1335
Gabriel VII, Patriarch, **1133–1134**
  dates of patriarchy, 1918

and Pēṭros II, Ethiopian prelate, 1018
and restoration of Dayr Anbā Anṭūniyūs, 720, 722
and restoration of Dayr Anbā Būlā, 742
and Roman Catholic embassy, 952
writings copied by Jirjis Makramallāh al-Bahnasāwī, 1335
Gabriel VIII, Patriarch, **1135**
consecrated at Church of Abū Sayfayn, 550
and Coptic relations with Rome, 609–610, 797–798, 810, 1134
dates of patriarchy, 1918
as monk at Dayr Anbā Bishoi, 735
and Yūsuf Abū Daqn, 2364
Gabriel al-Durunki (priest-monk at Dayr Anbā Anṭūniyūs), 722
Gabriel ibn Kātib al-Qūḍiyyah, Bishop of Asyūt, 1131
Gaianites, 734, 790, 876, 1138, 2054, 2139, 2241
see also Gaianus; Julian, Bishop of Halicarnassus
Gaianus (rival patriarch of Alexandria), **1138**, 2054, 2104, 2241
see also Gaianites
Gaius, Emperor. *See* Caligula
Galactotrophousa
depicted in Coptic art, 531
see also Virgo lactans
Galba, Emperor, patriarch under, 1913
Galerius, Emperor, 904, 906, 907, 1869
patriarch under, 1914
visit to Egypt, 2063, 2066
Gallery, 210
Gallielaion. *See* Oil of exorcism
Gallienus, Emperor, 909, 910, 1869
patriarch under, 1914
tolerance of Christians, 1936
Gallus, Emperor, 909
and Julian the Apostate, 1380
patriarch under, 1914
vision of the Holy Cross, 1244
Galtier, Emile Joseph, **1138**
Games, wooden, 2339, *2340*
Gangra, Council of (circa 340), **1138**, 1543
Garden of the Monks. See Apophthegmata patrum
Garimā, Ethiopian saint, 1046
Garments, sacred. *See* Liturgical vestments
Gaselee, Stephen, **1138**
Gaul, 252–253, 255, 1381
Gayet, Albert Jean Marie Philippe, 847, **1138–1139**, 1481
Gebhard, Johannes, 1921
Gelasius, Bishop of Caesarea, 2069
Gelasius I, Patriarch of Constantinople, 43
Gelasius, Saint, 2083
Gemination, vocalic. *See Appendix*
Genesis and Ecclesiastes (Didymus), 900
Geneva, University of, 1400
Gentilly, Synod of (767), 1112
Genuflection, **1139**
Geographic Society, 1993
Geography, dialectal. *See Appendix*
Geometric designs, in paintings at Bāwīṭ, 372
George (martyr). *See* Jirjis al-Muzāḥim
George, Bishop of Pelusium, 1089
George, Saint, 230, **1139–1140**, 1555, 2083
churches dedicated to, 686, 782, 784, 788, 820, 821, 1131, 1140, 1975
cycle of collected manuscript, 1782
and Horus myth, 248–249, 1762
iconography of, 248–250
monasteries dedicated to, 709, 824, 826, 830, 848, 850, 1658
in Nubian church art, 1812
pilgrimages linked with, 1968, 1970, 1971, 1973
portraits of, 726, 727
relics of, 1131
George of Alexandria (martyr), 1555
George of Alexandria, Bishop, 1380, 1381
George the Ascetic (martyr), 1555
George of Cappadocia. *See* George, Saint
George the Copt. *See* Jirjis al-Qibṭī
George of Makouria, King, 1099, 1271
George of Scetis. *See* Abraham and George of Scetis, Saints
Georgia, Russia, 2243–2244
Georgius (Arian bishop of Alexandria), 98, 101, 102, 1869
Geradamus, 1150
Gérdios (Coptic weaving term), 2221
Germanicus (Roman imperial prince), 2061–2062, 2066
German Institute, 842
German State Library, Berlin, 1893
Germanus, Bishop, 910
Germany
Coptic churches in, 1623
Coptic collections in, 1701, 1703–1704
papyrus collection in, 1892–1893
see also State Museum of Berlin
Gerspach, Edouard, 257
Ghālī (19th-century Coptic finance minister), **1141**, 1334, 1636, 1692, 2059
Ghālī, Boutros. *See* Boutros Ghālī
Ghali, Mirrit B., 1299
Gharbiyyah Province
Dayr Mār Mīnā in, 833
Dayr al-Maymah in, 837–838
Dimayrah in, 902–903
Dinūshar in, 903
monasteries in, 1651–1652
Ghillebert de Lannoy, 720, 722, 1977
Ghost trap, 1508
Ghubriyāl. *See* Gabriel
Ghubriyāl, Kāmil Ibrāhīm, 1743
Ghubriyāl, Riyāḍ, 1465, 1466
Ghuzz
plunder of Damrū, 689
plunder of Dayr Anbā Shinūdah (Suhāj), 764
Giambattista, Eliano, Father, 1134
Gildo, Count, 921
Gilles de Loche, 1977
Ginusi (martyr), 1555
Girdle, 342, 1476–1477, 1535
Girgis, V. A., 2022
Girgis Mattha, **1141**
Giuliano Cesarini, Cardinal, 1119
Giversen, S., 1894
Giyorgis I, Ethiopian prelate, 1006
Giyorgis II, Ethiopian prelate, 1008–1009
Giyorgis of Gāseḉhā, Ethiopian Saint, 1051–1052

Giza, **1141–1142**
Dayr al-Aḥmar in, 716–717
Dayr al-Muḥarraqah in, 841–842
Dayr Nahyā in, 843
Franciscan seminary in, 1123
see also Monasteries of the Lower Ṣaʿīd
Gjmoumi. *See* Ashmūn
Glass, Coptic, **1142–1147**, *1143-1147*
Islamic influence on, 1312
lamps, 1144–1145
in Louvre Museum, 1483
luster painting, 1146, 1311, 1312
preservation of, 280
religious uses, 1146–1147
restoration. *See* Art preservation
tableware and storage vessels, 1143–1144
technique, 1142–1143
window and wall decorating, 1145–1146
see also Art, historiography of Coptic
Glazing techniques, ceramic, 486–487, 510
Gloria in excelsis, **1147**, 1732
Gnapheus (Coptic textile term), 2221
Gnômès, and the *Arabic Canons of Nicaea*, 1789–1790
Gnosis, **1147–1148**, 1157, 1163, 1300, 1520
abraxas (word with numerical value), 14
apocryphons as source for understanding, 160, 172
in Jung Codex, 569
scholarship on, 2032, 2033
Gnostic Christians. *See* Gnosticism
Gnosticism, **1148–1151**, 1453
abstinence practice, 17
Allogenes text, 105
in the Apocalypse of Adam, 156–157, 166
in the Apocalypse of James, First, 157–158
in the Apocalypse of James, Second, 158–159
in the Apocalypse of Paul, 159–160
in the Apocalypse of Peter, 160–161
and the Apocryphon of James, 169
and *Authentikos logos*, 304
Basilides, 356–357
in Byzantine Alexandria, 101
on celibacy, 1543
Celsus on, 479
Cerinthus on Incarnation, 1288
Clement of Alexandria on, 103, 470, 562–563
in *Concept of Our Great Power*, 583
and Coptic literature, 1450–1451
Coptic translation of Plato's *Republic*, 1958
and *Dialogue of the Savior*, 897–898
Dialogue of the Savior, 897–898
and docetism, 917
Egyptian influence on, 1150
and *Eugnostos the Blessed*, 1068–1069
and *Exegesis on the soul*, 1081
Gabriel, Archangel, in literature of, 1135
Gnosis concept, 1147–1148, 1157, 1163; *see also Gnosis*
and *Gospel of Mary*, 1155
and *Gospel of Philip*, 1155–1156
and *Gospel of Thomas*, 1162, 1163
and *Gospel of Truth*, 1163–1164
Greek and Coptic-speaking adherents, 1177
Heracleon, 1219–1220
and Homoeans and *homoiousion* term, 1252, 1253
and *Hypostasis of the Archons*, 1261
and Hypsiphrone, 1262
and *Interpretation of Knowledge*, 1301
and *Letter of Peter to Philip*, 1446
link with monasticism, 1229, 1661
and liturgical music, 1732, 1735
magical spells, 1503
Marsanes, prophet, 1547
Melchizedek and, 1583–1584
in Nag Hammadi Codices, 1771–1773; *see also* Nag Hammadi Library
On the Origin of the World scripture, 1842–1844
papyri in Coptic Museum (Old Cairo), 608
and *Paraphrase of Shem*, 1901–1902
Plotinus refutation of, 1982
and *Second Treatise of the Great Seth*, 2117–2118
Sethian, 1154, 1222, 2117–2118, 2259–2260
seven "magic vowels", 1732, 1735
and the *Sophia of Jesus Christ*, 1068–1069
and *Testimony of Truth*, 2209–2210
and *Thought of Norea*, 2257
and *Three Stelae of Seth*, 2259–2260
and *Thunder, Perfect Mind*, 2260
and *Treatise on the Resurrection*, 2275
and *Trimorphic Protennoia*, 2276–2277
and *Tripartite Tractate*, 2277
and *Valentinian Exposition*, 2295–2296
and Valentinus, 157–158, 2296–2297
and *Zostrianus*, 2371–2372
see also Apocalypse headings; Manichaeism
Gobidlaha, Dado, and Caxo, Saints, **1151–1152**, 1555
Goblets, 1601–1603
God-bearer. *See Theotokos*
Goethe, Johann, 1149
Gold dinars, 574, 575–576, 709
Goldsmiths, 1595, 1604
Gondophernes, King of Malabar, 1635
Good Friday, 1104, **1152–1153**, 1252, 1904
candles, 446
and Holy Saturday, 1247–1249
lectern placement, 1435
music, *1720*, 1721, 1729
Good news. *See* Gospel headings
Gordian. *See* Epimachus and Gordian (martyrs)
Gordianus III, Emperor, patriarch under, 1914
Gorst, Sir Aldon, 1466, 1627
Gospel. *See* Egerton Gospel; Evangeliary; Evangelist; Gospels; specific names
Gospel book, 1474
Gospel casket, **1153**, 1474

Gospel of the Egyptians, **1153–1154**
and Gospel of Thomas, 1163
and *Zostrianus*, 2372
Gospel of the Hebrews, 1163, 1619
Gospel of Mary, 897, **1155**
Gospel of Philip, 897, **1155–1157**, 1164
and *Authentikos logos*, 309
and *Valentinian Exposition*, 2296
Gospels
Arabic translations, 282, 1464
in Bohairic dialect, 2138
Gospel of Saint John, 1078, 1148
on Last Supper, 1060–1061
on the nature of Christ, 524
parchment manuscript, 1885
Gospel of Saint Luke, 1078, 1157, 1160, 1161, 1163, 2195
commentary on, 1456
Lord's Prayer, 1480
parchment manuscript, 1885
Gospel of Saint Mark, 1078, **1157–1162**, 1529, 1530–1531, 1532, 1910, 2195
commentary on, 1456
parchment manuscript, 1885
see also Secret Gospel of Saint Mark
Gospel of Saint Matthew, 1078, 1157, 1160, 1161, 1163, 1544, 1881, 2195
on events of Holy Saturday, 1247
linked with Ebionites, 930
Lord's Prayer, 1480
reading for altar consecration, 108
Gospels, synoptic, **1157**, **2195**
see also Gospel of Saint Luke; Gospel of Saint Matthew; Gospel of Saint Mark
Gospel of Thomas, 897–898, **1162–1163**, 1981, 2032
on Ebionites, 929–930
and Gospel of Mary, 1155
and Gospel of Philip, 1156
Gospel of Truth, 569, 1151, **1163–1164**
in Jung Codex, 569
and Valentinus, 2297
Gothic War, 2020
Goths, conversion of, 2285
Goutinos (monk), 317
Government
Egyptian provincial reforms, 2007–2009, 2022–2023
Murqus Simaykah service, 1700
pagarch system, 1871–1872
patriarchal selection approval, 1911
political parties, 1986–1996
political party leadership, 1747–1748
Rizq Agha service, 2059
Roman emperors in Egypt, 2061–2063
Roman intervention in, 2064
see also Mamluks and Copts; Mūhammad ʿAlī dynasty; Political thought in modern Egypt; Roman Empire; Taxation; specific personal names, titles, and related subjects
Graeco-Roman. *See* Greco-Roman headings
Graf, Georg, **1165**, 1735, 2019
Graf, Theodor, 1389
Graffin, René, **1165**
Graffiti, **1165**
at al-Dayr, 695
at Dayr al-Bahri, 780, 781
at Kellia, 2129
medical, 1888
Nubian, 1172
at Shams al-Dīn, 2126–2127
at al-Shaykh Ḥasan, 2129
at al-Shaykh Ṣaʿid, 2130
see also Inscriptions
Grammars, Coptic, 34, 1266, 1268, 1302, 2148
Granite, Coptic sculpture in, 2113
Grapow, Hermann, **1165**
Gratian, Emperor, patriarch under, 1914
Graves. *See* Burial rites and practices; Cemeteries; Mummification; Stela; Tombs
Gravestones. *See* Stela; Tombs
Graziani, Rodolfo, 1041, 1042
Great Britain
Anglican Church in Egypt, 133
Coptic art influence in, 252
Coptic churches in, 1623–1624
Coptic collections in, 1707–1710
Coptic influences in the British Isles, 416–419
Coptic Street (London), 611–612
and Egyptian political relations, 1989–1991
English saints, 418–419
occupation of Egypt, 1627–1628, 1637, 1693–1694, 1748
papyrus collections in, 1893–1894
see also names of specific institutions and museums
Great Doxology, 923
Great Intercessions, in Mass of the Catechumens, 1564
Great Lent, 1102, 1437
see also Lent
Great Persecution (303–312), 88, 906–907, 919, 921
see also Diocletian, Emperor; Diocletian Era
Great Power. *See* Concept of Our Great Power
Great Synagogue (Tamūh), 717
Greco-Roman influence on Coptic art and architecture, 261–269, *262*, *263*, *264*, *265*
Greco-Roman Museum, Alexandria, 74, 75, 1891
Greece
Coptic collections in, 1710
monasticism in, 1663
Greek accounting practices. *See* Accounts and accounting, history of Coptic
Greek Church of Saint George, 320
Greek correspondence, 968–969
Greek culture. *See* Hellenism
Greek deities, 1865
see also specific names
Greek fathers (patristics), 1920, 1921, 1982
Greek language, **1165–1169**, 1175, 1176, 1178
accounting, 53
acrostics, 1986
in Alexandria, 97
Apostles' Creed in, 178
archives, 526
Bible manuscripts. *See* Bible manuscripts, Greek
and Coptic legal sources, 1438
and Coptic literature, 1450–1451, 1453–1455, 1456
and Coptic music, 1731–1732
Didache manuscript, 898–899
Egyptian papyri, 1889
Egypt in late antiquity, 946

Greek language (*cont.*)
foreign influences on, 1169
Hesychius of Alexandria dictionary, 1227
influence on Demotic and Coptic languages, 1169
inscriptions in, 327–328, 1171, 1290, 1291, 1292
Isidorus of Pelusium's letters, 1309
legends of martyrs in, 1550
Life of Paul of Thebes in, 1926
Liturgy of Saint Mark, 1539–1540
Lives of Pachomius, Saint, 1860–1861, 1862, 1863
medieval Nubian clergy use of, 1813, 1816, 1817
Mysteries of Greek Letters treatise, 1749–1750
Nonnos of Panopolis epics, 1799
papyri, 1166, 1890–1896, 1898, 1900
Physiologos, 1965–1966
post-Arab conquest use in Egypt, 189
Procopius' works in, 2020
Psalis in, 1727
Pseudo-Macarius homilies, 2027, 2028
spread and changes in Egypt, 1165–1167
see also Alphabet, Greek; Toponymy, Coptic
Greek language in Christian Nubia, **1171–1173**
Greek Monastery. *See* Dayr al-Rūmī; Dayr al-Rūmāniyyah
Greeks in Egypt, **1174–1178**
impact on Alexandria, 97–98, 99, 100
Melchites and Copts, 1583
numerals in Coptic system, 1820–1822
philosophy, 1958
see also Hellenism
Greek towns in Egypt, 413, **1179–1181**
Greek transcriptions. *See* *Appendix*
Green, M., 1895
Gregorian calendar. *See* Calendar, Gregorian
Gregorios, Bishop of al-Qays, 709
Gregory, Saint. *See* Liturgy of Saint Gregory
Gregory I (Gregory the Great), Pope (Rome), 71, 921, 1339, 1921
Gregory II, Patriarch, **1182**, 2047
Gregory of Damietta, Metropolitan, 1613–1614
Gregory of Dumyāṭ, Bishop, 926
Gregory the Illuminator, Saint and Patriarch of Armenia, **1183**, 1555
Gregory of Kois, Bishop, 2092–2093
Gregory of Nazianzus, Saint, 114, **1183–1184**, 1308, 1309, 1619, 1921, 2083
anaphora, 71, 124–125, 1066, 1733
on angels, 132
on Athanasius I, 298
on *communicatio idiomatum*, 578
consecration and translation of, 398–399
and Constantinople, First Council of, 594, 2263
and Didymus the Blind, 900
on Easter designation, 1104
encomia, 1196
and Evagrius Ponticus, 1076
on *filioque*, 1115
and Julian the Apostate, 1380
on *Kyrie eleison*, 1420
on meaning of candles, 446
and Origen, 471, 1854, 1855
patristic writings, 1921
Rufinus translations of, 2068
Gregory of Nyssa, Saint, 114, 1183, **1184–1185**, 2083
and the Anomoeans, 142
on celibacy, 476
collected homilies of, 1778
on *communicatio idiomatum*, 578
and eschatology, 973
on eucharistic divine transformation, 1058, 1059
and *filioque* justification, 1115
on immersion, 1286
Isidorus of Pelusium correspondence with, 1308
on orientation toward the East during prayers, 1846
patristic writings, 1921
philosophical writings, 1958
and Theophilus, Patriarch, 2249
see also Canons of Gregory of Nyssa
Gregory al-Sīnāwītī (the Sinaite). *See* Gregory II, Patriarch
Gregory Thaumaturgus, 1577
Gregory Theodorus, 1848
Gregory the Theologian. *See* Gregory of Nazianzus, Saint
Griffith, Francis Llewellyn, 110, 1091, **1185**
and Girgis Mattha, 1141
and Nubian archaeology, medieval, 1804
on Nubian languages and literature, 1815
and Nubian mural art in churches, 1811
Griffith Institute, Oxford University, 895
Groff, William N., **1185**
Grohmann, Adolf, **1185–1186**, 1389
Grossmünster, Zurich, Switzerland, 1082, *1083*, 1110, 2057
Guardian angel, **1186**
Abbaton, 2
Gubbā, Ethiopian saint, 1046
Guidi, Ignazio, **1186–1187**
Guild. *See* Confraternity
Guillaumont, Antoine, 694, 1397, 1398
Guimet, Emile Etienne, **1187**, 1481
Guimet Museum, Lyons, France, 1482

H

Haase, Felix, **1189**
Hawāwīsh, al-, monasteries near, 713
Ḥabachī, Bānūb, 1541
Habakkuk, 1618
Ḥabashī, Sābā, 1993
Ḥabīb Jirjis, 933, **1189**, 1464, 2354
Hābū, pharaonic temple of, 196
Ḥaddād, Nicola, 1996
Hades, **1189–1190**, 1900
and Holy Saturday, 1247
see also Judgment, Last
Hadrā of Aswan, Saint, 130, 745, **1190**, 2083
see also Dayr Anbā Hadrā
Hadrā of Benhadab, Saint, **1190–1191**, 1922, 2083

Hadrian, Emperor
  Antinoopolis founding by, 142, 1170, 1181
  martyrdom of daughter, 1552
  patriarch under, 1913, 1914
  temples, 863
  visit to Egypt, 2062, 2065, 2066
Hadrian I, Pope (Rome), 1112
Haffāz, 696
Ḥafiẓ, al-, Caliph, 1097–1098, 1099, 1128–1129
Ḥafn, 1528
Ḥafṣ ibn al-Walīd al-Ḥaḍramī, Caliph, 1410
Hage (village), 771
Hagiographa, in Jewish canon, 2109
Hagiography, Coptic, **1191–1197**, 1921
  on anachoresis, 120
  on Cycle of Diocletian martyrs, 153
  National Library (Paris) manuscripts, 1777–1782
  Synaxarion as primary source of, 2174
  see also Cycle
Haile Selassie I, Emperor of Ethiopia, 235, 1041, 1042, **1197–1199**, 1628, 1909, 2363
  and conference of Oriental Orthodox churches, 1845–1846
  and Cyril II, Patriarch, 6744
Hail Mary, **1199**
Ḥajar Danfīq, Dayr al-Ṣalīb, 859
Ḥājir Idfū, **1200**, **1200**
  see also Dayr al-Malāk Mīkhā'īl (Idfū)
Ḥākim Bi-Amr-Illāh Abū ʿAlī Manṣūr, al-, 94, 843, 854, 1104, **1200–1203**, 1517, 1524, 1525, 1776
  and Abū al-ʿAlā' Fahd ibn Ibrahim, 17–18
  and Abū al-Fadl ʿĪsā ibn Nastūrus, 18–19
  and Church of al-Muʿallaqah (Old Cairo), 558
  and Epiphany tanks, 968
  Isḥāq ibn Ibrāhīm ibn Nasṭās and, 1306
  and Pbow basilica destruction, 1927, 1929
  persecutions under, 1097, 1201, 2313–2314
  Zacharias, Patriarch, 2367
Ḥakīm, Tawfīq al-, 1995
Halkin, F., 1445
Hall, Henry Reginald Holland, 780, **1203**, 1585
Hall, Stuart G., 1585
Hallelujah. *See* Alleluia
Halo. *See* Nimbus
Hamai of Kahyor, Saint (martyr), **1203–1204**, 1555
Ḥamal. *See* Eucharistic bread
Hamburg Papyrus, 380–381, **1204–1205**, 1893
Ḥamīdāt, Al-, **1205**
Ḥammām (Bedouin), 1538
Ḥammām (village), 806
Ḥamzah, ʿAbd al-Qādir, 1990
Handbags, 645
Hand cymbals. *See* Cymbals
Hands, laying-on of. *See* Laying-on of hands
Hands, washing of, 8–9, 1469
Ḥannā, Murqus, 1466
Hanna Herkel. *See* Haraglī, Jean
Ḥannā Ṣalīb Saʿd, **1206**, 1591
Haraglī, Jean, **1206**
Hardy, Edward R., **1206**
Ḥārit al-Rūm (Old Cairo), **1206–1207**, 1647, 2046
  church restoration, 2315
  convents, 2325
  icons of Asṭāsī al-Rūmī at, 293–294
  patriarchal residence, 1348, 1913, 2000
Ḥārit Zuwaylah (Old Cairo), 23, **1207–1209**, 1647, 1963
  and al-ʿAdhrā' church, 322–323
  church blessing, 404
  church closures and burial prohibitions, 1128
  church of Mercurius of Caesarea, 1594
  convents, 2325
  and flight into Egypt, 1118
  icons of Asṭāsī al-Rūmī at, 294
  patriarchal seat and residence, 1133, 1344, 1348, 1913
Harmīnā, Saint, 808, **1209**, 1255, 2084
Harmonics (Claudius Ptolemy), 1731
Harnack, Adolf von, 1452, 1921
Haroeris (pagan deity), 1418
Harp, 1734, 1738, 1740
Harp of the Believing Faith. *See* Jacob of Sarūj
Ḥarrāniyyah, tapestry workshops at, 2051
Harūn, Apa, monastery of, 1652
Harwāj (martyr), 1555
Ḥasaballāh, Bishop of Shanshā, **1209–1210**
Ḥasab-Allāh al-Bayādī, Muʿallim, 722
Ḥasan (son of al-Ḥāfiz), 1129
Ḥasan ʿAbd al-Rāziq Pasha, 1987
Ḥasan al-ʿAṭṭār, Shaykh, 1654, 1994
Hasina. *See* Menas and Hasina (martyrs)
Hassān ibn Thābit, 1528
Hathor (pagan deity), 816, 817, 853, 1740, 1874
  Isis fusion with, 1752
  temple at Dandarah, 690, *691*
Hatshepsut (pagan deity), 1874
  temple excavations, 227
  temple of, 779, 780, 781, 786
Hātūr (third month of Coptic calendar), 438, 440, 2176–2177
Hauser, Walter, **1210**
  Ḥawāshī al-Ṣafawiyyah (al-Ṣafī ibn al-ʿAssāl), 2076
Hawtharah, Caliph, 1411
Hawwārah, **1210–1211**, *1210*
Hawwāriyyah, 718, **1211–1212**, *1211*
  basilica of, 213
Hay, R., 780
Haykal. *See* Altar; Sanctuary
Haykal, Muḥammad Ḥusayn, 1995
Haykal al-taqdimah. *See* Prothesis
Headdress, Coptic women, 641–642
Healings in Coptic literature, **1212–1214**
  by laying-on of hands, 1433
  see also Unction of the sick, Holy Sacrament of the
Heaven, **1214**
  see also Paradise
Heavenly Hymn, 1565
Hebbelynck, Adolphe, **1215**, 1749, 1895
Hebrews. *See* Jews and Judaism; Old Testament
Hebrews in the Furnace, in Coptic art, 388–390
Hefele, Karl Joseph, **1215**
Hegel, George, 1149
Hegumenos, **1215–1216**
  and appointment of Theophilos I, Archbishop, 2247

Hegumenos (*cont.*)
archimandrite differentiation, 192, 193
in ecclesiastical hierarchy, 1229, 2015
Jirjis Makramallāh al-Bahnasāwī, 1335
and John V, Patriarch, 1340
al-Makīn Jirjis, 1513
Makramallāh, 1515
provost and, 2024
of Scetis, 2103
Yacobos II, Archbishop, 2349
Yūsāb II, Patriarch, 2363
see also Proestos
Hegumenos, ordination of a, **1216**
Heinkel, Dettlof, 720
Helena, Saint and Empress (mother of Constantine), 660, 1243, 1377, 1378, 1971, 1972
Helias. *See* Elias
Helias, Bishop (martyr), 1555
Heliogabalus, Emperor, patriarch under, 1914
Hell
in Coptic theology, 974
see also Hades
Hellenism
Alexander Romance, 2059
Alexandria as center of, 91, 95–96, 100, 2065
and Arianism, 231
decline in Egypt, 946
and development of Alexandrian theology, 103–104, 1866
Judaism and, 1957
see also Greek headings
Helwan. *See* Ḥilwān
Henein Makarious. *See* Makāryus Ḥunayn
Hengstenberg, Wilhelm, **1217**
Henoch, 1867
Henoticon (Instrument of Unity), **1217–1218**, 2370
Acacian Schism and, 43, 44, 45, 47, 55, 1671, 1672
Acephaloi opposition to, 55
Armenian church acceptance, 234
and Eutyches anathematization, 1075
John I and, 1337
Mark II and, 1534
Peter III Mongus and, 1948
Philoxenus of Mabbug and, 1962
Severus of Antioch on, 2124
and Timothy Salofaciolus, 2269
Henry I of Germany, 1572
Henry II of Germany, 1113
Henschenius, G., 56
Hephaestus (pagan deity), 1768
Heraclas, Saint and Patriarch, **1219**, 2084
and Catechetical School of Alexandria, 472
and conversion of Dionysius the Great, 909
dates of patriarchy, 1914
as Demetrius I successor, 893
and Origen, 1847
Heracleas and Philemon (martyrs), 1555
Heracleon, 356–357, 1151, **1219–1220**
Heracleopolis Magna. *See* Ahnās
Heracleopolis Parva, 1648
Heracles, 73
Heraclides, Saint (martyr), **1220–1221**, 1555
Heraclius (general), 1938, 1940
Heraclius, Emperor
acceptance of Monenergist creed, 1676
and Arab conquest of Egypt, 184
Chalcedon dogma, 837
ecthesis formula, 682, 931, 1666, 1678
fast of, 1093–1094, 1095
and liberation of the cross, 660, 1243
patriarch under, 1915
Herai, Saint, **1221**
see also Ter and Erai, Saints
Herais (martyr), 892
Heraiscus, 283, **1221–1222**, 1868
Herakleides of Tamiathis/Dumyāṭ, Bishop, 925
Herakleopolis. *See* Ahnās
Hercules
depicted in Coptic art, 1761, *1762*
see also Amazons
Herculia (Egyptian province), 905
Heresiologists, 1921
Heresy, **1222**
Agnoetae, 70–71
anointing of heretics, 138–139
Apollinarianism, 173–174
Būkhīshā sect on passion of Jesus, 94–95
Damian countermeasures, 688, 689
Didascalia on, 899
Dionysius the Great on, 911
docetism, 917
in Dumyāṭ, 925
Ethiopian, 984–987, 1012–1013, 1052–1053
Eutychianism, 1075
evaluation of Arius' beliefs, 232
on immersion and baptism, 1286
on Incarnation, 1288
Jerome, Saint, efforts against, 1323
Leo I the Great and, 1440–1442
Manichaeism, 1519–1522
Maximus, patriarch, and, 1585
Monarchianism, 1637–1638
Pelagianism, 1929–1930
in Pentapolis, 1934
Sabellianism, 911, 2072
Subordinationism, 1484
see also Arianism; Ethiopian heresies and theological controversies
Hermas, **1223**
and Acts of Peter and Twelve Apostles, 62–63
as apostolic father, 180
on guardian angels, 1186
on immersion and baptism, 1186
patristic writings, 1920
Hermeneutics, canonical, 2110
Hermes Trismegistus–Thoth, 284, 917, 1150, **1223–1224**, 1617, 1867, 1868
Hermetic texts. *See Asclepius 21–29*; *Discourse on the Eighth and Ninth*; *The Prayer of Thanksgiving*
Hermitage, **1224–1225**
Eastern desert, 1649–1650
Gharbiyyah Province, 1652
of Isnā, 1660
Jabal Tafnīs, 1316–1317
Kellia grouping, 1398–1400
Kom Namrūd, 1418
Hermitage Museum. *See* State Hermitage Museum, Leningrad
Hermitages, Theban, **1225**, 1656
Hermit dress. *See* Costume of the religious

Hermits
Abraham and George of Scetis, Saints, 12–13
Abraham of Minūf, Saint, 13
Agathon, Saint, 3
Ammonius of Tūnah, 114
anachoresis, 118–120
and anchorite monasticism, 129–130, 1662
al-ʿAraj tombs, 189–190
Arsenius of Scetis and Ṭurah, 240–241
at burning bush site, 1682
cells and chambers, 1403
Daniel, 691–692
and Dayr Abū Daraj, 1649, 697
and Dayr Abū Fānah, 698
and Dayr Abū Ḥinnis, 701, 703
and Dayr Anbā Anṭūniyūs, 728, 1649
and Dayr Anbā Būlā, 1649
and Dayr Anbā Maqār, 749, 754
and Dayr al-Bakhīt, 786
and Dayr Epiphanius, 800, 801, 802
and Dayr al-Jabrāwī, 811
and Dayr Mār Mīnā (Gharbiyyah), 833
and Dayr al-Malāk Mīkhā'īl (Jirjā), 826
and Dayr Qubbat al-Hawā, 850
and Dayr Rīfah, 855–856
and Dayr al-Sanad, as center for, 860
and Dayr al-Sāqiyah as center for, 861
and Dayr Yuḥannis, 883
Didymus the Blind, 900
and early British Christian converts, 417–418
income-producing work, 802
Isaiah of Scetis, 1305–1306
Isḥāq, 772
and Jabal al-Silsilah region, 1656–1657
in Jabal Tafnīs region, 314, 1316–1317
John Sabas, 1369
and Kharjah (great oasis), 1658
laura, 1428
lodgings, 477–478; *see also* Caves; Cell; Hermitage; Laura
Macarius the Egyptian, 1491
at Meir, 1582–1583
monks as, 1667
Moses, 691–692
Murqus al-Antūnī, 1699
Nubian, 1818
Palaemon, Saint, 1876
Palamon, 1876
Paphnutius, Saint, 1882–1883
Patāsius, 1908
Paul of Tamma, Saint, 1923–1925
Paul of Thebes, 1925–1926
Phis, 1963
in Qalamūn, 758
at quarries of Shaykh Ḥasan, 1654
Qurnat Marʿī, 2040–2041
Rufinus history of Coptic, 2068
seven ascetics of Tūnah, 2122
in Suhāj area, 761–762
Timotheus, Saint, 2262–2263
women as, 1663
see also Anchorite; Caves; Cell; Reclusion
Hermolaus, 1882
Hermonthis. *See* Armant
Hermopolis Magna. *See* Ashmūnayn, al-
Hermopolis Mikra (the Lower). *See* Damanhūr
Hermopolis Parva. *See* Damanhūr
Herod, King, 533, 1117, 1395
Herodotus, 1165, 1166, 1174, 1686
Herpaese and Julianus, Saints, **1225–1226**
Hesychia, 1662
Hesychian Bible, **1226**
Hesychius (monk of Saint Sabas), 2046
Hesychius, Bishop, **1226**
and Egyptian Bible text, 382, 1226
Hesychius of Alexandria, **1226–1227**
Heuser, Gustav, **1227**, 2022
Hexameron (Pseudo-Epiphanius of Cyprus), collection of, 1782
Hexapla and Tetrapla (Origen), **1227–1228**, 1848, 1852, 1853
Hibat-Allāh ʿAbd-Allāh ibn Saʿīd al-Dawlah al-Qibṭī, **1228**
Hibat-Allāh ibn ʿAssal, Al-. *See* Awlād al-ʿAssāl
Hickmann, Hans, 1730, 1731, 1732, 1739, 1740, 1741–1742, 1743
Hides and skins
preservation of, 280
see also Leatherwork, Coptic
Hieracas of Leontopolis, **1228–1229**
and authorship of *Testimony of Truth*, 2210
possible Coptic texts of, 1451
Hierakion, camp of. *See* Dayr al-Jabrāwī
Hierarchy, church, **1229–1230**, 2015–2016
see also specific titles
Hieroglyphs
Coptic language used to decipher, 614
see also Rosetta Stone
High Council. *See* Consultative Council
Higher Institute for Arabic and Islamic Studies, 1993
Higher Institute of Coptic Studies (Cairo), 563, 933, **1230**, 1629–1630, 2091
and the Clerical College, 564
music department, 1737
and Yassa ʿAbd al-Masīḥ, 2353
Hijāb. *See* Iconostasis
Hijābs (amulets), Nubian, 1814
Ḥijāzah
Dayr Abū al-Sayfayn (Qūṣ) near, 711, 1657
pilgrimages to, 1972
Hilaria (martyr), 1552, 1555
Hilaria, Saint, 749, **1230–1231**, 2084
Hilarion (eunuch). *See* Hilaria, Saint
Hilarion, Saint (fourth-century monk), **1232**, 1664, 2084
Hilarius, Pope, 1441
Hilary, Bishop of Arles, 1440, 1921
Ḥilwān, 708, **1232–1235**, *1233*, *1234*, 1303
Ḥinnis, Abū. *See* Dayr Abū Ḥinnis
Hintze, F., 1893
Hippolytus (Roman presbyter), **1235–1236**, 1637
on baptism, 182
on Nativity, 1102
and Origen, 470–471
patristic writings, 1921
see also Apostolic Tradition; *Canons of Hippolytus*
Hippolytus (Sethian), 1902
Hisāb-dobia. *See* Accounts and accounting; Bookkeeping
Ḥisbah, **1236–1237**
Ḥishāh, Caliph, 87

Ḥiṣn, 1237
Historia Augusta, 1961
Historia ecclesiastica (Eusebius), 8, 84, 911, 1070–1071, 1323, 1455, 1530, 1920
Sozomen continuation of, 2145
Theodoret continuation of, 2236
see also Eusebius of Caesarea
Historia ecclesiastica (Rufinus translation), 2068
Historia lausiaca (Palladius), 3, 88, 894, 1238, 1876, 1877, 1878
on Antinoopolis, 144
on Dayr Abū Ḥinnis, 701
on monasteries for women, 1663
on Paul the Simple, 1923
Historia monachorum in Aegypto, 330, 894, **1237–1238**
on Ammonas, Saint, 113
on Ammonius, 114
on anchorites at Achoris, 2261
and Bāwīṭ and, 362
on Dayr Abū Ḥinnis, 701
hegumenos title in, 1215
and Isaac, Disciple of Apollo, 1304
on John of Lycopolis, 809, 1238, 1363, 1364
on Macarius Alexandrinus, 1490
on Paphnutius, 1884
on Paul the Simple, 1923
on proliferation of monks, 1662
Rufinus and, 2069
Historians
Abrīm al-Qibṭī, Anbā, 14
Abū al-Fakhr al-Masīḥī, 19
Abū al-Makārim, 23
Abū Shākir ibn al-Rāhib, 33
Chronicon orientale, 548
Eusebius of Caesarea, 1070–1071
History of the Patriarchs of Alexandria, 1238–1241
Ibn al-Biṭrīq, Saʿīd, 1265–1266
Isidhūrus, 1307
Josephus Flavius, 1375–1376
al-Makīn, ibn al-ʿAmīd, 1513
Manassā Yūḥannā, 1518
al-Maqrīzī, Taqīy al-Dīn, 1525
Mawhūb ibn Manṣūr ibn Mufarrij al-Iskandarānī, 1573–1574
Mīkhāʾīl Shārūbīm, 1630, 1631
Neale, John Mason, 1784–1785
Neander, Johann August Wilhelm, 1784–1785
Olympiodorus of Thebes, 1840
Palladius, 1876–1877
papyrology, 1888–1889
Philostorgius, 1958–1959
Procopius, 2019–2020
Puech, Henri-Charles, 2032–2033
Rémondon, Roger, 2057
Rufinus, 2068–2069
Socrates, 2142
Sozomen, 2145
al-Ṣuqāʿi Faḍl Allāh ibn Fakhr, 2160
Theodoret, 2236
theological literature, 1920–1921
Yaʿqūb Nakhlah Rufaylah, 2353
Yūsuf Abū Daqn, 2364–2365
Historiography. *See* Art, historiography of Coptic
History of Churches and Monasteries. See Abū al-Makārim
History of the Church (Sozomen), 666, 1455, 2145
History of the Coptic Nation, 1466
History of the Coptic Patriarchs. See History of the Patriarchs of Alexandria
History of the Holy Eastern Church (Neale), 1784
History of Joseph the Carpenter, 1136, 1372–1373
Coptic version, 1372–1373
The History of the Copts under the Domination of the Turk and Abyssinian Emperors (Yūsuf Abū Daqn), 2364
History of the Patriarchs of Alexandria, **1238–1241**, 2101
on Abraham, Saint and Patriarch, 10, 11
on Anastasius, 125, 126
on Andronicus, 131
on Asyūṭ, 296–297
on Athanasius II, 302
on Athanasius III, 303
authorship, 1239–1241, 1460, 1461, 1573–1574
and Bagham Ibn Baqūrah al-Ṣawwāf, 329
and Barbīsh, 349
and Bashmūr, 349
and Benjamin II, 377–378
on bishops from al-Faramā, 1089
on Bucalis, 134
and Būrah, 425
and Būsh, 427
on censer and incense use, 1471
and churches at Babylon, 323
on the Crusades, 664–665
on Damallū, 686
Damian discourse on the Logos in, 689
Damrū mention, 689, 690
on Dān'ēl, Ethiopian prelate, 1002
Daqahlah mention, 693
on Dayr Anbā Shinūdah, 762, 764
on Dayr Apa Anūb, 770
on Dayr al-ʿAsal, 782
on Dayr al-Fakhūrī, 802
on Dayr Mart Maryam, 835
on Dayr al-Muḥarraq, 840
on Dayr Nahyā, 843
on Dayr al-Shamʿ, 863
on Demetrius I, 892
and Dionysius the Great, 909, 911
on Dioscorus I, 915
on Enaton monasteries, 956
on Epimachus of Pelusium, Saint, 965–966
on Fiqṭor, Ethiopian prelate, 1002–1003
on flight into Egypt, 842
on Giyorgis I, Ethiopian prelate, 1006
on Giyorgis II, Ethiopian prelate, 1008–1009
on Ḥilwān, 1232
on icons, 1278
on Idkū, 1280
on Isaac the Deacon, 1304
on John I, 1337
on John III, 808
on John IV, 1338
on John V, 1340
on John IX, 1344
on John X, 1344
on John XI, 1344
on John XII, 1346
on John XIV, 1347
on John XVII, 1349
on John XVIII, 1350
on John of Nikiou, Bishop, 1366–1367
on Julian the Apostate, 1382
on the Kellia, 1397–1398
on Macarius II, 1487, 1488
on Marwān II, 695–696

on Mikā'ēl I, Ethiopian prelate, 1006–1007
on Mikā'ēl II, Ethiopian prelate, 1007–1008
on miracles, 707
on monasteries, 698
in National Library (Paris), 1781
on Origen, 1851
on patrology, 1921
on persecutions under Mamluks, 1343
on Peter VII, 1950
and Qurrah, 358–359
on relics of John the Baptist, 1355
on Sāwiros, Ethiopian prelate, 1005–1006
on Scetis monasteries, 782
on Tall Atrīb, 2200
on Tamnūh, 2201
and Ṭanbidā, 2201
on Theodorus, Patriarch, 2237
on Theophanes, Patriarch, 2247
on Yoḥannes I, Ethiopian prelate, 1001
and Yuḥannā, 2356

History of the Patriarchs of the Egyptian Church. *See History of the Patriarchs of Alexandria*
Hiw, **1242–1243**
Dayr Mār Mīnā, 833–834
and toponymy, Coptic, 2272
Ḥizb al-Aḥrār al-Dustūriyyīn. *See* Liberal Constitutional Party
Ḥizb al-Dīmūqrāṭī al-Miṣrī, al. *See* Egyptian Democratic Party
Ḥizb al-Hay'ah al-Sa'Diyyah. *See* Sa'dist Party
Ḥizb al-Iṣlāḥ 'Alā al-Mabādi' al-Dustrūriyyah. *See* Reform Party on Constitutional Principles
Ḥizb al-Ittiḥād. *See* Union Party
Ḥizb al-Miṣrī, al-. *See* Egyptian Party
Ḥizb al-Sha'b. *See* People's Party
Ḥizb al-Ummah. *See* Nation's party
Ḥizb al-Waṭanī. *See* Nationalist Party
Hiziqyāl. *See* Ezekiel (Hiziqyāl) (monk)
The Holy Book of the Great Invisible Spirit. *See Gospel of the Egyptians*
The Holy City, on Dayr al-Sulṭān, 872
Holy Communion. *See* Communion; Eucharist
Holy Cross Day, **1243–1244**
Holy Ghost. *See* Holy Spirit
Holy Horseman, as Christian subject in Coptic art, 538
Holy Land
custody of, 1122
pilgrims' assistance agency, 2049
Saladin's reconquest of, 1536
see also Crusades, Copts and the: Jerusalem, Coptic See of; Mount Sinai Monastery of Saint Catherine; Palestine
Holy Land, Coptic churches in the, **1244–1247**
see also Jerusalem, Coptic See of
Holy Light. *See* Apparition of the Holy Light
Holy Matrimony. *See* Marriage
Holy Mother. *See Theotokos*; Virgin Mary; Virgin Mary, Apparition of the
Holy Myron. *See* Chrism
Holy Oil. *See* Chrism
Holy Roman Emperors, 1572
Holy Saturday, **1247–1249**
Holy Sepulcher
and Coptic Good Friday celebration, 1153
reopened for pilgrimages (1426), 1130
Holy Spirit, 1437, 1446, 2028
Arianism on, 230
confirmation to receive, 585–586
descent on the disciples, 1105–1106, 1529
epiclesis, 964, 1566–1567
filioque controversy, 1112–1116
gnosticism on, 2256
and laying-on of hands, 1432, 1433
theological homilies on, 1183, 1184
Holy Spirit, Coptic doctrine of the, **1249–1250**
Holy Synod. *See* Synod, Holy
Holy Thursday. *See* Maundy Thursday
Holy Trinity. *See* Trinitarianism; Trinity
Holy Week, 1095, 1102, 1103–1104, **1251–1252**, 1904
fasting, 1152
footwashing, 1107–1108, 1426–1427
and genuflection, 1139
Kiss of Peace prohibition during, 1416
lectern placement, 1435
lectionary for, 1437
Lord's Prayer during, 1481
music for, 1715, 1721
patriarchal residence, 1912
use of ambo during, 111
see also Easter; Good Friday; Holy Saturday; Maundy Thursday; Palm Sunday; Resurrection
Homer, 1889
Homiletic cycles, 666–668
Homilies
of Amphilochius of Iconium, 115–116
of Andrew of Crete, 130–131
of Demetrius of Antioch, 894
on flight into Egypt, 669–670
Gnostic Christian, 898
of Gregory of Nazianzus, 1183, 1184
Interpretation of Knowledge, 1301
of Jacob of Sarūj, 1319, 1781, 1738
of John Chrysostom, 352, 1135, 1778, 1779, 2053, 2054
manuscripts in National Library, Paris, 1778
of Origen, 1847, 1852–1853
of Peter I, 1945–1946
of Proclus, 1356, 1454, 2017–2018
Pseudo-Cyril of Alexandria, 681, 2025–2026
Pseudo-Macarius, 2027–2028
al-Ṣafī ibn al-'Assāl works on, 276
on Saint Luke's Gospel (Origen), 1847
of Severian of Jabalah, 2122–2123
of Theophilus, Patriarch, 2252
see also Cycle; Encomia; Literature, Coptic; Manuscripts
Homoeans, **1252–1253**, 2119
Homoiousion, 84, 127, 141, **1253**, 1677, 2096

Homoiousion (*cont.*)
adopted by semi-Arians, 2119
Homoousion, 84, 127, 141, 1070, **1253–1254**, 1575, 1677
Athanasius I and, 298
and Constantine I and, 590
Marcellus support, 1526
Nicaea, Council of, on, 590, 1791
in Nicene Creed, 1792, 1793
Origen on, 1849
Honorius, Emperor, 789–790, 891
Honorius I, Pope (Rome), 1666, 1667, 1679
Hopfner, T., 1891
Hop of Ṭūkh, Apa and Saint, **1254**, 2084
Hor, **1254**
Hor, Apa (martyr), 722, 1553, 1555, 1974, 1975
Hor, Apa and Saint, **1255**, 2084
Hor of Abraḥat, Saint, 771, **1255**, 1963, 2084
Horapollon, **1255–1256**
and Asclepiades, 283
and Chairemon of Alexandria, 512
and Hellenization, 1168
Heraiscus relationship, 1221–1222
Horizontal loom, 2215
Hormisdas, Pope (Rome), and Acacian schism, 45, 46, 47, 1383
Horner, George W., **1257**
Horologion. *See* Canonical hours, Book of
Horseman
depicted in Coptic embroidery, *2223*
depicted on ornamental comb, *2337*
Parthian, depiction in Coptic art, 538, 1259
terra-cotta, *503*
woodwork, *2340*
Horseshoe arch, 211
Horsiesios, Saint, 32, **1257**, 1448, 1664, 1861, 1862, 1864, 2084
Coptic texts of, 1451–1452
as desert father, 894
and Pachomius, 1257, 2240
papyrus collection of letters, 1894
and Pbow, 1927
and Petronius, 1952, 2240
and Pisentius of Hermonthis, 1978
and Theodorus of Alexandria as interpreter, 2238
and Theodorus of Tabennēsē, 2240
Horus (pagan deity), 134, 243, 244, 281, 1502, 1503, 1505, 1590, 1752
depicted in Coptic art, 1259, 1761–1762
and iconography of George, Saint, 248–249
iconography of, 248–249, *249*
linked with Damanhūr (town), 686
temples built to, 262
Hosanna, **1258**
Hosius, Bishop of Cordova, 83, 84
Hōs (song of praise), 63, 1725–1726, *1725*, 1727, 1729, 1732, 2255, 2321
Hulwān, 1653
Humbert of Silva Candida, 1113
Ḥunayn, Ibrāhīm, 1466
Ḥunayn ibn Isḥāq, 1922
Hungary, Coptic collections, 1710
Hunting in Coptic art, **1258–1259**
Huntington, Robert, 791, **1260**, 1977
Ḥusayn, Ṭahā, 1995, 1996
Ḥusein Kamil, Sultan, 1694
Hussein, King of Jordan, 873, 874
Hydraulis (water organ), 1740
Hymn of Golgotha, 1152
"The Hymn of the Angels" (Great Doxology), 923
Hymns
Arian, 1733
canonical hours, 1724
cantors and, 137–138
for consecration of patriarchs, 1909, 1910
Difnār, 1728
doxologies, 923, 1727–1728
influences on Coptic, 1731–1732
instruments accompanying, 1739
lōbsh, 1479
Mass of the Faithful, 1565–1566
Psalis, 1726, 1727, *1728*
Psalmodia, 448, 1725, 2024
Theotokion, 1724, 1726, 1727, 2254–2255
Trisagion, 2278
the Twelve Virtues, 2310
unpublished manuscripts, 1986
Wāham, 2323
Hymns, authors of. *See* Music, Coptic
Hymn of the Savior (Clement of Alexandria), 1732
Hypatia (philosopher), 100, 1308, 1870, 2192
Hypostasis, 1106, **1260**, 1575
and hypostatic union, 1262
and Incarnation, 1287
Nicene Creed definition of, 300
Origen on, 1848
Hypostasis of the Archons, **1261**
and *On the Origin of the World*, 1842–1844
Hypostatic union, **1262**
Hypotyposeis (Theognostus), 911
Hypsiphrone, **1262**
Hyvernat, Henri Eugène Xavier Louis, **1263**, 1448

I

IAC. *See* International Association for Coptic Studies
Iamblichus, **1265**
Iaō Sabaōth Adōnai Eloi, 1503
Ibas (Antiochene theologians), 1672
Ibas of Edessa, 515
Ibn Abī Uṣaybiʻah, 1525
Ibn Abū al-Faḍā'il ibn Farūj, 710
Ibn al-ʻAmīd. *See* Makīn, ibn al ʻAmīd al-
Ibn al-ʻAssāl. *See* Ṣafī ibn al-ʻAssāl, al-
Ibn al-Batrīq, ʻIsa. *See* Ibn al-Biṭrīq, ʻĪsā
Ibn al-Batrīq, Saʻīd. *See* Ibn al-Biṭrīq, Saʻīd
Ibn al-Bishr al-Kātib. *See* Mufaḍḍal ibn Mājid ibn al-Bishr, al-
Ibn al-Biṭrīq, ʻĪsā, **1265**, 1266
Ibn al-Biṭrīq, Saʻīd (Eutychius), **1265–1266**, 1460
and Book of Epact, 410
on Church of Saint Michael, 1617
and Constantinople, Second Council of, 595
on Nubian evangelization, 1801–1802
on patriarchal election, 1911
on patriarchal seat, 1912

Sāwīrus ibn al-Muqaffa' and, 2101
Ibn al-Dahīrī, Bishop of Damietta, **1266**
Ibn al-Ḥabḥāb, Viceroy, 87
Ibn al-Ḥāmid, 711
Ibn Ḥawqal, **1266**, 1271
on 'Alwā, 110
and Babīj, 317
and Bashmūr, 349
and Beja tribes, 373
on medieval Nubia, 1804
Ibn al-'Ibrī. *See* Bar Hebraeus
Ibn Kabar, 20, 21, **1267–1268**, 1272, 1273
on Agathon of Ḥomṣ, 67–68
and Barlām and Yuwāṣaf, 346
and Butrus Sāwīrus al-Jamīl, 431
on canon law, 450
on *Canons of Epiphanius*, 456–457
on *Canons of Hippolytus*, 458
on *Canons of Saint John Chrysostom*, 460
on the Church of al-Mu'allaqah (Old Cairo), 558
on Dayr Mār Jirjis, 831
on Dayr Shahrān, 862
on feasts of the Virgin Mary, 2256
on Gregory of Nyssa, 457
on ingredients of holy chrism, 521–522
and Jirjis ibn al-Qass Abī al-Mufaḍḍal, 1332
and mysticism, 908–909
on Pseudo-Macarius homilies, 2028
and *tafsīr*, 2198
works of, 1463–1464
on Yūḥannā ibn Sāwīrus, 2357
and Yūsāb, Bishop (thirteenth century), 2359
See also Misbāh al-Zulmah (Ibn Kabar)
Ibn Kātib Qayṣar, 1266, **1268**
commentary on Revelation in Paris, 1777
Ibn Khaldūn, on Makouria, 1514–1515
Ibn Laqlaq. *See* Cyril III ibn Laqlaq
Ibn Mammātī, works by, 1461–1461
Ibn Mammātī dynasty, **1268–1269**
Ibn Nafrā, Bishop, consecrated at Dayr al-Sham', 863
Ibn Nūḥ. *See* 'Abd al-Masīḥ, known as Ibn Nūḥ
Ibn Qannā (monk), 1097
Ibn Qayyim al-Jawziyyah, **1269–1270**
Ibn al-Rāhib, 1513
Ibn Rajā', 1959–1960
Ibn Sabbā', collected encyclopedias of, 1779
Ibn al-Ṣā'igh ("son of the goldsmith"), **1270–1271**
Ibn Salīm al-Aswānī, 344, 1266, **1271–1272**
on 'Alwā, 110
and Baṭn al-Ḥajar, 361–362
and Beja tribes, 373
on Greek language use by Nubian clergy, 1813
and Jabal 'Adda, 1315
on Makouria, 921–922, 1514
on medieval Nubia, 1804
on Menarti, 1587–1588
on Nobatia, 1798
on Nubian languages and literature, 1815
on Soba, 2141
Ibn Sibā', Yuḥannā ibn Abī Zakariyyā, 1272, 1464
Ibn Taymiyyah, Taqī al-Dīn Aḥmad, 1269
Ibn Ṭūlūn, Aḥmad, Caliph, 1412–1413, 2280–2281
Ibn Tūlūn, Khumārawayh, 1413
Ibrāhīm (son of Prophet Muḥammad), 1528
Ibrāhīm, Jindī, 1465, 2010
Ibrāhīm Bey, 1274, 1411, 1688
Ibrāḥīm ibn 'Awn, the Nestorian, 1273, 1779
Ibrāhīm ibn 'Īsā, 1273
Ibrāhīm ibn Sim'ān, 1515
Ibrāhīm ibn Sulaymān al-Najjār al-Mīrī, 1273
Ibrāhīm al-Jawharī, **1274**, 1313, 1688
building start, 1538–1539
and Dayr Anbā Anṭūniyūs renovation, 720
and Dayr Anbā Maqār reconstruction, 753, 1121
and Ḥārit Zuwaylah chapel, 1208
and Jirjis al-Jawharī, 1332
and the Mamluks, 1857
Ibrāhīm al-Kurdī, 1536
Ibrāhīm al-Nāsikh (icon painter), *1278*, 1279
Ibrāhīm Pasha, 1141, 1248, 1950
Ibrāhīm al-Suryānī (alias Abrām), 1134
Ibrāhīm al-Tūkhī. *See* John XVI
Ibrīm. *See* Qaṣr Ibrīm
Ibscher, Hugo, **1274–1275**
Ibṭū, **1275**
Ibyār, 833
Iconoclasm, **1275–1276**, 1277
Asṭāsī al-Rūmī icon production during controversy, 293
Cyril IV, Patriarch, and, 1278
role of Ethiopia, 984–985
Iconography
of Asṭāsī al-Rūmī (Eustathius the Greek), 293–294
and dating of artifacts, 694
figurines, 500–502
and hunting theme in Coptic art, 1259
of Mark, Apostolic Saint, 1532
metalwork, 1606–1607
of resist-dyed textiles, 2227–2230, *2228–2230*
under Mark III patriarchy, 1536
of woven textiles, 2221–2227, *2222–2227*
see also Art and architecture, Coptic; Biblical subjects in Coptic art; Christian subjects in Coptic art; Christ, Triumph of; Icons; Mythological subjects in Coptic art; Symbols in Coptic art
Iconography, Greco-Roman. *See* Art survivals from ancient Egypt
Iconostasis, 211–212
at Bāwīṭ, 364–366
and candelabrum, 1469
of Church of Saints Sergius and Wachas (Alexandria), 94
Icons, Coptic, **1276–1279**, *1277–1279*
at Bāwīṭ, 368–371
at Dayr Anbā Būlā, 743–744
and Good Friday service, 1152
Iconoclastic controversy, 1275–1276
of Menas, Saint, 1588–1589
of Mercurius of Caesarea, Saint, 1593–1594
of Virgin Mary, *2309*
see also Figurines
Ideler, Julius Ludwig, **1280**

Idfā, 762, **1280**
Idfū
monasteries near, 825, 1657
monastery libraries, 1449
Panine and Paneu martyrdom near, 1880
pharaonic-style temples at, 196, 1865
tombstone material, 1295
Idiolect. *See Appendix*
Idiophones, 1739–1740, *1739*, *1740*
Idkū, **1280–1281**
Ignatius of Antioch, Saint and Bishop, **1281–1282**, 1555, 1980
as apostolic father, 180
on *Communicatio idiomatum*, 578
on consubstantiation, 597
on the Eucharist, 1057
on feasts, 1101
on Incarnation, 1287
on the offertory, 1824
and origin of antiphonal chanting, 148
patristic writings, 1920
and Polycarp, 1997
on priesthood, 2016
Ignatius IX, Patriarch of the Syrians, 1131
Ihnasiyyah al-Madinah. *See* Ahnās
Ikhnāway al-Zallāqah, 1652
Ikhshids. *See* Tulunids and Ikhshids, Copts under the
Iliad (Homer), 1889
Illness. *See* Communion of the sick; Healings in Coptic literature; Medicine; Unction of the sick
Illumination, Coptic, 267–268, 277–278, **1282–1284**, *1282–1284*
Abū al-Munā manuscripts, 29
Adoration of the Magi depiction, 527
baptism of Jesus depiction, 530
influence on Irish manuscripts, 252–253
see also Christian subjects in Coptic art
Ilyās Buqṭur, **1284–1285**
Images, religious. *See* Icons, Coptic; Iconoclasm
Imhotep (pagan deity), 1874
Immaculate Conception, **1285**
Immersion, **1285–1286**
Imperial cult. *See* Persecutions
Imperial Library of Vienna (Austria), 2049
ʿInān, Muḥammad ʿAbdallāh, 1996
ʿInānī, ʿAlī al-, 1996
Incarnation, 6, **1287–1290**
Damian on, 689
and Gabriel, Archangel, 1136
Origen on, 1849–1850
Proclus homily on, 2017
al-Ṣafī ibn al-ʿAssāl on, 2077, 2078
Incense, **1290**, 1469–1472, 2013
censers, *1599*, 1599–1601, *1600*
for consecration of patriarchs, 1909
and Holy Saturday, 1249
and Lord's Prayer, 1481
music for offerings of, 1715–1729, 1739
for spells, 1500, 1504, 1507
Incense box, 1474
Incident of the Churches. *See* Waqʿat al-Kanāʾis
India, Coptic missionaries in, 892, 1635–1636, 1881
Infant baptism. *See* Baptism
Inheritance. *See* Wills and inheritance
In Honor of Longinus (Basil of Oxyrhynchus), 360
In Isaiam I (Demetrius of Antioch), 894
Innocent I, Pope (Rome), 1930, 2247
Innocent III, Pope (Rome), 1635
Innocentius of Maronia, 1674
Insanity. *See* Madness
Inscriptions, 257, **1290–1296**
at al-Bagawāt, 328–329
on Gospel caskets, 1153
gravestone formulas, 1294–1295
in Greek language, 1171, 1290
icon, 1279
of the Kellia, 1407–1408
Nubian medieval, 1814–1815
of Roman visitors to Egypt, 2066
at al-Shaykh Ḥasan, 2129
see also Graffiti
Installatio of the Archangel Gabriel, 1136
Installatio Michaelis Archangeli, 1136
Institut catholique, 925
Institute for Antiquity and Christianity, Claremont, California, and the Nag Hammadi Codices, 1771
Institute of Christian Oriental Research, Washington, D.C., 1896
Institute of Coptic Studies, at Anbā Ruways Monastery, 129
Institute for Papyrology, Heidelberg, Germany, 1893
Institute of Religious and Ecclesiastical Art, Utrecht, 1620
Institut français d'archéologie orientale du Caire, 843, 924, 927, 1398, 1419, 1452, 1516, 1561
Coptic-language printing press, 1302
papyrus collection, 1892
Sauneron, Serge, 2100
Instruments, liturgical, 1595–1596
Instruments, medical, *1579*, *1580*, 1581, 1605
Instruments, musical, 1604–1605, *1605*, 1733, 1734, 1738–1739
Intaglios, 1509
Intercession
for the dormant, 889
icon formula of, 1279
ṭubḥ for litany of, 2279
and use of candles, 446
Interdict, **1299**, 1931
ancient correspondence on, 401
and *audientia episcopalis*, 308
Interlacing motifs (art), 251–253
International Association for Coptic Studies (IAC), **1299–1300**, 1890
International Congresses of Coptic Studies, **1300–1301**
Interpretation of Knowledge, **1301**
Intersected cross, 252
Invocation of the Holy Spirit. *See* Epiclesis
Ioulei, Apa, 824
Ioule and Pteleme (martyrs), 1555
Iovia (Egyptian province), 905
Iqāmat al-Ḥujjah al-Bāhirah ʿalā Hadm Kanāʾis Miṣr wa-al-Qāhirah ("Presentation of the Clear Proof for the Necessary Destruction of the Churches of Old and New Cairo"), 687
ʿIqd al-Madhbah. *See* Architectural elements of churches
Iqlādiyūs Labīb, **1302**

and printing of Bohairic-Coptic Bible, 564
Īrā'i. *See* Ter and Erai, Saints
Iraq, Coptic churches in, 1621
Ireland
art, Coptic influence on, 251–254, 418–419
Coptic influence in, 416–419
Coptic monks in, 253–254
Irish harp, 1734, 1740
monasticism, 253, 417–418
papyrus collection, 1894
saints, 418
Irenaeus, 917, 2157
on the Carpocratian sect, 460–461
on genuflection, 1139
on the Gospels, 1158, 1159, 1164
on Nativity, 1102
patristic writings, 1921
on Polycarp, 1997
Irenaeus of Scetis, Saint, 2084
Irene. *See* Eirene (martyr)
Irene, Empress, 1275
Irish art, 251–254, 418–419
Irish harp, 1734, 1740
Irrigation aqueducts, Dayr Abū Qarqūrah, 709
'Iryān Jirjis Muftāḥ, **1302–1303**, 1737, 1962
Isaac (hermit), 772
Isaac (Old Testament) depiction in Coptic art, 382–383, 726, 727, 778–779, 793
Isaac, Coptic Testament of. *See* Coptic Testament of Isaac
Isaac, disciple of Apollo, **1304**
Isaac, Patriarch, 12, 427, **1303**, 2084
Coptic texts on, 1456
dates of patriarchy, 1915
and Dayr Maṭrā, 837
disciples of, 13
and Ḥilwān, 1233
and John of Nikiou, 1366
Isaac, Saint (Kellia), **1304**, 1397, 2084
Isaac of al-Aqlāli. *See* Isaac, Saint (Kellia)
Isaac the Deacon, **1304**
Isaac al-Difrāwī (martyr), 806
Isaac of Hūrīn, Saint, 1972, 2084
Isaac of Panopolis (painter), 804
Isaac the Presbyter, Saint, 2084
Isaac of al-Qalālī. *See* Isaac, Saint
Isaac of Qalamūn, **1304**, 1455
Isaac of Scetis, Saint, 2084
Isaac of Shammā (martyr), 1555
Isaac of Tiphre, Saint, **1304–1305**, 1555
Isaiah, 22
Ascension of, 166
Isaiah the Hermit. *See* Isaiah of Scetis, Saint
Isaiah of Scetis, Saint (Isaiah the Hermit), 795, 1304, **1305–1306**, 2084
Isaiah the Solitary. *See* Isaiah of Scetis, Saint
'Īsā ibn Nasṭūrus, 1097
'Īsā ibn Zur'ah, collected works of, 1779
Ischurion (soldier-martyr), 1964
Ischyras, Bishop, 1527
Isḥāq, Adīb, 1994, 1995
Isḥāq, Apa. *See* Isaac (hermit)
Isḥaq al-Hūrīnī, Saint. *See* Isaac of Hūrīn, Saint
Isḥāq ibn Ibrāhīm ibn Nasṭās, **1306**
as grandson of Nasṭās ibn Jurayj, 1775–1776
wine prescription, 1524–1525
Isḥāq al-Mu'taman ibn al-'Assāl, on Coptic liturgical music, 1735
Ishkirūn, Saint, relic of, 758–759
Ishnīn al-Naṣārā, 1653, 1972
Ishshīd Muḥammad ibn Tughj, and Epiphany celebration, 1103
Isidhūrus, Bishop and Abbot, **1307**
Isidhūrus (monk), 1120
Isidore of Takinash, 1089
Isidorus, Saint (Isidore of Antioch), **1307**, 1555
Isidorus and Bandilaus (martyrs), 1555
Isidorus the Confessor, 686, 817
Isidorus of Hermopolis, Saint, 2084
Isidorus of Pelusium, Saint, 1089, **1308–1310**, 2084
and archimandrite title, 193
on Isidorus of Scetis, Saint, 1310
and Theophilus, Patriarch, 2247, 2249–2250
Isidorus of Scetis, Saint, 114, **1310**, 1427, 2084
Isidorus of Takināsh (martyr), 1555
Isis (pagan deity), 134, 243, 244, 281, 863, 1292, 1502, 1503, 1505, 1752, 1865, *1866*, 1867, 1868, 1870, 1874
Abūṣīr Banā and, 36
cult and temple at Philae, 265, 1954
destruction of shrine to, 1608, 1609
iconography of, 259531
Nubian worship of, 1801
nursing Horus. *See Isis lactans*
Isis lactans, 243, 244, 281, 531
Iskandar, Najīb, 1993
Iskandariyyah, al-, 90, 92
Iskārūs, Tawfīq, 1466
Iskhiron, Saint, 1972
Iskhīrūn, Abū, 735
Islam
Abraam I, Saint, relations with, 10
Ahl al-Dhimmah designation, 72–73
bans on Coptic pilgrimages, 1538
Christian apologetic literature in reaction to, 5
and Christian encounters under Mamluks, 2317
consort of Prophet Muḥammad, 1528
Copt conversions under Khā'īl I, 1411
Coptic conversions during Peter V patriarchy, 1949
Coptic conversions under Umayyad administration, 2288–2289
Coptic historical work, 1525
and Coptic monuments, 693–694
and Coptic press, 2010–2012
and Egyptian nationalist movement, 1987–1988, 1989
and Egyptian national unity, 950–951
and Egyptian religious reform movement, 1995–1996
and Epiphany celebration, 1103
Ethiopian prelate conversion to, 1028–1030
expansion in Egypt, 936–941
Fatimid-Coptic relations, 1097–1099
French relationships, 1417, 1591
ḥisbah concept, 1236–1237

Islam (*cont.*)
influences on Coptic art, 1310–1312
Jirjī al-Simʿānī debate with, 1331–1332
and *jizyah* tax, 1336
and *kharāj* tax, 1413–1414
law commentary, 1269–1270
martyrs recanting from, 1570
Nubian conversion to, 1802–1804
opposition to images of living things, 1276
and pagarch office, 1871
persecution of Copts (thirteenth-century), 1267, 1268, 1343
persecution of Copts (fourteenth-century), 750, 1343–1344, 1949, 2313–2316
persecution of Copts (15th-century), 1129, 1130
and personal status laws, 1941–1943
Qūṣ settlements, 2044
scholarship, 687, 1695–1696
societal influence on Coptic family, 1087
Waqʿat al-Kanāʾis (Incident of the Churches), 2313–2316
Waqʿat al-Naṣārā (Christian encounter), 2316–2319
see also Pan-Islamism; Umayyads, Copts under the
Islamic Benevolent Society, 1993
Islamic influences on Coptic art, **1310–1312**
Islamic law, 951, 1269–1270
Islam and the Principles of Government (al-Rāziq), 1996
Island of Michael, 1588
Island of Philae. *See* Philae
Ismāʿīl, Khedive, 1637, 1693
see also Muḥammad ʿAlī dynasty
Ismāʿīliyyah
Coptic Catholic church, 1123
Franciscan church, 1123
Isnā, **1312**
ceramics of, 480, 487, *489*
church dedicated to Gabriel, Archangel, 1137
hermit cells at, 477
inscriptions found at, 764, 1291, 1293
martyrs at, 866, 868, 870
monasteries near, 772, 856, 866–870, 1656, 1657
monastic paintings at, 1660
mural paintings at, 1872, 1873
pharaonic-style temples at, 1865
pilgrimages to, 1972
stelae from, 2149, 2151
tombstone material and shape, 1295
Israel, State of
Coptic collections, 1710
and status of Dayr al-Sulṭān, 874
see also Holy land; Jerusalem, Coptic See of
Issac of Nineveh, collected works of, 1778, 1779
Istifhām Baʿd al-Istibhām, al-, **1312–1313**
Italy
Coptic collections, 1710–1711
intervention in Ethiopia, 1041–1044, 1198
papyrus collections, 1894–1895
see also Rome
Iṭfīḥ, **1313**
mosque-building, 685
prosopography of, 2022
Ivory and bone carving, Coptic, **405–407**, *406*, *407*
Iyyasus Mo'a, Ethiopian saint, 1048–1049
ʿIzbat al-Aqbāt, 808
ʿIzbat Dayr al-Ḥadīd, 805
ʿIzbāwiyyah, pilgrimages to, 1972

J

Jabal Abū Dukhkhān, 1650
Jabal Abū Fūdah, 717, 834, 853
Jabal ʿAddā, **1315**, 2037
Dotawo documents, 922–923
Nobatian eparchal residence at, 1798
and Nubian archaeology, medieval, 1805
Jabal al-Aḥmar, al-, 2000
Jabal Bishwāw. *See* Dayr Mār Buqṭur (Qamūlah)
Jabal Jarād, 1659
Jabal al-Kaff. *See* Dayr al-ʿAdhrā' (Samālūṭ)
Jabal Khashm al-Quʿūd, **1315–1316**
Jabal Mūsā. *See* Mount Sinai
Jabal Qaṭṭār, 1650
Jabal Qusqām. *See* Pilgrimages
Jabal al-Silsilah, **1316**, 1656–1657
Jabal Tafnīs, hermitages of, 314, **1316–1317**
Jabal al-Ṭārif (Nag Hammadi), **1317**, 1657, 1771
Jabal al-Ṭayr (Khargah), **1317**, 1658
Asṭāsī al-Rūmī icons at, 293–294
Dayr al-ʿAdhrā' near, 715, *715*
pilgrimages to, 1969
Jabal al-Ṭayr (Samālūṭ). *See* Pilgrimages
Jablonski, Paul Ernst, **1318**, 1424, 2107
Jacob (Old Testament), 845, 1137, 1186, 1618
see also Testament of Jacob
Jacob, Saint and Patriarch, **1318**, 2084
dates of patriarchy, 1916
and Simon II, 2139
Yuḥannā as biographer, 2356
Jacob, Bishop of Memphis, 1587
Jacob Baradaeus, **1318–1319**
consecration by Theodosius I, 1675, 2241
and Damian, 589, 688
death site, 1650
and monophysitism in Syrian and Mesopotamian chuches, 1675, 1676
and Paul the Black, 1923
and Theodora, Empress, 1319, 1386, 1675, 2235
Jacobites
conflict with Melchites in Alexandria, 93–94
al-Istifhām baʿd al-Istibhām addressed to, 1312
see also Jacob Baradaeus; Monophysitism; Syrian Orthodox church
Jacob of Sarūj, **1319–1320**, 1727, 1781, 1783
Jacob the Sawn. *See* James Intercisus
Jacob the Soldier. *See* James of Amadjudj (martyr)
Jadal bayn al-Mukhālif-waal-Naṣrānī, al- (Eutychius), 1460
Jaffa. *See* Holy Land
Jahshiyārī, Abū ʿAbd Allāh, al-, **1320**
Jakob, Apa (Dayr Apa Phoibammon), 780–781

Jama. *See* Memnonia
Jamāl al-Dīn (Mamluk amir), 1570
James, Apostle and Saint
  Apocryphon of, 169–170, 569
  apostolic see, 181
  and *Gloria in excelsis*, 1147
  and the Transfiguration, 1108–1109
  see also Apocalypse of James, First and Second
James, Saint (James the Ascetic), **1320–1321**, 2084
James of Amadjudj (martyr), 1555
James of Antioch, Saint, 2084
James Bar 'Adai. *See* Jacob Baradaeus
James Intercisus, Saint (martyr), 324, **1321**, 1556
James (Jacob) and John (martyrs), 1555
James the Persian. *See* James Intercisus, Saint (martyr)
James of Sarūj. *See* Jacob of Sarūj
James of Scetis, Saint, **1321–1322**, 2084
Jam'iyyah Asdiqa' al-Kitab al-Muqaddas. *See* Friends of the Bible, Society of the
Jam'iyyah al-Iṣlāḥ al-Qibṭī. *See* Coptic Reform Society
Jam'iyyah al-Khayriyyah (Coptic Benevolent Society), 374, 1693
Jam'iyyat Aṣdiqā' al-Kitāb al-Muqaddas, 374–375
Jam'iyyat al-Ikhlāṣ, 375
Jam'iyyat al-Nash'ah al-Qibṭiyyah, 374
Jam'iyyat Thamarat al-Tawfīq, 375
Jammā, al-. *See* Madīnat Hābū; Memnonia
Jamoul (martyr), 1556
Jamu. *See* Memnonia
Japan, Coptic collections in, 1711
Jared, Ethiopian saint, 1047
Jarīdah, al- (publication), 1994
Jarnus, al-, 1653
Jars and jugs
  ceramic, 490–492
  metalwork, 1602–1603
  water, 2320
Jason (mythological subject), depicted in Coptic art, 1762–1763
Jawhar, General, 1097, 1099, 1271
Jawharah al-Nafīsah fī 'Ulum al-Kanīsah, al- (Ibn Sibā'), 1272, 1464
Jawhar al-Siqilī (the Sicilian), 1632, 1913
Jāwīsh, Shaykh 'Abd al-Azīz, 1465, 1988–1989
Jawlī, al-. *See* Dayr al-Jawlī
Jawsaq. *See* Keep
Jawziyyah School (Damascus), 1269
Jazīrat al-Dayr (Island of the Monastery). *See* Dayr al-Rūmāniyyah
Jeme. *See* Madīnat Hābū; Memnonia
Jerasimus, Saint (martyr), 1552, 1559
Jeremiah, Apocryphon of, 170–171
Jeremiah, Saint, 22, 166, 1254, **1322–1323**, 2084
  depicted in Coptic art, 270, 532–533
  see also Dayr Apa Jeremiah; *Paralipomena Jeremiou*
Jericho. *See* Holy Land
Jernstedt, Peter Viktorovich, **1323**, 1895
Jerome, Saint, **1323**, 1921, 2084
  on candle use in churches, 445
  on celibacy, 476
  Dayr Anbā Būlā founded in memory, 741, 742
  and Didymus the Blind, 900
  and Eusebius of Caesarea, 1070–1071
  and Hilarion, Saint, 1232, 1664
  and Horsiesios, Saint, 1257
  on John the Baptist burial site, 1355
  on *Kyrie eleison*, 1420
  on Monastery of the Metanoia, 1608
  on multiple marriages, 1545
  and Origen, 471–472
  and Pamphilus, Saint, 1879
  on Paul of Thebes, 1925–1926
  on priesthood, 2016
  Rufinus *Apology* and, 2068–2069
  Rule of Pachomius translation by, 1662, 1663, 1861–1862, 1863
  on Saturday fast, 2098
  theological literary history by, 1920
  and Theophilus, Patriarch, 2247, 2250, 2252
Jersey City, New Jersey, 1621
Jerusalem, Coptic See of, 180, **1324–1329**, 1613, 1614
  and Acacian schism, 45
  apostolic succession, 181
  barring of Coptic pilgrimages to, 1615
  Coptic collections, 1710
  Coptic Good Friday celebration, 1153
  Dayr al-Sulṭān, 872–874
  founding of monasteries in, 1663
  keep construction, 1395
  library, 1447
  Saladin's reconquest of, 1536
  Sophia, Saint, tradition of, 2143–1244
  see also Eastern Orthodox churches; Holy Land, Coptic churches in the
Jesuits and the Coptic church, 1132, **1329–1330**
  Ethiopian controversies, 986–987, 995–997
  influence in Ethiopia, 1021
  Jullien, Michel Marie, 1382–1383
  Kircher, Athanasius, 1415
  Sicard, Claude, 2136–2137
  see also Bollandists
Jesus, bath of the infant. *See* Christian subjects in Coptic art
Jesus Christ
  Advent, 63
  Agnus Dei, 70
  Ascension, 1105
  and asceticism, 1306
  and atonement, 306–307
  on baptism, 336–337, 1285
  baptism of, 967
  blessing style, 403–404
  Candlemas feast, 1106–1107
  on celibacy, 476
  and Christian Pasch, 1904
  crucifixion, fasts to commemorate, 1096
  crucifixion, Qur'anic theory of, 95
  and death of Joseph, 1697
  depiction in Coptic art, 270; *see also subhead* paintings of
  and Eucharist, 1107
  fasts, 1095–1096

Jesus Christ (*cont.*)
first miracle, 1107
and fraction rite, 1121
and Gabriel, Archangel, 1136
on guardian angel, 1186
icons of, 368–369, 1276, 1277–1278
Incarnation, 1287–1290
and laying-on of hands, 1432, 1433
Lord's Prayer, 1480–1481
and magical spells, 1500, 1503
and Mark, Apostolic Saint, 1529
and marriage, 1542, 1544
Melchizedek and, 1583–1584
Nativity, 1102–1103
pagan literature on, 1868
paintings of, 727, 747, 778, 794, 868, 869, 1660, 1875, 2004–2006, *2006*
Palm Sunday, 1103–1104
and Paradise, 1900–1901
power of binding and loosing, 1932
and priesthood, 2015
Resurrection, 1104–1105
and Revelation, 61–63
and symbolism of manual cross, 1472
and Thomas, disciple, 1108
Transfiguration, 1108–1109
see also Athanasian Creed; Christian subjects in Coptic art; Christ, nature of; Christology; Flight into Egypt; Good Friday; Gospel headings; Nicene Creed
Jewelry, 1605–1607, *1606*
Coptic colored glass-inlaid crosses, 1146
Jews and Judaism
Abraham, Saint and Patriarch, relations with, 11
as *Ahl al-Dhimmah*, 72, 655–656; *see also subhead* Muslim discriminatory measures
Alexandrian ascetics, 1661
Alexandrian community, 91, 97, 1175, 1180, 1865, 1866
and Alexandrian gnosticism, 1147, 1148, 1149–1150
Alexandrian rebellion, 97, 1947, 2016
altars, 106
anointing, 137
Antichrist concept and, 143
apologetic directed at, 2357
apologists, 176
atonement concept, 306–307
baptism at Dayr Anbā Anṭūniyūs, 721
Bar Hebraeus, 345–346
and canon of the Scripture, 2109
Coptic music and, 148–149, 1731
and Cyril I, 672
and eschatology, 973
Ethiopian prohibitions against, 991–993
Evodius of Rome homilies against, 1078–1079
Great Synagogue (Tamūh), 717
heaven concept, 1214
Hellenization in Egypt, 1167, 1175
jizyah tax on, 1336
Josephus Flavius, 176, 1375–1376
magical spells, 1508
Muslim discriminatory measures, 655–656, 939, 1202, 1343, 1348
New Testament explanation addressed to, 1273
Old Testament feasts, 1101
and paganism, 1868
Paraphrase of Shem and, 1902
Pascha (Passover), 1903
Philo of Alexandria, 1956–1957
religious impact in Egypt, 1865–1866
ritual purification ceremonials, 8–9
Roman poll tax and, 2203
Saturday as sabbath, 2098
scriptural proof texts disputes, 1227
and Youth of Egypt membership, 2354
see also Law, Mosaic; Old Testament; Therapeutae
Jibrīl ibn Bukhtīshū' ibn Jūrjīs, 1922
Jihād, al- (publication), 1990
Jilbānah, Saint, 700
Jimyānah, Saint. *See* Dimyānah, Saint
Jirjā, **1330–1331**
monasteries in region of, 825–826, 861–862, 1656, 1657
Jirjā and Upper Ṣa'īd, See of, 1614
Jirjis, Mār. *See* George, Saint
Jirjis Abū al-Faḍā'il ibn Luṭfallāh, 1462
Jirjis al-Muzāḥim. *See* George, Saint
Jirjis ibn al-'Amīd, 1095
Jirjis ibn al-Qass abī al-Mufaḍḍal, 1270, 1271, **1332**
Jirjī al-Sim'ānī, 461, **1331–1332**
Jirjis al-Jawharī, 1141, **1332–1334**, 1417, 1515, 1539, 1688, 1692, 2351
and Ibrāhīm al-Jawharī, 1274
Jirjis al-Jawharī al-Khanānī, **1334–1335**
Jirjis Makramallāh al-Bahnasāwī, **1335**, 1515
Jirjis al-Muzāḥim, Saint (martyr), 902–903, **1335–1336**, 1556
Jirjis Philūthāwus 'Awaḍ
church law compendium, 1942
on Dayr al-Sham', 865
Jirjis al-Qibṭī (George the Copt), 1700
Jizyah (poll tax), 303, 622, 636, 656, 665, 1097, **1336**, 2134–2135
abolition of, 1636
on *Ahl al-Dhimmah*, 72
Alexander II and, 86, 87
and Arab conquest of Egypt, 187, 189
and Baqṭ Treaty, 343
as factor in Islamization of Egypt, 937, 1411
and Gabriel II's patriarchy, 1129
and Gabriel V's patriarchy, 1130
and Gabriel VII's patriarchy, 1134
and *ḥisbah*, 1236–1237
Ibn Qayyim al-Jawziyyah commentary, 1269
increases during Theodorus patriarchy, 2237
increases under Badr al-Jamālī, 325
in Makouria, 1514
Job, Testament of, 164
Joel, King of Dotawo, 923
Johannes de Turrecremata (Juan de Torquemada), Cardinal, 1119
Johannes Gallicus Marinesis, Cardinal, 1119
Johann Georg, **1336**

Johannine Christology, 2157
John, Apostle and Saint
on celibacy, 476
church at Dayr Abū Ḥinnis, 701
church at Dayr al-Majmaʿ, 820, *821*
on confession and penitence, 585
feast day, 882, 2084
and Good Friday, 1104
and Michael, Archangel, 1618, 1619
monasteries dedicated to, 883
monastery of, 748, 861, 1656
Polycarp and, 1997
as Transfiguration witness, 1108–1109
see also Apocryphon of John; Revelation, Book of; Dayr al-Sāqiyah; Gospel of John
John, Hegumenos of Raithou, 2050
John, Hegumenos of Scetis, 12, **1362**
John, Saint and Bishop of Armant, **1353–1354**
John I, Saint and Patriarch, **1337**, 2084
and Acacian schism, 44
dates of patriarchy, 1915
John II, Saint and Patriarch, **1337**, 2084
and Acacian schism, 44, 45, 46
and churches in Babylon, 318
dates of patriarchy, 1915
at the Enaton, 956–957
and John I, 1337
John III, the Merciful, Saint and Patriarch, 70, 94, 709, **1337–1338**, 1939, 1966, 2084
dates of patriarchy, 1915
Isaac the Deacon as biographer of, 1304
and John of Nikiou, 1366
and John of Parallos, 1368
as monk–priest at Dayr al-Ikhwah, 808
panegyric by, 1456
successor, 1303
John IV, Saint and Patriarch, 334, **1338–1339**
dates of patriarchy, 1916
feast day, 2084
and Mark II, 1533
Yuḥannā as biographer of, 2356
John V, Patriarch, **1340–1341**, 1534, 1912
dates of patriarchy, 1917
and Mikā'ēl I, Ethiopian prelate, 1007
and Murqus ibn Qanbar reforms, 1699
John VI, Saint and Patriarch, **1341–1342**, 1391
and Būlus al-Būshī, 423
and Crusaders' occupation of Būrah, 425
dates of patriarchy, 1917
and Giyorgis II as metropolitan of Ethiopia, 1009
and Khā'īl translation, 399
and Mikā'ēl II, Ethiopian prelate, 1007
and Yesḥaq I, Ethiopian prelate, 1008
John VII, Patriarch, 33, **1342–1343**
burial site, 848
dates of patriarchy, 1917
and Yūsāb, Bishop (13th-century), 2359
John VIII, Patriarch, **1343–1344**
burial at Dayr Shahrān, 862
and Church of al-Muʿallaqah (Old Cairo), 558
consecrated by Ḥasaballāh, 1210
dates of patriarchy, 1917
patriarchal seat change and residence, 1208, 1913
successor, 1344
and Yūsāb, Bishop (13th-century), 2359
John IX, Patriarch, 377, **1344**
burial site, 848
dates of patriarchy, 1917
John X, Patriarch, **1344**
dates of patriarchy, 1918
John XI, Patriarch, **1344–1345**
consecration of Ethiopian prelates, 1014
and Coptic relations with Rome, 609
dates of patriarchy, 1918
and Dayr al-Maghṭis, 819
John XII, Patriarch, 1119, 1131, **1346**
and Coptic relations with Rome, 1347
dates of patriarchy, 1918
successor, 1346
John XIII, Patriarch, 1612, **1346–1347**, 1647, 1974
dates of patriarchy, 1918
on pillage of Dayr Anbā Anṭūniyūs, 722
writings copied by Jirjis Makramallāh al-Bahnasāwī, 1335
John XIV, Patriarch, **1347**
and Coptic relations with Rome, 952, 1329–1330
dates of patriarchy, 1918
John XV, Patriarch, 1022, **1347–1348**
dates of patriarchy, 1919
John XVI, Patriarch, 30, 1206, 1273, **1347–1348**, 1975
church restorations under, 713
and communion of the sick, 580
and Coptic relations with Rome, 610
dates of patriarchy, 1919
and Jesuits in Egypt, 1330
and Mārqos IV, Ethiopian prelate, 1027
as monk of Dayr Anbā Anṭūniyūs, 722
and restoration of Dayr Anbā Būlā, 742, 743
and Sinodā, Ethiopian prelate, 1025
successor, 1949
John XVII, Patriarch, **1348–1350**
Bisūrah al-Ḥarīrī manuscripts on, 403
consecration at Church of Abū Sayfayn, 550
and Coptic relations with Rome, 610–611
dates of patriarchy, 1919
as monk at Dayr Anbā Būlā, 742
successor, 1538
and Yoḥannes III, Ethiopian prelate, 1029
John XVIII, Patriarch, **1350**
consecration of Jūsāb, Bishop (18th-century), 2360
dates of patriarchy, 1919
John XIX, Patriarch, **1351**
and Coptic Community Council, 580
dates of patriarchy, 1919
and Ethiopian church autocephaly, 980, 1198, 1041–1043
Ethiopian visit, 1041
as first bishop elected as patriarch, 399, 1911
and Haile Selassie I, 1198

John XIX, Patriarch (*cont.*)
and Isidhūrus pardon, 1307
and Italian intervention in Ethiopia, 1041–1043, 1198
as monk at Dayr al-Baramūs, 791
and Qērelos III, Ethiopian prelate, 1040, 1042
and Sarjiyūs, Malatī, 2097
and School for Monks (Alexandria), 564
and Yūsāb II, 2363
John of Alexandria (martyr), 31, 1554
John the Almoner, Patriarch of Cyprus (Melchite), 184, 720, 721, 1641–1642
John of Antioch, Bishop, 55, 960, **1354**
and bishop's translation, 399
and Nestorius, 1786
John Arkaph, 1584
John of Ashmūn Ṭanāḥ (martyr), 1556
John of Asyūṭ, Bishop, on martyrs of Isnā, 866
John the Baptist, Saint, 71, **1354–1356**, 1477
birth of, 1102
churches dedicated to, 792
in Coptic literature, 1356
cult of, 1355
Feast of Commemoration. *See* Festal days, monthly
Gabriel, Archangel, and, 1135
and immersion, 1286
martyrium of, 1610, 1611, 1646
place in Coptic church, 1355–1356
Proclus homily on, 2018
Raphael, Archangel, and, 2054
relics of, 93
sanctuary of, 751
John of Biclarum, 921, 1513
on the evangelization of Nubia, 1801–1802
John the Black. *See* John Kāmā, Saint
John Calybites, **1357**
John Cassian. *See* Cassian, Saint John
John Chrysostom, Saint and Patriarch of Constantinople, **1357–1359**
on ablution, 9
on anamnesis, 121
on angels, 132
Antioch schism mediation, 2249
on asterisk as eucharistic vessel, 1065
Canons of Saint John Chrysostom, 459–460
on celibacy, 476
collected homilies of, 1778, 1779
Coptic translations, 1454
and cross-carrying, 1468
and Cyril I, 672
on deaconesses, 888
and Demetrius, cycle of, 667
and Demetrius of Antioch, 893
encomia as part of Coptic hagiography, 1196
on Eucharist, 597, 1056–1057, 1059–1060
and Eustathius of Thrace, 1073
on Feast of the Ascension, 1105
feast day, 2084
on Gospel of Saint Mark, 1159
on Holy Cross manifestation, 1243
homily on Basil the Great, 352
homily on Gabriel, Archangel, 1136
homily on Raphael, Archangel, 2053, 2054
on immersion, 1286
and Isidorus of Pelusium, 1308, 1309, 1310
and Jirjis al-Jawharī al-Khanānī (copyist), 1335
and John the Faster, 1339–1340
on Last Judgment, 1379
liturgies of, 1540
on Michael, Archangel, 1618, 1619
and Origenist monks, 113–114, 2250
Palladius defense of, 1877
patristic writings, 1921
Proclus on, 2018
relics, 2017
and al-Ṣafī ibn al-ʿAssāl revision of homilies of, 2075
and Severian of Jabalah, 1136, 1619, 2122, 2123
and Sophia, Saint, 2143–2144
and Tall Brothers, 916, 2250
Theodorus of Mopsuestia relationship, 2238
and Theophilus, Patriarch, 2247, 2250–2251, 2252
and tradition of Victor Stratelates, Saint, 2303
on unction of the sick, 139, 2291–2292
John of Claudiopolis, Bishop of Isauria, 2124
John Climacus (John the Cilician), 2050
John Colobos, Saint, **1359–1361**, 1448
on Ababius, 1
Arabic tradition of, 1361–1361
and Arsenius of Scetis and Ṭurah, 240
and Athanasius of Clysma (martyr), 305
and Bishoi, 734, 795
churches dedicated to, 701, 1426
Coptic tradition of, 1359–1361
death in Clysma, 565
feast day, 2084
and James of Scetis, Saint, 1321
and John Kāmā, Saint, 1363
monasteries of, 770, 809
as paragon of virtue and obedience, 1668
and Pshoi of Scetis, 2029
relics, 720, 753
and Shenute, 2029
and Three Hebrews in the Furnace, 2258
John the Confessor, Saint, 2084
John of Damanhūr (martyr), 688, 1554
John of Damascus, Saint, 71, 1735, 1985, 2046
John the Dwarf. *See* John Colobos, Saint
John of Ephesus, 921, **1362**, 1676
on the evangelization of Nubia, 1797, 1801–1802, 1807
on Longinus, 1480
on monophysitism, 1673–1674
and Sophia, 1384–1385
John the Faster, Saint and Patriarch of Constantinople, **1339–1340**
feast day, 2084
John of Gaza, Saint, 2084
John of the Golden Gospel, Saint, 2084
John the Grammarian of Caesarea, 1455
John of Heraclia (martyr), 1556
John Jejunator. *See* John the Faster, Saint
John of Jerusalem, Saint and Bishop, 1930, 2084

John Kāmā, Saint, 701, 749, **1362–1363**
in Ethiopia, 991
feast day, 2084
marital chastity of, 1543
John of Laqqānah, Bishop, 1426
John the Little. *See* John Colobos, Saint
John of Lycopolis, Saint, 296, **1363–1365**, 1976, 2029, 2084
and Bessarion, Saint, 379
Coptic texts on, 1455
and Dayr al-ʿIẓām, 809
Historia monachorum in Aegypto on, 809, 1238, 1363, 1364
at Lycopolis, 296
Palladius and, 1876
reclusion of, 2055–2056
John of Madīnat al-Fayyūm, Bishop, 1126
John of Mayuma, Bishop, **1366**, 1670, 2033
on early liturgical music practices, 1733, 1735
texts by, 1455
John of Montenero, 1114, 1116
John Moschus, 1467, 1560, 1662, 2050
John of Nikiou, Bishop, 37, **1366–1367**, 1676, 1794, 2060
as archimandrite, 193
chronicle of Arab conquest of Egypt, 183, 184, 186, 187, 188
on Church of Saint Michael, 1617
on the Covenant of ʿUmar, 655
on Eikoston, 951
and Jeremiah, Saint, 1322
on Mīt Damsīs, 1971
and Simon I, 2138–2139
and taxation, 358–359
and Theognosta, Saint, 2244
and Theophilus, Patriarch, 2247, 2248
and Timothy II Aelurus, Patriarch, 2264
on treaty of Alexandria (641), 187, 683
writings translated into Ethiopic, 977
John "of the Cells", 1948
John of Pake, **1367**
John of Parallos, Saint, 838, 871, **1367–1368**, 1456, 1618, 1619, 1626
feast day, 2084
John Paul II, Pope (Rome), on doctrines of Nestorius and Eutyches, 1786
John of Petra, Abbot, 1662 1662
John of Phanidjoit (martyr), 1556
John Philoponus, 29, 100
John and Piammônas of Diolkos, 908
John the Presbyter, **1368–1369**
and Life of Pisentius, Saint, 1368, 1455–1456
John of Psenhowt (martyr), 1556
John Rufus. *See* John of Mayuma
John Rylands Library, Manchester, England, 901, 1893
John of Ṣā, Bishop, 925
John of Sabarou (martyr), 1552
John Sabas, **1369**
John of Sais, Bishop, and monks of the Kellia, 1397–1398
John of Sanhūt, Saint (martyr), 882, 1556, 1626
John the Scribe. *See* Cyril V, Patriarch
John of Shmūn, Bishop, **1369**
on Bishoi and Shinūdah, 737
panegyrics by, 1456
John the Short. *See* John Colobos, Saint
John the Soldier (martyr), 1467, 1556
Johnson, D. W., 1573
John and Symeon, **1370**
John Talaia, 43, 1609, 1610, 2269
John of Tella, 1673–1674
John of Würzburg, 872
Jomard, Edmé Franois, 1284
Jonah, depiction in Coptic art, 386, *387*
Jonah, Fast of, **1094**
Jonas, Apa, festal date of, 840
Joore (martyr), **1370**, 1556
Jordan
Coptic churches in, 1621
and Dayr al-Sulṭān, 873–874
Jordan River, 1246
Jordanus, Bishop of Quilon, 1635–1636
Joseph (martyr). *See* Joshua and Joseph (ascetics and martyrs)
Joseph (Old Testament), 1868
depiction in Coptic art, 387–388, *388*
Egyptian sites connected with, 1976
and lecanoscopy, 1507
Joseph, Saint, **1370**
Joseph of Arsinoë, Bishop, 760
Joseph the Bishop, Saint, 2084
Joseph of Bishwāw, Saint, **1371**, 1374, 2084
Joseph the Carpenter, Saint, **1371–1374**
apocryphal accounts, 1372–1373
cult of, 1373–1374
and Dayr al-Janādlah, 705
feast day, 2084
and Gabriel and Michael, Archangels, 1136
and mummification, 1697
New Testament accounts, 1371–1372
see also Flight into Egypt
Joseph of Fuwwah, Bishop, 1126
Joseph of Tsenti, Saint, **1374**
Josephus Flavius, 176, **1375–1376**
Joshua (Old Testament), 1618
in Arabic versions, 1830–1831
Testament of. *See* Testament of Joshua
Joshua and Joseph (ascetics and martyrs), 1556
Josippon, 1375
Journals. *See* Press, Coptic; Press, Egyptian; specific titles
Jovian, Emperor, **1376–1377**
patriarch under, 1914
Jowett, William, 133
J. Paul Getty Museum, Malibu, California, 2003, *2005*
Jubilee Year, 1101
Judaism. *See* Jews and Judaism
Judaizing Christians. *See* Ebionites
Judas Cyriacus, Saint and Bishop of Jerusalem, **1377–1378**, 2085
Judas Iscariot, 897, 1416
Judges (Old Testament), Arabic versions, 1831–1832
Judgment, Last, **1378–1379**
Abbaton's role, 2
agnoetism and, 70–71
and eschatology, 974
and Hades, 1189–1190
and prayer for the dead, 889
see also Afterlife; Paradise
Jugs. *See* Glass, Coptic; Jars and jugs; Metalwork, Coptic; Water jugs and stands
Julian, Bishop of Halicarnassus, 70, 876, **1379**, 1455, 1674
doctrinal position, 547, 734

Julian, Bishop of Halicarnassus (*cont.*)
and Eutyches, 1075
Gaianus advocacy of doctrine, 1138
and Justin I, Emperor, 1384
and monophysitism, 1673
on the nature of Christ, 547, 1288, 2125, 2241
and Severus of Antioch, 2125
and Timothy III, 2268
see also Gaianites; Gaianus
Julian, Emperor, 1868
Against the Galileans, 177
and Libanius, 1447
patriarch under, 1914
Julian, Evangelist, **1380**, 1480
and Nubian conversion, 1797, 1801–1802, 1807
Julian, Proconsul of Tripoli, 1443
Julian, Saint and Patriarch, **1380**, 1999, 2085
dates of patriarchy, 1914
successor, 891–892
Juliana (martyr), 1552–1553, 1556
Julian the Apostate, Emperor, **1380–1382**
and Cyril I, 673
and martyrdom of Allādyūs, 1551
and martyrdom of Eusignius, 1071–1072, 1555
and martyrdom of Judas Cyriacus, 1377
martyrs under, 1556, 1557; *see also* specific names
Mercurius of Caesarea and death of, 1382, 1592, 1593
monastery establishment during reign of, 720
and paganism, 1869
persecutions of Christians by, 300, 1937
and profaning tomb of John the Baptist, 1355
succeeded by Jovian, 1376
Julian calendar. *See* Calendar, Julian
Julian and his mother (martyrs), 1556
Julianists. *See* Julian, Bishop of Halicarnassus
Julianus, Chaldean Oracles, 516
Julitta (Julietta), Saint (martyr), 671, 1554
icon of, *1278*
Julius, Bishop of Puteoli, 1441
Julius I, Pope (Rome), 523, 1442, 1669, 1670, 1672
Julius of Aqfahṣ, 1, 2, 152, 1556, 1865
Cycle of, 445
martyrdom in Atrīb, 307
Julius Caesar, 235
Jullien, Michel Marie, 806, 852, 856, **1382–1383**, 2197
Jung, Carl, 1149
Jung Codex. *See* Codex Jung
Junia (martyr), 1552
Junker, Hermann, 656, 815, **1383**
Jupiter (pagan deity), 889, 890, 904, 905, 1866
Justin I, Emperor, **1383–1384**
and Apion family, 155–156
and Chalcedon dispute, 46–47, 1673, 1674
patriarch under, 1915
Justin II, Emperor, 688, **1384–1385**
John of Ephesus on reign of, 1362
and monophysites, 1675, 1676
patriarch under, 1915
Justinian, Emperor, **1385–1386**, 1648, 2008
and Abraham of Farshūṭ, 11–12
and Abūṣīr, 34
and Acacian schism, 46, 47
and Anastasia, 125
Annunciation, Feast of the, 290
and Apion family, 155–156
and Athanasius of Clysma cult, 305–306
and *audientia episcopalis*, 308
and canons of Epiphanius, 456
and Codex Justinianus, 569–570, 1385
and Constantinople, Second Council of, 595–596
Henoticon edict, 1218, 1674
hymn ascribed to, 1733
and John of Ephesus missions, 1362
and Justin I, Emperor, 1383
and Justin II, Emperor, 1384–1385
military reforms, 136, 237–238
and monophysitism, 1319, 1673, 1674, 1676
Moses of Abydos prophecy on, 1679–1680
and Mount Sinai Monastery of Saint Catherine, 1681, 1682, 2325
patriarch under, 1915
and Pentapolis administration, 1934
Procopius history of, 2019–2020
and Qifṭ renaming, 2038
and Raithou monasteries, 2050
reforms of, 2007–2008, 2023; *see also subhead* military reforms
on sale of monasteries, 1639, 1640
and taxation in Roman Eqypt, 2205
and Theodorus of Mopsuestia, 2239
and Timothy II Aelurus, Patriarch, 2264
and wife, Theodora, 2234–2235
Justin Martyr, 1638
as apologist, 176, 177–178
on Easter designation, 1104
and "godly monarch" concept, 1957
on immersion, 1286
Justus, Patriarch, **1386**, 2085
dates of patriarchy, 1913
Justus, Saint (martyr), 2085, **1386–1387**, 1556, 2085, 2209
Juvenal, Patriarch of Jerusalem, 290, 515, 1440, 1670, 2242

K

Ka, festival of Union of, 438
Kaau, Saint, paintings of, 727
Kacmarcik manuscript, copying of, 722
Kāfī, al- (Mīkhā'īl Shārūbīm), 1630–1631
Kafr Ayyūb, pilgrimages to, 1972
Kafr Damrū (village), 689–690
Kafr al-Dayr, 1655, 1656
pilgrimages to, 1972–1973
Kafr Dimayrah al-Iadīd. See Dimarah
Kafr al-Shaykh. *See* Maḥallat Dānyāl
Kaft al-Dawwār, Coptic Catholic church, 1123
Kahle, Paul Eric, 902, 1389
Kahyor, monasteries at, 1654
Kainopolis. *See* Qinā
Kalabsha. *See* Talmīs
Kalamōn. *See* Qalamūn

Kallileion. *See* Anointing; Catechumen, oil of the
Kallinikos, Bishop, 1089
Kalūj. *See* Bajūj (martyr)
Kamāl, Aḥmad, on Dayr Abū Līfah, 704
Kamil Murad. *See* Murad Kamil
Kanebo. *See* Museums, Coptic collections in
Kansu, 1519
Kaou (martyr), 1556
Kaphalas. *See* Paphnutius of Scetis, Saint
Karabacek, Joseph von, 1389
Karanis, **1390**
glassmaking, 1143–1144
Kararah. *See* Qarārah
Kārimī Guild, **1391**
Karma, monastic murals at, 1874
Karm Abū Mena, 1936–1937
Karm al-Akhbāriyyah, **1391–1392**
Karmūz, catacomb at, 1873
Karnak in the Christian period, **1392–1394**, *1392*, *1393*, *1394*
end to institutionalized paganism in, 1870
monasteries near, 1657
pharaonic-style temples at, 1392, *1392*, 1865
Kasios. *See* Katīb al-Qals
Kassa Asrate Stele, 1394
Kata meros. *See* Lectionary
Kātib al-Miṣrī, al-. *See* Fakr al-Dawlah
Katīb al-Qals, 1650
Katochoi (recluses), 2055–2056
Kaufmann, Carl Maria, **1394**
Kaunakopoiós (*kaunakoplókos*) (Coptic weaving term), 2221
Kavād II Sērōē, 1940
Kawjar al-Rūmī, 810
Kawkab al-Sharq (publication), 1990
Kaysān ibn ʿUthmān ibn Kaysān, **1395**, 2079
Keep, **1395–1396**
Dayr Anbā Bishoi (Suhāj), 736, 740
Dayr Anbā Ṣamū'īl (Qalamūn), 760
Dayr al-Baramūs, 792
Kellia, 1395, 1404
Keimer, Ludwig, 1396
Kellia, 1395, **1396–1409**
altars, 106, 107
Ammonius and, 113
Amun, Saint, and, 119
architecture compared with Ḥilwān, 1234
ceramics of, *See* Ceramics, Coptic
complexes of churches, 552, 553, 1404–1405, 1406–1407
construction materials, 1401–1402
and Coptological studies, 615
and Damanhūr bishopric, 687
in "Desert of Scetis," 2102
earliest churches at, 552, 553
Egyptian archaeological activity, 1406–1407
epigraphy, 1407–1408
Evagrius Ponticus and, 1076–1077
excavations, 414, 694, 724, 1398–1406, 1658
French archaeological activity, 1398–1400, 1402
hegumenos title used at, 1216
hermit cells at, 477
history of site, 1397–1398
inscriptions found at, 1291, 1407–1408
and Jabal Khashm al-Quʿud identification, 1316
keeps, 1395, 1396
khizānahs found at, 1415
as laura of hermitages, 1224–1225
in Letters of Saint Antony, 150
and Macarius Alexandrinus, Saint, 1489–1490
monastic life, 1662
mural paintings at, 1408–1409, 1659, 1660, 1872, 1873, 1874, 1875, 1876, 1877
and Nitria monastery, 1794–1796
Palladius at, 1876, 1877
Swiss archaeological activity, 1400–1406
two-bay hall development, 1404
Kells, Book of. *See* British Isles and Ireland, Coptic influences in the
Kemal Atatürk, 1996
Kenya, Coptic churches in, 1622
Kenyon, Frederic George, 1410
Kephalaia, 1891
Kerygmata (Damian), 1455
Keys, 1604, *1604*
Khā'īl I, Patriarch, 24, 37, 93, 350, 1205, **1410–1412**, 1589, 1678, 1950
and bishop's translation, 399
chosen at Bilbeis, 391
dates of patriarchy, 1915
feast day, 2085
and Mīnā I, 1631
as monk at Dayr Anbā Anṭūniyūs, 721
Yūḥannā the Deacon biography of, 2356–2357
Khā'īl II, Patriarch, **1412**, 2085
dates of patriarchy, 1916
Yuḥannā biography of, 2356
Khā'īl III, Patriarch, 903, **1412–1413**
dates of patriarchy, 1916
held for ransom, 2280–2281
Khālīl Bey (Mamluk amir), 1538
Khandaq, al-, **1413**
see also Dayr al-Khandaq
Kharā'ib al-Nāmus. *See* Dayr al-Nāmūs
Kharāj (land tax), 636, 656, **1413–1414**, 2093
Alexander II and, 86, 87
and Arab conquest of Egypt, 189
on communal property, 72, 85–87
Ibn Qayyim al-Jawziyyah on, 1269
impact on Copts, 72, 1410, 1412
increases during Shenute I patriarchy, 2134–2135
and Jacob, Saint, 1318
and *jizyah* tax, 1336
John IV payment, 1338
Macarius II policy, 1487
Khargah. *See* Kharjah
Kharjah (great oasis), monasteries near, 1317, 1658–1659
Khartoum. *See* Sudan, Copts in the
Khashm al-Quʿūd, 1658
Khaṭṭ al-Hamayūnī, al. See Personal status law
Khāyla Malakot of Shewa, 1590
Khidmat al-Shammās. *See The Services of the Deacon*
Khirbat al-Filūsiyyah, **1414**, 1650
Khirbitah, **1415**
Khizānah, **1415**, 1418
Khonai, shrine to Michael the Archangel, 1616
Khosrow textile (Antinoopolis), 2097–208
Khumarawayh, Caliph, 2281

Khune. *See* Kounes, Governor of Aswan
Khūrus, 212–213, 218, 221, 223, 552, 553, 554, 555, 661
  and altar location, 107
  Dayr Anbā Maqār, 753, *754*
  Dayr Anbā Shinudah, 769
Khuṣus, al- (Coptic center), 703
Khūzi (martyr), 1552
Kīlānī, Muḥammad Sayyid, 1465
Kilns, pottery, 481–482
Kings, anointing of, 139
Kircher, Athanasius, 1248, 1330, **1415**, 1748, 1967, 2052
Kirillus, Anbā, Bishop of Asyūṭ, 1270
Kiss of Peace (*aspasmos*), 63, **1416**
Kitāb Akhbār al-Zamān (Yūḥannā al-Ḥādhiq al-Qibṭī)), 2357
Kitāb al-Burhān fī al-Qawānīn (Book of Evidence in Laws) (Abū Shākir ibn al-Rāhib), 33, 1463
Kitāb al-Hādī fī Ma'rifat al-Samādī (Qusṭanṭīn), 2046
Kitāb al-Hudā (Canons of Clement), 456
Kitāb al-'Ilm wa-al-'Amal (Yūḥannā ibn Sāwīrus), 2357–2358
Kitāb al-Īḍāh (Severus of al-Ashmūnayn), 1779
Kitāb al-Istidlāl. See Book of Dialectic
Kitāb Jalā' al-'Uqūl fi'Ilm al-Uṣūl, 1464
Kitāb al Khūlājī al-Muqaddas, 1464
Kitāb al-Majāmi', 1463
Kitāb Miṣbāḥ al-Ẓulmah fī Īḍāḥ al-Khidmah. See Misbāḥ al-Ẓulmah (Ibn Kabar)
Kitāb Qawānin al-Dawāwīn, 1461
Kitāb al-Ru'ūs, 1779
Kitāb al-Shifā' (Buṭrus ibn al-Rāhib), 1779
Kitāb al-Shifā fī Kashf ma-Istatara min Lāhūt al-Masīḥwa-Ikhtafā, 1463
Kitāb al-Sulūk li-Ma'rifat Duwal al-Mulūk (Maqrīzī), 1525
Kitāb al-Tawārīkh. See Book of Chronicles
Kitāb al-Ṭurūḥāt wa-al-Abṣāliyyāt, 1464
Kitchener, Lord, 1466
Kiyahk (fourth month of Coptic calendar), 438, 441
  in the Copto-Arabic Synaxarion, 2178–2179
Kléber, Jean-Baptiste, 1333, **1416–1417**, 2351
Kneeler-penitents, 1932
Kneeling. *See* Genuflection
Knowledge Society, 1993
Kohl, boxes for, 2337–2338
Koine, 1166, 1168, 1169
  see also Greek language
Koinonia (community), 1664, 1859–1860, 1861, 1862, 1952
  see also Monasticism, Pachomian; Pachomius, Saint
Kom Abū Billū. *See* Tarnūt
Komēte (patrician), 1679
Kom Gu'aif. *See* Naucratis
Kom Namrūd, 1224, **1418**
Kom Ombo, **1418**, 1865
Kom al-Rāhib, **1418–1419**
Konkhistēs (Coptic textile term), 2221
Kootwyck, Iohann van, 1647
Koptos. *See* Qifṭ
Korakion (Millenarian), 911
Kothos (pagan deity), 1870
Koui (Khui), Governor of Aswan, tomb of, 850
Koukoullion (bishop's hood), 1476
Kounes (Khune), Governor of Aswan, tomb of, 850, 851
Krajon and Amun, Saints, **1419**, 1556
Krall, Jakob, **1419**
Krestodolu I, Ethiopian prelate, 1020
Krestodolu II, Ethiopian prelate, 1024–1025
Krestodolu III, Ethiopian prelate, 1028, 1349
Krikoris Vegayasayr (Armenian bishop), 234
Kubāniyyah, al-, 815–816
Kuentz, Charles, 1419
Kühnel, Ernst, **1419–1420**
Kula al-Hamra, al-. *See* Hermitages, Theban
Kunnāsh al-Thurayyā, 1922
Kurum al-Tuwal. *See* 'Amriyyah
Kush, Empire of, 110, **1420**
  and Nubians, 1797, 1800
  threat by Beja tribes, 373
Kutlah al-Wafdiyyah, al-. *See* Wafdist bloc
Kuttāh. *See* Scriptorium
Kutulus (martyr), 1553
Kuwait, Coptic church in, 1621
Kyprianos, spells of, 1506–1507
Kyriakos Mīkhā'īl. *See* Mīkhā'īl, Kyriakos
Kyrie eleison, **1420–1421**, 1469, 1569, 2013, 2014
  in the Book of Canonical Hours, 446–449
  for consecration of patriarchs, 1909–1910
  in Coptic Good Friday service, 1152
Kyrillos. *See* Ethiopian Prelates
Kyrillus. *See* Cyril
Kyrollos. *See* Cyril

L

Labib, Claudius. *See* Iqlādiyūs Labīb
Labib, Subhi Yanni, **1423**
Labib Ḥabachi, **1423**
Labla. *See* Monasteries of the Fayyūm
Labor contracts, 1429
Lacaron, Saint, **1423–1424**
  see also Krajon and Amun
Lacau, Pierre, 694, **1424**
Lacbat. *See* Aqbāṭ, al-
La Croze-Veyssière, Mathurin, **1424**, 2324
Lactantius
  criticism of Diocletian's policies, 906
  on incense use, 1472
Ladder of Divine Ascent (John Climacus), 2050
Ladeuze, Paulin, **1424**, 1452
Ladles, 1603
Laetentur coeli, 1119
Laferrière, P.-H., study of Dayr Anbā Anṭūniyūs, 726
L'Africain, Jean Léon, 826
Lagarde, Paul Anton de, **1424–1425**, 2067
Laḥn (musical term), 63, **1425**, 1722, 1727, 1729
  and *wāham*, 2313
Laḥn Idrībī, 1722
Laḥn Sinjārī, 1722
Lake Bardawil, 1650
Lake al-Burullus, 818, 837
Lake al-Ḥabash, 848, 881
Lake al-Manzalah, 1648–1649
Lake Mareotis, 24, 1526, 1527, 1931
Lake Maryūt, 34, 837

Lālibalā (community), 975, **1425–1426**
Lālibalā, Ethiopian king and saint, 1008, 1047–1048
Lalibela. *See* Lālibalā
Lamp of Darkness (Ibn Kabar). *See Misbāḥ al-Ẓulmah* (Ibn Kabar)
Lamps
altar lights, 109–110
dolphin-shaped, *2169*
glass, 1144–1145, *1144*
metalwork, 1596–1598, *1597*
terra-cotta, 494–497
see also Candles
Lanapourgós (Coptic weaving term), 2221
Lanários (Coptic weaving term), 2221
Lance tips, 1605
Land acquisitions, monastic, 1642
Land tax. *See Kharāj*
Land tenure, under Umayyad administration, 2287–2288
Lane-Poole, Stanley, 1733–1734
Language, Coptic
Abū Shākir ibn al-Rāhib, 33–34
Arab conquest of Egypt and decline in use of, 1460
Arabic-Coptic dictionary, 1302
Athanasius' Copto-Arabic grammar, 2045
Champollion, Jean François, scholarship, 516, 614
Coptic melody relationship, 1730–1731, 1734–1735
decline of, 1459, 1464
dialects, 1389
dictionary, 1424
grammars, 1266, 1268, 1302, 2045
Greek characters use, 1167, 1169
Ibn Kabar lexical work, 1267
inscriptions in, 1290–1296, 1408
inscriptions in the Kellia, 1408
Iqlādiyūs Labīb studies and promotion of, 1302
ʿIryān Jirjis Muftāḥ modernization efforts, 1302–1303
Life of Paul of Thebes in, 1926
linguistics, 33–34
literature in, 1450–1459
liturgical texts in, 1734–1735
Lives of Pachomius in, 1860, 1861–1862, 1863
magical words, 1500–1502
medieval Nubian clergy use of, 1813, 1816
as medium for Christianization, 1167, 1169, 1177
modern studies of, 1630
monasticism and diffusion of, 1168
Old Testament translations, 1836–1838
papyrus collections, 1890–1896
papyrus discoveries, 1898–1900
patristics and, 1920–1921
Plato's *Republic* translation, 1981
role in Alexandria, 101
Rückert, Friedrich, studies, 2067
spoken, 604–606
teachers of, 1962
see also Appendix; Bohairic dialect; Coptic language, spoken; Literature, Coptic; Literature, Copto-Arabic; Sahidic dialect; Toponymy, Coptic
Languages. *See* Arabic language; Dictionaries; Grammars; Greek language; Language, Coptic; Latin language; Meroitic language; Nubian languages and literature
Lantschoot, A. van, 1965–1966
Laodicea, Council of, on observances during Lent, 2099
Laographia (poll tax), Alexandrian exemptions, 1180
Laqqān, 1107–1108, 1252, **1426–1427**
Laqqānah, **1427**
bishopric of Damanhūr union with, 686
Lascaris, Theodore, 1114
Lascarpis. *See* Yaʿqub, General
Last Judgment. *See* Judgment, Last
Last Supper
and fraction rite, 1121
leavened vs. unleavened bread at, 1060–1061
Later Prophets, in Jewish canon, 2108
Latin fathers (patristics), 1920
Latin language
Egyptian papyri, 1889
impact on Greek language in Egypt, 1167–1168, 1169, 1176
Jerome, Saint, biblical translations into, 1323
Life of Paul of Thebes in, 1926
Life and Rules of Pachomius translation, 1663, 1861, 1862, 1863
papyrus collections, 1890
patristics in, 1920
Rufinus' translation and writings, 1237–1238, 2068–2069
Latopolis. *See* Isnā
Latrocinium. *See* Ephesus, Second Council of
Latson, Apa, saint, **1427**, 2085
Lāuntiyūs (Valentinus), 1577
Laura, **1428**
and Dayr al-Jabrāwī, 810, 811, 812
diaconia center, 896
keep construction, 1395–1396
and the monastery of Oktokaidekaton, 1826–1827
see also Hermitage
Laurentius, Saint, monasteries dedicated to, 850
Lausiac History (Palladius), 1733, 1862
on Ansinā (Antinoopolis), 142–143
on Scetis monks, 2103
Law
Codex Justinianus, 569–570, 905
Codex Theodosianus, 571
defensor ecclesiae, 891
dikaion term, 902
Dioscorus of Aphrodito, 916
on monastery assets, 1640
Muslim interpretations, 687
prefect's administration of, 2009
register, 1089
Law, canon. *See* Canon law
Law, Coptic, **1428–1431**
legal sources, 1438
Schiller, A. Arthur, as specialist in, 2106
Steinwenter, Artur, as historian of, 2149
Law, Egyptian, on Coptic Waqf, 2319
Law, Islamic, 951

Law, Islamic (*cont.*)
Ibn Qayyim al-Jawziyyah encyclopedia on, 1269–1270
Law, Mosaic
ablution prescribed by, 8–9
Augustine, Saint, on, 1930
on confession, 585–585
Law of obligations, 1429–1430, 1641
Law of persons, 1428–1429
Law of things, 1429
Laying-on of hands, **1432–1433**, 1910
at bishop's consecration, 397
Lay members of church. *See* Archon
Layton, B., 1893
Lead collars. *See* Alexander, II
Leases, 1429
Leatherwork, Coptic, **1433**
in Louvre Museum, 1483
pen cases, 1933
preservation, 280
see also Bookbinding
Leavened bread, and Eucharist, 1060–1061
Lebanon
Coptic churches in, 1621
monasteries, 877
Lebna Dengel, 1016–1017
Lecanoscopy, 1507–1508
Lectern, **1434–1435**
Lectionary, **1435–1437**, 1449
for Church of Muʿallaqah, 1775
and evangeliary, 1077
Ibrāhīm ibn Sulaymān al-Najjār al-Mīrī copies, 1273
manuscripts in National Library, Paris, 1778
Mass of the Catechumens, 1562
Leda, depicted in Coptic art, 1763
Leeder, S. H., 1466
Lefebvre, Gustave
on Dayr Anbā Bākhūm, 729
students of, 694
Lefort, Louis Théophile, **1437**, 1448, 1453
on Letter of Ammon, 1445
on Life of Pachomius, 1860, 1861, 1863
Mark II homily discovery, 1534
Left Bank (Nile). *See* Monasteries of the Upper Ṣaʿīd
Legal procedure, Coptic, 1430–1431
Legal sources, Coptic, **1438**
Legion. *See* Army, Roman
LeGrain, Georges, **1439**
Leiden, University of, 1424
Leipoldt, Johannes, 614, **1439**, 1452
Lemm, Oskar Eduardovich von, **1439**, 14448
Lenormant, Charles, **1440**
Lent
Dionysius the Great on, 912
fasting during, 1093, 1094–1095
fasting on Saturday during, 2098, 2099
and genuflection, 1139
lectionary for, 1437
Palm Sunday and, 1103–1104
see also Good Friday; Great Lent; Maundy Thursday
Leo III, Emperor, edict banning images, 1275, 1276, 1277
Leo I, Emperor
patriarch under, 1915
and relics of the Three Hebrews in the Furnace, 2259
and Timothy Aelurus, 1441, 1671, 2264
Zeno as successor, 2369
Leo V, Emperor, 1275
Leo I the Great, Pope (Rome), **1440–1442**
and Chalcedon, Council of, 512, 513–515
Christology, 1670, 1671, 1672
on *communicatio idiomatum*, 578
as Coptic saint, 2085
and Dioscorus I, 525, 913, 914, 915
and Ephesus, Second Council of, 961–962
and Ephesus, Third Council of, 962
and Eutyches, 1074–1075
and Henoticon, 1218
and paschal controversy, 1906
and Pulcheria, 2033
and Theophilus, Patriarch, 2247, 2251
and Timothy II Aelurus, Patriarch, 2264, 2267
see also Tome of Leo
Leo II, Pope (Rome), on *filioque*, 1112–1113
Leo IV the Khazar, Emperor, 1275
Leonidas (martyr and Origen's father), 892, 1846, 1936
Leontius of Antioch, and Lucian of Antioch, 1484
Leontius of Byzantium, 1455, 1676
Leontius of Tripoli, Saint (martyr), **1442–1444**, 1556
Leprosy, 1581
Lepsius, Karl Richard, 717, **1444**
Le Quien, Michel, **1444**
Leroy, Jules, 726, 868, **1444**
Letronne, Jean Antoine, **1444–1445**
Letter of Ammon, 894, **1445**
on Antinoopolis, 144
and Theodorus of Alexandria, Saint, 2238
Letter of Peter to Philip, **1446**
and *Interpretation of Knowledge*, 1301
Letters. *See* Epistolography
Letters (Dionysius), 911–912
Letters of synods. *See* Synods, letters of
Lewata (Berber tribe), 1652
Libanius, 1308, **1447**
Libānos (Maṭṭā), Ethiopian saint, 1045
Libellus de processione Spiritus Sancti, 1115
Liberal Constitutional Party, 1991–1992
Liberal Socialists Center, 1991
Libraries, **1447–1449**
Alexandria, 100, 1447
Bodmer (Bibliotheca Bodmeriana), 404
in colophons, 577
Dayr Anbā Anṭūniyūs, 723
Dayr Anbā Maqār, 749, 750
Dayr Anbā Ṣamū'īl of Qalamūn, 758
Dayr Anbā Shinūdah, 763
Dayr al-Malāk Mīkhā'īl, 824
Dayr Nahyā, 843
Dayr al-Suryān, 876, 877, 878
monastic medical literature, 1578–1579
Nag Hammadi Library, 1771–1773
patriarchal, 1532
travelers' interest in, 1977
see also Archives; Literature, Coptic; Manuscripts; Museums, Coptic collections in; specific libraries
Library of the Coptic Patriarchate, 901

Library of Karl Marx University (Leipzig), 1893
Libri Carolini (790), 1112
Libya
  Coptic churches in, 1621
  see also Pentapolis
Libyan massif. *See* Western Desert
Lichtheim, M., 2022
Licinius, Emperor, 588–589, 1869
  conflict with Constantine, 81
  Neocaesarea, Council of, in reign of, 1785
  patriarch under, 1914
  persecutions under, 1937
Licinius (Roman officer), 1558
Līf, Abū. *See* Dayr Abū al-Līf
Lifāfah, 1472
Life of Abba Paul, the Holy Anchorite (Amélineau), 1926
Life of Basil (Amphilochius), 1593
Life of Dioscorus (Theopistus of Alexandria), 2254
Life of Eusebius of Samosata, 1593
Life of Hilarion, 1664
Life of Isidore (Damascius), 1221, 1222
Life of Longinus, on the Enaton, 955, 956
Life of Patape, 1907–1908
Life of Phib, 1953
Life of Pisentius (John the Presbyter), 1368, 1455–1456
Life of Poemen, 1983–1984
Life of Saint Antony (Athanasius), 101, 116, 119, 300, 302, 728, 1663
  on anachoresis, 119
  circulated in Gaul, 255
  collected manuscript of, 1782
  on devil as black, 248
  Latin translation in Ireland, 418
Life of Saint Jimyānah/Dimyānah (John of Parallos), 871
Life of Saint Pachomius, 1663, 1859, 1860–1861, 1952, 2207
  collected manuscripts of, 1782
  Letter of Ammon, 1445
  on Theodorus of Tabennēsē, 2240
Life of Saint Paul the First Hermit (Jerome), 1925–1926
Life of Saint Sabas, 894
Life of Samū'īl of Qalamūn, 758
Life of Shenute, 898
Lighting equipment. *See* Candles; Lamps
Lime, 1402
Limestone, Coptic sculpture in, 2113, 2115
Linen, use in Coptic textiles, *2211*, 2211–2212
Lingua aegyptiaca restituta: Scala Magna, hoc est nomenclator aegyptiaco-arabicus. See Scala Magna
Linguistics, Coptic, 33–34
  see also Appendix; Language, Coptic; specific dialects
Linoplygtēs (Coptic textile term), 2221
Linoúphos (Coptic weaving term), 2221
Lintels, wooden, 2342–2344, *2343*
Liqānos, Ethiopian saint, 1047
Listener-penitents, 1932
Literacy, under Roman administration of Egypt, 1168
Literary, scholarly, and religious offices or titles. *See* Copts in late medieval Egypt
Literature. *See* Apocalyptic literature; Apocryphal literature; Ethiopian Christian literature; Literature, Coptic; Literature, Copto-Arabic; Literature, Nubian; Literature, pagan Christian; Poetry; specific languages and works
Literature, Christian, patristics, 1920–1921
Literature, Coptic, **1450–1459**
  on Alexander I, 84–85
  beginnings of, 1450–1452
  cycle, 666–668
  Eusebius of Caesarea, 1070–1071
  fourth- and fifth-century translations, 1453–1454
  Gabriel, Archangel in, 1136–1137
  Gabriel II, Patriarch, contribution, 1129
  Gregory of Nazianzus's works, 1183–1184
  Gregory of Nyssa's works, 1184–1185
  healings in, 1212–1214
  on John the Baptist, 1356
  John Chrysostom's works, 459–460, 1356, 1357–1359, 1454
  Life of Pachomius, 1860
  Mark II homily, 1534
  on martyrdom of Philotheus of Antioch, 1961
  on martyrs, 1881
  medical, 1578–1579, 1581, 1582
  on Michael, Archangel, 1618–1619
  Mīkhā'īl, Bishop of Atrīb and Malīj, 1626
  ninth-to-eleventh-century decline, 1458–1459
  Patrologia orientalis, 1921
  poetry, 1985–1986
  Proclus' works, 1356, 1454, 2017–2019
  romances, 2059–2060
  seventh- and eighth-century, 1458–1458
  Shenute texts, 1452–1453
  sixth-century, 1454–1455
  tradition of Victor Stratelates, Saint, 2303–2304
  see also Cycles; Hagiography; Homilies; Language, Coptic; Papyri, Coptic literary; Poetry; Scholars
Literature, Copto-Arabic, **1460–1467**
  Abū Isḥāq ibn Faḍlallāh works, 19–20
  Abū Shākir ibn al-Rāhib's works, 33–34
  first works in Arabic language, 19–20
  al-Maqrīzī works, 1268–1269
  modern Egyptian liberal trends in, 1995
  al-Ṣafī ibn al-'Assāl, 2075–2079
  Sawīrus ibn al-Muqaffa', 2100–2102
  tradition of Victor Stratelates, Saint, 2305–2308
Literature, Ethiopian Christian. *See* Ethiopian Christian literature
Literature, Greek. *See* Greek language
Literature, Nubian, 1815–1816
Literature, pagan classical
  Libanius, 1447
  Physiologos stories, 1965–1966
Lithargoel, 61–62
Lithazomenon and Saint Peter's Bridge (monasteries), **1467**
Liturgical insignia, **1468–1469**
Liturgical instruments, **1469–1474**
  for ablution, 9
  deacon's role, 885
  Eucharistic, 1063–1066

Liturgical instruments (*cont.*)
metalwork, *1595*, 1595–1596
wood coffers for, 2329–2330, *2330*
Liturgical vestments, **1475–1479**
for bishop's consecration, 395–396
for consecration of patriarchs, 1910
Muslim restrictions, 1130
used in Epiphany, Liturgy of the, 967–968
see also Costume of the religious
Liturgy
ablution during, 9
Arabic translations, 1464
Coptic commentary on, 1267, 1272
deacon as response leader, 885
epiclesis, 964
Epiphany, 967–968; *see also subheads* Mass of the Catechumens; Mass of the Faithful
Epiphany, 967–968
Ethiopian, 987–990, 997–998
eucharistic, 120–121, 1058–1060
fraction in, 1121
Gabriel, Archangel in, 1137
and genuflection, 1139
Gloria in excelsis and, 1147
Good Friday, 1152–1153
for *hegumenos* ordination, 1216
Holy Saturday, 1247–1249, 1249
hosanna use in, 1258
hymn of the Twelve Virtues, 2310
Incarnation references, 1287
Kyrie eleison in baptism, 343
language of, 1134
Lord's Prayer in, 1480–1481
marriage service, 1543–1545
Mass of the Catechumens, 1562–1565
Mass of the Faithful, 1565–1568
of matins, 1568–1569
music and, 1715–1729, 1743, 2058
Nubian, 1816–1817
penitents and, 1932
physical accessories, 1434–1437
prayers of absolution in, 16–17
prayers for the dead in, 889
and Psalmodia, 2024
on Saturday, 2099–2100
seasons and, 443–444
Sunday worship, 2159
Trisagion, 2278–2279
and *Typikon of Saint Sabas*, 2046
see also Anaphora headings; Feasts; Hail Mary
Liturgy of Saint Basil, 1540, 1715, 1716, 1721, *1716–1723*, 1733, 1737, 1742
Liturgy of Saint Cyril, 1716
Liturgy of Saint Gregory, 120–121, 967–968, 1715–1716
Liturgy of Saint Mark, 120–121, 1539–1540
see also Liturgy of Saint Cyril
Lives of the Eastern Saints (John of Ephesus), 1362
The Lives of the Desert Fathers, 1238
Lives of Pachomius, 1663, 1782, 1859, 1860–1861, 1928, 1952, 2207
Lives of the Prophets, 166
see also Paralipomena Jeremiou
Livinus (Franciscan martyr), 1122
Le Livre des perles enfouies. See Book of the Hidden Pearls
Liwā', al- (publication), 1748, 2011
Loans. *See* Law, Coptic: Law of obligations; Private Law
Lōbsh (musical term), 63, 900, **1479**, 1726, 1727
and *tafsīr*, 2199
and Theotokion, 2255
and *Wāṭus*, 2320
Lōbsh Adām, 1479
Lōbsh Wāṭus, 1479
Logia, 1531
Logos
in Alexandrian theology, 103–104
Apollinarianism and, 173–174
Arius and Arianism on, 232, 240
Authentikos Logos, 309
Damian discourse on, 689
Origen on, 103, 1638, 1790–1791, 1848, 1849–1850
Philo on, 1957
see also Christ, nature of; Gnosticism
Longinus (martyr). *See* Paul, Longinus, and Zeno (martyrs)
Longinus, Bishop, 688, **1479–1480**, 1948
and Beja tribes, 373
and conversion of 'Alwā, 110
and conversion of Nubia, 1797, 1801–1802
and Theodosius I, 2241
Longinus of Enaton, Saint, 360, 955, 956–957, 1196
feast day, 2085
Looms, Coptic textile, 2215–2217
Lord's Day. *See* Sunday
Lord's Prayer, 122, 123, 124, **1480–1481**, 1568, 1569
and *apa* title, 152
in Book of Canonical Hours, 446–449
Evagrius Ponticus Coptic paraphrase, 1077
music for, 1721
Lord's Supper. *See* Eucharist
Lot, 1618
Louis IX, saint and king of France, 314–315, 925, 1524
Louis the German, 1110
Louis the Pious, 1110
Louvain, University of, 1424, 1452
Louvre Museum, Paris, France, 1139, 1452, **1481–1483**, 1509, 1588, 1589, 1596, 1598, 1601
letters of Pisentius in, 1979
papyrus collection, 1892
pen cases at, 1933
see also Art, historiography of Coptic
Love charms, 1504–1506
Lower Ṣa'īd, monasteries of, 1652–1653
Lucas, Paul, 1973, 1977
Lucchesi, E., 1892
Lucian of Antioch, **1484**
and Arius, 231, 1790
and the school of Antioch, 231–232
Lucianus, 2245
Lucilianus and four companions (martyrs), 1556
Lucinius, Governor, 1554
Lucius (Arian presbyter), 1947
Lucius of Enaton. *See* Enaton, The
Lucius Septimius Severus. *See* Septimius Severus
Luke, Apostle and Saint
on the Ascension of Christ, 244
see also Gospel of Saint Luke
Lusterware, *1146*, 1146, *1147*, 1311, 1312
Lute, 1740–1741, *1741*

Luṭfallāh (archon), 722, 1949–1950
Luther, Martin (and Lutheranism), 578, 597, 2110
Luxor, **1484**
castrum of, 237, 465–466, *466*
Coptic churches on temple sites, 1870
martyrs at, 1553
monasteries near, 717, 785–786, 1657
monastic murals at, 1874
stelae from, 2149
tombstone material, 1295
Luxor temples, 196, **1484–1485**, 1870, 1865
Lūzah al-Asyūṭī, Naṣr, 1465
Lycopolis. *See* Asyūṭ
Lycopolitan dialect
in Old Testament, Coptic translations of, 1837–1838
see also Appendix
Lyons, Second Council of (1274), 1114, 1115

M

Maʿādī, pilgrimages to, 1973
Mabarī, Shaykh, tomb of, 853
Macarius, homilies of Pseudo-. *See* Pseudo-Macarius, homilies of
Macarius I, Saint and Patriarch, **1487**
and consecration of holy chrism, 521
dates of patriarchy, 1916
and Ethiopian prelates, 1002
feast day, 2085
Macarius II, Saint and Patriarch, **1487–1488**, 1652
in Azarī, 315–316
burial, 1128
dates of patriarchy, 1917
feast day, 2085
and Mikā'ēl I, Ethiopian prelate, 1006
Macarius III, Patriarch, **1488–1489**, 1911
dates of patriarchy, 1919
on divorce, 1943
and Ethiopian church autocephaly, 980–981
and Ethiopian prelates, 1043
as monk at Dayr Anbā Bishoi, 735
and performance of Liturgy of Saint Cyril, 1716
and Sarjiyūs, Malatī, 2011, 2096, 2097
successor, 2363
Macarius, Saint (martyr son of Basilides), 892, **1489**, 1556
Macarius Alexandrinus, Saint, 1876, **1489–1490**, 1491, 2085, 2239
as desert father, 894
and Evagrius Ponticus, 1076
and Kellia community, 1397
Paphnutius of Scetis as disciple of, 1883, 1884
Macarius the Canonist, **1490–1491**
canonical collection of, 1780
and *Canons of Epiphanius*, 456–457
and *Canons of Hippolytus*, 458
and canons of Nicaea, 1789
and Octateuch of Clement, 1824
Macarius the Egyptian, Saint, **1491**
and Antony, Saint, 150
and Bessarion, Saint, 2082
churches dedicated to, 1969
and Dayr al-Baramūs, 789, 790
as desert father, 894
and Evagrius Ponticus, 1076
feast day, 2085
and Gregory of Nyssa writings, 1184
and homily of Amphilochius of Iconium, 115
and Macarius Alexandrinus, 1490
and Maximus and Domitius, Saints, 1576–1577, 1967
monastic settlement, 748–756
and Onophrius, Saint, 1842
and Pambo, Saint, 1878
Paphnutius the Hermit as disciple of, 1883
and Poemen, Saint, 1983–1984
and Pseudo-Macarius, 2027–2028
on respect for one's body, 958–959
and Scetis, 2102–2103
and Silvanus of Scetis, Saint, 2087, 2137
as subject in Coptic art, 270, 1842
see also Dayr Anbā Maqār
Macarius the Great. *See* Macarius the Egyptian, Saint
Macarius of Nikiou, Bishop, 1794, 1794
Macarius the Painter. *See* Macarius II, Saint and Patriarch
Macarius of Scetis. *See* Macarius the Egyptian, Saint
Macarius of Tkow, Saint and Bishop, **1492–1494**
on the Assumption, 290
Dioscorus encomium on, 400
feast day, 2085
funeral of, 1610, 1611
martyrdom, 1556, 1617
on Michael, Archangel, 1618
and Monastery of the Metanoia, 1609
panegyric, 1455, 1882
Maccabees, Books of the, 166
MacCoull, L. S. B., 1895, 1896, 2022
Macedonia. *See* Greek headings
Macedonius, Patriarch of Constantinople, 43, 44, 1672–1674
Macrina, Saint, 1468
Macrobius, Saint and Bishop, **1494**
and Dayr Abū Maqrūfah and Dayr al-Janādlah, 704, 705
feast day, 2085
martyrdom, 1494, 1556
panegyric on, 1456
Madamūd, **1494–1495**, *1495*
Madaris al-Aqbat al-Kubra. *See* Education
Madīnat Ghurān, excavations, 1651
Madīnat Hābū, 53, **1496–1497**, *1496*, 1586, 2022
ampullae from, 534
Dayr al-Amīr Tadrūs, 717, 1656
Dayr al-Rūmī, 856–857, 1656
Dayr al-Shahīd Tadrus al-Muḥārib, 862
hermitages found nearby, 1225
pharaonic temple of, 196
Madīnat Māḍī, **1497–1499**, *1497*
monastery of Saint George at, 824
papyrus discoveries, 1899
Madness, theme of simulated, 1541
Madonna and Child. *See* Virgin Enthroned
Maghāgha, Dayr al-Jarnūs, 813

Magic, **1499–1508**
abraxas (word with numerical value), 14
Gabriel, Archangel, role, 1137
Gnostic vowels, 1732, 1735
Iamblichus defense of, 1265
in Islamic period, 1504–1506
Plotinus refutation of, 1982
spell elements, 1502–1504
Stegemann, Viktor, texts on Coptic, 2148
Magical objects, **1509–1510**
Nubian *hījabs*, 1814
see also Amulets
Magician, 1500
Magnentius (Diocletian courtier), 1140
Magnus Maximus, Emperor, 1964
Maḥallah al-Kubrā, al-, **1510**
Maḥallat Abū ʿAlī, **1510**
Maḥallat al-Amīr, **1511**
Maḥallat Dāniyāl, patriarchal residence at, 1633, 1912, 1959
Maḥallat Minūf, **1511**
Maḥammah, al-, 1118
Maharati (martyr), 1556
Māhir, Aḥmad, 1992, 1993
Maḥmūd Sulaymān Pasha, 1987
Maiestas Domini (icon), 778, *1278*
Majallah al-Jadīdah, al- (journal), 2088
Majlā ibn Nasṭūrus, 1097
Majlis Milli, al-. *See* Community Council, Coptic
Majmaʿ (term), 819
Majmūʿ al-Mubārak, al-, 1513
Majmūʿ al-Ṣafawī, al- (al-Ṣafī ibn al-ʿAssāl), 1106, 1462, 1545, 2076
Majmūʿ Uṣūl al-Dīn (Compendium of the Fundamentals of Religion), **1511**
Makārī al-Suryānī, Father. *See* Samuel, Bishop
Makarius Salib. *See* Salippe Mikarius
Makāryus Ḥunayn, **1511–1512**
Makhūrah (Mareotis), **1512–1513**
Makīn, ibn al-ʿAmīd, al- (thirteenth century), 977, 1463, **1513**
Makīn Jirjis, al- (*hegumenos*), **1513**
Makin Jirjis ibn al-ʿAmīd, al- (fourteenth century), collected histories of, 1780–1781
Makouria, 38, 923, 1420, **1513–1515**, 1588
and 'Alwā, 110
and Banū al-Kanz, 336
and *Baqṭ* treaty, 343
Beja tribe attacks, 373
Chalcedon conversion, 1675
Dongola as capital, 921–922
Jabal ʿAddā fortress, 1315
and Nobatia, 1797, 1798, 1800
and Nubian evangelization, 1801, 1813
and Nubian Islamization, 1802, 1803
and Nubian languages and literature, 1815–1816
Shibāb al-Dīn Aḥmad Nuwayrī on, 2136
Tafa settlement, 2198
travel writing on, 1271–1272
Makram Aghā, 1636
Makramallāh the *Hegumenos*, 1335, **1515**
Makram Ebeid, 1466, **1515–1516**, 1990, 1993, 2011
Malabar. *See* India
Malachi, 22
Malāk Mīkhā'īl of Sibirbāy, al-, 1969
Malan, S. C., 1525
Malaṭī Yūsuf, **1516**, 1539
Malchion (Antiochean theologian), 1575
Malīḥ, Abū al-, 1268
Malīj, **1516**, 1655
Malik al-Kāmil ibn ʿĀdil, al-, sultan, 833, 1524, 1691, 1749
Malik al-Muʿazzam, al-, 1691
Malik al-Nāṣir Ṣalāḥ al-Dīn, al-, 1691
Mālik al-Ṣāliḥ Ṣalāḥ al-Dīn Ḥajjī, al-, 1548
Malinine, Michel, **1516**
Mallawī, Dayr Abū Ḥinnis at, 701–703
Mallidis. *See* Manqabād
Mallon, Marie Alexis, **1516**
Mama (martyr), 1556
Mamluks, **1517–1518**, 1856, 1857
ʿAlwā and, 110
Būlus al-Ḥabīs rescue of Dhimmis, 424–425, 1517
Christian tensions and encounters, 2317–2319
Ibrāhīm al-Jawharī, 1857
Islamization and, 940, 2313–2319
Jirjis al-Jawharī role, 1332–1333
Makouria and, 1514
Mark VII patriarchy, 1538
Matthew I patriarchy, 1570
occupations, offices, and titles under. *See* Copts in late medieval Egypt
patriarchs and rulers, 1917–1918
persecutions, 941, 1343, 1517–1518, 1535, 1949, 2314–2316
Peter VI patriarchy, 1949–1950
Rizq Agha and, 2059
Waqʿat al-Kanāʾis (Incident of the Churches), 2313–2316
Waqʿat al-Naṣārā (Christian encounter), 2316–2319
see also French expedition in Egypt
Man-, as prefix to place-names, 2273
Manār, al- (publication), 1996
Manārah al-Miṣriyyah, al- (publication), 2010
Manassā Yūḥannā, **1518**
Manasseh, Saint, 11, **1518**, 2085
Mandaean gnostics, 917
Mandal. See Lecanoscopy
Mandorla. *See* Symbols in Coptic Art
Mandouze, A., 2022
Mani
canon of sacred writings, 1149, 1519, 1520, 1521
and Maximus the Confessor, 1575
papyrus discoveries, 1899
see also Manichaeism
Manichaeism, **1519–1522**
abstinence practice, 17
Alexander of Lycopolis and, 87–88
in Alexandria, 98–99
on celibacy, 1543
Diocletian edict against, 905, 1936
and gnosticism, 1149, 1150, 1151, 1162
Greco-Coptic adherents, 1177
Hieracas of Leontopolis and, 1229
Maximus the Confessor and, 1575
Neoplatonism and, 1982
and origins of monasticism in Egypt, 1661

papyri collections and discoveries, 519, 1885, 1889, 1894
Sarapion of Tmuis work attacking, 2096
on Satan, 1184
scholarship on, 2032, 2033
Le Manichéisme, son fondateur, sa doctrine (Puech), 2032
Manqabād, **1523**
Manqabādī, Nabīl al-, 730
Manqabādī, Tadrus Shinudah al-, 2011
Manṣah, al-. *See* Psoï
Manshūbiyyas (dwellings for groups of monks), 749
Mansi, Giovanni Domenico, 347, **1523–1524**
Manṣūr, ʿAbdallah, **1524**
Manṣūr, Boktor, 1524
Manṣūr, Mikhā'īl, 1467
Manṣūr, Yūssuf, 1737
Manṣūrah, al-, **1524**, 1648, 2270
Manṣūr ibn Sahlān ibn Muqashshir, 6, **1524–1525**
Manṣūrī, Muṣṭafā Ḥasanayn al-, 1996
Manṣūr Qalāwūn, king of Egypt, 1630
Manṣūr al-Tilbānī, 872
Manual cross. *See* Cross, manual
Manufacturing techniques, Coptic textiles, 2213–2218, *2216–2218*
Manuscripts
of ʿAbdallāh ibn Mūsā, 3–4
of ʿAbd al-Masīḥ, 5
of Abū Isḥāq ibn Faḍlallāh, 19–20
Abū al-Munā acquisitions, 29
of Agathon of Ḥomṣ, 67–68
archives, 226–227
Bodmer Papyrus, 380–382
cataloging of Coptic, 1138, 1700
Chester Beatty collection, 380–381, 382, 518–519
codex, 565–566
codex cover, *409*
codicology, 572–573
colophon, 577
copied by Abīb ibn Naṣr, 8
copied by Abū al-Munā, 30
copied by Abū Naṣr ibn Hārūn ibn ʿAbd al-Masīḥ, 31
copied by Abū Saʿīd ibn Sayyid al-Dār ibn Abī al-Faḍl al-Masīḥī, 32
copied by Anṭūniyūs Mulūkhiyyah, 151–152
copied by Gregory II, patriarch, 1182
copied by Ibrāhīm ibn Sulaymān al-Najjār al-Mīrī, 1273
copied by Ibrāhīm ibn Simʿān, 1515
copied by Jirjis ibn al-Qass Abī al-Mufaḍḍal, 1270
copied by Tūmā ibn al-Najīb Lutfallāh, 2281–2282
copied by Tūmā ibn al-Ṣā'igh, 1270
Coptic literature, 1450–1459
copying at Dayr al-Baramūs, 791
copying at Dayr Durunkah, 799
from Dayr Anbā Sāwīrus, 760
from Dayr al-Malāk Mīkhā'īl, 824
from Dayr al-Nasṭūr, 848
difnār, 901
Dumyāṭ as copying center, 926
of early Greek musical notation, 1731–1732
Egerton Gospel, 933–934
Gabriel II as copyist, compiler, and translator, 1129
Greek Bible, 380–382
Hamburg Papyrus, 380–382, 1204–1205
illuminated. *See* Illumination, Coptic
Liturgy of Saint Mark texts, 1539–1540
in Louvre Museum, 1483
Macarius the Canonist collection, 1490–1491
modern, at Dayr Anbā Maqār, 756
Oxyrhynchus Papyri, 1857–1858
Petersen scholarship, 1951
Pietro delle Valle collection, 1967
preservation, 279
restoration by Ibscher, Hugo, 1274–1275
from Scetis, 748
see also Archives; Bookbinding; Libraries; Nag Hammadi Library; National Library, Paris; Papyri, Coptic headings; Papyrus collections; Papyrus discoveries; Scribes; Scriptorium; specific titles
Manyal Shīḥah, pilgrimages to, 1973
Manzalah, al-, 1648
see also Monasteries of the province of Daqahliyyah
Maqārah, Abba. *See* Macarius II
Maqārah, Anbā. *See* Macarius I
Maqārah of Scetis. *See* Macarius the Egyptian, Saint
Maqrīzī, Taqīy al-Dīn al-, **1525**
on Armenian and Coptic churches, 234
on Babylonian churches, 318
on *Baqṭ* treaty, 343, 1099
on Christodoulus, 546–547
on churches in Hiw, 1242–1243
on Church of Saint Michael, 1617
on church in Ṭanbidā, 2201
on convents, 2325
on Coptic Christian tensions and encounters under the Mamluks, 2317–2319
on Coptic revolts, 50
on Cyril III ibn Laqlaq, Patriarch, 675
on Dayr Abū al-Sayfayn (Tamwayh), 712
on Dayr Anbā Anṭūniyūs, 722
on Dayr Anbā Bishoi, 738
on Dayr Anbā Helias, 748
on Dayr Anbā Shinūdah, 764
on Dayr Apa Anūb, 770
on Dayr Apa Hor, 770–771
on Dayr al-Arman, 782
on Dayr al-ʿAskar, 783
on Dayr Bālūjah, 788
on Dayr Durunkah, 799
on Dayr al-Jūʿ, 814
on Dayr al-Khādīm location, 145
on Dayr al-Maghṭis
on Dayr al-Malāk Mīkhā'īl, 823
on Dayr Mār Mīnā (Jabal Abū Fūdah), 834
on Dayr al-Maymah (Gharbiyyah), 835, 837
on Dayr al-Muḥarraq, 840
on Dayr al-Muṭṭin, 842–843
on Dayr al-Qurqāṣ, 852
on Dayr al-Sabʿat Jibāl, 857
on Dayr Sitt Dimyānah, 870–871
on Durunkah, 926–927
on the Enaton, 957–958
family and accomplishments, 1268–1269

Maqrīzī, Taqīy al-Dīn al- (*cont.*)
on Feast of the Martyr, 1548
on Feast of Saint John, 882
on Gabriel V, Patriarch, 1131
on Ibn Mammātī, 1462
and Ibn Salīm al-Aswānī's Nubian account, 1271
on Idfā, 1280
on Islamic persecutions of Copts. *See subhead* on persecution of Copts
on Islamization of Egypt, 938
on John VI, 1341
on Mamluk persecutions. *See subhead* on persecution of Copts
on Mareotis, 1527
on Nawrūz, 1784
on persecution of Copts, 1343, 1535, 1949, 2314–2316
Maqṣūrah, 213
Maqta'. *See* Altar-board
Marāghah, Dayr al-Malāk Mīkhā'īl, 826
Mar'ah al-Jadīdah, al- (Amīn), 1994
Mār Awjīn (Eugene), 565
Marble, Coptic sculpture in, 2113, 2115
Mār Buqṭūr. *See* Dayr Abū al-Sayfayn
Marcel, Jean-Joseph, **1526**, 1696
Marcellus, Bishop of Ancyra, 178, **1526**, 1791
Marcellus, Saint (Scetis ascetic), 2085
Marcian, Emperor, 914, 1441, 1670, 2033
and Chalcedon, Council of, 512–513, 514, 515
patriarch under, 1915
Marcianus, Patriarch, **1526**
dates of patriarchy, 1914
Marcinus, Emperor, patriarch under, 1914
Marcion (Docetist), 917, 1148
Marco Polo, 1635
Marcus. *See* Mark I, Apostolic Saint and Patriarch
Marcus (monk), 692
Marcus (Roman governor), 903
Marcus Aurelius, Emperor
patriarch under, 72, 1914
visit to Egypt, 2062
Marcus Aurelius Antoninus. *See* Caracalla, Emperor
Marea. *See* Hawāriyyah
Mareotis, **1526–1527**
see also Makhūrah; Maryūt
Mareotis, Coptic paintings at, **1527–1528**
Marian Homily I (Proclus), 2017
Mariette, A., 780
Marina, Saint, 2085
Maris of Chalcedon, 84, 1484
Mariyyah the Copt, **1528**
Mār Jirjis. *See* George, Saint
Mark, Liturgy of Saint, 120–121, **1539–1540**
Mark, Secret Gospel of. *See* Secret Gospel of Saint Mark
Mark I, Apostolic Saint and Patriarch, **1528–1533**
Alexandrian apostolic succession from, 181
anaphora used in Ethiopian liturgy, 988
and Anianus, 133
on Ascension of Christ, 244
burial site, 92
and the Catechetical School of Alexandria, 469, 474
churches dedicated to, 92, 1532–1533; *see also* specific churches
contribution to Coptic church, 1532–1533
dates of patriarchy, 1913
and Dayr Asfal al-Arḍ, 783
and Divine Liturgy of the Eucharist, 120–121
as Evangelist Mark, 1078
feast day, 2085
as first patriarch of Coptic Church, 134, 2193
introduction of Christianity into Egypt, 103, 1866
and Jerusalem, 1324
and John of Shmūn writings, 1369
Liturgy of. *See* Liturgy of Saint Cyril; Liturgy of Saint Mark
martyrdom and relics, 546, 678, 1131, 1531–1532, 1556, 1573, 1646, 1910
and Metropolitan See of Pentapolis, 1612
Monastery of Mark the Evangelist (Qurnat Mar'ī), 2042
paintings of, 1532
panegyrics on, 1456
relics. *See subhead* martyrdom and relics
relics returned to Anbā Ruways Cathedral, 678
sanctuary of, 751
Venetian acquisition of relics of, 1131
see also Cathedral of Saint Mark; Gospel of Saint Mark; Mark, Liturgy of; Secret Gospel of Saint Mark
Mark II, Saint and Patriarch, 427, **1533–1534**
and Barsanuphians, 347
and Church of the Savior (Alexandria), 94
dates of patriarchy, 1916
and Enaton visit requirement, 958
and Eucharist heresy, 1057
feast day, 2085
Nabarūh residency, 1769
successor, 1318
Yuḥannā biography of, 2356
and Yūsāb I, 2362
Mark III, Saint and Patriarch, **1534–1536**
and Basṭah church, 361
on canon law, 450
Coptic texts of, 1456, 1461
dates of patriarchy, 1917
and Dayr al-Nasṭūr, 848
feast day, 2085
successor, 1341
Mark IV, Patriarch, **1536–1537**
dates of patriarchy, 1918
and Jirjis ibn al-Qass Abi al-Mufaḍḍal, 1332
Mark V, Patriarch, **1537**
dates of patriarchy, 1919
Mark VI, Patriarch, **1537**
dates of patriarchy, 1919
as monk at Dayr Anbā Anṭūniyūs, 722
Mark VII, Patriarch, **1537–1538**
and Coptic relations with Rome, 610–611
dates of patriarchy, 1919
death at Dayr al-'Adawiyyah church, 713
and Ethiopian prelate, 1029–1030
as monk at Dayr Anbā Būlā, 742
successor, 1350
Mark VIII, Patriarch, 1274, **1538–1539**
dates of patriarchy, 1919
liturgical music, 1736
as monk at Dayr Anbā

Anṭūniyūs, 723
patriarchal residence, 1913
and property of Jirjis al-Jawharī, 1334
successor, 1950
Mark of Ephesus, 1114
Mark the Evangelist. *See* Mark I, Apostolic Saint and Patriarch
Mark of al-Faramā, Bishop, 1089
Mark ibn Qanbar, collected commentaries of, 1776–1777
Mark the Mad (monk), 1931
Mark (Murqus) of the Beheirah, Bishop, 1911
Markos, Apa, 2042
Marks, funerary. *See* Portraiture
Mark the Simple, Saint, **1540–1541**, 2085
Mār Minā Cultural Association, **1541**
Mārqos I, Ethiopian prelate, 1016–1017
Mārqos II, Ethiopian prelate, 1019
Mārqos III, Ethiopian prelate, 1022–1023
Mārqos IV, Ethiopian prelate, 1026–1027
Marqūrah. *See* Mercurius of Caesarea
Mār Qūrus, 1593
Marquṣ, Bishop of Damietta, **1541–1542**, 2046
Marqus, Bishop of Qūsqām and al-Qūsiyyah, 840
Marquṣ, Bishop of Sinai, 2046
Marqus al-Anṭūnī, 30, **1542**
Marqus ibn Qanbar, 1652
Marriage, **1542–1546**
in ancient Egyptian, 1086
and anointing, 139
church-state legal issues, 1941, 1942–1943
Coptic, 1087
Coptic ceremonial celebration on Saturday or Sunday, 2159
Coptic ceremony, 1543–1545
Coptic customs, 1545–1546
Coptic law and legal documents, 1428, 1438
as Coptic sacrament, 1107, 1542–1543, 2139
digamy (remarriage) practice, 901, 1545
and excommunication grounds, 1079
Greek–Egyptian, prohibited, 1180, 1181
Lord's Prayer in Services of Engagement and Betrothal, 1481
ritual books for, 1729
Roman law on, 905
Valentinian theory, 1156–1157
see also Betrothal customs; Celibacy; Divorce
Marriage at Cana, Feast of the, 1107, 1542–1543
The Marriage Sacrament in the Eastern Church (papal encyclical), 1942
Marrou, H. I., 2022
Marṣafā, **1546**
Marṣafī, Shaykh Ḥusayn al-, 1994
Marsa Maṭruḥ. *See* Paraetonium
Marsanes, **1547**, 2372
Marseille, France, Coptic congregations in, 1623
Martha the Egyptian, Saint, 2085
Martin I, Pope (Rome), 1112
Martin of Braga, 418
Martin Luther University (Halle-Wittenberg), 1893
Martin of Tours, Saint, 253
Martyr, Feast of the, **1547–1548**
Martyr Church. *See* Abū Mīnā
Martyrdom, **1548–1549**
Didascalia on, 899
Stephen as first, 885, 2153
see also Martyrology; Martyrs, Coptic
Martyria (Christian woman of Antioch), 1117
Martyrium of the Apostle Simon, 1136
Martyrium and monastery of Saint Colluthus, 701, 702
Martyrium of Paese and Thecla, 1136–1137
Martyrius, Patriarch of Jerusalem, 43
Martyrology, **1549–1550**
Donatist acceptance of role in church, 920
shrines, 1976
Stephen as first Christian martyr, 885, 2153
Synaxarion as source, 2173–2190
Martyrs, Coptic, **1550–1559**
Abāmūn of Tarnūṭ, 1
Abāmūn of Ṭūkh, 1–2
Acta Alexandrinorum, 56, 1889
Agathon and his brothers, 66–67
in Alexandria, 890
in Anṣinā, 142
Arianus, 230–231
Ascla, 283
Besamon, 379
burial rites, 425
canonization, 449
in Canopus (Abūqīr), 32
Copres, 598
Coptic hymns for, 1728
Cosmas and Damian, 636–640
Cyriacus and Julitta, 671
Damanhūr al-Waḥsh, 688
Dayr Abū Anūb, 696
Dayr Abū Bifām, 297, 696
Dayr Abū Ḥinnis, 701, 702
Dayr Abū Mūshā, 708
Dayr al-Amīr Tadrūs, 718
Dayr Anbā Abshāy, 718, 719
Dayr Anbā Bākhūm, 730
Dayr Anbā Bisādah, 732
Dayr Anbā Maqār, 718
Dayr Asfal al-Arḍ, 783
Dayr Buqṭur of Shū, 797
Dayr Mār Jirjis al-Hadīdī, 831
Dayr al-Shamʿ, 863
Dayr al-Shuhadā' (Isnā), 865, 866, 868, 870
Demetrius of Antioch on, 893–894
in Dimayrah, 902–903
Dimyānah, 903
and Diocletian's persecutions, 905–908, 1937
during Dionysius the Great's patriarchy, 909–910, 911
in Durunkah, 927
Elias, *1282*
Epima, 965, 965
Epimachus of Pelusium, 965–966
era of, 434, 972
Eusebius, 1069–1070
Eusignius, 1071–1072
al-Faramā association, 1089
in the Fayyūm, 845
feasts of the, 1101
Febronia, 1109–1110
Felix, 1110
forty monks at Raithou, 2049, 2050
forty-nine elders of Scetis, 1120–1121
Gabriel, Archangel, and, 136–137
George, Saint, and, 1140

Martyrs *(cont.)*
Gobidlaha, Dado, and Caxo, 1151–1152
Gregory the Illuminator, 1183
hagiographers, 1921
Hamai of Kahyor, 1203–1204
Heraclides, 1220–1221
Herai, 1221
of Herakleopolis, 73–74
Herpaese, 1225–1226
Hesychius, 1226
iconoclastic measures and, 1275
Isaac of Tiphre, 1304–1305
Isidorus, 1307
James, Saint and Disciple, 1109
James Intercisus, 1321
James the Persian, 324
Jirjis al-Muzāḥim, Saint, 1335–1336
John and Symeon, 1370
Joore, 1370
Julianus, 1225–1226
Justus, 1386–1387
and al-Khandaq, 1413
Krajon and Amun, 1419
Lacaron, 1423–1424
Leontius of Tripoli, 1442–1444
Lucian of Antioch, 1484
Macarius, 1489
Macrobius, 1494
in Mareotis, 1526–1527
Mark, 1531–1532
Menas of al-Ashmūnayn, 1589
Menas the Miracle Maker, 24, 1589–1590, 1937
Mercurius of Caesarea, 1592–1594
Michael, Archangel, and, 1619
Moses the Black, 1681
Mui, 1696
in Nikiou, 1793
Olympius, 1840
Paese and Tecla, 1865
Pamphilus, 1879
Panesneu, 1880
Panine and Paneu, 1880–1881
Pantaleon, 1881–1882
Patape, 1907–1908
Peter I, Patriarch, and, 1117, 1467
Philotheus of Antioch, 1960–1961
Phoibammon of Preht, 1963–1965
Pisura, 1980
poetry on, 1985, 1986
Polycarp, 1997–1998
Psote of Psoï, 2030, 2031–2032
Ptolemaus church in Dinūshar, 903
recanters from Islam, 1570
Regula, 2057
and Roman persecutions, 892, 1935–1937; *see also* Persecutions
seven ascetics of Tūnah, 2122
Stephen, 2153
at Sunbāt, 2159
Symeon, 1370
Tecla. *See* Paese and Tecla
Ter and Erai, 2209
Theban Legion, 2231–2233
Theodorus, 2237–2238
Til, 2261
Tolemaus, 2271
Ursus of Solothurn, 2292–2293
Victor of Shū, 2302
Victor Stratelates, 2303–2308
see also Cycle; Persecutions; Pilgrimages; Saints, Coptic
The Martyrs of Palestine (Eusebius), 1071, 1549
Marucchi, Orazio, **1559**
Marutha (Takritan), 876
Marwān II (Umayyad caliph), 37, 695, 1411
Mary (mother of Mark), 1529
Mary, Mother of God. *See* Annunciation; *Theotokos*; Virgin Mary
Mary of Alexandria, Saint, **1560**, 1085
Mary the Egyptian, Saint, **1560**, 2085
as anchorite, 129, 130
site of repentance, 1324
and Zosimus, Saint, 2087
Mary Magdalene, 897, 1155
Mār Yuhannā, 881
Maryūṭ
Dayr Abū Mīnā, 706–707
kilns at, 481
pilgrimages to, 1968, 1970
see also ʿAbū Mīnā; ʿAmriyyah; Mareotis
Mashat al-mardā. *See* Unction of the sick
Mashtūl, **1561**
Maṣīl, **1561**
Maximus (martyr), 1556
Masjid al-Shaykh ʿAbādah, 1528
Masks. *See* Portraiture, Coptic
Maspero, Gaston Camille Charles, 112, 1448, **1561**, 1900
and Crum, Walter Ewing, 661
and historiography of Coptic art, 255–256, 1700
students of, 414, 1184
Maspero, Jean (Jacques) Gaston, 694, 1482, **1561–1562**, 1891, 1967
Massacre of the Innocents, depicted in Coptic art, 533
Mass of the Catechumens, **1562–1565**
Mass of the Faithful, 1562, **1565–1568**
Mastema. *See* Satan
Maṭariyyah
pilgrimages to, 1970, 1973, 1977
tree at, 1118
Mātēwos, Ethiopian prelate, 1038–1040, 1591
Matins, Liturgy of, **1568–1569**
Mātrā. *See* Batra (martyr)
Matrilineal succession, 1514
Matrimony. *See* Betrothal customs; Marriage
Maṭṭā. *See* Libānos (Maṭṭā), Ethiopian saint
Matthew, Apostle and Saint, 897
see also Gospel of Saint Matthew
Matthew I, Patriarch, **1569–1570**
and Bartalomēwos, Ethiopian prelate, 1013
burial site, 815
dates of patriarchy, 1918
and Dayr Abū Fānah, 698
as monk at Dayr Anbā Antšuniyūs, 722
prophecy on successor, 1130
relics removed from Birmā, 392
Matthew II, Patriarch, **1571**
dates of patriarchy, 1918
successor, 1133
Matthew III, Patriarch, **1571**, 1975, 610
consecration of Ethiopian prelates by, 1022, 1023
dates of patriarchy, 1919
as monk at Dayr al-Baramūs, 791
patriarchal residence, 1913
Matthew IV, Patriarch, **1571**, 1913
and Coptic relations with Rome, 610
dates of patriarchy, 1919

and Ethiopian prelates, 1024, 1025
as last patriarch residing in Ḥārit Zuwaylah, 1208
as monk at Dayr al-Baramūs, 791
profession of faith, 1780
successor, 1347
and Vansleb (Wansleben), Johann Michael, 2299
Matthew the Poor, Saint, 802, **1571-1572**
Coptic accounts of, 1455
Encomia on, 1196
feast day, 2085
Matthias. *See* Timothy and Matthias (martyrs)
Maṭūnah (martyr), 1556
Maundy Thursday, **1107-1108**, 1426, 1904
and chrism consecration, 522
lectern placement, 1435
music for, 1721
Maurice, Emperor, 125-126, 688, 1676
patriarch under, 1915
Mauritius, Saint, 1082, 1110, **1572**, 2085, 2231-2233
Mausoleums. *See* Tombs
Mawāʿiẓ wa-al-Iʿtibār fī Dhikr al-Khiṭaṭ wa-al-Athār, al- (al-Maqrīzī), 1525
Mawhūb ibn Manṣūr ibn Mufarrij al-Iskandarānī, 782, 1239, **1573-1574**
Maxentius, Emperor, 919-920
Maximian, Bishop of Ravenna, 915
Maximian, Emperor
persecutions of, 907, 1082, 1110, 1552, 1936, 1937, 1943, 2057
and Theban Legion martyrdom, 2231
and uprisings in Gaul, 904
Maximinus, Emperor
patriarch under, 1914
persecutions of, 912, 1937
Maximus, Saint and Patriarch, 93, **1574-1575**
dates of patriarchy, 1914
feast day, 2085
Maximus the Confessor (monk), **1575-1576**, 1678
Maximus and Domitius, Saints, **1576-1578**, 1491, 1967, 2085
Arabic tradition of, 1577-1578
Coptic tradition of, 789-790, 1576-1577
Mazār al-Sayyidah al-ʿAdhrāʾ (rock church), 853
Mazmūr Idrībī (Psalm Idrībī), melody, 1722
Measurement. *See* Metrology, Coptic
Medallions. *See* Ampulla
Medamud, Dayr Anbā Bākhūm near, 729-730
Medhane Alem (savior of the world) (Lālibalā church), 1425
Medical instruments, *1579*, *1580*, 1581, 1605
Medicine, **1578-1582**
Abū Ḥulayqah, 19, 2055
Ahrūn ibn A'yan al-Qass, 77
in Alexandria, 91, 2065
Coptic, Sahān ibn ʿUthmān ibn Kaysān and, 2079-2080
Cosmas and Damian, 636-640, 1213
at Dayr Apa Hor, 771-772
healings in Coptic literature, 1212-1214
Ibn al-Biṭrīq brothers, 1265-1266
Ibrāhīm ibn ʿĪsā, 1273
instruments. *See* Medical instruments
Isḥāq ibn Ibrāhīm ibn Nasṭās, 1306
Kaysān ibn ʿUthmān ibn Kaysān, 1395
magic spells, 1504
Manṣūr ibn Sahlān ibn Muqashshir, 1524
al-Mufaḍḍal ibn Mājid ibn al-Bishr, 1689
Muhadhdhab al-Dīn Abū Saʿīd ibn Abī Sulaymān, 1691
Muwaffaq al-Dīn Abu Shākir ibn Abī Sulaymān Dāwūd, 1749
Naguib Mahfouz, 1773
Nasṭās ibn Jurayj, 1775-1776
Olympius, Saint, 1840
onions to ward off disease, 2126
papyri, 1886-1888
Paul of Aigina, 1922
Raphael, Archangel, as patron of, 2053, 2054
Rashīd al-Dīn Abū Saʿīd, 2055
Sahlān ibn ʿUthmān ibn Kaysān, 2079-2080
Saʿīd ibn Ṭufayl, 2080
see also Birth rites and customs; Pilgrimages
Meinardus, O.
on churches at Dayr al-Malāk Mīkhāʾīl (Naqādah), 827
on Dayr al-Malāk Mīkhāʾīl, 823
on Dayr al-Muḥarraq, 841
Melania the Elder, 1663, 1877, 1878, 1884
Melania the Younger, 2017
Melas (anchorite), 1650
Melchites and Copts, **1583**
in Alexandria, 90-92, 93-94, 95
Canon of Clement, 445
conflict in Cathedral Church of the Jacobites, 93-94
and Greek language in Egypt, 1177
Ibn al-Biṭrīq patriarchy, 1265-1266
monks, 720
Murqus ibn Qanbar, 1699-1700
and Nubian evangelization, 1797, 1801-1802, 1813
Qusṭanṭīn ibn Abī al-Maʿālī ibn Abī al-Fatḥ Abū al-Fatḥ, 2046-2047
Melchizedek
depicted in Coptic art, 383, 793-794, *793*
Hieracas of Leontopolis on, 1229
paintings of, 793-794, *793*
Meletius. *See* Melitius, Bishop of Lycopolis
Melisma (Coptic musical characteristic), 1721, 1732
Melitian schism, 37, 919, **1584**, 1585
Alexander I and, 81-84
in Alexandria, 97, 99
and Arianism, 591-592, 1878
and Athanasius, 590
and Constantine of Asyūṭ, 591
Damian and, 689
Hesychius and, 1226
Nicaea, Council of, and, 81, 84, 1792
and Roman persecutions, 1935
and Sabellianism, 2072
Melitius, Bishop of Antioch
Christology of, 1376
and Constantinople, First Council of, 594
Melitius, Bishop of Lycopolis, 296, 1584, **1585**
and Alexander I, 81, 84

Melitius, Bishop of Lycopolis (*cont.*)
and appointments of bishops, 686
and Hesychius, 1226
Peter I and, 1585, 1943, 1944, 1945
see also Melitian schism
Melito of Sardis, **1585–1586**
Coptic translations, 1451
and "godly monarch" concept, 1957
Melodies. *See Adām*; Music, Coptic; *Oktoechos*; *Wāṭus*
Memnon, Bishop of Ephesus, 960
Memnon, colossuses of, 2065–2066
Memnonia, **1586**
Memnonion of Strabo, 729
Memoirs (Paul of Aigina), 1922
Memphis, **1586–1587**
as capital of Egypt, 95
end to institutionalized paganism in, 1870
Greek population, 1166
katochoi (recluses), 2055–2056
Roman travelers in, 2065
Memphitic. *See Appendix*
Menander, 1889
Menandros, sentences of, 2119
Ménard, René, 1730, 1743
Menarti, **1587–1588**
Nubian monastery at, 1817
Menas (Dayr Apa Apollo superior), **1588–1589**
icons at Bāwīṭ, 370–371, 1588
Menas (Greek martyr), 1556
Menas I. *See* Mīnā, Saint and Patriarch
Menas (town), as pilgrimage way station, 2066
Menas, Patriarch of Constantinople, 1674
Menas, Saint (soldier martyr under Diocletian), 1936–1937
Menas, Saint and Bishop of Pshati
feast day, 2085
panegyrics by, 1456
Menas, Saint and Bishop of Tmuis, **1589**
and Damrū, 689
as monk at Dayr Anbā Anṭūniyūs, 721
Menas the Ascetic. *See* Menas of al-Ashmūnayn, Saint
Menas of al-Ashmūnayn, Saint (martyr), 1556, **1589**
Menas and Hasina (martyrs), 1557
Menas the Miracle Maker, Saint, 955, 1411, 1541, **1589–1590**
ampullae, 116–118, 534, 537, 541
churches dedicated to, 116–117, 808, 833
depicted in Coptic art, 270, 534, 535, 1527, 2004–2005, *2006*
feast day, 1557, 2085
monasteries dedicated to, 833, 834, 853, 1622, 1974
and Nikiou, 1793, 1794
see also Abū Mīnā
Menelik II, Emperor of Ethiopia, 1039, **1590–1591**
Mennas, Bishop of Memphis, 1587
Mennufer. *See* Memphis
Menophantus of Ephesus, and Lucian of Antioch, 1484
Menou, Jacques François ʿAbdallah, **1591–1592**
Mensurius of Carthage, Bishop, 919–920
Menuthis, paganism in, 1870
Mercurius (monk painter), 737–738, 764, 804, 1291, 1589
Mercurius, Saint (ascetic and recluse), 833, 2085
Mercurius of Caesarea, Saint, 1557, **1592–1594**, 2085
and Church of Abū Sayfayn (Old Cairo), 11, 549–551
churches dedicated to, 92, 710, 711, 713, 741, 743, 757, 814, 839, 1427, 1593–1594, 1613
cycle manuscripts, 1782
feast day, 1557, 2085
linked with Julian the Apostate's death, 1382
monasteries of, 825, 1653, 1654
in Nubian liturgy, 1816–1817
portraits of, 726
relics at Dayr al-Amīr Tadrūs, 718
Mercurius and Ephraem (martyrs), 1557
Mercurius at Shahrān. *See* Dayr Shahrān
Merkabah mysticism, 1148
Meroë (Kush capital city), 1420
Meroites, and Qaṣr Ibrīm, 2036, 2037
Meroitic language, 1170–1171, 1185, 1420
Merovingians, 1572
Meshach, 1092
Mesodialect. *See Appendix*
Mesokemic. *See Appendix*
Mesopotamia, 1663, 1675
Messalian movement, 2027
Metadialect. *See Appendix*
Metalwork, Coptic, **1594–1607**
earliest works, 269
on Gospel caskets, 1153
in Louvre Museum, 1483
preservation of, 280
techniques, 1595
see also Art, historiography of Coptic
Metanoia, Monastery of the (Canopus), 32, 850, **1608–1611**, 1646, 1861, 1862, 2066
post-Chalcedon, 1609–1610
Metras, Saint (martyr), 837
Metrology, Coptic, 53, **1611**
Metropolitan, **1611–1612**
as *abun*, 30
authority over bishops, 190
in ecclesiastical hierarchy, 2015
in Nubian church organization, 1813
ordained by bishop, 2193, 2194
role in church hierarchy, 1229
Metropolitan Museum of Art, New York City, 780, 800, 1210, 1714, 1895
Metropolitan Sees, **1612–1614**
Micah, 22
Michael. For names not found here, *see also* Khā'īl; Mīkhā'īl
Michael I. *See* Khā'īl I, saint and Patriarch
Michael II. *See* Khā'īl II, Patriarch
Michael IV, Saint and Patriarch, 761, 863, 1099, **1614–1615**
and Church of al-Muʿallaqah (Old Cairo), 558
and Church of Sitt Maryam, 320
dates of patriarchy, 1917
feast day, 2085
and Giyorgis I, Ethiopian prelate, 1006
Michael V, Patriarch, **1615–1616**, 1912
birthplace, 1970
dates of patriarchy, 1917
and Dayr al-Shamʿ, 863
feast day, 2085
and Mikā'ēl I, Ethiopian

prelate, 1006–1007
successor, 1340
Michael VI, Patriarch, **1616**
dates of patriarchy, 1918
Michael VIII Palaeologos, 1114
Michael III. *See* Khā'īl III, Patriarch
Michael, Bishop of Damietta. *See* Mīkhā'īl, Bishop of Damietta; *Nomocanon* (Michael of Damietta)
Michael, Bishop of Ṣandafā, 819
Michael, Saint and Bishop of Naqādah, 2085
Michael the Archangel, Saint, 1, 93, 190, 1092, **1616–1619**
and Anatolius, Saint, 128
and Anub, Saint, 152
in Apocryphon of Jeremiah, 170
and Ari, Saint, 229
and the Assumption of the Virgin Mary, 292, 293
churches dedicated to, 92, 93, 355, 1617–1618
confraternities of, 586–587
in the Coptic *Testament of Isaac*, 612
and Cosmas and Damian, Saints, 639
depicted in Coptic art, 250, 270, 794, 868, 869
and Elias of Samhūd, Saint, 953
and Epima, Saint, 965
feast of, 1111
funerary customs, 1125
and Gabriel, Archangel, 1136
iconography of, 250
investiture in Heaven, 1618–1619
and Isidorus martyrdom, 1307
and John of Parallos homily, 1368
and Lacaron, Saint, 1424
in magical texts, 1501, 1502
monasteries dedicated to, 1974
in Nubian church art, 1812
in Nubian liturgy, 1816
in Nubian medieval inscription, 1805
patron of church at Banī Kalb, 335
Peter I Encomium on, 1946
and Satan, 1184
in Testament of Abraham, 164
in Testaments of the Patriarchs, 164
and Victor Stratelates, Saint, 2304, 2306
see also Chapel of the Archangel Michael; Dayr al-Malāk Mīkhā'īl
Michael bar Elias, *Chronicle*, 97–98
Michael Cerularius, 1113
Michael of Damietta (twelfth-century "new" martyr), 1557
Michael al-Ghamrī, Bishop of Samannūd, 1131
Michael of Qamūlah, Saint, 2085
Michael the Syrian, on Nubian evangelization, 1801–1802
Michalowski, Kazimierz, 613, 1091, 1092, **1620**, 1812
Michigan papyrus of Acts. *See* Acts, Michigan papyrus of
Middle Egyptian dialect
in Old Testament, Coptic translations of, 1837–1838
see also Appendix; Oxyrhynchite dialect
Middle Platonism, and Origen, 1847
Middle Ṣa'īd, monasteries of, 1654–1655
Miedema, Rein, **1620**
Migne, Jacques-Paul, **1620**
Migration, Coptic, **1620–1624**
Mikā'ēl I, Ethiopian prelate, 1006–1007
Mikā'ēl II, Ethiopian prelate, 1007–1008
Mikā'ēl III, Ethiopian prelate, 1013–1014
Mikā'ēl IV, Ethiopian prelate, 1023–1024
Mikhā'īl I, Archbishop of Jerusalem, 1325
Mīkhā'īl I, II, III, patriarchs. *See* Khā'īl I, II, III
Mīkhā'īl IV, V. *See* Michael IV, Michael V
Mīkhā'īl, Bishop of Asyūt, 755
Mīkhā'īl, Bishop of Atrīb and Malīj, 1–2, 458–459, **1625–1627**
on *cheirotonia*, 517
on Maximus and Domitius, Saints, 1577–1578
Mīkhā'īl, Bishop of Damietta, 1613, **1624–1625**
and blessing styles, 404
on *Canons of Gregory of Nyssa*, 457
collected *Nomocanon* of, 1781
on communion of the sick, 580
on incense, 1290
nomocanon of, 1129
opposition to Murqus ibn Qanbar, 1624, 1625, 1699
succeeded by Butrus Sāwīrus al-Jamīl, Bishop, 431
Mīkhā'īl, Bishop of Dumyāṭ, 926
Mikhail, Kyriakos, **1627–1628**
Mīkhā'īl 'Abd al-Sayyid, **1628**, 1993
Mīkhā'īl al-Baḥrāwī, **1628**
Mīkhā'īl ibn Buṭrus, **1629**
Mīkhā'īl ibn Danashtarī. *See* Michael V, Patriarch
Mīkhā'īl ibn Ghāzī, 1629
Mīkhā'īl ibn Ya'qūb 'Ubayd al-Miṣrī, 1630
Mīkhā'īl Jirjis, Mu'allim, **1629–1630**, 1737, *1737*, 1742
Mīkhā'īl of Miṣr (al-Fusṭāṭ), Bishop, 1533
Mīkhā'īl al-Miṣrī (monk), **1630**
Mīkhā'īl Shārūbīm, **1630–1631**
and British occupation of Egypt, 419
private collection in Coptic Museum (Old Cairo), 608
Milan, Edict of (313), 81, 208, 298, 588–589, 902
Mileham, G. S., 1091
Milik al-Kāmil, al-, Sultan, 1121
Military. *See* Army, Roman; Castrum; Costume, military; Warriors in Coptic art
Military–executive offices in Mamluk state. *See* Copts in late medieval Egypt
Milius (martyr), 1557
Millenarians, 911
Millet, 1087, **1631**
Milner, Lord, 1990, 1991, 2074
Milvian Bridge, battle of (312), 81, 588, 1869
Mīnā, al-, 895
Mīnā, Bishop of Sanabū, 1631
Mīnā I, Saint and Patriarch, **1631–1632**
dates of patriarchy, 1916
feast day, 2085
and Yuḥannā, 2356
Mīnā II, Patriarch, **1632–1633**, 1912
and chrism consecration, 521

Mina II, Patriarch (*cont.*)
dates of patriarchy, 1916
and Ethiopian prelates, 1001
successor, 10
Mīnā, Saint. *See* Menas the Miracle Maker, Saint
MināS, Ethiopian prelate, 1000–1001
Mīnā the Solitary. *See* Cyril VI, Patriarch
Minbar, al- (publication), 1990
Mingarelli, A., 1895
Minor Doxology, 923–924
Minshā'at al-Shaykh. *See* Dayr al-Zāwiyah
Minshāh, al-. *See* Psoï
Mint. *See* Coinage in Egypt
Minṭāsh (Mamluk amir), 1570
Minūfiyyah Province, monasteries in, 1655
Minūf al-Suflā. *See* Maḥallat Minūf
Minūf al-'Ulyah, **1633**, 2362
Minyā, **1634**
Dayr Abū Sarabām at, 709–710
Dayr Apa Hor at, 770–771
hermitages in, 1654
memorial to Abū Fīs at, 716
See also Ṣanabū
Minyā al-Qamḥ, pilgrimages to, 1973
Minyat al-Shammās, Dayr al-Sham', 863
Minyat al-Sudān, Dayr al-'Adawiyyah, 712
Miracles
Basil, Saint, 115–116
at Dayr Abū Mūsā, 707
at Dayr al-Maghṭis, 818
at Dayr al-Muḥarraq, 840
Demetrius of Antioch on, 893–894
first of Jesus Christ, 1107
in Gregory V patriarchy, 1130–1131
healings in Coptic literature, 1212–1213
and laying-on of hands, 1433
of Marqus al-Anṭūnī, 1542
of Maximus and Domitius, 1576–1577, 1578
of Mercurius of Caesarea, 1592, 1593
of Michael the Archangel, 1618
of Moses of Abydos, 1680
moving of Muqaṭṭam hill, 1095
of Pantaleon, 1882
of Patāsius, 1908
in Peter VII patriarchy, 1950
of Phoibammon of Preht, 1964
of Pshoi of Scetis, 2029
at Qalamūn, 758
of Thomas, Apostle and Saint, 1635
Virgin Mary, apparition of The, 681, 840, 871, 969, 2308–2310, *2309*
Miracles of Ptolemy, on Dayr Anbā Shinūdah, 765
Miracula Coluthi, 893
Miracula Victoris (Demetrius of Antioch), 894
Mirhom, 'Azīz, 1996
Miṣr al-Qāhirah, 1312
Mirrors, 1509, 1606, *1607*
supported by wood frame, 2338
Mirzā, 'Azīz, 2011
Miṣā'īl, Saint, **1634**, 2085
Mīsas, Dayr Abū Mūsā at, 707
Misbāḥ al-Ẓulmah (Ibn Kabar), 1267, 1272, 1463–1464, 1634, 1735
on Books of Chronicles, 1827
on Canons of Epiphanius, 456–457
on canons of Nicaea, 1789
on Ezra, 1829
manuscript in Paris, 1779
on *Nomocanon* of Gabriel II ibn Turayk, 1799
on Ruth, 1835
Miṣr, al- (publication), 1465, 1989, 1990, 1994, 2011, 2020, 2198
Miṣr, Metropolitan See of, 761, 1613, 1912
Miṣr Bank, 1694
Misrā (twelfth month of Coptic calendar), 439, 2189–2190
Mission archéologique française de Caire, 693
Missionaries
Anglican in Egypt, 133
in India, 1635–1636, 1881
liturgy spread by early Coptic, 1733
Longinus, 1479–1480
Manichaean, 1520, 1521
Mark, Saint, 1529–1530
monophysites, 1673, 1674–1675
Nubian evangelization, 1801–1802
Nubian Islamization, 1802–1804
Protestant in Egypt, 1693
Roman Catholic to Copts, 1330, 1349, 1538
Theban Legion in Switzerland, 2231–2233
Ulphilas, Apostle to the Goths, 2285
see also Evangeliary
Missionaries in India, Coptic, **1635–1636**, 1881
Mississippi Coptic Codex I. *See* Crosby Schøyen Codex
Missoria, 1607
Mistrīḥ, Vincentio, 1464
Mīt Damsīs
churches dedicated to Saint George at, 1140
pilgrimages to, 1968, 1970–1971
Miter, 1469, 1476, 1477
Mithra (pagan deity), 1617–1618, 1866
Mithraism, Michael the Archangel's link with, 1617–1618
Mīt Rahīnah, 1586
Mīt Shammās, Dayr al-Sham' at, 865
Modalist Monarchians, 1637, 1638
on nature of Christ, 547
see also Monarchianism; Sabellianism
Modern Egypt, Copts in, **1636–1637**
political thought, 1993–1996
Moftah, Ragheb, 1730, 1737–1738, 1742, 1743
Monarchianism, **1637–1338**
Eusebius of Caesarea opposition to, 1070–1071
and *homoiousion* controversy, 1253
Sabellianism and, 2072
Monarchs. *See* Kings, anointing of; specific names
Monasteries
abbots, 2–3
in Alexandria, 95; *see also* specific names
Anbā Orion, 12
in Anṣinā, 142
Arab conquest impact on, 693–694
archives, 227–228
attitudes toward music in, 1733
canonical hours, 1724
Church of Saint George (Jerusalem), 1327–1328

and Coptic literature, 1458–1459
in Damanhūr bishopric, 687
dedicated to Phoibammon, 1964–1965
deuterarios term, 895
diaconia term, 896
in Diolkos province, 908
donation of children to, 918–919
donations to, 1430
in Durunkah, 927
economic activities of
and Egyptian economy, 1643–1645
income-producing work, 802
and *oikonomos*, 1825–1826
outlays, 1642–1643
economic influence of, 1676, 1677
Eikoston, 951
the Enaton, 954–958, *957*
at Faras, 1090
Fārshūt, 12
Farshūṭ vicinity, 1093
Fatimid rule impact on, 1098
Fayyūm as early center, 1100
of free monks ("sarabaïtes"), 702
ḥiṣn fortification, 1237
inscriptions found at, 1291, 1292
involuntary reclusion, 2055
at Karnak, *1393*, 1393
keep construction, 1395–1396
Kellia grouping, 1396–1409
khizānah (hiding place), 1415
laura, 1428
libraries, 1448, 1977
library of medical literature, 1578–1579, 1886–1888
Lithazomenon and Saint Peter's Bridge, 1467
al-Makārim listing of, 1462
Maqrīzī history on, 1525
medical papyri, 1886–1888
most isolated in Egypt, 758
mummification, 1697
murals in, 1873–1874, 1875
of Nitria, 1794–1796
nursing practices, 1581–1582
Oktokaidekaton, 1826–1827
paintings, 1659–1660
in Pbow, 126, 1927–1929
in Pempton region, 1931
Persian conquests of, 1938, 1939
in Philae, 1955–1956
pilgrims and travelers to, 1976–1977
Pisentius of Hermonthis founding, 1978
proestos term, 2021
provost, 2024
Raithou, 2050
restorations by Gabriel VII, Patriarch, 1133
in Scetis, 2102–2106
Takinash, 2199
Tall Atrīb, 2199–2200
Tamnūh, 2201
Ṭanbidā, 2201
Theotokos duplicates, 714
travelers' interest under Roman empire, 2066
vigils, 2308
see also Dayr headings; Ethiopian monasticism; Hermitage; Hermitages, Theban; Monasticism; Monasticism, Pachomian; Monks; Nubian monasticism; specific monasteries
Monasteries, economic activities of, **1638–1645**
Monasteries, Nubian. *See* Nubian monasteries
Monasteries in and around Alexandria, **1645–1646**
Monasteries in and around Cairo, **1646–1647**
Monasteries in the Beheirah Province, **1646**
Monasteries in Cyprus, **1647–1648**
Monasteries in the Daqahliyyah Province, **1648–1649**
Monasteries of the Eastern Desert, **1649–1650**, 1659
Monasteries of the Eastern Desert of the Delta and Sinai, **1650**
Monasteries of the Fayyūm, **1650–1651**
Monasteries in the Gharbiyyah Province, **1651–1652**
Monasteries of the Lower Ṣaʿīd, **1652–1654**
Monasteries of the Middle Ṣaʿīd, **1654–1655**
Monasteries in the Minūfiyyah Province, **1655**
Monasteries in the Qalyūbiyyah Province, 835, **1655**
Monasteries of the Sharqiyyah Province, **1655–1656**
Monasteries of the Upper Ṣaʿīd, **1656–1658**, 1659
Monasteries of the Western Desert, **1658–1659**
Monastery of the Abyssinians, 1654
Monastery of Anbā Ḥiziqyāl. *See* Dayr Anbā Ḥiziqyāl
Monastery of Andrew. *See* Dayr Abū al-Līf
Monastery of Apa Harūn, 1652
Monastery of Apollo. *See* Bāwīṭ
Monastery of the Archangel Michael (Sopehes), 1449
Monastery of the Armenians. *See* Dayr al-Arman
Monastery of the Bones. *See* Dayr al-ʿIẓām
Monastery of the Brothers. *See* Dayr al-Ikhwah
Monastery of the Brothers of Siyalah. *See* Dayr al-Ikhwah
Monastery of Brucheum (Alexandria), 1646
Monastery of Canopus. *See* Metanoia, Monastery of the
Monastery of the Crosses. *See* Dayr Abū Fānah
Monastery of Enaton. *See* Enaton, The
Monastery of the Epiphany. *See* Dayr Ebifania
Monastery of the Ethiopians. *See* Dayr al-Muḥarraq
Monastery of the Exchange. *See* Dayr al-Maymūn
Monastery of Ezekiel. *See* Dayr al-Sāqiyah
Monastery of the Forty Saints (Alexandria), 1646
Monastery of the Greeks. *See* Dayr Anbā Bākhūm; Dayr al-Rūmī
Monastery of Heraclius. *See* Dayr al-Quṣayr (Ṭurah)
Monastery of the Hermits, 38
Monastery of the Holy Cross. *See* Dayr al-Ṣalīb
Monastery of the Holy Virgin at al-ʿAdawiyyah. *See* Dayr al-ʿAdawiyyah
Monastery of Hunger. *See* Dayr al-Jūʿ
Monastery of the Island. *See* Dayr al-Rūmāniyyah
Monastery of John Colobos, 734, 790, 2103, 2105

Monastery of John Kama, 1270, 2104
Monastery of John the Short. *See* Monastery of John Colobos
Monastery of Mark the Evangelist, 2041, 2042
Monastery of the Martyrs. *See* Dayr al-Shuhadā'
Monastery of Matthew the Poor. *See* Dayr al-Fakhūrī
Monastery of the Metanoia. *See* Metanoia, Monastery of the
Monastery of Michael and Cosmas, 1588
Monastery of the Mother of God (Alexandria), 1646
Monastery of the Mountain of the Bird. *See* Dayr al-ʿAdhrā (Samālūṭ)
Monastery of the Mule. *See* Dayr al-Quṣayr (Turah)
Monastery of al-Nūr, 1653
Monastery "of the Mother of God of the Syrians", 876
Monastery of Saint John. *See* Dayr al-Sāqiyah
Monastery of Pachomius. *See* Dayr Anbā Bākhūm
Monastery paintings, Coptic, **1659–1660**
  Dayr Anbā Hadrā, 747
Monastery of Pamin, 1649
Monastery of the Patrician, 125, 955, 1931
Monastery of Paul the Leper (Alexandria), 1646
Monastery of the Pool. *See* Dayr al-Maghṭis
Monastery of the Potter. *See* Dayr al-Fakhūrī
Monastery of the Pulley. *See* Dayr al-ʿAdhrā' (Samālūṭ); Dayr Mār Mīnā (Jabal Abū Fūdah)
Monastery in the quarter of the Ethiopians. *See* Dayr bi'l-Habash
Monastery of Saint Antony. *See also* Dayr Anbā Anṭūniyūs
Monastery of Saint Antony (Famagusta), 1647
Monastery of Saint Antony (Nairobi), 1622
Monastery of Saint Antony (Nicosia), 1648
Monastery of Saint Catherine. *See* Mount Sinai Monastery of Saint Catherine
Monastery of Saint Elias. *See* Dayr Anbā Helias
Monastery of Saint Epima of Pshante, 824
Monastery of Saint Gabriel. *See* Dayr al-Naqlūn
Monastery of Saint George, 824, 1649, 1653
  see also Dayr Mār Jirjis
Monastery of Saint Jeremiah (Saqqara). *See* Dayr Apa Jeremiah
Monastery of Saint John the Baptist. *See* Holy Land, churches of the
Monastery of Saint John Kama, 1270, 2104
Monastery of Saint Macarius. *See* Dayr Anbā Maqār
Monastery of Saint Macarius (Klima), 1647
Monastery of Saint Macarius (Platani), 1647–1648
Monastery of Saint Mark (Alexandria), 1646
Monastery of Saint Menas, 707
Monastery of Saint Menas the Recluse. *See* Dayr Mār Mīnā (Gharbiyyah)
Monastery of Saint Michael (Hamūlī), 1619
Monastery of Saint Paul. *See* Dayr Anbā Būlā
Monastery of Saint Simeon. *See* Dayr Anbā Hadrā
Monastery of Saint Sinuthius. *See* Dayr Anbā Shinūdah
Monastery of Saint Victor. *See* Dayr al-Jabrāwī
Monastery of Samuel. *See* Dayr al-Sanad
Monastery of the Seven Mountains. *See* Dayr al-ʿIẓām (Asyūṭ); Dayr al-Sabʿat Jibāl
Monastery of Shenute. *See* Dayr al-Ṣalīb
Monastery of Stone. *See* Dayr al-Ḥajar
Monastery of the Tabennesiotes. *See* Metanoia, Monastery of the
Monastery of the Tigers. *See* Dayr Anbā Būlā
Monastery of the Town. *See* Dayr al-Madīnah
Monastery of the Vine-Dresser. *See* Dayr Nahyā
Monastery of the Virgin, 7, 704, 927; *see also* Dayr al-ʿAdhrā
Monastery of the Virgin of Baramūs, 790
Monasticism
  British Isles, 417–418
  Ethiopian, 990–994
  Nubian, 1817–1818
  twentieth-century revival of, 1668
Monasticism, Egyptian, **1661–1664**
  anachoresis, 118–120, 1320–1321, 1661, 1958
  Antony of Egypt influence on, 150
  Apophthegmata patrum on, 177–178
  cell, 477–478
  Coptic influence on, 101
  and Coptic language diffusion, 1168, 1177
  Coptic text translations on, 1454
  desert fathers and, 894; *see also* Desert fathers
  early beginnings in Dalās, 685
  Ebionite influence on, 930
  Evagrius Ponticus works on, 1076–1077
  al-Faramā as center, 1089
  Gangra, Council of, on asceticism, 1138
  Historia monachorum in Aegypto on, 1237–1238, 2068–2069
  in Mareotis, 1527
  martyrs and, 1881
  Melitian, 1584
  in Memphis, 1587
  as model in other areas, 1663–1664
  origins, 1661–1664
  Palladius text on, 1876–1877
  proestos term, 2021
  reclusion as fundamental element of, 2055–2056
  refectory elements and usage, 2056
  Roman papal acceptance of, 299
  and Roman taxation, 2204
  see also Asceticism; Anachoresis; Anchorites; Dayr headings; Desert fathers; Hermitage; Hermits; Monk; Monasteries; specific personal and place names

Monasticism, Pachomian, 26, 32, 41, 78–80, 126, 1661, 1662–1663, **1664–1665**
Abraham of Farshūṭ and, 11
anchorite contrasted with, 725
cell, 477
and Claudius, Saint, 561
convents, 1663, 1822, 1860, 2325
and Cornelius as "ancient brother," 635
definition, 1667
deuterarios term, 895
diaconia term, 896
in Diolkos province, 908
and Hamai of Kahyor, Saint, 1204
Horsiesios and, 1257
and Joseph of Tsenti, Saint, 1374
Monastery of the Metanoia, 1608, 1610–1611
monastery sites, 1657
mourning rites, 1686
numbers of monks, 1662–1663
oikonomos at, 1826
opposition to, 1138
organization of, 1664–1665
Pachomius as founder, 1661, 1664, 1859–1863
Pachomius the Younger, 1864
Palladius on, 1877
Paphnutius and, 1882
Pbow, 1926–1929
Petronius, Saint, and, 1952
and pilgrimages, 1973–1974
proestos term, 2021
Pseudo-Macarius homilies addressed to, 2027
at Raithou, 2049–2050
refectory as standard architectural element, 2056
Rules of Saint Pachomius, 1861–1862
Souros, 2144
Tabennēsē site, 2197
and Theodorus of Tabennēsē, 2239–2240
and Victor of Tabennēsē, 2308
see also Pbow
Monastic vestments. *See* Monks, vestments
Mond, R., 861
Monde Copte, Le (publication), **1666**
Monenergism, 1666, 1676
Monk, **1667–1668**
see also Dayr headings; Hermits; Monasticism; Monasteries; specific names
Monks
abbots, 2–3
Abraham of Farshūṭ, 11–12
anchorite way of life compared with cenobite, 724–725
in church hierarchy, 1229
Coptic in Ireland, 253
Coptic texts on, 1455
Cornelius, 635
Ethiopian, 747–748
and genuflection, 1139
iconoclastic measures against, 1275
manshūbiyyas dwellings, 749
Moses of Abydos, 1679–1681
Moses the Black, 1681
Paphnutius, 1882
Paphnutius of Pbow, 1883–1884
Paphnutius of Scetis, 1884
and patriarchal election, 1911
as patriarchs, 1999
portraits in Old Church of Dayr Anbā Anṭūniyūs, 727
Pshoi of Scetis, 2029–2030
simulating madness for God, 1541
tasks and trades, 1641–1643
total number in the Wādī Habīb area in the year, 1088, 2135
vestments, 650–655, 1477
Victor, 2301
Victor of Tabennēsē, 2308
see also Anchorites; Desert fathers; Hermitage; Hermits; Monasticism; specific names
Monneret de Villard, Ugo, **1668–1669**
on Nubian archaeology, medieval, 1804
and Nubian church art, 1811
and Tamīt, 2200
Monophysitism, **1669–1677**
Acacian schism, 42–47, 1671–1672
Alexandrian, 101, 102
and Arab conquest of Egypt, 188
and Assumption, 290
and Chalcedon, Council of, 512–515, 663–664
and Christian subjects in Coptic art, 528
Christology, 547, 548, 679
and *communicatio idiomatum*, 578
consolidation of, 1672–1673, 1675
and Constantinople, Second Council of, 596
and Copts, 599–600
and Dyophysites in Alexandria, 97, 99
and ecthesis edict, 682
and Egypt in late antiquity, 100, 944–947
in Ethiopia, 986–987
and Greek-speakers in Egypt, 1177
and iconoclasm, 1275, 1276
influence on Coptic education, 931–932
and Jacob Baradaeus, 1318–1319
and Jacob of Sarūj, 1319–1320
John of Ephesus writings on, 1362
and Julian, Bishop of Halicarnassus, 1379
and Justin II, Emperor, 1384–1385
and Justinian, Emperor, 1385
Longinus, 1480
and Makourian Christian conversion, 1513
missions, 1674–1675
monasteries' economic impact, 1676, 1677
monenergism and, 1666–1667
on nature of Christ. *See* *subhead* Christology
and Nubian evangelization, 1797, 1800, 1801–1802, 1813, 1817
and Nubian liturgy, 1817
and Paul the Black patriarchy, 1922–1923
and persecution, 125–126, 165, 1676
and Peter III Mongus patriarchy, 1947–1948
and Philoxenus of Mabbug, 1672–1673, 1961–1962
pre-Chalcedon, 1669–1670
Roman Empire relations, 1675–1677; *see also* specific rulers
and Sabellianism, 2072
and Scetis monks, 2104
Severan/Alexandrian rift, 1673

Monophysitism (*cont.*)
and Severus of Antioch, 1673, 1674, 2123–2125
and Theodora, Empress, 2234
and Theodoret, 2236
Theodosians, 2240–2241
and Timothy II Aelurus, Patriarch, 2264, 2266–2267
see also Acacian schism; Cyril I, Saint; Monotheletism
Monotheletism, **1678**
and Constantinople, Third Council of, 595–597
and ecthesis edict, 682, 932
monenergist merger with, 1667
Mons Porphyrites, 1649
Monte Corvino, 1635
Months of Coptic calendar. *See* Calendar, months of Coptic; specific months
Monuments
dating of, 693–694
Dayr Qubbat al-Hawā, 851–852
Morenz, Siegfried, 614, 1439, **1678**, 2186
Morgan, J. Pierpont, 824
Morgan Library. *See* Pierpont Morgan Library, New York City
Morning Offering of Incense, music with, 1719, 1721, 1739
Morning prayer. *See* Matins, Liturgy of, 1568
Mosaic law. *See* Law, Mosaic
Mosaics, Copto-Muslim, 311
Moschus, John. *See* John Moschus
Moses (hermit). *See* Daniel and Moses
Moses (monk of Scetis), Cassian on, 462
Moses (Old Testament)
Apocalypse of, 165
and fasting as spiritual preparation, 1095
and liturgical instruments, 1469, 1470
pagan deity linked with, 1868
Philo on, 1957
and site of Mount Sinai Monastery of Catherine, 1681
Testament of, 163
Moses, Bishop of Awsīm, 843, 1631, **1678–1679**
Moses of Abydos, **1679–1681**
as archimandrite, 193
as desert father, 894
monasteries linked with, 707, 729
Moses of Balyanā, Coptic accounts of, 1455
Moses the Black, Saint, **1681**
Anbā Bishoi confused with, 738
as anchorite, 129, 130
as black man, 248
depicted in wall paintings, 727
martyrdom, 1557
monastery of, 707, 708
Zacharias of Scetis and, 1681, 2369
Moses of Nisibis, abbot of Dayr al-Suryān, 876
Moses of Qifṭ, 1368, 1455
Moses and Sarah (martyrs), 1557
Moslem Brotherhood, 951
Mosques
ʿAmr at al-Fusṭāṭ, 92
al-Aqmar, 810, 814
Dayr Abū Sayfayn (Old Cairo), 711
at Dongola, 922
Jerusalem, 1098, 1099
Mountain of Isis. *See* Dayr al-Kubāniyyah
Mountain of the Palm. *See* Dayr al-ʿAdhrā' (Samālūṭ)
Mount Casios. *See* Katīb al-Qals
Mount of Olives, 1446
Mount Sinai Monastery of Saint Catherine, 1539, 1593, **1681–1685**, *1682*, *1683*, *1684*, *1685*, 1900, 1903
capital at, 777
and Catherine, Saint, 2325
Codex Sinaiticus discovered at, 570–571
keeps in lauras of, 1395, 1396
as laura of hermitages, 1224–1225
manuscript microfilming project, 2353
manuscripts of hymn and psalm texts found at, 1735
oldest icons from, 1277
pilgrimages to, 1976
Qusṭanṭīn ibn Abī al-Maʿālī ibn Abī al-Fatḥ Abū al-Fatḥ retirement to, 2046, 2047
Mount Tabor, Jesus Christ's transfiguration on, 1109
Mourner–penitents, 1932
Mourning in early Christian times, 1125, **1686**
Mouseion (Alexandria), 1167
Muʿallaqah Church. *See* Church of al-Muʿallaqah
Muʿaqqab, **1687**, 2198
Muʿayyad, al- (publication), 1465, 1466, 1988, 2011
Muʿayyad, al-, Sultan, 1130
Mubārak, Ḥusnī, president of Egypt, 1991
Mubāshirūn, **1687–1688**
Mudji. *See* Thecla and Mudi (martyrs)
Mufaḍḍal ibn Mājid ibn al-Bishr, al-, **1689**
Muftāḥ, Rāghib, 1630
Muhadhdhab Abū al-Malīḥ Zakariyyā, 1268
Muhadhdhab al-Dīn Abū Saʿīd ibn Abī Sulaymān, **1691**
Muḥammad, Prophet of Islam, 72, 184–185, 1331
Coptic consort of, 1528
Muḥammad ʿAdbū, Shaykh al-Islam, 1465
Muḥammad ʿAlī, Viceroy, 1691–1692
Muḥammad ʿAlī dynasty, **1691–1694**
and administrative organization of Egypt, 935
and Consultative Council founding, 598
Coptic education under, 932
Copts under, 2314
and Cyril V, Patriarch, 677
Ghālī as finance minister, 1141
Jirjis al-Jawharī and, 1334
Republican Party opposition, 1987
Rizq Agha and, 2059
and societal modernization, 1993
Muḥammad Bey al-Alfī, 1141
Muḥammad Bey Zadeh, 1538
Muḥammad ibn Zakariyyā al-Rāzī, 1922
Muḥammad Ramzī, **1695**
Muhdī, Muḥammad al-, **1695–1696**
Muḥtasib, al-. *See* al-Ḥisbah
Mui, Saint (martyr), 1557, **1696**
Muʿizz, al-, Caliph
and Abraham, Saint and Patriarch, 10, 11
Fatimid dynasty policies, 1095, 1097, 1098, 1099, 1632–1633
Mukhtār, Maḥmūd, 1995
Mumarah. *See* Censer

Mummification, **1696–1697**, 1865, 1868
funerary portraiture, 2001–2003
Mummy labels, **1698**
Munā, al-. *See* Kellia
Munā al-Amīr, Dayr al-Amīr Tadrūs, 718
Munier, Adolphe Henri, **1698**
Dayr Abū Līfah inscriptions, 704
Muqaddimah, *See Appendix*
Muqaṭṭaʿ, al-. *See* James Intercisus
Muqaṭṭam hill (Cairo), moving of, 1095
Muqawqas, al-. *See* Cyrus al-Muqawqas
Muqtaṭaf, al- (publication), 1996
Murād Bey, 1274
Murad Kamil, 1197, 1206, 1230, **1698–1699**
Murals. *See* Painting, Coptic mural
Muratorian Canon, 1158
Muriel. *See* Abbaton
Murqus. *See also* Mark; Marqos
Murqus, Archbishop of Alexandria, 893
Murqus al-Anṭūnī, Saint, 722, 1621, **1699**
Murqus of Beḥeira, Metropolitan, 1614
Murquṣ Ḥannā, 1990
Murqus ibn Qanbar, **1699–1700**
and blessings, 404
and *Book of Spiritual Medicine* authorship, 1626
death at Dayr al-Quṣayr, 854
and *al-Durr al-Thamīn* authorship, 926
exiled to Dayr Anbā Anṭūniyūs, 722
Mīkhā'īl, Bishop of Damietta, as adversary, 1624–1625
Murqus ibn Zarʿah. *See* Mark III, Saint and Patriarch
Murqusiyyah, patriarchal residence at, 1913
Murqus al-Mashriqī al-Mallāwanī, **1700**
Murqus of Maṭāy, Abūnā, 1737
Murqus Simaykah, **1700**, 1892
Coptic collections, 256
Murray, Margaret Alice, **1700–1701**
Musa (martyr), 1553
Mūsā, Salāmā, 1995, 1996
Mūsā al-Aswad. *See* Moses the Black, Saint
Museum of Art and History, Fribourg, Switzerland, 1603, 1604
Museum of Fine Arts, Budapest, Hungary, 4
Museums, Coptic collections in, **1701–1715**
at Dayr Anbā Maqār, 756
Louvre, 1481–1483
State Museum of Berlin, 2146–2147
see also Art, historiography of Coptic; Papyrus collections; names of specific countries, museums, types of art and artifacts
Mūshā (site), 708, 797
Music, Coptic, **1715–1744**
Adām and *Wāṭus*, 63, 1722, 1724, 2320–2321
antiphon, 148–149
canonical hours, 1724, 1733
canticles, 1729, 1733
cantors, 460, 564, 1732, 1736–1738, 1742
chanters and singers, 1629–1630
characteristic phenomenon, 1721
corpus and present practice, 1715–1729
description of corpus, 2024
in Epiphany, Liturgy of the, 967–968
history, 1731–1736
for Holy Week, 1251
hymns, 900–901, 2254–2255
instruments. *See* Musical instruments
laḥn, 1425, 1722
language relationship to melody, 1730–1731
liturgical prayer of Trisagion, 2017
musicologists, 1741–1742, 1743–1744
nonliturgical, 1744
oral tradition of, 1730
and poetry, 1985–1986
Psalmodia service, 1725–1729
responsory, 2058
transcriptions in Western notations, 1742–1744
wāham, 2313
Wāṭus, 2320–2321
Musical instruments, 1604–1605, *1605*, 1732, 1738–1739
Clement of Alexander's disapproval of, 1733
Coptic link with Irish harp, 1734, 1740
wooden, 2333–2334, *2334*
see also specific kinds
Musicologists, 1741–1742, 1743–1744
Muslim Brethren (*al-Ikhwān al-Muslimūn*), 1694, 1996
Muslim Brotherhoods, 1991, 2313–2316
Muslim Copts. *See* Copts in late medieval Egypt
Muslims. *See* Islam
Muṣṭafā Fahmī Pasha, 1693
Muṣṭafā Kāmil, **1747–1748**, 1987–1988, 1994, 2011, 2322, 2333
Muṣṭafā al-Naḥḥās, 1515–1516, 2323
Mustanṣir, al-, Caliph, 324, 1097, 1099, 1574
Musṭurud, pilgrimages to, 1968, 1970
Mu'taman Abū Isḥāq Ibrāhīm ibn al-ʿAssāl, 1266, 1268, 1511, **1748**, 2356
Mutawakkil, al-, Caliph, 1412
Muwaffaq al-Dīn Abu Shākir ibn Abī Sulaymān Dāwūd, **1749**
Muwaffaq al-Din ibn Saʿid al-Dawlah. *See* Ḥibat Allāh ʿAbd-allāh Ibn Saʿīd al-Dawlah al-Qibṭī
Muyser, Jacob Louis Lambert, **1749**, 1975
Myers, O. H., 861
Myron procession, 1474
see also Chrism
Mystagogia (Photius), 1113
Mysteries of Greek Letters (treatise), **1749–1750**
Mysticism
and Coptic doctrine of the Holy Spirit, 1249
of desert fathers, 113
of Dionysius (Saint Denis of Paris), 908
and gnosticism, 1149–1151
of Philo of Alexandria, 1957
of Plotinus, 1982
symbolic interpretation of Greek letters, 1749–1750
see also Magic

Mythological subjects in Coptic art, 265–266, 281–282, 1659, 1660, **1750–1768**
Amazons, 1750–1751
Aphrodite, 1752–1753, *1752*, *1753*
Apollo and Daphne, 1753–1754, *1754*
Ariadne, 1754, *1755*
Bellerophon and the Chimera, 1754–1755
dancers, 1755–1757, *1756*
Daphne, 1753–1754, *1754*, 1757–1758, *1758*
Dionysus, 1758–1760, *1759*, *1760*
Hercules, 1761, *1762*
historiography, 258–260
Horus, 1761–1762
and hunting theme, 1259
Jason, 1762–1763
Leda, 1763
Nereids, *1763*, 1763–1764, *1763*, *1764*
Nile God, *1764*, 1765–1765, *1765*
Nilotic scenes, 1765–1766, *1766*
pastoral scenes, 1766–1767
seasons, 1767
Thetis, 1767–1768, *1768*
Three Graces, 1768
see also Symbols in Coptic art

N

Nabarūh, **1769**
Nabataeans, traces at Dayr Abū Daraj, 697
Nabdūnah, **1769**
Naber. *See* Onophrius, Saint
Nabis, Bishop, **1769–1770**
Nabraha, Saint, 1557, **1770**
Nadīm, ʻAbdallāh al-, 1994, 1995
Nag Hammadi, **1770**
see also Jabal al-Ṭaārif
Nag Hammadi codices, 1149–1150, 1300
Dayr Anbā Palaemon, 757
Dayr Mār Mīnā, 833–834
see also Nag Hammadi Library; specific names
Nag Hammadi Library, **1770–1773**, *1771*, *1772*, 1892, 1893, 1899
Acts of Peter and the Twelve Apostles, 61
Allogenes, 105
Apocrypha of John, *1771*
Apocryphon of James, 169
Asclepius 21–29, 284
Authentikos Logos, 1153
Book of Thomas the Contender, 411–412
Codex Jung, 568–569
Dialogue of the Savior, 897
and Encratites, 958–959
Eugnostos the Blessed, 1068–1069
Exegesis on the Soul, 1080–1081
Gnostic codices linked with Upper Egyptian monastic setting, 1453
Gospel of the Egyptians, 1153
Gospel of Philip, 1156
Gospel of Thomas, 1162, *1771*
Gospel of Truth, 1164
Hypostasis of the Archons, 1261
Hypsiphrone, 1262
Interpretation of Knowledge, 1301
Letter of Peter to Philip, 1446
Marsanes (Codex X), 1547
Melchizedek, 1583
and Pachomius the Younger, 1864
Paraphrase of Shem, 1901
Plato's *Republic* excerpt, 1981
Prayer of the Apostle Paul, 2007
Prayer of Thanksgiving, 2007
and Puech, Henri-Charles, 2032
Second Treatise of the Great Seth, 2117–2118
Sentences of Sextus, 2119–2120
sixth tractate, 916–917
Sophia of Jesus Christ, 1068–1069
Teachings of Silvanus, 2207–2208
Testimonium veritatis (*Testimony of Truth*), 1229, 2209–2210
Thought of Norea, 2257
Three Stelae of Seth, 2259–2260
Thunder, Perfect Mind, 2260
Treatise on the Resurrection, 2275
Trimorphic Protennoia, 2276
Tripartite Tractate, 2277
Valentinian Exposition, 2295–2296
Zostrianus, 2371–2372
Naguib, Muḥammad, 1123
Naguib Mahfouz, **1773**
Naharua (martyr), 1557
Naḥḥās, Musṭafā al-, 1989, 1990, 1991, 1992–1993
Nahj al-Sabīl fī al-Radd ʻalā man Qadaḥa al-Injīl, al-, 1463
Nahyā. *See* Dayr Nahyā
Naj ʻAbū ʻAzīzah, 740
Najʻ al-Dayr (village of the monastery), 825, 826–827, 861, 1657
see also Dayr al-Shahīd Phīlūthāwaus
Najʻ al-Ḥajar, **1773–1774**
Najʻ Qurquṭān, 1658
Najʻ al-Shinshifī, 781
Nakhlah, Rufā'īl, 1465, 1467
Nakīṭī. *See* Nicetas (martyr)
Names
magical elements, 1500–1501
place names (Coptic toponomy), 2271–2274
Nanaia (pagan deity), 1866
Naos, 213, 221, 222
Nāou (martyr), 1552
Napata (Kush capital city), 1420
Napoleon Bonaparte, 1206, 1284, 1416, 1417, 1511, 1526, 1591, 1688, 1977
and Jirjis al-Jawharī, 1332–1334
Napoleon III, Emperor, 1481
Napoleonic Wars, 1512
Naqādah, **1774**
monasteries at, 747, 819, 827, 860, 1656
Naqʻ al-Ghalal wa nafʻ al-ʻalal (al-Mufaḍḍal), 1689
Naqīzah, **1774–1775**
Naqlūn, al-, shrine dedicated to Gabriel, Archangel, 1137
Nāqūs (term), 1738–1739
Narcissus, Saint, 2085
Narses, King of Persia, 906, 2344
Narses (Persarmenian general), 2341
Narthex, 213–214, 222
Nāshi' al-Akbar, al-, al-Ṣafī ibn al-ʻAssāl reply to, 2077
Nash Papyrus, **1775**
Nasīm Abū Sa'd ibn ʻAbd al-Sayyid, 8, **1775**
Nāṣir ibn Qalawūn, al-, Sultan, 935, 940, 1517–1518
Nasser, Gamal Abdel, president of Egypt, 948–949, 1637, 1971
Nastaruh (Nastarāwah), **1775**
Nastās ibn Jurayj, 1306, **1775–1776**
Natalius, Bishop, 1638

Nathaniel, Saint, 2085
National Antiquities Museum, Leiden, 4, 227, 1895
National Democratic Party, 1991
Nationalist Party (al-Ḥizb al-Waṭanī), 1627, 1748, 1987–1988, 1992, 2322–2323
National Library, Cairo, 1993
National Library, Naples, 1894
National Library, Paris, Arabic manuscripts of Coptic provenance in, 876, **1776–1783**, 1862
  Abū Shākir ibn al-Raāhib autographed work, 33
  life of Paul of Tamma, 1925
National Library, Vienna, 1891
  see also Papyrus collections
National Marcan Library, Venice, 1895
National Museum, Pisa, 1894
National Museum, Warsaw, 1091
Nation's Party, 1748, 1987, 1988–1989, 1991, 1994, 1995
Nativity
  and Advent, 63
  depicted in Coptic art, 534–536, *535*
  Fast of the, 1095–1096
  Feast of the, 1102–1103
  festal day, 1111
  Gabriel, Archangel, and, 1136
  iconography in Church of al-Mu'allaqah (Old Cairo), 559
  Proclus homilies on, 2017, 2018
Natural disasters, 1633
Nature of Christ. *See* Christ, nature of; Christology
Nau, François-Nicolas, 1435, **1783**
  on Dayr al-Sultān, 872
  and Graffin, René, 1165
Naucratis, **1783–1784**
  cult of Homeric gods, 1865
  Greek colony at, 1166, 1174, 1179, 1180
Nave, 215, 552–553
Naville, A., 780
Nawaha. *See* Monasteries of the province of Daqahliyyah
Nawasā, 1648
Nawāy, 1654
Nawrūz, **1784**, 2198
Nāzim, Maḥmūd Ramzī, 1466
Naẓm al-Jawhar (Ibn al-Biṭrīq), 1266
Neale, John Mason, **1784**
Neander, Johann August Wilhelm, **1784–1785**
Nebuchadnezzar II, King of Assyria, 1618, 2060
Necklaces, 1606
Necropolis painting. *See* Funerary customs, murals, and portraiture
Nehemiah, and Old Testament, Arabic versions of the, 1832–1833
Nelson-Atkins Gallery of Art, Kansas City, Missouri, 1598
Neo-Arianism, 230
Neocaesarea, Council of (313–c. 321), **1785**
  on *chorepiscopus*, 521, 1785
Neoplatonism
  Alexander of Lycopolis and, 87–88
  Ammonius Saccas and, 470, 1981
  anti-Manichaeism, 1521
  apologia countering, 177
  Asclepiades, 283
  Chaldean Oracles and, 516
  Egyptian pagan converts, 1868
  gnosticism and, 1151
  Heraiscus, 1221–1222
  Horapollon, 1255–1256
  Iamblichus and, 1265
  and Julian the Apostate, 1380
  Plotinus and, 1981–1982
  Synetius and, 2192
Nepos, Bishop of Arsinoë, 845, 911
Nereids
  depicted in Coptic art, *267*, 1763–1764, *1763*, *1764*
  depicted in tapestry, *274*, *2227*
Nero, Emperor Titus Claudius, **1785**
  as Antichrist, 143, 1785
  intent to visit Egypt, 2062
  patriarch under, 1913
Nerva, Emperor, patriarch under, 1913
Nestorianism
  as Antichrist, 143
  apologetic literature, 5
  Armenian church rejection of, 234
  Cosmas Indicopleustes and, 640–641
  Eutyches and, 913, 1074–1075, 1786
  John Sabas, 1369
  Leo I the Great, opposition to, 1440, 1441
  on nature of Christ, 547, 913, 1575, 1669, 1785–1786, 1787
  and Obicini, Thomas, 1823
  patriarch selection procedure and, 1999
  and Severus of Antioch, 2124, 2125
  Timothy II Aelurus, Patriarch, rejection of, 2267
Nestorians and Copts, **1785–1786**
  Ephesus, First Council of, 959–960
  see also Nestorianism; Nestorius
Nestorius, Patriarch of Constantinople, 45, 127–128, 1671, 1674, **1786–1787**
  and Celestinus, 475
  and Cyril I, Patriarch, 671–674, 1669
  and Ephesus, First Council of, 959–960, 1786, 1787
  and Eutyches, 1440–1441
  and hypostatic union, 1262
  influence on Ethiopian theology, 984
  John of Antioch support for, 1354
  places of exile, 858, 1786–1787
  Proclus and, 2017, 2018
  rejection of *Theotokos*, 2255
  Shenute, Saint, and, 1787, 2131–2132
  Theodoret and, 2236
  Theodotus of Ancyra and, 2242
  see also Nestorianism; Nestorians and Copts
Netherlands
  Coptic collections in, 1711
  papyrus collection in, 1895
Netherworld, 1499
  see also Hades
Netra, Bishop of Pharan, 1952
Newark Museum. *See* Museums, Coptic collections in
Newlandsmith, Ernest, 1730, 1737, 1742, 1743
New Moon Feast, 1101
New Schaff-Herzog Encyclopedia of Religious Knowledge, 1529
Newspapers and periodicals. *See* Press, Coptic; Press, Egyptian; specific titles
New Testament
  abba (term) in, 3

New Testament (*cont.*)
Acts, Michigan papyrus of, 58
anathema in, 127
apologia in, 176
on apostolic succession, 181
Arabic translation, 1462
on baptism vs. circumcision, 1106
Bodmer papyri, 1885
candelabra representing, 1469
canon of, 2109–2110
canticles, 1729
Chester Beatty manuscripts, 518
Christology, 523–524, 545
Codex Alexandrinus, 566–567
commentary on, 926; *see also* Scholars; Theologians; specific personal names and works
Didascalia use of, 899
Didymus on, 900
early Christian feasts, 1101
early versions of, 567, 568, 569–570, 572
Eusebius of Caesarea commentary, 1071
Fayyūm Gospel fragment, 1100
Gabriel, Archangel, in, 1135, 1136
genuflection as practice in, 1139
Gospel casket, 1474
Hexapla and Tetrapla, 1227–1228
Ibrāhīm ibn ʿAwn explication for Jews, 1273
icons inspired by, 1276
illumination, Coptic, 1283
Joseph the Carpenter in, 1371–1372
lectionary, 1435
Lucian recension, 1484
Michael, Archangel in, 1616
in monastery libraries, 1448, 1449
on nature of Christ. *See subhead* Christology
Origen on. *See Hexapla and Tertrapla*; Origen, writings of
on pagan gods, 1867
papyrus collection, 1895
and Paraphrase of Shem, 1902
on Satan, 248
themes in Coptic poetry, 1985, 1986
Theodoret on, 2236
see also Gospel headings
New Testament, Coptic versions of the, 104, 1451, 1462, **1787–1789**
New *Wafd* Party, 1991
New Year
in Copto-Arabic Synaxarion, 2174
and Holy Synod session, 2193
New Year's Day, Coptic. *See* Nawrūz
New York Historical Society, papyrus collection, 1895
Nicaea, Arabic Canons of, **1789–1790**
Nicaea, Council of (325), 74, 81, 82, 93, 127, 142, 913, 1526, **1790–1792**
Alexander I and, 83, 84–85
and Apostles' Creed, 179
on archdeacon rank, 191
and Arianism controversy, 83, 230, 232, 589–590
and Athanasius I, 298, 590
background and description of, 83
and baptism, 337
and bishop elections, 394, 1934
bishop's consecration and affirmation of, 396
and bishop's translation, 398
and canons of Coptic law, 450
and *Canons of Hippolytus*, 458
on catechumens instruction, 474
Cathedral Church of the Jacobites (Alexandria) and, 93
Christology, 525, 547, 1669
on communion of the sick, 579–580
and Constantinople, First Council of, 594
on Coptic church organization, 2193–2194
Coptic text on, 1455
on deacons' privileges and obligations, 886
and Easter date-setting, 81, 1104–1105, 1904–1905
on eparchy, 959
and Ephesus, First Council of, 959–960
Eusebius of Caesarea at, 1070–1071
five bishops named Hesychius at, 1226
Gregory the Illuminator and, 1183
Homoeans opposition, 1252
and *homoousion* controversy, 1253
and Indian missions, 1635
and Melitian schism, 1584, 1585
metropolitan designation, 1612
on nature of Christ. *See subhead* Christology
participants, 1089
patristic writings and, 1920
on Pope in Coptic church, 1998
and Zeno, Emperor, 2370
see also Nicene Creed
Nicaea, Second Council of (787), 1112
cult of images sanction at, 1275
Nicanor, first deacon, 885
Nicene–Constantinopolitan Creed, 1564
filioque added to, 1112–1116
Nicene Creed, 83–84, 179, 590, 913, 914, 960, 1551, 1638, 1671, 1676, **1792–1793**
Abu al-Majd commentary on, 21–23
Arian dissent, 83, 1253–1254
Athanasius I and, 300–301
Constantinople, First Council, on, 593–595
and Constantinople, Third Council of, 596
filioque addition, 1112
homoousion in, 1253
on Incarnation, 1287
and Nicaea, Council of, 1791, 1792–1793
on subordinationism, 2156–2157
Nicephorus, Patriarch of Jerusalem, 1098
Nicetas (martyr), 1557, 1939
Niche, 215–216, *215*
Nicholas, Bishop of Myra, 1557
Nicholas I, Pope (Rome), 1113
Nicholas V, Pope (Rome), 1119
Nicodemus, Abbot, 1119
Nicolaus of Antioch (first deacon), 885
Nicomedia, 906
Nicosia, Cyprus, 1647
"Night of the Bridegroom" (marriage custom), 1546
"Night of the Henna" (marriage custom), 1545
Nika Revolt (532), 2234

Nikiou, **1793–1794**
Persian destruction of, 132
Nikolaus, Bishop, 1136
Nile deity, depiction in Coptic art, 1765–1765, *1764*, *1765*, *1795*
Nile flooding
Michael the Archangel role, 1618
Nilometer, 1794
prayers for waters, 443–444
and Shamm al-Nasim, 2126
Nile River
and calendologia, 444–445
consecration of waters of, 1182
as Coptic art theme, 1765–1766, *1764*, *1765*
cult of, 1869
Epiphany link with Egyptian festivals of, 1103
and Feast of the Martyr, 1547–1548
Menarti island, 1587–1588
miracles associated with, 1950
Philae island, 1954–1956
travelers' interest in, 2065
see also Monasteries of the Lower Ṣa'īd; Monasteries of the Middle Ṣa'īd; Monasteries of the Upper Ṣa'īd; Nile deity; Nile flooding; Nile valley
Nile valley, agriculture in, 440–443
Nilometer, **1794**, *1795*
at Dayr al-Jarnūs (Maghāgha), 813
Nilopolis, as early bishopric, 1866
Nilotic scenes. *See* Mythological subjects in Coptic art
Nimbus, as symbol in Coptic art, 2171
Nine Saints (Ethiopia), 990–991, 1045–1047
Nineveh, Fast of. *See* Jonah, Fast of
Niqyūs, 833, 850
Nisibis, monasticism in, 1664
Nitira. *See* Netra, Bishop of Pharon
Nitria, **1794–1796**
Ammon at, 1445
Amun as first monk to settle in, 119
Armenian monks, 234
"Desert of Scetis" location, 2102
Dioscorus in, 915–916
and Kellia site location, 1397, 1401
as laura of hermitages, 1224–1225
Macarius Alexandrinus in, 1490
monasteries and monastic life, 113, 687, 1662
Palladius in, 1876, 1877
Pambo, Saint in, 113, 1877–1878
papyrus collection, 1893–1894
recluses in, 2055
Theophilus, Patriarch, and monks of, 916, 2247, 2249–2250
Niẓām, al- (publication), 1990
Noah, 1542
Nob, Apa. *See* Anub, Saint
Nob, Apa (the Confessor), 1552, **1796**, 1878
Noba, **1797**
Nobatia, 905, **1797**, 1800
and Banū al-Kanz, 336
and Dotawo, 923
and Faras, 1090
Ibn Salīm on, 1587–1588
Julian the Evangelist missions, 1380
and Kush ancient traditions, 1420
language use, 1171
Longinus's missions, 1479–1480
Monophysite missions, 1675
and Nubian evangelization, 1801–1802
and Nubian languages and literature, 1815–1816
Qaṣr Ibrīm royal residence, 2037
see also Nubia
Nobatia, eparch of, **1798**
Jabal 'Addā, 1315
Nob of Samannūd, Apa, 1969
Noetus, 1638
Nofar, Anbā, 129, 130
Nome capitals, Egyptian, 1175, 1177, 1179
Nomocanon (Gabriel II ibn Turayk), 1799
on *Canons of Hippolytus*, 458
on *Canons of Saint John Chrysostom*, 459
Nomocanon (Michael of Damietta), 1625
on *Canons of Gregory of Nyssa*, 457
on *Canons of Hippolytus*, 458
on canons of Nicaea, 1789
on *Canons of Saint John Chrysostom*, 459
on frequency of masses, 554
on *Nomocanon* of Gabriel II ibn Turayk, 1799
Nomocanon (Mīkhā'īl I), 1624
Nomocanon (al-Ṣafī ibn al-'Assāl), on *Canons of Clement*, 456 1780, 1783, 2075, 2076
on *Canons of Hippolytus*, 458
on *Canons of Saint John Chrysostom*, 459
on *Nomocanon* of Gabriel II ibn Turayk, 1799
Nomocanons, Copto-Arabic, **1799**
authorship, 1089
copied by Yūḥannā al-Maqsī, 2358
copying of, 1270, 1271
Gabriel II, Patriarch, canons in, 458, 459, 1129, 1799
Nonnos, Bishop of Heliopolis, 1753
Nonnos of Panopolis, 914, 942, 1759, **1799**
compendium of mythology, 1865
influence on Christodoros of Coptos, 544
influence on Pamprepios, 1879
Norea. *See Thought of Norea*
Normans, 1099
North Basilica of Abū Mīnā. *See* Abū Mīnā; Ampulla
North Church at Bāwīṭ, *365*
Notation, musical
Coptic oral tradition, 1730
Greek, 1731–1732
Western, transcriptions of Coptic music in, 1742–1744
Novatianism, and Cyril I, Saint, 672, 912
Nūb, Dayr Apa Anūb, 770
Nūb the Confessor, Apa, 333, 1504
Nubia, 38, **1800**
archives, 227
Ayyubid invasion, 2037
and Ballana kingdom, 332
and Beja tribes, 373
Christian conversion. *See* Nubia, evangelization of
church as Coptic church ally, 688
conquest of Kush empire, 1420
Dongola, 921–922
Dotawo, 922–923
evangelization of, 333

Nubia (*cont.*)
  fall to Banū al-Kanz, 1955
  Faras, 1090
  Fatimids relations, 1099
  Greek language use in, 1171–1173
  Griffith's studies of, 1185
  Ibn Ḥawqal on, 1266
  Ibn Salīm al-Aswānī diplomatic mission to, 1271–1272
  and Isis cult, 1954
  Island of Michael, 1588
  Jabal ʻAddā fortress, 1315
  Khā'īl I and, 1411
  pharaonic-style temples at, 1865
  Qaṣr Ibrīm settlement, 2036–2037
  and Sai Island, 2080–2081
  and Saladin, 1536
  study of medieval archaeology and philology in, 1185
  Tamīt, 2200–2201
  tombstone material, 1295
  see also ʻAlwā; Makouria; Noba; Nobatia
Nubia, evangelization of, 1380, 1420, 1675, **1801–1802**
  Julian the Evangelist missions, 1380
  Longinus' missions, 1480
  and Theodora, Empress, 2234
  see also Nubian Christian survivals
Nubia, Islamization of, **1802–1804**
Nubian archaeology, medieval, **1804–1806**
  at Soba in ʻAlwā, 2142
Nubian ceramics, **1806–1807**, *1807*
Nubian Christian architecture, **1807–1810**, *1808*, *1809*, *1810*
  and Byzantine cross-in-square building, 661
  octagon-domed church in, 1823
  and Tamīt, 2200
Nubian Christian survivals, **1811**
Nubian church art, **1811–1812**
  Faras murals, 1091
  pictures of ecclesiastical and royal dress, 1820
  see also Faras murals
Nubian church organization, **1813**
  Qaṣr Ibrīm center, 2037
Nubian inscriptions, medieval, **1814–1815**
Nubian languages and literature, 1185, **1815–1816**, 1818
Nubian liturgy, **1816–1817**
Nubian monasteries, **1817–1818**
Nubians, 110, **1818–1819**
  see also ʻAlwā; Makouria; Noba; Nobatia
Nubian studies, 615, 616, 617
Nubian textiles, **1819–1820**
Nuʻman ibn al-Mundhir, al- (al-Mundaras), 688
Numbers, Coptic, 1820–1822
  manuscript of comparative table of, *1821*
Numenius, 1868
Numerian, 904
Numerianus, Emperor
  patriarch under, 1914
  persecutions of, 1552, 1556
Numerical system, Coptic, **1820–1822**, *1821*
  see also Accounts and accounting, history of Coptic
Numidia, Donatism in, 920–921
Numitius (martyr), 1556
Nun, **1822**
  see also Women's religious communities; specific convents
Nuqrāshī, Maḥmūd Fahmī al-, 1992–1993
Nūr, al- (publication), 2198
Nūr al-Dīn, 1099
Nursing, 1581–1582
Nuwayrī, al- (Island of Michael), 1588
Nyssa. *See* Gregory of Nyssa, Saint

O

Oak, Council of the (403), 2249
Oasis
  al-ʻAraj, 189–190
  and monasteries of the Western Desert, 1658–1659
  Pharan, 1952–1953
  Siwa, 2141
  see also Dākhlah Oasis
Oaths, in Coptic legal documents, 1430
Obicini, Thomas, **1823**
Objects and instruments. *See* Instruments; Liturgical instruments; Metalwork, Coptic; specific kinds
Oblations, 1121, 1641–1642
Obrimius. *See* Primus
Octagon-domed church, **1823–1824**
Octateuch of Clement, **1824**
Octavian Augustus, Emperor, 2061, 2064, 2066
Oengus. *See* Aengus, Saint
Offering, and pilgrimages, 1968
Offering of Incense. *See* Incense
Offertory, **1824–1825**
Of the Master and the Disciple (Murqus ibn Qanbar), 1626
Ogdoas, 1735
Ogier VIII, 720
Oikonomos, **1825–1826**
  in charge of sacristy, 219
Oil, Holy. *See* Chrism
Oils, sacramental
  anointing, 137–140
  of catechesis, 137
  cruets to hold, 1473
  of exorcism, 137
Oktoechos (John of Damascus), 1735, 1985, 1986
Oktokaidekaton, 118, 951, **1826–1827**
Old Cairo. *See* Fusṭāṭ, al-
Old Coptic. *See Appendix*
Old Testament
  anthropomorphism references in, 143
  apocrypha in Coptic tradition, 161–166
  apologia in, 176
  on apostolic succession, 181
  atonement in, 306–307
  Bodmer papyri, 1885
  candelabra representing, 1469
  canon of, 2109–2110
  canticles, 1729
  cantors in, 460
  censer in, 1470
  Codex Alexandrinus, 566–567
  commentary on, 926
  confession in, 584–585
  Coptic art subjects from, 726, 1660, 1875
  Didascalia use of, 899
  Didymus on, 900
  early versions of, 567, 568, 569, 572
  on Egypt, 1867
  feasts, 1101
  and flight into Egypt, 1117, 1118

Gabriel, Archangel, in, 37, 1135, 1136
genuflection as practice in, 1139
Greek language version, 1167
guardian angel concept in, 1186
Hexapla and Tetrapla (Origen), 1227–1228
icons of subjects from, 1276
illumination, Coptic, 1283
as Jewish canon, 2109
Lagarde text, 1424–1425
lectionary, 1435
Michael, Archangel, in, 1616
in monastery libraries, 1448, 1449
Nubian church art subjects in, 1092
Origen on. *See Hexapla and Tetrapla*; Origen, writings of
origin of chanting in, 148
papyrus collections, 1894, 1895
papyrus discoveries, 1900
Philo on, 1957
Raphael, Archangel, in, 2052–2053, 2054
sacred garments, 1475
on Satan, 248
themes in Coptic poetry, 1985
Theodoret on, 2236
Three Hebrews in the Furnace, 2257–2259
translation into Coptic, 104, 1836–1838
see also Bible; Scripture, canon of the
Old Testament, Arabic versions of the, **1827–1835**
Murqus ibn Qanbar commentary, 1699–1700
Old Testament, Coptic translations of, **1836–1838**
contrastive texts, 104
O'Leary, De Lacy Evans, 815, **1840**
as Coptic hagiographer, 1192
on Coptic music, 1726, 1732, 1733
on Coptic saints and martyrs, 1551, 2081
Olympiodorus of Thebes, **1840**
Olympius, Saint (martyr), 697, 1557, **1840**, 1882
Oman, Coptic churches in, 1621
Omar Toussoun, 1397, 1658, **1841**
Omega. *See* Alpha and omega
Omophorion, 1477
On the Deaths of the Persecutors (De mortibus persecutorum), 906
On Ephesians (Origen), 1847
On First Principles (Origen), 2157
On the Holy Spirit (Didymus), 900
Onias (high priest), 1866
On the Incarnation of the Word (De incarnatione Verbi) (Athanasius I), 1288–1290
Onions, in Shamm al-Nasīm festivities, 2126
The Only-Begotten (hymn), 1732, 1733
"On nature" (Dionysius), 911
Onophrius, Saint, **1841–1842**
as desert father, 894, 1953
encomium by Pisentius on, 1979
feast day, 2085
monastery of, 805
and Paphnutius the Hermit, 863, 1841–1842, 1883
Paphnutius of Scetis's life of, 1884
and Timotheus, Saint, 2262
Onopus, 86
On the Origin of the World, 1261, **1842–1844**, 1261
On Prayer (Origen), 1847, 1852, 1855
On the Priesthood (John Chrysostom), 459
"On the Promises" (Dionysius), 911
On Temptations (Dionysius), 911
On the Trinity (Didymus), 900
Ophilus of Alexandria, 840
Ophites, 1222
Ophthalmology, 1922
Oracles, Chaldaean. *See* Chaldaean Oracles
Oracula sibyllina, 1169
Oral tradition of Coptic music, 1730
Orant
depicted in Coptic art, 536–538, *536*, *537*
see also Figurines
Orarion, 1477
Oratory (room), 1403, 1404
Order of the Golden Fleece, 1572
Order Province of the Orient. *See* Franciscans in Egypt
Order of Saint Maurice, 1572
Ordination, clerical, **1844–1845**
of archdeacon, 887–888
of deacon, 885, 886–887
and education of clergy, 564
laying-on of hands and, 1432
of priest, 2013–2015
Ordo (Gabriel V), 1131
contents of, 1132
Organ (musical instrument), 1740
Oriens Christianus, **1845**
Oriental fathers (patristics), 1920
Orientalists. *See* Scholars; specific names
Oriental Orthodox churches, 235, **1845–1846**
and the monasteries of Scetis, 2104, 2105
see also Constantinople; Jerusalem
Orientation toward the East, 216, 221, **1846**
Origen, 1448, **1846–1855**, 1885, 1921
and Alexandrian theology, 103–104
and Catechetical School, 100–101, 470–472, 474, 892, 893
on Celsus, 478–479, 1847, 1854
and Coptic education, 931–932
in Copto-Arabic tradition, 1851–1852
in defense of the faith, 176–177
and Demetrius I, dispute with, 892–893, 1847
Didymus the Blind's support of, 900
Dionysius the Great as student of, 909, 911
on Ebionites, 929–930
and eschatology, 973
and Ethiopian theology, 984
and Eusebius of Caesarea, 1070–1071
and Evagrius Ponticus, 1076–1077
and exegesis, 104
and *gnosis*, 1150, 1151
and "godly monarch" concept, 1957
on Gospel of Saint Mark, 1161
Gregory of Nazianzus writings on, 1183
Heraclas, Saint, as student of, 1219
and Heracleon, 1219–1220

Origen (*cont.*)
and Hesychius, 1226
Hexapla and Tetrapla, 1227–1228
history of theology, 232
on *homoousion*, 1253
and hypostasis controversy, 1260
Jerome, Saint, and, 1323
in Jerusalem, 1324
Justinian, Emperor, condemnation of, 1386
Kellia monks and, 113–114
library in Caesarea, 1447
on liturgical music, 1733
on Logos, 1790–1791, 1848, 1849–1850
on marriage, 1542
on monarchianism, 1638
on musical instruments, 1738
on Nativity, 1102
Pachomian–Shenutean differences on, 1453
on paganism in Egypt, 1867
Pamphilus, Saint, defense of, 1879
and Pantaenus, 1881
and papyrus discoveries, 854, 1899
and penance terms, 1945
on Raphael, Archangel, 2053
Rufinus' translations of, 2068
Scetis monks and, 2103
and *Sentences of Sextus*, 2120
on subordinationism, 471, 2157
and *Teachings of Silvanus*, 2207
and Theophilus, Patriarch, 143, 916, 2250–2252
on *Theotokos*, 2255
on unction of the sick, 139, 2291
writings of, 1852–1855; *see also Commentaries on Corinthians*; *Commentary on Saint John's Gospel*; *De principiis*; *Hexapla*; *On Ephesians*; *On Prayer*: *Philocalia*
Origenist controversies, **1855–1856**
Origenist monks
Antony of Egypt and, 150
and Gregory of Nyssa's works, 1185
in Kellia, 113, 1397
Pambo, Saint, and, 1878
Original Sin, 1930
and Atonement, 306–307
and Immaculate Conception doctrine, 1285
and Incarnation, 1287–1288
Orlandi, Tito, 1299, 1448, 1894
Orphans, *Didascalia* on, 899
Orphics, 1150
Orsenuphis (soldier–martyr), 1964
Oṣ, Ethiopian saint, 1047
Osiris (pagan deity), 1761, 1866, 2002
and agriculture, 442
and burial rites, 283
and Coptic magic, 1501, 1502, 1505, 1506
festivals of, 438
iconography of, 245, 259
sanctuary and temple at Abūṣīr (Taposiris Magna), 34, *36*, 465
temple at Abydos, 38–42
see also Mythological subjects in Coptic art
Ossius, Bishop of Córdoba, 232, 1253, 1791
Ostracine. *See* Khirbat al-Filūsiyyah
Ostracon, 1290, **1856**
and Coptic correspondence, 970–971
in Louvre, 1483
medical, 1887
Nubian medieval, 1814
preservation of, 279–280
from temple of Hatsehpsut, 227
text of *Hōs* Three, *1726*
see also Papyrus collections
Otho, Emperor, patriarch under, 1913
Ottomans, Copts under the, **1856–1857**
and administrative organization of Egypt, 935
and Egyptian finances, 1274
impact on Copto-Arabic literature, 1464–1465
Jirjis al-Jawharī role, 1334
millet system, 1087
Qaṣr Ibrīm fortification, 2037
Ouarshufah. *See* Barsanuphius (martyr)
Ouēlários (Coptic weaving term), 2221
Ousia
Origen on, 1848
as synonym of hypostasis, 1260
see also Homoeans; *Homoiousion*; *Homoousion*
Ouspensky, Porphyry, 2049
Oxford University, 1091, 2030
papyrus collection, 1894
Oxyrhynchite dialect
New Testament in, 1788
see also Appendix
Oxyrhynchus
cult of Homeric gods, 1865
family life in, 1086–1087
Latson, Apa, from, 1427
monasteries in, 1653, 1654–1655, 1662
pagarch, 1871
Paphnutius the Hermit in, 1883
papyrus discoveries, 1898–1900
Persian troops in, 1939
Roman sacrifices at, 890
Oxyrhynchus Papyri, 330, 1531, **1857–1858**
Oẓ, Ethiopian saint, 1047

P

Pachomian monasticism. *See* Monasticism, Pachomian
Pachomius Basilica. *See* Pbow.
Pachomius, Lives of. *See Life of Saint Pachomius*; Lives of Pachomius
Pachomius, Saint, 88, 119, 1619, **1859–1863**, 1876, 1969
and Abraham of Minūf, Saint, 13–14
abstinence practice, 17
altar dedications, 711
and *amma* term, 2, 3
on Antinoopolis, 144
and Apa Hor the Ascetic, 2084
as archimandrite, 193
army service, 649
and Bakhānis-Tmoushons, 331
biographies of, 1663, 1860–1861; *see also Life of Saint Pachomius*; Lives of Pachomius
as cenobitic monasticism founder, 1138, 1661–1662, 1664–1665
churches dedicated to, 730
convent establishment, 1663, 1822, 2325
Coptic language texts of, 1168, 1451–1452, 1453, 1859
on Coptic medicine, 1578
on costume of the religious, 652, 654
and Dayr al-Shuhadā', 868

depicted in Coptic art, 270, 727, 754
as desert father, 894
disciples of, 635, 2055, 2144
and Elias of Samhūd, 953
feast day, 2085
as *hegumenos*, 1215
and Horsiesios, Saint, 1257
influence on Ethiopian monasticism, 990
instructions of, 1862–1863
Isnā birthplace, 1312
and Julian the Apostate's death, 1382
and Letter of Ammon, 1445
letters of, 1863
monasteries of, 729, 731, 757, 802, 803, 825, 840–841, 1654, 1656, 1657, 1658, 1661–1663, 1973–1974, 2197; *see also* Monasticism, Pachomian
and monastery libraries, 1448
and Palamon, Saint (fourth century), 2086
personal characteristics, 2240
and Petronius, Saint, 1952, 2086
rules of, 32, 119, 1861–1862
and Shenutean monasticism, 1453
Souros as disciple of, 635, 2144
Tabennēsē as site of first monastery, 2197
and Theodorus of Alexandria, Saint, 2238
and Theodorus of Tabennēsē, Saint, 2239
use of *ḥiṣn* (protective walls) around monastery, 1237
see also Monasticism, Pachomian; Pbow

Pachomius of Tabennēsē. *See* Pachomius, Saint

Pachomius the Younger, 1204, **1864**

Pachomius al-Muḥarraqī, Abūnā, 1719

Paese and Tecla, Saints, **1865**
martyrdoms of, 841, 1557, 2054

Paganism and Christianity in Egypt, 946, **1865–1870**
Abydos site, 38–40
Alexandria, 97–98, 99, 100
altars, 105–106
Canopus as pagan center, 31
Chaldean Oracles, 516
Coptic bone and ivory carvings, 405–406
Decius, Emperor, and, 889–991
Horus linked with legend of Saint George, 1762
Isis cult at Philae, 1954
Julian the Apostate and, 1380–1382
Luxor and Luxor temples, 1484–1485
martyrs. *See subhead* persecutions
Nonnos of Panopolis influence, 1799
Nubians and, 1818
persecutions, 1935–1937, 1943, 1944–1945, 1960–1961
poetry, 1879
Theodosius I, Emperor, antipagan measures, 1869, 1870, 2248
Theophilus, Patriarch, temple destruction, 31–32, 134, 2248
uprising against Peter II, 1947
see also Mythological subjects in Coptic art; Temples; specific names of deities

Pagarch, **1871–1872**, 2023
and Arab conquest of Egypt, 189
archives of, 226
archives of Papas and, 228–229
and taxation in Roman Eqypt, 2205

Paint, 1872

Painted ceramics, Coptic, 484–486

Painting, Coptic mural, **1872–1875**
from ʿAbdallāh Nirqī excavation, 4
ʿAlam Shaltāt, 1874
Arab conquest impact on, 275–276
Bāwīṭ, 272–273, 367–368
church at Dayr al-Fakhūrī, 804
as church decoration, 739
in churches, 1874–1875
Copt-Muslim frescoes, 1311
Dayr Anbā Anṭūniyūs, 726–727
Dayr Anbā Būlā, 743–744
Dayr Anbā Hadrā, 746, 747, 747
Dayr Anbā Maqār, 753–754, *754*
Dayr Anbā Ṣamū'īl of Qalamūn, 760
Dayr Anbā Shinūdah, 764
Dayr Apa Jeremiah (Saqqara), 777–779, 1659, 1660
Dayr al-Baramūs, *793*, 793–794, *794*
Dayr Shuhadā', 868–869
Faras murals, 1090–1091, *1091*
frescoes of Church of Saint Antony, 722
fresco technique, 1872
funerary murals, 1873
and Greek language use in Christian Nubia, 1171
inscriptions as legends for, 1291
Karm al-Akhbāriyyah, 1391–1392
in Kellia rooms, 1408–1409
Mareotis, 1527–1528
medieval Nubian, discovery of, 1185
in monasteries, 1659–1660, 1873–1874, 1875
saint portraits, 2004
in secular buildings, 1873
techniques, 1872–1873
see also Monastery paintings

Paintings
Coptic styles of, 267–268, 272–273
Ethiopian Orthodox Church, 998
oldest known of cherubim, 751
see also Art and architecture, Coptic; Art, historiography of; Icons; Portraiture

Pakhoras. *See* Faras

Pakire (artist-monk), 804

Palaemon, Saint (hermit), **1876**, 2086

Palamon, Saint (fourth century)
church of, 757
feast day, 2086
monasteries dedicated to, 1973–1974
Pachomius as disciple, 1859
see also Dayr Anbā Palaemon

Palamon, Saint, 1427, **1876**

Palanque, (Henri Amedée) Charles, **1876**

Palau-Ribes Collection (Barcelona), 1895

Paleography. *See Appendix*

Palestine
Acacian schism and, 45
monasticism origins in, 1663
see also Holy Land; Jerusalem, Coptic See of; Mount Sinai Monastery of Saint Catherine

Palettes (arm bands), *1606*

Palladius, 88, 894, **1876–1877**
on *abba* and *amma* terms, 3
and costume of the religious, 650, 652
and Cronius of Nitria, 2083
on Dayr Abū Ḥinnis, 701
desert fathers term use by, 894
on Didymus the Blind, 900
on Evagrius Ponticus, 1076–1077
Historia lausiaca compared with *Historia monachorum in Aegypto*, 1238
on Isaac, Saint, 1304
on Jabal Khashm al-Quʿūd, 1316
and John of Lycopolis, 1363, 1365
on Kellia, 1397
Lausiac History, 7
and Macarius Alexandrinus, 1490
on monasteries for women, 1663
as monk in Pempton region, 1931
on monks' hymn-singing, 1733
on Nitria, 1796
on numbers of Pachomian monks, 1662
Pachomian document ("Rule of the Angel"), 1862
on Pambo, Saint, 1877, 1878
on Paphnutius, 1884
on Paul the Simple, 1923
on Sarapion, 2094, 2095
and Theophilus, Patriarch, 2247, 2250
see also Historia lausiaca
Palladius (pagan prefect), uprising against Peter II, 1947
Palladius, Abbā (Thessalonian monk), 1467
Palladius, Bishop of Helenopolis, on flight into Egypt, 1118
Palm Sunday, **1103–1104**
and Anaphora of Saint Gregory, 124–125
cross with tapers, 1469
and events of Holy Week, 1251
Hosanna use on, 1258
pilgrimages to Dayr al-Muḥarraq, 840
Pambo, Saint, 113, 1076, 1733, **1877–1878**
and Ammonius of Kellia, 2082
feast day, 2086
and Hilaria, Saint, 1230–1231
and monasteries in Nitria, 1795
Pamīn. *See* Poemen, Saint
Pamin, Saint, 1553, 1649, **1878**, 2269
Pamio (scribe), 1961
Pamo. *See* Pambo, Saint
Pamphilus, Saint, **1879**
in defense of Origen, 471, 1071
and Eusebius of Caesarea, 1070, 1071
martyrdom, 1557
Pamprepios of Panopolis, **1879**
and Hellenization, 1168
and Nonnos of Panopolis, 1799
Pamun and Sarmata (martyrs), 1557
Pandektēs, 77
Panegyric of Saint Michael (Theophilus of Alexandria), 1782
Panels, wooden, *2345–2346*, 2345–2347
Panephysis, 1648
Panesneu, Saint (martyr), **1880**, 1557
Paneu. *See* Panine and Paneu, Saints
Panine and Paneu, Saints, 40, **1880–1881**
in Idfā, 1280
and Psote of Psoï, 2032
Pan-Islamism, 1995, 1996
Pano. *See* Pambo, Saint
Panoplia (Michael Cerularius), 1113
Panopolis. *See* Akhmīm
Pantaenus, **1881**
and Alexandrian theology, 103–104
and the Catechetical School of Alexandria, 469, 474
and Coptic education, 931–932
Indian missions, 892, 1635, 1881
Pantaleon (Christian governor of Antioch), 1307
Pantaleon, Saint (martyr), **1881–1882**, 1557, 1840
Pantalēwon (Pantaleon), Ethiopian saint, 1046
Paolo da Lodi, Friar, 1122
Papacy. *See* Pope; Roman Catholic church; specific names
Papadopoulos, Chrysostomos, on Dayr al-Sulṭān, 873
Papas, archives of, 228–229
Paper, medical manuscripts, 1887–1888
Paphnutius, Bishop of Upper Thebaid ("martyr without bloodshed)", 1557
Paphnutius, Saint (tenth-century monk and bishop), **1882**, 2086
Paphnutius the Hermit, Saint, 727, **1882–1883**, 2262
account of journey in the desert, 120, 1882
death and relics at Dayr al-Shamʿ, 863, 1883
as desert father, 894
feast day, 1557, 2086
and Onophrius, Saint, 1841–1842
Paphnutius Kephalas. *See* Paphnutius of Scetis, Saint
Paphnutius of Pbow, Saint, 1557, **1883–1884**, 2086
Paphnutius of Scetis, Saint, 1883, **1884**
and Cassian, John, 462
feast day, 2086
and Theophilius on anthropomorphism, 1884, 2103
Paphnutius of Tabennēsē, Saint (fifth century), **1882**, 2086
and Monastery of the Metanoia, 1609
Papias, Bishop of Hierapolis, 1531
Papohé. *See* Phib
Papylas (martyr), 1557
Papyri, Coptic
Acts, Michigan papyrus of, 58
Chester Beatty collection, 519
Dayr Apa Jeremiah (Saqqara) find, 773
Dayr Apa Phoibammon find, 780
Dayr al-Ḥammām find, 806
Dayr al-Quṣayr (Ṭurah) find, 854
Fayyūm Gospel fragment, 1100
Ibscher, Hugo, restoration of, 1274–1275
Karanis find, 1390
magical texts, 1501–1502, *1500, 1501, 1502*
on medicine, 1578, 1579, 1581
as source material for arabization of Egypt, 937
see also Manuscripts

Papyri, Coptic literary, **1884–1885**, 1889
examples of *Hōs*, 1726, *1726*
Papyri, Coptic medical, **1886–1888**, 1889
Papyri, Greek language, 1166, 1890–1896, 1898, 1900
Papyri, Manichaean, 2106
Papyrology, **1888–1889**, 2107
Wessely, Carl Franz Josef, 2321
Wilcken, Ulrich, 2322
Papyrus
preservation and restoration of, 279, 1274–1275
see also Bookbinding; Manuscripts
Papyrus Berolinensis (Coptic codex), 1149
Papyrus collections, 1885, **1890–1896**
Akhmīm fragments, 80
archives, 226–227
Beatty, Chester, 380–382, 518–519, 1899–1900
Bodmer, Martin, 404–405
Maspero catalogue, 1562
Nash Papyrus, 1775, 1775
Rainer Papyrus, 1100, 2049
Schubart, Wilhelm, studies, 2107
Vienna, University of, 1389
Papyrus discoveries, **1898–1900**
archives, 226–227
and Coptological studies, 615
Nag Hammadi codices, 1771
Oxyrhynchus Papyri, 1857–1858
Papyrus Egerton. *See* Egerton Gospel
Papyrus Institute, Florence, 1894
Parable, of faith and the mustard seed, 11
Parabolani, and Cyril I, Saint, 671–673
Paraclete, 1520
Paradise, **1900–1901**
see also Heaven
Paradise (Enanisho), 2, 3
Paradise of Orthodoxy, 1089
Paraetonium, as Greek town in Egypt, 1180
Paralipomena Jeremiou, 166
Paralipomena Pachomius, 1860, 1861
Parallos. *See* Burullus, al-
Paramelle, Joseph, 1749
Paramone, **1901**
and fasting, 2099
Paraphrase of Seth (Hippolytus), 1902
Paraphrase of Shem, **1901–1902**
as Old Testament apocrypha, 166
used by Basilides, 356–357
Parchasinus (Roman legate), 914
Parchment, **1902–1903**
codex, 565–566
medical manuscripts, 1886–1887
preservation of, 279
Parekklesia, **1903**
added to Dayr Anbā Bishoi, 735
in Church of Mār Mīnā, 320
Church of Saint Antony, 725
Paris, France. *See* Louvre Museum; National Library
Paris, Treaty of, 1941
Parmenas (first deacon), 885
Parmenian, Bishop, 920
Parmenides (Plato), 1981
Paromeos. *See* Dayr al-Baramūs
Parthey, Gustav Friedrich Constantin, **1903**
Parthian horseman, 538, *538*, 1259
Parties, political. *See* Political parties
Pascha, **1903–1904**
holy chrism use during, 521
see also Passover
Paschal controversy, 81, 84, 436, 892, 1792, 1904, **1905–1906**, 1997
Book of Epact and Demetrius I, 409–411, 1104
Paschal lamb, 1060, 1904
Passions of martyrs. *See* Cycle; Martyrs, Coptic; specific martyrs
Passion Week, 1095
Passover, 1095, 1101, 1152, 1792, 1903–1904, 1905
anamnesis relationship, 120
and Last Supper, 1060–1061
see also Eucharist; Pascha
Pastophorium, 216
Pastoralism, depicted in Coptic art, 1766–1767
Pastoral staff, 1468, *1468*
Patape, Bishop of Qifṭ, 1557, **1907–1908**
Patāsius, Saint, **1908**, 2086
Paten, as Eucharistic vessel, 1065
Paten veil. *See* Eucharistic Veils
Paterae, 1596, *1596*
Patermuthius, Saint, **1908**, 2086
Patriarch, **1909**
biographies by Abū Shākir ibn al-Rāhib, 1463
chrism consecration by, 522
chronology of, 33
Egyptian taxation of, 1414
as head of ecclesiastical hierarchy, 2015, 2193–2194
History of the Patriarchs of Alexandria, 1238–1241
Holy Synod, 2193–2194
liturgical insignia, 1468–1469
liturgical vestments, 1476–1477
problems in late antiquity, 944
selection of, 1999
see also Pope in the Coptic church; Patriarchs; specific names
Patriarch, consecration of, **1909–1910**, 1912, 2000
Patriarchal deputy, **1911**
Patriarchal election, **1911–1912**
Patriarchal Library, Alexandria, 1532
Patriarchal residences, 92, 689–690, **1912–1913**, 1999–2000
Patriarchs (Old Testament), apocrypha of the, 163–164
Patriarchs, Testaments of. *See* Testaments of the patriarchs
Patriarchs of the See of Saint Mark
Abilius, 8
Abraham, 10–11
Achillas, 55–56
Agathon of Alexandria, 65–66
Agrippinus, 72, 72
Alexander I, 81–85
Alexander II, 85–87
Anastasius, 125–126
Andronicus, 131–132, 131–132
Anianus, 133–134
Athanasius I, 298–302
Athanasius II, 302
Athanasius III, 302–303
Benjamin I, 375–377
Benjamin II, 377–378
Cerdon, 511
Cyril I, 671–675
Cyril II, 675–676
Cyril III ibn Laqlaq, 677
Cyril IV, 677–679
Cyril V, 679
Cyril VI, 679–681
Damian, 688–689

Patriarchs of the See of Saint Mark (*cont.*)
Dioscorus I, 912–915
Dioscorus II, 915
Eumenius, 1069
Gabriel I, 1127
Gabriel II ibn Turayk, 1127–1129
Gabriel IV, 1129–1130
Gabriel V, 1130–1132
Gabriel VII, 1133–1134
Gabriel VIII, 1135
Gabriel VI, 1133
Gaianus (rival), 1138
Isaac, 1303
Jacob, 1318
John I, 1337
John II, 1337
John III, the Merciful, 1337
John IV, 1338–1339
John V, 1340–1341
John VI, Saint, 1341–1342
John VII, 1342–1343
John VIII, 1343–1344
John IX, 1344
John X, 1344
John XI, 1344–1345
John XII, 1346
John XIII, 1346–1347
John XIV, 1347
John XV, 1347–1348
John XVII, 1348–1350
John XVIII, 1350
John XIX, 1351
Julian, 1380
Justus, 1386
Khā'īl I, 1410–1412
Khā'īl II, 1412
Khā'īl III, 1412–1413
Maqrīzī history on, 1525
Marcianus, 1526
Mark I as first, 1528–1533
Mark II, 1533–1534
Mark III, 1534–1536
Mark IV, 1536–1537
Mark V, 1537
Mark VI, 1537
Mark VII, 1537–1538
Mark VIII, 1538–1539
Matthew I, 1569–1570
Matthew II, 1571
Matthew III, 1571
Matthew IV, 1571
Maximus, 1574–1575
Michael IV, 1614–1615
Michael V, 1615–1616
Michael VI, 1616
Mīnā I, 1631–1632
Mīnā II, 1632–1633
Peter I, 1943–1946
Peter II, 1947
Peter III Mongus, 1947–1948
Peter IV, 1948
Peter V, 1948–1949
Peter VI, 1949–1950
Peter VII, 1950
Philotheus, 1959–1950
portraits at Old Church Dayr Anbā Anṭūniyūs, 726
Simon I, 2138–2139
Simon II, 2139
Theodorus, 2237
Theodosius I, 2241
Theodosius II, 2241–2242
Theonas, 2244–2246
Theophanes, 2247
Theophilus, 2247–2252
Timothy I, 2263
Timothy II Aelurus, 2263–2267
Timothy III, 2268
Yūsāb I, 2362–2363
Yūsāb II, 2362
Zacharias, 2367–2368
see also History of the Patriarchs
Patrician Monastery. *See* Monastery of the Patrician
Patristics, **1920–1921**
collection, 1778
Patrologia Orientalis, **1921**
Patrologia Orientalis edition. *See* Synaxarion, Copto-Arabic
Patrology, **1921**
see also Patristics
Paul, Apostle and Saint
and ablution, 9
on anathema, 127
and Antony, Saint, 1733
on celibacy, 476
churches and monasteries dedicated to, 849, 854
on circumcision, 1106
and creation of bishops, 2015
depiction in Coptic art, 529
early Christian feast observance, 1101
on Egyptian worship, 1867
epistles on deacons, 885
on Good Friday, 1104
on heaven, 1214
on interpretation of the Resurrection, 1104
on Kiss of Peace, 1416
laqqān use on feast day of, 1426
and laying-on of hands, 1432, 1433
and Mark, Saint, 1529, 1530
on marriage, 1542, 1544, 1545
and matins, 1568–1569
on the nature of Christ, 524
on Paradise, 1901
on Phoebe, deaconess, 888
prayer of, 2007
and Thecla, Saint, 540–541
on types, 2283
see also Apocalypse of Paul; Dayr Anbā Būlā
Paul IV, Pope (Rome), 1134
Paul of Aigina, **1922**, 77
Paul of Akhmīm, Bishop, 762
Paul of Bahnasā, Bishop, **1922**
Paul of Benhadab, Saint, **1922**, 2086
Paul the Black, Patriarch of Antioch, **1922–1923**
consecrated by Jacob Baradaeus, 1319
Damian and, 688, 689
Paulinus of Aquileia, 1112
Paulinus of Nola, Bishop, 1930
Paul, Longinus, and Zeno (martyrs), 1557
Paul of Mendes, 1965
Paul and Salfana (martyrs), 1557
Paul of Samosata, Bishop of Antioch, 911, 1484, 1575, 1638
Paul the Simple, Saint, 2–3, 727, **1923**, 2086
wall paintings of, 727
Paul the Solitary. *See* Būlus al-Ḥabīs, Saint
Paul the Syrian (martyr), 1557
Paul of Tamma, Saint, 154, 362, 1557, **1923–1925**, 2029, 2262
Paul of Thebes, Saint, **1925–1926**
and anachoresis, 120, 129, 130, 1661
churches dedicated to, 721, 741, 742
and Dayr Anbā Būlā site, 741
as desert father, 894
feast day, 2086
paintings of, 754
Paulus Orosius, 1930
Pbow, **1926–1929**, 1657
Abraham of Farshūṭ as archimandrite, 11–12
archaeology, 1927–1929
and Bakhānis-Tmoushons, 331

and church architecture in Egypt, 552–553
history of, 1926–1927
Pachomian monastic center at, 1657, 1665, 1860
Paphnutius, Saint, of, 1883–1884
and Stephen of Hnēs, 2154
Theodorus of Tabennēsē and, 2239
and Victor of Tabennēsē, 2308
see also Monasticism, Pachomian
The Pearl of Great Value. *See Durr al-Thamīn, al*
Pectoral crosses, 1468
Peeters, Paul, 1445, **1929**
Pehke, 707, 1679
Peiresc, Nicolas Claude de Fabri, Seigneur de, **1929**, 1977
Peisouchos (crocodile god), 1390
Pejosh. *See* Bajush (martyr)
Pelagianism, **1929–1930**
condemned by Ephesus, First Council of, 959–960, 1930
Cyril I, Saint and, 673
Jerome, Saint and, 1323
Pelagia, Saint, 2086
Pelagius, 1929–1930
Pelagius II, Pope (Rome), 1339
Pellegrini, Astorre, **1931**
Pelusium. *See* Faramā, al-
Pelusium, Isidorus, Saint, 1308–1310
Pemdje. *See* Bahnasā, al-
Pempton, 125, **1931**
Penalization, **1931–1932**
anathema, 127–128
and *audientia episcopalis*, 308
excommunication, 1079–1080
Penance, **1932**, 1945
and absolution, 15–16
Phib, Saint, associated with, 1954
and unction of the sick, 2291
Pen cases, **1933**, 1961
Pendants, 1606
Pendektēs (Akhrūn), 77
Pendeme. *See* Qaṣr Ibrīm
Penitence. *See* Absolution; Confession and penitence
Pentapolis, 1529, 1638, **1933–1935**
metropolitan see of, 1612–1613
Paraetonium as capital, 1180
Pentateuch
Arabic versions of, 1833–1834
collected manuscripts of, 1776–1777
in Jewish canon, 2108
Philo philosophical thought based on, 1957
Pentecost, **1105–1106**
and Coptic doctrine of the Holy Spirit, 1250
and Fast of the Apostles, 1093
and genuflection, 1139
Gnostic version of, 1446
lectionary for, 1437
Letter of Peter to Philip on, 1446
pilgrimages to Dayr al-Muḥarraq, 840
People of the covenant. *See Ahl al-Dhimmah*
People's Party, 1992
Pepin, F., 854
Pepin the Short, 1112
Percussion instruments, 1732, 1738–1739
see also specific kinds
Periodicals. *See* Press, Coptic; Press, Egyptian; specific titles
Persecutions, **1935–1937**
Alexander II patriarchy and, 86–87
in Alexandria, 99, 100
by Arianus, 230–231
Canonical Letter provisions, 1944–1945, 1946
Constantine I halt to, 588
Cosmas II patriarchy and, 636–637
by Cyrus al-Muqawqas, 188, 682–683, 682
by Decius, Emperor, 889–890
destruction of Christian manuscripts, 1885
by Diocletian. *See* Diocletian, Emperor
Eusebius of Caesarea chronicle, 1071
by al-Ḥākim Bi-Amr-Illāh Abū ʻAlī Manṣūr, 1201–1203, 2313–2314
imagery of, 1961
Islamic (fifteenth-century), 1129, 1130
Islamic (fourteenth-century), 750, 1343–1344, 1949
Islamic (thirteenth-century), 1267, 1268
by Mamluks, 941, 1343, 1517–1518, 1535, 1949, 2313–2316
by Maximian, Emperor, 1082, 1110, 2057
Melchite, 188
of Monophysites, 590, 1674, 1676, 1923
by Nero, Emperor, 1785
Peter I and, 1943, 1944–1945
by Romans, 892–893, 903, 909–910, 912, 1110, 1548–1549, 1550–1559, 1868–1869, 1935–1937, 2231–2233; *see also* names of specific emperors
Saladin's anti-Coptic decrees, 1535
see also Great Persecution; Martyrology; Martyrs, Coptic
Persia, Christian martyrs in, 1151–1152
Persians in Egypt, **1938–1940**
and administrative organization, 946–947
impact on Alexandria, 131–132
influences on Coptic art, 2097–2098
Nawrūz celebration, 1784
Pisentius on, 1979
see also Arab conquest of Egypt
Personal status courts, 1941–1942
Personal status law, **1941–1943**
Pertinax, Emperor, patriarch under, 1914
Pesaḥ. *See* Pascha
Pesenetai. *See* Khandaq, al-
Peter (fourteenth-century scribe), 927
Peter, Apostle and Saint
Act of Peter, 57
Acts of Peter and the Twelve Apostles, 57
Apocalypse of, 160–161
in Apocryphon of James, 169
apostolic see, 181
churches and monasteries dedicated to, 849, 854
and funerary stelae, 705
on Good Friday, 1104
and Gospel of Saint Mark, 1158, 1159, 1161
and Holy Spirit, 1446
on Incarnation, 1287–1288
on Kiss of Peace, 1416
laqqān use on feast day of, 1426
and Mark, Saint, 1529, 1530–1531
and Mary Magdalene's spiritual leadership, 1155

Peter, Apostle and Saint (*cont.*)
and Michael, Archangel, 1618
monasteries dedicated to, 1467
and origin of antiphonal chanting, 148
paintings of, 529, 869
and penitence, 584
on salvation, 1285
and Transfiguration, 1108–1109
see also Apocalypse of Peter
Peter I, Archbishop of Jerusalem. *See* Jerusalem, Coptic See of
Peter I, Patriarch, 55, 81, **1943–1946**
and Achillas, 81
and Arius, 231
Canonical Letter on persecutions, 1944–1945, 1946
dates of patriarchy, 1914
and Diocletian's persecutions, 907
encomiums honoring, 400, 1117
on Eucharist, 1061
excommunication of Arius, 231
execution of, *See subhead* martyrdom
homilies and letters of, 1617, 1945–1946
and Lithazomenom and Saint Peter's Bridge, 1467
martyrdom, 1557, 1869, 1937, 1945, 2031
and Melitian schism, 1584, 1585
and Melitius, 609, 1585
on Michael the Archangel, 1617
and Theonas, 2246
on Wednesday and Friday fasting, 1096
Peter II, Saint and Patriarch, **1947**
dates of patriarchy, 1914
feast day, 2086
successor, 2263
Peter III Mongus, Patriarch, **1947–1948**
and Acacian schism, 42–47, 55
anathematized by Severus of Antioch, 2124
as anti-Chalcedonian, 2370
dates of patriarchy, 1915
and Henoticon edict, 1218, 1534, 1670, 1671
and Monastery of the Metanoia, 1608, 1609
as successor to Timothy II Aelurus, 2266
and Timothy Salofaciolus as patriarch, 2269
Peter IV, Patriarch, **1948**
Damian and, 688
dates of patriarchy, 1915
at Dayr Ebifania, 800
and the Enaton, 95, 956–957
feast day, 2086
and John of Parallos, 1368
and Paul the Black, 1923
residence and refuge outside of Alexandria, 94
Peter V, Patriarch, **1948–1949**
consecrated at Church of Abū Sayfayn, 550
dates of patriarchy, 1917
Peter VI, Patriarch, 399, 427, 1348, **1949–1950**
dates of patriarchy, 1919
and Ethiopian prelates, 399, 1028, 1032
as monk at Dayr Anbā Būlā, 742
Peter VII, Patriarch, 1248, 1614, **1950**
dates of patriarchy, 1919
and Ethiopian prelates, 1034, 1035
as monk at Dayr Anbā Anṭūniyūs, 723
and Sa'd Mīkhā'īl 'Abdū, 2073
Tādrus al-Mashriqī history of, 2197
Peter of Akhmīm. *See* Pshoi, Saint
Peter of Apamea, 2124
Peter the Ascetic. *See* Peter of Scetis, Saint
Peter Callinicus, Patriarch of Antioch, 688, 689
Peter de Lusignan. *See* Pierre de Lusignan
Peter the Elder. *See* Peter the Presbyter, Saint
Peter the Fuller, Patriarch of Antioch, 1218, 1671
Peter the Great, Saint, 2086
Peter the Iberian, 44, 1218, 1672
Peter Mongus. *See* Peter III Mongus
Peter the Presbyter, Saint, 1922, **1951**, 2086
Peter al-Sadamanti. *See* Buṭrus al-Sidmantī
Peter of Scetis, Saint, **1951**, 2086
Petersen, Theodore, **1951**
Petra. *See* Jabal Khashm al-Qu'ūd
Petraeus, Theodor, **1951**
Petrie, W. A. F., 786, 806, 1726
Petronius, Saint, **1952**
feast day, 2086
as Pachomius's successor, 1664
and Pbow, 1927
and Theodorus of Tabennēsē, 2240
Pēṭros I, Ethiopian prelate, 1001–1002
Pēṭros II, Ethiopian prelate, 1018–1019
Pēṭros III, Ethiopian prelate, 1020–1021
Pēṭros IV, Ethiopian prelate, 1038
Peyron, Amedeo Angelomaria, 1952
Phantasiasts
on Incarnation, 1288
see also Julian, Bishop of Halicarnassus
Pharan (oasis), **1952–1953**, 1976
Pidjimi, Saint, at, 1966, 1967
Pharos, island of, 90, 93, 96, 101
Pharos Lighthouse, 90
Pherme. *See* Jabal Khashm al-Qu'ud
Phib, Saint, 1551, **1953–1954**, 2086
and Bāwīṭ founding, 362, 843
see also Apollo of Bāwīṭ, Saint
Philae, 1657, **1954–1956**
castrum of, 236, 467
inscriptions found at, 1292
memorial stone, 1294
monasticism, 1955–1956
as pagan sanctuary, 1178
pharaonic-style temples at, 1865
worship of Isis at, 107, 1801; *see also* Temple of Isis
Philas, Saint, 2086
Phileas, Bishop of Tmuis, 907, 1937
Philemon. *See* Apollonius and Philemon; Heracleas and Philemon
Philip (first deacon), 885
Philip. *See* Gospel of Philip
Philip, Apostle and Saint
on Good Friday, 1104
and Holy Spirit, 1446
Philip, Saint. *See* Philas, Saint
Philip of Anatolia, Bishop, **1956**
Philip the Arabian, Emperor, 889
Philip of Damanhūr (martyr), 1554
Philip the Good of Burgundy, 1572

Philipps Library, Cheltenham, England, 1893
Philippus, Bishop of Memphis, 1587
Philippus, Emperor, 909
 patriarch under, 1914
Philip of Side, 2016–2017
Philo of Alexandria, 103, 104, 1865, **1956–1957**
 apologists in tradition of, 175
 Eusebius on, 1530
 on Judaism, 176
 and Origen, 1850
Philocalia (Origen), 1853, 1854
Philology. *See* Language, Coptic; other specific languages
Philopater. *See* Mercurius of Caesarea, Saint
Philoponoi. *See* Confraternity
Philoponus, 916
Philosophers
 Alexander of Lycopolis, 87–88
 Alexandrian in late antiquity, 100
 Asclepiades, 283, 283
 Celsus, 478–479
 Chairemon of Alexandria, 512
 Heraiscus, 1221–1222
 Horapollon, 1255–1256
 Philo of Alexandria, 1956–1957
 Plotinus, 1981–1982
 Synesius, 2192
 see also Catechetical School of Alexandria
Philosophy, **1958**
 and Alexandrian theology, 103–104
 Arabic, 6
 at the Enaton, 956
 eschatology, 973–974
 see also Philosophers; specific philosophies, e.g., Platonism
Philostorgius, **1958–1959**
Philotheus, Patriarch, **1959–1960**
 and Damrū, 689
 dates of patriarchy, 1916
 and Ethiopian prelates, 1002
 language of liturgy under, 1134
 Life of Latson, 1427
 and Paphnutius, Saint, 1882
 patriarchal residence, 1912
Philotheus of Antioch, Saint, **1960–1961**
 martyrdom, 1557, 2054
 monasteries dedicated to, 848, 861, 862, 1657
 pilgrimages to sanctuary of, 1974
Philoxenus of Mabbug, **1961–1962**
 and Acacian schism, 44
 monophysitism, 1672–1673
 and Severus of Antioch, 2124
Philūthāwus Ibrāhīm al-Baghdādī, 1630, **1962–1963**
 role in Coptic education, 563, 931–933
Phis, Saint, **1963**, 2086
Phocas (martyr). *See* Fugas
Phocas, Emperor, 126, 688, 1676
 patriarch under, 1915
Phoebammon. *See* Phoibammon of Preht (martyr)
Phoebe (deaconess), 888
Phoibammon, Bishop of Qifṭ, 1769–1770, 2039
Phoibammon, Saint. *See* Abū Bifām, Saint; Dayr Apa Phoibammon; Phoibammon of Preht (martyr)
Phoibammon of Preht (martyr), 13, 296, 370, 965, 1093, 1557, **1963–1965**
 and donation of children, 918
 martyrdom, 696, 1557
Phonen, King, 1171
Phonology. *See Appendix*
Photius, 917
 on *filioque*, 1113, 1115, 1116
 and Pamphilus, Saint, 1879
Phragonis. *See* Afrājūn, al-
Phrim. *See* Qaṣr Ibrīm
Phyloxenite. *See* Bahīj
Physicians. *See* Medicine, Coptic
Physiologos, 1337, **1965–1966**
Piamot of Dumyāṭ, Bishop, 925
Piankoff, Alexandre, **1966**
Pidjimi, Saint, 129–130, 1117, **1966–1967**, 2086
Piehl, Karl Fredrik, **1967**
Pier. *See* Pillar
Pierius ("Origen the Younger"), 907, 2246
Pierpont Morgan Library, New York City, 48, 824, 1136, 1449, 1592
 papyrus collection, 1895, 1899
Pierre de Lusignan, 1537, 1569
Pietro delle Valle, **1967**, 1894
Pihebs (martyr), 1557
Pihur, Pisura, and Asra (martyrs), 1557
Pilasters, wooden, *2345*, 2345
Pilate. *See* Filatis (martyr)
Pilgrimages, **1968–1975**
 Abū Mīnā as center for, 24–29
 Abydos, 38–42
 ban on access to Holy Sepulcher, 1130
 bans on Coptic, 1615
 famous, 1969–1971
 inscriptions attesting, 1291
 Islamic sites, 1528
 length and dates of, 1968
 Muslim interference with, 1538
 Rabitat al-Quds (agency), 2049
 secular aspect of, 1968–1969
 seven specific aspects of, 1968
 sites, 1971–1975
 to Abraam I, Saint, gravesite, 10
 to Abū Mīnā, 24, 1550, 1969
 to Abū Tīj, 38
 to burning bush site, 1682, 1683
 to Dayr Abū Isḥāq
 to Dayr al-ʿAdhrā', 714
 to Dayr Anbā Bisādah, 732
 to Dayr Anbā Palaemon, 757
 to Dayr Anbā Shinūdah, 765
 to Dayr al-ʿAzab, 784
 to Dayr Durunkah, 799
 to Dayr al-Maghṭis, 818–819
 to Dayr al-Malāk Mīkhā'īl, 823
 to Dayr Mār Jirjis al-Jadīdī, 832
 to Dayr Mār Mīnā (Gharbiyyah), 833
 to Dayr Mār Mīnā (Jabal Abū Fūdah), 834
 to Dayr al-Muḥarraq, 840
 to Dayr Sitt Dimyānah, 872, 903
 to Dayr Yūḥannā, 882
 to Egyptian monasteries, 2066
 to Kafr al-Dayr, 1656
 to martyrs' sanctuaries, 1550
 to Mazār al-Sayyidah al-ʿAdhrā' (rock church), 853
 to Qaṣr Ibrīm, 2037
 to Saint Dimyānah residence site, 903
 to tomb of Marqus al-Antūnī, 1699
 to tomb of Psote of Psoï, 2030
Pilgrims and travelers in Christian Egypt, **1975–1977**
 Pococke, Richard, 1983
Pillar, 217
Pillar of the Faith. *See* Cyril I, Saint and Patriarch
Pimandjoili, **1977**
Pinon, Carlier du, 1977
Pior, Saint, 894, 2086

Piriminius, on Apostles' Creed, 178
Piroou and Athom (martyrs), 695, 971, 1089, 1558
Pisentius, Saint and Bishop of Armant (seventh century), **1978**, 2086
Pisentius, Saint and Bishop of Hermonthis (Armant) (fourth–fifth century), 1353–1354, **1978**, 2086
Pisentius, Saint and Bishop of Qifṭ (Coptos), 703, 779, 1448, 1892, **1978–1980**
  archive of, 227
  Coptic works on, 1455–1456
  correspondence of, 401–402
  depicted in Coptic art, 727
  feast day, 2086
  John the Presbyter life of, 1368
  monastery of, 757, 819–821
  and Persian conquest of Egypt, 1939
  see also Pseudo-Pisentius of Qifṭ
Pispir, 838
Pistis Sophia, 897, 1148–1149, 1155
Pisura. *See* Pihur, Pisura, and Asra (martyrs)
Pisura, Saint and Bishop of Maṣīl (martyr), 1558, **1980**
Pitchers. *See* Water vessels
Pitiryon, Saint, 2086
Pius IX, Pope (Rome), 1373
Pius XII, Pope (Rome), 1942
Piusammon, Bishop of Nikiou, 1793–1794
Pjol, Anbā, 1974, **1981**
  and Dayr Anbā Shinūdah founding, 378–379
  and Shenute, Saint, 737, 762
Place names. *See* Toponymy, Coptic
Plagues, 86, 910, 1130, 1536–1537, 1633, 1867, 2045, 2242
  see also Black Death
Plain weaving, Coptic textiles, 2217
Plants, in paintings at Bāwīṭ, 371
Plaques, bone and ivory carvings, 406
Plated boxes, 1605
Plates and Dishes. *See* Ceramics, Coptic; Metalwork, Coptic; Tableware
Plato, 1957, 1981
  see also Platonism; Plato's *Republic*
Platonism, 1147, 1148, 1149, 1519, 1547
  Celsus, 478–479
  Christian apologia and, 176
  see also Neoplatonism
Plato's *Republic*, 1149, **1981**
  Coptic translation, 1958
Plerophoria (John of Mayuma), 1670, 1735
Pliny the Elder, 1902
Plotinus, 1868, **1981–1982**
  doctrine of soul's divinity, 1265
Ploumários (Coptic textile term), 2221
Plutarch (martyr), 892
Pochan, André, 704
Pococke, Edward, 1266
Pococke, Richard, 1349, 1977, **1983**
Poebarumon, Saint, 1137
Poemen, Saint, 3, 862, **1983–1984**
  feast day, 2086
  hypothesis of two, 1983
  and John Colobos, 1360, 1360, 1668
  on Sisoēs, 2141
Poemen and Eudoxia. *See* Benjamin and Eudoxia (martyrs)
Poetry, **1985–1986**
  in ʿAbd al-Masīḥ manuscript, 5
  by Abū Ḥulayqah, 19
  Alexandrian in late antiquity, 100
  Chaldean Oracles, 516
  Christodoros of Coptos, 544
  Copto-Arabic, 1465–1466, 1467
  by Dioscorus of Aphrodito, 916
  Greek-language Egyptian, 1177–1178
  Nonnos of Panopolis epic, 1799
  pagan, 1879
  translations into German, 2067
Poggibonsi, 1977
Poikiltēs (Coptic textile term), 2221
Poland, Coptic collections, 1711
Polemon, 1638
Polish Center of Mediterranean Archaeology, 1091
Political activity, modern Coptic. *See* Coptic Reform Society; Political parties
Political parties, **1986–1993**, 1994, 2322–2324
  and Egyptian national unity, 950–951
  Muṣṭafā Kāmil, 1747–1748
  Saʿd Zaghlūl, 2074–2075
Political thought in modern Egypt, 1636–1637, **1993–1996**
  democratic trend, 1995
  Makram Ebeid, 1515–1516
  Mikhail, Kyriakos, 1627–1628
  national liberal trend, 1994–1995
  religious political trend, 1995–1996
  Saʿd Zaghlūl, 2074
  Salāmah Mūsā, 2088–2089
  socialist trend, 1996
  Wissa Wassef, 2322–2324
Poll tax. *See Jizyah*
Polycarp, Saint and Bishop of Smyrna, 1558, 1905, **1997–1998**
  as apostolic father, 180
  and Ignatius of Antioch letters, 1281, 1282
  letters of, 1997–1998
  life of, 1997
  patristic writings, 1920
Polycrates of Ephesus, Bishop, 1585, 1905
Pompey's Pillar (Alexandria), 96
Pool of the Ethiopians, 796
Pope in the Coptic church, **1998–1999**
  as bishop of Alexandria and Cairo, 2193
  and bishop's consecration, 395–398
  and Coptic monasteries, 2194
  Heraclas, Saint, and first use of title, 1219
  as patriarch of Alexandria, 2193
  patriarch title interchangeable with, 1909
  see also Patriarch; Patriarchs; specific names
Porch, 217
Porcher, Ernest, **2000–2001**
Porphyrius, predictions of, 1867, 1868
Porphyry (Coptic sculpture), 2113, 2114–2115
Porphyry (martyr), 1558
Porphyry (pupil of Plotinus), 1265, 1981

Portais, Father, 1972
Portraiture, Coptic, **2001–2006**
of bishops, 402–403
bust of Mark, Saint, 529
of monastic founders, 1660
paintings of Mark, Saint, 1532
Portugal, Coptic collections in, 1711
Posidonios. *See* Dayr Posidonios
Posniakoff, Basil, 2050
Postumian
on Dayr Anbā Anṭūniyūs, 721
on Dayr Anbā Būlā, 742
on Dayr al-Maymūn, 838
Potamioena (martyr), 892
Potstands. *See* Ceramics, Coptic, specific types
Potter's Oracle, 1169
Pottery. *See* Ceramics, Coptic
Pousei, Bishop of Philae, 1955
Pouto. *See* Ibṭū
Praecepta (Pachomius), 1862
Pratum spirituale (John Moschus), 2050
Praxeas, 1638
"Prayer of Abū Tarbū," 1507
Prayer of the Apostle Paul, **2007**
in the Jung Codex, 569
Prayerbooks. *See* Euchologion
Prayer of Esaias, 1732–1733
Prayer of Reconciliation, 121, 1416
Prayers
of absolution, 15–16
ashiyah, 311
in the Book of Canonical Hours, 446–449, 1724
as center of Pachomian monastic life, 1665
compline (sleep), 582–583, 900
of confirmation, 138
for consecration of altar, 108–109
for consecration of patriarchs, 1909–1910
copied for amulets, 1504
for the dead, 889
Didache on, 898
fraction, 71
and genuflection, 1139
Good Friday, 1152–1153
Hail Mary, 1199
Kyrie eleison use in, 1421
morning, 71, 1568–1569
morning incense, 2013
of the ninth hour (collect of None), 71
of oblation, 71
of offertory. *See* Offertory
for ordination of priests, 2013–2015
orientation toward the East during, 1846
reconciliation, 121, 1416
Saladin's decrees against, 1535
for the seasons, 443–444
of Thanksgiving, 1715, 2007, 2126
tombstone inscription formulas, 1294–1295
ṭubḥ, 2279
vespers, 2301
vigil, 2308
see also Eucharistic literature; Hail Mary; Liturgy; Lord's Prayer
Prayer of Thanksgiving, 1715, **2007**
Pre-Coptic. *See Appendix*
Prefect, **2007–2009**, 2022
powers of, 2008–2009
qualifications, appointment, and term of office, 2008
Pregnancy and birth. *See* Birth rites and customs
Preht (Abrahat), 771, 795
Phoibammon of, 1963–1965
see also Dayr al-Barshah
Premnis. *See* Qaṣr Ibrīm
Pre-Old Coptic. *See Appendix*
Presbyterian National Church. *See* Coptic Evangelical Church
Presbyters
in ecclesiastical hierarchy, 2015, 2016
see also Hegumenos
Presbytery, 217–218, 220
Prescription books (medical), 1578–1579, 1581, 1582
"Presentation of the Clear Proof for the Necessary Destruction of the Churches of Old and New Cairo," 687
Presentation of the Virgin In The Temple, Feast of the. *See Theotokos*, Feast of the
Preservation of art. *See* Art preservation
Preservation of manuscripts, Nag Hammadi codices, 1771–1772
Press, Coptic, 1988, 1989, **2010–2013**
Le Monde Copte, 1666
Tādrus Shinudah al-Manqabādī, 2197–2198
see also specific publications
Press, Egyptian, 1990–1991, 1993, 2088
Pretiosa margarita de scientiis ecclesiasticis, 1464
Priest, ordination of, **2013–2015**
Priesthood, **2015–2016**, *2015*
Agathon of Ḥomṣ on essence of, 68
blessing styles, 404
celibacy, 84
in church hierarchy, 1229
clerical instruction, 564–565
defrocking of, 308, 891
see also Bishop; related subjects
"The Priest of Abū Sarjah." *See* Sanī Abū al-Majd Buṭrus ibn Qannā, al-
Prima. *See* Qaṣr Ibrīm
Primis. *See* Qaṣr Ibrīm
Primus, Patriarch, 1913, **2016**
Printing press
for Coptic-language publications, 1302
first Coptic, 932
French expedition, 1526
Migne, Jacques-Paul, 1620
Prisca (wife of Diocletian), 2246
Private law, Coptic, 1428–1430
Probus, Emperor, patriarch under, 1914
Procession, at bishop's consecration, 396
Processional cross, 1468
Prochorus, 885
Proclus (composer) (421–485), 1731, 1868
Proclus, Saint and Patriarch of Constantinople, **2016–2019**
contested election as bishop of Cyzicus, 399, 2016–2017
Coptic translation of homilies, 1356, 1454, 2017–2018
and the *Cycle of John Chrysostom and Demetrius*, 667
feast day, 2086
Proclus of Cyzicus. *See* Proclus, Saint and Patriarch of Constantinople

Procopius, **2019–2020**
on Theodora, Empress, 2234, 2235
Procopius of Alexandria (martyr), 1558
Procopius of Gaza, 907
Proestos, 192, **2021**
and *hegumenos*, 1215
and *oikonomos*, 1826
Professions of Copts in late medieval Egypt, 1616
Prognostications. *See* Calendologia
Propaganda Edition, and Old Testament, Arabic versions of the, 1828–1829, 1830, 1831–1832
Property law. *See* Law of things; Law of obligations
Property tax. *See Kharāj*
Prophets, Lives of the. *See* Lives of the prophets; Paralipomena Jeremiou
Propylon. *See* Prothyron
Proselytization. *See* Evangeliary; Evangelist; Missionaries
Prosopographia Arsinoitica (Diethart), 2022
Prosopographie chrétienne du Bas-Empire (Marrou et al.), 2022
Prosopography, **2021–2022**
in colophons, 577
inscriptions' importance, 1291
The Prosopography of the Later Roman Empire A.D. 260–640 (Jones et al.), 2021–2022
Protennoia, 2276–2277
Proterius (Melchite patriarch), 1441–1442, 1583, 1906
assassination site, 94
opposition to, 1670
Protestantism
American missionaries in Egypt, 1693
Anglican church in Egypt, 133
Coptic Evangelical church, 603–604
see also Luther, Martin
Prothesis, 218
Prothyron, 218
Protodialect. *See Appendix*
Protomartyr. See Stephen, Saint
Protonike, Empress, 1377–1378
Protopriests. *See Hegumenos*
Provincial organization of Egypt, 943–944, 959, 2007–2009, **2022–2023**
Provost, **2024**
Psalmodia, 900, 924, 1687, 1724–1729, *1728*, 1736, **2024**
during Lent, 2099
Lord's Prayer, 1481
and *sab'ah wa-arba'ah*, 2017
and Theotokion, 2255
Virgin-censer analogy, 1470
and *Wāṭus*, 2320
see also Lōbsh Adām
Psalms
for altar consecration, 108
canonical hours for reading, 1724
collected manuscripts of, 1777
for consecration of patriarchs, 1909, 1910
in Coptic Good Friday Service, 1152
Coptic magic's use of, 1504
Coptic translations, 1451
guardian angel concept in, 1186
Holy Week readings, 1251
musical setting, 2024
Psalter, 1731
Psammetichos I, 1165
Psammetichos II, 1166
Pseudo-Athanasius, Canons of. *See* Canons of Pseudo-Athanasius
Pseudo-Clement of Rome, collection of *Book of Rolls*, 1777, 1783
Pseudo-Cyril of Alexandria, 681, **2025–2026**
Pseudo-Demetrius of Phaleron, 1731, 1732
Pseudo-Epiphanius of Cyprus, collected works, 1782
Pseudo-Macarius, homilies of, 722, **2027–2028**
Pseudo-Pisentius of Qifṭ, 360, **2028**
Pseudo-Proclus, 2018
Pshoi, Saint (Akhmīm), **2028–2029**, 2082, 2086
Pshoi of Jeremiah, 1924, 1925
Pshoi of Scetis, 1974, **2029–2030**
and Life of Maximus and Domitius, Saints, 1576
monasteries associated with, 734, 736–737, 738, 795
and Paul of Tamma, 1924, 1925
pilgrimages to burial site, 1974
and Shanashā, 2127
and vigil legend, 2308
Pshoi of Ṭūd, Saint, **2030**, 2086
Psobt-m-p-hoi. *See* Khandaq, al-
Psoï, 732, 1657, **2030–2031**
Dayr Yuḥannis at, 883
as Greek town in Egypt, 1175, 1179, 1180–1181
pilgrimages to, 1973
Psote of Psoï, Saint and Bishop, 1980, 2030, **2031–2032**
Aswan church of, *294*, *295*
martyrdom, 1558
and Panine and Paneu, 1880
relics in Dayr Anbā Bisādah, 732, 1657
role in Coptic hagiography, 1193
tomb of, 733
see also Dayr Anbā Bisādah
Pteleme. *See* Ioule and Pteleme (martyrs); Ptolemy of Dandarah (martyr)
Ptolemaeus, 688, 1151
Ptolemais
cult of Homeric gods, 1865
shrines, 1976
Ptolemais Hermiou. *See* Pso
Ptolemeus the Martyr, church dedicated to, 903, 1412
Ptolemic temples, Dayr al-Madīnah on site of, 816, 817–818
Ptolemy, Saint and Bishop of Minūf, 2086
Ptolemy of Dandarah (martyr), 1558
Ptolemy dynasty, 1166, 1175–1176, 1179, 1180–1181
and administrative organization of Egypt, 934
and Alexandria, 95, 97, 103
Dionysiac cult, 1758, 1760
Publications. *See* Press, Coptic; Press, Egyptian; specific titles
Public law, Coptic, 1430
Publius Licinius Valerianus. *See* Valerian, Emperor
Puech, Henri-Charles, **2032–2033**
Pulcheria, Empress, **2033**
and the Assumption of Mary, 292, 290
and Chalcedon, Council of, 513–514, 1441, 1442, 1670, 2033
and Dioscorus I, 914

Pulpit. *See* Ambo
Punishment, ecclesiastical. *See* Excommunication; Penalization
Purgatory, 974, 1125
see also Hades
Purification ritual. *See* Ablution
Pushkin Museum, Moscow, 1895
Pusi, Bishop of Philae, 1295
Putti, 1765–1766, *1766*
Pyramids, 34, 2065
Pyrrhus, Patriarch of Constantinople, 1678
Pythagoras, 1867–1868

Q

Q (source of Gospels of Saint Matthew and Saint Luke), 1163
Qafri (Nubian), 762
Qāhirah, al-, 1633
Qalamūn, al-, 758, 1658, 2311
Qal'at al-Bābayn, **2035**
Qallīn, 752, **2036**
Qalyūb, **2036**
Qalyūbiyyah Province, monasteries in, 1655
Qamūlah
monasteries at, 827–828, 829–830, 1656, 1658
pilgrimages to, 1973–1974
Qāmūs al-Jughrāfī lil-Bilād al-Miṣrīyyah, al- (Muḥammad Ramzī), 1695
Qarārah, **2036**
Qarfūnah. *See* Dayr Durunkah
Qartasā (village), 688
Qāsim ibn'Ubayd Allāh, al-, 762, 764
Qaṣr Fārisī (Persian Castle), 1939
Qaṣr Ibrīm, **2036–2037**
as administrative center, 1315
and Ballana kingdom, 332
and Baqṭ, 344
and Beja tribes, 373
and bishopric of Faras, 1090, 1091
as capital of Nobatia, 1797, 1798
Dotawo documents at, 922
as episcopal see of Nubia, 1813
letters on the eparchs of Nobatia found at, 1798
and Nubian archaeology, medieval, 1805
Nubian archives of, 227, 1675, 1816–1817
and Nubian Christian architecture, 1807–1809
and Nubian evangelization, 1802
and Nubian inscriptions, medieval, 1815
and Nubian languages and literature, 1815–1816
and Nubian studies, 615
Qaṣr Nisīmah, **2038**
Qaṣr Qarūn, 465, *466*, 1873
Qaṣr al-Ṣayyād
monasteries near, 1657
pilgrimages to, 1973
see also Jabal al-Ṭarīf
Qaṣr al-Sham', **2038**, 1647
and Babylon, 317
church of Mercurius of Caesarea, 1594
Church of al-Mu'allaqah at, 557–560
Qaṣr Waḥeida, 1399–1400, 1404, 1406
Qaṣr al-Wizz, 1090, 1817–1818
Qaṭamārus. *See* Lectionary
Qays, al-, 709, **2038**
Qena, monasteries in, 1657
Qērelos I, Ethiopian prelate, 1009
Qērelos II, Ethiopian prelate, 1032–1033
Qērelos III, Ethiopian prelate, 1040–1042
Qiblī Qamūlah. *See* Qamūlah
Qibriyūs, Saint, monastery of, 850
Qifṭ, 98, 1374, **2038–2040**, 2043
and Ballāṣ, 333
martyrdoms in, 1907
monasteries in region of, 787–788, 1657–1658
Qinā, **2040**
Qiryāquṣ, Metropolitan of the Pentapolis, 1612–1612
Quartodeciman controversy, 1791–1792
Quasten, Johannes, 1921
Qubbah, 332
see also Dome
Quecke, H., 1863, 1894, 1895
Quibell, Annie A., 2040
Quibell, James Edward, 560, 777, **2040**
Qulqās (vegetable), 1103
Qulzūm, al-. *See* Clysma
Qummuṣ. *See Hegumenos*
Qummuṣ Sarjiyūs. *See* Sarjiyūs, Malatī
Qumrān sect, 143
Didache compared with writings of, 898
Qumriyyah (mother superior), 1652
Qūnā (martyr), 1558
Qūqām, as stopping place in flight into Egypt, 840
Qurnah, 800
Qurnat Mar'ī, 849, 857, 1656, **2040–2042**, *2041*
history, 2040–2041
Monastery of Mark the Evangelist, 2042
Qurrah ibn Sharīk (Shurayk), 86, 187
Qūṣ, 66, 67, **2043–2045**, 66, 67
monasteries in, 711, 819–820, 657, 1658
Qusṭanṭīn ibn Abī al-Ma'ālī ibn Abī al-Fatḥ Abū al-Fatḥ, 1182, **2046–2047**
Quṣūr el-'Abīd, 1400
Quṣūr 'Īsā, 1400, 1401, 1402, 1404–1405, 1406–1407, 1408
Quṣūr el-'Izeila, 1395, 1400, 1402, 1404, 1405, 1407, 1408
Quṣūr el-Ruba'īyāt, 1398–1399, 1401, 1402, 1404, 1408
Qutruz, Sultan, 1517
Quzmān, Iskandar, 1467
Quzmān of Ṭaḥā and his companions (martyrs), 1558

R

Rabbinical teaching, *Didache* compared with, 898
Rabitat al-Quds, **2049**
Rāfi'ī, 'Abdal-Raḥmān al-, 2010
Rāfi'ī, Amīn al-, 1990
Rainer, Archduke, **2049**
papyri collection (Vienna), 1100, 2049, 2321
Raithou, **2049–2050**
and Pharan oasis, 1952
as pilgrimage site, 1976
Rampart. *See Ḥiṣn*
Ramses II, 1485
Ramses III, 53, 1586
Ramses VI, tomb of, 2066

Ramses Wissa Wassef, **2051**
Ramshausen, Franciscus Wilhelm von, **2052**
Ramzī, M., on Dayr al-Ṭurfah, 882
Ramzi Tadrus. *See* Literature, Copto-Arabic
Ranke, Hermann, 656, **2052**
Raoue (Coptic term), 695
Raphael, Archangel, 101, 190, **2052–2054**
Rashīd (Rosetta), 925, **2054**
  Franciscan friary, 1122, 1123
  French governors, 1591
Rashīd al-Dīn Abū Saʿīd, **2055**
Rashīd Riḍā, Muḥammad, 1996
Rās Tafari Makonnen, 1041
Rās Zaʿfarānah, 741
Ratramnus of Corbie, 1113, 1115
Rāyah, al-. *See* Raithou
Rayramūn, al-, Dayr al-Malāk Mīkhā'īl, 828–829, 1654
Rāzī, Fakhr al-Dīn al-, al-Ṣafī ibn al-ʿAssāl reply to, 2077
Rāziq, ʿAlī Abd, al-, 1996
Readers, in ecclesiastical hierarchy, 1229, 2016
Reading. *See* Lectionary; Libraries
Rebecca (martyr), 66–67
Recared (Visigoth king), 1112
Recension, characteristics of the Egyptian. *See* Canons, Apostolic
Reclusion, **2055–2056**
  Pidjimi, Saint, 1966–1967
  women practitioners, 88, 1663
Redline Bookstore, 1628
Red Monastery. *See* Dayr Anbā Bishoi (Suhāj)
Refectory, 735–736, **2056**
Reform Party on Constitutional Principles (Ḥizb al-Iṣlāḥ ʿAlā al-Mabādi' al-Dustrūriyyah), 1988
The Refutation of Allegorists (Nepos), 911
Refutation and Apology (Dionysius), 911
Regula, Saint, 1082, 1110, 1558, **2057**, 2086, 2232
Relics
  at Dayr Apa Anūb, 770
  of Elisha, Prophet, 1646
  of John of Sanhūt, 1626
  kept in wood coffers, 2329–2330
  of Mark, Apostle and Saint, 1521–1532, 1573, 1646, 1910
  of Mercurius of Caesarea, 1592, 1594
  at Monastery of the Metanoia, 1608
Reliefs
  preservation of Coptic, 280
  woodworking, 2327
  see also Sculpture in stone
Religio licita, Christianity as, 308
Religious History (Theodoret), 2236
Rémondon, Roger, **2057**
Renaudin, Paul, **2057**
Renaudot, Eusebe, 298, **2057**
Repentance. *See* Confession and penitence
Reply to Jaqfarī (al-Ṣafī ibn al-ʿAssāl), 2078–2079
Reply to Ṭabarī (al-Ṣafī ibn al-ʿAssāl), 2078
Republic (Plato). *See* Plato's *Republic*
Republican Party (Egypt), 1987
Respima (martyr), 1558
Responses, melodies of Copic. *See* Music, Coptic, description
Responsory, **2058**
Resurrection
  Abbaton's presence, 2
  in the Apocryphon of James, 169
  Easter commemoration, 1104–1105, 2159–2160; *see also* Easter
  fasts prior to feast of, 1093, 1095
  Holy Saturday and, 1247–1249
  monthly feastal day commemoration, 1111
  and mummification, 1697
  Sunday commemoration, 2098, 2159
  Treatise on the Resurrection (gnostic tractate), 2275
Resurrection of the dead. *See* Hades; Judgment, Last
Return aisle, church, 218
Revelation, Book of
  on altar lights, 109
  authorship, 911
  in canon of Scripture, 2109
  reading on Holy Saturday, 1249
Revelation 4
  tetramorph depiction in Coptic art, 539–540
  in Triumph of Christ, 525
  on the twenty-four elders, 541
Revillout, Charles Eugene, 58, 1481, 1892, **2058**
Revue d'histoire ecclésiastique (publication), 1424
Revue égyptologique (publication), 2058
Rhakotiṣ, 97
Rháptēs (Coptic textile term), 2221
Rhenish State Museum, Trier, 1598
Rhinokorua, 1650
Rhyme, 1986
Ricci, Seymour Montefiore Robert Rosso de, **2059**
Riḍwān, Vizier, 1097
Right Bank. *See* Monasteries of the Upper Ṣaʿīd
Rings, 1607
Risālah al-Masīḥiyyah, al- ("the Christian message"), 1098
Risālat al-Bayān al-Azhar (Ibn Kabar), 1464
Rites and sacraments
  baptism, 336–338
  baptism, liturgy of, 339–342
  burial, 425–426
  communion, 578–579
  in Ethiopian Orthodox Church, 997–998
  Eucharist, 1056–1061
  interdict, 1299
  marriage, 1542–1546
  unction of the sick, 2291–2292
  see also Birth rites and customs; Sacrament; specific sacraments
Ritual books, 1728–1729
River Jordan, 1246
Rizq Agha, **2059**
Robertson, Marian, 1730, 1743
Robinson, J. M., 1899
Rock churches, 716, 747, 770, 771, 798, 853, 1656
  Lālibalā, 1425–1426, *1426*
Rodriguez, Christophore, Father, 1134
Roger I (Norman), 1099
Roman Catholic church
  absolution in, 15
  and Acacian schism, 42–47
  Acta sanctorum, 56–57
  Agnus Dei in, 70
  bishopric, 911
  canonization in, 449
  and canon law, 449–550
  canon of Scripture, 2108

and Chalcedon, Council of, 1670, 1671, 1673, 1674
concomitance in, 584
control of Jerusalem, 1615
Coptic church relations with, 609–611, 913, 914, 1134, 1141; *see also* Trent, Council of
Dominicans in Egypt, 918
Easter date-setting, 1906
and Ethiopian controversies, 986–987
and Ethiopian prelates, 1028–1030, 1033–1036
fan use, 1474
Franciscans in Egypt, 1121–1123
gnosticism and, 1151
Iconoclastic controversy, 1275
Immaculate Conception doctrine, 1285
and Jerome, Saint, biblical translation, 1323
Jesuits and the Coptic Church, 1329–1330
John XVII, Patriarch, and proselytizing by, 1349
and Last Judgment, 1379
on Mark, Saint, 1529
missions in Ethiopia, 1028–1030, 1036–1037
missions in India, 1635–1636
missions to Copts, 1538
on nature of Christ, 523
papal supremacy precedent, 1440
patriarch title, 1909
return of Saint Mark's relics by, 1532
Rūfa'īl al-Ṭūkhī, 2067–2068
and trinitarian controversies, 1638
and Ya'qub, General, 2351
and Yūsuf Abū Daqn, 2364
see also Acacian schism; Nicaea, Council of; Rome
The Romance of Julian the Apostate, 1593
Romances, Coptic, **2059–2060**
Roman emperors in Egypt, **2061–2063**, 2066
see also names of specific emperors
Roman Empire
administration of Egypt under, 934, 959, 2007–2009, 2022–2023
Alexandria under, 95–99
Antinoopolis founding, 1179
army in Egypt, 235–238
Babylonian fortress, 317–318, *318*
boule, 413–414
castrum (military camp), 464–468, 1485
Christian martyrs, 1548–1549, 1550–1559
conflict during Alexander I patriarchy, 81
Decius, 889–891
Diocletian, 904–908
division of, 942
and Egypt in late antiquity, 942–947
impact on Hellenized Egypt, 1167–1168, 1176–1177, 1179, 1180–1181
Jovian's restoration of Christianity, 1376–1377
Manichaeism in, 1519, 1521
Maximus patriarchy under, 1575
Mercurius of Caesarea, 1592–1594
Monarchianism in, 1638
and monophysitism, 1675–1677
pagarch system, 1871–1872
patriarchs under, 1913–1915
Pelagianism heresy, 1929–1930
persecution of Christians, 892–893, 903, 909–910, 912, 1110, 1868–1869, 1935–1937; *see also* specific emperors
provincial art, 1873
provincial organization of Egypt, 959
Pulcheria, Empress, 2033
religion in Europe under, 1865–1870
and Scetis monasteries, 789–790
taxation policies in Egypt, 98, 237–238, 904, 905, 945, 2009, 2202–2206
temples, 690, *691*, 863
and Theban Legion, 2231–2233
see also Byzantine Empire; Constantinople; Roman emperors in Egypt; specific personal and place names
Roman soldiers. *See* Army, Roman; Castrum
Roman travelers in Egypt, **2064–2066**
Romanus. *See* Victor Stratelates, Saint
Romanus II, Emperor, 1098
Rome
as apostolic see, 180
apostolic succession, 181
Coptic relations with. *See* Coptic relations with Rome
sack of, 1930
see also Roman Catholic church; Roman Empire
Roof, 218
saddleback, 220
Roosevelt, Theodore, 1466
Ropemaking, 1640
Rösch, Friedrich, **2067**
Rosenthal, Joseph, 1996
Rosetta. See *Rashīd*
Rosetta Stone, 516, 2054
Rose al-Youssef (publication), 1991
Rossi, Francesco, 1894, **2067**
Rosweyde, H., 56, 405
Roy, Martha, 1726
Royal Ontario Museum of Archaeology, Toronto, 1891
Rubbaytah. *See* Provost
Rückert, Friedrich, **2067**
Rudwān ibn Walkhasī, 1129
Rūfa'īl al-Ṭūkhī, 1349, **2067–2068**
and Coptic relations with Rome, 610
ordained as Catholic priest, 1122
as printer of Coptic books, 610, 614, 1349
Rufaylah, Ya'qūb Nakhlah, 1466
Rufinus, **2068–2069**
on Athanasius I, 298
on Canopus, 31
on Ethiopian conversion to Christianity, 312–313
and founding of Jerusalem monasteries, 1663
on Nitria, 1796
and *Sentences of Sextus*, 2120
as student of Didymus the Blind, 472, 900
on Temple of Serapis, 134
and Theophilus, Patriarch, 2252
translation of Pamphilus, 1879
Rufus of Shotep, commentary on Gospels of Mark and Luke, 1456
Rukn al-Dīn Baybars-Jashankīr, 1464
"Rule of the Angel" (Pachomian document), 1862

Rules of Pachomius, 32, 119, 1661–1662, 1663, 1861–1862
Rural Diaconate, 2091
Russia
and the Coptic Church, 1950
Theognosta, Saint, and Christianization of Georgia, 2243–2244
see also Union of Soviet Socialist Republics
Ruth, in Arabic versions of the Old Testament, 1835
Ruthwell Cross, 419
Ruways, Anbā. *See* Anbā Ruways
Ruzayqāt, al- (Armant), **2069**

S

Ṣā (son of Miṣrā'im), 1652
Saad, Zaki Yusef, 708, **2071**
Sābā, 1089, 1750
Saba, Saint, 45, 1182
Sab'ah wa-arba'ah, **2071**
and *tafsīr*, 2198
and Theotokion, 2255
Sābā ibn Tādurus al-Ḥawrānī (deacon), 2047
Sabas, John, collected works of, 1779
Sābā Yāsā, 1182, **2071**
on residence of Gregory II, Patriarch, 1182
Sabbath
differing meanings for Christians and Jews, 2098–2100
Ethiopian controversy, 1050–1051
Old Testament, 1101
Saturday as, 2098
Sunday as, 2159
vigil associated with, 2308
Sabellianism, 1638, 1934, **2072**
Alexander I and, 82
Arius's opposition to, 231
Dionysius the Great and, 911
Eusebius of Caesarea's opposition to, 1070
and hypostasis controversy, 1260
Sabellius the Libyan, 911, 1638, 1944, 2072
see also Sabellianism
Sabinus, prefect of Alexandria, 909
Sacrament, **2072**
absolution and, 15
baptism, 336–338
baptism, liturgy of, 339–342
Communion, Holy, 578–579
confirmation, 585–586
Dialogue of the Savior on, 898
Eucharist, 1056–1061
and excommunication, 1079–1080
given to children, 2072
Gospel of Philip on, 1156
holy orders, 2013–2015
interdict against administering, 1299
marriage, 1542–1543
and penance, 584–585
unction of the sick, 2291–2292
see also under individual sacraments
Sacrament, reservation of the blessed, **2073**
Sacramental oils. *See* Oils, sacramental
Sacrifice, Eucharist as, 1058–1060
Sacrificial altars, 106
Sacristy, 219
Sacrorum conciliorum nova et amplissima collectio. *See Amplissima*
Sacy, Antoine Isaac Silvestre de, **2073**
Sadamant, pilgrimages to, 1974
Sadamant-Fayyūm, Dayr Mār Jirjis, 831
Sadat, Anwar al-, president of Egypt, 582, 707, 756, 948–949, 1516, 1991, 2091
Saddleback roof, 220
Sādij, al-, 114
Sādiq Attallāh, Mu'allim, 1737
Sa'dist Party, 1992–1993
Sa'd Mīkhā'īl 'Abdū, **2073–2074**
Sa'd Zaghlūl, 375, 1466, 1515, 1628, **2074–2075**
and British occupation of Egypt, 421–422
and political thought in modern Egypt, 1990, 1991, 1992, 1994
on status of Copts, 950–951
and Wissa Wassef, 2323
Ṣafī Abū al-Faḍā'īl ibn al-'Assāl, al-, 310–311, 1748
Ṣafī al-Dīn 'Abd Allāh ibn 'Alī ibn Shukr, vizier, 1269
Ṣafī ibn al-'Assāl, al-, 1089, 1096, **2075–2079**
and Butrus ibn 'Abd al-Sayyid, 428
on canon law, 1942, 2076
on circumcision, 1106
on Great Lent fasting, 1095
on Holy Saturday, 1247
on laying-on of hands, 1432–1433
on marriage, 1545
Nomocanon of, 1780, 1783, 2075, 2076
on offertory, 1824
works of, 1463, 1464, 2076–2079
works translated into Ethiopic, 977
and Yūḥannā al-Maqsī, 2358
Sahidic dialect
Alexander's encomium on Peter I, 1943, 1944, 1945
Cambyses Romance in, 2060
Canons, Apostolic, 451
canons, ecclesiastical, 454
inscriptions in, 1296
Life of Pachomius, 1860, 1861
magical texts, 1501
manuscripts, 1885
New Testament in, 1787–1788
in Old Testament, Coptic translations of, 1836–1838
poetry, 1986
see also Appendix
Sahlān ibn 'Uthmān ibn Kaysān, **2079–2080**
Saht (Coptic textile term), 2221
Ṣahyūn Wālid (Akhmīm), 1122
Ṣa'īd, **2080**
Sa'īd, Khedive, 676, 1692–1693
Sa'īd ibn Batrīq. *See* Ibn al-Biṭrīq, Sa'īd
Sa'īd ibn al-Biṭrīq. *See* Ibn al-Biṭrīq, Sa'īd
Sa'īd ibn Ṭufayl, **2080**
Sai Island, **2080–2081**
as episcopal see of Nubia, 1813
see also Nubian church organization
Saint Andrew's Church (Jericho), 1245
Saint Catherine's Church (Alexandria), 1123
Saint Didymus Institute for the Blind (Cairo). *See* Didymus Institute for the Blind
Saint Mark's Cathedral. *See* Cathedral of Saint Mark

Saint Mary and Saint Mark (Paris), 1623
Saint Maurice-en-Valais (city), 1572
Saint-Paul-Girard, Louis, **2081**
Saint Peter's Bridge monastery. *See* Lithazomenon and Saint Peter's Bridge
Saint Peter's Cathedral (Rome), 1572
Saints
  Ababius, 1
  Abāmūn of Tarnūt, 1
  Abāmūn of Ṭūkh, 1–2
  Abilius, 8
  Abraam I, 10
  Abraham, 10–11
  Abraham and George of Scetis, 12–13
  Abraham of Minūf, 13–14
  Achillas (monk), 56
  Achillas (patriarch), 55–56
  Acta Sanctorum, 56–57
  Agathon, 64–65
  Agathon and his brothers, 66–67
  Agathon the Stylite, 68–69
  Alexandra, 88
  Ammonas, 113
  Amun, 119
  Anastasia, 125
  Anatolius, 128
  Anbā Ruways, 128
  anchorites, 129
  Antony of Egypt, 149–151
  Apaiule and Tolemaeus, 153
  Archellides, 192
  Ari, 229
  Arianus, 230–231
  Arsenius of Scetis and Ṭurah, 240–241
  Ascla, 283
  Barsanuphius, 348
  Barsūm the Naked, 348–349
  Basil, 351–351
  Besamon, 379
  Bessarion, 379
  Būlus al-Ḥabīs, 424–425
  Camoul, 445
  canonization, 449
  Cassian, John, 461–463, 461–463
  Celadion, 475
  Claudius, 561
  commemoration of, 1567
  Copres, 598
  Coptic hymns for, 1728
  Cyriacus and Julitta, 671
  Cyril I, 671–675
  difnār hymns on, 900–901
  Dimyānah, 903
  Dioscorus I, 912–915
  Domitius, 1576–1578
  Elias of Bishwāw, 952–953
  Elias of Samhūd, 953
  English, 418–419
  Ephraem Syrus, 963
  Epima, 965
  Epimachus of Pelusium, 965–966
  Erai, 2209
  Ethiopian, 1044–1055; *see also* Synaxarion, Ethiopian
  Euphrosyna, 1069
  Eusebius, 1069–1070
  Eusignius, 1071–1072
  Eustathius and Theopista, 1072–1073
  Exuperantius, 1082
  al-Faramā association, 1089
  feasts, 1101
  Febronia, 1109–1110
  Felix, 1110
  Fīs, 1116
  Gabra Masqal, 1047–1048
  Gabriel, Archangel, appearance to, 1137
  Gāseçhā, 1051–1052
  George, 1137–1138
  Giyorgis, 1051–1052
  Gregory the Illuminator, 1183
  Gregory of Nazianzus, 1183–1184
  Gregory of Nyssa, 1184–1185
  Hadrā of Aswan, 1190
  Hadrā of Benhadab, 1190–1191
  hagiographers, 1921
  Hamai of Kahyor, 1203–1204
  Harmīnā, 1209
  Heraclas, 1219
  Heraclides, 1220–1221
  Herai, 1221
  Herpaese and Julianus, 1225–1226
  Hilaria, 1230–1231
  Hilarion, 1232
  Hop of Ṭūkh, 1254
  Hor of Abraḥat, 1255
  Horsiesios, 1257
  Iconoclastic controversy, 1275
  icons of, 1276, 1278
  Ignatius of Antioch, 1281–1282
  illuminated manuscript depiction of, 1283
  Irish, 418–419
  Isaac, 1304
  Isaac of Tiphre, 1304–1305
  Isaiah of Scetis, 1305–1306
  Isidorus of Antioch, 1307
  Isidorus of Scetis, 1310
  Jacob, 1318
  James, 1320–1321
  James Intercisus, 1321
  James of Scetis, 1321–1322
  Jeremiah, 1322–1323
  Jerome, 1323
  Jirjis al-Muzāḥim, 1335–1336
  John, Bishop of Armant, 1353–1354
  John I, 1337
  John II, 1337
  John III, 1337
  John IV, 1338–1339
  John VI, 1341–1342
  John the Baptist, 1354–1356
  John Chrysostom, 1357–1359
  John Colobos, 1359–1361
  John the Faster, 1339–1340
  John Kāmā, 1362–1363
  John of Lycopolis, 1363–1365
  John of Parallos, 1367–1368
  Joseph, 1370
  Joseph of Bishwāw, 1371
  Joseph the Carpenter, 1371–1374
  Joseph of Tsenti, 1374
  Judas Cyriacus, 1377–1378
  Julian, 1380
  Justus, 1386–1387
  Macarius, 1489
  Macarius Alexandrinus, 1490
  Macarius the Egyptian, 1491
  Manasseh, 1518
  Mark, 1528–1533
  Mark II, 1533–1534
  Mark III, 1534–1536
  Mark the Simple, 1540–1541
  Mary of Alexandria, 1560
  Mary the Egyptian, 1560
  Mass of the Faithful commemoration, 1567
  Matthew the Poor, 1571–1572
  Mauritius, 1572
  Maximus, 1576–1578
  Menas, 1589
  Menas of al-Ashmūnayn, 1589
  Menas the Miracle Maker, 1589–1590
  Mercurius of Caesarea, 1592–1594

Michael the Archangel, 1616–1619
Michael IV, 1614–1615
Miṣā'īl, 1634
Moses the Black, 1681
Mui, 1696
Nob, Apa, 1796
Olympus, 1840
Onophrius, 1841–1842
Pachomius, 1859–1863
Paese, 1865
paintings in church, Dayr al-Baramūs, 794
paintings in Main Church, Dayr Apa Jeremiah, 778, 1660
paintings in monasteries, 1660
paintings in Old Church, Dayr Anbā Anṭūniyūs, 727
Palaemon, 1876
Palamon, 1876
Pambo, 1876–1877
Pamin, 1878
Pamphilus, 1879
Panesneu, 1880
Panine and Paneu, 1880–1881
Pantaleon, 1881–1882
Paphnutius, 1882
Paphnutius the Hermit, 1882–1883
Paphnutius of Pbow, 1883–1884
Paphnutius of Scetis, 1884
Patāsius, 1908
Patermuthius, 1908
Paul of Benhadab, 1922
Paul the Simple, 1923
Paul of Tamma, 1923–1925
Paul of Thebes, 1925–1926
Peter II, 1947
Peter the Presbyter, 1951
Peter of Scetis, 1951
Petronius, 1952
Phib, 1953–1954
Philotheus of Antioch, 1960–1961
Phis, 1963
Pidjimi, 1966–1967
pilgrimages to sites of, 1968–1975
Pisentius of Armant, 1978
Pisentius of Hermonthis, 1978
Pisentius of Qifṭ, 1978–1980
Pisura, 1980
Poemen, 1983–1984
poetry on, 1985, 1986
Polycarp, 1997–1998
portraits of, 2004
Proclus, 2016
Pshoi, 2028–2029
Pshoi of Ṭūd, 2030
Psote of Psoï, 2031–2032
Regula, 2057
Samuel of Benhadab, 2091–2092
Samū'īl of Qalamūn, 2092–2093
Sarapamon of Scetis, 2094–2095
Sarapion of Tmuis, 2095–2096
Severian of Jabalah, 2122
Shenufe, 2130–2131
Shenute, 2131–2133
Silvanus of Scetis, 2137
Simon I, 2138–2139
Simon II, 2139
Sophia, 2143–2144
Takla Hāymānot, 1049–1050
Tecla, 1865
Ter and Erai, 2209
Theodora, 2235
Theodorus, 2237–2238
Theodorus of Alexandria, 2238
Theodorus of Pherme, 2239
Theodorus of Tabennēsē, 2239–2240
Theodosius I, 2241
Theognosta, 2243–2244
Theophilus, 2253–2254
Thomas, 2256
Timotheus, 2262–2263
Timothy I, 2263
Tolemaus, 2271
Ursus of Solothurn, 2292–2293
Verena, 2299–2301, *2301*
Victor of Shū, 2302
Victor Stratelates, 2303–2308
Victor of Tabennēsē, 2308
Yūsāb I, 2362
Zacharias, Bishop, 2368
Zar'a Yā'qob, 1052–1053
see also Hagiography, Coptic; Martyrs
Saints, Coptic, **2081–2087**
Copto-Arabic Synaxarion list of, 2172–2190
Synaxarion list of, 2173–2190
Synaxarion as source of knowledge of, 1044–1045
The Saints of Egypt in the Coptic Calendar (O'Leary), 1551, 2081
Sakhā, 66, **2087–2088**
Sakhirun of Qallīn (martyr), 1558
Saklabaoth, 1618
Saklas (pagan deity), 1154
Saladin, 872, 1534–1535, 1536, 1097, 1615
see also Ayyubid Dynasty and the Copts
Ṣalaḥ al-Dīn. *See* Saladin
Salāmā I, Ethiopian prelate, 312–313, 990–991
Salāmā II, Ethiopian prelate, 1011–1012
Salāmā III, Ethiopian prelate, 1033–1036
Salāmā IV, Metropolitan, 1590
Salāmah, Albert Barsūm, 1911
Salāmah Mūsā, 1996, 2011, **2088–2089**
Salāmūnī, al-, pilgrimages to, 1974
Salfana. *See* Paul and Salfana (martyrs)
Ṣalīb (new martyr), 1558
Ṣalīb Sāmī, 1991
Ṣaliḥ ibn Qalā'ūn, al-, Sultan, 750
Sāliḥ Sālaḥ al-Dīn. *See* Saladin
Salīm, Bakhkhāsh, 1626
Sālim ibn Yūsuf al-Sibā'ī al-Itfāwī, **2089**
Salippe, Mikarius, **2089–2090**
Salome (mother of Zebedee's children), 1117
Salvation
Gnostic Christian homily on, 898
Origen on, 1849
Samālūṭ
Dayr Abū Bifām at, 696–697
Dayr al-'Adhrā' at, 715–716
Samannūd, 36, 925, **2090**
Sāmī Gabrā, 1230, **2090**
Samson, 1618
Samuel, A. E., 1895
Samuel, Bishop, 1624, **2090–2091**
and Cyril VI, 707
role in Coptic education, 933
and Yūsāb II, 2363
Samuel of Benhadab, Saint, 2086, **2091–2092**, 2086
Samuel of Kalamun. *See* Samū'īl of Qalamūn, Saint
Samuel Koui (the Small), 826
Samuel the Recluse, Anbā, 1504
Ṣamū'īl of Qalamūn, Saint, 1216, 1362, 1448, **2092–2093**
feast day, 2086
monasteries, 707, 758, 759, 845, 1130
and Takinash, 2092–2093, 2199

see also Dayr Anbā Ṣamū'īl of Qalamūn
Ṣamū'īl al-Suryānī, 1462
Ṣanabū, **2093–2094**
monasteries around, 1654
Sanad, al-, 1656
Sanctuary
askinah, 288
and candelabrum, 1469
communion table, 580
in Egyptian church architecture, 220–221, 552–553
Sanctuary of Philotheus (Antioch), 893
Sanctus, 1731
Sandals and shoes, 646, 1433
Sanders, H. A., 1895
Sandstone, Coptic sculpture in, 2115
Sandstorm, 1487
Sanhirā, pilgrimages to, 1974
Sanhūt, Bishop of Miṣr, 760–761
Sanī Abū al-Majd Buṭrus ibn al-Muhadhdhib Abū al-Faraj, al-, 1085
Sanqūriyyah, al-, pilgrimages to, 1974
Sansno, Saint, 2087
Sanutios. *See* Shute I, Saint
Saqqara
and Coptic scupture in stone, 2112, 2115, 2116
Dayr Apa Jeremiah in, 772, 773, 776–777, 1659, 1660
decorations of monastery cells at, 525, 555, 556
inscriptions found at, 1293, 1294, 1295
monastery mural painting, 1873, 1874
pilgrims and travelers to, 1976
remains and representations of Coptic clothing. *See* Costume, civil
Sara, Saint, 2087, **2094**
Sarabaïtes (free monks), 702
Sarabām. *See* Dayr Abū Sarabām
Saragossa, Council of, on regulations for nuns, 1822
Sarah. *See* Bahnām and Sarah (martyrs); Benam and Sarah (martyrs); Moses and Sarah (martyrs)
Sarah and her children (martyrs), 1558
Sarapamon, Bishop of Beheira and al-Minūfiyyah, 686
Sarapamon, Bishop of Minufiyyah, 1950
Sarapamon of Nikiou, 955, 1793
Sarapamon of Scetis, Saint, 1558, 2087, **2094**
Sarapion, **2094–2095**
see also Serapion
Sarapion, Saint (martyr from Bīnūsah), 1558, **2120–2121**
Sarapion of Tmuis, Saint and Bishop, 1491, 2095, **2095–2096**
anaphora of, 1539
anti-Manichaeism, 1522, 2096
as disciple of Antony, Saint, 149, 2096
feast day, 2087
Sarcophagus, wooden, 2330–2331
Sardica, Council of (351), 1089
Sarjiyūs, Malaṭī, 1465, 1466, **2096–2097**
conflict with Yūsāb II, Patriarch, 2011, 2097, 2363
Sarmata. *See* Pamun and Sarmata (martyrs)
Sarrāj al-Warrāq, al-, 1085
Sasht (Coptic textile term), 2221
Sassanid Empire. *See* Persians in Egypt
Sassanid influences on Coptic art, **2097–2098**
Sasso, François, Father, 1330
Satan
and Antichrist, 143
Gabriel, Archangel, power over, 1136
Gregory of Nazianzus on sin of, 1184
Michael, Archangel, power over, 1617, 1618–1619
Raphael, Archangel, power over, 2053
see also Demons; Devil
Saturday, 1901, **2098–2100**
Holy Saturday, 1247–1249
Saturn (pagan deity), 1617
Sauneron, Serge, **2100**
Savery Codex. *See* Crosby Schøyen Codex
Savoyards, 1572
Sawādah
Dayr Apa Hor at, 770–771
pilgrimages to, 1974
Sawām'ah Sharq, al-, Dayr Anbā Bākhūm, 730–731
Sāwiros, Ethiopian prelate, 1005–1006
Sāwīrus ibn al-Muqaffa', 19, 21, 1573, **2100–2102**
Abraham, Saint and Patriarch and, 11
on al-Afrājūn, 64
and Alexander's encomium on Peter I, 1943, 1944
on the Arab conquest of Eqypt, 183–189
and Bashmuric revolts, 350
and blessings, 404
and Book of Epact, 410
collected works of, 1779
on the Crusades, 664–665
al-Durr al-Thamīn, 926
and Egyptian conscription of Christian sailors, 2286
and *History of the Patriarchs of Alexandria*, 1239
and John of Shmūn, 1369
on Primus, 2016
on Saturdays during Lent, 2099
and Theophilus, Patriarch, 2247
and the Three Hebrews in the Furnace, 2258–2259
and al-Wāḍih ibn Rajā', 2311
works by, 1460, 1461, 1779
and Yuḥannā, 2356
Sayce, Archibald Henry, 856, 1090, **2102**
Sayfayn, Abū. *See* Dayr Abū Sayfayn; Mercurius of Caesarea, Saint
Sayyid, Aḥmad Luṭfī, al-, 1994, 1995, 1996
Sayyid, Mīkhā'īl 'Abd, al-, 1995, 2010
Scala magna (Kircher), 1415, 1267, 1748
Scarves, 643–644
Scenas Mandras, castrum of, 465
Scetis, 113, 120, **2102–2106**
Abraham and George of, Saints, 12–13
Agathon of Alexandria and monastic cell construction, 65
Amun, Saint, and, 119
Apophthegmata patrum on monks of, 177–178
Arsenius, Saint, 240–241
Bedouin plunder of, 1534
Bessarion, Saint, of, 379
Cassian, John, on monks of, 462–463
and Damanhūr bishopric, 687

Scetis (*cont.*)
Damian as monk at, 688
Daniel of, 1648
Daniel, Saint, of, 692
Dayr Abū Mūsā al-ʿAswad, 708
Dayr Anbā Anṭūniyūs, 720, 722
Dayr Anbā Bishoi, 734–736
Dayr Anbā Helias, 747–748
Dayr Anbā Maqār, 748–756
Dayr Apa Ȧnūb, 770
Dayr al-Arman, 782
Dayr al-Baramūs, 789–794
Dayr al-Suryān in, 876–881
Dayr Yuḥannis Kama at, 883
Ēwosṭātēwos, Ethiopian saint, of, 1050–1051
forty-nine martyrs of. *See* Forty-nine martyrs of Scetis
Gabriel I, Saint and Patriarch in monastaries of, 1127
Hilaria, Saint, at, 1230–1231
Isaiah the Hermit at, 1305–1306
Jabal Khashm al-Quʿūd link with, 1316
John Colobos at, 1360
John Colobos and Bishoi flight from, 701, 795
John Kāmā of, 1362
and Kellia site location, 1397, 1401
Krajon and Amun martyrdom at, 1419
as laura of hermitages, 1224–1225
Macarius Alexandrinus in, 1490
Macarius the Egyptian in, 1491
monasteries, 707, 714, 727, 835, 841, 1658, 1659
monastery libraries, 1449
monastic life, 1662
monastic population, 1663
monks and anthropomorphism, 143
Moses the Black in, 707, 708
and Nitria monastery, 1794–1796
Palladius at, 1877
papyrus discoveries, 1900
parekklesia, 1903
Peter of, 1951
Poemen and brothers as monks at, 1983, 1984
Pshoi of, 2029–2030
recluses in, 2055
Rufinus history of hermits of, 2068
Samū'īl of Qalamūn expulsion from, 2092
Silvanus of, 2137
Theodorus of Pherme of, 2239
Theophilus, Patriarch, and monks of, 2247, 2249–2250
travel reports of monasteries, 1977
al-Wāḍih ibn Rajā' in, 2311
Zacharias, Saint, in, 2368
Scevophilacion. *See* Pastophorium
Schäfer, Heinrich, **2106**
Schema. *See* Bishop, consecration of
Schermann, Theodor, **2106**
Schiller, A. Arthur, 1895, 1438, **2106**
Schism. *See* Acacian schism; Chalcedon, Council of; Donatism; Melitian schism
Schmidt, Carl, 1149, 1899, **2106–2107**
Scholarios, 1114
Scholars
ʿAbd al-Masīḥ al-Isrā'īli al-Raqqī, 5–7
ʿAbd al-Masīḥ Ṣalīb al-Masūʿdī, 7
Acta sanctorum, 56–57
Amélineau, Emile Clement, 112
Assemani family, 289
Bachatly, Charles, 323
Bajūrī, Shaykh Ibrāhīm, al-, 330–331
Balestri, Giuseppe, 332
Bardenhewer, Otto, 345
Barns, John Wintour Baldwin, 347
Basset, René, 360
Bell, Harold Idris, 374
Bilabel, Friedrich, 390–391
Bodmer, Martin, 404–405
Boeser, Pieter Adriaan Art, 405
Borgia, Stefano, 412
Bourguet, Pierre du, S. J., 414
Bouriant, Urbain, 414–415
Breccia, A. Evaristo, **416**
Brightman, Frank Edward, 416
Bruce, James, 422
Brugsch, Heinrich Ferdinand Karl, 422
Budge, Ernest Alfred Thompson Wallis, 422–423
Burmester, Oswald Hugh Edward, 427
Burkitt, Francis Crawford, 426
Butcher, Edith L., 428
Butler, Alfred Joshua, 428
Černý, Jaroslav, 511
Champollion, Jean François, 516
Chassinat, Emile Gaston, 516–517
Chiftichi, Yuḥanna, 519–520
Cledat, Jean, 561
Cramer, Maria, 656–657
Curzon, Robert, 663–665
al-Damanhūrī, Shaykh Ahmad, 687
Daressy, Georges Emile Jules, 693
Daumas, Franois, 694–695
Dévaud, Eugène Victor, 895
Didymus the Blind, 900
Dominicans in Egypt, 918
Drescher, James Anthony Bede, 924
Drioton, (Chanoine) Etienne, 924
Dulaurier, Jean Paul, 925
Erichsen, Wolja, 972–973
Erman, Adolf, 973
Evelyn-White, Hugh Gerard, 1078
Evetts, Basil Thomas Alfred, 1078
Fortescue, Adrian, 1120
Galtier, Emile Joseph, 1138
Girgis Mattha, 1141
Graf, Georg, 1165
Graffin, René, 1165
Grapow, Hermann, 1165
Griffith, Francis Llewellyn, 1185
Groff, William N., 1185
Grohmann, Adolf, 1185–1186
Guidi, Ignazio, 1186–1187
Haase, Felix, 1189
Ḥabib Jirjis, 1189
hagiography, 1191
Hall, Henry Reginald Holland, 1203
Ḥanna Ṣalib Saʿd, 1206
Hardy, Edward R., 1206
Hauser, Walter, 1210
Hebbelynck, Adolphe, 1215
Hefele, Karl Joseph, 1215
Hengstenberg, Wilhelm, 1217
Heuser, Gustav, 1227
Horner, George W., 1257
Huntington, Robert, 1260
Hyvernat, Henri Eugène Xavier Louis, 1263
Ibn Kabar, 1267–1268
Ibn Kātib Qayṣar, 1268

Ibn Qayyim al-Jawziyyah, 1269–1270
Ibn Sibā', Yuḥannā ibn Abī Zakariyyā, 1272
Ideler, Julius Ludwig, 1280
Ilyās Buqṭur, 1284–1285
Iqlādiyūs Labīb, 1302
'Iryān Jirjis Muftāḥ, 1302–1303
Jablonski, Paul Ernst, 1318
Jernstedt, Peter Viktorovich, 1323
Johann Georg, 1336
Jullien, Michel Marie, 1382–1383
Junker, Hermann, 1383
Kahle, Paul Eric, 1389
Karabacek, Joseph von, 1389
Keimer, Ludwig, 1396
Kenyon, Frederic George, 1410
Kircher, Athanasius, 1415
Krall, Jakob, 1419
Kuentz, Charles, 1419
Kühnel, Ernst, 1419–1420
Labib Habachi, 1423
Labib, Subhi Yanni, 1423
Lacau, Pierre, 1424
Lanormant, Charles, 1440
Lefort, Louis Théophile, 1437
Legrain, Georges, 1439
Leipoldt, Johannes, 1439
Lemm, Oskar Eduardovich Von, 1439
Lepsius, Karl Richard, 1444
Le Quien, Michel, 1444
Leroy, Jules, 1444
Letronne, Jean Antoine, 1444–1445
Lucian of Antioch, 1484
Malinine, Michel, 1516
Mallon, Marie Alexis, 1516
Marcel, Jean-Joseph, 1526
Marucchi, Orazio, 1559
Maspero, Gaston, 1561
Maspero, Jean (Jacques), 1561–1562
Michalowski, Kazimierz, 1620
Miedema, Rein, 1620
Migne, Jacques-Paul, 1620
Monneret de Villard, Ugo, 1668–1669
Morenz, Siegfried, 1678
Muḥammad Ramzī, 1695
al-Muhdī, Muḥammad, 1695–1696
Munier, Adolphe Henri, 1698
Murad Kamil, 1698–1699
Murray, Margaret Alice, 1700–1701
musicologists, 1741–1742, 1743–1744
Muyser, Jacob Louis Lambert, 1749
Nau, François-Nicolas, 1783
Obicini, Thomas, 1823
Oriens Christianus, 1845
Palanque, (Henri Amedée) Charles, 1876
papyrologists, 1888–1889
Parthey, Gustav Friedrich Constantin, 1903
patristics, 1920–1921
Peeters, Paul, 1929
Peiresc, Nicolas Claude de Fabri, 1929
Pellegrini, Astorre, 1931
Petersen, Theodore, 1951
Petraeus, Theodor, 1951
Peyron, Amedeo Angelomaria, 1952
Piankoff, Alexandre, 1966
Piehl, Karl Fredrik, 1967
Porcher, Ernest, 2000–2001
prosopography use by, 2021–2022
Puech, Henri-Charles, 2032–2033
Quibell, James Edward, 2040
Qusṭanṭīn ibn Abī al-Ma'ālī ibn Abī al-Fatḥ Abū al-Fatḥ, 2046–2047
Ramshausen, Franciscus Wilhelm von, 2052
Ranke, Hermann, 2052
Rémondon, Rogert, 2057
Renaudin, Paul, 2057
Renaudot, Eusebe, 2057
Revillout, Charles Eugene, 2058
Ricci, Seymour Montefiore Robert Rosso de, 2059
Rösch, Friedrich, 2067
Rossi, Francesco, 2067
Rückert, Friedrich, 2067
Rūfa'īl al-Ṭūkhī, 2067–2068
Rufinus, 2068–2069
Saad, Zaki Yusef, 2071
Sacy, Antoine Isaac Silvestre de, 2073
Sauneron, Serge, 2100
Sayce, Archibald Henery, 2102
Schäfer, Heinrich, 2106
Schermann, Theodor, 2106
Schiller, A. Arthur, 2106
Schmidt, Carl, 2106–2107
Scholtz, Christian, 2107
Schubart, Wilhelm, 2107
Schwartze, Moritz Gotthilf, 2107
Sethe, Kurt Heinrich, 2121
Seyffarth, Gustavus, 2125
Sicard, Claude, 2136–2137
Simon, Jean, 2140
Spiegelberg, Wilhelm, 1245
Stegemann, Viktor, 2148
Steindorff, Georg, 2148
Steinwenter, Artur, 2149
Stern, Ludwig, 2155–2156, 2155–2156
Strothmann, Rudolph, 2156
Strzygowski, Josef, 2156
Tattam, Henry, 2202
Teza, Emilio, 2230
Thompson, Henry Francis Herbert, 2257
Till, Walter Curt Franz Theodor Karl Alois, 2261
Tischendorf, Konstantin von, 2269
Tisserant, Eugne, 2270
Turaev, Boris Alexandrovitch, 2282
Van Lantschoot, Arnold, 2298
Vansleb (Wansleben), Johann Michael, 2299
Villecourt, Louis, 2308
Wessely, Carl Franz Joseph, 2321
Whittemore, Thomas, 2321
Wiesmann, Hermann, 2321
Wiet, Gaston, 2321
Wilcken, Ulrich, 2322
Wilke, David, 2322
Woide, Charles Godfrey, 2324
Worrell, William Hoyt, 2348
Wüstenfeld, Ferdinand, 2348
Ya'qūb Nakhlah Rufaylah, 2353
Yassa 'Abd al-Masīḥ, 2353
Yūsuf Abū Daqn, 2364–2365
Zoega, Georg (Jorgen), 2371
see also *Coptological studies; Historians; Philosophers; Theologians*
Scholtz, Christian, 1424, **2107**
School of Alexandria. See *Catechetical School of Alexandria*
Schools, Coptic. See *Education, Coptic; specific institutions*
Schubart, Wilhelm, **2107**
Schwartze, Moritz Gotthilf, 1424, **2107**

Schweinfurth, G., 1396
Screen. See *Cancelli*
Screens, wooden, 2334, 2335
Scribes
  Abū Shākir ibn al-Rāhib, 33–34
  accounting, 52–54
  Caraccioli, Clement, 461
  from Durunkah, 927
  pen cases, 1933
  Yuḥannā, 2356
  see also Manuscripts; Scriptorium
Scriptores historiae Augustae, 904
Scriptorium, 577, **2108**
  role in Coptic education, 931–932
  see also Manuscripts
Scripture, canon of the, **2108–2111**
  see also Bible; New Testament; Old Testament
Scrofula, 771, 1975
Sculpture, 266–267, 271–272
  at Ahnās, 74–76, 2112, 2116
  Arab conquest impact on, 275–276
  at al-Ashmūnayn, 74, 287–288
  at Bāwīṭ, 74, 374, 66
  figurines, 1607
  in Louvre Museum, 1483
  portraiture, Coptic, 2006
  preservation of, 280
  at Saqqara, 74
  in State Museum of Berlin, 2146–2147
  statuary, 2147–2148
  stone relief of Shenute, *2132*
  of the Virgin Enthroned, 543–544
  in woodworking, 2327
  see also Architectural sculpture; Christian subjects in Coptic art; Metalwork, Coptic; Sculpture in stone
Sculpture in stone, Coptic, **2112–2117**, *2114*, *2115*, *2116*, *2149*
  see also Architectural sculpture; Sculpture; Statuary; Stela
"Seal of the Martyrs" (Peter I), 81
Seals
  rings, 1607
  wooden, 2334, *2335–2336*
  see also Ceramics, Coptic; Stamps
Seasons
  Coptic calendar and liturgy for, 443–444
  depicted in Coptic art, 1767
  Shamm al-Nasīm spring festival, 2126
Sebaste, martyrdoms at, 1558, 1593
Second Coming
  and orientation toward the East, 1846
  Origen on, 1850
  see also Judgment, Last
Second Henoticon of 571, 1676
Second Treatise of the Great Seth, **2117–2118**
  and *Gospel of the Egyptians*, 1154
Secret Gospel of Saint Mark, **2118–2119**
  Carpocrates and, 461
Secret History (Procopius), 2019, 2020
Secundus, Bishop of Tigisis, 84, 920
See of Saint Mark. *See* Alexandria; Patriarchs of the See of Saint Mark
Ṣeḥmā, Ethiopian saint, 1047
Semi-Arians, **2119**
Sem'on, Ethiopian prelate, 1021–1022
Senouthios. *See* Shenute
Sent. *See* Isnā
Sentences of Menandros, **2119**
Sentences of Sextus, **2119–2120**
Septimius Severus, Emperor, 1179, 1180, 1868
  and Alexandria, 97
  patriarch under, 1914
  persecutions under, 892, 1846, 1936
  visits to Egypt, 2062, 2066
Septuagint, 1865, 1867
Serapeum (Alexandria), 31–32, 100, 101, 134, 1869–1870, 2065, 2248
  destruction of, 946
Seraphim. *See* Cherubim and seraphim
Serapion. *See* Sarapion, Saint
Serapion of Antioch, Bishop, 917
Serapion Sindonita. *See* Sarapion
Serapis (pagan deity), 1531, 1867, 1868, 1869, 1936
  popularity in Canopus, 31
  Roman emperors' veneration of, 2062, 2063
  see also Serapeum (Alexandria)
Sergius, Patriarch of Constantinople, 1666, 1667
Sergius of Atrīb (martyr), 1558
Sergius and Bacchus (martyrs), 1558
The Services of the Deacon (ritual book), 1729. 1737
Seth (pagan deity), 1154, 1503, 1761
Seth (son of Adam), 1154, 1503
  see also Sethianism
Seth, Apa, 763, **2121**
Sethe, Kurt Heinrich, **2121**
Sethianism, 1154, 1222, 2117–2118, 2259–2260
Seti I, temple of at Abydos, 39–40, 41
Settlements. *See* Excavations; Toponymy, Coptic; Towns and settlements; specific names
Seven Ascetics of Tūnah, **2122**
Seven Smaller Intercessions, 1567
Severan dynasty, 2062–2063
Severian of Jabalah (Gabala), Saint, 1138, **2122–2123**
  feast day, 2087
  homily on Gabriel, Archangel, 1136
  homily on Michael, Archangel, 1619
  and Nestorian influence on Cosmas Indicopleustes, 640
Severians. *See* Severus; Theodosians
Severianus. *See* Severian of Jabalah (Gabala), Saint
Severus (martyr), 892
Severus, Emperor. *See* Septimius Severus, Emperor
Severus Alexander, Emperor, 2063
Severus of Antioch, 592, 732, 876, 1455, 1931, **2123–2125**
  and Acacian schism, 44, 45, 55; *see also subheads* Christological dispute; monophysitism
  Athanasius of Antioch biography of, 304
  in the *Christian Topography*, 640
  Christological dispute with Julian of Halicarnassus, 70, 1379, 2125
  Coptic texts on, 304, 1455

and Dioscorus II, Patriarch, 45–46, 915
doctrinal position, 734
Encomia, 1193, 1196
and Eutyches, 1075
and Flavius Apion, 155
hymn ascribed to, 1733
on Isidorus of Pelusium, 1308
and John II, Patriarch, 1337
and Justin I, Emperor, 1383
on Michael, Archangel, 1618
and monophysitism, 734, 1442, 1672–1673, 1674, 1675, 2263
Moses of Abydos prophecy on, 1679–1680
and Oktokaidekaton monastery, 1826–1827
on Philotheus, Saint, 1961
portraits of, 726
relics and shrine of, 95, 1976
and Scetis monks, 2104
and Theodosius I, Patriarch, 2241
and Timothy III, Patriarch, 2268
see also Dayr Anbā Sāwīrus
Severus of al-Ashmūnayn. *See* Sāwīrus ibn al-Muqaffaʿ
Sextus, sentences of, 2119–2120
Seyffarth, Gustavus, **2125**
Shabehmōt, **2126**
Shadrach, 1092
Shaft. *See* Column
Shahrān. *See* Dayr Shahrān
Shalān ibn ʿUthmān, Abū al-Ḥasan, 1395
Shamlah. *See* Taylasān
Shamm al-Nasīm, **2126**
Shams al-Dīn, **2126–2127**
plan of church at, *2127*
Shamul (martyr), 1558
Shanashā, 1209, **2127–2128**
Shapur, King of Persia, 14, 1519, 1558
Shapurakan (Mani), 1521
Shaqalqīl, pilgrimages to, 1974
Shaqq al-haykal, niches, 216, 221
Sharaf al-Dīn Hibat-Allāh ibn Sāʿid al-Fā'izī, 1517
Shārah (Shārāt). *See* Theotokion
Shard. *See* Ostracon
Sharqiyyah Province, monasteries in, 1655–1656
Sharūnah, **2128**
Shaṭa, 1649
Shats. *See* Khandaq, al-
Shawār (Muslim governor), 2043–2044
Shaw, George Bernard, 1996, 2088
Shawls, 642–643
linen and tapestry, *2223*
Shawl of Sabine, 1754, 1755
Shaykh ʿAbādah. *See* Antinoopolis; Ḥafn
Shaykh ʿAbd al-Qurnah, 1078, **2128**, *2129*
monastery explored by Evelyn-White, Hugh Gerard, 1078
tombs used as hermitages, 1225
see also Dayr Epiphanius
Shaykh Abū al-Barakāt ibn Abī Saʿīd, al-, 1535
Shaykh Ḥasan, al-, **2129**
Shaykh al-Islam. *See* Bajūrī, Shaykh Ibrāhīm, al-
Shaykh Ṣaʿid, al-, **2130**
Shekenda, King, 1514
Shem (son of Noah), 1901–1902
Paraphrase of, 166
Shenesēt, 1859, 1860
Shen-hīn. *See* Lecanoscopy
Shenouda III, Patriarch, **2130**
collected works of, 1782
consecration of Beirut, Lebanon, church, 1621
and Coptic Community Council, 582
and Coptic relations with Rome, 611
and Coptic youth movements, 2355
dates of patriarchy, 1919
and Dayr al-Suryān, 879
on divorce, 1943
establishment of Coptic eparchy in France, 1623
and Ethiopian church autocephaly, 982
on funerary customs, 1125
on Mark, Saint, 1529
on patriarchal election, 1911
and personal status laws, 1942
and Rabitat al-Quds, 2049
reestablishment of See of Pentapolis, 1613
selection method, 1999
Shenoute. *See* Shenute
Shenufe, Saint, 307, 1526, 1558, 1585–1587, **2130–2131**
Shenute (fourteenth-century scribe), 927
Shenute (seventh-century "new martyr"), 1558
Shenute I, Patriarch, 1527, **2133–2135**
and al-Balyanā, 333
and al-Batanūn, 361
condemnation of *cheirotonia*, 517
dates of patriarchy, 1916
and destruction of Tall Atrīb, 2200
feast day, 2087
and monastery wall construction, 750, 1237
Sāwīrus biography of, 1461
successor, 1412–1413
and Yuḥannā as scribe and biographer, 2356
Shenute II, Patriarch, **2135**
and Church of Abū Sayfayn, 550
Damrū residence, 689
dates of patriarchy, 1917
and al-Faramā bishopric, 1089–1090
selection method, 1999
Shenute, Saint, **2131–2133**, *2132*
and Abū Bishāi, 738
antipaganism, 1868, 1870
as archimandrite, 193, 378
on birth of Moses of Abydos, 1679, 1680
and convents, 1663, 1822
Coptic texts of, 1452–1453, 1456
Dayr Abū Sayfayn church dedicated to, 710
depicted in Coptic art, 538–540, 727, *2132*
as desert father, 894
feast day, 2087
and Greek philosophy, 1958
Grohmann's studies of, 1186
and John of Lycopolis, 1365
and Joseph, Saint, 1370
life of, 737, 762, 781
and medicine, 1886
monasteries of, 729, 1661
and monastery libraries, 1448
on mourning, 1686
and Nestorius, 1787
numbers of monks under, 1662–1663
and Pachomian monasticism, 1453, 1664
and *Physiologos*, 1966

Shenute, Saint (*cont.*)
and Pidjimi, Saint, 1966–1967, 2086
on pilgrimage abuses, 1968
pilgrimages to burial site of, 1969–1970
Pjol and, 1974, 1981
poetry on, 1985, 1986
prophecy of, 707, 1679
and Pshoi, Saint, 2029
relics, 764
on the Resurrection, 1697
and Seth, 2121
and Thomas, Saint, 2256
and Victor of Tabennēsē, 2308
writings in Coptic language, 1168
and Zenobios, 2371
see also Dayr Anbā Shinūdah
Shenutean idiom. *See Appendix*
Shenute the Archimandrite. *See* Shenute, Saint
Shenute of Bahnasā (martyr), 1558
Shenute of Hermopolis (seventh-century notary), archive of, 226
Shenuti (recluse), 1648
Sheol. *See* Afterlife
The Shepherd of Hermas, 62, 63, 898, 1223
Shewa, 1590
Shibāb al-Dīn Aḥmad Nuwayrī, **2136**
Shihāt, 377, 1135
Shinshif. *See* Naj' al-Shinshifī
Shinūdah, Anbā. *See* Dayr Anbā Shinūdah; Shenute, Saint
Shipbuilding centers, Alexandria, 89
Shīrkūh. *See* Ghuzz
Shirt. *See* Liturgical vestments
Shoes. *See* Sandals and shoes
A Short History of the Copts and Their Church (Maqrīzī), 1525
Shotep. *See* Shuṭb
Shtit (Coptic textile term), 2221
Shube (martyr), 1558
Shubrā Nabāt (Shubrā Damrū) (village), 689–690
Shukrallāh Jirjis, **2136**
Shukrī, 'Abd al-Raḥmān, 1466
Shumayyil, Shiblī, 1996
Shuṭb, 797, **2136**
Shute I, Saint, 2087
Shuttle. *See* Textiles, Coptic, manufacturing techniques
Sibirbāy, 1969, **2136**
Sibylla, 1136, 1867
Sibylline Oracles, 899, 1867
Sicard, Claude, 1330, 1977, **2136–2137**
on Antinoopolis, 145
on Dayr Anbā Anṭūniyūs, 722
on Dayr Anbā Bākhūm, 729–730
on Dayr al-Baramūs, 791
on Dayr al-Jabrāwī
on Dayr al-Malāk Mīkhā'īl (Jirjā), 825
Sicily, 182, 1099
Sickness. *See* Communion of the sick; Healings in Coptic literature; Medicine; Unction of the sick
Sīdārūs, Gabriel, 1206, **2137**
Siderius, Bishop of Palaebisca and Hydrax, 1612
Ṣidfā, pilgrimages to, 1974
Sidhom Bishāy (new martyr),1558
Sidon, Council of (511), 1962
Ṣidqī Pasha, Ismā'īl, 1992
Sign of the Cross. *See* Holy Cross Day
Sign of life, Egyptian. *See* Ankh
Silk, used in Coptic textiles, 2212–2213, *2213–2214*
Silko, King, 1171
Silvanus, Teachings of. *See* Teachings of Silvanus
Silvanus of Scetis, Saint, 1733, 2087, **2137**, 2369
Silver, 576, 1599
Simaikah, Marcos. *See* Murqus Simaykah
Sim'ān ibn Abī Naṣr al-Ṭamadā'ī, **2138**
Simeon (new martyr), 1558
Simeon, Saint, 745, 1633, 1778, 2087
see also Dayr Anbā Hadrā
Simeon the Armenian (martyr), 1558
Simeon the elder, 1106–1107
Simeon the Potter of Geshir, Theotokia melodies ascribed to, 1726–1727
Simeonstift Coptic Collection. *See* Museums, Coptic collections
Simeon the Stylite. *See* Pseudo-Macarius, homilies of; Simeon, Saint
Simon, Apostle and Saint, 57
Simon, Jean, **2140**
Simon I, Saint and Patriarch, 20, 85, 93, **2138–2139**
and bishops of Nikiou, 1794
dates of patriarchy, 1915
feast day, 2087
as monk at the Enaton, 958
and ordination of Zacharias as bishop, 2368
Simon II, Saint and Patriarch, **2139**
dates of patriarchy, 1916
feast day, 2087
and Yoḥannes I, Ethiopian prelate, 1001
Yuḥannā as biographer, 2356
Simon the Mad, Saint, collected miracles of, 1783
Simon Simeionis, 1977
Simony. *See Cheirotonia*
Simon the Zealot, Saint, relics, 764
Simplicius, Pope (Rome), 42, 43, 1218, 1671
Simyen Mountains, 1425
Sin. *See* Absolution; Atonement; Confession and penitence; Original sin; Penance
Sina (martyr), 1089, 1558
Sinai Peninsula
Christian pilgrimages and travelers in, 1976
Pharan oasis, 1952–1953
Raithou, 2049–2050
on route of flight into Egypt, 1118
Sinān Pasha, 1134
Sinbillāwayn, al-, 1648
Singing. *See* Cantors; Chant; Choral singing; Hymns; Music, Coptic
Sinhira. *See* Pilgrimages
Sinhūt, Bishop of Miṣr, 1615
Sinjār, 1722, **2140**
Sinodā, Ethiopian prelate, 1025–1026
Sinuthius, Saint, monastery of. *See* Dayr Anbā Shinūdah
Siricus, Pope, 2249
Sirmium, Council of (359), 1089
Sirri, Ḥusayn, 1990
Siryāqūs
Dayr Apa Hor, 771–772
pilgrimages to, 1974–1975
Sisinnius, Saint, paintings of, 727
Sisoēs, Abbā, 758, **2141**
Sistrum (musical instrument), 1740, *1740*

Siti, King of Dotawo, 922
Sitt Dimyānah. *See* Dayr Sitt Dimyanah
Sitt al-Mulk, 18, 1097, 1098, 1201
Sitt Rifqah, 1971
Siwa (oasis), 1659, **2141**
Sixtus III, Pope, 1440
Siyar al-Bīʿah al-Muqaddasah. See History of the Patriarchs of Alexandria
Skin diseases, 1579–1580
Skins. *See* Hides and skins
Slaves, Nubian in Egypt, 1099
Sleep, prayer of. *See* Compline
Sleeves, 1477–1478
Slippers, 1478
Smaller Church in the Febrius (Pharos island), 93
Smith, Morton, 2118, 2119
Smyrna
  martyrs, 1997–1998
  sacrifice to Roman gods at, 890
Sne. *See* Isnā
Snuffer, 1598
Soba, **2141–2142**
  as capital of the Nubian kingdom of ʿAlwā, 110, 111, 1797
  as episcopal see of Nubia, 1813
  and Nubian archaeology, medieval, 1804
Socialism, 1996, 2088–2089
Socialist Action Party, 1991
Socialist Party, 1996
Socialist Union, 1991
Société d'archéologie copte. *See* Society of Coptic Archaeology
Société française des fouilles archéologiques, 1482
Société royale de géographie de l'Egypte, 1698
Society of the Bollandists. *See* Bollandists
Society of Coptic Archaeology (Cairo), 1700, 1891, 1892, **2142**
  and Bachatly, Charles, 323
  and excavation of Dayr Apa Phoibammon, 779
  and Omar Toussoun, 1841
  and Sāmī Gabrā, 2090
Society of Jesus. *See* Jesuits and the Coptic Church
Socks, 646
Socrates (church historian), 2068, **2142**
  on Athanasius I, 298
  on feast of the Ascension, 1105
  on Gallus Caesar's vision of the Holy Cross, 1244
  on Helena, Empress, discovery of Holy Cross of Christ, 1243
  on Jovian, Emperor, 1376
  and Sozomen, 2145
  supplemented by Theodoret, 2236
  on Theophilus, Patriarch, 2247, 2248, 2250, 2252
Soknopaiou Nesos, 1390
Soldier–martyrs, 1964
Sol Invictus (pagan deity), 1617
Sollerius, Jean Baptiste, 1330
Solomon (Old Testament)
  as author of *Physiologos*, 1966
  and guardian angel concept, 1186
  poetry on, 1985, 1986
  Psalms of, 166
Solomon, King of Nubia, 1099
Solon (anchorite), 1650
Son of Grace, Ethiopian doctrinal conflict, 1033
Songs, nonliturgical, 1744
Songs of Isis and Nephthys, 1732
Song of the Three Young Men in the Furnace, 4
Sophia (gnosticism), 1148, 1150, 1151, 1156
Sophia (martyr and mother of Eudamon and Epistamon), 1558
Sophia (wife of Christian governor of Antioch), 1307
Sophia, Empress (Justin II), 1384, 1676
Sophia, Saint, **2143–2144**
  compared with Hilaria, Saint, 1231
  feast day, 1558
  relics, 95, 783
The Sophia of Jesus Christ. See Eugnostos the Blessed and the Sophia of Jesus Christ
Sophronius, 1467, 1560, 1666, 1676, 1667, 1678
Sossianus Hierocles, 907, 1937, 2009
Soul
  Authentikos Logos on, 309
  exegisis on the, 1080–1081
  preexistence, Ethiopian controversy, 985–986
  preexistence, creed of, 900, 2118
  see also Sophia (gnosticism)
Souros, 635, **2144**
Soviet Union. *See* Russia; Union of Soviet Socialist Republics
Sozomen, 2068, **2145**
  on Athanasius I, 298
  on Eucharistic fast, 1063
  on flight into Egypt, 841
  on Jabal Khashm al-Quʿūd, 1316
  on Mareotis monks, 1527
  on Temple of Serapis, 134
  and Theodoret, 2236
  on Theophilus, Patriarch, 2247
  and Timothy I, Patriarch, 2263
Sozousa, 1934
Spain, papyrus collection, 1895
Spells. *See* Magic
Speos Artemidos. *See* Banī Ḥasan and Speos Artemidos
Sphinx, 2065
Spiegelberg, Wilhelm, **2145**
Spindles and spindle whorls, wooden, 2335, *2336*
Spinning, in manufacture of Coptic textiles, 2213–2214
Spirit. *See* Holy Spirit
Spiritual Homilies, 1491
Spoon
  Coptic metalwork, 1603
  as Eucharistic vessel, 1065–1066
Sprang, used in manufacture of Coptic textiles, 2218
Spring
  Shamm al-Nasīm feast, 2126
  see also Easter; Pascha
Springs. *See* Water supply
Staatliches Museum (Berlin), 2060
Stack, Sir Lee, 1990
Staff, pastoral. *See* Liturgical insignia
Stamps
  terra-cotta, 498–499
  wooden bread, State Museum of Berlin collection of, 2147
State Hermitage Museum, Leningrad, USSR, 1601, 1895
State Library, Berlin, 1892
State Museum of Berlin, 74, **2146–2147**
  papyrus collection, 1893, 1899
  pen cases at, 1933
State of the Provinces, on Dayr Abū Maqrūfah, 704
State and University Library, Hamburg, Germany, 1893

State and University Library of
Lower Saxony, Göttingen,
Germany, 1893
Statuary, **2147–2148**, *2148*
military, 649–650, *649*,
2147–2148
see also Ceramics, Coptic;
Sculpture in stone
Stefanski, E., 2022
Stegemann, Viktor, **2148**
Steindorff, Georg, 405, 780, 973,
1165, **2148**
Steiner, Rudolf, 1149
Steinwenter, Arthur, 902, 1438,
2149
Stela, **2149–2152**, *2149–2152*,
2161
at al-Duwayr, 928
Epimachus of Pelusium,
965–966
inscriptions, 1293
in Louvre Museum, 1483
symbols, 2161–2162
wood, 2335–2336
see also Tombs
Stephanite. *See* Esṭifānosites
Stephanos of Ahnāsyah, Bishop,
illuminated manuscript,
1282
Stephanus (architect), 1682
Stephen, Saint, **2153**
churches dedicated to, 1870
as deacon, 885
depicted in Coptic art, 869
feast day, 2087
martyrdom, 1558
Stephen of Hnēs, Bishop, 1455,
2154
Stephen the Theban, **2154–2155**
Stephen the Younger, Saint
(martyr), 1275
Stern, Ludwig, **2155–2156**
Steward. *See* Oikonomos
Stewart, Randall, 1891
Sticharion, 1478–1479, *1478*
Stippourgós (Coptic weaving
term), 2221
Stoicism, 512, 1148, 1957
Stone. *See* Sculpture in stone,
Coptic; specific types
Stoppers, ceramic, 499
Strabo, 95–96, 1613
Stratelates. *See* Theodorus
Stratelates, Saint; Victor
Stratelates, Saint
Strothmann, Rudolph, **2156**
Strzygowski, Josef, **2156**
Stucco
Coptic sculpture in, 2113
Copto-Muslim art, 1311
Subakhmimic. *See Appendix*
Subdeacon, **2156**
in church hierarchy, 1229
Subdialects. *See Appendix*
Subordinationism, **2156–2157**,
1484
Arianism link with, 231–232
Origen on, 471
Suchos (god), 1418
Sudan, 1990, 1992, 2097
see also Beja tribes; Nubia
headings
Sudan, Catholic Copts in the,
2157–2158
Sudan, Coptic Evangelical Church
in the, **2158**
Sudan, Copts in the, **2158**
Sudan Antiquities Service, 1588
Sudan National Museum, 1091
Suez, Franciscan church in, 1123
Suez Canal, 1636, 1637, 1692
Suhāj
Dayr Anbā Bishoi, 736–740,
1654
Dayr Anbā Shinūdah, 761–770,
767, 1654
monasteries in region of, 884,
1650–1651
Sullam. See Appendix
*Sullam al-Kabīr, al-. See Scala
Magna*
*Sullam al-Muqaffā wa-al-Dhahab
al-Muṣaffā, al-* (Abū Isḥāq),
1748
Sultan al-Nāsir Muḥammad ibn
Qalawūn, 1517–1518
Summa theologiae (Abū Isḥāq ibn
al-ʿAssāl), 21, 1779
Sunbāṭ, **2159**
pilgrimages to, 1971
Sunday, 1901, **2159–2160**
consecration of patriarch on,
1909
Easter, 1904, 1905
lectionary for, 1435–1436, 1437
Palm Sunday, 1103–1104
service for ordination of priest,
2013–2015
Sunday School movement, 933,
2090, 2091, 2355
Sunday of Thomas, feast of, 1108
Sunni Islam, 1097
Ṣuqāʿi Faḍl Allāh ibn Fakhr, al-,
2160
Surety, 1430
Suriel, Archangel, 190, **2160**
Surūr ibn Jirjā, Archdeacon of
Alexandria, 1960
Suryāl. *See* Suriel, Archangel
Suryāl, Father Ṣalīb, 1623
Susinius, Saint, 2087
Suwwāh (Arabic term). *See*
Anchorites
Swinburne, Thomas de,
1976–1977
Swiss Reformation, 1110
Switzerland
archaeological activity in the
Kellia, 1400–1406
Bibliotheca Bodmeriana
(Bodmer Library), 404
Coptic churches in, 1624
Coptic collections, 1711–1712
Egyptology, 895
Mauritius, Saint, veneration,
1572
papyrus collection, 1895
sites of veneration, 1110
Theban Legion, 1082,
2231–2233
Syllabication. *See Appendix*
Symbols in Coptic art, 270, 293,
1259, **2160–2171**, *2161–2171*
alpha and omega, 2160–2163
conch shell, 2163–2164
cross, 2164–2165
dolphins, 2168–2169
eagle, 2167–2169
fish, 2170–2171
nimbus, 2171
see also Cross, Triumph of the
Symeon. *See* Pseudo-Macarius,
homilies of, 2028
Symeon (martyr). *See* John and
Symeon
Symmachus, Pope (Rome), 44, 45
Symphronius. *See* Panine
Synaxarion, Copto-Arabic,
2171–2190
authorship, 1626–1627
and lectionary, 1435
source of knowledge about
saints, 1044–1045, 2173–2190
on *Theotokos*, 2256
translation into Ge'ez, 722
word *apa* in, 152
see also Hagiography, Coptic
Synaxarion, Ethiopian, **2190–2191**
Syncletica, **2192**
Synesius, Bishop of Ptolemais,
100, 1612, 1935, **2192**, 2247

Synod, Holy, **2193–2194**
and bishop's consecration, 395
patriarchal deputies in, 1911
see also Patriarch headings
Synodicon (Damian), 1455
Synod of Diospolis, 1930
Synods, letters of, **2194**
Synod of Tyre, 1962
Synoptic Gospels, **1157**, **2195**
see also Gospel of Saint Luke; Gospel of Saint Matthew; Gospel of Saint Mark
Synthronon, 221–222
Syria
and Acacian schism, 45, 46
anaphora of Saint Basil, 121–123
Ignatius IX, Patriarch, consecration in Egypt, 1131
influences on Coptic art, 2195
Mark II, Patriarch, relations with, 1533, 1534
monasteries, 876, 877, 878
monasticism origins in, 1663
monastic practices in, 1662
monophysites, 547–548, 1675, 1676, 1677
and origin of *Gospel of Thomas*, 1163
Syriac language
inscriptions in, 1290
Philoxenus of Mabbug's writings, 1962
Syriacos, Saint, 2087
Syrian influences on Coptic art, **2195**
Syrian Orthodox church
and Jacob Baradaeus, 1318–1319
and monophysitism, 547–548, 1675, 1676, 1677
see also Jacobites
Syrian, the. *See* Ephraem Syrus, Saint

T

Tabennēsē, 1976, **2197**
Pachomian monastery, 685, 1657, 1662, 1859–1860, 1973–1974
Paphnutius at, 1882
and Pbow, 1927
Victor of, Saint, 2308
women's monastery founded at, 1663
Tabennesiotes. *See* Metanoia, Monastery of the; Monasticism, Pachomian
Tab'ī, Muhammad al-, 1991
Tablet loom, for manufacture of Coptic textiles, 2216, *2216*, 2217
Tableware
ceramic, 487–499
glass, 1143–1144, *1143*, *1144*, *1147*
see also Missoria
Tacitus, Emperor, patriarch under, 1914
Tādrus. *See* Theodorus of Tabennēsē, Saint
Tadrus, Ramzī, 1466
Tādrus al-Mashriqī, **2197**
Tādrus Shinudah al-Manqabādī, **2197–2198**
Tadrus al-Shuṭbī (martyr), 1974
Tafa, **2198**
as episcopal see of Nubia, 1813, 2200
Tafsīr, 1687, **2198–2199**
Taharqa temple, 2036, 2037
Taḥrīr al-Mar'ah (Amīn), 1994
Ṭaḥṭāwī, Rifā'ah al-, 1994
Taifa. *See* Tafa
Tāj. *See* Miter
Tāj al-Riyāsah Abū Isḥāq ibn Faḍlallāh, 20
Takināsh, 758, **2199**
Taklā, Abūnā, *The Services of the Deacon*, 1729, 1737
Takla Hāymānot, Ethiopian saint, 1049–1050
Takla Haymot, chapel of. *See* Church of al-Mu'allaqah (Old Cairo)
Takritans, at Dayr al-Suryān, 876, 877
Talā'ī ibn Ruzzayj, 761
Tall al-'Amarnah, **2199**
Tall Atrīb, 307, 1620, **2199–2200**
Tall Brothers, 113, 916, 1357, 2249–2251
see also Ammonius; Dioscorus; Eusebius; Euthymius
Tall al-Faramā. *See* Faramā, al-
Talmīs, **2200**
Ṭambūq, 1648
Tamerlane (Timur), impact on Dayr al-Suryān, 877
Tamīt, **2200–2201**, *2201*
example of Byzantine cross-in-square building at, 661
Tamnūh, **2201**
Tamūh, Dayr al-Aḥmar at, 716
Tamulawus, King (Greek island), 2253
Tamwayh, Dayr Abū al-Sayfayn at, 709–710
Tanaithis, 1657
Ṭanbidā, 1653, **2201**
Tapers, cross and, 1469
Tapestries, 264, 273, 1483
of Coptic icons, *2222–2230*, *2309*
Coptic weaving, 2217
dancers depicted in, *277*, *2230*
Ḥarrāniyyah workshops, 2051
Icon of the Virgin, 542, 543
Nilometer depicted in, 1794, *1795*
Parthian horseman depicted in, *538*
portraiture, *2005*, 2006
State Museum of Berlin collection, 2146–2147
Triumph of the Cross, 658–659, *659*
see also Symbols in Coptic art; Textiles, Coptic
Taposiris Magna. *See* Abūṣīr (Tapisiris Magna)
Taqī al-Dīn Abū al-Baqā' Ṣaliḥ ibn al-Ḥusayn al-Ja'farī, al-Ṣafī ibn al-'Assāl reply to, 2078–2079
Tarānīm (songs), 1744
Tarasius of Constantinople, Patriarch, 1112, 1115
Tarbū, Abū, 1507
Ṭarḥ, 1479, 1726
hōs paraphrase, 1727
and *sab'ah wa-arba'ah*, 2017
and *ṭubḥ*, 2279
and *wāṭus*, 2320
Tārīkh Baṭārikat al-Iskandariyyah al-Qibṭ. See *History of the Patriarchs*
Tārīkh al-Kanā'is wa-al-Adyurah. *See* Abū al-Makārim; *Churches and Monasteries of Egypt and Neighboring Countries*
Tarmīnah (martyr), 1653
Tarnūṭ, 1, **2202**
Tarsikários (Coptic weaving term), 2221
Tartīb mashat al-mulūk. *See* Kings, anointing of
Tasempoti. *See* Sunbāt

Tattam, Henry, 1148, **2202**
Ṭawfīq. *See* Muḥammad ʿAlī dynasty
Tawfīq Coptic Society, 374, 933, 1465, 2198
Tawqīʿāt al-Mūsīqiyyah li-Maraddāt al-Kanīsah al-Murqusiyyah, al- (Ghubriyāl), 1743
Taxation
accounting, 50, 52
apostolic canons on, 453
Arab conquest of Egypt and, 72, 85–86, 185, 1430
Blemmyes, 228
in Byzantine period in Alexandria, 98
of Dayr Anbā Maqār, 749–750
of *dhimmis*, 72
by French in Egypt, 1417
Ibn Qayyim al-Jawziyyah on, 1269
and islamization of Egypt, 937–938
land and communal property (*kharāj*), 72, 85–86, 87, 189, 636, 656, 1413–1414, 2093, 2134–2135
Mamluk dynasty, 1517
of monasteries, 1643
Moses of Awsīm resistance to, 1679
mubāshirūn (officials), 1687–1688
pagarch role in, 1871–1872
poll (*jizyah*), 72, 85–87, 187, 189, 303, 622, 636, 656, 665, 2134–2135
Roman. *See* Taxation in Roman Egypt
and Shenute I, 2134–2135
Umayyad administration, 2287–2288
Taxation in Roman Egypt, 98, 237–238, 904, 905, 945, 2009, **2202–2206**
annona civica, 135
annona militaris, 135–136; *see also* Army: Roman
boule, 414
Tayaban (martyr), 1553
Taylasān, 1479
Tbow, **2207**
Petronius's founding of monastery at, 1952
The Teaching of the Apostles. See *Didache*
Teachings of Silvanus, **2207–2208**
Tebtunis. *See* Monasteries of the Fayyūm; Umm al-Barakāt
Tebtynis. *See* Umm al-Barakāt
Tecla, Saint. *See* Paese and Tecla, Saints
Television, 1088
Tell Idfū, ceramics of. *See* Ceramics, Coptic
Temple of Amun, 1484–1485
Temple of Hathor, 816, 817, 1656, 1874
Temple of Hatshepsut, 1874
see also Dayr al-Bahri
Temple of Imhotep, 1874
Temple of Isis, 107, 1292, 1801, 1870, 1874, 1954, *1954*
Temple in Jerusalem, Pentecost and, 1446
Temple of Karnak, 1392–1394, 1484
Temple of Kom Ombo, 1418
Temple of Luxor, 1870
Temple of Month, 1494
Temples
altars, 106
churches built on sites of, 1292, 1870, 1874, 1954
Dandarah, 690, *691*
Hawwārah, 1210–1211
Jewish (Leontopolis), 1866
pharaonic-style, 1865
Taharqa, 2036, 2037
Ṭūd as cultic center, 2279–2280
Temples, Egyptian, 1496–1499
Temple of Seti I, 1874
Temples of Nectanebo II, 1653
Ten Canons. See Nomocanon
Tentyra. *See* Dandarah
Ter and Erai, Saints (martyrs), 1117, 1221, 1558, **2209**
Termoute. *See* Patermuthius, Saint
Terra-cotta. *See* Ceramics, Coptic
Tertullian (apologist), 176, 177–178, 917, 1548, 1638
on abstinence practice, 17
on consubstantiality, 1253
on immersion, 1286
on incense use, 1472
on Last Judgment, 1379
on Nativity date, 1102
patristic writings, 1920, 1921
on prayers for the dead, 889
on remarriage of widows (digamy), 901
Tes. *See* Akhmīm
Tesmine. *See* Akhmīm
Testament of Abraham, 163, 164
Testament of Isaac, 164
Testament of Isaac, Coptic version of. *See* Coptic Testament of Isaac
Testament of Jacob, 164
Testament of Job, 164
Testament of Joshua, 164
Testament of Moses, 164
Testaments of the Patriarchs, 163–164
Testamentum Domini, in the Octateuch of Clement, 1824
Testimony of Truth, 1301, **2209–2210**
Tetraconch, 222
Tetradite, 688
Tetramorph, depicted in Coptic art, 539–540
Tetrapla. See Hexapla and Tetrapla
Tēwodros II, Emperor, 1590
Textiles, Coptic, 268–269, 273, 276, **2210–2230**, *2211*, *2213–2214*, *2216–2218*, *2222–2230*
Amazons depicted in, 1751–1752
Arab conquest of Egypt impact on, 1311
clothing. *See* Costume, civil; Costume, military; Costume of the religious
dancers depicted in, 1756–1757
Dionysus portraits, 1760
historiography of, 255–258
Louvre Museum collection of, 255–258, 1483
measurement, 1611
monastic weavers, 1641
Nubian, 1819–1820
pastoral scenes depicted in, 1766–1767
portraiture, 1760, 2001
preservation of, 279
production of fabrics, 2220–2221
Sassanid artistic influence, 2097–2098
and spindles and spindle whorls, 2335
State Museum of Berlin collection of, 2146–2147
see also Symbols in Coptic art; Tapestries
Textiles, Nubian, 1819–1820

Textiles preservation. *See* Art preservation
Teza, Emilio, **2230**
Thais. *See* Sarapion
Thalassius, Prefect of Illyricum, 2017
Thaleia (Arius), 82, 230, 232, 1253, 1733
Thanksgiving, prayer of, 1715, 2007, 2126
Tharwat, ʿAbd al-Khalīq, 1990
Thebaid, the. *See* Ṣaʿīd
Theban hermitages. *See* Hermitages, Theban
Theban Legion, 1110, 1936, **2231–2233**, *2232–2233*
  and Exuperantius, Saint, 1082
  martyrdom, 1082, 1555, 1558, 1559, 2057
  and Mauritius, Saint, 1572
  and Regula, Saint, 2086
  and Ursus of Solothurn, 2292
  and Verena, Saint, 2087, 2299
  and Victor of Solothurn and Geneva, Saint, 2302
Thebes
  end to institutionalized paganism in, 1870
  hermitages, 1225
  Luxor and, 1484
  monasteries dedicated to Phoibammon at, 1964–1965
  monasteries in region of, 1656, 1657
  monastic murals at, 1874
  papyrus collections, 1893, 1895
  Persian occupation of, 1939
  prosopography, 2022
  Roman travelers in, 2065
Thecla, Saint
  church of, 1652
  depicted in Coptic art, 540–541
  martyrdom, 540, 892, 1558
  relics and miracles of, 544, 1774
Thecla and Mudi (martyrs), 1559
Thekla al-Ḥabishī (monk–painter), 753–754
Themistius (Alexandrian deacon), 70–71
Thenaud, Jean, 722, 1977, 2050
Theoclas, Saint. *See* Heraclas, Saint
Theoclia (martyr), 1559
Theodora (fourth-century martyr), 31, 1554
Theodora, Empress, 944, 1046, 1682–1682, **2234–2235**
  and Abraham of Farshūṭ, 11–12
  and Anastasia, 125
  and Jacob Baradaeus, 1319, 1386, 1675, 2235
  and Monophysites, 1386, 1674, 1675
  and Nubian evangelization, 1801
  Procopius on, 2019, 2234, 2235
  and Theodosius I, Patriarch, 2241
  and Timothy III, Patriarch, 2268
Theodora, Saint (fifth century), **2235**, 2087
  and Oktokaidekaton monastery, 1826
Theodora, Saint (third century), 2087
Theodore (missionary), 1480
Theodore I, Pope (Rome), 1678
Theodore. *See* Theodorus
Theodoret, Bishop of Cyrrhus, 515, 914, 1672, 2068, **2235–2237**
  on Athanasius I, 298
  and Justinian, Emperor, 1386
  and Theophilus, Patriarch, 2247
Theodorus (recluse), 2055
Theodorus, Bishop of Pentapolis, 1559
Theodorus, Emperor (Ethiopia), 1693
Theodorus, Patriarch, 1589, **2237**
  dates of patriarchy, 1915
  feast day, 2087
  successor, 1410–1412
  and Tamnūh, 2201
Theodorus, Saint, **2237–2238**
Theodorus of Alexandria, Saint, 32, 1952, 2087, **2238**
Theodorus Anatolius (martyr), 1559, 2238
Theodorus of Antioch (fictitious), 2032, 2268
Theodorus Balsamon, 1540
Theodorus the General. *See* Theodorus Stratelates, Saint
Theodorus of Mopsuestia, 597, 2017, 1672, **2238–2239**
  on *communicatio idiomatum*, 578
  and Constantinople, Second Council of, 595
  and Cyril I, 673
  Justinian, Emperor, condemnation of, 1386, 2239
  on Kiss of Peace, 1416
  on the nature of Christ, 547
  opposition to Apollinarius, 174
  Theodoret history of, 2236
  and Theophilus, Patriarch, 2249
Theodorus the Oriental, paintings of, 726, 727
Theodorus of Pherme, Saint, 56, 2087, **2239**
Theodorus of Shotep. *See* Theodorus Stratelates, Saint
Theodorus Stratelates, Saint, 727, 796–797, 1559, 1609, **2237–2238**
  relics at Dayr al-Amīr Tadrūs, 718
Theodorus of Tabennēsē, Saint, 1257, 1448, 1864, 1927, **2239–2240**
  Coptic texts of, 1451–1452
  as desert father, 894
  distinguished from Theodorus of Alexandria, Saint, 2238
  feast day, 2087
  founding of monasteries for women, 1663, 1822
  and Letter of Ammon, 1445, 2030
  as Pachomian disciple, 1664, 1860, 1861, 1862
  papyrus collection of letters, 1894
  personal characteristics, 2240
Theodorus and Timothy (martyrs), 1559
Theodosia of Alexandria (martyr), 1554, 1559
Theodosians (Severians), 734, 790, 876, **2240–2241**
Theodosius (martyr), 1553
Theodosius (tax collector), 66
Theodosius I, Emperor
  on age of deaconesses, 888
  antipaganism, 1869, 1870, 2248
  and Constantinople, First Council of, 593–595
  and Henoticon edict, 1218
  and Maximus and Domitius, 789–790, 1577
  and miracles of Phoibammon of Preht, 1963
  patriarch under, 1914
  and Raphael, Archangel, 2054
  and Theodorus of Mopsuestia, 2238

Theodosius I, Emperor (*cont.*)
and Theophilus, Patriarch, 2248, 2251
Thessalonica, edict of (380), 1947
Theodosius II, Emperor
and Chalcedon, Council of, 512–513
Codex Theodosianus, 571
and Elias, 748
Ephesus, First Council of, 959–960
and Ephesus, Second Council of, 913, 961–962, 1441, 1670
and Eutyches, 913, 1074–1075
on Holy Chrism ingredients, 522
Olympiodorus of Thebes on, 1840
patriarchs under, 1914–1915
and Proclus, 2017
Pulcheria as regent, 2033
and Scetis monks, 1120
and Victor of Tabennēsē, 2308
Theodosius I, Saint and Patriarch, **2241**
Alexandrian church restoration, 93
Cosmas Indicopleustes and, 640
dates of patriarchy, 1915
and Dayr Anbā Maqār, 749
deposition and return, 1674, 1675
feast day, 2087
and Gaianus as rival patriarch, 1138
homily on Michael, Archangel, 1619
and Julian, Evangelist, 1380
and Longinus' missions, 1480
Moses of Abydos prophecy on, 1679–1680
and Severus of Antioch, 2104
and Theodosians, 2240–2241
Theodosius II, Patriarch, 94, 558, 1209, **2241–2242**, 2359
burial site, 848
and the chrism at Church of Abū Sayfayn, 550
dates of patriarchy, 1917
as monk at Dayr Abū Fānah, 698
Theodosius of Jerusalem, Bishop, **2242**, 2303
Theodota (martyr), 1554
Theodotus (Dynamic Monarchian), 1638
Theodotus (martyr and disciple of Athanasius), 1559
Theodotus (martyr under Valerian), 1552
Theodotus of Ancyra, Bishop, **2242–2243**
Theodoxia (fourth-century martyr), 31, 1554
Theodulf of Orleans, 1115
Theognius of Nicaea, 84, 1484
Theognosta, Saint, 2087, **2243–2244**, 2087
Theologians
Abū Shākar ibn al-Rāhib, 33
Agathonicus of Tarsus, 69–70
Clement of Alexandria, 562–563
Draguet, René, 924
Duchesne, Louis, 925
Eusebius of Caesarea, 1070–1071
Hardy, Edward R., 1206
Hippolytus, 1235–1236
Horner, George W., 1257
Jablonski, Paul Ernst, 1318
John Chrysostom, 1357–1359
John of Parallos, Saint, 1367–1368
Leipoldt, Johannes, 1439
Lucian of Antioch, 1484
Mansi, Giovanni Domenico, 1523–1524
Origen, 1846–1855
patristics, 1920–1921
Schermann, Theodor, 2106
Seyffarth, Gustavus, 2125
Theodorus of Mopsuestia, 2238–2239
Theodosius I, Saint and Patriarch, 2241
Tischendorf, Konstantin von, 2269
Wilke (Wilkius, Wilkins), David, 2322
see also Apologist; Scholars
Theology
Alexandrian, 103–104
Catechetical School of Alexandria, 469–472
Clerical College (Cairo), 563–564
see also Chalcedon, Council of; Christology; Heresy; other specific councils and aspects
Theonas (recluse), 2055
Theonas, Patriarch, **2244–2246**
and Achillas, 55
and Alexandrian churches, 93, 102, 588
dates of patriarchy, 1914
and Manichaean asceticism, 88
and Peter I as successor, 1936, 1937
Theonas of Libya (dissenter), 84
Theone (martyr), 1559
Theopemptos of Antioch, panegyric on Victor Stratelates, Saint, 2306
Theophanes, Patriarch, **2247**
dates of patriarchy, 1916
and Ethiopian prelates, 1002
successor, 1632
Theophanes the Chronicler, 2017, 2020, 2264
Theophila (martyr), 1
Theophilos I, Archbishop of Jerusalem, 1246–1247, 1325, 2049, **2247**
Theophilus, Patriarch, 1978, **2247–2252**
and Ammonius of Kellia, 113, 686
anthropomorphism rejection by, 143, 154, 1884, 2103, 2249–2250
and Antioch schisms, 2248–2249
and Bostra affair, 2249
church-building and consecrations by, 24, 93, 94, 101, 1969, 2248
collected works, 1782
and consecration of Holy Chrism, 521
cycle of, 667
and Cyril I, 671
dates of patriarchy, 1914
and Dioscorus, 915–916
feast day, 2087
and Gregory of Nyssa, 1185
and Hadrā of Aswan, 1190
and John the Baptist, 1355
and John Chrysostom, 1357, 2250–2251, 2252
and Kellia monks, 1076, 1397
Letter of Ammon to, 1445
on miracles of George, Saint, 592
and Monastery of the Metanoia, 1608, 1611
and Nikiou, 1793
and Origenist teachings, 471–472, 916, 2249–2250, 2252

and Pachomian monks, 1861
pagan attacks on, 1869–1870
on Raphael, Archangel, 2053
reputation, 2252
and Scetis monks, 2103, 2249
Serapeum destruction order, 31–32, 134, 2248
on Three Hebrews in the Furnace, 2258
writings, 2251–2252
Theophilus, Saint (monk), **2253–2254**, 2087
Theophylact. *See* Cosmas
Theophylact, Archbishop of Ochrida, 1113
Theopista, Saint (2nd century). *See* Eustathius and Theopista
Theopista, Saint, and Macarius, Bishop of Nikiou, 1794
Theopista and Dorotheus, and Michael, Archangel, 1618, 1619
Theopiste (daughter of Zeno), 1230–1231
Theopiste (fourth-century martyr), 31, 1554
Theopistus of Alexandria, **2254**
Theotokion, 900, 1687, 1724, 1726, 1727, 1728, 1986, **2254–2255**
doxology, 924
lōbsh as conclusion for, 1479
and *tafsīr*, 2198
Virgin analogy with censer, 1470
and *wāṭus*, 2320
Theotokos, 514, 528, 672, 883, 2026, **2255**
Annunciation and, 528–529
Basil the Great catechesis, 351–352
Chalcedon, Council of, on, 514, 2255
communicatio idiomatum on, 578
and Constantinople, 1276
controversy over term, 475
Coptic position on, 101, 1785
Cyril I on, 270, 672
Dayr Apa Jeremiah wall paintings, 78
Dioscorus on, 525
Ephesus, First Council on, 960
Henoticon on, 1217–1218
intercession of, 108
John of Antioch on, 1354
mentioned at bishop's consecration, 396
monasteries dedicated to, 714, 876
Monophysite, 1669
Nestorian opposition, 960
Nestorius on, 672
Proclus sermon on, 2017, 2018
Theodoret on, 2236
see also Annunciation; Christ, nature of; Christology
Theotokos, Feasts of the, **2256**
Therapeutae (Jewish ascetics), 1661
antiphon use, 148–149
and origin of antiphonal chanting, 148
Therenoutis. *See* Tarnūṭ
Theriac of the Understanding in the Science of the Fundamentals, 20–21
Thessalonica, Edict of (380), 1947
Thetis, depicted in Coptic art, 1767–1768, *1768*
Theurgy. *See* Magic
Thévenot, Jean de, 791, 1977
Thiqah ibn al-Duhayrī. *See* Ibn al-Dahīrī
Thmius. *See* Tmuis
Thmonē as loanword in place-names, 2273
Thomas, Apostle and Saint
and Assumption of Mary, 292
and missions in India, 708, 1635
Pseudo-Cyril of Alexandria homily on, 2025–2026
Thomas, Bishop of Damascus (new martyr), 1559
Thomas, Saint, **2256**
churches dedicated to, 835–836, *835*
and Dayr al-Janādlah, 705
feast of, 1108
Thomas, Sunday of, 1108
Thomas Aquinas, Saint, 1115, 1186
Thomas of Shinshif (hermit), 781
Thompson, Henry Francis Herbert, **2257**
Thoth (pagan deity), 917, 1617
in Coptic calendar, 438
and Nawrūz name derivation, 1784
shrine at al-Ashmūnayn (Hermopolis Magna), 285
Thought of Norea (gnostic tractate), **2257**
"Three Chapters" controversy, 1676
Three Graces, depicted in Coptic art, 1768
Three Hebrew Children (martyrs). *See* Three Hebrews in the Furnace
Three Hebrews in the Furnace, 4, 1553, 1634, **2257–2259**
Three Risen Saints. *See* Exuperantius, Saint; Felix, Saint; Regula, Saint
Three Stelae of Seth, **2259–2260**, 2007
and *Gospel of the Egyptians*, 1154
and *Valentinian Exposition*, 2295
and *Zostrianus*, 2372
Three Youths, sanctuary of (Dayr Anbā Māqar), 752
Thuʿbān al-Rāhib, al-. *See* al-Sanī Abū al-Majd Buṭrus ibn al-Muhadhdhib Abū al-Faraj
Thunder, Perfect Mind, **2260**
Thursday. *See* Maundy Thursday
Tibarcius. *See* Valerianus and Tibarcius
Tiberius II, Emperor, 125–126, 688, 1675, 2061–2062
patriarch under, 1915
Tiberius Julius Alexander (prefect of Egypt), 2061
Ṭiḥnā al-Jabal, **2260–2261**
Tīj. *See* Abū Tīj
Til, Apa (martyr), 1089, 1559, **2261**
Till, Walter Curt Franz Theodor Karl Alois, 1891, 1894, 2022, **2261**
life of Zenobios, 2371
work on Coptic law, 1438
Tilodj. *See* Pispir
Timā, Dayr Abū Bifām at, 697
Timolaus (martyr), 1559
Timon, first deacon, 885
Timotheos I, Archbishop of Jerusalem, 358, 1245–1246, 1325, **2262**
and Haile Selassie I, 1198
Timotheus (pupil of Dionysius the Great), 909
Timotheus the Egyptian. *See* Timothy of Memphis (martyr)
Timotheus, Saint, 1883, 2087, **2262–2263**

Timothy (martyr), 1553
see also Theodorus and Timothy (martyrs)
Timothy, Bishop of Antinoopolis (martyr without bloodshed), 1559
Timothy, Bishop of Ephesus, 1432, 2015
Timothy, Bishop of Qaṣr Ibrīm, 829
Timothy I, Saint and Patriarch, **2263**
on Abbaton, 2
dates of patriarchy, 1914
feast day, 2087
Timothy II Aelurus ("the Cat"), Patriarch, 24, 1609, **2263–2267**
and Abū Mīnā church completion, 94, 2248
and Acacian schism, 42–47
Christology, 2266–2267
Coptic–Melchite split and disputed patriarchal succession, 1583, 1670, 1671, 1947, 1948, 2268
dates of patriarchy, 1915
as Dioscorus's successor, 915, 1441, 1442
and Eikoston monks, 951
and Enaton monks, 956–957
and Ephesus, Third Council of, 962
exile of, 525
and family of Zeno, Emperor, 2369–2370
feast day, 2087
and *History of the Patriarchs* authorship, 1239
John of Mayuma on, 1366
life, 2264–2266
on Michael, Archangel, 1618–1619
writings, 2266
Timothy III, Patriarch, **2268**
and Cosmas Indicopleustes, 640, 2268
dates of patriarchy, 1915
Justin I, Emperor and, 1384
and Severus of Antioch, 2125
Theodosius I and, 2241
Timothy and Matthias (martyrs), 1559
Timothy of Memphis (martyr), 1559
Timothy Salofaciolus ("Wobble-Cap"), Patriarch, 42, 43, 1442, 1609, 1671, 1947, 2265, **2268–2269**
Tinnis, **2269**
Tiridates, King of Armenia, 1183
Tirsā, **2269**
Tiryāq al-'Uqūl fī Ilm al-Uṣūl, 1464
Tischendorf, Konstantin von, 1893, 1900, **2269**
Tisserant, Eugène, **2270**
Titkooh. *See* Bāwīṭ
Titus, Bishop of Crete, 1432, 2015
Titus, Emperor
and Josephus Flavius, 1375
patriarch under, 1913
visit to Egypt, 2062, 2066
Tkow, paganism in, 1870
Tmone. *See* Minyā
Tmoone as loanword in place-names, 2273
Tmoushons. *See* Bakhānis-Tmoushons
Tmuis, 1648, **2270**
Tobias, 2052–2053, 2054
Tobit, 2052–2053, 2054
Toilet articles, 2336–2338, *2337–2339*
Tokoa. *See* Menarti
Toledo, Third Synod of (589), 1112
Tolemaeus, Saint (martyr), 1559, **2271**
see also Apaiule and Tolemaeus, Saints
Tomb of the Martyr. *See* Abū Mīnā
Tombs
architecture and decoration of. *See* Sculpture in stone, Coptic
Banī Ḥasan, 334–335
Catherine of Alexandria, Saint, 1683
Dayr al-'Adhrā', 715
Dayr Anbā Bisādah, 733
Dayr Anbā Ḥiziqyāl, 748
Dayr Apa Jeremiah (Saqqara), 776
Dayr al-Madīnah, 817–818
Dayr al-Misaykrah, 840
Dayr al-Muṭṭin, 843
Dayr Qubbat al-Hawā, 850, 851, *851*
Dayr al-Quṣayr, 853
Dayr Rīfah, 855–856
hermits' at Asyūt, 114
inscriptions, 1291, 1292, 1293–1296
inscriptions, Nubian, 1814–1815
inscriptions of visitors from Roman period, 2066
Jabal al-Ṭārif, 1657, 1771
Meir, 1583–1583
Menas the Miracle Maker, 24
mural paintings, 1873
Nag Hammadi codices find, 1771
oldest Coptic tombstones, 1294
pharaonic at Abydos, 39
pharaonic at Ahnās, 73–76
Phib, Saint, 1954
al-Shaykh Ṣa'id, 2130
Speos Artemidos, 334–335
see also Cemeteries; Reclusion; Stela
Tome of Leo, 514, 578, 961, 1075, 1441
and Acacian schism, 44–46, 1384
and Chalcedon, Council of, 514–515, 1441, 1442, 1675
communicatio idiomatum doctrine, 578
and Constantinople, Second Council, on, 595
Dioscorus I and, 913, 914, 915
Henoticon and, 1218
and monophysitism, 1670, 1671, 1672, 1674
Pulcheria and, 2033
Samū'īl of Qalamūn and, 2092
Tambūq monastery rejection of, 1648
Tome of Proclus, 2017
Tome of Union (633), 1667
Tomus of Lyons, 692
Tools, for woodworking, 2326
Topography
Christian Topography, 640–641, 1635
al-Maqrīzī study, 1525
Toponymy, Coptic, **2271–2274**
Topos (place), 153
Topos al-Malak Mikhā'īl (Idfū). *See* Dayr al-Malāk Mikhā'īl (Idfū)
Topos al-Qiddīs Yuḥannis. *See* Dayr al-Sāqiyah
Torah, 2109, 2111
Toronto, Canada, 1621

Tóth, Margit, 1741, 1743
Toulon, France, Coptic congregations in, 1623
Toussoun, Omar. *See* Omar Toussoun
Tower. *See* Keep
Tower of Palaemon, 749
Towns and settlements
'Abdallāh Nirqī, 4
Abū Mīnā, 24–25
Abūṣīr, 34
Abūṣīr Banā, 36–37
Abūṣīr al-Malaq, 37
Abū Tīj, 38
Aflāqah, 64
Agharwah, 70
Ahnās, 73–76
Aphrodito, 153–154
Aqbāṭ, 182–183
Aqfahṣ, 183
Ashmūn Ṭanāh, 288
Aswan, 294–296
Atrīs, 307–308
Awsīm, 311–312
Azarī, 315–316
Babīj, 317
al-Bagawāt, 326–329, *327*, *328*
Bahīj, 330
Bahjūrah, 330
Bakhānis-Timoushons, 331
al-Ballaṣ, 333
al-Banāwān, 334
Banī Kalb, 335
Barbīsh, 349
Bilad, 391
Biljāy, 391
Birmā, 392
Būrah, 425
al-Burullus, 427
Būsh, 427
Clysma, 565
confraternities in, 586–587
Dahlak, 685
Dahshūr, 685
Dalās, 685
Damallū, 686
Damanhūr, 686–687
Damanhūr al-Waḥsh, 688
Damrū, 689–690
Dandarah, 690–691
Daqādūs, 692
Daqahlah, 693
al-Dayr, 695
Dayr Rīfah, 855–856
Dimayrah, 902–903
Dinūshar, 903–904
Dūsh, 927–928
al-Duwayr, 928
Egyptian nome capitals, 1175, 1177, 1179
Elephantine, 951–952, *952*
Faras, 1090–1091
Farshūṭ, 1092–1093
Fīshah, 1117
Greek towns in Egypt, 1179–1181
Ḥājir Idfū, 1200
at Hawwārah, 1210–1211
at Hawwāriyyah, *1211*, 1211–1212
Ḥilwān, 1233
Jabal 'Addā, 1315
Jabal Khashm al-Qu'ūd, 1315–1316
Jabal al-Silsilah, 1316
Jirjā, 1330–1331
Karanis, 1390
Karm al-Akhbāriyyah, 1391–1392
al-Khandaq, 1413
Khirbat al-Filūsiyyah, 1414
Khirbitah, 1415
Kom Ombo, 1418
Kom al-Rāhib, 1418–1419
Laqqānah, 1426
Madamūd, 1494–1495
Maḥallat Abū 'Alī, 1510
Maḥallat al-Amīr, 1511
Maḥallat Minūf, 1511
Makhūrah, 1512–1513
Malīj, 1516
Marṣafā, 1546
Mashtūl, 1561
Maṣīl, 1561
Meir, 1582–1583
Memnonia, 1586
Menarti, 1587–1588
Nabarūh, 1769
Nag Hammadi, 1770
Naqīzah, 1774–1775
Nastaruh, 1775
Psoï, 2030–2031
Qarārah, 2036
Qaṣr Ibrīm, 2036–2037
Qūṣ, 2043–2045
Raithou, 2049–2050
Sakhā, 2087–2088
Shams al-Dīn, 2126–2127
Shanashā, 2127–2128
Sharūnah, 2128
Shuṭb, 2136
Sibirbāy, 2136
Sinjār, 2140
Sunbāṭ, 2159
Tabennēsē, 2197
Tafa, 2198
Tall al-'Amarnah, 2199
Talmīs, 2200
Tamīt, 2200–2201, *2201*
Tarnūṭ, 2202
Tbow, 2207
Ṭiḥnā al-Jabal, 2260–2261
Tirsā, 2269
Tuṭūn, 2283
Umm al-Barakāt, 2289–2291, *2290*
Umm Dabadīb, 2291
see also Boule; Cities; Dayr headings; Fortresses; Greek towns in Egypt; Toponymy, Coptic
Toys and games
wooden, 2339, *2340*
see also Ceramics, Coptic; Metalwork, Coptic; Ceramics, Coptic
Tractatus in Joannem Evangelium (Augustine), 1115
Trajan, Emperor, patriarch under, 1913
Transept. *See* Basilica
Transfiguration, Feast of the, 1108–1109
Transformation, Divine, 1058
Transitus Mariae, 1618, 1619
Transmigration of souls, 1521
Travelers in Egypt, 1975–1977
Pietro delle Valle, 1967
Roman, 2064–2066
see also Pilgrimages' Pilgrims and travelers in Christian Egypt
Treadle loom, Coptic textiles, 2215–2216
Treaties. *See* name, inverted
Treatise on the Resurrection, 569, **2275**
Treatise of the Ten Fundamentals (al-Ṣafī ibn al-'Assāl), 2078
Trees. *See* Woodworking, Coptic
Trent, Council of (1545–1547)
on the canon of the Old and New Testaments, 2110
Gabriel VII, Patriarch, and, 1134
Triadelphus, Bishop of Prosopites, 1793
Triadon (poem), 1986

Triangle (musical instrument), 1738, 1739
Tribelon, 222
Tribune. *See* Synthronon
Triconch, 222–223
Trīmitários (Coptic weaving term), 2221
Trimorphic Protennoia, **2276–2277**
Trinitarian theology, 688, 1637–1638, 2241
  Coptic influence in Alexandria, 101
  Dionysius on, 911
  doxologies, 923
  Origen, 1848–1850
Trinity
  'Abd al-Masīḥ al-Isrā'īli al-Raqqī on, 6
  and Alexander I, 82
  in Alexandrian theology, 103–104
  and the Anomoeans, 141–142
  and Apostles' Creed, 178–179
  Damian on, 689
  and *filioque*, 1114–1116
  and Nicene Creed, 82–84
  Origen on the, 1848–1849, 1850, 1855
  see also Trinitarian theology
Tripartite Tractate, 569, 1151, **2277**
  and *Valentinian Exposition*, 2296
Triphiou. *See* Suhāj
Tripoli, 1098
Trisagion, 1732, 2017, **2278–2279**
  and Acacian schism, 45
  and consecration of church and altar, 108, 109, 548, 549
Tritheism. *See* Trinitarian theology
Triumphal arch, 223–224
Triumph of Christ. *See* Christ, Triumph of
Troparia, 1724
Trullo, Council of (691), 71, 918
Tsenti, monastery of, 757
Ṭūbah (fifth month of Coptic calendar), 438–439, 441
  Assumption of Mary celebration, 289–290
  in the Copto-Arabic Synaxarion, 2179–2180
Ṭubḥ, **2279**
  and *Wāṭus*, 2321
Ṭūd, **2279–2280**, *2280*
Ṭūkh, 1, 2
Ṭūkhī, Raphael, and Arabic versions of Old Testament, 1829, 1830, 1832, 1834–1835
Ṭukh al-Naṣārā, pilgrimages to, 1975
Ṭūkh Ṭanbishā, pilgrimages to, 1975
Tulunids and Ikhshids, Copts under the, **2280–2281**
  see also Abbasids
Tūmā ibn al-Najīb Luṭfallāh al-Mahallī, **2281–2282**
Tūmā ibn al-Ṣā'igh, 1270
Tūnah, 1649
  seven ascetics of, 2122
Tunics, 644, *645*, 648
Tunis. *See* Arsenal of Tunis
Ṭūr, al-, 2050
Turaev, Boris Alexandrovitch, **2282**
Ṭurah
  Dayr al-Quṣayr, 853–855
  papyrus discoveries, 1899
Ṭurah, Saint, hymns attributed to, 1726
Tūrānshāh, 1536
Turicum. *See* Zurich
Turkey
  Coptic collections, 1712
  see also Constantinople; Ottomans, Copts under the; Tulunids and Ikhshids, Copts under the
Tūt (first month of Coptic calendar), 438, 440
  in the Copto-Arabic Synaxarion, 2174–2175
  and Nawrūz (Coptic New Year's Day), 1784
Tuṭūn, **2283**
  scriptoria of, 1651
Twelve Anathemas of Cyril, 1671
  and Armenian church, 234
Twelve Apostles, as portrayed in Coptic art, 529
Twelve Patriarchs, Testament of the, 163
The Twelve Virtues, 2310
Twenty-Four Elders, depicted in Coptic art, 541–542
"The Two Ways", 898
Tyloplókos, tylophántēs (Coptic weaving term), 2221
Types, **2283–2284**
Typikon of Saint Sabas (Qusṭanṭīn translation), 1182, 2046–2047
Typology. *See* Types
Typos of Constans II, 1678
Typos tes plerophorias (Anastasius). *See* Formula of Satisfaction

U

Udrunkah. *See* Durunkah
Uigurs, Kingdom of the, 1519
Ulphilas, **2285**
Ulysses, 1867
'Umar. *See* Covenant of 'Umar
'Umar (Bey) Ghaytās, 1538
'Umar ibn Abd al-'Azīz, 86–87
Umar Tussun. *See* Omar Toussoun
Umayyad fleet, Coptic contribution to, **2286**
Umayyads, Copts under the, **2286–2289**
  and Alexandria, 88, 89, 91
  and Islamic-influenced Coptic art, 1311, *1311*
  and Islamization of Egypt, 937
Ummanah, al-. *See* Nation's Party
Umm al-Barakāt, **2289–2291**, *2290*
Umm Dabadīb, **2291**
Unction of Christ, Ethiopian controversy, 986–987, 1023–1028
Unction of the sick, Holy Sacrament of the, **2291–2292**
  and anointing with oil, 139
  use of candles in, 446
Undergarments, 645
UNESCO, 1300, 1771–1772, 1955, 2032
Uniatism. *See* Coptic Catholic Church
Union of Christ dispute. *See* Unction of Christ
Unionist Progressive party, 1991
Union party, **1992**
Union of Soviet Socialist Republics
  Coptic collections, 1712
  papyrus collection, 1895
  see also Russia
United Arab Emirates, Coptic churches in, 1621
United Kingdom. *See* British Isles; Great Britain
United Nations Educational, Scientific and Cultural Organization. *See* UNESCO
United States of America
  Coptic churches in, 1621–1622

Coptic collections, 1712–1715
papyrus collection, 1895–1896
Universe. *See Christian Topography* (Cosmas Indicopleustes)
Universität der Rheinisch-Westfälischen Akademie of Cologne, 1892
Université Paul Valéry, Montpellier, 694
University College, London, 1893
University of Florence, 1894
University Library (Freiburg im Breisgau), 1892
University Library (Giessen), 1893
University Library (Graz), 1891
University Library (Heidelberg), 1893
University Library (Louvain), 1891
University Library (Strasbourg), 1892
University Library (Turin), 1894
University Library (Würzburg), 1893
University of Michigan Library, 1895
University of Mississippi, 1900
Unleavened bread, and Eucharist, 1060–1061
Upper Egypt. *See* Ṣaʿīd
Upper Ṣaʿīd
monasteries of, **1656–1658**, 1659
Qūṣ as administrative center of, 2043
Uqṣur, al-. *See* Luxor
Uqsurayn, al-. *See* Luxor
ʿUrābī revolution (1881–1882), 1637, 1693, 1995
Urban VIII, Pope (Rome), 610, 611
Ūrī. *See* Ari (martyr)
Ursus of Solothurn, Saint, 1559, 2232, **2292–2293**, 2302
Usaghnīyūs. *See* Eusignius (martyr)
Uṣūl Muqaddīmat Sullam al-Lughah al-Qibṭiyyah, 1463

V

Valais, canton of, 1572
Valens, Emperor, 1650, 1947, 1956
patriarch under, 1914
Valentinian I, Emperor, 790, 1576, 1577, 1578
Valentinian II, Emperor, 1577
patriarch under, 1914
Valentinian III, Emperor, 1440
Valentinian Exposition, **2295–2296**
Valentinians. *See* Valentinus
Valentinus, 1731, 1866, **2296–2297**
and Basilides, 357
and gnosticism, 1147, 1148, 1150, 1151, 1156
and *Gospel of Philip*, 1157
and *Gospel of Truth*, 1151, 1164
and Heracleon, 1219
as heretic, 1222
myth of fall of Sophia linked with *Authentikos Logos*, 309
Valeria (daughter of Diocletian), 2246
Valerian, Emperor, 1869, **2297–2298**
patriarch under, 1914
persecutions of, 909, 910, 1552, 1575, 1785, 1936
Valerianus and Tibarcius (martyrs), 1559
Valesius (martyr), 1559
Valley of the Kings, festival of, 439
Valley of the Nile. *See* Nile valley
Van Lantschoot, Arnold, 1895, **2298**
Van Moorsel, Paul, 726
Vansleb (Wansleben), Johann Michael, 23, 30, 613, 1462, 1892, 1977, **2299**
on Antinoopolis, 145
on Asyūṭ, 297
on Būsh, 427
contribution to Coptological studies, 613
on Dayr Anbā Anṭūniyūs, 722
on Dayr Anbā Bishoi, 738
on Dayr Anbā Shinūdah, 765
on Dayr al-Quṣayr, 853
on Durunkah, 926
Vasco da Gama, 1636
Vatatzes, John, 1114
Vatican Arabic 123, 722
Vatican Coptic 9, on pillage of Dayr Anbā Anṭūniyūs, 722
Vatican Library, 6, 30, 31, 876
Assemani family and, 289
papyrus collections, 1894–1895
Vatican Museum, Coptic textile collection. *See* Museums, Coptic collections in
Vault, 224–225
Veil, custom of women wearing, 641, 650
Veils. *See* Eucharistic veils
Veneration. *See* Icons, Coptic; Saints
Venice, and relics of Mark, Saint, 1532
Verena, Saint, 2087, 2232, **2299–2301**, *2301*
Vertical loom, Coptic textiles, 2215
Vespasian, Emperor, 2061, 2062
and Josephus Flavius, 1375
patriarch under, 1913
Vespers, **2301**
Vestments. *See* Liturgical vestments
Vestry. *See* Architectural elements of churches: Sacristy
Viaud, Gérard, 1975
Victor (uncle of Anbā Yūnā), 744
Victor (martyr), 1559
Victor, Anbā, 861, **2301**
festal date of, 840
Victor of Asyūṭ. *See* Victor of Shū
Victor, Decius, and Eirene (martyrs), 1559
Victor the General. *See* Victor Stratelates, Saint
Victoria and Albert Museum, London, 255
Victor of Pbow. *See* Victor of Tabennēsē
Victor of Rome, 1905
Victor of Shū, Saint (martyr), 296, 370, 708, **2302**
churches dedicated to, 797
confused with tribunal of Victor Stratelates, 2305
feast day, 1559, 2087
pilgrimages, 1971
Victor of Solothurn and Geneva, Saint, 1159, 2232, **2302–2303**
and Ursus of Solothurn, Saint, 2293
and Verena, Saint, 2300
Victor Stratelates, Saint, 1159, **2303–2308**, **2303–2308**
Celestinus of Rome panegyric on, 2305–2306
Cyriacus, Bishop, panegyric on, 670, 2305
Demetrius of Antioch on, 2306–2307
Demetrius of Antioch panegyric on, 2305
and Eusebius, 1070

Victor Stratelates, Saints (*cont.*)
Michael of Atrīb and Malīj on, 2306
monasteries of, 810, 1657–1658, 2307–2308
Theopemptos of Antioch panegyric on, 2306
Victor of Tabennēsē, Saint, 1455, **2308**
Victor of Tunnuna, 1609
Vienna, University of, 1389, 1419
Vienna Academy of Sciences, 815
Vies des saints pères des déserts (d'Andilly), 894
Vigil, **2308**
Village of the Monastery. *See* Naj' al-Dayr
Villecourt, Louis, 1735, **2308**
Villoteau, Guillaume André, 1742
Virgil, 1867
Virgin Enthroned (Virgin and Child)
depicted in Coptic art, 270, *277*, 281, 542–544, 868, 869, 1660
in Nubian church art, 1812
see also Virgo Lactans
Virgin Mary
Annunciation, 1102
apparitions of. *See* Virgin Mary, apparition of the
chapels dedicated to, 754
churches dedicated to, 704–705, 710, 716, 721, 741, 806, 813, 815, 820, *821*, 856, 924, 1118, 1975
encomium on, 1956
Fast of the Virgin Mary, 1096
Feast of the Virgin, 1111
Gabriel, Archangel, and, 1135
Hail Mary, 1199
iconography, 243–244, 1276, *1279*
icons at Bāwīṭ, 368–369
and Immaculate Conception, 1285
and Incarnation, 1287–1290
incense as analogy for, 1470
intercessional character of, 1107
manuscript collection on, 1778
miraculous appearances of. *See* Virgin Mary, apparition of the
monasteries dedicated to, 714, 715–716, 734, 799, 835
as Mother of God. *See* *Theotokos*
paintings of, 1875
pilgrimage centers in Egypt, 1968, 1969, 1970, 1972, 1973
portraits of, 726–727, 778, *794*
Pseudo-Cyril of Alexandria homily on, 2025–2026
Theotokia (hymns to), 1724, 1726, 1727, 1986
see also Annunciation; Assumption; Flight into Egypt; Joseph the Carpenter, Saint; *Theotokos*; Virgin Enthroned
Virgin Mary, apparition of the, 681, 840, 871, 1969, **2308–2310**, *2309*
Virgins, communities of. *See* Nuns: Women's religious communities
Virgo lactans, 243–244, 531, 543
Virtues, the Twelve, **2310**
Virtues of Saint Macarius, 1984
Visio Isaiae, Coptic translations, 1451
Vitae patrum (Rosweyde), 56
Vita Gregorii Thaumaturgi (Gregory of Nyssa), 1184
Vitalian, 45
Vita Pauli. See Life of Saint Paul the First Hermit
Vitellius, Emperor, patriarch under, 1913
Vitruvius (Roman architect), 1872
Vocabulary. *See Appendix*
Vocalise (Coptic musical characteristic), *1720*, 1721, 1732
Vocal music. *See* Cantors; Choral singing; Hymns
Volbach, W. F., 256, 257
Volusianus, 2017
Vows, and pilgrimages, 1968
Voyage nouveau de la Terre Sainte (Nau), on Dayr al-Sulṭān, 872
Vulgate, 1323

W

Wādī 'Arabah, 728
Wādī bīr al-'Ayn, Dayr al-Sab'at Jibāl, 857
Wādī Ghazālī, 1817–1818
Wādī Habīb. *See* Scetis
Wādī Hannebah, hermitages, 728
Wāḍih ibn Rajā', al-, **2311**
and al-Sāwīrus ibn al-Muqaffa', 2102
Wādī al-Jilbānah, 700
Wādī al-Mulūk, Dayr al-Sab'at Jibāl, 857–858
Wādī al-Nakhlah, 795
Wādī Natfah, hermitages, 728
Wādī al-Naṭrūn
Dayr al-Suryān in, 876–881
Dayr Yuḥannis, al-Qaṣīr at, 883–884
Dayr Yuḥannis Kama at, 883
keep construction, 1395–1396
see also Scetis
Wādī al-Nīl (publication), 1990
Wādī al-Rayyān, 755, 755, **2311**
Wadī' Sa'īd (Dawūd al-Maqārī), 1307
Wādī Sarjah, **2312**
deuterarios term, 895
Monastery of the Virgin near, 704
Wādī Shaykh 'Alī, **2312–2313**
Wa-al-Durr al-Farīd fīmā ba'd Tārīkh ibn al- 'Amīd (al-Assāl), 1463
Wafdist bloc, 1993
Wafd al-Miṣrī, al- (publication), 1990
Wafd party, 1515, 1516, 1628, 1989–1991, 1993, 2323
Sa'd Zaghlūl leadership, 2074–2075
Wāham, **2313**
Wahbī, Tadrus, 1465, 1467
Walīd ibn 'Abd al-Malik, al-, Caliph, 86
Walīd ibn Yazīd, al-, Caliph, 1410–1411
Wall decorations
Coptic glass, 1145–1146
see also Painting, Coptic mural
Walters Art Gallery, Baltimore, Maryland, 1599, 1600, 1601
Wansleben, Johann. *See* Vansleb (Wansleben), Johann Michael
Waqā'ī' al-Miṣriyyah (publication), 1993, 1074
Waq'at al-Kanā'īs, **2313–2316**
Waq'at al-Naṣārā, **2316–2319**
Waqf, Coptic, **2319**
Warp-weighted loom, Coptic textiles, 2215
Warriors in Coptic art, 649–650, **2319–2320**
Warshanūfyus. *See* Barsanuphius (martyr)
Warshenufe, Saint, 2087
Wars (Procopius), 2019, 2020

Washing. *See* Ablution; Feet, washing of; Hands, washing of
Wāṣif, ʿAwaḍ, 1466
Wāṣif Buṭrus Ghālī, 1990
Wāsīlīdas. *See* Basilidas (martyr)
Wassef, Wissa. *See* Wissa Wassef
Wasserkirche (Zurich), 1082, 1110, 2057
Waṭan, al- (publication), 1465, 1466, 1628, 1989, 1993–1996, 2010–2012
Water
  into wine, 1107
  liturgical instruments for, 1469
  for spells, 1500
  see also Ablution; Baptism; Immersion
Water jugs and stands, 491–492, 2148, **2320**
Water supply
  irrigation aqueducts at Dayr Abū Qarqūrah, 709
  Karanis, 1390
  in keep, 1396
  Kellia site, 1401
  spring at Dayr Abū Ḥalbānah spring, 700
  spring at Dayr Anbā Anṭūniyūs, 725
  spring at Dayr al-Sabʿat Jibāl, 857, 858
  spring of Saint Antony, 721
  well at Dayr al-Jarnūs (Maghāgha), 813
  well at Dayr al-Malāk Mīkhā'īl (Qamūlah), 827
Water vessels. *See* Water jugs and stands
Wāṭus, 63, 1425, 1479, 1722, 1724, 1726, 1727, 1728, **2320–2321**
  hymns for, 901
  and Ṭubh, 2279
Weather, in the Nile Valley, 440–443
Weaving, 1641
  combs and shuttles, 2340–2341, *2341*
  techniques in manufacture of Coptic textiles, 2217–2218
  see also Tapestries
Weddings. *See* Betrothal customs; Marriage
Wednesday and Friday fast days, 1096
Week, seven-day. *See* Calendar, Coptic; Days of the week; specific days
Weights and balances, 1603–1604, *1605*
  boxes made of wood, 2328
Wessely, Carl Franz Joseph, 1891, **2321**
  Shenute text-editing, 1452
West Bank. *See* Monasteries of the Upper Ṣaʿīd
Western Desert, monasteries of the, 1658–1659
Wheat crop. *See* Annona
White Monastery of Shenute (Suhāj). *See* Dayr Anbā Shinūdah
Whitsunday. *See* Pentecost
Whittemore, Thomas, **2321**
  visit to Dayr Anbā Anṭūniyūs, 726
Widows
  Didascalia on, 899
  digamy (remarriage), 901
Wiesmann, Hermann, **2321**
Wiet, Gaston, **2321**
Wilcken, Ulrich, **2322**
Wilke (Wilkius, Wilkins), David, 1424, **2322**
Wills and inheritance, 1429, 1941
Window glass, 1145
Wine
  amphorae, 490–491
  Dionysius as god of, 1758
  Eucharistic, 1066
  Feast of the Martyr, 1548
  as medicine, 1524–1527
  miracle of water into, 1107
  offertory, 1824–1825
  Saladin's prohibitions against, 1535
  storage, *2330*
Wisdom literature, *Didache* compared with, 898
Wissa Wassef, 1466, 1738, 2988, 2051, **2322–2324**
Woide, Charles Godfrey, 1424, 1428, 2324
Women
  absolution in baptism, 339
  Alexandra, Saint, 88
  Anastasia, Saint, 125
  Bayt al-Niṣā' (reserved area in church), 373, 703
  birth rites and customs, 393–393
  Catherine, Saint, Mount Sinai Monastery of, 1681–1685
  communion regulations, 579
  Coptic education of, 932, 933
  Coptic equality measures for, 1465
  Coptic headdress, 641
  Coptic ideals, 1086–1087
  deaconess, 888
  Dimyānah and her forty virgins, 903
  doctors, 1581
  Erai, Saint, 2209
  Eudoxia, Saint, 1067
  Euphemia, Saint, 1073
  Euphrosyna, Saint, 1069
  Febronia, Saint, 1109–1110
  first full-time Egyptologist, 1701
  funerary customs, 1124
  and gnosticism, 1081, 1148, 1150, 1155
  Herai, Saint, 1221
  Hilaria, Saint, 1230–1231
  Mariyyah the Copt, 1528
  martyrs, 903, 1552–1553, 1554, 1555, 1556, 1558, 1559; *see also* specific names
  Mary of Alexandria, 1560
  Mary the Egyptian, 1560
  mourning customs, 1686
  Nabdūnah, 1769
  personifying soul in Gnostic literature, 1081
  Pulcheria, 2033
  recluses, 88, 1663, 2055
  Regula, Saint, 2057
  rights in ancient Egypt, 1086
  rights in modern Egypt, 1088, 1944
  role in Ethiopian church, 1044–1045
  Salāmah Mūsā on equal rights for, 2089
  Sara, Saint, 2094
  Sophia, Saint, 2143–2144
  Syncletica, 2192
  Theodora, Empress, 2235
  Theognosta, Saint, 2243–2244
  Theopista, Saint, 1072–1073
  veil-wearing, 641–650
  Verena, Saint, 2299–2301, *2301*
  see also Betrothal customs; Birth rites and customs; Costume, civil; Marriage; Widows; Women's religious communities
Women's religious communities, 1663, **2324–2325**

Women's religious communities (*cont.*)
amma in, 2, 3
Anastasia, Saint, founding, 125
convent and nunnery organization, 1663
at Dayr Abū Sayfayn (Old Cairo), 710
at Dayr al-Banāt, 788–789, *789*
Dimyānah and her forty virgins, 903
al-Ḥamīdāt, 1205
Moses of Abydos founding, 707
nuns, 1822
origins in Egypt, 1663
Pachomian community, 1663, 1822, 1860, 2325
Woodwork, Coptic, **2325–2347**, *2328–2346*
altar ban, 580
painted icons, 293
portraiture, 2001
preservation of wood, 279
under Muslim rule, 1311, 1312
see also Art, historiography of Coptic
Wool, used in Coptic textiles, 2212–2213, *2213*
Word, Liturgy of the. *See* Catechumens, Liturgy of the
Words, magical, 1500–1502
World Chronicle (John of Nikiou), 2060
World Council of Churches, 2091
World War I, 1694
Worrell, William Hoyt, 1895, **2348**
Writing surfaces. *See* Ostracon; Papyrus; Parchment
Wüstenfeld, Ferdinand, **2348**

X

Xenedochou. *See* Pimandjoili
Xois. *See* Sakhā

Y

Yacobos II, Archbishop of Jerusalem, 1245, 1325. **2349**
Yacoub, Jacob. *See* Ya'qub, General
Yaḥyā, 'Abd al-Fattāḥ, 1992
Yaḥyā ibn 'Adī, 6, 1779
Yaḥyā ibn Sa'īd al-Anṭākī, 1266, 1460, 1524
Yalbogha al-Sāmirī, 1570
Yale University
Nag Hammadi Codices, 1771
papyrus collection, 1895
Yā'qob, Ethiopian prelate, 1011
Ya'qūb, Abū. *See* Isḥāq ibn Ibrāhīm ibn Nastās
Ya'qūb, General, 1511–1512, 1524, 1539, **2349–2352**
and Chiftichi, Yuḥanna, 520
and Coptic Legion, 1417
and Egyptian national identity, 948
and French expedition in Egypt, 1284
and Jirjis al-Jawharī, 1333
and Menou, Jacques, 1591
and Salippe, Mikarius, 2089
and Shukrallāh Jirjis, 2136
and Sīdārūs, Gabriel, 2137
Ya'qūb Ḥannā, 1688
Ya'qūb ibn Killīs, 11
Ya'qūb Nakhlah Rufaylah, 415, **2353**
Yārēd, Ethiopian saint, 1047
Yashu'. *See* Joshua and Joseph (ascetics and martyrs)
Yassa 'Abd al-Masīḥ, 1700, 1727, **2353**
Yazīd II, Caliph, 87
Year. *See* Calendar, Coptic
Yeken, 'Adlī, 1990, 1991
Yem'atā, Ethiopian saint, 1046
Yemen, 1134
Yesḥaq, Ethiopian saint, 1046
Yesḥaq I, Ethiopian prelate, 1008
Yesḥaq II, Ethiopian prelate, 1015–1016
Yoḥannes I, Ethiopian prelate, 1001
Yoḥannes II, Ethiopian prelate, 1010
Yoḥannes III, Ethiopian prelate, 1028–1030
Yoḥannes IV, Emperor, 1590–1591
Yosāb I, Ethiopian prelate, 1017–1018
Yosāb II, Ethiopian prelate, 1030–1032
Youel, 105
Youna (martyr), 1554
Young, D. W., 1448
Young, Thomas, 1445
Young Egypt (*Miṣr al-Fatāh*), 1694
Youssef, Faṭmah al-, 1991
Youth of Egypt, **2354**
Youth movements, **2354–2355**
Ypantēs (Coptic textile term), 2221
Yu'annā. *See* Junia (martyr)
Yu'annis, *see also* John
Yu'annis, Anbā (head of Dayr Anbā Maqār), 69, 749
Yu'annis, Bishop of Asyūṭ, **2355**
Yu'annis, Bishop of Durunkah, 927
Yu'annis, Bishop of Miṣr, 1613
Yu'annis, Bishop of Samnnūd, 1748
Yu'annis, Metropolitan of al-Minūfiyyah, 1614
Yūḥannā. *See also* Dayr Yuḥannis headings; John
Yuḥannā (scribe), **2356**
Yūḥannā, Bishop of Samannūd, 686, **2355–2356**
Yuḥannā al-Armānī al-Qudsī (icon painter), *1278*, 1279
Yūḥannā the Deacon, **2356–2357**
Yūḥannā al-Ḥādhiq al-Qibṭī (Mu'allim), **2357**
Yuḥānnā ibn Abī Zakāriyyā ibn Sibā, 1735
Yuḥannā ibn Māsāwayh, 1273
Yūḥannā ibn Moesis. *See* Yūḥannā the Deacon
Yūḥannā ibn Sāwīrus, **2357–2358**
Yūḥannā ibn Zakariyyā ibn Abi Siba'. *See* Ibn Sibā' Yūḥannā Ibn Abī Zakariyyā
Yūḥannā al-Maqsī, **2358**
Yūḥannā ibn Ṣā'id, 1573
Yuhannis, Bishop of Asyūṭ, 297
Yuḥannis ibn Buqṭur al-Dimyāṭī, **2358**
Yūnā, Anbā, 744, 805
Yūnus ibn Kadrān, 1615, 1616
Yusāb, Bishop of Damanhūr, 686
Yūsāb, Bishop of Akhmīm (13th century), **2359**
Yūsāb, Bishop of Akhmīm (15th century), **2359–2360**
Yūsāb, Bishop of Akhmīm (18th century), **2360–2361**
Yūsāb I, Archbishop of Jerusalem, 1325
Yūsāb I, Saint and Patriarch, 361, **2362–2363**
and Church of al-Mu'allaqah (Old Cairo), 558
and Church of Sitt Maryam, 320
dates of patriarchy, 1916
feast day, 2087

and first portable altar, 144
and the Martyr Church at Abū Mīnā, 94
successor, 1412
and Yoḥannes I, Ethiopian prelate, 1001
Yuḥannā biography of, 2356
Yūsāb II, Patriarch, 1911, **2363**
dates of patriarchy, 1919
and Ethiopian church autonomy, 981–982, 1043–1044, 1613
and Haile Selassie I, 1198
and Sarjiyūs, Malaṭī, 2011, 2097
translation as bishop, 399
Yūsāb of Qifṭ, Saint, 2087
Yustus Marāghī, 1122
Yūsuf Abū Daqn, **2364–2365**
Yūsuf al-Qibṭī, **2365**
Yūsuf the Syrian (recluse), 1128

Z

Zacharias I, Archbishop of Jerusalem, 1325
Zacharias, Patriarch, **2367–2368**
and church restorations, 94, 558
and continued use of Coptic language, 1734
Damrū residence, 689
dates of patriarchy, 1916
and Dayr Shahrān restoration, 862
feast day, 2087
Zacharias, Saint and Bishop of Ṣā, 12, 2087
Zacharias, Saint and Bishop of Sakhā, 12, 840, 1456, 2087, **2368**
Zacharias of Scetis, 1681, **2369**
Zadok and his companions (martyrs), 1559
Zaghlūl, Sa'd. *See* Sa'd Zaghlūl
Zagwē dynasty, 1425
Ẓāhir, Caliph, 1097, 1098, 1099
Zambia, Coptic church in, 1622
Zamikā'ēl, Ethiopian saint, 1046
Zamikā'ēlites, 985
Zananīq, 1650
Zanetti, U., 1435, 1626
Zanufius, Saint, 2087
Zar'a Yā'qob, King of Ethiopia, 1052–1053, 1054
Zawditu, Empress, 1040, 1041
Zāwiyah, al- (village), 884
Zaytūn, Apparition of the Virgin Mary at, 2308–2309
Zechariah, 1102, 1135
Zechariah (Didymus), 900
Zechariah, Bishop of Sakhā, 840
Zechariah, Patriarch of Jerusalem, and Holy Cross, 1243
Zeno (martyr). *See* Paul, Longinus, and Zeno (martyrs)
Zeno, Emperor, **2369–2370**
Alexander of Lycopolis on, 87–88
endowment of Dayr Anbā Maqār, 749, 1642
as father of Hilaria, Saint, 1230
Henoticon edict. *See* Henoticon
and Monophysites, 1671, 1673
patriarch under, 1915
and Timothy Salofaciolus, Patriarch, 1671, 2269
Zenobios, 762, **2371**
Zephaniah, Apocalypse of, 165
Zephyrinus, Bishop of Rome, 1638
Zeus Ammonios (desert oracle), 1180
Zimbabwe, Coptic church in, 1622
Ziniyyah. *See* Coptic language, spoken
Ziyādah ibn Yaḥyā ibn al-Rāsī, 2079
Zo, Empress, 1099
Zoega, Georg (Jorgen), **2371**
Zoilus (scribe), 1467
Zoroaster (pagan deity), 1520, 1617
Zosima, Anbā, 130
Zosimus, Saint (monk–priest from Palestine)
on *Apophthegmata patrum*, 177
feast day, 2087
and Mary the Egyptian, 1560
Zosimus of Panopolis, 1735, **2371**
Zostrianus, 2295, **2371–2372**
Zubayr ibn al-'Awwām, al-, 186
Zubdat al-Fikrah fī Tārīkh al-Hijrah, 1464
Zukayr (Yu'annis), 1573
Zūnī, 22
Zurich, Switzerland, 1082, 1110, 2057
see also Switzerland; Theban Legion